PRENTICE HALL
LITERATURE

GRADE 12
Part 2

COMMON CORE EDITION ©

Upper Saddle River, New Jersey

Boston, Massachusetts

Chandler, Arizona

Glenview, Illinois

PEARSON

Cover Art: (Bkgd) ©Ted Mead/Getty Images, (L) ©James Forte/Getty Images, (B) (c) Tom Merton/OJO Images/ Getty Images, (TL, BC) (c)Blaine Harrington III/CORBIS, (CR) (c)Uli Wiesmeier/zefa/CORBIS.

Taken from:

Prentice Hall Literature, The British Tradition, Common Core Edition
Copyright © 2012 by Pearson Education, Inc.
Published by Prentice Hall
Upper Saddle River, New Jersey 07458

This special edition published in cooperation with Pearson Learning Solutions.

All trademarks, service marks, registered trademarks, and registered service marks are the property of their respective owners and are used herein for identification purposes only.

Pearson Learning Solutions, 501 Boylston Street, Suite 900, Boston, MA 02116
A Pearson Education Company
www.pearsoned.com

Printed in the United States of America

2 16

000200010271275795

CW

Acknowledgments appear on page R82, which constitutes an extension of this copyright page.

SAT is a registred trademark of the College Entrance Examination Board. ACT is a trademark owned by ACT, Inc.

Wikipedia® is a registered trademark of the Wikimedia Foundation, Inc., ‹http://www.wikimediafoundation.org›

iPod® and Mac® are registered trademarks of Apple Inc.

Use of the trademarks implies no relationship, sponsorship, endorsement, sale, or promotion on the part of Pearson Education, Inc., or its affiliates.

Common Core State Standards © Copyright 2010. National Governors Association Center for Best Practices and Council of Chief State School Officers. All rights reserved.

"Understanding by Design" is registered as a trademark with the United States Patent and Trademark Office by the Association for Supervision of Curriculum Development (ASCD). ASCD claims exclusive trademark rights in the terms "Understanding by Design" and the abbreviation "UbD".

Pearson Education has incorporated the concepts of the Understanding by Design methodology into this text in consultation with Grant Wiggins, one of the creators of the Understanding by Design methodology. The Association for Supervision of Curriculum Development (ASCD), publisher of the "Understanding by Design Handbook" co-authored by Grant Wiggins, has not authorized, approved or sponsored this work and is in no way affiliated with Pearson or its products.

ISBN-13: 978-1-256-33185-8
ISBN-10: 1-256-33185-6

Contributing Authors

The contributing authors guided the direction and philosophy of Pearson Prentice Hall Literature. Working with the development team, they helped to build the pedagogical integrity of the program and to ensure its relevance for today's teachers and students.

Grant Wiggins, Ed.D., is the President of Authentic Education in Hopewell, New Jersey. He earned his Ed.D. from Harvard University and his B.A. from St. John's College in Annapolis. Grant consults with schools, districts, and state education departments on a variety of reform matters; organizes conferences and workshops; and develops print materials and Web resources on curricular change. He is the coauthor, with Jay McTighe, of Understanding by Design and The Understanding by Design Handbook, the award-winning and highly successful materials on curriculum published by ASCD. His work has been supported by the Pew Charitable Trusts, the Geraldine R. Dodge Foundation, and the National Science Foundation. *The Association for Supervision of Curriculum Development (ASCD), publisher of the "Understanding by Design Handbook" co-authored by Grant Wiggins and registered owner of the trademark "Understanding by Design", has not authorized, approved, or sponsored this work and is in no way affiliated with Pearson or its products.*

Jeff Anderson has worked with

struggling writers and readers for almost 20 years. Anderson's specialty is the integration of grammar and editing instruction into the processes of reading and writing. He has published two books, *Mechanically Inclined: Building Grammar, Usage, and Style into Writer's Workshop* and *Everyday Editing: Inviting Students to Develop Skill and Craft in Writer's Workshop,* as well as a DVD, *The Craft of Grammar.* Anderson's work has appeared in *English Journal.* Anderson won the NCTE Paul and Kate Farmer Award for his *English Journal* article on teaching grammar in context.

Arnetha F. Ball, Ph.D., is a

Professor at Stanford University. Her areas of expertise include language and literacy studies of diverse student populations, research on writing instruction, and teacher preparation for working with diverse populations. She is the author of *African American Literacies Unleashed* with Dr. Ted Lardner, and *Multicultural Strategies for Education and Social Change.*

Sheridan Blau is Professor of

Education and English at the University of California, Santa Barbara, where he directs the South Coast Writing Project and the Literature Institute for Teachers. He has served in senior advisory roles for such groups as the National Board for Professional Teaching Standards, the College Board, and the American Board for Teacher Education. Blau served for twenty years on the National Writing Project Advisory Board and Task Force, and is a former president of NCTE. Blau is the author of *The Literature Workshop: Teaching Texts and Their Readers,* which was named by the Conference on English Education as the 2004 Richard Meade Award winner for outstanding research in English education.

William G. Brozo, Ph.D., is a Professor of Literacy at George Mason University in Fairfax, Virginia. He has taught reading and language arts in junior and senior high school and is the author of numerous texts on literacy development. Dr. Brozo'z work focuses on building capacity among teacher leaders, enriching the literate culture of schools, enhancing the literate lives of boys, and making teaching more responsive to the needs of all students. His recent publications include *Bright Beginnings for Boys: Engaging Young Boys in Active Literacy* and the *Adolescent Literacy Inventory.*

Doug Buehl is a teacher, author, and

national literacy consultant. He is the author of *Classroom Strategies for Interactive Learning* and coauthor of *Reading and the High School Student: Strategies to Enhance Literacy;* and *Strategies to Enhance Literacy and Learning in Middle School Content Area Classrooms.*

Jim Cummins, Ph.D, is a profes-

sor in the Modern Language Centre at the University of Toronto. He is the author of numerous publications, including *Negotiating Identities: Education for Empowerment in a Diverse Society.* Cummins coined the acronyms BICS and CAPT to help differentiate the type of language ability students need for success.

Harvey Daniels, Ph.D., has been

a classroom teacher, writing project director, author, and university professor. "Smokey" serves as an international consultant to schools, districts, and educational agencies. He is known for his work on student-led book clubs, as recounted in *Literature Circles: Voice and Choice in Book Clubs & Reading Groups* and *Mini Lessons for Literature Circles.* Recent works include *Subjects Matter: Every Teacher's Guide to Content-Area Reading* and *Content Area Writing: Every Teacher's Guide.*

Jane Feber taught language arts in Jacksonville, Florida, for 36 years. Her innovative approach to instruction has earned her several awards, including the NMSA Distinguished Educator Award, the NCTE Edwin A. Hoey Award, the Gladys Prior Award for Teaching Excellence, and the Florida Council of Teachers of English Teacher of the Year Award. She is a National Board Certified Teacher, past president of the Florida Council of Teachers of English, and the author of *Creative Book Reports* and *Active Word Play*.

Danling Fu, Ph.D., is Professor of Language and Culture in the College of Education at the University of Florida. She researches and provides inservice to public schools nationally, focusing on literacy instruction for new immigrant students. Fu's books include *My Trouble is My English* and *An Island of English* addressing English language learners in the secondary schools. She has authored chapters in the *Handbook of Adolescent Literacy Research* and in *Adolescent Literacy: Turning Promise to Practice*.

Kelly Gallagher is a full-time English teacher at Magnolia High School in Anaheim, California. He is the former co-director of the South Basin Writing Project at California State University, Long Beach. Gallagher wrote *Reading Reasons: Motivational Mini-Lessons for the Middle and High School, Deeper Reading: Comprehending Challenging Texts 4-12,* and *Teaching Adolescent Writers.* Gallagher won the Secondary Award of Classroom Excellence from the California Association of Teachers of English—the state's top English teacher honor.

Sharroky Hollie, Ph.D., is an assistant professor at California State University, Dominguez Hills, and an urban literacy visiting professor at Webster University, St. Louis. Hollie's work focuses on professional development, African American education, and second language methodology. He is a contributing author in two texts on culturally and linguistically responsive teaching. He is the Executive Director of the Center for Culturally Responsive Teaching and Learning and the co-founding director of the Culture and Language Academy of Success, an independent charter school in Los Angeles.

Dr. Donald J. Leu, Ph.D., teaches at the University of Connecticut and holds a joint appointment in Curriculum and Instruction and in Educational Psychology. He directs the New Literacies Research Lab and is a member of the Board of Directors of the International Reading Association. Leu studies the skills required to read, write, and learn with Internet technologies. His research has been funded by groups including the U.S. Department of Education, the National Science Foundation, and the Bill & Melinda Gates Foundation.

Jon Scieszka founded GUYS READ, a nonprofit literacy initiative for boys, to call attention to the problem of getting boys connected with reading. In 2008, he was named the first U.S. National Ambassador for Young People's Literature by the Library of Congress. Scieszka taught from first grade to eighth grade for ten years in New York City, drawing inspiration from his students to write *The True Story of the 3 Little Pigs!, The Stinky Cheese Man,* the *Time Warp Trio* series of chapter books, and the *Trucktown* series of books for beginning readers.

Sharon Vaughn, Ph.D., teaches at the University of Texas at Austin. She is the previous Editor-in-Chief of the *Journal of Learning Disabilities* and the co-editor of *Learning Disabilities Research and Practice.* She is the recipient of the American Education Research Association SIG Award for Outstanding Researcher. Vaughn's work focuses on effective practices for enhancing reading outcomes for students with reading difficulties. She is the author of more than 100 articles, and numerous books designed to improve research-based practices in the classroom.

Karen K. Wixson is Dean of the 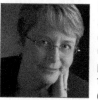 School of Education at the University of North Carolina, Greensboro. She has published widely in the areas of literacy curriculum, instruction, and assessment. Wixson has been an advisor to the National Research Council and helped develop the National Assessment of Educational Progress (NAEP) reading tests. She is a past member of the IRA Board of Directors and co-chair of the IRA Commission on RTI. Recently, Wixson served on the English Language Arts Work Team that was part of the Common Core State Standards Initiative.

The selections in this book are presented through the lens of three Essential Questions:

What is the relationship between literature and place?

How does literature shape or reflect society?

What is the relationship of the writer to tradition?

Resources

Rebels and Dreamers
The Romantic Period (1798 to 1832)

PHLit Online!
www.PHLitOnline.com

Interactive resources provide personalized instruction and activities online.

PART TWO: **LYRIC POETRY**

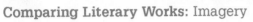

PART THREE: **THE REACTION TO SOCIETY'S ILLS**

Progress and Decline

The Victorian Period (1833 to 1901)

PART FOUR: **GLOOM AND GLORY**

PHLit Online!
www.PHLitOnline.com

Interactive resources provide personalized instruction and activities online.

A Time of Rapid Change

The Modern and Postmodern Periods (1901 to Present)

Reading for Information: Analyzing Functional and Expository Texts

PHLit Online!
www.PHLitOnline.com

Interactive resources provide personalized instruction and activities online.

Literature

► Poetry

Informational Text—Literary Nonfiction

▶ Historical and Literary Background

▶ The British Tradition—Reading in the Humanities

Informational Text—Literary Nonfiction

▶ Literature in Context—Reading in the Content Areas

▶ World Literature Connections

Comparing Across World Literature

World Literature Connection

▶ Literary History

▶ Writing Workshops

▶ Communications Workshops

▶ Vocabulary Workshops

SAT PREP ACT Test-Taking Practice

The Common Core State Standards will prepare you to succeed in college and your future career. They are separated into four sections—Reading (Literature and Informational Text), Writing, Speaking and Listening, and Language. Beginning each section, the College and Career Readiness Anchor Standards define what you need to achieve by the end of high school. The grade-specific standards that follow define what you need to know by the end of your current grade level.

Common Core Reading Standards

College and Career Readiness Anchor Standards

Key Ideas and Details

1. Read closely to determine what the text says explicitly and to make logical inferences from it; cite specific textual evidence when writing or speaking to support conclusions drawn from the text.

2. Determine central ideas or themes of a text and analyze their development; summarize the key supporting details and ideas.

3. Analyze how and why individuals, events, and ideas develop and interact over the course of a text.

Craft and Structure

4. Interpret words and phrases as they are used in a text, including determining technical, connotative, and figurative meanings, and analyze how specific word choices shape meaning or tone.

5. Analyze the structure of texts, including how specific sentences, paragraphs, and larger portions of the text (e.g., a section, chapter, scene, or stanza) relate to each other and the whole.

6. Assess how point of view or purpose shapes the content and style of a text.

Integration of Knowledge and Ideas

7. Integrate and evaluate content presented in diverse formats and media, including visually and quantitatively, as well as in words.

8. Delineate and evaluate the argument and specific claims in a text, including the validity of the reasoning as well as the relevance and sufficiency of the evidence.

9. Analyze how two or more texts address similar themes or topics in order to build knowledge or to compare the approaches the authors take.

Range of Reading and Level of Text Complexity

10. Read and comprehend complex literary and informational texts independently and proficiently.

Grade 12 Reading Standards for Literature

Key Ideas and Details

1. Cite strong and thorough textual evidence to support analysis of what the text says explicitly as well as inferences drawn from the text, including determining where the text leaves matters uncertain.

2. Determine two or more themes or central ideas of a text and analyze their development over the course of the text, including how they interact and build on one another to produce a complex account; provide an objective summary of the text.

3. Analyze the impact of the author's choices regarding how to develop and relate elements of a story or drama (e.g., where a story is set, how the action is ordered, how the characters are introduced and developed).

Craft and Structure

4. Determine the meaning of words and phrases as they are used in the text, including figurative and connotative meanings; analyze the impact of specific word choices on meaning and tone, including words with multiple meanings or language that is particularly fresh, engaging, or beautiful. (Include Shakespeare as well as other authors.)

5. Analyze how an author's choices concerning how to structure specific parts of a text (e.g., the choice of where to begin or end a story, the choice to provide a comedic or tragic resolution) contribute to its overall structure and meaning as well as its aesthetic impact.

6. Analyze a case in which grasping point of view requires distinguishing what is directly stated in a text from what is really meant (e.g., satire, sarcasm, irony, or understatement).

Integration of Knowledge and Ideas

7. Analyze multiple interpretations of a story, drama, or poem (e.g., recorded or live production of a play or recorded novel or poetry), evaluating how each version interprets the source text. (Include at least one play by Shakespeare and one play by an American dramatist.)

8. (Not applicable to literature)

9. Demonstrate knowledge of eighteenth-, nineteenth-, and early-twentieth-century foundational works of American literature, including how two or more texts from the same period treat similar themes or topics.

Range of Reading and Level of Text Complexity

10. By the end of grade 12, read and comprehend literature, including stories, dramas, and poems, at the high end of the grades 11–CCR text complexity band independently and proficiently.

Grade 12 Reading Standards for Informational Text

Key Ideas and Details

1. Cite strong and thorough textual evidence to support analysis of what the text says explicitly as well as inferences drawn from the text, including determining where the text leaves matters uncertain.

2. Determine two or more central ideas of a text and analyze their development over the course of the text, including how they interact and build on one another to provide a complex analysis; provide an objective summary of the text.

3. Analyze a complex set of ideas or sequence of events and explain how specific individuals, ideas, or events interact and develop over the course of the text.

Craft and Structure

4. Determine the meaning of words and phrases as they are used in a text, including figurative, connotative, and technical meanings; analyze how an author uses and refines the meaning of a key term or terms over the course of a text (e.g., how Madison defines *faction* in *Federalist* No. 10).

5. Analyze and evaluate the effectiveness of the structure an author uses in his or her exposition or argument, including whether the structure makes points clear, convincing, and engaging.

6. Determine an author's point of view or purpose in a text in which the rhetoric is particularly effective, analyzing how style and content contribute to the power, persuasiveness, or beauty of the text.

Integration of Knowledge and Ideas

7. Integrate and evaluate multiple sources of information presented in different media or formats (e.g., visually, quantitatively) as well as in words in order to address a question or solve a problem.

8. Delineate and evaluate the reasoning in seminal U.S. texts, including the application of constitutional principles and use of legal reasoning (e.g., in U.S. Supreme Court majority opinions and dissents) and the premises, purposes, and arguments in works of public advocacy (e.g., *The Federalist*, presidential addresses).

9. Analyze seventeenth-, eighteenth-, and nineteenth-century foundational U.S. documents of historical and literary significance (including The Declaration of Independence, the Preamble to the Constitution, the Bill of Rights, and Lincoln's Second Inaugural Address) for their themes, purposes, and rhetorical features.

Range of Reading and Level of Text Complexity

10. By the end of grade 12, read and comprehend literary nonfiction at the high end of the grades 11–CCR text complexity band independently and proficiently.

Common Core Writing Standards

College and Career Readiness Anchor Standards

Text Types and Purposes

1. Write arguments to support claims in an analysis of substantive topics or texts, using valid reasoning and relevant and sufficient evidence.

2. Write informative/explanatory texts to examine and convey complex ideas and information clearly and accurately through the effective selection, organization, and analysis of content.

3. Write narratives to develop real or imagined experiences or events using effective technique, well-chosen details, and well-structured event sequences.

Production and Distribution of Writing

4. Produce clear and coherent writing in which the development, organization, and style are appropriate to task, purpose, and audience.

5. Develop and strengthen writing as needed by planning, revising, editing, rewriting, or trying a new approach.

6. Use technology, including the Internet, to produce and publish writing and to interact and collaborate with others.

Research to Build and Present Knowledge

7. Conduct short as well as more sustained research projects based on focused questions, demonstrating understanding of the subject under investigation.

8. Gather relevant information from multiple print and digital sources, assess the credibility and accuracy of each source, and integrate the information while avoiding plagiarism.

9. Draw evidence from literary or informational texts to support analysis, reflection, and research.

Range of Writing

10. Write routinely over extended time frames (time for research, reflection, and revision) and shorter time frames (a single sitting or a day or two) for a range of tasks, purposes, and audiences.

Grade 12 Writing Standards

Text Types and Purposes

1. Write arguments to support claims in an analysis of substantive topics or texts, using valid reasoning and relevant and sufficient evidence.

   a. Introduce precise, knowledgeable claim(s), establish the significance of the claim(s), distinguish the claim(s) from alternate or opposing claims, and create an organization that logically sequences claim(s), counterclaims, reasons, and evidence.

   b. Develop claim(s) and counterclaims fairly and thoroughly, supplying the most relevant evidence for each while pointing out the strengths and limitations of both in a manner that anticipates the audience's knowledge level, concerns, values, and possible biases.

   c. Use words, phrases, and clauses as well as varied syntax to link the major sections of the text, create cohesion, and clarify the relationships between claim(s) and reasons, between reasons and evidence, and between claim(s) and counterclaims.

   d. Establish and maintain a formal style and objective tone while attending to the norms and conventions of the discipline in which they are writing.

   e. Provide a concluding statement or section that follows from and supports the argument presented.

2. Write informative/explanatory texts to examine and convey complex ideas, concepts, and information clearly and accurately through the effective selection, organization, and analysis of content.

   a. Introduce a topic; organize complex ideas, concepts, and information so that each new element builds on that which precedes it to create a unified whole; include formatting (e.g., headings), graphics (e.g., figures, tables), and multimedia when useful to aiding comprehension.

   b. Develop the topic thoroughly by selecting the most significant and relevant facts, extended definitions, concrete details, quotations, or other information and examples appropriate to the audience's knowledge of the topic.

   c. Use appropriate and varied transitions and syntax to link the major sections of the text, create cohesion, and clarify the relationships among complex ideas and concepts.

   d. Use precise language, domain-specific vocabulary, and techniques such as metaphor, simile, and analogy to manage the complexity of the topic.

   e. Establish and maintain a formal style and objective tone while attending to the norms and conventions of the discipline in which they are writing.

   f. Provide a concluding statement or section that follows from and supports the information or explanation presented (e.g., articulating implications or the significance of the topic).

3. Write narratives to develop real or imagined experiences or events using effective technique, well-chosen details, and well-structured event sequences.

   a. Engage and orient the reader by setting out a problem, situation, or observation and its significance, establishing one or multiple point(s) of view, and introducing a narrator and/or characters; create a smooth progression of experiences or events.

   b. Use narrative techniques, such as dialogue, pacing, description, reflection, and multiple plot lines, to develop experiences, events, and/or characters.

   c. Use a variety of techniques to sequence events so that they build on one another to create a coherent whole and build toward a particular tone and outcome (e.g., a sense of mystery, suspense, growth, or resolution).

   d. Use precise words and phrases, telling details, and sensory language to convey a vivid picture of the experiences, events, setting, and/or characters.

   e. Provide a conclusion that follows from and reflects on what is experienced, observed, or resolved over the course of the narrative.

Production and Distribution of Writing

4. Produce clear and coherent writing in which the development, organization, and style are appropriate to task, purpose, and audience.

5. Develop and strengthen writing as needed by planning, revising, editing, rewriting, or trying a new approach, focusing on addressing what is most significant for a specific purpose and audience.

6. Use technology, including the Internet, to produce, publish, and update individual or shared writing products in response to ongoing feedback, including new arguments or information.

Research to Build and Present Knowledge

7. Conduct short as well as more sustained research projects to answer a question (including a self-generated question) or solve a problem; narrow or broaden the inquiry when appropriate; synthesize multiple sources on the subject, demonstrating understanding of the subject under investigation.

8. Gather relevant information from multiple authoritative print and digital sources, using advanced searches effectively; assess the strengths and limitations of each source in terms of the task, purpose, and audience; integrate information into the text selectively to maintain the flow of ideas, avoiding plagiarism and overreliance on any one source and following a standard format for citation.

9. Draw evidence from literary or informational texts to support analysis, reflection, and research.

   a. Apply *grades 11–12 Reading standards* to literature (e.g., "Demonstrate knowledge of eighteenth-, nineteenth-, and early-twentieth-century foundational works of American literature, including how two or more texts from the same period treat similar themes or topics").

   b. Apply *grades 11–12 Reading standards* to literary nonfiction (e.g., "Delineate and evaluate the reasoning in seminal U.S. texts, including the application of constitutional principles and use of legal reasoning [e.g., in U.S. Supreme Court Case majority opinions and dissents] and the premises, purposes, and arguments in works of public advocacy [e.g., *The Federalist*, presidential addresses]").

Range of Writing

10. Write routinely over extended time frames (time for research, reflection, and revision) and shorter time frames (a single sitting or a day or two) for a range of tasks, purposes, and audiences.

ⓒ Common Core Speaking and Listening Standards

College and Career Readiness Anchor Standards

Comprehension and Collaboration

1. Prepare for and participate effectively in a range of conversations and collaborations with diverse partners, building on others' ideas and expressing their own clearly and persuasively.

2. Integrate and evaluate information presented in diverse media and formats, including visually, quantitatively, and orally.

3. Evaluate a speaker's point of view, reasoning, and use of evidence and rhetoric.

Presentation of Knowledge and Ideas

4. Present information, findings, and supporting evidence such that listeners can follow the line of reasoning and the organization, development, and style are appropriate to task, purpose, and audience.

5. Make strategic use of digital media and visual displays of data to express information and enhance understanding of presentations.

6. Adapt speech to a variety of contexts and communicative tasks, demonstrating command of formal English when indicated or appropriate.

Grade 12 Speaking and Listening Standards

Comprehension and Collaboration

1. Initiate and participate effectively in a range of collaborative discussions (one-on-one, in groups, and teacher-led) with diverse partners on *grades 11–12 topics, texts, and issues,* building on others' ideas and expressing their own clearly and persuasively.

   a. Come to discussions prepared, having read and researched material under study; explicitly draw on that preparation by referring to evidence from texts and other research on the topic or issue to stimulate a thoughtful, wellreasoned exchange of ideas.

   b. Work with peers to promote civil, democratic discussions and decision-making, set clear goals and deadlines, and establish individual roles as needed.

   c. Propel conversations by posing and responding to questions that probe reasoning and evidence; ensure a hearing for a full range of positions on a topic or issue; clarify, verify, or challenge ideas and conclusions; and promote divergent and creative perspectives.

   d. Respond thoughtfully to diverse perspectives; synthesize comments, claims, and evidence made on all sides of an issue; resolve contradictions when possible; and determine what additional information or research is required to deepen the investigation or complete the task.

2. Integrate multiple sources of information presented in diverse formats and media (e.g., visually, quantitatively, orally) in order to make informed decisions and solve problems, evaluating the credibility and accuracy of each source and noting any discrepancies among the data.

3. Evaluate a speaker's point of view, reasoning, and use of evidence and rhetoric, assessing the stance, premises, links among ideas, word choice, points of emphasis, and tone used.

Presentation of Knowledge and Ideas

4. Present information, findings, and supporting evidence, conveying a clear and distinct perspective, such that listeners can follow the line of reasoning, alternative or opposing perspectives are addressed, and the organization, development, substance, and style are appropriate to purpose, audience, and a range of formal and informal tasks.

5. Make strategic use of digital media (e.g., textual, graphical, audio, visual, and interactive elements) in presentations to enhance understanding of findings, reasoning, and evidence and to add interest.

6. Adapt speech to a variety of contexts and tasks, demonstrating a command of formal English when indicated or appropriate. (See grades 11–12 Language standards 1 and 3 for specific expectations.)

©Common Core Language Standards

College and Career Readiness Anchor Standards

Conventions of Standard English

1. Demonstrate command of the conventions of standard English grammar and usage when writing or speaking.

2. Demonstrate command of the conventions of standard English capitalization, punctuation, and spelling when writing.

Knowledge of Language

3. Apply knowledge of language to understand how language functions in different contexts, to make effective choices for meaning or style, and to comprehend more fully when reading or listening.

Vocabulary Acquisition and Use

4. Determine or clarify the meaning of unknown and multiple-meaning words and phrases by using context clues, analyzing meaningful word parts, and consulting general and specialized reference materials, as appropriate.

5. Demonstrate understanding of figurative language, word relationships, and nuances in word meanings.

6. Acquire and use accurately a range of general academic and domain-specific words and phrases sufficient for reading, writing, speaking, and listening at the college and career readiness level; demonstrate independence in gathering vocabulary knowledge when considering a word or phrase important to comprehension or expression.

Grade 12 Language Standards

Conventions of Standard English

1. Demonstrate command of the conventions of standard English grammar and usage when writing or speaking.
   a. Apply the understanding that usage is a matter of convention, can change over time, and is sometimes contested.
   b. Resolve issues of complex or contested usage, consulting references (e.g., *Merriam-Webster's Dictionary of English Usage, Garner's Modern American Usage*) as needed.

2. Demonstrate command of the conventions of standard English capitalization, punctuation, and spelling when writing.
   a. Observe hyphenation conventions.
   b. Spell correctly.

Knowledge of Language

3. Apply knowledge of language to understand how language functions in different contexts, to make effective choices for meaning or style, and to comprehend more fully when reading or listening.

    a. Vary syntax for effect, consulting references (e.g., Tufte's *Artful Sentences*) for guidance as needed; apply an understanding of syntax to the study of complex texts when reading.

Vocabulary Acquisition and Use

4. Determine or clarify the meaning of unknown and multiple-meaning words and phrases based on *grades 11–12 reading and content,* choosing flexibly from a range of strategies.

    a. Use context (e.g., the overall meaning of a sentence, paragraph, or text; a word's position or function in a sentence) as a clue to the meaning of a word or phrase.

    b. Identify and correctly use patterns of word changes that indicate different meanings or parts of speech (e.g., *conceive, conception, conceivable*).

    c. Consult general and specialized reference materials (e.g., dictionaries, glossaries, thesauruses), both print and digital, to find the pronunciation of a word or determine or clarify its precise meaning, its part of speech, its etymology, or its standard usage.

    d. Verify the preliminary determination of the meaning of a word or phrase (e.g., by checking the inferred meaning in context or in a dictionary).

5. Demonstrate understanding of figurative language, word relationships, and nuances in word meanings.

    a. Interpret figures of speech (e.g., hyperbole, paradox) in context and analyze their role in the text.

    b. Analyze nuances in the meaning of words with similar denotations.

6. Acquire and use accurately general academic and domain-specific words and phrases, sufficient for reading, writing, speaking, and listening at the college and career readiness level; demonstrate independence in gathering vocabulary knowledge when considering a word or phrase important to comprehension or expression.

Introductory Unit

COMMON CORE
Workshops

Building Academic Vocabulary

Writing an Objective Summary

Comprehending Complex Texts

Analyzing Arguments

Common Core
State Standards

Reading Literature 2, 4
Reading Informational Text 2, 4, 6, 8, 9
Writing 1.a, 1.b, 1.e, 9, 9.b
Language 6

Building Academic Vocabulary

Academic vocabulary is the language used in school, on standardized tests, and—often—in the business world. Academic terms are more formal and specific than the informal vocabulary most people use among friends and family members. Success in school and later in work requires a clear understanding of different types of academic language. The Common Core State Standards require that you acquire and use grade-appropriate academic words and phrases.

Technical Domain-Specific Academic Vocabulary The literary concepts you will learn throughout this book are one type of academic language. These words are specific to the content area—the subject or discipline—of literature. Other disciplines, such as social studies, the sciences, mathematics, and the arts, have their own academic vocabularies. Some content-area words cross disciplines, or have different meanings when applied to different areas of study.

Technical words are an even more specialized type of domain-specific academic vocabulary. These are words and phrases, such as the following, that identify a precise element in the content area and usually do not appear in other disciplines:

Science: pipette; genome
Music: clef; libretto

Critical Reading and Thinking Terms Many academic terms define modes of thinking, discussing, or writing about ideas. In this book, these words appear in the Critical Reading questions at the ends of the selections. Such academic terms also appear in instructions and writing prompts.

 Common Core State Standards

Language 6. Acquire and use accurately general academic and domain-specific words and phrases, sufficient for reading, writing, speaking, and listening at the college and career readiness level; demonstrate independence in gathering vocabulary knowledge when considering a word or phrase important to comprehension or expression.

A Note on Etymology

Etymology is the branch of linguistics that deals with word origins and the development of languages. Etymologists trace the history of a word in its own language, and then to even earlier sources in other, more ancient languages. Knowledge of a word's etymology will contribute to your understanding of its meaning and help you determine the meaning of other words that share its history. Etymological information for content-area words appears in the charts on the following pages.

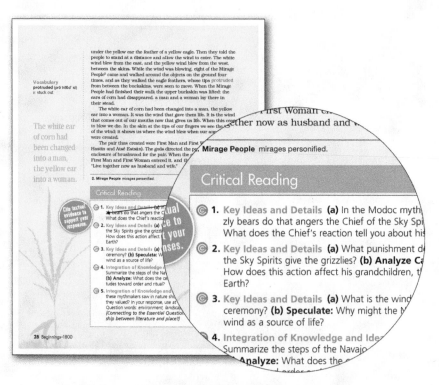

Technical Domain-Specific Academic Vocabulary

Knowledge of technical content-area academic words, and the roots and affixes that compose them, will help you in all your school courses. As you review the charts below, recognize words that apply to content areas other than those specified here.

Technical Domain-Specific Academic Vocabulary: Science

Term	Meaning	Root/Affix
Accelerate	*v.* increase speed	Latin root *-celer-* = swift Words with the same root: accelerator *n.*; celerity *n.*
Catalyst	*n.* something that acts to bring about a result	Latin root *-cata-* = down; away Words with the same root: cataclysm *n.*; catapult *n.*
Chlorophyll	*n.* green pigment found in plant cells	Greek root *-chloro-* = green Words with the same root: chlorine *n.*; chlorosis *n.*
Chromosome	*n.* strand of proteins that carries the genes of a living creature	Greek prefix *chromo-* = color; pigment Words with the same prefix: chromatic *adj.*; chromate *n.*
Cytoplasm	*n.* colorless substance of a cell; outside the nucleus	Greek suffix *-plasm* = molded; formed Words with the same suffix: bioplasm *n.*; protoplasm *n.*
Entropy	*n.* lack of order which increases over time in a system	Greek root *-tropos-* = turning; deviation Words with the same root: tropical *adj.*; trophy *n.*; heliotrope *n.*
Enzyme	*n.* chemical substance produced by living cells that causes changes in other chemicals	Greek suffix *-zyme* = leavening (an agent that causes fermentation) Words with the same suffix: vitazyme *n.*; microzyme *n.*
Mitosis	*n.* method of cell division	Greek suffix *-osis* = action; process Words with the same suffix: prognosis *n.*; psychosis *n.*
Thermometer	*n.* instrument for measuring temperature	Greek root *-therme-* = hot Words with the same root: thermonuclear *adj.*; thermostat *n.*
Viscous	*adj.* having a thick and sticky fluid consistency	Latin prefix *visco-* = sticky Words with the same prefix: viscometer *n.*; viscosity *n.*

Ordinary Language: Ice cubes placed in water will begin to break down.

Academic Language: Ice cubes placed in water will begin the process of entropy.

Exploring Academic Vocabulary: Science

The word *thermometer* combines the Greek roots *-therme-*, which means "heat," and *-metr-*, which means "measure." Using this knowledge, determine the meaning of the following words derived from the same roots:

dynameter   **odometer**   **hypothermia**   **thermography**

Then, use a dictionary to confirm the definitions you proposed. If a general dictionary is not sufficient, consult a specialized science dictionary to find the information you need. Explain how the meaning of each word relates to those of its Greek origins.

Technical Domain-Specific Academic Vocabulary: Mathematics

Term	Meaning	Root/Affix
Correlate	v. show mutual relationship between items	Latin prefix cor- = together; with Words with the same prefix: correspond v.; corrosion n.
Exponent	n. symbol placed above and to the right of a number or letter to show how many times that quantity is to be multiplied by itself	Latin suffix -ponent = to put; place; set Words with the same suffix: component n.; proponent n.
Inflection	n. change of a curve or arc from convex to concave or the reverse	Latin root -flectere- = to bend Words with the same root: reflection n.; deflect v.
Logarithm	n. power to which a base must be raised to produce a given number	Greek prefix logos- = word; speech; reason Words with the same prefix: logic n.; logotype n.
Statistics	n. numerical facts or data	Latin root -stat- = condition; position; state Words with the same root: statistical adj.; static adj.
Permutation	n. one of the ways in which a set of things can be arranged or ordered	Latin root -mutare- = change Words with the same root: mutable adj.; mutation n.
Estimate	v. calculate approximately	Middle French root -estimer- = value; appraise Words with the same root: estimation n.; esteem v.
Graphic	adj. relating to the use of diagrams, graphs, curves	Greek root -graph- = writing; drawing Words with the same root: telegraph n.; biography n.; autograph n.
Configure	v. construct; arrange	Latin root -figura- = shape; form; figure Words with the same root: disfigure v.; effigy n.

Ordinary Language: We arranged the numerical information in different charts.

Academic Language: We incorporated statistical data into charts.

Exploring Academic Vocabulary: Mathematics

The word *correlate* is built on the Latin prefix *cor-* (also *com-* or *con-*), which means "with" or "together." Using this knowledge, determine the meaning of the following words derived from the same prefix:

correspond   **concert**   **compress**   **congruent**

Then, use an online or print dictionary to confirm the definitions you proposed. Explain how the meaning of each word relates to that of its Latin ancestor.

Technical Domain-Specific Academic Vocabulary: Social Studies

Term	Meaning	Root/Affix
Corporation	*n.* organization of many people authorized to act as a single person	Latin root -*corpus*- = body Words with the same root: corporeal *adj.*; incorporate *v.*
Demography	*n.* study of human populations	Greek prefix *demos*- = people Words with the same prefix: demographic *n.*; democracy *n.*
Economy	*n.* system by which a country's money and goods are used and produced	Greek suffix -*nomy* = law; received knowledge Words with the same suffix: economy *n.*; taxonomy *n.*
Invest	*v.* give money to a company in order to receive a profit	Latin root -*vestire*- = dress; clothe Words with the same root: vestment *n.*; investigation *n.*
Admiral	*n.* high-ranking naval officer	Arabic root -*amir*- = leader Words with the same root: emirate *n.;* admiralship *n.*
Curfew	*n.* law requiring a population to stay indoors at a stated hour	Old French root -*covrir*- = to cover Words with the same root: covert *adj.*; coverlet *n.*
Lieutenant	*n.* someone who substitutes for another person of greater authority	Old French root -*lieu*- = place Word with the same root: milieu *n.*
Absolutism	*n.* system of government in which a ruler has unlimited power	Latin prefix *ab*- = away; from Words with the same prefix: absolve *v.*
Civic	*adj.* of a city, citizens, or citizenship	Latin root -*civ*- = citizen Words with the same root: civilian *n.*; civilization *n.*

Ordinary Language: The government urges citizens to put money into local businesses.

Academic Language: The government urges citizens to invest in local businesses.

Exploring Academic Vocabulary: Social Studies

The word *economy* is built on the Greek suffix –*nomy*, which means "law; body of received knowledge." Using this knowledge, determine the meaning of the following words derived from the same suffix:

taxonomy   autonomy   astronomy   gastronomy

Then, use an online or print dictionary to confirm the definitions you proposed. Explain how the meaning of each word relates to that of its Greek ancestor.

Technical Domain-Specific Academic Vocabulary: Technology

Term	Meaning	Root/Affix
Gigabyte	*n.* unit of storage capacity in a computer system equal to 1,073,741,824 bytes	Greek prefix *giga-* = giant Words with the same prefix: gigahertz *n.*; gigantic *adj.*
Macro	*n.* single computer instruction that represents a sequence of operations	Greek prefix *macro-* = long, tall, deep, large Words with the same prefix: macrobiotic *adj.*; macrocosm *n.*
Pixel	*n.* smallest unit of an image on a television or computer screen	Old French suffix *–el* = small one Words with the same suffix: satchel *n.*; model *n.*
Processor	*n.* central part of a computer that does the calculations needed to deal with the information it is given	from Latin root *-cedere-* = to go Words with the same root: proceed *v.*; recede *v.*
Simulation	*n.* situation that produces conditions that are not real but appear real	Latin root *-sim-* = like derived through Indo-European base *sem-/som-* = same; as one Words with the same root: ensemble *v.*; simultaneous *adj.*
Streaming	*n.* method of transmitting data so that it can be delivered and received in a steady stream	German root *-strom-* = current; river Words with the same root: mainstream *n.*; streamline *v.*
Transmitter	*n.* equipment that sends out radio or television signals	Latin prefix *trans-* = across Words with the same prefix: transportation *n.*; transcontinental *adj.*
Debug	*v.* find and correct defects	Latin prefix *de-* = down; from Words with the same prefix: defuse *v.*; defrost *v.*
Export	*v.* in computers, to save data in a format usable by another program	Latin root *-portare-* = to carry Words with the same root: import *v.*; airport *n.*
Binary	*adj.* made up of two parts or things; twofold	Latin root *-bin-* = together; double Words with the same root: binocular *n.*; binomial *n.*

Ordinary Language:
I asked the technician to clean up my computer.

Academic Language:
I asked the technician to debug my operating system.

Exploring Academic Vocabulary: Technology

The word *simulation* comes from the Latin root *-sim-,* which means "like." This Latin root derives from the Indo-European base *sem-/som-,* which means "same; as one." Using your knowledge of these origins, determine the meaning of the following words derived from the same roots:

resemble   **facsimile**   **verisimilitude**   **semblance**

Then, use a dictionary to confirm the definitions you proposed. Explain how the meaning of each word relates to that of its Indo-European base.

Technical Domain-Specific Academic Vocabulary: The Arts

Term	Meaning	Root/Affix
Allegro	*adv.* faster than allegretto but not so fast as presto	Latin root -*alacer-*/-*alacris-* = lively; brisk Words with the same root: allegretto *adj.*; *adv.*; alacrity *n.*
Alignment	*n.* arrangement in a straight line	Old French root -*lignier-* = to line Words with the same root: align *v.*; realign *v.*
Craftmanship	*n.* skill used in making handmade objects	Middle English suffix -*schipe*; derived through Anglian suffix -*scip* = state; condition; quality Words with the same suffix: friendship *n.*; dictatorship *n.*
Decrescendo	*n.* gradual decrease in volume	Old French *creissant*; derived through Latin root -*crescere-* = come forth; spring up; grow; thrive Words with the same root: crescent *n.*; increase *v.*
Baritone	*n.* male singing voice lower than a tenor and higher than a bass	Latin root -*tonus-* = sound; tone Words with the same root: monotone *n.*; intonation *n.*
Medium	*n.* material or technique used in art	Latin root -*medius-* = middle Words with the same root: media *n.*; mediate *v.*; median *adj.*
Musicality	*n.* sensitivity to, knowledge of, or talent for music	Latin suffix -*ity* = quality; state; or degree Words with the same suffix: normality *n.*; publicity *n.*
Technique	*n.* method or procedure in rendering an artistic work	Indo-European prefix *tek-* = shape; make Words with the same prefix: technical *adj.*; technician *n.*
Tempo	*n.* speed at which a composition is performed	Latin root -*tempus-* = time Words with the same root: temporal *adj.*; temporary *adj.*

Ordinary Language: The dancers moved in a perfectly straight line.

Academic Language: The dancers moved in perfect alignment on stage.

Exploring Academic Vocabulary: The Arts

The word *craftsmanship* is built on the Anglian suffix –*scip*, which means "state, condition, quality." Using this knowledge, determine the meaning of the following words derived from the same suffix:

musicianship   **readership**   **friendship**   **partnership**

Then, use an online or print dictionary to confirm the definitions you proposed. Explain how the meaning of each word relates to that of its Anglian ancestor.

Vocabulary Across Content Areas

You might recognize words that apply to content areas other than those specified in the charts on the previous pages. For example, notice how the word *accelerator* relates to two different content areas:

Science: accelerator *n.* nerve or muscle that speeds up a body function

Automotive Technology: accelerator *n.* device, such as the foot throttle of an automobile, for increasing the speed of a machine

While the objects referred to in each definition are different, both of their functions relate to the Latin root *–celer–,* meaning "swift." As you read texts for school, recognize similarities in roots or affixes among words in different content areas. This will help you better understand specific terms and make meaningful connections among topics.

Academic Vocabulary: Critical Thinking Terms

Throughout this book, you will encounter academic vocabulary related to the process of critical thinking. Unlike content-area vocabulary, these words apply equally in all school studies. Being familiar with these academic vocabulary words will be useful as you approach high-stakes standardized tests such as the SAT and ACT. Academic vocabulary will also aid you as you encounter business materials in the workplace.

Term (verb form)	Meaning	Root/Affix
Advocate	Speak or write in support of	Latin root *-voc-* = speak; call Related words: advocate *n.*; advocacy *n.*
Anticipate	Prepare for or signal something	Latin prefix *ante-* = before Related words: anticipatory *adj.*; anticipation *n.*
Arrange	Put into order or sequence	Old French root *-rang-* = rank Related words: arrangement *n.*
Assess	Determine importance; size; or value	Latin root *-sed-/-sess-* = sit Related words: assessment *n.*
Categorize	Place in related groups	Greek prefix *kata-/cata-* = down; against Related words: category *n.*; categorical *adj.*
Compare	Examine in order to discover similarities	Latin root *-par-* = equal Related words: comparison *n.*; comparable *adj.*
Conclude	Determination reached through logical reasoning	Latin root *-clud-* = shut Related words: conclusion *n.*; conclusive *adj.*
Contrast	Examine in order to discover differences	Latin prefix *con-/com-* = with; together Related words: contrastable *adj.*
Debate	Discuss opposing reasons; argue	French root *-batre-* = to beat Related words: debatable *adj.*

Term (verb form)	Meaning	Root/Affix
Deduce	Infer from a general principle	Latin root -*duc*- = to lead Related words: deduction *n.*; deductive *adj.*
Defend	Maintain or support in the face of argument	Latin root -*fend*- = to strike; push Related words: defense *n.*; defendant *n.*
Describe	Represent in words	Latin root -*scrib*- = to write Related words: description *n.*; descriptive *adj.*
Design	Create; fashion or construct according to plan	Latin root -*sign*- = to mark Related words: design *n.*; designer *n.*
Devise	Form in the mind by new combinations of ideas; invent	Latin root -*vid*- = to separate Related words: devisable *adj.*
Differentiate	Recognize a difference	Latin suffix -*ate* = act Related words: different *adj.*; differentiation *n.*
Evaluate	Determine significance, worth, or condition through careful study	Old French root -*val*- = worth; value Related words: evaluation *n.*; evaluative *adj.*
Format	Arrange according to a design or plan	Latin root -*form*- = form, shape Related words: format *n.*; formation *n.*
Generalize	Draw a larger principle from details	Latin root -*genus*- = stock; kind Related words: generalization *n.*
Hypothesize	Develop a theory about	Greek prefix *hypo*- = under, beneath Related words: hypothesis *n.*; hypothetically *adv.*
Illustrate	Give examples that support an idea	Latin root -*lus*- = brighten; illuminate Related words: illustration *n.*; illustrative *adj.*
Interpret	Explain the meaning of	Latin root -*inter*- = between Related words: interpretation *n.*; interpreter *n.*
Investigate	Make a systematic examination	French root -*vestige*- = mark; trace; sign Related words: investigation *n.*; investigative *adj.*
Paraphrase	Express in one's own words what another person has said or written	Greek prefix *para*- = beside Related words: paraphraser *n.*
Predict	Foretell on the basis of observation, experience, or reason	Latin root -*dic*- = speak, tell, say Related words: prediction *n.*; predictable *adj.*
Refute	Prove an argument or statement false or wrong	Latin root -*fut*- = beat Related words: refutable *adj.*; refutably *adv.*
Sort	Put in place according to kind, class, or nature	Old French root -*sortir*- = allot; assort Related words: sorter *n.*
Speculate	Use evidence to guess what might happen	Latin root -*spec*- = look at; view Related words: speculation *n.*; speculative *adj.*
Structure	Create a general plot or outline	Latin root -*struct*- = to build; assemble Related words: structure *n.*; structural *adj.*
Validate	Prove to be factual or effective	Latin root -*val*- = be strong Related words: valid *adj.*; validity *n.*

Ordinary Language:
She explained the meaning of the story's symbols.

Academic Language:
She interpreted the meaning of the story's symbols.

Writing an Objective Summary

The ability to write objective summaries is important in college course work and in many careers, such as journalism, business, law, various medical fields, social work, and research. Writing an effective objective summary involves recording the key ideas of a text as well as demonstrating your understanding of the text.

Characteristics of an Objective Summary

An effective objective summary is a concise, overview of a text. Following are important elements of an objective summary:

- It is **focused,** relaying the main theme or central idea of a text. It includes specific, relevant details that support that theme or central idea and leaves out unnecessary supporting details.
- It is **brief,** although the writer must be careful to balance brevity and thoroughness and not misrepresent the text by eliminating important parts.
- It is **accurate.** It captures the essence of the longer text it is describing.
- It is **objective.** The writer should refrain from inserting his or her own opinions, judgments, reactions, or personal reflections into the summary.

Remember that an objective summary is *not* a collection of sentences or paragraphs copied from the original source. It is *not* a long retelling of every event, detail, or point in the original text. Finally, a good summary does *not* include evaluative comments, such as the reader's overall opinion of or reaction to the text.

Checklist for Writing an Objective Summary

Before writing an objective summary, be sure you are well acquainted with the text.

- **Understand the entire passage.** You must clearly understand the text's meaning, including any advanced or technical terminology. In your summary, refer to details from the beginning, middle, and end of the text.
- **Prioritize ideas and details.** Determine the main or central ideas of a text and identify the key supporting details. Make sure you recognize which details are less important so that you do not include them in your objective summary.
- **Identify the author's audience and purpose.** Knowing what the author intended to accomplish in the text as well as what audience it was designed to reach will help you summarize accurately.

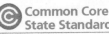

Common Core State Standards

Reading Informational Text
2. Determine two or more central ideas of a text and analyze their development over the course of the text, including how they interact and build on one another to provide a complex analysis; provide an objective summary of the text.

Reading Literature
2. Determine two or more themes or central ideas of a text and analyze their development over the course of the text, including how they interact and build on one another to produce a complex account; provide an objective summary of the text.

INFORMATIONAL TEXT

Model Objective Summary

Note the key elements of an effective objective summary, called out in the sidenotes. Then, write an objective summary of a text you have recently read. Review your summary, and delete any unnecessary details, opinions, or evaluations.

Summary of "The Story of an Hour"

"The Story of an Hour" by ~~the under-appreciated~~ Kate Chopin is a short story about a woman who is told her husband is dead. Set in the late nineteenth century, the story takes place in the home of Mrs. Louise Mallard.

Because of Mrs. Mallard's heart condition, her sister Josephine tells her the news gently. Richards, a family friend, had been in the newspaper office when a telegram was received that told of a railroad disaster, and Brently Mallard was listed as dead. Mrs. Mallard immediately takes in the news and begins to weep, heading to her room alone.

She sits in an armchair and looks out the window. She notices signs of life everywhere, which contrast with her loss. ~~It is so very sad.~~

Then a thought begins to come to her as she looks at the blue patches in the sky. She breathes heavily as she struggles with the full comprehension of the thought that is trying to possess her, but she gives in. She whispers the word: "Free." She repeats the word over and over. Her eyes brighten, her heart beats quickly, and her body relaxes.

She decides that she will cry at the dead body of the man who loved her, but she welcomes the years beyond that. She looks forward to living independently. The thought of freedom is exhilarating.

Josephine begs her to open the door, but Louise refuses.

She imagines the days ahead and prays that her life will be long, remembering that the day before she had dreaded the thought of a long life. She finally lets her sister in ~~and holds her tight around her waist~~. Together they go downstairs to meet Richards.

Brently Mallard, alive and unharmed, then walks through the front door. He was unaware of the accident at the railroad and surprised at the cry of his wife.

The doctors said her weak heart could not stand such joy; they called it the "joy that kills."

A one-sentence synopsis highlighting the theme or central idea of the story can be an effective start to a summary. Relating the setting of the text gives the summary context.

Opinions should not be included in an objective summary.

These sentences are too detailed and too interpretative to be included in an objective summary. More appropriate would be a simpler statement, such as, "Suddenly a thought came to her."

Eliminate unnecessary details.

The writer includes the last phrase in the story because the irony is a key element of the story.

Comprehending Complex Texts

As you prepare for higher education and the workplace, you will be required to read increasingly complex texts. A complex text features one or more of the following qualities:

- challenging vocabulary
- long, complex sentences
- figurative language
- multiple levels of meaning
- unfamiliar settings and situations

The selections in this textbook provide you with a range of readings in many genres. Some of these texts will be quite accessible, while others will be, and should be, more challenging. In order to comprehend and interpret complex texts, practice the reading strategies described here.

Strategy 1: Multi-draft Reading

Good readers develop the habit of rereading texts in order to comprehend them completely. Similar to listening to a song over and over in order to better understand the lyrics and relive the emotional experience, returning to a text enables readers to more fully enjoy and comprehend it. To fully understand a text, try this multi-draft reading strategy:

1st Reading

The first time you read a text, read to gain its basic meaning. If you are reading a narrative text, look for the basics of the plot, character, and setting. If the text is nonfiction, look for central ideas. If you are reading poetry, read first to get a sense of speaker, topic, and mood.

2nd Reading

During your second reading of a text, look for deeper meaning by applying your literary analysis skills. Focus on the artistry or effectiveness of the writing. Look for text structures. Think about why the author chose those organizational patterns. Examine the author's use of language and its effect. For example, consider the effect of rhyme, figurative language, or words with distinct connotations.

3rd Reading

In this reading, search for multiple levels of meaning, considering historical and cultural context. Now is the time to compare and contrast the text with others of its kind you have read. Consider it in the context of its genre, and make connections between texts. You may also make connections between the text and your own experiences. After your third reading, you should be able to evaluate the text's overall effectiveness and its central idea or theme.

**Common Core
State Standards**

Reading Literature
4. Determine the meaning of words and phrases as they are used in the text, including figurative and connotative meanings; analyze the impact of specific word choices on meaning and tone, including words with multiple meanings or language that is particularly fresh, engaging, or beautiful.

Reading Informational Text
4. Determine the meaning of words and phrases as they are used in a text, including figurative, connotative, and technical meanings; analyze how an author uses and refines the meaning of a key term or terms over the course of a text (e.g., how Madison defines *faction* in *Federalist* No. 10).

9. Analyze seventeenth-, eighteenth- and nineteenth-century foundational U.S. documents of historical and literary significance (including the Declaration of Independence, the Preamble to the Constitution, the Bill of Rights, and Lincoln's Second Inaugural Address) for their themes, purposes, and rhetorical features.

Independent Practice

As you read this poem by John Keats, practice the multi-draft reading strategy by completing a chart like the one below.

On the Grasshopper and Cricket
by John Keats

The poetry of earth is never dead:

When all the birds are faint with the hot sun,

And hide in cooling trees, a voice will run

From hedge to hedge about the new-mown mead;

That is the Grasshopper's—he takes the lead

In summer luxury—he has never done

With his delights; for when tired out with fun

He rests at ease beneath some pleasant weed.

The poetry of earth is ceasing never:

On a lone winter evening, when the frost

Has wrought a silence, from the stove there shrills

The Cricket's song, in warmth increasing ever,

And seems to one in drowsiness half lost,

The Grasshopper's among some grassy hills.

Multi-Draft Reading Chart

	My Understanding
1st Reading Look for key ideas and details that reveal basic meaning.	
2nd Reading Read for deeper meanings. Look for ways in which the author used text structures and language to create effects.	
3rd Reading Integrate knowledge and ideas. Consider cultural and historical context and genre. Connect the text to your own experience.	

Strategy 2: Close Read the Text

Complex texts require close reading and a careful analysis of the writer's choice of words, phrases, and sentences. An awareness of literary and rhetorical techniques and elements, such as parallelism, symbolism, analogy, and text structure, contributes to a deep understanding of a complex text. However, a starting point for close reading is comprehension, which is the foundation for interpretation and analysis. Use the following tips to comprehend the text:

Tips for Close Reading

1. **Break down long sentences into parts.** Look for the subject of the sentence and its verb. Then identify which parts of the sentence modify, or give more information about, its subject.

2. **Reread passages.** When reading complex texts, be sure to reread passages to confirm that you understand their meaning. Look for rhetorical devices and persuasive techniques.

3. **Look for context clues,** such as
   a. Restatement of an idea. For example, in this sentence, *small* restates the adjective *diminutive*.

      She received only a **diminutive** sum, but she was able to make the small amount last the rest of the month.

   b. Definition of sophisticated words. In this sentence, the word *depravity* defines the verb *turpitude*.

      The **turpitude**, or depravity, of the young character in the film stunned the audience to silence.

   c. Examples of concepts and topics. In the following sentence, the underlined text provides examples of words that suggest the meaning of the adjective *melancholy*.

      The **melancholy** territory of gothic literature includes gloomy settings, eerie occurrences, and emotionally troubled characters.

   d. Contrasts of ideas and topics.

      Their **banter** evolved into a serious conversation.

4. **Identify pronoun antecedents.** If long sentences contain pronouns, reread the text to make sure you know to what the pronouns refer. The pronoun *it* in the following sentence refers to the infinitive phrase *to protest injustices,* not to the government.

   The government should assume that **it** is not harmful to protest injustices. (The government should assume that to protest injustices is not harmful.)

5. **Look for conjunctions,** such as *and, or, however, accordingly,* and *yet,* to help you understand relationships between ideas.

6. **Paraphrase,** or restate in your own words, passages of difficult text in order to check your understanding. Remember that a paraphrase is essentially a word-for-word restatement of an original text; it is not a summary.

INFORMATIONAL TEXT

Close-Read Model

As you read this document, take note of the sidenotes that model ways to unlock meaning in the text.

from "Defending Nonviolent Resistance" by Mohandas K. Gandhi

Affection cannot be manufactured or regulated by law. If one has an affection for a person or system, one should be free to give the fullest expression to his disaffection, so long as he does not contemplate, promote, or incite to violence. But the section under which Mr. Banker [a colleague in nonviolence] and I are charged is one under which mere promotion of disaffection is as crime. I have studied some of the cases tried under it, and I know that some of the most loved of India's patriots have been convicted under it. I consider it a privilege, therefore, to be charged under that section. I have endeavored to give in their briefest outline the reasons for my disaffection. I have no personal ill will against any single administrator, much less can I have any disaffection toward the king's person. But I hold it to be a virtue to be disaffected toward a government which in its totality has done more harm to India than any previous system. India is less manly under the British rule than she ever was before. Holding such a belief, I consider it to be a sin to have affection for the system. And it has been a precious privilege for me to be able to write what I have in the various articles, tendered in evidence against me.

In fact, I believe that I have rendered a service to India and England by showing in non-cooperation the way out of the unnatural state in which both are living. In my humble opinion, non-cooperation with evil is as much a duty as is cooperation with good. But in the past, non-cooperation has been deliberately expressed in violence to the evildoer. I am endeavoring to show to my countrymen that violent non-cooperation only multiplies evil and that as evil can only be sustained by violence, withdrawal of support of evil requires complete abstention from violence. Nonviolence implies voluntary submission to the penalty for non-cooperation with evil. I am here, therefore, to invite and submit cheerfully to the highest penalty that be inflicted upon me for what in law is a deliberate crime and what appears to me to be the highest duty of a citizen. The only course open to you, the judge, is either to resign your post, and thus dissociate yourself from evil if you feel that the law you are called upon to administer is an evil and that in reality I am innocent, or to inflict on me the severest penalty if you believe that the system and the law you are assisting to administer are good for the people of this country and that my activity is therefore injurious to the public weal.

Note rhetorical devices, such as Gandhi's use of antithesis—connecting contrasting ideas—here.

The conjunction *But* indicates a contrasting idea: Gandhi has no ill will toward a single person, but he does have disaffection toward the totality of the government.

Look for antecedents. The antecedent of the first *it* comes after the pronoun: *to be disaffected toward a government...* The antecedent of the second *it* is *government*.

Search for context clues. The words in blue are context clues that help you figure out the meaning of the word that appears in yellow.

Break down this long sentence into parts. The text highlighted in yellow conveys the basic meaning of the sentence. The text highlighted in blue provides additional information.

Strategy 3: Ask Questions

Be an attentive reader by asking questions as you read. Throughout this program, we have provided questions for you following each selection. Those questions are sorted into three basic categories that build in sophistication and lead you to a deeper understanding of the texts. Here is an example from this textbook:

Some questions are about **Key Ideas and Details** in the text. You will need to locate and cite explicit information in the text or draw inferences from what you have read.

Some questions are about **Craft and Structure** in the text. To answer these questions, you will need to analyze how the author developed and structured the text. You will also look for ways in which the author artfully used language and how those word choices impacted the meaning and tone of the work.

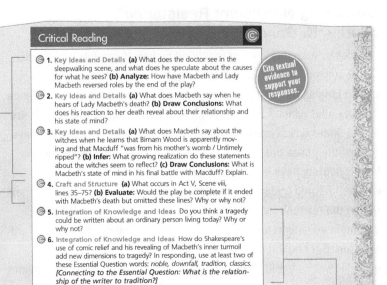

Critical Reading

1. Key Ideas and Details (a) What does the doctor see in the sleepwalking scene, and what does he speculate about the causes for what he sees? **(b) Analyze:** How have Macbeth and Lady Macbeth reversed roles by the end of the play?

2. Key Ideas and Details (a) What does Macbeth say when he hears of Lady Macbeth's death? **(b) Draw Conclusions:** What does his reaction to her death reveal about their relationship and his state of mind?

3. Key Ideas and Details (a) What does Macbeth say about the witches when he learns that Birnam Wood is apparently moving and that Macduff "was from his mother's womb / Untimely ripped"? **(b) Infer:** What growing realization do these statements about the witches seem to reflect? **(c) Draw Conclusions:** What is Macbeth's state of mind in his final battle with Macduff? Explain.

4. Craft and Structure (a) What occurs in Act V, Scene viii, lines 35–75? **(b) Evaluate:** Would the play be complete if it ended with Macbeth's death but omitted these lines? Why or why not?

5. Integration of Knowledge and Ideas Do you think a tragedy could be written about an ordinary person living today? Why or why not?

6. Integration of Knowledge and Ideas How do Shakespeare's use of comic relief and his revealing of Macbeth's inner turmoil add new dimensions to tragedy? In responding, use at least two of these Essential Question words: *noble, downfall, tradition, classics.* *[Connecting to the Essential Question: What is the relationship of the writer to tradition?]*

Cite textual evidence to support your responses.

Some questions are about the **Integration of Knowledge and Ideas** in the text. These questions ask you to evaluate a text in many different ways, such as comparing texts, analyzing arguments in the text, and using many other methods of thinking critically about a text's ideas.

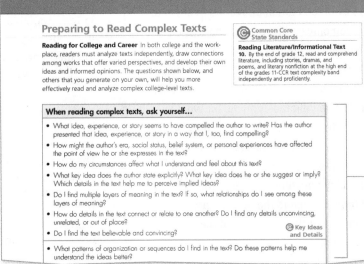

Preparing to Read Complex Texts

Reading for College and Career In both college and the workplace, readers must analyze texts independently, draw connections among works that offer varied perspectives, and develop their own ideas and informed opinions. The questions shown below, and others that you generate on your own, will help you more effectively read and analyze complex college-level texts.

Common Core State Standards

Reading Literature/Informational Text
10. By the end of grade 12, read and comprehend literature, including stories, dramas, and poems, and literary nonfiction at the high end of the grades 11-CCR text complexity band independently and proficiently.

When reading complex texts, ask yourself...

- What idea, experience, or story seems to have compelled the author to write? Has the author presented that idea, experience, or story in a way that I, too, find compelling?
- How might the author's era, social status, belief system, or personal experiences have affected the point of view he or she expresses in the text?
- How do my circumstances affect what I understand and feel about this text?
- What key idea does the author state explicitly? What key idea does he or she suggest or imply? Which details in the text help me to perceive implied ideas?
- Do I find multiple layers of meaning in the text? If so, what relationships do I see among these layers of meaning?
- How do details in the text connect or relate to one another? Do I find any details unconvincing, unrelated, or out of place?
- Do I find the text believable and convincing?

Key Ideas and Details

- What patterns of organization or sequences do I find in the text? Do these patterns help me understand the ideas better?

As you read independently, ask similar types of questions to ensure that you fully enjoy and comprehend any text you choose to read. We have provided sets of questions for you on the Independent Reading pages at the end of each unit.

Ⓒ INFORMATIONAL TEXT

Model

In this example of a complex text, the call-out boxes show questions that an attentive reader might ask while reading.

The Preamble of the United States Constitution

We the people of the United States, in order to form a more perfect union, establish justice, insure domestic tranquility, provide for the common defense, promote the general welfare, and secure the blessings of liberty to ourselves and our posterity, do ordain and establish this Constitution for the United States of America.

Sample questions:

Key Ideas and Details What is the purpose of the Preamble? What is the purpose of the Constitution?

INFORMATIONAL TEXT

Independent Practice

The Bill of Rights

Amendment I Congress shall make no law respecting an establishment of religion, or prohibiting the free exercise thereof; or abridging the freedom of speech, or of the press, or the right of the people peaceably to assemble, and to petition the Government.

Amendment II A well regulated Militia, being necessary to the security of a free State, the right of the people to keep and bear Arms, shall not be infringed.

Amendment III No Soldier shall, in time of peace be quartered in any house, without the consent of the Owner, nor in time of war, but in a manner to be prescribed by law.

Amendment IV The right of the people to be secure in their persons, houses, papers, and effects, against unreasonable searches and seizures, shall not be violated, and no Warrants shall issue, but upon probable cause, supported by Oath or affirmation, and particularly describing the place to be searched, and the persons or things to be seized.

Amendment V No person shall be held to answer for a capital, or otherwise infamous crime, unless on a presentment or indictment of a Grand Jury . . . nor shall any person be subject for the same offence to be twice put in jeopardy of life or limb, nor shall be compelled in any criminal case to be a witness against himself . . . nor shall private property be taken for public use, without just compensation.

Amendment VI In all criminal prosecutions, the accused shall enjoy the right to a speedy and public trial, by an impartial jury of the State and district wherein the crime shall have been committed . . . to be confronted with the witnesses against him . . . and to have the assistance of counsel for his defense.

Amendment VII In Suits at common law, where the value in controversy shall exceed twenty dollars, the right of trial by jury shall be preserved . . .

Amendment VIII Excessive bail shall not be required, nor excessive fines imposed, nor cruel and unusual punishments inflicted. . . .

Craft and Structure What is the effect of parallel structure here? How does this pattern help me follow the ideas and argument? What attitude does the author project?

Integration of Knowledge and Ideas What other U.S. documents have themes similar to those found in the Preamble and the Bill of Rights?

Analyzing Arguments

The ability to evaluate an argument, as well as to make one, is critical for success in college and in the workplace.

What Is an Argument?

Chances are you have used the word *argument* to refer to a disagreement between people. A second definition of *argument* is to present one side of a controversial or debatable issue. Through this type of argument, the writer logically supports a particular belief, conclusion, or point of view. A good argument is supported with reasoning and evidence.

Purposes of Argument

There are three main purposes for writing a formal argument:

- to change the reader's mind about an issue
- to convince the reader to accept what is written
- to motivate the reader to take action, based on what is written

---

Elements of Argument

Claim (assertion)—what the writer is trying to prove
Example: The penny should be abolished.

Grounds (evidence)—the support used to convince the reader
Example: There is no profit derived from manufacturing pennies; they actually cost consumers money.

Justification (reasons)—the link between the grounds and the claim; why the grounds are credible
Example: As a unit of currency, pennies are widely viewed as being obsolete.

Evaluating Claims

When reading or listening to an argument, critically assess the claims that are made. Analyze the argument to identify claims that are based on fact or that can be proved true. Also evaluate evidence that supports the claims. If there is little or no reasoning or evidence provided to support the claims, the argument may not be sound or valid.

**Common Core
State Standards**

Language
6. Acquire and use accurately grade-appropriate general academic and domain-specific words and phrases, sufficiently for reading, writing, speaking, and listening at the college and career readiness level; demonstrate independence in gathering vocabulary knowledge when considering a word or phrase important to comprehension or expression.

Reading Informational Text
6. Determine an author's point of view or purpose in a text in which the rhetoric is particularly effective, analyzing how style and content contribute to the power, persuasiveness, or beauty of the text.

INFORMATIONAL TEXT

Model Argument

from Philadelphia, and Its Solitary Prison
by Charles Dickens

In the outskirts, stands a great prison, called the Eastern Penitentiary: conducted on a plan peculiar to the state of Pennsylvania. The system here is rigid, strict, and hopeless solitary confinement. I believe it, in its effects, to be cruel and wrong.

In its intention, I am well convinced that it is kind, humane, and meant for reformation; but I am persuaded that those who devised this system of Prison Discipline, and those benevolent gentlemen who carry it into execution, do not know what it is that they are doing. I believe that very few men are capable of estimating the immense amount of torture and agony which this dreadful punishment, prolonged for years, inflicts upon the sufferers; and in guessing at it myself, and in reasoning from what I have seen written upon their faces, and what to my certain knowledge they feel within, I am only the more convinced that there is a depth of terrible endurance in it which none but the sufferers themselves can fathom, and which no man has a right to inflict upon his fellow-creature.

I hold this slow and daily tampering with the mysteries of the brain, to be immeasurably worse than any torture of the body: and because its ghastly signs and tokens are not so palpable to the eye and sense of touch as scars upon the flesh; because its wounds are not upon the surface. . . I hesitated once, debating with myself, whether, if I had the power of saying 'Yes' or 'No,' I would allow it to be tried in certain cases, where the terms of imprisonment were short; but now, I solemnly declare, that with no rewards or honours could I walk a happy man beneath the open sky by day, or lie me down upon my bed at night, with the consciousness that one human creature, for any length of time, no matter what, lay suffering this unknown punishment in his silent cell, and I the cause, or I consenting to it in the least degree.

It seems to me that the objection that nothing wholesome or good has ever had its growth in such unnatural solitude, and that even a dog or any of the more intelligent among beasts, would pine, and mope, and rust away, beneath its influence, would be in itself a sufficient argument against this system. But when we recollect, in addition, how very cruel and severe it is, and that a solitary life is always liable to peculiar and distinct objections of a most deplorable nature, which have arisen here, and call to mind, moreover, that the choice is not between this system, and a bad or ill-considered one, but between it and another which has worked well, and is, in its whole design and practice, excellent; there is surely more than sufficient reason for abandoning a mode of punishment attended by so little hope or promise, and fraught, beyond dispute, with such a host of evils.

The introduction sets the stage for the argument that follows, narrowing the focus from the prison to the system of solitary confinement.

Claim: Solitary confinement is cruel and wrong.

Dickens addresses the counterclaim, stating that the intentions of the system were good, and he assumes that the gentlemen do not know how cruel they are being.

Evidence provided includes that people underestimate the unfathomable suffering from the punishment; the punishment is torture. Dickens draws this conclusion based on what he has seen.

Justification: Basic human rights prohibit cruel, inhumane, or unusual punishment.

Dickens reasons that this punishment is worse than physical torture because no one can see the wounds; he also offers the testimony that he would not assent to this punishment in any case.

The last paragraph summarizes the arguments, and the final sentence restates the claim and asks for action: abandon this mode of punishment.

The Art of Argument: Rhetorical Devices and Persuasive Techniques

Rhetorical Devices

Rhetoric is the art of using language in order to make a point or to persuade listeners. Rhetorical devices such as the ones listed below are accepted elements of argument. Their use does not invalidate or weaken an argument. Rather, the use of rhetorical devices is regarded as a key part of an effective argument.

Rhetorical Devices	Examples
Repetition The repeated use of words, phrases, or sentences	Stop the violence! We want to avoid violence! Stop the violence!
Parallelism The repeated use of similar grammatical structures	The strength of the army, the reach of the navy, and the speed of the air force are considered the source of national pride in the military.
Rhetorical Question Calls attention to the issue by implying an obvious answer	Shouldn't civilized nations avoid cruel punishments, even for the most heinous crimes?
Sound Devices The use of alliteration, assonance, rhyme, or rhythm	The **so**und of the **cr**ow**d** protesting **ou**tside the gate drifted to the **in**mate's ear and **l**ifted his spirits.
Simile and Metaphor Compares two seemingly unlike things or asserts that one thing *is* another	The **words** in the book became a **salve** for her wounded soul.

Persuasive Techniques

Persuasive techniques are often found in advertisements and in other forms of informal persuasion. Although techniques like the ones below are sometimes found in formal arguments, they should be avoided in formal arguments.

Persuasive Techniques	Examples
Bandwagon Approach/Anti-Bandwagon Approach Appeals to a person's desire to belong; encourages or celebrates individuality	Don't be the only one without one! Be the first to own our brand.
Emotional Appeal Evokes people's fear, anger, or desire	Our choices today will ensure the health and prosperity of our children! Of our children's children!
Endorsement/Testimony Employs a well-known person to promote a product or idea	These famous authors, actors, politicians, and CEOs are alumnae of our university!
Loaded Language The use of words that are charged with emotion	It is a crisis of unfathomable proportions.
"Plain Folks" Appeal Shows a connection to everyday, ordinary people	I enjoy a good ol' burger and fries, just like everyone else.
Hyperbole Exaggerates to make a point	I'd give my right arm to end the abuse and neglect of animals.

© EXEMPLAR TEXT

Model Speech

The excerpted speech below includes examples of rhetorical devices and persuasive techniques.

Speech on Conciliation with America, by Edmund Burke

. . . The proposition is peace. Not peace through the medium of war; not peace to be hunted through the labyrinth of intricate and endless negotiations; not peace to arise out of universal discord, fomented from principle, in all parts of the empire; not peace to depend on the juridical determination of perplexing questions, or the precise marking the shadowy boundaries of a complex government. It is simple peace, sought in its natural course and in its ordinary haunts.

Let the colonies always keep the idea of their civil rights associated with your government—they will cling and grapple to you, and no force under heaven will be of power to tear them from their allegiance. But let it be once understood that your government may be one thing and their privileges another, that these two things may exist without any mutual relation - the cement is gone, the cohesion is loosened, and everything hastens to decay and dissolution. As long as you have the wisdom to keep the sovereign authority of this country as the sanctuary of liberty, the sacred temple consecrated to our common faith, wherever the chosen race and sons of England worship freedom, they will turn their faces towards you . . . Slavery they can have anywhere. It is a weed that grows in every soil . . . But until you become lost to all feeling of your true interest and your natural dignity, freedom they can have from none but you. This is the commodity of price, of which you have the monopoly . . . Deny them this participation of freedom, and you break that sole bond which originally made, and must still preserve, the unity of the empire . . . It is the spirit of the English constitution which, infused through the mighty mass, pervades, feeds, unites, invigorates, vivifies, every part of the empire, even down to the minutest member.

Is it not the same virtue which does every thing for us here in England? Do you imagine, then, that it is the Land-Tax Act which raises your revenue? that it is the annual vote in the Committee of Supply, which gives you your army? or that it is the Mutiny Bill which inspires it with bravery and discipline? No! surely, no! It is the love of the people; it is their attachment to their government, from the sense of the deep stake they have in such a glorious institution, which gives you your army and your navy, and infuses into both that liberal obedience without which your army would be a base rabble and your navy nothing but rotten timber . . .

We ought to elevate our minds to the greatness of that trust to which the order of Providence has called us. By adverting to the dignity of this high calling, our ancestors have turned a savage wilderness into a glorious empire, and have made the most extensive and the only honorable conquests, not by destroying, but by promoting the wealth, the number, the happiness of the human race. Let us get an American revenue as we have got an American empire. English privileges have made it all that it is; English privileges alone will make it all it can be.

The repetition of the word *peace* emphasizes its importance, while the paragraph provides a growing, defining context for the term.

This metaphor compares slavery to a weed. Burke uses the metaphor to explain why slavery does not create allegiance to a government.

The alliteration, besides adding to the rhythm of the speech, reinforces the relationship between parts and the whole.

This rhetorical question applies the previous conclusions about the empire to England.

The parallelism in these rhetorical questions builds momentum and leads to the emphatic answer: No!

The strongly rhythmic parallelism in the final sentence provides a memorable conclusion.

Analyzing Legal Meanings and Reasoning

Reading historical and legal texts requires careful analysis of both the vocabulary and the logical flow of ideas that support a conclusion.

Understanding Legal Meanings

The language of historical and legal documents is formal, precise, and technical. Many words in these texts have specific meanings that you need to understand in order to follow the flow of ideas. For example, the second amendment to the U.S. Constitution states that "A well regulated militia being necessary to the security of a free State, the right of the People to keep and bear arms shall not be infringed." To understand this amendment, it is important to know that in this context *militia* means "armed forces," *bear* means "carry," and *infringed* means "denied." To understand legal meanings:

- Use your knowledge of word roots to help you understand unfamiliar words. Many legal terms use familiar Greek or Latin roots, prefixes, or suffixes.

- Do not assume that you know a word's legal meaning: use a dictionary to check the meanings of key words to be certain that you are applying the correct meaning.

- Paraphrase the text to aid comprehension. Replace difficult words with synonyms to make sure you follow the logic of the argument.

Delineating Legal Reasoning

Works of public advocacy, such as court decisions, political proclamations, proposed laws or constitutional amendments, use careful reasoning to support conclusions. These strategies can help you understand the legal reasoning in an argument:

- State the **purpose** of the document in your own words to help you focus on the writer's primary goal.

- Look for the line of reasoning that supports the **arguments** presented. To be valid and persuasive, key arguments should be backed up by clearly stated logical analysis. Be aware of persuasive techniques, such as citing facts and statistics, referring to expert testimonials, and using emotional language with strong connotations.

- Identify the **premises,** or evidence, upon which a decision rests. In legal texts, premises often include **precedents,** which are earlier examples that must be followed or specifically overturned. Legal reasoning is usually based on the decisions of earlier trials. Be sure you understand precedents in order to identify how the court arrived at the current decision.

Common Core State Standards

Reading Informational Text

4. Determine the meaning of words and phrases as they are used in a text, including figurative, connotative, and technical meanings; analyze how an author uses and refines the meaning of a key term or terms over the course of a text.

8. Delineate and evaluate the reasoning in seminal U.S. texts, including the application of constitutional principles and use of legal reasoning and the premises, purposes, and arguments in works of public advocacy.

Writing

9. Draw evidence from literary or informational texts to support analysis, reflection, and research.

9.b. Apply *grades 11–12 Reading Standards* to literary nonfiction.

INFORMATIONAL TEXT

Model Court Decision

Note the strategies used to evaluate legal meanings and reasoning in this Supreme Court decision from 1954 regarding the legality of segregated, "separate, but equal" schools for black and white students.

---

from *Brown v. Board of Education of Topeka,* Opinion of the Supreme Court by Chief Justice Earl Warren

We come then to the question presented: Does segregation of children in public schools solely on the basis of race, even though the physical facilities and other "tangible" factors may be equal, deprive the children of the minority group of equal educational opportunities? We believe that it does.

In *Sweatt v. Painter,* in finding that a segregated law school for Negroes could not provide them equal educational opportunities, this Court relied in large part on "those qualities which are incapable of objective measurement but which make for greatness in a law school." In *McLaurin v. Oklahoma State Regents,* the Court, in requiring that a Negro admitted to a white graduate school be treated like all other students, again resorted to intangible considerations: ". . . his ability to study, to engage in discussions and exchange views with other students, and, in general, to learn his profession." Such considerations apply with added force to children in grade and high schools. To separate them from others of similar age and qualifications solely because of their race generates a feeling of inferiority as to their status in the community that may affect their hearts and minds in a way unlikely ever to be undone. The effect of this separation on their educational opportunities was well stated by a finding in the Kansas case by a court which nevertheless felt compelled to rule against the Negro plaintiffs: Segregation of white and colored children in public schools has a detrimental effect upon the colored children. The impact is greater when it has the sanction of the law, for the policy of separating the races is usually interpreted as denoting the inferiority of the negro group. A sense of inferiority affects the motivation of a child to learn. Segregation with the sanction of law, therefore, has a tendency to [retard] the educational and mental development of negro children and to deprive them of some of the benefits they would receive in a racially integrated school system. Whatever may have been the extent of psychological knowledge at the time of *Plessy v. Ferguson,* this finding is amply supported by modern authority. Any language in *Plessy v. Ferguson* contrary to this finding is rejected.

We conclude that, in the field of public education, the doctrine of "separate but equal" has no place. Separate educational facilities are inherently unequal.

The word tangible comes from the Latin root meaning "to touch." In this decision, the court contrasts tangible, measurable features with intangible features that are difficult to measure.

The court cites two precedents: earlier cases relating to unequal education opportunities for black students.

Here's one way you might break down the ideas in this sentence when you paraphrase: Segregating black students just because of their race makes them feel as if they are less valued by our society. This separation can have a permanent negative influence on their character.

*The conclusion makes the **purpose** of the decision clear: to overturn the precedent established by Plessy v. Ferguson. The **argument** describes the reasons why the Court no longer considers the reasoning in that earlier case to be valid.*

Writing About Legal Meanings

Write a detailed analysis of the phrase "segregation with the sanction of law" in the *Brown v. Board of Education of Topeka* decision. Explain the definitions of the terms as they are used in this context and explain how this phrase relates to the courts decision to outlaw "separate but equal" education.

Composing an Argument

Common Core State Standards

Writing

1.a. Introduce precise, knowledgeable claim(s), establish the significance of the claim(s), distinguish the claim(s) from alternate or opposing claims, and create an organization that logically sequences claim(s), counterclaims, reasons, and evidence.

1.b. Develop claim(s) and counterclaims fairly and thoroughly, supplying the most relevant evidence for each while pointing out the strengths and limitations of both in a manner that anticipates the audience's knowledge level, concerns, values, and possible biases.

1.e. Provide a concluding statement or section that follows from and supports the argument presented.

Choosing a Topic

You should choose a topic that matters to people—and to you. The topic should be debatable or controversial to some degree.

Confirm that you can make an arguable claim. Ask yourself:

1. What am I trying to prove? What ideas do I need to get across?
2. Are there people who would disagree with my claim? What counterclaims would they make?
3. Do I have evidence to support my claim? Is my evidence sufficient and relevant?

If you are able to state what you want to prove and answered "yes" to questions 2 and 3, you have an arguable claim.

Introducing the Claim and Establishing Its Significance

Before you begin writing, determine how much your audience already knows about your chosen topic. Then, provide only as much background information as necessary to introduce your claim. If there are issues surrounding your topic, you will need to clarify them for your audience and narrow the focus to your specific claim. Remember that you are not writing a summary of the topic—you are crafting an argument. Once you have provided context for your argument, you should clearly state your claim, or thesis.

Developing Your Claim With Reasoning and Evidence

Now that you have made your claim, you must support it with evidence, or grounds, and reasons for your claim. A good argument should have at least three solid pieces of evidence to support the claim. Evidence can range from personal experience to researched data or expert opinion. Knowing your audience's knowledge level, concerns, values, and possible biases can help you decide what kind of evidence will have the strongest impact. Make sure your evidence is up to date and comes from a credible source. Always credit your sources.

You should also address opposing counterclaims within the body of your argument. Consider points you have made or evidence you have provided that a person might challenge. Decide how best to refute these counterclaims. One technique for defusing an opponent's claims is to agree with selected parts of them.

Writing a Concluding Statement or Section

Restate your claim in the conclusion of your argument, and summarize your main points. The goal of a concluding section is to provide a sense of closure and completeness to an argument. Make your concluding statement strong enough to be memorable and to leave the reader thinking.

Practice

Exploring both sides of an issue can be a good way to start planning an argument. Complete a chart like the one below to help you plan your own argument.

Topic:	
Issue: _____ _____	
Claim:	Counterclaim:
Grounds (Evidence): 1._____ 2._____ 3._____	Grounds (Evidence): 1._____ 2._____ 3._____
Justification: 1._____ 2._____ 3._____	Justification: 1._____ 2._____ 3._____

When you have completed the chart and developed your own, precise claim, consider the following questions:

1. Who is your audience? What type of evidence can you use to best convince those who do not agree with your claim?

2. Is your evidence strong and difficult to dispute? If not, how can you strengthen it or find better evidence?

3. How will you refute the counterclaim? Are there any parts of the counterclaim you agree with?

Media Literacy Handbook

INTRODUCTION: Today, messages are transmitted across a variety of media modes, such as film, television, radio, and the Internet. As you interact with these messages each day—in images, advertisements, movies, and an array of different contexts—it is important to consider the potential influences of the medium.

- What is the intention of the message?
- How is it communicated?
- How do specific elements of the medium—such as color, image, or font—help convey the message?
- Why might the creator of the message have selected this medium?

These are the key issues of media literacy, the study of messages in the media and their impact.

Camera Shots and Angles
Filmmakers create camera shots and sequences to help them tell stories. Some shots capture an entire scene; others zoom in on specific characters.

Special Effects

Filmmakers use special effects to create on-screen illusions that bring the imagination to life.

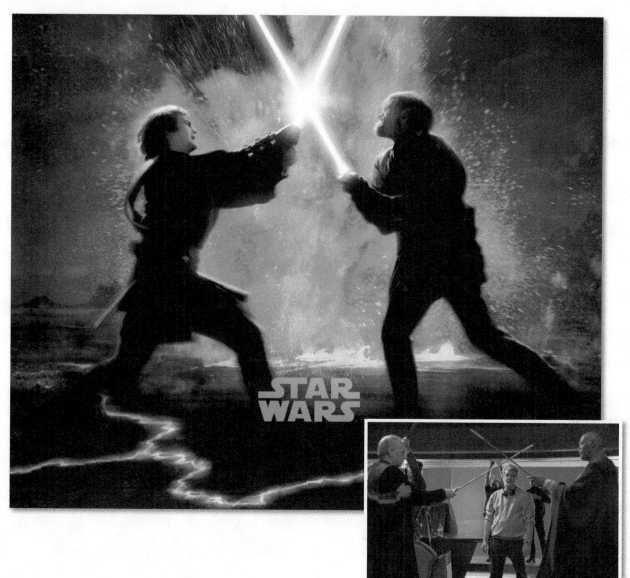

Questions About Film Techniques

- What effect is created by the choice of camera angle shown in the image at left? Choose another camera angle and explain how that shot might convey a different message than the one shown here.

- Study the images above. In what way does the use of special effects make the film better for viewers?

Media Literacy Handbook

Focus and Framing
A sharp focus captures all details in a photographic image. A softer focus lessens the amount of detail that can be seen. The framing of elements within a photograph directs the eye toward a portion of the image.

Lighting and Shadow
Lighting techniques are used in photography to enhance mood and direct the viewer's focus.

Special Techniques

Most images you see today have been manipulated or changed in some way. Even a small change—such as an added graphic element or a difference in shading—can alter the mood of an image.

FROM LUCY: ENGLAN' LADY

James Berry

Questions About Graphics and Photos

- What would be the effect if the image at left used a sharp focus instead of a combination of a sharp and soft focus?

- In what way does the use of color and light create mood in the photo at left?

- What special techniques were applied to the original photograph shown above right? What effect does the use of special techniques create?

Persuasive Techniques
Advertisements use carefully selected visual elements and specific language to appeal to the viewer's emotions.

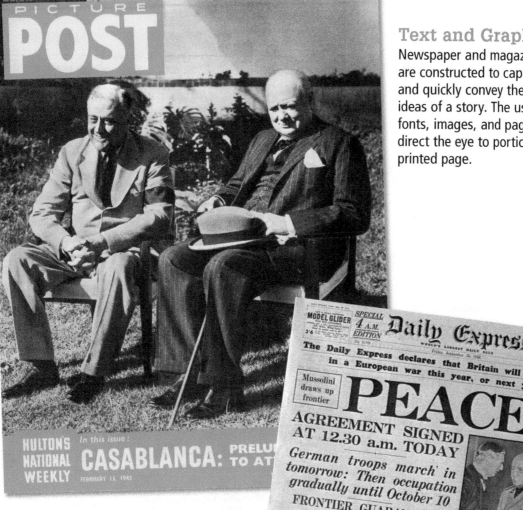

Text and Graphics

Newspaper and magazine layouts are constructed to capture the eye and quickly convey the important ideas of a story. The use of type fonts, images, and page space direct the eye to portions of the printed page.

Questions About Print Media

- What image or graphic dominates the advertisement at left? In what way does the use of language in the ad enhance its message?

- Which of the above grabs your attention: the image or the graphic on the magazine cover? Explain.

- What do you notice first on the newspaper's front page? What overall effect does the use of type size and fonts create?

How is this book organized?

- **There are six chronological units, starting with Native American beginnings and extending to the present.**
- **Each unit has an introduction that offers multiple perspectives on the history, culture, and literature of the time period.**

A *"Snapshot"* shows you key people, places, and innovations. ▶

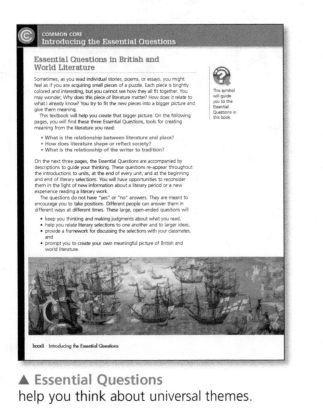

▲ **Essential Questions** help you think about universal themes.

Historical Background summarizes key events of the era. ▼

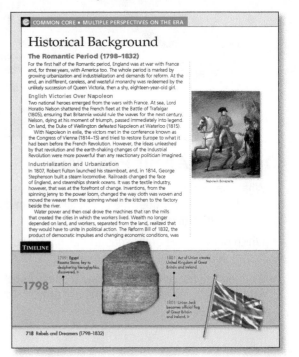

How are the literary selections organized?

- **Each unit contains literary selections from the time period.**
- **Each selection has features to help you better understand the literature.**

Before You Read teaches you important skills and vocabulary. ▶

Vocabulary

averred (ə vʉrd′) v. stated to be true (p. 824)

sojourn (sō′ jʉrn) v. stay for a while (p. 831)

expiated (eks′ pē āt′ id) v. atoned for, especially by suffering (p. 838)

▲ **Author Biography** tells you about the author's life.

◀ **While You Read questions** help you apply the skills as you read.

After You Read helps you practice the skills you have learned. ▶

Skills Practice

Special Features Bring British and World Literature to Life and Show Why They Matter Today

Extended Study brings you closer to an author's world or allows you to explore a literary movement or genre in great depth. ▶

▲ **Illustrations** help you visualize literary history.

Themes Across Centuries, Genres, or Cultures features essays by today's writers on the topic of the classics. ▼

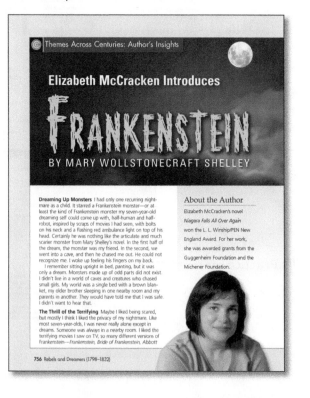

Contemporary Connections links the classics to today. ▶

THE STORY BEHIND THE DOCUMENTS

Lord John Russell (1792–1878) was the British statesman who introduced the Reform Bill of 1832 in Parliament. A champion of reform, Lord Russell was a leading member of the Whig party when it came to power in 1830 with Lord Grey as prime minister. Some years later, after the Whigs had evolved into the Liberal party, Russell himself served twice as Britain's prime minister. Among his later achievements was passage of a law limiting factory labor to ten hours a day.

Sir Robert Peel (1788–1850) helped lead the Tory party opposition to the Reform Bill of 1832. Peel later served as prime minister twice: first from 1834 to 1835 and later, after reorganizing the Tories as the modern Conservative party, for a much longer period in the 1840s. In 1829, while serving as home secretary in a Tory administration, he established London's police force, whose members are nicknamed "bobbies" in his honor.

Thomas Babington Macaulay (1800–1859) was a well-known nineteenth-century historian and literary critic. Trained as a lawyer, he was also a Whig member of Parliament who, like Lord Russell, spoke in favor of the Reform Bill of 1832. Macaulay first won literary fame with an essay on John Milton. His influential five-volume *History of England* (1849–1861) offered a Whig interpretation of British history, stressing the value of gradual democratic reform.

The Industrial Revolution brought great change to Britain. Large chunks of the population shifted from rural areas to newly emerging urban centers, where the middle class grew and prospered. Britain's political landscape, however, had not changed with the times. Sparsely populated rural areas lost disproportionately large representation, while booming new industrial cities like Manchester had none. Some seats in Parliament were completely controlled by a single nobleman or by small self-interested groups. Additionally, landholding and financial restrictions kept much of the population from voting. The result was a Parliament that strongly favored the interests of landowners at the expense of everyone else. The Reform Bill of 1832—often called the First Reform Bill—was an attempt to correct that situation.

▶ **Primary Source: Photography** How does the arrangement of seats in the House of Commons suggest the idea of opposed parties? **[Analyze]**

SPEECH IN FAVOR OF REFORM
Lord John Russell

BACKGROUND When the Whigs came to power in 1830, the number one issue on the party's agenda was reform of Britain's election system. To that end, Lord Russell first proposed the Reform Bill on March 1, 1831. The Tory party opposed the bill, with Sir Robert Peel speaking effectively against it. Extracts from both these speeches are presented here.

On the second reading, the bill passed Parliament's House of Commons by just one vote. Recognizing the need for a greater majority, Lord Grey, the Whig prime minister, dissolved Parliament and called for a new election. The Whigs now won many more seats, and the Reform Bill readily passed in the House of Commons—but it was still rejected in Parliament's other chamber, the House of Lords. Finally, the prime minister forced King William IV to name several new members to the House of Lords—members sympathetic to the reform—and in July of 1832 the bill passed both Houses of Parliament and became law.

Interior of the Devolved Chamber House of Parliament, Westminster, United Kingdom

Lord John Russell's Speech in Favor of Reform

◀ **Primary Sources** features real documents that made history, and supports in-depth research projects.

Comparing Literary Works
Poetry of William Wordsworth • Lyric Poetry from Around the World

Comparing Lyric Poetry from Around the World

Lyric Poetry Lyric poetry began in song. In fact, the word *lyric* comes from *lyre*, the harplike instrument that ancient Greek poets like Sappho played to accompany their lyric poems. Even before the Greeks, however, people were singing poems expressing faith, love, sorrow, joy, and other strong emotions. Love lyrics survive from ancient Egypt's New Kingdom (c. 1570–1070 b.c.). The philosopher Confucius is said to have compiled the *Book of Songs*, collecting Chinese poetry written as early as 1100 b.c.

Lyric poetry typically has these characteristics:
• It is brief and concise.
• It is communicated by a single speaker expressing personal emotions and observations.
• It uses vivid images to convey ideas and evoke emotions.
• It is musical, often employing rhyme, alliteration, and repetition and following a pattern of rhythm (called meter) or a pattern of syllables.

For lyric poems that you read, fill in a chart like this one. Then, use your charts to answer comparison-and-contrast questions about the poems.

	"The World Is Too Much With Us"	"I Have Visited Again"
Form and/or lines	Petrarchan sonnet; 14 lines	
Speaker	Lover of nature	
Observations	Society is too materialistic; nature's beauty is unappreciated	
Emotions	Unhappiness with society; joy and wonder in nature	
Images	Vivid sights and sounds of wild and pagan sea	
Sound devices	Rhyme, meter, some alliteration, assonance	

Gather Vocabulary Knowledge

These lyric poets use words such as *fathomless*, *treacherous*, and *splendor*. Use a **dictionary** to find each word's part of speech and definition. Then, employ the following references (printed or electronic) to explore these words:
• **History of Language:** Use a history of English to research each word's etymology, or origins.
• **Book of Quotations:** Use a collection of quotations to find a statement containing some of the words. In a paragraph, explain the nuances in meaning that are evident from the context of the quotation.

Comparing References Compare and contrast what you learn about the words from these specialized references.

Common Core State Standards

Reading Literature
5. Analyze how an author's choices concerning how to structure specific parts of a text contribute to its overall structure and meaning as well as its aesthetic impact.

Language
4.c. Consult general and specialized reference materials, both print and digital, to find the pronunciation of a word or determine or clarify its precise meaning, its part of speech, its etymology, or its standard usage.

◀ **Reading for Information** feature nonfiction texts you will encounter in daily life.

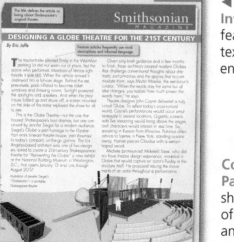

The title defines the article as being about Shakespeare's original theater.

Feature Article
Smithsonian
MAGAZINE

DESIGNING A GLOBE THEATRE FOR THE 21ST CENTURY
By Eric Jaffe

Feature articles frequently use vivid descriptions and informal language.

The tractor-trailer planted firmly in the Wal-Mart parking lot did not seem out of place, but the actors who performed *Merchant of Venice* right beside it sure did. When the vehicle arrived it deployed into a full-size stage. Behind the set, pneumatic pods inflated to become ticket windows and dressing rooms. Sunlight poured into the playhouse. And when the playhouse folded up and drove off, a screen mounted on the side of the trailer replayed the show for all to see.

This is the Globe Theatre—not the one that housed Shakespeare's best dramas, but one conceived by Jennifer Siegal for a modern audience. Siegal's Globe is part homage to the Elizabethan era's itinerant theatre troupe, part showcase to today's compact, on-the-go gizmos. The late Angeles-based architect was one of two design on asked to create a 21st-century Shakespearean theatre for "Reinventing the Globe," a new exhibit at the National Building Museum in Washington, D.C., that opens January 13 and runs through August 2007.

Given only brief guidance and a few months to finish, these architects created modern Globes that challenge conventional thoughts about dramatic performances and the spaces that accommodate them, says Martin Moeller, the exhibition's curator. "When the words stay the same but all else changes, you realize how much power the words have," he says.

Theatre designer John Coyne delivered a truly virtual Globe. To reflect today's cross-cultural world, Coyne's performances would occur simultaneously in several locations. Gigantic screens with live streaming would hang above the stages, and characters would interact in real time. So, speaking in Russian from Moscow, Polonius offers advice to Laertes in New York; standing oceans away, Hamlet pierces Claudius with a venom-tipped sword.

Michele (pronounced Mikeleh) Saee, who did not have theatre design experience, modeled a Globe that would capture an actor's fluidity in the structure itself. He proposed saucing the movements of an actor throughout a performance.

Illustration of Jennifer Siegal's "Globetrotter"—a portable Shakespearean theater.

Comparing Literature Past and Present shows the continuity of ideas, themes, and styles. ▶

Essential Questions in British and World Literature

Sometimes, as you read individual stories, poems, or essays, you might feel as if you are acquiring small pieces of a puzzle. Each piece is brightly colored and interesting, but you cannot see how they all fit together. You may wonder, Why does this piece of literature matter? How does it relate to what I already know? You try to fit the new pieces into a bigger picture and give them meaning.

This textbook will help you create that bigger picture. On the following pages, you will find these three Essential Questions, tools for creating meaning from the literature you read:

- **What is the relationship between literature and place?**
- **How does literature shape or reflect society?**
- **What is the relationship of the writer to tradition?**

On the next three pages, the Essential Questions are accompanied by descriptions to guide your thinking. These questions re-appear throughout the introductions to units, at the end of every unit, and at the beginning and end of literary selections. You will have opportunities to reconsider them in the light of new information about a literary period or a new experience reading a literary work.

The questions do not have "yes" or "no" answers. They are meant to encourage you to take positions. Different people can answer them in different ways at different times. These large, open-ended questions will

- keep you thinking and making judgments about what you read,
- help you relate literary selections to one another and to larger ideas,
- provide a framework for discussing the selections with your classmates, and
- prompt you to create your own meaningful picture of British and world literature.

This symbol will guide you to the Essential Questions in this book.

What is the **relationship** between literature and *place?*

From the beginning, England's geography captured the imagination of its writers. Over a thousand years ago, a monk named Bede began a section of his history, "Britain, formerly known as Albion, is an island in the ocean . . ." As you read the selections in this book, think about how England's island existence and dependence on the sea influenced its literature.

The imagination can shape the perception of a place, and writers play a major part in that imagining. How have different generations of England's writers re-imagined their country? How have they shaped remembered or even unreal places, such as a perfect pastoral community that exists only on the pages of a book?

As you read, watch how writers invest places with reality and invent places with imagination. Stay attuned to the variety of responses to the Essential Question: What is the relationship between literature and place?

Thematic Vocabulary

To help as you explore this Essential Question, use words like these:

boundary	**colonize**	**conquest**
destruction	**empire**	**geography**
immigrant	**isolation**	**mobility**
nature		

"This blessed plot, this earth, this realm, this England."

—William Shakespeare, *Richard II*

How does **literature** shape or reflect *society?*

We know why we need farmers, carpenters, and doctors, but why do we need writers? Also, how do writers interact with the culture to produce literature that entertains, informs, persuades, challenges, and moves readers?

The writers who create British literature are a vital part of British society. They help to produce its culture, and they are the products of that culture. They are the entertainers who amuse, the critics who confront, and the teachers who share wisdom. Every day, writers celebrate Britain, define it, defy it, and tell its story. As you read this textbook and keep asking this Essential Question, you will become aware of the many relationships between Britain and its writers.

Thematic Vocabulary

To help as you explore this Essential Question, use words like these:

capitalism	**dissatisfaction**	**ideal**	**independence**
industry	**loyalty**	**modernization**	
order	**revolution**	**values**	

"No man is an island, entire of itself; every man is a piece of the continent, a part of the main." —John Donne, *Meditation 17*

What is the **relationship** of the writer to *tradition?*

The past is not past. It is a living part of the present, and tradition is its embodiment. Literary tradition is the record of how men and women imaginatively responded to their times, what they believed was important and beautiful. It is the record of how they chose to express that beauty, the forms and styles and words and images they used. Tradition is the biography of literature.

Every British writer is, in some way, a product of the British literary tradition and a participant in it. As you keep asking this Essential Question throughout this book, you will be getting to the core of what gives British literature its unique character.

Thematic Vocabulary

To help as you explore this Essential Question, use words like these:

authentic	**conventional**	**interpretation**
monarchy	**philosophy**	**piety**
propriety	**reform**	**struggle**
transformation		

"Let me imagine . . . what would have happened had Shakespeare had a wonderfully gifted sister, called Judith, let us say."

—Virginia Woolf, *A Room of One's Own*

LITERARY MAP OF THE BRITISH ISLES

0 Miles   50   100   150   200
0 Km   50   100   150   200   250   300

ENGLAND

Bath Jane Austen writes

Cambridge Alfred, Lord Tennyson studies

Canterbury Destination of Chaucer's pilgrims

Chalfont St Giles John Milton completes *Paradise Lost*

Dorchester Inspiration for Thomas Hardy's Wessex

Dover Matthew Arnold's *Dover Beach*

Haworth The Brontë sisters write

Oxford Samuel Johnson studies

Portsmouth Charles Dickens born

Southwold George Orwell takes his pen name from the river Orwell

Stratford-upon-Avon William Shakespeare born

Tilbury Elizabeth I appears before her troops

Tintagel Legendary birthplace of King Arthur

York W.H. Auden born

SCOTLAND

Ayrshire Robert Burns writes
Dunsinane Macbeth slain

English-Scottish Border
Setting of many early ballads

IRELAND

Dublin James Joyce, Jonathan Swift and William Butler Yeats born
Clonmel Laurence Sterne writes

NORTHERN IRELAND

Londonderry Seamus Heaney born

WALES

Swansea Dylan Thomas born

Atlantic Ocean

Outer Hebrides

Orkney Islands

NORTH SEA

Scottish Highlands

Dunsinane

SCOTLAND

Glasgow

★ EDINBURGH

Ayrshire

English-Scottish Border

Londonderry

NORTHERN IRELAND (U.K.) ★ BELFAST

IRELAND

Galway

DUBLIN

Clonmel

Isle of Man

IRISH SEA

CELTIC SEA

Newcastle upon Tyne

ENGLAND (U.K.)

Haworth   York

Liverpool

Manchester   Sheffield

Nottingham

WALES (U.K.)

Burmingham

Cambridge   Southwold

Stratford-upon-Avon

Tintern Abbey

Swansea

Cardiff

Bristol

Bath

Oxford

Chalfont St Giles

Tilbury

Canterbury

Dover

Thames River

★ LONDON

Bristol Channel

Portsmouth

Dorchester

Tintagel

Plymouth

Isle of Wight

English Channel

Strait of Dover

FRANCE

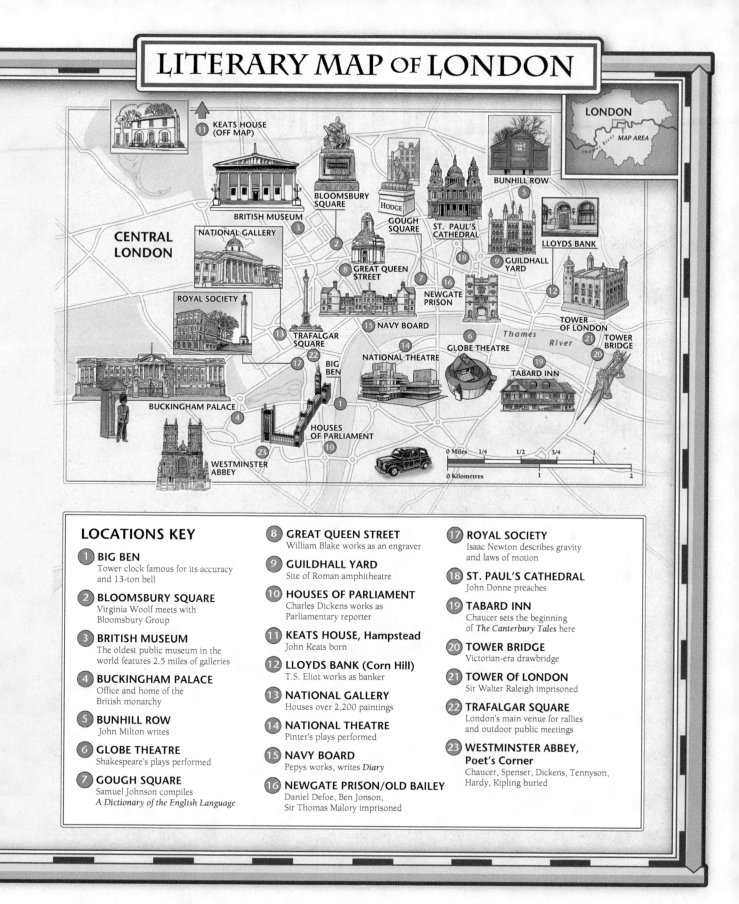

LITERARY MAP of LONDON

KEATS HOUSE (OFF MAP) 11

LONDON
MAP AREA
Thames River

BUNHILL ROW

BLOOMSBURY SQUARE

GOUGH SQUARE
HODGE

ST. PAUL'S CATHEDRAL

BRITISH MUSEUM

LLOYDS BANK

CENTRAL LONDON

NATIONAL GALLERY

GUILDHALL YARD

GREAT QUEEN STREET

ROYAL SOCIETY

NEWGATE PRISON

TOWER OF LONDON

TRAFALGAR SQUARE

NAVY BOARD

Thames River

TOWER BRIDGE

BIG BEN

NATIONAL THEATRE

GLOBE THEATRE

BUCKINGHAM PALACE

TABARD INN

HOUSES OF PARLIAMENT

WESTMINSTER ABBEY

| 0 Miles | 1/4 | 1/2 | 3/4 | 1 |
| 0 Kilometres | | 1 | | 2 |

LOCATIONS KEY

1 BIG BEN
Tower clock famous for its accuracy and 13-ton bell

2 BLOOMSBURY SQUARE
Virginia Woolf meets with Bloomsbury Group

3 BRITISH MUSEUM
The oldest public museum in the world features 2.5 miles of galleries

4 BUCKINGHAM PALACE
Office and home of the British monarchy

5 BUNHILL ROW
John Milton writes

6 GLOBE THEATRE
Shakespeare's plays performed

7 GOUGH SQUARE
Samuel Johnson compiles *A Dictionary of the English Language*

8 GREAT QUEEN STREET
William Blake works as an engraver

9 GUILDHALL YARD
Site of Roman amphitheatre

10 HOUSES OF PARLIAMENT
Charles Dickens works as Parliamentary reporter

11 KEATS HOUSE, Hampstead
John Keats born

12 LLOYDS BANK (Corn Hill)
T.S. Eliot works as banker

13 NATIONAL GALLERY
Houses over 2,200 paintings

14 NATIONAL THEATRE
Pinter's plays performed

15 NAVY BOARD
Pepys works, writes *Diary*

16 NEWGATE PRISON/OLD BAILEY
Daniel Defoe, Ben Jonson, Sir Thomas Malory imprisoned

17 ROYAL SOCIETY
Isaac Newton describes gravity and laws of motion

18 ST. PAUL'S CATHEDRAL
John Donne preaches

19 TABARD INN
Chaucer sets the beginning of *The Canterbury Tales* here

20 TOWER BRIDGE
Victorian-era drawbridge

21 TOWER Of LONDON
Sir Walter Raleigh imprisoned

22 TRAFALGAR SQUARE
London's main venue for rallies and outdoor public meetings

23 WESTMINSTER ABBEY, Poet's Corner
Chaucer, Spenser, Dickens, Tennyson, Hardy, Kipling buried

Rebels and Dreamers

The Romantic Period

Unit

4

PHLit Online!
www.PHLitOnline.com

Hear It!
- Selection summary audio
- Selection audio

See It!
- Author videos
- Essential Question video
- Get Connected videos
- Background videos
- More about the authors
- Illustrated vocabulary words
- Vocabulary flashcards

Do It!
- Interactive journals
- Interactive graphic organizers
- Grammar tutorials
- Interactive vocabulary games
- Test practice

"But oh! that deep Romantic chasm which slanted / Down the green hill, athwart a cedarn cover! / A savage place! as holy and enchanted / As e'er beneath a waning moon was haunted . . ."

—*Samuel Taylor Coleridge*

Snapshot of the Period

During the Romantic period, all the attitudes and assumptions of eighteenth-century classicism and rationalism were dramatically challenged, in part by social and political upheavals. The French Revolution, which began on July 14, 1789, shook the established order in the name of democratic ideals. Fearing the events in France, the English ruling class also felt threatened by unrest at home. British authorities tried to repress workers' efforts to organize, going so far as to kill a number of peaceful demonstrators in Manchester (1819). Another type of revolution, the Industrial Revolution, boosted the growth of manufacturing but also brought poverty and suffering for those who worked or failed to find work in slum-ridden cities. British Romantic writers responded to the climate of their times. For many of them, the faith in science and reason, so characteristic of eighteenth-century thought, no longer applied in a world of tyranny and factories.

RECENT EVENT at MANCHESTER.

▶ In 1819, thousands of workers and their families demonstrated peacefully at St. Peter's Fields in Manchester to protest desperate economic conditions and to gain parliamentary reforms. Soldiers dispersed the crowd, injuring about 500 people and killing 11.

As you read the selections in this unit, you will be asked to think about them in view of three key questions:

What is the **relationship** between literature and *place?*

How does literature **shape or reflect** *society?*

What is the relationship of the **writer** to *tradition?*

Integration of Knowledge and Ideas In the image below, the cracked façade and the pictures whirling out of it dramatize the way in which Romantic values challenged earlier Neoclassical beliefs in order and balance. Which of these Romantic values, described in the captions, are still influential today? Which seem historically interesting but no longer directly relevant to us today?

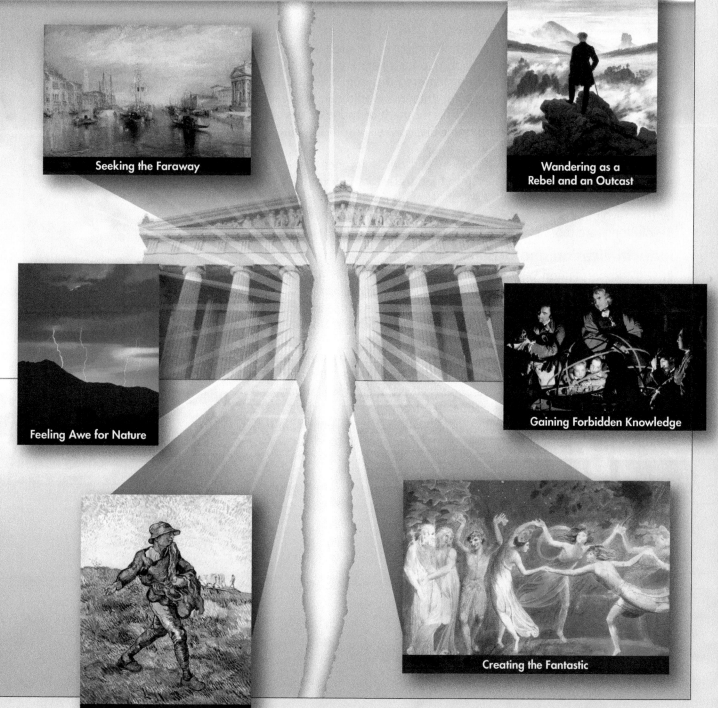

Seeking the Faraway

Wandering as a Rebel and an Outcast

Feeling Awe for Nature

Gaining Forbidden Knowledge

Honoring the Common Person

Creating the Fantastic

Historical Background

The Romantic Period (1798–1832)

For the first half of the Romantic period, England was at war with France. At home, the period was marked by growing urbanization and industrialization and demands for reform. At the end, a wasteful monarchy was redeemed by the succession of a shy, eighteen-year-old girl, Victoria.

English Victories Over Napoleon

Revolutionary France, led by Napoleon Bonaparte, declared war on Britain in 1793. In the ensuing conflict, two national heroes emerged for England. At sea, Lord Horatio Nelson shattered the French fleet at the Battle of Trafalgar (1805), ensuring that Britannia would rule the waves for the next century. Nelson, dying at his moment of triumph, passed immediately into legend. On land, the Duke of Wellington defeated Napoleon at Waterloo (1815).

With Napoleon in exile, the victors met in the conference known as the Congress of Vienna (1814–15) and tried to restore Europe to what it had been before the French Revolution. However, the ideas unleashed by that revolution and the earth-shaking changes of the Industrial Revolution were more powerful than any reactionary politician imagined.

Industrialization and Urbanization

In 1807, Robert Fulton launched his steamboat, and, in 1814, George Stephenson built a steam locomotive. Railroads changed the face of England, and steamships shrank oceans. It was the textile industry, however, that was at the forefront of change. Inventions, from the spinning jenny to the power loom, changed the way cloth was woven and moved the weaver from the spinning wheel in the kitchen to the factory.

Water power and then coal drove the machines that ran the mills that created the cities in which the workers lived. Wealth no longer depended on land, and workers, separated from the land, realized that they would have to unite in political action. The Reform Bill of 1832, the product of democratic impulses and changing economic conditions, was

Napoleon Bonaparte

1799: Egypt
Rosetta Stone, key to deciphering hieroglyphics, discovered. ▶

1801: Act of Union creates United Kingdom of Great Britain and Ireland.

1798

1801: Union Jack becomes official flag of Great Britain and Ireland. ▶

a first step in extending the right to vote. It increased the voting rolls by 57 percent, but the working classes and some members of the lower middle classes were still unable to vote. In 1833, after the period ended, Parliament abolished slavery in the British Empire.

An Out-of-Touch Monarchy

The struggle for increased political rights was a difficult one. Those in power and those who wanted reform collided tragically at St. Peter's Field, Manchester, in 1819. Workers had assembled in a peaceful demonstration for economic and political reform. A cavalry charge killed eleven and wounded many women and children. Called the Peterloo Massacre, the incident inspired Shelley to write "England in 1819" which opens: "An old, mad, blind, despised and dying King."

Cruelly accurate, the line describes George III, who had been declared insane in 1811. His son, named Prince Regent, was designated to rule in his place (a regent substitutes for a ruler). This gave the period its name, The Regency, and the Regent's conduct gave it its scandalous reputation.

Extravagant, obese, separated from his wife in an ugly and very public marital quarrel, he was unaware of the great changes taking place around him. The Regent became George IV in 1820. In 1830, he was succeeded by his brother William, who had ten illegitimate children with his common-law wife, but no legitimate heir. When William died in 1837, the daughter of his younger brother was next in the royal line.

That daughter, Victoria, was determined to restore morality and dignity to the throne. She became the queen and then the symbol of an era in which political reform and industrial might made England the most powerful country in the world.

Key Historical Theme: Political Oppression vs. Political Reform

- Conservative European rulers tried to roll back revolutionary ideas.
- In England, industrialization prompted workers to organize.
- Police killed peacefully protesting workers in Manchester in 1819.
- The Reform Bill of 1832 extended the right to vote but not to the working classes.

1803: United States
Louisiana Territory purchased from France.

1804: Germany
Beethoven composes *Symphony No. 3.*

◄ **1804: France**
Napoleon crowns himself emperor.

1805

▲ 1805: Battle of Trafalgar.

Essential Questions Across Time

The Romantic Period (1798–1832)

 What is the relationship between literature and *place?*

English Romanticism was born in and inspired by a real place—the Lake District. (See the feature on the next page.) However, since Romanticism defines itself by opposition to the commonplace and familiar, much of the literature of the period is also set in exotic and faraway locations.

How did Romantics emphasize strange and faraway places?

In poetry, the Romantics took readers to distant lands, both real and imaginary. For example, Samuel Taylor Coleridge's Ancient Mariner sails around Cape Horn to the edge of Antarctica, which was just then being explored. He returns to narrate his strange adventures. In Coleridge's "Kubla Khan," the fabulous emperor dwells in a place that has come to symbolize luxury and mystery: Xanadu. Similarly, Percy Bysshe Shelley's poem "Ozymandias" takes us to "an antique land," the Egypt of the pharaohs, which had recently been invaded and plundered by Napoleon.

What worlds became refuges from the smoky cities?

Whether or not they wrote of exotic lands, the Romantic poets all sought something beyond this world, turning to nature and the imagination for transcendence. The worlds they explored were alternatives to the spreading stain of the cities; to what the poet William Blake called the "dark, Satanic mills," factories that seemed to chew up people.

The Lake District William Wordsworth, who settled in the beautiful Lake District—far from the urban blight of London, Manchester, and Birmingham—wrote of the natural world in a religious way. A "worshipper of Nature," he saw the landscape bathed in a heavenly light.

ESSENTIAL QUESTION VOCABULARY

These Essential Question words will help you think and write about literature and place:

exotic (eg zöt´ ik) *adj.* foreign; strange or different in a way that is striking

secular (sek´ yə lər) *adj.* relating to worldly things as opposed to religion

residential (rez´ ə den´ shəl) *adj.* characterized by private homes

---

TIMELINE

1806: Germany
Prussia declares war on France.

1807: United States
Fulton's steamboat navigates Hudson River. ▼

1805

1806: Western Europe
Official end of Holy Roman Empire.

Going Beyond Wordsworth was a native of the Lake District; he had climbed its mountains and rowed across its lakes. He saw ideal beauty in the land that spread out before him. However, when Shelley writes of the skylark and John Keats of the nightingale, they are not concerned with describing these birds in their natural settings. Each celebrates the song and the flight of a bird that lures the poet beyond the bounds of earth.

The urban world the Romantics fled was not, as Wordsworth discovered, completely bleak. Wordsworth, poet of nature and the countryside, had a moment of stunned revelation when, at dawn on a clear September morning, he saw London from Westminster Bridge. "Earth," he wrote, "has not anything to show more fair . . ."

The City Improved—or Blighted London had indeed been improved. The architect John Nash contributed to the secular beautification of London as Christopher Wren had to the ecclesiastical, with the rebuilding of St. Paul's Cathedral after the Great Fire of 1666. Nash built the Brighton Pavilion, modeled in part on India's Taj Mahal, another example of the period's taste for the exotic and fantastic.

Bath, a city forever connected with Regency novelist Jane Austen, created its beautiful crescents, or curved streets, during this time. However, these Regency splendors were the exception. What the novelist Charles Dickens would later call "Coketown," a dirty, soul-destroying city, stands for the world from which the Romantic poets struggled to escape.

The BRITISH TRADITION

CLOSE-UP ON GEOGRAPHY

The Lake District, Cradle of Romanticism

The cradle of English Romanticism is the Lake District. Located in the northwest of England, this picturesque region contains some of the country's most impressive mountains and lakes. The Romantic poet William Wordsworth was born in the Lake District, wandered there as a boy, lived there as a man, and wrote poems inspired by its beauty. In the following passage, Wordsworth captures the mystery and thrill of his boyhood climbing expeditions in the region.

> . . . Oh! at that time,
> While on the perilous ridge I hung alone,
> With what strange utterance did the loud dry wind
> Blow through my ears! the sky seemed not a sky
> Of earth, and with what motion moved the clouds.
> —from *The Prelude*

1812: **United States**
War with Britain declared.

1812

▲ 1810: **South America**
Simón Bolívar leads rebellion against Spanish rule.

1812: Byron publishes *Childe Harold's Pilgrimage.* ▶

721

How does literature **shape or** reflect *society?*

The French Revolution hit Europe like a tidal wave. The Industrial Revolution, which owes so much to inventor James Watt's improvements to the steam engine, is still shaping the world today. The social history of the period is the story of how people in general, and writers in particular, reacted to the shocks of these revolutions.

How did political and industrial revolutions affect society?

"Bliss was it in that dawn to be alive . . ." In his autobiographical epic, *The Prelude*, William Wordsworth looks back on the heady days when he and the French Revolution were young. Europe, he says, was "thrilled with joy" at the prospect of "human nature seeming born again." (Book 6, lines 340–342) More personally and poignantly: "Bliss was it in that dawn to be alive, / But to be young was very Heaven." (Book 11, lines 108–109)

Disillusionment Sets In The Revolution, however, turned blindly destructive, and England and France went to war. The young poet's bliss faded quickly, as did that of many who had such hope in the beginning. Napoleon's crowning himself emperor ended any belief that human nature had been born again.

Trying to Bring Back the Old Order In the aftermath of Napoleon's defeat, those in power were determined that human nature would not be reborn, and that the old order would be restored—the privileged few would continue to rule. However, the forces of democratic reform had been unleashed and could not be suppressed.

Ideas That Would Not Die The original message of the Revolution, the one that had thrilled Wordsworth, was that people were to be free in their personal lives and free to choose their government—that all people were equally "citizens." Although the later course of the Revolution might have distorted these ideas, the ideas themselves would not die.

> ### ESSENTIAL QUESTION VOCABULARY
>
> These Essential Question words will help you think and write about literature and society:
>
> **privileged** (priv´ ə lijd) *adj.* having rights or advantages denied to others
>
> **institution** (in´ stə tōō´ shən) *n.* established law, custom, or practice
>
> **industrial** (in dus´ trē əl) *adj.* of or connected with industries or manufacturing

TIMELINE

1813: Jane Austen publishes *Pride and Prejudice.*

1814: George Stephenson constructs first successful steam locomotive. ▶

1812

1813: Mexico independence declared.

◀ **1815: Belgium** Napoleon defeated at Waterloo.

In England, a group of men and women, mostly Quakers, led by William Wilberforce, were determined that one ancient social institution would be abolished. Thanks to them, slavery was ended in England and in the empire.

The Reform Bill of 1832 was another part of the peaceful revolution that transformed England. It extended the right to vote to many males previously disqualified by lack of wealth. The 1832 bill was a step in a century-long journey that, in the end, gave all citizens voting rights.

The Application of Power to Work Revolutions are about power, and the Industrial Revolution was about the application of power to work: the creation of machines that work while human beings feed and "tend" them.

Unfortunately, the mills—and the cities that grew up around them—crushed and destroyed many who came from the countryside looking for new opportunities. Economic progress exacted an enormous human price.

How did writers react to revolutionary changes?

Direct Responses Some writers directly addressed the problems of their changing world. Mary Wollstonecraft, a witness to the French Revolution, urged a radical transformation of society in her *Vindication of the Rights of Woman*. Among other social institutions, she criticized "a false system of education" geared to make women marriageable rather than knowledgeable.

The BRITISH TRADITION

THE CHANGING ENGLISH LANGUAGE BY RICHARD LEDERER

The Romantic Age

During the Romantic Age, Britannia ruled the waves, and English ruled much of the land. As British ships traveled throughout the world, they left the language of the mother country in their wake but also came home from foreign ports laden with cargoes of words from other languages freighted with new meanings for English speakers.

The biggest and fattest unabridged English dictionaries hold more than 600,000 words, compared to German in second place with 185,000 words. One reason we have accumulated the world's largest and most varied vocabulary is that English continues to be the most hospitable and democratic language that has ever existed, unique in the number and variety of its borrowed words.

The following are words that became part of the English language as a result of England's great economic expansion.

Africa *banana, boorish, chimpanzee, gorilla, gumbo,* and *zebra*

Asia *gingham, indigo, mango,* and *typhoon*

Australia *boomerang* and *kangaroo*

India *bandanna, bungalow, calico, cashmere, china, cot, curry, juggernaut, jungle, loot, nirvana, polo, punch* (beverage), *thug,* and *verandah*

1816: France
René Laënnec invents stethoscope. ▼

1818: Mary Wollstonecraft Shelley publishes *Frankenstein, or the Modern Prometheus.* ▲

1819: Peterloo Massacre in Manchester.

1819

Blake made his readers look at the reality of child labor in "The Chimney Sweeper." Lord Byron spoke "In Defense of the Lower Classes" when Parliament debated using the death penalty against protesting unemployed weavers. This rebellious aristocrat, who would later die in the Greek War of Independence, declared, "I have been in some of the most oppressed provinces of Turkey; but never . . . did I behold such squalid wretchedness as I have seen since my return, in the very heart of a Christian country."

Shelley's poem "Men of England" later became the anthem of the British Labour Party:

> Men of England, wherefore plough
> For the lords who lay ye low?
> Wherefore weave with toil and care
> The rich robes your tyrants wear?

Other Ways Some writers reminded people of other ways of being. Nature in the poetry of Wordsworth is not the artificial world of pastoral poetry. His nature is a cleaner, greener world in which human nature can be, if not reborn, at least restored. He writes in "Tintern Abbey": "Nature never did betray / The heart that loved her."

Revolution on a Page Not only that, Wordsworth's focus on common people and their language was a translation of the political goals of the French Revolution—"liberty, equality, fraternity"—into literature. If revolution had turned to terror on the stage of history, it still might be successful on the page.

An Era of Change The people of the time faced unprecedented changes. No political order could ever again be seen as unchangeable. That all people should be free and free to choose their leaders were ideas whose time had come. That economic progress could only be had at the cost of blighting the world was an idea to be challenged.

Some writers spoke out against the ills they saw; others looked inward or far away to see worlds that might be. Human nature was not born again, but human beings were changed profoundly.

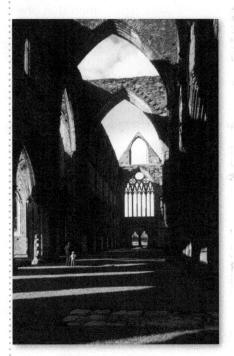

Tintern Abbey

TIMELINE

1819: Percy Bysshe Shelley writes "Ode to the West Wind."

1820: John Keats publishes "Ode on a Grecian Urn." ▶

1819

1819: First steamship crosses Atlantic. ▶

What is the relationship of the **writer** to *tradition?*

No writer of the period called himself or herself "Romantic," but later critics applied the term because they saw consistent themes and attitudes in the literature. *Romantic* in this sense does not mean love stories. It means everything that is the opposite of the drab, the ordinary, the conventional, the routine, the predictable, and the expected.

The Faraway and Exotic Romantic literature can be realistic, as in Scottish poet Robert Burns's "To a Louse," but the emphasis is on the faraway and exotic, as in the Xanadu of Coleridge's "Kubla Khan" and the fantastic and supernatural of his *The Rime of the Ancient Mariner*.

In what ways did Romantics reject previous traditions?

Discarding Eighteenth-Century Forms Romantics were by nature rebellious, unhappy with and unwilling to settle for the status quo. They cast aside the literary forms and subjects that had dominated the previous century—no more conventions and artificialities, satires and heroic couplets. Such forms were to be swept away, as the French Revolution had swept away powdered wigs and knee breeches. Prefigured by Burns and Blake, the new literature was to be authentic and sincere.

Using Ordinary Speech The use of ordinary speech in Romantic literature gave it its authentic feel. The poems of Burns and Joanna Baillie, written in Scottish dialect, proved to be popular with people of the common, or uneducated, class. Romantics achieved sincerity by revealing their personal thoughts and feelings. For example, Wordsworth charts the development of his consciousness with sincerity in *The Prelude*.

Political Rebels Writers were also rebelling against a political order that had, after victory over Napoleon's tyranny, itself become reactionary and repressive. They rebelled against an economic system that turned men, women, and children into factory "hands." They idolized seventeenth-century writer John Milton, in whom they saw a poet who stood up to kings and valued poetry for its prophetic strain.

1825: **Russia** Bolshoi Ballet founded. ▶

1826

◀ 1825: Horse-drawn buses begin operating in London.

What poetical traditions did the Romantics revive?

The Sonnet Romantic poets revived the sonnet, which had virtually disappeared after Milton. Wordsworth used it as a political form in "London, 1802" and Shelley as a visionary form in "Ozymandias" and in "Ode to the West Wind," which is made up of linked sonnets.

The Ode In addition, the Romantics brought to perfection one of the oldest forms of poetry—the ode. Odes were written by Wordsworth, Coleridge, Shelley and, most notably, twenty-four-year-old John Keats.

What mysterious literary figure did the Romantics create?

The Byronic Hero Lord Byron embodies in his life the spirit of the age. A handsome, club-footed aristocrat who scorned the rules of society, he was described as "mad, bad and dangerous to know." Byron created in his person and in his characters the Byronic Hero—mysterious, brooding, threatening. That hero is the distant ancestor of today's mysterious outsiders, whether in film, literature, or the graphic novel.

What prose genres did the Romantics invent?

The leading novelists of the period were Jane Austen and Sir Walter Scott. Austen created a kind of comic novel that focused on the manners of middle-class people, depicting the follies and foibles of families. Her insights into human behavior and her comic touches have inspired today's directors to make film versions of Austen's *Emma* and *Pride and Prejudice*. Scott, regarded as the inventor of the historical novel, took readers back into the history, myths, and legends of England and Scotland. A best seller of his time and the creator of an enduring genre, he fed the Romantic hunger for the distant and the exotic.

The Gothic Mary Shelley wrote *Frankenstein*, influenced by the relatively new tradition of the horror-filled Gothic novel. Doctor Frankenstein, in creating his monster, acts out the great Romantic theme of going beyond the limit. The novel reveals the disquieting shadow cast by science and reason. Frankenstein's monster, in his immense solitude, also seems to warn of a darker side of Romantic ideals—of a humanity that, seeking to redefine itself, is, instead, cut off from its origins.

> **ESSENTIAL QUESTION VOCABULARY**
>
> These Essential Question words will help you think and write about the writer and tradition:
>
> **conventional** (kən ven´ shə nəl) *n.* usually an adjective, it refers as a noun to whatever follows rules and is not original
>
> **routine** (rōō tēn´) *n.* regular, customary procedure
>
> **foibles** (foi´ bəlz) *n.* small weaknesses in character

TIMELINE

1829: Robert Peel establishes Metropolitan Police in London. ▶

1826

1827: System for purifying London water installed.

1830: Liverpool–Manchester railway opens. ▼

Jane Austen, Movie Star

At first glance, Jane Austen, a nineteenth-century novelist, seems an improbable box-office draw.

She never married, lived with her mother and sister, and died at age 41. Her novels lack sensation of the kind that modern audiences might be thought to crave. They mostly depict the lives of well-brought-up young ladies as they embark on the marriage-go-round.

Yet, since the 1990s, there have been literally dozens of successful film adaptations of Austen's books.

Some have been faithful to the original setting of her works, such as the 2005 *Pride and Prejudice* starring Keira Knightley. Other movies, such as *Clueless*, have transplanted plot and characters to more contemporary settings.

In 2007, the film *Becoming Jane* was made about Austen's own life, a fact that would certainly have brought a wry smile to her face.

As Hollywood has discovered, Austen's portrayal of human nature hits the mark every time. Her heroes and heroines may wear top hats and layers of petticoats. They may ride sedately in horse-drawn carriages. However, in their king's English, they speak directly to today's audiences, who see in these characters' dilemmas and decisions reflections of their own.

1831: Michael Faraday demonstrates electromagnetic induction. ▶

◀ **1831: United States** Edgar Allan Poe publishes *Poems*.

1832

1832: First Reform Act extends voting rights.

Recent Scholarship

ELIZABETH McCRACKEN

TALKS ABOUT THE TIME PERIOD

Creating a Legend

Mary Shelley wasn't the first person to imagine creating a living being out of something dead. The subtitle of *Frankenstein—The Modern Prometheus*—refers to the mythological Greek titan who made men out of clay. In a famous Jewish myth, a learned rabbi creates a creature out of clay to protect the Jewish people. Throughout the eighteenth century, inventors created increasingly complicated automata—early robots—who could eat, make musical instruments, and even play chess. People have always been fascinated by trying to create life, or the appearance of it, using nonliving material.

Science Explained

But Mary Shelley was the first writer to explain the notion of someone creating an actual living, breathing being using scientific methods. She was the product of her times. The eighteenth century was a time of enormous scientific discovery, including the work of Isaac Newton, the father of modern physics; the chemist Antoine Lavoisier; and Benjamin Franklin, with his experiments into electricity. Scientists and philosophers of the eighteenth century spoke of "The New Science," meaning that the universe could be understood by human beings who observed the natural world.

About the Author

Born in in 1966 in Boston, Massachusetts, to editor/writer parents, Elizabeth McCracken worked full time as a librarian until 1995. She draws on her love of that profession in the novel *The Giant's House: A Romance* (1996), which was a National Book Award finalist for fiction. Other works include the notable collection of short works, *Here's Your Hat, What's Your Hurry* (1993).

PROMETHÉE

Part of the Natural World

In the early nineteenth century, writing and science became more aligned than ever before. Percy Shelley was a passionate student of all the sciences. His college room was filled with his experiments. John Keats studied as a doctor. The "Dr. Darwin" mentioned in Mary Shelley's introduction is Charles's grandfather, Erasmus Darwin, who was not only a doctor, botanist, and inventor, but also a best-selling poet. William Wordsworth, Lord Byron, Percy Shelley, and John Keats all read Darwin and took what they learned about the natural world and applied it to their poetry. To be a human being was to be part of the natural world, and to write about nature, you had to study it very carefully. When the Romantic poets wrote about nature, they were also writing about the human condition. We are nature, and nature is us.

And, Mary Shelley might suggest, we better not mess with it. *Frankenstein* is filled with real and imagined science, but one of the reasons it's been popular for so long is that, at the dawn of modern science, Mary Shelley talked about how it was both exciting and dangerous. Before writing *Frankenstein*, Mary Shelley had had a child who died a few days after birth, and in her journal she writes of a dream in which the baby "came to life again . . . it had only been cold . . . and we rubbed it before the fire, and it lived." She knew the pain of wanting to bring something that was dead back to life, and then she wrote a book about the dangers.

Frankenstein had many children—characters from *Blade Runner, Robocop,* and *The Terminator,* clones and androids in any number of science fiction novels. You give something life, and then it goes amuck. Even now, when people argue about the latest scientific advances—transplants of animal organs, artificial organs, and of course cloning—*Frankenstein* is often the cautionary tale. We are nature, and nature is us, and we can never hope to completely master it.

▶ **Critical Viewing** In what way is a figure like this one a "Son of Frankenstein"?

© **Research and Technology: Synthesizing Information**

As Elizabeth McCracken points out, Mary Shelley's *Frankenstein* influenced many horror movies about scientists going too far in their investigations. Working with a partner, create an **annotated filmography** of such films. Entitled "Frankenstein's Children," your filmography should include this information for each entry: title of movie, year of release, director, main actors, plot summary, and relationship to the Frankenstein theme of meddling with nature. For your research, use books on film and online resources like the Internet Movie Database. Consider using a simple *database* or *Excel chart* for your filmography and *integrating it into a word-processed document.*

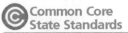

Integrate and Evaluate Information

1. Use a chart like the one shown to determine the key ideas expressed in the Essential Question essays on pages 720–726. Fill in two ideas related to each Essential Question and note the authors most closely associated with each concept. One example has been done for you.

Essential Question	Author	Key Concept
Literature and Place		
Literature and Society		
Writer and Tradition	William Wordsworth	Using ordinary speech

2. How do the visual sources in this section—artifacts, paintings, photographs, and illustrations—add to your understanding of the ideas expressed in words? Cite specific examples.

3. The Romantic period was characterized by innovation and a rejection of tradition. Sometimes these innovations led to positive changes and a greater degree of freedom. Other times, they created new problems. Choose one innovation or change that emerged during this period and describe the various perspectives of those it affected. Who gained something from the change? Who lost something or was harmed by it? Cite evidence from the multiple sources presented on pages 718–726 in your answer.

4. Address a Question According to Elizabeth McCracken, the Romantic poets understood that "we are nature, and nature is us." What do you think McCracken means by this? In your view, is this idea mostly honored or ignored in today's world? Integrate information from this textbook and other sources to support your ideas.

Speaking and Listening: Press Conference

Romantic poets challenged earlier literary practices. With a group, stage a **press conference** in which Wordsworth; his sister, Dorothy; and Coleridge answer questions about their Romantic beliefs. The questioners are journalists who pose challenging queries like these:

- Why do Romantics reject refined language?
- Why do Romantics promote dangerous revolutionary ideas?
- Why are Romantics prejudiced against cities?

Solve a Research Problem: This assignment requires you to integrate information and distinguish nuances in Romantic beliefs. To prepare, research Romantic ideas about language, politics, and nature. Identify print and media sources that provide reliable information about Romanticism. Consider using various types of sources, including

- **primary sources,** or the poets' written works; and

- **secondary sources,** or books and articles about this era.

Create a list of sources you used to prepare.

Common Core State Standards

Reading Informational Text
7. Integrate and evaluate multiple sources of information presented in different media or formats as well as in words in order to address a question or solve a problem.

Speaking and Listening
1. Initiate and participate effectively in a range of collaborative discussions with diverse partners on *grades 11–12 topics, texts, and issues,* building on others' ideas and expressing their own clearly and persuasively.

1.c. Propel conversations by posing and responding to questions that probe reasoning and evidence; ensure a hearing for a full range of positions on a topic or issue; clarify, verify, or challenge ideas and conclusions; and promote divergent and creative perspectives.

ESSENTIAL QUESTION VOCABULARY

Use these words in your responses:

Literature and Place
exotic
secular
residential

Literature and Society
privileged
institution
industrial

The Writer and Tradition
conventional
routine
foibles

Fantasy and Reality

Connecting to the Essential Question These poets have a sharp eye for people's behavior in social situations. As you read, consider what these poets observe and say about the social customs and attitudes of their time. Noting this information will help you answer the Essential Question: **How does literature shape or reflect society?**

Literary Analysis

Dialect is the language, and particularly the speech habits, of a specific social class, region, or group. A dialect may vary from the standard form of a language in grammar, in pronunciation, and in the use of certain expressions. In literature, dialect helps achieve these goals:

- Establishing character, mood, and setting
- Adding "texture" or charm for readers who do not speak the dialect

By using dialect, Burns and Baillie broke with tradition and made their work accessible to the common folk who spoke that dialect. Their use of dialect also adds a sense of authenticity and freshness to the poems. As you read, note the ways in which the poets infuse the dialect with poetic effects.

Comparing Literary Works In addition to using dialect, Romantic poets like Burns and Baillie also introduced subjects drawn from everyday life. This shift away from lofty topics was part of the artistic rebellion known as *Romanticism*. As you read, compare how effectively these poets write about daily life in the language of common folk. Consider factors such as their ability to convey *mood,* or emotional atmosphere, and *meaning*.

Reading Strategy

Preparing to Read Complex Texts Even if you do not know Scottish dialect, you can **analyze information from text features** to interpret words. As you read, pay attention to features such as footnotes and apostrophes indicating missing letters in a word. Use a chart like the one shown to help you translate the dialect.

Vocabulary

dominion (də min′ yən) *n.* rule; authority (p. 735)

impudence (im′ pyoo dəns) *n.* lack of shame; rudeness (p. 737)

winsome (win′ səm) *adj.* having a charming appearance or way (p. 741)

discretion (di skresh′ ən) *n.* good judgment; prudence (p. 742)

inconstantly (in kän′ stənt lē) *adv.* changeably; in a fickle way (p. 742)

Common Core State Standards

Reading Literature
4. Determine the meaning of words and phrases as they are used in the text, including figurative and connotative meanings; analyze the impact of specific word choices on meaning and tone, including words with multiple meanings or language that is particularly fresh, engaging, or beautiful.

Footnotes	
sleekit[3]	**3.** sleek
Missing Letters	
woo'd, a'	wooed, all

PHLit
Online!
www.PHLitOnline.com

Robert Burns

(1759–1796)

Author of "To a Mouse" • "To a Louse"

Known as "The Voice of Scotland," Robert Burns wrote his first verse when he was fifteen. It was a love poem to a girl named Nellie, who was helping the Burns family with the harvest on their farm in Scotland. "Thus with me," Burns later wrote, "began Love and Poesy."

Poor But Learned Beginnings Burns was born at Alloway, in Ayrshire. Although poverty kept him from a full formal education, with his father's encouragement he read widely, studying the Bible, Shakespeare, and Alexander Pope. His mother, though herself illiterate, instilled in him a love of Scottish folk songs, legends, and proverbs.

Literary Triumph In 1786, Burns published his first collection of poems, *Poems, Chiefly in the Scottish Dialect*, through a small local press. The collection, which included "To a Mouse," was a huge success, applauded by critics and country folk alike. The new literary hero was invited to the Scottish capital, where he was swept into the social scene and hailed as the "heaven-taught plowman." When he died, thousands of people from all social levels followed his coffin to the grave.

A Lasting Contribution Although Burns died while just in his thirties, having suffered for years from a weak heart, his brief career resulted in a lasting contribution to literature. Burns's poems, written for the most part in dialect, are marked by their natural, direct, and spontaneous quality. Burns certainly drew on the ballad tradition of Scotland, but while some of the poet's work had its origins in folk tunes, "it is not," as critic James Douglas writes, "easy to tell where the vernacular ends and the personal magic begins."

*"My heart's in
the Highlands . . ."*

TO A MOUSE

On Turning Her up in Her Nest with the Plow, November, 1785

Robert Burns

BACKGROUND

Before Robert Burns published his poetry, works of literature were almost always modeled on the classics, in which structure, grammar, and vocabulary were polished and complex. Robert Burns ignored these conventions and boldly put poetry in the hands of the people, writing in their language, Scottish dialect, and using common folk as subject matter.

Wee, sleekit,[1] cow'rin', tim'rous beastie,
O, what a panic's in thy breastie!
Thou need na start awa sae hasty,
    Wi' bickering brattle![2]
5 I wad be laith[3] to rin an' chase thee
    Wi' murd'ring pattle![4]

I'm truly sorry man's dominion
Has broken Nature's social union,
An' justifies that ill opinion,
10   Which makes thee startle,
At me, thy poor, earth-born companion,
    An' fellow-mortal!

I doubt na, whyles,[5] but thou may thieve;
What then? poor beastie, thou maun[6] live!
15 A daimen icker in a thrave[7]
    'S a sma' request:
I'll get a blessin' wi' the lave,[8]
    And never miss't!

Thy wee bit housie, too, in ruin!
20 Its silly wa's[9] the win's are strewin'!
An' naething, now, to big[10] a new ane,
    O' foggage[11] green!
An' bleak December's winds ensuin',
    Baith snell[12] an' keen!

25 Thou saw the fields laid bare and waste,
An' weary winter comin' fast,
An' cozie here, beneath the blast,
    Thou thought to dwell,
Till crash! the cruel coulter[13] past
30   Out through thy cell.

Vocabulary
dominion (də min′ yən)
n. rule; authority

Spiral Review
Conceit In what ways does the poem build a conceit about the mouse as the speaker's companion or equal?

Reading Strategy
Analyzing Text Features
Use context clues and nearby footnotes to determine the meaning of "win's" in line 20.

Reading Check
How does the speaker uncover the mouse?

---

1. **sleekit** sleek.
2. **Wi' . . . brattle** with a quick pattering sound.
3. **wad be laith** would be loath.
4. **pattle** paddle for cleaning a plow.
5. **whyles** at times.
6. **maun** must.
7. **A . . . thrave** an occasional ear of grain in a bundle.
8. **lave** rest.
9. **silly wa's** feeble walls.
10. **big** build.
11. **foggage** rough grass.
12. **snell** sharp.
13. **coulter** plow blade.

That wee bit heap o' leaves an' stibble,
Has cost thee mony a weary nibble!
Now thou's turned out, for a' thy trouble,
    But[14] house or hald,[15]
35 To thole[16] the winter's sleety dribble,
    An' cranreuch[17] cauld!

But, Mousie, thou art no thy lane,[18]
In proving foresight may be vain:
The best laid schemes o' mice an' men
40   Gang aft a-gley,[19]
An' lea'e us nought but grief an' pain,
    For promised joy.

Still thou art blest, compared wi' me!
The present only toucheth thee:
45 But, och! I backward cast my e'e
    On prospects drear!
An' forward, though I canna see,
    I guess an' fear!

BUT, MOUSIE,

thou art no
thy lane,
In proving
foresight may
be vain:

14. **But** without.
15. **hald** property.
16. **thole** withstand.
17. **cranreuch** (krən′ rəkh) frost.
18. **no thy lane** not alone.
19. **Gang aft a-gley** go often awry.

Critical Reading

Cite textual evidence to support your responses.

1. **Key Ideas and Details (a)** For what reason does the speaker apologize to the mouse? **(b) Infer:** How does the speaker feel about the grain the mouse steals? **(c) Interpret:** What does the speaker's reaction show about his ideas of justice?

2. **Key Ideas and Details (a) Infer:** What has happened to the mouse's attempt to prepare for winter? **(b) Interpret:** Which two famous lines in the poem express the poem's theme? **(c) Paraphrase:** Restate the theme in your own words.

3. **Key Ideas and Details (a) Interpret:** What comparison does the speaker draw between himself and the mouse in the last stanza? **(b) Evaluate:** Do you agree with the speaker about the mouse's advantage? Explain.

4. **Integration of Knowledge and Ideas** What value do you place on foresight? Explain.

5. **Craft and Structure** Does dialect add to the quality of folk-wisdom in the poem, or does it distract from the meaning? Explain.

To a Louse

On Seeing One on a Lady's Bonnet At Church

Robert Burns

◀ **Critical Viewing**
In what way are this lady's pose and costume similar to those of the lady in the poem? Explain. **[Connect]**

Ha! whare ye gaun, ye crowlin' ferlie!¹
Your impudence protects you sairly:²
I canna say but ye strunt³ rarely,
    Owre gauze and lace;
5 Though faith! I fear ye dine but sparely
    On sic a place.

Ye ugly, creepin', blastit wonner,⁴
Detested, shunned by saunt an' sinner,
How dare ye set your fit⁵ upon her,

Vocabulary
impudence (im′ pyo͞o dəns)
n. lack of shame; rudeness

Reading Check

Where is the louse crawling?

---

1. **crowlin' ferlie** crawling wonder.
2. **sairly** wondrously.
3. **strunt** strut.
4. **blastit wonner** blasted wonder.
5. **fit** foot.

The Literature of Scotland
Burns's dialect poems were part of a long struggle over Scottish identity. From the late thirteenth century to the middle of the sixteenth century, the Lowlands area of Scotland—Burns's native region—frequently warred with England. A distinctive culture blossomed in the region, yielding famous ballads such as "Barbara Allan."

When Scotland united with England in 1707, important Scottish authors of the time, such as economist Adam Smith, wrote in English as the English spoke it. However, there was a backlash, and Scotland was swept by a literary enthusiasm for things distinctly Scottish. In the poems of Burns, Baillie, and others, as well as in a new passion for collecting the old ballads, the Scottish past reasserted itself even as it faded.

Connect to the Literature

Read aloud lines 7–12. What effect does the Scottish dialect of selected words have on the entire stanza?

10   Sae fine a lady?
Gae somewhere else, and seek your dinner
    On some poor body.

Swith![6] in some beggar's haffet[7] squattle;[8]
There ye may creep, and sprawl, and sprattle[9]
15 Wi' ither kindred, jumping cattle,
    In shoals and nations:
Whare horn nor bane[10] ne'er dare unsettle
    Your thick plantations.

Now haud[11] ye there, ye're out o' sight,
20 Below the fatt'rels,[12] snug an' tight;
Na, faith ye yet![13] ye'll no be right
    Till ye've got on it,
The vera tapmost, tow'ring height
    O' Miss's bonnet.

25 My sooth! right bauld ye set your nose out,
As plump and gray as onie grozet;[14]
O for some rank, mercurial rozet,[15]
    Or fell,[16] red smeddum,[17]
I'd gie you sic a hearty dose o't,
30   Wad dress your droddum![18]

I wad na been surprised to spy
You on an auld wife's flannen toy;[19]
Or aiblins some bit duddie boy,[20]
    On's wyliecoat;[21]

6. **Swith** swift.
7. **haffet** locks.
8. **squattle** sprawl.
9. **sprattle** struggle.
10. **horn nor bane** comb made of horn or bone.
11. **haud** hold.
12. **fatt'rels** ribbon ends.
13. **Na, faith ye yet!** "Confound you!"
14. **onie grozet** (gräz´ it) any gooseberry.
15. **rozet** (räz´ it) rosin.
16. **fell** sharp.
17. **smeddum** powder.
18. **Wad . . . droddum** "would put an end to you."
19. **flannen toy** flannel cap.
20. **Or . . . boy** or perhaps on some little ragged boy.
21. **wyliecoat** (wī´ lē kōt´) undershirt.

35　But Miss's fine Lunardi![22] fie,
　　　　How daur ye do't?

　　O, Jenny, dinna toss your head,
　　An' set your beauties a' abread![23]
　　Ye little ken what cursèd speed
40　　　　The blastie's[24] makin'!
　　Thae[25] winks and finger-ends, I dread,
　　　　Are notice takin'!

　　O wad some Pow'r the giftie gie us
　　To see oursels as ithers see us!
45　It wad frae monie a blunder free us
　　　　And foolish notion:
　　What airs in dress an' gait wad lea'e us,
　　　　And ev'n devotion!

What airs in dress an' gait wad lea'e us, And ev'n devotion!

---

22. **Lunardi** balloon-shaped bonnet, named for Vincenzo Lunardi, a balloonist of the late 1700s.
23. **abread** abroad.
24. **blastie's** creature's.
25. **Thae** those.

Critical Reading

1. **Key Ideas and Details** **(a)** What is the louse doing? **(b)** What does the speaker command it to do instead? **(c) Interpret:** What social assumptions about cleanliness does the speaker's command reflect?

2. **Key Ideas and Details** **(a) Draw Conclusions:** What impression of Jenny does the speaker create? **(b) Analyze:** How do the references to her clothing and the contrast between her and "some poor body" contribute to this impression?

3. **Key Ideas and Details** **(a) Infer:** In lines 37–42, why does the speaker warn Jenny against tossing her head? **(b) Infer:** What is the reaction of others in the church to Jenny's gesture? **(c) Draw Conclusions:** Why is the contrast between this gesture and the progress of the louse particularly embarrassing?

4. **Integration of Knowledge and Ideas** **(a) Interpret:** Paraphrase the generalization that the speaker makes in the last stanza. **(b) Evaluate:** Do you agree that we would profit if we could "see oursels as ithers see us"? Explain.

5. **Integration of Knowledge and Ideas** Do you think caring about the impression we make on others is foolish vanity? Explain.

Cite textual evidence to support your responses.

Joanna Baillie (1762–1851)

Author of "Woo'd and Married and A' "

When Joanna Baillie's (bā´ lēz) *Plays on the Passions* was published anonymously in 1798, it created a great literary sensation in London. Debates raged over which famous man of letters had written the plays. It was not until 1800 that the true author was revealed—an unassuming thirty-eight-year-old Scottish woman named Joanna Baillie. Even her literary friends were astounded, and she became an instant celebrity.

A Gregarious Tomboy Born in Lanarkshire, Scotland, the daughter of a minister, young Joanna Baillie was a tomboy who loved horseback riding and who resisted the stern moral education given by her father. She blossomed when she and her sister, Agnes, were sent away to boarding school in 1772. Joanna Baillie became an outgoing leader who led the other girls on boisterous outdoor adventures and staged plays that she herself wrote.

A Spinster's Life in London When Baillie's father died in 1778, the family depended on the kindness of a wealthy uncle for support. He provided the two sisters with a lifetime income. When their brother married in 1791, the sisters and their mother started a household of their own. They began a busy social life amid London's bustling literary scene, welcoming many important writers of the day into their home.

Success and Critical Acclaim With Baillie's literary success, the two sisters were able to travel, and they often returned to Scotland to visit Sir Walter Scott, who helped in the production of Baillie's plays. Best known in her day for her dramatic works, Baillie also wrote poetry. Like her fellow Scot, Robert Burns, she wrote poems in the dialect of her homeland, many of them on nature and rustic manners.

> **"Pampered vanity is a better thing perhaps than starved pride."**

Woo'd and Married and A'

Joanna Baillie

The bride she is winsome and bonny,
  Her hair it is snooded[1] sae sleek,
And faithfu' and kind is her Johnny,
  Yet fast fa' the tears on her cheek.
5 New pearlins[2] are cause of her sorrow,
  New pearlins and plenishing[3] too;
The bride that has a' to borrow
  Has e'en right mickle[4] ado.
    Woo'd and married and a'!
10   Woo'd and married and a'!
  Is na' she very weel aff
    To be woo'd and married at a'?

Her mither then hastily spak,
  "The Lassie is glaikit[5] wi' pride;
15 In my pouch I had never a plack[6]
  On the day when I was a bride.
E'en tak to your wheel and be clever,
  And draw out your thread in the sun;
The gear[7] that is gifted it never
20 Will last like the gear that is won.
    Woo'd and married and a'!
    Wi' havins and toucher[8] sae sma'!
  I think ye are very weel aff
    To be woo'd and married at a'."

---

1. **snooded** bound up with a ribbon.
2. **pearlins** lace trimmings.
3. **plenishing** furnishings.
4. **mickle** much.
5. **glaikit** foolish.
6. **plack** farthing; a small coin equal to one fourth of a penny.
7. **gear** wealth or goods.
8. **havins and toucher** possessions and dowry.

Vocabulary
winsome (win´ səm) *adj.*
having a charming
appearance or way

Literary Analysis
Dialect What feelings
or qualities does the use of
dialect add to the mother's
advice to her daughter?

Reading
Check
What is the mother's opinion
about her daughter's
marriage?

The Village Wedding, (detail) Sir Luke Fildes, Christopher Wood Gallery, London

25 "Toot, toot," quo' her gray-headed faither,
        "She's less o' a bride than a bairn,[9]
    She's ta'en like a cout[10] frae the heather,
        Wi' sense and discretion to learn.
    Half husband, I trow, and half daddy,
30   As humor inconstantly leans,
    The chiel maun be patient and steady[11]
            That yokes wi' a mate in her teens.
                A kerchief sae douce[12] and sae neat
                O'er her locks that the wind used to blaw!
35 I'm baith like to laugh and to greet[13]
            When I think of her married at a'!"

    Then out spak the wily bridegroom,
            Weel waled[14] were his wordies, I ween,
    "I'm rich, though my coffer be toom,[15]
40   Wi' the blinks o' your bonny blue e'en.[16]
    I'm prouder o' thee by my side,

---

 9. bairn child.
10. cout colt.
11. The chiel maun . . . steady The man must be patient and steady.
12. douce respectable.
13. greet weep.
14. waled chosen.
15. toom empty.
16. e'en eyes.

Though thy ruffles or ribbons be few,
Than if Kate o' the Croft were my bride
Wi' purfles[17] and pearlins enow.
45   Dear and dearest of ony!
          Ye're woo'd and buikit[18] and a'!
And do ye think scorn o' your Johnny,
And grieve to be married at a'?"

She turn'd, and she blush'd, and she smiled,
50   And she looked sae bashfully down;
The pride o' her heart was beguiled,
          And she played wi' the sleeves o' her gown.
She twirled the tag o' her lace,
          And she nipped her boddice sae blue,
55   Syne blinkit sae sweet in his face,
          And aff like a maukin[19] she flew.
          Woo'd and married and a'!
Wi' Johnny to roose[20] her and a'!
She thinks hersel very weel aff
60   To be woo'd and married at a'!

---

17. purfles embroidered trimmings.
18. buikit "booked"; entered as married in the official registry.
19. maukin hare.
20. roose praise.

Critical Reading ©

© 1. Key Ideas and Details (a) How does the bridegroom respond to his bride's unhappiness? **(b) Analyze Cause and Effect:** Describe the effect the bridegroom's words have on his young bride. **(c) Draw Conclusions:** How would you describe the personality of the bridegroom?

© 2. Key Ideas and Details (a) Which speaker succeeds in changing the bride's outlook? **(b) Draw Conclusions:** Judging from the final stanza, do you think the marriage will be a happy one? Explain.

© 3. Integration of Knowledge and Ideas Do you think the poet is unkind to the young bride, or does she show insight into people? Explain.

© 4. Integration of Knowledge and Ideas What are the poets' attitudes toward the behaviors they describe in these poems? In your response, use at least two of these Essential Question words: *traditional, role, spirit.* [*Connecting to the Essential Question: How does literature shape or reflect society?*]

Cite textual evidence to support your responses.

Literary Analysis

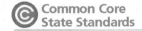

1. **Craft and Structure** What does the use of **dialect** in the poems by Burns suggest about the speaker's social status?

2. **Craft and Structure** What does dialect contribute to the setting of Joanna Baillie's "Woo'd and Married and A'"?

3. **Craft and Structure** Find at least two examples in "To a Mouse" of the following pronunciation patterns for Scottish English: **(a)** Final consonants are dropped, and **(b)** the letter *o* is replaced by either *ae* or *a*.

4. **Craft and Structure** How would the overall effect of these poems have been different if they had been written in Standard English?

5. **Comparing Literary Works** Using a chart like the one shown, analyze the subject matter of the poems in this grouping.

Poem	Subject	Message

6. **Comparing Literary Works** **(a)** Which poem conveys a message that applies most generally? Explain. **(b)** Which poem conveys a message that applies only to some people? Explain.

7. **Comparing Literary Works** Do you think the use of everyday subjects in these poems limits the messages they convey? Explain.

8. **Integration of Knowledge and Ideas** The use of everyday subjects in poetry is our inheritance from poets like these. What subject matter, if any, would you be surprised to find in poetry today? Explain.

Reading Strategy

9. List and define ten words in dialect that appear in these poems. For each, explain how you **analyzed information from text features** to interpret it.

10. **(a)** Choose one stanza from a Burns or Baillie poem, and translate it into Standard English. **(b)** Compare and contrast the original with your version, indicating what has been gained or lost in the translation.

11. **(a)** Use text aids to write one or two lines of poetry in Scottish dialect. **(b)** Does dialect work better for poetry meant to be read aloud? Why or why not? **(c)** What are the pros and cons of writing poetry in dialect?

12. How could a mass medium like television, aimed at a nation of common folk, cause the dialects spoken by common folk to vanish?

Common Core State Standards

Language
5.b. Analyze nuances in the meaning of words with similar denotations. *(p. 745)*

Writing
1.b. Develop claim(s) and counterclaims fairly and thoroughly, supplying the most relevant evidence for each while pointing out the strengths and limitations of both in a manner that anticipates the audience's knowledge level, concerns, values, and possible biases. *(p. 745)*

Integrated Language Skills

ⓒ Vocabulary Acquisition and Use

Word Analysis: Anglo-Saxon Suffix -some

Baillie calls the bride in her poem *winsome*, meaning "charming." The Anglo-Saxon suffix *-some* means "tending to" or "tending toward being." Literally, *winsome* means "tending to win over or to delight." Use this meaning of the suffix to infer the meaning of each of these words. If necessary, use a *dictionary* to check your educated guesses.

1. awesome
2. handsome
3. lithesome
4. loathsome
5. tiresome
6. worrisome

Then, invent your own new adjective using the suffix *-some*, and explain how the suffix helps create the word's meaning.

Vocabulary: Synonyms

Synonyms are words that share similar denotations, or dictionary definitions. Write the letter of the word that is the best synonym of each word from the vocabulary list on page 732. Then, use a dictionary to explain any nuances in meaning between the synonyms in each pair.

1. dominion: **(a)** incapability **(b)** rule **(c)** pride
2. impudence: **(a)** rudeness **(b)** shyness **(c)** test
3. winsome: **(a)** competitive **(b)** bold **(c)** attractive
4. discretion: **(a)** quiet **(b)** caution **(c)** gratitude
5. inconstantly: **(a)** changeably **(b)** emptily **(c)** sadly

Writing

ⓒ Argumentative Text Both Burns and Baillie use dialect, the distinctive language of a group's everyday speech, in their poems. Suppose you have been invited to speak at a literary festival on the use of dialect in literature. Prepare a three- to five-minute **editorial** speech in which you argue that using dialect is or is not a valuable literary technique.

Prewriting Develop a list of claims both for and against using dialect. Based on those claims, decide which position you will take. Use your list of claims to develop an outline for your speech. Be sure to include the opposing arguments, or counterclaims, in your outline; use the ones you favor to refute them.

Drafting Draft your speech following your outline. Present evidence for your position by using examples from the Burns and Baillie poems. Use persuasive techniques such as *appeals to authority*, *appeals to emotion*, *rhetorical questions,* and *irony* to make your speech more persuasive.

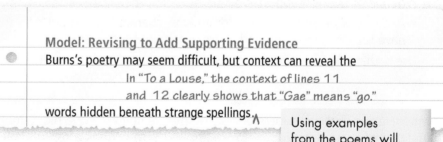

Model: Revising to Add Supporting Evidence

Burns's poetry may seem difficult, but context can reveal the
        In "To a Louse," the context of lines 11
        and 12 clearly shows that "Gae" means "go."
words hidden beneath strange spellings.

Using examples from the poems will support your claims.

Revising Rehearse your delivery, timing yourself and focusing on *performance details*. Make sure the arguments and evidence you present are clear and convincing. Revise the text to fix any trouble spots you find.

Connecting to the Essential Question Like many modern-day artists, Blake pointed out to his audience the misery of fellow humans. As you read, identify passages in which Blake seems to focus on social ills. Doing so will help you answer the Essential Question: **How does literature shape or reflect society?**

Literary Analysis

Blake was a poet who had one eye on mystical visions and the other on the real social ills around him. His mystical visions were based on a perception of **archetypes**—plot patterns, character types, or ideas with emotional power and widespread appeal. Critics argue that archetypes reveal in symbolic form universal truths about humanity. Blake often expressed such archetypes in paired poems, like "The Lamb" and "The Tyger."

Blake is perhaps less well known for his **social commentary**—his criticism of the ills caused by the Industrial Revolution and political tyranny. This Blake, author of "The Chimney Sweeper," had his eye not on the clouds but on urban slums and on the factories in which men, women, and children labored for long hours and little pay.

Comparing Literary Works As you read, compare and contrast these two thematic approaches in Blake's poems: the archetypal visions and the social commentary.

Reading Strategy

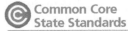 **Preparing to Read Complex Texts** Applying critical perspectives will help you better understand Blake's complex vision of society. As you read, use the following perspectives as ways of understanding Blake's use of archetypes and social commentary:

- *Historical and political perspective*: look for details that suggest economic or political oppression.
- *Archetypal perspective*: look for images, characters, and patterns that have universal meaning and a strong emotional charge.

Use a chart like the one shown to apply both of these perspectives.

Vocabulary

vales (vālz) *n.* valleys; depressed stretches of ground (p. 748)

immortal (i môrt´ əl) *adj.* living or lasting forever; not dying (p. 749)

symmetry (sim´ ə trē) *n.* balanced, beautiful form; the beauty resulting from such balance (p. 749)

aspire (ə spīr´) *v.* have high ambitions; yearn or seek after (p. 749)

sinews (sin´ yo̅o̅z) *n.* tendons (p. 749)

sulk (sulk) *v.* show resentment by refusing to interact with others (p. 752)

Common Core State Standards

Reading Literature
2. Determine two or more themes or central ideas of a text and analyze their development over the course of the text, including how they interact and build on one another to produce a complex account.

Image or Detail

Archetypal Perspective?

Historical Perspective?

PHLit Online!
www.PHLitOnline.com

William Blake

(1757–1827)

Author of "The Lamb" • "The Tyger" • "The Chimney Sweeper" • "Infant Sorrow"

"I must create a system or be enslaved by another man's." So spoke William Blake, an artist and poet who strove in his work to break free from the patterns of thought that defined common experience. As if to underscore the difference between his views and the ordinary, he claimed that mystical visions were the source of his inspiration.

Finding His Way Blake's visions began when, at the age of four, he thought he saw God at his window. Four years later, Blake said, he saw a tree filled with angels. While Blake's "spells" might have seemed a cause for concern, Blake's parents were followers of the mystical teachings of Emanuel Swedenborg, a Swedish spiritualist. They believed that their son had a "gift of vision" and did all they could to nurture this gift.

Blake's father was a poor Londoner who owned a small hosiery shop. He sent Blake to drawing school, and Blake pursued his own education at home through wide reading. He became an engraver's apprentice and then went on to study at the Royal Academy.

Striking Out on His Own Formal study did not last long, however. The rebellious Blake left the school and eventually set up his own print shop. He was to live most of his days eking out a living as an engraver, barely making enough to support himself and his wife, Catherine.

Innocence and Experience When Blake was thirty-two, he published *Songs of Innocence*, a series of poems that he had composed when he was younger. In these poems, Blake suggested that by recapturing the wonderment of childhood, we can achieve the goal of true self-knowledge and integration with the world. In 1794, he brought out a companion to *Songs of Innocence*, entitled *Songs of Experience*.

A Mature Vision Exploring the darker side of life, *Songs of Experience* reflected Blake's growing disillusionment and more mature vision. He came to believe that a return to innocence was not, at least by itself, sufficient for people to attain true self-awareness. Blake's credo was that there must be a fusion of innocence and experience.

Blake's talent was barely recognized by his peers or by the public during his lifetime. Despite the lack of recognition, Blake filled his seventy years with constant creative activity. Years after his death, he came to be regarded as one of the most important poets of his time.

From a manuscript of "The Lamb" by William Blake, Lessing J. Rosenwald Collection, Library of Congress, Washington, D.C.

▲ **Critical Viewing**
What view of nature is expressed by the style of Blake's drawing? **[Infer]**

Vocabulary
vales (vālz) *n.* valleys; hollows; depressed stretches of ground

Literary Analysis
Archetypes What types of people or human conditions does a lamb usually represent?

The Lamb

William Blake

BACKGROUND Blake illustrated his poems with striking, integrated designs. These illustrations seem to swirl through the words and become part of their meaning. Blake claimed that many of the images he drew as illustrations were likenesses of his inner visions. They have a childlike feeling and are very different from the strict, formal styles of his time.

> Little Lamb who made thee
> Dost thou know who made thee
> Gave thee life & bid thee feed.
> By the stream & o'er the mead;
> 5   Gave thee clothing of delight,
> Softest clothing wooly bright;
> Gave thee such a tender voice,
> Making all the vales rejoice!
> Little Lamb who made thee
> 10   Dost thou know who made thee
>
> Little Lamb I'll tell thee,
> Little Lamb I'll tell thee!
> He is called by thy name,
> For he calls himself a Lamb:
> 15   He is meek & he is mild,
> He became a little child:
> I a child & thou a lamb,
> We are called by his name.
> Little Lamb God bless thee.
> 20   Little Lamb God bless thee.

The TYGER

William Blake

Vocabulary

immortal (i môrt′əl)
adj. living or lasting forever; not dying

symmetry (sim′ ə trē)
n. balanced form; the beauty resulting from such balance

aspire (ə spīr′) *v.* have high ambitions; yearn or seek after

sinews (sin′ yo͞oz)
n. tendons

Literary Analysis
Social Commentary
To what type of worker does Blake compare the tiger's creator?

Tyger Tyger, burning bright,
In the forests of the night;
What immortal hand or eye,
Could frame thy fearful symmetry?

5 In what distant deeps or skies
Burnt the fire of thine eyes!
On what wings dare he aspire?
What the hand, dare seize the fire?

And what shoulder, & what art,
10 Could twist the sinews of thy heart?
And when thy heart began to beat,
What dread hand? & what dread feet?

What the hammer? what the chain,
In what furnace was thy brain?
15 What the anvil? what dread grasp,
Dare its deadly terrors clasp?

When the stars threw down their spears
And water'd heaven with their tears:
Did he smile his work to see?
20 Did he who made the Lamb make thee?

Tyger, Tyger burning bright,
In the forests of the night:
What immortal hand or eye,
Dare frame thy fearful symmetry?

The Tyger.

Tyger Tyger. burning bright,
In the forests of the night;
What immortal hand or eye.
Could frame thy fearful symmetry.

In what distant deeps or skies.
Burnt the fire of thine eyes?
On what wings dare he aspire?
What the hand, dare sieze the fire?

And what shoulder, & what art,
Could twist the sinews of thy heart?
And when thy heart began to beat,
What dread hand? & what dread feet?

What the hammer? what the chain,
In what furnace was thy brain?
What the anvil? what dread grasp.
Dare its deadly terrors clasp!

When the stars threw down their spears
And water'd heaven with their tears:
Did he smile his work to see?
Did he who made the Lamb make thee?

Tyger Tyger burning bright,
In the forests of the night;
What immortal hand or eye.
Dare frame thy fearful symmetry.

▲ **Critical Viewing**
Compare and contrast the tiger's expression with the poem's image
of the animal. **[Compare and Contrast]**

THE Chimney Sweeper

William Blake

When my mother died I was very young,
And my father sold me while yet my tongue,
Could scarcely cry weep weep weep weep.
So your chimneys I sweep & in soot I sleep.

5   There's little Tom Dacre, who cried when his head
That curl'd like a lambs back, was shav'd, so I said.
Hush Tom never mind it, for when your head's bare,
You know that the soot cannot spoil your white hair.

And so he was quiet, & that very night,
10 As Tom was a sleeping he had such a sight,
That thousands of sweepers Dick, Joe, Ned & Jack
Were all of them lock'd up in coffins of black

And by came an Angel who had a bright key,
And he open'd the coffins & set them all free.
15 Then down a green plain leaping laughing they run
And wash in a river and shine in the Sun.

Then naked & white, all their bags left behind,
They rise upon clouds, and sport in the wind.
And the Angel told Tom if he'd be a good boy,
20 He'd have God for his father & never want joy.

And so Tom awoke and we rose in the dark
And got with our bags & our brushes to work.
Tho' the morning was cold, Tom was happy & warm,
So if all do their duty, they need not fear harm.

▲ **Critical Viewing**
Compare and contrast Blake's image of a chimney sweeper in his engraving with the image he creates in his poem. **[Compare and Contrast]**

Reading Strategy
Applying Critical Perspectives
Which details in this poem suggest economic oppression? Which details have a strong emotional charge?

INFANT
Sorrow

William Blake

My mother groand!¹ my father wept.
Into the dangerous world I leapt,
Helpless, naked, piping loud;
Like a fiend hid in a cloud.

5 Struggling in my father's hands,
Striving against my swaddling bands;
Bound and weary, I thought best
To sulk upon my mother's breast.

---

1. **groand** groaned; an example of Blake's often eccentric spelling.

▲ **Critical Viewing**
Does the relationship of mother and child in the engraving match that in the poem? Explain. **[Connect]**

Vocabulary
sulk (sulk) *v.* show resentment by refusing to interact with others

Cite textual evidence to support your responses.

Critical Reading

1. Integration of Knowledge and Ideas In what ways do "The Lamb" and "The Tyger" represent opposite sides of human existence?

2. Key Ideas and Details (a) How does the child in the first stanza of "The Chimney Sweeper" get his job? **(b) Interpret:** What do these events suggest about the life of a chimney sweep?

3. Integration of Knowledge and Ideas In "Infant Sorrow," is the infant's final reaction characteristic of the way people deal with frustration? Explain.

4. Integration of Knowledge and Ideas How do these poems prompt you to rethink assumptions about society? Use two of these Essential Question words in your response: *modify, responsibility, justice.* **[Connecting to the Essential Question: How does literature shape or reflect society?]**

Literary Analysis

1. Key Ideas and Details "The Lamb" and "The Tyger" come, respectively, from Blake's paired books *Songs of Innocence* and *Songs of Experience*. **(a)** Why is the lamb, as Blake presents it, an **archetype,** or universal symbol, of innocence? **(b)** Why is the tiger an archetype of experience? **(c)** Does Blake have a good reason for presenting archetypes in pairs? Explain.

2. Craft and Structure Blake uses a great deal of repetition in "The Lamb" and "The Tyger." Do you think this repetition increases the archetypal power of the images in these poems? Why or why not?

3. Integration of Knowledge and Ideas (a) How does the archetypal symbolism of "The Lamb" add to your understanding of the second stanza of "The Chimney Sweeper"? **(b)** How does the symbolism of "The Lamb" help you understand "Infant Sorrow"?

4. Comparing Literary Works (a) Using a chart like the one shown, compare the **social commentary** presented in "The Chimney Sweeper" with that in "Infant Sorrow." **(b)** Does the ending of each poem confirm or challenge the poem's perspective? Explain.

Who Is Suffering?	Why?	Significance to Time Period

5. Analyze Visual Information Explain the humor of the cartoon below.

Reading Strategy

6. Apply an archetypal perspective in reading these poems. **(a)** Can you find examples of archetypal symbols in each of them? Why or why not? **(b)** Which poems are best explained by an archetypal perspective? Support your choices with references to the poems.

7. Apply a historical perspective in reading these poems. **(a)** Can you find references to social ills in each of them? Why or why not? **(b)** Which of the poems are best explained by a historical perspective? Support your choices by making specific references to the poems.

8. Consider how you can blend the archetypal and historical perspectives in reading these poems. For example, could the archetypal "fire" in "The Tyger" be linked with the fires of the oppressive factories of the Industrial Revolution? Explain.

"WHAT IMMORTAL HAND OR EYE COULD FRAME THY FEARFUL SYMMETRY?" ▶

Common Core State Standards

Writing
2.a. Introduce a topic; organize complex ideas, concepts, and information so that each new element builds on that which precedes it to create a unified whole; include formatting, graphics, and multimedia when useful to aiding comprehension. *(p. 754)*

Language
3.a. Vary syntax for effect, consulting references for guidance as needed. *(p. 755)*

4.a. Use context as a clue to the meaning of a word or phrase. *(p. 754)*

© Vocabulary Acquisition and Use

Word Analysis: Latin Root -spir-

In "The Tyger," Blake uses the word *aspire*, meaning "to yearn or seek after." *Aspire* contains the Latin root -spir-, meaning "breath" or "life." When you aspire to something, you "live for it." Many scientific words that have to do with breathing contain the root -spir-. Look up the meaning of each word below. Then, write a definition of your own for each word, incorporating the meaning of -spir-.

1. respiration
2. respirator
3. transpiration
4. aspirate
5. spiracle
6. spirometer

Vocabulary: Context Clues

For each item below, explain how a context clue, or a hint from surrounding words, helps you identify the meaning of the italicized vocabulary word.

1. We traveled through *vales* and over hills.
2. The *symmetry* of the animal's body—two bright eyes, four strong and balanced legs—made it look graceful and powerful.
3. Even though it is a lofty goal, the students *aspire* to attend a top college.
4. After spraining her ankle, the runner received a massage of her muscles and *sinews*.
5. You are not going to *sulk* because we ordered pizza instead of burgers, are you?
6. His work is *immortal*; it will always be read.

Writing

© **Explanatory Text** Write an **essay** on "The Tyger" and "The Chimney Sweeper," applying an archetypal analysis to the former and a social analysis to the latter. Support your analysis with diagrams of archetypes and of social forces.

Prewriting In your thesis, express Blake's vision in each work, and explain whether it is archetypal or social. Also, sketch a diagram that will help readers picture Blake's visions—for "Tyger," it might be a web showing qualities associated with an archetypal symbol and for "Chimney Sweeper," a diagram showing the effects of industrialization.

Drafting Analyze the perspective presented in each poem and show how it affects literary elements such as *tone, imagery,* and *setting.* Refine your diagrams and include *accurate and detailed references* to the texts to support your work.

Revising Review your essay, circling particularly striking details or ideas. Consider moving these details to the beginning or end of a paragraph to add emphasis. Be sure that your diagrams clearly support your analysis.

Model: Revising Placement for Emphasis

The tiger burns with the fires of passion and ambition and perhaps of cruelty. Can one and the same world contain the innocent lamb and the terrors of the tiger? Therefore, Blake seems to suggest, both the world and its creator contain more power and mystery than we care to admit.

At the beginning of the paragraph, the circled sentence will lend greater emphasis.

Conventions and Style: Using Introductory Phrases and Clauses

One way to improve your writing style is to vary your sentence structure. For example, instead of using a subject, you can use phrases and clauses to introduce a sentence. A **phrase** is a group of words that acts as one part of speech but that lacks a subject and a verb. A **clause** is a group of words that has a subject and a verb.

Varying Sentence Beginnings

Blake was writing simple poems by the age of twelve.
By the age of twelve, Blake was writing simple poems. (prepositional phrase)

He read widely at home and was able to get an education on his own.
Reading widely at home, he was able to get an education on his own. (participial phrase)

Blake entered the Royal Academy to continue his studies.
To continue his studies, Blake entered the Royal Academy. (infinitive phrase)

Blake's parents believed him although his visions were unusual.
Although Blake's visions were unusual, his parents believed him. (subordinate clause)

Punctuation Tip Use a comma after introductory elements, except when they are very brief and omitting a comma would not cause confusion.

Practice Revise each sentence by using the italicized part as an introductory phrase or clause. Hint: In some cases, you will need to make slight changes to the original wording.

1. Blake developed his own unique etching process *to print his works.*
2. He could produce only a few books *since the printing process took so long.*
3. Blake's illustrations were *characterized by a childlike mood* and differed from the more formal styles of the time.
4. Blake describes the magnificence of the tiger *in this powerful poem.*
5. The speaker *answers his own question* and says that Christ made the lamb. (Change *answers* to *answering.*)
6. The reader must understand symbolism *to appreciate these poems.*
7. The father sold the boy as a chimney sweep *after the mother died.*
8. Little Tom is *comforted by his friend's words* and has a dream about an angel.
9. The angel opens all the coffins *with his special, bright key.*
10. The boys *rise up into the clouds* and fly toward heaven. (Change *rise* to *rising.*)

© Writing and Speaking Conventions

A. Writing Use each phrase or clause to begin a sentence.

1. during his lifetime
2. working as an engraver
3. to support himself
4. after the boy had a dream

   Example: during his lifetime
   Sentence: During his lifetime, Blake's talent went virtually unnoticed.

B. Speaking Write and present to the class a paragraph contrasting the lamb and the tiger. Use at least four phrases or clauses to begin sentences.

PH WRITING COACH
Further instruction and practice are available in *Prentice Hall Writing Coach.*

Elizabeth McCracken Introduces

FRANKENSTEIN

BY MARY WOLLSTONECRAFT SHELLEY

Dreaming Up Monsters I had only one recurring nightmare as a child. It starred a Frankenstein monster—or at least the kind of Frankenstein monster my seven-year-old dreaming self could come up with, half-human and half-robot, inspired by scraps of movies I had seen, with bolts on his neck and a flashing red ambulance light on top of his head. Certainly he was nothing like the articulate and much scarier monster from Mary Shelley's novel. In the first half of the dream, the monster was my friend. In the second, we went into a cave, and then he chased me out. He could not recognize me. I woke up feeling his fingers on my back.

I remember sitting upright in bed, panting, but it was only a dream. Monsters made up of odd parts did not exist. I didn't live in a world of caves and creatures who chased small girls. My world was a single bed with a brown blanket, my older brother sleeping in one nearby room and my parents in another. They would have told me that I was safe. I didn't want to hear that.

The Thrill of the Terrifying Maybe I liked being scared, but mostly I think I liked the privacy of my nightmare. Like most seven-year-olds, I was never really alone except in dreams. Someone was *always* in a nearby room. I liked the terrifying movies I saw on TV, so many different versions of Frankenstein—*Frankenstein, Bride of Frankenstein, Abbott*

About the Author

Elizabeth McCracken's novel *Niagara Falls All Over Again* won the L. L. Winship/PEN New England Award. For her work, she was awarded grants from the Guggenheim Foundation and the Michener Foundation.

and *Costello Meet Frankenstein*. I liked fairy tales with dark woodcuts of dense forests that might hide any number of monsters. Fear was the only room I had to myself. When I read awful books—ghost stories as I got older, then true crime books about murderers, cannibals, disasters at sea—the safe suburban world around me disappeared, and I was alone and strangely happy.

Where Do Great Characters Come From?

I certainly never had to wonder what Mary Shelley says she was so often asked: "How I, then a young girl, came to think of, and to dilate upon, so very hideous an idea." Young girls—young boys, too, of course—love hideous ideas. My dream about a Frankenstein monster impressed me, because my own brain had come up with it—even if I'd ripped off most of the details. He scared me. He belonged to me. My dream-self wanted to go back to it, the way I would reread a particularly terrifying book. When I woke up in my own solid, real, boring bedroom, all the objects surrounding me were briefly as frightening as the dead fingers that had brushed my back.

It's the same reason I became a fiction writer. I wanted to make up people, and then, later, I wanted to wonder where they came from.

▶ **Critical Viewing**
Which details in this image of Frankenstein's monster convey terror? Explain. **[Analyze]**

Critical Reading

Ⓒ 1. **Key Ideas and Details (a)** What types of frightening movies and books did McCracken enjoy as a child? **(b) Connect:** What does her enjoyment of these tales suggest about her relationship to "the safe suburban world around" her?

Ⓒ 2. **Key Ideas and Details** What do you think McCracken means when she says, "I liked the privacy of my nightmare"?

Ⓒ 3. **Integration of Knowledge and Ideas** Do you agree or disagree with McCracken's statement that young people "love hideous ideas"? Why or why not?

As You Read *Introduction to* Frankenstein . . .

4. Look for the inspiration that helped Mary Shelley write *Frankenstein*.

5. Note the connections between Shelley's fiction and the real-life foundations of her novel.

Connecting to the Essential Question Readers of Gothic literature like Mary Shelley's *Frankenstein* were looking for suspense and thrills. As you read, identify some of the dark, mysterious images Shelley describes. Finding such images will help you answer the Essential Question: **What is the relationship of the writer to tradition?**

Literary Analysis

The novel *Frankenstein* is a classic example of **Gothic literature,** a *sub-genre* of literature that takes the reader from the reasoned order of the everyday world into the dark world of the supernatural. Gothic litera-ture, popular in the late eighteenth and early nineteenth centuries, is set in dark castles or towers or in other places with a disquieting, mysterious atmosphere. As you read, note Gothic characteristics in Shelley's work.

The popularity of this form was due in part to the new **Romantic movement** in literature. Romantics rejected two central beliefs of the 18th-century Enlightenment: that reason is the most important human faculty and that its application can fully explain the world. Instead, Romantics put their faith in imagination and the healing powers of nature. They viewed imagination in the following terms:

- It is a creative force comparable to that of nature.
- It is the fundamental source of morality and truth, enabling people to sympathize with others and to picture the world.

As you read, notice how Shelley's account of the creative process reflects the high value the Romantics placed on imagination.

Reading Strategy

Preparing to Read Complex Texts Involved readers naturally try to **make predictions,** or reasoned guesses, about what will happen next in a literary work. As you read, use *text features*, such as titles, background notes, side notes, clues in the text, and your *background knowledge* to make and confirm predictions. Employ a chart like the one shown to record your predictions.

Vocabulary

appendage (ə pen´ dij) *n.* something added on (p. 761)

ungenial (un jē´ nyəl) *adj.* disagreeable; characterized by bad weather (p. 761)

acceded (ak sēd´ id) *v.* yielded (to); agreed (p. 762)

platitude (plat´ ə tōōd´) *n.* statement lacking originality (p. 762)

phantasm (fan´ taz´ əm) *n.* ghost; figment of the imagination (p. 763)

incitement (in sīt´ mənt) *n.* act of urging; encouragement (p. 764)

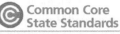

Common Core State Standards

Reading Informational Text
3. Analyze a complex set of ideas or sequence of events and explain how specific individuals, ideas, or events interact and develop over the course of the text.

Clue

"Some volumes of ghost stories . . . fell into our hands."

Prediction

Shelley found the idea for *Frankenstein* in another story.

New Information

"'We will each write a ghost story,' said Lord Byron. . ."

Revision

She found her idea while competing in a contest that the stories inspired.

www.PHLitOnline.com

Mary Wollstonecraft Shelley

(1797–1851)

Author of *Frankenstein*

Writing was in Mary Shelley's blood. Her mother, Mary Wollstonecraft Godwin (who died at Mary's birth), wrote one of the first feminist books ever published, *A Vindication of the Rights of Woman*. Her father, William Godwin, was a leading reformer, author, and political philosopher.

Four years after his wife's death, Godwin married a widow, Mary Jane Claremont, whom his daughter grew to resent bitterly. It was agreed that to ease the situation in the tense household, the girl, now fourteen, would go to live in Dundee, Scotland, in the home of William Baxter, her father's friend. After two years in Scotland, she returned.

Upon her return, Mary Shelley (then still named Godwin) met her future husband, Percy Bysshe Shelley. He was a radical young poet who had become William Godwin's admirer. Mary, only sixteen, fell in love with Shelley, and the two ran away together to the continent and later married.

Eventually, the couple settled in Italy, where they lived blissfully for an all-too-short time. (Their great friend, Lord Byron, also lived in Italy.) Within a few years, the Shelleys suffered the death of two of their children. Then, in 1822, only eight years after Mary Shelley had first met him, Percy Shelley drowned. His death left the twenty-four-year-old Mary and their two-year-old son penniless.

After Percy's death, Mary returned to England, where she continued writing to support herself and her son. She produced several other novels, including *The Last Man* (1826), a tale of a great plague that destroys the human race.

At the age of forty-eight, Mary Shelley became an invalid. She died six years later of a brain tumor.

Introduction to

Frankenstein

Mary Wollstonecraft Shelley

BACKGROUND In Greek mythology, Prometheus was one of the Titans—a race of giants who were said to have existed before humans and who engaged the gods in battle. Later myths say Prometheus created the first human beings. During the Romantic Era, Prometheus drew renewed attention. Percy Bysshe Shelley wrote a verse play about Prometheus entitled *Prometheus Unbound*. The complete title of Mary Shelley's novel about a doctor who attempts to create a man is *Frankenstein, or the Modern Prometheus*.

The Publishers of the Standard Novels, in selecting *Frankenstein* for one of their series, expressed a wish that I should furnish them with some account of the origin of the story. I am the more willing to comply, because I shall thus give a general answer to the question, so very frequently asked me: "How I, then a young girl, came to think of, and to dilate upon, so very hideous an idea?" It is true that I am very averse to bringing myself forward in print; but as my account will only appear as an appendage to a former production, and as it will be confined to such topics as have connection with my authorship alone, I can scarcely accuse myself of a personal intrusion. . . .

In the summer of 1816, we[1] visited Switzerland, and became the neighbors of Lord Byron. At first we spent our pleasant hours on the lake or wandering on its shores; and Lord Byron, who was writing the third canto of *Childe Harold*, was the only one among us who put his thoughts upon paper. These, as he brought them successively to us, clothed in all the light and harmony of poetry, seemed to stamp as divine the glories of heaven and earth, whose influences we partook with him.

But it proved a wet, ungenial summer, and incessant rain often confined us for days to the house. Some volumes of ghost stories, translated from the German into French,[2] fell into our hands. There was "The History of the Inconstant Lover,"[3] who, when he thought to clasp the bride to whom he had pledged his vows, found himself in the arms of the pale ghost of her whom he had deserted. There was the tale of the sinful founder of his race,[4] whose miserable doom it was to bestow the kiss of death on all the younger sons of his fated house, just when they reached the age of promise. His gigantic, shadowy form, clothed like the ghost in Hamlet, in complete armor but with the beaver[5] up, was seen at midnight, by the moon's fitful beams, to advance slowly along the gloomy avenue. The shape was lost beneath the shadow of the castle walls; but soon a gate swung back, a step was heard, the door of the chamber opened, and he advanced to the couch of the blooming youths, cradled in healthy sleep. Eternal sorrow sat upon his face as he bent down and kissed the foreheads of the boys, who from that hour withered like flowers snapped upon the stalk. I have not seen these stories since then, but their incidents are as fresh in my mind as if I had read them yesterday.

---

1. **we** Mary Shelley, her husband Percy Bysshe Shelley, and their two children.
2. **volumes . . . French** *Fantasmagoriana*, or *Collected Stories of Apparitions of Specters, Ghosts, Phantoms, Etc.*, published anonymously in 1812.
3. **"The History . . . Lover"** The true name of the story is "The Dead Fiancée."
4. **the tale . . . race** "Family Portraits."
5. **beaver** hinged piece of armor that covers the face.

A View of Chamonix and Mt. Blanc

◀ **Critical Viewing**
Based on the second paragraph of her essay, do you think Shelley might have liked this image? Why? **[Speculate]**

Vocabulary
appendage (ə pen′ dij) *n.* something added on

ungenial (un jē′ nyəl) *adj.* disagreeable; characterized by bad weather

Elizabeth McCracken
Scholar's Insight
Mary Shelley turned nineteen in the summer of 1816, and while I do think—I hope!—that writers get better as they get older, there's also the fact that you can only write your first novel once. That the mix of ambition and fear and, yes, youth, may make it more exciting and fully realized than the books you write when you know what you're doing.

Reading Check
What has the author set out to explain?

Elizabeth McCracken
Scholar's Insight
A good ghost story stays
in your head forever. I've
never gotten over a book of
New England ghost stories
I had as a child, including
one story about a man who
buried his murder victim
at the base of a tree, only
to find that the next year's
apples all had a clot of
blood in the center of them.

Vocabulary

acceded (ak sēd´ id) *v.*
yielded (to); agreed

platitude (plat´ ə tōōd´)
n. statement lacking
originality

Literary Analysis
Gothic Literature
What elements of the
Gothic tradition are
incorporated in the
image of a shape "lost
beneath the shadow of
the castle walls"?

Reading Strategy
Making Predictions
By what means do you
think Shelley will find a
story idea?

"We will each write a ghost story," said Lord Byron; and his proposition was acceded to. There were four of us.[6] The noble author began a tale, a fragment of which he printed at the end of his poem of Mazeppa. Shelley, more apt to embody ideas and sentiments in the radiance of brilliant imagery, and in the music of the most melodious verse that adorns our language, than to invent the machinery of a story, commenced one founded on the experiences of his early life. Poor Polidori had some terrible idea about a skull-headed lady, who was so punished for peeping through a keyhole—what to see I forget—something very shocking and wrong of course; but when she was reduced to a worse condition than the renowned Tom of Coventry,[7] he did not know what to do with her, and was obliged to despatch her to the tomb of the Capulets,[8] the only place for which she was fitted. The illustrious poets also, annoyed by the platitude of prose, speedily relinquished their uncongenial task.

I busied myself to *think of a story*—a story to rival those which had excited us to this task. One which would speak to the mysterious fears of our nature and awaken thrilling horror—one to make the reader dread to look round, to curdle the blood, and quicken the beatings of the heart. If I did not accomplish these things, my ghost story would be unworthy of its name. I thought and pondered—vainly. I felt that blank incapability of invention which is the greatest misery of authorship, when dull Nothing replies to our anxious invocations. *Have you thought of a story?* I was asked each morning, and each morning I was forced to reply with a mortifying negative. . . .

Many and long were the conversations between Lord Byron and Shelley, to which I was a devout but nearly silent listener. During one of these, various philosophical doctrines were discussed, and among others the nature of the principle of life and whether there was any probability of its ever being discovered and communicated. They talked of the experiments of Dr. Darwin. (I speak not of what the Doctor really did or said that he did, but, as more to my purpose, of what was then spoken of as having been done by him), who preserved a piece of vermicelli in a glass case till by some extraordinary means it began to move with voluntary motion. Not thus, after all, would life be given. Perhaps a corpse would be reanimated: galvanism[9] had given token of such things. Perhaps the component parts of a creature might be manufactured, brought together, and endued with vital warmth.

---

6. **four of us** Byron, the two Shelleys, and John William Polidori, Byron's physician.
7. **Tom of Coventry** "Peeping Tom" who, according to legend, was struck blind for looking at Lady Godiva as she rode naked through Coventry.
8. **tomb of the Capulets** the place where Romeo and Juliet died.
9. **galvanism** use of electric current to induce twitching in dead muscles.

> I saw the *hideous* phantasm of a man stretched out, and then, on the working of some powerful engine, show signs of life and stir with an uneasy, half vital motion.

Night waned upon this talk, and even the witching hour had gone by, before we retired to rest. When I placed my head on my pillow, I did not sleep, nor could I be said to think. My imagination, unbidden, possessed and guided me, gifting the successive images that arose in my mind with a vividness far beyond the usual bounds of reverie. I saw—with shut eyes but acute mental vision—I saw the pale student of unhallowed arts kneeling beside the thing he had put together. I saw the hideous phantasm of a man stretched out, and then, on the working of some powerful engine, show signs of life and stir with an uneasy, half vital motion. Frightful must it be, for supremely frightful would be the effect of any human endeavor to mock the stupendous mechanism of the Creator of the world. His success would terrify the artist; he would rush away from his odious handiwork, horror-stricken. He would hope that, left to itself, the slight spark of life which he had communicated would fade; that this thing, which had received such imperfect animation, would subside into dead matter; and he might sleep in the belief that the silence of the grave would quench forever the transient existence of the hideous corpse which he had looked upon as the cradle of life. He sleeps; but he is awakened; he opens his eyes; behold the horrid thing stands at his bedside, opening his curtains, and looking on him with yellow, watery, but speculative eyes.

I opened mine in terror. The idea so possessed my mind, that a thrill of fear ran through me, and I wished to exchange the ghastly image of my fancy for the realities around. I see them still: the very room, the dark parquet,[10] the closed shutters, with the moonlight struggling through, and the sense I had that the glassy lake and white high Alps were beyond. I could not so easily get rid of my hideous phantom: still it haunted me. I must try to think of something else. I recurred to my ghost story—my tiresome unlucky ghost story! O! if I could only contrive one which would frighten my reader as I myself had been frightened that night!

---

10. **parquet** (pär kā´) flooring made of wooden pieces arranged in a pattern.

Elizabeth McCracken
Scholar's Insight
Nothing is worse than wanting to write something but not knowing what. I think it's common for stories to come into your head when you *think* you've given up trying, and are thinking about something else entirely.

Vocabulary
phantasm (fan´ taz´ əm) *n.* ghost; figment of the imagination

Elizabeth McCracken
Scholar's Insight
What surprised me most when I first read *Frankenstein* was that the monster could speak and yearn and accuse. Shelley's Victor Frankenstein did a better job making a creature than the movie version suggested. I've always wondered why they kept him silent in the film.

Reading Check
That night, what does Mary Shelley imagine?

Vocabulary

incitement (in sīt´ mənt)
n. act of urging;
encouragement

Elizabeth McCracken
Scholar's Insight
Death and grief must have
been more than mere words
to Mary Shelley when she
started writing *Frankenstein*
at the age of eighteen. Her
mother died five days after
Mary's birth, and Mary's
first child died after being
born prematurely. Still, Percy
Shelley's death five years
after the book's publication
redefined those words. The
book is, as its author says,
a ghost story based on a
hideous idea, but it's also
a love letter: terrifying,
but built during a time of
tender memory.

Swift as light and as cheering was the idea that broke in
upon me. "I have found it! What terrified me will terrify others, and I need only describe the specter which had haunted
my midnight pillow." On the morrow I announced that I had
thought of a story. I began that day with the words, *It was on
a dreary night of November,* making only a transcript of the
grim terrors of my waking dream.

At first I thought but of a few pages—of a short tale—but
Shelley urged me to develop the idea at greater length. I certainly did not owe the suggestion of one incident, nor scarcely of one train of feeling, to my husband, and yet but for his
incitement, it would never have taken the form in which it
was presented to the world. From this declaration I must
except the preface. As far as I can recollect, it was entirely
written by him.

And now, once again, I bid my hideous progeny go forth
and prosper. I have an affection for it, for it was the offspring
of happy days, when death and grief were but words, which
found no true echo in my heart. Its several pages speak
of many a walk, many a drive, and many a conversation,
when I was not alone; and my companion was one who, in
this world, I shall never see more. But this is for myself: my
readers have nothing to do with these associations.

What terrified
me will *terrify*
others, and I need
only describe
the specter which
had haunted my
midnight pillow.

Cite textual
evidence to
support your
responses.

Critical Reading

1. **Key Ideas and Details (a)** What special set of
   circumstances inspired the four friends to attempt
   to write ghost stories? **(b) Compare and Contrast:**
   Compare the difficulty Shelley has with the reason her
   companions give up their efforts.

2. **Key Ideas and Details (a)** What gives Shelley her
   idea for a story? **(b) Connect:** What does the intensity
   of her vision suggest about her reaction to Dr. Darwin's
   experiments?

3. **Integration of Knowledge and Ideas** **Make a
   Judgment:** In your opinion, has later history borne out
   Shelley's dread of science? Explain.

4. **Integration of Knowledge and Ideas** Why does
   Shelley's use of a dream to write her novel confirm
   Romantic beliefs about the imagination? In your response,
   use at least two of these Essential Question words:
   *imagination, reason, intuition. [Connecting to the
   Essential Question: What is the relationship of the
   writer to tradition?]*

Literary Analysis

1. Key Ideas and Details Which characteristics of the **Gothic tradition**—horror, supernatural elements, medieval elements—do the ghost stories described by Shelley in her third paragraph share? List examples in a chart like the one shown.

Gothic Characteristic	Example in Shelley

2. Key Ideas and Details In which passage does Shelley describe a connection between the world of reason and a terrifying supernatural world?

3. Integration of Knowledge and Ideas Explain why Shelley's idea for *Frankenstein* fits the Gothic tradition.

4. Integration of Knowledge and Ideas Compare the ingredients of Gothic tales with those used in current horror movies and books.

5. Integration of Knowledge and Ideas **(a)** How does Shelley respond to the discussion of Darwin's experiments? **(b)** How does her response confirm an assumption of the **Romantic movement**—that the power of imagination is similar to that of nature's creative force?

6. Integration of Knowledge and Ideas **(a)** Contrast Shelley's first efforts to find an idea with her final inspiration. **(b)** How does this contrast reflect the Romantic tendency to value imagination above reason?

7. Integration of Knowledge and Ideas What "truth" does Shelley's imagined vision suggest about the dangerous possibilities of science?

8. Integration of Knowledge and Ideas Are there areas of scientific investigation in which human beings should not become involved? Explain.

9. Analyzing Visual Information Use your knowledge of *Frankenstein* to explain the humor of the cartoon shown on this page.

Reading Strategy

10. Explain whether you were able to **make predictions** as to how Shelley would be affected by the discussion of Darwin's experiments.

11. Based on clues in the Background note, predict what will happen to Victor Frankenstein in the novel. Explain your reasoning.

©The New Yorker Collection, 1995, Danny Shanahan, from *cartoonbank.com*. All Rights Reserved.

"Remember how big and clunky the first ones were?" ▶

© Vocabulary Acquisition and Use

Word Analysis:
Relate New Words to Familiar Vocabulary

You can often infer the meaning of unfamiliar words by relating them to words you know. For instance, *phantasm*, meaning "figment of the mind," is similar to *fantasy*. Both refer to the imagination. Sometimes, you can use parts from more than one word. The prefix *bi-* ("two") and the root *-ped-* ("foot," as in *pedestrian*, "someone who walks") can help you see that *biped* means "creature with two feet." Infer the meaning of the numbered words by relating them to familiar words. Use a dictionary to confirm your inferences.

1. ambidextrous, *adj.*
2. autodidact, *n.*
3. fallacy, *n.*
4. perfervid, *adj.*
5. retrogression, *n.*
6. somnambulate, *v.*

Vocabulary: Synonyms

A *synonym* is a word that has the same, or similar, meaning as another word. Write a complete sentence to answer each question that follows. In your answer, replace each underlined word with a synonym from the vocabulary list on page 758.

1. Was the king's offer of a royal office a sufficient <u>spur</u> to the noble to change sides?
2. Did the audience accept the tired <u>clichés</u> of the speaker uncritically?
3. Did the <u>attachment</u> in the rear of the car affect its speed?
4. How did the audience react when the <u>ghost</u> of Hamlet's father appeared?
5. Did the dean easily <u>agree</u> to her promotion to college president?
6. Have you ever seen such a sarcastic host or one so <u>disagreeable</u>?

Writing

© **Narrative Text** Typically, monster stories are told from the perspective of the humans confronting the monster. Ask yourself what the monsters think about their treatment, and write a brief **autobiography** of a monster. Choose one you know from literature or film, or invent a new monster. Outline the *sequence of events* in the monster's whole life or focus on events in one episode. Remember to write using the pronoun "I," show the *significance of events*, and gain readers' sympathy, as an autobiography would aim to do.

Prewriting Outline the plot of your narrative. Remember to think about the incidents from the monster's point of view.

Drafting Write your narrative in a serious or humorous way. Use concrete sensory details to add impact. If appropriate, pace the presentation of action to build suspense or sympathy.

Revising Revise your draft to make sure you maintain the monster's point of view and voice. Add figurative language to make your descriptions more vivid.

Model: Revising to Add Figurative Language

like a threatening eye

As the full moon rose, my skin suddenly began to tingle. I saw hair sprouting along my arms.

Using figurative language such as similes makes the description more vivid.

Conventions and Style: Subject-Verb Agreement Problems

Subject-verb agreement means that you use a singular verb with a singular subject and a plural verb with a plural subject, even when a phrase or clause comes between the subject and verb. The antecedent of a relative pronoun determines its agreement with a verb.

Example:
The *publishers* of Mary Shelley's first novel *make* a request.

Example:
The *writer, who is* one of several similar authors, gets the idea while vacationing.

Sentences with inverted order may contain agreement problems. Check the agreement by putting the sentence in normal word order.

Examples:
There *are* constant *rainstorms* in summer.
The *rainstorms* in summer *are* constant.

Sentences with collective nouns or indefinite pronouns may require singular or plural verbs. Titles are always singular.

Examples:
The *group listens* to ghost stories. [group acting as a unit]
The *group* then *writes* their own stories [group acting as individuals]
All of the guests *are* up late.
Romeo and Juliet is a play.

Practice Choose the verb in parentheses that agrees with the subject of each sentence.

1. Lord Byron, who is the Shelleys' neighbor, (proposes, propose) writing ghost stories.
2. Everyone present (agrees, agree) to the idea immediately.
3. Philosophical discussions between Lord Byron and Mary Shelley's husband (includes, include) mentions of Dr. Darwin.
4. There (was, were) experiments by Dr. Darwin, reportedly with a noodle in a glass.
5. The talk that has kept Mary Shelley up late (makes, make) it impossible for her to sleep when she does retire for the night.
6. Before her closed eyes (appears, appear) a series of images.
7. A student, pale and kneeling, (watches, watch) in horror as the creature that he has created (comes, come) to life.
8. When the student wakes, both watery eyes of the creature (is, are) staring at him.
9. Today, the audience for movies based on *Frankenstein* (is, are) huge.
10. *Frankenstein*, one of her many novels, (is, are) Mary Shelley's best-known work.

© Writing and Speaking Conventions

A. **Writing** Complete each sentence by writing a verb that agrees with the subject. Two sentences require more than one answer.

1. Each of the three men _____ quick to give up the task.
2. Mary Shelley, who _____ determined, does not quit.
3. All of Mary Shelley's energy _____ focused on her story.
4. There _____ conversations, but Mary Shelley only _____.
5. The student, who creates the monster, _____ and then _____.

B. **Speaking** Write and present to the class a paragraph to describe Shelley's imaginings. Use an inverted sentence and two sentences with clauses between the subject and verb.

PH WRITING COACH

Further instruction and practice are available in *Prentice Hall Writing Coach*.

FRANKENSTEIN
Past & Present

In a way, it was the weather that created the monster. The year was 1816, and Mary Wollstonecraft Godwin had traveled to Lake Geneva in Switzerland with her husband-to-be, Percy Bysshe Shelley, to visit their close friend, the poet Lord Byron. The group of friends was forced by the cold and dreary weather to stay indoors, so Lord Byron challenged everyone to a contest to tell the scariest ghost story. Young Miss Wollstonecraft was the hands-down winner. Her story, published anonymously at first, became the novel *Frankenstein*, which has been called a first in the now long-established mad scientist genre.

The influence of Mary Shelley's book went far beyond literature. *Frankenstein* spawned an entire film library, from British director James Whale's 1931 version for Universal that added the "Dr." to Frankenstein's name, to Mel Brooks's hilarious 1974 spoof *Young Frankenstein*, to the 2006 *Saturday Night Live* skit "The Curse of Frankenstein" with British actor Hugh Laurie, star of the popular TV medical drama *House*.

Saturday Night Live

It has been "live from New York" since 1975. Just like Frankenstein, *Saturday Night Live* has created its own place in our culture. When executive producer Lorne Michaels began *SNL* in 1975, he wanted it raw, not polished, more like improv than sitcom. He got his wish, as the show has endured with an amazing array of talented cast members, from John Belushi to Will Ferrell to Tina Fey, who went on from *SNL* to become creator and star of *30 Rock*, a sitcom about a show amazingly like *SNL*.

Saturday Night Live Transcripts
Season 32: Episode 4
06d: Hugh Laurie / Beck

The Curse of Frankenstein

HEAD VILLAGER, Hugh Laurie
FRANKENSTEIN'S MONSTER, Bill Hader
VILLAGER #1, Amy Poehler
VILLAGER #2, Kristen Wiig
VILLAGER #3, Fred Armisen
DRACULA, Jason Sudeikis

ANNOUNCER: [over title graphic] We now return to The Late Night Movie: "The Curse of Frankenstein." They still do these late night movie things, right?

[dissolve to exterior, Frankenstein's castle]

[dissolve to stock footage, villagers running through the night with torches ablaze]

[cut to exterior, main door of Frankenstein's castle, as the villagers scream with a collective force]

HEAD VILLAGER: Hold it, everyone! He's right in there! Dr. Frankenstein! Give us your answer!

[the villagers begin screaming again, as Frankenstein's Monster steps through the door]

VILLAGER 1: There he is! The Monster!

FRANKENSTEIN'S MONSTER: Whoa, whoa, whoa, hey, hey, oh!! You guys looking for *Frankenstein?*

CROWD: YES!!!!

FRANKENSTEIN'S MONSTER: [holds up his stitched hands] You guys got the wrong house!

HEAD VILLAGER: What do you mean, we got the wrong house?

VILLAGER #1: YEAH?!! WHAT DO YOU MEAN?!!

FRANKENSTEIN'S MONSTER: SHUT UP!! [they silence] You got the wrong house! Frankenstein lives, uh—[points behind the villagers] Yeah, he lives over *there.* Across the moor.

HEAD VILLAGER: Across the *moor?*

FRANKENSTEIN'S MONSTER: Yeah, yeah, yeah, yeah, yeah! It's, uh—a big castle . . . uh, it's got those, uh—[snaps fingers] oh, what do you call it, those white trees out front, uh—

HEAD VILLAGER: You mean birch trees?

FRANKENSTEIN'S MONSTER: Yeah. Whatever.

HEAD VILLAGER: [embarrassed] Well. Sorry about that.

[Frankenstein's Monster shrugs vacantly]

HEAD VILLAGER: WRONG HOUSE!! ACROSS THE MOOR!!

[the villagers run back in the opposite direction from which they came]

[stock footage of villagers running through the night]

[cut to villagers standing at Dracula's door]

DRACULA: He said *what*?! *I'm* Frankenstein?! [chuckles, as he files his fingernails] I'm sorry, guys—I think someone's messin' with ya'. I'm *Dracula*! See? [shows off his outfit] Cape. Fangs. Widow's peak. Frankenstein's, uh . . . way back *that* way. [points back in the direction the villagers just came from] Across the *moor.*

HEAD VILLAGER: Back *that* way? We just *came* from there. He said Frankenstein lives *here*!

VILLAGER #1: *Yeah!*

VILLAGER #2: Yeah, he said Frankenstein lives HERE!!

[all the villagers join in the chorus]

DRACULA: Hold on, hold on, hold on—what did this guy look like?

VILLAGER #1: He was TALL!

DRACULA: Right, right, okay—what else?

VILLAGER #2: He had BOLTS in his neck!

DRACULA: Uh-huh. What else?

VILLAGER #3: He was *gree-ee-ee-eennnn*!

DRACULA: Okay. Tall guy, green, bolts in his neck—yeah, I hate to break it to you, but *that's* Frankenstein!

HEAD VILLAGER: Okay . . . well, alright. I believe we've made a bit of a mistake. Sorry to trouble you! [to the villagers] Across the moor!!

CROWD: ACROSS THE MOOR!!

[the villagers run back in the opposite direction from which they came]

[stock footage of villagers running through the night]

[cut to villagers standing at Frankenstein's door]

FRANKENSTEIN'S MONSTER: Well, uh . . . he's a *li-ar*! That's what!

HEAD VILLAGER: Well . . . what about the *bolts* in your neck?

FRANKENSTEIN'S MONSTER: Oh, great, thanks a lot! I almost forgot about that *spinal injury* I had when I was four-years old! Thanks for bringing back *those* rosy memories! Hey—my dog died last year, why don't you make a few jokes about *that*?!

VILLAGER #1: He's a mon-sterrrr!!

[all the villagers join in the chorus]

FRANKENSTEIN'S MONSTER: Hey, now we're *name-calling*! What am I, in the 7th grade, all of a sudden! . . . How do you like that?

HEAD VILLAGER: Well, how do we know you're *not* Frankenstein's Monster?

FRANKENSTEIN'S MONSTER: How do I know *you're* not Frankenstein's Monster, you freakin' genius?! I mean—[glances at villager stepping too close with a lit torch] Hey, dude—get that fire away from me. Alright? I mean, *you* could be a monster, you know? You got the weird hat, the patchy beard—you know? I mean, you look like a monster to *me*!

VILLAGER #1: [to Head Villager] Well, maybe *you're* the monster!

[all the villagers join in the chorus]

HEAD VILLAGER: [shakes his head] I'm not the monster! [points to Frankenstein's Monster] Look at 'im! He's got a square head and green skin!

FRANKENSTEIN'S MONSTER: Oh, great—now it's a *racial* thing! You know what? You guys are a bunch of fascists! [villager with a lit torch again steps too close] *Seriously*, du-ude! Get that fire away from me! [to the crowd] Here's the deal: I'm a cobbler. I make shoes, and I hang out with my kids. You want to lynch me for *that*—be my guest!

HEAD VILLAGER: Well, I'm sorry. We—we shouldn't have jumped to conclusions. We'll leave you alone.

FRANKENSTEIN'S MONSTER: Uh—how about, apology *not* accepted, Weird Beard! I mean, let a guy live his life, would you? You know what I mean? I mean, it—[his arm suddenly falls off and hits the stone steps] Uhhhhhh—

CROWD: *KILL HIM!!!*

[the villagers storm forward]

[cut to title graphic]

ANNOUNCER: We'll be back with more of The Late Night Movie. I *swear* they haven't done these things in, like, twenty years . . .

[fade]

Critical Reading

1. **(a)** What is confusing the villagers? **(b) Interpret:** In what way is their confusion a humorous comment on monster movies in general?

2. What is surprising and humorous about the way in which Frankenstein's monster talks?

Use this question to focus a group discussion of "The Curse of Frankenstein":

3. What, if anything, should you know about the Frankenstein story to appreciate the humor of this skit?

Lyric Poetry

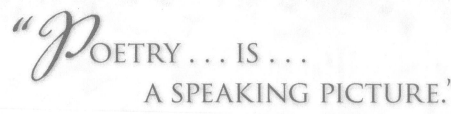

"POETRY ... IS ...
A SPEAKING PICTURE."

— SIR PHILIP SIDNEY

Defining Lyric Poetry

Lyric poetry expresses the personal thoughts and feelings of a single speaker. Lyric poems often have musical effects and a songlike structure.

Types of Lyric Poems While lyric poems do not have to follow a specific form, many do. The following are traditional lyric forms:

- **Ode:** a serious, often intensely emotional poem that honors a person or thing. In an ode, the speaker directly addresses the subject.
- **Elegy:** a solemn and formal poem about death. The speaker may mourn a person or a more abstract loss, such as the passing of youth.
- **Sonnet:** a 14-line poem with a formal structure, specific meter, and rhyme scheme

Sound Devices and Figurative Language In addition to the descriptive, sensory language called **imagery,** one of the most distinctive qualities of poetry is its use of sound devices and figurative language.

Sound devices are patterns of words that use the innate sounds of language to create musical effects. They include the following types:

- **Rhyme:** repetition of sounds at the ends of words, as in _brake_ and _lake_
- **Consonance:** repetition of final consonant sounds in stressed syllables that have different vowel sounds, as in _speak_ and _break_
- **Repetition:** repeated use of sounds, words, phrases, or sentences

Figurative language is language that is used imaginatively rather than literally. Figurative language includes the following figures of speech:

- **Simile:** comparison of two unlike things using the words _like_ or _as_
- **Metaphor:** comparison of two apparently unlike things without using _like_ or _as_
- **Oxymoron:** juxtaposing two opposite or contradictory words to reveal a surprising truth

Close Read: Sound Devices and Figurative Language
These literary elements appear in the Model text at right.

Sound Device—Alliteration: repetition of initial identical consonant sounds in accented syllables	Figurative Language—Personification: giving human traits to nonhuman things
Example: "All powers of swiftness, subtlety, and strength..." (William Wordsworth)	_Example: "These waters, rolling from their mountain springs / With a soft inland murmur..." (William Wordsworth)_
Sound Device—Assonance: repetition of similar vowel sounds in accented syllables	Figurative Language—Apostrophe: a figure in which the speaker addresses an absent person
Example: "One shade the more, one ray the less..." (Lord Byron)	_Example: "Milton! thou shouldst be living at this hour: / England has need of thee..." (William Wordsworth)_

Model

About the Text Pablo Neruda (1904–1973) was one of Chile's most popular poets. In 1971, he was awarded the Nobel Prize in Literature.

"Ode to My Suit" by Pablo Neruda (translated by Margaret Sayers Peden)

Every morning, suit,
you are waiting on a chair
to be filled
by my vanity, my love,
my hope, my body.
Still
only half awake
I leave the shower
to shrug into your sleeves,
my legs seek
the hollow of your legs,
and thus embraced
by your unfailing loyalty
I take my morning walk,
work my way into my poetry;
from my windows I see
the things,
men, women,
events and struggles
constantly shaping me,
constantly confronting me,
setting my hands to the task,
opening my eyes,
creasing my lips,
and in the same way,
suit,
I am shaping you,
poking out your elbows,
wearing you threadbare,
and so your life grows
in the image of my own.
In the wind
you flap and hum
as if you were my soul,
in bad moments

you cling
to my bones,
abandoned, at nighttime
darkness and dream
people with their phantoms
your wings and mine.
I wonder
whether some day
an enemy
bullet
will stain you with my blood,
for then
you would die with me,
but perhaps
it will be
less dramatic,
simple,
and you will grow ill,
suit,
with me,
grow older
with me, with my body,
and together
we will be lowered
into the earth.
That's why
every day
I greet you
with respect and then
you embrace me and I forget you,
because we are one being
and shall be always
in the wind, through the night,
the streets and the struggle,
one body,
maybe, maybe, one day, still.

Apostrophe The speaker talks directly to his suit. This use of apostrophe establishes both tone, or emotional attitude, and meaning: the suit is far more than a suit. It is a being for whom the speaker feels admiration and affection.

Personification The poem as a whole is based on personification. The speaker attributes human emotion and actions to an inanimate suit. The speaker is actually addressing an aspect of his own being, but doing so through the mechanism of the personified suit.

Assonance Repeated vowel sounds are less obvious than rhyme. However, along with other sound devices, they create musical qualities and connections among words.

Alliteration In both of the highlighted examples, repetition of the initial consonant sounds helps to link words and stir emotion.

William Wordsworth
(1770–1850)

Writing poetry may seem like a quiet, meditative activity, a matter of words, not deeds—hardly the scene of upheavals and crises. Yet in 1798, when Wordsworth and his friend Samuel Taylor Coleridge published the first edition of *Lyrical Ballads,* a revolution shook the world of poetry. Together, Wordsworth and Coleridge rejected all the traditional assumptions about the proper style, words, and subject matter for a poem.

A Revolution in Poetry

As Wordsworth announced in the Preface to the 1802 edition of the book, "There will . . . be found in these volumes little of what is usually called poetic diction; I have taken as much pains to avoid it as others ordinarily take to produce it; . . ."

Gone were the flowery language, the wittily crafted figures of speech, the effusive praise, and the tragic complaints that had defined poetry in the past. In their place, Wordsworth offered an intensified presentation of ordinary life and nature using common language. Wordsworth's revolution took literature in a dramatic new direction, building the movement known as Romanticism.

The Lake District

Wordsworth's revolution was rooted in his early love for nature. Born in the beautiful Lake District of England, Wordsworth spent his youth roaming the countryside. In later years, too, he found peace and reassurance in the gentle hills and serene lakes of this landscape. This region of northwestern England became the cradle of the Romantic Movement, inspiring many personal commentaries and poetic tributes.

Revolution and Love

By the time Wordsworth was thirteen, both his parents had died. Nonetheless, he was able to pursue his education and entered Cambridge University in 1787. After graduating, he traveled through Europe, spending considerable time in France. There, he embraced the ideals of the newly born French Revolution—ideals that stressed social justice and individual rights. Growing emotionally as well as intellectually, Wordsworth fell in love with Annette Vallon.

Disillusionment and Crisis

Wordsworth's involvement with the Revolution and with Vallon ended abruptly when lack of funds and family pressure forced him to return home. Two months later, in 1793, England declared war on France, and the Revolution became increasingly violent. His dreams of liberty betrayed, Wordsworth lapsed into a depression. His beloved sister, Dorothy, and fellow poet Samuel Taylor Coleridge helped him through this crisis.

From Politics to Art

In 1798, Wordsworth published *Lyrical Ballads* with Coleridge. With the publication of this work, Wordsworth translated his revolutionary hopes from politics to literature. His democratic ideals appeared in his use of the language of ordinary people rather than specialized "poetic" words.

Poetry

Critics agree that Wordsworth's greatest work is his autobiography in poetry, *The Prelude*. Wordsworth completed a version of this poem in 1799, which he expanded considerably by 1805. As he wrote to a friend, *The Prelude* told the story of "the growth of my own mind." The poem is not always factually accurate, but, as noted by critic Stephen Gill, in its combination of "satire and narrative, description and meditation, the visionary and the deliberately banal," it was unique.

Eventually, Wordsworth's radical new approach to poetry gained acceptance, while he himself grew more conservative in his politics. A new generation of Romantics, more radical than Wordsworth and Coleridge, arose. Wordsworth's position was secure, however: we remember him as the father of English Romanticism.

WORDSWORTH'S
Mountain Legacy

*W*hich of these two sets of words would you probably choose to describe Mount Whitney, Mount McKinley, the Rockies, the Alps, or the Himalayas?

massy heaps, disfigurations of the Earth's face, scars, pimples, protuberances, warts

snow-mantled peaks, spectacular beauty, breath-taking scenery, towering spires

The first set of words may seem like a joke to you. Who ever described majestic mountains as if they were ugly? The answer is that many writers did, before William Wordsworth and the Romantic movement changed forever the way we look at and experience lofty peaks. The unflattering terms are not invented. They come from descriptions of mountains written in the centuries leading up to Romanticism. The second group of words comes from web sites describing today's national parks and mountain resorts.

As a boy and later as a man, Wordsworth wandered through England's Lake District, climbing mountains like Scafell Pike and Helvellyn and learning to appreciate their power and beauty. As a young man, he hiked across the Alps, whose awe-inspiring scenery made a deep impression on him.

Most important, Wordsworth expressed in poems his feelings about mountains. Today, these descriptions are part of his mountain legacy to us. Because of what he and others wrote centuries ago, we travel to national parks to view impressive peaks, vacation and camp out in the mountains, and hike on mountain trails.

. . . Oh! when I have hung
Above the raven's nest, by knots of grass
And half-inch fissures in the slippery rock . . .
. . . oh, at that time
While on the perilous ridge I hung alone . . .

— *from The Prelude, Book I*

. . . in the mountains did he *feel* his faith.
All things responsive to the writing, there
Breathed immortality, revolving life,
And greatness still revolving; infinite:
There littleness was not; the least of things
Seemed infinite . . .

— *from The Excursion, Book I*

Before You Read

Poetry of William Wordsworth

Connecting to the Essential Question Today's rock musicians and environmentalists are descendants of the Romantic movement Wordsworth helped to found. As you read, find passages that show Wordsworth rebelling against eighteenth-century poetic traditions. Identifying these passages will help you answer the Essential Question: **What is the relationship of the writer to tradition?**

Literary Analysis

Romanticism was a late-eighteenth-century European literary movement. While the earlier Neoclassical writers, such as Pope and Johnson, favored reason, wit, and outward elegance, the works of many Romantic poets include these elements:

- Simplicity or directness of language
- The expression of spontaneous, intensified feelings
- Responses to nature that lead to a deeper awareness of self

English Romanticism began with William Wordsworth. The **lyric,** a poem in which a single speaker expresses personal emotions and observations, was particularly suited to his vision.

Comparing Literary Works The Romantics adopted a new and freer **diction,** or choice of words. As you read, notice that Wordsworth's poetry favors simple words but that his work also relies heavily on abstract terms. Compare the different types of words Wordsworth chooses—whether specific and concrete like *sycamore* or abstract like *a sense sublime*.

Reading Strategy

Preparing to Read Complex Texts You can better understand a work by **evaluating the influence of the historical period** on it. Wordsworth lived in an age of political and social revolutions, and he himself helped bring about a revolution in literature. The relationship between Wordsworth's literary ideas and social and political change are evident in the details in these poems. As you read, use a chart like the one shown to identify the revolutionary *political and philosophical assumptions* that color the view of life in his work.

Vocabulary

recompense (rek´ əm pens´) *n.* payment for something (p. 783)

roused (rouzd) *v.* stirred up (p. 786)

presumption (prē zump´ shən) *n.* audacity; nerve (p. 787)

anatomize (ə nat´ ə mīz´) *v.* to dissect in order to examine structure (p. 788)

sordid (sôr´ did) *adj.* dirty (p. 790)

stagnant (stag´ nənt) *adj.* motionless; foul (p. 791)

Common Core State Standards

Reading Literature
4. Determine the meaning of words and phrases as they are used in the text, including figurative and connotative meanings; analyze the impact of specific word choices on meaning and tone, including words with multiple meanings or language that is particularly fresh, engaging, or beautiful.

Historical Ideas

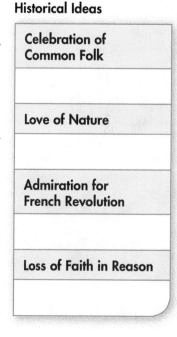

Celebration of Common Folk
Love of Nature
Admiration for French Revolution
Loss of Faith in Reason

PHLit
Online!
www.PHLitOnline.com

Lines Composed a Few Miles Above

Tintern Abbey

William Wordsworth

BACKGROUND This poem was written in 1798 during Wordsworth's second visit to the valley of the River Wye and the ruins of Tintern Abbey, once a great medieval church, in Wales. Wordsworth had passed through the region alone five years earlier. This time he brought his sister along to share the experience.

Five years have past; five summers, with the length
Of five long winters! and again I hear
These waters, rolling from their mountain springs
With a soft inland murmur. Once again
5   Do I behold these steep and lofty cliffs,
That on a wild secluded scene impress
Thoughts of more deep seclusion; and connect
The landscape with the quiet of the sky.
The day is come when I again repose
10 Here, under this dark sycamore, and view
These plots of cottage ground, these orchard tufts,
Which at this season, with their unripe fruits,
Are clad in one green hue, and lose themselves
'Mid groves and copses. Once again I see
15 These hedgerows, hardly hedgerows, little lines
Of sportive wood run wild: these pastoral farms,
Green to the very door; and wreaths of smoke
Sent up, in silence, from among the trees!
With some uncertain notice, as might seem
20 Of vagrant dwellers in the houseless woods,
Or of some hermit's cave, where by his fire
The hermit sits alone.
                              These beauteous forms,
Through a long absence, have not been to me
As is a landscape to a blind man's eye:
25 But oft, in lonely rooms, and 'mid the din
Of towns and cities, I have owed to them
In hours of weariness, sensations sweet,
Felt in the blood, and felt along the heart;
And passing even into my purer mind,
30 With tranquil restoration—feelings too
Of unremembered pleasure: such, perhaps,
As have no slight or trivial influence
On that best portion of a good man's life.
His little, nameless, unremembered, acts
35 Of kindness and of love. Nor less, I trust,
To them I may have owed another gift,
Of aspect more sublime; that blessed mood,
In which the burthen[1] of the mystery,
In which the heavy and the weary weight

Literary Analysis
Romanticism and the Lyric
How do the sensory observations Wordsworth includes reflect what you know about Romanticism?

◄ **Critical Viewing**
What elements in this painting help it capture awe and excitement comparable to Wordsworth's on his return to the Wye? **[Connect]**

☑ Reading Check
Name two sights that strike Wordsworth on his return to the Wye.

1. **burthen** burden.

Literary Analysis
Romanticism and the Lyric
How do the images in
lines 40–49 reflect Romantic
ideas of the relation between
nature and the soul?

40 Of all this unintelligible world
Is lightened—that serene and blessed mood,
In which the affections gently lead us on—
Until, the breath of this corporeal frame[2]
And even the motion of our human blood
45 Almost suspended, we are laid asleep
In body, and become a living soul;
While with an eye made quiet by the power
Of harmony, and the deep power of joy,
We see into the life of things.

                If this
50 Be but a vain belief, yet, oh! how oft—
In darkness and amid the many shapes
Of joyless daylight; when the fretful stir
Unprofitable, and the fever of the world,
Have hung upon the beatings of my heart—
55 How oft, in spirit, have I turned to thee,
O sylvan[3] Wye! thou wanderer through the woods,
How often has my spirit turned to thee!

       And now, with gleams of half-extinguished thought,
With many recognitions dim and faint,
60 And somewhat of a sad perplexity,
The picture of the mind revives again;
While here I stand, not only with the sense
Of present pleasure, but with pleasing thoughts
That in this moment there is life and food
65 For future years. And so I dare to hope,
Though changed, no doubt, from what I was when first

Reading Strategy
**Understanding the
Historical Period**
What changing attitude
about the importance
of reason is reflected in
Wordsworth's contrast of
childhood with adulthood?

▼ **Critical Viewing**
How is the landscape in
this photograph similar to
the setting Wordsworth
describes? **[Connect]**

---

2. corporeal (kôr pór´ ē əl) **frame** body.
3. sylvan (sil´ vən) wooded.

I came among these hills; when like a roe[4]
I bounded o'er the mountains, by the sides
Of the deep rivers, and the lonely streams,
70 Wherever nature led: more like a man
Flying from something that he dreads, than one
Who sought the thing he loved. For nature then
(The coarser pleasures of my boyish days,
And their glad animal movements all gone by)
75 To me was all in all—I cannot paint
What then I was. The sounding cataract
Haunted me like a passion; the tall rock,
The mountain, and the deep and gloomy wood,
Their colors and their forms, were then to me
80 An appetite; a feeling and a love,
That had no need of a remoter charm,
By thought supplied, nor any interest
Unborrowed from the eye. That time is past,
And all its aching joys are now no more,
85 And all its dizzy raptures. Not for this
Faint[5] I, nor mourn nor murmur; other gifts
Have followed; for such loss, I would believe,
Abundant recompense. For I have learned
To look on nature, not as in the hour
90 Of thoughtless youth; but hearing oftentimes
The still, sad music of humanity,
Nor harsh nor grating, though of ample power
To chasten and subdue. And I have felt
A presence that disturbs me with the joy
95 Of elevated thoughts; a sense sublime
Of something far more deeply interfused,
Whose dwelling is the light of setting suns,
And the round ocean and the living air,
And the blue sky, and in the mind of man;
100 A motion and a spirit, that impels
All thinking things, all objects of all thought,
And rolls through all things. Therefore am I still
A lover of the meadows and the woods
And mountains; and of all that we behold
105 From this green earth; of all the mighty world
Of eye, and ear—both what they half create,
And what perceive; well pleased to recognize
In nature and the language of the sense,
The anchor of my purest thoughts, the nurse,

---

4. roe type of deer.
5. Faint lose heart.

The BRITISH TRADITION

The Evolution of the Self
On returning to the Wye, Wordsworth discovers his own deeper self in experiences of nature bound together by memory. His discovery contributed to a new, Romantic idea of the self. For the Romantics, the self was a journey of self-discovery, not a collection of personal quirks or facts. The Romantic poet set out to recover his or her deeper self through nature, memory, and lyric poetry. For the Romantics, writing a poem became an act of discovery and self-definition.

This Romantic idea of the self—always divided yet always recovering itself—inspired later works such as Tennyson's *In Memoriam, A.H.H.* Centuries later, Wordsworth's vision of the self and its journey still resonates in modern culture.

Connect to the Literature

In lines 88–93, what does the speaker learn about himself and his world?

Vocabulary
recompense (rek´ əm pens´)
n. payment in return for something

Reading Check

What natural sights inspire in Wordsworth a sense of the unity of things—of "something far more deeply interfused, . . ."?

Spiral Review
Point of View
In lines 112–121, how does the use of first-person point of view shape what we know of the speaker's sister?

Literary Analysis
Romanticism and Diction
Does Wordsworth use simple or difficult words to describe old age? Are they specific or general?

110 The guide, the guardian of my heart, and soul
Of all my moral being.

                      Nor perchance,
If I were not thus taught, should I the more
Suffer[6] my genial spirits[7] to decay;
For thou art with me here upon the banks
115 Of this fair river; thou my dearest Friend,[8]
My dear, dear Friend, and in thy voice I catch
The language of my former heart, and read
My former pleasures in the shooting lights
Of thy wild eyes. Oh! yet a little while
120 May I behold in thee what I was once,
My dear, dear Sister! and this prayer I make
Knowing that Nature never did betray
The heart that loved her; 'tis her privilege,
Through all the years of this our life, to lead
125 From joy to joy; for she can so inform
The mind that is within us, so impress
With quietness and beauty, and so feed
With lofty thoughts, that neither evil tongues,
Rash judgments, nor the sneers of selfish men,
130 Nor greetings where no kindness is, nor all
The dreary intercourse of daily life,
Shall e'er prevail against us, or disturb
Our cheerful faith, that all which we behold
Is full of blessings. Therefore let the moon
135 Shine on thee in thy solitary walk;
And let the misty mountain winds be free
To blow against thee: and, in after years,
When these wild ecstasies shall be matured
Into a sober pleasure; when thy mind
140 Shall be a mansion for all lovely forms,
Thy memory be as a dwelling place
For all sweet sound and harmonies; oh! then,
If solitude, or fear, or pain, or grief,
Should be thy portion, with what healing thoughts
145 Of tender joy wilt thou remember me,
And these my exhortations! Nor, perchance—
If I should be where I no more can hear
Thy voice, nor catch from thy wild eyes these gleams
Of past existence—wilt thou then forget
150 That on the banks of this delightful stream
We stood together; and that I, so long
A worshipper of Nature, hither came

Reading Strategy
Understanding the Historical Period How do the lines "let the misty mountain winds be free / To blow against thee" reflect Romantic beliefs and assumptions?

---

6. **Suffer** allow.
7. **genial spirits** creative powers.
8. **Friend** his sister Dorothy.

Tintern Abbey, J. M. W. Turner, © British Museum

Unwearied in that service: rather say
With warmer love—oh! with far deeper zeal
155 Of holier love. Nor wilt thou then forget,
That after many wanderings, many years
Of absence, these steep woods and lofty cliffs,
And this green pastoral landscape, were to me
More dear, both for themselves and for thy sake!

▲ **Critical Viewing**
Compare the appreciation of light and sky shown by Romantic painter J. M. W. Turner with Wordsworth's descriptions in the poem.
[Compare and Contrast]

Critical Reading ©

1. **Key Ideas and Details** (a) How long has it been since the poet visited Tintern Abbey? (b) **Infer:** At what time of year does the poet make his second visit to the area? How do you know?

2. **Key Ideas and Details** (a) How have the poet's memories of his first visit helped him? (b) **Interpret:** In line 36 of the poem, the poet mentions "another gift" that his contact with this rural scene bestowed upon him. Briefly describe this gift.

3. **Key Ideas and Details** Explain the difference in the poet's attitude on his first and on his second visit to Tintern Abbey.

4. **Integration of Knowledge and Ideas** (a) What wish for his sister does the poet express toward the end of the poem? (b) **Connect:** What connection can you see between this wish, Wordsworth's thoughts in lines 22–31, and his hopes in lines 62–65?

5. **Integration of Knowledge and Ideas** Does Wordsworth express a deep truth about our relationships with nature, or are his reactions exaggerated? Explain.

Cite textual evidence to support your responses.

BACKGROUND In 1790, Wordsworth witnessed the early, optimistic days of the French Revolution. The country seemed on the verge of achieving true freedom from outdated, oppressive feudal institutions. Caught up in the revolutionary fervor, Wordsworth felt he was seeing "France standing on the top of golden hours." The war between England and France (declared in 1793) and the violent turn taken by the French Revolution, known as the Reign of Terror (1793–1794), dashed Wordsworth's hopes.

from THE Prelude

WILLIAM WORDSWORTH

O pleasant exercise of hope and joy!
For mighty were the auxiliars which then stood
Upon our side, us who were strong in love!
Bliss was it in that dawn to be alive,
5 But to be young was very Heaven! O times,
In which the meager, stale, forbidding ways
Of custom, law, and statute, took at once
The attraction of a country in romance!
When Reason seemed the most to assert her rights
10 When most intent on making of herself
A prime enchantress—to assist the work,
Which then was going forward in her name!
Not favored spots alone, but the whole Earth,
The beauty wore of promise—that which sets
15 (As at some moments might not be unfelt
Among the bowers of Paradise itself)
The budding rose above the rose full blown.
What temper at the prospect did not wake
To happiness unthought of ? The inert
20 Were roused, and lively natures rapt away!
They who had fed their childhood upon dreams,
The play-fellows of fancy, who had made
All powers of swiftness, subtlety, and strength
Their ministers,—who in lordly wise had stirred
25 Among the grandest objects of the sense,
And dealt with whatsoever they found there

Vocabulary
roused (rouzd)
v. stirred up

786

▲ **Critical Viewing** Compare and contrast the impression of the French Revolution conveyed by this poem to the one conveyed by this picture. **[Compare and Contrast]**

As if they had within some lurking right
To wield it;—they, too, who of gentle mood
Had watched all gentle motions, and to these
30   Had fitted their own thoughts, schemers more mild,
And in the region of their peaceful selves;—
Now was it that *both* found, the meek and lofty
Did both find helpers to their hearts' desire,
And stuff at hand, plastic as they could wish,—
35   Were called upon to exercise their skill,
Not in Utopia,—subterranean fields,—
Or some secreted island, Heaven knows where!
But in the very world, which is the world
Of all of us,—the place where, in the end,
40   We find our happiness, or not at all!

But now, become oppressors in their turn,
Frenchmen had changed a war of self-defense
For one of conquest, losing sight of all
Which they had struggled for: now mounted up,
45   Openly in the eye of earth and heaven,
The scale of liberty. I read her doom,
With anger vexed, with disappointment sore,
But not dismayed, nor taking to the shame
Of a false prophet. While resentment rose
50   Striving to hide, what nought could heal, the wounds
Of mortified presumption, I adhered

Vocabulary
presumption (prē zump´ shən) *n.* audacity; nerve

✓ **Reading Check**

To which two kinds of people did the Revolution appeal?

from The Prelude **787**

More firmly to old tenets, and, to prove
Their temper, strained them more; and thus, in heat
Of contest, did opinions every day
55 Grow into consequence, till round my mind
They clung, as if they were its life, nay more,
The very being of the immortal soul.

I summoned my best skill, and toiled, intent
To anatomize the frame of social life,
60 Yea, the whole body of society
Searched to its heart. Share with me, Friend! the wish
That some dramatic tale, endued with shapes
Livelier, and flinging out less guarded words
Than suit the work we fashion, might set forth
65 What then I learned, or think I learned, of truth,
And the errors into which I fell, betrayed
By present objects, and by reasonings false
From their beginnings, inasmuch as drawn
Out of a heart that had been turned aside
70 From Nature's way by outward accidents,
And which are thus confounded,[1] more and more
Misguided, and misguiding. So I fared,
Dragging all precepts, judgments, maxims, creeds,
Like culprits to the bar; calling the mind,
75 Suspiciously, to establish in plain day
Her titles and her honors; now believing,
Now disbelieving; endlessly perplexed
With impulse, motive, right and wrong, the ground
Of obligation, what the rule and whence
80 The sanction; till, demanding formal *proof*,
And seeking it in every thing, I lost
All feeling of conviction, and, in fine,
Sick, wearied out with contrarieties,
Yielded up moral questions in despair.

Vocabulary
anatomize (ə naťə mīz′)
v. to dissect in order to examine structure

---

1. **confounded** (kən found′ id) *adj.* confused; mixed together indiscriminately; bewildered

Critical Reading

Cite textual evidence to support your responses.

1. **Key Ideas and Details (a)** With what phrase does the speaker describe the early days of the French Revolution? **(b) Generalize:** What basic values does his reaction reflect? **(c) Interpret:** What role did reason seem to play in the Revolution?

2. **Key Ideas and Details (a)** What change in the course of the French Revolution caused a conflict in Wordsworth? **(b) Interpret:** What two reactions to this turn of events does Wordsworth describe?

3. **Key Ideas and Details (a) Interpret:** What does Wordsworth say happened to him when his heart "had been turned aside / From Nature's way"? **(b) Interpret:** At the end of the excerpt, how has Wordsworth resolved his conflict?

Critical Commentary

"The White Knight's Song"
Lewis Carroll

Lewis Carroll was the pseudonym of Charles Lutwidge Dodgson, the English author who wrote Alice's Adventures in Wonderland.

Writers with a well-defined style and beliefs are the most tempting to parody, especially if they do not show much humor themselves. Wordsworth fit these requirements, and therefore was a tempting target for Lewis Carroll, author of *Alice in Wonderland*. Carroll parodied Wordsworth's famous poem "Resolution and Independence," which contains the following account of a meeting with a strange old man:

> *. . . I saw a Man before me unawares:*
> *The oldest man he seemed that ever wore gray hairs. . . .*
>
> *Like a sea-beast crawled forth, that on a shelf*
> *Of rock or sand reposeth, there to sun itself;*
>
> *Such seemed this Man, not all alive or dead,*
> *Nor all asleep—in his extreme old age . . .*

The poet then asks this old man, who has been staring at the "muddy water" of a pond, "What occupation do you there pursue?" The man responds as follows:

> *He told, that to these waters he had come*
> *To gather leeches, being old and poor:*
> *Employment hazardous and wearisome!*
> *And he had many hardships to endure:*
> *From pond to pond he roamed, from moor to moor . . .*

Carroll parodied this encounter in "The White Knight's Song":

> *I'll tell thee everything I can:*
>   *There's little to relate.*
> *I saw an aged, aged man,*
>   *A-sitting on a gate.*
>
> *"Who are you, aged man?" I said*
>   *"And how is it you live?"*
> *And his answer trickled through my head*
>   *Like water through a sieve.*
> *He said, "I look for butterflies*
>   *That sleep among the wheat:*
> *I make them into mutton-pies*
>   *And sell them in the street. . . .*

Ⓒ **Key Ideas and Details** How does the old man Wordsworth meets in "Resolution and Independence" make his living? In Carroll's parody of Wordsworth's poem, how does the "aged man" make his living?

Parody, a composition that imitates and makes fun of another, is actually a humorous form of literary criticism. In order to ridicule a writer's style, a parodist has to understand and reproduce it accurately enough for the reader to recognize. The parodist then exaggerates some aspect of the style or subject to make the reader laugh. The result is a caricature, rather than a portrait—recognizable, but silly.

David Levine's caricature of William Wordsworth

The World Is Too Much With Us

William Wordsworth

▲ **Critical Viewing**
Do you agree with
Wordsworth that an
image such as this one
"moves us not"? Explain.
[Make a Judgment]

Vocabulary
sordid (sôr´ did) *adj.* dirty

The world is too much with us; late and soon,
Getting and spending, we lay waste our powers:
Little we see in Nature that is ours;
We have given our hearts away, a sordid boon![1]
5 This Sea that bares her bosom to the moon;
The winds that will be howling at all hours,
And are upgathered now like sleeping flowers;
For this, for everything, we are out of tune;
It moves us not.—Great God! I'd rather be
10 A Pagan suckled in a creed outworn;
So might I, standing on this pleasant lea,[2]
Have glimpses that would make me less forlorn;
Have sight of Proteus[3] rising from the sea;
Or hear old Triton[4] blow his wreathèd horn.

---

1. **boon** favor.
2. **lea** meadow.
3. **Proteus** (prō´ tē əs) in Greek mythology, a sea god who could change his appearance at will.
4. **Triton** in Greek mythology, a sea god with the head and upper body of a man and the tail of a fish.

London, 1802

William Wordsworth

Milton![1] thou should'st be living at this hour:
England hath need of thee: she is a fen[2]
Of stagnant waters: altar, sword, and pen,
Fireside, the heroic wealth of hall and bower,
5 Have forfeited their ancient English dower
Of inward happiness. We are selfish men;
Oh! raise us up, return to us again;
And give us manners, virtue, freedom, power.
Thy soul was like a Star, and dwelt apart:
10 Thou hadst a voice whose sound was like the sea:
Pure as the naked heavens, majestic, free,
So didst thou travel on life's common way,
In cheerful godliness; and yet thy heart
The lowliest duties on herself did lay.

Vocabulary
stagnant (stag´ nənt)
adj. motionless; foul

---

1. Milton seventeenth-century English poet John Milton.
2. fen (fen) *n.* area of low, flat, marshy land.

Critical Reading

1. **Key Ideas and Details (a)** In "The World Is Too Much With Us," what activities cause people to exhaust their "powers"? **(b) Interpret:** What does the speaker mean by the "world"?

2. **Key Ideas and Details (a)** According to the speaker, with what are we "out of tune"? **(b) Interpret:** Why is being out of tune with these experiences such a loss?

3. **Key Ideas and Details (a)** According to "London, 1802," what is England like? **(b) Analyze:** What lacks or missing qualities have caused this condition? **(c) Interpret:** How would Milton's return help?

4. **Integration of Knowledge and Ideas** What qualities do you find in Wordsworth's poems that make him a poetic rebel? In your response, use at least two of these Essential Question words: *traditional, interpretation, rebellious.* [*Connecting to the Essential Question: What is the relationship of the writer to tradition?*]

Cite textual evidence to support your responses.

After You Read

Poetry of William Wordsworth

Literary Analysis

1. Key Ideas and Details Identify a passage from the poems that illustrates Wordsworth's idealized view of nature.

2. Key Ideas and Details Find a passage that reflects the **Romantic** belief in the dignity and importance of ordinary people and common language.

3. Integration of Knowledge and Ideas Romantic **lyrics** focus on the speaker's personal development. What lessons from Wordsworth's growth might readers adopt?

4. Integration of Knowledge and Ideas Using a chart like the one shown, find examples in the poems of **diction** that is specific and simple, abstract but simple, or abstract and difficult. Then, summarize your results.

Specific and Simple: "steep and lofty cliffs"

Abstract but Simple: "clad in one green hue"

Abstract and Difficult: "tranquil restoration"

5. Comparing Literary Works Wordsworth's subjects in these poems range widely, from natural scenes to politics to modern life. Does his diction vary to match his subject? Support your answer with details from the poems.

6. Comparing Literary Works Identify two passages, each from a different poem, whose diction would have seemed revolutionary to Neoclassical poets. Then, explain your choices.

Reading Strategy

7. (a) What do the hopes described in *The Prelude* tell you about the *political and philosophical assumptions* of the **historical period** in which Romanticism was born? **(b)** What do lines 66–84 suggest about the Romantics' view of reasoning not guided by the heart? Explain.

8. Imagine that you are a Neoclassical writer—a sociable city-dweller who writes polished, witty, rational verse. Explain how you might react to lines 76–80 of "Tintern Abbey."

9. Would Wordsworth have appreciated modern technology such as computers and the Internet? Support your answer by referring to the political and philosophical assumptions of Romanticism.

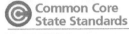

Common Core State Standards

Language
4.b. Identify and correctly use patterns of word changes that indicate different meanings or parts of speech. *(p. 793)*

5.b. Analyze nuances in the meanings of words with similar denotations. *(p. 793)*

© Vocabulary Acquisition and Use

Word Analysis: Forms of *anatomize*

The verb *anatomize*, meaning "cut into constituent parts," or "dissect," comes from the Greek word *atomos*, meaning "that which cannot be cut further; the smallest part." In *anatomizing* society, Wordsworth attempts to dissect it into the parts that make it up. Several scientific words come from this Greek word. Explain how, as the use of the root changes, each word has a different function or meaning.

1. atom
2. anatomy
3. anatomical
4. atomizer

Root words are modified when affixes are attached. Identify four words with the root *-string-* or *-strict-* ("to draw tight") and explain how each differs in meaning.

Vocabulary: Synonyms

A *synonym* is a word that has the same, or a similar, meaning as another word. Write the letter of the word that is the best synonym of each word from the vocabulary list on page 779. Then, write an original sentence using each vocabulary word.

1. recompense: **(a)** assistance, **(b)** penitence, **(c)** reward
2. roused: **(a)** angered, **(b)** stirred, **(c)** interfered
3. presumption: **(a)** audacity, **(b)** flattery, **(c)** attractive
4. anatomize: **(a)** address, **(b)** dissect, **(c)** respect
5. sordid: **(a)** dirty, **(b)** organized, **(c)** reclassified
6. stagnant: **(a)** direct, **(b)** foul, **(c)** repugnant

Using Resources to Build Vocabulary

Epic Style: Words for Nature

Words have **denotations,** which are their basic meanings, and also **connotations,** which are the feelings or ideas associated with them. For instance, *tired* and *spent* both denote a loss of physical energy from exertion, but *spent* suggests a more extreme state, in which all stamina or tolerance for a difficult situation is gone.

Poets use connotations to add depth and richness to their poems. Wordsworth reveals his feelings for nature through these words from "Tintern Abbey" that he uses to describe it:

> sublime (lines 37, 95)
>
> power (line 47)
>
> harmony (line 48)
>
> spirit (line 100)

Use a print or electronic *dictionary* or *thesaurus* to find synonyms of these words. Explain how the connotation of each word differs from that of at least one synonym.

PERFORMANCE TASKS
Integrated Language Skills

Writing

Argumentative Text Literary critic Harold Bloom expressed the following insight into Wordsworth's work: "The fear of mortality haunts much of Wordsworth's best poetry, especially in regard to the premature mortality of the Imagination and the loss of its creative joy."

Do you agree or disagree with this evaluation? Prepare an **essay** that refutes or supports Bloom's view.

Prewriting Begin by carefully rereading the poems by Wordsworth in the text.

- After finishing each poem, think about Wordsworth's attitudes toward the loss of imaginative power.
- Note the *imagery, figures of speech, personification,* and *sounds* in the poems that *evoke readers' emotions* and relate to the *theme* of "premature mortality of the Imagination."
- Write a sentence or two to serve as the *thesis* of your essay, and develop an outline that shows how you will support your thesis.

Drafting Write a draft of your essay that follows your outline.

- In the opening paragraph, remember to quote or paraphrase Bloom's insight; to state your thesis clearly, agreeing or disagreeing with Bloom; and to offer a brief explanation of your position.
- Be sure to support your thesis in the body of the essay, making *detailed and accurate references* to the text of Wordsworth's poems.
- Conclude the essay by summarizing what you proved.

Revising Revise your essay to make it clear and effective:

- Review your draft, making sure you have details to support your points. Where they are lacking, find them in the text and add them.
- Determine whether the opening paragraph, in particular, engages the reader's interest as well as setting forth your thesis.
- Check quotations to be sure they are accurate and properly referenced.
- Read the essay carefully to make sure it is grammatically correct and all words are spelled correctly.

Common Core State Standards

Writing

1.a. Introduce precise, knowledgeable claim(s), establish the significance of the claim(s), distinguish the claim(s) from alternate or opposing claims, and create an organization that logically sequences claim(s), counterclaims, reasons, and evidence.

1.e. Provide a concluding statement or section that follows from and supports the argument presented.

9.a. Apply *grades 11–12 Reading standards* to literature.

Language

1. Demonstrate command of the conventions of standard English grammar and usage when writing or speaking. *(p. 795)*

5.a. Interpret figures of speech in context and analyze their role in the text.

Model: Revising to Clearly State Your Position

Much of Wordsworth's work seems to focus on the transience

, however,

of time. Close reading of his poetry ∧ suggests that rather than a fear of mortality, his work presents a celebration of life.

> Using conjunctions signals agreement or disagreement.

Conventions and Style: Pronoun-Antecedent Agreement Problems

To write effectively, avoid vague or confusing sentences by using pronouns correctly. Remember that a **pronoun** stands for a noun. The noun is the **antecedent.**

Example: *Wordsworth's* poetry shows *his* love of nature.

Problems in Agreement

Avoid **unintended shifts in person or gender.** It is easy to make accidental errors.

Shift in Person William Wordsworth visited Tintern Abbey, where you saw the ruins.
Revised William Wordsworth visited Tintern Abbey, where he saw the ruins.

Shift in Gender Dorothy Wordsworth, the poet's sister, was himself a very good writer.
Revised Dorothy Wordsworth, the poet's sister, was herself a very good writer.

Watch out for **indefinite pronouns**, such as *all, few, most,* and *none.* Some of them can be either singular or plural.

Most of his *poetry* is read for *its* images.

Most of his *poems* are read for *their* images.

Be sure it is clear to which nouns your pronouns refer.

Unclear Reference Triton and Proteus were sea gods. He was part man and part fish.
Revised Triton was part man and part fish. He and Proteus were sea gods.

Practice Rewrite each sentence, correcting the problem in antecedent and pronoun agreement.

1. Milton and Wordsworth were both English poets. He wrote "London, 1802."
2. There is a poem about the French Revolution in my textbook, but I cannot find it.
3. Poets write of meadows and woods. They are inspiring.
4. Nature is loyal to those who cherish her as it accompanies them through life.
5. The French people lost sight of the reason it fought the French Revolution.
6. Much of the abbey is in ruins, but their former grandeur remains today.
7. Although he has been away five years, the poet remembers the hills for her beauty.
8. One of the landscapes certainly will make their impression.
9. England was going in the wrong direction. They had forgotten manners. They had forgotten freedom.
10. People were interested in worldly things, and you were ignoring nature.

© Writing and Speaking Conventions

A. Language Use each pronoun to write a sentence with correct pronoun and antecedent agreement. Choose from these antecedents: *nature, world, beliefs, England, Wordsworth, hope and joy, poets.*

1. he   **2.** it   **3.** they   **4.** her   **5.** its

Example: its
Sentence: The *world* offers us *its* beauty to appreciate.

B. Writing As Wordsworth's sister, write a brief letter to Wordsworth after your visit together to Tintern Abbey. Describe the landscape and what you enjoyed about the visit. Use at least two examples of pronoun-antecedent agreement.

PH WRITING COACH
Further instruction and practice are available in *Prentice Hall Writing Coach.*

THE *Muse's* CHILDREN:
LYRIC POETS IN WORLD LITERATURE

Erato—LYRIC POETRY IS NAMED FOR THE LYRE, A STRINGED INSTRUMENT USED BY THE ANCIENT GREEKS TO ACCOMPANY RECITATIONS OF POETRY. THE GREEKS DEPICTED THE GODDESS ERATO, SHOWN HERE PLAYING THE LYRE, AS THE MUSE OR PATRON OF LYRIC POETRY.

TU FU
(712–770) CHINESE

ONO KOMACHI
(c. 820–c. 900) JAPANESE

CHARLES BAUDELAIRE
(1821–1867) FRENCH

ALEXANDER PUSHKIN
(1799–1837) RUSSIAN

Comparing Literary Works

Poetry of William Wordsworth •
Lyric Poetry from Around the World

Comparing Lyric Poetry from Around the World

Lyric Poetry Lyric poetry began in song. In fact, the word *lyric* comes from *lyre*, the harplike instrument that ancient Greek poets like Sappho played to accompany their lyric poems. Even before the Greeks, however, people were singing poems expressing faith, love, sorrow, joy, and other strong emotions. Love lyrics survive from ancient Egypt's New Kingdom (c. 1570–1070 B.C.). The philosopher Confucius is said to have compiled the *Book of Songs*, collecting Chinese poetry written as early as 1100 B.C.

Lyric poetry typically has these characteristics:

- It is brief and concise.
- It is communicated by a single speaker expressing personal emotions and observations.
- It uses vivid images to convey ideas and evoke emotions.
- It is musical, often employing rhyme, alliteration, and repetition and following a pattern of rhythm (called meter) or a pattern of syllables.

For lyric poems that you read, fill in charts like this one. Then, use your charts to answer comparison-and-contrast questions about the poems.

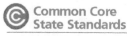

**Common Core
State Standards**

Reading Literature
5. Analyze how an author's choices concerning how to structure specific parts of a text contribute to its overall structure and meaning as well as its aesthetic impact.

Language
4.c. Consult general and specialized reference materials, both print and digital, to find the pronunciation of a word or determine or clarify its precise meaning, its part of speech, its etymology, or its standard usage.

	"The World Is Too Much With Us"	**"I Have Visited Again"**
Form and/or lines	Petrarchan sonnet; 14 lines	
Speaker	Lover of nature	
Observations	Society is too materialistic; nature's beauty is unappreciated.	
Emotions	Unhappiness with society; joy and wonder in nature	
Images	Vivid sights and sounds of wild and pagan sea	
Sound devices	Rhyme, meter, some alliteration, assonance	

Ⓒ Gather Vocabulary Knowledge

These lyric poets use words such as *fathomless, treacherous,* and *splendor.* Use a **dictionary** to find each word's part of speech and definition. Then, employ the following references (printed or electronic) to explore these words:

- **History of Language:** Use a history of English to research each word's etymology, or origins.
- **Book of Quotations:** Use a collection of quotations to find a statement containing one of the words. In a paragraph, explain the nuances in meaning that are evident from the context of the quotation.

Comparing References Compare and contrast what you learn about the words from these specialized references.

Alexander Pushkin (1799–1837)

Author of "I Have Visited Again"

Russian author Alexander Pushkin was born in Moscow into an aristocratic family. As a youth, he led a life of relative privilege and wrote with a skill that would hint at his eventual fame. While working in government service in St. Petersburg, he aroused suspicion by associating with political rebels and writing poems advocating government changes. In 1820, the government acted upon its suspicions by reappointing Pushkin to a post in a remote province in southern Russia. During the five years Pushkin spent there, he enhanced his reputation as a writer and began working on his masterpiece, the verse novel *Yevgeny Onegin* (1833). Unfortunately, his unrestrained and sometimes violent behavior resulted in his dismissal from civil service in 1824 and banishment to his family's estate.

Though isolated and unhappy on the estate, Pushkin channeled most of his energy into his writing. He spent much of his time interacting with the peasants who lived on the estate, learning about their lifestyles, and incorporating their legends and folklore into a number of his finest poems.

Acts of Rebellion Pushkin was allowed to return to Moscow in 1826. After marrying Natalya Goncharova in 1831, Pushkin grudgingly returned to government service. In a final act of rebellion, Pushkin entered into a duel that cost him his life.

Charles Baudelaire (1821–1867)

Author of "Invitation to the Voyage"

Charles Baudelaire (shàrl bōd ler´) was one of the most colorful, startling, and innovative poets of the nineteenth century. Attempting to break away from the Romantic tradition, Baudelaire created poems that are objective rather than sentimental. Many of his works celebrate the city and the artificial rather than nature.

As a youth, Baudelaire rebelled against his family to pursue a career as a writer. To dissuade him from such a dissolute life, they sent him on an ocean voyage to India. Instead of completing the voyage, he returned to France to claim his share of his late father's fortune. Soon, extravagant living drove him into debt, a problem that would plague him for the rest of his life.

Baudelaire published short stories, translated works by Edgar Allan Poe into French, and both wrote and collected poems for *Flowers of Evil* (1857), which would become his signature work. Although his talents were not widely recognized during his lifetime, Baudelaire's reputation blossomed posthumously, and he came to be considered one of the finest nineteenth-century poets.

I Have Visited Again

Alexander Pushkin, translated by D. M. Thomas

BACKGROUND Initially, Alexander Pushkin found the inspiration to write in the politics of his homeland. His rebellious writings, as well as his unruly behavior, resulted in banishment to his family estate. Such a personality seems distantly related to the speaker of the gentle words and images in "I Have Visited Again." In this poem, the speaker revisits the estate to find that time and nature have hardly stood still in the intervening years.

Comparing Lyric Poetry
How is the speaker's experience here similar to that of the speaker in Wordsworth's "Lines Composed a Few Miles Above Tintern Abbey"? Do the two speakers share similar views of nature? Explain.

. . . I have visited again
That corner of the earth where I spent two
Unnoticed, exiled years. Ten years have passed
Since then, and many things have changed for me,
5   And I have changed too, obedient to life's law—
But now that I am here again, the past
Has flown out eagerly to embrace me, claim me,
And it seems that only yesterday I wandered
Within these groves.

                              Here is the cottage, sadly
10   Declined now, where I lived with my poor old nurse.
She is no more. No more behind the wall
Do I hear her heavy footsteps as she moved
Slowly, painstakingly about her tasks.

15   Here are the wooded slopes where often I
Sat motionless, and looked down at the lake,
Recalling other shores and other waves . . .
It gleams between golden cornfields and green meadows,
A wide expanse; across its fathomless waters
20   A fisherman passes, dragging an ancient net.
Along the shelving banks, hamlets are scattered
—Behind them the mill, so crooked it can scarcely
Make its sails turn in the wind . . .

                              On the bounds

Vocabulary
ancestral (an ses′ trəl) *adj.*
inherited

morose (mə rōs′) *adj.*
gloomy; sullen

25   Of my ancestral acres, at the spot
Where a road, scarred by many rainfalls, climbs
The hill, three pine-trees stand—one by itself,
The others close together. When I rode
On horseback past them in the moonlit night,
30   The friendly rustling murmur of their crowns
Would welcome me. Now, I have ridden out
Upon that road, and seen those trees again.
They have remained the same, make the same murmur—
But round their ageing roots, where all before
35   Was barren, naked, a thicket of young pines
Has sprouted; like green children round the shadows
Of the two neighboring pines. But in the distance
Their solitary comrade stands, morose,
Like some old bachelor, and round its roots
40   All is barren as before.

I greet you, young
And unknown tribe of pine-trees! I'll not see
Your mighty upward thrust of years to come
When you will overtop these friends of mine
45 And shield their ancient summits from the gaze
Of passers-by. But may my grandson hear
Your welcome murmur when, returning home
From lively company, and filled with gay
And pleasant thoughts, he passes you in the night,
50 And thinks perhaps of me . . .

And I have changed too,
obedient to life's law—

Critical Reading

1. Key Ideas and Details (a) Identify four familiar landmarks in the poem that have changed over the years. **(b) Infer:** How has the speaker changed in a similar fashion?

2. Key Ideas and Details (a) In stanza three, what thoughts occupy the speaker while he looks down at the lake? **(b) Infer:** What does the speaker mean by "other shores"? **(c) Hypothesize:** Why might the speaker have yearned to be in another place?

3. Craft and Structure (a) Where does the "unknown tribe of pine-trees" grow? **(b) Speculate:** What role will those pines play in the future? **(c) Interpret:** What do those pines symbolize?

4. Integration of Knowledge and Ideas Novelist Thomas Wolfe commented on how our lives change by saying that we "can't go home again," a theme shared by "I Have Visited Again." Do you agree or disagree with such a claim? Explain your answer.

Cite textual evidence to support your responses.

INVITATION TO THE VOYAGE

CHARLES BAUDELAIRE
translated by Richard Wilbur

BACKGROUND There is little doubt that Charles Baudelaire's ocean voyage to India was a significant event in his life. Although the journey was cut short—lasting only eight months instead of eighteen—the experience clearly inspired him as a poet. The voyage, his desire for a life of ease and luxury, and his yearning to escape reality all find expression in his poem "Invitation to the Voyage."

> My child, my sister, dream
> How sweet all things would seem
> Were we in that kind land to live together
> And there love slow and long,
> 5   There love and die among
> Those scenes that image you, that sumptuous[1] weather.
> Drowned suns that glimmer there
> Through cloud-disheveled[2] air
> Move me with such a mystery as appears
> 10   Within those other skies
> Of your treacherous eyes
> When I behold them shining through their tears.

---

1. **sumptuous** (sump′ choo əs) *adj.* magnificent or splendid.
2. **disheveled** (di shev′ əld) *adj.* disarranged and untidy.

There, there is nothing else but grace and measure,
Richness, quietness, and pleasure.

15   Furniture that wears
      The luster of the years
Softly would glow within our glowing chamber,
      Flowers of rarest bloom
      Proffering their perfume
20 Mixed with the vague fragrances of amber;
      Gold ceilings would there be,
      Mirrors deep as the sea,
The walls all in an Eastern splendor hung—
      Nothing but should address
25   The soul's loneliness,
Speaking her sweet and secret native tongue.

There, there is nothing else but grace and measure,
Richness, quietness, and pleasure.

      See, sheltered from the swells
30   There in the still canals
Those drowsy ships that dream of sailing forth;
      It is to satisfy
      Your least desire, they ply
Hither through all the waters of the earth.
35   The sun at close of day
      Clothes the fields of hay,
Then the canals, at last the town entire
      In hyacinth and gold:
      Slowly the land is rolled
40 Sleepward under a sea of gentle fire.

There, there is nothing else but grace and measure,
Richness, quietness, and pleasure.

Vocabulary
proffering (prāf′ ər iŋ)
v. offering

Comparing Lyric Poetry
How is the landscape
described here unlike the
landscape described in
Pushkin's poem? What
feelings does the speaker of
each poem seem to have for
the landscape he describes?

Critical Reading

1. **Key Ideas and Details** **(a)** Which details describe the "kind land"
   in "Invitation to the Voyage"? **(b) Interpret:** What impression of
   the land do these details convey?

2. **Integration of Knowledge and Ideas** How does the world
   described in "Invitation to the Voyage" compare to your ideal
   world?

Cite textual evidence to support your responses.

Chinese Poets

BOOK OF SONGS

The Book of Songs, also known as *The Book of Odes*, is an anthology of 305 ancient Chinese poems. The poems come from many different regions of China. Most of them were originally folk songs describing people's daily activities. Others, like "Thick Grow the Rush Leaves," focus on love or courtship. All of the songs were originally set to music.

TU FU (712–770)

Author of "Jade Flower Palace"

Tu Fu (dōō′ fōō′) is regarded as the supreme craftsman of Chinese shih (shĭ) poetry. In all of his poetry—poems dealing with social issues and those that focus on his personal experiences—Tu Fu shows a command of language and a mastery of the shih form. As a result, his poems are admired as much for their form as for their content.

Early in Tu Fu's career, China was relatively peaceful, but later the poet witnessed a major rebellion, the destruction of the capital city, and an invasion by tribes from the northwest. In his poems, Tu Fu gives some of the most vivid accounts of war and destruction in all of Chinese literature.

Japanese Poets

KI TSURAYUKI (died c. 945)

The chief aide of Emperor Daigo (dī′ gō′), Ki Tsurayuki (kē tsōōr′ ī ōō kē) was one of the leading poets, critics, and diarists of his time. Tsurayuki deserves much of the credit for assembling an anthology of over eleven hundred poems of the Heian (hā′ än′) Age. In addition, his *Tosa Diary* helped to establish the Japanese tradition of the literary diary.

ONO KOMACHI (c. 820–c. 900)

A great beauty with a strong personality, Ono Komachi (ō′ nō′ kō′ mä′ chē′) was an early tanka (tän′ kə) poet whose poems are characterized by their passion and energy. Few details of Ono Komachi's life are known.

PRIEST JAKUREN (1139?–1202)

Jakuren (jä′ kōō′ ren′) was a Buddhist priest and prominent tanka poet whose poems are filled with beautiful yet melancholic imagery. After entering the priesthood at the age of twenty-three, Jakuren spent much of his time traveling the Japanese countryside, writing poetry and seeking spiritual fulfillment.

FROM **THE BOOK OF SONGS**

Thick Grow the Rush Leaves

TRANSLATED BY ARTHUR WALEY

Thick grow the rush leaves;
Their white dew turns to frost.
He whom I love
Must be somewhere along this stream.
5   I went up the river to look for him,
But the way was difficult and long.
I went down the stream to look for him,
And there in mid-water
Sure enough, it's he!

10   Close grow the rush leaves,
Their white dew not yet dry.
He whom I love
Is at the water's side.
Up stream I sought him;
15   But the way was difficult and steep.
Down stream I sought him,
And away in mid-water
There on a ledge, that's he!

Very fresh are the rush leaves;
20   The white dew still falls.
He whom I love
Is at the water's edge.
Up stream I followed him;
But the way was hard and long.
25   Down stream I followed him,
And away in mid-water
There on the shoals is he!

▼ **Critical Viewing**
How is the river in this painting similar to or different from the one in the poem, along which "the way was difficult and long"?
[Compare and Contrast]

Jade Flower Palace

TU FU

TRANSLATED BY KENNETH REXROTH

Vocabulary

scurry (skʉr´ ē) *v.* to run hastily; to scamper

pathos (pa´ thəs´) *n.* quality that evokes sorrow or compassion

imperceptibly (im´ pər sep´ tə blē) *adv.* without being noticed

The stream swirls. The wind moans in
The pines. Gray rats scurry over
Broken tiles. What prince, long ago,
Built this palace, standing in
5   Ruins beside the cliffs? There are
Green ghost fires in the black rooms.
The shattered pavements are all
Washed away. Ten thousand organ
Pipes whistle and roar. The storm
10 Scatters the red autumn leaves.
His dancing girls are yellow dust.
Their painted cheeks have crumbled
Away. His gold chariots
And courtiers are gone. Only
15 A stone horse is left of his
Glory. I sit on the grass and
Start a poem, but the pathos of
It overcomes me. The future
Slips imperceptibly away.
20 Who can say what the years will bring?

▶ **Critical Viewing** How is the building in this photo different from the palace described in "Jade Flower Palace"? How is the girl in the drawing on the facing page like the "dancing girls" found in the poem? **[Connect]**

All three of the following poems are tanka. The tanka is the most prevalent verse form in traditional Japanese literature. In the original Japanese, each tanka consists of five lines of five, seven, five, seven, and seven syllables. Tanka usually tell a brief story or express a single thought or insight, usually relating to love or nature.

Priest Jakuren

TRANSLATED BY GEOFFREY BOWNAS

One cannot ask loneliness
How or where it starts.
On the cypress-mountain,[1]
Autumn evening.

Ki Tsurayuki

TRANSLATED BY GEOFFREY BOWNAS

When I went to visit
The girl I love so much,
That winter night
The river blew so cold
5   That the plovers[2] were crying.

---

1. **cypress-mountain** Cypress trees are cone-bearing evergreen trees, native to North America, Europe, and Asia.
2. **plovers** (pluv´ ərz) *n.* wading shorebirds with short tails, long, pointed wings, and short, stout beaks.

Ono Komachi

TRANSLATED BY GEOFFREY BOWNAS

Comparing Lyric Poetry
In which of the three tanka does the translator best retain the original syllabification?

Was it that I went to sleep
Thinking of him,
That he came in my dreams?
Had I known it a dream
5   I should not have wakened.

Critical Reading

Cite textual evidence to support your responses.

© 1. **Craft and Structure (a)** In "Thick Grow the Rush Leaves," which images in each stanza are repeated with slight variations? **(b) Infer:** What activity on the river do the images help capture? **(c) Interpret:** How do images help convey the speaker's feelings?

© 2. **Key Ideas and Details (a)** In "Jade Flower Palace," what remains of the long-gone prince's "glory"? **(b) Compare and Contrast:** In what way does this image contrast with the speaker's description of what used to be in the palace? **(c) Draw Conclusions:** What point might the speaker be making through this contrast?

© 3. **Craft and Structure (a)** What is the setting of Tsurayuki's poem? **(b) Infer:** What does the speaker's willingness to face that setting suggest about the depth of his love?

© 4. **Key Ideas and Details (a)** What question does the speaker of Ono Komachi's poem ask? **(b) Infer:** What do her question and her response to that question suggest about her feelings toward the man in her dreams?

After You Read

Poetry of William Wordsworth • Lyric Poetry from Around the World

Comparing Lyric Poetry

1. Key Ideas and Details Compare "Thick Grow the Rush Leaves" to the first two tanka poems by Japanese writers. **(a)** What is similar and different about the feelings each poem expresses? **(b)** In which poem does imagery most effectively capture those feelings? Explain.

2. Key Ideas and Details (a) Compare and contrast the passage of time in "Tintern Abbey," the selection from *The Prelude*, "Jade Flower Palace," and "I Have Visited Again." **(b)** In which two poems are the speakers' experiences of the passage of time most similar? Explain.

3. Craft and Structure Of the translations presented here, which lyric poems do you find the most musical? Cite examples from the poems to support your evaluation.

Timed Writing

Explanatory Text: Essay

Many of the lyric poems you have read in this section include descriptions of natural settings.

Assignment: Choose two poems by different authors that have vivid descriptions of nature. Write an **essay** in which you *compare and contrast* the two poems by addressing these questions. **[40 minutes]**

- What is the theme or central insight expressed in each poem?
- For each poem, how does the description of nature support the theme?
- What images does each speaker use to describe nature?
- For each poem, what feelings does the description of nature evoke?

As you write, follow the conventions of a strong explanatory essay. Organize your ideas logically. You might focus on the features of one poem and then the features of the other, or you might focus on points of similarity and difference, moving back and forth between the two poems.

5-Minute Planner

Complete these steps before you begin to write:

1. Read the assignment carefully. List key words and phrases.
2. To focus your analysis, scan the poems for evidence that relates to the questions.
3. Create a rough outline for your essay.
4. Reread the prompt, and draft your essay.

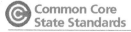 **Common Core State Standards**

Writing

2. Write informative/ explanatory texts to examine and convey complex ideas, concepts, and information clearly and accurately through the effective selection, organization, and analysis of content.

10. Write routinely over extended time frames and shorter time frames for a range of tasks, purposes, and audiences.

USE ACADEMIC VOCABULARY

As you write, use academic language, including the following words or their related forms:

correspond
insight
musicality
perspective

For more on academic language, see the vocabulary charts in the introduction to this book.

Analyzing Functional and Expository Texts

Government Report • Travel Guide

About the Texts

A **government report** is an account of work or a study completed by a government agency. These types of reports often include a description of events or an analysis of an issue; an explanation of how an issue affects different groups; and a description of problems, with proposed solutions, often including actions taken or planned by the government.

A **travel guide** is a document that provides information to people who are planning a trip to a particular destination. Travel guides generally provide an overview of an area and then go into detail about specific attractions, transportation, food, and lodging.

Reading Strategy

Reports and guides provide information in a logical order. Often, the textual information in these types of documents is supplemented by graphics, such as charts and photographs. Graphics may clarify the structure of the text and make it easier to read. They may also make the text more attractive and engaging. As you study these documents, **analyze information from charts, graphs, and illustrations** by evaluating these features:

- a heading or title of a graph that defines its information
- labels that classify different elements of charts and graphs
- captions explaining symbols and images

Use a checklist like the one shown to assess graphics in these texts. Analyze and evaluate how well these structures complement information presented verbally. Consider whether the graphic elements clarify ideas and make the text more interesting or useful to readers.

Features	Yes/No	Content
Graph and chart titles	☐ / ☐	
Graph and chart labels	☐ / ☐	
Photos or images	☐ / ☐	
Captions	☐ / ☐	
Explanations of symbols	☐ / ☐	

Common Core State Standards

Reading Informational Text
5. Analyze and evaluate the effectiveness of the structure an author uses in his or her exposition or argument, including whether the structure makes points clear, convincing, and engaging.

Language
4.d. Verify the preliminary determination of the meaning of a word or phrase. *(p. 817)*

Content-Area Vocabulary

These words may also appear in other subject-area texts:

district (dis´ trikt) *n.* a given area or selected geographical section on a map

trade (trād) *n.* the buying and selling of goods or services

policies (päl´ ə sēz´) *n.* plans of action by a government, business, or political party

geological (jē´ ə läj´ ik əl) *adj.* of or related to the structure of the earth

LAKE DISTRICT
National Park Authority

EDUCATION SERVICE TRAFFIC MANAGEMENT

The Lake District National Park is an area of outstandingly beautiful and varied landscape and the scenery is the reason most people give for visiting the Lake District (62%, 1994 All Parks Visitor Survey).

The Lake District remained relatively isolated until the 19th century when new railways allowed the large urban populations of Northwest England to visit the area easily. Both trade and early tourism flourished. In the 1940s, it was recognised that areas such as the Lake District would benefit from some kind of special protection. The Lake District was designated a National Park in 1951 to conserve and enhance its special landscape while providing opportunities for the public to enjoy that landscape. At this time, it was expected that "walkers, cyclists, riders and students of nature" would be the main users of the National Park rather than motorists, although National Parks were intended for all to enjoy.

Since then, car ownership has increased and now the vast majority of visitors come by car. Today, over 12 million people visit the National Park annually (staying for 22 million days) while 42,000 people live in the National Park. 89% of visitors come to the National Park by private motor vehicle.

The Lake District National Park Authority (LDNPA) and Cumbria County Council (CCC) have a number of automatic traffic counters around the National Park to help understand traffic movements. Traffic is greatest during the summer months when most visitors come to the National Park and mid-mornings and late afternoons can be exceptionally busy. In recent years, the rate of increase of traffic has slowed down, with recorded increases being largely confined to main roads such as the A591.

The heading "Lake District" and the words "Traffic Management" in the report's heading reveal the focus and purpose of the report.

This paragraph establishes the focus of the report on the issue of car traffic in the park.

Traffic Issues

Large volumes of traffic can lead to a number of issues, especially in an area like the Lake District where roads are often narrow.

- **Pollution:** Motor vehicles emit various pollutants which may reach high levels in certain weather conditions, especially within towns.

- **Noise:** 'Peace and Quiet' is often given as a reason for visiting, so this is an issue, especially when considering development.

- **Visual intrusion:** Lines of parked cars can detract from the natural beauty of the National Park.

- **Congestion:** Congestion can be a problem in certain areas and towns at peak times of day and the year.

- **Reducing visitor traffic:** Traffic Management aims to minimize the impact of traffic and encourage visitors to use public transport rather than private cars.

- **Parking:** A balance needs to be found between provision of parking for visitors and locals and impact on the landscape.

- **Hazards to vulnerable road users:** Walkers, cyclists and horse riders should be at ease on the roads in the Lake District. Actual and perceived hazards to these road users should be minimized.

The traffic problems are clearly described in this bulleted list.

The graph's clear title, different colors, and sidebar labels make information easy to interpret.

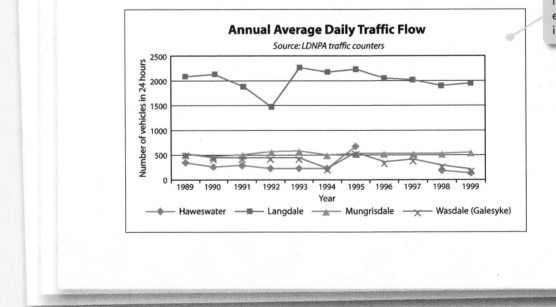

Annual Average Daily Traffic Flow

Source: LDNPA traffic counters

Number of vehicles in 24 hours — Year

Haweswater   Langdale   Mungrisdale   Wasdale (Galesyke)

Traffic Management in the National Park

The guiding principle underpinning the **policies** of the LDNPA towards transport and traffic is that demand should be managed in order to:

- minimize its impact on the landscape
- improve the quality of life for local residents
- improve the quality of enjoyment for visitors
- encourage use of sustainable means of travel

The policies of the LDNPA are set out in the Lake District National Park Management Plan. These clearly state that increasing road capacity is not an appropriate solution to traffic management in the National Park. Instead, traffic management policy is to tailor traffic to existing roads.

A balance of interests is needed between the purposes of the National Park, local people and visitors to ensure the special qualities of the National Park are not compromised. For example, in 1966 the Lake District Special Planning Board published a "Report on Traffic in the Lake District National Park" suggesting that in the future it might become necessary to restrict all except local traffic along secondary routes. Objections were raised by local residents of Langdale and Borrowdale concerning the impact of these closures on the tourism trade.

> This paragraph addresses the different groups the traffic problem and proposed solutions affect.

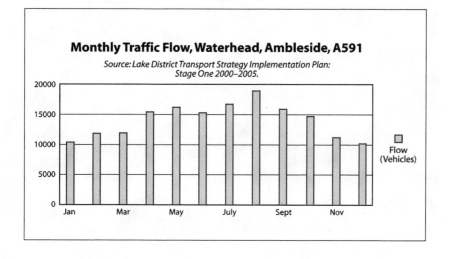

Monthly Traffic Flow, Waterhead, Ambleside, A591
Source: Lake District Transport Strategy Implementation Plan: Stage One 2000–2005.

The North Country

Exploring Lancashire and the Lakes

The lake district's natural scenery outweighs any of its man-made attractions. Its natural features are the result of **geological** upheavals over millennia (see pp 340–41), and four of its peaks are more than 1,000 m (3,300 ft). Human influences have left their mark too: the main activities are quarrying, mining, farming and tourism.

The Lakes are most crowded in summer when activities include lake trips and hill-walking. The best bases are Keswick and Ambleside, while there are also good hotels on the shores of Windermere and Ullswater and in the Cartmel area.

Lancashire's Bowland Forest is an attractive place to explore on foot, with picturesque villages. Further south, Manchester and Liverpool have excellent museums and galleries.

This picture and caption give readers a clearer understanding of the area's "natural scenery" described in the text.

View over Crummock Water, north of Buttermere, one of the quieter Western Lakes

Preserved docks and Liver Building, Liverpool

This section giving visitors information on traveling to different sites is supplemented by the map on the following page.

Getting Around

For many, the first glimpse of the Lake District is from the M6 near Shap Fell, but the A6 is a more dramatic route. You can reach Windermere by train, but you need to change at Oxenholme, on the mainline route from Euston to Carlisle. Penrith also has rail services and bus links into the Lakes. L'al Ratty, the miniature railway up Eskdale, and the Lakeside & Haverthwaite railway, which connects with the steamers on Windermere, make for enjoyable outings. Regular buses link all the main centres where excursions are organized. One of the most enterprising is the Mountain Goat minibus, in Windermere and Keswick.

Lancaster, Liverpool and Manchester are on the main rail and bus routes and also have airports. For Blackpool, you need to change trains in Preston. Wherever you go in the area, one of the best means of getting around is on foot.

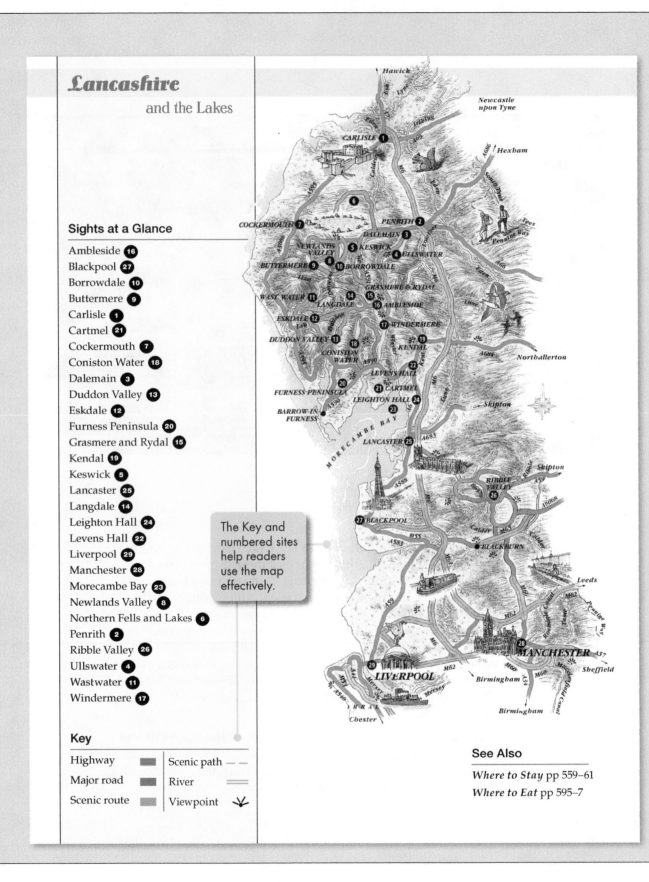

Lancashire
and the Lakes

Sights at a Glance

Ambleside 16
Blackpool 27
Borrowdale 10
Buttermere 9
Carlisle 1
Cartmel 21
Cockermouth 7
Coniston Water 18
Dalemain 3
Duddon Valley 13
Eskdale 12
Furness Peninsula 20
Grasmere and Rydal 15
Kendal 19
Keswick 5
Lancaster 25
Langdale 14
Leighton Hall 24
Levens Hall 22
Liverpool 29
Manchester 28
Morecambe Bay 23
Newlands Valley 8
Northern Fells and Lakes 6
Penrith 2
Ribble Valley 26
Ullswater 4
Wastwater 11
Windermere 17

Key

Highway		Scenic path	- - -
Major road		River	= =
Scenic route		Viewpoint	↓

The Key and numbered sites help readers use the map effectively.

See Also

Where to Stay pp 559–61
Where to Eat pp 595–7

Critical Reading

1. Key Ideas and Details **(a)** Based on the government report, what major change has taken place since 1951 in the way visitors tour the Lake District? **(b)** What problems has this change caused? **(c)** What solutions does the report propose?

2. Key Ideas and Details **(a)** Based on the travel guide, what are various transportation options in the Lake District? **(b)** Which option does the guide state is best? **(c)** How does the information in the government report support the opinion expressed in the travel guide?

3. Craft and Structure For each document, note at least one way in which its structure and organization reflect and support its content.

4. Craft and Structure **(a)** For each document, note a statement or fact presented verbally that is supported or enhanced by one or more graphics. **(b)** For each document, do the graphic elements make the ideas clearer and more engaging? Why or why not?

5. Content-Area Vocabulary (a) The word *policy* derives from the Greek root *-polis-/-polit-*, which means "city." Explain how the meaning of the root informs the meaning of *policy*. **(b)** Define the following words derived from the same root: *political, police,* and *cosmopolitan*. Use a dictionary to verify your definitions.

Timed Writing

Informative Text [40 minutes]

Format
In an **analytical essay,** you break a topic into smaller elements and show how these elements relate to the idea or ideas you are discussing.

Although these documents have different purposes, they are about the same place. Write a brief **analytical essay** in which you use both documents to tell visitors what to expect on a trip to the Lake District. To accomplish your goal, **synthesize ideas and make logical connections** between the texts. Support your ideas with textual evidence, including evidence from the graphs and the map.

Academic Vocabulary
When you **synthesize and make logical connections,** you combine ideas and relate texts logically.

5-Minute Planner

Complete these steps before you begin to write.

1. Read the prompt carefully. Underline key words.

2. Draft a thesis that clearly responds to the prompt.

3. Scan the text for details that relate to the prompt. **TIP** Your scan will help provide the evidence you need to support your points.

4. Reread the prompt, and draft your essay.

The Rime of the Ancient Mariner • Kubla Khan

Connecting to the Essential Question Romantics like Coleridge wrote about strange and faraway places. As you read, note details in the settings of these poems that seem unusual, even dreamlike. Finding such details will help you answer the Essential Question: **What is the relationship between literature and place?**

Literary Analysis

Unlike *lyric poetry*, which expresses the thoughts and feelings of a speaker, **narrative poetry** tells a story. Narrative poems feature the storytelling elements of character, plot, and setting, but organize them with poetic structures. Romantics admired the storytelling of folk ballads, so it is no wonder Coleridge uses a *ballad stanza* (*abcb*) in much of his narrative poem *The Rime of the Ancient Mariner.* He also uses these **poetic sound devices** to heighten the music and *evoke emotions*:

- **Alliteration,** a repeated consonant sound at the beginnings of words: "The fair <u>b</u>reeze <u>b</u>lew, the white <u>f</u>oam <u>f</u>lew, . . ."
- **Consonance,** repeated similar final consonant sounds in stressed syllables with dissimilar vowel sounds: ". . . fie<u>nd</u> / . . . behi<u>nd</u>"
- **Assonance,** a repeated vowel sound in stressed syllables with dissimilar consonant sounds: "The western w<u>a</u>ve was all afl<u>a</u>me."
- **Internal rhyme,** the use of rhymes within a poetic line: "With heavy th<u>ump</u>, a lifeless l<u>ump</u>, . . ."

Comparing Literary Works Notice how, in both poems, the rhythms propel you forward. At the same time, Coleridge uses sound devices; *archaic,* or old-fashioned, words such as *eftsoons* ("immediately"); and exotic place names ("Xanadu") to create a riveting fantasy.

Reading Strategy

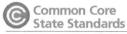 **Preparing to Read Complex Texts** By **comparing and contrasting sound devices** in two of his poems, you can understand how Coleridge evokes a range of moods. As you read, use a chart like the one shown to compare the effects of sound devices in the two poems.

Vocabulary

averred (ə vʉrd´) *v.* stated to be true (p. 824)

sojourn (sō´ jʉrn) *v.* stay for a while (p. 831)

expiated (eks´ pē āt´ id) *v.* atoned for, especially by suffering (p. 838)

reverence (rev´ ər əns) *n.* deep respect (p. 845)

sinuous (sin´ yo͞o əs) *adj.* bending; winding (p. 847)

tumult (to͞o´ mult´) *n.* noisy commotion (p. 848)

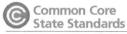 Common Core
State Standards

Reading Literature
5. Analyze how an author's choices concerning how to structure specific parts of a text contribute to its overall structure and meaning as well as its aesthetic impact.

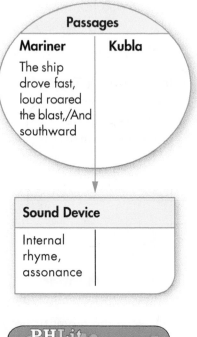

Passages	
Mariner	**Kubla**
The ship drove fast, loud roared the blast,/And southward	

Sound Device	
Internal rhyme, assonance	

www.PHLitOnline.com

Samuel Taylor Coleridge

(1772–1834)

Author of *The Rime of the Ancient Mariner* • "Kubla Khan"

The poetry of Samuel Taylor Coleridge stands at the place where real life slips into dreams and facts are reborn as fantasies. More than any other Romantic poet, he dared to journey inward—deep into the world of the imagination.

Early Fantasies Coleridge was born in Ottery St. Mary on the Devon coast of England, the last of ten children. At an early age, he retreated into a world of books and fantasy. When he was nine, his father died, and Coleridge was sent to school in London. Later, he went to Cambridge University.

Utopian Plans At Cambridge, Coleridge's hunger for new ideas led him into radical politics. He became a friend of the poet Robert Southey. Inspired by the early promise of the French Revolution, the two men planned to form a settlement in Pennsylvania based on their utopian political ideas. The plan collapsed, however, when Southey's aunt refused to fund their project.

A Literary Breakthrough In 1795, Coleridge and his wife, Sara Fricker, moved to Somerset, where he became a friend of poet William Wordsworth. In 1798, the two poets published *Lyrical Ballads*, a joint collection of their works. The four poems that make up Coleridge's contribution to the volume include his masterpiece *The Rime of the Ancient Mariner.* The collection of poems slowly gained critical attention. In the end, it caused a revolution in poetic style and thought, firmly establishing the movement known as Romanticism.

Success and Difficulty As Coleridge's fame grew, he suffered increasingly from asthma and rheumatism. He began to rely heavily on pain-killers, which dulled his creative powers. He sought relief from pain in the warmer climates of Malta and Italy. His travels, however, did not relieve his pain and caused the collapse of his marriage.

Though the end of his life was troubled, Coleridge left a great legacy in poetry and literary criticism. Above all, he helped establish the importance of the imagination in literature and in life.

> "Poetry:
> the best words
> in the best order."

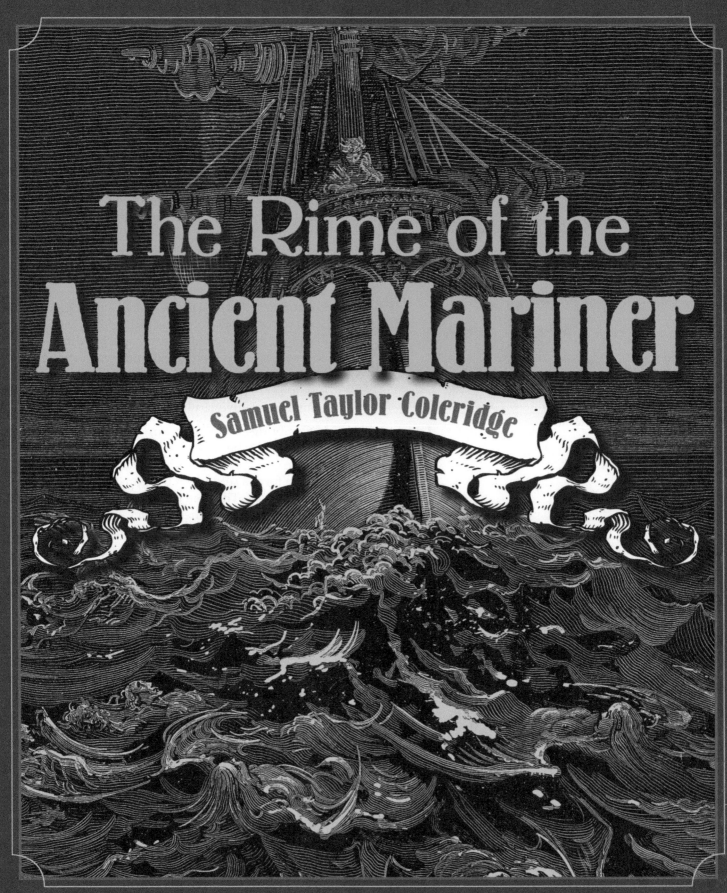

The Rime of the Ancient Mariner

Samuel Taylor Coleridge

Coleridge used dreams as the basis of many of his great poems. "The Rime of the Ancient Mariner" was based on a dream reported by his friend John Cruikshank. Starting with the dream as raw material, Coleridge and Wordsworth began to elaborate upon it. Wordsworth suggested that the act that would drive the entire poem was a crime committed at sea. Using this idea and his own lively imagination, Coleridge wrote a poem that has chilled and enthralled audiences to this day. (The margin notes in italics were written by the poet.)

Argument

How a Ship having passed the Line[1] was driven by storms to the cold Country towards the South Pole: and how from thence she made her course to the tropical Latitude of the Great Pacific Ocean; and of the strange things that befell: and in what manner the Ancyent Marinere came back to his own Country.

◀ **Critical Viewing**
Identify two elements in this engraving that create a gloomy, suspense-filled atmosphere. **[Analyze]**

Part I ●━━━━━

An ancient Mariner meeteth three Gallants bidden to a wedding feast and detaineth one.

It is an ancient Mariner,
And he stoppeth one of three.
"By thy long gray beard and glittering eye,
Now wherefore stopp'st thou me?"

5 "The Bridegroom's doors are opened wide,
And I am next of kin;
The guests are met, the feast is set:
May'st hear the merry din."

The Wedding Guest is spellbound by the eye of the old seafaring man and constrained to hear his tale.

He holds him with his skinny hand,
10 "There was a ship," quoth he.
"Hold off! unhand me, graybeard loon!"
Eftsoons[2] his hand dropped he.

He holds him with his glittering eye—
The Wedding Guest stood still,

Literary Analysis
Poetic Sound Devices
What examples of internal rhymes and assonance can you find in lines 5–8?

Reading
Check
What effect does the ancient Mariner have on the Wedding Guest?

---

1. Line Equator.
2. Eftsoons immediately.

Engraving by Gustave Doré for "The Rime of the Ancient Mariner" by Samuel Taylor Coleridge © 1970 by Dover Publications, Inc.

▶ **Critical Viewing**
From the expression on the Wedding Guest's face (figure on far left), what can you infer about his reaction to the ancient Mariner?
[Infer]

15 And listens like a three years' child:
    The Mariner hath his will.

    The Wedding Guest sat on a stone:
    He cannot choose but hear;
    And thus spake on that ancient man,
20 The bright-eyed Mariner.

    "The ship was cheered, the harbor cleared,
    Merrily did we drop
    Below the kirk,[3] below the hill,
    Below the lighthouse top.

25 "The Sun came up upon the left,
    Out of the sea came he!
    And he shone bright, and on the right
    Went down into the sea.

    "Higher and higher every day,
30 Till over the mast at noon[4]—"
    The Wedding Guest here beat his breast,
    For he heard the loud bassoon.

    The bride hath paced into the hall.
    Red as a rose is she;

The Mariner tells how the ship sailed southward with a good wind and fair weather till it reached the Line.

The Wedding Guest heareth the bridal music; but the Mariner continueth his tale.

---

3. kirk church.
4. over . . . noon The ship has reached the equator.

35 Nodding their heads before her goes
    The merry minstrelsy.

    The Wedding Guest he beat his breast,
    Yet he cannot choose but hear;
    And thus spake on that ancient man
40 The bright-eyed Mariner.

    "And now the Storm blast came, and he
    Was tyrannous and strong:
    He struck with his o'ertaking wings,
    And chased us south along.

45 "With sloping masts and dipping prow,
    As who pursued with yell and blow
    Still treads the shadow of his foe,
    And forward bends his head,
    The ship drove fast, loud roared the blast,
50 And southward aye[5] we fled.

    "And now there came both mist and snow.
    And it grew wondrous cold;
    And ice, mast-high, came floating by,
    As green as emerald.

55 "And through the drifts the snowy clifts[6]
    Did send a dismal sheen;
    Nor shapes of men nor beasts we ken[7]—
    The ice was all between.

    "The ice was here, the ice was there,
60 The ice was all around;
    It cracked and growled, and roared and howled,
    Like noises in a swound![8]

    "At length did cross an Albatross,
    Thorough[9] the fog it came;
65 As if it had been a Christian soul,
    We hailed it in God's name.

    "It ate the food it ne'er had eat,[10]
    And round and round it flew.

---

5. aye ever.
6. clifts icebergs.
7. ken knew.
8. swound swoon.
9. thorough through.
10. eat (et) old form of *eaten*.

The ship driven by a storm toward the South Pole.

The land of ice, and of fearful sounds, where no living thing was to be seen.

Till a great sea bird, called the Albatross, came through the snow-fog, and was received with great joy and hospitality.

Literary Analysis
Poetic Sound Devices
What archaic word-form appears in lines 37–40?

Reading Strategy
Comparing and Contrasting Sound Devices Find one line in lines 51–54 that contains the long and the short sound of the same vowel. What emphasis does this alternation create?

Reading Check

In the Mariner's tale, what happens to the ship shortly after it sets out?

> The ice did split with a thunder-fit;
> 70 The helmsman steered us through!

▶ Critical Viewing
Based on the details of this
illustration, how would you
characterize the Albatross?
[Connect]

"And a good south wind sprung up behind;
The Albatross did follow,
And every day, for food or play,
Came to the mariner's hollo!

75 "In mist or cloud, on mast or shroud,[11]
It perched for vespers[12] nine;
Whiles all the night, through fog-smoke
     white,
Glimmered the white Moonshine."

"God save thee, ancient Mariner!
80 From the fiends, that plague thee thus!—
Why look'st thou so?"[13] "With my crossbow
I shot the Albatross."

And lo! the Albatross proveth a bird of good omen, and followeth the ship as it returned northward through fog and floating ice.

The ancient Mariner inhospitably killeth the pious bird of good omen.

Part II ●━━━

"The Sun now rose upon the right:[14]
Out of the sea came he,
85 Still hid in mist, and on the left
Went down into the sea.

"And the good south wind still blew behind,
But no sweet bird did follow.
Nor any day for food or play
90 Came to the mariners' hollo!

"And I had done a hellish thing,
And it would work 'em woe:
For all averred, I had killed the bird
That made the breeze to blow.

95 Ah wretch! said they, the bird to slay,
That made the breeze to blow!

"Nor dim nor red, like God's own head,
The glorious Sun uprist;[15]
Then all averred, I had killed the bird
100 That brought the fog and mist.
'Twas right, said they, such birds to slay,
That bring the fog and mist.

His shipmates cry out against the ancient Mariner for killing the bird of good luck.

But when the fog cleared off, they justify the same, and thus make themselves accomplices in the crime.

Reading Strategy
Comparing and Contrasting Sound Devices How does the use of alliteration and internal rhyme in lines 91–94 give a fatal feeling to the Mariner's deed?

Vocabulary
averred (ə vʉrd´) v. stated to be true

---

11. shroud *n.* ropes stretching from the ship's side to the masthead.
12. vespers evenings.
13. God . . . so spoken by the Wedding Guest.
14. The Sun . . . right The ship is now headed north.
15. uprist arose.

Engraving by Gustave Doré for "The Rime of the Ancient Mariner" by Samuel Taylor Coleridge © 1970 by Dover Publications, Inc.

"The fair breeze blew, the white foam flew,
The furrow[16] followed free;
105 We were the first that ever burst
Into that silent sea.

"Down dropped the breeze, the sails
        dropped down,
'Twas sad as sad could be;
And we did speak only to break
110 The silence of the sea!

"All in a hot and copper sky,
The bloody Sun, at noon,
Right up above the mast did stand,
No bigger than the Moon.

115 "Day after day, day after day,
We stuck, nor breath nor motion;
As idle as a painted ship
Upon a painted ocean.

"Water, water, everywhere,
120 And all the boards did shrink;
Water, water, everywhere,
Nor any drop to drink.

"The very deep did rot: O Christ!
That ever this should be!
125 Yea, slimy things did crawl with legs
Upon the slimy sea.

"About, about, in reel and rout[17]
The death fires[18] danced at night;
The water, like a witch's oils,
130 Burned green, and blue and white.

"And some in dreams assurèd were
Of the Spirit that plagued us so;
Nine fathom deep he had followed us
From the land of mist and snow.

135 "And every tongue, through utter drought,
Was withered at the root;
We could not speak, no more than if
We had been choked with soot.

---

16. **furrow** ship's wake.
17. **rout** disorderly crowd.
18. **death fires** St. Elmo's fire, a visible electrical discharge from
    a ship's mast, believed by sailors to be an omen of disaster.

Reading Strategy
Comparing and Contrasting Sound Devices How does the repetition of words in lines 115–119 contribute to the image of the stilled ship?

Reading Strategy
Comparing and Contrasting Sound Devices What effect does the increased concentration of sound devices in lines 127–130 have?

The fair breeze continues; the ship enters the Pacific Ocean, and sails northward, even till it reaches the Line. The Ship hath been suddenly becalmed.

And the Albatross begins to be avenged.

A Spirit had followed them; one of the invisible inhabitants of this planet, neither departed souls nor angels. They are very numerous, and there is no climate or element without one or more.

Engraving by Gustave Doré for "The Rime of the Ancient Mariner" by Samuel Taylor Coleridge © 1970 by Dover Publications, Inc.

◀ **Critical Viewing**
What effects does the artist, Gustave Doré, use to capture the eerie mood of the poem? **[Analyze]**

The shipmates, in their sore distress, would fain throw the whole guilt on the ancient Mariner: in sign whereof they hang the dead sea bird round his neck.

"Ah! well a-day! what evil looks
140 Had I from old and young!
Instead of the cross, the Albatross
About my neck was hung.

Part III

The ancient Mariner beholdeth a sign in the element afar off.

"There passed a weary time. Each throat
Was parched, and glazed each eye.
145 A weary time! a weary time!
How glazed each weary eye,
When looking westward, I beheld
A something in the sky.

"At first it seemed a little speck,
150 And then it seemed a mist;
It moved and moved, and took at last
A certain shape, I wist.[19]

"A speck, a mist, a shape, I wist!
And still it neared and neared:
155 As if it dodged a water sprite,
It plunged and tacked and veered.

Reading Strategy
Comparing and Contrasting Sound Devices What poetic effect does Coleridge use in lines 149–153 to build suspense?

Reading Check

What causes the sailors to suffer?

---

19. wist knew.

"With throats unslaked, with black lips baked,
We could nor laugh nor wail;
Through utter drought all dumb we stood!
160 I bit my arm, I sucked the blood,
And cried, A sail! a sail!

"With throats unslaked, with black lips baked,
Agape they heard me call:
Gramercy![20] for joy did grin,
165 And all at once their breath drew in,
As they were drinking all.

"See! see! (I cried) she tacks no more!
Hither to work us weal;[21]
Without a breeze, without a tide,
170 She steadies with upright keel!

"The western wave was all aflame.
The day was well nigh done!
Almost upon the western wave
Rested the broad bright Sun;
175 When that strange shape drove suddenly
Betwixt us and the Sun.

"And straight the Sun was flecked with bars,
(Heaven's Mother send us grace!)
As if through a dungeon grate he peered
180 With broad and burning face.

"Alas! (thought I, and my heart beat loud)
How fast she nears and nears!
Are those *her* sails that glance in the Sun,
Like restless gossameres?[22]

185 "Are those *her* ribs through which the Sun
Did peer, as through a grate?
And is that Woman all her crew?
Is that a Death? and are there two?
Is Death that woman's mate?

190 "*Her* lips were red, *her* looks were free,
Her locks were yellow as gold;
Her skin was as white as leprosy,

Engraving by Gustave Doré for "The Rime of the Ancient Mariner" by Samuel Taylor Coleridge © 1970 by Dover Publications, Inc.

Literary Analysis
Poetic Sound Devices How does the line "Hither to work us weal" give the sense that these events are taking place in a strange, distant era?

▶ **Critical Viewing**
What reactions to the sighting of the other ship would you expect from the sailors? Can you find such reactions in the engraving? Explain. **[Connect]**

At its nearer approach, it seemeth him to be a ship; and at a dear ransom he freeth his speech from the bonds of thirst.

A flash of joy:

And horror follows. For can it be a ship that comes onward without wind or tide?

It seemeth him but the skeleton of a ship.

And its ribs are seen as bars on the face of the setting Sun.

The Specter Woman and her Death-mate, and no other on board the skeleton ship.

Like vessel, like crew! Death and Life-in-Death have diced for the ship's crew, and she (the latter) winneth the ancient Mariner.

20. **Gramercy** (grə mur′ sē): great thanks.
21. **work us weal** assist us.
22. **gossameres** floating cobwebs.

The Nightmare Life-in-Death was she,
Who thicks man's blood with cold.

195 "The naked hulk alongside came,
And the twain were casting dice;
'The game is done! I've won! I've won!'
Quoth she, and whistles thrice.

"The Sun's rim dips; the stars rush out:
200 At one stride comes the dark;
With far-heard whisper, o'er the sea,
Off shot the specter bark.

No twilight within the courts of the Sun.

"We listened and looked sideways up!
Fear at my heart, as at a cup,
205 My lifeblood seemed to sip!
The stars were dim, and thick the night,
The steersman's face by his lamp
      gleamed white;
From the sails the dew did drip—
Till clomb[23] above the eastern bar
210 The hornèd[24] Moon, with one bright star
Within the nether tip.

At the rising of the Moon,

"One after one, by the star-dogged Moon,[25]
Too quick for groan or sigh,
Each turned his face with a ghastly pang,
215 And cursed me with his eye.

One after another,

"Four times fifty living men,
(And I heard nor sigh nor groan)
With heavy thump, a lifeless lump,
They dropped down one by one.

His shipmates drop down dead.

220 "The souls did from their bodies fly—
They fled to bliss or woe!
And every soul, it passed me by,
Like the whizz of my crossbow!"

But Life-in-Death begins her work on the ancient Mariner.

Part IV ●━━━━

"I fear thee, ancient Mariner!
225 I fear thy skinny hand!
And thou art long, and lank, and brown,
As is the ribbed sea sand.

The Wedding Guest feareth that a Spirit is talking to him;

---

23. clomb climbed.
24. hornèd crescent.
25. star-dogged Moon omen of impending evil to sailors.

"I fear thee and thy glittering eye,
And thy skinny hand, so brown."
230 "Fear not, fear not, thou Wedding Guest!
This body dropped not down.

But the ancient Mariner assureth him of his bodily life, and proceedeth to relate his horrible penance.

"Alone, alone, all, all alone,
Alone on a wide wide sea!
And never a saint took pity on
235 My soul in agony.

He despiseth the creatures of the calm,

"The many men, so beautiful!
And they all dead did lie:
And a thousand thousand slimy things
Lived on; and so did I.

And envieth that they should live, and so many lie dead.

240 "I looked upon the rotting sea,
And drew my eyes away;
I looked upon the rotting deck,
And there the dead men lay.

"I looked to heaven, and tried to pray;
245 But or²⁶ ever a prayer had gushed,
A wicked whisper came, and made
My heart as dry as dust.

"I closed my lids, and kept them close,
And the balls like pulses beat;
250 For the sky and the sea and the sea and the sky
Lay like a load on my weary eye,
And the dead were at my feet.

But the curse liveth for him in the eye of the dead men.

"The cold sweat melted from their limbs,
Nor rot nor reek did they;
255 The look with which they looked on me
Had never passed away.

In his loneliness and fixedness he yearneth towards the journeying Moon, and the stars that still sojourn, yet still move onward; and everywhere the blue sky belongs to them,

"An orphan's curse would drag to hell
A spirit from on high;
But oh! more horrible than that
260 Is the curse in a dead man's eye!
Seven days, seven nights, I saw that curse,
And yet I could not die.

"The moving Moon went up the sky,
And nowhere did abide:

---

26. or before.

Reading Strategy

Comparing and Contrasting Sound Devices How does repetition in lines 240–243 emphasize the starkness of the Mariner's situation—the fact that he has "no way out"?

Vocabulary

sojourn (sō´ jᵊrn) *v.* stay for a while

Reading Check

What has happened to the other sailors?

265 Softly she was going up,
And a star or two beside—

"Her beams bemocked the sultry main,[27]
Like April hoarfrost spread;
But where the ship's huge shadow lay,
270 The charmèd water burned alway
A still and awful red.

"Beyond the shadow of the ship,
I watched the water snakes:
They moved in tracks of shining white,
275 And when they reared, the elfish light
Fell off in hoary flakes.

"Within the shadow of the ship
I watched their rich attire:
Blue, glossy green, and velvet black,
280 They coiled and swam; and every track
Was a flash of golden fire.

"O happy living things! no tongue
Their beauty might declare:
A spring of love gushed from my heart,
285 And I blessed them unaware;
Sure my kind saint took pity on me,
And I blessed them unaware.

"The selfsame moment I could pray;
And from my neck so free
290 The Albatross fell off, and sank
Like lead into the sea.

Part V

"Oh sleep! it is a gentle thing,
Beloved from pole to pole!
To Mary queen the praise be given!
295 She sent the gentle sleep from Heaven,
That slid into my soul.

"The silly[28] buckets on the deck.
That had so long remained,
I dreamed that they were filled with dew;
300 And when I awoke, it rained.

---

27. **main** open sea.
28. **silly** empty.

and is their appointed rest, and their native country and their own natural homes, which they enter unannounced, as lords that are certainly expected and yet there is a silent joy at their arrival.

By the light of the Moon he beholdeth God's creatures of the great calm.

Their beauty and their happiness.

He blesseth them in his heart.

The spell begins to break.

By grace of the holy Mother, the ancient Mariner is refreshed with rain.

Spiral Review
Imagery How does Coleridge's pattern of imagery in lines 270–276 help set the tone of the poem?

Literary Analysis
Poetic Sound Devices
What does the connection of the two events in lines 288–291 add to the fairy-tale quality of the story?

▶ **Critical Viewing**
How does Coleridge's description of the creatures of the great calm compare and contrast with the artist's representation of them?
[Compare and Contrast]

Literary Analysis
Poetic Sound Devices
Which repeated consonant
sound in lines 303–304
creates alliteration?

"My lips were wet, my throat was cold,
My garments all were dank;
Sure I had drunken in my dreams,
And still my body drank.

305 "I moved, and could not feel my limbs:
I was so light—almost
I thought that I had died in sleep,
And was a blessèd ghost.

"And soon I heard a roaring wind:
310 It did not come anear;
But with its sound it shook the sails,
That were so thin and sere.[29]

"The upper air burst into life!
And a hundred fire flags sheen,[30]
315 To and fro they were hurried about!
And to and fro, and in and out,
The wan stars danced between.

"And the coming wind did roar more loud,
And the sails did sigh like sedge;[31]
320 And the rain poured down from one
    black cloud;
The Moon was at its edge.

"The thick black cloud was cleft, and still
The Moon was at its side:
Like waters shot from some high crag,
325 The lightning fell with never a jag,
A river steep and wide.

"The loud wind never reached the ship,
Yet now the ship moved on!
Beneath the lightning and the Moon
330 The dead men gave a groan.

"They groaned, they stirred, they all uprose,
Nor spake, nor moved their eyes;
It had been strange, even in a dream,
To have seen those dead men rise.

Literary Analysis
Poetic Sound Devices
Find an example of
assonance—the repetition of
vowel sounds in unrhymed
syllables—in lines 331–334.

*He heareth sounds
and seeth strange
sights and commo-
tions in the sky and
the element.*

*The bodies of the
ship's crew are
inspired[32] and the
ship moves on;*

---

29. sere dried up.
30. fire flags sheen the aurora australis, or southern
     lights, shone.
31. sedge *n.* rushlike plant that grows in wet soil.
32. inspired inspirited

335   "The helmsman steered, the ship moved on:
Yet never a breeze up-blew;
The mariners all 'gan work the ropes,
Where they were wont[33] to do;
They raised their limbs like lifeless tools—
340 We were a ghastly crew.

"The body of my brother's son
Stood by me, knee to knee;
The body and I pulled at one rope,
But he said nought to me."

345 "I fear thee, ancient Mariner!"
"Be calm, thou Wedding Guest!
'Twas not those souls that fled in pain,
Which to their corses[34] came again,
But a troop of spirits blessed:

But not by the souls of the men, nor by demons of earth or middle air, but by a blessed troop of angelic spirits, sent down by the invocation of the guardian saint.

350 "For when it dawned—they dropped their arms,
And clustered round the mast;
Sweet sounds rose slowly through
    their mouths,
And from their bodies passed.

Literary Analysis
Poetic Sound Devices
Find an example of alliteration—the repetition of initial consonant sounds—in lines 350–353.

"Around, around, flew each sweet sound,
355 Then darted to the Sun;
Slowly the sounds came back again,
Now mixed, now one by one.

"Sometimes a-dropping from the sky
I heard the skylark sing;
360 Sometimes all little birds that are,
How they seemed to fill the sea and air
With their sweet jargoning![35]

"And now 'twas like all instruments,
Now like a lonely flute;
365 And now it is an angel's song,
That makes the heavens be mute.

Reading Check

What happens to the bodies of the Mariner's shipmates?

"It ceased; yet still the sails made on
A pleasant noise till noon,
A noise like of a hidden brook
370 In the leafy month of June,

---

33. wont accustomed.
34. corses corpses.
35. jargoning singing.

That to the sleeping woods all night
Singeth a quiet tune.

"Till noon we quietly sailed on,
Yet never a breeze did breathe;
375 Slowly and smoothly went the ship,
Moved onward from beneath.

"Under the keel nine fathom deep,
From the land of mist and snow,
The spirit slid; and it was he
380 That made the ship to go.
The sails at noon left off their tune,
And the ship stood still also.

"The Sun, right up above the mast,
Had fixed her to the ocean:
385 But in a minute she 'gan stir,
With a short uneasy motion—
Backwards and forwards half her length
With a short uneasy motion.

"Then like a pawing horse let go,
390 She made a sudden bound:
It flung the blood into my head,
And I fell down in a swound.

Reading Strategy
Comparing and Contrasting Sound Devices How does the alliteration in lines 373–376 enhance the description of the boat's smooth progress?

▶ **Critical Viewing**
Which details convey the mood of hopelessness in this illustration? **[Analyze]**

The lonesome Spirit from the South Pole carries on the ship as far as the Line, in obedience to the angelic troop, but still requireth vengeance.

The Polar Spirit's fellow demons, the invisible inhabitants of the element, take part in his wrong; and two of them relate, one to the other, that penance long and heavy for the ancient Mariner hath been accorded to the Polar Spirit, who returneth southward.

"How long in that same fit I lay,
I have not to declare;
395 But ere my living life returned,
I heard and in my soul discerned
Two voices in the air.

"'Is it he?' quoth one, 'Is this the man?
By him who died on cross,
400 With his cruel bow he laid full low
The harmless Albatross.

"'The spirit who bideth by himself
In the land of mist and snow,
He loved the bird that loved the man
405 Who shot him with his bow.'

"The other was a softer voice,
As soft as honeydew:
Quoth he, 'The man hath penance done,
And penance more will do.'

Part VI ●━━━━

FIRST VOICE
410 "'But tell me, tell me! speak again,
Thy soft response renewing—
What makes that ship drive on so fast?
What is the ocean doing?'

SECOND VOICE
"'Still as a slave before his lord,
415 The ocean hath no blast;
His great bright eye most silently
Up to the Moon is cast—

"'If he may know which way to go;
For she guides him smooth or grim.
420 See, brother, see! how graciously
She looketh down on him.'

FIRST VOICE
"'But why drives on that ship so fast,
Without or wave or wind?'

SECOND VOICE
"'The air is cut away before,
425 And closes from behind.

The Mariner hath been cast into a trance; for the angelic power causeth the vessel to drive northward faster than human life could endure.

Literary Analysis
Poetic Sound Devices How do the two voices contribute to Coleridge's creation of a dream world?

Literary Analysis
Poetic Sound Devices What instance of assonance can you find in lines 414–417?

Reading Check

What do the two voices discuss?

Engraving by Gustave Doré for "The Rime of the Ancient Mariner" by Samuel Taylor Coleridge
© 1970 by Dover Publications, Inc.

▶ **Critical Viewing**
How closely can you connect this illustration to the events in the poem? Is the image being portrayed from the Ancient Mariner's point of view? Why or why not?
[Connect]

"'Fly, brother, fly! more high, more high!
Or we shall be belated:
For slow and slow that ship will go,
When the Mariner's trance is abated.'

430   "I woke, and we were sailing on
As in a gentle weather:
'Twas night, calm night, the moon was high;
The dead men stood together.

"All stood together on the deck,
435   For a charnel dungeon[36] fitter;
All fixed on me their stony eyes,
That in the Moon did glitter.

"The pang, the curse, with which they died,
Had never passed away;
440   I could not draw my eyes from theirs,
Nor turn them up to pray.

"And now this spell was snapped; once more
I viewed the ocean green,
And looked far forth, yet little saw
445   Of what had else been seen—

---

36. **charnel dungeon** vault where corpses or bones are deposited.

The super-natural motion is retarded; the Mariner awakes, and his penance begins anew.

The curse is finally expiated.

Vocabulary
expiated (ĕkʹ spē āt ́ əd)
v. atoned; made amends for, especially by suffering

"Like one, that on a lonesome road
Doth walk in fear and dread,
And having once turned round
　　walks on,
And turns no more his head;
450　Because he knows, a frightful fiend
Doth close behind him tread.

"But soon there breathed a wind
　　on me,
Nor sound nor motion made:
Its path was not upon the sea,
455　In ripple or in shade.

"It raised my hair, it fanned my cheek
Like a meadow-gale of spring—
It mingled strangely with my fears,
Yet it felt like a welcoming.

460　"Swiftly, swiftly flew the ship,
Yet she sailed softly too:
Sweetly, sweetly blew the breeze—
On me alone it blew.

"Oh! dream of joy! is this indeed
465　The lighthouse top I see?
Is this the hill? is this the kirk?
Is this mine own countree?

"We drifted o'er the harbor bar,
And I with sobs did pray—
470　O let me be awake, my God!
Or let me sleep alway.

"The harbor bay was clear as glass,
So smoothly it was strewn!³⁷
And on the bay the moonlight lay,
475　And the shadow of the Moon.

"The rock shone bright, the kirk
　　no less,
That stands above the rock;
The moonlight steeped in silentness
The steady weathercock.

480　"And the bay was white with
　　silent light,

*And the ancient
Mariner beholdeth
his native country.*

---

37. strewn spread.

The BRITISH TRADITION

The Tradition of Fantasy

Coleridge's *Rime of the Ancient Mariner*—written in a dreamlike language, set in an indeterminate past, and filled with supernatural events—is part of the British tradition of fantasy literature. Writers of works of fantasy set out to create a realm distinct from the everyday world of their readers—a never-never land ruled by strange laws.

The fantasy tradition began as long ago as Sir Thomas Malory's *Morte d'Arthur* (p. 185), which is set in a vanished past that had become a myth by Malory's own day. The idea of a vanished past fascinated writers long after Malory, reappearing in the work of Alfred, Lord Tennyson, who resorted to Arthurian and mythological elements in many poems, as in "The Lady of Shalott" (p. 963).

Fantasy writers like Coleridge use strange settings and supernatural tales to break the spell of ordinary life. By plunging us into a wild, unfamiliar world, they remind us that human imagination can always envision worlds beyond the one into which we are born—a power that enables scientific discoveries and social reforms as well as great poetry.

Connect to the Literature

What images in lines 480–499 contribute to the fantastical atmosphere in the poem?

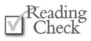
Reading Check

What familiar things does the Mariner suddenly see from the ship?

Till rising from the same,
Full many shapes, that shadows were,
In crimson colors came.

"A little distance from the prow
485 Those crimson shadows were:
I turned my eyes upon the deck—
Oh, Christ! what saw I there!

"Each corse lay flat, lifeless and flat,
And, by the holy rood!³⁸
490 A man all light, a seraph³⁹ man,
On every corse there stood.

"This seraph band, each waved
    his hand:
It was a heavenly sight!
They stood as signals to the land,
495 Each one a lovely light;

"This seraph band, each waved
    his hand,
No voice did they impart—

38. rood cross.
39. seraph angel.

Engraving by Gustave Doré for "The Rime of the Ancient Mariner" by Samuel Taylor Coleridge
© 1970 by Dover Publications, Inc.

The angelic spirits leave the dead bodies,

And appear in their own forms of light.

▶ **Critical Viewing**
What event from the poem does this engraving represent? **[Connect]**

No voice; but oh! the silence sank
Like music on my heart.

500 "But soon I heard the dash of oars,
I heard the Pilot's cheer;
My head was turned perforce away
And I saw a boat appear.

"The Pilot and the Pilot's boy,
505 I heard them coming fast:
Dear Lord in Heaven! it was a joy
The dead men could not blast.

"I saw a third—I heard his voice:
It is the Hermit good!
510 He singeth loud his godly hymns
That he makes in the wood.
He'll shrieve[40] my soul, he'll
    wash away
The Albatross's blood.

Part VII

"This Hermit good lives in that wood
515 Which slopes down to the sea.
How loudly his sweet voice he rears!
He loves to talk with marineres
That come from a far countree.

"He kneels at morn, and noon,
    and eve—
520 He hath a cushion plump:
It is the moss that wholly hides
The rotted old oak-stump.

"The skiff boat neared; I heard them talk.
'Why, this is strange, I trow![41]
525 Where are those lights so many and fair,
That signal made but now?'

"'Strange, by my faith!' the Hermit said—
'And they answered not our cheer!
The planks looked warped! and see those sails,
530 How thin they are and sere!
I never saw aught like to them,
Unless perchance it were

The Hermit of the Wood,

Approacheth the ship with wonder.

40. **shrieve** (shrēv) absolve from sin.
41. **trow** believe.

Reading Strategy
Comparing and Contrasting Sound Devices These lines are less crowded with sound devices than the lines describing the Mariner's nightmarish sea journey. How does this shift in language match the shift in mood?

Literary Analysis
Poetic Sound Devices Which word in lines 523–526 might Coleridge have borrowed from medieval tales of knights?

Reading Check

What does the Mariner think the Hermit will do for him?

"'Brown skeletons of leaves that lag
My forest brook along;
535   When the ivy tod[42] is heavy with snow,
And the owlet whoops to the wolf below,
That eats the she-wolf's young.'

"'Dear Lord! it hath a fiendish look'
(The Pilot made reply)
540   'I am a-feared'— 'Push on, push on!'
Said the Hermit cheerily.

"The boat came closer to the ship,
But I nor spake nor stirred;
The boat came close beneath the ship,
545   And straight[43] a sound was heard.

"Under the water it rumbled on,
Still louder and more dread:
It reached the ship, it split the bay;
The ship went down like lead.

550   "Stunned by that loud and dreadful sound,
Which sky and ocean smote,
Like one that hath been seven days drowned
My body lay afloat;
But swift as dreams, myself I found
555   Within the Pilot's boat.

"Upon the whirl, where sank the ship,
The boat spun round and round;
And all was still, save that the hill
Was telling of the sound.

560   "I moved my lips—the Pilot shrieked
And fell down in a fit;
The holy Hermit raised his eyes,
And prayed where he did sit.

"I took the oars; the Pilot's boy,
565   Who now doth crazy go,
Laughed loud and long, and all the while
His eyes went to and fro.
'Ha! ha!' quoth he, 'full plain I see,
The Devil knows how to row.'

---

42. tod bush.
43. straight immediately.

Reading Strategy
Comparing and Contrasting Sound Devices Which poetic effects contribute to the impact of lines 556–559?

▶ **Critical Viewing**
Identify the Pilot, the Mariner, and the Hermit in this engraving. **[Connect]**

Engraving by Gustave Doré for "The Rime of the Ancient Mariner" by Samuel Taylor Coleridge © 1970 by Dover Publications, Inc.

570 "And now, all in my own countree,
I stood on the firm land!
The Hermit stepped forth from the boat,
And scarcely he could stand.

"'O shrieve me, shrieve me, holy man!'
575 The Hermit crossed his brow.⁴⁴
'Say, quick,' quoth he, 'I bid thee say—
What manner of man art thou?'

"Forthwith this frame of mine was wrenched
With a woeful agony,
580 Which forced me to begin my tale;
And then it left me free.

"Since then, at an uncertain hour,
That agony returns:
And till my ghastly tale is told,
585 This heart within me burns.

"I pass, like night, from land to land;
I have strange power of speech;
That moment that his face I see,
I know the man that must hear me:
590 To him my tale I teach.

"What loud uproar bursts from that door!
The wedding guests are there:
But in the garden bower the bride
And bridemaids singing are:
595 And hark the little vesper bell,
Which biddeth me to prayer!

"O Wedding Guest! this soul hath been
Alone on a wide wide sea:
So lonely 'twas, that God himself
600 Scarce seemèd there to be.

"O sweeter than the marriage feast,
'Tis sweeter far to me,
To walk together to the kirk
With a goodly company!—

605 "To walk together to the kirk,
And all together pray,
While each to his great Father bends,

44. crossed his brow made the sign of the cross on his forehead.

Reading Strategy
Comparing and Contrasting Sound Devices What effect does the alliteration in line 590 featuring *tale*—a word that appears in each of the preceding two stanzas—have?

The ancient Mariner earnestly entreateth the Hermit to shrieve him; and the penance of life falls on him.

And ever and anon throughout his future life an agony constraineth him to travel from land to land;

Old men, and babes, and loving friends
And youths and maidens gay!

And to teach, by his own example, love and reverence to all things that God made and loveth.

610 "Farewell, farewell! but this I tell
To thee, thou Wedding Guest!
He prayeth well, who loveth well
Both man and bird and beast.

"He prayeth best, who loveth best
615 All things both great and small;
For the dear God who loveth us,
He made and loveth all."

The Mariner, whose eye is bright,
Whose beard with age is hoar,
620 Is gone; and now the Wedding Guest
Turned from the bridegroom's door.

He went like one that hath been stunned
And is of sense forlorn:
A sadder and a wiser man,
625 He rose the morrow morn.

Critical Reading ©

Cite textual evidence to support your responses.

© **1. Key Ideas and Details** **(a)** On what occasion does the Mariner tell his story? **(b) Interpret:** Why do you think Coleridge chose this occasion for the poem?

© **2. Key Ideas and Details** **(a)** What contradictory connections does the crew make between the Albatross and the weather? **(b)** What does the Mariner do to the Albatross? **(c) Infer:** Why does the Mariner wear the Albatross around his neck?

© **3. Key Ideas and Details** **(a)** What happens to the Mariner's shipmates after the appearance of the Specter Woman and her Death-mate? **(b) Generalize:** What might this symbolize about the effect of guilt on an individual's perceptions of and relations with others?

© **4. Craft and Structure** **(a) Infer:** Why does the Albatross finally fall from the Mariner's neck? **(b) Interpret:** What do you think the Albatross symbolizes? Find evidence to support your answer.

© **5. Integration of Knowledge and Ideas** **(a)** What is the Mariner's lifelong penance? **(b) Analyze:** How does his story affect his listener? **(c) Draw Conclusions:** What larger lesson about human life might his story suggest?

KUBLA KHAN

Samuel Taylor Coleridge

Box and Cover, Ming Dynasty, first half of 16th century, lacquer, black; mother of pearl; wood; fabric. H. 4 in. The Seattle Art Museum

▲ **Critical Viewing**
How do Coleridge's poetic images compare with the details on this sixteenth-century Chinese box cover? **[Compare and Contrast]**

BACKGROUND

Coleridge claimed to have dreamed his poem "Kubla Khan" line for line after falling asleep while reading a passage from a work about the founder of the great Mongol dynasty. Upon awakening, he transcribed the lines as fast as he could. When he was interrupted by a visitor, however, the lines in his head disappeared, never to be remembered. As a result, Coleridge was unable to complete the poem.

In Xanadu[1] did Kubla Khan
A stately pleasure dome decree:
Where Alph,[2] the sacred river, ran
Through caverns measureless to man
5   Down to a sunless sea.
So twice five miles of fertile ground
With walls and towers were girdled round;
And there were gardens bright with sinuous rills,[3]
Where blossomed many an incense-bearing tree;
10 And here were forests ancient as the hills,
Enfolding sunny spots of greenery.

But oh! that deep romantic chasm which slanted
Down the green hill athwart[4] a cedarn cover![5]
A savage place! as holy and enchanted
15 As e'er beneath a waning moon was haunted
By woman wailing for her demon lover!
And from this chasm, with ceaseless turmoil seething,
As if this earth in fast thick pants were breathing,
A mighty fountain momently was forced;

Vocabulary
sinuous (sin´ yoo əs)
adj. bending; winding

Reading Strategy
Comparing and Contrasting Sound Devices What alliteration in lines 15–16 helps you hear the cries of the haunted woman?

---

1. **Xanadu** (zan´ ə doo) indefinite area in China.
2. **Alph** probably derived from the Greek river Alpheus, the waters of which, it was believed in Greek mythology, joined with a stream to form a fountain in Sicily.
3. **rills** brooks.
4. **athwart** across.
5. **cedarn cover** covering of cedar trees.

▶ **Critical Viewing**
Which details in this work of art convey the same sense of luxury as the poem does? **[Connect]**

Vocabulary
tumult (tōō´ mult´) *n.* noisy commotion

Literary Analysis
Poetic Sound Devices
Find examples of assonance and alliteration in lines 31–34.

20 Amid whose swift half-intermitted burst
    Huge fragments vaulted like rebounding hail,
    Or chaffy grain beneath the thresher's flail;
    And 'mid these dancing rocks at once and ever
    It flung up momently the sacred river.
25 Five miles meandering with a mazy motion
    Through wood and dale the sacred river ran,
    Then reached the caverns measureless to man,
    And sank in tumult to a lifeless ocean:
    And 'mid this tumult Kubla heard from far
30 Ancestral voices prophesying war!
        The shadow of the dome of pleasure
        Floated midway on the waves;
        Where was heard the mingled measure
        From the fountain and the caves.
35 It was a miracle of rare device.[6]
    A sunny pleasure dome with caves of ice!

_____

6. device design.

A damsel with a dulcimer[7]
In a vision once I saw:
    It was an Abyssinian[8] maid,
40   And on her dulcimer she played,
    Singing of Mount Abora.[9]
    Could I revive within me
    Her symphony and song,
    To such a deep delight 'twould win me,
45 That with music loud and long,
    I would build that dome in air,
    That sunny dome! those caves of ice!
    And all who heard should see them there,
    And all should cry, Beware! Beware!
50 His flashing eyes, his floating hair!
    Weave a circle round him thrice,
    And close your eyes with holy dread,
    For he on honeydew hath fed,
    And drunk the milk of Paradise.

---

7. dulcimer (dul´ sə mər) *n.* stringed musical instrument played with small hammers.
8. Abyssinian (ab ə sin´ ē ən) Ethiopian.
9. Mount Abora probably Mount Amara in Abyssinia.

Critical Reading

1. **Key Ideas and Details (a)** Describe the pleasure dome and its setting. **(b) Analyze:** What makes the pleasure dome and its setting seem beautiful? What makes them sinister?

2. **Integration of Knowledge and Ideas (a)** What comes from the chasm, and what are its effects? **(b) Draw Conclusions:** The pleasure dome might be thought of as a work of art. What does the existence of the chasm on the site of the dome suggest about the relationship between constructive and "chaotic," or "wild," forces in art?

3. **Integration of Knowledge and Ideas (a)** What does the "holy dread" experienced by "all who heard" suggest about the power of art? **(b) Connect:** What connection can you find between this "dread" and the existence of the chasm at the site of the dome?

4. **Integration of Knowledge and Ideas** In what ways do the settings of these poems demonstrate the Romantics' rejection of the dreariness of everyday places and activities? In your response, use at least two of these Essential Question words: *exotic, fantastic, faraway.* [*Connecting to the Essential Question: What is the relationship between literature and place?*]

Cite textual evidence to support your responses.

Literary Analysis

@ **1. Craft and Structure** What **sound device** does Coleridge use in the line "It cracked and growled, and roared and howled . . ." (*The Rime of the Ancient Mariner,* line 61)?

@ **2. Craft and Structure** Find an example of **alliteration** in lines 9–12 of *The Rime of the Ancient Mariner.*

@ **3. Craft and Structure** Which words in the following line create an **internal rhyme**: "Whiles all the night through fog smoke white..."? (*The Rime of the Ancient Mariner,* line 77)

@ **4. Craft and Structure (a)** Identify an example of **consonance** in lines 51–54 of *The Rime of the Ancient Mariner.* **(b)** Identify an example of **assonance** in the same lines.

@ **5. Craft and Structure** What device dominates the first stanza of "Kubla Khan"? Give three examples.

@ **6. Craft and Structure (a)** What mood do lines 472–483 of *The Rime of the Ancient Mariner* create? **(b)** What poetic devices contribute to this mood? Explain.

7. Comparing Literary Works Using a chart like the one shown, explain how the characteristics of Coleridge's poetry, including its subjects, settings, events, and uses of language, suit the fantastic subjects he addresses. In discussing his uses of language, specifically consider sound devices.

Poem: _____

Subject	Setting	Events	Language	Why Suitable?

@ **Common Core State Standards**

Reading Literature
9. Demonstrate knowledge of eighteenth-, nineteenth-, and early-twentieth-century foundational works of American literature, including how two or more texts from the same period treat similar themes or topics. (*p. 851*)

Writing
2.b. Develop the topic thoroughly by selecting the most significant and relevant facts, extended definitions, concrete details, quotations, or other information and examples appropriate to the audience's knowledge of the topic. (*p. 851*)
2.d. Use precise language, domain-specific vocabulary, and techniques such as metaphor, simile, and analogy to manage the complexity of the topic. (*p. 851*)
9.a. Apply grades 11–12 Reading standards to literature. (*p. 851*)

Reading Strategy

8. Compare and contrast sound devices in these poems by answering these questions. **(a)** Identify the mood, or feeling, that Coleridge evokes in lines 1–12 of *The Rime of the Ancient Mariner* and lines 1–11 of "Kubla Khan." **(b)** How do the sound devices and archaic words used in each poem allow Coleridge to create these moods?

9. (a) Identify four words in "Kubla Khan" that contribute to the poem's exotic, or strange and faraway, atmosphere. **(b)** Do archaic words in *The Rime of the Ancient Mariner* also make the setting of this poem seem exotic? Why or why not?

10. Which of these two poems uses sound devices to create a greater variety of moods? Quote specific passages to support your points.

Integrated Language Skills

Ⓖ Vocabulary Acquisition and Use

Word Analysis: Latin Root -journ-

The verb *sojourn*, meaning "to visit for a while," contains the root *-journ-*, derived from French and Latin words meaning "day." In French, the root appears in such words and phrases as *bonjour* ("good day") and *soup du jour* ("soup of the day"). Explain how this root contributes to the meaning of each of these words. If you are unsure of the meaning of any of these words, you may consult a dictionary. Then use each word in an original sentence.

1. adjourn
2. journal
3. journalism
4. journey
5. journeyman

Vocabulary: Antonyms

An antonym is a word that has the opposite meaning of another word. *Freezing* and *boiling* are antonyms, as are *happy* and *sad*. For each word from the vocabulary list on page 818, choose the correct antonym. Then, write an original sentence using both the word and its antonym.

1. averred: **(a)** claimed, **(b)** denied, **(c)** wished
2. sojourn: **(a)** depart, **(b)** rest, **(c)** visit
3. expiated: **(a)** atoned, **(b)** sinned, **(c)** sold
4. reverence: **(a)** contempt, **(b)** hope, **(c)** respect
5. sinuous: **(a)** dark, **(b)** narrow, **(c)** straight
6. tumult: **(a)** peace, **(b)** pleasure, **(c)** wealth

Writing

Ⓖ **Explanatory Text** Coleridge was not the only nineteenth-century poet to fascinate readers with a mysterious symbolic bird. Find a copy of "The Raven" by the American author Edgar Allan Poe, and read it carefully. Then, write an **essay** comparing the Albatross in *The Rime of the Ancient Mariner* with Poe's Raven as poetic symbols.

Prewriting Gather details about the Albatross and the Raven, grouping them under headings such as "Appearance," "Actions," and "Influence." Remember that symbols are concrete images that stand for a cluster of ideas. For each specific quality or relationship you list in your chart, give the general ideas it suggests.

Drafting As you draft, discuss each category in your chart, linking the details you have listed to your conclusions about the symbolic meaning of each bird. Then, compare the two symbols. Support your ideas with quotations from the works.

Model: Revising for Vivid, Precise Language

The sailors praise the Albatross for bringing good weather,

a deadly calm

then blame it for bringing ~~bad weather.~~ The Polar Spirit also

wreaks vengeance through extended drought and fast winds.

~~uses weather for its vengeance.~~

Vivid words and details make the analysis more interesting and precise.

Revising Review your draft to identify flat, unexciting language. Replace such language with vivid, specific descriptions or claims. Make sure that all quotations are accurate and properly cited.

Connecting to the Essential Question Like some Romantic poets, you may react with awe to nature's dramatic effects—a snow-covered mountain or a towering waterfall. As you read, note the feelings that the ocean calls up in the speaker of Byron's "Apostrophe to the Ocean." Identifying these feelings will help as you consider this Essential Question: **What is the relationship between literature and place?**

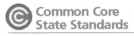
Common Core State Standards

Reading Literature
4. Determine the meaning of words and phrases as they are used in the text, including figurative and connotative meanings.

Literary Analysis

Poetry often uses **figurative language,** or language not meant to be taken literally, to evoke emotions and state ideas in an imaginative way:

- **Similes**—direct comparisons of dissimilar things using the words *like* or *as:* "Her eyes glowed like the moon."
- **Metaphors**—comparisons in which one thing is identified with another, dissimilar thing: "All the world's a stage."
- **Personification**—giving human qualities to nonhuman subjects: "The trees danced in the wind."

Comparing Literary Works In two of these poems, Byron uses figurative language to express the *sublime*—a Romantic sense of overwhelming power and beauty in nature that escapes understanding. As you read, compare the impressions of nature's sublime beauty and power expressed in the first two lyrics with the sense of human limitations expressed in *Don Juan*.

Reading Strategy

 Preparing to Read Complex Texts When you do not understand a difficult passage, **question** yourself to *repair your comprehension*. For example, to figure out the subject of a passage, ask yourself "Whom is the speaker talking about?" Begin your questions with *who, what, where, when,* and *why*. Use a chart like the one shown to ask and answer questions as you read.

Passage
She walks in beauty, like the night Of cloudless climes and starry skies;...

Questions
1. *Who* is she? 2. *What* is her relationship with the speaker? 3. To *what* does the speaker compare her?

Vocabulary

arbiter (är′ bət ər) *n.* judge; umpire (p. 858)

torrid (tôr′ id) *adj.* very hot; scorching (p. 859)

retort (ri tôrt′) *v.* to respond with a clever answer or wisecrack (p. 861)

credulous (krej′ ℴℴ ləs) adj. willing to believe; naive (p. 862)

copious (kō′ pē əs) adj. abundant; plentiful (p. 862)

avarice (av′ ə ris) n. greed; great desire to have wealth (p. 862)

www.PHLitOnline.com

Lord Byron *(1788–1824)*

Author of "She Walks in Beauty" • "Apostrophe to the Ocean" • *Don Juan*

As famous for the life he led as for the poems he wrote, George Gordon, Lord Byron, came from a long line of handsome but irresponsible aristocrats. Byron lived life in the "fast lane" and was looked on with disapproval by most of his contemporaries.

From Rags to Riches Byron was born in London to a poor but noble family. His father, a handsome ladies' man, died when Byron was just three years old. At the age of ten, Byron inherited his great-uncle's title, baron. He and his mother moved from Scotland to Nottingham, where Byron lived for a time in the ruins of the family hall. When he was seventeen, he left home to attend Trinity College at Cambridge.

A Zest for Life While at Cambridge, Byron made friends, played sports, and spent money. After graduating, he traveled to out-of-the-way corners of Europe and the Middle East. Byron returned home bearing two sections of a book-length poem entitled *Childe Harold's Pilgrimage*, which depicted a young hero not unlike himself—moody, sensitive, and reckless. The work was well received, and Byron became an overnight sensation.

For a time, Byron was the darling of London society. Byron became a celebrity, a public figure of literary genius who in turn thrilled and scandalized his contemporaries. "Mad, bad, and dangerous to know" was Lady Caroline Lamb's famous description of Lord Byron.

The Byronic Hero Although Byron could be quite charming and friendly, his admirers insisted on associating him with the dark, brooding hero, impassioned by a cause, whom he so often described. Because of this persona, or adopted personality, readers throughout the nineteenth century saw Byron as the quintessential Romantic poet.

Italy and Tragedy Byron's fame and infamy grew. When his marriage to Annabella Milbanke broke up, the resulting scandal drove Byron from England in 1816. He would never return to the country of his birth.

A Budding Revolutionary In 1823, Byron, a champion of liberty, joined a group of revolutionaries seeking to free Greece from Turkish rule. Soon after, while training Greek rebel troops, Byron died of a rheumatic fever. To this day he is revered in Greece as a national hero.

She
Walks in
Beauty

George Gordon,
Lord Byron

BACKGROUND Lord Byron became so identified with the rebellious heroes he created—brooding figures whose ironic attitude and hidden sorrow only added to their charm—that this kind of figure became known as a Byronic hero. Such heroes are a staple of Romantic literature. They survive in modern times as a Hollywood or rock-and-roll star.

The Byronic attitude may be ironic, but Byron the poet was certainly capable of direct, sincere appreciation of beauty, as this poem demonstrates.

> She walks in beauty, like the night
>   Of cloudless climes and starry skies;
> And all that's best of dark and bright
>   Meet in her aspect and her eyes:
> 5 Thus mellowed to that tender light
>   Which heaven to gaudy day denies.
>
> One shade the more, one ray the less,
>   Had half impaired the nameless grace
> Which waves in every raven tress,
> 10   Or softly lightens o'er her face;
> Where thoughts serenely sweet express
>   How pure, how dear their dwelling place.
>
> And on that cheek, and o'er that brow,
>   So soft, so calm, yet eloquent,
> 15 The smiles that win, the tints that glow,
>   But tell of days in goodness spent,
> A mind at peace with all below,
>   A heart whose love is innocent!

Literary Analysis
Figurative Language
With what kind of poetic comparison does Byron capture the reader's imagination in the opening lines?

◄ **Critical Viewing**
How does the rendering of this woman suggest some of the qualities that Byron attributes to his cousin in the poem? **[Analyze]**

Critical Reading ©

© 1. **Key Ideas and Details** **(a)** To what does the speaker compare the lady's beauty? **(b) Interpret:** What might "that tender light" in line 5 be?

© 2. **Integration of Knowledge and Ideas** **(a) Connect:** In lines 11–18, what is the woman's appearance said to reveal about her character? **(b) Compare and Contrast:** How is the focus of the last six lines different from the focus of the opening lines? **(c) Draw Conclusions:** Does Byron's portrayal emphasize the spiritual or the physical aspect of the lady? Explain.

Cite textual evidence to support your responses.

FROM
CHILDE HAROLD'S PILGRIMAGE
APOSTROPHE TO THE *Ocean*

Geⱺrge Gⱺrdⱺn,
Lⱺrd Byrⱺn

Reading Strategy
Questioning
List three questions you
might ask after reading
the first stanza.

There is a pleasure in the pathless woods,
There is a rapture on the lonely shore,
There is society, where none intrudes,
By the deep sea, and music in its roar;
5 I love not man the less, but nature more,
From these our interviews, in which I steal
From all I may be, or have been before,
To mingle with the universe, and feel
What I can ne'er express, yet cannot all conceal.

10 Roll on, thou deep and dark blue ocean—roll!
Ten thousand fleets sweep over thee in vain;
Man marks the earth with ruin—his control
Stops with the shore; upon the watery plain
The wrecks are all thy deed, nor doth remain

15 A shadow of man's ravage, save¹ his own,
    When, for a moment, like a drop of rain,
    He sinks into thy depths with bubbling groan,
    Without a grave, unknelled, uncoffined, and unknown.

    His steps are not upon thy paths—thy fields
20 Are not a spoil for him—thou dost arise
    And shake him from thee; the vile strength he wields
    For earth's destruction thou dost all despise,
    Spurning him from thy bosom to the skies,
    And send'st him, shivering in thy playful spray
25 And howling, to his gods, where haply² lies
    His petty hope in some near port or bay,
    And dashest him again to earth—there let him lay.³

▲ **Critical Viewing**
How does this painting capture the sublime nature of the ocean? **[Analyze]**

Reading
Check

According to the speaker, what impact does humanity's power have on the ocean?

The armaments which thunderstrike the walls
Of rock-built cities, bidding nations quake,
30   And monarchs tremble in their capitals,
The oak leviathans,[4] whose huge ribs make
Their clay creator[5] the vain title take
Of lord of thee, and arbiter of war—
These are thy toys, and, as the snowy flake,
35   They melt into thy yeast of waves, which mar
Alike the Armada's[6] pride or spoils of Trafalgar.[7]

Thy shores are empires, changed in all save thee—
Assyria, Greece, Rome, Carthage, what are they?
Thy waters washed them power while they were free,
40   And many a tyrant since; their shores obey
The stranger, slave, or savage: their decay
Has dried up realms to deserts—not so thou,
Unchangeable, save to thy wild waves' play.
Time writes no wrinkle on thine azure brow;
45   Such as creation's dawn beheld, thou rollest now.

---

4. **leviathans** (lə vī´ ə thənz) monstrous sea creatures, described in the Old Testament. Here the word means giant ships.
5. **clay creator** human beings.
6. **Armada's** refers to the Spanish Armada, defeated by the English in 1588.
7. **Trafalgar** battle in 1805 during which the French and Spanish fleets were defeated by the British fleet led by Lord Nelson.

UNCHANGEABLE,
SAVE TO THY
WILD WAVES' *play.*

Thou glorious mirror, where the Almighty's form
Glasses[8] itself in tempests: in all time,
Calm or convulsed—in breeze, or gale, or storm,
Icing the pole, or in the torrid clime
50   Dark-heaving—boundless, endless, and sublime;
The image of eternity, the throne
Of the Invisible; even from out thy slime
The monsters of the deep are made: each zone
Obeys thee; thou goest forth, dread, fathomless,[9] alone.

55   And I have loved thee, ocean! and my joy
Of youthful sports was on thy breast to be
Borne, like thy bubbles, onward; from a boy
I wantoned with thy breakers—they to me
Were a delight: and if the freshening sea
60   Made them a terror—'twas a pleasing fear,
For I was as it were a child of thee,
And trusted to thy billows far and near,
And laid my hand upon thy mane—as I do here.

Vocabulary
torrid (tôr´ id) *adj.* very
hot; scorching

---

8. Glasses mirrors.
9. fathomless (fath´ əm lis) *adj.* too deep to be measured or understood.

Critical Reading

1. Key Ideas and Details (a) What natural settings does the speaker describe in the first lines? **(b) Interpret:** What attitude toward nature do his descriptions reveal?

2. Craft and Structure (a) In an apostrophe, a speaker addresses an absent person or personified quality or idea. Whom or what is the speaker addressing from line 10 on? **(b) Infer:** What is the speaker's attitude toward the subject he is addressing?

3. Key Ideas and Details (a) How does the ocean treat such human things as cities and warships? **(b) Compare and Contrast:** What contrast between the ocean and human governments does the speaker make in lines 37–45? **(c) Draw Conclusions:** In what sense is the ocean a power that dwarfs all human endeavors?

4. Key Ideas and Details (a) Interpret: In lines 46–54, what qualities make the ocean a reflection of "the Almighty's form"? **(b) Generalize:** What attitude toward nature do the lines encourage?

5. Integration of Knowledge and Ideas Is the sea still as mysterious and powerful today as it was in Byron's day? Explain.

Cite textual evidence to support your responses.

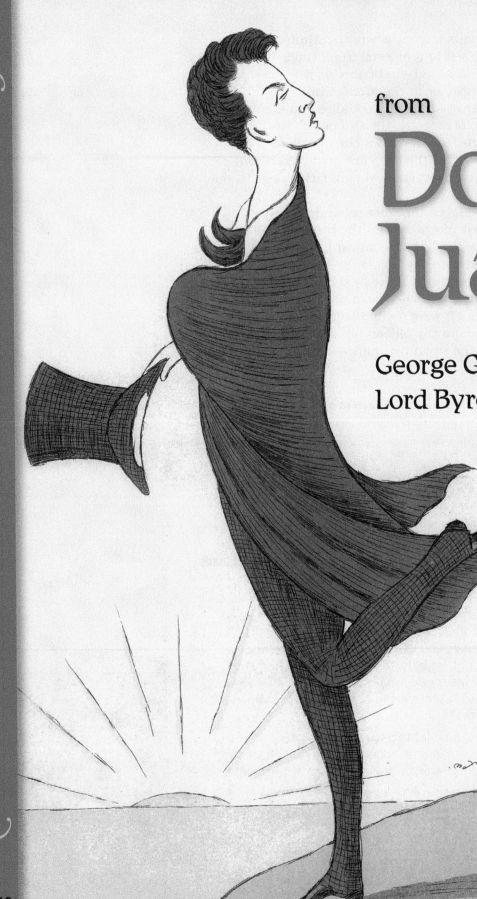

from

Don Juan

George Gordon, Lord Byron

Lord Byron, Shaking the Dust of England off His Shoes, from "The Poet's Corner" pub. William Heinemann, 1904 (engraving by Max Beerbohm) Central Saint Martin's College of Art and Design

BACKGROUND Though it is unfinished, *Don Juan* (jōō´ ən) is regarded as Byron's finest work. A mock epic described by Shelley as "something wholly new and relative to the age," it satirizes the political and social problems of Byron's time.

Traditionally Don Juan, the poem's hero, is a wicked character driven by his obsession with beautiful women. In Byron's work, Don Juan is an innocent young man whose physical beauty, charm, and spirit prove to be alluring to ladies. As a result, he finds himself in many difficult situations.

During periodic pauses in the story, the narrator drifts away from the subject. In these digressions the narrator comments on the issues of the time and on life in general. In this excerpt the narrator sets aside the adventures of his hero to reflect on old age and death.

> But now at thirty years my hair is gray
> (I wonder what it will be like at forty?
> I thought of a peruke[1] the other day)—
> My heart is not much greener; and in short, I
> 5 Have squandered my whole summer while 'twas May,
> And feel no more the spirit to retort; I
> Have spent my life, both interest and principal,
> And deem not, what I deemed, my soul invincible.
>
> No more—no more—Oh! never more on me
> 10 The freshness of the heart can fall like dew,
> Which out of all the lovely things we see
> Extracts emotions beautiful and new,
> Hived in our bosoms like the bag o' the bee:
> Think'st thou the honey with those objects grew?
> 15 Alas! 'twas not in them, but in thy power
> To double even the sweetness of a flower.
>
> No more—no more—Oh! never more, my heart,
> Canst thou be my sole world, my universe!
> Once all in all, but now a thing apart,
> 20 Thou canst not be my blessing or my curse:
> The illusion's gone forever, and thou art
> Insensible,[2] I trust, but none the worse,
> And in thy stead I've got a deal of judgment,
> Though heaven knows how it ever found a lodgment.

Vocabulary
retort (ri tôrt´) *v.* respond with a clever answer or wisecrack

◄ **Critical Viewing**
What traits of the poem's narrator does this famous caricature of Byron share? **[Interpret]**

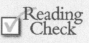
Reading Check
What type of experience will the speaker no longer undergo?

---

1. peruke (pə rōōk´) wig.
2. insensible (in sen´ sə bəl) *adj.* unable to feel or sense anything; numb.

Vocabulary

credulous (krej´ ᴏᴏ ləs) *adj.*
willing to believe; naive

copious (kō´ pē əs) *adj.*
abundant; plentiful

avarice (av´ ə ris) *n.* greed

World LITERATURE CONNECTION

Byron's Influence on World Literature

Byron's work was translated into many languages, and his fame quickly spread through Europe and beyond. Although the British dismissed Byron because of his wild life, the rest of Europe considered him the most important English poet. They were taken with the dark, brooding heroes described in his poems and were inspired by his life. Byron was a man of action. He made speeches in the House of Lords, defending the rights of workers and religious minorities. He traveled widely and he put his life on the line for liberty, joining the Greek revolutionaries in their fight against Turkish rule.

At a time when much of the world was embroiled in political and economic upheaval, writers found in Byron a model for passionate political and literary engagement. Byron's followers included some of the leading European and Russian poets: Alexander Pushkin and Mikhail Lermontov in Russia, Adam Mickiewicz in Poland, Heinrich Heine in Germany, Alfred de Musset in France, and José de Espronceda in Spain.

Connect to the Literature

What evidence of engagement with the world beyond Britain can you find in Byron's poems?

25 My days of love are over; me no more
The charms of maid, wife, and still less of widow
Can make the fool of which they made before—
In short, I must not lead the life I did do;
The credulous hope of mutual minds is o'er,
30 The copious use of claret is forbid too,
So for a good old-gentlemanly vice,
I think I must take up with avarice.

Ambition was my idol, which was broken
Before the shrines of Sorrow and of Pleasure;
35 And the two last have left me many a token
O'er which reflection may be made at leisure:
Now, like Friar Bacon's brazen head, I've spoken,
"Time is, Time was, Time's past,"[3] a chymic[4] treasure
Is glittering youth, which I have spent betimes—
40 My heart in passion, and my head on rhymes.

What is the end of fame? 'tis but to fill
A certain portion of uncertain paper:
Some liken it to climbing up a hill,
Whose summit, like all hills, is lost in vapor;
45 For this men write, speak, preach, and heroes kill,
And bards burn what they call their "midnight taper,"
To have, when the original is dust,
A name, a wretched picture, and worse bust.

What are the hopes of man? Old Egypt's King
50 Cheops erected the first pyramid
And largest, thinking it was just the thing
To keep his memory whole, and mummy hid:
But somebody or other rummaging
Burglariously broke his coffin's lid:
55 Let not a monument give you or me hopes,
Since not a pinch of dust remains of Cheops.

But I, being fond of true philosophy,
Say very often to myself, "Alas!
All things that have been born were born to die,
60 And flesh (which Death mows down to hay) is grass;
You've passed your youth not so unpleasantly,
And if you had it o'er again—'twould pass—
So thank your stars that matters are no worse,
And read your Bible, sir, and mind your purse."

---

3. Friar Bacon's . . . Time's past In Robert Greene's comedy *Friar Bacon and Friar Bungay* (1594), these words are spoken by a bronze bust, made by Friar Bacon.
4. chymic (kim´ ik) alchemic: counterfeit.

65 But for the present, gentle reader! and
    Still gentler purchaser! the bard—that's I—
    Must, with permission, shake you by the hand,
    And so your humble servant, and good-bye!
    We meet again, if we should understand
70 Each other; and if not, I shall not try
    Your patience further than by this short sample—
    'Twere well if others followed my example.

    "Go, little book, from this my solitude!
    I cast thee on the waters—go thy ways!
75 And if, as I believe, thy vein be good,
    The world will find thee after many days."[5]
    When Southey's read, and Wordsworth understood,
    I can't help putting in my claim to praise—
    The four first rhymes are Southey's, every line:
    For God's sake, reader! take them not for mine!

---

5. **Go . . . days** lines from the last stanza of Robert Southey's (1774–1843)
Epilogue to *The Lay of the Laureate.*

Critical Reading

1. **Key Ideas and Details (a)** What subject does the speaker consider in the opening lines? **(b) Analyze:** How would you describe the mood of the speaker's reflections?

2. **Key Ideas and Details (a)** What does the speaker say was the focus of his youth? **(b) Interpret:** In lines 33–40, why does the speaker call "glittering youth" "chymic," or counterfeit, treasure?

3. **Key Ideas and Details (a) Draw Conclusions:** What do lines 65–80 suggest about Byron's attitude toward his own epic poem? **(b) Connect:** Is this attitude consistent with his "true philosophy"? Explain.

4. **Integration of Knowledge and Ideas** Identify a modern character who shares the disillusioned attitude of Byron's speaker.

5. **Integration of Knowledge and Ideas** Which poems express a sense of the sublime, a feeling of fear and wonder inspired by nature? Use at least two of these Essential Question words in your answer: *majestic, capture, preserve.* *[Connecting to the Essential Question: What is the relationship between literature and place?]*

Cite textual evidence to support your responses.

What are the hopes of man?

Literary Analysis

1. **Craft and Structure** Use a chart to list examples from the poems of **figurative language,** finding at least one example each of **simile, metaphor,** and **personification.** Show how each example suggests a number of different associations for what is being described.

Figurative Language	What Is Being Described	Associations Suggested

2. **Craft and Structure** **(a)** Identify the simile in lines 10–18 of "Apostrophe to the Ocean." **(b)** What does the comparison suggest about the drowning man?

3. **Craft and Structure** Identify and interpret the types of figurative language in the following lines: **(a)** "Thou glorious mirror, where the Almighty's form / Glasses itself. . . ." **(b)** "The freshness of the heart can fall like dew, . . ."

4. **Craft and Structure** In "Apostrophe to the Ocean," what effect does the personification of the ocean have on the poem as a whole?

5. **Craft and Structure** In *Don Juan*, the speaker says he "squandered [his] whole summer while 'twas May." **(a)** What type of figurative language is in this line? **(b)** What meaning does the comparison convey?

6. **Comparing Literary Works** **(a)** In "She Walks in Beauty," how does Byron use figures of speech and imagery of the night to convey the mysterious, endless power of Lady Horton's beauty? **(b)** Identify three images or figures of speech suggesting the sublime power of nature in "Apostrophe to the Ocean."

7. **Comparing Literary Works** Compare the feelings associated with infinite power or mystery in these two poems.

8. **Comparing Literary Works** In what ways does Byron express the opposite of the sublime in the excerpt from *Don Juan*? Cite specific passages, figures of speech, and images to support your point.

Reading Strategy

9. **(a)** List the questions you asked as you read Byron's poems and the answers you found. **(b)** Did *repairing your comprehension* by **questioning** make your reading more active or focused? Explain.

10. Ask and answer a series of questions to uncover the meaning of lines 9–16 of the excerpt from *Don Juan*.

11. **(a)** In what ways might you apply a questioning strategy to a poem's title before you even begin to read it? **(b)** What questions could you ask and answer about the titles of Byron's poems?

Common Core State Standards

Writing

3.c. Use a variety of techniques to sequence events so that they build on one another to create a coherent whole and build toward a particular tone and outcome. *(p. 865)*

3.d. Use precise words and phrases, telling details, and sensory language to convey a vivid picture of the experiences, events, setting, and/or characters. *(p. 865)*

Language

4.a. Use context as a clue to the meaning of a word or phrase. *(p. 865)*

Integrated Language Skills

Vocabulary Acquisition and Use

Word Analysis: Latin Suffix -ous

The suffix -ous means "full of." The root of the word credulous, cred-, means "belief." Therefore, credulous means "full of belief" or "overly willing to believe." Strenuous exercise is "exercise that requires great exertion," or exercise that is "full of strain." Use the meaning of -ous to define the listed terms, checking a dictionary if necessary. Then, write an original sentence using each word.

1. furious
2. glorious
3. porous
4. plenteous
5. portentous
6. spacious
7. barbarous
8. querulous

Vocabulary: Context

An unfamiliar word's context—words, phrases, or sentences around it—can provide clues to its meaning. Identify the meaning of each italicized vocabulary word below and explain how the context makes that meaning clear.

1. Unable to agree on anything, the two brothers constantly relied on their sister as an *arbiter*.

2. The creek bed became dry after weeks of *torrid* weather.

3. The author's witty *retorts* to the host's questions left the audience laughing.

4. Unable to see her faults, he was always *credulous* with regard to her excuses.

5. The dutiful student filled the pages with *copious*, or plentiful, notes.

6. *Avarice* compelled him to accumulate wealth; selfishness led him to keep it all.

Writing

Narrative Text Write an **interior monologue**—words a character speaks to himself or herself—in which a modern Byronic hero tells his or her story. This type of hero is a brooding loner who may feel impassioned by a cause. If you like, use a real-life celebrity as a model.

Prewriting Jot down some opinions that a Byronic hero might hold today. Think about your hero's circumstances and how he or she might feel about them. Then, list words and phrases that convey this attitude.

Drafting Structure your monologue as the tale of a *sequence of events* that leads to your hero's strongest expression of his or her attitude. As you draft, use precise words to describe the character's feelings.

Revising Read through your draft and think about its *dramatic effect*. Rearrange or change words to intensify the dramatic effect.

Model: Revising to Structure Ideas for Effect

If I am a great actor, it is because my life has been great—not perfect. The films of my long career form an exhibition of my

mistakes, and crimes
flaws, crimes and mistakes.

Rearranging strengthens the dramatic effect by putting the more powerful word last.

Connecting to the Essential Question Romantic poets like Shelley were rebels who wanted to overthrow tyrants and bring in a new age of equality and justice. As you read, note which passages reveal Shelley as a political rebel. Finding such passages will help as you consider the Essential Question: **How does literature shape or reflect society?**

Literary Analysis

Imagery is descriptive language that re-creates sensory experience. Writers may use imagery to create metaphors and other figures of speech. Poetic imagery has these characteristics:

- It appeals to any or all of the five senses.
- It often creates patterns supporting a poem's theme.

The process of interpreting imagery requires you to make inferences, or educated guesses, about meaning. For example, in "Ode to the West Wind," Shelley uses wind images that appeal to sight, sound, and touch. Even though the poet does not explicitly state a theme, these images and their patterns suggest his message.

By gathering together powerful images of the west wind or of a skylark, Shelley links these natural beings to the strivings of his own spirit. His images all depict concrete objects, such as leaves in the wind. Yet they also stir up longings and dreams. In the **Romantic philosophy** of the imagination, an image connects what is "outside" the mind with what is "inside," linking nature and spirit. As you read, think about the deeper meanings Shelley's imagery suggests.

Reading Strategy

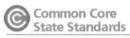
Common Core State Standards

Reading Literature
1. Cite strong and thorough textual evidence to support analysis of what the text says explicitly as well as inferences drawn from the text, including determining where the text leaves matters uncertain.

Preparing to Read Complex Texts You can better understand an author's poetry by **comparing and contrasting elements** from different texts. For example, you might contrast the desert images of "Ozymandias," which suggest the bleakness of tyranny, with the wind images of "Ode to the West Wind," which suggest political rebellion. Use a chart like the one shown to compare the imagery in different poems by Shelley.

Imagery	Poem

Vocabulary

verge (vʉrj) *n.* edge; rim (p. 870)

sepulcher (sep′ əl kər) *n.* tomb (p. 870)

impulse (im′ puls) *n.* force driving forward (p. 872)

blithe (blīth) *adj.* cheerful (p. 873)

profuse (prō fyo͞os′) *adj.* abundant; pouring out (p. 873)

satiety (sə tī′ ə tē) *n.* state of being filled with enough or more than enough (p. 875)

PHLit Online!
www.PHLitOnline.com

Percy Bysshe Shelley (1792–1822)

Author of "Ozymandias" • "Ode to the West Wind" • "To a Skylark"

When he died in a boating accident at 29, Percy Bysshe (bish) Shelley was eulogized by his fellow poet Lord Byron as "without exception the best and least selfish man I ever knew."

A Loner and Rebel Born into the British upper classes, Shelley was raised on a country estate in Sussex. He attended the finest schools, including the prestigious boarding school Eton, but he was never able to settle into the routine of a student. Instead, he spent most of his time wandering the countryside and performing private scientific experiments. At Oxford University, he became a friend of Thomas Jefferson Hogg, a student whose political views were as strong as his own. When, with Hogg's encouragement and support, Shelley published the radical tract *The Necessity of Atheism*, both he and Hogg were expelled from the university.

Love and Art The expulsion estranged Shelley from his father. Instead of going home, Shelley headed for London. There, he met Harriet Westbrook. An unhappy schoolgirl, Westbrook persuaded him to elope, and they married.

Shelley's development as a poet was already under way. In 1813, he had completed "Queen Mab," his first important poem. The work explored ideas of social justice that Shelley had encountered in the philosopher William Godwin's *Political Justice*.

Turmoil, Romance, and Tragedy Shelley's marriage, meanwhile, was in trouble. Harriet felt that she could not keep up with her husband. Then, Shelley fell in love with Mary Wollstonecraft Godwin, daughter of William Godwin and the feminist Mary Wollstonecraft. After Harriet's tragic death in 1816, Shelley married his beloved Mary Godwin.

A Poet and an Outcast His radical politics, his tract about atheism, his separation from his first wife—all helped make Shelley an outcast from England. He and Mary eventually settled in Italy, where Lord Byron, another famous exile, lived.

Shelley wrote many of his finest works in Italy, including "Ode to the West Wind" and "To a Skylark." His early death there, however, meant that he never saw his dreams of social progress come true.

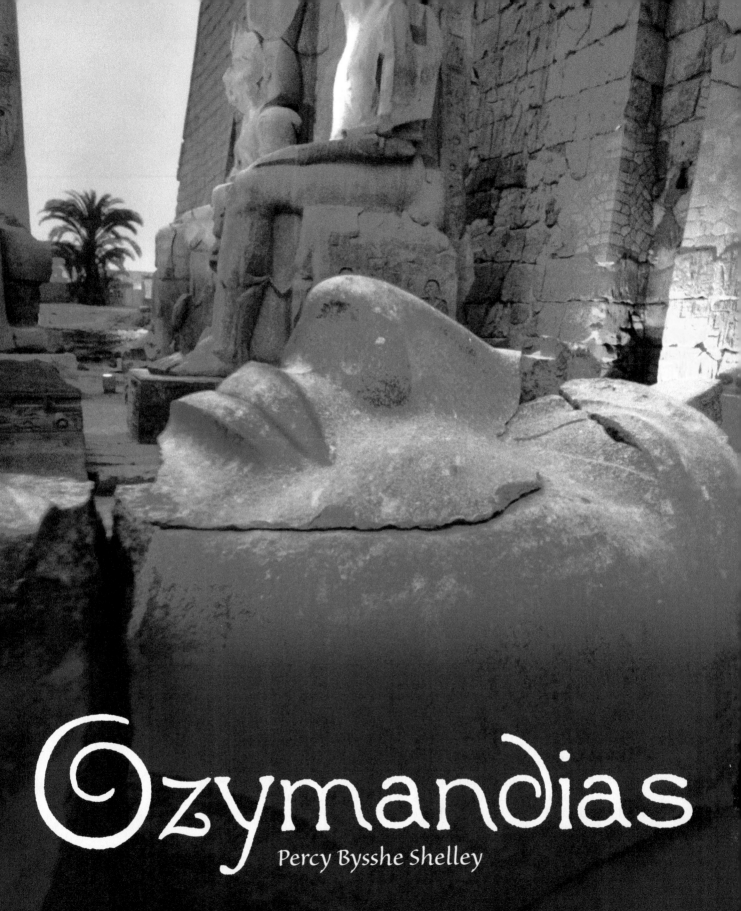

Ozymandias

Percy Bysshe Shelley

Background The Ozymandias of Shelley's poem is based on an actual Egyptian pharaoh, Ramses II ("Ozymandias" was his name in Greek). Ramses II ruled during the thirteenth century B.C. and figures in the biblical story of Moses. He sponsored ambitious building projects and called for huge statues of himself to be built. According to an ancient story, one of these colossal statues was inscribed with this boast about his bold deeds: "I am Ozymandias, king of kings; if anyone wishes to know what I am and where I lie, let him surpass me in some of my exploits."

I met a traveler from an antique land
Who said: Two vast and trunkless legs of stone
Stand in the desert. Near them, on the sand,
Half sunk, a shattered visage[1] lies, whose frown,
5 And wrinkled lip, and sneer of cold command,
Tell that its sculptor well those passions read
Which yet survive, stamped on these lifeless things,
The hand that mocked them and the heart that fed:
And on the pedestal these words appear:
10 "My name is Ozymandias, king of kings:
Look on my works, ye Mighty, and despair!"
Nothing beside remains. Round the decay
Of that colossal wreck, boundless and bare,
The lone and level sands stretch far away.

◄ **Critical Viewing**
How is this Egyptian statue like and unlike the one in the poem? **[Compare and Contrast]**

---

1. visage (viz´ ij) *n.* face.

Critical Reading

1. **Key Ideas and Details (a)** How would you describe the expression on the face of Ozymandias? **(b) Infer:** What does his expression suggest about the kind of ruler he was?

2. **Key Ideas and Details (a) Interpret:** What attitude is conveyed by the words on the pedestal? **(b) Compare and Contrast:** Compare this attitude with the opening images of the poem. **(c) Analyze:** In what sense is the inscription ironic?

3. **Integration of Knowledge and Ideas (a) Draw Conclusions:** What is the message of this poem? **(b) Apply:** Do you think that the message is pertinent to today's world? Why or why not?

Cite textual evidence to support your responses.

Ode to the West Wind

Percy Bysshe Shelley

I

O wild West Wind, thou breath of Autumn's being,
Thou, from whose unseen presence the leaves dead
Are driven, like ghosts from an enchanter fleeing,

Yellow, and black, and pale, and hectic red,
5   Pestilence-stricken multitudes: O thou,
Who chariotest to their dark and wintry bed

The wingèd seeds, where they lie cold and low,
Each like a corpse within its grave, until
Thine azure sister of the Spring[1] shall blow

10 Her clarion[2] o'er the dreaming earth, and fill
(Driving sweet buds like flocks to feed in air)
With loving hues and odors plain and hill:

Wild Spirit, which art moving everywhere;
Destroyer and preserver; hear, oh, hear!

II

15 Thou on whose stream, 'mid the steep sky's commotion,
Loose clouds like earth's decaying leaves are shed,
Shook from the tangled boughs of Heaven and Ocean,

Angels[3] of rain and lightning: there are spread
On the blue surface of thine aery surge,
20 Like the bright hair uplifted from the head

Of some fierce Maenad,[4] even from the dim verge
Of the horizon to the zenith's height,
The locks of the approaching storm. Thou dirge

Of the dying year, to which this closing night
25 Will be the dome of a vast sepulcher,
Vaulted with all thy congregated might

Literary Analysis
Imagery To which sense does the image in lines 18–23 mostly appeal?

Vocabulary
verge (vʉrj) *n.* edge; rim

sepulcher (sep´ əl kər) *n.* tomb

---

1. **sister of the Spring** the wind prevailing during spring.
2. **clarion** *n.* trumpet producing clear, sharp tones.
3. **angels** messengers.
4. **Maenad** (mē´ nad) a priestess of Bacchus, the Greek and Roman god of wine and revelry.

Of vapors, from whose solid atmosphere
Black rain, and fire, and hail will burst: oh, hear!

III

Thou who didst waken from his summer dreams
30 The blue Mediterranean, where he lay,
Lulled by the coil of his crystalline streams,

Beside a pumice[5] isle in Baiae's bay,[6]
And saw in sleep old palaces and towers
Quivering within the wave's intenser day,

35 All overgrown with azure moss and flowers
So sweet, the sense faints picturing them!
For whose path the Atlantic's level powers

Cleave themselves into chasms, while far below
The sea-blooms and the oozy woods which wear
40 The sapless foliage of the ocean, know

Thy voice, and suddenly grow gray with fear,
And tremble and despoil themselves: oh, hear!

IV

If I were a dead leaf thou mightest bear;
If I were a swift cloud to fly with thee;
45 A wave to pant beneath thy power, and share

---

5. **pumice** (pum´ is) *n.* volcanic rock.
6. **Baiae's** (bā´ yēz) **bay** site of the ancient Roman resort near Naples, parts of which
lie submerged.

▲ **Critical Viewing**
Which elements in this
painting match Shelley's
evocation of the west wind
in lines 1–8? **[Connect]**

Reading Strategy
Comparing Imagery
Contrast the images in lines
29–36 with those in lines
12–14 of "Ozymandias."

Reading
Check

In the first three sections,
what does the speaker
ask the West Wind to do?

The impulse of thy strength, only less free
Than thou, O uncontrollable! If even
I were as in my boyhood, and could be

The comrade of thy wanderings over Heaven,
50 As then, when to outstrip thy skyey speed
Scarce seemed a vision; I would ne'er have striven

As thus with thee in prayer in my sore need.
Oh, lift me as a wave, a leaf, a cloud!
I fall upon the thorns of life! I bleed!

55 A heavy weight of hours has chained and bowed
One too like thee: tameless, and swift, and proud.

Literary Analysis
Imagery and Romantic Philosophy How do the images in lines 57–63 imply a connection between the speaker and nature?

V

Make me thy lyre,[7] even as the forest is:
What if my leaves are falling like its own!
The tumult of thy mighty harmonies

60 Will take from both a deep, autumnal tone,
Sweet though in sadness. Be thou, Spirit fierce,
My spirit! Be thou me, impetuous one!

Drive my dead thought over the universe
Like withered leaves to quicken a new birth!
65 And, by the incantation of this verse,

Scatter, as from an unextinguished hearth
Ashes and sparks, my words among mankind!
Be through my lips to unawakened earth

The trumpet of a prophecy! O Wind,
70 If Winter comes, can Spring be far behind?

---

7. lyre Aeolian (ē ō′ lē ən) lyre, or wind harp, a stringed instrument that produces musical sounds when the wind passes over it.

Critical Reading

1. **Key Ideas and Details (a)** What season does the poet associate with the west wind? **(b) Interpret:** What feelings does Shelley create around the west wind in sections II and III?

2. **Key Ideas and Details (a)** What does the speaker ask of the wind in section IV? **(b) Infer:** What change in his life prompts this question?

3. **Key Ideas and Details (a)** What does the final line of the poem mean? **(b)** How does it tie together the poem?

Woman and Bird in Moonlight, 1949, Joan Miro, Tate, London/Art Resource, NY. © Copyright ARS, NY

To a Skylark

Percy Bysshe Shelley

▲ **Critical Viewing** Which details in this painting capture the freedom and independence of Shelley's skylark? **[Connect]**

Hail to thee, blithe spirit!
    Bird thou never wert,
That from heaven, or near it,
    Pourest thy full heart
5 In profuse strains of unpremeditated art.

    Higher still and higher,
    From the earth thou springest
Like a cloud of fire;
    The blue deep thou wingest,
10 And singing still dost soar, and soaring ever singest.

    In the golden lightning
    Of the sunken sun,
O'er which clouds are brightening,
    Thou dost float and run;
15 Like an unbodied joy whose race is just begun.

Vocabulary
blithe (blīth) *adj.* cheerful
profuse (prō fyōōs´) *adj.*
abundant; pouring out

Reading Check

To what type of cloud does
Shelley compare the skylark?

To a Skylark **873**

The pale purple even[1]
    Melts around thy flight;
Like a star of heaven,
    In the broad daylight
20 Thou art unseen, but yet I hear thy shrill delight,

    Keen as are the arrows
    Of that silver sphere,[2]
Whose intense lamp narrows
    In the white dawn clear,
25 Until we hardly see—we feel that it is there.

    All the earth and air
    With thy voice is loud,
As, when night is bare,
    From one lonely cloud
30 The moon rains out her beams, and Heaven is overflowed.

    What thou art we know not;
    What is most like thee?
From rainbow clouds there flow not
    Drops so bright to see,
35 As from thy presence showers a rain of melody.

    Like a poet hidden
    In the light of thought,
Singing hymns unbidden,
    Till the world is wrought
40 To sympathy with hopes and fears it heeded not:

    Like a highborn maiden
    In a palace tower,
Soothing her love-laden
    Soul in secret hour
45 With music sweet as love, which overflows her bower:

    Like a glowworm golden
    In a dell of dew,
Scattering unbeholden
    Its aerial hue
50 Among the flowers and grass, which screen it from the view!

    Like a rose embowered
    In its own green leaves,

---

1. even evening.
2. silver sphere the morning star.

By warm winds deflowered,[3]
    Till the scent it gives
55 Makes faint with too much sweet those heavy-wingèd thieves.[4]

    Sound of vernal[5] showers
        On the twinkling grass,
    Rain-awakened flowers,
        All that ever was
60 Joyous, and clear, and fresh, thy music doth surpass:

    Teach us, sprite or bird,
        What sweet thoughts are thine:
    I have never heard
        Praise of love or wine
65 That panted forth a flood of rapture so divine.

    Chorus Hymeneal,[6]
        Or triumphal chant,
    Matched with thine would be all
        But an empty vaunt,
70 A thing wherein we feel there is some hidden want.

    What objects are the fountains[7]
        Of thy happy strain?
    What fields, or waves, or mountains?
        What shapes of sky or plain?
75 What love of thine own kind? what ignorance of pain?

    With thy clear keen joyance
        Languor cannot be;
    Shadow of annoyance
        Never came near thee;
80 Thou lovest—but ne'er knew love's sad satiety.

    Waking or asleep,
        Thou of death must deem[8]
    Things more true and deep
        Than we mortals dream,
85 Or how could thy notes flow in such a crystal stream?

    We look before and after,
        And pine for what is not;
    Our sincerest laughter

Reading Strategy
Comparing Imagery
Compare the images in lines 51–55 with those in lines 35–36 of "Ode to the West Wind."

Vocabulary
satiety (sə tī´ ə tē) *n.* state of being filled with enough or more than enough

Reading Check
Through what sense or senses does the speaker perceive the Skylark?

With some pain is fraught;
90 Our sweetest songs are those that tell of saddest thought.

Yet if[9] we could scorn
    Hate, and pride, and fear;
If we were things born
    Not to shed a tear,
95 I know not how thy joy we ever should come near.

Better than all measures
    Of delightful sound,
Better than all treasures
    That in books are found,
100 Thy skill to poet were,[10] thou scorner of the ground!

Teach me half the gladness
    That thy brain must know,
Such harmonious madness
    From my lips would flow,
105 The world should listen then, as I am listening now.

_____

9. if even if.
10. were would be.

Critical Reading

1. Key Ideas and Details (a) In the first stanza, what does the poet claim the skylark is not? **(b) Interpret:** What point is he making? **(c) Analyze:** How do the images of light in lines 6–35 reinforce the point?

2. Key Ideas and Details (a) To what four things does the speaker compare the bird in lines 36–55? **(b) Analyze:** What quality or power does each comparison suggest that the bird's song has?

3. Key Ideas and Details (a) What comparisons does the poet make between human song and the skylark's? **(b) Analyze:** Based on these comparisons, what does the speaker conclude about similarities and differences between the bird's life and human life?

4. Craft and Structure What does the speaker's use of the phrase "harmonious madness" (line 103) suggest about the difference between the skylark's song and human poetry?

5. Integration of Knowledge and Ideas In what ways does the sculpture in "Ozymandias" represent tyranny and the wind in "Ode to the West Wind" rebellion? In your response, use at least two of these Essential Question words: _independence, conform, limits._ _[Connecting to the Essential Question: How does literature shape or reflect society?]_

Cite textual evidence to support your responses.

SHELLEY AND SCIENCE

Percy Bysshe Shelley was well educated in the science of his day. As a schoolboy, he studied with Adam Walker, a scientist who lectured on natural history, electricity, and meteorology. Later, Shelley, who was an avid reader, followed the latest scientific discoveries with great interest. For example, he read the work of meteorologist Luke Howard and incorporated Howard's theories of cloud formation into his poem "The Cloud":

This cloud sketch is by Luke Howard (1772–1864). Howard kept precise records of the weather in London for forty years and created a classification system for clouds that we still use today. His writings transformed the science of meteorology and inspired Shelley's poem "The Cloud."

> . . . I am the daughter of Earth and Water,
>   And the nursling of the Sky;
> I pass through the pores of the ocean and shores;
>   I change, but I cannot die.

CONNECT TO THE LITERATURE

What evidence of scientific influence can you find in the poems you have read by Shelley?

Literary Analysis

1. **Key Ideas and Details** Imagine filming the **imagery** of "Ozymandias." **(a)** Compare the camera placement you would use for lines 4–5, lines 9–11, and the final line. **(b)** Explain how each image helps convey Shelley's message.

2. **Craft and Structure (a)** In "Ode to the West Wind," find three images indicating the power of the wind, and explain to which senses each appeals. **(b)** How do these images support Shelley's message of renewal?

3. **Craft and Structure (a)** How do descriptions of sounds in "To a Skylark" *evoke emotions* by suggesting the bird's "unbodied joy"? **(b)** How does sound show the defect in human joy in lines 86–90?

4. **Comparing Literary Works** Compare Shelley's images of the statue, the west wind, and the skylark. **(a)** Which paints the strongest sensory picture of the object described? Explain. **(b)** Which provides the clearest sense of the ideas and feelings connected with the object? Explain.

5. **Comparing Literary Works** Using a chart like the one shown, compare two poems where an image connects the speaker with nature.

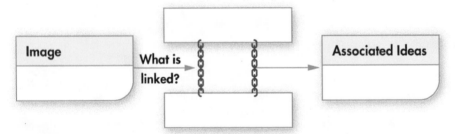

6. **Comparing Literary Works** In **Romantic philosophy,** the imagination connects nature and spirit. **(a)** What images in sections IV and V of "Ode to the West Wind" suggest such a connection? **(b)** Show how Shelley's use of *personification*—treating nonhuman things as if they were human—in two poems also helps link nature and spirit.

7. **Analyzing Visual Information** Using your knowledge of "Ozymandias," explain the humor of the cartoon shown on this page.

Reading Strategy

8. **Compare elements** in Shelley's poems by contrasting the desert imagery of "Ozymandias" with the wind imagery of "Ode to the West Wind." How does each of these patterns of imagery reveal Shelley as a political rebel?

9. **(a)** Using imagery from each poem, contrast the oppressive heaviness of the tyrant in "Ozymandias" with the lightness and ease of the bird in "To a Skylark." **(b)** To what extent do you think Shelley identifies the skylark with imagination itself? Explain.

"My name is Ozymandias, king of kings: Look on my works, ye Mighty, and despair!" ▼

© Vocabulary Acquisition and Use

Word Analysis: Latin Root -puls-

The Latin root -puls- means "push or drive." It is the base of some common words that are also used for *scientific concepts.* Using your knowledge of the root -puls-, write the definition of each numbered word below. Verify your definitions by checking a *dictionary.* Then, write three original sentences, each using a different word on the list.

1. compulsion
2. expulsion
3. impulse
4. propulsion
5. pulse
6. repulse

Vocabulary: Analogies

Analogies show the relationships between pairs of words. Complete each analogy using a word from the vocabulary list on page 866. In each, your choice should create a word pair that matches the relationship between the first two words given. Then, explain your answers.

1. *Penalty* is to *punishment* as _____ is to *brink.*
2. _____ is to *push* as *halt* is to *stop.*
3. *Sad* is to _____ as *ill* is to *healthy.*
4. *Glare* is to *sunlight* as _____ is to *fullness.*
5. _____ is to *building* as *dirge* is to *music.*
6. *Speed* is to *velocity* as _____ is to *excessive.*

Writing

© **Explanatory Text** In lyric poems like "Ode to the West Wind," Shelley drew on the scientific and historical knowledge of his time. Develop a **research plan** for a report on Shelley's use of scientific or historical knowledge—or both—in his poetry. Include a *narrowed topic* to be investigated, *questions* to be answered, a *bibliography* of properly cited sources you will consult, and *annotations* stating the *appropriateness and objectivity* of each source.

Prewriting Use *creative research strategies* to formulate questions and develop a bibliography. Consider interviewing librarians and Shelley scholars. Also consider scanning biographies of Shelley and footnoted editions of his work to uncover scientific and historical influences.

Drafting Based on your reading, identify a narrow topic that could be answered adequately in a short paper. List your sources. Scan introductions, tables of contents, or opening paragraphs of the sources to see how appropriate and reliable each might be. Write specific annotations commenting on the relevance and objectivity of each.

Revising Review your questions to make sure they are clear and focused. Study your bibliography to make sure that you follow the format requested by your teacher.

Model: Making Evaluations Specific

Shelley, Mary. *Notes to the Complete Poetical Works of Percy Bysshe Shelley.* Sydney, Australia: ReadHowYouWant.com, 2006. Comments by his wife might show what reading in history and science Shelley had done.

Use specific information in your evaluations for clarity.

Connecting to the Essential Question Keats adapted the ode—a poetic form designed to broadcast public concerns—to express personal emotions. As you read, note which lines in the odes reveal personal emotions. Locating these lines will help you answer the Essential Question: **What is the relationship of the writer to tradition?**

Literary Analysis

An **ode** is a lyric poem, characterized by heightened emotion, that pays respect to a person or thing, usually directly addressed by the speaker.

- The **Pindaric ode** (named for the ancient Greek poet Pindar) uses groups of three stanzas, one of which differs in form from the other two. Pindar's odes celebrated victors at the Olympic Games.
- Roman poets later developed the **Horatian ode** (also called homostrophic), which contains only one type of stanza.
- The **irregular ode** has no set pattern.

Keats created his own form of the ode, using ten-line stanzas of iambic pentameter (lines containing ten beats with a repeated pattern of weak-strong). Often those stanzas begin with a heroic quatrain (four lines rhymed *abab*) followed by a sestet (six lines rhymed in various ways). As you read, note the various formal structures Keats uses in his odes.

Comparing Literary Works In his odes, Keats follows the tradition of paying respect to something. Yet his odes reveal as much about him as they do about his subjects. As you read, compare the ways in which his odes dramatize a conflict in the speaker. Also, analyze how, in each case, the conflict is brought on by longings for what is unobtainable.

Reading Strategy

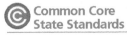 **Preparing to Read Complex Texts** You can **determine the main idea** of a passage by *paraphrasing* it—restating it in your own words. Doing so will not only help you clarify the meaning of the specific passage but will also help you see how the ideas in a work connect and develop. Use a chart like the one shown to paraphrase difficult passages in Keats's poems.

Vocabulary

ken (ken) *n.* range of sight or knowledge (p. 883)

surmise (sər mīz´) *n.* guess; assumption (p. 883)

gleaned (glēnd) *v.* collected bit by bit, as when gathering stray grain after a harvest (p. 885)

teeming (tēm´ iŋ) *adj.* filled to overflowing (p. 885)

vintage (vin´ tij) *n.* wine of fine quality (p. 887)

requiem (rek´ wē əm) *n.* musical composition honoring the dead (p. 888)

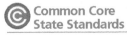
Original
"When I have fears that I may cease to be…"
Paraphrase
"When I am afraid that I may die…"

www.PHLitOnline.com

John Keats (1795–1821)

Author of "On First Looking into Chapman's Homer" • "When I Have Fears That I May Cease to Be" • "Ode to a Nightingale" • "Ode on a Grecian Urn"

Although he died at age twenty-five, Keats left his indelible mark on literature, and this makes us wonder what more he might have accomplished had he lived longer.

A Defender of Worthy Causes Unlike his contemporaries Byron and Shelley, John Keats was not an aristocrat. Instead, he was born to working-class Londoners. As a child, he received attention for his striking good looks and his restless spirit. Keats developed a reputation for fighting, but always for a worthy cause. It was not until he and his school-master's son, Charles Cowden Clarke, became friends that Keats developed an interest in poetry and became an avid reader.

From Medicine to Poetry In 1815, Keats began studying medicine at a London hospital. He had already begun writing poetry, but he earned his pharmacist's license before abandoning medicine for the literary world. In 1818, he published his first major work, *Endymion*, a long poem that the critics panned. Despite the critical rejection, Keats did not swerve from his new career.

A Year of Sorrow and Joy The year 1818 was significant for Keats in other ways as well. He lost his brother Tom to tuberculosis, but he also met the light of his life, Fanny Brawne, to whom he became engaged. The next year, 1819, was a period of feverish creativity. In just nine months, fired by grief, new-found love, and his own encroaching illness, Keats wrote the poems for which he is most famous, including "The Eve of St. Agnes," "La Belle Dame sans Merci," and his odes. Each is recognized as a masterpiece.

An Early Death Keats's engagement to Fanny and his burst of creativity might have been the prelude to a happy, productive life. Instead, Keats found his health deteriorating. Recognizing that like his brother, he had tuberculosis, Keats moved to Italy, hoping that the warmer climate would reverse the disease. Sadly, that hope proved false, and, in 1821, his battle with tuberculosis ended with his death.

Despite his early death, John Keats remains one of the major influences in English poetry.

On First Looking into Chapman's Homer

John Keats

BACKGROUND Romantic poets such as Byron, Shelley, and Keats admired the culture of ancient Greece and derived inspiration from its art and literature. Keats's "Ode on a Grecian Urn" (p. 890), for instance, shows his tendency to associate ideas about beauty with antiquities, such as the beautifully adorned vases that ancient Greek society produced.

When Keats was twenty-one, his friend and former schoolmate, Charles Cowden Clarke, introduced him to a translation of Homer by Elizabethan poet George Chapman. The two men spent the evening reading this book, and early the next morning Keats presented this sonnet to Clarke.

Much have I traveled in the realms of gold,
    And many goodly states and kingdoms seen;
    Round many western islands have I been
Which bards in fealty to Apollo[1] hold.
5 Oft of one wide expanse had I been told
    That deep-browed Homer ruled as his demesne;[2]
    Yet did I never breathe its pure serene[3]
Till I heard Chapman speak out loud and bold:
Then felt I like some watcher of the skies
10 When a new planet swims into his ken;
Or like stout Cortez[4] when with eagle eyes
    He stared at the Pacific—and all his men
Looked at each other with a wild surmise—
    Silent, upon a peak in Darien.[5]

Reading Strategy
Paraphrasing
Paraphrase lines 5–6, paying special attention to the metaphor of a "demesne."

Vocabulary
ken (ken) *n.* range of sight or knowledge

surmise (sər mīz´) *n.* guess; assumption

---

1. **Apollo** in Greek and Roman mythology, the god of music, poetry, and medicine.
2. **demesne** (di mān´) realm.
3. **serene** clear air.
4. **Cortez** Here, Keats was mistaken. The Pacific was discovered in 1513 by Balboa, not Cortez.
5. **Darien** (der´ ē ən) the Isthmus of Panama.

◀ **Critical Viewing** How does this image of ships convey the feeling of exploration Keats describes in this sonnet? **[Connect]**

When I Have Fears That I May Cease to Be

John Keats

When I have fears that I may cease to be
    Before my pen has gleaned my teeming brain,
Before high-piled books, in charactery,[1]
    Hold like rich garners[2] the full ripened grain;
5 When I behold, upon the night's starred face,
    Huge cloudy symbols of a high romance,
And think that I may never live to trace
    Their shadows, with the magic hand of chance;
And when I feel, fair creature of an hour,
10   That I shall never look upon thee more,
Never have relish in the fairy power
    Of unreflecting love—then on the shore
Of the wide world I stand alone, and think
Till love and fame to nothingness do sink.

---

1. **charactery** written or printed letters of the alphabet.
2. **garners** storehouses for grain.

Vocabulary

gleaned (glēnd) *v.* collected from bit by bit, as when gathering stray grain after a harvest

teeming (tēm´ iŋ) *adj.* filled to overflowing

◀ **Critical Viewing** From this rendering of Keats, how would you characterize him? **[Infer]**

Critical Reading

1. **Key Ideas and Details (a)** In "On First Looking into Chapman's Homer," what feelings about Chapman's translation do lines 9–14 convey? **(b) Draw Conclusions:** How does the comparison of reading to a journey support these feelings?

2. **Key Ideas and Details (a)** In lines 1–4 of "When I Have Fears," what does the speaker fear he will not accomplish before he dies? **(b) Interpret:** In lines 5–12, what is he concerned about missing? **(c) Evaluate:** Do the last lines offer a convincing resolution to such fears? Explain.

3. **Integration of Knowledge and Ideas** What words describe Keats's character as revealed in these two poems?

4. **Integration of Knowledge and Ideas** Are most young people today as anxious about and thrilled by the future as Keats? Explain.

Cite textual evidence to support your responses.

Ode to a Nightingale

John Keats

BACKGROUND Keats composed the following ode in 1819, while living in Hampstead with his friend Charles Brown. Brown wrote the following description about how the ode was composed: "In the spring of 1819 a nightingale had built her nest near my house. Keats felt a tranquil and continued joy in her song; and one morning he took his chair from the breakfast table to the grass plot under the plum tree, where he sat for two or three hours. When he came into the house, I perceived he had some scraps of paper in his hand, and these he was quietly thrusting behind the books. On inquiry, I found those scraps, four or five in number, contained his poetic feeling on the song of our nightingale."

I

My heart aches, and drowsy numbness pains
    My sense, as though of hemlock[1] I had drunk,
Or emptied some dull opiate to the drains
    One minute past, and Lethe-wards[2] had sunk:
5 'Tis not through envy of thy happy lot,
    But being too happy in thine happiness,—
        That thou, light-winged Dryad[3] of the trees,
            In some melodious plot
Of beechen green, and shadows numberless,
10   Singest of summer in full-throated ease.

II

O, for a draft[4] of vintage! that hath been
    Cooled a long age in the deep-delved earth,
Tasting of Flora[5] and the country green,
    Dance, and Provençal[6] song, and sunburnt mirth!
15 O for a beaker full of the warm South,
    Full of the true, the blushful Hippocrene,[7]
        With beaded bubbles winking at the brim,
            And purple-stained mouth;
That I might drink, and leave the world unseen,
20   And with thee fade away into the forest dim:

III

Fade far away, dissolve, and quite forget
    What thou among the leaves hast never known,
The weariness, the fever, and the fret
    Here, where men sit and hear each other groan;
25 Where palsy shakes a few, sad, last gray hairs,
    Where youth grows pale, and specter-thin, and dies;[8]
        Where but to think is to be full of sorrow
            And leaden-eyed despairs,
    Where Beauty cannot keep her lustrous eyes,
30   Or new Love pine at them beyond tomorrow.

---

1. **hemlock** poisonous herb.
2. **Lethe-wards** toward Lethe, the river of forgetfulness in Hades, the underworld, in classical mythology.
3. **Dryad** (drī´ əd) in classical mythology, a wood nymph.
4. **draft** drink.
5. **Flora** in classical mythology, the goddess of flowers, or the flowers themselves.
6. **Provencal** (prō´ vən säl´) pertaining to Provence, a region in Southern France, renowned in the late Middle Ages for its troubadours, who composed and sang love songs.
7. **Hippocrene** (hip´ ō krēn´) in classical mythology, the fountain of the Muses on Mt. Helicon. From this fountain flowed the waters of inspiration.
8. **youth . . . dies** Keats is referring to his brother, Tom, who had died from tuberculosis the previous winter.

Birds on a Flowering Plum Branch Attributed to Ma Lin, ink and colors on silk, S Song dynasty (13th c.), The Gotoh Museum

◄ **Critical Viewing**
Compare the mood of this painting with that of stanza III. **[Compare and Contrast]**

Vocabulary
vintage (vin´ tij) *n.* wine of fine quality

Reading Strategy
Paraphrasing
Restate lines 11–14 in your own words.

Literary Analysis
The Ode Which passages in stanza III seem to express Keats's deep personal feelings? Explain.

Reading Check

What does the speaker wish to do along with the nightingale?

Pablo Neruda's Odes

Keats is considered the master of the 19th-century English ode. However, the master of the 20th-century ode is Pablo Neruda, who wrote in Spanish.

Neruda was born in Chile in 1904. At sixteen, he was already a published poet. As he grew older, Neruda realized that many of the uneducated poor in Latin America would have trouble understanding his ornate, complicated poems. Yet he wanted to reach everyone. "Poetry is like bread," he said. "It should be shared by all."

So Neruda began writing poems with short lines and vivid images. These new poems were tributes to everyday objects: a hat, a pair of socks, an onion, a tomato. Neruda called them odes. He described a watermelon as "a jewel box of water," and he described fire as "jumpy and blind but with studded eyes." Eventually, Neruda achieved his goal: hundreds of thousands of Spanish-speaking people, rich and poor, came to know and love his poetry.

Connect to the Literature

What sort of people do you think John Keats imagined would read "Ode to a Nightingale?"

Vocabulary
requiem (rek´ wē əm)
n. musical composition honoring the dead

IV

Away! away! for I will fly to thee,
    Not charioted by Bacchus[9] and his pards,
But on the viewless[10] wings of Poesy,[11]
    Though the dull brain perplexes and retards:
35 Already with thee! tender is the night,
    And haply[12] the Queen-Moon is on her throne,
      Clustered around by all her starry Fays;[13]
      But here there is no light,
    Save what from heaven is with the breezes blown
40   Through verdurous[14] glooms and winding mossy ways.

V

I cannot see what flowers are at my feet,
    Nor what soft incense hangs upon the boughs,
But, in embalmed[15] darkness, guess each sweet
    Wherewith the seasonable month endows
45 The grass, the thicket, and the fruit-tree wild;
    White hawthorn, and the pastoral eglantine;[16]
      Fast fading violets covered up in leaves;
      And mid-May's eldest child,
    The coming musk-rose, full of dewy wine,
50   The murmurous haunt of flies on summer eves.

VI

Darkling[17] I listen; and, for many a time
    I have been half in love with easeful Death,
Called him soft names in many a mused[18] rhyme,
    To take into the air my quiet breath;
55 Now more than ever seems it rich to die,
    To cease upon the midnight with no pain,
      While thou art pouring forth thy soul abroad
        In such an ecstasy!
    Still wouldst thou sing, and I have ears in vain—
60   To thy high requiem become a sod.

---

9. **Bacchus** (bak´ əs) in classical mythology, the god of wine, who was often represented in a chariot drawn by leopards ("pards").
10. **viewless** invisible.
11. **Poesy** poetic fancy.
12. **haply** perhaps.
13. **Fays** fairies.
14. **verdurous** green-foliaged.
15. **embalmed** perfumed.
16. **eglantine** (eg´ lən tīn´) sweetbrier or honeysuckle.
17. **Darkling** in the dark.
18. **mused** meditated.

VII

Thou wast not born for death, immortal Bird!
No hungry generations tread thee down;
The voice I hear this passing night was heard
In ancient days by emperor and clown:
65   Perhaps the selfsame song that found a path
Through the sad heart of Ruth,[19] when, sick for home,
She stood in tears amid the alien corn;
The same that ofttimes hath
Charmed magic casements, opening on the foam
70   Of perilous seas, in fairylands forlorn.

VIII

Forlorn! the very word is like a bell
To toll me back from thee to my sole self!
Adieu! the fancy cannot cheat so well
As she is famed[20] to do, deceiving elf.
75   Adieu! adieu! thy plaintive anthem fades
Past the near meadows, over the still stream,
Up the hillside; and now 'tis buried deep
In the next valley-glades:
Was it a vision, or a waking dream?
80   Fled is that music:—Do I wake or sleep?

19. **Ruth** in the Bible (Ruth 2:1–23), a widow who left her home and went to Judah to work in the corn (wheat) fields.
20. **famed** reported.

Past the near meadows,
over the still stream,
Up the hillside;
and now 'tis buried deep

Critical Reading

Cite textual evidence to support your responses.

1. **Key Ideas and Details** **(a)** How does the speaker describe his emotional state in stanza I? **(b) Infer:** What appears to have brought on this state?

2. **Key Ideas and Details** **(a)** What wish does the speaker express in lines 19–20? **(b) Compare and Contrast:** What differences does he see between the bird's life and his own that cause him to wish this?

3. **Craft and Structure** **(a) Analyze:** What is the viewpoint from which the speaker describes his surroundings in stanza V? **(b) Connect:** How does this viewpoint reflect the speaker's wish in line 21?

4. **Craft and Structure** **(a) Analyze:** How does stanza VII "answer" stanza VI? **(b) Synthesize:** What similarity between death and immortality does the speaker imply?

5. **Integration of Knowledge and Ideas** By writing a poem full of extreme feeling, is Keats just being dramatic, or is writing such a poem a way of making peace with strong feelings? Explain.

ODE ON A GRECIAN URN

JOHN KEATS

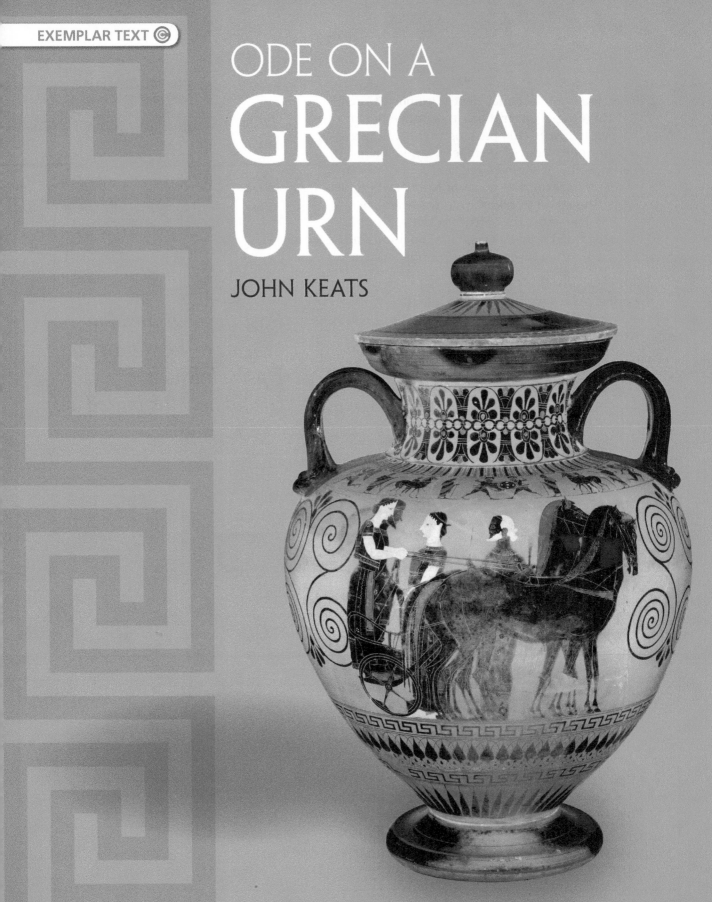

I

Thou still unravished bride of quietness
    Thou foster child of silence and slow time,
Sylvan[1] historian, who canst thus express
    A flowery tale more sweetly than our rhyme:
5 What leaf-fringed legend haunts about thy shape
    Of deities or mortals, or of both,
      In Tempe[2] or the dales of Arcady?[3]
    What men or gods are these? What maidens loath?[4]
    What mad pursuit? What struggle to escape?
10   What pipes and timbrels?[5] What wild ecstasy?

II

Heard melodies are sweet, but those unheard
    Are sweeter; therefore, ye soft pipes, play on;
Not to the sensual[6] ear, but, more endeared,
    Pipe to the spirit ditties of no tone:
15 Fair youth, beneath the trees, thou canst not leave
    Thy song, nor ever can those trees be bare;
      Bold Lover, never, never canst thou kiss,
Though winning near the goal—yet, do not grieve;
    She cannot fade, though thou hast not thy bliss,
20   Forever wilt thou love, and she be fair!

III

Ah, happy, happy boughs! that cannot shed
    Your leaves, nor ever bid the Spring adieu;
And, happy melodist, unwearied,
    Forever piping songs forever new;
25 More happy love! more happy, happy love!
    Forever warm and still to be enjoyed,
      Forever panting, and forever young;
All breathing human passion far above,
    That leaves a heart high-sorrowful and cloyed,
30   A burning forehead, and a parching tongue.

IV

Who are these coming to the sacrifice?
    To what green altar, O mysterious priest,
Lead'st thou that heifer lowing at the skies,
    And all her silken flanks with garlands dressed?

---

1. **Sylvan** rustic, representing the woods or forest.
2. **Tempe** (tem´ pē) beautiful valley in Greece that has become a symbol of supreme rural beauty.
3. **Arcady** (är´ kə dē) region in Greece that has come to represent supreme pastoral contentment.
4. **loath** unwilling.
5. **timbrels** tambourines.
6. **sensual** involving the physical sense of hearing.

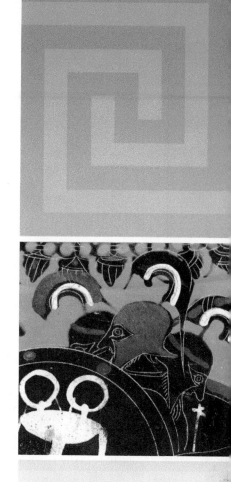

Literary Analysis
The Ode
What two figures on Keats's urn are directly addressed in stanza II?

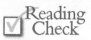

Reading
Check

Describe two scenes depicted on the urn.

◀ **Critical Viewing**
What stories can you see in the picture above and in the picture decorating the urn to the left? **[Speculate]**

Literary Analysis
The Ode
What do the speaker's
questions reveal about his
feelings or personality?

35 What little town by river or seashore,
        Or mountain-built with peaceful citadel,
            Is emptied of this folk, this pious morn?
    And, little town, thy streets forevermore
        Will silent be; and not a soul to tell
40   Why thou art desolate, can e'er return.

                            V

    O Attic[7] shape! Fair attitude! with brede[8]
        Of marble men and maidens overwrought,[9]
    With forest branches and the trodden weed;
        Thou, silent form, dost tease us out of thought
45 As doth eternity: Cold[10] Pastoral!
        When old age shall this generation waste,
            Thou shalt remain, in midst of other woe
    Than ours, a friend to man, to whom thou say'st,
        "Beauty is truth, truth beauty,"—that is all
50   Ye know on earth, and all ye need to know.

___

7. **Attic** Attica was the region of Greece in which Athens was located; the art of the region
   was characterized by grace and simplicity.
8. **brede** interwoven pattern.
9. **overwrought** adorned with.
10. **Cold** unchanging.

Critical Reading

Cite textual
evidence to
support your
responses.

1. **Key Ideas and Details** **(a)** Describe the scenes in stanzas I and II. **(b) Infer:** Why might the lover in stanza II grieve? **(c) Interpret:** Why does the speaker advise him not to grieve?

2. **Key Ideas and Details** **(a)** Which items are called "happy" in stanza III? **(b) Infer:** What is the reason for their happiness?

3. **Key Ideas and Details** **Infer:** What do the speaker's comments on these painted scenes indirectly suggest about real life?

4. **Key Ideas and Details** **(a) Interpret:** In line 49, what is the "truth" represented by the scenes on the urn? **(b) Connect:** How is this truth connected to the fact that the urn will remain after "old age shall this generation waste"? **(c) Make a Judgment:** Is the truth of the urn the "whole truth"? Explain.

5. **Integration of Knowledge and Ideas** In what ways are these poems traditional odes? In what ways has Keats personalized them? In your response, use at least two of these Essential Question words: *authentic, conventional, interpretation.* *[Connecting to the Essential Question: What is the relationship of the writer to tradition?]*

Literary Analysis

1. Craft and Structure **(a)** Identify the rhyme scheme of stanza I of "Ode on a Grecian Urn." **(b)** Is this rhyme scheme used throughout the poem? **(c)** Classify the **ode** as **Pindaric, Horatian,** or **irregular.** Then, explain your choice.

2. Craft and Structure What phrase does Keats use to directly address his subject in stanza I of "Ode to a Nightingale"? Identify another such phrase in the poem.

3. Key Ideas and Details **(a)** What do Keats's two odes honor? **(b)** Would you say he treats his subjects with heightened emotion? Why or why not?

4. Integration of Knowledge and Ideas What artifacts of today would speak most to the future about our culture, as the urn speaks of ancient Greece? Why?

5. Comparing Literary Works **(a)** Compare the speaker's attitude—wonder? fear? longing?—in each ode. **(b)** In each, an object or event represents something that the speaker desires but does not and perhaps cannot possess. Support this generalization with details from the poems.

6. Comparing Literary Works Both "Ode to a Nightingale" and "Ode on a Grecian Urn" show a speaker caught between eternal beauty and the realities of life. Using a chart like the one shown, collect details from each ode that compare the relationship between the eternal and the world of time.

Speaker's Attitude

Eternal World

World of Time

7. Comparing Literary Works Explain how each ode contributes to the idea that a person's self is defined by his or her deepest conflicts.

8. Comparing Literary Works In what ways are Keats's two sonnets as dramatic as his odes? Cite specific passages to support your points.

Reading Strategy

9. Paraphrase lines 9–10 from "Chapman's Homer."

10. Paraphrase at least one passage that you find difficult in stanza VII of "Ode to a Nightingale."

11. Suppose you are telling a friend about Keats's sonnet "When I Have Fears." Paraphrase lines of the poem to explain to your friend exactly what Keats fears.

Common Core State Standards

Writing
9.a. Apply *grades 11–12 Reading standards* to literature. [RL.11-12.5] *(p. 894)*

Language
5. Demonstrate understanding of figurative language, word relationships, and nuances in word meanings. *(p. 894)*

Integrated Language Skills

© Vocabulary Acquisition and Use

Word Analysis: Multiple Meanings

Some words have both a literal and a figurative meaning. Literally, *vintage* is "wine of a particular place and season." Figuratively, though, the word *vintage* means "of a particular era" or "best of its class." As you can see, the figurative meaning draws on the literal one. Identify the figurative meaning of each word below and explain how it is related to the literal meaning. Consult a dictionary to verify your answers. Then, write two sentences for each word, one illustrating the literal meaning and one the figurative.

1. lamb, *n.*
2. varnish, *v.*
3. flak, *n.*
4. mouthpiece, *n.*
5. dim, *adj.*

Vocabulary: Sentence Completion

Using words from the vocabulary list on page 880, complete the sentences below. Use each word once. If necessary, change its form. Then, write original sentences with each word.

1. The storage room was _____ with supplies.
2. Despite the evidence, he remained convinced that his initial _____ was correct.
3. At the funeral, the organist played a mournful _____.
4. There are many mysteries beyond our _____.
5. The wine collector carefully organized his bottles according to _____.
6. At harvest time, the birds _____ stray grain from the reaped fields.

Writing

© **Explanatory Text** Critics David Perkins and Walter Jackson Bate have pointed to the dramatic quality of Keats's odes, a quality also found in his lyrics. Write an **essay** analyzing how Keats uses *imagery, personification, figures of speech,* and *sound* to structure his poems, setting up dramatic situations and evoking readers' emotions. Bear in mind that drama springs from internal or external conflicts.

Prewriting Take notes on the poems, recording examples of the kinds of dramatic images and situations Keats presents. Annotate your notes to show how he evokes emotions. Then, use your notes to formulate a thesis statement.

Drafting Write your essay, explaining the techniques Keats uses and the effects they have. To make your essay more coherent, organize it to follow the sequence of ideas in your thesis statement.

Model: Annotating Notes

Words or Passage	Comment
"Looked at each other with a wild surmise— / Silent, upon a peak in Darien." ("Chapman's Homer," lines 13–14)	Dramatic image: men stunned into silence by what they see.

Taking specific notes will help your writing flow more easily.

Revising Revise your draft to make sure you have organized it well, clearly stated your points, and supported your ideas with *accurate and detailed references* to the text.

The Reaction to Society's Ills

Primary Sources

Parliamentary Debate
Speech by Lord John Russell
Speech by Sir Robert Peel

Letter
Thomas Babington Macaulay to Thomas Flower Ellis

Common Core State Standards

Reading Informational Text
4. Determine the meaning of words and phrases as they are used in a text, including figurative, connotative, and technical meanings; analyze how an author uses and refines the meaning of a key term or terms over the course of a text.
6. Determine an author's point of view or purpose in a text in which the rhetoric is particularly effective, analyzing how style and content contribute to the power, persuasiveness, or beauty of the text.

About the Text Forms

A **debate** is a formal argument in which speakers with opposing views try to persuade an audience to support their positions. Debates follow rules, especially if they take place in a legislative body like Parliament.

Those who viewed parliamentary proceedings might provide an eyewitness account of them in a **letter.** Such a communication can provide insights into public opinion as well as the writer's own views.

Reading Strategy

A speaker or author arguing for a position may use *rhetorical devices.*
Analyzing rhetorical devices like these will help you understand how authors try to make their case:

- *charged language and imagery:* words that carry strong emotional associations and stir up the audience's feelings
- *parallelism:* similar ideas expressed in similar grammatical forms
- *dramatic alternatives:* the posing of sharply contrasting alternatives
- *allusions:* references to well-known people, places, and events

As you read, notice how the two debaters and Macaulay use rhetorical devices to clarify their ideas, make them memorable, and engage the audience's emotions.

To fully appreciate rhetoric, first clarify the meaning of the writer's words:

- Be sensitive to word *connotations*—the positive or negative associations of words.
- Interpret words used in a *figurative sense,* such as *similes* (comparisons of unlike things using *like* or *as*).
- Consult references to determine the meaning of *technical terms*—terms specific to a discipline or profession, such as politics.

How does literature **shape or** reflect *society?*

Lord Russell and Sir Robert Peel were on opposite sides of the debate on the First Reform Bill. As you read, consider how the two served as spokesmen for different social interests. Also consider how the outcome of their argument, as reflected in Macaulay's letter, affected their society.

Note-Taking Guide

Primary source documents are a rich source of information for researchers. As you read these documents, use a note-taking guide like this one to organize relevant and accurate information.

1 Type of Document (check one)

☐ Newspaper   ☐ Letter   ☐ Diary   ☐ Map   ☐ Speech   ☐ Government Form

☐ Advertisement   ☐ Memorandum   ☐ Other (Specify) _____

2 Date of Document _____

3 Author _____

Author's Position _____

4 Original Audience _____

5 Purpose and Importance

  a How does the author try to persuade his audience? ◀·······················

  Write down two details that support your answer. _____

  _____

  b List two important ideas, statements, or observations from this document. ___

  _____

  _____

  c What does this document show about life in the time and place in which it

  was written? _____

  _____

  _____

Reading Strategy

Analyzing Rhetorical Devices As you read, analyze rhetorical devices that authors of public documents, or of private documents relating to public issues, use to support their positions.

This guide was adapted from the **U.S. National Archives** document analysis worksheet.

Vocabulary

measure (mezh´ ər) *n.* a bill, resolution, or something else proposed or enacted to improve a situation (p. 900)

grievances (grēv´ əns əz) *n.* circumstances that cause people to complain (p. 900)

electors (ē lek´ tərz) *n.* those who vote (p. 900)

constituency (kən stich´ ōō ən sē) *n.* the people making up a body of voters (p. 901)

extravagant (ek strav´ ə gənt) *adj.* going beyond reasonable limits; excessive (p. 902)

reverence (rev´ ər əns) *n.* deep respect (p. 902)

inauspicious (in´ ô spi´ shəs) *adj.* not promising a good outcome; unfavorable (p. 904)

orthodox (ôr´ thə däks´) *adj.* conforming to established beliefs (p. 907)

THE STORY BEHIND THE DOCUMENTS

Lord John Russell

Sir Robert Peel

Thomas Babington Macaulay

Lord John Russell (1792–1878) was the British statesman who introduced the Reform Bill of 1832 in Parliament. A champion of reform, Lord Russell was a leading member of the Whig party when it came to power in 1830 with Lord Grey as prime minister. Some years later, after the Whigs had evolved into the Liberal party, Russell himself served twice as Britain's prime minister. Among his later achievements was passage of a law limiting factory labor to ten hours a day.

Sir Robert Peel (1788–1850) helped lead the Tory party opposition to the Reform Bill of 1832. Peel later served as prime minister twice, first from 1834 to 1835 and later, after reorganizing the Tories as the modern Conservative party, for a much longer period in the 1840s. In 1829, while serving as home secretary in a Tory administration, he established London's police force, whose members are nicknamed "bobbies" in his honor.

Thomas Babington Macaulay (1800–1859) was a well-known nineteenth-century historian and literary critic. Trained as a lawyer, he was also a Whig member of Parliament who, like Lord Russell, spoke in favor of the Reform Bill of 1832. Macaulay first won literary fame with an essay on John Milton. His influential five-volume *History of England* (1849–1861) offered a Whig interpretation of British history, stressing the value of gradual democratic reform.

The Industrial Revolution brought great change to Britain. Large chunks of the population shifted from rural areas to newly emerging urban centers, where the middle class grew and prospered. Britain's political landscape, however, had not changed with the times. Sparsely populated rural areas had disproportionately large representation, while booming new industrial cities like Manchester had none. Some seats in Parliament were completely controlled by a single nobleman or by small self-interested groups. Additionally, landholding and financial restrictions kept much of the population from voting. The result was a Parliament that strongly favored the interests of landowners at the expense of everyone else. The Reform Bill of 1832—often called the First Reform Bill—was an attempt to correct that situation.

▶ **Primary Source: Photography** How does the arrangement of seats in the House of Commons suggest the idea of opposed parties? **[Analyze]**

SPEECH IN FAVOR OF REFORM

Lord John Russell

BACKGROUND When the Whigs came to power in 1830, the number one issue on the party's agenda was reform of Britain's election system. To that end, Lord Russell first proposed the Reform Bill on March 1, 1831. The Tory party opposed the bill, with Sir Robert Peel speaking effectively against it. Extracts from both those speeches are presented here.

On the second reading, the bill passed Parliament's House of Commons by just one vote. Recognizing the need for a greater majority, Lord Grey, the Whig prime minister, dissolved Parliament and called for a new election. The Whigs now won many more seats, and the Reform Bill readily passed in the House of Commons—but it was still rejected in Parliament's other chamber, the House of Lords. Finally, the prime minister forced King William IV to name several new members to the House of Lords—members sympathetic to the reforms—and in July of 1832 the bill passed both Houses of Parliament and became law.

Interior of the Commons Chambers Houses of Parliament, Westminster, United Kingdom

Vocabulary

measure (mezh´ ər) *n.* a bill, resolution, or something else proposed or enacted to improve a situation

grievances (grēv´ əns əz) *n.* circumstances that cause people to complain

Reading Strategy

Analyzing Rhetorical Devices Identify the emotionally charged language in the first paragraph of Russell's speech.

An announcement for the first election following the passage of the Reform Bill

AN ACCOUNT

OF

The Proceedings

AT THE

ELECTION OF MEMBERS

FOR THE BOROUGH OF

BURY ST. EDMUND'S,

DEC. 13 AND 14, 1832;

BEING THE FIRST ELECTION FOR THE BOROUGH SINCE THE PASSING OF THE
"ACT FOR AMENDING THE REPRESENTATION OF THE PEOPLE."

BURY ST. EDMUND'S:
PRINTED AND PUBLISHED BY WALTER B. FROST.

MDCCCXXXIII.

I come now to the utmost difficult part of this subject—the explanation of the measure, which, representing the King's Ministers,[1] I am about to propose to the House. . . . The chief grievances of which the people complain are these;—First, the nomination of Members by individuals. Second, the Elections by close Corporations;[2] third, the Expense of Elections. With regard to the first—the nomination by individuals—it may be exercised in one of two ways; either over a place containing scarcely any inhabitants, and with a very extensive right of election, or over a place of wide extent and numerous population, but where the franchise[3] is confined to very few residents. . . . We have addressed ourselves to both these evils, because we have thought it essential to apply a remedy to both; but they must, of course, be dealt with in different ways. With regard to Boroughs[4] where there are scarcely any inhabitants, . . . , it would be evidently a mere farce to take away the right from the person exercising it, and to give it to the borough; and the only Reform that can be justly recommended is, to deprive the borough of its franchise altogether. . . .

But, as I have already said, we do not mean to allow that the remaining boroughs should be in the hands of select Corporations—that is to say, in the possession of a small number of persons, to the exclusion of the great body of the inhabitants, who have property and interest in the place represented. . . . We therefore propose that the right of voting shall be given to householders paying rates[5] for, or occupying a house of, the yearly value of £10. and upwards. Whether he be the proprietor, or whether he only rent the house, the person rated will have the franchise, upon certain conditions hereafter to be named. At the same time, it is not intended to deprive the present electors of their privilege to vote, provided they be resident.

With regard to non-residence, we are of the opinion that it produces much expense, that it is the cause of a great deal of bribery, and that it occasions such manifold and manifest evils, that electors who do not live in a place ought not to be permitted to retain their votes. . . .

Vocabulary

electors (ē lek´ tərz) *n.* those who vote

1. **King's Ministers** Having won the last election, members of Parliament from the Whig party become the King's ministers, taking charge of the different departments of government.
2. **close Corporations** small unelected groups of influential people who controlled all the votes in nearly 200 voting districts.
3. **franchise** (fran´ chīz´) *n.* the right to vote.
4. **Boroughs** (bʉr´ ōz) *n.* towns or voting districts that send members to Parliament.
5. **rates** *n.* local property taxes.

I now beg leave to direct the attention of the House to that part of the plan which relates to the expense of long-protracted Polls, and which, while it removes that evil also greatly facilitates the collection of the sense of the elective body. The names of electors are to be enrolled, by which means we hope that the disputes regarding qualification will be in a great measure avoided. We propose that all electors in counties, cities, towns, or boroughs, shall be registered. . . . These regulations are extremely simple, and will prevent all those vexatious and noisy scenes now so often witnessed, regarding disputed votes.

The means of ascertaining who are the electors being made thus easy, there will be no reason why the poll should be kept open for eight days, or for a longer period; and it is proposed that, nearly according to the present law, booths shall be erected for the voters of the different parishes, so that the whole poll may be taken in two days. . . . With respect to the manner of proceeding at Elections, we have it in view to introduce a measure which can hardly fail to be an improvement of the present system. Everybody knows, and must have lamented the enormous expense to which candidates are put in bringing voters to the poll. An election in Yorkshire has been known to cost nearly £150,000; and in Devonshire some of the electors are obliged to travel forty miles over rough cross-roads, which occupies one day; the next is consumed in polling, and the third in returning home; the whole scheme being a manifest source of vast expense, and most inconvenient delay. We propose, therefore, that the poll shall be taken in separate districts, into which the counties are to be divided, those districts to be arranged according to circumstances by the Magistrates at Quarter Sessions. . . .[6]

It is my opinion, therefore, that the whole measure will add to the constituency of the Commons House of Parliament, about half a million of Persons, and these all connected with the property of the country, having a valuable stake amongst us, and deeply interested in our institutions. They are the persons on whom we can depend in any future struggle in which this nation may be engaged, and who will maintain and support Parliament and the Throne in carrying that struggle to a successful termination. I think that those measures will produce a further benefit to the people, by the great incitement which it will occasion to industry and good conduct. For when a man finds, that by industrious exertion, and by punctuality, he will entitle himself to a place in the list of voters, he will have an additional motive to improve his circumstances, and to preserve his character amongst his neighbors. I think, therefore, that in adding to the constituency, we are providing for the moral as well as for the political improvement of the country. . . .

---

6. **Magistrates** (maj´ is trāts *or* trits) **at Quarter Sessions** judges in English local courts that sit four times a year.

Primary Sources
What do the details in Russell's next-to-last paragraph show about the actual process of holding elections in Russell's day?

Reading Strategy
Analyzing Rhetorical Devices How does the phrase "Everybody knows" help persuade the audience to accept the statement that follows?

Vocabulary
constituency (kən stich´ ōō ən sē) *n.* the people making up a body of voters

Reading
Check
To whom does Russell propose to give the right to vote?

SPEECH AGAINST REFORM

Sir Robert Peel

Vocabulary
extravagant (ek strav´ ə gənt) *adj.* going beyond reasonable limits; excessive

Reading Strategy
Analyzing Rhetorical Devices In referring to the recent revolution in France, to what emotion does Peel appeal? Explain.

I expected that the present ministers would bring in a reform bill on their acceptance of office; but I believe, in my conscience, that the concessions made by them to the popular demands have been far more extensive than was at all necessary. I was not prepared for so extravagant a measure, still less could I have thought that they would venture to bring in so large a measure of reform within three months after they had taken office, and while the country was yet agitated by the events of the French Revolution.[7]

No issue of this discussion can be satisfactory, for, decide as we may, there must be much irreparable evil. I may be obliged to submit by necessity to a plan of reform which I cannot successfully oppose; but believing, as I do, that the people of this country are grossly deceived, grossly deluded, in their expectations of the practical benefits they will derive from reform, I shall not be precluded from declaring my opinion, and opposing that reform as long as I can. . . .

I am satisfied with the constitution under which I have lived hitherto, which I believe is adapted to the wants and habits of the people. I deplore a disposition, which seems too prevalent, to innovate unnecessarily upon all the institutions of the country. I admit, that to serve the sovereign, and the public in an office of honor and dignity, is an object of honorable ambition; but I am ready to sacrifice that object, rather than incur the responsibility of advocating measures which, I believe on my conscience, will tend to the destruction of the best interests of the country. I will continue my opposition to the last, believing, as I do, that this is the first step, not directly to revolution, but to a series of changes which will affect the property, and totally change the character, of the mixed constitution of this country. . . .

Primary Source
Debate What position on the Reform Bill does Peel state in his last paragraph?

On this ground I take my stand, not opposed to a well-considered reform of any of our institutions which need reform, but opposed to this reform in our constitution, because it tends to root up the feelings of respect, the feelings of habitual reverence and attachment, which are the only sure foundations of government. . . .

Vocabulary
reverence (rev´ ər əns) *n.* deep respect

---

7. French Revolution a second revolution in France, which took place in 1830 and replaced the reactionary monarch Charles X with Louis-Philippe, Duke of Orleans.

▲ **Primary Source: Artifact** Why might this ceremonial mace, which is carried into the House of Commons each day, be an effective symbol of the authority of the Crown and Parliament? **[Analyze]**

▲ **Primary Source: Art** In the 18th century, British artist William Hogarth created a series of paintings satirizing corrupt politicians. Which details in this depiction of a tavern dinner attended by Whig candidates serve Hogarth's satiric purpose? **[Infer]**

ON THE PASSING OF THE REFORM BILL

Thomas Babington Macaulay

BACKGROUND Macaulay was elected to Parliament in 1830, when his party, the Whigs, began the fight to pass the First Reform Bill. A talented writer and orator, he was in an excellent position to report on the great debate that was raging over the bill. The following letter, written to his good friend and fellow lawyer Thomas Flower Ellis, describes the excitement of the Reform Bill's passage—by just one vote—in Parliament's House of Commons.

Vocabulary
inauspicious (in´ ô spi´ shəs) *adj.* not promising a good outcome; unfavorable

Primary Source
What are two subjects you might learn something about by reading this letter?

Dear Ellis,

I have little news for you, except what you will learn from the papers as well as from me. It is clear that the Reform Bill must pass, either in this or in another Parliament. The majority of one does not appear to me, as it does to you, by any means inauspicious. We should perhaps have had a better plea for a dissolution if the majority had been the other way. But surely a dissolution under such circumstances would have been a most alarming thing. If there should be a dissolution now there will not be that ferocity in the public mind which there would have been if the House of Commons had refused to entertain the Bill at all.—I confess that, till we had a majority, I was half inclined to tremble at the storm which we had raised. At present I think that we are absolutely certain of victory, and of victory without commotion.

Such a scene as the division of last Tuesday I never saw, and never expect to see again. If I should live fifty years the impression of it will be as fresh and sharp in my mind as if it had just taken place. It was like seeing Caesar stabbed in the Senate House,[1] or seeing Oliver taking the mace from the table, a sight to be seen only once and never to be forgotten. The crowd overflowed the House in every part. When the strangers were cleared out and the doors locked we had six hundred and eight members present, more by fifty five than

---

1. Caesar (sē´ zər) **stabbed in the Senate House** Emperor Julius Caesar, assassinated in the legislative council of ancient Rome.

ever were at a division before. The Ayes and Noes were like two vol-
lies of cannon from opposite sides of a field of battle. When the opposition went out into the lobby,—an operation by the by which took
up twenty minutes or more,—we spread ourselves over the benches
on both sides of the House. For there were many of us who had not
been able to find a seat during the evening. When the doors were
shut we began to speculate on our numbers. Everybody was despond-
ing. "We have lost it. We are only two hundred and eighty at most. I
do not think we are two hundred and fifty. They are three hundred.
Alderman Thompson has counted them. He says they are two hundred and ninety-nine." This was the talk on our benches. I wonder
that men who have been long in parliament do not acquire a better
coup d'œil[2] for numbers. The House when only the Ayes were in it
looked to me a very fair house,—much fuller than it generally is even

▲ **Primary Source
Art** Does Hogarth's
portrayal of voters attending
the polling booth for an
election suggest that the
electoral process is fair?
Why or why not? **[Infer]**

**Reading
Check**

What scene does Macaulay
describe in his letter?

---

2. coup d'œil (kŌŌ dĕy´) glance.

Vocabulary Connection

Government Terms

The following terms in the selection refer to British government:

Parliament the bicameral (two-house) legislative body of Britain

dissolution dismissal of Parliament in order to hold new elections; if major legislation fails, the prime minister resigns and Parliament is dissolved.

House of Commons the house of Parliament made up of elected members and led by the prime minister

House of Lords the house of Parliament whose membership is hereditary or by appointment

mace the symbol of the authority of the Speaker of the House of Commons. By demanding the removal of the mace in 1653, Puritan leader Oliver Cromwell (1599–1658) overrode Parliamentary authority and became virtual dictator of England.

Ayes and Noes respectively, votes in favor of and votes against a bill

tellers those appointed to count votes in Parliament

Connect to the Literature

What effect does a knowledge of the terminology have on your ability to understand the message of this work? Explain.

METROPOLITAN
BOROUGHS.

on debates of considerable interest. I had no hope however of three hundred. As the tellers passed along our lowest row on the left hand side the interest was insupportable,—two hundred and ninety-one:—two hundred and ninety-two:—we were all standing up and stretching forward, telling with the tellers. At three hundred there was a short cry of joy, at three hundred and two another—suppressed however in a moment. For we did not yet know what the hostile force might be. We knew however that we could not be severely beaten. The doors were thrown open and in they came. Each of them as he entered brought some different report of their numbers. It must have been impossible, as you may conceive, in the lobby, crowded as they must have been, to form any exact estimate. First we heard that they were three hundred and three—then the number rose to three hundred and ten, then went down to three hundred and seven. Alexander Baring told me that he had counted and that they were three hundred and four. We were all breathless with anxiety, when Charles Wood who stood near the door jumped on a bench and cried out, "They are only three hundred and one." We set up a shout that you might have heard to Charing Cross[3]—waving our hats—stamping against the floor and

---

3. Charing Cross London neighborhood some distance from the Houses of Parliament.

clapping our hands. The tellers scarcely got through the crowd:—for the house was thronged up to the table, and all the floor was fluctuating with heads like the pit of a theater. But you might have heard a pin drop as Duncannon read the numbers. Then again the shouts broke out—and many of us shed tears—I could scarcely refrain. And the jaw of Peel fell; and the face of Twiss[4] was as the face of a damned soul; and Herries[5] looked like Judas taking his neck-cloth off for the last operation. We shook hands and clapped each other on the back, and went out laughing, crying, and huzzaing into the lobby. And no sooner were the outer doors opened than another shout answered that within the house. All the passages and the stairs into the waiting rooms were thronged by people who had waited till four in the morning to know the issue. We passed through a narrow lane between two thick masses of them; and all the way down they were shouting and waving their hats; till we got into the open air. I called a cabriolet—and the first thing the driver asked was, "Is the Bill carried?"—"Yes, by one." "Thank God for it, Sir." And away I rode to Grey's Inn—and so ended a scene which will probably never be equalled till the reformed Parliament wants reforming; and that I hope will not be till the days of our grandchildren—till that truly orthodox and apostolical person Dr. Francis Ellis[6] is an archbishop of eighty.

---

4. **Twiss** Horace Twiss, another Tory who opposed the bill.
5. **Herries** J. C. Herries, another Tory who opposed the bill.
6. **Francis Ellis** six-year-old son of Thomas Ellis.

◄ **Critical Viewing**
The map shows London electoral boroughs as defined by the Reform Bill. Based on your knowledge of the bill, what can you assume about the voters in these boroughs? **[Apply]**

Vocabulary
orthodox (ôr´ thə däks´) *adj.* conforming to established beliefs

Critical Reading

1. **Key Ideas and Details** **(a)** To what two historic events does Macaulay compare the scene of division he witnessed in Parliament? **(b) Interpret:** What do these comparisons stress about the scene?

2. **Craft and Structure** **(a)** What was the outcome of the vote in the House of Commons for the Reform Bill, as reported by Macaulay? **(b) Analyze:** In what ways does he make the procedure exciting and dramatic?

3. **Integration of Knowledge and Ideas** **(a)** According to Macaulay, what was happening outside the House of Commons during and after the vote? **(b) Infer:** What do these details suggest about the public's view of the vote on the Reform Bill?

Cite textual evidence to support your responses.

Parliamentary Debate • Letter

Comparing Primary Sources

Refer to your Note-Taking Guide to complete these questions.

1. (a) In his opening paragraph, what approach does Sir Robert Peel take to convince others not to support the Reform Bill? **(b)** In contrast, what basic approach does Lord Russell outline in his opening paragraph? **(c)** Which approach seems more effective to you? Why?

2. (a) Using a chart like the one below, compare the language that Russell and Peel use in their speeches. Explain the meaning of technical terms and figurative language and the connotations of charged language. **(b)** In your opinion, which man uses language more persuasively? Why?

Type of Language	Lord John Russell	Sir Robert Peel
Precise (including technical) language		
Charged language		
Imagery and figurative language		
Parallelism		

3. (a) Which rhetorical devices does Macaulay use? **(b)** Compare and contrast his use of these devices with that of the debaters. Does his purpose differ from theirs? Explain.

© Vocabulary Acquisition and Use

Using Context Clues Revise each sentence so that the underlined word is used in a logical way.

1. The miser was typically quite <u>extravagant</u> with his money.

2. Most people show <u>reverence</u> for fools.

3. Her broad grin signaled an <u>inauspicious</u> outcome.

Content-Area Vocabulary For each item, choose the lettered word closest in meaning to the vocabulary word. Explain your answers.

1. electors: **(a)** candidates **(b)** voters **(c)** choices **(d)** elite

2. orthodox: **(a)** disobedient **(b)** spiritual **(c)** open-minded **(d)** conservative

3. grievances: **(a)** complaints **(b)** listings **(c)** armor **(d)** funerals

4. measure: **(a)** conclusion **(b)** question **(c)** remedy **(d)** contract

5. constituency: **(a)** candidates **(b)** voters **(c)** democracy **(d)** election

Etymology Study *Orthodox* combines the Greek word part *ortho-*, which means "straight," with the Greek word *doxa*, meaning "opinion." Someone or something that is *orthodox* conforms to the "straight" or established opinion. Why do you think certain dentists are called *orthodontists?*

Common Core State Standards

Reading Informational Text
8. Delineate and evaluate the reasoning in seminal U.S. texts, including the application of constitutional principles and use of legal reasoning and the premises, purposes, and arguments in works of public advocacy. *(p. 909)*

Writing
7. Conduct short as well as more sustained research projects to answer a question or solve a problem; narrow or broaden the inquiry when appropriate; synthesize multiple sources on the subject, demonstrating understanding of the subject under investigation. *(p. 909)*

9. Draw evidence from literary or informational texts to support analysis, reflection, and research. *(p. 909)*

Language
4.a. Use context as a clue to the meaning of a word or phrase.

Research Task

Topic: The Reform Bill Debate

The debate about reform was a battle between Britain's past and future. Greater representation in Parliament would mean greater economic benefits and more rights for many people, especially city dwellers.

Assignment: Stage a debate on the Reform Bill. Several students should take the roles of debating lords and members of the press, and others should act as the "commoners" who evaluate and judge the proceedings.

The debate on the Reform Bill

Plan your research, gather sources, and synthesize information. As a participant or an evaluator, list questions you need to answer, such as "What were the basic positions on reform?" Then, consult reliable primary and secondary sources, including the speeches and letter on pages 899–907, to gather and synthesize the answers.

Evaluate arguments. Review the arguments for and against reform, noting their strengths and weaknesses. Broaden the debate by consulting important United States works on government, such as the first section of Thomas Paine's *Common Sense*. Compare American arguments with those of the reformers. Debaters may incorporate or answer the strongest of them.

Listen responsively and frame inquiries. Listen carefully and respond effectively, whether as a debater or a member of the press. Take notes to identify the positions taken and the evidence in support of those positions.

Assess persuasiveness and formulate sound arguments. Identify each speaker's strong and weak arguments based on content; diction, or word choice; rhetorical strategies, such as appeals to logic or emotion; and delivery. Use a chart like the one shown.

Model: Questioning a Speaker's Appeal to Logic

Fact	Speaker's Conclusion	My Question
Recent French Revolution	Too soon for major reform in England	Why? Maybe time is just right.

Speak clearly. As a debater, communicate your ideas effectively by using rhetorical devices such as appeals to logic and emotion. Make eye contact and control your speaking rate and volume. Pause for effect. Enunciate words clearly and use purposeful gestures.

RESEARCH TIP

As you do your own research, keep asking yourself, "Is this information my opponent can use against me?" Keep an index of facts and arguments that are "pro and con" (for and against) each issue.

Use a checklist like the one shown to ensure that you have prepared as well as possible.

Research Checklist

☐ Have I answered the basic questions about issues and positions?

☐ Have I gathered information from reliable sources?

☐ Have I organized the information in a useful way?

☐ Have I formulated sound arguments?

☐ Have I anticipated counter-arguments?

Connecting to the Essential Question These authors address issues of women's role in society. As you read, find comments that suggest which of these two authors was more advanced for her time. Identifying such comments will help you answer the Essential Question: **How does literature shape or reflect society?**

Literary Analysis

Social commentary is writing or speech that offers insights into society. Social commentary can be *unconscious*, as when a writer points to a problem caused by social customs without explicitly challenging those customs. The commentary is *conscious* when a writer directly attributes a problem to social customs. As you read these selections, *analyze the political assumptions* about women they expose, consciously or unconsciously.

Comparing Literary Works Austen and Wollstonecraft address widely different audiences for different purposes—Austen writes advice to her niece, and Wollstonecraft seeks to persuade the general reader. Both, however, use **persuasive techniques** that take the following forms:

- *Logical appeals:* arguments based on sound reasoning
- *Ethical appeals:* appeals to authority that establish credibility
- *Emotional appeals:* arguments that engage the reader's feelings

As you read, consider each author's purpose for writing. Then, identify how the persuasive appeals each writer uses reflect and support that purpose.

Reading Strategy

Tone

Reasonable, but also expresses impatience

Background

Author supported equal rights.

Clues in Title

Vindication means "justification."

Writer's Purpose

Effect on Meaning

Preparing to Read Complex Texts To **analyze the author's purpose,** or goals, use background knowledge and clues, such as the work's title. Then, determine how the purpose *affects the meaning* of passages. (Wollstonecraft's purpose explains her "indignation" in the first sentence.) Use a chart like the one shown.

Vocabulary

amiable (ā´ mē ə bəl) *adj.* friendly; agreeable (p. 914)

vindication (vin´ də kā´ shən) *n.* act of providing justification or support for (p. 917)

fastidious (fas tid´ ē əs) *adj.* particular; difficult to please (p. 917)

specious (spē´ shəs) *adj.* deceptively attractive or valid; false (p. 917)

fortitude (fôrt´ ə tōōd´) *n.* courage; strength to endure (p. 918)

gravity (grav´ i tē) *n.* weight; seriousness (p. 918)

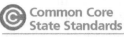

Common Core State Standards

Reading Informational Text
6. Determine an author's point of view or purpose in a text in which the rhetoric is particularly effective, analyzing how style and content contribute to the power, persuasiveness, or beauty of the text.

PHLit Online! www.PHLitOnline.com

Jane Austen *(1775–1817)*

Author of "On Making an Agreeable Marriage"

Modest about her own genius, Jane Austen lived a quiet life devoted to her family. Although she never married, she nonetheless explored love, beauty, and marriage in her six novels, which include *Pride and Prejudice, Emma,* and *Sense and Sensibility.*

A Reserved Life Austen was born in Steventon, Hampshire, the daughter of a clergyman. The seventh of eight children, she was educated largely at home by her father. In her teens, Austen began writing parodies and skits to amuse her family.

An Anonymous Novelist As an adult, Austen put her gift for keen observation to work in her novels. Capturing the absurdities of social life with satirical wit, she makes brilliant observations on human nature. Like most women writers of the time, Austen published anonymously. As her identity became more widely known, she was honored by the Prince Regent a few years before her death.

(1759–1797) Mary Wollstonecraft

Author of *A Vindication of the Rights of Woman*

Mary Wollstonecraft, the mother of writer Mary Wollstonecraft Shelley, is recognized as one of the first major feminists. She wrote revolutionary works attacking the restrictions on women's freedom and education. The movement for women's rights has been influenced by her writings ever since.

A Passionate Educator The daughter of a textile worker and sometime farmer, Mary Wollstonecraft grew up in poverty, yet she pursued an education. She worked at various times as a lady's companion and governess. With her sisters and a friend, she established a girls' school near London. In 1787, she wrote *Thoughts on the Education of Daughters,* criticizing the poor education given to most females of her day.

A Voice for Women In 1790, when the writer Edmund Burke attacked the French Revolution, Wollstonecraft defended it in *A Vindication of the Rights of Man.* Two years later, she produced her most important work, *A Vindication of the Rights of Woman,* a landmark book on women's rights.

On Making an AGREEABLE *Marriage*

Jane Austen

Marriage à la Mode: The Marriage Contract, 1743, William Hogarth, Reproduced by courtesy of the Trustees, National Gallery of Art, London

To Fanny Knight [1]

Friday 18–Sunday 20 November 1814

Chawton Nov: 18.—Friday

I feel quite as doubtful as you could be my dearest Fanny as to *when* my Letter may be finished, for I can command very little quiet time at present, but yet I must begin, for I know you will be glad to hear as soon as possible, & I really am impatient myself to be writing something on so very interesting a subject, though I have no hope of writing anything to the purpose.—I shall do very little more I dare say than say over again, what you have said before.—I was certainly a good deal surprised *at first*—as I had no suspicion of any change in your feelings, and I have no scruple in saying that you cannot be in Love. My dear Fanny, I am ready to laugh at the idea—and yet it is no laughing matter to have had you so mistaken as to your own feelings—And with all my heart I wish I had cautioned you on that point when first you spoke to me;—but tho' I did not think you then so *much* in love as you thought yourself, I did consider you as being attached in a degree—quite sufficiently for happiness, as I had no doubt it would increase with opportunity.—And from the time of our being in London together, I thought you really very much in love.—But you certainly are not at all—there is no concealing it.—What strange creatures we are!—It seems as if your being secure of him (as you say yourself) had made you Indifferent.—There was a little disgust I suspect, at the Races—& I do not wonder at it. His expressions then would not do for one who had rather more Acuteness, Penetration & Taste, than Love, which was your case. And yet, after all, I *am* surprised that the change in your feelings should be so great.—He is, just what he ever was, only more evidently & uniformly devoted to *you*. This is all the difference.—How shall we account for it?—My dearest Fanny, I am writing what will not be of the smallest use to you. I am feeling differently every moment, & shall not be able to suggest a single thing that can assist your Mind.—I could lament in one sentence & laugh in the next, but as to Opinion or Counsel I am sure none will [be] extracted worth having from this Letter.—I read yours through the very even[2] I received it—getting away by myself—I could not bear to leave off, when I had once begun.—I was full of curiosity & concern. Luckily Your Aunt C. dined at the other

---

1. **Fanny Knight** Fanny Austen Knight was the daughter of Austen's brother Edward.
2. **even** evening.

◄ **Critical Viewing** In what ways does William Hogarth's (1697–1764) satirical depiction of the signing of a wedding contract echo attitudes in Austen's letter? **[Compare and Contrast]**

He is just what he ever was, only more evidently & uniformly devoted to you.

Reading Skill
Analyzing the Author's Purpose What is Austen's purpose in claiming she has "no hope of writing anything to the purpose"?

Reading Check
What news from Fanny prompts Austen's reaction?

body else, I do not care.—Poor dear Mr J. P!³—Oh! dear Fanny, Your
mistake has been one that thousands of women fall into. He was the
first young Man who attached himself to you. That was the charm, &
most powerful it is.—Among the multitudes however that make the
same mistake with Yourself, there can be few indeed who have so little
reason to regret it;—*his* Character & *his* attachment leave you nothing
to be ashamed of.—Upon the whole, what is to be done? You certainly
have encouraged him to such a point as to make him feel almost
secure of you—you have no inclination for any other person—His situation in life, family, friends, & above all his Character—his uncom-
monly amiable mind, strict principles, just notions, good habits—*all*
that *you* know so well how to value, *All* that really is of the first
importance—everything of this nature pleads his cause most strongly.—You have no doubt of his having superior Abilities—he has proved
it at the University—he is I dare say such a Scholar as your agreeable, idle Brothers would ill bear a comparison with.—Oh! my dear
Fanny, the more I write about him, the warmer my feelings become,
the more strongly I feel the sterling worth of such a young Man & the
desirableness of your growing in love with him again. I recommend
this most thoroughly.—There *are* such beings in the World perhaps,
one in a Thousand, as the Creature You & I should think perfection,
where Grace & Spirit are united to Worth, where the Manners are
equal to the Heart & Understanding, but such a person may not come
in your way, or if he does, he may not be the eldest son of a Man of
Fortune, the Brother of your particular friend, & belonging to your
own County.—Think of all this Fanny. Mr J. P.– has advantages which
do not often meet in one person. His only fault indeed seems Modesty.
If he were less modest, he would be more agreeable, speak louder &
look Impudenter;—and is not it a fine Character, of which Modesty
is the only defect?—I have no doubt that he will get more lively &
more like yourselves as he is more with you;—he will catch your ways
if he belongs to you. And as to there being any objection from his
Goodness, from the danger of his becoming even Evangelical,⁴ I cannot admit *that.* I am by no means convinced that we ought not all to
be Evangelicals, & am at least persuaded that they who are so from
Reason & Feeling, must be happiest & safest.—Do not be frightened
from the connection by your Brothers having most wit. Wisdom is
better than Wit, & in the long run will certainly have the laugh on
her side; & don't be frightened by the idea of his acting more strictly
up to the precepts of the New Testament than others.—And now, my
dear Fanny, having written so much on one side of the question, I
shall turn round & entreat you not to commit yourself farther, & not

*My dear Fanny,
the more I write
about him the
warmer my
feelings become…*

---

3. **Mr J. P.** Fanny's suitor.
4. **Evangelical** of or relating to a group of earnest Church of England members active in social
   reform movements at the time of the letter.

to think of accepting him unless you really do like him. Anything is to be preferred or endured rather than marrying without Affection; and if his deficiencies of Manner &c &c[5] strike you more than all his good qualities, if you continue to think strongly of them, give him up at once.—Things are now in such a state, that you must resolve upon one or the other, either to allow him to go on as he has done, or whenever you are together behave with a coldness which may convince him that he has been deceiving himself.—I have no doubt of his suffering a good deal for a time, a great deal, when he feels that he must give you up;—but it is no creed of mine, as you must be well aware, that such sort of Disappointments kill anybody.—Your sending the Music was an admirable device,[6] it made everything easy, & I do not know how I could have accounted for the parcel otherwise; for tho' your dear Papa most conscientiously hunted about till he found me alone in the Din^g-parlor,[7] Your Aunt C. had seen that he had a parcel to deliver.—As it was however, I do not think anything was suspected.—We have heard nothing fresh from Anna. I trust she is very comfortable in her new home. Her Letters have been very sensible & satisfactory, with no *parade* of happiness, which I liked them the better for.—I have often known young married Women write in a way I did not like, in that respect.

You will be glad to hear that the first Edit: of M.P.[8] is all sold.— Your Uncle Henry is rather wanting me to come to Town, to settle about a 2^d Edit:—but as I could not very conveniently leave home now, I have written him my Will & pleasure, & unless he still urges it, shall not go.—I am very greedy & want to make the most of it;—but as you are much above caring about money, I shall not plague you with any particulars.—The pleasures of Vanity are more within your comprehension, & you will enter into mine, at receiving the *praise* which every now & then comes to me, through some channel or other.—

> *Anything is to be preferred or endured rather than marrying without Affection...*

---

5. &c &c et cetera (the & symbol, called an ampersand, stands for et, Latin for "and").
6. device trick; ruse; ploy.
7. Din^g-parlor dining room.
8. M.P. Austen's novel *Mansfield Park*.

Critical Reading

Ⓒ **1. Key Ideas and Details** What is the problem Austen is trying to help her niece resolve?

Ⓒ **2. Key Ideas and Details (a)** What qualities does Austen find in Mr. J. P.? **(b) Interpret:** What does she mean by "Wisdom is better than Wit"?

Ⓒ **3. Key Ideas and Details Summarize:** In one or two sentences, summarize Austen's advice to her niece about Mr. J. P.

Cite textual evidence to support your responses.

from A Vindication of the Rights of Woman

Mary Wollstonecraft

BACKGROUND British women in the eighteenth and early nineteenth centuries had few economic or legal rights. In most cases, a woman's property was legally her father's until she married, after which the property became her husband's. Women's education focused mainly on "ladylike" accomplishments such as sewing and music. Women who showed an interest in things beyond marriage and the home were generally regarded as unfeminine. Mary Wollstonecraft focuses on the deforming effects that inadequate education had on women of her time and indicates the larger social forces holding women back.

After considering the historic page,[1] and viewing the living world with anxious solicitude the most melancholy emotions of sorrowful indignation have depressed my spirits, and I have sighed when obliged to confess that either Nature has made a great difference between man and man,[2] or that the civilization which has hitherto taken place in the world has been very partial. I have turned over various books written on the subject of education, and patiently observed the conduct of parents and the management of schools; but what has been the result?—a profound conviction that the neglected education of my fellow creatures is the grand source of the misery I deplore, and that women, in particular, are rendered weak and wretched by a variety of concurring causes, originating from one hasty conclusion. The conduct and manners of women, in fact, evidently prove that their minds are not in a healthy state; for, like the flowers which are planted in too rich a soil, strength and usefulness are sacrificed to beauty; and the flaunting leaves, after having pleased a fastidious eye, fade, disregarded on the stalk, long before the season when they ought to have arrived at maturity. One cause of this barren blooming I attribute to a false system of education, gathered from the books written on this subject by men who, considering females rather as women than human creatures, have been more anxious to make them alluring . . . than affectionate wives and rational mothers; and the understanding of the sex has been so bubbled by this specious homage, that the civilized women of the present century, with a few exceptions, are only anxious to inspire love, when they ought to cherish a nobler ambition, and by their abilities and virtues exact respect . . . .

The education of women has of late been more attended to than formerly; yet they are still reckoned a frivolous sex, and ridiculed or pitied by the writers who endeavor by satire or instruction to improve them. It is acknowledged that they spend many of the first years of their lives in acquiring a smattering of accomplishments; meanwhile strength of body and mind are sacrificed to libertine[3] notions of beauty, to the desire of establishing themselves—the only way women can rise in the world—by marriage. And this desire making mere animals of them, when they marry they act as such children may be expected to act—they dress, they paint, and nickname God's creatures . . . . Can they be expected to govern a family with judgment, or take care of the poor babes whom they bring into the world?

---

1. **the historic page** the record of history.
2. **man and man** used here in the generic sense to mean "human being and human being."
3. **libertine** immoral.

The Literature of Protest
Mary Wollstonecraft writes in the tradition of protest in British literature. As early as the seventeenth century, the poet Amelia Lanier was speaking out for women's rights. In the nineteenth century, the Romantics were urging a fair distribution of wealth and power to the working classes. Twentieth-century poets, including Siegfried Sassoon, would chronicle the horrors of war. In the 1950s, the "angry young men," including Alan Sillitoe, would write grim portrayals of working-class lives. Wollstonecraft was an early voice in this tradition of protest.

Connect to the Literature
Identify four words that suggest Wollstonecraft's attitude of protest. Why do they convey this tone?

Vocabulary
vindication (vin′ də kā′ shən) *n.* act of providing justification or support for

fastidious (fas tid′ ē əs) *adj.* particular; difficult to please

specious (spē′ shəs) *adj.* deceptively attractive or valid; false

Reading Check
According to Wollstonecraft, for what does the "false system of education" train women?

If, then, it can be fairly deduced from the present conduct of the sex, from the prevalent fondness for pleasure which takes place of ambition and those nobler passions that open and enlarge the soul, that the instruction which women have hitherto received has only tended, with the constitution of civil society, to render them insignificant objects of desire—mere propagators of fools!—if it can be proved that in aiming to accomplish them, without cultivating their understandings, they are taken out of their sphere of duties, and made ridiculous and useless when the short-lived bloom of beauty is over, I presume that *rational* men will excuse me for endeavoring to persuade them to become more masculine and respectable.

Indeed the word masculine is only a bugbear;[4] there is little reason to fear that women will acquire too much courage or fortitude, for their apparent inferiority with respect to bodily strength must render them in some degree dependent on men in the various relations of life; but why should it be increased by prejudices that give a sex to virtue, and confound simple truths with sensual reveries?

Women are, in fact, so much degraded by mistaken notions of female excellence, that I do not mean to add a paradox when I assert that this artificial weakness produces a propensity to tyrannize, and gives birth to cunning, the natural opponent of strength, which leads them to play off those contemptible infantine[5] airs that undermine esteem even whilst they excite desire. Let me become more chaste and modest, and if women do not grow wiser in the same ratio it will be clear that they have weaker understandings. It seems scarcely necessary to say that I now speak of the sex in general. Many individuals have more sense than their male relatives; and, as nothing preponderates where there is a constant struggle for an equilibrium without it has[6] naturally more gravity, some women govern their husbands without degrading themselves, because intellect will always govern.

---

4. **bugbear** frightening imaginary creature, especially one that frightens children.
5. **infantine** infantile; childish.
6. **without it has** without having.

Critical Reading

1. **Key Ideas and Details** **Summarize:** According to the author, how do her society's notions of femininity encourage women to be childish and manipulative?

2. **Integration of Knowledge and Ideas** Which author expresses a more radical view of women for her day? In your response, use at least two of these Essential Question words: *independence, values, rebellious.* [Connecting to the Essential Question: How does literature shape or reflect society?]

Literary Analysis

1. Key Ideas and Details What unconscious **social commentary** does Austen's letter offer about the pressures that once limited women's choices?

2. Key Ideas and Details Which social and political assumptions about men and women does Wollstonecraft challenge in *A Vindication of the Rights of Woman*?

3. Key Ideas and Details Which assumptions about men's motives and desires does Wollstonecraft incorporate into her argument?

4. Comparing Literary Works Compare the kinds of appeals used by Wollstonecraft and Austen in a chart like the one shown.

Logic	Ethics	Emotion

5. Comparing Literary Works How does each writer's audience affect her choice of **persuasive techniques?**

Reading Strategy

6. Compare Wollstonecraft's and Austen's purposes in writing, explaining the clues you used to **analyze the author's purpose** in each work.

7. Explain how each author's purpose affected the meaning of a passage.

PERFORMANCE TASKS
Integrated Language Skills

Vocabulary Acquisition and Use

From the vocabulary list on page 910, find a **synonym**—a word with the same or similar meaning—or an **antonym**—a word with the opposite meaning—for each of these words. Then, write an original sentence using each antonym or synonym pair.

1. justification

2. lightness

3. false

4. disagreeable

5. picky

6. cowardice

Writing

Explanatory Text Relatives still give well-meaning advice today, but they are more likely to do so in **e-mails** than in letters.

- Rewrite Austen's letter to her niece as an e-mail, keeping her ideas.
- Update the word choices, syntax, and situation to reflect modern times. For example, consider how you would update this sentence to reflect modern usage: "I read yours through the very even I received it . . . I could not bear to leave off, when I had once begun."

Create a Multimedia Presentation

Multimedia Presentation Written text is only one communication tool. Ideas can be communicated through a wide variety of other media, including film, radio, television, digital technology, and the Internet. In a multimedia presentation, a writer organizes words, images, and sounds into a coherent, informative, and lively presentation of a topic. Follow the steps in this workshop to create your own multimedia presentation.

Assignment Research, draft, revise, and present a multimedia presentation on a topic that interests you.

What to Include Your presentation should have these elements:

- an effective combination of words, images, and sounds
- a clear, consistent organization
- a coherent, well-paced flow of sounds, images, and information
- a variety of media appropriate to each aspect of the topic
- a strong, memorable conclusion
- an overall length of ten to fifteen minutes

To preview the criteria on which your multimedia presentation may be assessed, see the rubric on page 927.

Media Types and Sources

Presentations can include existing media as well as media that you create yourself. When you generate your own media, you begin by using equipment (hardware) to produce the raw material. Then, you use computer programs (software) to edit the media into a final form.

You can use multimedia software to assemble your media elements. Ask your teacher which programs he or she recommends.

Common Core State Standards

Writing
2.a. Introduce a topic; organize complex ideas, concepts, and information so that each new element builds on that which precedes it to create a unified whole; include formatting, graphics, and multimedia when useful to aiding comprehension.

2.b. Develop the topic thoroughly by selecting the most significant and relevant facts, extended definitions, concrete details, quotations, or other information and examples appropriate to the audience's knowledge of the topic.

6. Use technology, including the Internet, to produce, publish, and update individual or shared writing products in response to ongoing feedback, including new arguments or information.

7. Conduct short as well as more sustained research projects to answer a question or solve a problem; narrow or broaden the inquiry when appropriate.

www.PHLitOnline.com

	Sources of Existing Media	Hardware to Generate New Media	Software to Edit Media
text	books, magazines, newspapers, Web sites, CD-ROMs, e-mails	keyboard; scanner; printer	word processor; multimedia software
photographs	books, magazines, newspapers, Web sites, CD-ROMs	digital camera; scanner; printer	photo-editing software
illustrations	books, magazines, newspapers, Web sites, CD-ROMs	keyboard; graphics tablet; scanner; printer	graphics programs
movies	television, DVDs, videos, Web sites, CD-ROMs	digital video camera	digital editor; animation software
sound	radio, CDs, Web sites, CD-ROMs	microphone; digital instruments	sound/music editor

Prewriting and Planning

Choosing Your Topic

Use one of these strategies to choose an appropriate topic:

- **Conduct a media flip-through.** Browse available sources, including magazines, television programs, and the Internet. As you scan for a topic, keep in mind that your presentation should include a variety of media.

- **List and itemize.** Start with a broad category that interests you, such as sports, travel, celebrities, or science. Then, jot down specific ideas that come to mind. Review your list, considering the media you might use to present your ideas. Choose a topic.

Broad Category	Nature
Specific Ideas	National Parks: Yosemite, Zion Canyon, Grand Canyon
Media	slides and video of the park, music, audio of animal sounds park visitors might hear, video interviews
Topic	Zion Canyon National Park: Yesterday and Today

Narrowing Your Topic

Consider time management. Choosing a specific topic can help make your research time more efficient and focused. If your topic is too broad, you might waste time viewing and collecting unnecessary media. For example, "Renaissance art" is too broad because it connects to an overwhelming supply of possible media elements. Instead, choose a specific focus, such as portrait painters or a particular painter, such as Raphael.

Gathering Details

Organize your material. After you have gathered a variety of media, outline your topic. Identify the media elements that best explain, illustrate, or set a mood for each aspect of your subject. Do a rough outline like the one shown, indicating where you expect to use each element.

Renaissance Portraits
I. Raphael
   portraits show individuality
Visuals:
   – portrait of *Castiglione*
Audio:
   – courtly music

II. Later Renaissance Art
   Titian (Venice)
Visuals:
   – map of Venice
Audio:
   – baroque music
   (Bach or Vivaldi)

Drafting

Shaping Your Presentation

Select and position media elements. Your report should present information through both text and media elements. Using a two-column planning chart will help you be sure that you achieve an effective balance.

Text	Audio and Video

Follow a logical flow and focus. Before you draft your presentation, try rehearsing it in your mind to make sure that the ideas follow a logical arc, or overall focus. It can be tempting to include too many media elements. Make sure that each of your elements is genuinely appropriate. Remember your target duration of ten to fifteen minutes. Create a timed outline to plan how much time you will devote to each media element.

Providing Elaboration

Consider variety and flow. As you draft, try to create a varied, interesting experience for your audience. Make sure that your presentation flows logically from idea to idea and that each media element supports the focus and mood. These tips will help you avoid some common problems.

> **Avoid:** a series of photographs showing the same scene from different angles
>
> **Improvement:** a photograph of a scene, followed by a map showing the scene's location
>
> **Avoid:** one song repeated throughout the entire presentation
>
> **Improvement**: shorter music clips that set specific moods

Clarify and frame your media. For each transition you make from your script to a multimedia element, include an explanation so listeners can follow the connection. Transitional clauses such as the following can help you introduce media elements:

- This photograph highlights…
- As this chart indicates…
- In this footage, the speaker makes it clear that…
- This audio clip demonstrates…
- Notice how this diagram connects to the photograph…

Imagine that your media elements are like quotations in a literature essay. Just as you would introduce a quotation, you must also introduce a media element and integrate it into your presentation.

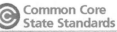
Common Core State Standards

Writing
2.c. Use appropriate and varied transitions and syntax to link the major sections of the text, create cohesion, and clarify the relationships among complex ideas and concepts.

Writers on Writing

Elizabeth McCracken On the Writing Process

Elizabeth McCracken is the author of "Creating a Legend" (p. 728).

I am a very inefficient writer. I do thousands of drafts and throw out a lot of pages. I keep a journal when I write, a place I can play around with ideas, and I often write a page in the voice of a minor character. I tried it with the librarian as I was writing *The Giant's House*. It turned out she wouldn't shut up. She was cranky and talkative and ended up narrating the entire story. The passage here is one of the oldest passages in the book, which is maybe why I'm fond of it. All around it, I tore out pages and pages and pages—I bet I write at least twice as many pages as ever gets into a book—and somehow it always worked.

"I keep a journal when I write, a place I can play around with ideas."

—*Elizabeth McCracken*

from *The Giant's House*

People think librarians are unromantic, unimaginative. This is not true. We are people whose dreams run in particular ways. Ask a mountain climber what he feels when he sees a mountain; a lion tamer what goes through his mind when he meets a new lion; a doctor confronted with a beautiful malfunctioning body. The idea of a library full of books, the books full of knowledge, fills me with fear and love and courage and endless wonder. I knew I would be a librarian in college as a student assistant at a reference desk, watching those lovely people at work. "I don't think there's such a book—" a patron would begin, and then the librarian would hand it to them, that very book.

I worried about what my fellow librarians would make of my librarian, who's pretty stereotypically uptight and tweedy. I tried to make up for it by making her very romantic.

I hear my sentences when I write them, and I love semi-colons—they're just another kind of music.

Sometimes phrases stick in my mind for years before they come out in a book.

Revising

Revising Your Overall Structure

Improve your pacing. Practice your presentation, noting places where your pacing feels too rapid, too slow, or incompatible with the technology you are using. You may need to add more text for clarity or cut a media element that makes your presentation feel choppy.

Student Model: Revising for Smooth Flow

(Cue AUDIO) The pose exhibits the man's elegant manner, his head and hands ~~(Show SLIDE C)~~ placed in the perfectly calm demeanor that a man of his stature would be expected to display *Show SLIDE C; pause, then back to* (Show SLIDE B)	AUDIO: selection from Bach's *Well-Tempered Clavier* SLIDE C: Detail of Castiglione's hands SLIDE B: Raphael's *Baldassare Castiglione* Full length

The student postpones showing Slide C to make the delivery smoother and to provide better pacing for the audience.

Revising Your Media

Evaluate your media and delivery. Rehearsal is vital for a successful presentation. Do a run-through, focusing on smooth oral delivery and accurate matching of media elements to ideas. Become comfortable with your script so that you can maintain eye contact with your audience and not read word for word.

Revise media elements. You may decide to improve media elements to make them more effective. Here are some common revisions:

- Shorten video segments that feel too long.
- Add labels or captions to art to emphasize important ideas.
- Crop photos to focus more closely on the subject.
- Adjust sound levels of audio narration or music.

Peer Review: Hold a test run for a small group. Ask them to use the Evaluation Form shown here. Talk with your viewers about elements that were confusing or ineffective and revise accordingly.

Evaluation

Rate from 1 to 5 (5 = very; 1 = not at all)

____ How clear is the overall focus?
____ How logical is the organization of ideas?
____ How appropriate are the media elements?
____ How smooth are transitions between elements?
____ How effectively is the running time used?

Which media element is most effective?
_____

Which media element is least effective?
_____

What change would most improve the presentation?
_____

Developing Your Style

Integrating Media

It is important that all of the media elements work together. Use a chart like the one shown to help you evaluate the integration of these elements.

Media Element	Idea It Expresses or Supports	Is the idea clear? If not, consider how you can improve the way you handle this element or if you should replace it with something else.
Audio interview with art expert	Titian was a perfectionist. It could take him 10 years to finish a painting.	Clear
Video of people in a museum	Renaissance portraits were made for the wealthy, but today anyone can see them in a museum.	Not very clear; add a line of narration to explain the connection.
Brass theme by Mussorgsky	Raphael's portraits have an elegant simplicity.	This point would be better made with another musical selection, perhaps something by Bach.

Find It in Your Reading

Read or review the Student Model on page 926.

   1. Locate elements of the presentation that work together.

   2. In particular, consider how the audio and video work together.

Apply It to Your Writing

Review the script for your multimedia presentation.

   1. Evaluate each media element you have included in your presentation. Ask yourself, "Why did I include this element?"

   2. Decide whether each element clearly connects to a key idea. Consider adding narration and text labels or changing the order of media elements in order to make the ideas clearer.

   3. Experiment with different combinations of images, music, and text. Preview combinations for a group and see if they work.

> **PH** **WRITING COACH**
>
> Further instruction and practice are available in *Prentice Hall Writing Coach.*

Raphael's Art of the Portrait

Text

[Cue AUDIO.] In the fifteenth and sixteenth centuries, art underwent a drastic change. [Cue VIDEO SLIDESHOW.] Each artist developed a unique style, sometimes blatantly trying to break the rules, other times creating innovative techniques. One common focus for Renaissance artists was the portrayal of individual personality. [Fade music.]

[Cue SLIDE A.] In the Early Renaissance, portraits remained somewhat formal. By the High Renaissance, though, there is a clear focus on the personality of the subject, as in this portrait by Raphael. [Cue SLIDE B; pause.] In this portrait, *Baldassare Castiglione,* every detail helps communicate the subject's inner self. The background remains a stately neutral shade, free of decoration, appropriate for a man such as Baldassare Castiglione, the author of a handbook on genteel behavior.

[Cue AUDIO.] The pose exhibits the man's elegant manner, his hands folded with the composure that a man of his stature would be expected to display. [Show SLIDE C; pause, then back to SLIDE B.]

[Cue MUSIC.] [Cue VIDEO SLIDESHOW.] As this painting attests, Renaissance painters discovered complex ways to give insight into the individuality of their subjects.

Audio and Video

AUDIO: brass theme from Mussorgsky's *Pictures at an Exhibition*
VIDEO: rapid dissolve from one slide to the next: Raphael's *Baldassare Castiglione* to Bronzio's *Portrait of a Young Man* to Titian's *Man with the Glove*

SLIDE A: timeline: Early / High Renaissance
SLIDE B: Raphael's *Baldassare Castiglione*

AUDIO: selection from Bach's *The Well-Tempered Clavier*
SLIDE C: detail of Castiglione's perfectly calm demeanor
SLIDE B

AUDIO: same as at opening
VIDEO SLIDESHOW: same as at opening

Dramatic theme music and a sampling of portraits establish the tone and topic of the presentation.

Transitions and pauses keep the flow of the presentation smooth.

Kate chooses music to reflect the melancholy mood of this portrait.

Information is consistently organized, with each new main idea illustrated by a slide.

Both the audiovisual and textual parts of Kate's conclusion are strong and memorable.

Editing and Proofreading

Check your presentation for errors in grammar, usage, punctuation, and spelling.

Focus on proper nouns and titles. Double-check the capitalization of names and places in your text elements, including labels and handouts.

Focus on spelling. Most words ending with the sound *seed* end with the spelling *cede,* as in *concede.* Three English words end in *ceed: exceed, proceed,* and *succeed.* Review your essay, circling words that end with this sound. Make sure your spelling of these words is correct.

Spiral Review: Conventions Earlier in this unit, you learned about correct subject-verb and pronoun-antecedent agreement. Check your presentation to make sure you have used these conventions correctly.

Publishing, Presenting, and Reflecting

Consider one of the following ways to share your writing:

Stage a showing. Deliver your multimedia presentation to your class. Speak slowly and confidently, and allow time for questions and answers.

Post your presentation. Create a final version of your report using multimedia software and post it to a class or school file-sharing site. If possible, invite visitors to post comments, and address readers' concerns or questions by posting updates with new information or additional arguments.

Reflect on your writing. Jot down your thoughts about the experience of creating a multimedia presentation. Answer these questions: What did you learn about presenting your ideas using audio and visual elements as well as words? What surprised you about presenting material to an audience?

Rubric for Self-Assessment

Evaluate your multimedia presentation using the following criteria and rating scale.

Common Core State Standards

Writing
5. Develop and strengthen writing as needed by editing, focusing on addressing what is most significant for a specific purpose and audience.
6. Use technology, including the Internet, to produce, publish, and update individual or shared writing products in response to ongoing feedback, including new arguments or information.

Language
2. Demonstrate command of the conventions of standard English capitalization, punctuation, and spelling when writing.
3. Apply knowledge of language to make effective choices for meaning or style.

PH WRITING COACH

Further instruction and practice are available in *Prentice Hall Writing Coach.*

Criteria	Rating Scale				
	not very				*very*
Focus: How clearly do all of your media elements present your topic?	1	2	3	4	5
Organization: How well do you organize the presentation of information?	1	2	3	4	5
Support/Elaboration: How well do you integrate video and audio elements to support each aspect of your topic?	1	2	3	4	5
Style: How coherent and well paced is the flow of sound, images, and information?	1	2	3	4	5
Conventions: How correct are the grammar, spelling, and punctuation in your presentation materials?	1	2	3	4	5

Communications Workshop

Analyze a Non-Print Political Advertisement

Common Core
State Standards

Speaking and Listening
3. Evaluate a speaker's point of view, reasoning, and use of evidence and rhetoric, assessing the stance, premises, links among ideas, word choice, points of emphasis, and tone used.

During an election year, you may see advertisements promoting political candidates in many different forms of media. Non-print political advertisements air on television, the radio, and the Internet. Because they reach a vast audience, these ads can exert great influence on voters' decisions.

Identify Purpose of Political Advertising

Learning how political ads are designed will help you make informed political choices. The goal of a political ad, like that of any ad, is to sell something. However, instead of selling a product, a political ad sells a candidate's ideas and image. Political ads create name recognition and cast a candidate in a favorable light—or, in an attack ad, cast an opponent in a negative light.

Negative Techniques Used in Political Ads

Campaign strategists determine advertising tactics based on their candidate's position in the polls. If a candidate is leading, strategists may simply tout his or her accomplishments. When a race is very close, you may see ads using **propaganda,** biased content that damages an opponent's credibility or image. Some ads use **wrong facts** to intentionally misrepresent an opponent's stance on an issue. Other times, ads use **logical fallacies,** appeals that sound convincing but are based on faulty reasoning.

Common Logical Fallacies

Ad Hominem	Bandwagon	Either-Or
Attacking a candidate's character	Appealing to popularity	Offering only two solutions (when more are possible)
"My opponent spent $400 on a day at the spa. How can she understand the issues facing the poor?"	"The police support our candidate. So should you!"	"You can elect our candidate or watch unemployment skyrocket. What's your choice?"

Persuasive Techniques

Other strategies used in a non-print political ad include the following:

- *Editing*: arranging images and sound to create certain effects. A TV clip edited to show a candidate shaking hands with rival politicians creates the impression that he or she can negotiate successfully.
- *Camera Angles:* the direction from which a camera operator shoots images. A low-angle shot makes a person appear tall and confident.
- *Camera Shots:* different ways of framing a subject on camera. A close-up may make an ad feel more personal and intimate.
- *Symbols:* images with positive or negative associations. An ad that depicts a candidate's family suggests he or she understands issues affecting voters with families.
- *Charged Language:* words that carry very positive or negative connotations. A candidate might describe an opponent as a "waffler" to make him or her seem inconsistent.
- *Tone:* the general attitude conveyed by the words used. A phrase like "rising to the challenge" helps create a positive tone.

Activities: Analyze Non-Print Political Ads

ⓒ **Comprehension and Collaboration** For both activities, use an evaluation form like the one shown below.

A. Watch a recent political ad on TV or online. Use the evaluation form to analyze the persuasive techniques included in the ad.

B. Using the Internet, find and analyze two opposing non-print political ads from a historical campaign.

Evaluating a Political Ad

Ad Title:_____

Name of Candidate:_____

Year of Production:_____

Primary Audience [pick one]:   *Sympathetic* □   *Neutral* □   *Hostile* □

What makes you think so?   Tone □   Language □   Images □
   Other _____

Visual and Sound Techniques: Angles □   Symbols □   Charged Language □
   Other _____

Negative Techniques: Yes □   No □
   If Yes, which ones? _____

How many of the claims made in this ad are true? Consult an unbiased
   source to find out._____

Etymology of Scientific, Medical, and Mathematical Terms

During the Renaissance, English scholars gained much of their knowledge on medicine, mathematics, and science from ancient Greek and Roman texts. As they absorbed information from these works, the English naturally adopted many of the words they found. From the Renaissance onward, scholars have used these classical languages to describe new scientific and mathematical discoveries.

Study these other affixes and roots commonly found in science and math.

Common Core State Standards

Language
4.a. Use context as a clue to the meaning of a word or phrase.
4.c. Consult general and specialized reference materials (e.g., dictionaries, glossaries, thesauruses), both print and digital, to find the pronunciation of a word or determine or clarify its precise meaning, its part of speech, its etymology, or its standard usage.

Prefixes	Roots	Suffixes
anthrop- (Greek): human *bio-* (Greek): life *cosmo-* (Greek): universe, world *epi-* (Greek): upon, over *equi-* (Latin): equal *geo-* (Greek): Earth *pseudo-* (Greek): false *quadr-* (Latin): four *thermo-* (Greek): heat	*angle* (Latin): intersecting lines *derma* (Greek): skin *morph* (Greek): form *photo* (Greek): light *pod* (Greek): foot *sphere* (Greek): ball, globe *stell* (Latin): star	*-al* (Latin): characterized by *-ar* (Latin): of or relating to, resembling *-ic* (Greek): of or relating to *-logy* (Greek): science, theory, study *-meter* (Greek): measure *-oid* (Greek): resembling, like *-phobia* (Greek): fear *-ty* (Anglo-Saxon): multiplied by ten

Practice

Directions: Combine the indicated affix or root with others from the chart to create additional terms related to science or math. Define them, using the meanings given in the chart. Check your definitions in a dictionary.

1. thermo
2. bio
3. geo
4. angle
5. sphere
6. anthrop

Directions: Provide an explanation for each question.

7. Why might an amoeba be called a *pseudopod?*
8. What is an *equilateral* triangle?
9. Why might a *photophobic* stay in the dark?
10. How can you protect your *epidermis?*

Vocabulary Acquisition and Use: Context Clues

Context clues are words or phrases that help readers clarify the meanings of unfamiliar words in a text. By using context clues, you can determine the word or words that complete a sentence. Sentence Completion questions appear in most standardized tests. In these types of questions, you are given sentences with one or more missing words. Your task is to choose the correct word or words to complete each sentence logically. Try this strategy: (1) Read the entire sentence and look for signal words that indicate whether a missing word is positive or negative. (2) Scan the answer choices and cross out those that do not fit your criteria. (3) Test the rest of the answer choices in the sentence.

Practice

This exercise is modeled after the Sentence Completion exercises that appear in the Critical Reading section of the SAT.

Directions: Each of the following sentences is missing one or two words. Choose the word or set of words that best completes each sentence.

> **Test-Taking Tip**
> Eliminate words you know are wrong. Test the rest in the sentence to determine what fits best.

1. William Blake studied painting at the Royal Academy yet was not considered one of the ___?___ of art in his time.
   A. sepulchers
   B. roused
   C. arbiters
   D. torrid
   E. morose

2. Blake was a visionary, but he lived in ___?___ conditions, often at the edge of poverty.
   A. sordid
   B. vintage
   C. orthodox
   D. copious
   E. ancestral

3. He existed on meager sales and the ___?___ of his patrons.
   A. reverence
   B. symmetry
   C. mundane
   D. fortitude
   E. recompense

4. Some of Blake's illustrations are childlike and ___?___ while others are marked by ___?___ and darkness.
   A. incitement . . . sinuous
   B. presumption . . . amiable
   C. winsome . . . pathos
   D. avarice . . . ungenial
   E. platitudes . . . teeming

5. Blake used ___?___ brushwork in his precise watercolors to create apocalyptic images, including ___?___, and otherworldly creatures, giving shape to his poetic vision.
   A. stagnant . . . vindications
   B. expiated . . . discretions
   C. blithe . . . requiems
   D. acceded . . . discretions
   E. fastidious . . . phantasms

Test-Taking Practice

Reading Test: Long Reading Passages

The **long reading passages** of standardized tests present more substantial texts that require extended concentration. Passages can be as long as 850 words and can present narrative, persuasive, and expository styles. You should spend more time on answering the questions than reading the passages. You must read purposefully to cover the material, to which you can later return for details.

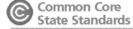
Common Core
State Standards

RI.11-12.1, RI.11-12.2,
RI.11-12.3, RI.11-12.4,
RI.11-12.6; L.11-12.1,
L.11-12.2, L.11-12.3,
L.11-12.4.a
[For the full wording of
the standards, see the
standards chart in the
front of your textbook.]

Practice

The following exercise is modeled after the SAT Long Passage Critical Reading section. This section usually includes 48 questions.

Directions: Read the following passage, taken from *A Vindication of the Rights of Woman* by Mary Wollstonecraft. Then, choose the best answer to each question.

> Indeed the word *masculine* is only a bugbear; there is little reason to fear that women will acquire too much courage or fortitude, for their apparent inferiority with respect to bodily strength must render them in some degree dependent on men in the various relations of life; but
> 5   why should it be increased by prejudices that give a sex to virtue, and confound simple truths with sensual reveries?
>   Women are, in fact, so much degraded by mistaken notions of female excellence, that I do not mean to add a paradox when I assert that this artificial weakness produces a propensity to tyrannize and gives
> 10 birth to cunning, the natural opponent of strength, which leads them to play off those contemptible infantine airs that undermine esteem even whilst they excite desire. Let me become more chaste and modest, and if women do not grow wiser in the same ratio it will be clear that they have weaker understandings. It seems scarcely necessary to say that
> 15 I now speak of the sex in general. Many individuals have more sense than their male relatives; and, as nothing preponderates where there is a constant struggle for an equilibrium without it has naturally more gravity, some women govern their husbands without degrading themselves, because intellect will always govern.

Strategy

Identify opinions.

- **Scan the passage.** Notice "I" statements and charged language. These may indicate opinions.

- **Determine point of view.** Identify what the author wants readers to feel, understand, or do.

- Use this information to guide your answer choices.

1. Which of the following is the best statement of the overall purpose of the author's commentary in this passage?
   A. Most men are stronger than women and thus dominate.
   B. Some women dominate because they are smarter.
   C. Women are held back by a fear of their powers.
   D. Women should become more chaste and modest toward men.
   E. Men fear that women will gain too much strength and courage.

2. Which of the following persuasive techniques does the author employ?
   A. anticipating objections of her male readers and countering them
   B. suggesting that all women believe as she does and so should the reader
   C. offering questionable statistics and facts that support only her opinion
   D. challenging established opinions of both men and women of her day
   E. resorting to name-calling and mud-slinging to provoke male readers

3. In line 2, the word *fortitude* means
   A. attractiveness
   B. intelligence
   C. resistance
   D. weakness
   E. strength

4. Which social issue is this author attempting to address?
   A. forces in society that hold women back
   B. the struggle for equality among women
   C. men using physical force against women
   D. peer pressure on young women of the day
   E. career versus motherhood for young women

5. Which of the following quotations from the passage show the author attempting to persuade her audience?
   A. ". . . their apparent inferiority with respect to bodily strength . . ."
   B. ". . . I now speak of the sex in general . . ."
   C. ". . . there is a constant struggle for an equilibrium . . ."
   D. "Let me become more chaste and modest . . ."
   E. ". . . but why should it be increased by prejudices . . ."

6. Which choice best expresses the main idea of the first paragraph?
   A. Women have very little reason to fear men and should take comfort in their own feminine nature.
   B. Women will never be masculine, but their weaknesses should not be multiplied by turning them into virtues.
   C. Men are prejudiced against the virtues of women and have none of their own.
   D. Women will gradually gain power and courage, which poses a threat to men.
   E. Women lack strength and virtue, and always will.

Grammar and Writing: Improving Sentences

Improving Sentences exercises often appear in the writing sections of standardized tests. The test items show five different versions of a sentence. Your job is to choose the most effective version. This type of exercise tests your ability to recognize and correct flaws in grammar, usage, and sentence structure.

Practice

This exercise is modeled after the Improving Sentences portion of the SAT Writing Section. The full test has 25 such questions.

Directions: Part or all of each of the following sentences is underlined; beneath each sentence are five ways of phrasing the underlined portion. Choice A will always be the same as the original wording; B–E are different options. If you consider the original sentence to be the most effective sentence, select choice A; otherwise, select one of the other choices.

> ### Strategy
>
> ***Rely on your "ear."***
> Say possible choices quietly to yourself and let your natural "ear" for proper grammar distinguish what sounds correct.

1. John Keats's great poem "When I Have Fears" <u>represent his finest work and delight</u> millions of readers.
   - **A.** represent his finest work and delight
   - **B.** represents his finest work and delight
   - **C.** represents his finest work and delights
   - **D.** represent his finest work and delights
   - **E.** have represented his finest work and have delighted

2. <u>Readers of Wordsworth are lovers</u> of Romantic ideals.
   - **A.** Readers of Wordsworth are lovers
   - **B.** One of the readers of Wordsworth are lovers
   - **C.** Readers of Wordsworth is lovers
   - **D.** Reader of Wordsworth is a lover
   - **E.** Readers of Wordsworth is a lover

3. There <u>were, it seems in the varied life of Samuel Coleridge, few accomplishments</u> he didn't achieve.
   - **A.** were, it seems in the varied life of Samuel Coleridge, few accomplishments
   - **B.** were, it seem in the varied life of Samuel Coleridge, few accomplishments
   - **C.** were, it seems, in the varied life of Samuel Coleridge, few accomplishments
   - **D.** are, it seem in the varied life of Samuel Coleridge, few accomplishments
   - **E.** are, it seems in the varied lives of Samuel Coleridge, few accomplishments

4. Lord Byron, while at school, <u>have made friends, has played sports, and spends</u> money like a wastrel.
   A. have made friends, has played sports, and spends
   B. has made friends, has played sports, and has spent
   C. have made friends, have played sports, and spends
   D. made friends, played sports, and spent
   E. make friends, play sports, and spend

5. Percy Bysshe Shelley, <u>born into the British upper classes, were expelled from Oxford University with a friend and were forced</u> to live apart from his family.
   A. born into the British upper classes, were expelled from Oxford University with a friend and were forced
   B. born into the British upper classes, was expelled from Oxford University with a friend and were forced
   C. born into the British upper classes, was expelled from Oxford University with a friend and forced
   D. birthed into the British upper classes, were expelled from Oxford University with a friend and were forced
   E. born into the British upper classes, was expelled from Oxford University with a friend and was forced

6. <u>It were a tragedy that John Keats, like many poets, dies so young and writes</u> his major works in the space of only two years.
   A. It were a tragedy that John Keats, like many poets, dies so young and writes
   B. It was a tragedy that John Keats, like many poets, dies so young and writes
   C. It was a tragedy that John Keats, like many poets, died so young and wrote
   D. It was a tragedy that John Keats, like many poets, dies so young and writes
   E. It is a tragedy that John Keats, like many poets, dies so young and writes

7. *The Prelude*, which many students <u>memorize, and "Ozymandias" are poetry any reader loves</u> for a lifetime.
   A. memorize, and "Ozymandias" are poetry any reader loves
   B. memorizes, and "Ozymandias" are poetry any reader loves
   C. memorize, and "Ozymandias" is poetry any reader loves
   D. memorize, and "Ozymandias" is poetry any reader love
   E. memorize, and "Ozymandias" is poetry any readers loves

⏱ Timed Writing: Position Statement [25 minutes]

Mary Wollstonecraft wrote about the condition of women in the late eighteenth century. At that time few women enjoyed a formal education, and all women lacked basic legal rights. Things are entirely different today.

Write an essay in which you discuss whether education is the key to liberation for an oppressed group of people. You are free to take any side of the issue, but be sure to back up your opinions with observations and reasoning. This assignment is similar to the Essay portion of the SAT Writing Section.

> **Academic Vocabulary**
>
> Your **observations** come from things you have noticed or witnessed. You do not have to cite experts or recognized sources of research to include your observations in your essay.

Performance Tasks

Directions: *Follow the instructions to complete the tasks below as required by your teacher. As you work on each task, incorporate both general academic vocabulary and literary terms you learned in this unit.*

> **Common Core State Standards**
>
> RL.11-12.1, RL.11-12.2, RL.11-12.4, RL.11-12.5; RI.11-12.5, RI.11-12.6; W.11-12.2.a, W.11-12.4, W.11-12.9.a; SL.11-12.1.a, SL.11-12.1.d, SL.11-12.4, SL.11-12.6; L.11-12.3.a
> [For the full wording of the standards, see the standards chart in the front of your textbook.]

Writing

Task 1: Literature [RL.11-12.1, W.11-12.2.a, W.11-12.9.a]
Draw Inferences

*Write an **essay** in which you cite textual evidence to support inferences drawn from a poem in this unit.*

- Explain which poem you chose. Identify the poem's explicit meaning or key idea. Quote from the text to support your point.
- Identify any ideas or emotions that the speaker suggests but does not explicitly state. Cite details from the poem that help you draw inferences about the speaker's unstated ideas or feelings. Explain how you tied these details together to see connections that suggest implicit meanings.
- Discuss ideas or emotions the poem leaves uncertain or open to interpretation. Consider the reasons for and effects of this ambiguity.
- Organize your ideas so that each new idea builds on the one that precedes it to create a unified whole.

Task 2: Literature [RL.11-12.4, W.11-12.9.a]
Analyze the Impact of Word Choice

*Write an **essay** in which you analyze the impact of word choice in a poem from this unit.*

- Choose a poem in which the word choice is particularly interesting to you. Explain which poem you chose and why you chose it.
- Identify at least two words in the poem that carry connotative meanings that are essential to the poet's overall meaning. Explain the shades of meaning each word contributes to the poem as a whole.

- Explain the cumulative, or combined, impact these words have on the tone of the poem.
- Consider how word choices with similar denotations but different connotations would alter the meaning and tone of the poem.

Task 3: Literature [RL.11-12.5, W.11-12.4, L.11-12.3.a]
Analyze Text Structure

*Write an **essay** in which you analyze how a poet's choice of structure adds to the overall meaning and aesthetic impact of a poem in this unit.*

- Choose a poem from this unit in which the structure, or form, plays a key role in developing meaning. Explain which poem you chose and why.
- Analyze how the poet's choices of structure in sections of the poem contribute to the structure of the poem as a whole. Consider line length, rhyme scheme, and stanza lengths and divisions.
- Connect the author's choices concerning structure to the meaning as well as to the aesthetic, or artistic and emotional, impact of the poem.
- Clearly develop and organize your ideas while maintaining an appropriate, consistent style and tone in your writing.
- Vary your sentence length and structure to add interest and sophistication to your writing.

Speaking and Listening

Task 4: Literature [RL.11-12.2, SL.11-12.4]
Analyze Development of Theme

*Deliver an **oral presentation** in which you analyze the development of two or more themes in a poem in this unit.*

- State which poem you chose and briefly explain why you chose it.
- Clearly state the themes of your chosen poem. Discuss specific ways in which the author develops each theme throughout the poem. Identify specific details, figurative language, and images that contribute to the expression of each theme.
- Explain how the themes interact and build on one another as the poem progresses.
- Be sure to develop your ideas fully and present them in logical order.
- As you present, demonstrate your command of the conventions of Standard English grammar and usage. Choose language that expresses ideas precisely and concisely, eliminating wordiness.

Task 5: Informational Text [RI.11-12.6, SL.11-12.6]
Determine the Author's Point of View

*Deliver an **oral presentation** in which you examine the author's point of view, rhetoric, and style in a nonfiction work from this unit.*

- Introduce the work you chose. Explain the author's purpose, topic, and central idea.
- Describe the author's point of view. Explain how the author's stance affects his or her discussion of the topic and helps to shape the central idea.
- Discuss specific aspects of the author's rhetoric and style, explaining how they contribute to the power or persuasiveness of the text. Cite details and examples from the text to support your position.
- Be aware of your own uses of rhetoric and style. Use formal English appropriate to an academic discussion.

Task 6: Informational Text [RI.11-12.5, SL.11-12.1.a, SL.11-12.1.d]
Analyze Ideas or Events

*Participate in a **small-group discussion** in which you analyze the structure of an author's exposition or argument in a nonfiction work from this unit.*

- As a group, choose a nonfiction work from this unit. Prepare for the discussion by working independently to conduct your own analysis of the work.
- Identify the structure the author uses to present ideas. Consider whether the structure involves a formal pattern of organization, such as comparison-and-contrast, or combines various patterns.
- Evaluate the clarity and logic of the structure. Consider how the structure helps or hinders readers' understanding and whether it makes ideas more convincing and engaging.
- Discuss your ideas in a small group. Respond thoughtfully to each other's ideas, and work to resolve any contradictions in your interpretations.

 What is the relationship of the writer to tradition?

The Voice of a Romantic The voice of the Romantic writer is personal, passionate, and dedicated to expressing a personal imaginative vision. That personal vision colors the writer's reflections.

Assignment Write a **composition** in the voice of a Romantic. You may choose the voice of a particular author or any writer of the time. Use the form of an essay, a book introduction, or a letter to a friend.

Featured Titles

In this unit, you have read a variety of literature from the Romantic period. Continue to read works related to this era on your own. Select books that you enjoy, but challenge yourself to explore new topics, new authors, and works offering varied perspectives or approaches. The titles suggested below will help you get started.

LITERATURE

Frankenstein
Mary Shelley

Novel This classic story presents an epic battle between man and monster. Frankenstein, a medical student, fashions a creature from the body parts of the dead and brings it to life, setting in motion a chain of events that brings him to the brink of madness.

[Shelley's introduction to Frankenstein *appears on page 760 in this book. Build knowledge by reading the entire work.]*

Pride and Prejudice
Jane Austen   EXEMPLAR TEXT ©

Novel The setting is the English countryside in the eighteenth century, a world of comfortable homes, tidy fortunes, and respectable families. In this world, Mr. Darcy, handsome and wealthy, would seem to be the ideal match for the charming and pretty Elizabeth Bennet. Their courtship is one of the most treasured love stories of English literature.

The Portable Romantic Poets
Edited by W. H. Auden and Norman Holmes Pearson

Anthology This volume includes works by celebrated British and American poets, such as Robert Burns, William Wordsworth, and Edgar Allan Poe, as well as works by lesser-known writers.

[Poems by Burns and Wordsworth appear earlier in this unit. Build knowledge by reading additional works by these poets.]

The Complete Poetry and Prose of William Blake
Edited by David V. Erdman

Anthology All of Blake's great poetry, including *Songs of Innocence and Experience* and *The Marriage of Heaven and Hell*, appear in this volume. Also included are early poems and many illuminating letters.

[Poems by Blake appear on pages 748–752 of this book. Build knowledge by reading additional poems by Blake.]

INFORMATIONAL TEXT

Historical Texts

A Defence of Poetry and Other Essays
Percy Bysshe Shelley

Essays First published in 1821, "A Defence of Poetry" proclaimed a revolutionary idea—that poets are active political forces, or "the unacknowledged legislators of the world." In these essays, Shelley reflects on the art of poetry.

[Poems by Shelley appear on pages 868–876 of this book. Build knowledge by reading Shelley's essays.]

From Montrose to Culloden: Bonnie Prince Charlie & Scotland's Romantic Age
Sir Walter Scott

History Scott, one of the nineteenth century's most popular novelists, wrote these stories for his grandson. The historical tales bring to life Scotland's colorful and romantic history and feature memorable characters such as Bonnie Prince Charlie and the Duke of Cumberland.

Contemporary Scholarship

The Mirror and the Lamp: Romantic Theory and the Critical Tradition
M. H. Abrams
Oxford University Press, 1971

Scholarship Abrams explains a powerful contrast in the history of literary criticism. Pre-Romantic writers regarded literature as a mirror that reflects the real world. The Romantics, however, saw literature as a lamp that projects the writer's soul.

Romantic Poetry: Recent Revisionary Criticism
Edited by Karl Kroeber and G. Ruoff

Anthology These up-to-date essays reflect key critical views on the English Romantic poets: Blake, Wordsworth, Coleridge, Byron, Shelley, and Keats.

Preparing to Read Complex Texts

Reading for College and Career In both college and the work-place, readers must analyze texts independently, draw connections among works that offer varied perspectives, and develop their own ideas and informed opinions. The questions shown below, and others that you generate on your own, will help you more effectively read and analyze complex college-level texts.

Ⓒ **Common Core State Standards**

Reading Literature/Informational Text
10. By the end of grade 12, read and comprehend literature, including stories, dramas, and poems, and literary nonfiction at the high end of the grades 11-CCR text complexity band independently and proficiently.

When reading complex texts, ask yourself...

- What idea, experience, or story seems to have compelled the author to write? Has the author presented that idea, experience, or story in a way that I, too, find compelling?

- How might the author's era, social status, belief system, or personal experiences have affected the point of view he or she expresses in the text?

- What key idea does the author state explicitly? What key idea does he or she suggest or imply? Which details in the text help me to perceive implied ideas?

- Do I find multiple layers of meaning in the text? If so, what relationships do I see among these layers of meaning?

- How do details in the text connect or relate to one another? Do I find any details unconvincing, unrelated, or out of place?

- Do I find the text believable and convincing?

Ⓒ **Key Ideas and Details**

- What patterns of organization or sequences do I find in the text? Do these patterns help me understand the ideas better?

- What do I notice about the author's style, including his or her diction, uses of imagery and figurative language, and syntax?

- Do I like the author's style? Is the author's style memorable?

- What emotional attitude does the author express toward the topic, the story, or the characters? Does this attitude seem appropriate?

- What emotional attitude does the author express toward me, the reader? Does this attitude seem appropriate?

- What do I notice about the author's voice—his or her personality on the page? Do I like this voice? Does it make me want to read on?

Ⓒ **Craft and Structure**

- Is the work fresh and original?

- Do I agree with the author's ideas entirely or are there elements I find unconvincing?

- Do I disagree with the author's ideas entirely, or are there elements I can accept as true?

- How do the concerns, values, and assumptions of my own era shape my response to the text?

- Based on my knowledge of British literature, history, and culture, does this work reflect the British tradition? Why or why not?

Ⓒ **Integration of Ideas**

Progress and Decline

The Victorian Period

"It was the best of times, it was the worst of times . . . we were all going direct to Heaven, we were all going direct the other way . . ."

- Charles Dickens, from A Tale of Two Cities

PHLit
Online!
www.PHLitOnline.com

Hear It!
- Selection summary audio
- Selection audio

See It!
- Author videos
- Essential Question video
- Get Connected videos
- Background videos
- More about the authors
- Illustrated vocabulary words
- Vocabulary flashcards

Do It!
- Interactive journals
- Interactive graphic organizers
- Grammar tutorials
- Interactive vocabulary games
- Test practice

Snapshot of the Period

The Crystal Palace, on the facing page, is a symbol of Victorian optimism and Victorian faith in progress, technology, and empire. It is true that this period witnessed dramatic technological advances, rapid industrialization, the growth of cities, political reforms, and the development of Britain into a worldwide empire. It is equally true that this era witnessed the spread of poverty, a division of Britain into two nations—one prosperous and the other poverty stricken—and advances in philosophy and science that threatened long-held beliefs. Above all, Victorians were aware that they were living—as a writer of the time put it—"in an age of transition." An old social and political order, dating back to medieval times, was being transformed into a modern democracy. The poet Matthew Arnold expressed the unease of this transition when he described himself as "Wandering between two worlds . . ."

This English cartoon of 1843 reflects the sharp contrast between the rich and the poor. The cartoon was inspired by a government report on the horrific state of workers in coal mines.

As you read the selections in this unit, you will be asked to think about them in view of three key questions:

What is the **relationship**
   between literature and *place?*

How does literature **shape or**
   reflect *society?*

What is the relationship
   of the **writer** to *tradition?*

Integration of Knowledge and Ideas The Crystal Palace (shown here), designed by Sir Joseph Paxton for Britain's Great Exhibition of 1851, was a large structure made of iron and glass. Stunningly advanced for its time, this "palace" housed exhibitions dramatizing the themes of empire and progress. If you were designing a Crystal Palace for today, what materials would you use, what would the structure look like, and what kind of exhibitions would it house?

Interior of the Crystal Palace; notice the glass and iron vaulted roof, advanced for its time.

Displays from Tunis, North Africa; Tunisia, whose capital is Tunis, was a French colony, but Britain was poised to expand its colonial holdings in Africa.

The machinery section; new and powerful machines testified to the Victorian belief in progress.

The stained glass gallery; the Victorian fascination with the Middle Ages prompted an interest in the art of the medieval church, including stained-glass windows.

Historical Background

The Victorian Period (1833–1901)

Queen Victoria's reign (1837–1901) was marked by triumphs and tragedies. The consequences of some of them, like the mixed legacy of imperialism, were felt well beyond her century.

Shy and diminutive, the young queen set out to restore the reputation of the monarchy. Her marriage in 1840 to her first cousin, Albert of Saxe-Coburg and Gotha, whom she loved dearly, was a model of respectability. That quality, respectability, became a very important concept in her time.

Tragedies and Triumphs of Empire

The first blight on her reign came in 1845, when the potato crop failed in Ireland. The Famine grew worse until by 1849, half the population of Ireland had died or gone into exile. The British government did little or nothing for this quarter of the "United Kingdom." The events and the legends of the Famine fueled the hatred and violence in the relations between the British and the Irish for more than a hundred and fifty years.

The high point of Victoria's reign was the Great Exposition in the Crystal Palace, organized by her husband, the Prince Consort, in 1851. Built in a wholly new style, with iron girders holding over a million feet of glass panels, the building was the cathedral of commerce and empire. A combination of world's fair and industrial show, the Exposition trumpeted to the world the achievements of manufacturing England, colonizing England, and self-satisfied England.

Two works published during Victoria's reign proved as powerful as any of the machinery assembled for the Great Exposition. In 1848, as England watched while revolutions convulsed Europe, Karl Marx published *The Communist Manifesto*. This pamphlet warned that there was "a spectre haunting Europe." That "spectre" was communism, with its prophecy of political revolution. The other book, the work of a gentleman scientist who had seen evidence for biological evolution during his long sea voyage on the *H.M.S. Beagle*, was *On the Origin of Species*. Supporters and attackers alike

Queen Victoria

TIMELINE

1833: Slavery abolished in British empire.

1837: Victoria becomes queen. ▶

1839: Michael Faraday offers general theory of electricity. ▼

1832

1836 North America The Alamo falls to the Mexican army. ▶

knew that after Charles Darwin's work, our sense of ourselves and our place in the world would never be the same.

The reform impulse gathered strength throughout the period. Laws regulated the worst abuses of child labor in mills and mines. The Second Reform Bill of 1867 further extended the franchise. The Elementary Education Act of 1870, passed in part to ensure an educated electorate, provided for the education of all children between five and twelve, the first step toward education for all. Nevertheless, poverty continued to be a major problem, especially in rapidly growing cities.

In 1871, Germany, newly unified and serving notice that it was a powerful force in European politics, crushed the French army and occupied Paris. Ominously, Germany began to build a fleet with which to challenge the Royal Navy.

Celebrating Empire

In 1876, Victoria was proclaimed Empress of India. England purchased the Suez Canal from the bankrupt French company that had built it and now had a vital sea link to the vast sub-continent. Few questioned whether it was appropriate for a constitutional monarch to be the Empress of a country half-a-world away. In 1887, Victoria celebrated her Golden Jubilee as queen and the nation rejoiced in fifty years of progress, prosperity and peace. The theme of the Diamond Jubilee in 1897 was The Empire.

When Victoria died in 1901, her eldest son became King Edward VI. His reign proved to be the "Indian summer" of Victorian England. The rise of Germany, France's desire to revenge the defeat of 1871, and squabbles over colonies formed clouds over Europe that would soon thicken and loose the deluge of war that would sweep away all vestiges of Victorian stability.

Key Historical Theme: Imperial Britain

- Under Victoria, Britain's empire expanded, and Britain celebrated progress, prosperity, and peace.
- Darker stories linked to Britain's empire included the Irish Famine, widespread poverty at home, and the rise of Germany as a competing imperial power.

1841 South Pacific
New Zealand becomes
a British colony.

1844 United States
Samuel F.B. Morse sends first
message over a long-distance
telegraph line. ▶

1846

◀ **1843:** William Wordsworth
becomes poet laureate.

◀ **1845: Ireland**
Irish Potato Famine begins.

Essential Questions Across Time

The Victorian Period (1833–1901)

What is the **relationship** between **literature** and *place?*

What was the reach of the United Kingdom's empire?

Imagine a map of the world in 1897, Queen Victoria's Diamond Jubilee year, her sixtieth as queen. The British Empire, centered in the United Kingdom of Great Britain and Ireland, covered the globe. Starting from Great Britain (England, Scotland, and Wales), take an imaginary tour of the Empire. Sail a little to the west to reach Ireland. Then, sail across the Atlantic Ocean, to the vast expanse of Canada. Next, sail southward to the islands of the Caribbean. Continuing southward, pass the Falkland Islands and, rounding Cape Horn at the tip of South America, cross the Pacific Ocean to reach New Zealand and Australia. Traveling northward, dock at the beautiful harbor of Hong Kong. Then, turn southward to reach India, which includes what we now know as India, Pakistan, and Bangladesh. Traveling westward brings you to Africa, where there is almost enough continuous British territory for someone to dream of a railroad connecting Cape Town in South Africa with Cairo in Egypt. Finally, your tour takes you through the British-owned Suez Canal to the Mediterranean, past Gibraltar, and northward back to Britain.

The British flag flew over forty percent of the earth's land, and the Royal Navy patrolled and controlled all the oceans of the world.

How was the spirit of empire reflected in Victorian literature?

Restless Spirit The poem "Ulysses," by Victorian poet Alfred, Lord Tennyson, makes no mention of England or empire, yet it still captures the spirit that produced an empire. Ulysses is the wandering hero of Homer's

> ### ESSENTIAL QUESTION VOCABULARY
>
> These Essential Question words will help you think and write about literature and place:
>
> **empire** (em´ pīr´) *n.* extensive territory and many peoples under the control of a single country or power
>
> **conquest** (kän´ kwest´) *n.* act of taking control of a people or territory, especially in war
>
> **missionary** (mish´ ən er´ ē) *n.* religious person who cares for others, usually in another country, and tries to teach them his or her religion

TIMELINE

1846

1848 Belgium
Marx and Engels publish *The Communist Manifesto.* ▶

1848: Women begin attending University of London.

1853 Eastern Europe
Crimean War begins. ▶

1854 Japan
Trade with West reopened. ▶

Odyssey who finally makes it home and reclaims his kingdom. In later legends, he is depicted as having had so many adventures that he cannot settle down to ordinary life. In these legends, he sails beyond the Pillars of Hercules, the Straits of Gibraltar, into the unknown sea. In Dante's medieval epic, the *Divine Comedy*, Ulysses is in hell, punished for his sin of going beyond an established boundary. To go beyond a limit—in Dante's structured, medieval world—was a grave sin. In Tennyson's fluid Victorian world, to accept a limit was a grave sin. The restless spirit that can never stop exploring, glorified in Tennyson's poem, is the spirit that created an empire.

Even a novel like Charlotte Brontë's *Jane Eyre*, set entirely in England, is connected with empire. When Jane Eyre grows up, she rejects one suitor who wants her to go with him as a missionary to India. She falls in love with the dark, brooding, Byronic Mr. Rochester, who has come back from Jamaica with a fortune and a terrible secret.

Empire's Poet The poet of empire was Rudyard Kipling. Born to British parents in India, he made that country, which he loved, vivid to his countrymen in poems and his panoramic novel *Kim*. Kipling delighted in describing British soldiers, the "Tommies," the thin, red line of heroes who carried the empire on their shoulders. In "The Widow at Windsor," one of those soldiers speaks of his pride and his problems in her service. "Recessional" is Kipling's own solemn warning against the arrogance of power.

The BRITISH TRADITION

CLOSE-UP ON ART

The Values of Empire and the Values of Art

While the British empire thrived on progress and expansion, an avant-garde group of Victorian painters sought purity and inward focus by moving backward in time. This group, founded by the painter and poet Dante Gabriel Rossetti (1828–1882), called itself the Pre-Raphaelite Brotherhood. Its members found inspiration in the Gothic style of the Middle Ages, before the time of the Renaissance painter Raphael (hence the group's name). Rossetti is known especially for his portraits of women, such as the one shown here. These portraits emphasize color, texture, and an earthy or sadly spiritual feminine beauty.

Critical Viewing Could this portrait by Rossetti, entitled *Day Dream*, be regarded as a comment on the Victorian belief in empire and progress? Why or why not?

1855: London sewers modernized after outbreak of cholera.

◄ **1857 India** Sepoy Mutiny against British.

1859: Charles Darwin publishes *On the Origin of Species*. ▲

1860

How does literature **shape or reflect** *society?*

"It was the best of times, it was the worst of times…." That is how Charles Dickens begins his novel of the French Revolution, *A Tale of Two Cities*. He goes on to say that this is also true of Victorian England. He knew what he was talking about, and it is helpful to follow Dickens's words as a guide to the contradictions of Victorian society:

". . . it was the age of wisdom, it was the age of foolishness, it was the epoch of belief, it was the epoch of incredulity, it was the season of Light, it was the season of Darkness, it was the spring of hope, it was the winter of despair, we had everything before us, we had nothing before us, we were all going direct to Heaven, we were all going direct the other way . . ."

How did literature reflect Victorian contradictions?

"best of times" Sydney Smith's essay "Progress in Personal Comfort" lists some of the creature comforts invented in his lifetime. More important, however, is the attitude behind the essay: Life is getting better for more and more people. That optimistic spirit helped England make peaceful progress while Europe was torn by revolutions, assassinations, and war.

"worst of times" In the Irish Famine, two million people starved to death although there was food enough to feed them. From 1899 to 1902, the British fought the Dutch settlers of South Africa in the Boer War. The British army herded the women and children of the Boer guerillas into barbed-wire enclosures, thereby helping to invent the concentration camp.

"wisdom . . . foolishness" Wisdom includes Michael Faraday's experiments in electricity and Joseph Lister's introduction of sterile surgery. Matthew Arnold wrote essays urging his fellow citizens to enrich their minds with the same zeal with which they enriched their bank accounts.

Charles Dickens

TIMELINE

1861 Russia
Emancipation
of serfs.

1865 Austria
Gregor Mendel
proposes laws
of heredity. ▶

1860

1860: Florence Nightingale
founds school for nurses. ▲

1861 United States
Civil War begins. ▶

1865: London
Fire Department
established.

There were two varieties of foolishness. One was creative, a relief from the smug self-satisfaction of the time. Examples of this healthy foolishness are the operettas of W. S. Gilbert and Arthur Sullivan, with their amusing patter, and Lewis Carroll's fantastic tale *Alice in Wonderland* and his nonsense poem "Jabberwocky."

Unhealthy foolishness included using the Thames as an open sewer until one typhoid outbreak in 1861 killed Albert, Victoria's beloved Prince Consort. It also included sending British troops to fight in the Crimea so ill-fed, ill-clothed, and ill-led that the war is best remembered in Tennyson's poem "The Charge of the Light Brigade," which celebrates a suicidal cavalry charge.

"belief . . . incredulity" Problems of belief haunted the Victorians. At the very moment they wanted to think they were God's chosen people, they faced serious challenges to their belief in that God. Historical and scientific investigations undermined literal interpretations of the Bible, but it was Darwin who was the real villain for believers. Newton had distanced God from the universe; more frighteningly, Darwin seemed to distance God from human life.

"hope . . . despair" It is the spring of hope in Elizabeth Barrett Browning's Sonnet 43; it is the winter of despair in Matthew Arnold's "Dover Beach." It is the season of light in Gerard Manley Hopkins's "God's Grandeur"; it is the season of darkness in Emily Brontë's "Remembrance."

The BRITISH TRADITION

THE CHANGING ENGLISH LANGUAGE, BY RICHARD LEDERER

Euphemisms: The Fig Leaves of Language

Prudishness reached its golden age in the straitlaced Victorian era. Take the widely read *Lady Gough's Book of Etiquette*. Among Lady Gough's pronouncements was that under no circumstances should books written by male authors be placed on shelves next to books written by "authoresses." Married writers, however, such as Robert and Elizabeth Barrett Browning could be shelved together without impropriety.

So delicate were Victorian sensibilities that members of polite society would blush at the mention of anything physical. Instead of being *pregnant*, women were in a delicate condition, in a family way, or *expectant*. Their children were not born; rather, they were *brought by the stork* or *came into the world*.

Such words and expressions are called *euphemisms* (from two Greek roots that mean "pleasant speech," "words of good omen"). A euphemism is a mild, indirect word or phrase used in place of one that is more direct or that may have an unpleasant connotation for some people. Using a euphemism is "calling a spade a heart" . . . or "telling it like it isn't."

In the Victorian Age, prudery extended even to animals and things. *Bull* was considered an indecent word, and the proper substitute was *he cow*, *male cow*, or (gasp!) *gentleman cow*. Victorian standards were so exacting that Victorians could not refer to something as vulgar as legs. They had to call them *limbs*, even when talking about the legs on a chicken or a piano. Instead of asking for a leg of chicken, they would ask for dark meat, and they even went so far as to cover up piano legs with little skirts!

1869: Debtors' prisons abolished.

1872: Ballot Act in Britain introduces voting by secret ballot.

1874

◀ **1869 Egypt**
Suez Canal, linking the Mediterranean Sea and the Red Sea, completed.

1872: First international soccer game, England vs. Scotland. ▶

◄ **Critical Viewing**
In this scene from Charles Dickens's autobiographical novel *David Copperfield*, young David (shown at the center) is on a journey from Yarmouth to London. To what extent does the illustrator sentimentalize David? To what extent does the illustrator show David struggling to survive in a hostile world?
[Interpret]

There was light and hope in The Crystal Palace; despair and darkness in the fetid slums with contaminated water.

"going direct to Heaven . . . going direct the other way" Nowhere is paradox more apparent than in the era's treatment of children. The Victorians frequently sentimentalized their children as little angels. However, in the novels of Dickens and Brontë and many others, we meet orphans and abandoned children struggling to survive in a hostile world. Often we see these children in school where the adults view them as, to use Dickens's phrase, "going direct the other way" unless they are rigorously and painfully kept in line.

All ages have their paradoxes, but the Victorians more than most felt, again in Dickens's words: ". . . we had everything before us, we had nothing before us."

ESSENTIAL QUESTION VOCABULARY

These Essential Question words will help you think and write about literature and society:

zeal (zēl) *n.* intense enthusiasm

smug (smug´) *adj.* narrowly self-satisfied; overly contented

undermined (un´ dər mīnd) *v.* injured or weakened, especially in ways that are not immediately obvious

TIMELINE

1876 United States
Alexander Graham Bell patents telephone. ▶

1874

1875: Public Health Act is passed in Britain.

What is the relationship of the writer to *tradition?*

Literature turned inward in the Victorian period. As the Empire expanded and people talked of progress and prosperity, there was a brooding, melancholic tone to much of Victorian writing. Writers also used old forms in new ways or created new forms. Poets adapted traditional forms like the elegy and the sonnet to address contemporary questions of belief. Robert Browning's dramatic monologue, a new poetic form more vital than many stage plays of the era, reflected an up-to-date understanding of psychology. Novelists developed a genre created in an earlier century and found an eager audience. Published in serial form in magazines, novels generated the same excitement as popular TV sitcoms do today.

How did poets repurpose traditional forms and subjects?

An Elegy with Up-to-Date Themes Tennyson's *In Memoriam, A.H.H.,* his elegy for his friend Arthur Hallam, speaks to the problem of belief and doubt that was central to the age. In this poem, Tennyson struggles to come to terms with Hallam's death at the age of twenty-two, asking whether a benevolent God or an indifferent nature directs the universe. About ten years before Darwin, he writes of "nature red in tooth and claw." One of the most impressive aspects of this elegy is its engagement with the latest scientific discoveries. By the end of the poem, however, Tennyson has regained his belief and declares his faith in a divine plan for the universe.

Old and New Like the Pre-Raphaelite painters and many other artists of the era, Tennyson was fascinated by the Middle Ages. However, he combines this traditional subject with up-to-date concerns. In his epic poem *Idylls of the King*, which retells the story of King Arthur, he warns his contemporaries about what can happen to a powerful kingdom like Victoria's Britain.

A melancholy that is the opposite of faith in empire and progress informs Matthew Arnold's "Dover Beach." The speaker stands at the edge of the island kingdom and contemplates the chaos encroaching on the world. He hopes, almost desperately, that a personal relationship will survive that chaos.

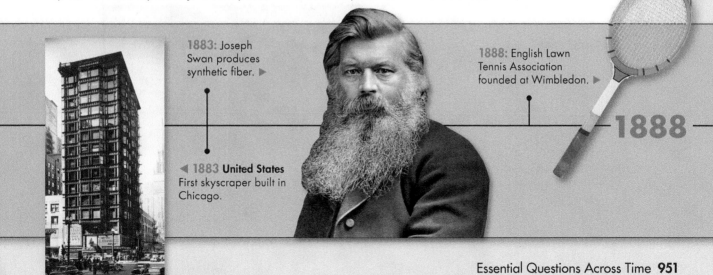

1883: Joseph Swan produces synthetic fiber. ▶

◀ **1883 United States** First skyscraper built in Chicago.

1888: English Lawn Tennis Association founded at Wimbledon. ▶

1888

The Sonnet In Sonnet 43, Elizabeth Barrett Browning states her belief in the power of love, more positively than Matthew Arnold. She adds a distinctively Victorian note of piety, reverence, and religious belief to her love poem. Victorian poets were as committed to the sonnet as were the Romantics, and none more so than Gerard Manley Hopkins. A Catholic convert and Jesuit priest, he experimented boldly with the form. In "God's Grandeur," a traditional sonnet enhanced by experiments with meter, he proclaims his faith in a divine presence in the world.

What literary forms did the Victorians invent or perfect?

The Dramatic Monologue Robert Browning, Elizabeth Barrett's husband, perfected the dramatic monologue. In this poetic form, a character is speaking to a silent listener and in the process revealing more about himself than he realizes. Browning's strange and chilling speakers are the British cousins of Edgar Allan Poe's mad narrators in stories like "The Cask of Amontillado" and "The Tell-Tale Heart."

The Novel The dramatic monologue takes readers into the mind of a character, as does the popular Victorian genre, the novel. This genre was as central to the Victorian period as the drama was to the Elizabethan. Usually published serially in magazines, each new installment of a novel was eagerly awaited by all levels of society. The novel's social commentary and realistic descriptions presented the Victorians to themselves.

The great theme of these novels is education: the depiction of a hero or heroine learning how to secure a proper place in society.

Note of Melancholy At the end of the era, A. E. Housman does not react as Tennyson did to the premature death of a young man. He does not seek the meaning of such a death in cosmic terms. Rather, in "To an Athlete Dying Young," he offers ironic consolation.

In an age of prosperity and progress, pride and power, England's poets and novelists reminded their countrymen that empires crumble, individuals are fragile and vulnerable, and death awaits us.

> **ESSENTIAL QUESTION VOCABULARY**
>
> These Essential Question words will help you think and write about the writer and tradition:
>
> **chaos** (kā äs´) *n.* disorder and formlessness
>
> **piety** (pī´ ə tē) *n.* devotion to religious duties
>
> **reverence** (rev´ ər ens) *n.* feeling of deep respect, love, and awe

TIMELINE

1888

1890: First English electrical power station opens in Deptford.

1890 United States
First entirely steel-framed building erected in Chicago.

1894 Asia
Sino-Japanese War begins. ▲

The BRITISH TRADITION

CONTEMPORARY CONNECTION

The Brontës: Fantasy Forerunners

For today's readers, the name Brontë evokes two renowned classics, Emily Brontë's *Wuthering Heights* and her sister Charlotte's *Jane Eyre*. Less known is the fact that the Brontës—three sisters, including Anne, as well as their brother, Branwell—were among the pioneer writers of fantasy.

As children, the Brontës lived with their widowed clergyman father in a bleak and isolated region of northern England. Perhaps as a result of their isolation, they immersed themselves in a world of make-believe. Inspired by their play with Branwell's toy soldiers, they invented the lands of Angria and Gondal as settings for their fantasies.

They peopled their make-believe empires with fictional characters and real-life heroes, such as the Duke of Wellington, Napoleon, and various Arctic explorers. Also, they recorded the elaborate adventures of their characters in books, using tiny handwriting that adults needed a magnifying glass to read.

The Brontë children may not have intended their childhood tales to be widely read. These fantasies have been published, however, and have even inspired well-known authors. Not long ago, Joan Aiken published a book entitled *Dangerous Games* that, as she says, uses "bits and pieces" of the Brontës' Angria.

1896 **Greece**
First modern
Olympics held. ▶

1898 **France**
Marie and Pierre Curie
discover radium.

1901: Queen Victoria dies.

1901

◀ 1896 **Austria**
Sigmund Freud
first uses the term
"psychoanalysis."

1900 **China**
Boxer Rebellion
against foreign
influence. ▶

953

Recent Scholarship

Growing up in Colonial Jamaica

James Berry

A British Colonial Child

I grew up as a British colonial child in Jamaica, British West Indies. I was made to feel that there was something special about being British: You were born into honoring the British flag and feeling that the British way of life was best. Yet you also knew in a strange way that there was something alien and inferior about you. I came to realize that this was to do with race. Because we were a black people, we knew that we were different from the rulers of our island, who were white.

We sang songs in praise of Britain, like "Land of Hope and Glory," which glorified Britain's colonial past and power. And once a year, on Empire Day, we sang "Rule Britannia," with its line: "Britons never, never, never shall be slaves." We sang with fervor because Britishness seemed to offer a sense of safety and belonging. But we also knew that our ancestors *had* been slaves and had been enslaved by the British.

As a child growing up, you had these two different histories to contend with. You felt and knew that your colonial existence was strongly influenced by your slave history. It made you feel almost an outsider in the world because there was nowhere you could appeal to.

Schooling

It was the British way of life that constructed our schooling. We received a good, basic education in ordinary subjects like English language, arithmetic, biology, history, and geography. The maps we used showed British territories colored in red, and we were proud of that. We were made to learn a little verse about Queen Victoria setting us free.

Our reading books were not based on Africa or Jamaica. They brought us the culture of the British Isles; the stories and poems in them were all British. Many of the poems were from the eighteenth or nineteenth centuries—they had all the weight of grand English usage.

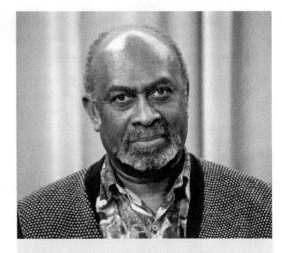

About the Author

Born and raised in rural Jamaica, James Berry (b. 1925) now lives in London. His poetry and prose are enriched by both Creole language and more formal English. In 1993, Berry won the Coretta Scott King Award Honor Book and the Boston Globe–Horn Book Award for *Ajeeman and His Son,* a work of historical fiction set in Jamaica. Berry's books of poetry include *Fractured Circles* and *Lucy's Letters and Loving.*

Most Jamaican children spoke our island dialect every day at home, but if you spoke dialect at school, teachers would shame you. They would say, "This is not a place for bad talk." Speaking English properly was tremendously respected and was connected to further education.

The Mother Country

We grew up with the idea that all the best things came from England. On Sundays, my father liked to ride to church on an English saddle that he had sent to England for. People would save up to order shoes and wedding suits from England.

At church on Sundays, we prayed for the King and the Royal Family. These were our hopeful figureheads, possible sources of influence. On Empire Day, at school, we were issued with tins of sweets with pictures of the King on them. England was our mother country.

Our Jamaican colonial history is different from that of many other colonial peoples because our own mother country sold our ancestors as slaves, and we grew up disconnected from Africa. In this kind of situation, a country takes a long time to recover from its own history. But this history has given Jamaicans a unique status in the world: a connection with Europe as well as a link back to Africa.

"This is not a place for bad talk."

© Speaking and Listening: Collaboration

James Berry discusses the positive and negative effects of British colonialism on Jamaica. With a partner, develop a research **plan for a presentation** on the pros and cons of colonialism for Jamaicans like Berry. In formulating your plan, take the following steps:

- Review Berry's essay, listing the pros and cons of colonialism from his perspective.
- Formulate *clear research questions* to explore this topic further.
- Develop *research strategies* that would help you answer these questions; consider such sources as *oral histories*, *interviews*, and *autobiographies*.
- Review sources, *evaluating them for objectivity or bias* and taking preliminary notes on your topic.

After reviewing sources, discuss what you have learned with your partner. Drawing on your reading, decide on a preliminary thesis. Present your plan and thesis to the class and ask for comments and suggestions for improving it.

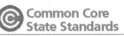

Integrate and Evaluate Information

1. Use a chart like the one shown to determine the key ideas expressed in the Essential Question essays on pages 946–952. Fill in two ideas related to each Essential Question and note the authors most closely associated with each concept. An example has been provided for you.

Essential Questions	Key Concepts	Key Author
Place and Literature		
Literature and Society	pride in and cautions about empire	Rudyard Kipling
Writer and Tradition		

2. "It was the best of times, it was the worst of times," wrote Victorian novelist Charles Dickens. Review the images on pages 940–955, and choose one that evokes the "best" of this period and one that evokes the "worst." Describe each image and explain its significance.

3. When Queen Victoria celebrated her Diamond Jubilee in 1897, the theme was "The Empire." Which British citizens would have agreed that the Empire was a cause for celebration? Which citizens might have disagreed? Explain, citing evidence from the multiple sources on pages 942–953, as well as from other sources, such as online encyclopedias.

4. **Address a Question:** In his essay on pages 954–955, James Berry portrays Jamaican culture as a complex intersection of British tradition and local history. Choose an aspect of Jamaican culture, such as the Jamaican dialect of English. Integrating ideas from Berry's essay as well as from other sources, such as online encyclopedias, explain how the element reflects the intersection of—or struggle between—cultures.

Speaking and Listening: Multimedia Presentation

The British Empire was at its height in 1851, when the Crystal Palace was built. Create and deliver a **multimedia presentation** on the Palace, analyzing what its innovative construction and displays implied about Britain's place in the world.

Solve a Research Problem: To create an effective multimedia presentation, combine text, images, and sound from sources like these:

- TV documentaries
- Internet sites
- videos
- Victorian newspapers
- history books
- magazines

Formulate a plan to find and assemble the media you need. Determine how to access each type of source listed above. Then, select and use media strategically. Choose only pieces that clearly illustrate your points, and create pacing by distributing them evenly through the report.

Common Core State Standards

Reading Informational Text

7. Integrate and evaluate multiple sources of information presented in different media or formats as well as in words in order to address a question or solve a problem.

Speaking and Listening

1.a. Come to discussions prepared, having read and researched material under study; explicitly draw on that preparation by referring to evidence from texts and other research on the topic or issue to stimulate a thoughtful, well-reasoned exchange of ideas. (p. 955)

5. Make strategic use of digital media in presentations to enhance understanding of findings, reasoning, and evidence and to add interest.

ESSENTIAL QUESTION VOCABULARY

Use these words in your responses:

Literature and Place
empire
conquest
missionary

Literature and Society
zeal
smug
undermine

The Writer and Tradition
chaos
piety
reverence

Relationships

Before You Read

Connecting to the Essential Question *In Memoriam, A.H.H.* is a poem Tennyson wrote in memory of his best friend, Arthur Hallam. As you read, note the ideas Tennyson explores as a result of his friend's death. This focus will help you answer the Essential Question: **How does literature shape or reflect society?**

Literary Analysis

The **speaker** in a poem—the person who "says" its words—is not necessarily the poet. Speakers fall into the following categories:

- Fictional or real
- Generalized (not described in specific detail) or with a specific identity

As you read, determine the identity of each speaker and analyze the speaker's conflict and motivation.

Comparing Literary Works Some of Tennyson's speakers have histories—they have undergone a change or suffered a loss. Using such speakers, he dramatizes different experiences of time, including the following:

- A perpetual present, in which nothing significant changes
- Restless movement from past achievement into an unknown future
- The loss of the past

Consider whether each poem creates its own "time"—a moment in which the speaker sums up the past, making way for the future.

Reading Strategy

 Preparing to Read Complex Texts **Analyzing an author's philosophical assumptions and beliefs** will help you understand the meaning of a poem. For example, Tennyson's speaker in "Ulysses" expresses a desire "to seek a newer world." The speaker's restless drive to explore suggests that Tennyson, like many Victorians, valued progress. Use what is stated explicitly, or directly, in the text as the basis for making inferences about the author's assumptions and beliefs. As you read, use a chart like the one shown to identify the author's beliefs.

Vocabulary

chrysalis (kris′ l is) *n.* the third stage in the development of a moth or butterfly (p. 961)

diffusive (di fyoō′ siv) *adj.* tending to spread out (p. 962)

prosper (präs′ pər) *v.* thrive (p. 962)

waning (wān′ iŋ) *v.* gradually dimming or weakening (p. 967)

prudence (prood′ ns) *n.* careful management of resources; economy (p. 972)

furrows (fʉr′ ōz) *n.* grooves, such as those made by a plow (p. 972)

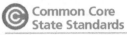 **Common Core State Standards**

Reading Literature
1. Cite strong and thorough textual evidence to support analysis of what the text says explicitly as well as inferences drawn from the text, including determining where the text leaves matters uncertain.

Assumption/Belief		
Progress and exploration are valuable.		

Supporting Detail	Supporting Detail
"Ulysses," lines 6–7	

Supporting Detail	
"Ulysses," lines 31–32	

PHLit Online!
www.PHLitOnline.com

Author of *In Memoriam, A.H.H.* • "The Lady of Shalott" • "Tears, Idle Tears" • "Ulysses"

Tennyson was born in the rural town of Somersby in Lincolnshire, the fourth of twelve children. He was a sensitive boy who was charmed by the magical words "far, far away." His father, a clergyman, had a large library and supervised Tennyson's early education, predicting that his son would be "the greatest Poet of the Time." At the same time, Tennyson's father was extremely bitter, having been disinherited by his own father. His anger poisoned the atmosphere of the Tennyson household. As a teenager, Alfred was probably eager to escape to Cambridge University.

The Power of Friendship At first, Tennyson was disappointed by Cambridge. Then, he met the young man who became his closest friend, Arthur Henry Hallam. They were often together, and Hallam intended to marry Tennyson's sister Emily. In 1830, with Hallam's encouragement, Tennyson published *Poems, Chiefly Lyrical.*

A Stunning Tragedy In 1833, however, Hallam died suddenly, leaving a void in Tennyson's life that nearly destroyed him. Soon after Hallam's death, Tennyson began working on a series of short poems that considered questions of death, religious faith, and immortality. This series, which grew over seventeen years into an extended elegy for his friend, was published in 1850 under the title *In Memoriam, A.H.H.*

National Honor The elegy so impressed Prince Albert that in 1850, he encouraged Queen Victoria to appoint Tennyson the poet laureate of England, replacing the recently deceased Wordsworth.

In 1884, Queen Victoria made Tennyson a baron, and so added the title of Lord to his name.

Land, Literature, Long Life When royalties from *In Memoriam, A.H.H.* began to flow in, Tennyson bought a farm on the Isle of Wight. There, he and his wife Emily Sellwood raised two children. Tennyson continued to publish poems into his eighties.

ALFRED, LORD **TENNYSON**

(1809–1892)

The Stages of Life, Caspar David Friedrich, Museum der Bildenden Kunst, Leipzig

FROM In Memoriam, A.H.H.

ALFRED, LORD TENNYSON

1

▲ **Critical Viewing** This painting, *The Stages of Life*, suggests that life is like a voyage. How would the speaker in the poem react to such a comparison? Explain. **[Speculate]**

I held it truth, with him who sings
    To one clear harp in divers[1] tones,
    That men may rise on stepping stones
Of their dead selves to higher things.

5 But who shall so forecast the years
    And find in loss a gain to match?
    Or reach a hand through time to catch
The far-off interest of tears?

---

1. **divers** (dī′ vərz) *adj.* varied; having many parts.

Let Love clasp Grief lest both be drowned,
10   Let darkness keep her raven gloss.
        Ah, sweeter to be drunk with loss,
To dance with death, to beat the ground,

Than that the victor Hours should scorn
        The long result of love, and boast,
15   "Behold the man that loved and lost,
But all he was is overworn."

7

Dark house, by which once more I stand
        Here in the long unlovely street,
        Doors, where my heart was used to beat
20 So quickly, waiting for a hand,

A hand that can be clasped no more—
        Behold me, for I cannot sleep,
        And like a guilty thing I creep
At earliest morning to the door.

25 He is not here; but far away
        The noise of life begins again,
        And ghastly through the drizzling rain
On the bald street breaks the blank day.

82

I wage not any feud with Death
30   For changes wrought on form and face;
        No lower life that earth's embrace
May breed with him, can fright my faith.

Eternal process moving on,
        From state to state the spirit walks;
35   And these are but the shattered stalks,
Or ruined chrysalis of one.

Nor blame I Death, because he bare
        The use of virtue out of earth;
        I know transplanted human worth
40 Will bloom to profit, otherwhere.

For this alone on Death I wreak
        The wrath that garners in my heart;
        He put our lives so far apart
We cannot hear each other speak.

He put our lives so far apart
We cannot hear each other speak.

Literary Analysis
The Speaker in Poetry
What do you learn about the speaker in lines 21–24?

Reading Strategy
Analyzing Philosophical Beliefs In lines 29–44, what does the poet suggest about the consolations of faith and philosophy?

Vocabulary
chrysalis (kris´ l is)
n. the third stage in the development of a moth or butterfly

Reading Check

What are two of the main feelings Tennyson conveys in these stanzas?

I prosper, circled with thy voice;
I shall not lose thee though I die.

130

45 Thy voice is on the rolling air;
   I hear thee where the waters run;
   Thou standest in the rising sun,
And in the setting thou art fair.

What art thou then? I cannot guess;
50   But though I seem in star and flower
     To feel thee some diffusive power,
I do not therefore love thee less.

My love involves the love before;
   My love is vaster passion now;
55   Though mixed with God and Nature thou,
I seem to love thee more and more.

Far off thou art, but ever nigh;
   I have thee still, and I rejoice;
   I prosper, circled with thy voice;
60 I shall not lose thee though I die.

Vocabulary
diffusive (di fyoo′ siv) *adj.*
tending to spread out

prosper (präs′ pər) *v.*
thrive

Critical Reading

Cite textual evidence to support your responses.

1. **Key Ideas and Details (a)** In section 1, what idea does the speaker say he once held as truth but now doubts?
   (b) Interpret: The speaker rejects this truth in favor of a new view of grief. Paraphrase this view.

2. **Key Ideas and Details (a)** By what place is the speaker standing in section 7? **(b) Interpret:** What effect does the loss of his friend have on the scene?

3. **Integration of Knowledge and Ideas** Contrast the facts that, in section 82, the speaker says do not anger him with the one fact that does.

4. **Integration of Knowledge and Ideas (a) Interpret:** Explain the paradox in line 57: "Far off thou art, but ever nigh."
   (b) Connect: How does section 130 answer the speaker's one reason for anger in section 82?

Progress and Decline (1833–1901)

The Lady of
SHALOTT

ALFRED, LORD TENNYSON

PART I

On either side the river lie
Long fields of barley and of rye,
That clothe the wold[1] and meet the sky;
And through the field the road runs by
5   To many-towered Camelot,[2]
And up and down the people go,
Gazing where the lilies blow[3]
Round an island there below,
      The island of Shalott.

10   Willows whiten, aspens quiver,
Little breezes dusk and shiver
Through the wave that runs forever
By the island in the river
      Flowing down to Camelot.
15   Four gray walls, and four gray towers,
Overlook a space of flowers,
And the silent isle imbowers
      The Lady of Shalott.

The Lady of Shalott, (detail), John
Waterhouse, The Tate Gallery, London

Literary Analysis
The Speaker in Poetry
What does setting this poem
in the days of King Arthur
suggest about the poet's
attitude toward the past?

---

1. **wold** rolling plains.
2. **Camelot** legendary English town where King Arthur had his court and Round Table.
3. **blow** bloom.

The Lady of Shalott, John Waterhouse, The Tate Gallery, London

▲ **Critical Viewing**
What symbols of the Lady of Shalott's occupation and eventual fate are in this painting? Explain why they are significant. **[Interpret]**

By the margin, willow-veiled,
20 Slide the heavy barges trailed
By slow horses; and unhailed
The shallop⁴ flitteth silken-sailed
        Skimming down to Camelot:
But who hath seen her wave her hand?
25 Or at the casement seen her stand?
Or is she known in all the land,
        The Lady of Shalott?

Only reapers, reaping early
In among the bearded barley,
30 Hear a song that echoes cheerly,
From the river winding clearly,
        Down to towered Camelot:
And by the moon the reaper weary,
Piling sheaves in uplands airy,
35 Listening, whispers, "'Tis the fairy
        Lady of Shalott."

---

4. **shallop** light, open boat.

PART II

There she weaves by night and day
A magic web with colors gay.
She has heard a whisper say,
40   A curse is on her if she stay
       To look down to Camelot.
She knows not what the curse may be,
And so she weaveth steadily,
And little other care hath she,
45   The Lady of Shalott.

And moving through a mirror[5] clear
That hangs before her all the year,
Shadows of the world appear.
There she sees the highway near
50   Winding down to Camelot:
There the river eddy whirls,
And there the surly village churls,[6]
And the red cloaks of market girls,
       Pass onward from Shalott.

55   Sometimes a troop of damsels glad,
An abbot on an ambling pad,[7]
Sometimes a curly shepherd lad,
Or long-haired page in crimson clad,
       Goes by to towered Camelot;
60   And sometimes through the mirror blue
The knights come riding two and two:
She hath no loyal knight and true,
       The Lady of Shalott.

But in her web she still delights
65   To weave the mirror's magic sights,
For often through the silent nights
A funeral, with plumes and lights
       And music, went to Camelot:
Or when the moon was overhead,
70   Came two young lovers lately wed;
"I am half sick of shadows," said
       The Lady of Shalott.

---

5. mirror Weavers placed mirrors in front of their looms, so that they could view the progress of their work.

6. churls (churlz) *n.* farm laborers; peasants.

7. pad easy-paced horse.

Literary Analysis
The Speaker in Poetry
Is the speaker who tells the Lady of Shalott's story also a character in the poem? How can you tell?

Reading Check

What does the Lady of Shalott do with her time?

A Crisis of Faith

When the grief-stricken Tennyson of *In Memoriam* pushes away the comforting philosophies of his day, or when he turns to the mythic past in "The Lady of Shalott," he reflects a broader crisis of faith that rocked Victorian society. The Industrial Revolution and its teeming urban masses had pushed aside the traditional bond between peasant and lord. The comfortable rhythms of a farming society had given way to surging spirals of economic boom and bust. Meanwhile, such intellectual developments as Charles Darwin's theory of evolution challenged religious beliefs.

In the midst of these social and intellectual changes, Victorian artists asked whether their cultural resources —religion, science, art—were still sufficient to guide their lives. From Tennyson to Matthew Arnold to T. S. Eliot to Philip Larkin, the theme of a fractured culture, unable to answer its own questions, persists to this day.

Connect to the Literature

In what way might the isolated Lady of Shalott find the sight of Sir Lancelot a crisis of faith?

PART III

A bow-shot from her bower eaves,
He rode between the barley sheaves,
75 The sun came dazzling through the leaves,
And flamed upon the brazen greaves[8]
    Of bold Sir Lancelot.
A red-cross knight[9] forever kneeled
To a lady in his shield,
80 That sparkled on the yellow field,
    Beside remote Shalott.

The gemmy[10] bridle glittered free,
Like to some branch of stars we see
Hung in the golden Galaxy.[11]
85 The bridle bells rang merrily
    As he rode down to Camelot:
And from his blazoned baldric[12] slung
A mighty silver bugle hung,
And as he rode his armor rung,
90   Beside remote Shalott.

All in the blue unclouded weather
Thick-jeweled shone the saddle leather,
The helmet and the helmet feather
Burned like one burning flame together,
95   As he rode down to Camelot.
As often through the purple night,
Below the starry clusters bright,
Some bearded meteor, trailing light,
    Moves over still Shalott.

100 His broad clear brow in sunlight glowed;
On burnish'd hooves his war horse trode;
From underneath his helmet flowed
His coal-black curls as on he rode,
    As he rode down to Camelot.
105 From the bank and from the river
He flashed into the crystal mirror,
"Tirra lirra," by the river
    Sang Sir Lancelot.

---

8. **greaves** armor that protects the legs below the kneecaps.
9. **red-cross knight** refers to the Redcrosse Knight from *The Faerie Queene* by Edmund Spenser. The knight is a symbol of holiness.
10. **gemmy** jeweled.
11. **Galaxy** the Milky Way.
12. **blazoned baldric** decorated sash worn diagonally across the chest.

She left the web, she left the loom,
110　She made three paces through the room,
She saw the waterlily bloom,
She saw the helmet and the plume,
　　She looked down to Camelot.
Out flew the web and floated wide;
115　The mirror cracked from side to side;
"The curse is come upon me," cried
　　The Lady of Shalott.

PART IV

In the stormy east wind straining,
The pale yellow woods were waning,
120　The broad stream in his banks complaining,
Heavily the low sky raining
　　Over towered Camelot;
Down she came and found a boat
Beneath a willow left afloat,
125　And round about the prow she wrote
　　The Lady of Shalott.

And down the river's dim expanse
Like some bold seër in a trance,
Seeing all his own mischance—
130　With a glassy countenance
　　Did she look to Camelot.
And at the closing of the day
She loosed the chain, and down she lay;
The broad stream bore her far away,
135　　The Lady of Shalott.

Lying, robed in snowy white
That loosely flew to left and right—
The leaves upon her falling light—
Through the noises of the night
140　　She floated down to Camelot:
And as the boathead wound along
The willowy hills and fields among,
They heard her singing her last song,
　　The Lady of Shalott.

145　Heard a carol, mournful, holy,
Chanted loudly, chanted lowly,
Till her blood was frozen slowly,
And her eyes were darkened wholly,
　　Turned to towered Camelot.

Literary Analysis
The Speaker in Poetry
How does the speaker create the sense that a decisive moment has arrived?

Vocabulary
waning (wān′ iŋ) *v.* gradually becoming dimmer or weaker

Reading Check
What does the Lady of Shalott do once she sees Sir Lancelot?

The Lady of Shalott **967**

150   For ere she reached upon the tide
The first house by the waterside,
Singing in her song she died,
     The Lady of Shalott.

Under tower and balcony,
155   By garden wall and gallery,
A gleaming shape she floated by,
Dead-pale between the houses high,
     Silent into Camelot.
Out upon the wharfs they came,
160   Knight and burgher, lord and dame,
And round the prow they read her name,
     The Lady of Shalott.

Who is this? and what is here?
And in the lighted palace near
165   Died the sound of royal cheer;
And they crossed themselves for fear,
     All the knights at Camelot:
But Lancelot mused a little space;
He said, "She has a lovely face;
170   God in his mercy lend her grace,
     The Lady of Shalott."

Critical Reading

Cite textual evidence to support your responses.

© **1. Key Ideas and Details (a)** What does the Lady spend her time doing? Why? **(b) Interpret:** Why does the Lady glimpse only "shadows of the world"? **(c) Interpret:** Why might an artist share the complaint the Lady makes in lines 71–72?

© **2. Key Ideas and Details (a)** What does the Lady do after seeing Sir Lancelot in the mirror? **(b) Analyze:** How does the long description of Sir Lancelot make the knight seem like the real-life embodiment of a vision? **(c) Draw Conclusions:** Given this description of Lancelot, explain why the Lady might be said to leave her room in pursuit of her visions.

© **3. Key Ideas and Details (a) Draw Conclusions:** What does the fact that the Lady dies before meeting Lancelot suggest about her love for him? **(b) Make a Judgment:** Do you agree with Tennyson's implication that we can never realize our fantasies? Why or why not?

© **4. Integration of Knowledge and Ideas** The poem suggests that the life of the imagination isolates one from reality. Do modern media outlets, such as television and the Internet, suggest otherwise? Explain.

TEARS, *Idle* TEARS

ALFRED, LORD TENNYSON

BACKGROUND *The Princess* (1847) is a long narrative poem that contains a number of songs. Some of these songs, including the one that follows, are considered to be among the finest of Tennyson's lyrics.

> Tears, idle tears, I know not what they mean,
> Tears from the depth of some divine despair
> Rise in the heart, and gather to the eyes,
> In looking on the happy autumn fields,
> 5 And thinking of the days that are no more.
>
> Fresh as the first beam glittering on a sail,
> That brings our friends up from the underworld,
> Sad as the last which reddens over one
> That sinks with all we love below the verge;
> 10 So sad, so fresh, the days that are no more.
>
> Ah, sad and strange as in dark summer dawns
> The earliest pipe of half-awakened birds
> To dying ears, when unto dying eyes
> The casement slowly grows a glimmering square;
> 15 So sad, so strange, the days that are no more.
>
> Dear as remembered kisses after death,
> And sweet as those by hopeless fancy feigned
> On lips that are for others; deep as love,
> Deep as first love, and wild with all regret;
> 20 O Death in Life, the days that are no more.

Reading Check

What is the speaker's reaction to the thought of "the days that are no more"?

ALFRED, LORD TENNYSON

Ulysses

BACKGROUND In this poem, Tennyson extends the story of Ulysses (yoo lis´ ez´), the hero of Homer's epic the *Odyssey*. Homer's writing ends after Ulysses' triumphant return home to Ithaca. Years later, Tennyson tells us, the hero has grown restless. Although he had been away for twenty long years—ten fighting in the Trojan War and another ten on a long and adventure-filled voyage back—Ulysses finds that he is contemplating yet another journey.

It little profits that an idle king,
By this still hearth, among these barren crags,
Matched with an aged wife, I mete and dole[1]
Unequal[2] laws unto a savage race,
5 That hoard, and sleep, and feed, and know not me.
I cannot rest from travel; I will drink
Life to the lees.[3] All times I have enjoyed
Greatly, have suffered greatly, both with those
That loved me, and alone; on shore, and when
10 Through scudding drifts the rainy Hyades[4]
Vexed the dim sea. I am become a name;
For always roaming with a hungry heart
Much have I seen and known—cities of men
And manners, climates, councils, governments,
15 Myself not least, but honored of them all—
And drunk delight of battle with my peers,
Far on the ringing plains of windy Troy.
I am a part of all that I have met;
Yet all experience is an arch wherethrough
20 Gleams that untraveled world, whose
      margin fades
Forever and forever when I move.
How dull it is to pause, to make an end,
To rust unburnished, not to shine in use!
As though to breathe were life. Life piled on life
25 Were all too little, and of one to me
Little remains; but every hour is saved
From that eternal silence, something more,
A bringer of new things; and vile it were
For some three suns to store and hoard myself,

Ulysses, 1827, Jean-Auguste-Dominique Ingres, National Gallery of Art, Washington, D.C.

---

1. mete and dole measure and give out.
2. unequal unfair.
3. lees sediment.
4. Hyades (hī´ ə dēz´) group of stars whose rising was assumed to be followed by rain.

Literary Analysis
The Speaker in Poetry
Who is speaking the words of this poem? How can you tell?

◄ **Critical Viewing**
Compare the character of Ulysses conveyed by this painting with the speaker in the poem. **[Compare and Contrast]**

Reading
Check

What has Ulysses encountered on his travels?

Reading Strategy
Analyzing Philosophical
Beliefs What do lines 22-32
suggest about Tennyson's
philosophical beliefs?

Vocabulary
prudence (prōōd´ ns) *n.*
careful management of
resources; economy

30 And this gray spirit yearning in desire
To follow knowledge like a sinking star,
Beyond the utmost bound of human thought.
    This is my son, mine own Telemachus,
To whom I leave the scepter and the isle[5]
35 Well-loved of me, discerning to fulfill
This labor, by slow prudence to make mild
A rugged people, and through soft degrees
Subdue them to the useful and the good.
Most blameless is he, centered in the sphere
40 Of common duties, decent not to fail
In offices of tenderness, and pay
Meet[6] adoration to my household gods,
When I am gone. He works his work, I mine.
    There lies the port; the vessel puffs her sail;
45 There gloom the dark broad seas. My mariners,
Souls that have toiled and wrought, and thought with me—
That ever with a frolic welcome took
The thunder and the sunshine, and opposed
Free hearts, free foreheads—you and I are old;
50 Old age hath yet his honor and his toil;
Death closes all; but something ere the end,
Some work of noble note, may yet be done,
Not unbecoming men that strove with Gods.
The lights begin to twinkle from the rocks;
55 The long day wanes; the slow moon climbs; the deep
Moans round with many voices. Come, my friends,
'Tis not too late to seek a newer world.
Push off, and sitting well in order smite
The sounding furrows; for my purpose holds

Vocabulary
furrows (fŭr´ ōz) *n.* narrow
grooves, such as those made
by a plow

---

5. isle Ithaca, an island off the coast of Greece.
6. meet appropriate.

HOW DULL IT IS TO PAUSE, TO MAKE AN END,

TO RUST UNBURNISHED, NOT TO **SHINE IN USE!**

60 To sail beyond the sunset, and the baths
    Of all the western stars, until I die.
    It may be that the gulfs will wash us down;
    It may be we shall touch the Happy Isles,[7]
    And see the great Achilles,[8] whom we knew.
65 Though much is taken, much abides; and though
    We are not now that strength which in old days
    Moved earth and heaven, that which we are, we are—
    One equal temper of heroic hearts,
    Made weak by time and fate, but strong in will
70 To strive, to seek, to find, and not to yield.

---

7. **Happy Isles** Elysium, or the Islands of the Blessed: in classical mythology, the place heroes went after death.
8. **Achilles** (ə kil′ ēz′) Greek hero of the Trojan War.

Critical Reading

1. **Key Ideas and Details (a)** What three comparisons in "Tears, Idle Tears" describe "the days that are no more"? **(b) Analyze:** What contrast does each comparison involve? **(c) Interpret:** What feelings does the line "Deep as first love, and wild with all regret" capture?

2. **Key Ideas and Details (a)** In "Ulysses," how does Ulysses describe his situation? **(b) Compare and Contrast:** How does this situation contrast with his previous experiences? **(c) Draw Conclusions:** What is Ulysses' attitude toward his experiences?

3. **Key Ideas and Details (a)** According to lines 58–61, what is Ulysses' purpose? **(b) Draw Conclusions:** What are Ulysses' feelings about aging? **(c) Draw Conclusions:** What is his attitude toward life in general?

4. **Integration of Knowledge and Ideas** What values do you think Tennyson celebrates in his poetry? Explain using two of these Essential Question words: *universe, rationalism, curiosity, challenge.* *[Connecting to the Essential Question: How does literature shape or reflect society?]*

Cite textual evidence to support your responses.

After You Read

**from *In Memoriam, A.H.H.*•
The Lady of Shalott • *Tears,
Idle Tears* • *Ulysses***

Literary Analysis

**Common Core
State Standards**

1. Craft and Structure (a) Who is the **speaker** of *In Memoriam, A.H.H.*? **(b)** Tennyson wrote the poem in direct response to his friend's death. How does the speaker's conflict reflect one that Tennyson might have felt?

2. Craft and Structure (a) Who is the speaker of "The Lady of Shalott"? **(b)** Is the speaker fictional or real, generalized or specific? Explain.

3. Integration of Knowledge and Ideas Why might Tennyson have identified the situation of a poet with the Lady's situation?

4. Key Ideas and Details (a) Describe the conflict faced by the speaker in "Ulysses." **(b)** Does Tennyson see Ulysses as heroic or as selfish and self-justifying? Support your answer by quoting from the poem.

5. Integration of Knowledge and Ideas Use a chart like the one shown to compare Ulysses' view of time with the Lady of Shalott's view.

	Past	Present	Future
Ulysses	Remembers it with satisfaction: "I am a part of all that I have met"		
The Lady of Shalott	Considers it identical with the present: "There she weaves by night and day"		

6. Integration of Knowledge and Ideas Compare the speaker's relationship with the past in "Tears, Idle Tears" and in *In Memoriam, A.H.H.*

7. Comparing Literary Works Which did Tennyson value more—the timeless world of poetry or the perishable real world? Support your view.

Reading Strategy

8. Analyze the philosophical assumptions and beliefs Tennyson expresses in *In Memoriam, A.H.H.* What attitudes toward faith and hope can you detect?

9. Tennyson's work is considered to be reflective of the Victorian period. What philosophical assumption about the spiritual condition of Victorian society is demonstrated in "The Lady of Shalott"?

10. Tennyson lived in an age that accepted the idea of progress, believing the acquisition of knowledge would lead to a better world. Identify two passages in "Ulysses" that support this belief. Explain your choices.

Writing
2. Write informative/explanatory texts to examine and convey complex ideas, concepts, and information clearly and accurately through the effective selection, organization, and analysis of content. *(p. 975)*

Language
4.a. Use context as a clue to the meaning of a word or phrase. *(p. 975)*

Integrated Language Skills

© Vocabulary Acquisition and Use

Word Analysis: Literal and Figurative Meanings

Many words have both a literal meaning and a figurative one. This is a broader or more symbolic meaning that often draws on the literal meaning. For instance, a *chrysalis* is the stage in the life of a butterfly in which the insect grows in a cocoon before emerging as an adult butterfly. Tennyson, in *In Memoriam, A.H.H.,* uses the word figuratively to refer to stages of human life. His image has a richer meaning, though. In the cocoon, the chrysalis changes from caterpillar to butterfly, just as death may transform a person from physical to spiritual life. Identify the literal and figurative meanings of these other words Tennyson uses:

1. doors (*In Memoriam, A.H.H.,* line 19)
2. bald (*In Memoriam, A.H.H.,* line 28)
3. lees ("Ulysses," line 7)
4. hungry ("Ulysses," line 12)
5. shine ("Ulysses," line 23)

Vocabulary: Context

The context of a word—the lines or phrases around it—can provide clues to the meaning of an unfamiliar word. Identify the contextual meaning of each italicized vocabulary word below and explain how context makes that meaning clear.

1. As the sun rose, its *diffusive* light reached into all the shadows of the night, revealing sharp edges and colors.
2. His popularity *waning,* the actor could no longer command starring roles.
3. When the *chrysalis* turns into the adult butterfly, the empty cocoon remains behind.
4. Her natural *prudence* prevented her from taking any rash action.
5. The *furrows* on his parents' foreheads showed their anxiety.
6. After launching the new business, she worked day and night to ensure it would *prosper.*

Writing

© **Informative Text** Arthur Hallam's death had a decisive influence not only on Tennyson's life but also on his poetry. Writing *In Memoriam, A.H.H.* gave Tennyson the money he needed to buy his own land. Write a **biographical essay** that recounts the details of Tennyson's life and work, examining the *cause-and-effect relationships* between them.

Prewriting Research Tennyson's life and work. Outline the main events of his life and make a chart of his main accomplishments and literary themes. Take notes on ways his life and work affected each other.

Draft Draft your essay, following the *correct sequence of events* and locating incidents in specific places where they occurred. In your draft, explore the significance of major events in Tennyson's life, clarifying the way his life influenced his work and vice versa.

Revising Read through your draft to make sure that you present the correct sequence of events and clearly explain cause-and-effect relationships. Be sure that you have ample evidence or solid reasoning to claim such a relationship. If not, revise your text to support your claim.

Model: Charting Cause-and-Effect Relationships

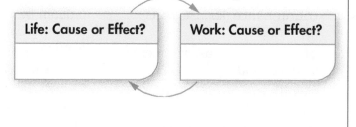

Life: Cause or Effect?	Work: Cause or Effect?

Connecting to the Essential Question Robert Browning's monologues were innovative in adapting dramatic devices to poetry. As you read, notice what makes these poems dramatic. This will help you address the Essential Question: **What is the relationship of the writer to tradition?**

Literary Analysis

Robert Browning perfected the **dramatic monologue,** in which a single character delivers a speech. His monologues contain these elements:

- A speaker who indirectly reveals his or her situation and character
- A silent listener, addressed by the speaker and implied in what the speaker says

Browning's decision to write "My Last Duchess" as a dramatic monologue allows him to develop a dramatic, tension-filled scene in which the reader does not immediately understand who is speaking, who is being addressed, and what has happened to the "last Duchess." Further, having only the duke speaking highlights his egotism. As you read, consider other ways that using the form of a dramatic monologue allows the author to develop the narrative and convey meaning.

Comparing Literary Works Robert Browning's monologues capture the rhythms of speech through **run-on lines**—lines whose natural flow goes past line endings:

> But to myself they turned (since none puts by
> The curtain I have drawn for you, but I)

He and Elizabeth Barrett also use **end-stopped lines,** which end just where a speaker would pause. Compare the poets' use of these devices.

Reading Strategy

Preparing to Read Complex Texts You can better understand the theme of a poem if you **compare and contrast speakers in multiple poems.** For example, you might gain insights into the selfish, possessive love of the speaker in one poem if you compare it to the deep, abiding love of the speaker in another. Use a diagram like the one shown to compare and contrast speakers in these poems.

Vocabulary

countenance (koun´ tə nəns) *n.* face (p. 979)

officious (ə fish´ əs) *adj.* meddlesome (p. 980)

munificence (myoo nif´ ə səns) *n.* lavish generosity (p. 980)

dowry (dou´ rē) *n.* property brought by a woman's family to her husband upon their marriage (p. 980)

eludes (ē loodz´) *v.* avoids or escapes (p. 981)

sullen (sul´ ən) *adj.* brooding; morose; sulky (p. 982)

Common Core State Standards

Reading Literature
3. Analyze the impact of the author's choices regarding how to develop and relate elements of a story or drama.

"My Last Duchess"

"Sonnet 43"

www.PHLitOnline.com

Robert Browning

(1812–1889)

Author of "My Last Duchess" • "Life in a Love" • "Porphyria's Lover"

Young Robert Browning's best teacher may not have been a person, but his father's 6,000-book library. Although he had little schooling, he eagerly devoured those books, hungry for knowledge about history, art, and literature.

Inspiration and Discouragement By the time he was a teenager, Browning had decided to make poetry his life's pursuit. He published his first book, *Pauline*, at the age of twenty-one. Success was a while coming, though. A long and highly personal poem modeled after Shelley's work, *Pauline* did not sell a single copy.

Discouraged, Browning tried his hand at something less personal, a long dramatic poem called *Paracelsus*. He also wrote a play. His work still failed to attract much public notice, and his reputation was eclipsed by that of his wife, the poet Elizabeth Barrett Browning, whom he had married in 1846.

Lasting Fame In 1869, eight years after Elizabeth's death, the publication of *The Ring and the Book* turned Browning's career around. This long poem, based on an actual trial, tells the story of a murder in a series of dramatic monologues, or speeches by characters. *The Ring and the Book* achieved wide recognition for its author. It demonstrated the unique elements that Browning contributed to nineteenth-century poetry: a more down-to-earth, less "poetic" language and a renewal of the dramatic monologue, a literary form ideally suited to reveal character.

Today, Browning ranks with Tennyson as one of the great Victorian poets. His shorter dramatic monologues, such as "My Last Duchess," and "Porphyria's Lover," remain favorites of many.

My Last Duchess

Robert Browning

Background *This poem, set in the sixteenth century in a castle in northern Italy, is based on events from the life of the duke of Ferrara, a nobleman whose first wife died after just three years of marriage. Following his wife's death, the duke began making arrangements to remarry. In Browning's poem, the duke is showing a painting of his first wife to an agent who represents the father of the woman he hopes to marry.*

That's my last Duchess painted on the wall,
Looking as if she were alive. I call
That piece a wonder, now: Frà Pandolf's[1] hands
Worked busily a day, and there she stands.
5 Will't please you sit and look at her? I said
"Frà Pandolf" by design, for never read
Strangers like you that pictured countenance
The depth and passion of its earnest glance,
But to myself they turned (since none puts by
10 The curtain I have drawn for you, but I)
And seemed as they would ask me, if they durst,[2]
How such a glance came there; so, not the first
Are you to turn and ask thus. Sir, 'twas not
Her husband's presence only, called that spot

---

1. Frà Pandolf's work of Brother Pandolf, an imaginary painter.
2. durst dared.

15 Of joy into the Duchess' cheek: perhaps
    Frà Pandolf chanced to say "Her mantle laps
    Over my lady's wrist too much," or "Paint
    Must never hope to reproduce the faint
    Half-flush that dies along her throat"; such stuff
20 Was courtesy, she thought, and cause enough
    For calling up that spot of joy. She had
    A heart—how shall I say?—too soon made glad,
    Too easily impressed; she liked whate'er
    She looked on, and her looks went everywhere.
25 Sir, 'twas all one! My favor at her breast,
    The dropping of the daylight in the West,
    The bough of cherries some officious fool
    Broke in the orchard for her, the white mule
    She rode with round the terrace—all and each
30 Would draw from her alike the approving speech,
    Or blush, at least. She thanked men—good! but thanked
        Somehow—I know not how—as if she ranked
    My gift of a nine-hundred-year-old name
    With anybody's gift. Who'd stoop to blame
35 This sort of trifling? Even had you skill
    In speech—(which I have not)—to make your will
    Quite clear to such an one, and say, "Just this
    Or that in you disgusts me; here you miss,
    Or there exceed the mark"—and if she let
40 Herself be lessoned so, nor plainly set
    Her wits to yours, forsooth,[3] and made excuse,
    —E'en then would be some stooping; and I choose
    Never to stoop. Oh sir, she smiled, no doubt,
    Whene'er I passed her; but who passed without
45 Much the same smile? This grew; I gave commands;
    Then all smiles stopped together. There she stands
    As if alive. Will 't please you rise? We'll meet
    The company below, then. I repeat,
    The Count your master's known munificence
50 Is ample warrant that no one just pretense
    Of mine for dowry will be disallowed;
    Though his fair daughter's self, as I avowed
    At starting, is my object. Nay, we'll go
    Together down, sir! Notice Neptune,[4] though,
55 Taming a sea horse, thought a rarity,
    Which Claus of Innsbruck[5] cast in bronze for me!

---

3. **forsooth** in truth.
4. **Neptune** in Roman mythology, the god of the sea.
5. **Claus of Innsbruck** imaginary Austrian sculptor.

Life in a Love

Robert Browning

Escape me?
    Never—
    Beloved!
While I am I, and you are you,
5   So long as the world contains us both,
       Me the loving and you the loth,
While the one eludes, must the other pursue.
My life is a fault at last, I fear:
It seems too much like a fate, indeed!
10 Though I do my best I shall scarce succeed.
But what if I fail of my purpose here?
It is but to keep the nerves at strain,
To dry one's eyes and laugh at a fall,
And, baffled, get up and begin again,—
15 So the chase takes up one's life, that's all.
While, look but once from your farthest bound
At me so deep in the dust and dark,
No sooner the old hope goes to ground
Than a new one, straight to the self-same mark,
20 I shape me—
    Ever
    Removed!

Reading Strategy
Compare and Contrast Speakers How is the speaker's attitude toward his beloved in this poem like and unlike the attitude toward his former wife of the speaker in "My Last Duchess"?

Vocabulary
eludes (ē lōōdz´) *v.* avoids or escapes

Critical Reading

©

1. Key Ideas and Details (a) What complaint does the speaker make about his first wife in lines 13–24 of "My Last Duchess"? **(b) Infer:** How did he respond to her behavior? **(c) Support:** Explain what has happened to the duchess, indicating where in the poem this is revealed.

2. Key Ideas and Details (a) To what new subject does the speaker turn in his last remark? **(b) Draw Conclusions:** What does this change of subject reveal about his character?

3. Key Ideas and Details (a) What does the speaker of "Life in a Love" do as his beloved eludes him? **(b) Interpret:** What causes his behavior?

4. Integration of Knowledge and Ideas Is the speaker's "love" truly love? Explain.

Cite textual evidence to support your responses.

PORPHYRIA'S LOVER

Robert Browning

Vocabulary
sullen (səl´ ən) *adj.*
brooding; morose; sulky

The rain set early in tonight,
    The sullen wind was soon awake,
It tore the elm-tops down for spite,
    And did its worst to vex the lake:
5   I listened with heart fit to break.
When glided in Porphyria; straight
    She shut the cold out and the storm,
And kneeled and made the cheerless grate
    Blaze up, and all the cottage warm;
10   Which done, she rose, and from her form
Withdrew the dripping cloak and shawl,
    And laid her soiled gloves by, untied
Her hat and let the damp hair fall,
    And, last, she sat down by my side
15   And called me. When no voice replied,
She put my arm about her waist,
    And made her smooth white shoulder bare,
And all her yellow hair displaced,
    And, stooping, made my cheek lie there,
20   And spread, o'er all, her yellow hair,
Murmuring how she loved me—she
    Too weak, for all her heart's endeavor,
To set its struggling passion free
    From pride, and vainer ties dissever,

► **Critical Viewing**
Does the subject of this
painting seem to be in
love, as Porphyria is? Why
or why not? **[Infer]**

983

25 And give herself to me for ever.
    But passion sometimes would prevail,
        Nor could tonight's gay feast restrain
    A sudden thought of one so pale
        For love of her, and all in vain:
30   So, she was come through wind and rain.
    Be sure I looked up at her eyes
        Happy and proud; at last I knew
    Porphyria worshipped me; surprise
        Made my heart swell, and still it grew
35   While I debated what to do.
    That moment she was mine, mine, fair,
        Perfectly pure and good: I found
    A thing to do, and all her hair
        In one long yellow string I wound
40   Three times her little throat around,
    And strangled her. No pain felt she;
        I am quite sure she felt no pain.
    As a shut bud that holds a bee,
        I warily oped her lids: again
45   Laughed the blue eyes without a stain.
    And I untightened next the tress
        About her neck; her cheek once more
    Blushed bright beneath my burning kiss:
        I propped her head up as before,
50   Only, this time my shoulder bore
    Her head, which droops upon it still:
        The smiling rosy little head,
    So glad it has its utmost will,
        That all it scorned at once is fled,
55   And I, its love, am gained instead!
    Porphyria's love: she guessed not how
        Her darling one wish would be heard.
    And thus we sit together now,
        And all night long we have not stirred,
60   And yet God has not said a word!

Reading Strategy
Compare and Contrast Speakers From the contrast between the speaker's words and actions, what can you conclude about his mental state?

Critical Reading   ©

Cite textual evidence to support your responses.

© **1. Craft and Structure** Does this monologue have such dramatic elements as conflict, resolution, dialogue, and stage directions? Explain.

© **2. Craft and Structure** What makes the last line especially dramatic? Explain.

(1806–1861)

ELIZABETH BARRETT Browning

Author of Sonnet 43

Like her future husband, young Elizabeth Barrett had no formal education. However, her zest for knowledge spurred her to learn eight languages on her own. By the time she was ten, she had read plays by Shakespeare, passages of *Paradise Lost,* and histories of England, Greece, and Rome. The oldest of eleven children in an upper-middle-class family, she began writing poetry as a child. By the time she reached adulthood, she had published two volumes of verse.

Frailty and Romance Elizabeth Barrett's frail health, caused by a spinal injury, made her something of a recluse. But her poetry attracted much attention, including that of Robert Browning, who wrote her a letter of appreciation. After five months of correspondence, she and Browning met and fell in love. Her father objected to their romance, but Elizabeth and Robert married in 1846 and ran away to Florence, Italy, where they had a son they nicknamed Pen and lived in happy exile. In Italy, Elizabeth Barrett took an interest in politics and wrote denunciations of slavery in the United States. She died in Florence in 1861.

Shifting Reputations It is hard for us to believe today, when Robert Browning's reputation is so great, that Elizabeth was the more famous poet during her lifetime. Her love story in verse, *Aurora Leigh* (1857), was so popular that the income from it helped support the Brownings. Also popular was her *Sonnets from the Portuguese,* a sequence of forty-four love poems written to her husband. Sonnet 43, which comes from this collection, has appeared in countless anthologies and has assured her place in the history of English poetry.

Sonnet 43

ELIZABETH BARRETT BROWNING

Reading Strategy
Compare and Contrast Speakers Compare and contrast the love expressed here with the speaker's love for Porphyria in "Porphyria's Lover." What, if anything, do the two types of love have in common? How are they different?

How do I love thee? Let me count the ways.
I love thee to the depth and breadth and height
My soul can reach, when feeling out of sight
For the ends of Being and ideal Grace.
5 I love thee to the level of every day's
Most quiet need, by sun and candlelight.
I love thee freely, as men strive for Right;
I love thee purely, as they turn from Praise.
I love thee with the passion put to use
10 In my old griefs, and with my childhood's faith.
I love thee with a love I seemed to lose
With my lost saints—I love thee with the breath,
Smiles, tears, of all my life!—and, if God choose,
I shall but love thee better after death.

Critical Reading

Cite textual evidence to support your responses.

1. Key Ideas and Details **(a)** In Sonnet 43, what question does the speaker ask? **(b) Paraphrase:** Briefly summarize the speaker's answers to her own question.

2. Integration of Knowledge and Ideas Cite a popular song that praises love, and compare its language, attitude, and images with those of Sonnet 43.

3. Integration of Knowledge and Ideas Which speakers in these poems are most dramatic? Explain, using three of these Essential Question words: *psychological, emotional, motivation, rationalize, confront. [Connecting to the Essential Question: What is the relationship of the writer to tradition?]*

Literary Analysis

 1. Craft and Structure (a) Who delivers the **dramatic monologue** in "My Last Duchess," and who is the listener? **(b)** How can you tell when the listener interacts with the speaker? Give an example.

2. Key Ideas and Details (a) Cite two lines in which the speaker reveals something negative about himself. **(b)** Basing your answer on this monologue, do you think the speaker's next marriage will be successful? Explain.

3. Key Ideas and Details (a) Who are the speaker and the listener in "Life in a Love"? **(b)** Do they interact with each other? Explain.

4. Key Ideas and Details (a) Characterize the speaker in "Porphyria's Lover." **(b)** Whom do you think he might be addressing?

5. Craft and Structure (a) Use a chart like the one shown to analyze the places at which a speaker would naturally pause in lines 14–22 of "My Last Duchess." **(b)** How does the lack of **end-stopped lines** and the use of **run-on lines** and pauses within lines create a conversational rhythm?

Line 14:	Her hus-	-band's pre-	-sence on-	-ly, called	that spot
Natural Pauses	no pause	no pause	no pause	**pause**	no pause

6. Craft and Structure Use a similar chart to analyze the rhythms of Elizabeth Barrett Browning's Sonnet 43.

7. Comparing Literary Works (a) Compare the rhythms of speech in the two poems. **(b)** Which rhythm is more dramatic? Explain. **(c)** Which better captures general feelings in a memorable manner?

8. Analyzing Visual Information What qualities in Robert Browning's work earned it the popularity suggested by this Victorian cartoon?

Reading Strategy

9. Compare and contrast the speakers' behavior in "My Last Duchess" and "Porphyria's Lover." What is similar about their actions? What is different about the reasons for their actions?

10. (a) What is similar about the mental state of the speakers in all three poems by Robert Browning? Cite details to support your comparisons. **(b)** How do the tones or attitudes of all three speakers differ?

TRUE LITERARY EXCLUSIVENESS.

"Don't you admire Robert Browning as a poet, Mr. Fitzsnook?" "I used to, once; but everybody admires him now, don't'cherknow—so I've had to give him up!"▶

TRUE LITERARY EXCLUSIVENESS.

Common Core State Standards

Writing

1. Write arguments to support claims in an analysis of substantive topics or texts, using valid reasoning and relevant and sufficient evidence. *(p. 988)*

1.d. Establish and maintain a formal style and objective tone while attending to the norms and conventions of the discipline in which they are writing. *(p. 988)*

Language

4.b. Identify and correctly use patterns of word changes that indicate different meanings or parts of speech. *(p. 988)*

© Vocabulary Acquisition and Use

Word Analysis: Latin Suffix -ence

The Latin suffix -ence means "quality of," or "state of being." Words with this ending are often nouns that are closely related to adjectives. The adjective *munificent*, for example, means "very generous." Replacing the suffix -ent with -ence yields the noun *munificence,* "the state of being very generous." Write the noun forms of each of these words and then write an original sentence using each word.

1. innocent   **4.** permanent

2. intelligent   **5.** prominent

3. obedient   **6.** insistent

Vocabulary: Analogies

In an analogy, the relationship between two words is explained by comparing it to the relationship between two other words. Discern the meaning of the words from the vocabulary list on page 976 by using each word once to complete these analogies. Explain each choice.

1. *Building* is to *edifice* as *escapes* is to _____.

2. _____ is to *husband* as *gift* is to *charity*.

3. *Dialogue* is to *play* as _____ is to *portrait*.

4. *Silence* is to *noise* as _____ is to *happy*.

5. _____ is to *annoying* as *attentive* is to *pleasing*.

6. *Starting* is to *stopping* as _____ is to *greed*.

Writing

© **Argumentative Text** The duke in "My Last Duchess" has proposed marriage to another woman. Her father has hired you, a detective, to investigate the duke's history and character. Your task is to write a **report** to the father recommending whether he should allow the marriage to take place.

Prewriting Begin by reviewing the poem, noting what it reveals about the duke's character and first marriage. Draw from it as many facts as you can; infer others that you think are logical outgrowths of the duke's character. Think about the steps you might take to verify these facts so that you can detail those actions in your report. Speculate about what might have caused the duke's behavior.

Drafting Write your report using the *format* a detective might employ. For instance, you might state the date of the assignment and the subject. Include technical words that a detective might use, such as *surveillance, eyewitnesses, suspicions,* or *charges*. Keep in mind that you are a professional working for a client. Choose words, such as *suspect,* that create a formal, businesslike tone, rather than informal words such as *guy*.

Model: Revising to Add Transitional Words

As a result of my observations,
I have concluded the duke is a <u>cruel and dangerous</u>
    Therefore,
man. ~~and~~ I advise you to <u>reject</u> his proposal to marry your daughter.

Transitional words and phrases highlight causes and effects.

Revising Review your draft, drawing arrows between observations and the conclusions they support. Where needed, add missing transitional words to clarify causes and effects.

Focus on Literary Forms:
The Novel

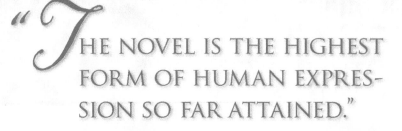

"THE NOVEL IS THE HIGHEST FORM OF HUMAN EXPRESSION SO FAR ATTAINED."

—D. H. LAWRENCE

Defining the Novel

A novel is a long work of prose fiction. As a genre, the novel is comparatively recent, though it has roots in the narratives of earlier ages. The length of a novel allows a writer great scope, and from its beginnings, the novel tended to survey—and sometimes criticize—a society, a social class, or a way of life as a whole. The English novel began with the work of writers such as Henry Fielding in the eighteenth century and reached full flower during the Victorian era with such classics as *Hard Times* and *David Copperfield* by Charles Dickens.

Types of Novels While novels need not belong to a specific type, many do. The following are traditional types:

- **Picaresque Novel:** relates the adventures of a traveling hero in episodic form
- **Historical Novel:** features characters and events from history
- **Novel of Manners:** shows the effects of social customs on individuals
- **Social Novel:** presents a large-scale portrait of an age, showing the influence of social and economic conditions on characters and events
- *Bildungsroman* **(Novel of Growth):** traces a protagonist's passage to adulthood

Literary Elements Nearly all novels contain certain basic literary elements, including **plot,** or an ordered sequence of events; **setting,** or the specific time and place of the action; **characters,** or the people who take part in the action; and a **theme,** or the insight into life conveyed by the work. In addition, as the novel developed historically, it emphasized or led to innovations in the literary elements shown in the chart below.

Close Read: Novelistic Literary Elements

These literary elements are called out in the Model text at right.

Narrative Technique: the way in which a writer tells a story. **Example:** *In* Mrs. Dalloway, *Virginia Woolf tells the story through the thoughts of her characters.*	**Philosophical Themes:** general ideas about existence and values. **Example:** *In* Crime and Punishment, *Fyodor Dostoyevsky's main character tries to apply new philosophical ideas, rejecting traditional morality.*
Social Commentary: writing that poses questions about or suggests criticisms of life in a society. **Example:** *In* Oliver Twist, *Charles Dickens's portrayal of the plight of a poor orphan is a call for reforms in England's treatment of its poor.*	**Realistic Description:** writing that attempts to accurately capture life in its details. **Example:** *In* The Jungle, *Upton Sinclair described industrial conditions in his day with grim accuracy.*

Model

About the Text The Russian novelist Fyodor Dostoyevsky (1821–1881), is noted for keen psychological portraits, including that of Raskolnikov in *Crime and Punishment.*

from Crime and Punishment
Fyodor Dostoyevsky (translated by Constance Garnett)

On an exceptionally hot evening early in July a young man came out of the garret in which he lodged in S. Place and walked slowly, as though in hesitation, towards K. bridge.

He had successfully avoided meeting his landlady on the staircase. His garret was under the roof of a high, five-storied house and was more like a cupboard than a room. The landlady who provided him with garret, dinners, and attendance, lived on the floor below, and every time he went out he was obliged to pass her kitchen, the door of which invariably stood open. And each time he passed, the young man had a sick, frightened feeling, which made him scowl and feel ashamed. He was hopelessly in debt to his landlady, and was afraid of meeting her....

This evening, however, on coming out into the street, he became acutely aware of his fears.

"I want to attempt a thing *like that* and am frightened by these trifles," he thought, with an odd smile. "Hm... yes, all is in a man's hands and he lets it all slip from cowardice, that's an axiom. It would be interesting to know what it is men are most afraid of. Taking a new step, uttering a new word is what they fear most.... But I am talking too much. It's because I chatter that I do nothing. Or perhaps it is that I chatter because I do nothing. I've learned to chatter this last month, lying for days together in my den thinking...of Jack the Giant-killer. Why am I going there now? Am I capable of *that*? Is *that* serious? It is not serious at all. It's simply a fantasy to amuse myself; a plaything! Yes, maybe it is a plaything."

The heat in the street was terrible: and the airlessness, the bustle and the plaster, scaffolding, bricks, and dust all about him, and that special Petersburg stench, so familiar to all who are unable to get out of town in summer—all worked painfully upon the young man's already overwrought nerves. The insufferable stench from the pot-houses, which are particularly numerous in that part of the town, and the drunken men whom he met continually, although it was a working day, completed the revolting misery of the picture. An expression of the profoundest disgust gleamed for a moment in the young man's refined face. He was, by the way, exceptionally handsome, above the average in height, slim, well-built, with beautiful dark eyes and dark brown hair. Soon he sank into deep thought, or more accurately speaking into a complete blankness of mind; he walked along not observing what was about him and not caring to observe it. From time to time, he would mutter something, from the habit of talking to himself, to which he had just confessed. At these moments he would become conscious that his ideas were sometimes in a tangle and that he was very weak; for two days he had scarcely tasted food.

Realistic Description The details in this passage realistically depict a poor young man's life, without apology or an attempt to "dress things up."

Narrative Technique The interior monologue, or direct representation of a character's thoughts, in this passage helps to advance the plot: The young man is plotting something that will require daring. It also helps to develop his character: he is beset by doubts and confusion.

Philosophical Themes Here, Dostoevsky hints at key philosophical questions in the novel: What are the limits on a person's freedom of choice? Are these limits valid—a matter of morals—or invalid—a matter of fear?

Social Commentary Details in this passage point to the inhuman, alienating conditions in the city and prompt questions about the society that has created these conditions.

Literary History: Dickens's World

"Dickens compounded characters of peculiar turns of speech and singular mannerisms, some endearing, *some frightening.*"

The Curious Workshop of Charles Dickens: Making Myths

Even if you have never read a novel by Charles Dickens, you have encountered his work. Characters such as the miser Ebenezer Scrooge and the orphan Oliver Twist stepped out from Dickens's books long ago to take up a life as old friends in musicals and cartoons. The very word *Dickensian* conjures obscure city streets populated by leering villains, honest clerks, wide-eyed innocents, and a host of knotty eccentrics.

Defining Dickens This generalized picture of Dickens and his works is based on his novels and Christmas stories, most published in serial form in magazines. Dickens's popularity in his own lifetime was enormous. With his first major effort, *The Pickwick Papers* (1836–1837), and for decades after, he held Victorian England spellbound, raptly awaiting the publication of the next chapter of *Oliver Twist* (1837–1839) or *Great Expectations* (1860–1861). When his character Little Nell of *The Old Curiosity Shop* (1840–1841) died, England was torn by grief.

Reformer and Myth-Maker In Dickens's lifetime, the Industrial Revolution left England overcrowded with the new working class, living in slums and riddled with epidemic fatal diseases. Dickens's stories of hard times and injured innocents challenged the forces that smothered compassion and nursed vice in the new society.

A Curious Workshop Yet Dickens does more than tell stories about social injustice. The most distinctive characteristic of his work might be its mythical or fairy tale–like quality. In the shadow of the factories choking London with smoke and slums, Dickens set up a workshop of the imagination, where he developed new myths of crime and redemption.

"A Perpetual Summer of Being Themselves" There are no John Smiths or Jane Joneses among Dickens's characters. From Samuel Pickwick to Wilkins Micawber to Uriah Heep, each character's name is a distinctive concoction of syllables, a two-word poem. The names reflect the quirkiness of the characters themselves. From the Rumplestiltskin-like Daniel Quilp of *The Old Curiosity Shop* to the hopelessly optimistic Mr. Micawber of *David Copperfield* (1849–1850), Dickens compounded characters of peculiar turns of speech and mannerisms, some endearing, some frightening.

Wicked Woods, Safe Havens Under Dickens's fairy-tale pen, the economic and social challenges of Victorian times reappear as a grotesque landscape, the literary equivalent of the woods in which a wicked witch lives. Here is Dickens's description of landscape surrounding a new railroad:

> Everywhere were bridges that led nowhere; thoroughfares that were wholly impassable; Babel towers of chimneys, wanting half their height; temporary wooden houses and enclosures, in the most unlikely situations; carcasses of ragged tenements, and fragments of unfinished walls and arches, and piles of scaffolding, and wildernesses of bricks, and giant forms of cranes, and tripods straddling above nothing. There were a hundred thousand shapes and substances of incompleteness. . . *(Dombey and Son, 1846–1848).*

Yet Dickens also creates islands of safety and refuge, such as the permanently beached boat in which David Copperfield finds happiness with the Peggoty family. In settings such as these, both Dickens's social criticism and his childlike attunement to the fairy-tale dimension of life have a place.

Dickens and Victorian England Dickens ruled over the imagination of Victorian England as a kind of father figure, by turns jolly and stern. He amuses his readers even while reprimanding their faults. Though there is much that is simply sentimental in Dickens, there are also depths of realism, an unflagging faith in redemption, and the eternal exuberance in human variety. Modern readers can still warm themselves at the cheerful glow of his work.

Speaking and Listening: Discussion

> **© Comprehension and Collaboration** **Message Art** Dickens was a brilliant novelist and social critic who blended scathing critiques of Victorian society with first-class literary entertainment.
>
> With a group, discuss your thoughts about how modern writers, musicians, and entertainers convey messages of social or political reform. Use these questions to guide your discussion:
>
> • Of the writers, musicians, and entertainers you know, which ones use their art to send a message? What are their messages?
>
> • What effect, if any, do popular entertainers' social or political messages have on others?
>
> • Do you think artists have a responsibility to make public their social or political messages? Explain.
>
> Choose a point person to share your thoughts with the class.

PHLit Online!
www.PHLitOnline.com

CHARLES *Dickens*

(1812–1870)

No writer since Shakespeare has occupied as important a place in popular culture as Charles Dickens. His novels have held a special appeal for critics and the public alike. They have also been dramatized time and again in plays and films.

A CHILDHOOD OF HARDSHIP

Born in Portsmouth on England's southern coast, Dickens had a generally unhappy childhood. His father was sent to debtors' prison, and the boy was sent to a "prison" of his own—a factory in which he worked long hours pasting labels. Similar experiences, dramatizing the ills of the newly industrialized society, were to figure prominently in Dickens's novels.

THE BIRTH OF A WRITER

As a young man, Dickens held jobs as a stenographer in the courts and as a reporter for London newspapers. At twenty-one, he began to apply his keen powers of observation to producing humorous literary sketches of everyday life in London. A collection of these, *Sketches by Boz* (1836), earned him a small following, but his first novel, *The Pickwick Papers* (1837), made him the most popular writer of his day. Closely following were *Oliver Twist* (1839) and *Nicholas Nickleby* (1839).

A SERIOUS NOVELIST

The young Dickens reveled in the variety and peculiarity of the human character. Memorable characters like the charming Mr. Pickwick and the evil Fagin abound in his early work, but they are perhaps more like cartoons or natural forces than full-blooded characters. Dickens shows his growing mastery of characterization in *Dombey and Son* (1848) and *David Copperfield* (1850), novels of greater psychological depth. Throughout his work, Dickens offers his distinctive brand of social criticism, which is especially prominent in his masterpiece *Hard Times* (1854).

SERIALIZATION

Many of Dickens's novels, beginning with *The Pickwick Papers,* were published serially in magazines—a common method of writing and producing fiction at the time. Monthly installments often ended with uncertain or dangerous situations, leaving readers eagerly awaiting the next installment.

IMMENSE POPULARITY

Dickens developed an avid following, and he thrived on the support of the public. He was widely read in Europe and the United States. Always fond of theater, he gave dramatic public readings from his novels. In 1842, he crossed the Atlantic for a five-month lecture tour in the United States. The American public welcomed him enthusiastically but were less happy with him when he criticized social issues in the United States.

Without doubt, Dickens was the preeminent nineteenth-century novelist. He was both imaginative and prolific. Despite his criticism of his age, he wrote to please his audience. So deeply did he affect his audiences, in fact, that the view of life in his novels has become a part of English tradition.

Dickens's
Characters—And
Their Words—Live On!

"Bah, humbug!"

"Shake me up, Judy"

"Very 'Eavy... Very 'Umble'"

Scrooged!

What's in a name, Juliet asked in Shakespeare's *Romeo and Juliet*. She was making the point that names do not reveal anything about a person. Well, don't tell that to Charles Dickens. For him, there was a world of meaning in the names he gave his characters—989 in all. In fact, many of the names Dickens coined and the odd phrases he put into characters' mouths are still used today.

- Ever been Scrooged? Even if you are unfamiliar with *A Christmas Carol*, Dickens's tale about a miserly man whose experiences with three spirits on Christmas Eve change him into a kind and generous soul, you probably know how it feels to be the victim of someone else's stinginess. One of the unreformed Scrooge's favorite phrases, "Bah, humbug!," is still used today to express a Scrooge-like view of the world.

- Ever hear the optimistic phrase, "Something will turn up," used in a sarcastic way? If so, the speaker may be ironically quoting the ne'er-do-well Wilkins Micawber, a character from Dickens's autobiographical novel *David Copperfield*. Based on Dickens's father, Micawber was a perennial optimist, despite the evidence of reality.

- Ever listen to the music of the band Uriah Heep? The title of the band's first album, "Very 'Eavy . . . Very 'Umble," quotes a characteristic phrase spoken by the devious, obsequious clerk Uriah Heep, another character from *David Copperfield*. Young David memorably describes Heep as someone "who had hardly any eyebrows, and no eyelashes, and eyes of a red brown, so unsheltered and unshaded, that I remember wondering how he went to sleep." To this day, it is an insult to be called a falsely humble Uriah Heep.

These are just a few of the Dickens characters whose vivid names and twitchy phrases are still part of pop culture today.

Before You Read | from *Hard Times*

Connecting to the Essential Question In *Hard Times*, Dickens criticizes education that is based on rote learning instead of imagination. As you read, notice how Dickens describes the educational approaches he is criticizing. Focusing on these descriptions will help you answer the Essential Question: **How does literature shape or reflect society?**

**Common Core
State Standards**

**Reading Literature
3.** Analyze the impact of the author's choices regarding how to develop and relate elements of a story or drama.

Literary Analysis

The novel, a long work of fiction, became popular in the nineteenth century, a period of disturbing social and economic changes. Like other novelists of the time, Dickens included social criticism in his works, calling attention to the **ethical and social influences** that resulted in society's ills. In *Hard Times*, Dickens focuses on misguided educational practices. Through his characters and situations, Dickens reveals his own *philosophical assumptions*. As you read, notice how Dickens turns incidents into dramatizations—and criticisms—of ethical and social issues.

Reading Strategy

Preparing to Read Complex Texts **Analyzing an author's purpose** will help you understand how specific incidents relate to *meaning* in a novel. In *Hard Times*, note how Dickens develops elements such as characterization, setting, and dialogue to reveal the ethical and social influences that he is criticizing. Also note Dickens's use of comic exaggeration to achieve his purpose. Use a chart like the one shown to help you analyze Dickens's purpose and the meaning it reveals.

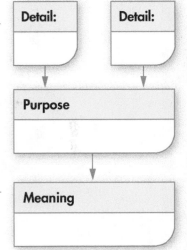

Vocabulary

monotonous (mə nät′ ən əs) *adj.* without variation (p. 999)

obstinate (äb′ stə nət) *adj.* stubborn; dogged (p. 999)

deficient (di fish′ ənt) *adj.* lacking an essential quality (p. 1001)

adversary (ad′ vər ser ē) *n.* opponent; enemy (p. 1002)

indignant (in dig′ nənt) *adj.* outraged; filled with righteous anger (p. 1002)

approbation (ap′ rə bā shən) *n.* official approval (p. 1002)

etymology (et′ ə mol′ ə jē) *n.* the study of word origins (p. 1004)

syntax (sin′ taks) *n.* the study of sentence structure (p. 1004)

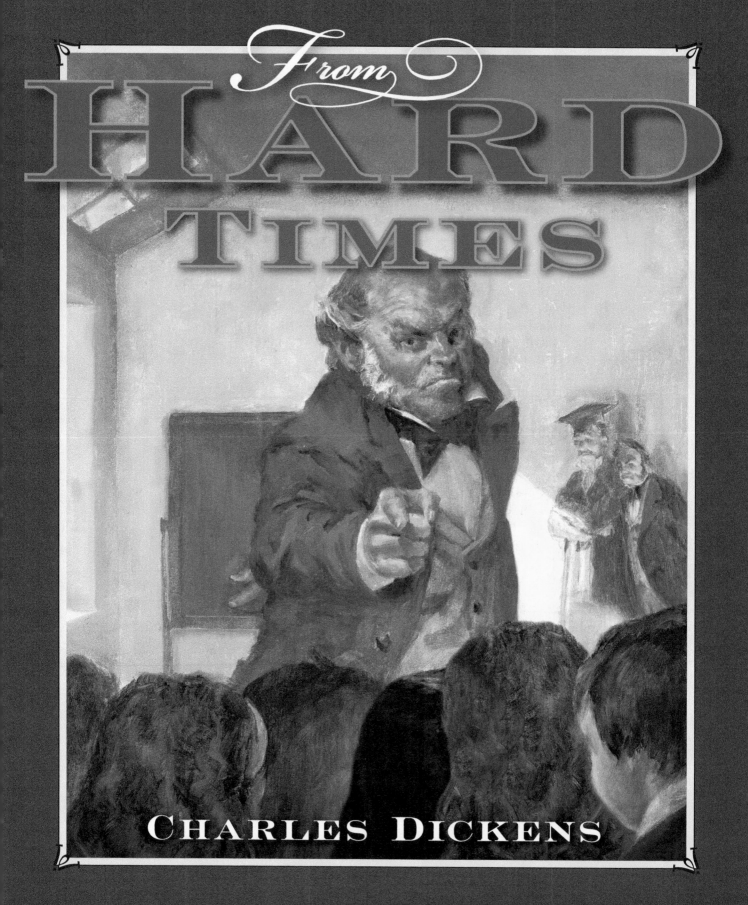

From HARD TIMES

CHARLES DICKENS

BACKGROUND OF THE MANY BELIEFS IN HIS SOCIETY WITH WHICH DICKENS TOOK ISSUE, THE UTILITARIANISM OF PHILOSOPHER JEREMY BENTHAM (1748–1832) PARTICULARLY IRRITATED HIM. BENTHAM BELIEVED THAT STATISTICS AND LOGIC COULD BE APPLIED TO ALL HUMAN AFFAIRS, AND HE VIEWED HUMAN BEINGS AS ESSENTIALLY INTERESTED ONLY IN THEIR OWN HAPPINESS. HE SAW THE PURPOSE OF SOCIETY AS "THE GREATEST HAPPINESS FOR THE GREATEST NUMBER," WITH HAPPINESS CALCULATED IN TERMS OF INDIVIDUAL PLEASURES AND PAINS. DICKENS BELIEVED UTILITARIANISM DISCOUNTED OR EVEN SOUGHT TO NEGATE VIRTUES LIKE IMAGINATION AND SYMPATHY. IN *HARD TIMES*, DICKENS USED HIS CHARACTER MR. GRADGRIND TO POKE FUN AT THIS PHILOSOPHY.

Artist rendering of cover of first edition of *Hard Times*

CHAPTER 1
THE ONE THING NEEDFUL

"Now, what I want is, Facts. Teach these boys and girls nothing but Facts. Facts alone are wanted in life. Plant nothing else, and root out everything else. You can only form the minds of reasoning animals upon Facts: nothing else will ever be of any service to them. This is the principle on which I bring up my own children, and this is the principle on which I bring up these children. Stick to Facts, sir!"

The scene was a plain, bare, monotonous vault of a schoolroom, and the speaker's square forefinger emphasized his observations by underscoring every sentence with a line on the schoolmaster's sleeve. The emphasis was helped by the speaker's square wall of a forehead, which had his eyebrows for its base, while his eyes found commodious cellarage in two dark caves, overshadowed by the wall. The emphasis was helped by the speaker's mouth, which was wide, thin, and hard set. The emphasis was helped by the speaker's voice, which was inflexible, dry, and dictatorial. The emphasis was helped by the speaker's hair, which bristled on the skirts of his bald head, a plantation of firs to keep the wind from its shining surface, all covered with knobs, like the crust of a plum pie, as if the head had scarcely warehouse-room for the hard facts stored inside. The speaker's obstinate carriage, square coat, square legs, square shoulders—nay, his very neckcloth, trained to take him by the throat with an unaccommodating grasp, like a stubborn fact, as it was—all helped the emphasis.

"In this life, we want nothing but Facts, sir; nothing but Facts!"

The speaker, and the schoolmaster, and the third grown person present, all backed a little, and swept with their eyes the inclined plane of little vessels, then and there arranged in order, ready to have imperial gallons of facts poured into them until they were full to the brim.

Vocabulary
monotonous (mə nät´ ən əs)
adj. without variation

obstinate (äb´ stə nət)
adj. stubborn; dogged

◀ **Critical Viewing**
Judging from the details in this illustration, what was school like in England during Victorian times? **[Speculate]**

☑ Reading Check
What does Gradgrind aim to do for students?

The Nineteenth-Century Novel

In the nineteenth century, technological advances allowed newspaper and magazine publishers to print large runs at affordable prices. For the first time, this made reading material widely available to the middle classes. For these publications, writers contributed fiction that was serialized in weekly or monthly issues. British authors Charles Dickens, George Eliot, William Thackeray and Thomas Hardy, French authors Honoré de Balzac and Victor Hugo, and Russian authors Fyodor Dostoyevsky and Leo Tolstoy wrote their novels as serials.

Connect to the Literature

How do you think contemporary readers might have responded to the weekly installments of *Hard Times*, which Dickens joked were "teaspoon" servings?

Literary Analysis
Ethical and Social Influences What outlook is Dickens criticizing through Gradgrind's identification of Sissy Jupe by a number?

CHAPTER 2
MURDERING THE INNOCENTS

Thomas Gradgrind, sir. A man of realities. A man of fact and calculations. A man who proceeds upon the principle that two and two are four, and nothing over, and who is not to be talked into allowing for anything over. Thomas Gradgrind, sir—peremptorily Thomas—Thomas Gradgrind. With a rule and a pair of scales, and the multiplication table always in his pocket, sir, ready to weigh and measure any parcel of human nature, and tell you exactly what it comes to. It is a mere question of figures, a case of simple arithmetic. You might hope to get some other nonsensical belief into the head of George Gradgrind, or Augustus Gradgrind, or John Gradgrind, or Joseph Gradgrind (all suppositious, non-existent persons), but into the head of Thomas Gradgrind—no, sir!

In such terms Mr. Gradgrind always mentally introduced himself, whether to his private circle of acquaintance, or to the public in general. In such terms, no doubt, substituting the words "boys and girls," for "sir," Thomas Gradgrind now presented Thomas Gradgrind to the little pitchers before him, who were to be filled so full of facts.

Indeed, as he eagerly sparkled at them from the cellarage before mentioned, he seemed a kind of cannon loaded to the muzzle with facts, and prepared to blow them clean out of the regions of childhood at one discharge. He seemed a galvanizing apparatus, too, charged with a grim mechanical substitute for the tender young imaginations that were to be stormed away.

"Girl number twenty," said Mr. Gradgrind, squarely pointing with his square forefinger, "I don't know that girl. Who is that girl?"

"Sissy Jupe, sir," explained number twenty, blushing, standing up, and curtseying.

"Sissy is not a name," said Mr. Gradgrind. "Don't call yourself Sissy. Call yourself Cecilia."

"It's father as calls me Sissy, sir," returned the young girl in a trembling voice, and with another curtsey.

"Then he has no business to do it," said Mr. Gradgrind. "Tell him he mustn't. Cecilia Jupe. Let me see. What is your father?"

"He belongs to the horse-riding, if you please, sir."

Mr. Gradgrind frowned, and waved off the objectionable calling with his hand.

"We don't want to know anything about that, here. You mustn't tell us about that, here. Your father breaks horses, don't he?"

"If you please, sir, when they can get any to break, they do break horses in the ring, sir."

"You mustn't tell us about the ring, here. Very well, then. Describe your father as a horsebreaker. He doctors sick horses, I dare say?"

"Oh yes, sir."

"Very well, then. He is a veterinary surgeon, a farrier and horse-breaker. Give me your definition of a horse."

(Sissy Jupe thrown into the greatest alarm by this demand.)

"Girl number twenty unable to define a horse!" said Mr. Gradgrind, for the general behoof of all the little pitchers. "Girl number twenty possessed of no facts, in reference to one of the commonest of animals! Some boy's definition of a horse. Bitzer, yours."

The square finger, moving here and there, lighted suddenly on Bitzer, perhaps because he chanced to sit in the same ray of sunlight which, darting in at one of the bare windows of the intensely white-washed room, irradiated Sissy. For, the boys and girls sat on the face of the inclined plane in two compact bodies, divided up the center by a narrow interval; and Sissy, being at the corner of a row on the sunny side, came in for the beginning of a sunbeam, of which Bitzer, being at the corner of a row on the other side, a few rows in advance, caught the end. But, whereas the girl was so dark-eyed and dark-haired, that she seemed to receive a deeper and more lustrous color from the sun when it shone upon her, the boy was so light-eyed and light-haired that the self-same rays appeared to draw out of him what little color he ever possessed. His cold eyes would hardly have been eyes, but for the short ends of lashes which, by bringing them into immediate contrast with something paler than themselves, expressed their form. His short-cropped hair might have been a mere continuation of the sandy freckles on his forehead and face. His skin was so unwhole-somely deficient in the natural tinge, that he looked as though, if he were cut, he would bleed white.

"Bitzer," said Thomas Gradgrind. "Your definition of a horse."

"Quadruped. Graminivorous. Forty teeth, namely twenty-four grinders, four eye-teeth, and twelve incisive. Sheds coat in the spring; in marshy countries, sheds hoofs, too. Hoofs hard, but requiring to be shod with iron. Age known by marks in mouth." Thus (and much more) Bitzer.

"Now girl number twenty," said Mr. Gradgrind. "You know what a horse is."

She curtseyed again, and would have blushed deeper, if she could have blushed deeper than she had blushed all this time. Bitzer, after rapidly blinking at Thomas Gradgrind with both eyes at once, and so catching the light upon his quivering ends of lashes that they looked like the antennae of busy insects, put his knuckles to his freckled fore-head, and sat down again.

The third gentleman now stepped forth. A mighty man at cutting and drying, he was; a government officer; in his way (and in most other people's too), a professed pugilist; always in training, always with a sys-tem to force down the general throat like a bolus,[1] always to be heard of at the bar of his little Public-office, ready to fight all England. To continue

---

1. **bolus** small, round mass, often of chewed food.

"GIRL NUMBER TWENTY UNABLE TO DEFINE A HORSE!"

Vocabulary
deficient (di fish´ ənt)
adj. lacking an essential quality

Spiral Review
Plot How would you summarize the events of *Hard Times* up to this point in the plot?

Reading Check

What type of answer to his question does Gradgrind accept?

Vocabulary
adversary (ad´ vər ser´ ē)
n. opponent; enemy

Reading Strategy
Analyzing the Author's Purpose What does the reaction of the class hint about Dickens's purpose in this scene?

in fistic phraseology, he had a genius for coming up to the scratch, wherever and whatever it was, and proving himself an ugly customer. He would go in and damage any subject whatever with his right, follow up with his left, stop, exchange, counter, bore his opponent (he always fought All England[2]) to the ropes, and fall upon him neatly. He was certain to knock the wind out of common sense, and render that unlucky adversary deaf to the call of time. And he had it in charge from high authority to bring about the great public-office Millennium, when Commissioners should reign upon earth.

"Very well," said this gentleman, briskly smiling, and folding his arms. "That's a horse. Now, let me ask you girls and boys, Would you paper a room with representations of horses?"

After a pause, one half of the children cried in chorus, "Yes, sir!" Upon which the other half, seeing in the gentleman's face that Yes was wrong, cried out in chorus, "No, sir!"—as the custom is, in these examinations.

"Of course, No. Why wouldn't you?"

A pause. One corpulent slow boy, with a wheezy manner of breathing, ventured the answer, Because he wouldn't paper a room at all, but would paint it.

"You *must* paper it," said Thomas Gradgrind, "whether you like it or not. Don't tell *us* you wouldn't paper it. What do you mean, boy?"

"I'll explain to you, then," said the gentleman, after another and a dismal pause, "why you wouldn't paper a room with representations of horses. Do you ever see horses walking up and down the sides of rooms in reality—in fact? Do you?"

"Yes, sir!" from one half. "No, sir!" from the other.

"Of course no," said the gentleman, with an indignant look at the wrong half. "Why, then, you are not to see anywhere, what you don't see in fact; you are not to have anywhere, what you don't have in fact. What is called Taste, is only another name for Fact."

Thomas Gradgrind nodded his approbation.

"This is a new principle, a discovery, a great discovery," said the gentleman. "Now, I'll try you again. Suppose you were going to carpet a room. Would you use a carpet having a representation of flowers upon it?"

There being a general conviction by this time that "No, sir!" was always the right answer to this gentleman, the chorus of No was very strong. Only a few feeble stragglers said Yes; among them Sissy Jupe.

"Girl number twenty," said the gentleman, smiling in the calm strength of knowledge.

Sissy blushed, and stood up.

"So you would carpet your room—or your husband's room, if you were a grown woman, and had a husband—with representations of flowers, would you," said the gentleman. "Why would you?"

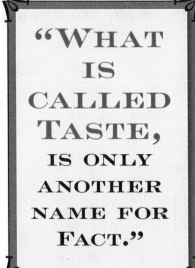

"WHAT IS CALLED TASTE, IS ONLY ANOTHER NAME FOR FACT."

Vocabulary
indignant (in dig´ nənt)
adj. outraged; filled with righteous anger

approbation
(ap´ rə bā´ shən) *n.* official approval

---

2. fought All England fought according to the official rules of boxing.

"If you please, sir, I am very fond of flowers," returned the girl.

"And is that why you would put tables and chairs upon them, and have people walking over them with heavy boots?"

"It wouldn't hurt them, sir. They wouldn't crush and wither if you please, sir. They would be the pictures of what was very pretty and pleasant, and I would fancy—"

"Ay, ay, ay! but you mustn't fancy," cried the gentleman, quite elated by coming so happily to his point. "That's it! You are never to fancy."

"You are not, Cecilia Jupe," Thomas Gradgrind solemnly repeated, "to do anything of that kind."

"Fact, fact, fact!" said the gentleman. And "Fact, fact, fact!" repeated Thomas Gradgrind.

"You are to be in all things regulated and governed," said the gentleman, "by fact. We hope to have, before long, a board of fact, composed of commissioners of fact, who will force the people to be a people of fact, and of nothing but fact. You must discard the word Fancy altogether. You have nothing to do with it. You are not to have, in any object of use or ornament, what would be a contradiction in fact. You don't walk upon flowers in fact; you cannot be allowed to walk upon flowers in carpets. You don't find that foreign birds and butterflies come and perch upon your crockery. You never meet with quadrupeds going up and down walls; you must not have quadrupeds represented upon walls. You must use," said the gentleman, "for all these purposes, combinations and modifications (in primary colors) of mathematical figures which are susceptible of proof and demonstration. This is the new discovery. This is fact. This is taste."

The girl curtseyed, and sat down. She was very young, and she looked as if she were frightened by the matter of fact prospect the world afforded.

"Now, if Mr. M'Choakumchild," said the gentleman, "will proceed to give his first lesson here, Mr. Gradgrind, I shall be happy, at your request, to observe his mode of procedure."

Mr. Gradgrind was much obliged. "Mr. M'Choakumchild, we only wait for you."

So, Mr. M'Choakumchild began in his best manner. He and some one hundred and forty other schoolmasters, had been lately turned at the same time, in the same factory, on the same principles, like so many pianoforte legs. He had been put through an immense

Literary Analysis
Ethical and Social Influences What point about imagination does Dickens make through the teacher's literal-minded understanding?

▼ **Critical Viewing**
What does this picture of Sissy suggest about her relationship with her classmates and Gradgrind? **[Infer]**

Reading Check

Why does the third gentleman object to horses on wallpaper and flowers on rugs?

Vocabulary
etymology (ət´ ə məl´ ə jē)
n. the study of word origins

syntax (sin´ taks) *n.* the
study of sentence structure

variety of paces, and had answered volumes of head-breaking questions. Orthography, etymology, syntax, and prosody, biography, astronomy, geography, and general cosmography, the sciences of compound proportion, algebra, land-surveying and leveling, vocal music, and drawing from models, were all at the ends of his ten chilled fingers. He had worked his stony way into Her Majesty's most Honorable Privy Council's Schedule B, and had taken the bloom off the higher branches of mathematics and physical science, French, German, Latin, and Greek. He knew all about all the Water Sheds of all the world (whatever they are), and all the histories of all the peoples, and all the names of all the rivers and mountains, and all the productions, manners, and customs of all the countries, and all their boundaries and bearings on the two-and-thirty points of the compass. Ah, rather overdone, M'Choakumchild. If he had only learnt a little less, how infinitely better he might have taught much more!

He went to work in this preparatory lesson, not unlike Morgiana in the Forty Thieves:[3] looking into all the vessels ranged before him, one after another, to see what they contained. Say, good M'Choakumchild. When from thy boiling store, thou shalt fill each jar brim full by and by, dost thou think that thou wilt always kill outright the robber Fancy lurking within—or sometimes only maim him and distort him!

---

3. **Morgiana in the Forty Thieves** In the tale "Ali Baba and the Forty Thieves," Ali Baba's clever servant, Morgiana, saves him from the thieves who are hiding in large jars.

> **"IF HE
> HAD ONLY
> LEARNT
> A LITTLE
> LESS...
> HE
> MIGHT
> HAVE
> TAUGHT
> MUCH
> MORE!"**

Cite textual evidence to support your responses.

Critical Reading

1. **Key Ideas and Details (a)** What does Mr. Gradgrind believe is the key to all learning? **(b) Connect:** In what ways does he put this belief into practice? **(c) Interpret:** What attitude does the description of the children as "little pitchers" reflect?

2. **Integration of Knowledge and Ideas (a) Compare and Contrast:** Compare and contrast Sissy's and Bitzer's performances in the classroom. **(b) Analyze:** With whom does Dickens expect the reader to sympathize? Why?

3. **Integration of Knowledge and Ideas** What values does Dickens believe a system of education should teach? Explain, using two of these Essential Question words: *imagination, sympathy, conform, society, fact. [Connecting to the Essential Question: How does literature shape or reflect society?]*

Critical Commentary

"Charles Dickens"
George Orwell

George Orwell (1903–1950), an important author in his own right (see p. 1317), wrote a brilliant and highly readable essay on Charles Dickens. In the essay, Orwell comments specifically on the criticism of Victorian education that Dickens made in Hard Times *and elsewhere.*

. . . Except for the universities and the big public schools, every kind of education then existing in England gets a mauling at Dickens's hands. . . . But as usual, Dickens's criticism is neither creative or destructive. He sees the idiocy of an educational system founded on the Greek lexicon and the wax-ended cane; on the other hand, he has no use for the new kind of school that is coming up in the 'fifties and 'sixties, the "modern" school, with its gritty insistence on "facts." What, then, *does* he want? As always, what he appears to want is a moralized version of the existing thing—the old type of school, but with no caning, no bullying or underfeeding, and not quite so much Greek.

Orwell also explains how he visualizes Dickens and what he values most about him.

When one reads any strongly individual piece of writing, one has the impression of seeing a face somewhere behind the page. It is not necessarily the actual face of the writer. . . . What one sees is the face that the writer *ought* to have. Well, in the case of Dickens I see a face that is not quite the face of Dickens's photographs, though it resembles it. It is the face of a man of about forty, with a small beard and a high color. He is laughing, with a touch of anger in his laughter, but no triumph, no malignity. It is the face of a man who is always fighting against something, but who fights in the open and is not frightened, the face of a man who is *generously angry*—in other words, of a nineteenth-century liberal, a free intelligence, a type hated with equal hatred by all the smelly little orthodoxies which are now contending for our souls.

> "Charity begins at home, and justice begins next door."

▼ **Critical Viewing** Does this caricature of Dickens by David Levine capture any of the qualities Orwell discusses? Why or why not? **[Connect]**

© **Key Ideas and Details** According to Orwell, what kind of a school does Dickens favor? What picture of Dickens does Orwell have in mind as he reads the Victorian author?

After You Read from *Hard Times*

Literary Analysis

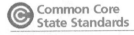

Common Core
State Standards

Language
4.c. Consult general and specialized reference materials, both print and digital, to find the pronunciation of a word or determine or clarify its precise meaning, its part of speech, its etymology, or its standard usage. *(p. 1007)*

4.d. Verify the preliminary determination of the meaning of a word or phrase. *(p. 1007)*

1. **Key Ideas and Details (a)** In the selection from *Hard Times,* which details make the setting vivid? **(b)** How do they contribute to a criticism of the **ethical and social influences** of the time?

2. **Key Ideas and Details (a)** Summarize the viewpoint that Dickens criticizes. **(b)** Do you think there is a positive side to this viewpoint that Dickens may have neglected or deliberately ignored? Why or why not?

3. **Craft and Structure (a)** Identify three examples in which Dickens uses comic exaggeration to criticize Gradgrind and his fellows. **(b)** What does Dickens accomplish through his use of exaggeration, both in characterization and in the character's words? Use a chart like the one shown to examine Dickens's techniques.

Passage	Intended Effect on Reader	Intended Message	Enjoyment Value

4. **Integration of Knowledge and Ideas (a)** Identify the passage that you think is most effective in conveying Dickens's message about education. **(b)** Which details in this passage reveal the writer's desire to convey a message? Explain.

Reading Strategy

5. Choose an example of each of the following elements that help clarify the **author's purpose,** explaining your choice:
   (a) the name of a character
   (b) a character's statement or dialogue
   (c) a description of a place

6. **(a)** If Sissy and Bitzer grew up and became writers, which character would write social criticism and which might not? Explain. **(b)** What does your answer suggest about Dickens's purpose in including both characters?

7. **(a)** What conclusion does Dickens want the reader to draw about the three adults in the classroom? **(b)** What conclusions does Dickens want the reader to draw about the kind of children this type of education will produce?

8. If Dickens were alive today, what purpose or purposes might he have in writing about contemporary educational practices? Explain.

Integrated Language Skills

⊚ Vocabulary Acquisition and Use

Word Analysis: Greek Prefix *mono-*

The Greek prefix *mono-* means "single" or "alone." Thus, someone who speaks in a *monotonous* way talks in a single, unchanging manner, without varying tone or subject. The prefix is used to form many common words as well as some scientific and technical words. Explain how the prefix *mono-* contributes to the meaning of each of these words. Use a dictionary to confirm the meaning of a word if you are unsure.

1. monochromatic
2. monogamy
3. monologue
4. monopoly
5. monorail
6. monotreme

Write two original sentences using these or any other words with the prefix *mono-*.

Vocabulary: Antonyms

Antonyms are words with opposite or nearly opposite meanings. *Bitter* and *sweet* are antonyms, as are *night* and *day*. For each of the following vocabulary words, identify an antonym. Then, write an original sentence using the word and its antonym.

Example: reality
Antonym: fantasy
Sentence: Gradgrind did not believe in fantasy or the imagination, only in his cold, hard reality.

1. monotonous
2. obstinate
3. deficient
4. adversary
5. indignant
6. approbation

Using Resources to Build Vocabulary

Words for a Utilitarian Perspective
Charles Dickens gives Thomas Gradgrind a particular vocabulary that emphasizes his interest in only the utilitarian aspects of life. Near the beginning of the passage, he declares, "Facts alone are wanted in life." Review this list of utilitarian words that Dickens puts in Gradgrind's mouth—or thoughts.

reason	inflexible
observation	calculation
weigh	mechanical

Use a print or an electronic dictionary to find the **connotations** of these words. Connotations are ideas or emotions associated with a word. Then, use a print or an electronic dictionary or a thesaurus to find antonyms—words with the opposite connotation, such as *illogic* for *reason*. Explain why each word you choose is a suitable antonym.

PERFORMANCE TASKS
Integrated Language Skills

Writing

Informative Text The excerpt from *Hard Times* presents a vivid picture of a Victorian school. Were the attitudes and methods used by Gradgrind typical of the period, or was Dickens painting an extreme picture? Answering that question requires a historical investigation.

Compile an **annotated bibliography** of works that could be used in a research paper on the topic. An annotated bibliography includes not only full bibliographic information on sources but also notes that describe the kinds of information each source can offer and an evaluation of its usefulness. In your bibliography, include works with different perspectives, and include both primary sources (books from Victorian times) and secondary sources (those from later periods).

Prewriting Use both print materials and the Internet to locate sources. You might ask a librarian for help in finding appropriate sources.

- Use relevant keywords like *education, Victorian,* and *Britain* to search for sources. Be sure to locate both primary and secondary sources.

- Scan the table of contents, introduction, first chapter, or other key elements of each source to learn what it says about the subject. Consider its scope, what type of education it addresses; its validity, how authoritative the observations seem to be; and its reliability, how free or absent of bias it is.

- Find a copy of the style guide, such as the MLA style guide, that your teacher wants you to use for presenting the bibliographic information for each source.

Drafting Write a draft of your annotated bibliography.

- Prepare an entry for each source you consulted, styling it properly according to the style guide.

- Add an annotation that addresses the scope, reliability, and validity of each source. Use your annotations to show the different perspectives you can gain from this variety of sources.

Revising Review your bibliographical entries for both format and content.

- Be sure the entries conform to the correct style. If not, make any needed changes.

- Review the annotations to make sure they clearly assess each work's usefulness.

Common Core State Standards

Writing

2. Write informative/ explanatory texts to examine and convey complex ideas, concepts, and information clearly and accurately through the effective selection, organization, and analysis of content.

8. Gather relevant information from multiple authoritative print and digital sources, using advanced searches effectively; assess the strengths and limitations of each source in terms of the task, purpose, and audience; integrate information into the text selectively to maintain the flow of ideas, avoiding plagiarism and overreliance on any one source and following a standard format for citation.

> **Model: Drafting Annotations for Primary Sources**
> Timkins, Charles. *School Days.* London: Chapman, 1868.
> Timkins's memoir narrates his life in a boarding, or private, school. It reveals the loneliness felt by the boys, the brutality of some teachers, and the tough academic standards students had to meet. Limited in scope to just one school but full of anecdotes.

The annotation shows the unique insight provided by this source.

Conventions and Style Shifts in Verb Tense

Use **verb tenses** in a logical sequence to show when actions happen in relation to one another. **Avoid shifting tenses** when the actions occur at the same time.

> **Shifted Tenses:** Mr. Gradgrind points to Sissy and asked her name.
> **Correct:** Mr. Gradgrind pointed to Sissy and asked her name.
> **Correct:** Mr. Gradgrind points to Sissy and asks her name.

Note the different forms of verb tenses:

Present:	wants, is wanting, does want, have wanted, have been wanting
Past:	wanted, was wanting, did want, had wanted, had been wanting
Future:	will want, will be wanting, will have wanted, will have been wanting

When actions occur at different times, use the sequence of tenses that indicates the correct times.

> **Mr. Gradgrind had learned Sissy's name, but he still called her "girl number twenty."**

Participle forms (*wanting, wanted, having wanted*) and infinitive forms (*to want, to have wanted*) can also indicate time. Use the form that indicates the timing in relation to the main verb.

Practice Decide whether a sentence uses verb tenses correctly. If it is correct, write *correct*. If it is incorrect, rewrite the sentence correctly

1. Bitzer had learned the definition of a horse, and so he recites it when called on.
2. The gentleman hopes commissioners of fact forced people to use only facts.
3. Once the children learn facts, they will be educated.
4. Having stated his beliefs about facts, Gradgrind begins to call on students.
5. The gentleman had been listening, but then he joins in the examining of students.
6. Half the class had called out "yes" before they see that the gentleman expected "no."
7. Sissy hadn't known the definition of *horse*, but she will be speaking up again.
8. In Mr. Gradgrind's opinion, children are like pitchers to have been filled with facts.
9. Educated with facts, the schoolmaster wanted to see what the children knew.
10. The schoolmaster had learned too many facts, and he is a poorer teacher as a result.

ⓒ Writing and Speaking Conventions

A. Writing Use the two verbs in a sentence showing actions that happen at the same time. Use the tense given in parentheses.

1. ask, answer (*present*)
2. weigh, measure (*future*)
3. frown, wave (*past*)
4. fill, hold (*present*)

    Example: ask, answer
    Sentence: The adults ask questions, and the children answer.

B. Speaking Write and present to the class a persuasive argument in which you either agree or disagree with Mr. Gradgrind's point of view about education. Be sure to avoid shifts in verb tense and to include support for your argument.

PH WRITING COACH

Further instruction and practice are available in *Prentice Hall Writing Coach.*

The Novelist as Social Critic

John Steinbeck
(1902–1968)

Doris Lessing
(b. 1919)

Anton Chekhov
(1860–1904)

Émile Zola
(1840–1902)

Charles Dickens
(1812–1870)

Charlotte Brontë
(1816–1855)

Comparing Literary Works

from *Hard Times* by Charles Dickens
• "An Upheaval" by Anton Chekhov

Comparing Social Criticism in Fiction

Social Criticism

In the nineteenth century, **social criticism** began to appear much more frequently in fiction. Writers like Charles Dickens and Anton Chekhov told stories that brought societal ills to public awareness. Slavery, unsafe work or living conditions, colonialism, the class system, injustices in the judicial and education systems—these are some of the issues that authors have criticized over the years. Social criticism often takes these forms:

- **Realism:** Reveals social ills by showing how life is really lived
- **Satire:** Ridicules individuals, institutions, groups, and so on
- **Utopian fiction:** Shows a perfect society, forcing readers to see what needs improvement in their own society
- **Dystopian fiction:** Depicts a dreadful society, forcing readers to see the dangers to which current social ills may lead

Some social criticism is **explicit,** stated directly in the work. More often in fiction, however, it is **implicit,** with readers expected to infer the criticisms based on the work's details. As you read "An Upheaval," compare it to the selection from *Hard Times,* using a chart like this to list your inferences.

**Common Core
State Standards**

Reading Literature
1. Cite strong and thorough textual evidence to support analysis of what the text says explicitly as well as inferences drawn from the text, including determining where the text leaves matters uncertain.

Language
6. Demonstrate independence in gathering vocabulary knowledge when considering a word or phrase important to comprehension or expression.

"An Upheaval"		*Hard Times*	
Details	**Criticisms**	**Details**	**Criticisms**

Gather Vocabulary Knowledge

Chekhov uses related forms of the words *shame, resentment,* and *dismay.* Use a **dictionary** to find each word's part of speech and definition. Then, employ the following references to further explore these words:

- **History of English:** Use this work to research each word's origin. Explain the word's emergence in English.
- **Book of Quotations:** Use this resource to find a quotation containing one of the words. Then, explain nuances in meaning that are evident from the context of the quotation.

Comparing References Compare and contrast what you learn about the words from these specialized references.

(1860–1904)

ANTON CHEKHOV

Anton Chekhov (än tôn′ chek′ ôf) is one of only a few major writers who also studied and practiced medicine. By applying to his writing the same type of compassion and objectivity that are required of a good doctor, Chekhov was able to establish himself as one of the dominant figures in Russian Realism.

Beginnings The grandson of a serf who had purchased his freedom, Chekhov was born in the small coastal town of Taganrog in southern Russia. After the failure of his father's grocery business, his family moved to Moscow, while he remained in Taganrog to complete his schooling. In 1879, he moved to Moscow to be with his family, and he enrolled in medical school. As a medical student, he began writing comic sketches and light short stories to earn extra money to help support his family.

Devoted to Writing While helping to care for his elderly parents, offering medical treatment to local peasants, and becoming involved in community affairs, Chekhov managed to continue writing prolifically throughout the six years he lived in Melikhovo, a village south of Moscow. Among the most notable short stories that he produced during this period are "Ward Number Six" (1892), the story of a doctor who is ironically committed to the same grim, depressing mental ward that he had previously directed; and "An Anonymous Story" (1893) and "Peasant" (1897), two harshly realistic sketches of Russian peasant life. During this period, Chekhov also wrote one of his finest plays, *The Seagull* (1896), which focuses on the conflict between different generations of people.

Poor Health and High Acclaim Toward the end of the nineteenth century, Chekhov's physical condition began to rapidly deteriorate. No longer able to withstand the cold climate of Melikhovo, he was forced to move to Yalta, a coastal resort on the Black Sea. His ill health did not impair his literary output, however, and in the final years of life he was able to produce two critically acclaimed plays, *The Sisters* (1901) and *The Cherry Orchard* (1904).

"YOU MUST TRUST AND BELIEVE IN PEOPLE OR LIFE BECOMES IMPOSSIBLE."

AN UPHEAVAL

BY ANTON CHEKHOV

TRANSLATED BY CONSTANCE GARNETT

BACKGROUND THE INDUSTRIAL REVOLUTION WAS SLOW IN COMING TO RUSSIA, BUT BY CHEKHOV'S DAY, TIMES WERE CHANGING. IN 1861, CZAR ALEXANDER II FREED THE SERFS—PEASANTS BOUND TO THE LAND SINCE MEDIEVAL TIMES—THOUGH MOST FREED SERFS REMAINED DESPERATELY POOR PEASANTS. STILL, AS THE NATION MOVED FROM AN AGRARIAN TO AN INDUSTRIAL ECONOMY, NEW OPPORTUNITIES AROSE FOR SOME WHOSE PARENTS OR GRANDPARENTS HAD NOT BEEN WELL BORN. HOWEVER, AMONG THE GENTRY, THOSE WHO COULD NOT ADAPT TO THE CHANGING ECONOMY WERE FINDING IT HARD TO STAY AFLOAT ECONOMICALLY.

**Comparing Social
Criticism** What explicit
commentary does this
paragraph contain about
the treatment of those in
dependent positions?

MASHENKA PAVLETSKY, a young girl who had only just finished her studies at a boarding school, returning from a walk to the house of the Kushkins, with whom she was living as a governess, found the household in a terrible turmoil. Mihailo, the porter who opened the door to her, was excited and red as a crab.

Loud voices were heard from upstairs.

"Madame Kushkin is in a fit, most likely, or else she has quarrelled with her husband," thought Mashenka.

In the hall and in the corridor she met maidservants. One of them was crying. Then Mashenka saw, running out of her room, the master of the house himself, Nikolay Sergeitch, a little man with a flabby face and a bald head, though he was not old. He was red in the face and twitching all over. He passed the governess without noticing her, and throwing up his arms, exclaimed:

"Oh, how horrible it is! How tactless! How stupid! How barbarous! Abominable!"

Mashenka went into her room, and then, for the first time in her life, it was her lot to experience in all its acuteness the feeling that is so familiar to persons in dependent positions, who eat the bread of the rich and powerful, and cannot speak their minds. There was a search going on in her room. The lady of the house, Fedosya Vassilyevna,[1] a stout, broad-shouldered, uncouth woman with thick black eyebrows, a faintly perceptible moustache, and red hands, who was exactly like a plain, illiterate cook in face and manners, was standing, without her cap on, at the table, putting back into Mashenka's work-bag balls of wool, scraps of materials, and bits of papers. . . . Evidently the governess's arrival took her by surprise, since, on looking round and seeing the girl's pale and astonished face, she was a little taken aback, and muttered:

"*Pardon.* I . . . I upset it accidentally. . . . My sleeve caught in it . . ."

And saying something more, Madame Kushkin rustled her long skirts and went out. Mashenka looked round her room with wondering eyes, and, unable to understand it, not knowing what to think, shrugged her shoulders, and turned cold with dismay. What had Fedosya Vassilyevna been looking for in her workbag? If she really had, as she said, caught her sleeve in it and upset everything, why had Nikolay Sergeitch dashed out of her room so excited and red in the face? Why was one drawer of the table pulled out a little way? The moneybox, in which the governess put away ten kopeck pieces[2] and old stamps, was open. They had opened it, but did not know how to shut it, though they had scratched the lock all over. The whatnot[3]

---

1. **Fedosya Vassilyevna** Russian names traditionally include a patronymic, or father's name, with the ending *-evich/-ovich* meaning "son of" or *-evna/-ovna* meaning "daughter of"; *Fedosya Vassilyevna*, for example, means "Fedosya, daughter of Vassily."
2. **kopeck pieces** coins each worth a tenth of a **rouble** (roo´ bəl), the chief currency of Russia.
3. **whatnot** n. set of open shelves used to display miscellaneous items.

with her books on it, the things on the table, the bed—all bore fresh traces of a search. Her linen-basket, too. The linen had been carefully folded, but it was not in the same order as Mashenka had left it when she went out. So the search had been thorough, most thorough. But what was it for? Why? What had happened? Mashenka remembered the excited porter, the general turmoil which was still going on, the weeping servant-girl; had it not all some connection with the search that had just been made in her room? Was she not mixed up in something dreadful? Mashenka turned pale, and feeling cold all over, sank on to her linen-basket.

A maidservant came into the room.

"Liza, you don't know why they have been rummaging in my room?" the governess asked her.

"Mistress has lost a brooch worth two thousand," said Liza.

"Yes, but why have they been rummaging in my room?"

"They've been searching every one, miss. They've searched all my things, too. They stripped us . . . and searched us . . . God knows, miss, I never went near her toilet-table, let alone touching the brooch. I shall say the same at the police-station."

"But . . . why have they been rummaging here?" the governess still wondered.

"A brooch has been stolen, I tell you. The mistress has been rummaging in everything with her own hands. She even searched Mihailo, the porter, herself. It's a perfect disgrace! Nikolay Sergeitch simply looks on and cackles like a hen. But you've no need to tremble like that, miss. They found nothing here. You've nothing to be afraid of if you didn't take the brooch."

"But Liza, it's vile . . . it's insulting," said Mashenka, breathless with indignation. "It's so mean, so low! What right had she to suspect me and to rummage in my things?"

"You are living with strangers, miss," sighed Liza. "Though you are a young lady, still you are . . . as it were . . . a servant. . . . It's not like living with your papa and mamma."

Mashenka threw herself on the bed and sobbed bitterly. Never in her life had she been subjected to such an outrage, never had she been so deeply insulted. . . . She, well-educated, refined, the daughter of a teacher, was suspected of theft; she had been searched like a street-walker! She could not imagine a greater insult. And to this feeling of resentment was added an oppressive dread of what would come next. All sorts of absurd ideas came into her mind. If they could suspect her of theft, then they might arrest her . . . and search

Vocabulary
rummaging (rum´ ij iŋ) *v.* thoroughly searching through

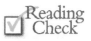

Reading Check

What is happening in the household where Mashenka is governess?

An Upheaval **1015**

▶ **Critical Viewing** This nineteenth century Russian painting depicts a governess arriving at a merchant's house. What social commentary might the artist be offering? **[Interpret]**

"THEY WILL BELIEVE THAT I COULD NOT BE A THIEF!"

Comparing Social Criticism What social criticism about the plight of young working women does Chekhov imply in this paragraph?

Vocabulary
kindred (kin´ drəd) *n.* family; relatives

her, then lead her through the street with an escort of soldiers, cast her into a cold, dark cell with mice and wood-lice, exactly like the dungeon in which Princess Tarakanov[4] was imprisoned. Who would stand up for her? Her parents lived far away in the Provinces; they had not the money to come to her. In the capital she was as solitary as in a desert, without friends or kindred. They could do what they liked with her.

"I will go to all the courts and all the lawyers," Mashenka thought, trembling. "I will explain to them, I will take an oath. . . . They will believe that I could not be a thief!"

Mashenka remembered that under the sheets in her basket she had some sweetmeats, which, following the habits of her schooldays, she had put in her pocket at dinner and carried off to her room. She

---

4. **Princess Tarakanov** daughter supposedly born to Russia's Empress Elizabeth (1709–1761) in a secret marriage to a commoner.

felt hot all over, and was ashamed at the thought that her little secret was known to the lady of the house; all this terror, shame, resentment, brought on an attack of palpitation of the heart, which set up a throbbing in her temples, in her heart, and deep down in her stomach.

"Dinner is ready," the servant summoned Mashenka.

"Shall I go, or not?"

Mashenka brushed her hair, wiped her face with a wet towel, and went into the dining-room. There they had already begun dinner. At one end of the table sat Fedosya Vassilyevna with a stupid, solemn, serious face; at the other end Nikolay Sergeitch. At the sides there were the visitors and the children. The dishes were handed by two footmen in swallowtails[5] and white gloves. Everyone knew that there was an upset in the house, that Madame Kushkin was in trouble, and everyone was silent. Nothing was heard but the sound of munching and the rattle of spoons on the plates.

The lady of the house, herself, was the first to speak.

"What is the third course?" she asked the footman in a weary, injured voice.

"*Esturgeon à la russe*,"[6] answered the footman.

"I ordered that, Fenya," Nikolay Sergeitch hastened to observe. "I wanted some fish. If you don't like it, *ma chère*,[7] don't let them serve it. I just ordered it. . . ."

Fedosya Vassilyevna did not like dishes that she had not ordered herself, and now her eyes filled with tears.

"Come, don't let us agitate ourselves," Mamikov, her household doctor, observed in a honeyed voice, just touching her arm, with a smile as honeyed. "We are nervous enough as it is. Let us forget the brooch! Health is worth more than two thousand roubles!"

"It's not the two thousand I regret," answered the lady, and a big tear rolled down her cheek. "It's the fact itself that revolts me! I cannot put up with thieves in my house. I don't regret it—I regret nothing; but to steal from me is such ingratitude! That's how they repay me for my kindness. . . ."

They all looked into their plates, but Mashenka fancied after the lady's words that every one was looking at her. A lump rose in her throat; she began crying and put her handkerchief to her lips.

"*Pardon*," she muttered. "I can't help it. My head aches. I'll go away."

And she got up from the table, scraping her chair awkwardly, and went out quickly, still more overcome with confusion.

"It's beyond everything!" said Nikolay Sergeitch, frowning. "What need was there to search her room? How out of place it was!"

Vocabulary
palpitation (pal′ pə tā′ shən) *n.* rapid fluttering of the heart

Comparing Social Criticism What do the presence of "footmen in swallowtails" and so many other servants show about the Kushkin household?

Reading Check

What did Mashenka hide in her basket?

---

5. **footmen in swallowtails** servants whose uniforms include full dress coats with long tapering tails in the back.

6. ***Esturgeon à la russe*** Russian sturgeon, the fish whose salted eggs are served as the costly Russian appetizer known as caviar.

7. ***ma chère*** (mä châr′) French for "my dear."

Comparing Social Criticism What does the disagreement about whether Mashenka's room should be searched reveal about attitudes toward social class in late-nineteenth-century Russia?

Spiral Review
Conflict There is disagreement about whether or not Mashenka's room should be searched. What does this reveal about ideas regarding social class in late-nineteenth-century Russia?

"I don't say she took the brooch," said Fedosya Vassilyevna, "but can you answer for her? To tell the truth, I haven't much confidence in these learned paupers."

"It really was unsuitable, Fenya. . . . Excuse me, Fenya, but you've no kind of legal right to make a search."

"I know nothing about your laws. All I know is that I've lost my brooch. And I will find the brooch!" She brought her fork down on the plate with a clatter, and her eyes flashed angrily. "And you eat your dinner, and don't interfere in what doesn't concern you!"

Nikolay Sergeitch dropped his eyes mildly and sighed. Meanwhile Mashenka, reaching her room, flung herself on her bed. She felt now neither alarm nor shame, but she felt an intense longing to go and slap the cheeks of this hard, arrogant, dull-witted, prosperous woman.

Lying on her bed she breathed into her pillow and dreamed of how nice it would be to go and buy the most expensive brooch and fling it into the face of this bullying woman. If only it were God's will that Fedosya Vassilyevna should come to ruin and wander about begging, and should taste all the horrors of poverty and dependence, and that Mashenka, whom she had insulted, might give her alms![8] Oh, if only she could come in for a big fortune, could buy a carriage, and could drive noisily past the windows so as to be envied by that woman!

But all these were only dreams, in reality there was only one thing left to do—to get away as quickly as possible, not to stay another hour in this place. It was true it was terrible to lose her place, to go back to her parents, who had nothing; but what could she do? Mashenka could not bear the sight of the lady of the house nor of her little room; she felt stifled and wretched here. She was so disgusted with Fedosya Vassilyevna, who was so obsessed by her illnesses and her supposed aristocratic rank, that everything in the world seemed to have become coarse and unattractive because this woman was living in it. Mashenka jumped up from the bed and began packing.

"May I come in?" asked Nikolay Sergeitch at the door; he had come up noiselessly to the door, and spoke in a soft, subdued voice. "May I?"

"Come in."

He came in and stood still near the door. His eyes looked dim and his red little nose was shiny. After dinner he used to drink beer, and the fact was perceptible in his walk, in his feeble, flabby hands.

"What's this?" he asked, pointing to the basket.

"I am packing. Forgive me, Nikolay Sergeitch, but I cannot remain in your house. I feel deeply insulted by this search!"

"I understand. . . . Only you are wrong to go. . . . Why should you? They've searched your things, but you . . . what does it matter to you? You will be none the worse for it."

---

8. alms (ämz) *n.* money, food, clothing, etc., given as charity to the poor.

Mashenka was silent and went on packing. Nikolay Sergeitch pinched his moustache, as though wondering what he should say next, and went on in an ingratiating voice:

"I understand, of course, but you must make allowances. You know my wife is nervous, headstrong; you mustn't judge her too harshly."

Mashenka did not speak.

"If you are so offended," Nikolay Sergeitch went on, "well, if you like, I'm ready to apologize. I ask your pardon."

Mashenka made no answer, but only bent lower over her box. This exhausted, irresolute man was of absolutely no significance in the household. He stood in the pitiful position of a dependent and hanger-on, even with the servants, and his apology meant nothing either.

"H'm . . . You say nothing! That's not enough for you. In that case, I will apologize for my wife. In my wife's name. . . . She behaved tactlessly, I admit it as a gentleman. . . ."

Nikolay Sergeitch walked about the room, heaved a sigh, and went on:

"Then you want me to have it rankling here, under my heart. . . . You want my conscience to torment me. . . ."

"I know it's not your fault, Nikolay Sergeitch," said Mashenka, looking him full in the face with her big tearstained eyes. "Why should you worry yourself?"

"Of course, no. . . . But still, don't you . . . go away. I entreat you."

Mashenka shook her head. Nikolay Sergeitch stopped at the window and drummed on a pane with his fingertips.

"Such misunderstandings are simply torture to me," he said. "Why, do you want me to go down on my knees to you, or what? Your pride is wounded, and here you've been crying and packing up to go; but I have pride, too, and you do not spare it! Or do you want me to tell you what I would not tell at Confession? Do you? Listen; you want me to tell you what I won't tell the priest on my deathbed?"

Mashenka made no answer.

"I took my wife's brooch," Nikolay Sergeitch said quickly. "Is that enough now? Are you satisfied? Yes, I . . . took it. . . . But, of course, I count on your discretion. . . . For God's sake, not a word, not half a hint to any one!"

Mashenka, amazed and frightened, went on packing; she snatched her things, crumpled them up, and thrust them anyhow into the box and the basket. Now, after this candid avowal on the part of Nikolay Sergeitch, she could not remain another minute, and could not understand how she could have gone on living in the house before.

Vocabulary
ingratiating
(in grā′ shē āt′ iŋ) *adj.* trying to win someone's favor or good opinion

Reading Check
What does Nikolay Sergeitch confess?

"I WILL APOLOGIZE FOR MY WIFE. IN MY WIFE'S NAME..."

Comparing Social Criticism What do these details suggest about marriage among people of the Kushkins' economic class? How does Mrs. Kushkin's situation contrast with Mashenka's?

"And it's nothing to wonder at," Nikolay Sergeitch went on after a pause. "It's an everyday story! I need money, and she . . . won't give it to me. It was my father's money that bought this house and everything, you know! It's all mine, and the brooch belonged to my mother, and . . . it's all mine! And she took it, took possession of everything. . . . I can't go to law with her, you'll admit. . . . I beg you most earnestly, overlook it . . . stay on. *Tout comprendre, tout pardonner.*[9] Will you stay?"

"No!" said Mashenka resolutely, beginning to tremble. "Let me alone, I entreat you!"

"Well, God bless you!" sighed Nikolay Sergeitch, sitting down on the stool near the box. "I must own I like people who still can feel resentment, contempt, and so on. I could sit here forever and look at your indignant face. . . . So you won't stay, then? I understand. . . . It's bound to be so. . . . Yes, of course. . . . It's all right for you, but for me—wo-o-o-o! . . . I can't stir a step out of this cellar. I'd go off to one of our estates, but in every one of them there are some of my wife's rascals . . . stewards, experts, damn them all! They mortgage and remortgage. . . . You mustn't catch fish, must keep off the grass, mustn't break the trees."

"Nikolay Sergeitch!" his wife's voice called from the drawing-room. "Agnia, call your master!"

"Then you won't stay?" asked Nikolay Sergeitch, getting up quickly and going toward the door. "You might as well stay, really. In the evenings I could come and have a talk with you. Eh? Stay! If you go, there won't be a human face left in the house. It's awful!"

Nikolay Sergeitch's pale, exhausted face besought her, but Mashenka shook her head, and with a wave of his hand he went out.

Half an hour later she was on her way.

---

9. *Tout comprendre, tout pardonner* (too͞´ kən prän´ dr too͞´ pär´ də nā´) a French proverb meaning "To understand all, to forgive all."

Critical Reading

1. **Key Ideas and Details (a)** Why is Mashenka's room searched? **(b) Infer:** Why does the search upset her?

2. **Key Ideas and Details (a)** What does Fedosya Vassilyevna say about her confidence in Mashenka? **(b) Infer:** Based on her remarks and behavior, what sort of person is Fedosya Vassilyevna?

3. **Integration of Knowledge and Ideas (a) Compare and Contrast:** In taking the brooch, how does Nikolay Sergeitch show himself to be unlike Mashenka? **(b) Analyze:** Why is it ironic that he has taken the brooch?

Cite textual evidence to support your responses.

After You Read | from *Hard Times* • *An Upheaval*

Comparing Social Criticism

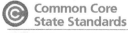

Common Core State Standards

Writing

1. Write arguments to support claims in an analysis of substantive topics or texts, using valid reasoning and relevant and sufficient evidence.

1. Key Ideas and Details (a) What is similar about the plight of the schoolchildren in *Hard Times* and Mashenka in "An Upheaval"? **(b)** What is different about their backgrounds?

2. Key Ideas and Details (a) How does sticking to a particular social philosophy play a role in the behavior of the teachers in *Hard Times* and the behavior of Mashenka in "An Upheaval"? **(b)** In what way are the two philosophies nearly opposite?

3. Key Ideas and Details (a) Where in each selection do characters have trouble communicating? **(b)** What does each selection suggest about the importance of and barriers to communication in society?

4. Integration of Knowledge and Ideas What role does the title of the work play in stressing the social criticisms that each selection contains?

Timed Writing

Argumentative Text: Essay

Both Dickens and Chekhov take issue with ethical and social influences prevalent in their times.

Assignment: In an **essay,** compare and contrast the means that each author uses to express criticism of his society.
[40 minutes]

Address these questions, citing details from the selections to support your ideas:

- What main social criticisms does each selection make?
- Which selection uses more realism in its social criticism?
- Which writer uses more satire in his social criticism?
- Which text is more effective in its social criticism?

5-Minute Planner

Complete these steps before you begin to write:

1. Read the assignment carefully. Identify key words and phrases.

2. Weigh the similarities and differences between the two selections.
TIP As you scan the texts, jot down quotations or details that you might use in your essay.

3. Create a rough outline for your essay.

4. Reread the prompt, and draft your essay.

Analyzing Functional and Expository Texts

Web Site Home Page • Brochure

About the Texts

A **Web site** consists of text and media that is divided into pages and accessed online, via a computer. A **Web site home page** is the opening page of a Web site. Serving as a table of contents, the home page displays links or connections to other pages on the site. In addition, it may provide information on the site's purpose and sponsoring organization.

A park or museum **brochure** is a pamphlet with information about an attraction, including contact and admission information. It also usually includes a map to guide visitors, historical background, and images meant to excite interest.

Reading Strategy

You can **predict the content and purpose** of home pages and brochures by scanning these *text features:*

- Simple section headings
- Introductions providing basic background information
- Sidebars, or sections of information presented in a column down the side of a page
- Captions or explanations of graphics

Once you have used text features to learn how a document is organized, you can more effectively use the text. To *evaluate the effectiveness of a document's organization,* consider how easy it is to follow the sequence of information and to locate specific items. Use a chart like this one to guide your review of the documents.

Checklist	Questions	Responses
☐ Introduction	How helpful is the overview provided?	
☐ Links or Headings	What ordering or subdivision of information do these present? Is this order logical?	
☐ Layout	How is information arranged on the page? Is this layout effective?	
☐ Graphics	How clear is the purpose for and labeling of graphics?	

Common Core State Standards

Reading Informational Text
5. Analyze and evaluate the effectiveness of the structure an author uses in his or her exposition or argument, including whether the structure makes points clear, convincing, and engaging.

Language
4.d. Verify the preliminary determination of the meaning of a word or phrase.

Content-Area Vocabulary

These words appear in the selections that follow. They may also appear in other content-area texts.

manuscripts (man´ yoo skripts´) *n.* the unpublished versions of a written work

agricultural (ag´ ri kul´ chərəl) *adj.* pertaining to farming

tenant (ten´ ənt) *adj.* of or for someone who rents property

(The site's URL appears here.)

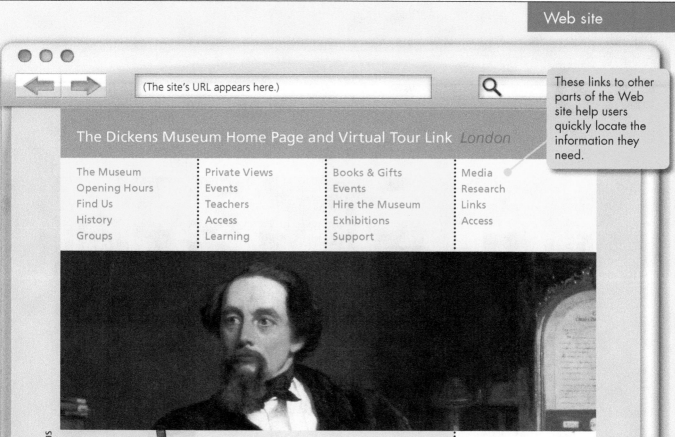

The Dickens Museum Home Page and Virtual Tour Link *London*

These links to other parts of the Web site help users quickly locate the information they need.

The Museum	Private Views	Books & Gifts	Media
Opening Hours	Events	Events	Research
Find Us	Teachers	Hire the Museum	Links
History	Access	Exhibitions	Access
Groups	Learning	Support	

The front of 48 Doughty Street.

© Adam Woolfitt/CORBIS

The Museum

The Charles Dickens Museum in London is the world's most important collection of material relating to the great Victorian novelist and social commentator. The only surviving London home of Dickens (from 1837 until 1839) was opened as a Museum in 1925 and is still welcoming visitors from all over the world in an authentic and inspiring surrounding. On four floors, visitors can see paintings, rare editions, **manuscripts**, original furniture and many items relating to the life of one of the most popular and beloved personalities of the Victorian age.

Gifts and Books
Here you will find gifts for all the family as well as a wide range of books by or about Charles Dickens.

Support
Click here to find out how you can support the Museum in its many educational, conservational and curatorial activities.

Events
For our program of events and educational activities, please click here.

Hire the Museum
The Museum can be hired for private functions, performances, soirees, book launches and many other social occasions. Click here to find out more.

This introduction provides a short history of the museum and a brief description of its holdings. To the left, you can see a photograph of the museum's entrance.

(The site's URL appears here.)

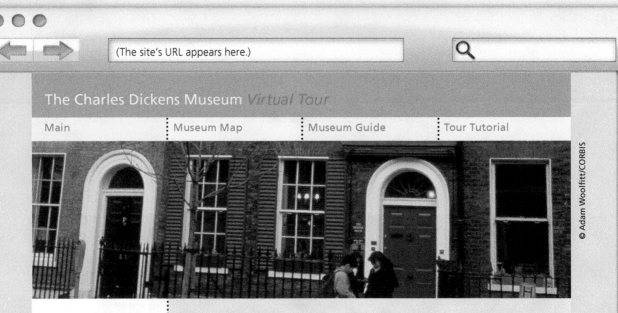

© Adam Woolfitt/CORBIS

The Charles Dickens Museum *Virtual Tour*

Main | Museum Map | Museum Guide | Tour Tutorial

Basement
Library
Still room
Main Hallway
Wash House
Wine Cellar
Stairs to Ground Floor

Ground Floor
Front Hallway
Dining Room
Morning Room
Back Parlour
Stairs to First Floor

First Floor
Drawing Room
Study
Stairs to Second Floor

Second Floor
Dressing Room
Charles and Catherine
  Bedroom
Mary Hogarth Room

Users can take a virtual tour of the museum by clicking on the links in the left column. The text in the main column provides background on the tour.

Welcome to the Virtual Tour of the Charles Dickens Museum!

What follows is a photographic tour of the former home of Charles Dickens, located at 48 Doughty Street, London. You can explore the house much as you would in an actual visit, going between rooms and focusing on items that catch your interest. This tour is meant to provide to you a feeling of actually exploring the house, from the comfort of any computer with access to the Internet.

As you make your way about the house you may notice some glare from light fixtures and windows present in pictures. This is a result of the fact that the purpose is to provide an accurate account of what a visitor to the actual museum experiences, and glare and reflections would be present in a real-life visit. It is also important to note that since the museum is constantly acquiring new items related to Charles Dickens, not everything currently on display at the museum will be present in this virtual tour. This tour was created during March and April of 2005, and since then some items may have been added, moved or removed.

The requirements to view this tour are minimal. It relies on providing an immersive experience through the use of pictures and text. File sizes are small enough so that visitors with low speed connections should be able to view it without problems, but please be patient, especially when viewing the panoramic photos.

To the left of this main section, you will see a column of links. These links will allow you to jump to specific rooms within the museum, and will be visible no matter what page within the tour you are currently viewing. If you are unsure of where to begin, you can start in The Morning Room and then follow the links at the bottom of each room's page. If you require more help making your way through the museum, check the tutorial which is also linked at the top.

The tour was developed at no cost to the museum by four college students in an effort to help The Charles Dickens Museum comply with the Disability Discrimination Act. Enjoy your visit!

© 2005 Charles Dickens Museum

ANDALUSIA

home of Flannery O'Connor

Milledgeville, Georgia

Andalusia is open on Monday, Tuesday and Saturday from 10:00 a.m. to 4:00 p.m. or by appointment. Guided trolly tours can be arranged by calling the Milledgeville, Baldwin County Visitors Center at 1-800-653-1804

2628 N. Columbia Street (Hwy 441 N)
Milledgeville, Georgia
www.andalusiafarm.org   478-454-4029

Where was Flannery O'Connor born?

Flannery O'Connor was born in Savannah, Georgia on March 25, 1925, the only child of Edward F. O'Connor, Jr. and Regina Cline O'Connor.

Where did Flannery O'Connor attend school and college?

O'Connor attended St. Vincent's Grammar School and Sacred Heart Parochial School in Savannah, Georgia; St. Joseph's Parochial School and North Fulton High School in Atlanta, Georgia; Peabody High School and Georgia State College for Women in Milledgeville, Georgia; and the State University of Iowa in Iowa City.

How long did Flannery O'Connor live at Andalusia?

Flannery O'Connor lived at Andalusia with her mother, Regina Cline O'Connor, from early 1951 until Flannery's death in 1964. She completed all her published books while living here.

Why is the farm called Andalusia?

In the fall of 1946, before the death of Dr. Bernard Cline, Flannery O'Connor met on a bus to Atlanta a descendant of the original Hawkins family that owned Andalusia. It was the descendant who told her the original name of the place in the 19th century was Andalusia. She wrote her mother, and when her uncle Bernard heard of it, he was pleased and liked the name. From then on the name was Andalusia.

What happened to Flannery's peacocks?

None of the descendants of O'Connor's domestic flock has survived at the farm. Regina Cline O'Connor gave two pair of peafowl to Stone Mountain Mansion, one pair to Our Lady of Perpetual Help Cancer Home in Atlanta, and another pair to the Monastery of the Holy Spirit near Conyers, Georgia.

Publications by Flannery O'Connor:

Wise Blood — 1952

A Good Man Is Hard To Find — 1955

The Violent Bear It Away — 1960

Everything That Rises Must Converge — 1965

Mystery and Manners — 1969

The Complete Stories, winner of the 1971 National Book Award for Fiction.

The Habit of Being — 1979, winner of the National Book Critics Circle Award.

Flannery O'Connor: Collected Works (Library of America) — 1988

Andalusia is the picturesque farm where American author Flannery O'Connor lived from 1951 until her death from lupus in 1964. Listed on the National Register of Historic Places, Andalusia is brought to life on many occasions in O'Connor's published letters. In the 1950s Andalusia was a dairy farm operated by O'Connor's mother, Regina Cline O'Connor. The **agricultural** setting of Andalusia provided for O'Connor not only a place to live and write, but also a landscape in which to set her fiction.

The farm complex consists of the 19th century Main House, Jack and Louise Hill's house (the home of farm workers), the cow barn, an equipment shed, the milk-processing shed, an additional smaller barn, a parking garage, a water tower, an old well house (storage), a horse stable, a pump house, several small **tenant** houses, a small pond, and nature trails.

Flannery O'Connor did not live a reclusive life at Andalusia. She traveled for various speaking engagements and made frequent visits into town for dining, social events, and to attend Mass regularly at Sacred Heart Catholic Church. She routinely wrote every morning until noon in her downstairs bedroom/study and spent her afternoons and evenings tending to her peafowl and other domestic birds or entertaining visitors.

The brochure provides background information about the house and the author.

Andalusia is located just north of the shopping center on Hwy 441 North of Milledgeville

The map helps visitors planning a trip to the site.

Critical Reading

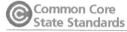

1. Key Ideas and Details (a) Based on the Web site home page, where could you access views of Dickens's study? **(b)** How do the links at the top of the home page help visitors navigate the Web site?

2. Key Ideas and Details (a) Where in the brochure can you find information about O'Connor's publications and awards? **(b)** Where can you find contact information for the organization that sponsors the site?

3. Craft and Structure (a) How does the structure of each text, including the graphic elements, make points clear and engaging? **(b)** Which text has a more effective structure? Explain.

4. Content-Area Vocabulary (a) The word *tenant* derives from the Latin verb *tenere,* which means "to hold." Explain how the meaning of the Latin verb informs the meaning of *tenant.* **(b)** Define the following words derived from the same Latin verb: *tenable* and *tenacious.* Use a dictionary to verify your definitions.

Common Core State Standards

Writing

2. Write informative/explanatory texts to examine and convey complex ideas, concepts, and information clearly and accurately through the effective selection, organization, and analysis of content.

⏱ Timed Writing

Explanatory Text [40 minutes]

Format

In an **analytical essay,** you present a clear thesis statement in an introductory paragraph and develop it in the body, following a clear organization.

Write an **analytical essay** in which you explain the types of information preserved and published by museums and parks focused on authors' lives. Carefully select and organize information from the Web site home page and the museum brochure to support your explanation. Gather and develop ideas by **synthesizing ideas and making logical connections** between the Web site and the brochure.

Academic Vocabulary

When you **synthesize ideas and make logical connections,** you combine related ideas, focusing on ways in which they reinforce or build on one another, to reach new conclusions.

5-Minute Planner

Complete these steps before you begin to write.

1. Read the prompt carefully, and underline key words.

2. Scan the text for details that relate to the prompt. **TIP** As you consider the various types of information available at museums and parks, consider the types of information that a visitor might gather by inspecting an author's home in person, as well as information that the museum or park might provide in printed materials.

3. Before writing, create an outline to guide you.

4. Reread the prompt, and begin drafting your essay.

Before You Read | from *Jane Eyre*

Connecting to the Essential Question In *Jane Eyre*, Charlotte Brontë criticizes harsh boarding schools like the one she attended as a girl. As you read, look for details that criticize conditions at the Lowood School. Doing so will help you answer the Essential Question: **How does literature shape or reflect society?**

Literary Analysis

Works of fiction often reflect the author's philosophy—his or her assumptions about human nature and our relationships to each other and society. Such **philosophical assumptions** may influence the way the author develops and relates the elements of the story, including characters, settings, and events. For example, Charlotte Brontë develops Jane Eyre's character by contrasting the reactions that Jane and Helen Burns have to their harsh treatment at the Lowood School:

> **Jane**: "When we are struck at without a reason, we should strike back again very hard. . . . so hard as to teach the person who struck us never to do it again."

> **Helen**: " . . . Love your enemies; bless them that curse you; do good to them that hate you and despitefully use you. . . . Life appears to me to be too short to be spent in nursing animosity or registering wrongs."

When characters' philosophies conflict, the author may be criticizing one and accepting the other or may see some merit in both. As you read, consider the philosophical assumptions that drive Brontë's narrative.

Reading Strategy

Preparing to Read Complex Texts To **analyze the author's assumptions,** apply information you have about the author and time period to details in the selection itself. For example, if you consider the novel's presentation of the Lowood School along with the strong Victorian belief in social reform and Charlotte Brontë's experience, you can better understand the assumptions the author makes about such schools. As you read, use a chart like the one shown to help you analyze the author's assumptions.

Vocabulary

obscure (əb skyoor´) *adj.* not easily seen; not generally known (p. 1031)

comprised (kəm prīzd´) *v.* consisted of; included (p. 1031)

sundry (sun´ drē) *adj.* various, miscellaneous (p. 1031)

tumult (too´ mult) *n.* noise caused by a crowd (p. 1032)

truculent (truk´ yə lənt) *adj.* cruel; fierce (p. 1036)

Common Core State Standards

Reading Literature
3. Analyze the impact of the author's choices regarding how to develop and relate elements of a story or drama.

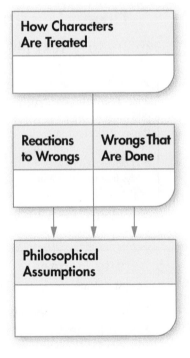

How Characters Are Treated

| Reactions to Wrongs | Wrongs That Are Done |

Philosophical Assumptions

www.PHLitOnline.com

Charlotte Brontë
(1816–1855)

Author of *Jane Eyre*

Charlotte Brontë was part of a renowned literary family: Her sisters Anne and Emily were also writers. Their father, an Anglican clergyman, moved his family to the moors in Yorkshire in 1820, and the children were educated largely at home. Raised without their mother, who had died in 1821, the sisters, together with their brother Branwell, led a rich fantasy life that nurtured their artistic development.

Early Failure With three of her sisters, Charlotte briefly attended a boarding school. Her experiences there provided material for the critical descriptions of boarding-school life at Lowood in *Jane Eyre*. Charlotte spent several years as a teacher, first of her own siblings and then at another school that she herself had briefly attended. She found this job difficult and unappealing, and in 1844 attempted to open her own school near her family home. The school's failure was quick and definite: No pupils enrolled.

Success In 1846, the three sisters published a volume of poems under the pseudonyms Currer, Ellis, and Acton Bell, but the book had little success. Charlotte had also written a novel, *The Professor,* but the book failed to find a publisher. Charlotte persevered, however, and when *Jane Eyre* was published in 1847, it met with immediate popular success.

Personal Struggle The final years of Charlotte Brontë's life were clouded by tragedy. Her brother died in 1848, and Emily and Anne died soon after. Despite her loneliness, Charlotte found the strength to complete the novels *Shirley* (1849) and *Villette* (1853). She married Arthur Bell Nicholls, her father's curate, and died about nine months later.

FROM **JANE EYRE**

Charlotte Brontë

CHAPTER 6

The next day commenced as before, getting up and dressing by rushlight; but this morning we were obliged to dispense with the ceremony of washing: the water in the pitchers was frozen. A change had taken place in the weather the preceding evening, and a keen northeast wind, whistling through the crevices of our bedroom windows all night long, had made us shiver in our beds, and turned the contents of the ewers to ice.

Before the long hour and a half of prayers and Bible reading was over, I felt ready to perish with cold. Breakfast time came at last, and this morning the porridge was not burnt; the quality was eatable, the quantity small; how small my portion seemed! I wished it had been doubled.

Reading Strategy
Analyzing an Author's Assumptions Which details suggest Brontë thinks schools like Lowood are in need of reform?

In the course of the day I was enrolled a member of the fourth class, and regular tasks and occupations were assigned to me: hitherto, I had only been a spectator of the proceedings at Lowood, I was now to become an actor therein. At first, being little accustomed to learn by heart, the lessons appeared to me both long and difficult: the frequent change from task to task, too, bewildered me; and I was glad, when, about three o'clock in the afternoon, Miss Smith put into my hands a border of muslin two yards long, together with needle, thimble, etc., and sent me to sit in a quiet corner of the school room, with directions to hem the same. At that hour most of the others were sewing likewise; but one class still stood round Miss Scatcherd's chair reading, and as all was quiet, the subject of their lessons could be heard, together with the manner in which each girl acquitted herself, and the animadversions or commendations of Miss Scatcherd on the performance. It was English history; among the readers, I observed my acquaintance of the verandah; at the commencement of the lesson, her place had been at the top of the class, but for some error of pronunciation or some inattention to stops, she was suddenly sent to the very bottom. Even in that obscure position, Miss Scatcherd continued to make her an object of constant notice: she was continually addressing to her such phrases as the following:—

"Burns" (such it seems was her name: the girls here, were all called by their surnames, as boys are elsewhere), "Burns, you are standing on the side of your shoe, turn your toes out immediately." "Burns, you poke your chin most unpleasantly, draw it in." "Burns, I insist on your holding your head up: I will not have you before me in that attitude," etc. etc.

A chapter having been read through twice, the books were closed and the girls examined. The lesson had comprised part of the reign of Charles I, and there were sundry questions about tonnage and poundage, and ship-money, which most of them appeared unable to answer; still, every little difficulty was solved instantly when it reached Burns: her memory seemed to have retained the substance of the whole lesson, and she was ready with answers on every point. I kept expecting that Miss Scatcherd would praise her attention; but, instead of that, she suddenly cried out:—

"You dirty, disagreeable girl! you have never cleaned your nails this morning!"

Burns made no answer: I wondered at her silence.

"Why," thought I, "does she not explain that she could neither clean her nails nor wash her face, as the water was frozen?"

My attention was now called off by Miss Smith, desiring me to hold a skein of thread: while she was winding it, she talked to me from time to time, asking whether I had ever been at school before, whether I could mark, stitch, knit, etc.; till she dismissed me, I could not pursue my observations on Miss Scatcherd's movements. When I returned to my seat, that lady was just delivering an order, of which I did not catch the import; but Burns immediately left the class, and

Vocabulary
obscure (əb skyoor′) adj. not easily seen; not generally known

comprised (kəm prīzd′) v. consisted of; included

sundry (sun′ drē) adj. various, miscellaneous

Reading Check

How has the narrator's role at Lowood changed?

Literary Analysis
Author's Philosophical Assumptions What does Miss Scatcherd's reaction suggest about Brontë's assumptions regarding an ideal teacher-student relationship?

Ⓒ
Spiral Review
Point of View How does the novel's first-person narration affect the reader's connection with Jane?

Vocabulary
tumult (tōō′ mult) *n.* noise caused by a crowd

going into the small inner room where the books were kept, returned in half a minute, carrying in her hand a bundle of twigs tied together at one end. This ominous tool she presented to Miss Scatcherd with a respectful courtesy; then she quietly, and without being told, unloosed her pinafore, and the teacher instantly and sharply inflicted on her neck a dozen strokes with the bunch of twigs. Not a tear rose to Burns's eye; and, while I paused from my sewing, because my fingers quivered at this spectacle with a sentiment of unavailing and impotent anger, not a feature of her pensive face altered its ordinary expression.

"Hardened girl!" exclaimed Miss Scatcherd, "nothing can correct you of your slatternly habits: carry the rod away."

Burns obeyed: I looked at her narrowly as she emerged from the book closet; she was just putting back her handkerchief into her pocket, and the trace of a tear glistened on her thin cheek.

The play-hour in the evening I thought the pleasantest fraction of the day at Lowood: the bit of bread, the draught of coffee swallowed at five o'clock had revived vitality, if it had not satisfied hunger; the long restraint of the day was slackened; the school room felt warmer than in the morning: its fires being allowed to burn a little more brightly to supply, in some measure, the place of candles, not yet introduced; the ruddy gloaming,[1] the licensed uproar, the confusion of many voices gave one a welcome sense of liberty.

On the evening of the day on which I had seen Miss Scatcherd flog her pupil, Burns, I wandered as usual among the forms and tables and laughing groups without a companion, yet not feeling lonely: when I passed the windows, I now and then lifted a blind and looked out; it snowed fast, a drift was already forming against the lower panes; putting my ear close to the window, I could distinguish from the gleeful tumult within, the disconsolate moan of the wind outside.

Probably, if I had lately left a good home and kind parents, this would have been the hour when I should most keenly have regretted the separation: that wind would then have saddened my heart; this obscure chaos would have disturbed my peace: as it was I derived from both a strange excitement, and reckless and feverish, I wished the wind to howl more wildly, the gloom to deepen to darkness, and the confusion to rise to clamor.

Jumping over forms, and creeping under tables, I made my way to one of the fire-places: there, kneeling by the high wire fender, I found Burns, absorbed, silent, abstracted from all round her by the companionship of a book, which she read by the dim glare of the embers.

"Is it still 'Rasselas'?"[2] I asked, coming behind her.

"Yes," she said, "and I have just finished it."

And in five minutes more she shut it up. I was glad of this.

---

1. ruddy gloaming glowing twilight; the sunset.
2. Rasselas *The History of Rasselas, Prince of Abyssinia*, a moralizing novel by Samuel Johnson.

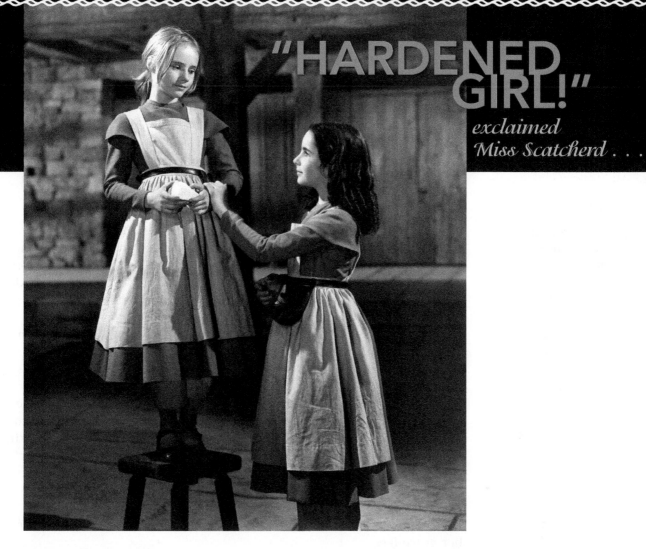

"HARDENED GIRL!" *exclaimed Miss Scatcherd . . .*

"Now," thought I, "I can perhaps get her to talk." I sat down by her on the floor.

"What is your name besides Burns?"

"Helen."

"Do you come a long way from here?"

"I come from a place further north; quite on the borders of Scotland."

"Will you ever go back?"

"I hope so; but nobody can be sure of the future."

"You must wish to leave Lowood?"

"No: why should I? I was sent to Lowood to get an education; and it would be of no use going away until I have attained that object."

"But that teacher, Miss Scatcherd, is so cruel to you?"

"Cruel? Not at all! She is severe: she dislikes my faults."

"And if I were in your place I should dislike her: I should resist her; if she struck me with that rod, I should get it from her hand; I should break it under her nose."

▲ **Critical Viewing**
How well does this still from a movie version of *Jane Eyre* match your vision of Jane and Burns? Explain.
[Evaluate]

Reading Check

How does Burns react to her beating by Miss Scatcherd?

"Probably you would do nothing of the sort: but if you did, Mr. Brocklehurst would expel you from the school; that would be a great grief to your relations. It is far better to endure patiently a smart which nobody feels but yourself, than to commit a hasty action whose evil consequences will extend to all connected with you—and, besides, the Bible bids us return good for evil."

"But then it seems disgraceful to be flogged, and to be sent to stand in the middle of a room full of people; and you are such a great girl: I am far younger than you, and I could not bear it."

"Yet it would be your duty to bear it, if you could not avoid it: it is weak and silly to say you *cannot bear* what it is your fate to be required to bear."

I heard her with wonder: I could not comprehend this doctrine of endurance; and still less could I understand or sympathize with the forbearance she expressed for her chastiser. Still I felt that Helen Burns considered things by a light invisible to my eyes. I suspected she might be right and I wrong; but I would not ponder the matter deeply: like Felix,[3] I put it off to a more convenient season.

"You say you have faults, Helen: what are they? To me you seem very good."

"Then learn from me, not to judge by appearances: I am, as Miss Scatcherd said, slatternly; I seldom put, and never keep, things in order; I am careless; I forget rules; I read when I should learn my lessons; I have no method; and sometimes I say, like you, I cannot *bear* to be subjected to systematic arrangements. This is all very provoking to Miss Scatcherd, who is naturally neat, punctual, and particular."

"And cross and cruel," I added; but Helen Burns would not admit my addition: she kept silence.

"Is Miss Temple as severe to you as Miss Scatcherd?"

At the utterance of Miss Temple's name, a soft smile flitted over her grave face.

"Miss Temple is full of goodness; it pains her to be severe to anyone, even the worst in the school: she sees my errors, and tells me of them gently; and, if I do anything worthy of praise, she gives me my meed liberally. One strong proof of my wretchedly defective nature is

---

3. Felix in the Bible, governor of Judea who released Paul from prison and deferred his trial until a more "convenient season" (Acts 24:25).

Literary Analysis
Author's Philosophical Assumptions What do Jane's thoughts suggest about the author's assumptions regarding the relative importance of obedience and independence?

". . . it is weak and silly to say you
CANNOT BEAR
what it is your fate to be required to bear."

that even her expostulations, so mild, so rational, have not influence to cure me of my faults; and even her praise, though I value it most highly, cannot stimulate me to continued care and foresight."

"That is curious," said I: "it is so easy to be careful."

"For *you* I have no doubt it is. I observed you in your class this morning, and saw you were closely attentive: your thoughts never seemed to wander while Miss Miller explained the lesson and questioned you. Now, mine continually rove away: when I should be listening to Miss Scatcherd, and collecting all she says with assiduity,[4] often I lose the very sound of her voice; I fall into a sort of dream. Sometimes I think I am in Northumberland, and that the noises I hear round me are the bubbling of a little brook which runs through Deepden, near our house;—then, when it comes to my turn to reply, I have to be wakened; and, having heard nothing of what was read for listening to the visionary brook, I have no answer ready."

"Yet how well you replied this afternoon."

"It was mere chance: the subject on which we had been reading had interested me. This afternoon, instead of dreaming of Deepden, I was wondering how a man who wished to do right could act so unjustly and unwisely as Charles the First sometimes did; and I thought what a pity it was that, with his integrity and conscientiousness, he could see no farther than the prerogatives of the crown. If he had but been able to look to a distance, and see how what they call the spirit of the age was tending! Still, I like Charles—I respect him—I pity him, poor murdered king! Yes, his enemies were the worst: they shed blood they had no right to shed. How dared they kill him!"

Helen was talking to herself now: she had forgotten I could not very well understand her—that I was ignorant, or nearly so, of the subject she discussed. I recalled her to my level.

"And when Miss Temple teaches you, do your thoughts wander then?"

"No, certainly, not often; because Miss Temple has generally something to say which is newer to me than my own reflections: her language is singularly agreeable to me, and the information she communicates is often just what I wished to gain."

"Well, then, with Miss Temple you are good?"

"Yes, in a passive way: I make no effort; I follow as inclination guides me. There is no merit in such goodness."

"A great deal: you are good to those who are good to you. It is all I ever desire to be. If people were always kind and obedient to those who are cruel and unjust, the wicked people would have it all their own way: they would never feel afraid, and so they would never alter, but would grow worse and worse. When we are struck at without a reason, we should strike back again very hard; I am sure we should—so hard as to teach the person who struck us never to do it again."

---

4. assiduity (as´ ə dyo͞o´ ə tē) *n.* constant care and attention; diligence.

Reading Strategy
Analyzing an Author's Assumptions To what extent is Brontë criticizing or supporting the ideas Helen shares about Charles the First? Explain.

Reading Check

What faults does Helen Burns attribute to herself?

"You will change your mind, I hope, when you grow older: as yet you are but a little untaught girl."

"But I feel this, Helen: I must dislike those who, whatever I do to please them, persist in disliking me; I must resist those who punish me unjustly. It is as natural as that I should love those who show me affection, or submit to punishment when I feel it is deserved."

". . . Love your enemies; bless them that curse you; do good to them that hate you and despitefully use you."

"Then I should love Mrs. Reed, which I cannot do; I should bless her son John, which is impossible."

In her turn, Helen Burns asked me to explain; and I proceeded forthwith to pour out, in my way, the tale of my sufferings and resentments. Bitter and truculent when excited, I spoke as I felt, without reserve or softening.

Helen heard me patiently to the end: I expected she would then make a remark, but she said nothing.

"Well," I asked impatiently, "is not Mrs. Reed a hard-hearted, bad woman?"

"She has been unkind to you, no doubt; because, you see, she dislikes your cast of character, as Miss Scatcherd does mine: but how minutely you remember all she has done and said to you! What a singularly deep impression her injustice seems to have made on your heart! No ill usage so brands its record on my feelings. Would you not be happier if you tried to forget her severity, together with the passionate emotions it excited? Life appears to me too short to be spent in nursing animosity or registering wrongs. We are, and must be, one and all, burdened with faults in this world: but the time will soon come when, I trust, we shall put them off in putting off our corruptible bodies; when debasement and sin will fall from us with this cumbrous frame of flesh, and only the spark of the spirit will remain,—the impalpable principle of life and thought, pure as when it left the Creator to inspire the creature: whence[5] it came it will return; perhaps again to be communicated to some being higher than man—perhaps to pass through gradations of glory, from the pale human soul to brighten to the seraph![6] Surely it will never, on

Vocabulary
truculent (truk´ yə lənt) *adj.*
cruel; fierce

Literary Analysis
Author's Philosophical Assumptions Does the author favor one girl's argument over the other's? Explain.

---

5. whence the place from which.

the contrary, be suffered to degenerate from man to fiend? No; I cannot believe that: I hold another creed; which no one ever taught me, and which I seldom mention; but in which I delight, and to which I cling: for it extends hope to all: it makes Eternity a rest—a mighty home, not a terror and abyss. Besides, with this creed, I can so clearly distinguish between the criminal and his crime; I can so sincerely forgive the first while I abhor the last: with this creed revenge never worries my heart, degradation never too deeply disgusts me, injustice never crushes me too low: I live in calm, looking to the end."

Helen's head, always drooping, sank a little lower as she finished this sentence. I saw by her look she wished no longer to talk to me, but rather to converse with her own thoughts. She was not allowed much time for meditation: a monitor, a great rough girl, presently came up, exclaiming in a strong Cumberland accent—

"Helen Burns, if you don't go and put your drawer in order, and fold up your work this minute, I'll tell Miss Scatcherd to come and look at it!"

Helen sighed as her reverie fled, and getting up, obeyed the monitor without reply as without delay.

---

6. **seraph** angel of the highest order.

Critical Reading

1. **Key Ideas and Details** **(a)** For what offense does Miss Scatcherd punish Helen Burns? **(b) Infer:** When punished, why does Helen make every effort to hold back tears?

2. **Key Ideas and Details** **(a)** Which teacher does Helen particularly like? **(b) Analyze:** Why does Helen find that there is "no merit" in being good in this teacher's class?

3. **Key Ideas and Details** Describe Jane's personality in a few sentences.

4. **Integration of Knowledge and Ideas** **(a) Compare and Contrast:** Compare Jane's and Helen's reactions to mistreatment. **(b) Make a Judgment:** Do you think each has something to teach the other? Explain.

5. **Integration of Knowledge and Ideas** Might Helen and Jane be seen as two sides of the author's personality? Why or why not?

6. **Integration of Knowledge and Ideas** How do you think Brontë would like to reform schools like Lowood? In your response, use at least two of these Essential Question words: *education, independence, leadership. [Connecting to the Essential Question: How does literature shape or reflect society?]*

Cite textual evidence to support your responses.

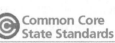

Literary Analysis

1. Integration of Knowledge and Ideas **(a)** Use a chart like the one shown to compare and contrast the two philosophies espoused by Jane and Helen in this excerpt. **(b)** Which do you think best reflects the underlying **philosophical assumptions** that Brontë brings to this story? Explain.

Character's view	of Miss Scatcherd's actions	of education		Assumption
			→	

2. Integration of Knowledge and Ideas **(a)** Based on their behavior, what different teaching philosophies do Miss Temple and Miss Scatcherd follow? **(b)** How does the author seem to feel about each teacher's philosophy? Cite details from the selection to support your evaluation.

Reading Strategy

3. (a) Begin to **analyze the author's assumptions** in this selection by identifying three details Brontë uses to describe the setting. **(b)** What assumptions about children and education do these details suggest?

4. Early Victorian society taught that women should be docile, domestic creatures with little concern for larger issues. Do Brontë's assumptions seem to agree with that view? Cite details to support your evaluation.

PERFORMANCE TASKS
Integrated Language Skills

Vocabulary Acquisition and Use

For each word, choose the letter of its synonym, and explain your choice.

1. **tumult:** **(a)** ache **(b)** cruelty **(c)** satisfaction **(d)** excitement
2. **comprised:** **(a)** included **(b)** suggested **(c)** pried **(d)** attached
3. **truculent:** **(a)** forgetful **(b)** ferocious **(c)** driven **(d)** peaceful
4. **obscure:** **(a)** murky **(b)** noisy **(c)** arrogant **(d)** attentive
5. **sundry:** **(a)** shiny **(b)** outdoor **(c)** withered **(d)** diverse

Writing

Informative Text Write the **school conduct report** that Miss Scatcherd might have written about Helen Burns. From the selection, infer Miss Scatcherd's feelings about Helen. Then, set up a formal report with the Lowood School heading, your name (Miss Scatcherd), a date at the top, and an evaluation section that includes grades and comments in categories such as schoolwork, personal hygiene, posture, and effort.

Common Core State Standards

Writing
2. Write informative/explanatory texts to examine and convey complex ideas, concepts, and information clearly and accurately through the effective selection, organization, and analysis of content.

The Empire and Its Discontents

Connecting to the Essential Question Matthew Arnold sees the world in terms of private loyalties, and Rudyard Kipling sees it in terms of public duties. As you read, notice Arnold's private settings and compare and contrast them with Kipling's public arenas. Doing so will help you answer the Essential Question: **What is the relationship between literature and place?**

Literary Analysis

Poems contain emotional thoughts and thoughtful emotions. With thought and emotion so closely linked, the **mood,** or feeling, that a poem calls up is bound to be related to its **themes**, or messages about life, and to its *aesthetic impact*—its intended *emotional effect* on the reader. Read poetry with your feelings and you will find your way to its ideas.

In "Dover Beach," for example, the crash of waves brings "The eternal note of sadness in." This mood of sadness contributes to an important theme of the poem, which concerns a world with "neither joy, nor love, nor light." This theme interacts with other themes in the poem, such as the loss of certainty and faith, to produce a work with rich layers of meaning.

Comparing Literary Works The *"sound" of language* contributes to the mood and the intended effect on the reader. Compare the sounds of Arnold's and Kipling's language and consider their effects on the reader.

Reading Strategy

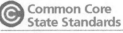 **Preparing to Read Complex Texts** **Connecting a poem to the historical period** will help you better understand its mood and themes. The Victorian era was marked by scientific progress, material prosperity, and British global domination, yet each success brought fresh anxieties with it:

- Scientific progress brought a greater questioning of religious faith.
- Material prosperity for some brought greater poverty for others.
- Expansion of Britain's empire brought heavy responsibilities as well as political and cultural tensions that often resulted in warfare.

Use a diagram like this to relate the poems to their historical period.

Vocabulary

tranquil (traŋ′ kwil) *adj.* calm; serene; peaceful (p. 1042)

cadence (kād′ əns) *n.* measured movement (p. 1042)

turbid (tʉr′ bid) *adj.* muddy or cloudy; not clear (p. 1043)

dominion (də min′ yən) *n.* rule; control (p. 1046)

contrite (kən trīt′) *adj.* willing to repent or atone (p. 1046)

awe (ô) *n.* mixed feeling of reverence, fear, and wonder (p. 1046)

Common Core State Standards

Reading Literature
2. Determine two or more themes or central ideas of a text and analyze their development over the course of the text, including how they interact and build on one another to produce a complex account.

Historical Background

The 1897 "Diamond Jubilee" celebrates the British Empire.

"Recessional" Mood/Themes

The speaker prays for the British Empire while recognizing its greatness is likely temporary.

PHLit Online!
www.PHLitOnline.com

MATTHEW ARNOLD

Author of "**Dover Beach**"

Much of Matthew Arnold's poetry concerns a theme as relevant today as it was in the nineteenth century: the isolation of individuals from one another and from society. In fact, in the 1960s, the American novelist Norman Mailer used a modified quotation from Arnold's poem "Dover Beach" for the title of his book about a Vietnam War protest, *Armies of the Night.*

A Social Conscience While attending Oxford University, Arnold developed the social conscience that was to guide his career as a public servant, poet, and literary critic. In 1851, he became Inspector of Schools, and in performing this job he did much to improve education throughout Great Britain. All the while, he remained a poet at heart, although his first two collections, published in 1849 and 1852, met with little success.

Literary Achievement Arnold's literary fortunes changed in 1853 when he published *Poems,* with its long preface that established him as a major critic. *New Poems*, published in 1867, contained Arnold's celebrated "Dover Beach."

A Return to Culture After completing this collection, Arnold believed that he had said everything he could in poetry. From that point on he wrote prose, such as the social criticism of the essays in *Culture and Anarchy* (1869). In this book, he attacks Victorian complacency and materialism, arguing that culture should open our minds to what is true and valuable. Arnold's idea of culture still influences critics today.

"CULTURE IS TO KNOW THE BEST THAT HAS BEEN SAID AND THOUGHT IN THE WORLD."

DOVER BEACH

MATTHEW ARNOLD

▲ **Critical Viewing**
Does this photograph capture the "eternal note of sadness" Arnold describes? Explain. **[Support]**

Vocabulary
tranquil (traṇ´ kwil) *adj.* calm; serene; peaceful

cadence (kād´ əns) *n.* measured movement

The sea is calm tonight.
The tide is full, the moon lies fair
Upon the straits;[1] on the French coast the light
Gleams and is gone; the cliffs of England stand,
5   Glimmering and vast, out in the tranquil bay.
Come to the window, sweet is the night air!

Only, from the long line of spray
Where the sea meets the moon-blanched land,
Listen! you hear the grating roar
10   Of pebbles which the waves draw back, and fling,
At their return, up the high strand,[2]
Begin, and cease, and then again begin,
With tremulous cadence slow, and bring
The eternal note of sadness in.

---

1. straits Straits of Dover, between England and France.
2. strand shore.

15   Sophocles[3] long ago
Heard it on the Aegean,[4] and it brought
Into his mind the turbid ebb and flow
Of human misery; we
Find also in the sound a thought,
20   Hearing it by this distant northern sea.

The Sea of Faith
Was once, too, at the full, and round earth's shore
Lay like the folds of a bright girdle furled.
But now I only hear
25   Its melancholy, long, withdrawing roar,
Retreating, to the breath
Of the night wind, down the vast edges drear
And naked shingles[5] of the world.

Ah, love, let us be true
30   To one another! for the world, which seems
To lie before us like a land of dreams,
So various, so beautiful, so new,
Hath really neither joy, nor love, nor light,
Nor certitude, nor peace, nor help for pain;
35   And we are here as on a darkling[6] plain
Swept with confused alarms of struggle and flight,
Where ignorant armies clash by night.

Vocabulary
turbid (tur´ bid) *adj.* muddy or cloudy; not clear

Reading Strategy
Connecting to the Historical Period How does the doubt expressed in lines 21–28 reflect the historical period in which the poem was written?

Literary Analysis
Mood as a Key to Theme How do the feelings that the final stanza evokes relate to its message in lines 29–30?

---

3. **Sophocles** (säf´ ə klēz´) Greek tragic dramatist (496?–406 B.C.).
4. **Aegean** (ē jē´ ən) arm of the Mediterranean Sea between Greece and Turkey.
5. **shingles** *n.* beaches covered with large, coarse, waterworn gravel.
6. **darkling** *adj.* in the dark.

Critical Reading ©

© 1. **Key Ideas and Details** **(a)** Where are the speaker and his "love," and what do they hear and see? **(b) Interpret:** Why do you think the scene suggests to the speaker "the eternal note of sadness"?

© 2. **Key Ideas and Details** **(a)** What does the speaker say has happened to "The Sea of Faith"? **(b) Interpret:** What does he mean by this remark?

© 3. **Key Ideas and Details** **(a)** In the last stanza, what does the speaker say that he and his "love" should do? **(b) Draw Conclusions:** What problem does the speaker believe that they can alleviate if they follow his urging?

© 4. **Integration of Knowledge and Ideas** Is Arnold's message in the final stanza a satisfactory response to "human misery" today? Why or why not?

Cite textual evidence to support your responses.

Rudyard Kipling

(1865–1936)

Author of **"Recessional"** • **"The Widow at Windsor"**

Rudyard Kipling's works are known for their celebration of the British Empire, yet they also warn of the costs of world dominion. While praising the benefits of imperialism, he emphasizes the responsibility of the British to bring their "civilized" ways to other parts of the world.

Early Success Kipling was born to British parents in India, one of Britain's largest colonies. At the age of six, he was placed by his parents in a foster home in England, and later, at a chaotic boarding school. One critic speculates that the theme of self-preservation in Kipling's work was inspired by experiences at the boarding school that tested his courage. Kipling would later immortalize his school days in a collection of stories called *Stalky and Co.* (1899). In 1882, Kipling returned to India to work as a journalist. During the next seven years, he published a number of witty poems and stories, and by the time he returned to England in 1889, he was a celebrity.

Kipling's Achievements Kipling is known as a Victorian author because he produced his best work before the death of Queen Victoria in 1901. In its great variety, that work includes poetry, short stories, and novels. Some of his books, such as *The Jungle Books* (1894, 1895), *Captains Courageous* (1897), and *Kim* (1901), have become children's classics.

For years, Kipling was the most popular English poet, and in 1907 he became the first English writer to receive the Nobel Prize for Literature.

RECESSIONAL[1]

Rudyard Kipling

▲ **Critical Viewing**
Does the Diamond
Jubilee, shown here,
seem to reflect the pride
against which Kipling
warns? Explain. **[Connect]**

*Queen Victoria's Diamond Jubilee
procession in London in 1897*

Recessional **1045**

The
Diamond Jubilee
March.

Composed by
J. Ord Hume.

Piano Solo 4/-

London
E. Ascherberg & Co.
46 Berners Street, W.

New York E. Schuberth & Co.

BACKGROUND In 1897, a national celebration called the "Diamond Jubilee" was held in honor of the sixtieth anniversary of Queen Victoria's reign. The occasion prompted a great deal of boasting about the strength and greatness of the empire. Kipling responded to the celebration by writing this poem, reminding the people of England that the British empire might not last forever.

> God of our fathers, known of old—
>   Lord of our far-flung battle-line—
> Beneath whose awful Hand we hold
>   Dominion over palm and pine—
> 5 Lord God of Hosts, be with us yet,
> Lest we forget—lest we forget!
>
> The tumult and the shouting dies—
>   The Captains and the Kings depart—
> Still stands Thine ancient Sacrifice,
> 10   An humble and a contrite heart.[2]
> Lord God of Hosts, be with us yet,
> Lest we forget—lest we forget!
>
> Far-called, our navies melt away—
>   On dune and headland sinks the fire[3]—
> 15 Lo, all our pomp of yesterday
>   Is one with Nineveh[4] and Tyre![5]
> Judge of the Nations, spare us yet,
> Lest we forget—lest we forget!
> If, drunk with sight of power, we loose
> 20   Wild tongues that have not Thee in awe—
> Such boasting as the Gentiles use

Vocabulary

dominion (də min′ yən) *n.* rule; control

contrite (kən trīt′) *adj.* willing to repent or atone

awe (ô) *n.* mixed feeling of reverence, fear, and wonder

1. **Recessional** hymn sung at the end of a religious service. [footnote in title, previous page]
2. **An . . . heart** allusion to the Bible (Psalms 51:17) "The sacrifices of God are a broken spirit: a broken and contrite heart, O God, thou wilt not despise."
3. **On . . . fire** Bonfires were lit on high ground all over Britain as part of the opening ceremonies of the Jubilee celebration.
4. **Nineveh** (nin′ ə ve) ancient capital of the Assyrian Empire, the ruins of which were discovered buried in desert sands in the 1850s.
5. **Tyre** (tīr) once a great port and the center of ancient Phoenician culture, now a small town in Lebanon.

Or lesser breeds without the Law—[6]
Lord God of Hosts, be with us yet,
Lest we forget—lest we forget!

25 For heathen heart that puts her trust
  In reeking tube[7] and iron shard[8]—
All valiant dust that builds on dust,
  And guarding calls not Thee to guard—
For frantic boast and foolish word,
30 Thy mercy on Thy People, Lord!

---

6. **Such boasting . . . Law** allusion to the Bible (Romans 2:14) "For when the Gentiles, which have not the law, do by nature the things contained in the law, these, having not the law, are a law unto themselves."
7. **tube** barrel of a gun.
8. **shard** fragment of a bombshell.

Literary Analysis
Mood as a Key to Theme
How does the refrain "Lest we forget," create a mood and support the poem's theme?

Critical Reading

1. **Key Ideas and Details** **(a)** To whom is this poem addressed? **(b) Interpret:** For whom is the message of the poem really meant?

2. **Key Ideas and Details** **(a)** What is the literal meaning of the title of the poem? **(b) Interpret:** What double meaning is contained in the title? **(c) Analyze:** How is this ambiguity appropriate to the mood of the poem?

3. **Key Ideas and Details** **(a)** Paraphrase the first stanza of the poem. **(b) Analyze:** According to this stanza, what is the relationship between God and empire? Explain.

4. **Key Ideas and Details** **(a)** In lines 15 and 16, what happens to "our pomp of yesterday"? **(b) Infer:** What qualities and actions does the speaker condemn? **(c) Draw Conclusions:** What is the theme of the poem?

5. **Integration of Knowledge and Ideas** Britain is no longer an empire. Does this fact bear out Kipling's warning? Explain.

6. **Integration of Knowledge and Ideas** Is Kipling condemning the very existence of the British empire, or is he advocating a more humble approach to the responsibilities of empire? Explain.

Cite textual evidence to support your responses.

The Widow at Windsor

Rudyard Kipling

▲ **Critical Viewing**
What elements of this portrait of Queen Victoria do you think the speaker of the poem might point out? Explain. **[Connect]**

'Ave you 'eard o' the Widow at Windsor
    With a hairy gold crown on 'er 'ead?
She 'as ships on the foam—she 'as millions at 'ome,
    An' she pays us poor beggars in red.
5   (Ow, poor beggars in red!)
There's 'er nick on the cavalry 'orses,
    There's 'er mark on the medical stores—
An' 'er troops you'll find with a fair wind be'ind
    That takes us to various wars.
10   (Poor beggars!—barbarious wars!)
    Then 'ere's to the Widow at Windsor,
        An' 'ere's to the stores an' the guns,
    The men an' the 'orses what makes up the forces
        O' Missis Victorier's sons.
15   (Poor beggars! Victorier's sons!)

Walk wide o' the Widow at Windsor,
    For 'alf o' Creation she owns:

We'ave bought 'er the same with the sword an' the flame,
  An' we've salted it down with our bones.
20   (Poor beggars!—it's blue with our bones!)
Hands off o' the sons o' the widow,
  Hands off o' the goods in 'er shop.
For the kings must come down an' the emperors frown
  When the Widow at Windsor says "Stop!"
25   (Poor beggars!—we're sent to say "Stop!")
    Then 'ere's to the Lodge o' the Widow,
      From the Pole to the Tropics it runs—
    To the Lodge that we tile with the rank an' the file,
      An' open in form with the guns.
30   (Poor beggars!—it's always they guns!)

We 'ave 'eard o' the Widow at Windsor,
  It's safest to leave 'er alone:
For 'er sentries we stand by the sea an' the land
  Wherever the bugles are blown.
35   (Poor beggars!—an' don't we get blown!)
    Take 'old o' the Wings o' the Mornin',
    An' flop round the earth till you're dead;
But you won't get away from the tune that they play
  To the bloomin' old rag over'ead.
40   (Poor beggars!—it's 'ot over'ead!)
    Then 'ere's to the sons o' the Widow,
      Wherever, 'owever they roam.
    'Ere's all they desire, an' if they require
      A speedy return to their 'ome.
45   (Poor beggars!—they'll never see 'ome!)

Literary Analysis
Mood as a Key to Theme
What do the remarks in parentheses suggest about the speaker's attitude toward the empire?

Critical Reading

© **1. Key Ideas and Details (a)** Who is the "Widow at Windsor"? **(b) Infer:** What is surprising about the speaker's decision to use this description?

© **2. Key Ideas and Details (a)** Who is the speaker of this poem? **(b) Analyze:** Would you describe the speaker's tone as disloyal or disrespectful? Explain.

© **3. Key Ideas and Details (a)** What various remarks of the speaker's appear in parentheses? **(b) Make a Judgment:** How would the poem be different if the remarks in parentheses were deleted? Why?

© **4. Integration of Knowledge and Ideas** What comment is the speaker making about the extent and power of the British Empire? Use two of these Essential Question words in your answer: *authority, consequence, domination. [Connecting to the Essential Question: What is the relationship between literature and place?]*

Cite textual evidence to support your responses.

Literary Analysis

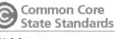

Common Core State Standards

Writing

1. Write arguments to support claims in an analysis of substantive topics or texts, using valid reasoning and relevant and sufficient evidence. *(p. 1051)*

1.a. Introduce precise, knowledgeable claim(s), establish the significance of the claim(s), distinguish the claim(s) from alternate or opposing claims, and create an organization that logically sequences claim(s), counterclaims, reasons, and evidence. *(p. 1051)*

1. Craft and Structure Fill in a chart like the one shown here by describing the **mood** evoked by images from "Dover Beach." Then, using what you have written as a clue, state the **theme** of the poem.

Image	Where It Appears	Mood It Evokes

2. Craft and Structure Review Arnold's descriptions of the night throughout "Dover Beach" and his use of the word "night" in line 37. Do you think his mood is ultimately pessimistic or optimistic? Explain.

3. Craft and Structure Explain how the mood of sternness and solemnity in "Recessional" relates to the theme of the poem.

4. Craft and Structure Basing your answer on the concluding two lines of each stanza in "Recessional," what conclusion can you draw about Kipling's theme?

5. Craft and Structure Use the mood in "The Widow at Windsor" to explain which of these sentences best describes the theme of the poem: **(a)** Maintaining the Empire seems ridiculous to soldiers who must do it. **(b)** Maintaining the Empire is a deadly serious game, played at the expense of soldiers.

6. Comparing Literary Works Compare and contrast the effect of the sounds of words and lines of Arnold's and Kipling's poetry. **(a)** Which poet's work is more slow and somber? **(b)** Which poet's work is more clipped and lively? **(c)** Explain how the sound of the language contributes to the mood of each poem and to the poets' aesthetic purposes.

7. Analyzing Visual Information Use your knowledge of Arnold's "Dover Beach" to explain the humor of the cartoon on this page.

©The New Yorker Collection, 1988, J. B. Handelsman, from *cartoonbank.com*. All Rights Reserved.

Reading Strategy

8. Connect Arnold's work to the historical period by considering how the phrases "ignorant armies" and "darkling plain" in "Dover Beach" might relate to advances in science and the decline of faith.

9. (a) What do Kipling's parenthetical remarks in "The Widow" reveal about the historical period? **(b)** What does Kipling achieve by describing the Empire from the point of view of a common soldier?

10. Relate "Recessional" and "The Widow at Windsor" to the historical period by explaining how the poems reflect different perspectives on the responsibilities and dangers that come with empire.

"Here as on a darkling plain swept with confused alarms of struggle and flight, where ignorant armies clash by night, Matthew Arnold, News." ▶

Integrated Language Skills

ⓒ Vocabulary Acquisition and Use

Word Analysis: Word-Phrase Relationships

Some words have special meaning when used in phrases. *Dominion,* for instance, means "control." The phrase *dominion over,* which Kipling uses in "Recessional," suggests a responsibility for the beings that the person with dominion controls. Contrast the meanings of each of these words and the phrases in which they also appear. Then, write an original sentence using the phrase.

1. attend; attend on
2. awe; in awe of
3. closed; closed down
4. move; move on
5. see; see through
6. stand; stand by

Vocabulary: Antonyms

Antonyms are words with opposite meanings. *Love* and *hate* are antonyms. For each word from the vocabulary list on page 1040, choose the antonym. Then, write an original sentence using both the word and its antonym.

1. awe: **(a)** attrition **(b)** contempt **(c)** reverence
2. turbid: **(a)** clear **(b)** confused **(c)** separated
3. tranquil: **(a)** calm **(b)** rational **(c)** restless
4. contrite: **(a)** incomplete **(b)** respectful **(c)** unrepentant
5. cadence: **(a)** tempo **(b)** unevenness **(c)** vigor
6. dominion: **(a)** obedience **(b)** rule **(c)** sway

Writing

ⓒ **Argumentative Text** Critic Walter E. Houghton writes that the Victorian Age was characterized by "widespread doubt about the nature of man, society, and the universe." Using *evidence* from the poems by Arnold and Kipling, write an **essay** to support or refute this general observation.

Prewriting Review the poems, using a chart like the one shown to gather evidence about the *theme* of Victorian doubt or self-confidence. Note uses of imagery, language, or stylistic devices that illustrate or contradict the doubts that Houghton cites. Based on your examples, decide whether you agree or disagree with Houghton's claim.

Drafting Begin your draft by summarizing Houghton's point and stating your position for or against it. Support your generalizations with evidence from Arnold's and Kipling's poems. Consider organizing your response by devoting a paragraph to each selection.

Model: Gathering Details

Poem:			
	Images	**Mood(s)**	**Theme(s)**
Doubt			
Self-confidence			

Revising Review your draft, highlighting generalizations and looking for supporting details for each. Where details are lacking, provide them. Make sure that all quotations are accurate and properly referenced. Also, be sure you have *acknowledged and refuted opposing arguments.*

James Berry Introduces
"From Lucy: Englan' Lady," "Time Removed," and "Freedom"

On Growing Up British The poems in this selection reflect my different heritages: my Jamaican upbringing, my British identity, and to some extent, my African background. I was one of the peoples "of palm and pine" who grew up under the dominion of the British Empire that is the subject of Kipling's "Recessional" (p. 1045). As pompous as it sounds, Kipling's poem foresees some of the dangers of power and pomp and their likely end—those at the top will have to climb down. Empires are humbled, but sometimes, out of that, new relationships are made and changes happen.

Looking at England from a Caribbean Perspective When I grew up, the British Empire was fading fast, but my Caribbean people had become part of the British way of life. My poem "From Lucy: Englan' Lady" is one of a group of poems that I wrote in Caribbean Creole language and in the voice of Lucy, a Caribbean woman living in England.

Like Lucy, most people who came to Britain in the 1950s were royalists with a natural respect for the Royal Family. To them, the Queen was just like the church. Lucy treats the Queen like an ancient institution, something that will always be there, but at the same time she feels sympathy for her as a woman, for the hard time she has keeping up a show. She feels the Queen belongs to her, so she has a right to comment on her.

About the Author

James Berry has won numerous awards for his work as a poet, novelist, and short-story writer. Among his awards and honors are the Signal Poetry Award in 1989 for *When I Dance* and the Order of the British Empire in 1990.

Lucy represents the uncritical, unwavering admiration that so many ordinary people feel for royalty. She comes from the poverty-stricken context of the Caribbean, yet she would give her life for an institution that does nothing positive for her.

Traveling Back to Jamaica The poem "Time Removed" was one I wrote after I'd been in England for some years and following a visit I made back to Jamaica. I was saddened by how little had happened during my absence. My surroundings seemed to be more broken-down and less well maintained than before I went away.

Because I had a wider experience of life now, I could see what was not being done. In England, I had felt a kind of awe for all the work that had gone on over centuries to shape and tame the land. There was a sense of a managed landscape that was kept up and renewed continually through organization and the application of knowledge and skill. In Jamaica, the landscape and the roads were still very undeveloped.

▼ **Critical Viewing**
Which details in this photograph reflect Berry's recollections in his essay? **[Interpret]**

" *I was saddened by how little had happened during my absence.* "

The end of the poem is the intricate part. The image of my father's horse stands for a dying way of life. It's what my father had left me, an old-fashioned place and a stuck way of life. The place that I loved called out to me, neighing like a half-dead horse. I think that's why I called the poem "Time Removed"—because, although I was removed from the time of my childhood, I still felt part of it in a helpless way. The poem is a kind of sigh of pain for the inequalities I'd become more aware of.

The Poetry of Letting Go "Freedom" was a response to protest poems I'd been reading, which were full of negative interpretations of black people's history. It was also an argument, an outcry against the backwardness I was born in and the inadequate political solutions that had been found for it. I was sick and tired of Jamaican leaders harping on in a helpless way about the terrible things Europeans had done to them. They were always hanging onto hurt instead of applying themselves in a positive way to change things.

I think you have to free yourself from your own pain and past. It's no good spending your energy on righteous indignation. For us to create something for ourselves as Caribbean people, we have to go beyond that, let go of a destructive past and create new structures. I hoped for a renaissance among Caribbean people. That's what my poems wanted to do—to stir people and show positive visions of possible futures.

Critical Reading

1. **Key Ideas and Details** **(a)** According to Berry, what often happens to those individuals or empires that reach the peak of their power? **(b) Interpret:** What changes in the relationship between the Empire and Jamaica might Berry have wanted after Britain's power diminished?

2. **Key Ideas and Details** **(a)** What reason does Berry give for naming his poem "Time Removed"? **(b) Apply:** What kind of inequalities around you echo Berry's concerns for Jamaica?

As You Read "From Lucy: Englan' Lady," "Time Removed," and "Freedom" . . .

3. **Key Ideas and Details** Look for images of Jamaica that Berry describes in his essay.

4. **Integration of Knowledge and Ideas** Note instances where Berry uses his poems to voice his frustration with Britain's treatment of Jamaica.

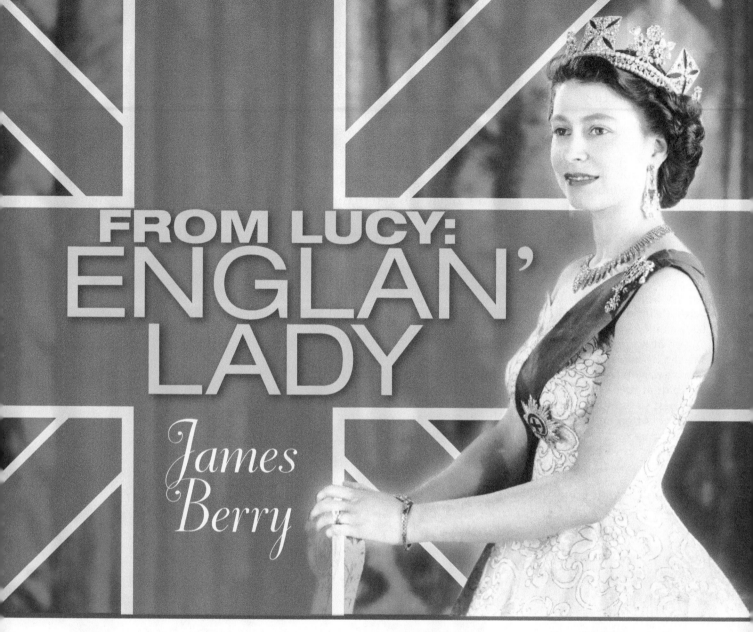

FROM LUCY: ENGLAN' LADY

James Berry

Queen Elizabeth II

You ask me 'bout the lady. Me dear,
old center here still shine
with Queen. She affec' the place
like the sun: not comin' out oft'n
5 an' when it happ'n everybody's out
smilin' as she wave a han'
like a seagull flyin' slow slow.

> **James Berry**
> **Author's Insight** Lucy has been asked by Leela, her friend back home, whether she has seen the Queen. Every time I go back to the Caribbean people ask me that!

James Berry
Author's Insight Lucy connects the Queen with her feeling of the ancient power of British history and with the vast metropolitan character of London.

An' you know she come from
dust free rooms an' velvet
10 an' diamond. She make you feel
this on-an'-on[1] town, London,
where long long time deeper than mind.[2]
An' han's after han's[3] die away,
makin' streets, putt'n' up bricks,
15 a piece of brass, a piece of wood
an' plantin' trees: an' it give
a car a halfday job gett'n' through.

An' Leela, darlin', no, I never
meet the Queen in flesh. Yet
20 sometimes, deep deep, I sorry for her.
Everybody expec' a show
from her, like she a space touris'
on earth. An' darlin', unless
you can go home an' scratch up[4]
25 you' husban', it mus' be hard
strain keepin' good graces for
all hypocrite faces.

Anyhow, me dear, you know what
ole time people say,
30 "Bird sing sweet for its nest."[5]

James Berry
Author's Insight Lucy imagines the Queen at home, where she can be herself and behave naturally—just as a bird at home in its own nest sings most sweetly. I often end my Lucy poems with a Jamaican proverb.

"BIRD SING SWEET FOR ITS NEST"

---

1. **on-an'-on** extraordinary.
2. **deeper . . . mind** more than can be comprehended.
3. **han's after han's** many generations.
4. **scratch up** lose your temper at.
5. **"Bird . . . nest"** Jamaican proverb, referring to the nightingale's habit of singing loudest near its nest. It means, "Those closest to home are the most contented."

Freedom

James Berry

Freedom is not
  a helpless grasping
  at a source of hurt
  or an outpour of oneself
5 to fixed ends others started

Freedom is not
  a hiding in the dust
  of righteous indignation
  or a merging with shadows

10 Freedom is not
  a becoming the model
  of destructive echoes
  or a walking in the hands of ghosts

Freedom is not
15 a reframing of oneself
  in the walls of the old prison
  or a becoming the tyrant's chain

Freedom is not
  excursions of energy
20 to nowhere
  driven and controlled
  by someone else's motivation

Freedom is
  a letting go like trees grow
25 a native self unravelling
  an adventure of a new
  self because of oneself

James Berry
Author's Insight This poem works through a series of images which all in some way suggest a failure to let go of a history of hurt and oppression.

James Berry
Author's Insight My argument in this poem is that people can continue their own imprisonment; if you live with hate and the desire for revenge, you replace one set of chains with another.

James Berry
Author's Insight This last verse sums up the adventure of living and striving to become more.

Time

REMOVED

James Berry

I go on and on in England
and walk no ground untrodden.

Landscapes are checkered —
tamed out of new years
5   and recurring generations.

Compulsive hands have shaped
bordered fields
out of scrub,
rivers' faces with bridge,
10   edifices for trees towering
lands now railed and tarred.

Animals are not bony and bare.
Wheels quicken time —
through a late summer
15   staying fresh as spring.

And here
just as jungles hold my love
every whiff of air evokes a time
like the horse my father left
20   and I after ten years away
found the greyhaired skeleton
neighing to me,
like these days do,
in memories too overlaid to touch.

James Berry
Author's Insight When I
first rode through England on
a train I was extraordinarily
moved by the organization
and variety of the landscape,
like an ordered checkerboard
of fields with different
colored crops.

◄ **Critical Viewing**
How do the two landscapes
in these photographs
dramatize the contrast that
Berry makes in the poem?
[Connect]

James Berry
Author's Insight Coming
from the Caribbean, I
wasn't used to the change
of seasons. I'd thought that
grass would go brown and
dry up in late summer, but it
stayed green all year round.

Critical Reading ©

1. **Key Ideas and Details (a)** According to Lucy, in what kind
   of environment does the Queen live? **(b) Summarize:** What
   challenges does Lucy think the Queen faces as a result of her
   position? **(c) Analyze:** How do Lucy's perceptions humanize
   the Queen?

   Cite textual evidence to support your responses.

2. **Key Ideas and Details (a) Interpret:** In your own words,
   explain the meaning of lines 18–22 in "Freedom."
   (b) Support: Provide an example that illustrates your point.

3. **Integration of Knowledge and Ideas** In "Time Removed,"
   Berry writes in lines 3–5 that the landscapes around us are "tamed
   out" by each new generation. Do you think the landscape around
   you is improved by each generation or compromised by it? Provide
   examples to support your response.

CONNECTING VICTORIAN THEMES

Colin Meloy, frontman for lit-rock band The Decemberists, admits he reads a lot of Victorian novels. They have informed his writing style. His lyrics are often couched in the doubts and melancholy of the Victorians, harking back to the era's concerns about the passing of the natural world and the isolation ushered in by the new industrial age. Specifically, Meloy's "Eli, the Barrow Boy" lyrics echo the themes of love and loss in Matthew Arnold's "Dover Beach" as well as the working class voices in Kipling's poems.

COLIN MELOY SONGWRITER

Music is a necessity to Colin Meloy, something "that drives me completely," he says. He is the main songwriter for the indie group The Decemberists, whose music has been described as lit-rock. Meloy's background in literature qualifies him for the "lit" side of that description. He has a Master of Fine Arts (MFA) in creative writing and considers himself a writer of fictional song stories. The songs on the album *Picaresque,* for example, tell stories that seem to come straight out of Victorian Literature 101.

Sometimes, Meloy has to defend himself against charges of using too many big words! "I don't want to be the person who sends everyone to the diction-ary when they're listening to music," he said in a 2004 interview, "just because I think that pop music should be a populist thing."

ELI, THE BARROW BOY

Eli, the barrow boy of the old town
Sells coal and marigolds
And he cries out all down the day

Below the tamaracks he is crying.
"Corncobs and candlewax for the buying!"
All down the day

"Would I could afford to buy my love a fine robe
Made of gold and silk Arabian thread
But she is dead and gone and lying in a pine grove
And I must push my barrow all the day.
And I must push my barrow all the day."

Eli, the barrow boy—when they found him
Dressed all in corduroy, he had drowned in
The river down the way.

They laid his body down in the church yard
But still when the moon is out
With his push cart he calls down the day:

"Would I could afford to buy my love a fine robe
Made of gold and silk Arabian thread
But I am dead and gone and lying in a church ground
But still I push my barrow all the day.
Still I must push my barrow all the day."

"CORNCOBS AND CANDLEWAX FOR THE BUYING!"

Critical Reading

1. **(a)** What does Eli do to make a living? **(b) Summarize:** What is the story behind the poem?

2. **Compare and Contrast:** In what ways do the setting, characters, and details in these lyrics echo those of Victorian literary works? Explain.

Use this question to focus a group discussion of "Eli, The Barrow Boy":

3. What might a contemporary music group gain by connecting with literature from the past?

Primary Sources

Newspaper Article
Progress in Personal Comfort

Advertisement
Cook's Railroad Advertisement

Common Core State Standards

Reading Informational Text

1. Cite strong and thorough textual evidence to support analysis of what the text says explicitly as well as inferences drawn from the text, including determining where the text leaves matters uncertain.

3. Analyze a complex set of ideas or sequence of events and explain how specific individuals, ideas, or events interact and develop over the course of the text.

About the Text Forms

A **newspaper article** is any short piece of prose writing that appears in a newspaper. It may contain straight news, opinions about recent events, or a combination of both.

An **advertisement** is a persuasive piece that attempts to sell people a product or service. Before the invention of radio and television, printed advertisements were the major means of publicizing products. Such advertisements appeared in a variety of formats, including leaflets, newspaper advertisements, billboards, posters, and product labels.

Reading Strategy

Analyze the techniques of media messages in advertisements and persuasive newspaper articles by focusing on the following *modes of persuasion:*

- **Logical:** presents factual evidence and arguments that make sense

- **Faulty:** presents arguments that upon close study are not fully sound

- **Deceptive:** presents intentionally misleading information

- **Emotional:** uses status symbols, peer pressure, patriotism, humor, or other appeals to the reader's emotions and desires

Look for these modes of appeal as you read or view the primary sources. To help you identify and analyze appeals in these modes,

- summarize what the text explicitly says

- draw conclusions about what the text implies, or suggests

- analyze the sequence of and interrelationships between ideas. For example, do they follow a logical order? Do they build on one another?

Support your summary and your analysis by citing relevant quotations and other details from the text.

How does literature **shape or** reflect *society?*

Both the newspaper article and the advertisement reflect changes to society in Victorian times. As you read, consider what each document reveals about its times and how each relates to the other.

PHLit
Online!
www.PHLitOnline.com

Note-Taking Guide

Primary source documents are a rich source of information for researchers. As you read these documents, use a note-taking guide like the one shown to organize relevant and accurate information.

1 Type of Document (check one)
☐ Newspaper Article   ☐ Letter   ☐ Diary   ☐ Speech   ☐ Map
☐ Government Document   ☐ Advertisement   ☐ Memorandum   ☐ Other

2 Date of Document _____

3 Author _____
Author's Position _____

4 Original Audience _____

5 Purpose and Importance

   a Does this document or image have a persuasive purpose?_____
_____

     What techniques does it use to accomplish this purpose? Logical argument?
Appeals to emotion? Attractive images?_____
_____

   b List two important ideas, statements, or observations from this document.
_____
_____

   c What does this document show about life in the time and place in which it
was composed? _____
_____

> **Reading Strategy**
> **Analyzing Media Messages** Identifying a source's persuasive goals, target audience, and techniques is a key to analyzing its message.

This guide was adapted from the **U.S. National Archives** document analysis worksheet.

Vocabulary

depredation (dep´ rə dā´ shən) *n.* act or instance of robbing or laying waste (p. 1065)

Macadam (mə kad´ əm) *n.* road surfacing made of small stones bound with adhesive (p. 1065)

fracture (frak´ chər) *n.* a broken bone (p. 1065)

pulp (pulp) *n.* a soft, formless mass (p. 1065)

gout (gout) *n.* a type of arthritis characterized by painful attacks in the hands and especially the feet (p. 1066)

bilious (bil´ yəs) *adj.* suffering from or caused by too much bile or another liver problem (p. 1066)

privations (prī vā´ shənz) *n.* instances of being deprived; losses or absences of something (p. 1066)

THE STORY BEHIND THE DOCUMENTS

Sydney Smith

THE
EDINBURGH REVIEW,
OR
CRITICAL JOURNAL:
FOR
OCT. 1802......JAN. 1803.

TO BE CONTINUED QUARTERLY.

JUDEX DAMNATUR CUM NOCENS ABSOLVITUR.
PUBLIUS SYRUS.

VOL. I.

Edinburgh:

PRINTED BY D. WILLISON, CRAIG'S CLOSE,
FOR ARCHIBALD CONSTABLE, EDINBURGH;
AND T. N. LONGMAN & O. REES,
LONDON.

1803.

Volume I of *The Edinburgh Review,*
co-founded by Sydney Smith

Sydney Smith (1771–1845) was an influential writer and preacher of his time. In 1802, he helped found the *Edinburgh Review,* a popular journal to which he frequently contributed articles. Many of these articles express progressive viewpoints on issues such as parliamentary reform, prisons, slavery, and religious freedom. Ordained in the Church of England, Smith nevertheless was a tireless champion of Catholic Emancipation, arguing that Roman Catholics should enjoy equal rights in Britain, at a time when many Britons still thought they should not.

The *Edinburgh Review,* which was published from 1802 to 1929, was a forerunner of today's magazines and journals. It was especially known for its progressive commentaries on politics and its criticism of literary works. Contributors to the journal included famous authors such as the essayist William Hazlitt and the historian Thomas Babington Macaulay (a letter of whose appears in this textbook). The relatively large circulation of this journal—13,500 in 1818—testifies to the growing interest in ideas and literature.

A pioneer of the modern travel industry, **Thomas Cook** (1808–1892) was a devout Baptist who organized his first tour to bring people to a meeting of the temperance movement, a movement to discourage the use of alcoholic beverages. Soon Cook was booking railway excursions all over Britain. He eventually expanded his tours to include Europe, the Middle East, and even North America. In 1872, he led a round-the-world tour that is said to have inspired Jules Verne's novel *Around the World in 80 Days.*

Smith's journal and Cook's tours are both evidence of the growth of Victorian Britain's middle class. An increasingly prosperous and literate middle class meant a greater audience for books, magazines, and newspapers. Having more money and leisure time also meant that middle-class Victorians could see a bit more of the world, enjoying the relatively safe and comfortable travel adventures that a Cook's tour provided.

New publications and new means of travel are just two examples of the kind of progress that Victorian Britain valued. Sydney Smith's newspaper article celebrates the innovations, large and small, that contributed to progress in the area of personal comfort—umbrellas, gas streetlights, and adhesive postage stamps, to name just a few. The great strides in transportation that Smith also describes—steamships, better roads, and most of all, railways—were the cornerstone of the new tourist industry promoted in Thomas Cook's advertisement.

Thomas Cook

PROGRESS IN
PERSONAL COMFORT

Sydney Smith

It is of some importance at what period a man is born. A young man, alive at this period, hardly knows to what improvements of human life he has been introduced; and I would bring before his notice the following eighteen changes which have taken place in England since I first began to breathe in it the breath of life—a period amounting now to nearly seventy-three years.

Gas[1] was unknown: I groped about the streets of London in all but the utter darkness of a twinkling oil lamp, under the protection of watchmen in their grand climacteric,[2] and exposed to every species of depredation and insult.

I have been nine hours in sailing from Dover to Calais before the invention of steam. It took me nine hours to go from Taunton to Bath, before the invention of railroads, and I now go in six hours from Taunton to London! In going from Taunton to Bath, I suffered between 10,000 and 12,000 severe contusions,[3] before stone-breaking Macadam was born.

I paid £15 in a single year for repairs of carriage-springs on the pavement of London; and I now glide without noise or fracture, on wooden pavements.

I can walk, by the assistance of the police, from one end of London to the other, without molestation; or, if tired, get into a cheap and active cab, instead of those cottages on wheels, which the hackney coaches[4] were at the beginning of my life.

I had no umbrella! They were little used, and very dear. There were no waterproof hats, and *my* hat has often been reduced by rains into its primitive pulp.

---

1. gas coal gas, piped under the streets of London and used in streetlights after 1814.
2. climacteric (klī mak´ tər ik) *n.* a major turning point in life, referring here to old age.
3. contusions (kən tyoo´ or too´ zhənz) *n.* bruises.
4. cheap and active cab . . . hackney coaches Faster two-wheeled hansom cabs replaced hackney coaches as London's typical vehicles for hire to travel short distances.

Primary Sources:
Newspaper Article What does the article reveal to be the contrasting attitudes of younger and older Victorians toward the progress it describes?

Reading Strategy
Analyzing Media Messages Identify the logical reasoning and emotional appeals in the third paragraph.

Vocabulary
depredation (dep´ rə dā´ shən) *n.* act or instance of robbing or laying waste

Macadam (mə kad´ əm) *n.* road surfacing made of small stones bound with adhesive

fracture (frak´ chər) *n.* a broken bone

pulp (pulp) *n.* a soft, formless mass

Primary Sources

Newspaper Article

Why do you think Smith does not relate the detailed history of the inventions he cites?

Vocabulary

gout (gout) *n.* a type of arthritis that especially affects the feet

bilious (bil′ yəs) *adj.* having a digestive ailment caused by too much bile or another liver problem

privations (prī vā′ shənz) *n.* losses or absences of something

I could not keep my smallclothes in their proper place, for braces were unknown.[5] If I had the gout, there was no colchicum. If I was bilious, there was no calomel. If I was attacked by ague, there was no quinine.[6] There were filthy coffee houses instead of elegant clubs. Game could not be bought. Quarrels about uncommuted tithes[7] were endless. The corruption of Parliament, before Reform, infamous.[8] There were no banks to receive the savings of the poor. The Poor Laws were gradually sapping the vitals of the country; and whatever miseries I suffered, I had no post to whisk my complaints for a single penny[9] to the remotest corners of the empire; and yet, in spite of all these privations, I lived on quietly, and am now ashamed that I was not more discontented, and utterly surprised that all these changes and inventions did not occur two centuries ago.

I forgot to add, that as the basket of stage coaches, in which luggage was then carried, had no springs, your clothes were rubbed all to pieces. . . .

---

5. **smallclothes . . . braces were unknown** There were no suspenders to hold up his trousers.
6. **gout . . . quinine** (kwī′ nīn′) Colchicum, calomel, and quinine were new, more effective medications used to treat the medical conditions mentioned. *Ague* (ā′ gyoo′) is an old word for a fever accompanied by chills—the kind of fever that recurs in people suffering from malaria.
7. **uncommuted tithes** (tī*th*z) Beginning with the Tithe Act of 1836, taxes paid to the Church of England in the form of produce were "commuted," or changed to, an equivalent payment in money.
8. **The corruption . . . infamous** Before passage of the Reform Bill of 1832, the House of Commons was dominated by a small number of wealthy, corrupt landowners.
9. **I had no post . . . single penny** Penny postage, in the form of an adhesive stamp, was first introduced to Britain in 1840.

Critical Reading

Cite textual evidence to support your responses.

1. Key Ideas and Details **(a)** How old was Smith when he wrote this newspaper article? **(b) Infer:** Why does he think a young man would "hardly know" the value of the improvements he describes?

2. Key Ideas and Details **(a) Classify:** What are two improvements in public safety and two in public transportation that Smith reports? **(b) Generalize:** What general picture does he draw of life before the various inventions and changes he describes?

3. Integration of Knowledge and Ideas **(a) Assess:** Does Smith consider the possibility that people in the future might find his world uncomfortable? Explain. **(b) Generalize:** What does Smith's attitude toward the past, present, and future show about human attitudes toward progress in general?

TECHNOLOGICAL ADVANCES
IN THE NINETEENTH CENTURY

As Sydney Smith describes, during the nineteenth century, technology developed at a rapid pace and changed people's lives in important ways. This timeline shows a few of these advances.

▲ 1824
Englishman **Joseph Aspin** patented Portland Cement, made from hydraulic lime. In 1843, cement was used to build the Thames Tunnel, the world's first underwater tunnel.

▼ 1835
Fox Talbot, an English chemist, published an article on his discovery of the paper negative, preparing the way for modern photography.

▲ 1862
French scientist **Louis Pasteur** discovered that, by heating milk, one could kill many harmful organisms in it, thus extending its shelf life. He called the process "pasteurization."

▲ 1895
The Frenchman **Louis Lumière** invented a portable all-in-one motion-picture camera, film processing unit, and projector called the Cinématographe, which began the era of motion pictures.

▶ 1834
The Analytic Engine—designed by **Charles Babbage,** a British scientist and mathematician—is a forerunner of modern digital computers.

▼ 1877
The cylinder phonograph, the earliest method of recording sound, was developed by **Thomas Edison.** Soon after, he recorded the voice of Alfred, Lord Tennyson.

CONNECT TO THE LITERATURE

How would you describe Sydney Smith's attitude toward the changes he witnessed during his lifetime?

RAILROAD ADVERTISEMENT

BACKGROUND This Victorian advertisement for a Cook's tour was aimed at Britain's growing middle class.

Reading Strategy
Analyzing Media Messages For each of the following elements, indicate the intended audience, the message, and the method of persuasion:

- The use of a woman as the central figure
- The woman's position, body language, and dress
- Other images
- Featured words

Primary Source
Advertisement
What does this advertisement try to persuade people to do?

Critical Reading

©

© **1. Key Ideas and Details (a)** Where does the ad say a Cook's tour will take you? **(b) Infer:** Why do you think the word *anywhere* is underlined?

© **2. Integration of Knowledge and Ideas (a) Apply:** If this ad were used today, how would a contemporary reader react to it? Explain, citing specific elements of the ad. **(b) Evaluate:** Have the techniques of print advertising changed very much since Victorian times? Explain, giving examples in support.

Cite textual evidence to support your responses.

Newspaper Article • Advertisement

Comparing Primary Sources

Refer to your Note-Taking Guide to answer these questions.

1. **(a)** Summarize the **newspaper article.** Support your answer with quotations from the text. **(b)** What attitudes and ideas does Smith implicitly promote? Explain, citing relevant details. **(c)** Explain how the main ideas in the article reinforce one another.

2. **(a)** What does the appearance of the people in the **advertisement** show about the background, class, and interests of its audience? **(b)** Which details in Smith's article appeal to a similar audience? Organize details in a diagram like the one shown.

Details of People Pictured in Ad

↓

Likely Audience

Details in Newspaper Article

↓

Likely Audience

3. Write a paragraph comparing the modes of persuasion used in the two sources.

© Vocabulary Acquisition and Use

New Vocabulary Is each statement true or false? Explain.

1. A generous philanthropist will often engage in *depredation*.
2. The *pulp* of the tooth is the hard enamel on the outside.
3. Someone camping in the wild is likely to experience *privations*.

Content-Area Vocabulary Use the italicized vocabulary words to help you answer each question. Then, explain your answer.

1. A person with *gout* would probably **(a)** cough a lot **(b)** sleep a lot **(c)** rest his or her feet on a cushion.
2. A person would most likely feel *bilious* after **(a)** eating **(b)** resting **(c)** trying on shoes.
3. To heal a *fracture*, a person would most likely need **(a)** a cast **(b)** a flu shot **(c)** a warm drink.
4. Supplying new *Macadam* would be the job of **(a)** a chef **(b)** a road builder **(c)** a travel agent.

Etymology Study Macadam is named for John Macadam, the engineer who developed it. Use a dictionary to trace the etymology of these words based on a person's name: *boycott, maverick, silhouette, watt.*

Common Core State Standards

Writing
7. Conduct short as well as more sustained research projects to answer a question or solve a problem; narrow or broaden the inquiry when appropriate; synthesize multiple sources on the subject, demonstrating understanding of the subject under investigation. *(p. 1070)*

8. Gather relevant information from multiple authoritative print and digital sources, using advanced searches effectively; assess the strengths and limitations of each source in terms of the task, purpose, and audience; integrate information into the text selectively to maintain the flow of ideas, avoiding plagiarism and overreliance on any one source and following a standard format for citation. *(p. 1070)*

Language
6. Acquire and use accurately general academic and domain-specific words and phrases, sufficient for reading, writing, speaking, and listening at the college and career readiness level; demonstrate independence in gathering vocabulary knowledge when considering a word or phrase important to comprehension or expression.

Research Task

Topic: The Theme of "Progress" in the Media

In the centuries separating Victorian England from the present, the idea of progress—measured with terms such as "faster," "farther," and "easier"—has acquired a large shadow side. Concerned about everything from pollution to poor diet to cell phones, people today may associate progress with threats to the environment, to health, and even to civility. These days, "progress" may even mean taking a step back.

Assignment: Present a research report in which you analyze the treatment of the theme of "progress" in a television and a print advertisement. Then, evaluate how these media reflect cultural and social views different from those in Sydney Smith's essay and in the Cook's tour advertisement.

Gather sources. Use television recordings, newspapers, magazines, and online and library sources to locate and review possible ads for your report. Narrow or broaden your search as needed to ensure that you find the material you need efficiently. Keep accurate notes of the sources of all material.

Develop questions to guide analysis. Analyzing your chosen advertisements should involve answering questions like these:

- What is the purpose of and audience for the ad?
- What media techniques does the ad use to convey the theme of progress?
- What view of progress—positive, negative, or mixed—does the advertisement present?

Synthesize information. Review each ad, analyzing individual elements such as words, images, graphic elements, and sounds. Create a chart like the one shown to help synthesize your insights.

Model: Synthesizing Information in Media

Words	Images	Graphics	Sounds
Simpler and *purer* suggest progress —away from "progress"!	Images of an elderly farmer suggest tradition.	Logo of a mill suggests return to the past.	Theme played on banjo suggests simpler times.

Conclusion: Ad suggests that the product helps consumers escape the confusion and stress of "progress" to return to simpler times.

Organize and present ideas. Present your analysis of the ads and your comparison of the social and cultural views they reflect with the views found in Smith's essay and the Cook's tour advertisement. To ensure flow, select the strongest examples for each point you make. Avoid plagiarism, citing your sources for images and ideas.

RESEARCH TIP

Pay close attention to the denotations, or literal meanings, and the connotations, or emotional associations, of words used in the ads. Note what individual words literally mean and what connotations they take on in the context of the ads.

Use a checklist like the one shown to evaluate your work.

Research Checklist

- ☐ Have I answered all the questions in my guidelines for analysis?
- ☐ Have I fully analyzed the words and the images?
- ☐ Have I evaluated the impact of the graphics and the sounds?
- ☐ Have I articulated the overall meaning of each ad?
- ☐ Have I successfully compared the social and cultural views reflected in the ads with the views of optimistic Victorians?

Gloom and Glory

Before You Read

Remembrance • The Darkling Thrush • "Ah, Are You Digging on My Grave?"

Connecting to the Essential Question Brontë and Hardy express the feeling of not being at home in the world. As you read, note the ways in which the speakers in these poems indicate dissatisfaction with the places in which they find themselves. Doing so will help you think about the Essential Question: **What is the relationship between literature and place?**

Literary Analysis

Poets have a number of ways of addressing a reader's expectations. **Stanzas,** for instance, are repeated groupings of two or more verse lines with a definite pattern of line length, rhythm, and, frequently, rhyme. The **stanza structure** of a poem is the pattern of stanzas from which it is built. While stanza structure creates an expectation of a regular pattern, **irony** challenges expectations by creating a contradiction between reality and appearance or between what is said and what is meant.

Both stanza structure and irony may set up and then fulfill or not fulfill expectations. In reading these poems, for example, notice these patterns:

- The arrangement of the first stanza leads you to expect a similar arrangement in the others.
- Irony surprises you by not fulfilling expectations.

Comparing Literary Works Brontë's and Hardy's poems deal in different ways with the theme of absence—the sense of something missing. Compare the ways in which the speakers in these poems feel about an absence and succeed or fail in handling it.

Reading Strategy

Preparing to Read Complex Texts Many poetic stanzas express a single main idea, as paragraphs do in prose. You can **analyze the pattern of stanzas** and how it affects the meaning and aesthetic impact of the poem if you notice how each stanza builds on the preceding one. Use a chart like this one to understand the logical progression of stanzas in each poem.

Vocabulary

obscure (ăb skyo͞or´) *v.* make difficult to see (p. 1076)

languish (laŋ´ gwish) *v.* become weak; suffer from longing (p. 1076)

rapturous (rap´ chər əs) *adj.* filled with joy and love; ecstatic (p. 1076)

gaunt (gônt) *adj.* thin and bony, as from great hunger or age (p. 1080)

terrestrial (tə res´ trē əl) *adj.* relating to the earth or to this world (p. 1080)

prodding (präd´ iŋ) *adj.* poking, jabbing, seeking (p. 1081)

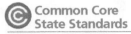

Common Core State Standards

Reading Literature
5. Analyze how an author's choices concerning how to structure specific parts of a text contribute to its overall structure and meaning as well as its aesthetic impact.

"Remembrance"

Stanza 1
Speaker had a true love who died and whom she may be forgetting.

Stanza 2

Etc.

PHLit Online!
www.PHLitOnline.com

Emily Brontë
(1818–1848)

Author of "Remembrance"

Although some literary critics of the time attacked Emily Brontë for the violent passions expressed in her novel *Wuthering Heights* (1847), her dark Romanticism is now regarded as the essence of her genius.

A Writer's Beginnings Brontë grew up in the Yorkshire moorlands, a barren wasteland in the north of England, where her father was a clergyman. When Emily was just three, her mother died. Emily and her sisters, Charlotte and Anne, were educated at home for the most part and were often on their own.

Homesickness In 1835, Charlotte became a teacher at a school some distance from her home. Emily accompanied her as a pupil, but she quickly returned home. Three years later, she took a teaching position herself but resigned after six months.

Several years later, Charlotte and Emily devised another plan to support themselves as teachers. They would establish and run a school for girls in their own town of Haworth. To learn the skills they needed for this enterprise, they traveled to Brussels, Belgium. There, many people they met admired Emily for her Romantic temperament. However, Emily became homesick again and, after learning of her aunt's death, went home for good.

A Career Cut Short As adults, the three sisters published a book of poetry. The twenty-one poems that Emily contributed are considered the best of the collection. Emily's first and only novel, *Wuthering Heights*, was published in 1847. It tells the story of a tragic love affair played out against the mysterious landscape of the Yorkshire moors. The book is now considered a classic.

Wuthering Heights is the culminating expression of Emily's fiery imagination. A year after the book was published, she died of tuberculosis.

1074

REMEMBRANCE

Emily Brontë

The Soul of the Rose, 1908, John William Waterhouse, Private Collection/Julian Hartnoll, London, UK

BACKGROUND Victorian poets wrote in many voices and many styles. Some writers, like Emily Brontë, are classified as Romantic because they explore and celebrate the human soul, the wildness of nature, and the powers of the imagination. Thomas Hardy, however, focused on the victimization of ordinary people by social and natural forces.

Cold in the earth, and the deep snow piled above thee!
Far, far removed, cold in the dreary grave!
Have I forgot, my Only Love, to love thee,
Severed at last by Time's all-wearing wave?

5 Now, when alone, do my thoughts no longer hover
Over the mountains, on that northern shore;
Resting their wings where heath and fern-leaves cover
Thy noble heart for ever, ever more?

Cold in the earth, and fifteen wild Decembers
10 From those brown hills have melted into spring—
Faithful indeed is the spirit that remembers
After such years of change and suffering!

Sweet Love of youth, forgive if I forget thee
While the World's tide is bearing me along:

◀ **Critical Viewing**
In what ways might the woman in this painting represent the poem's speaker? **[Analyze]**

Reading Check
What is troubling the poem's speaker?

Vocabulary
obscure (äb skyo͞or′)
v. make difficult to see

15 Other desires and other hopes beset me,
Hopes which obscure but cannot do thee wrong.

No later light has lightened up my heaven,
No second morn has ever shone for me:
All my life's bliss from thy dear life was given—
20 All my life's bliss is in the grave with thee.

But when the days of golden dreams had perished
And even Despair was powerless to destroy,
Then did I learn how existence could be cherished,
Strengthened and fed without the aid of joy;

25 Then did I check the tears of useless passion,
Weaned my young soul from yearning after thine;
Sternly denied its burning wish to hasten
Down to that tomb already more than mine!

Vocabulary
languish (laŋ′ gwish)
v. become weak; suffer from longing

rapturous (rap′ chər əs)
adj. filled with joy and love; ecstatic

And even yet, I dare not let it languish,
30 Dare not indulge in Memory's rapturous pain;
Once drinking deep of that divinest anguish,
How could I seek the empty world again?

Critical Reading

Cite textual evidence to support your responses.

1. **Key Ideas and Details (a)** How long ago did the speaker's love die? **(b) Interpret:** What does the speaker mean by, "No later light has lightened up my heaven"?

2. **Key Ideas and Details (a)** What does the speaker plan to do? **(b) Interpret:** Why is the speaker afraid to give in to his or her old feelings?

3. **Key Ideas and Details (a) Draw Conclusions:** In your own words, express the basic conflict of the poem's speaker. **(b) Analyze:** How does the speaker handle this conflict?

4. **Integration of Knowledge and Ideas** Can it be desirable in some circumstances to lead an existence "without . . . joy"? Explain.

5. **Integration of Knowledge and Ideas** In ancient times, lyric poems like this one were accompanied by music. Which of these types of music would make the best accompaniment for this poem: country, jazz, folk, rock, or rap? Explain your choice.

Thomas Hardy

(1840–1928)

Author of "The Darkling Thrush" •
"Ah, Are You Digging on My Grave?"

Thomas Hardy, who was unusual in being both a great novelist and a great poet, was born in Dorset, a region of southwest England. He used this region as the basis for the imaginary county of Wessex that is the setting of many of his novels.

Early Life The son of a stonemason, Hardy grew up in a rural cottage near a tract of wasteland. He received a fine education at a local school, although he never went on to study at a university. As a teenager, he began working for a local architect, and he eventually became a draftsman for an architect who specialized in churches.

While on a business trip to Cornwall, at the southwestern tip of England, Hardy met the woman who later became his first wife. She encouraged him in his literary activities, and soon he committed himself entirely to writing.

The Novelist When Hardy's early poetry did not gain notice, he turned to writing novels. *Far From the Madding Crowd* was the first to gain success.

Hardy used his fiction writing to elaborate his own pessimistic view of life. In tragic novels like *Tess of the D'Urbervilles* (1891) and *Jude the Obscure* (1895), he showed the difficulty people experience when trying to rise above their circumstances.

The Poet The bleakness of Hardy's fiction disturbed readers, and the response to *Jude the Obscure* was so hostile that Hardy abandoned fiction and returned to writing poetry, a form of writing he had pursued in the 1860s.

A Poetic Legacy Hardy's poetry marks a transition from Victorian verse to the Modernist movement of the twentieth century. In his use of strict meter and stanza structure, Hardy was unmistakably Victorian. However, his nonpoetic language and odd rhymes, his devotion to English characters and the English countryside, and his fatalistic outlook inspired twentieth-century poets like Philip Larkin.

"**Time changes** everything except something within us which is always surprised **by change.**"

The Darkling¹ Thrush

THOMAS HARDY

▶ **Critical Viewing**
How does the thrush shown in this painting provide a hopeful contrast to the bleak winter landscape?
[Interpret]

I leant upon a coppice gate²
    When Frost was specter-gray,
And Winter's dregs made desolate
    The weakening eye of day.
5   The tangled bine-stems³ scored the sky
    Like strings of broken lyres,
And all mankind that haunted nigh
    Had sought their household fires.

The land's sharp features seemed to be
10   The Century's corpse⁴ outleant,
His crypt the cloudy canopy,
    The wind his death-lament.
The ancient pulse of germ⁵ and birth
    Was shrunken hard and dry,
15 And every spirit upon earth
    Seemed fervorless as I.

---

1. **darkling** *adj.* in the dark.
2. **coppice** (kop´ is) **gate** gate leading to a thicket, or small wood.
3. **bine-stems** twining stems.
4. **Century's corpse** This poem was written on December 31, 1900, the last day of the nineteenth century.
5. **germ** seed or bud.

At once a voice arose among
    The bleak twigs overhead
In a full-hearted evensong
20   Of joy illimited;
An aged thrush, frail, gaunt, and small,
    In blast-beruffled plume,
Had chosen thus to fling his soul
    Upon the growing gloom.

25 So little cause for carolings
    Of such ecstatic sound
Was written on terrestrial things
    Afar or nigh around,
That I could think there trembled through
30   His happy good-night air
Some blessed Hope, whereof he knew
    And I was unaware.

Vocabulary

gaunt (gônt) *adj.* thin and bony, as from great hunger or age

terrestrial (tə res′ trē əl) *adj.* relating to the earth or to this world

Critical Reading

Cite textual evidence to support your responses.

1. **Key Ideas and Details** **(a)** In which season and time of year is this poem set? **(b) Classify:** In the first two stanzas, what details and images does Hardy use to convey the mood of the setting?

2. **Key Ideas and Details** **(a)** What does the speaker suddenly hear and see in the third stanza? **(b) Compare and Contrast:** How does the mood in the third stanza differ from that in the first two?

3. **Integration of Knowledge and Ideas** **(a)** Summarize what the speaker says in the final stanza. **(b) Draw Conclusions:** Do you agree with critics who assert that Hardy longs to believe there is reason for hope but does not really think so? Why or why not?

4. **Integration of Knowledge and Ideas** If Hardy had seen the end of the twentieth century, do you think he would have felt the same way that he did at the end of the nineteenth? Explain.

"Ah, Are You Digging on My Grave?" Thomas Hardy

"Ah, are you digging on my grave
    My loved one?—planting rue?"
—"No: yesterday he went to wed
One of the brightest wealth has bred.
5 'It cannot hurt her now,' he said,
    'That I should not be true.'"

"Then who is digging on my grave?
    My nearest dearest kin?"
—"Ah, no: they sit and think, 'What use!
10 What good will planting flowers produce?
No tendance of her mound can loose
    Her spirit from Death's gin.'"[1]

"But some one digs upon my grave?
    My enemy?—prodding sly?"
15 —"Nay: when she heard you had passed the Gate
That shuts on all flesh soon or late,
She thought you no more worth her hate,
    And cares not where you lie."

---

1. gin *n.* trap.

Reading Strategy
Analyzing Patterns of Organization What pattern do you see developing in these first stanzas?

Vocabulary
prodding (präd´ iŋ)
adj. poking; jabbing; seeking

Reading Check
Who is the speaker of this poem?

The Greek Anthology

Hardy was not the first poet to write in the voice of a deceased person. Many of the poems in *The Greek Anthology,* compiled in the tenth century, are ancient Greek epitaphs written in the voice of the person who died. Like most well-educated people in nineteenth-century Britain, Hardy owned a copy of *The Greek Anthology.* He probably spent hours poring over the little tombstone poems, which commemorate the lives of men, women, children, and even dogs.

Connect to the Literature

Do you think Hardy expresses traditional sentiments about remembering the dead? Why or why not?

"Then, who is digging on my grave?
20   Say—since I have not guessed!"
—"O it is I, my mistress dear,
Your little dog, who still lives near,
And much I hope my movements here
        Have not disturbed your rest?"

25 "Ah, yes! *You* dig upon my grave . . .
        Why flashed it not on me
That one true heart was left behind!
What feeling do we ever find
To equal among human kind
30   A dog's fidelity!"

"Mistress, I dug upon your grave
        To bury a bone, in case
I should be hungry near this spot
When passing on my daily trot.
35 I am sorry, but I quite forgot
        It was your resting-place."

Critical Reading

Cite textual evidence to support your responses.

1. **Key Ideas and Details (a)** In each of the first three stanzas, who does the speaker think is digging? **(b) Infer:** What do the responses tell you about the people thought to be digging?

2. **Key Ideas and Details (a)** Who is actually digging on the grave? **(b) Draw Conclusions:** What point about human vanity and self-esteem is Hardy making in this poem?

3. **Integration of Knowledge and Ideas** How do the places in which the Hardy's speakers find themselves limit their knowledge? Use two of these Essential Question words in your answer: *pessimism, insignificant, humorous, ironic. [Connecting to the Essential Question: What is the relationship between literature and place?]*

Literary Analysis

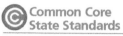 **Common Core State Standards**

1. Craft and Structure **(a)** Complete a chart like the one shown to determine whether each poem uses a consistent **stanza structure.** **(b)** Summarize the pattern of stanzas in each of these poems.

Stanza	Number of lines	Rhyme scheme	Meter
1			
2			
3			

2. Craft and Structure What is ironic about the phrases "rapturous pain" and "divinest anguish" in the final stanza of "Remembrance"?

3. Craft and Structure Explain how repetition in the stanza structure of "Ah, Are You Digging on My Grave?" contributes to Hardy's ironic—and aesthetic—purpose.

4. Craft and Structure **(a)** How do lines 25–30 of "Ah, Are You Digging on My Grave?" disappoint a reader's expectations for an established stanza structure? **(b)** How does the last stanza use **irony** to disappoint a character's expectations in a drastic way?

5. Integration of Knowledge and Ideas Compare and contrast the types of absence that these poems address.

6. Integration of Knowledge and Ideas Which of the three speakers seems to experience the sorrow of loss most keenly? Why?

7. Integration of Knowledge and Ideas Which speaker seems best able to handle the absence of a sign of remembrance or hope? Explain.

8. Analyzing Visual Information What qualities of Hardy's poetry—for example, its moods and themes—does the artist capture in the caricature of Hardy on this page? Explain.

Reading Strategy

9. Analyze the pattern of stanzas in "Remembrance" to show how the speaker gradually works out an answer to the question in the first stanza.

10. Explain the function of each stanza in "The Darkling Thrush."

11. (a) In "The Darkling Thrush," which stanza introduces a shift in meaning? Explain. **(b)** In "Ah, Are You Digging on My Grave?," what important shift in meaning occurs between the last two stanzas?

Common Core State Standards

Writing
2.b. Develop the topic thoroughly by selecting the most significant and relevant facts, extended definitions, concrete details, quotations, or other information and examples appropriate to the audience's knowledge of the topic. *(p. 1084)*

5. Develop and strengthen writing as needed by planning, revising, editing, rewriting, or trying a new approach, focusing on addressing what is most significant for a specific purpose and audience. *(p. 1084)*

Language
5. Demonstrate understanding of figurative language, word relationships, and nuances in word meaning. *(p. 1084)*

Integrated Language Skills

Vocabulary Acquisition and Use

Word Analysis: Latin Root -terr(a)-

The Latin root -terr(a)- comes from the Latin word for "earth." *Terrestrial*, which contains this root, means "of the earth" or "of this world." Write the definition for each -terr(a)- word below based on the meaning of the root. Explain how you arrived at your meaning. Then, write an original sentence for each of the words.

1. extraterrestrial
2. subterranean
3. terrace
4. terrain
5. territory

Vocabulary: Analogies

In an analogy, the relationship between two words is compared to the relationship between two other words. To complete these analogies, choose the word from the vocabulary list on page 1072 that creates a word pair that matches the relationship in the other pair. Explain your choices.

1. *Explain* is to *clarify* as _____ is to *conceal.*
2. _____ is to *ecstasy* as *miserable* is to *depression.*
3. _____ is to *emaciated* as *vigorous* is to *fitness.*
4. *Arrival* is to *departure* as _____ is to *heavenly.*
5. *Withdrawn* is to *shy* as *pushy* is to _____.
6. *Longing* is to _____ as *sympathy* is to *assist.*

Writing

Informative Text Brontë's and Hardy's poems deal in different ways with the theme of absence, the sense of something missing, whether that is a loved one, a sign of hope, or the knowledge that people remember the speaker. Write a **comparative analysis** in which you examine the ways in which the speakers in these poems feel about an absence and succeed or fail in handling it.

Prewriting Review the poems, using a chart to take notes on how each speaker perceives and responds to absence. Note uses of *imagery, language, or stylistic devices* that reveal the speaker's feelings. Review your examples to determine whether the speakers' attitudes and feelings are more similar or different. Then develop a thesis statement that expresses your view.

Drafting Begin your draft by stating your thesis. As you write, support your generalizations with quotations from Brontë's and Hardy's poems. Consider analyzing all the similarities first and then the differences if you think the differences are more important—and vice versa.

Model: Revising to Signal Similarities and Differences

The speaker in Hardy's "Ah, Are You Digging on My Grave?" learns that family and friends have gone on with their lives.

In contrast,

Brontë's speaker points out that she lives "without the aid of joy" in an "empty world."

Use of expressions like in *the same way* or in *contrast* calls attention to key similarities and differences.

Revising Review your draft, making sure that you signal similarities and differences. Make sure that all quotations are accurate and properly referenced.

Conventions and Style: Active, Not Passive, Voice

When you write, you can make your sentences more energetic and powerful by using active-voice verbs. A verb is in the **active-voice** when the subject is the doer of the action. A verb is in the **passive voice** when it receives the action of the verb.

The active voice is more direct and concise than the passive voice. However, the passive voice can be appropriate and effective in the following situations:

- You wish to emphasize the receiver of the action rather than the doer.

Hope was symbolized by the tiny thrush.

- The doer of the action is not known or is unimportant to your meaning.

The poem had been written on the last day of the nineteenth century.

The passive voice is constructed from the past participle of the main verb and a form of the verb *be.* Review these examples of active and passive voice.

	Active	**Passive**
Present	is digging, digs	is dug, is being dug
Past	dug, was digging, had dug	was dug, was being dug, had been dug
Future	will dig, will have dug	will be dug, will have been dug

Practice Identify whether the verb in each sentence is in the active or passive voice. If a sentence in the passive voice should be in the active voice, rewrite it. If the passive voice is appropriate, explain why.

1. Fires were hurried to by people who wanted to sit by them on a winter night.
2. A tiny bird was heard to sing in the middle of the gloomy evening.
3. The branches of a tree are compared to the broken strings of a musical instrument by the speaker.
4. The bird's joy cannot be understood.
5. The speaker, surprised by the joyful singing, believes that something giving hope is known by the bird.
6. The woman buried in the grave was not mourned by her loved one.
7. Flowers won't be planted by relatives.
8. The dead one was disturbed by the digging.
9. The dead are quickly forgotten by the living.
10. Can anyone overlook the faithfulness expressed by a friendly dog?

© Writing and Speaking Conventions

A. Writing Use each subject-verb pair in a sentence with the verb in the active voice.

1. **S:** poet, **V:** lean   3. **S:** voice, **V:** sing   5. **S:** thrush, **V:** know
2. **S:** relatives, **V:** plant   4. **S:** dog, **V:** disturb

   Example: S: poet, **V:** lean.
   Sentence: The poet leans on a gate and sees a winter landscape.

B. Speaking Write and present to the class a brief scene for a play based on the poem "Ah, Are You Digging on My Grave?" Describe the setting, list the character(s) in your scene, and include at least one speech written in the active voice.

> **PH** **WRITING COACH**
> Further instruction and practice are available in *Prentice Hall Writing Coach.*

Connecting to the Essential Question Hopkins coined words and invented new rhythms for his poetry. As you read, notice how Hopkins is innovative and Housman is traditional. This distinction will help you explore the Essential Question: **What is the relationship of the writer to tradition?**

Literary Analysis

Poetry with a regular **rhythm,** or movement, is **metrical verse,** which is divided into combinations of syllables called **feet.** The following are types of feet and the pattern of stressed and unstressed syllables they contain:

- **Iambic:** unstressed, stressed, as in *the time*
- **Trochaic:** stressed, unstressed, as in *grandeur*

Lines with three, four, and five feet are **trimeter, tetrameter,** and **pentameter,** respectively. Iambic pentameter, for example, is a five-foot line with iambic feet. Housman uses regular meters like iambic and trochaic tetrameter, but Hopkins invents rhythms like these:

- **Counterpoint rhythm:** two opposing rhythms appear together; for example, two trochaic feet in an iambic line:
  The world is charged with the grandeur of God.
- **Sprung rhythm:** all feet begin with a stressed syllable and contain a varying number of unstressed syllables. Sprung rhythm creates densely stressed lines with many echoing consonant and vowel sounds.

As you read, notice which words the poets choose to stress. Consider why the authors may have placed special emphasis on these words and determine if such emphasis adds to the meaning of the poems.

Comparing Literary Works Beauty and mortality are two connected themes these poets explore. Analyze how these themes interact.

Reading Strategy

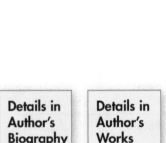

Preparing to Read Complex Texts **Analyzing the author's beliefs** will help you understand the ideas and feelings in the poems. Consider details in the author's biography along with details of the poems. Use a diagram like this to analyze the poets' beliefs.

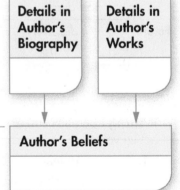

Vocabulary

Common Core State Standards

Reading Literature
5. Analyze how an author's choices concerning how to structure specific parts of a text contribute to its overall structure and meaning as well as its aesthetic impact.

grandeur (gran´ jər) *n.* splendor; magnificence (p. 1089)

smudge (smŭj) *n.* a smear or stain of dirt (p. 1089)

brink (brĭngk) *n.* edge (p. 1089)

blight (blīt) *n.* condition of withering (p. 1090)

lintel (lĭn´ tl) *n.* horizontal bar above a door (p. 1092)

rue (rōō) *n.* sorrow; regret (p. 1093)

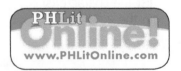
www.PHLitOnline.com

GERARD MANLEY HOPKINS

(1844–1889)

Author of "God's Grandeur" • "Spring and Fall: To a Young Child"

Although he was the most innovative poet of the Victorian period, Hopkins never published a collection of his work during his lifetime. It was not until 1918 that his work was published and a generation of poets could read and be influenced by his startling poetry.

Devotion to God and Nature This quietly rebellious poet was born just outside London, the oldest of nine children in a prosperous middle-class family. Although physically slight, he would perch fearlessly at the top of a tree and sway in the wind while observing the landscape. He began to write poetry in grammar school, a practice he continued at Oxford University, where he studied the classics.

During his third year at Oxford, Hopkins decided to become a Catholic priest in the Jesuit order—a decision that dismayed his parents, who were devout Anglicans. The discipline of Hopkins's religious vocation was sometimes at odds with his writing of verse. He temporarily gave up poetry but continued to keep detailed notebooks that recorded his fascination with words and his love of nature.

Inscape In the mid-1870s, while studying theology in Wales, he began to write poetry again, stimulated by the Welsh language and encouraged by his religious mentor. Somewhat earlier, Hopkins had found in the medieval theologian Duns Scotus a verification of his own ideas about the individuality of all things. Hopkins called this precious individuality *inscape*, and he tried to capture it in highly original poems like "God's Grandeur." He also experimented with new rhythms in his verse.

From early 1884 on, he taught at a Jesuit college in Dublin. There, he died of typhoid fever just before his forty-fifth birthday. Although in many ways he was not typical of the other poets of his age, he is now considered one of the greatest Victorian poets.

GOD'S GRANDEUR

GERARD MANLEY HOPKINS

BACKGROUND Surprisingly, when Gerard Manley Hopkins died, none of his obituaries mentioned that he was a poet and only a few friends were aware of this fact. One of these friends was Robert Bridges, an Oxford classmate and later the British poet laureate. Bridges had corresponded with Hopkins and took an interest in his experiments with rhythm. It was through Bridges's efforts that a volume of Hopkins's poetry was published for the first time in 1918. Today, Bridges is little known, but his once-obscure friend Gerard Manley Hopkins is a famous Victorian poet.

The world is charged with the grandeur of God.
　　It will flame out, like shining from shook foil;¹
　　It gathers to a greatness, like the ooze of oil
Crushed.² Why do men then now not reck his rod?³
5　Generations have trod, have trod, have trod;
　　And all is seared with trade; bleared, smeared with toil;
　　And wears man's smudge and shares man's smell: the soil
Is bare now, nor can foot feel, being shod.

And for all this, nature is never spent;
10　There lives the dearest freshness deep down things;
And though the last lights off the black West went
　　Oh, morning, at the brown brink eastward, springs—
Because the Holy Ghost over the bent
　　World broods with warm breast and with ah! bright wings.

1. foil n. tinsel.
2. crushed squeezed from olives.
3. reck his rod heed God's authority.

Vocabulary
grandeur (gran´ jər)
n. splendor; magnificence

smudge (smŭj) n. a smear
or stain of dirt

brink (brĭngk) n. edge;
margin

◄ **Critical Viewing** How
does this painting reflect
Hopkins's ideas in "God's
Grandeur"? **[Apply]**

SPRING AND FALL:
TO A YOUNG CHILD
GERARD MANLEY HOPKINS

Literary Analysis
Rhythm and Meter
Identify a visual clue that proves that this poem is written in sprung rhythm.

Vocabulary
blight (blīt) *n.* condition of withering

Márgarét, áre you gríeving
Over Goldengrove unleaving?
Leáves, líke the things of man, you
With your fresh thoughts care for, can you?
5   Áh! ás the heart grows older
It will come to such sights colder
By and by, nor spare a sigh
Though worlds of wanwood[1] leafmeal[2] lie;
And yet you wíll weep and know why.
10 Now no matter, child, the name:
Sórrow's spríngs áre the same.
Nor mouth had, no nor mind, expressed
What heart heard of, ghost[3] guessed:
It ís the blight man was born for,
15 It is Margaret you mourn for.

---

1. **wanwood** (wän' wood) pale wood.
2. **leafmeal** ground-up decomposed leaves.
3. **ghost** spirit.

Critical Reading

> Cite textual evidence to support your responses.

1. **Key Ideas and Details (a)** According to Hopkins in "God's Grandeur," what has been the impact on nature of humanity's behavior? **(b) Analyze:** What opposition or conflict does he explore in lines 1–8 of "God's Grandeur"? **(c) Draw Conclusions:** How does Hopkins resolve that opposition?

2. **Key Ideas and Details (a)** What makes Margaret unhappy in "Spring and Fall"? **(b) Interpret:** Explain how the poem's speaker suggests that Margaret will both outgrow and not outgrow this sadness.

3. **Key Ideas and Details (a)** According to the speaker, how will Margaret change as she grows older? **(b) Draw Conclusions:** What lesson does the speaker offer to Margaret in this poem?

4. **Integration of Knowledge and Ideas** Judging by "God's Grandeur," would Hopkins support the ecology movement if he were alive today? Explain.

A. E. Housman

(1859–1936)

Author of "To an Athlete Dying Young" • "When I Was One-and-Twenty"

A man of solitary habits and harsh self-discipline, Housman was also capable of creating delicately crafted poems, full of gentle regret.

Challenges of Youth Housman grew up in Worcestershire, a region northwest of London. His childhood came to an end on his twelfth birthday, when his mother died. Later, at Oxford University, his despair over an unrequited love darkened his life still further. Perhaps because of this double grief, his poetry has bitter undertones.

Upon leaving Oxford, where he had studied classical literature and philosophy, Housman went to work in the Patent Office. Determined to prove himself in the classics, he studied Greek and Latin at night and wrote scholarly articles. In 1892, his hard work paid off when he was appointed to a position as professor of Latin at University College in London.

Literary Success Although Housman spent most of his life engaged in teaching and in scholarly pursuits, he is most remembered for three slender volumes of poetry that are as romantic and melancholy as any ever written. His first and most famous collection of verse, *A Shropshire Lad* (1896), has as its central character a young man named Terence. In later years, Housman claimed, ironically, that he had "never spent much time" in Shropshire.

Housman's image is that of an emotionless intellectual, but his poems display deep feelings. In his view, the goal of poetry is to "transfuse emotion," not to transmit thought. A well-written poem, he maintained, should affect the reader like a shiver down the spine or a punch in the stomach.

To an Athlete Dying Young

A. E. Housman

The time you won your town the race
We chaired you through the marketplace;
Man and boy stood cheering by,
And home we brought you shoulder-high.

5   Today, the road all runners come,
Shoulder-high we bring you home,
And set you at your threshold down,
Townsman of a stiller town.

Smart lad, to slip betimes away
10 From fields where glory does not stay
And early though the laurel[1] grows
It withers quicker than the rose.

Eyes the shady night has shut
Cannot see the record cut,
15 And silence sounds no worse than cheers
After earth has stopped the ears:

Now you will not swell the rout
Of lads that wore their honors out,
Runners whom renown outran
20 And the name died before the man.

So set, before its echoes fade,
The fleet foot on the sill of shade.
And hold to the low lintel up
The still-defended challenge cup.

25 And round that early-laureled head
Will flock to gaze the strengthless dead,
And find unwithered on its curls
The garland briefer than a girl's.

Vocabulary
lintel (lĭn´ tl) *n.* horizontal
bar above a door

---

1. **laurel** symbol of victory.

When I Was One-and-Twenty

A. E. Housman

When I was one-and-twenty
    I heard a wise man say,
"Give crowns and pounds and guineas[1]
    But not your heart away;
5 Give pearls away and rubies
    But keep your fancy free."
But I was one-and-twenty,
    No use to talk to me.

When I was one-and-twenty
10   I heard him say again,
"The heart out of the bosom
    Was never given in vain;
'Tis paid with sighs a plenty
    And sold for endless rue."
15 And I am two-and-twenty,
    And oh, 'tis true, 'tis true.

Reading Strategy
Analyzing an Author's Beliefs In this poem, do the speaker's beliefs about youth correspond with the author's? Why or why not?

Vocabulary
rue (rōō) *n.* sorrow; regret

1. **crowns . . . guineas** denominations of money.

Critical Reading ©

1. **Key Ideas and Details (a)** In "To an Athlete," what are three advantages of dying young, according to the speaker?
   (b) Interpret: Does the speaker entirely mean what he says about these advantages? Explain.

2. **Key Ideas and Details (a)** In "When I Was One-and-Twenty," what advice does the speaker receive, and how does he react?
   (b) Interpret: What clues are there in the poem that Housman is mocking his speaker?

3. **Integration of Knowledge and Ideas** Which are more effective, Hopkins's inventive rhythms or Housman's more traditional ones? Explain, using two of these Essential Question terms: *meter, sprung rhythm, innovation.* [*Connecting to the Essential Question:* **What is the relationship of the writer to tradition?**]

Cite textual evidence to support your responses.

After You Read

God's Grandeur • Spring and Fall:
To a Young Child • To an Athlete Dying
Young • When I Was One-and-Twenty

Literary Analysis

1. Craft and Structure (a) Use scansion symbols (˘ ´) to identify the **feet** in line 5 of "God's Grandeur," inserting symbols over syllables on a slip of paper like the one shown below. **(b)** Explain how your scan demonstrates that the line uses **counterpoint rhythm.**

> **Generations have trod, have trod, have trod;...**

2. Craft and Structure "Spring and Fall" is written with **sprung rhythm.** Using the stresses in line 11, indicate how many feet that line has.

3. Craft and Structure (a) How does the counterpoint rhythm in line 5 of "God's Grandeur" support the meaning of the line? **(b)** In "Spring and Fall," how do the three stresses in line 11 reinforce the meaning of the line?

4. Craft and Structure (a) Show that in lines 1–8 of "To an Athlete," the **meter** includes five **iambic tetrameter** lines and three **trochaic tetrameter** lines. **(b)** How do the trochaic lines reinforce the idea of a "stiller town"?

5. Integration of Knowledge and Ideas (a) In "God's Grandeur," does Hopkins think the beauty of nature is enduring? Explain. **(b)** In "Spring and Fall," does he express the same perspective on the endurance of nature's beauty as he does in "God's Grandeur"? Explain.

6. Integration of Knowledge and Ideas Would the speakers in "Spring and Fall" and "To an Athlete" agree that deep sorrow is the right response to the realization that life and earthly beauty are fleeting? Explain.

7. Comparing Literary Works Which poem conveys the most compassionate view of human mortality—"Spring and Fall," "To an Athlete," or "When I Was One-and-Twenty"? Explain.

Reading Strategy

8. Analyze the author's beliefs by finding a passage in "God's Grandeur" that reflects Hopkins's love of nature. Then, explain your choice.

9. Find a passage in "To an Athlete" that reflects Housman's underlying sadness. Explain your choice.

10. Hopkins was inspired by his idea of "inscape"—that special individual quality that distinguished one person, object, or emotion from every other. Find a passage that reflects this belief, and explain how this passage conveys the idea of inscape.

11. Do you agree with Housman in "To an Athlete" that aging can bring only sadness to an athlete? Why or why not?

Common Core
State Standards

Writing
1. Write arguments to support claims in an analysis of substantive topics or texts, using valid reasoning and relevant and sufficient evidence. *(p. 1095)*

1.d. Establish and maintain a formal style and objective tone while attending to the norms and conventions of the discipline in which they are writing. *(p. 1095)*

Language
3. Apply knowledge of language to understand how language functions in different contexts, to make effective choices for meaning or style, and to comprehend more fully when reading or listening. *(p. 1095)*

Integrated Language Skills

ⓒ Vocabulary Acquisition and Use

Word Analysis: Coined Words

Hopkins's fascination with language can be seen in the way he coins, or invents, words. For example, he combines *wan*, meaning "pale," and *wood* to make *wanwood*, a new word to describe pale autumn trees. Similarly, he coins *leafmeal* to describe fallen dead leaves ground into a kind of meal. Imitate Hopkins and *create new words from familiar words* to replace each of these phrases. Use concrete or vivid words so that others will understand the meaning you are trying to convey.

1. the very end of summer
2. chilly mornings right after dawn
3. snow-covered lawns
4. tall, bare trees

Vocabulary: Analogies

Analogies compare the relationships between pairs of words. To complete these analogies, choose the word from the vocabulary list on page 1086 that creates a word pair that matches the relationship in the other pair. Explain your choices.

1. *Roof* is to *car* as _____ is to *doorway*.
2. _____ is to *squalor* as *summer* is to *winter*.
3. _____ is to *cliff* as *balcony* is to *building*.
4. *Joy* is to *happiness* as _____ is to *regret*.
5. *Remove* is to *stain* as *wash* is to _____.
6. *Starvation* is to *hunger* as _____ is to *damage*.

Writing

ⓒ **Argumentative Text** Hopkins's poetry was virtually unknown during his life. The poet became more widely read only after Robert Bridges, a long-time friend, had his work published in 1918, long after the poet's death. Take the role of Bridges in 1918 and write a **business letter** to a British publishing company recommending that the publisher issue a collected edition of the poetry of Hopkins.

Prewriting Review the background information about Hopkins's theory of sprung rhythm, his idea of inscape, and his use of coined words. Find passages from his poems that illustrate these ideas and Hopkins's unique poetic voice.

Drafting Use the proper format of a business letter, with the date, the name and address of a fictional publisher, salutation, body, and closing. In the body of your letter, give reasons why the publisher should issue the volume you propose. Explain Hopkins's ideas and cite passages from Hopkins's poetry that show his use of *imagery, figures of speech, and sound* to *evoke reader's emotions*.

Revising Review your letter to make sure that it is persuasive, and strengthen parts that need more emphasis. Use the formal language of business and not the less formal tone of everyday speech.

Model: Revising to Use Formal Language

In sum, Hopkins's poetry deserves to reach a wider public.

unique poetic voice

His awesome style must be heard.

The use of formal language in business letters establishes credibility.

Write a Report

Historical Investigation Conducting a historical investigation can help you analyze and evaluate the historical background of literary works. You can record your findings in a research report. Remember that an effective report does more than simply list facts: it synthesizes information from a variety of primary, secondary, and tertiary sources and connects ideas to present a coherent analysis, explaining any differences in sources. Follow the steps outlined in this workshop to write a historical investigation.

Assignment Write a **historical investigation report** on an event, figure, or topic that relates to the historical context of a work or works of literature.

What to Include Your research report should have these elements:

- A clear thesis statement, supported by a variety of formats and rhetorical strategies
- An analysis that supports and develops personal opinions, as opposed to restating existing information
- Incorporation of the complexities of and discrepancies in information from multiple sources, with anticipation and refutation of counter-arguments
- Proper documentation and listing of sources, using a style manual
- Sufficient length and complexity to address the topic

To preview the criteria on which your research report may be assessed, see the rubric on page 1107.

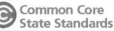

**Common Core
State Standards**

Writing

2. Write informative/explanatory texts to examine and convey complex ideas, concepts, and information clearly and accurately through the effective selection, organization, and analysis of content.

7. Conduct short as well as more sustained research projects to answer a question or solve a problem; narrow or broaden the inquiry when appropriate; synthesize multiple sources on the subject, demonstrating understanding of the subject under investigation.

8. Gather relevant information from multiple authoritative print and digital sources, using advanced searches effectively; assess the strengths and limitations of each source in terms of the task, purpose, and audience.

www.PHLitOnline.com

To get a feel for historical investigation, read this mentor text. Notice how Sir Frank Kermode combines factual information with his version of Shakespeare's perceptions.

from: Life in Elizabethan and Jacobean England

Inflation was unchecked but money flowed freely. Among the expensive luxuries of the day were ostentatious clothes and tobacco, a recent import from the New World. London was a perpetual bustle, noise and display. Imagine how a young man from the provinces, like Shakespeare, might react to it. Shakespeare's Stratford, though a sturdy community with its own guilds and its good grammar school, hardly offered adequate preparation for London, among other things a great port and the gateway to the larger world. The splendor of the river and the mansions lining its bank won the keen admiration of foreign visitors, who compared its magnificence with that of Paris and other great European cities.

WRITE GUY
Jeff Anderson, M. Ed.

What Do You Notice?

Read the highlighted sentence several times. Then, with a partner, discuss the qualities that make it special. You might consider the following elements:

- Word choice
- Sentence length
- Rhythm
- Structure

Share your group's observations with the class.

Prewriting and Planning

Choosing Your Topic

To choose a topic suitable for the research sources that are available to you, use one of the following strategies:

- **Notebook and Textbook Review** Reviewing school notebooks, textbooks, and writing journals, list topics that interest you. Also review the selections you have read in this textbook, and consider specific questions you have about the historical context for your favorite works.

- **Research Preview** When you have two good topic choices, spend 10–15 minutes researching each topic on the Internet or at the library. This quick research preview will help you identify how much information is available on each topic. Look for both primary and secondary sources.

  Primary sources: letters, diaries, interviews, eyewitness accounts
  Secondary sources: encyclopedias, nonfiction books, and articles

Narrowing Your Topic

Freewrite to find your focus. If your topic can be divided into significant subheads, each with its own focus, it is probably too broad. Using what you already know or have learned in preliminary research, write freely on your topic for two or three minutes. Review your writing and circle the most important or interesting idea. Continue this process until you arrive at a topic that is narrow enough for your paper.

Gathering Details

Do the research. Use both library and Internet resources to locate information. Evaluate sources for validity and reliability before citing them. Be especially critical of Internet sources, checking that the authors have followed careful academic procedures.

Use source cards and note cards. For every source you consult, create a source card with the author's name, title, publisher, city, and date of publication. Then, create a note card for each relevant fact or opinion. Write the general subject at the top. Then, write the fact or quotation, followed by a keyword, such as the author's name, that links the fact with its source.

Source Card
[Ament]
Ament, Phil. "Charles Babbage." The Great Idea Finder. 15 Jan. 2008 <http://www.ideafinder.com/history/inventors/babbage.htm>

Note card
[Babbage's importance]
he's often called the "Father of Computing"
Source: Ament

Drafting

Shaping Your Writing

Develop a thesis statement. Review your notes and draft a statement that reflects a theme in the material you have collected. Your thesis statement should introduce your topic and the point you will develop.

Establish your organizational plan. Decide whether you will present conclusions about your sources as part of your introduction, or build toward your conclusions throughout the paper. Use one of these plans.

Effective Methods of Organization		
Introduction	present historical context give thesis statement DRAW CONCLUSION	present historical context establish issue in thesis statement
Body	PROVE CONCLUSION present/analyze/compare sources	present/analyze/compare sources LEAD TO CONCLUSION
Closing	summarize	DRAW CONCLUSION

Write a powerful introduction and conclusion. Use your opening paragraph to introduce the issue, to define unfamiliar terms, and to clarify background details such as the time, place, and relevant social conditions. In your conclusion, emphasize the significance of your findings.

Maintain a formal style and objective tone. As you draft, choose words consistent with a formal style, such as *supplies*, rather than informal words, such as *stuff*. In addition, keep your tone objective. Rather than choosing words that express opinions, such as *outrageous*, choose objective words and phrases such as *widely condemned*.

Providing Elaboration

Handle your sources well. Follow these guidelines when presenting sources:

- Use a mix of paraphrases and direct quotations. Do not string quotations together without interpretation. Instead, frame your quotations so that a reader understands why you chose them.

- Describe and analyze your sources. Explain whether or not primary resources reflect consensus, or general agreement, about a topic. When primary resources offer different perspectives, try to account for these differences. If a writer's perspective is unique, explain it, if possible, by analyzing the writer's circumstances and motives.

- As you draft, underline sentences you will need to document. After you finish drafting, you can format the appropriate citations.

- Be aware of what constitutes *plagiarism*, especially in using media and digital sources. Clearly attribute the words and ideas of others.

Common Core State Standards

Writing

2.c. Use appropriate and varied transitions and syntax to link the major sections of the text, create cohesion, and clarify the relationships among complex ideas and concepts.

2.e. Establish and maintain a formal style and objective tone while attending to the norms and conventions of the discipline in which they are writing.

2.f. Provide a concluding statement or section that follows from and supports the information or explanation presented.

4. Produce clear and coherent writing in which the development, organization, and style are appropriate to task, purpose, and audience.

Developing Your Style

Check for Coherence

Examine your draft for coherence, the logical, smooth connections of ideas. Vary your syntax and consider adding transitional words and phrases to show the relationships between your thoughts.

Transitional Words and Phrases			
above all	aside from	however	on the whole
accordingly	because	in other words	otherwise
alternatively	consequently	instead	particularly
although	for example	likewise	similarly
as a result	for that reason	on the contrary	therefore
as well as	furthermore	on the other hand	usually

Integrate source material. Another aspect of a coherent report is the careful integration of source material. Be aware of discrepancies among sources and account for them. Also, connect paraphrases or quotations to the subject being discussed and show how they support your point.

Find It in Your Reading

Read the student model research report "Visionaries" on page 1104.

1. Identify and evaluate transitional words and phrases.
2. Analyze how the writer integrates information from other sources.

Try It in Your Writing

To check your sentences for coherence, follow these steps:

1. Circle any transitional words and phrases in your writing. Check that each transition is effective and appropriate.

2. Read each paragraph aloud, listening for how the ideas connect. Sudden shifts may indicate that a transition is needed.

3. Review sentences in which you present information from your research. For paraphrases, be sure you have not copied wording. For direct quotations, check that you have introduced and analyzed the quotation effectively.

PH WRITING COACH

Further instruction and practice are available in *Prentice Hall Writing Coach*.

Revising

Revising Your Overall Structure

Organize ideas effectively. Review the flow of ideas in your historical investigation report. This chart shows some common organizational methods you can use throughout your report or in specific sections. For example, you might follow an overall chronological order, but within one section, a problem/solution order may help you clarify an important relationship.

Common Core State Standards

Writing

5. Develop and strengthen writing as needed by planning, revising, editing, rewriting, or trying a new approach, focusing on addressing what is most significant for a specific purpose and audience.

Method	Description
Chronological	Discuss events in time order.
Cause/Effect	Analyze the causes and/or effects of an event.
Problem/Solution	Identify a specific problem or conflict and tell how it was or was not solved.
Parts to Whole	Relate elements of a single event or topic to a whole.
Order of Importance	Present your support from most to least important, or from least to most important.
Comparison and Contrast	When comparing two topics, discuss their similarities and then their differences, or discuss each topic separately.

Peer Review: Ask a partner to review your draft and describe your organizational plan. Did your partner identify the plan you intended to follow? Discuss how you can improve the flow of ideas throughout your report.

Revising Your Paragraphs

Place topic sentences effectively. Each key paragraph should contain a topic sentence and supporting details, but the topic sentence can appear in the first sentence, in the last sentence, or in the body of the paragraph.

Reread each paragraph in your essay. Place brackets around the topic sentence. Then, review the placement of each topic sentence, considering moving it for maximum impact.

Model: Revising Placement of Topic Sentence

Original: In contrast to Babbage and Da Vinci, Bill Gates has been able to directly affect the world in which he lives. He is a visionary of our own time. It seems that this man can literally predict future technology and then develop it.

Moving the topic sentence to the beginning of the paragraph presents a clearer focus.

Revised: A visionary of our own time is Bill Gates. In contrast to Babbage and Da Vinci, Gates has been able to directly affect the world in which he lives. It seems that this man can literally predict future technology and then develop it.

Writers on Writing

James Berry On Research-Based Writing

James Berry is the author of *"From Lucy: Englan' Lady"* (p. 1055).

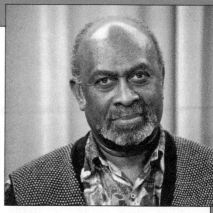

James Berry on Research-Based Writing

I deliberately set this novel of slavery in the period 1807–1840, so as to take in both the end of the slave trade and life after Emancipation. Writing it, for me, was like traveling through the experiences of my ancestors. My childhood home was only minutes from the ruins of a big slave plantation, so I grew up surrounded by landmarks of slavery. To learn more about these times, I read obsessively, consulting books, maps, and old pictures.

"To learn more about these times, I read obsessively. . . ."

—James Berry

from *Ajeemah and His Son*

Atu saw his father leaving, being taken away by a planter while he was held, already bought by another plantation owner. Led along, Ajeemah looked back, calling desperately, "Atu, my son Atu—freedom! Freedom! Or let us meet in the land of spirits!"

Two hours' ride from Kingston, in the back of the estate horse-drawn carriage with two other male slaves bought with him, and Ajeemah came to his big and busy New World sugar plantation. Nearly four hundred slaves lived and worked here.

Everybody stepped down from the carriage in the center of the estate work yard in a blaze of sunlight. The estate work yard buildings spread out like a little village. The huge windmill that powered the grinding of the sugarcane was near the millhouse where the cane was crushed and where its juice was taken and boiled into the wealth-making sugar, and also rum. Then in a close cluster there were the boiling house, curing house, distilling house and trash house. Ajeemah stared at the windmill; he'd never seen a windmill. He then glanced at the many workshop buildings, the animal houses and the overseer's and headmen's houses. And he could see, separated some good distance away, the huts—the slaves' quarters. . . .

I wanted to show here how family members could be separated forever at the kind of barbaric sales, called "scrambles," where purchasers rushed in and grabbed slaves to gain the right to buy them.

I researched in Jamaican libraries for pictures of how four broken-down old estates near my home would have looked when they were flourishing.

I used Eric Williams's *Capitalism and Slavery* as a reference in writing this book.

Just at the top of my lane were the ruins of an old slave estate. As a boy, I climbed up inside the windmill tower to look out over the landscape.

Providing Appropriate Citations

You must cite the source for the information and ideas you use in your report. In the body of your paper, include a footnote, an endnote, or a parenthetical citation to identify the source of each fact, opinion, and quotation. At the end of your paper, provide a bibliography or a Works Cited list, a list of all the sources you cite. Follow the format your teacher recommends, such as Modern Language Association (MLA) style or American Psychological Association (APA) style. See page 1103 for more information about how to prepare citations for different kinds of sources.

If you do not give credit for the information you found, you commit the serious offense of plagiarism, presenting someone else's work as your own. Plagiarism is stealing someone else's ideas, so it is both illegal and dishonest. It's easy to prevent this problem by fairly and thoroughly citing every source you use.

Deciding What to Cite

A fact that can be found in three or more reference sources is probably common knowledge and does not need to be cited. However, do cite facts and opinions that are not common knowledge. This chart distinguishes between common knowledge and facts that should be cited.

Common Core State Standards

Writing

8. Integrate information into the text selectively to maintain the flow of ideas, avoiding plagiarism and overreliance on any one source and following a standard format for citation.

Reading/Writing Connection

To read the complete student model, see page 1104.

Common Knowledge
• Charles Babbage was born in 1791 and died in 1871.   • He was a mathematician and a philosopher.   • He invented a machine called The Difference Engine.
Facts to be Cited
• Babbage's early computer greatly impressed some forward-thinking scientists as early as 1833.   Source: "Wonderful Machinery." *New York Weekly Messenger.* 13 Feb, 1833.   • Babbage was fascinated by machinery and even went backstage at the theater to find out how the staging was created.   Source: Lee, J.A.N. "Charles Babbage." 15 Jan. 2008.   <http://ei.cs.vt.edu/~history/Babbage.html>.

In your report, you will give credit for the following ideas, opinions, or theories presented by other writers:

- Any facts or statistics that are not common knowledge
- Direct quotations of spoken or written words
- Paraphrases of spoken or written words

Notice that you must still provide a citation even if you paraphrase someone else's ideas. It is appropriate to give credit to someone else's thoughts, whether or not you use his or her exact words. In general, it is a good idea to provide too many citations rather than too few.

Developing Your Style

Avoiding Plagiarism

Give proper credit. In a research paper, commonly known facts need not be credited. However, lesser-known facts, as well as quotations and the opinions of other writers, must be acknowledged with proper citations.

> ***Common knowledge:*** *Charles Babbage was a nineteenth-century British scientist.*
>
> ***Requires citation:*** *Charles Babbage planned a calculating machine with [describe the design].*

Never present someone else's ideas or words as though they were your own. To avoid plagiarism—the act of repeating other people's words or ideas without crediting them—follow these steps:

1. Avoid taking notes verbatim, or word for word. Instead, jot down a main idea. When you copy from a source, use quotation marks.

2. Have a partner read your draft and mark any statements that need documentation. Write legibly to avoid miscommunication.

3. Add credits and documentation, as needed.

Find It in Your Reading

Read or review the writing model on page 1104. Notice the way in which this writer gives credit to specific individuals whose ideas she uses.

Indicate the date you accessed information from an Internet site. Content and addresses at Web sites change frequently.

Sample Works-Cited List

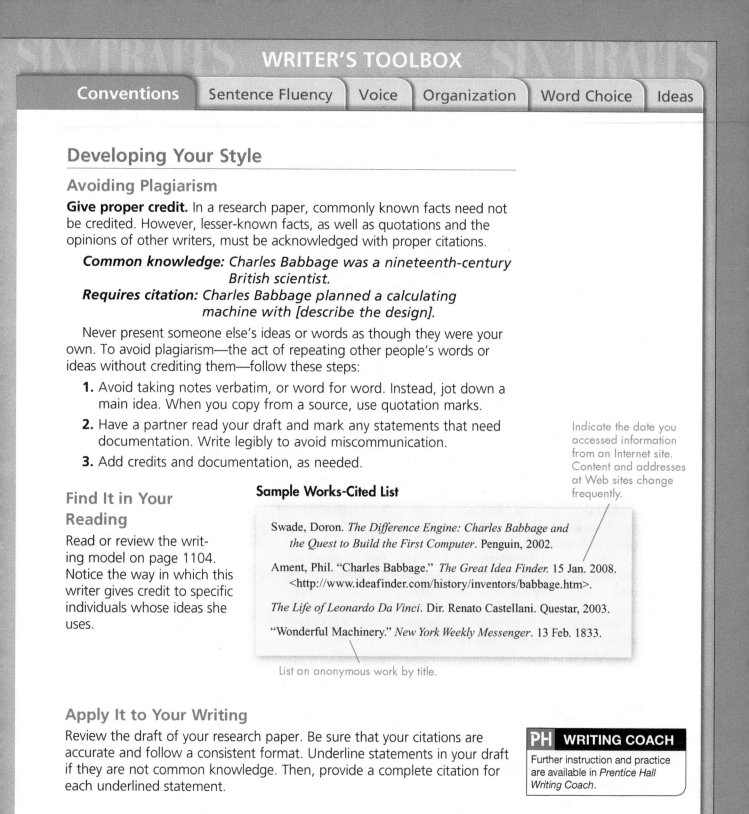

Swade, Doron. *The Difference Engine: Charles Babbage and the Quest to Build the First Computer*. Penguin, 2002.

Ament, Phil. "Charles Babbage." *The Great Idea Finder*. 15 Jan. 2008. <http://www.ideafinder.com/history/inventors/babbage.htm>.

The Life of Leonardo Da Vinci. Dir. Renato Castellani. Questar, 2003.

"Wonderful Machinery." *New York Weekly Messenger*. 13 Feb. 1833.

List an anonymous work by title.

Apply It to Your Writing

Review the draft of your research paper. Be sure that your citations are accurate and follow a consistent format. Underline statements in your draft if they are not common knowledge. Then, provide a complete citation for each underlined statement.

PH WRITING COACH
Further instruction and practice are available in *Prentice Hall Writing Coach*.

Visionaries

The world has seen many visionaries whose inventions and concepts would change the world forever and shape the way we live our lives today. Despite the fact that their ideas were not necessarily accepted right away, many people like Charles Babbage, Leonardo Da Vinci, and even Bill Gates, are now regarded as some of the most amazing minds the world has ever seen.

One who is not very well known but incredibly influential was Charles Babbage. He was born in 1791 and died in 1871 in the UK. Babbage was a well-known mathematician, philosopher, and engineer who invented the first computer and was so far ahead of the technology of his time that he was unable to complete his machine due to lack of sufficient machinery to build the parts needed. Babbage is now considered the "Father of Computing," but during the early 1800s—the period in which he lived—his plans for the first programmable computer seemed unattainable to most people despite his credibility as a leading mathematician and engineer (Ament). His life was so consumed by his work that even when he went to the theater "[He] went behind the scenes to look at the mechanism" (Lee). In the 1820s and 1830s it was impossible to build his precisely engineered Difference Engine with the technology available to him and the lack of funding that he experienced (Ament). However, more than a century later in the 1990s, several scientists decided to build his machine according to his original plans. The machine was made up of four thousand parts and weighed over three metric tons, but size was not the most impressive part (Ament). His Difference machine worked to perfection and effectively eliminated the high rate of human error in math problems, which was his original motivation for the project.

It's hard to imagine how different the world would be if Babbage had finished his machine and given us the first programmable computer. However, it was not until a century later in the 1940s that Howard Aiken created the Harvard Mark I Calculator, which is the first modern digital computer. Aiken used several ideas from Babbage's original design, including a push card and vacuum tube, both of which were unheard of at the time Babbage envisioned them.

Another visionary working past simpler innovation was Leonardo Da Vinci. Da Vinci is best known for his paintings that seem to pop off the canvas. He was one of the first painters to use the technique of perspective to achieve this type of picture, which was radically different from the flat paintings of the Middle Ages. He often used mathematics, geometry, and shading to help him plan out the perspective. His paintings show something else that is truly remarkable. They show no brush strokes because of his skill level as well as his use of oil paints while the rest of the painting world was using tempera paints (O'Connor 27).

However, Da Vinci's legacy is more than just his artwork. As he sketched and painted, Da Vinci often drew scientific instruments on the side of his paper. He had a fascination with studying the way things worked and most of

Nicole states her thesis in the opening paragraph.

Next, Nicole provides readers with general background on her subject.

Nicole provides readers with a sense of Babbage's accomplishments by linking them to modern computer technology.

Nicole cites sources on her Works Cited list properly, following MLA style.

all creating his own inventions, ranging from war machines to musical instruments (O'Connor 44). Soon his study and experimentation distracted him from his painting. He began to study the nature of light and how it affects shading and the inner workings of optics. As he studied the human body more closely, he found that human eyes received light rather than giving off particles, which was the common belief at the time. Through this experimentation, Da Vinci began to develop theories that linked sound waves and light. He also studied the way muscles work and greatly contributed to the medical science of his day. These concepts were well ahead of their time.

Da Vinci's study of the human body fit in perfectly with his inventions; he noted that joints were like hinges and muscles were like gears and levers. He was fascinated with the thought of motion and how things move. In fact, he once expressed the idea that "motion is the principle of all life" (O'Connor 58). Da Vinci devoted much of his study to how things could move by themselves. He drew several sketches of motors and flying machines that came from his study of the wings of a variety of birds. One of his sketches of his flying machines, called an aerial screw, resembles the modern-day helicopter.

Overall, Leonardo Da Vinci's devotion to the study of the human body, scientific observations, and inventions, and his ground-breaking artistic work became the foundation that many after him would build on.

Another visionary who has directly affected the world is Bill Gates. In contrast to Babbage and Da Vinci, Gates has been able to directly affect the world in which he lives. It seems that this man can literally predict future technology and then develop it.

In the 1980s, Bill Gate's company focused on producing products for individual computer use. Three years later, Microsoft developed a word-processing tool called Word that put words on the screen exactly how they would be printed on paper (Lesinski 41). Later, he made use of a piece of hardware called the mouse, which had been invented by Douglas C. Englebart and Bill English. At that time, the mouse was a breakthrough innovation that made interaction with a computer screen easier for many people.

This, however, was just the beginning. Gates's company went international as he continued to innovate and create new technology. The new technologies he developed have changed the way we communicate, do business, teach, and learn. Due to the contributions of Bill Gates, we can now use computers at home and at school. We can communicate with amazing speed. Recently, Microsoft has expanded into the creation of voice-activated technology to be put in cars. With this technology, driving may become safer and the number of accidents may be reduced. After so many years of creating and innovating, Bill Gates continues to influence the evolution of technology, bringing products to market that people before him could not even imagine.

It is hard to imagine how the world would be without Bill Gates and his contributions to technology. It is truly amazing that in a matter of seconds

Nicole provides specific information on Da Vinci's study of optics.

Notice how Nicole creates a transition between Gates and the previous "visionaries": "In contrast to Babbage and Da Vinci . . ." Such a transition makes the report more coherent.

Notice how Nicole uses language to show causes and effects: "Due to . . ."

anyone could pull up a Web site about Charles Babbage or Leonardo Da Vinci or communicate incredibly quickly with someone on the other side of the world.

There is no doubt that the world would be a different place if it were not for visionaries like these. These men were not afraid of the limitations of their time. They pursued the what-ifs their minds developed, imagining things that were science fiction in their day. For Babbage and Da Vinci, their ideas would be brought to fruition in future generations. Gates has been able to bring his imaginings from sketch to prototype to best-seller, consistently moving technology past what even he might have thought possible.

Nicole summarizes her report in the final paragraph.

Works Cited

Ament, Phil [pseudonym for employees at Vaunt Design Group, an Internet consulting company in Troy, Michigan]. "Charles Babbage." The Great Idea Finder. 4 May 2006. 15 Jan. 2008
    <http://www.ideafinder.com/history/inventors/babbage.htm>.

Lee, J.A.N. "Charles Babbage." History of Computing site. Department of Computer Science at Virginia Tech. Sep. 1994. 15 Jan. 2008.
    <http://ei.cs.vt.edu/~history/Babbage.html>.

Lesinski, Jeanne M. *Bill Gates*. Minneapolis: Lerner Publications, 2000.

O'Connor, Barbara. *Leonardo Da Vinci: Renaissance Genius*. Minneapolis: Carolrhoda Books, Inc., 2003.

Nicole provides a complete, detailed, and properly formatted list of all the works she has cited in her report.

Editing and Proofreading

Focus on quotations. Compare each direct quotation in your essay with its source. Make sure that you have recorded exactly what your source said or wrote. To avoid plagiarism, use quotation marks around words, phrases, and sentences that come directly from your sources.

Spiral Review: Conventions Earlier in this unit, you learned about verb tense (p. 1009) and active voice (p. 1085). Check your report to be sure you have used those conventions correctly.

Publishing, Presenting, and Reflecting

Consider one of the following ways to share your writing:

Prepare your Works-Cited list. Your paper is ready for presentation only after you add your Works-Cited list, which provides full bibliographical information on each source you cite. Identify the format your teacher prefers. Then, follow that accepted style to assemble your list. (For more information, see Citing Sources, pp. R21–R23.)

Apply principles of design. Make sure the text of your investigation is appealing to the eye. The lines should be evenly spaced, and the margins of the page should be even, not ragged.

Present your report orally. Use your report as the basis for an oral presentation. Be sure to rehearse well, using clear syntax and accessible diction.

Reflect on your writing. Jot down your thoughts on the experience of writing a research report. Begin by answering these questions:

- What have you learned in this workshop about differing points of view on the same event?
- What aspects of researching one topic in depth surprised you?

Rubric for Self-Assessment

Evaluate your reflective essay using the following criteria and rating scale:

Criteria	Rating Scale
	not very *very*
Focus: How clearly does your thesis statement guide your report?	1 2 3 4 5
Organization: How logical and well documented is your presentation?	1 2 3 4 5
Support/Elaboration: How well do you use a variety of primary and secondary sources to support your thesis?	1 2 3 4 5
Style: How clearly and effectively do you state your conclusions?	1 2 3 4 5
Conventions: According to an accepted format, how complete and accurate are your citations?	1 2 3 4 5

 Common Core State Standards

Writing
5. Develop and strengthen writing as needed by editing, focusing on addressing what is most significant for a specific purpose and audience.

Language
2. Demonstrate command of the conventions of standard English capitalization, punctuation, and spelling when writing.

PH WRITING COACH

Further instruction and practice are available in *Prentice Hall Writing Coach*.

Analyze and Evaluate Entertainment Media

Common Core
State Standards

Speaking and Listening
2. Integrate multiple sources
of information presented in
diverse formats and media
in order to make informed
decisions and solve problems,
evaluating the credibility and
accuracy of each source and
noting any discrepancies
among the data.

Our culture is saturated with **entertainment media**—movies, TV shows, music videos, and other programming designed primarily for enjoyment rather than for instruction or information. While providing entertainment is the core goal, these media also appeal to our values, offering representations of society that both reinforce those values and shape our perceptions of reality. As a consumer of media, you should determine whether the portrait of reality they present is flawed or misleading.

Evaluating Media Credibility

In addition to seeking the primary goal of entertaining audiences, entertainment media makers often influence viewers in these ways:

- *Informing them* and providing a new understanding of historical or current events. Dramatic interpretations of history or current issues, however, may not always be reliable factual accounts.

- *Persuading them* to accept particular viewpoints. By providing only certain perspectives or depicting groups or actions as positive or negative, media can present a *biased* view of an issue.

Entertainment media also cater to audiences' values. For instance, when they tell tales of families reunited, criminals punished, and underdogs who become winners, they are forming a picture of how we think life should be. In this way, they *transmit our own cultural values* back to us. You might envision the relationship between media and culture as a cycle:

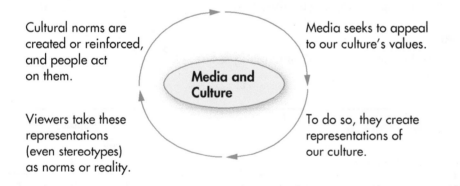

Cultural norms are created or reinforced, and people act on them.

Media seeks to appeal to our culture's values.

Media and Culture

Viewers take these representations (even stereotypes) as norms or reality.

To do so, they create representations of our culture.

Along with the transmission of values, however, come representations of groups of people. Scholars who study the media have examined the effects these representations have upon public perception. They have found that the way groups are portrayed in the media can create **stereotypes,** assumptions about race, gender, or religion that influence a person's attitude and behavior toward individuals who belong to certain groups.

Media Tools and Techniques

The makers of entertainment media use the following *editing techniques*:

- **Special Effects**—technological tricks of sight and sound that produce images, such as flying superheroes and roaming dinosaurs
- **Camera Angles**—the different positions from which a scene is recorded to create different effects
- **Reaction Shots**—close-up shots of an actor's face as he or she responds to another actor or to action in the script
- **Sequencing**—the arrangement of a story's events, such as chronological order or a series of flashbacks
- **Music**—sound added to visual sequences to complement the action or create a particular mood

Activities: Evaluate a Movie, TV Episode, or Skit

ⓒ **Comprehension and Collaboration** For both activities, use an evaluation form like the one shown below.

A. Find a movie, show, or skit you like to watch on television or the Internet. Examine the main ideas it presents and analyze how it conveys these ideas. Record your observations on a form like the one below.

B. Search the Internet to find episodes of a television show from the 1960s or 1970s. Consider how a particular group is represented in this show. Then, compare this representation with representations of the same group on television today. Share your observations with your class.

Evaluation Form

Type of Entertainment Media: Movie ☐ TV Episode ☐ Skit ☐

Name of Movie, Show, or Skit: _____

What story does this movie, episode, or clip tell? _____

What cultural values does it appeal to? Idealism ☐ Fear ☐ Family ☐
  Justice ☐ Other _____
  How does it appeal to these values? _____

Are there stereotypes in this representation? Yes ☐ No ☐
  If yes, what are they? _____

Identify techniques used in this film: Special effects ☐ Editing ☐
  Camera angles ☐ Reaction shots ☐ Sequencing ☐ Music ☐
  Explain the effect of two of these techniques. _____

  _____

Vocabulary Workshop

Idioms

Idioms are figurative expressions that do not mean what the words literally say. For example, describing the weather as *raining cats and dogs* means the rain is torrential. To recognize an idiom, you have to understand *word-phrase relationships*—to realize that in the phrase *raining cats and dogs,* the words have a figurative meaning rather than their usual literal ones.

Idioms can be effective tools in some kinds of writing to convey character or to evoke a particular time period or setting. For example, an American detective of the 1940s might jump in a taxi and growl to the driver, "Step on it." Idioms can also help set a particular mood or tone.

Relying on idioms consistently in your own writing is not always a good idea, however. Because they have been used so often, many of them have lost their originality. Look at the examples below. Note how replacing the idioms can help to communicate meaning in a more precise and lively way.

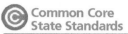

Common Core State Standards

Language
4.a. Use context as a clue to the meaning of a word or phrase.
5. Demonstrate understanding of figurative language, word relationships, and nuances in word meanings.

Idioms	Alternatives
After ten hours of driving in heavy traffic, the trucker <u>ran out of steam.</u>	❏ collapsed over his steering wheel. ❏ sighed and pulled into a rest stop. ❏ radioed his boss and told her he quit.
She was <u>down in the dumps.</u>	❏ too lethargic to get out of bed. ❏ apt to burst into tears if anyone looked at her the wrong way. ❏ in need of a friend to listen to her problems.

Practice

Directions: An analogy shows the relationship between sets of words. Each of the analogies below pairs a word with an idiomatic phrase. Complete each analogy with one of the lettered words provided, creating a pair that matches the other pair in the analogy. Then, write an explanation of the idiomatic expression and the relationships in each pairing.

1. upset : "bent out of shape" :: _____ : "under the weather"
   a. cloudy   **b.** sick   **c.** wet   **d.** forgetful

2. "jump the gun" : _____ :: "shoot the breeze" : deliberate
   a. run quickly   **b.** rush   **c.** chat   **d.** consider

3. "over the moon" : ecstatic :: "fit to be tied" : _____
   a. furious   **b.** delighted   **c.** sad   **d.** fastened

Vocabulary Acquisition and Use: Context Clues

Context clues are words or phrases that help readers clarify the meanings of unfamiliar words in a text. By using context clues, you can determine the word or words that complete a sentence. Sentence Completion questions appear in most standardized tests. In these types of questions, you are given sentences with one or more missing words. Your task is to use the context to choose the correct word or words to complete each sentence logically. Try this strategy: (1) Read the sentence. (2) Scan the answer choices. Find synonyms that are simple words or phrases for the choices. (3) Test the synonyms and determine which makes the most sense.

Practice

This exercise is modeled after the Sentence Completion questions that appear in the Reading Comprehension section of the SAT.

Directions: Each of the following sentences is missing one or two words. Choose the word or set of words that best completes each sentence.

Test-Taking Tip
Eliminate any words with similar meanings because a single correct answer choice should be obvious.

1. Charlotte Brontë's work might have remained ___?___ without the popular success of *Jane Eyre*.
   A. truculent
   B. obscure
   C. rapturous
   D. monotonous
   E. obstinate

2. Charlotte and her gifted siblings can be called ___?___ spirits.
   A. agricultural
   B. terrestrial
   C. gaunt
   D. rapturous
   E. kindred

3. Her close-knit family ___?___ six children and a widowed father.
   A. blanched
   B. eluded
   C. comprised
   D. assessed
   E. clasped

4. The ___?___ Charlotte witnessed at boarding school inspired her to write *Jane Eyre*.
   A. depredation
   B. contusion
   C. adversary
   D. approbation
   E. etymology

5. She would never ___?___ her days as a governess, for they led her to write a popular novel from which she would ___?___ .
   A. impel . . . profundity
   B. fracture . . . officious
   C. rue . . . prosper
   D. languish . . . deficient
   E. elude . . . diffusive

6. In the ___?___ years of her life she married, enjoying a brief time of happiness after the ___?___ of her siblings' deaths.
   A. waning . . . turmoil
   B. ingratiating . . . inculcation
   C. ravenous . . . rendezvous
   D. wily . . . malevolence
   E. gaudy . . . predilection

Test-Taking Practice

Reading Test: Prose Fiction

Some standardized tests include lengthy prose fiction reading passages drawn from novels and short stories. You will have to demonstrate your basic comprehension as well as your analytical skills. Questions will focus on topics such as main ideas, significant details, causes and effects, and themes. In addition, you may be asked to show understanding of words, statements, and the author's perspective.

 Common Core State Standards

RL.11-12.1, RL.11-12.3, RL.11-12.4; L.11-12.1, L.11-12.2, L.11-12.3
[For the full wording of the standards, see the standards chart in the front of your textbook.]

Practice

The following exercise is modeled after the ACT Reading Test, Prose Fiction section.

Directions: Read the following passage, taken from *Jane Eyre,* by Charlotte Brontë. Then, choose the best answer to each question.

It was English history: among the readers I observed my acquaintance of the verandah: at the commencement of the lesson, her place had been at the top of the class, but for some error of pronunciation, or some inattention to stops, she was suddenly sent to the very bottom.
5 Even in that obscure position, Miss Scatcherd continued to make her an object of constant notice: she was continually addressing to her such phrases as the following:—

"Burns" (such it seems was her name: the girls here were all called by their surnames, as boys are elsewhere), "Burns, you are
10 standing on the side of your shoe; turn your toes out immediately." "Burns, you poke your chin most unpleasantly; draw it in." "Burns, I insist on your holding your head up; I will not have you before me in that attitude," etc. etc.

A chapter having been read through twice, the books were closed
15 and the girls examined. The lesson had comprised part of the reign of Charles I, and there were sundry questions about tonnage and poundage and ship-money, which most of them appeared unable to answer; still, every little difficulty was solved instantly when it reached Burns: her memory seemed to have retained the substance
20 of the whole lesson, and she was ready with answers on every point. I kept expecting that Miss Scatcherd would praise her attention; but, instead of that, she suddenly cried out—

"You dirty, disagreeable girl! you have never cleaned your nails this morning!"
25 Burns made no answer: I wondered at her silence. "Why," thought I, "does she not explain that she could neither clean her nails nor wash her face, as the water was frozen?"

Strategy:

- **Underline time words,** such as dates and time of day, and **transition words,** such as "then," and "afterwards," to clarify sequence.

- As you read, **make a chronological list of the story's events.**

- Refer to your list as you answer the questions.

 PHLit Online!
www.PHLitOnline.com

1. Which of the following quotes from the passage demonstrates emotive language and not informative language?
   A. "there were sundry questions about tonnage and poundage"
   B. "she was suddenly sent to the very bottom"
   C. "'You dirty, disagreeable girl!'"
   D. "the girls here were all called by their surnames"

2. The author provides precise dialogue to increase the reader's understanding of her characters' motivations because she wants:
   F. readers to understand what Burns is really like.
   G. to show how the setting affects the characters.
   H. readers to experience the shock the narrator feels.
   J. to show how Burns forces Miss Scatcherd to act.

3. As it is used in line 9, the word *surnames* most nearly means:
   A. nicknames.
   B. last names.
   C. first names.
   D. official titles.

4. Which of the following would be included in a summary of this selection?

   I. Burns was an acquaintance of Jane's.
   II. The lesson they read was about Charles I.
   III. Burns did not mention the frozen wash water.

   F. I and II
   G. I only
   H. III only
   J. I, II, and III

5. Considering the events of the entire passage, it is most reasonable to infer that
   A. Jane would soon become a favorite of the teacher.
   B. Burns knew how to deal with Miss Scatcherd.
   C. Burns would one day be recognized as intelligent.
   D. Jane thought Burns deserved the way she was treated.

6. Which elements of the author's beliefs are demonstrated in her description of Miss Scatcherd's response to Burns's answers?
   F. Good students deserve praise.
   G. Boarding schools are good for character.
   H. Teachers need to be firm with their students.
   J. Cleanliness is an important personal trait.

7. The details and events in the passage suggest that the relationship between Jane and Burns would most accurately be described as:
   A. a misunderstanding.
   B. a rivalry.
   C. sympathetic.
   D. jealousy.

Grammar and Writing: Editing in Context

Editing-in-context segments appear in some standardized tests. They are made up of a passage with underlined and numbered areas, some of which contain errors in grammar, style, and usage. For each question, you must choose the best way to correct a given sentence.

Practice

This exercise is modeled after the ACT English Test.

Directions: For each underlined sentence or portion of a sentence, choose the best alternative. If an item asks a question about the underlined portion or a numbered sentence, choose the best answer to the question.

[1]

Boarding schools first began in England when boys <u>go</u> to a local monastery
                                                    1
for their education. Monks and lay staff would provide a variety of instruction
while <u>the boys' housing would be provided by the order that spon-</u>
<u>sored the monastery.</u> Often a local nobleman would make his estate avail-
      2
able to the sons of other nobles. <u>Employing a literate priest from the</u>
                                                                        3
<u>area.</u> These makeshift academies often became boarding houses for the elite.

[2]

In the twelfth century, <u>all Benedictine monasteries were ordered by the</u>
<u>Pope to provide what were known as "charity schools."</u> <u>Followed by</u>
                                    4
<u>what we know today as public schools.</u> Students <u>began to pay their</u>
                          5   6
<u>way and attended</u> in greater numbers than ever before.

[3]

Aristocratic families continued to favor private instruction in their homes.⁷
The great universities of Cambridge and Oxford provided models. As the British Empire began to expand, the boarding school became well established.⁸

1. **A.** NO CHANGE
   B. goes
   C. have gone
   D. went

2. Which of the following sentences would best make this statement more forceful?
   F. NO CHANGE
   G. the order that sponsored the monastery would provide the boys' housing.
   H. the boys' housing would be sponsored by the order the monastery provided.
   J. the order that sponsored the monastery would be provided by the boys' housing.

3. **A.** NO CHANGE
   B. attach it to previous sentence
   C. attach it to next sentence
   D. OMIT

4. **F.** NO CHANGE
   G. all Benedictine monasteries were ordered to provide what were known as "charity schools" by the Pope.
   H. the Pope ordered all Benedictine monasteries to provide what were known as "charity schools."
   J. the Pope was ordered by all Benedictine monasteries to provide what were known as "charity schools."

5. **A.** NO CHANGE
   B. These were soon followed by what we know today as public schools.
   C. Followed soon is what we know today as public schools.
   D. Public schools what we know today followed soon.

6. **F.** NO CHANGE
   G. began to pay their way and attending
   H. begin to pay their way and attend
   J. begin paying their way and attending

7. The writer wishes to add the following sentence without creating a run-on sentence:
   However, elite boarding schools also became fashionable.
   If added, this would best be placed:
   A. as part of the previous sentence, at its beginning, with new punctuation.
   B. as part of the previous sentence, at its end, joined by a semicolon and a conjunction.
   C. as part of the following sentence at its beginning joined by a comma.
   D. as is, standing alone as a sentence.

8. Which of these alternatives provides the most direct conclusion of Paragraph 3?
   F. To stay attuned to their own culture and attend boarding school, children of British administrators were sent back to England.
   G. Children of British administrators attended boarding school, going back to England and stay attuned to their own culture.
   H. Children of British administrators went back to England attending boarding school and staying attuned to their own culture.
   J. British administrators sent their children back to England to attend boarding school and stay attuned to their own culture.

⏱ Timed Writing: Position Statement [30 minutes]

Jane Eyre is sent to Lowood, a private boarding school, and has to deal with strict teachers and harsh conditions. Charlotte Brontë briefly attended a school like Lowood and clearly did not enjoy the experience. But for many students, boarding school life became a wonderful home away from home and a memorable academic experience.

Write an essay in which you discuss the benefits or drawbacks of boarding school. Support your opinions with sound reasoning, and try to anticipate and address counterarguments.

> **Academic Vocabulary**
>
> An essay often argues with itself by first presenting one way of looking at an issue, and then refuting that argument with another viewpoint.

Performance Tasks

**Common Core
State Standards**

RL.11-12.2, RL.11-12.3, RL.11-12.5;
RI.11-12.5; W.11-12.2, W.11-12.9.a,
W.11-12.4; SL.11-12.1, SL.11-12.4,
SL.11-12.6; L.11-12.3.a
[For the complete wording of the
standards, see the standards chart in
the front of your textbook.]

Directions: *Follow the instructions to complete the tasks below as required by your teacher. As you work on each task, incorporate both general academic vocabulary and literary terms you learned in this unit.*

Writing

Task 1: Literature [RL.11-12.2; W.11-12.2, W.11-12.9.a]

Analyze Development of Themes

*Write an **essay** in which you analyze the development of two themes in a work of fiction from this unit.*

- Choose a story or a novel excerpt from this unit that expresses multiple themes.

- Briefly summarize the story. Identify two themes that develop in the story.

- Analyze how the author introduces and develops those themes over the course of the story.

- Note ways in which the themes interact and build on one another, and discuss how this interaction creates deeper meaning.

- Use transitions to clearly show the relationships and interactions among story elements.

- Use active, not passive, voice.

- Accurately use academic vocabulary in your writing.

Task 2: Literature [RL.11-12.5; W.11-12.4; L.11-12.3.a]

Analyze Text Structure

*Write an **essay** in which you analyze how a poet's choice of structure adds to the overall meaning and aesthetic impact of a poem in this unit.*

- Choose a poem from this unit in which the structure, or form, plays a key role in developing the poem's meaning. Explain which poem you chose and why.

- Analyze how the poet's choices of structure in sections of the poem contribute to the structure of the poem as a whole. Consider line length, rhyme scheme, and meter, as well as stanza lengths and divisions.

- Connect the author's choices concerning structure to the meaning as well as to the aesthetic, or artistic and emotional, impact of the poem. Cite examples from the text to support your thinking.

- Develop and present your ideas while maintaining an appropriate, consistent style and tone in your writing.

- Vary your sentence length and structure to add interest and sophistication to your writing.

Task 3: Literature [RL.11-12.3; W.11-12.2, W.11.12.9.a]

Analyze Character Development

*Write an **essay** in which you analyze the impact of the author's choices regarding how to introduce and develop characters in a work of fiction from this unit.*

- State which fictional characters you will be discussing in your essay and the reasons for your choice.

- Describe each character, including the points at which important information is revealed. Determine what kinds of details the author provides about each character.

- Analyze the role each character plays in the story and explain each character's goals and motivations.

- Explain the connection between characters and theme.

- Sum up your analysis with a conclusion about how the author's choices regarding character development shaped the work of fiction.

- In your writing, use technical academic vocabulary, standard English grammar, and correct spelling.

Speaking and Listening

Task 4: Literature [RL.11-12.2, SL.11-12.6]
Analyze Related Themes

*Prepare and deliver an **oral presentation** in which you analyze two themes expressed in a literary work in this unit and the way in which those themes interact.*

- Select a work that expresses multiple, related themes. Briefly summarize the work and explain why you chose it.

- Explain how the author develops themes over the course of the work. Consider narrative elements such as plot, setting, and character. Also consider literary elements such as symbolism and imagery.

- Explain how the two themes interact and build on each other during the course of the work.

- Cite specific evidence from the text to support your points.

- As you present, use adequate volume and clear pronunciation. Demonstrate a command of formal English.

Task 5: Literature [RL.11-12.3; SL.11-12.1]
Analyze and Compare Speakers

Prepare and conduct a group discussion comparing speakers in two poems in this unit.

- Choose two poems with distinctive speakers that have a good basis for comparison.

- Analyze the speaker in each poem. Consider the choices the poet made as to the speaker. For example, the speaker may be real or fictional, specific or general. Determine each speaker's motivation and conflict. Draw inferences about the character of each speaker based on evidence from the poems.

- Prepare for the discussion. Create a list of questions designed to promote discussion. Make charts on which to record the main points that are brought up during the discussion.

- During the discussion, clarify or challenge ideas; respond thoughtfully to diverse perspectives; and propel conversation by posing and responding to questions.

Task 6: Informational Text [RI.11-12.5; SL.11-12.4]
Analyze Structure

*Prepare and deliver an **oral presentation** in which you analyze an author's use of text structure as part of exposition in a nonfiction work from this unit.*

- Select a work of nonfiction from this unit in which the structure helps to communicate the author's ideas or argument. Briefly explain why you chose this work.

- Define the text's structure. Explain how it enhances or helps to develop the author's ideas or argument. Consider how the text structure serves the author's purpose as well as how it might affect an audience.

- Be sure to provide examples from the text to support your points. Check the pronunciation of challenging words from the text.

- Present your ideas clearly and completely so that your listeners can follow your reasoning.

- While presenting, use formal English, good pronunciation, and adequate volume.

How does literature shape or reflect society?

Victorian Views in Today's World Which aspects of the Victorian Age have meaning and value for us now?

Assignment Imagine that you are compiling a book of Victorian wit and wisdom to be sold today. It will include nuggets of literature that reflect Victorian values. First, select some quotations you would include. Then, write a **preface to the book,** convincing the reader of the value and relevance of the quotations in today's world.

Featured Titles

In this unit, you have read a variety of British literature from the Victorian period. Continue to read works related to this era on your own. Select books that you enjoy, but challenge yourself to explore new topics, new authors, and works offering varied perspectives or approaches. The titles suggested below will help you get started.

LITERATURE

Wuthering Heights
Emily Brontë

Novel Set on the wild and windy moors of northern Yorkshire, *Wuthering Heights* tells the story of Heathcliff and Catherine, who are desperately in love. The thwarting of their love prompts Heathcliff to seek revenge.

[The poem "Remembrance" by Emily Brontë begins on page 1075. Build knowledge by reading a novel by this author.]

Jane Eyre
Charlotte Brontë   EXEMPLAR TEXT ©

Novel The title character in this classic novel endures many challenges that give readers insight into the life of a single, middle-class woman in Victorian Britain. After a lonely, difficult childhood, Jane Eyre becomes a governess at the home of Mr. Rochester, a man with a terrible secret.

[An excerpt from Jane Eyre *begins on page 1030 of this book. Build knowledge by reading the complete novel.]*

Hard Times
Charles Dickens

Novel While exposing the harsh realities of poverty in nineteenth-century England, Dickens tells the story of Thomas Gradgrind, a teacher and parent who believes facts alone are all that are needed in life. As life unfolds around him, his views change.

[An excerpt from Hard Times *begins on page 998 of this book. Build knowledge by reading the complete novel.]*

Crime and Punishment
Fyodor Dostoyevsky   EXEMPLAR TEXT ©

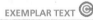

Novel Ex-student Raskolnikov is poor and starving. Though he thinks of himself as a good person, he rationalizes robbing and murdering an old woman by telling himself that she is morally corrupt. His actions soon begin to haunt him, however, and he is forced to face their consequences.

INFORMATIONAL TEXTS

Historical Texts

The Essays of Virginia Woolf
Virginia Woolf
Mariner Books, 1990

Essay This four-volume text includes essays written by Woolf from her early twenties until her death in 1941. Woolf's essays present a personal view of her life, as well as her views on women, writing, literature, and politics.

[Selected works by Virginia Woolf appear on page 1192 of this book. Build knowledge by reading the full text.]

Queen Victoria
Lytton Strachey
Nabu Press, 2010

Biography Get to know Britain's long-reigning and influential queen in this comprehensive and engaging biography—her willful childhood, her joyful marriage to Albert, her sorrow at his death, and her devotion to her servant John Brown.

Contemporary Scholarship

Dickens
Peter Ackroyd

Biography This award-winning biography describes in detail the life of famed British novelist Charles Dickens. Read about his difficult childhood and his rise to popular and critical acclaim as one of the most important writers of his time.

The Ghost Map
Steven Johnson
Riverhead, 2007

Scientific History It is the summer of 1854 and a devastating cholera outbreak has seized London. Dr. John Snow—whose ideas about contagious disease have been dismissed by the scientific community—is spurred into action when his neighbors begin dying.

Preparing to Read Complex Texts

Reading for College and Career In both college and the workplace, readers must analyze texts independently, draw connections among works that offer varied perspectives, and develop their own ideas and informed opinions. The questions shown below, and others that you generate on your own, will help you more effectively read and analyze complex college-level texts.

Common Core State Standards

Reading Literature/Informational Text
10. By the end of grade 12, read and comprehend literature, including stories, dramas, and poems, and literary nonfiction at the high end of the grade 11-CCR text complexity band independently and proficiently.

When reading analytically, ask yourself...

- What idea, experience, or story seems to have compelled the author to write? Has the author presented that idea, experience, or story in a way that I, too, find compelling?

- How might the author's era, social status, belief system, or personal experiences have affected the point of view he or she expresses in the text?

- How do my circumstances affect what I understand and feel about this text?

- What key idea does the author state explicitly? What key idea does he or she suggest or imply? Which details in the text help me to perceive implied ideas?

- Do I find multiple layers of meaning in the text? If so, what relationships do I see among these layers of meaning?

- How do details in the text connect or relate to one another? Do I find any details unconvincing, unrelated, or out of place?

- Do I find the text believable and convincing?

Key Ideas and Details

- What patterns of organization or sequences do I find in the text? Do these patterns help me understand the ideas better?

- What do I notice about the author's style, including his or her diction, uses of imagery and figurative language, and syntax?

- Do I like the author's style? Is the author's style memorable?

- What emotional attitude does the author express toward the topic, the story, or the characters? Does this attitude seem appropriate?

- What emotional attitude does the author express toward me, the reader? Does this attitude seem appropriate?

- What do I notice about the author's voice—his or her personality on the page? Do I like this voice? Does it make me want to read on?

Craft and Structure

- Is the work fresh and original?

- Do I agree with the author's ideas entirely, or are there elements I find unconvincing?

- Do I disagree with the author's ideas entirely, or are there elements I can accept as true?

- Based on my knowledge of British literature, history, and culture, does this work reflect the British tradition? Why or why not?

Integration of Ideas

A Time of Rapid Change

The Modern and Postmodern Periods

1901–Present

"Yesterday, we split the atom. . . . And because of this, the great dream and the great nightmare of centuries of human thought have taken flesh and walk beside us all, day and night."

— *Doris Lessing, from*

"The Small Personal Voice"

PHLit Online!
www.PHLitOnline.com

Hear It!
- Selection summary audio
- Selection audio

See It!
- Author videos
- Essential Question video
- Get Connected videos
- Background videos
- More about the authors
- Illustrated vocabulary words
- Vocabulary flashcards

Do It!
- Interactive journals
- Interactive graphic organizers
- Grammar tutorials
- Interactive vocabulary games
- Test practice

Snapshot of the Period

A Ride on the London Eye

England celebrated the new millennium with the London Eye, a 443-foot Ferris wheel beside the Thames (see page to the right). Picture this wheel as the symbol of a 2,000-year cycle in time. Looking out from it, we might view England's history—waves of invaders from the Romans to the Normans, performances at Shakespeare's Globe, the changing versions of London known to Dr. Johnson, Charles Dickens, and Virginia Woolf. From the top, we might see how England's empire stretched across the globe in the nineteenth century and how, in the twentieth, two world wars led to the loss of that empire. The ride over, we would step onto the soil of twenty-first-century England, once more a nation rather than an empire. It is a nation, however, whose language is spoken across the globe and whose literature is enriched by writers from St. Lucia to Singapore.

These two maps dramatize Britain's loss of its empire in the twentieth century.

British Empire, 1900

Britain Today

As you read the selections in this unit, you will be asked to think about them in view of three key questions:

What is the **relationship** between literature and *place?*

How does literature **shape or reflect** *society?*

What is the relationship of the **writer** to *tradition?*

Integration of Knowledge and Ideas As this London Eye timeline indicates, the end of the British empire was also marked by a renewal of English literature as writers from former colonies made—and are still making—important contributions to the tradition. During what postwar decade did Britain lose most of its colonies? What are three former colonies that have produced Nobel Prize-winning authors who write in English?

GAINING INDEPENDENCE

1947 India and Pakistan

1948 Burma (Myanmar); Sri Lanka

1957 Ghana

1960 Nigeria; Cyprus

1961 Sierra Leone; Tanzania

1962 Jamaica; Trinidad & Tobago; Uganda

1963 Kenya; Malaysia

1964 Malawi; Malta; Zambia

1965 The Gambia; Singapore

1966 Guyana; Botswana; Lesotho

NOBEL PRIZE WINNERS

Rabindrinath Tagore (India) 1913

William Butler Yeats (Ireland) 1923

Samuel Beckett (Ireland) 1969

Wole Soyinka (Nigeria) 1986

Nadine Gordimer (South Africa) 1991

Derek Walcott (St. Lucia) 1992

V.S. Naipaul (Trinidad) 2001

J.M. Coetzee (South Africa) 2003

Doris Lessing (Rhodesia/Zimbabwe) 2007

Historical Background

The Modern and Postmodern Periods (1901–Present)

At dusk on August 3, 1914, Sir Edward Grey, the British Foreign Secretary, clutching the telegram announcing the German invasion of Belgium, walked to the window, looked over a darkening London and said: "The lamps are going out all over Europe; we shall not see them lit again in our lifetime." The next day, Britain declared war on Germany.

World War I and Its Long-Lasting Effects

Many said that the war would be brief, with the troops coming home by Christmas. Instead, the war lasted four long years and 750,000 British soldiers never came home at all. World War I, and the flaws in the treaty with which it was finally settled, influenced much of what followed in the twentieth century.

Germany, for example, wanting to get Russia out of the war and thereby win a victory on the Western Front, transported Lenin to St. Petersburg. There, he led the Bolshevik Revolution that altered the course of Russian and European history.

The war also encouraged Irish nationalists to fight for independence in 1916 while the British army was engaged in France. Their attempted rebellion failed and deepened the hatred between the British and Irish. In 1922, the Irish achieved a measure of independence in the south, but fighting between Catholics and Protestants in the northern, British provinces prolonged the bloodshed for the rest of the century.

The Treaty of Versailles, which settled World War I, led to economic collapse and near-anarchy in Germany, paving the way for Hitler to exact revenge on the Allies.

The horrific slaughter of the war and the crippling effects of the Great Depression forced England into a passive role in the 1930s. Once the mightiest nation in the world, England looked on as a re-armed Germany amassed territory in Europe, and as Japan, perceiving Western powers as weak, occupied much of China.

World War I recruiting poster

TIMELINE

1901: Edward VII becomes king. ▶

1905: Germany Albert Einstein proposes theory of relativity. ▶

1901

1903: Orville and Wilbur Wright build first successful airplane.

1914: Britain enters World War I ▶

World War II and the Loss of the Empire

The aggression of Germany and Japan led inevitably to World War II. When Hitler's armies overran Europe, the English stood defiantly alone, shielded by the English Channel and the Royal Air Force. It was, Winston Churchill said, "their finest hour."

In 1942, Russia blunted the German advance, America was in the war, and the tide turned against the aggressors. After nearly six years of struggle, England emerged from the war victorious, battered, and impoverished.

England's former colonies became independent countries. The Indian subcontinent, where Gandhi had led an independence movement, was divided into the nations of India and Pakistan in 1947.

The imperial British lion gave a dying gasp in 1956 when Britain, France, and Israel invaded Egypt to keep control of the Suez Canal. However, the United States intervened, the Egyptians kept the Canal, and British troops came home to a country ashamed of its government's actions.

Suez was forgotten in the cultural upheaval of the nineteen sixties when British fashion and British rock musicians carried the flag around the world in a kind of cultural conquest. Also, writers from England's former colonies were engaged in their own re-conquest, enriching English literature.

As the century closed, the violence in Northern Ireland seemed to be ending. Also, England pondered its involvement with Europe, not accepting the common currency, the Euro, but cooperating in drilling a tunnel under the English Channel.

Do Sir Edward Grey's words still have a prophetic ring? Many thought the lamps came on again when the Berlin Wall fell. However, countries cobbled together in the aftermath of World War I—Yugoslavia and Iraq—have been the sites of bitter conflict.

The Spitfire fighter played a major role in defending Britain during World War II.

Key Historical Theme: Conflicts and the Loss of Empire

- England emerged victorious but weakened from World War I, which influenced events in Europe for years to come.
- England was on the winning side in World War II as well, but it was weakened further and gradually lost all its colonies.

1917: Austria
Sigmund Freud publishes *Introduction to Psychoanalysis*.

◀ **1920: India**
Mohandas Gandhi leads nonviolent protests.

1922: Irish Free State formed.

1917: Russia
Czar overthrown; Bolsheviks, led by Lenin, seize power. ▶

1918: Women over thirty achieve right to vote in Great Britain.

THE LITTLE REVIEW
Vol. V.   MARCH. 1918   No. 11
ULYSSES
JAMES JOYCE
Episode 1

◀ **1922:** James Joyce publishes *Ulysses*.

1922

Essential Questions Across Time

A Time of Rapid Change (1901–Present)

What is the relationship between literature **and** *place?*

England in the twentieth century is, of course, a geographic place—an island nation ravaged and rebuilt to an unprecedented degree. It is also a geopolitical place—a "mother country" that stood as a land of hope and glory to many citizens of her far-flung empire. Lastly, it is a place of imagination, a realm of letters and literature fed by the ever-changing English language.

In what ways are the "three Englands" reflected in literature?

The Land Itself The English landscape was untouched by the terrible destruction of World War I. However, the real devastation was human, as an entire generation of young men was wiped out. The physical and psychological damage of the war is documented in poems by soldier poets.

Postwar Growth and Materialism The most obvious change in the landscape after the war came with the automobile. More people could afford cars, and ribbons of highway covered the landscape. Accompanying this economic growth was a materialistic attitude on the part of many, perhaps inspired by the war's devastation. In his story "The Rocking-Horse Winner" (1926), D. H. Lawrence criticizes such materialism and reveals a stylish home as a place haunted by the need for "more money."

World War II and the Blitz The Blitz, from the German *blitzkrieg,* "lightning warfare," refers to the German bombing of English cities during World War II. Large sections of London were destroyed by bombs and rockets, but nothing could break what a song hailed as "London Pride." Elizabeth Bowen's story "The Demon Lover" reflects not so much the actual damage as

---

ESSENTIAL QUESTION VOCABULARY

These Essential Question words will help you think and write about literature and place:

generation (jen´ ər ā´ shən) *n.* all the people born and living at the same time

materialism (mə tir´ ē əl iz´ əm) *n.* belief in comfort, pleasure, and wealth as the highest values

colonial (kə lō´ nē əl) *adj.* of or relating to the colony or colonies of a mother country

---

TIMELINE

1922

1927: United States
Charles Lindbergh flies solo to Paris. ▼

1939: Europe
Hitler invades Poland; World War II begins. ▶

1939: Britain enters World War II. ▼

the psychological aftershocks of this assault. Her wartime London is truly a haunted place.

From the ashes, a new London emerged. Other changes were more problematic. The mill and mining country of the north was no longer the economic heart of the country. Wealth concentrated in the south as banking and technology took command. The economic divide between the rusting north and the booming south grew wider as the century ended. The poet Ted Hughes, a northerner, portrays in his work a vision of nature as both glorious and cruel. That vision may be related to the north-south divide.

The England of Hope and Glory In addition to an economic divide, Britain felt the effects of racial and colonial divisions. In V. S. Naipaul's story "B. Wordsworth," England is the distant land of hope and glory to those living in colonial Trinidad, but the dream may be an empty one.

Until 1950, the typical English man or woman was seen as fair-haired, blue eyed, and Anglican. When people of color, British citizens from the former colonies, began to move to England, the English had to deal with unprecedented diversity. In "Midsummer XXIII," Caribbean poet Derek Walcott writes about riots prompted by racial prejudice.

The Realm of the English Language Walcott also raises questions about the English language itself. To whom does the language and its literary tradition belong? Can writers from former colonies and elsewhere in the world find a home in that language and tradition? The evidence, starting with Walcott's own brilliant work, indicates that the answer is yes.

The BRITISH TRADITION

CLOSE-UP ON HISTORY

Planned Town, Unplanned Poet

Sir Ebenezer Howard (1850–1928) was a British social thinker who helped invent the concept of the suburbs. In *Garden Cities of Tomorrow* (1902), Howard described a new kind of planned town surrounded by a ring of farmland. This garden city, as he called it, would combine the advantages of a city with those of the country. Welwyn Garden City, one of the first examples, was built after World War I and inspired the "new towns" that the British government built after World War II. Howard's ideas also inspired Walt Disney's original design for the Experimental Prototype Community of Tomorrow (EPCOT) in Florida.

Unplanned by Howard was the fact that Glyn Maxwell, a talented young poet and playwright, would grow up in a planned town. Humorously calling himself the "Shakespeare of Welwyn Garden City," Maxwell often alludes to Welwyn in his poetry. He has also been known to stage what he calls "large pageant-like shows" in his parents' garden. Given Maxwell's skilled use of poetic forms, perhaps it is true that Sir Ebenezer's talent for planning influenced him after all.

1940: Winston Churchill becomes prime minister. ▶

1943

1941: United States Japan bombs Pearl Harbor; United States enters World War II. ▲

How does literature **shape or** reflect *society?*

In what ways did literature reflect new social freedoms?

Women as Bicyclists At the end of the nineteenth and beginning of the twentieth century, the craze for cycling swept England and the Continent. Cycling required a drastic change in the way women dressed. The new freedom in clothing was, however, only a part of the change in pre-World War I England. The strongest social movement of the time was the campaign for women's right to vote. The Suffragettes, women who crusaded for the vote, chained themselves to buildings and went on hunger strikes when arrested. Their victory was slow in coming, but by 1918 women over the age of thirty could vote.

Women as Writers The work of novelist Virginia Woolf revealed a new freedom that women were finding in literature as well. Woolf's experimental fiction broke new ground, and her nonfiction explored the social conditions that would help women succeed in the arts.

   The bicycle as product and the right to vote as principle were part of the century-long process of loosening the rigid rules of class, propriety, and morality that had bound the Victorians. This process applied to such areas as access to higher education, health care, marriage laws and customs for ordinary people and the monarchy, home ownership, pensions, and working conditions.

How did writers respond to social crises?

War and Social Change The war of 1914 put most questions of social change on hold, but the men who were "demobbed" (demobilized or discharged) and the women who had coped without them were not going to settle for the old ways. As soldier-poet Siegfried Sassoon wrote of one patrol, "night's misery is ended." However, the years-long "misery" of the war would not be forgotten by those who returned. The

TIMELINE

1945: Japan The United States drops atomic bombs on Hiroshima and Nagasaki. World War II ends as Japan surrenders. ▼

1948: Middle East Israel established.

1943

1947: India and Pakistan gain independence.

1949: China Mao Zedong establishes People's Republic. ▲

aristocracy would have to make do with many fewer servants as men and women found work in new industries (automotive), new jobs (radio), and new forms of entertainment (movies). Higher hemlines and shorter hair signaled that women were freer than ever.

Writers and Politics Then came the 1930s, called by poet W. H. Auden "a low dishonest decade." Auden and fellow poets Louis MacNeice and Stephen Spender responded to such crises as The Great Depression and the Spanish Civil War. In that conflict, the Communist and Fascist tyrannies sparred, foreshadowing the conflict that would come in World War II. Especially shocking was the Nazi-Soviet treaty, a cynical pretense at peace by the totalitarian powers. Men and women on the left and the right were sickened by the callousness of it. Left-wing writer George Orwell, who fought in Spain, would later attack totalitarianism of all kinds in books like *Animal Farm* and *1984*.

Speeches and Poems When war broke out, British Prime Minister Winston Churchill rallied the people for the supreme effort required of them. His radio broadcasts and other speeches—"I have nothing to offer but blood, toil, tears, and sweat"—were classics of their kind. The war indeed brought blood and tears, and the bombs and rockets made all the British combatants and casualties. Literary descendants of the World War I soldier poets, writers like Keith Douglas and Alun Lewis, recorded the cost of conflict.

The BRITISH TRADITION

THE CHANGING ENGLISH LANGUAGE, BY RICHARD LEDERER

Britspeak, A to Zed

At the end of World War II, Winston Churchill tells us, the Allied leaders nearly came to blows over a single word during their negotiations when some diplomats suggested that it was time to "table" an important motion. For the British, table meant that the motion should be put on the table for discussion. For the Americans it meant just the opposite—that it should be put on the shelf and dismissed from discussion.

This confusion serves to illustrate the truth of George Bernard Shaw's pronouncement that "England and America are two countries divided by a common language."

When an American exclaims, "I'm mad about my flat," he is upset about his tire. When a Brit exclaims, "I'm mad about my flat," she's not bemoaning the puncture of her "tyre"; she is delighted with her apartment. When a Brit points out that you have "a ladder in your hose," the situation is not as bizarre as you might at first think. Quite simply, you have a run in your stocking.

With the increasing influence of film, radio, television, and international travel, the two main streams of the English language are rapidly converging like the streets of a circus (British for "traffic circle"). Nonetheless, there are scores of words, phrases, and spellings about which Brits and Yanks still do not agree.

1955: United States
Martin Luther King, Jr., leads civil rights bus boycott. ▶

1961: Germany
Berlin Wall built.

1964: Vietnam
American involvement in the Vietnam War grows.

◀ **1957: Russia**
Sputnik I, first satellite, launched.

1963: United States
President John F. Kennedy assassinated. ▶

1964

As soon as the war had ended, however, Churchill was voted out of office and the returning veterans and the survivors of the bombings demanded a new kind of welfare state. Recovery was slow and England was struggling when the twenty-five-year-old Elizabeth became Queen in 1952. She reminded many of Victoria, another shy young woman who had become queen more than a century before, and suddenly things looked brighter.

The Rolling Stones in performance

How did music and literature respond to social changes?

Music and Literature in the Sixties Things were at their brightest in the next decade: the swinging sixties. The Greek philosopher Plato once said: "When the modes of music change, the walls of the city are shaken." The walls were rocked by the Beatles and the Rolling Stones. Not as famous as these songwriters and singers, poets like Ted Hughes and Peter Redgrove nevertheless opened their minds and their styles to a wide range of new influences.

The pendulum slowed in the eighties. Margaret Thatcher, a Conservative Party member and the first female prime minister, reversed many of the socio-economic changes of the previous twenty-five years. Early in her administration, the army and navy crushed Argentina's attempt to seize the Falkland Islands in the South Atlantic. This was the final flick of the imperial lion's tail. She was succeeded by fellow Conservative John Major, but the Labor Party came back into power with Tony Blair's election in 1997.

Literature Celebrates Diversity More capitalistic, more technological, and much more multiracial, the England of Tony Blair entered the twenty-first century in style. That style was maintained in literature as well, as Zadie Smith's acclaimed first novel, *White Teeth* (2000), welcomed the new millennium with a comic celebration of diversity.

> **ESSENTIAL QUESTION VOCABULARY**
>
> These Essential Question words will help you think and write about literature and society:
>
> **propriety** (prō prī´ ə tē) *n.* display of proper manners or behavior
>
> **aristocracy** (ar i stä´ krə sē) *n.* ruling class; nobility
>
> **fascism** (fash´ iz´ əm) *n.* type of government ruled by one party, which puts down all opposition

TIMELINE

1964

1967: The Beatles release *Sgt. Pepper's Lonely Hearts Club Band.* ▲

1969: United States Apollo 11 lands on moon. ▼

1975: North Sea oil production begins.

1972: Britain imposes direct rule on Northern Ireland.

What is the relationship of the writer to *tradition?*

In the twentieth century, the English literary tradition became more accessible and more inclusive. It was more accessible because inexpensive editions of books and the Internet made all of English literature instantly available for writers and readers. It was more inclusive because writers from the former colonies were now enriching the tradition.

How did writers connect with and renew traditions?

Poet as Prophet It was an "outsider," for example, who, following the examples of Romantic poets Blake and Shelley, continued the tradition of prophetic poetry. Irish poet William Butler Yeats summed up the fears of the century in "The Second Coming": "Things fall apart; the center cannot hold . . ."

New Uses for Traditional Forms Twentieth-century writers found new uses for traditional forms such as the sonnet. In twentieth-century hands, the sonnet dealt with experiences undreamed of by the Elizabethans. The radical change in subject matter and tone can be seen by comparing sonnets written by two different World War I poets. The young and dashing Rupert Brooke wrote, in "The Soldier," of the idealism that spurred many of his generation. However, Wilfred Owen's sonnet "Anthem for Doomed Youth" tells what happened when those idealistic young men encountered the turmoil of the Western Front: "What passing bells for those who die as cattle?"

Echoes of Romanticism Although Ted Hughes's lyric "The Horses" differs in many ways from William Wordsworth's "Tintern Abbey," we can still hear an echo of Wordsworth in Hughes's celebration of nature and his distrust of cities.

The Blossoming of the Modern Short Story The modern short story was invented in the nineteenth century. In the twentieth century, however, it became a global genre. Just a few examples will show how authors were setting their tales everywhere and anywhere in the world: James

◀ **1977: Africa**
Djibouti, last remaining
European colony, granted
independence.

1979: Iran
Ayatollah Khomeini
overthrows Shah. ▶

1985

◀ **1979:** Margaret
Thatcher becomes first
woman prime minister.

Joyce in the streets of Dublin, Joseph Conrad in the jungles of the Malay Archipelago, and Doris Lessing on the Rhodesian veldt.

The subjects of these stories are as varied as their settings. Joyce writes about the coming of age of an infatuated boy. D. H. Lawrence, in "The Rocking-Horse Winner, tells a chilling story of twisted love and destructive greed. Elizabeth Bowen's "The Demon Lover" links both of the World Wars in a few evocative pages. Doris Lessing and Nadine Gordimer deal with the thorny cultural and racial problems of a fading empire.

How did well-crafted poetry capture an unruly world?

A Sestina on "The Troubles" Poets Seamus Heaney, from Northern Ireland, and Derek Walcott, from St. Lucia, both use well-ordered poetry to express the world's disorder. In the sestina "Two Lorries," Heaney writes of the lingering violence in Ireland resulting from an incomplete separation, violence known as "the Troubles." At first glance, a sestina, with its intricate pattern of repeated end words, seems like the wrong form for capturing such a gritty reality. In this poet's hands, however, the repetitions evoke a repeated nightmare of violence that cannot be shaken.

In "Midsummer XXIII," Walcott writes about the violent racism experienced by people of color in "antic England." Like Heaney's, his poem is deeply rooted in the English poetic tradition—it is filled with allusions to earlier work—but also expresses bitter contemporary realities.

What happens to literary traditions in tumultuous times?

Traditions change, especially in times of conflict, but they also endure and connect a living present with a vital past. T. S. Eliot said that any individual talent is best understood in terms of the tradition within which that talent is working. Eliot, who served as an air-raid warden during the Blitz, wrote his poem "Little Gidding" during that dark time. This work links a perilous present to the literary past by invoking Shelley and Milton and the recently deceased Joyce and Yeats, a communion of writers. It invokes them at "the intersection of" a "timeless moment" that somehow contains both past and present—"the timeless moment" of a work of art.

TIMELINE

1989: Germany
Berlin Wall torn down; reunification of East and West Germany follows. ▶

1994: South Africa
Nelson Mandela elected president. ▶

1985

1986: Soviet Union
Nuclear accident occurs in Chernobyl. ▶

1991: Eastern Europe
Soviet Union dissolved.

CONTEMPORARY CONNECTION

George Orwell: More Relevant Than Ever!

Big Brother, Newspeak, and *doublethink* are words that probably sound familiar because you hear them frequently. They were all coined in the 1940s by British author George Orwell for his novel *1984* (published in 1949). After World War II, Orwell was alarmed by a trend toward repressive totalitarian rule. Believing that language is the first weapon dictators use to seize power, he employed his own words as a warning. In the futuristic tyranny portrayed in his novel, words are used to obscure and destroy meaning:

- The official language, *Newspeak,* has been stripped of meaning.

- The tyrannical ruler is deceptively named *Big Brother.*

- Dissenters face torture in the innocently named *Room 101.*

- Citizens are adept at *doublethink,* the ability to accept blatant contradictions, as in the government declaration "War is Peace."

Sixty years later, these terms and others coined by Orwell still ring true. In fact, Orwell's own name is used as an adjective, *Orwellian,* to describe this kind of abuse of language. Pundits, reporters, citizens, and bloggers alike use Orwell's words to criticize Orwellian practices. The year 1984 has come and gone, but Orwell's words live on.

1997: United Kingdom signs Kyoto Protocol against global warming.

2001: United States Hijacked planes crash into the World Trade Center in New York, the Pentagon in Washington, D.C., and a field in rural Pennsylvania. Thousands of lives are lost. ▶

Present

1997: Tony Blair becomes Prime Minister.

◀ **2004:** Tsunami devastates Southeast Asia.

Recent Scholarship

ANITA DESAI

The English Language Takes Root in India

The Portuguese, the Dutch, and the French all came to India as traders. So did the British, but they stayed to govern. To trade and to govern, you need a common language with the people. In the French colony of Pondicherry, people were taught French; in the Portuguese colony of Goa, Portuguese. In the rest of India, a few English people did learn some Indian languages—in order to compile dictionaries and to translate the Bible—but it was largely left to Indians to learn English if they wanted jobs or to do business. So schools were set up across the country to teach the English language and also its literature.

Two Languages and Two Worlds to Occupy

I went to such a school myself, Queen Mary's School for Girls in Old Delhi. I was taught to read and write English before my own language, Hindi, and my first books were of English nursery rhymes and fairy stories. This was curious because they had nothing at all to do with our Indian world—its plants and animals, its festivals and seasons—but they did provide me with a rich, imagined world, in addition to the one we lived in and knew. And at home, with our families and neighbors, we spoke our own language. So there were always two languages and two worlds to occupy.

About the Author

Introducing Anita Desai (b. 1937)
Born to a German mother and an Indian father, Desai spoke German at home in New Delhi, conversed in Hindi with friends, and learned English in school. Her works, written in English, often deal with the conflict between tradition and contemporary life.

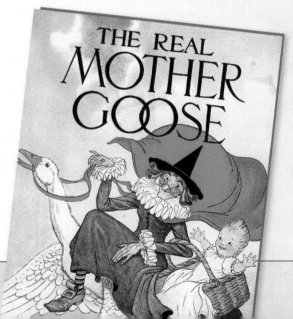

THE REAL MOTHER GOOSE

I went on to read the English classics—Jane Austen and George Eliot, Charles Dickens and Henry James—as well as other literatures translated into English. And all the time, I was writing my own books about my own world—but in this other language, English.

Expressing Indian Thoughts in This Foreign Language, English

There were other Indian writers in those years who were also doing so, while continuing to draw upon the rich Indian-language literatures. Each of us had to experiment to find out how to express Indian thoughts and experiences in this foreign language. Sometimes, we had to combine the languages if, say, we were describing an Indian ceremony or a meal for which there were no English words.

After India won independence in 1947, writing in English was looked on with scorn. The English were gone, so why were we still using their language? We found ourselves having to explain how, after three hundred years, a language could not simply vanish or be thrown aside. It had established roots in India and by now had a tradition—not as old as the literary traditions in the Indian languages but still, a living, growing one that belonged to our own complicated times.

A New Form of the Language: Indian English

Then, in 1980, a book called *Midnight's Children* by Salman Rushdie was published. It was based

Indian women cheer Lord and Lady Mountbatten, who are followed by Pandit Nehru, the Indian prime minister. This ceremony marks the British departure from India, a newly independent nation (June 25, 1948).

on our own themes—the fight for freedom and the birth of two nations, India and Pakistan—and used our own epics, the *Mahabharata* and the *Ramayana* as sources. But it was written in the polyglot language of the Indian streets, of newspapers and shop signs, the cinema and school grounds. It was a bold, noisy, loud, and funny language. Rushdie's work won the Booker Prize, which showed that the English, too, were ready to read this new form of their language—Indian English.

It gave many young writers in India the confidence to use Indian English. So things came together at last, and now there is as lively a literature in English as in Bengali and Tamil, Urdu and Hindi, to name just a few of the Indian languages. If you look into it, I think you will find it as crowded and colorful and bustling as an Indian market or fair.

© Speaking and Listening: Collaboration

Anita Desai describes the language she uses in her work as a new form of English—Indian English. With a group of classmates, develop a **presentation** on the varieties of English in your school or community. These varieties may include versions of English with different degrees of formality, types of English used by different age groups, and types of English influenced by other languages. Develop a *comprehensive flexible search plan,* using *clear research questions* and *strategies* like these:

- Oral histories—in-depth interviews with individuals
- Field studies—observation and notetaking in public places
- Surveys—use of questionnaires to obtain information from numbers of people

Take steps to ensure that your interviews, observations, and questionnaires are *objective* and *free from bias*—that they don't reflect prejudice against any language uses. Finally, summarize your findings in a presentation to your classmates.

Integrate and Evaluate Information

1. Use a chart like the one shown to determine the key ideas expressed in the Essential Question essays on pages 1126–1132. Fill in two ideas related to each Essential Question and note the author or group most closely associated with each concept. One example has been done for you.

Essential Question	Key Concept	Author or Group
Literature and Place	Bombing of England in WWII	Winston Churchill
Literature and Society		
Writer and Tradition		

2. For England, as for much of the world, the twentieth century was a time of dramatic social, political, and technological change. Choose three visual sources from this section, one reflecting each kind of change. Describe the image and explain its impact on England during this period.

3. In "The Second Coming," William Butler Yeats wrote that "Things fall apart; the center cannot hold...." How do these words describe the British Empire over the course of the twentieth century? Explain, citing evidence from the multiple sources presented on pages 1122–1133.

4. **Address a Question:** Anita Desai grew up speaking three different languages—German at home, Hindi with friends, and English at school. Even if you speak only one language, you probably use different versions of that language in various social contexts. Explain how you use different "languages" in your life, using information from "Britspeak, A to Zed" on page 1129 as well as other sources to support your ideas.

Speaking and Listening: Book Talk

Authors from former British colonies who write in English often use language that reflects their countries of origin. With a partner, prepare a **book talk** illustrating this idea. Choose four or five contemporary writers from countries such as India, Jamaica, Nigeria, Pakistan, and South Africa. Prepare a talk in which you discuss connections between the authors' cultural experiences and their writing.

Solve a Research Problem: This assignment requires you to research and synthesize a great deal of complex material. Work with your partner to formulate a research plan that includes the authors' writings, biographical materials, and reviews. Consult both print and electronic sources. For each author you cover, provide the following content:
- Name, with correct pronunciation; date of birth; native country
- Titles of one or two books, with brief summaries
- Clear explanation, using formal English, of the author's style, subject matter, and cultural influences
- Brief recitation from the author's work to show the influence of place

Common Core State Standards

Reading Informational Text
7. Integrate and evaluate multiple sources of information presented in different media or formats as well as in words in order to address a question or solve a problem.

Speaking and Listening
4. Present information, findings, and supporting evidence, conveying a clear and distinct perspective.
6. Adapt speech to a variety of contexts and tasks, demonstrating a command of formal English when indicated or appropriate.

ESSENTIAL QUESTION VOCABULARY

Use these words in your responses:

Literature and Place
generation
materialism
colonial

Literature and Society
propriety
aristocracy
fascism

Writer and Tradition
inclusive
evocative
allusions

Forging Modernism

Connecting to the Essential Question Yeats felt a deep connection to Ireland. As you read, note details in Yeats's poems that evoke a sense of place. Noticing these details will help you think about the Essential Question: **What is the relationship between literature and place?**

Literary Analysis

Yeats created a unique **philosophical system,** or set of ideas about fundamental truths, woven from his own insights and the ideas of many thinkers. To express his philosophy, Yeats used symbols. A **symbol** is an image, character, object, or action with these functions:

- It stands for something beyond itself, such as an abstract idea.
- It gives rise to a number of associations.
- It intensifies feelings and adds complexity to meaning by concentrating these associations together.

The swans in "The Wild Swans at Coole," for example, combine associations of beauty (they are attractive), purity (they are white), freedom (they are wild), and the eternal (they return every year). Over time, Yeats consistently used certain symbols to express his philosophical system, which is described in more detail in the graphic Literature in Context feature on page 1144. As you read, consider how this philosophy shapes the meaning of his poems, particularly "The Second Coming" and "Sailing to Byzantium."

Reading Strategy

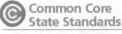

Preparing to Read Complex Texts As a poet, Yeats uses vivid language and rich symbols to make his philosophical arguments, relying on the emotional impact of specific word choices and symbolic images to convey meaning and "convince" his readers. As you read, **analyze Yeats's philosophical assumptions** by analyzing the emotional impact of his word choices and symbolic images. Use a chart like the one shown. To ensure you appreciate his word choice, consult a dictionary as needed to determine the connotations as well as the literal meaning of unfamiliar words.

Vocabulary

clamorous (klam´ ər əs) *adj.* loud and confused; noisy (p. 1142)

conquest (kän´ kwest´) *n.* the winning of the submission or affection of (p. 1143)

anarchy (an´ ər kē) *n.* absence of government; disorder (p. 1145)

conviction (kən vik´ shən) *n.* belief; faith (p. 1145)

paltry (pôl´ trē) *adj.* practically worthless; insignificant (p. 1147)

artifice (ärt´ ə fis) *n.* skill; the product of skill, especially a skillful deception (p. 1148)

Common Core State Standards

Reading Literature
4. Determine the meaning of words and phrases as they are used in the text, including figurative and connotative meanings; analyze the impact of specific word choices on meaning and tone, including words with multiple meanings or language that is particularly fresh, engaging, or beautiful.

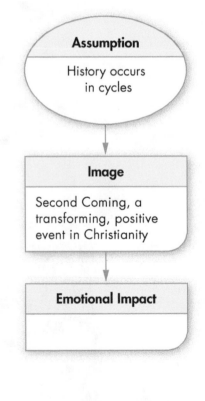

Assumption

History occurs in cycles

Image

Second Coming, a transforming, positive event in Christianity

Emotional Impact

PHLit
Online!
www.PHLitOnline.com

Author of **Poetry of William Butler Yeats**

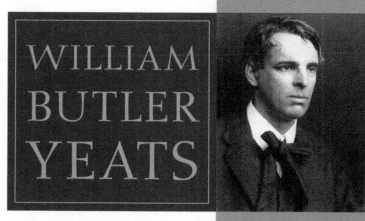

WILLIAM BUTLER YEATS

(1865–1939)

"THINGS FALL APART; THE CENTER CANNOT HOLD..."

The twentieth century was a time of change, marked by unprecedented world wars, revolutions, technological innovations, and a mass media explosion. Even as the winds of change threatened to sweep away old traditions, the Irish poet William Butler Yeats delved deep into his nation's mythological past for insight. Winner of the Nobel Prize for Literature in 1923, Yeats is generally regarded as one of the finest poets of the century. His return to the past helped earn him an abiding place in the future.

Born in Dublin, Ireland, Yeats was educated there and in London. His heart lay to the west, though, in County Sligo, where he spent childhood vacations with his grandparents. In the shadow of Sligo's barren mountains, the young Yeats was immersed in the mythology and legends of Ireland. This experience led to a lifelong enthusiasm for the roots of Irish culture.

Philosophical Influences After three years of studying painting in Dublin, Yeats moved to London to pursue a literary career. He became a friend of the poet Arthur Symons, who awakened his interest in the symbolic, visionary poetry of William Blake and the delicate, musical verse of the French Symbolists. Yeats's early poems show Symbolist influences as well as an affinity with the Pre-Raphaelites, a group of nineteenth-century British painters and writers who turned to medieval art as they strove for simplicity and beauty.

From Poetry to Plays to Poetry As the century turned, Yeats became interested in drama. He joined with his friend Lady Augusta Gregory in founding the Irish National Theatre Society. In 1892, Yeats had written *The Countess Cathleen,* a play that was to become one of his most popular dramatic works. With the acquisition and opening of the Abbey Theatre in Dublin, Yeats turned increasingly to writing plays. When Yeats returned to poetry, it was with a new voice, subtler and more powerful than the one he had used before. The poems in *The Tower* (1928) show Yeats at the height of his abilities. "Sailing to Byzantium" dates from this period of his work.

Ireland's Hero On his seventieth birthday, he was hailed by his nation as the greatest living Irishman. Though Yeats's quarrels with the tastes and politics of middle-class Ireland were often fierce, no one could deny his stature. He continued to write up until a day or two before his death in France. One of his last poems contains his famous epitaph: "Cast a cold eye / On life, on death. / Horseman, pass by!"

WHEN YOU ARE OLD

WILLIAM BUTLER YEATS

When you are old and gray and full of sleep,
And nodding by the fire, take down this book,
And slowly read, and dream of the soft look
Your eyes had once, and of their shadows deep;

5   How many loved your moments of glad grace,
And loved your beauty with love false or true,
But one man loved the pilgrim soul in you,
And loved the sorrows of your changing face;

And bending down beside the glowing bars,
10 Murmur, a little sadly, how Love fled
And paced upon the mountains overhead
And hid his face amid a crowd of stars.

The Lake Isle of Innisfree

WILLIAM BUTLER YEATS

I will arise and go now, and go to Innisfree,
And a small cabin build there, of clay and wattles[1] made:
Nine bean-rows will I have there, a hive for the honeybee,
And live alone in the bee-loud glade.

5   And I shall have some peace there, for peace comes dropping slow,
Dropping from the veils of the morning to where the cricket sings;
There midnight's all a glimmer, and noon a purple glow,
And evening full of the linnet's wings.[2]

I will arise and go now, for always night and day
10   I hear lake water lapping with low sounds by the shore:
While I stand on the roadway, or on the pavements gray,
I hear it in the deep heart's core.

---

1. **wattles** stakes interwoven with twigs or branches.
2. **linnet's wings** wings of a European singing bird.

Reading Strategy
Analyzing Philosophical Assumptions What kind of ideal life does Yeats envision in the first stanza?

Critical Reading ©

© 1. **Key Ideas and Details (a)** What "comes dropping slow" at Innisfree? **(b) Infer:** How does life at Innisfree contrast with the speaker's current life?

© 2. **Integration of Knowledge and Ideas Compare and Contrast:** Do you think that "Innisfree" and "When You Are Old" suggest that writing poetry is a way of compensating for disappointments? Why or why not?

Cite textual evidence to support your responses.

THE WILD SWANS AT COOLE

WILLIAM BUTLER YEATS

▲ **Critical Viewing**
Why might Yeats describe swans such as this one as "mysterious" and "beautiful"? **[Infer]**

Vocabulary
clamorous (klam′ ər əs) *adj.*
loud and confused; noisy

The trees are in their autumn beauty,
The woodland paths are dry,
Under the October twilight the water
Mirrors a still sky;
5   Upon the brimming water among the stones
Are nine-and-fifty swans.

The nineteenth autumn has come upon me
Since I first made my count;
I saw, before I had well finished,
10 All suddenly mount
And scatter wheeling in great broken rings
Upon their clamorous wings.

I have looked upon those brilliant creatures,
And now my heart is sore.
15   All's changed since I, hearing at twilight,
The first time on this shore,
The bell-beat of their wings above my head,
Trod with a lighter tread.

Unwearied still, lover by lover,
20   They paddle in the cold
Companionable streams or climb the air;
Their hearts have not grown old;
Passion or conquest, wander where they will,
Attend upon them still.

25   But now they drift on the still water,
Mysterious, beautiful;
Among what rushes will they build,
By what lake's edge or pool
Delight men's eyes when I awake some day
30   To find they have flown away?

Vocabulary
conquest (kän´ kwest´) *n.*
the winning of the sub-
mission or affection of

Literary Analysis
Symbolism What might
the swans symbolize?

Critical Reading

1. **Key Ideas and Details (a)** Where is the poem set? **(b) Interpret:** How does the time of year reflect the speaker's place in life? **(c) Analyze:** Which details suggest the passing of time?

2. **Key Ideas and Details (a)** When the speaker first counted the swans, what did they suddenly do? **(b) Interpret:** What reflection does the memory of their action prompt in the speaker?

3. **Key Ideas and Details (a) Infer:** What has changed in the speaker since he first heard the swans? **(b) Compare and Contrast:** How does the swans' condition contrast with that of the speaker?

4. **Integration of Knowledge and Ideas (a) Interpret:** The speaker says he will "awake some day / To find they have flown away?" What event might this flight represent for him? **(b) Draw Conclusions:** How does this imagined absence increase the poignancy of the sight of the swans?

5. **Integration of Knowledge and Ideas (a) Interpret:** In what way does the sight of the swans help the speaker measure the passage of time? **(b) Apply:** Compare this experience with another way in which people measure the passage of time.

Cite textual evidence to support your responses.

YEATS'S PHILOSOPHY

Yeats developed a philosophy that united his interest in history, art, personality, and society. His basic insight was that, in all these fields, conflicting forces are at work. In history, for example, as one kind of civilization grows and eventually dies, an opposite kind of civilization is born to take its place. Similarly, human personalities can be defined as opposites: the creative or subjective person versus the active or objective person.

Gyres
To visualize the conflict of opposites, Yeats uses gyres [jierz]. In two dimensions, these look like triangles.

Objectivity

Subjectivity

Circles and Wheels
Because Yeats wanted to imagine completion as well as conflict, he placed a circle around the two gyres. This circle he called The Great Wheel. He labeled it with compass points, qualities, and phases of the moon. He said this wheel is "every completed movement of thought or life."

However, Yeats pictured them as helixes, whirling forms of motion.

Interpenetrating gyres showed how two different forces struggled against one another, moving from left to right, and back again. This movement could describe the development of a personality or the rise and fall of civilizations.

Byzantium: Perfect Place and Time
For Yeats, the perfect era in the cycle was the Byzantine Empire in the early sixth century A.D. It stands for an escape from time's wheel because "in early Byzantium, maybe never before or since . . ., religious, aesthetic and practical life were one." Artists' work spoke directly to the people.

CONNECT TO THE LITERATURE

Does knowing some of Yeats's philosophical ideas help you better understand poems like "The Second Coming" and "Sailing to Byzantium"? Explain.

The Second Coming

WILLIAM BUTLER YEATS

BACKGROUND In 1925, Yeats published *A Vision*, a work that explained the mythology, symbolism, and philosophy that he strove to express in his poetry. Yeats believed that history occurs in two-thousand-year cycles, during which a particular civilization is born, grows, and decays. Each civilization then gives way to a new one that is the direct opposite of it. Yeats believed that the society of the early twentieth century was decaying and would lead to another sort of rebirth, very different from the birth of Christ. These ideas are vividly expressed in the poem "The Second Coming."

Turning and turning in the widening gyre
The falcon cannot hear the falconer;
Things fall apart; the center cannot hold;
Mere anarchy is loosed upon the world,
5   The blood-dimmed tide is loosed, and everywhere
The ceremony of innocence is drowned;
The best lack all conviction, while the worst
Are full of passionate intensity.[1]

---

1. **Mere . . . intensity** refers to the Russian Revolution of 1917.

Vocabulary
anarchy (an′ ər kē) *n.* absence of government; disorder
conviction (kən vik′ shən) *n.* belief; faith

Surely some revelation is at hand;
10 Surely the Second Coming is at hand.
The Second Coming! Hardly are those words out
When a vast image out of *Spiritus Mundi*[2]
Troubles my sight: somewhere in sands of the desert
A shape with lion body and the head of a man,[3]
15 A gaze blank and pitiless as the sun,
Is moving its slow thighs, while all about it
Reel shadows of the indignant desert birds.
The darkness drops again; but now I know
That twenty centuries[4] of stony sleep
20 Were vexed to nightmare by a rocking cradle,[5]
And what rough beast, its hour come round at last,
Slouches towards Bethlehem to be born?

---

2. *Spiritus Mundi* (spir´ i təs mōōn´ dē) Universal Spirit or Soul, in which the
   memories of the entire human race are forever preserved.
3. **A . . . man** the Sphinx, a monster in Greek mythology that posed a riddle to
   passing travelers and destroyed those who could not answer it. The answer
   to the riddle was "man."
4. **twenty centuries** historical cycle preceding the birth of Christ.
5. **rocking cradle** cradle of Jesus Christ.

Literary Analysis
Philosophical System
What elements of Yeats's philosophy does "The Second Coming" contain?

Critical Reading

Cite textual evidence to support your responses.

1. **Key Ideas and Details** (a) In the first two lines of the poem, why does the falcon not return to the falconer, as it ordinarily would? (b) **Analyze:** Why is the image of the falcon an effective introduction to Yeats's ideas about order and innocence?

2. **Key Ideas and Details** (a) At the beginning of the second stanza, what does the speaker believe is at hand? (b) **Interpret:** What era of history might the vision in lines 11–17 represent? Explain. (c) **Interpret:** In what sense did a past birth in Bethlehem bring this era to an end?

3. **Key Ideas and Details** (a) **Analyze:** What birth does the speaker predict will end the modern era? (b) **Draw Conclusions:** How does the traditional idea of the Second Coming differ from what the speaker is envisioning?

4. **Integration of Knowledge and Ideas** Yeats draws on his own theories of history for the theme and imagery of this poem. Why might the poem be appreciated even by readers who do not share his beliefs?

5. **Integration of Knowledge and Ideas** In your opinion, do any contemporary events bear out Yeats's vision of history? Explain.

SAILING TO BYZANTIUM

William Butler Yeats

I

That is no country for old men. The young
In one another's arms, birds in the trees
—Those dying generations—at their song,
The salmon-falls, the mackerel-crowded seas,
5   Fish, flesh, or fowl, commend all summer long
Whatever is begotten, born, and dies.
Caught in that sensual music all neglect
Monuments of unaging intellect.

II

An aged man is but a paltry thing,
10   A tattered coat upon a stick, unless
Soul clap its hands and sing, and louder sing
For every tatter in its mortal dress,
Nor is there singing school but studying
Monuments of its own magnificence;
15   And therefore I have sailed the seas and come
To the holy city of Byzantium.[1]

III

O sages standing in God's holy fire
As in the gold mosaic of a wall,[2]

Vocabulary
paltry (pôl′ trē) *adj.*
practically worthless;
insignificant

Reading Check

What does the speaker's age
motivate him to do?

---

1. **Byzantium** (bi zan′ shē əm) ancient capital of the Eastern Roman (or Byzantine) Empire
and the seat of the Greek Orthodox Church; today, Istanbul, Turkey. For Yeats, Byzantium
symbolized the world of art as opposed to the world of time and nature.
2. **sages . . . wall** wise men portrayed in mosaic on the walls of Byzantine churches.

                    Come from the holy fire, perne in a gyre,[3]
20   And be the singing-masters of my soul.
                    Consume my heart away; sick with desire
                    And fastened to a dying animal
                    It knows not what it is; and gather me
                    Into the artifice of eternity.

                    IV
25   Once out of nature I shall never take
                    My bodily form from any natural thing,
                    But such a form as Grecian goldsmiths make
                    Of hammered gold and gold enameling
                    To keep a drowsy Emperor awake;
30   Or set upon a golden bough to sing[4]
                    To lords and ladies of Byzantium
                    Of what is past, or passing, or to come.

Vocabulary
artifice (ärt′ ə fis) *n.* skill;
the product of skill,
especially a skillful deception

Reading Strategy
**Analyzing Philosophical
Assumptions** What does
the last stanza suggest about
the artist's relationship to
nature and time?

3. **perne . . . gyre** spin in a spiraling motion.
4. **To . . . sing** Yeats wrote, "I have read somewhere that in the Emperor's palace at Byzantium was a tree made of gold and silver, and artificial birds that sang."

Critical Reading

Cite textual evidence to support your responses.

1. Key Ideas and Details (a) What do the people and things of the country referred to in the first stanza "commend"? What do they "neglect"? **(b) Interpret:** What "country" is Yeats describing in the first stanza?

2. Key Ideas and Details (a) What is an "aged man," according to the second stanza? **(b) Interpret:** Why might the aged not belong to the "country" of the first stanza?

3. Key Ideas and Details (a) Interpret: In the third stanza, what does the speaker ask the sages to change in him? **(b) Draw Conclusions:** What does this request reveal about the speaker's faith in artistic production?

4. Integration of Knowledge and Ideas Make a Judgment: In your view, which is a "dream"—Byzantium or the world of what "is begotten, born, and dies"?

5. Integration of Knowledge and Ideas How is Yeats's poetry affected by both real and imagined places? Use at least three of these Essential Question words in your response: *ideal, locate, occur, affect, significance, constant.* *[Connecting to the Essential Question: What is the relationship between literature and place?]*

After You Read | *Poetry of William Butler Yeats*

Literary Analysis

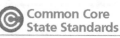
Common Core State Standards

Writing
1. Write arguments to support claims in an analysis of substantive topics or texts, using valid reasoning and relevant and sufficient evidence. *(p. 1150)*

5. Develop and strengthen writing as needed by planning, revising, editing, rewriting, or trying a new approach, focusing on addressing what is most significant for a specific purpose and audience. *(p. 1150)*

Language
4.d. Verify the preliminary determination of the meaning of a word or phrase. *(p. 1150)*

1. **Key Ideas and Details (a)** In "When You Are Old," Yeats refers to "Love" as a person. What ideas are traditionally associated with that character? **(b)** How does the behavior of Love in the poem compare to that traditional image?

2. **Craft and Structure (a)** What associations does the speaker in "The Lake Isle of Innisfree" build around the **symbol** of Innisfree? **(b)** Explain two things Innisfree might symbolize.

3. **Key Ideas and Details** Explain what the dry "woodland paths," "October twilight," and the "still sky" symbolize in "The Wild Swans at Coole."

4. **Key Ideas and Details** "The Second Coming" is a poem strongly influenced by Yeats's **philosophical system. (a)** In the poem, what events does Yeats connect to the end of one civilization and the beginning of another? **(b)** How does humanity respond to these times of crisis?

5. **Craft and Structure** Use a chart like the one below to compare the birds in the first and second stanzas of "The Second Coming." How do these symbols contribute to the meaning of the poem?

Symbol	Associations	Effect on Meaning
Falcon		

6. **Craft and Structure (a)** In "Sailing to Byzantium," what do the monuments in lines 8 and 14 symbolize? **(b)** Find two examples in this poem of Yeats's use of Byzantine art to symbolize perfection.

7. **Integration of Knowledge and Ideas** Based on Yeats's poems, do you think symbols based on personal associations, such as Innisfree, are more compelling than traditional symbols such as the Sphinx?

Reading Strategy

8. **(a)** What emotions does the speaker in "The Lake Isle of Innisfree" feel? **(b)** What does the speaker in "The Wild Swans at Coole" feel? **(c)** Explain how Yeats's word choice helps convey these feelings.

9. **Analyze Yeats's philosophical system** by assessing the emotional impact of his symbols. **(a)** Compare the emotional effect and meaning of the swans in "The Wild Swans at Coole" and the birds in "Sailing to Byzantium." **(b)** Based on those meanings, how do you think Yeats's attitude toward nature changed during his life?

10. How does Yeats use the symbol of the "gyre" in "The Second Coming" and "Sailing to Byzantium"?

11. Compare Yeats's idea of historical cycles with the scientific view of time.

Integrated Language Skills

© Vocabulary Acquisition and Use

Word Analysis: Words with the Greek Root -archy-

In "The Second Coming," Yeats uses the word *anarchy*. The word combines the prefix *an-*, meaning "not," and the Greek root *-archy*, which means "ruler." *Anarchy*, then, is the condition of having no ruler, or government. Use context to determine the meanings of the italicized words. Explain those meanings in a sentence. You may consult a dictionary to confirm the meanings.

1. In a *matriarchy*, mothers own the land and pass it on to their daughters.
2. The oldest surviving child of the king gains the throne in a *monarchy*.
3. In the army's *hierarchy*, each member obeys the orders of those with higher rank.
4. The Council of Ten was a powerful *oligarchy* that led a country of millions.
5. The family was a *patriarchy*, and the father's word had to be followed.

Vocabulary: Synonyms

A synonym is a word that has a meaning similar to that of another word. Replace each italicized word below with a synonym from the vocabulary list on page 1138. Use each vocabulary word only once. Then write two original sentences, each using one of the vocabulary words.

1. His *trickery* managed to convince the gullible victim.
2. *Chaos* resulted when the government leaders fled.
3. She had the power gained from certainty in her *beliefs*.
4. The *insignificant* sum was hardly sufficient recompense for the damage done.
5. With her final victory in the chess tournament, her *triumph* was complete.
6. The *noisy* crowd shouted the speaker down.

Writing

© **Argumentative Text** Critic Richard Ellmann writes that Yeats's poetry is based on the opposition between "the world of change" and a world of "changelessness." Write a **response** in which you find evidence of this opposition in Yeats's poems.

Prewriting Note uses of imagery, language, or ideas that represent change or changelessness. Review your examples to see if they mainly support or refute Ellmann's claim, and decide whether you agree or disagree with his view.

Drafting Begin your draft by summarizing Ellmann's position and stating your response to it. Support your generalizations with quotations from Yeats's writing. Introduce each quotation and explain how it supports the point you are making.

Revising Review your draft, highlighting generalizations and looking for supporting details. Where details are lacking, look back at Yeats's poems to find supporting details. Be sure that the titles of Yeats's poems and the quotations you use from them are accurate.

Model: Revising References to Be Accurate

In "The Wild Swans at Coole," Yeats laments that, for him

All's

at least, "All is changed."

Review of quotations ensures they are accurate.

Conventions and Style: Sentence Fragments and Run-ons

In most writing, except for dialogue in fiction, it is important to avoid sentence fragments and run-on sentences. A **sentence fragment** is an incomplete sentence punctuated as a sentence. It may be missing a subject, a verb, or both, and it fails to express a complete thought. Fragments are often phrases or subordinate clauses.

Fragment (lacking a verb): The lover old and gray sitting by the fire.

Add a verb: The lover grew old and gray sitting by the fire.

A **run-on sentence** is two or more sentences punctuated as one. **Fused sentences** and **comma splices** are two types of run-ons:

Fused sentence: The trees are beautiful in the fall the still water reflects the sky.

Corrected by rewriting: The trees are beautiful in the fall when the still water reflects the sky.

Comma splice: Many love a woman's beauty, few will love the inner person.

Corrected by adding a conjunction: Many love a woman's beauty, but few will love the inner person.

Punctuation Tip If the two parts of a run-on sentence are related, you can connect them with a semicolon.

Practice: Identify each of the following items as a fragment, a run-on, or a complete sentence. If an item is a fragment or a run-on, rewrite it.

1. The sound of water remains in the memory it gives calm in a cold, gray world.
2. Swans do not seem to weary from the cares of the world as humans do.
3. The swans swim across the water. Or take off and fly through the air.
4. On the still water, swans mysterious and lovely.
5. In fall, swans migrate. In noisy flight.
6. Things that live and breathe must one day die it is the way of the world.
7. When there is no order, things collapse disorder rules the world.
8. People grow old and worthless, monuments are timeless.
9. Art that captures the sound of birds hammered in gold. Lives on through time.
10. Yeats believed in historical cycles of twenty centuries.

© Writing and Speaking Conventions

A. **Writing** Find three fragments and two run-ons in the paragraph below. Rewrite the paragraph so that each sentence is complete.

A small cabin at Innisfree. The cabin is built of clay and sticks, the cabin provides shelter and peace. A place for a garden and hive for the bees. In the morning the cricket sings in the evening songbirds fill the air with music. Outside the water against the shore.

Example: A small cabin at Innisfree.

Rewritten: There's a small cabin at Innisfree.

B. **Speaking** Write and present to the class a brief explanation of whether you believe Yeats's predictions are proving true or false in the twenty-first century. Be sure to check your writing for fragments and run-ons.

PH WRITING COACH

Further instruction and practice are available in *Prentice Hall Writing Coach.*

Literary History: T. S. Eliot's World

Modernists like T. S. Eliot responded to an increasingly complex and fragmented world with art that was also complex, dark, and multifaceted.

Modernism and Beyond

At the beginning of the twentieth century, the world woke up and discovered that it had changed. Electricity, engines, telephones, radios—the globe crackled with new energy. Airplanes, machine guns, and chemical warfare enabled human beings to destroy each other with horrendous efficiency. The First World War (1914–1918) claimed twenty million lives. Disillusionment with politics and society was common.

In this climate of change and uncertainty, artists broke with the past and began to pursue new ideals and visions. They began to see themselves not just as preservers of culture but as creators of culture; they did not simply follow traditions, they created new ones. These dramatic trends in the arts in the early twentieth century are collectively known as Modernism (1890–1945).

Images of Modernism When you take a photograph, you record and preserve what is happening now. Modernism could be thought of as a complex response to what photographs imply. Some Modernists, such as the American poet Ezra Pound (1885–1972) and the British poet T. S. Eliot (1888–1965), wrote poetry as if they were taking snapshots of the world and then cutting and pasting them into collages. Eliot celebrated what he called objectivity in poetry. He relied on images, well chosen and artfully rendered, to encapsulate a feeling or perspective.

On the other hand, the British Modernist novelist Virginia Woolf (1882–1941) perfected techniques for conveying an individual's moment-by-moment experience. For Woolf, the mind is like a camera filming continuously. Her writing records what the moment looks like to an individual. A photograph shows us exactly what the world looks like; Woolf suggests that what the world looks like depends on who is looking.

Visual Arts Photography makes a good analogy for Modernist literary developments. It had a clear impact on painting. Photography now had the job of recording literal appearances, so artists were freed from the necessity of directly imitating the look of things. The revolutionary French painter Paul Cézanne (1839–1906) began to emphasize the canvas as a two-dimensional arrangement of form and color. His work led to the in-novations of Modernists such as Pablo Picasso (1881–1973), whose

Les Desmoiselles d'Avignon is the first Cubist painting—a picture in which multiple perspectives on the subject are depicted simultaneously.

Past, Present, and Future Time is a central theme of Modernism. To a photographer, every moment in time is equal to every other, another present to be captured. Yet Eliot was deeply preoccupied with the thought that the past and present are quite unequal. In a poem like "Journey of the Magi" (p. 1158), Eliot portrays the present as a time of despair, an emptiness left behind when the past has disappeared.

Making the New At the same time that Eliot seemed to mourn the past, Modernism also turned toward the future. Modernist fiction writers broke with traditional narrative methods. Describing how characters saw their lives became more important than constructing a traditional plot, and endings were sometimes unresolved. Modernist poets, too, favored experimentation over traditional forms and rhyme schemes. Their poems draw images from a variety of sources, such as history, everyday life, and other texts and cultures.

Beyond Modernism The Modernist literary movement climaxed in 1922, when both James Joyce's *Ulysses* and T. S. Eliot's *The Waste Land* were published. In ensuing decades, the arts took another turn in the developments known as Postmodernism, a movement that replaced the hopes Modernism placed on innovative artistic breakthroughs with a sometimes cynical questioning of the nature of art and perception. The Modernist legacy lives on, though, in the continuing drive for the new.

Speaking and Listening: Discussion

Comprehension and Collaboration Photography was invented in the nineteenth century and evolved aesthetically and technologically through the twentieth century. Today, photography is both an art form and a technology accessible to nearly everyone. With a group, discuss photography's changing role in art and culture. Use the list of questions provided to guide your discussion.

Prepare by researching photography as both popular hobby and art form. Assign group members to specific research tasks, using these questions to focus the work:

- How has digital technology changed photography?
- With the technology to retouch photographs, have we strayed completely from the Modernist idea that an image captures a moment forever?
- If anyone can take a picture, what makes photography an art form?

As a group, assign roles for the discussion, such as moderator and note-taker. Agree upon a set of rules to ensure all members participate fully. Choose a point person to share your conclusions with the class.

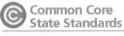

Before You Read

Preludes • Journey of the Magi • The Hollow Men

Connecting to the Essential Question T. S. Eliot broke dramatically with traditional poetry. As you read, notice details in Eliot's poems that show differences from traditional poetic themes, meter, or language. Doing so will help you think about the Essential Question: **What is the relationship of the writer to tradition?**

Literary Analysis

Modernism was an early-twentieth-century movement in the arts. The movement responded to the fragmented modern world created by industrialization, rapid transportation and communication, and a feeling of alienation caused by mass society and the growth of cities. Eliot led the movement for **Modernism in poetry,** which had several features:

- A new objectivity or impersonality in poetry, in which a work is built from images and allusions rather than from direct statements of thoughts and feelings
- A rejection of realistic depictions of life in favor of the use of images for artistic effect
- Critical attention to social conditions and the spiritual troubles of modern life, often accompanied by a sense of displacement and despair

As you read, look for details that reflect Modernism in Eliot's poems.

Reading Strategy

Preparing to Read Complex Texts Modernist writers found their society bleak and lifeless. They saw crowded cities as places of isolation and loneliness. They believed that the new emphasis on material goods and technology left people adrift spiritually, while factory work dehumanized them. Modernist works do not state these ideas directly. Instead, their emphasis on the oblique suggested meanings requiring readers to draw inferences, or interpret ideas, from images and details. As you read, use a chart like the one shown to **relate Eliot's literary works to the historical period** by identifying images that suggest the Modernist worldview.

Vocabulary

galled (gôld) *adj.* injured or made sore by rubbing or chafing (p. 1158)

refractory (ri frak´ tər ē) *adj.* hard to manage; stubborn (p. 1158)

dispensation (dis´ pən sā´ shən) *n.* religious system or belief (p. 1159)

supplication (sup´ lə kā´ shən) *n.* act of praying or pleading (p. 1164)

tumid (too´ mid) *adj.* swollen (p. 1165)

Common Core State Standards

Reading Literature
1. Cite strong and thorough textual evidence to support analysis of what the text says explicitly as well as inferences drawn from the text.

Speaking and Listening
1.a. Come to discussions prepared, having read and researched material under study.
1.b. Work with peers to promote civil, democratic discussions and decision making, set clear goals and deadlines, and establish individual roles as needed. *(p. 1162)*

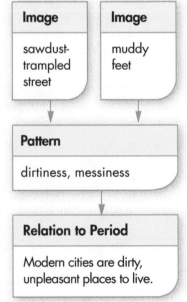

Image	Image
sawdust-trampled street	muddy feet

Pattern

dirtiness, messiness

Relation to Period

Modern cities are dirty, unpleasant places to live.

www.PHLitOnline.com

T. S. ELIOT

(1888–1965)

Author of "Preludes" • "Journey of the Magi" • "The Hollow Men"

T. S. Eliot was the most famous English poet of his time. He was also the most influential. His distinctive style and novel ideas affected not only poets, but also critics, fiction writers, playwrights, and even philosophers. From the 1920s on, he was a leader of the artistic movement called Modernism. Eliot and fellow Modernist Ezra Pound transformed English-language poetry, grounding their work in the power of images.

Crossing the Atlantic Born Thomas Stearns Eliot in St. Louis, Missouri, he was educated at Harvard University. He went on to study at Oxford University in England and at the Sorbonne in Paris. The outbreak of World War I in 1914 found Eliot in England, where he settled and eventually became a citizen.

In 1915, Eliot married the sensitive, intelligent, and witty Vivien Haigh-Wood. While writing poetry and critical reviews, Eliot taught school, worked for the banking firm of Lloyd's, and eventually took a position with a publishing company.

Early Work Because of its unconventional style, Eliot's earliest work was greeted with less than universal acclaim, although the American poet Ezra Pound was a vocal supporter from the beginning. Pound saw that Eliot spoke in an authentic new voice and offered an original, if bleak, vision. From *Prufrock and Other Observations* (1917) through *The Waste Land* (1922) and "The Hollow Men" (1925), Eliot portrayed the modern world as one of fragmented experiences and despair. Eliot may have been responding to World War I, an event that damaged the faith of many. At the same time, the war may have prompted readers to catch up with Eliot, who had written works such as "Preludes" and "The Love Song of J. Alfred Prufrock" before the war.

A Spiritual Rebirth Eventually, Eliot found an answer to despair in religion. In 1927, he joined the Church of England and became a devout Anglican. His new faith shaped the writing of "Journey of the Magi" (1927), *Ash Wednesday* (1930), and the *Four Quartets* (1935–1943).

As a literary critic, Eliot had a profound influence on his contemporaries. His re-evaluations of past poetry shaped the tastes of a generation. In 1948, Eliot received the Nobel Prize for Literature.

" WE SHALL NOT CEASE FROM EXPLORATION."

Preludes

T. S. ELIOT

I

The winter evening settles down
With smell of steaks[1] in passageways.
Six o'clock.
The burnt-out ends of smoky days.
5 And now a gusty shower wraps
The grimy scraps
Of withered leaves about your feet
And newspapers from vacant lots;
The showers beat
10 On broken blinds and chimney-pots,
And at the corner of the street
A lonely cab-horse steams and stamps.
And then the lighting of the lamps.

II

The morning comes to consciousness
15 Of faint stale smells of beer
From the sawdust-trampled street
With all its muddy feet that press
To early coffee-stands.
With the other masquerades
20 That time resumes,
One thinks of all the hands
That are raising dingy shades
In a thousand furnished rooms.

III

You tossed a blanket from the bed,
25 You lay upon your back, and waited;
You dozed, and watched the night revealing
The thousand sordid images
Of which your soul was constituted;

Literary Analysis
Modernism in Poetry
What fragmented images of city life appear in this stanza?

---

1. steaks In 1910, when this poem was composed, steaks were inexpensive and were commonly eaten by members of the lower class.

They flickered against the ceiling.
30 And when all the world came back
And the light crept up between the shutters
And you heard the sparrows in the gutters,
You had such a vision of the street
As the street hardly understands;
35 Sitting along the bed's edge, where
You curled the papers from your hair,
Or clasped the yellow soles of feet
In the palms of both soiled hands.

IV

His soul stretched tight across the skies
40 That fade behind a city block,
Or trampled by insistent feet
At four and five and six o'clock;
And short square fingers stuffing pipes,
And evening newspapers, and eyes
45 Assured of certain certainties,
The conscience of a blackened street
Impatient to assume the world.

    I am moved by fancies that are curled
Around these images, and cling:
50 The notion of some infinitely gentle
Infinitely suffering thing.

    Wipe your hand across your mouth, and laugh;
The worlds revolve like ancient women
Gathering fuel in vacant lots.

Reading Strategy
Relating Poetry to Historical Period
What view of modern life do the last lines in this stanza convey?

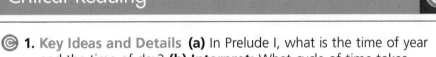

Critical Reading

1. **Key Ideas and Details (a)** In Prelude I, what is the time of year and the time of day? **(b) Interpret:** What cycle of time takes place from Prelude I to Prelude IV? **(c) Support:** What effect does the poet achieve by representing this complete cycle?

2. **Key Ideas and Details (a) Draw Conclusions:** What is the character of modern life as Eliot depicts it? **(b) Compare and Contrast:** Contrast this character with "The notion of some infinitely gentle / Infinitely suffering thing" (lines 50–51). **(c) Speculate:** Based on this contrast, what do you think the "thing" might be?

3. **Integration of Knowledge and Ideas** Think of a sight in a modern city that conveys joy. How might Eliot have reacted to that image?

Cite textual evidence to support your responses.

Preludes 1157

JOURNEY
OF THE MAGI

T. S. ELIOT

BACKGROUND "Journey of the Magi" is a dramatic monologue spoken by one of the wise men ("magi") who, according to the Bible, visited the infant Jesus. In the poem, the speaker uses modern conversational language to describe events, making vividly present the spiritual agony of a man who lived long ago.

"A cold coming we had of it,
Just the worst time of the year
For a journey, and such a long journey:
The ways deep and the weather sharp,
5   The very dead of winter."[1]
And the camels galled, sore-footed, refractory,
Lying down in the melting snow.
There were times we regretted
The summer palaces on slopes, the terraces,
10   And the silken girls bringing sherbet.
Then the camel men cursing and grumbling
And running away, and wanting their liquor and women,
And the night-fires going out, and the lack of shelters,
And the cities hostile and the towns unfriendly
15   And the villages dirty and charging high prices:
A hard time we had of it.

---

1. **"A . . . winter"** Adapted from a part of a sermon delivered by 17th-century Bishop Lancelot Andrewes: "A cold coming they had of it at this time of year, just the worst time of the year to take a journey, and specially a long journey in. The ways deep, the weather sharp, the days short, the sun farthest off . . . the very dead of winter."

At the end we preferred to travel all night,
Sleeping in snatches,
With the voices singing in our ears, saying
20 That this was all folly.

Then at dawn we came down to a temperate valley,
Wet, below the snow line, smelling of vegetation;
With a running stream and a water-mill beating the darkness,
And three trees on the low sky,
25 And an old white horse galloped away in the meadow.
Then we came to a tavern with vine-leaves over the lintel,
Six hands at an open door dicing for pieces of silver,
And feet kicking the empty wine-skins.
But there was no information, and so we continued
30 And arrived at evening, not a moment too soon
Finding the place; it was (you may say) satisfactory.

All this was a long time ago, I remember,
And I would do it again, but set down
This set down
35 This: were we led all that way for
Birth or Death? There was a Birth, certainly,
We had evidence and no doubt. I had seen birth and death,
But had thought they were different; this Birth was
Hard and bitter agony for us, like Death, our death.
40 We returned to our places, these Kingdoms,
But no longer at ease here, in the old dispensation,
With an alien people clutching their gods.
I should be glad of another death.

Vocabulary
dispensation (dis´ pən sā´
shən) *n.* religious system
or belief

Critical Reading

© 1. **Key Ideas and Details (a)** What event has the speaker in
"Journey of the Magi" gone to witness? **(b) Compare and
Contrast:** How does the description of the journey compare
to the description of the event? **(c) Interpret:** Why might the
speaker say so little about one and so much about the other?

Cite textual
evidence to
support your
responses.

© 2. **Key Ideas and Details** How has the event changed the
speaker's relation to his own people?

© 3. **Integration of Knowledge and Ideas (a) Compare and
Contrast:** In what way is Eliot's choice of details similar in the
first stanzas of "Preludes" and "Journey of the Magi"? **(b) Draw
Conclusions:** What do you think Eliot was trying to achieve in
each case?

Literary History: Eliot's "The Hollow Men"

"Eliot's allusions create a distinctive, dreamlike world for a reader to explore."

How "The Hollow Men" Was Written

In 1921, T. S. Eliot began a long poem called *The Waste Land*. He later used sections that had been edited out of *The Waste Land* as the basis for "The Hollow Men." He often worked this way, building a poem from pieces that had been written independently and using discarded fragments of one poem to create the next. He explained this process of working in an interview with Donald Hall (*The Paris Review*, No. 21):

Interviewer: Are any of your minor poems actually sections cut out of longer works? There are two that sound like "The Hollow Men."

Eliot: Oh, those were the preliminary sketches. Those things were earlier. Others I published in periodicals but not in my collected poems . . .

Interviewer: You seem often to have written poems in sections. Did they begin as separate poems? I am thinking of "Ash Wednesday," in particular.

Eliot: Yes, like "The Hollow Men," it originated out of separate poems. As I recall, one or two early drafts of parts of *Ash Wednesday* appeared in *Commerce* [magazine] and elsewhere. Then gradually I came to see it as a sequence. That's one way in which my mind does seem to have worked throughout the years poetically—doing things separately and then seeing the possibility of fusing them together, altering them, and making a kind of whole of them.

The Theme of "The Hollow Men"

It makes sense to assume that "The Hollow Men" and *The Waste Land* are thematically related. *The Waste Land*, as its title suggests, deals with a sense of emotional and spiritual barrenness after the destruction wrought by World War I. "The Hollow Men," published in 1925, also deals with a barren and empty (hollow) existence. It resembles *The Waste Land* in its use of literary allusions to convey this theme of barrenness and to compare the present with other historical eras.

Using Allusions to Interpret the Poem

Critics have identified four key allusions in the poem:

Joseph Conrad's "Heart of Darkness" Kurtz, referred to in a line introducing the poem, is a mysterious character in Conrad's "Heart of Darkness." He travels to the Belgian Congo on a mission to uplift and educate the Congolese people. However, he develops his own little kingdom in which he exercises absolute power over the people he intended to save. It is only when he is dying that he sees the "horror" of what he has done and how he has been, in Conrad's words, a "hollow sham," or fake. His tragic downfall exposes the hollowness of his noble ideals and of the whole colonial enterprise. That enterprise is supported by a host of administrators and clerks who are most like the speakers in Eliot's poem, a chorus of paralyzed nonentities: "We are the hollow men. . . ." Eliot may also be suggesting that this chorus includes his readers.

The Gunpowder Plot The hollow men are also like the effigies of Guy Fawkes, burned to commemorate the uncovering of the Gunpowder Plot of 1605. Fawkes himself was tortured until he revealed the names of his co-conspirators who plotted a powerful explosion that would destroy the king of England and Parliament. As Eliot writes at the end of the poem, "This is the way the world ends / Not with a bang but a whimper." Like Fawkes, so the speakers of Eliot's poem are as helpless and ineffective as straw dummies: "Leaning together / Headpiece filled with straw. Alas!"

Shakespeare's *Julius Caesar* This play deals with another conspiracy to betray a leader. Brutus, a high-minded Roman, is lured by flattery into a plot to assassinate the Roman ruler Julius Caesar. Section V of "The Hollow Men" quotes lines from Shakespeare's play in which Brutus experiences the nightmarelike emptiness of the time before the deed. Like Kurtz in Conrad's story, Brutus is a tragic figure, a self-deluded man who commits murder in the name of high ideals. In this sense, he too is a form of hollow man.

Dante's *Divine Comedy* Dante's medieval poems describe the three realms of the afterlife according to Roman Catholic belief: *Inferno, Purgatorio,* and *Paradiso*—hell, purgatory, and heaven. The speakers in Eliot's poem are being punished for their spiritual emptiness in a kind of inferno: a "dead land" (line 39); a "cactus land" (line 40); a "valley of dying stars" (line 54). It does not appear that these speakers will gain salvation, but Eliot uses images drawn from Dante's description of paradise to suggest the existence of higher realms: " . . . the perpetual star / Multifoliate rose . . .". (lines 63–64). In terms of Dante's work, "The Hollow Men" is like an inferno (a realm of punishment) that is almost without the promise of a purgatory or a paradise.

Eliot's Theory of Tradition

Eliot's allusions create a distinctive, dreamlike world for a reader to explore. They also reflect his theory of poetry. In an essay, Eliot compares the poet to a catalyst in a chemical reaction. A catalyst adds nothing of itself, but without it, the reaction will not take place. The poet's mind is the catalyst that causes images and feelings to combine in a poem, but the poem does not necessarily reflect the poet's own life. For Eliot, a tradition of past literature was a key source of ingredients for the reaction. Eliot's allusions reflect both of these values: impersonality and tradition.

Speaking and Listening: Discussion

© **Comprehension and Collaboration** An **allusion** is a device used by many creative artists, not just poets. Filmmakers and composers sometimes incorporate cinematic or musical allusions into their work to enrich the audience's experience. As "The Hollow Men" demonstrates, allusions add depth to a work but can also make it more difficult to understand.

With a group, discuss your thoughts about films and musical works that feature allusions. Set a twenty-minute time limit for the discussion, and use these questions to help you set clear goals:

- Identify a movie or song that alludes to or quotes from another source. What is that source, and what point does the artist make through the allusion?

- In what way does understanding allusions enhance your enjoyment of a work?

- Is it always necessary to fully understand an allusion? Explain.

Encourage each group member to participate. Remind participants to be courteous as they interact. Appoint one person to take notes on the ideas and issues presented. After the discussion, choose a point person to share your thoughts with the class.

THE HOLLOW MEN

T. S. ELIOT

BACKGROUND As in "Journey of the Magi," Eliot uses allusions at the beginning of "The Hollow Men" to help him contrast the past with the present. For example, "A penny for the Old Guy" is a traditional cry of children on Guy Fawkes Day. Fawkes was executed for attempting to blow up the king and Parliament on November 5, 1605. He is one of the "lost / Violent souls" of the past who contrast with the "hollow men" of today.

Mistah Kurtz[1]—he dead.

A penny for the Old Guy[2]

I

We are the hollow men
We are the stuffed men
Leaning together
Headpiece filled with straw. Alas!
5   Our dried voices, when
We whisper together
Are quiet and meaningless
As wind in dry grass

Le Maitre d'ecole. 1955, Rene Magritte, Photothèque R. Magritte-ADAGP / Art Resource, NY, © 1998 C. Herscovici, Brussels / Artists Rights Society (ARS), New York.

Reading Check

How does the speaker characterize the sounds made by the hollow men?

---

1. **Mistah Kurtz** character in Joseph Conrad's "Heart of Darkness" who hopes to improve the lives of native Africans, but who finds instead that he is corrupted by his power over them.
2. **A . . . Guy** traditional cry used by children on Guy Fawkes Day (November 5), celebrating the execution of a famous English traitor of the same name. The "Old Guy" refers to stuffed dummies representing Fawkes.

Or rats' feet over broken glass
10 In our dry cellar

Shape without form, shade without color,
Paralyzed force, gesture without motion;
Those who have crossed
With direct eyes, to death's other Kingdom[3]
15 Remember us—if at all—not as lost
Violent souls, but only
As the hollow men
The stuffed men.

II

Eyes I dare not meet in dreams
20 In death's dream kingdom
These do not appear:
There, the eyes are
Sunlight on a broken column
There, is a tree swinging
25 And voices are
In the wind's singing
More distant and more solemn
Than a fading star.
Let me be no nearer
30 In death's dream kingdom
Let me also wear
Such deliberate disguises
Rat's coat, crowskin, crossed staves
In a field[4]
35 Behaving as the wind behaves
No nearer—

Not that final meeting
In the twilight kingdom

III

This is the dead land
40 This is cactus land
Here the stone images
Are raised, here they receive
The supplication of a dead man's hand
Under the twinkle of a fading star.

3. **Those . . . kingdom** allusion to Dante's *Paradiso*, in which those "with direct eyes" are blessed by God in heaven.
4. **crossed . . . field** scarecrows.

SHAPE
WITHOUT FORM,
SHADE
WITHOUT COLOR

45 Is it like this
    In death's other kingdom
    Waking alone
    At the hour when we are
    Trembling with tenderness
50 Lips that would kiss
    Form prayers to broken stone.

                    IV

    The eyes are not here
    There are no eyes here
    In this valley of dying stars
55 In this hollow valley
    This broken jaw of our lost kingdoms

    In this last of meeting places
    We grope together
    And avoid speech
60 Gathered on this beach of the tumid river[5]

    Sightless, unless
    The eyes reappear
    As the perpetual star[6]
    Multifoliate rose[7]
65 Of death's twilight kingdom
    The hope only
    Of empty men.

                    V

    Here we go round the prickly pear
    Prickly pear prickly pear
70 *Here we go round the prickly pear*
    At five o'clock in the morning.[8]

    Between the idea
    And the reality
    Between the motion
75 And the act[9]
    Falls the Shadow

---

5. **river** from Dante's *Inferno*, the river Acheron, which the dead cross on the way to hell.
6. **star** traditional symbol for Christ.
7. **Multifoliate rose** rose with many leaves. Dante describes paradise as such a rose in his *Paradiso*. The rose is a traditional symbol for the Virgin Mary.
8. **Here . . . morning** adaptation of a common nursery rhyme. A prickly pear is a cactus.
9. **Between . . . act** reference to *Julius Caesar*, Act II, Scene i, 63–65: "Between the acting of a dreadful thing / And the first motion, all the interim is / Like a phantasma or hideous dream."

Vocabulary
tumid (too′ mid) *adj.* swollen

Reading Check
To what kingdoms does the speaker refer?

For Thine is the Kingdom[10]

Between the conception
And the creation
80   Between the emotion
And the response
Falls the Shadow

Life is very long[11]

Between the desire
85   And the spasm
Between the potency
And the existence
Between the essence
And the descent
90   Falls the Shadow

For Thine is the Kingdom

For Thine is
Life is
For Thine is the

95   *This is the way the world ends*
This is the way the world ends
This is the way the world ends
Not with a bang but a whimper.

Literary Analysis
Modernism in Poetry
How does Eliot's handling of the line from the Lord's Prayer reflect modernist techniques?

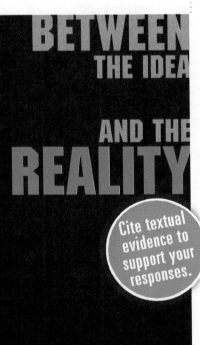

---

10. **For . . . Kingdom** from the ending of the Lord's Prayer.
11. **Life . . . long** Quotation from Joseph Conrad's *An Outcast of the Islands*.

Critical Reading

Cite textual evidence to support your responses.

1. **Craft and Structures** **(a)** Which words are used to describe the hollow men in the first ten lines? **(b) Infer:** What do the images of wind in Parts I and II suggest about the hollow men?

2. **Key Ideas and Details** **(a)** In Part V, what repeatedly "falls"? **(b) Interpret:** How is this action related to the poem's theme?

3. **Integration of Knowledge and Ideas** In what ways do Eliot's poems both break with tradition and connect to tradition? Use at least two of these Essential Question words in your response: *free verse, fragmentation, allusion, imagery*. *[Connecting to the Essential Question: What is the relationship of the writer to tradition?]*

After You Read
Preludes • Journey of the Magi • The Hollow Men

Literary Analysis

1. Craft and Structure Identify three images in the "Preludes" that suggest the **Modernist** view that modern life is empty. Explain your choices.

2. Craft and Structure What Modernist qualities characterize "The Hollow Men"? Use a chart like the one shown to help you in answering.

Passage	Fragmented Images/ Realistic Pictures	Critical of Modern Life?

3. Key Ideas and Details **(a)** What escape from modern despair does "Journey of the Magi" suggest? **(b)** What despair appears in the poem?

4. Craft and Structure **(a)** Quoting passages in support, identify two aspects of Modernism illustrated by the "Preludes." **(b)** Does "Journey of the Magi" also illustrate these aspects? Explain, quoting from the poem.

5. Craft and Structure Compare the use of *allusion*—brief references to literature—in "The Hollow Men" with the use of images in the "Preludes." How are they similar?

6. Integration of Knowledge and Ideas Which poem is easiest to relate to? Explain.

7. Integration of Knowledge and Ideas Why might Eliot have found it necessary to turn to past literature to make a point about what is missing in the present?

Reading Strategy

8. (a) What similarities are there in the way Eliot describes people in "Preludes" and "The Hollow Men"? **(b) Relate Eliot's work to the historical period** by determining what vision of modern life these similar images provide.

9. "The Journey of the Magi" is set in ancient times. What aspects of the poem reflect on Eliot's contemporary society? Explain your answer.

10. The Christian religion had been a source of spiritual comfort for the British for many centuries. Both "The Journey of the Magi" and "The Hollow Men" refer to Christian events or ideas. What does Eliot's treatment of these events or ideas suggest about his view of the role of Christianity in his society?

11. To what extent does Eliot's criticism of the hollow men apply to people today? Explain.

Common Core State Standards

Writing

2. Write informative/ explanatory texts to examine and convey complex ideas, concepts, and information clearly and accurately through the effective selection, organization, and analysis of content. *(p. 1168)*

4. Produce clear and coherent writing in which the development, organization, and style are appropriate to task, purpose, and audience. *(p. 1168)*

Language

3.a. Vary syntax for effect. *(p. 1169)*

5. Demonstrate understanding of figurative language, word relationships, and nuances in word meanings. *(p. 1168)*

PERFORMANCE TASKS
Integrated Language Skills

© Vocabulary Acquisition and Use

Word Analysis: Latin Root -fract-

The Latin root -fract- means "to break." A *refractory* animal is one that "breaks away," making it difficult to manage. A *fraction* is a part broken away from a larger whole. Explain how the root contributes to the meaning of the italicized words in these sentences.

1. When white light is *refracted* by a prism, it produces a spectrum.

2. Her motives were good, but she was guilty of an *infraction* of the rules.

3. Computer scenery may be formed of *fractals* so tiny you cannot see them.

4. The *fractured* bone needed time to mend.

Vocabulary: Analogies

In an analogy, the relationship between two words is explained by comparing it to the relationship between two other words. Discern the meaning of the words from the vocabulary list on page 1154 by using each word once to complete these analogies. Explain each choice.

1. *Thin* is to *slender* as _____ is to *bloated*.

2. *Emotional* is to *rational* as *obedient* is to _____.

3. *Order* is to *inferior* as _____ is to *superior*.

4. *Belief* is to _____ as *citizenship* is to *nation*.

5. *Medicine* is to *scraped* as *ointment* is to _____.

Writing

© **Informative Text** Eliot's poetry reflects the Modernist movement that swept through other arts as well. He uses words to achieve effects similar to those attained by such artists as Pablo Picasso and Paul Cézanne. Write a **multi-genre response** that responds to Eliot's Modernism in poetry. Analyze his techniques, showing how they contribute to a *comment on life*, and present the art of a Modernist painter, showing how he or she uses comparable devices.

Prewriting Review Eliot's poems to identify imagery, rhythms, and other techniques that reflect Modernism. Take notes on his Modernist themes as well. Using a history of art, find a Modernist work of art that shows comparable techniques or themes in visual form.

Drafting Begin with a thesis statement explaining your main point about Modernism in literature and art. Then, discuss the Modernist techniques in Eliot's poetry and write a caption for the work of art explaining similar Modernist techniques it uses.

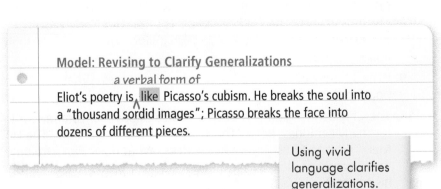

Model: Revising to Clarify Generalizations

a verbal form of

Eliot's poetry is ˄ like Picasso's cubism. He breaks the soul into a "thousand sordid images"; Picasso breaks the face into dozens of different pieces.

Using vivid language clarifies generalizations.

Revising Review your draft, highlighting generalizations. Where supporting details are lacking, look back at the poems or the artwork to find relevant support. Make sure that all quotations are accurate and properly referenced.

Conventions and Style: Transitional Expressions

To write coherently and smoothly, you must show how your ideas relate to one another. **Transitional expressions** can help you do this by making clear the connection between ideas.

Conjunctive adverbs make a transition between two independent clauses and show the relationship between the ideas in the clauses.

The examples demonstrate how conjunctive adverbs combine choppy sentences and make clear the relationship between ideas.

Choppy: The Magi's journey was long. It was at the worst time of year.

Conjunctive adverb: The Magi's journey was long; *moreover,* it was at the worst time of year.

Below is a chart of some common transitional expressions used as conjunctive adverbs.

Cause-effect	consequently, because of this
Time	in time, afterwards, at present
To illustrate	in other words, for instance
To add to	also, moreover, in addition
Compare	similarly, in like manner
Contrast	however, on the contrary

Punctuation Tip Remember to use a semicolon before the transitional expression.

Practice Rewrite each item using a conjunctive adverb to make a transition and show the relationship between the ideas.

1. Nighttime was dark and dismal. A new day dawned.
2. The modern world appeared lifeless. Former times seemed filled with emotion.
3. Cities, towns, and villages were unwelcoming. The travelers chose to keep on through the night.
4. The journey was long ago. The speaker would make it again.
5. The Magi returned to their homes. They no longer felt comfortable there.
6. Eliot alluded to Mistah Kurtz. He wanted to emphasize that power corrupts.
7. Hollow men had heads filled with straw. They were unthinking and unfeeling.
8. People spoke with dry voices. Their words were meaningless.
9. On Earth, people gathered but avoided speaking. They lived in a world of shadows.
10. Sightless eyes were symbols. They stood for emptiness.

Writing and Speaking Conventions

A. **Writing** Write an independent clause followed by a semicolon to fill each blank.

1. _____ that is, they had no shape or form.
2. _____ for this reason, he used the cactus image.
3. _____ in other words, it will go out with a quiet groan.

Example: _____ **that is, they had no shape or form.**

Complete Sentence: Eliot wrote of hollow men; that is, they had no shape or form.

B. **Speaking** Briefly explain to the class why Eliot's poems continue to have meaning. Include at least two conjunctive adverbs as transitional expressions.

PH WRITING COACH

Further instruction and practice are available in *Prentice Hall Writing Coach.*

Connecting to the Essential Question These poems reveal a profound sense of place. As you read, notice details in these poems that highlight the special character of the places being described. These observations will help you think about the Essential Question: **What is the relationship between literature and place?**

Literary Analysis

Allegory and pastoral are two subgenres of literature with a long tradition. They are called subgenres because these approaches to writing can be found in each major genre—poetry, prose, fiction, and drama.

- In an **allegory,** a writer uses symbolic characters to stand for abstract qualities or traits. In "In Memory of W. B. Yeats," for instance, Auden embodies poetry in a brief allegory. Allegories often teach a moral or lesson.

- In the **pastoral,** writers celebrate nature and those who live in the natural world. In this subgenre, farmers and shepherds are often seen as being wiser or more virtuous than city dwellers.

Comparing Literary Works Many modernist writers rejected traditional forms and styles. These poets may explore allegory or the pastoral not by embracing them but by rejecting them. As you read, look for both positive and negative attitudes.

Reading Strategy

Preparing to Read Complex Texts Both Auden poems address the role of art in the world. The speakers in the MacNeice and Spender poems react in different ways to the traditional pastoral world and the modern human-made one. You can enrich your understanding by **comparing and contrasting elements** that appear in the same poem or different poems. Comparing and contrasting MacNeice's and Spender's presentations of the natural world, for instance, highlights the different themes of their poems and how each poet develops them. As you read, use a chart like the one shown to record similarities and differences in the poems.

Vocabulary

sequestered (si kwes´ tərd) *adj.* kept apart from others (p. 1175)

topographical (täp´ ə graf´ i kəl) *adj.* representing the surface features of a region (p. 1180)

affinities (ə fin´ i tēz) *n.* family connections; sympathies (p. 1181)

prenatal (prē nāt´ əl) *adj.* existing or taking place before birth (p. 1181)

intrigues (in trēgz´) *v.* plots or schemes (p. 1183)

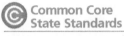

Common Core State Standards

Reading Literature
1. Cite strong and thorough textual evidence to support analysis of what the text says explicitly as well as inferences drawn from the text, including determining where the text leaves matters uncertain.

MacNeice on Nature

"The child's astonishment not yet cured"

Spender on Nature

"Leave your gardens"

Conclusion

MacNeice is tied to the place and the past; Spender rejects the natural for the new.

www.PHLitOnline.com

W. H. AUDEN

(1907–1973)

Author of **"In Memory of W. B. Yeats"** • **"Musée des Beaux Arts"**

Much as T. S. Eliot became established as the poetic voice of the 1920s, so Wystan Hugh Auden emerged as the voice of the 1930s. As a young poet, Auden was greatly influenced by Eliot's work, particularly *The Waste Land*. He soon developed his own poetic style, however, characterized by versatility, wit, and dazzling technique.

Born in York, England, Auden had early dreams of becoming an engineer but gravitated to poetry instead. His commitment to social justice and his opposition to fascism made him a poetic spokesperson for the political left. In 1939, Auden left England for the United States, where he taught at a number of universities. He became an American citizen in 1946. From 1956 to 1960, he taught at Oxford as professor of poetry.

Achievements in Poetry Auden's early poems, along with works by his friends Louis MacNeice and Stephen Spender, appeared in *Oxford Poetry*, a series of annual collections of verse by the university's undergraduates. Auden's first published collection, entitled *Poems*, appeared in 1930. Full of cryptic images and references, Auden's verse struck some readers of the day as impenetrable. His more straightfoward second collection, *On This Island* (1937), generated greater enthusiasm. In 1948, Auden won a Pulitzer Prize for the collection *The Age of Anxiety*.

A Versatile Poet Auden wrote equally well in the idiom of the street or in the archaic measures of *Beowulf*. His voice is original, achieving a kind of personable intimacy even as he makes polished pronouncements on the general human condition. With Yeats and Eliot, he is among the most highly regarded British poets of the twentieth century.

> "A REAL BOOK IS NOT ONE THAT WE READ, BUT ONE THAT READS US."

In Memory of
W. B. YEATS

W. H. AUDEN

1

He disappeared in the dead of winter:
The brooks were frozen, the airports almost deserted,
And snow disfigured the public statues;
The mercury sank in the mouth of the dying day.
5   O all the instruments agree
The day of his death was a dark cold day.

Far from his illness
The wolves ran on through the evergreen forests,
The peasant river was untempted by fashionable quays;[1]
10 By mourning tongues
The death of the poet was kept from his poems.

But for him it was his last afternoon as himself,
An afternoon of nurses and rumors;
The provinces of his body revolted,
15 The squares of his mind were empty,
Silence invaded the suburbs,
The current of his feeling failed: he became his admirers.

Now he is scattered among a hundred cities
And wholly given over to unfamiliar affections;
20 To find his happiness in another kind of wood
And be punished by another code of conscience.
The words of a dead man
Are modified in the guts of the living.

But in the importance and noise of tomorrow
25 When the brokers are roaring like beasts on the floor
        of the Bourse,[2]
And the poor have the sufferings to which they are
        fairly accustomed,

◀ **Critical Viewing**
Does this photograph of Yeats present him as the mortal man described in parts 1 and 2 of Auden's poem or as the great writer eulogized in part 3? Explain.
[Interpret]

Reading Strategy
Compare and Contrast Elements How does Auden use images of different locations to dramatize Yeats's death?

☑ Reading Check

According to the speaker, where is Yeats now?

---

1. **quays** (kēz) wharfs with facilities for loading or unloading ships.
2. **Bourse** (boors) Paris Stock Exchange.

And each in the cell of himself is almost convinced of
his freedom;
A few thousand will think of this day
As one thinks of a day when one did something
slightly unusual.
30 O all the instruments agree
The day of his death was a dark cold day.

2

You were silly like us: your gift survived it all;
The parish of rich women, physical decay,
Yourself; mad Ireland hurt you into poetry.
35 Now Ireland has her madness and her weather still,
For poetry makes nothing happen: it survives
In the valley of its saying where executives
Would never want to tamper; it flows south
From ranches of isolation and the busy griefs,
40 Raw towns that we believe and die in; it survives,
A way of happening, a mouth.

3

Earth, receive an honored guest;
William Yeats is laid to rest:
Let the Irish vessel lie
45 Emptied of its poetry.

Time that is intolerant
Of the brave and innocent,
And indifferent in a week
To a beautiful physique,

50 Worships language and forgives
Everyone by whom it lives;
Pardons cowardice, conceit
Lays its honors at their feet.

Time that with this strange excuse
55 Pardoned Kipling and his views,[3]
And will pardon Paul Claudel,[4]
Pardons him for writing well.

3. **Kipling . . . views** English writer Rudyard Kipling (1865–1936) was a supporter
of imperialism.
4. **pardon Paul Claudel** (klō del´) French poet, dramatist, and diplomat. Paul Claudel
(1868–1955) had antidemocratic political views, which Yeats at times shared.

Literary Analysis
Allegory How does Auden
create a mini-allegory, or
symbolic narrative, in lines
36–41 to describe the
creation and progress
of poetry?

In the nightmare of the dark
All the dogs of Europe bark,
60   And the living nations wait,
Each sequestered in its hate;

Intellectual disgrace
Stares from every human face,
And the seas of pity lie
65   Locked and frozen in each eye.

Follow, poet, follow right
To the bottom of the night,
With your unconstraining voice
Still persuade us to rejoice;

70   With the farming of a verse
Make a vineyard of the curse,
Sing of human unsuccess
In a rapture of distress;

In the deserts of the heart
75   Let the healing fountain start,
In the prison of his days
Teach the free man how to praise.

Vocabulary
sequestered (si kwes′ tərd)
adj. kept apart from others

FOLLOW, POET,

FOLLOW RIGHT

TO THE BOTTOM

OF THE *Night*

Critical Reading

1. **Key Ideas and Details** What does the speaker mean by saying Yeats "became his admirers"?

2. **Key Ideas and Details** What does the second section suggest about the sources and effects of poetry?

3. **Integration of Knowledge and Ideas (a) Interpret:** Considering the kind of fame great past poets enjoy, why does the speaker say that time "Worships language and forgives / Everyone by whom it lives . . ."? **(b) Synthesize:** What kind of poetry might "Sing of human unsuccess / In a rapture of distress . . ."?

4. **Integration of Knowledge and Ideas** Summarize the view of poetry presented in the poem.

5. **Craft and Structure** In phrases such as "ranches of isolation," Auden combines the abstract and the specific. Identify three other images that combine abstract ideas and concrete details.

6. **Craft and Structure** Is Auden's style suited to a poem of mourning? Explain.

Cite textual evidence to support your responses.

▲ **Critical Viewing** In this painting by Brueghel, which inspired Auden's poem, the drowning Icarus appears in the lower right. What is Brueghel implying about the place of suffering in life? [Interpret]

Musée des Beaux Arts[1]

W. H. Auden

About suffering they were never wrong,
The Old Masters: how well they understood
Its human position; how it takes place
While someone else is eating or opening a window or just
    walking dully along;
5   How, when the aged are reverently, passionately waiting
For the miraculous birth, there always must be
Children who did not specially want it to happen, skating

---

1. Musée des Beaux Arts Museum of Fine Arts in Brussels, Belgium, which contains
Brueghel's *Icarus*.

Reading Check

What did the Old Masters understand about suffering?

On a pond at the edge of the wood:
They never forgot

10 That even the dreadful martyrdom must run its course
Anyhow in a corner, some untidy spot
Where the dogs go on with their doggy life and the
      torturer's horse
Scratches its innocent behind on a tree.

In Brueghel's *Icarus*,[2] for instance: how everything turns away
15 Quite leisurely from the disaster; the ploughman may
Have heard the splash, the forsaken cry,
But for him it was not an important failure; the sun shone
As it had to on the white legs disappearing into the green
Water; and the expensive delicate ship that must have seen
20 Something amazing, a boy falling out of the sky,
Had somewhere to get to and sailed calmly on.

Literary Analysis
Allegory In what way does Brueghel's picture depict an allegorical landscape for Auden? What is the moral of this allegory?

---

2. **Brueghel's** (brü´ gəlz) *Icarus* (ik´ ə rəs) *The Fall of Icarus*, a painting by Flemish painter Pieter Brueghel (1525?–1569). In Greek mythology, Icarus flies too close to the sun. The wax of his artificial wings melts, and he falls into the sea.

Critical Reading

Cite textual evidence to support your responses.

1. **Key Ideas and Details** **(a)** Who are the "Old Masters"? **(b) Interpret:** What general device used by the Old Masters does the speaker discuss?

2. **Key Ideas and Details** **(a)** What disaster do the "ploughman" and the "ship" witness? **(b) Compare and Contrast:** How do their responses contrast with the gravity of the event?

3. **Key Ideas and Details** **(a) Infer:** What is the relation of the children to the important events near them? **(b) Connect:** Is the attitude of the ploughman to Icarus's fall similar? Explain.

4. **Key Ideas and Details** **(a) Analyze:** Look at Brueghel's *The Fall of Icarus* (p. 1176). What does the artist imply by showing only Icarus's legs in the right corner of the picture? **(b) Infer:** What does Brueghel, an Old Master, realize about the place of suffering in the world?

5. **Integration of Knowledge and Ideas** Consider these two statements: (1) *A person's suffering belongs to him or her in a way that not even pity can change.* (2) *Suffering gives meaning to innocent everyday life, and vice versa.* Which statement better captures the sense of the poem? Support your choice.

6. **Integration of Knowledge and Ideas** **(a) Apply:** Identify two examples of indifference to suffering today. **(b) Relate:** What might Auden say about them?

(1907–1963)

Louis MacNeice

Author of **"Carrick Revisited"**

Louis MacNeice was the son of a Protestant clergyman in
Belfast, Northern Ireland. A gifted youth, he began to write
poetry at age seven, about the time his mother died. His
first collection, *Blind Fireworks*, appeared in 1929, followed
six years later by *Poems*, the volume that established his
reputation. During the 1930s, MacNeice taught classical
literature. In 1941, he joined the British Broadcasting
Corporation, writing radio plays in verse.

   In a period when Auden and others embraced leftist
politics, MacNeice was unwilling to commit to a rigid
political program. He once dismissed Marxism by writing
that "the evil of the means obscures the good of the end."
Proudly Irish, he often returned to the island to enjoy its
land and people. At the same time, he lived most of his adult
life in England and tried to achieve a balance between the
pulls of those two places and Europe as a whole.

   T. S. Eliot praised MacNeice as a "poet of genius whose
virtuosity can be fully appreciated only by other poets."
Critics of his time viewed him less favorably, though. His
reputation has since shifted more toward Eliot's judgment.
Today, many consider MacNeice second only to Auden
among the poets of their generation. His poetry is restrained
and precise, with overtones of melancholy. It is the poetry of
a man who, as the poet Edwin Muir put it, "is never swept
off his feet."

> "The evil of the
> means obscures the
> good of the end."

Carrick Revisited

Louis MacNeice

Back to Carrick,[1] the castle as plumb assured
As thirty years ago—Which war was which?
Here are new villas, here is a sizzling grid
But the green banks are as rich and the lough[2] as hazily lazy
5 And the child's astonishment not yet cured.

Who was—and am—dumbfounded to find myself
In a topographical frame—here, not there—
The channels of my dreams determined largely
By random chemistry of soil and air;
10 Memories I had shelved peer at me from the shelf.

Fog-horn, mill-horn, corncrake and church bell
Half-heard through boarded time as a child in bed
Glimpses a brangle of talk from the floor below
But cannot catch the words. Our past we know
15 But not its meaning—whether it meant well.

---

1. Carrick shortened form of Carrickfergus, a town in Northern Ireland.
2. lough (läkh) lake, specifically Belfast Lough. Carrickfergus is situated on the northern shore of Belfast Lough.

Vocabulary
topographical (täp´ ə graf´ i kəl) *adj.* representing the surface features of a region

Literary Analysis
Pastoral In what way does the third stanza present childhood itself as a kind of pastoral?

Time and place—our bridgeheads into reality
But also its concealment! Out of the sea
We land on the Particular and lose
All other possible bird's-eye views, the Truth
20 That is of Itself for Itself—but not for me.

Torn before birth from where my fathers dwelt,
Schooled from the age of ten to a foreign voice,
Yet neither western Ireland nor southern England
Cancels this interlude; what chance misspelt
25 May never now be righted by my choice.

Whatever then my inherited or acquired
Affinities, such remains my childhood's frame
Like a belated rock in the red Antrim[3] clay
That cannot at this era change its pitch or name—
30 And the prenatal mountain is far away.

◀ Carrickfergus Castle, shown on the facing page, was built in 1177.

Vocabulary
affinities (ə fin´ i tēz) *n.* family connections; sympathies

prenatal (prē nāt´ əl) *adj.* existing or taking place before birth

---

3. Antrim county in Northern Ireland in which Carrickfergus is located.

Critical Reading

Cite textual evidence to support your responses.

1. **Key Ideas and Details** **(a)** Where does the speaker find himself at the beginning of the poem? **(b) Compare and Contrast:** According to the first stanza, what has changed and what has remained the same?

2. **Key Ideas and Details** **(a)** What discovery dumbfounds the speaker? **(b) Interpret:** What relationship does the speaker discover between the imagination—which enables us to picture ourselves in any circumstances—and the facts of his personal history?

3. **Key Ideas and Details** **(a) Interpret:** What effect do the specifics of the place have on the speaker's imagination? **(b) Interpret:** What does the speaker mean in saying "Our past we know / But not its meaning . . ."? **(c) Speculate:** What task concerning the past might MacNeice assign to poetry?

4. **Integration of Knowledge and Ideas** **(a) Interpret:** Why does the speaker call his childhood in Carrick an "interlude"? **(b) Draw Conclusions:** How is MacNeice's identity, as described in this poem, influenced by two cultures but separate from both?

5. **Integration of Knowledge and Ideas** Name two ways in which issues of identity are just as complex for people today.

Stephen Spender

(1909–1995)

Author of "Not Palaces"

No poet of the 1930s provided a more honest picture of the era between the wars than did Stephen Spender. Much of his early poetry deals with the world of the thirties, the "low dishonest decade"—in W. H. Auden's phrase—that saw many countries struggle with economic depression, experiment with extremist ideologies, and drift inexorably toward war. Yet Spender, never a pessimist, celebrates technology at the same time as he confronts the problems of industrial progress. While many of his poems had political themes, they also reflect his deeply personal responses to the world.

Born in London and educated at Oxford, Spender published his first important book, *Poems* (1933), while he was living in Germany. Early in life, Spender was politically active and—like many other young English college men of the time—embraced communism. He promoted antifascist propaganda in Spain during that country's civil war (1936–1939) but abandoned communism during World War II. In 1949, he joined with others in publishing a work that criticized communism called *The God That Failed*.

Even in his college years, Spender was more than a poet. It was he who published Auden's first collection of poems, privately printing an edition of thirty copies. Starting in the 1940s, Spender became a highly regarded literary critic and commentator. He later coedited the literary magazine *Horizon* and the political, cultural, and literary review *Encounter*. Along with writing poetry, Spender wrote short stories, a novel, verse plays, and volumes of criticism and essays. He continued working at poetry, though, publishing his last collection of poems a year before his death.

"I think continually of those who were truly great./Who, from the womb, remembered the soul's history..."

Not Palaces

Stephen Spender

BACKGROUND In this poem's unifying metaphor, Spender says that he will not build old-fashioned poems that are like palaces—beautiful, ornate structures remote from the masses. Instead, he hopes to build active, modern poetry, more like the steel and glass skyscrapers that began with the International and Bauhaus architectural styles of the 1920s and 1930s. These buildings create dynamic spaces by combining strikingly simple forms with superior industrial craftsmanship. Walter Gropius, the founder of the Bauhaus school, sought to integrate architecture and the other arts.

Not palaces, an era's crown
Where the mind dwells, intrigues, rests:
Architectural gold-leaved flower
From people ordered like a single mind,
5   I build: this only what I tell:
It is too late for rare accumulation,
For family pride, for beauty's filtered dusts;

Vocabulary
intrigues (in trēgz´)
v. plots or schemes

I say, stamping the words with emphasis,
Drink from here energy and only energy
10 To will this time's change.
Eye, gazelle, delicate wanderer,
Drinker of horizon's fluid line;
Ear that suspends on a chord
The spirit drinking timelessness;
15 Touch, love, all senses;
Leave your gardens, your singing feasts,
Your dreams of suns circling before our sun,
Of heaven after our world.
Instead, watch images of flashing glass
20 That strike the outward sense, the polished will,
Flag of our purpose which the wind engraves.
No spirit seek here rest. But this: No one
Shall hunger: Man shall spend equally;
Our goal which we compel: Man shall be man.

Reading Strategy
Compare and Contrast Elements Contrast Spender's definite rejection of pastoral images in lines 16–18 with MacNeice's mixed feelings about the pastoral of childhood.

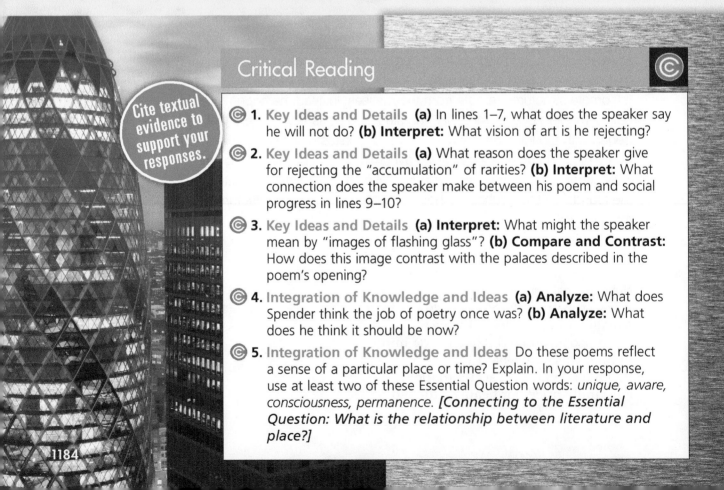

Cite textual evidence to support your responses.

Critical Reading

1. Key Ideas and Details (a) In lines 1–7, what does the speaker say he will not do? **(b) Interpret:** What vision of art is he rejecting?

2. Key Ideas and Details (a) What reason does the speaker give for rejecting the "accumulation" of rarities? **(b) Interpret:** What connection does the speaker make between his poem and social progress in lines 9–10?

3. Key Ideas and Details (a) Interpret: What might the speaker mean by "images of flashing glass"? **(b) Compare and Contrast:** How does this image contrast with the palaces described in the poem's opening?

4. Integration of Knowledge and Ideas (a) Analyze: What does Spender think the job of poetry once was? **(b) Analyze:** What does he think it should be now?

5. Integration of Knowledge and Ideas Do these poems reflect a sense of a particular place or time? Explain. In your response, use at least two of these Essential Question words: *unique, aware, consciousness, permanence. [Connecting to the Essential Question: What is the relationship between literature and place?]*

Literary Analysis

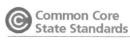
Common Core
State Standards

1. Craft and Structure Is it reasonable to say that Auden builds an **allegory** out of Yeats's work and life in the poem "In Memory of W. B. Yeats"? Explain.

2. Craft and Structure Auden uses similar images in lines 27 and 76–77 in "In Memory of W. B. Yeats." How do the differences in these two mentions help carry the meaning of the poem?

3. Craft and Structure Use a chart like the one shown to trace the use of **pastoral** images in "In Memory of W. B. Yeats," "Carrick Revisited," and "Not Palaces." Then, summarize the way each writer uses pastoral elements in his poems.

Poem	Pastoral Images	Poet's Attitude Toward Pastoral
"In Memory of W. B. Yeats"	Frozen brook; wolves running wild	
"Carrick Revisited"		
"Not Palaces"		

4. Key Ideas and Details (a) What does MacNeice say we gain from being born in a particular time and place? **(b)** What do we lose?

5. Comparing Literary Works Pastoral writers often look to the past, cherishing a time when life was simpler and sometimes portraying that time as a "golden age." **(a)** Does Auden reflect this perspective in "Musée des Beaux Arts"? Explain your answer. **(b)** Does Spender reflect this view in "Not Palaces"? Explain your answer.

Reading Strategy

6. (a) Compare and contrast Auden's portrayal of the contemporary world in "In Memory of W. B. Yeats" with Spender's view of the modern world in "Not Palaces." **(b)** With which of these views do you think MacNeice would most agree? Explain your answer.

7. (a) How do the language and tone of "Musée des Beaux Arts" and "Not Palaces" differ? **(b)** How do those differences contribute to the feeling and meaning of the poems?

8. Both "In Memory of W. B. Yeats" and "Carrick Revisited" question the connection between the particulars of an artist's life and his or her work. Compare their answers.

9. (a) Which of these poets believe that art in some sense rises above life? **(b)** Which do not? Explain, using examples. **(c)** With which poet's view of art do you agree? Why?

Integrated Language Skills

Ⓒ Vocabulary Acquisition and Use

Word Analysis: Greek Root -top-

The Greek root -top- means "place" or "surface." The word *topographical*, which MacNeice uses in "Carrick Revisited," means "relating to a map of the surface features of a place." Explain how the root contributes to the meaning of the italicized words in these sentences.

1. The nurse used a *topical* ointment on the bee sting to reduce the swelling.

2. The *topocentric* distances were all measured from the same point of origin.

3. Mapmakers use precise measures to learn the *topography* of a place.

4. *Topology* is only one branch of geography.

Vocabulary: Synonyms

A synonym is a word that has a meaning similar to that of another word. Answer each question below. In your answer, use a word from the vocabulary list on page 1170 that is a synonym for the italicized word in each question.

1. Were the *schemes* of the plotters successful?

2. Were the different conspirators *isolated* from each other or held together?

3. What kind of detail did the *elevation* map show?

4. Do experts agree on the importance of *prebirth* nutrition?

5. Did her *sympathies* affect what charities she gave to?

Writing

Ⓒ **Poem** Auden's poem "Musée des Beaux Arts" was inspired by a Brueghel painting. Choose another painting or a photograph and respond to it in a **poem** of your own. To convey one main impression, establish and maintain a strong, consistent tone. Demonstrate your understanding of the style of the poets in this collection by using the free verse and conversational tone of Auden or the more energetic, rhythmic style of Spender.

Prewriting Begin by choosing an artwork that you either admire or dislike. Jot notes about what the artwork shows—the use of shapes and colors—and how it makes you feel. Is the work dramatic and stirring? Or is it peaceful and calming? Review your notes, circling important details.

Drafting Choose a logical organization. You might begin with a physical description of the artwork and then reveal your emotional response to it. As you draft, concentrate on choosing natural, fresh, and vivid language that will result in a strong, consistent tone, whether that is wonder, amusement, or disappointment.

Revising Ask a partner to read your poem and share the main impression he or she received. Revise your poem if your partner's impression does not match the one you wanted to convey. Pay special attention to your word choice, revising language as needed to more clearly convey your intended impression.

Model: Revising to Add Descriptive Language

bold   mocking, laughing—
A blue stripe splits the canvas in two, ~~challenging the viewer,~~
"On which side are you?"

Flatly descriptive language is revised to portray stronger images.

Modernism in Fiction

Virginia Woolf

(1882–1941)

Virginia Woolf, one of the early practitioners of Modernism, was instrumental in revolutionizing modern fiction. Abandoning traditional plot and structure in fiction, she was one of the pioneers of the stream-of-consciousness technique. This device allows readers to tune in directly to the flow of thoughts and images in a character's mind.

A Literary Life

Born Virginia Stephen, Woolf came from a prim and proper Victorian family, but it was one in which literature was prized. Her father, the renowned editor Leslie Stephen, made sure that his daughter grew up surrounded by books. Woolf always knew that she wanted to be a writer. At the age of twenty-three, Woolf was writing articles and essays and contributing book reviews to the *Times Literary Supplement*.

Bloomsbury

After their father died in 1904, Virginia moved with her sister Vanessa and her brothers to a home in the Bloomsbury neighborhood of London. Their house became a meeting place for writers, artists, and thinkers, who gathered to discuss literature, art, and politics. This influential group, known as the Bloomsbury Group, generally rejected the values and morals of Victorianism, instead promoting artistic and personal freedoms.

In 1912, Virginia married Leonard Woolf, a member of this group, who was a journalist, author, and literary editor. Together they founded the Hogarth Press in 1917. Along with Virginia's works, they published the works of other notable writers, including T. S. Eliot, E. M. Forster, and Katherine Mansfield.

Revolutionizing Fiction

Woolf's first two novels were not unusual, but she soon established herself as one of the leading writers of Modernism. *Jacob's Room* (1922) shattered the conventions of fiction by telling the story of a young man's life entirely through an examination of his room. (She also uses this device in "The Lady in the Looking Glass: A Reflection.") Woolf continued to refine her fluid, inward-looking style with three more stream-of-consciousness novels—*Mrs. Dalloway* (1925), *To the Lighthouse* (1927), and *The Waves* (1931). In her more revolutionary works, she virtually abolishes a traditional plot, preferring to concentrate on what she called "an ordinary mind on an ordinary day." In *Mrs. Dalloway*, for example, there is little action. The central character, Clarissa Dalloway, spends a day in London preparing for an evening party. Her thoughts move from the present to the past and back to the present.

Depression and Tragedy

Throughout her life, Woolf suffered episodes of severe depression brought on by poor health. She had frequent periods when she was unable to focus enough to read or write. The turmoil of World War II worsened her depression. In 1941, she drowned in the River Ouse near the Woolfs' home in Sussex.

In addition to the considerable number of critical essays she produced in her life, Woolf wrote about fifteen novels. Today she is recognized as one of the greatest contributors to modern fiction.

Virginia Woolf
& Pop Culture

Who's afraid of Virginia Woolf? That punning question—based on the jingle, Who's Afraid of the Big Bad Wolf—was the title of a famous Edward Albee play. Part of the joke behind it is that the author of such sophisticated stream-of-consciousness novels as *Mrs. Dalloway* and *To the Lighthouse* does seem like a forbidding intellectual figure.

Surprisingly, however, this great Modernist author turns up frequently on the Internet. Apparently, no one on the World Wide Web is afraid of her.

Some Woolf sites, such as that of The Virginia Woolf Society, are devoted to a serious-minded discussion of her as an important literary figure. Others, however, blur the line between high and low culture, bringing the upper-class British author into the democracy of the Internet. Another way to view her online popularity would be to say that somehow she has entered into our culture's stream of consciousness.

One of the sites showing no fear of the Woolf is that of the Cosmic Baseball Association, a self-described art project that had the Bloomsbury author playing on one of the league's teams. A dispute between Woolf and her manager, however, led to her being traded.

As these Web shenanigans reveal, Woolf has gone beyond her role as a writer to become a cultural icon—a figure in whom many online constituencies see their own interests and obsessions reflected. In this respect, Woolf is not unlike Marilyn Monroe, another iconic female who has achieved immortality in the culture's stream of consciousness.

Marilyn Monroe, as depicted by Andy Warhol

Director Mike Nichols (left) and part of the cast of the film version of *Who's Afraid of Virginia Woolf* (1966): (from left to right, after Nichols) George Segal, Elizabeth Taylor, and Richard Burton

Nicole Kidman, playing Virginia Woolf in the film *The Hours* (2002)

Before You Read

The Lady in the Looking Glass ▪ from *Mrs. Dalloway* ▪ *Shakespeare's Sister*

Connecting to the Essential Question Think of a song you like. Freewrite about your associations with the song—your thoughts, your feelings, and why you like it. As you read, find details in the fictional selections by Virginia Woolf that differ from the traditional way of telling a story. This will help you think about the Essential Question: **What is the relationship of the writer to tradition?**

Literary Analysis

Searching for forms suited to modern experience, writers tested different **points of view,** the perspective from which a story is told.

- A **first-person** narrator tells his or her own story. With this technique, authors can probe the thoughts of the narrator.

- A **third-person** narrator tells what happened to others. An **omniscient third person** has the ability to reveal the thoughts of several characters. A narrator with **limited omniscience** sees only into the mind of one or few characters.

- **Stream-of-consciousness** narration follows the flowing, branching currents of thought in a character's mind.

Writers began using the stream-of-consciousness technique under the influence of the emerging science of psychology. As in psychology, the free association of ideas in stream-of-consciousness narration reveals the dynamic nature of people's minds. As you read, consider how Woolf uses this technique to develop character.

Reading Strategy

Preparing to Read Complex Texts Experimental works offer great rewards but also place demands on readers. If you lose your way in a stream-of-consciousness story, you can **repair your comprehension by asking questions** to restore your focus. Use a chart such as the one shown.

Vocabulary

suffused (sə fyo̅o̅zd´) *v.* spread throughout; filled (p. 1193)

transient (tran´ shənt) *n.* that which passes quickly (p. 1193)

upbraidings (up brād´ iŋz) *n.* words of disapproval; scoldings (p. 1194)

evanescence (ev´ ə nes´ əns) *n.* vanishing or tendency to vanish (p. 1196)

reticent (ret´ ə sənt) *adj.* silent; reserved (p. 1196)

vivacious (və vā´ shəs) *adj.* lively, spirited (p. 1199)

irrevocable (i rev´ ə kə bəl) *adj.* not possible to revoke or change (p. 1199)

escapade (es´ kə pād) *n.* a wild and reckless adventure (p. 1202)

 Common Core State Standards

Reading Literature
3. Analyze the impact of the author's choices regarding how to develop and relate elements of a story or drama.

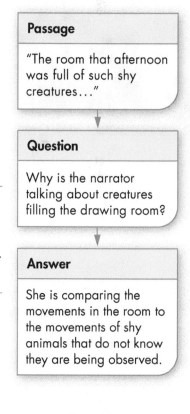

Passage

"The room that afternoon was full of such shy creatures…"

Question

Why is the narrator talking about creatures filling the drawing room?

Answer

She is comparing the movements in the room to the movements of shy animals that do not know they are being observed.

THE LADY IN THE LOOKING GLASS
A Reflection
Virginia Woolf

BACKGROUND Virginia Woolf was part of an artistic and intellectual circle called the Bloomsbury Group, named for the section of London where they met. The circle included Woolf's husband, her brother, her sister and brother-in-law, and such intellectual stars as novelist E. M. Forster and economist John Maynard Keynes. Like others in the Modernist movement, group members rejected tradition and sought new answers in their efforts to define artistic beauty and morality.

People should not leave looking glasses hanging in their rooms any more than they should leave open checkbooks or letters confessing some hideous crime. One could not help looking, that summer afternoon, in the long glass that hung outside in the hall. Chance had so arranged it. From the depths of the sofa in the drawing room one could see reflected in the Italian glass not only the marble-topped table opposite, but a stretch of the garden beyond. One could see a long grass path leading between banks of tall flowers until, slicing off an angle, the gold rim cut it off.

The house was empty, and one felt, since one was the only person in the drawing room, like one of those naturalists who, covered with grass and leaves, lie watching the shyest animals—badgers, otters, king-fishers—moving about freely, themselves unseen. The room that afternoon was full of such shy creatures, lights and shadows, curtains blowing, petals falling—things that never happen, so it seems, if someone is looking. The quiet old country room with its rugs and stone chimney pieces, its sunken bookcases and red and gold lacquer cabinets, was full of such nocturnal creatures. They came pirouetting across the floor, stepping delicately with high-lifted feet and spread tails and pecking allusive beaks as if they had been cranes or flocks of elegant flamingoes whose pink was faded, or peacocks whose trains were veiled with silver. And there were obscure flushes and darkening too, as if a cuttlefish had suddenly suffused the air with purple; and the room had its passions and rages and envies and sorrows coming over it and clouding it, like a human being. Nothing stayed the same for two seconds together.

But, outside, the looking glass reflected the hall table, the sunflowers, the garden path so accurately and so fixedly that they seemed held there in their reality unescapably. It was a strange contrast—all changing here, all stillness there. One could not help looking from one to the other. Meanwhile, since all the doors and windows were open in the heat, there was a perpetual sighing and ceasing sound, the voice of the transient and the perishing, it seemed, coming and going like human breath, while in the looking glass things had ceased to breathe and lay still in the trance of immortality.

Half an hour ago the mistress of the house, Isabella Tyson, had gone down the grass path in her thin summer dress, carrying a basket, and had vanished, sliced off by the gilt rim of the looking glass. She had gone presumably into the lower garden to pick flowers; or as it seemed more natural to suppose, to pick something light and fantastic and leafy and trailing, traveler's-joy, or one of those elegant sprays of convolvulus that twine round ugly walls and burst here and there into white and violet blossoms. She suggested the fantastic and the tremulous convolvulus rather than the upright aster, the starched zinnia, or her own burning roses alight like lamps on the straight posts of their rose trees. The comparison showed how very little, after all these years, one knew about her; for it is impossible that any woman of flesh and blood of fifty-five or sixty should be really a wreath or a tendril. Such comparisons are worse than idle and superficial—they are cruel even, for they come like the convolvulus itself trembling between one's eyes and the truth. There must be truth; there must be a wall. Yet it was strange that after knowing her all these years one could not say what the truth about Isabella was; one still made up phrases like this about convolvulus and traveler's-joy. As for facts, it was a fact that she was a spinster; that she was rich; that she had bought this house and collected with her own hands—often in the

Reading Strategy
Repairing Comprehension
Is your impression of the narrator clear? Ask a question to clarify your impression.

Vocabulary
suffused (sə fyo͞ozd′) v. spread throughout; filled

Vocabulary
transient (tran′ shənt) n. that which passes quickly

Reading Check
Where is the narrator?

most obscure corners of the world and at great risk from poisonous stings and Oriental diseases—the rugs, the chairs, the cabinets which now lived their nocturnal life before one's eyes. Sometimes it seemed as if they knew more about her than we, who sat on them, wrote at them, and trod on them so carefully, were allowed to know. In each of these cabinets were many little drawers, and each almost certainly held letters, tied with bows of ribbon, sprinkled with sticks of lavender or rose leaves. For it was another fact—if facts were what one wanted—that Isabella had known many people, had had many friends; and thus if one had the audacity to open a drawer and read her letters, one would find the traces of many agitations, of appointments to meet, of upbraidings for not having met, long letters of intimacy and affection, violent letters of jealousy and reproach, terrible final words of parting—for all those interviews and assignations had led to nothing—that is, she had never married, and yet, judging from the masklike indifference of her face, she had gone through twenty times more of passion and experience than those whose loves are trumpeted forth for all the world to hear. Under the stress of thinking about Isabella, her room became more shadowy and symbolic; the corners seemed darker, the legs of chairs and tables more spindly and hieroglyphic.

Suddenly these reflections were ended violently and yet without a sound. A large black form loomed into the looking glass; blotted out everything, strewed the table with a packet of marble tablets veined with pink and gray, and was gone. But the picture was entirely altered. For the moment it was unrecognizable and irrational and entirely out of focus. One could not relate these tablets to any human purpose. And then by degrees some logical process set to work on them and began ordering and arranging them and bringing them into the fold of common experience. One realized at last that they were merely letters. The man had brought the post.

There they lay on the marble-topped table, all dripping with light and color at first and crude and unabsorbed. And then it was strange to see how they were drawn in and arranged and composed and made part of the picture and granted that stillness and immortality which the looking glass conferred. They lay there invested with a new reality and significance and with a greater heaviness, too, as if it would have needed a chisel to dislodge them from the table. And, whether it was fancy or not, they seemed to have become not merely a handful of casual letters but to be tablets graven with eternal truth—if one could read them, one would know everything there was to be known about Isabella, yes, and about life, too. The pages inside those marble-looking envelopes must be cut deep and scored thick with meaning. Isabella would come in, and take them, one by one, very slowly, and open them, and read them carefully word by word, and then with a profound sigh of comprehension, as if she had seen to the bottom of everything, she would tear the envelopes to little bits and tie the letters together and lock the cabinet drawer in her determination to conceal what she did not wish to be known.

Vocabulary
upbraidings (up brād´ iŋz)
n. stern words of disapproval; scoldings

Literary Analysis
Point of View What effect does the narrator's attention to the workings of his or her own mind have on the narration?

▶ **Critical Viewing**
What aspects of this painting mirror the story's setting?
[Connect]

The thought served as a challenge. Isabella did not wish to be known—but she should no longer escape. It was absurd, it was monstrous. If she concealed so much and knew so much one must prize her open with the first tool that came to hand—the imagination. One must fix one's mind upon her at that very moment. One must fasten her down there. One must refuse to be put off any longer with sayings and doings such as the moment brought forth—with dinners and visits and polite conversations. One must put oneself in her shoes. If one took the phrase literally, it was easy to see the shoes in which she stood, down in the lower garden, at this moment. They were very narrow and long and fashionable—they were made of the softest and most flexible leather. Like everything she wore, they were exquisite. And she would be standing under the high hedge in the lower part of the garden, raising the scissors that were tied to her waist to cut some dead flower, some overgrown branch. The sun would beat down on her face, into her eyes; but no, at the critical moment a veil of cloud covered the sun, making the expression of her eyes doubtful—was it mocking or tender, brilliant or dull? One could only see the indeterminate outline of her rather faded, fine face looking at the sky. She was thinking, perhaps, that she must order a new net for the strawberries; that she must send flowers to Johnson's widow; that it was time she drove over to see the Hippesleys in their new house. Those were the things she talked about at dinner certainly. But one was tired of the things that she talked about at dinner. It

Literary Analysis
Point of View In what way does this paragraph illustrate the use of stream-of-consciousness narration?

Reading Check
What do the "marble tablets" turn out to be?

THE THOUGHT SERVED AS A CHALLENGE.

Isabella did not wish to be known—but she should no longer escape.

The Garden of Love, (detail), Walter Richard Sickert, The Fitzwilliam Museum, Cambridge

The Lady in the Looking Glass: A Reflection **1195**

AND THERE WAS NOTHING. *Isabella was perfectly empty. She had no thoughts. She had no friends.*

▲ **Critical Viewing**
Does the woman in this painting seem, like Isabella, to have "no thoughts"? Why or why not? **[Connect]**

Vocabulary
evanescence (ev´ ə nes´ əns) *n.* vanishing or tendency to vanish

reticent (ret´ ə sənt) *adj.* silent; reserved

was her profounder state of being that one wanted to catch and turn to words, the state that is to the mind what breathing is to the body, what one calls happiness or unhappiness. At the mention of those words it became obvious, surely, that she must be happy. She was rich; she was distinguished; she had many friends; she traveled—she bought rugs in Turkey and blue pots in Persia. Avenues of pleasure radiated this way and that from where she stood with her scissors raised to cut the trembling branches while the lacy clouds veiled her face.

Here with a quick movement of her scissors she snipped the spray of traveler's-joy and it fell to the ground. As it fell, surely some light came in too, surely one could penetrate a little farther into her being. Her mind then was filled with tenderness and regret. . . . To cut an overgrown branch saddened her because it had once lived, and life was dear to her. Yes, and at the same time the fall of the branch would suggest to her how she must die herself and all the futility and evanescence of things. And then again quickly catching this thought up, with her instant good sense, she thought life had treated her well; even if fall she must, it was to lie on the earth and molder sweetly into the roots of violets. So she stood thinking. Without making any thought precise—for she was one of those reticent people whose minds hold their thoughts enmeshed in clouds of silence—she was filled with thoughts. Her mind was like her room, in which lights advanced and retreated, came pirouetting and stepping delicately, spread their tails, pecked their way; and then her whole being was suffused, like the room again, with a cloud of some profound knowledge, some unspoken regret, and then she was full of locked drawers, stuffed with letters, like her cabinets. To talk of "prizing her open" as if she were an oyster, to use any but the finest and subtlest and most pliable tools upon her was impious and absurd. One must imagine—here was she in the looking glass. It made one start.

She was so far off at first that one could not see her clearly. She came lingering and pausing, here straightening a rose, there lifting a pink to smell it, but she never stopped; and all the time she became larger and larger in the looking glass, more and more completely the person into whose mind one had been trying to penetrate. One verified her by degrees—fitted the qualities one had discovered into this visible body. There were her gray-green dress, and her long shoes, her basket, and something sparkling at her throat. She came so gradually that she did not seem to derange the pattern in the glass, but only to bring in some new element which gently moved and altered the other objects as if asking them, courteously, to make room for her. And the letters and the table and the grass walk and the sunflowers which had been waiting in the looking glass separated and opened out so that she might be received among them. At last there she was, in the hall. She stopped dead. She stood by the table. She stood perfectly still. At once the looking glass began to pour over her a light that seemed to fix her; that seemed like some acid to bite off the unessential and superficial and to leave only the truth. It was an enthralling spectacle. Everything dropped from her—clouds, dress, basket, diamond—all that one had called the creeper and convolvulus. Here was the hard wall beneath. Here was the woman herself. She stood naked in that pitiless light. And there was nothing. Isabella was perfectly empty. She had no thoughts. She had no friends. She cared for nobody. As for her letters, they were all bills. Look, as she stood there, old and angular, veined and lined, with her high nose and her wrinkled neck, she did not even trouble to open them.

People should not leave looking glasses hanging in their rooms.

▼ **Critical Viewing**
Make an analogy comparing an unopened letter like this one with Isabella as seen by the narrator. **[Connect]**

Critical Reading

1. **Key Ideas and Details (a)** Where are the narrator and Isabella, respectively, at the opening of the story? **(b) Infer:** From what perspective does the narrator observe Isabella? **(c) Speculate:** Who might the narrator be? Explain.

2. **Key Ideas and Details (a)** Briefly describe the layout and furnishings of the room in the story. **(b) Summarize:** How does the looking glass "guide" the narrator to an understanding of Isabella? **(c) Interpret:** What does the last sentence of the story, repeated from the beginning, mean?

Cite textual evidence to support your responses.

from
MRS. DALLOWAY

Virginia Woolf

Mrs. Dalloway said she would buy the flowers herself. For Lucy had her work cut out for her. The doors would be taken off their hinges; Rumpelmayer's men were coming. And then, thought Clarissa Dalloway, what a morning—fresh as if issued to children on a beach.

What a lark! What a plunge! For so it had always seemed to her, when, with a little squeak of the hinges, which she could hear now, she had burst open the French windows and plunged at Bourton into the open air. How fresh, how calm, stiller than this of course, the air was in the early morning; like the flap of a wave; the kiss of a wave; chill and sharp and yet (for a girl of eighteen as she then was) solemn, feeling as she did, standing there at the open window, that something awful was about to happen; looking at the flowers, at the trees with the smoke winding off them and the rooks[1] rising, falling; standing and looking until Peter Walsh said, "Musing among the vegetables?"— was that it?—"I prefer men to cauliflowers"—was that it? He must have said it at breakfast one morning when she had gone out on to the terrace—Peter Walsh. He would be back from India one of these days, June or July, she forgot which, for his letters were awfully dull; it was his sayings one remembered; his eyes, his pocket-knife, his smile, his grumpiness and, when millions of things had utterly vanished—how strange it was!—a few sayings like this about cabbages.

She stiffened a little on the kerb,[2] waiting for Durtnall's van to pass. A charming woman, Scrope Purvis thought her (knowing her as one does know people who live next door to one in Westminster); a touch of the bird about her, of the jay, blue-green, light, vivacious, though she was over fifty, and grown very white since her illness. There she perched, never seeing him, waiting to cross, very upright.

For having lived in Westminster—how many years now? over twenty,—one feels even in the midst of the traffic, or waking at night, Clarissa was positive, a particular hush, or solemnity; an indescribable pause; a suspense (but that might be her heart, affected, they said, by influenza) before Big Ben strikes. There! Out it boomed. First a warning, musical; then the hour, irrevocable. The leaden circles dissolved in the air. Such fools we are, she thought, crossing Victoria Street. For Heaven only knows why one loves it so, how one sees it so, making it up, building it round one, tumbling it, creating it every moment afresh; but the veriest frumps,[3] the most dejected of miseries sitting on doorsteps (drink their downfall) do the same; can't be dealt with, she felt positive, by Acts of Parliament for that very reason: they love life. In

---

1. **rooks** crows.
2. **kerb** the curb.
3. **veriest frumps** most plain, unfashionable women.

◀ **Critical Viewing**
How do the bustle and vividness of this painting mirror the stream-of-consciousness narration of the story? **[Deduce]**

Vocabulary
vivacious (və vā′ shəs)
adj. lively, spirited

irrevocable (i re′ və kə bəl)
adj. not possible to revoke or change

Reading Check
Where does Mrs. Dalloway live?

people's eyes, in the swing, tramp, and trudge; in the bellow and the uproar; the carriages, motor cars, omnibuses,[4] vans, sandwich men shuffling and swinging; brass bands; barrel organs; in the triumph and the jingle and the strange high singing of some aeroplane overhead was what she loved; life; London; this moment of June.

---

4. omnibuses buses

▶ **Critical Viewing**
What might Mrs. Dalloway think about on a London street like this?
[Connect]

Critical Reading

Cite textual evidence to support your responses.

1. **Key Ideas and Details (a)** What does Mrs. Dalloway remember of Peter Walsh? **(b)** How does the narrator call into question Scrope Purvis's understanding of Mrs. Dalloway? **(c) Infer:** What do these comments suggest about the ability of one person to understand another?

2. **Key Ideas and Details (a)** What details suggest that Mrs. Dalloway has not been in the best of health? **(b) Infer:** How might that history affect her outlook on life?

3. **Key Ideas and Details (a) Summarize:** What happens in the passage? **(b) Draw Conclusions:** How important are those events?

4. **Integration of Knowledge and Ideas** How effectively do you think Woolf portrays the inner thoughts of Mrs. Dalloway?

Critical Commentary

from a Speech on Virginia Woolf
Michael Cunningham

Michael Cunningham

> *Michael Cunningham is an American writer whose Pulitzer Prize–winning novel* The Hours *features Virginia Woolf as a character. In this speech delivered at a PEN America Virginia Woolf tribute, Cunningham describes how, as a high-school student, he first fell in love with her work.*

Mrs. Dalloway is the first great book I ever read. I was fifteen . . . One day I . . . suddenly found myself standing beside the pirate queen of our school. She was beautiful and mean and smart, she had long red fingernails, and long straight hair. Fringe, pretty much everywhere. I found myself standing next to her, and I thought, "Uh oh, uh oh . . . Think fast, be suave, say something that will make her love you forever." So I said something that I thought then—and I think today—was very winning, about the poetry of Bob Dylan and Leonard Cohen. She was kind to me. . . . and said, "Well, yes, they're very good, but how do you feel about T. S. Eliot and Virginia Woolf?"

. . . I never expected I'd have to read either one of them. I went to the library, the Bookmobile, the little trailer where the books were. They didn't have any Eliot, but they did have one book of Woolf's, and it was *Mrs. Dalloway*. I took it out, and I took it home and read it, tried to read it, and I didn't know what was going on. In another way I did get it. I did get the depth and density, and the sentences, and it did turn on some little light inside my stupid skull.

Everybody who reads has a first book—maybe not the first book you read, but the first book that shows you what literature can be. Like a first kiss. And you read other books, you kiss other people, but especially for those who are romantically inclined, that first book stays with you. I felt wedded to *Mrs. Dalloway* in a way I've never felt about any other book. I finally, finally, finally grew up and wrote *The Hours*, in which I tried to take an existing work of great art and make another work of art out of it, the way a jazz musician might play improvisations on a great piece of music.

I learned so much from Woolf as a writer. I think what I learned most importantly was her conviction that the whole of human existence, while it is copiously contained in foreign wars and the death of kings, and the other big subjects for big novels, is also contained in every hour in the life of everybody, very much the way the blueprint for the whole organism is contained in every strand of its DNA. If you look with sufficient penetration, and sufficient art, at any hour in the life of anybody, you can crack it open. And get everything. Virginia Woolf understood that every character, no matter how minor, in a novel she wrote was visiting the novel, from a novel of his or her own, where he or she was the hero of another great tragic and comic tale.

ⓒ **Key Ideas and Details** What did Cunningham as a writer learn from reading Virginia Woolf?

Shakespeare's Sister

Virginia Woolf

Vocabulary
escapade (es′ kə pād)
n. a wild and reckless adventure

Be that as it may, I could not help thinking, as I looked at the works of Shakespeare on the shelf, that the bishop was right[1] at least in this; it would have been impossible, completely and entirely, for any woman to have written the plays of Shakespeare in the age of Shakespeare. Let me imagine, since facts are so hard to come by, what would have happened had Shakespeare had a wonderfully gifted sister, called Judith, let us say. Shakespeare himself went, very probably—his mother was an heiress—to the grammar school, where he may have learned Latin—Ovid, Virgil and Horace—and the elements of grammar and logic. He was, it is well known, a wild boy who poached[2] rabbits, perhaps shot a deer, and had, rather sooner than he should have done, to marry a woman in the neighborhood, who bore him a child rather quicker than was right. That escapade sent him to seek his fortune in London. He had, it seemed, a taste for the theater; he began by holding horses at the stage door. Very soon he got work in the theater, became a successful actor, and lived at the hub of the universe, meeting everybody, knowing everybody, practicing his art on the boards, exercising his wits in the streets, and even getting access to the palace of the queen. Meanwhile his extraordinarily gifted sister, let us suppose, remained at home. She was as adventurous, as imaginative, as agog to see the world as he was. But she was not sent to school. She had no chance of learning grammar and logic, let alone of reading Horace and Virgil. She picked up a book now and then, one of her brother's perhaps, and read a few pages. But then her parents came in and told her to mend the stockings or mind the stew and not moon about with books and papers. They would have spoken sharply but kindly, for they were substantial people who knew the conditions of life for a woman and loved their daughter—indeed, more likely than not she was the apple of her father's eye. Perhaps she scribbled some pages up in an apple loft on the sly, but was careful to hide them or set fire to them. Soon, however, before she was out of her teens, she was to be betrothed to the son

---

1. **the bishop was right** In the paragraph prior to this one, Woolf recalls that a bishop, whom she does not name, once wrote to a newspaper to say "it was impossible for any woman, past, present, or to come, to have the genius of Shakespeare."
2. **poached** hunted illegally.

of a neighboring wool-stapler. She cried out that marriage was hateful to her, and for that she was severely beaten by her father. Then he ceased to scold her. He begged her instead not to hurt him, not to shame him in this matter of her marriage. He would give her a chain of beads or a fine petticoat, he said; and there were tears in his eyes. How could she disobey him? How could she break his heart? The force of her own gift alone drove her to it. She made up a small parcel of her belongings, let herself down by a rope one summer's night and took the road to London. She was not seventeen. The birds that sang in the hedge were not more musical than she was. She had the quickest fancy, a gift like her brother's, for the tune of words. Like him, she had a taste for the theater. She stood at the stage door; she wanted to act,[3] she said. Men laughed in her face. The manager—a fat, loose-lipped man—guffawed. He bellowed something about poodles dancing and women acting—no woman, he said, could possibly be an actress. He hinted—you can imagine what. She could get no training in her craft. Could she even seek her dinner in a tavern or roam the streets at midnight? Yet her genius was for fiction and lusted to feed abundantly upon the lives of men and women and the study of their ways. At last—for she was very young, oddly like Shakespeare the poet in her face, with the same grey eyes and rounded brows—at last Nick Greene the actor-manager took pity on her; she found herself with child by that gentleman and so—who shall measure the heat and violence of the poet's heart when caught and tangled in a woman's body?—killed herself one winter's night and lies buried at some cross-roads where the omnibuses now stop outside the Elephant and Castle.

That, more or less, is how the story would run, I think, if a woman in Shakespeare's day had had Shakespeare's genius.

---

3. **she wanted to act** In Shakespeare's time, women were not allowed to act on stage. Men, dressed as women, played female roles.

Reading Strategy
Repairing Comprehension
If you were wondering whether these events actually occurred, what questions might you ask to clarify that point?

Like him, She had a taste for the theater.

Critical Reading ©

© 1. Key Ideas and Details (a) What details does Woolf include to give an identity to Shakespeare's sister? **(b) Infer:** What does she hope to accomplish by doing so?

© 2. Integration of Knowledge and Ideas Would Woolf say that the same obstacles blocking Shakespeare's sister existed in Woolf's own time?

© 3. Integration of Knowledge and Ideas How do the selections by Woolf reveal her to be a writer interested in changing tradition? In your response, use at least two of these Essential Question words: *convention, defy, credible, narrative, stream of consciousness.* *[Connecting to the Essential Question: What is the relationship of the writer to tradition?]*

Cite textual evidence to support your responses.

After You Read

The Lady in the Looking Glass • from *Mrs. Dalloway* • *Shakespeare's Sister*

Literary Analysis

© **1. Craft and Structure** Give three examples of the use of the **stream-of-consciousness** technique in "The Lady in the Looking Glass."

© **2. Craft and Structure (a)** How does the literal reflection of Isabella in the mirror serve as a climax for the narrator's mental reflections? **(b)** What does the climax reveal about Isabella?

© **3. Craft and Structure (a)** In the excerpt from *Mrs. Dalloway,* how does the focus of the narrator shift? **(b)** How does Woolf's choice of a narrative **point of view** make that shift possible?

© **4. Craft and Structure (a)** What is similar in writing style in all three selections? **(b)** What does Woolf gain by using this style?

© **5. Craft and Structure (a)** How would you describe Woolf's narrative voice in the essay "Shakespeare's Sister"? **(b)** How does that voice compare to those of the narrators of the other two selections? Use a chart like the one shown to list details about each narrator.

"The Lady in the Looking Glass"	*Mrs. Dalloway*	"Shakespeare's Sister"
Narrator has limited knowledge until end	Omniscient narrator	

© **6. Integration of Knowledge and Ideas** What does Woolf's use of the stream-of-consciousness technique show about how we construct a picture of another person?

7. Analyzing Visual Information In the caricature of Woolf on this page, what qualities of Woolf or her work does David Levine capture?

Reading Strategy

8. (a) In "The Lady in the Looking Glass," what **questions** about the narrator might you ask? **(b)** What answers does the story suggest?

9. (a) What impression did you have of Mrs. Dalloway after reading the first long paragraph in the passage? **(b)** What questions would you ask about her to confirm that impression? **(c)** Did you have the same impression after reading the entire passage?

10. (a) What did you think would happen to Shakespeare's sister when Woolf introduced her? **(b)** What questions might you have asked to anticipate the ending?

© **Common Core State Standards**

Language
4.d. Verify the preliminary determination of the meaning of a word or phrase. *(p. 1205)*

▲ David Levine caricature of Woolf from November 20, 1980

⊚ Vocabulary Acquisition and Use

Word Analysis: Latin Root -trans-

The Latin root -trans-, meaning "through" or "across," appears in the word *transient*, which Woolf uses in "The Lady in the Looking Glass." In that word, the root conveys the idea that an emotion or thought passes quickly, moving *through* a person rapidly. Use the meaning of -trans- to define these phrases that include the root.

1. transnational corporation
2. business transaction
3. transatlantic communication
4. transparent proceedings
5. transfer station
6. transformational experience

After defining the phrases, check your meanings by looking up the words in a dictionary.

Vocabulary: Sentence Completions

Use a word from the vocabulary list on page 1191 to complete each sentence, and explain your choice. Use each word only once.

1. The _____ hostess helped everyone at her party have a good time.
2. Constant _____ from his boss convinced the harried worker to resign.
3. The decisions of the Supreme Court are _____ and cannot be appealed.
4. How did the trickster manage to avoid the consequences of that particular _____?
5. The setting sun _____ the room with red-orange light.
6. The shy man was _____ to speak at the crowded meeting.
7. "It is just a passing fad, a _____ movement," declared the critic.
8. The preacher contrasted the _____ of worldly goods with the eternal nature of the spirit.

Using Resources to Build Vocabulary

Precise Words for Movement

Many words have synonyms, or other words with a similar meaning, but each word has a precise meaning. Woolf uses several words to describe the movements of light or objects in "The Lady in the Looking Glass":

> pirouetting (p. 1193)   trembling (p. 1193)
> pecking (p. 1193)   loomed (p. 1194)

Use a print or electronic dictionary or thesaurus to find synonyms of these words. State whether you think Woolf used the most effective word or whether you would recommend that she use one of the synonyms. Explain your reasoning.

PERFORMANCE TASKS

Integrated Language Skills

Writing

© Informative Text While a traditional omniscient third-person narrator can penetrate the thoughts of characters, the stream-of-consciousness technique gives the author an opportunity to show those thoughts in more complex ways. At the same time, this technique puts demands on readers. Choose a passage from "The Lady in the Looking Glass" or *Mrs. Dalloway* that you think is a good representative of the stream-of-consciousness technique. Then "translate" that passage into the style of a traditional omniscient third-person narrator. Finally, write a brief essay in which you state whether you prefer the original version or your "translation" and explain why.

Prewriting Begin by choosing a passage to "translate."

- Look for a passage that effectively presents the flow of the character's thoughts and feelings.
- Pick a passage that you found difficult to understand.

Drafting Write a "translation" of the passage that converts it to that of a traditional omniscient narrator.

- Remember that an omniscient narrator can reveal the inner thoughts of a character but does not use the fragmented words and phrases or association of ideas that mark stream-of-consciousness narration.
- Draft a brief **essay** that compares the two techniques. You might think about the different opportunities each gives to writers and the demands each places on readers. You might use a graphic organizer like the one below to take notes on the two points of view.

Revising Revise your essay to make it clear and effective:

- Review the draft of your "translation," making sure it is true to the traditional narrative style.
- Review the draft of your essay to ensure that you clearly state your position and cite evidence to support your points.
- Read both drafts carefully to make sure they are grammatically correct and all words are spelled correctly.

Common Core State Standards

Writing
2. Write informative/explanatory texts to examine and convey complex ideas, concepts, and information clearly and accurately through the effective selection, organization, and analysis of content.

Language
1. Demonstrate command of the conventions of standard English grammar and usage when writing or speaking. *(p. 1207)*
2.b. Spell correctly.

Conventions and Style: Parallel Structure

Good writers use **parallel structure,** or similar grammatical forms, to express similar ideas. Parallel structure gives your writing rhythm and emphasizes key ideas. To create parallel structure, use nouns with nouns, phrases with phrases, and clauses with clauses.

Look at the examples below. Notice that coordinating conjunctions (*and, or*) join items of equal importance.

Nonparallel: Look past the room *with its rugs, with its bookcases, and the night creatures that were dancing around.*	**Parallel:** Look past the room *with its rugs, with its bookcases, and with its dancing night creatures.*
Nonparallel: It was a fact *that Isabella was rich, and she took risks to collect objects.*	**Parallel:** It was a fact *that Isabella was rich and that she took risks to collect objects.*
Nonparallel: Isabella went into the garden *because of its flowers rather than because she wanted quiet.*	**Parallel:** Isabella went into the garden *because of its flowers rather than because of its quiet.*

As you edit your writing, check for parallel structure.

Practice Rewrite each item to correct the non-parallel structure.

1. Lights and shadows moved across the room, curtains blew, and there were petals that fell.
2. Rage, envy, and sorrowing seemed to fill the room.
3. Isabella went from the house, down the grass path, and she walked into the garden.
4. Isabella would choose a trailing plant rather than it was an upright, sturdy flower.
5. Because it was hot, the windows and doors were open, letting in sounds of life and to contrast with the scene in the mirror.
6. Isabella bought the house, traveled to far off places, and choosing furnishings.
7. The envelopes lay on the marble table, seeming to be out of order and not focusing.
8. Letters can reveal a person's past— appointments, dates not kept, and breaking promises.
9. She was seen in the looking glass, pausing, straightening a rose, and to lift a bloom to smell it.
10. Was her expression scornful or sensitive, shining or in a dull way?

Writing and Speaking Conventions

A. Writing Use the following items to write sentences with parallel structure:

1. feet, tails, beaks
2. of affection, of jealousy, of parting
3. marble-topped table, long grass path, the sunflowers
4. raising, looking, thinking

   Example: feet, tails, beaks

   Sentence: The birds lifted their feet, spread their tails, and tapped their beaks.

B. Speaking Consider the letters mentioned in "The Lady in the Looking Glass." Compose and present to the class a letter that might be written by the narrator who is imagining the contents of the drawers. Use at least three examples of parallel structure.

PH WRITING COACH

Further instruction and practice are available in *Prentice Hall Writing Coach.*

Stream-of-Consciousness
IN WORLD LITERATURE

Comparing Literary Works

"The Lady in the Looking Glass"
by Virginia Woolf • from *Pedro Páramo by*
Juan Rulfo • from *The Nine Guardians*
by Rosario Castellanos

Comparing Stream-of-Consciousness Narratives

Stream-of-Consciousness Narration

In the early twentieth century, writers like James Joyce and Virginia Woolf tried to capture all the layers of consciousness observed in the groundbreaking work of Austrian psychoanalyst Sigmund Freud—visual and auditory perceptions, associations, memories, dreams, unconscious impulses—all flowing through the mind in what psychologist William James called the stream of consciousness. **Stream-of-consciousness narration** has these traits:

- Whether it uses first- or third-person point of view, it presents the external world through one or more characters' impressions.
- It leaps abruptly to new mental associations.
- It may shift in time, presenting memories or flashbacks.
- It may include fantasy elements or even dreams.
- It may use symbols that can be interpreted to reveal character.
- It may use long sentences or irregular grammar or punctuation to capture the flow of thoughts.

As you read, use a form like the one shown to help you compare the stream-of-consciousness narration in these selections.

> Selection: _____
> Character(s) Portrayed: _____
> Leaps to New Associations: _____
> Time Shifts/Memories or Flashbacks: _____
> Fantasies or Dreams: _____
> Symbols and Interpretations: _____
> Unusual Grammar/Usage/Punctuation: _____

Ⓒ Gather Vocabulary Knowledge

Rulfo and Castellanos use related forms of the words *sweeping, swirling,* and *lashing.* Use a **dictionary** to find each word's part of speech and definition. Then, employ the following references to further explore these words:

- **History of Language:** Use a history of English to research each word's origins. Write a paragraph about the word's emergence in English.
- **Book of Quotations:** Use an online or print collection of quotations to find a quotation containing one of the words. In a paragraph, explain nuances in meaning that are evident from the context of the quotation.

Comparing References Compare and contrast what you learn about the words from these and other related references (printed or electronic), such as **books of roots and affixes.**

Ⓒ **Common Core
State Standards**

Reading Literature
3. Analyze the impact of the author's choices regarding how to develop and relate elements of a story or drama.

Language
4.c. Consult general and specialized reference materials, both print and digital, to find the pronunciation of a word or determine or clarify its precise meaning, its part of speech, its etymology, or its standard usage.

PHLit
Online!
www.PHLitOnline.com

JUAN RULFO (1918–1986)

The son of wealthy landowners, Juan Rulfo (hwän rōōl' fō) grew up at a time when violent rebellion was tearing the Mexican countryside apart. When his father was killed and his mother died soon after, he lived for a time in an orphanage before moving to Mexico City. There he held a variety of jobs and also wrote fiction and screenplays, drawing on the tormented landscape of his childhood to produce the story collection *The Burning Plain* and the short novel *Pedro Páramo*.

A Literary Pioneer Although he wrote only two major works, Rulfo's influence on Latin American literature has been enormous. One of the first Spanish-language writers to use stream-of-consciousness narration, he also blended reality and fantasy to pioneer the magical realism that became so popular in Latin American fiction. The great magical realist Gabriel García Márquez recognized his debt to Rulfo by including a line from *Pedro Páramo* in his famous novel *One Hundred Years of Solitude*.

ROSARIO CASTELLANOS (1925–1974)

Rosario Castellanos (rō sär' ē ō käs tel yä' nōs) grew up in the southern Mexican region of Chiapas, where her family owned sugar and coffee plantations. Here she saw firsthand the poverty of the indigenous Mayan population whose plight she would later portray in her writing. After graduating from college in Mexico City, she began publishing essays and poetry. She won fame with her novel *The Nine Guardians*, published in 1957.

Battling for Justice A champion of social and economic justice, Rosario Castellanos wrote with deep concern about women's rights and the rights of Mexico's indigenous peoples. She also held several government posts and, as a member of the National Indigenous Institute, worked to promote literacy in impoverished parts of the country. She was serving as Mexico's ambassador to Israel when she died in an accident there in 1974.

from
Pedro Páramo
Juan Rulfo

BACKGROUND To fulfill his mother's deathbed request of vengeance against the man who abandoned their family, Juan Preciado goes in search of his father, Pedro Páramo. He travels to Comala, his mother's home town, only to learn that his father has died years before. Comala itself is a ghost town—literally, for the reader gradually comes to realize that all of the people Preciado encounters there are ghosts. The book shifts point of view to some of those people; in the following passage, the voice talking is probably that of Doña Susanita, Pedro Páramo's last wife.

I am lying in the same bed where my mother died so long ago; on the same mattress, beneath the same black wool coverlet she wrapped us in to sleep. I slept beside her, her little girl, in the special place she made for me in her arms.

I think I can still feel the calm rhythm of her breathing; the palpitations and sighs that soothed my sleep. . . . I think I feel the pain of her death. . . . But that isn't true.

Here I lie, flat on my back, hoping to forget my loneliness by remembering those times. Because I am not here just for a while. And I am not in my mother's bed but in a black box like the ones for burying the dead. Because I am dead.

Vocabulary
palpitations
(pal´ pə tā´ shənz) *n.*
rapid beating of the heart

I sense where I am, but I can think. . . .

I think about the limes ripening. About the February wind that used to snap the fern stalks before they dried up from neglect. The ripe limes that filled the overgrown patio with their fragrance.

The wind blew down from the mountains on February mornings. And the clouds gathered there waiting for the warm weather that would force them down into the valley. Meanwhile the sky was blue, and the light played on little whirlwinds sweeping across the earth, swirling the dust and lashing the branches of the orange trees.

The sparrows were twittering; they pecked at the wind-blown leaves, and twittered. They left their feathers among the thorny branches, and chased the butterflies, and twittered. It was that season.

February, when the mornings are filled with wind and sparrows and blue light. I remember. That is when my mother died.

I should have wailed. I should have wrung my hands until they were bleeding. That is how you would have wanted it. But in fact, wasn't that a joyful morning? The breeze was blowing in through the open door, tearing loose the ivy tendrils.

Critical Reading

Cite textual evidence to support your responses.

1. **Key Ideas and Details (a)** What has happened to the narrator to cause her to lie in the black box? **(b) Infer:** What is the black box? **(c) Analyze:** Why does she pretend to be a little girl in her mother's bed?

2. **Key Ideas and Details (a) Compare and Contrast:** Contrast the narrator's attitude toward the morning her mother died with the attitude she thinks she is supposed to have. **(b) Analyze:** Why do you think she feels the way she does about the morning?

3. **Integration of Knowledge and Ideas (a) Interpret:** What does the passage suggest about death in general? **(b) Support:** Cite details to support your interpretation.

from
The Nine Guardians
Rosario Castellanos

BACKGROUND Set in the remote towns and countryside of 1930s Chiapas, Mexico, *The Nine Guardians* depicts the harsh poverty of the area's Mayan Indians and the changes to society brought about by government efforts to improve economic conditions. Most of the book is narrated by a nameless seven-year-old girl from a family of ranch owners, through whose eyes and mind we see the social landscape mixed together with the nursery tales and fantasies of childhood. In this passage from early in the book, the narrator walks through the nearby town with Nana, the devoted Indian servant who has cared for her since birth.

Nana leads me through the street by the hand. The pavements are flagstones, polished and slippery. The street is cobbled. Little stones are arranged like petals in a flower. From between the joints grows short grass which the Indians tear up with the points of their machetes.[1] There are carts drawn by sleepy bullocks;[2] and ponies that strike sparks with their hoofs; and old horses tied to posts by their halters. All day they remain there, heads hanging, ears sadly twitching. We've just passed one. I held my breath and pressed close to the wall, afraid that any minute the horse would bare its great yellow teeth—and he has such lots of them—and bite my arm. I'd be ashamed, because my arms are very skinny and the horse might laugh.

The balconies are forever staring into the street, watching it go uphill and down and the way it turns the corners. Watching the gentlemen pass with their mahogany canes; the ranchers dragging their spurs as they walk; the Indians running under their heavy burdens. And at all times the diligent trotting donkeys loaded with water in wooden tubs. It must be nice to be like the balconies, always idle, absent-minded, just looking on. When I'm grown up. . . .

Vocabulary
diligent (dil´ ə jənt) *adj.*
persevering and careful

---

1. **machetes** (mə shet´ *or* chet´ əz) *n.* large, heavy blades used for cutting down sugar cane, dense underbrush, or other plants.
2. **bullocks** (bool´ ə ks) *n.* bulls that have been neutered.

Comparing Stream-of-Consciousness Narration Do any details indicate that this is a child's stream of consciousness, unlike the stream-of-consciousness narratives of the mature women in *Pedro Páramo* and *Mrs. Dalloway*?

Now we begin climbing down Market Hill. The butchers' hatchets are ringing inside, and the stupid, sated flies are buzzing. We trip over the Indian women sitting on the ground weaving palm. They are talking together in their odd language, panting like hunted deer. And suddenly they let their sobs fly into the air, high-pitched, without tears. They always frighten me though I've heard them so often.

We skirt past the puddles. Last night came the first shower, the one that brings out the little ants with wings that go *tzisim*. We pass in front of the shops smelling of freshly dyed cloth. Behind the counter the assistant is measuring with a yard-stick. We can hear the grains of rice pattering against the metal scales. Someone is crumbling a handful of cocoa. And through the open street doors goes a girl with a basket on her head, and she screams, afraid that either the dogs or the owners will let fly at her:

"Dumplings—come buy!"

Nana urges me on. Now the only person in the street is a man with squeaking yellow shoes he can't have worn very often. A large door is wide open, and in front of the lighted forge[3] stands the blacksmith, dark from his trade. His chest shows bare and sweating as he hammers. An old maid opens her window just wide enough to watch us furtively. Her mouth is clamped tight as if she'd locked some secret in. She is sad because she knows her hair is turning white.

"Say how-do-you-do, child, she's a friend of your mother."

But we're already some distance off. The last few steps I almost run. I mustn't be late for school.

---

3. forge *n.* the place where a blacksmith heats metal and hammers it into shape.

Vocabulary

sated (sāt´ id) *adj.* with appetite satisfied; full from eating

furtively (fur´ tiv lē) *adv.* in a sneaky or secretive manner

Critical Reading

Cite textual evidence to support your responses.

1. **Key Ideas and Details (a)** Where is the narrator going? **(b) Infer:** Why does Nana accompany her? **(c) Infer:** What does the presence of Nana suggest about the social or economic standing of the narrator's family?

2. **Key Ideas and Details (a)** List some of the people, animals, or things the narrator observes as she walks through the town. **(b) Draw Conclusions:** From the details, what can you conclude the town is like?

3. **Key Ideas and Details (a)** With what emotions does the narrator react to the world around her? **(b) Evaluate:** Would you say she has a vivid imagination? Why or why not?

After You Read

The Lady in the Looking Glass •
from *Pedro Páramo* • from *The Nine Guardians*

Comparing Stream-of-Consciousness Narration

1. Craft and Structure In your estimation, in which of the three selections does the **stream-of-consciousness narration** best capture the way the human mind works? Cite examples to support your opinion.

2. Integration of Knowledge and Ideas **(a)** Contrast the point of view in the Woolf story with that of the selections by Rulfo and Castellanos. **(b)** Which narrative has the strongest sense of immediacy, making you feel as if you are there? Why?

3. Integration of Knowledge and Ideas **(a)** What do the narrator in Woolf's story and the narrators of the other two selections have in common? **(b)** What are some of their chief differences? **(c)** Which of the three characters seems most in touch with reality? Why?

Timed Writing

Informative Text: Analytical Essay

Each of these stream-of-consciousness narratives has to meet a challenge: how to use a character's thought processes, which are often chaotic, to convey a sense of the world around the character.

Assignment: Write an **analytical essay** in which you compare and contrast the ways in which the exterior world is conveyed in the three stream-of-consciousness narratives. **[40 minutes]**

Your essay should address these questions:

* Through whose eyes is the setting conveyed?

* What memories or other associations do the details of setting prompt in this person's mind?

* How do the character's perceptions and memories color your impression of the exterior world?

As you write, follow the conventions of a strong analytical essay:

* Advance a clear thesis statement.

* Support your ideas with relevant and substantial evidence and well-chosen details from the texts.

Remember to write legibly and use appropriate capitalization and punctuation conventions.

5-Minute Planner

Complete these steps before you begin to write:

1. Read the assignment carefully. Identify key words and phrases.

2. Weigh the similarities and differences in the ways in which each selection conveys the setting. **TIP** As you scan the texts, jot down quotations or details that you might use in your essay.

3. Create a rough outline for your essay.

4. Reread the prompt, and draft your essay.

Common Core State Standards

Writing
2. Write informative/explanatory texts to examine and convey complex ideas, concepts, and information clearly and accurately through the effective selection, organization, and analysis of content.

10. Write routinely over extended time frames and shorter time frames for a range of tasks, purposes, and audiences.

USE ACADEMIC VOCABULARY

As you write, use academic language, including the following words or their related forms:

approximates
clarify
coherent
emerge

For more on academic language, see the vocabulary charts in the introduction to this book.

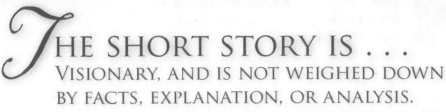

THE SHORT STORY IS . . .
VISIONARY, AND IS NOT WEIGHED DOWN BY FACTS, EXPLANATION, OR ANALYSIS.

— ELIZABETH BOWEN

Defining the Contemporary Short Story

A short story is a brief work of fiction that usually features a plot with a distinct beginning, middle, and end. In the late nineteenth century, most writers used a formulaic structure that involved a suspenseful climax and a dramatic ending. In the twentieth century, British writers like Virginia Woolf, Henry Green, and Katherine Mansfield strove to depict life more truthfully and modernized the short story. Later writers such as D. H. Lawrence, Graham Greene, and Doris Lessing continued to develop the form.

Literary Elements The short story and the novel share basic narrative elements:

- **Plot:** the ordered sequence of events that explores characters in conflict in many modern stories. The plot builds to a crucial moment in which the conflict is altered, but not necessarily resolved.
- **Conflict:** a struggle between opposing forces
- **Setting:** the time and place of a story's action
- **Character:** a person or creature that participates in the action of a story
- **Theme:** the central idea, message, or insight expressed in a story
- **Point of view:** the vantage point from which a story is told. In *first-person point of view*, the narrator is a character in the story who speaks in the first person. In *third-person point of view*, the narrator is a voice outside the action. A *third-person omniscient* narrator is all-knowing and can reveal all the characters' thoughts and feelings. A *third-person limited* narrator reveals only what a single character experiences, thinks, and feels.

Close Read: Literary Elements
These additional narrative elements appear in the Model text at right.

Irony: a discrepancy between appearance and reality, between what is said and what is meant, or between expectation and outcome Example: *"The scientist, who all the time had been leaning back in a big chair, sipping his coffee and smiling with skeptical good humor, chipped in and explained . . . about . . . the progress of science."* (Doris Lessing)	**Flashback:** a type of plot device in which a scene from the past interrupts an ongoing sequence of events Example: *"The young girl talking to the soldier in the garden had not ever completely seen his face. It was dark; they were saying goodbye under a tree."* (Elizabeth Bowen)
Dialogue: the words characters speak; dialogue may advance the story's action and show what characters are like Example: *"Oh!" said the boy. "Then what is luck, mother?"* *"It's what causes you to have money. . . ."* (D.H. Lawrence)	**Characterization:** the revelation of characters' personalities through descriptions of their appearances, feelings, thoughts, and actions Example: *"There was a woman who was beautiful, who started with all the advantages, yet she had no luck."* (D.H. Lawrence)

Model

About the Text One of the dominant figures in Russian Realism, Anton Chekhov (1860–1904) excelled at two literary forms: drama and the short story. His work is noted for both its compassion and objectivity.

from "Home"
by Anton Chekhov (translated by Constance Garnett)

"Someone came from the Grigoryevs' to fetch a book, but I said you were not at home. The postman brought the newspaper and two letters. By the way, Yevgeny Petrovitch, I should like to ask you to speak to Seryozha. To-day, and the day before yesterday, I have noticed that he is smoking. When I began to expostulate with him, he put his fingers in his ears as usual, and sang loudly to drown my voice."

Yvgeny Petrovitch Bykovsky, the prosecutor of the circuit court, who had just come back from a session and was taking off his gloves in his study, looked at the governess as she made her report, and laughed.

"Seryozha smoking . . ." he said, shrugging his shoulders. "I can picture the little cherub with a cigarette in his mouth! Why, how old is he?"

"Seven. You think it is not important, but at his age smoking is a bad and pernicious habit, and bad habits ought to be eradicated in the beginning."

"Perfectly true. And where does he get the tobacco?"

"He takes it from the drawer in your table."

"Yes? In that case, send him to me."

When the governess had gone out, Bykovsky. . . called up memories of the long past, half-forgotten time when smoking aroused in his teachers and parents a strange, not quite intelligible horror. . . . Yvegeny Petrovitch remembered the head-master of the high school, a very cultured and good-natured old man, who was so appalled when he found a high-school boy with a cigarette in his mouth that he turned pale, immediately summoned an emergency committee of the teachers, and sentenced the sinner to expulsion. . . .

"What am I to say to him, though?" Yvgeny Petrovitch wondered.

But before he had time to think of anything whatever his son Seryozha, a boy of seven, walked into the study. . . .

"Good evening, papa!" he said, in a soft voice, clambering on to his father's knee and giving him a rapid kiss on his neck. "Did you send for me?" . . .

"Natalya Semyonovna has just been complaining to me that you have been smoking. . . . Is it true? Have you been smoking?"

"Yes, I did smoke once. . . . That's true. . . ."

"Now you see you are lying as well," said the prosecutor, frowning to disguise a smile. "Natalya Semyonovna has seen you smoking twice. So you see you have been detected in three misdeeds: smoking, taking someone else's tobacco, and lying. Three faults."

Characterization The passage begins to develop Bilovsky's character—he is a successful lawyer who does not seem to view life, or child rearing, with too much gravity.

Dialogue The conversation between the governess and Bilovsky both reveals differences in the two characters' personalities and sets up the action that is to follow.

Flashback As Bilovsky prepares to scold his son, a flashback in the form of a memory interrupts the narrative. The information it provides helps readers understand Bilovsky's mild reaction to his son's behavior.

Irony The discrepancy between Bilovsky's feelings of amusement and his stern statements is ironic. The irony emphasizes both Bilovsky's understanding of his paternal role and the tenderness he feels toward his son.

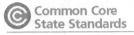

Before You Read

The Lagoon • Araby

Connecting to the Essential Question Conrad and Joyce tried to find new ways to explore language and human relationships. As you read, find details in these stories that show new approaches to storytelling. These details will help you think about the Essential Question: **What is the relationship of the writer to tradition?**

Common Core State Standards

Reading Literature
5. Analyze how an author's choices regarding how to structure specific parts of a text contribute to its overall structure and meaning as well as its aesthetic impact.

Literary Analysis

Both Conrad and Joyce use **plot devices** to achieve aesthetic effects as they relate the events of a story.

- In "The Lagoon," Conrad tells a **story within a story**—a tale told by a character within a framing fictional narrative.
- In "Araby," Joyce builds toward an **epiphany**—a character's sudden insight—which forms the climax of the story.

Comparing Literary Works Plot devices have a close connection with the **themes,** or central meaning, of a story. "The Lagoon" is told by a neutral narrator outside the story—but the story within this story is told in the first person, with passion. By juxtaposing these two points of view, Conrad reveals one of his themes: the relation of passion to the act of storytelling. Similarly, Joyce's epiphany depends on the contrast between the narrator's passion at the time of the story and his detachment later, when he tells the story. As you read, compare the implications that these plot devices have for the themes of the stories in which they are used.

Reading Strategy

Preparing to Read Complex Texts Plots are a sequence of causally connected events. That is, one event usually causes another, which in turn triggers yet another effect. The sequence continues until the action closes. **Identifying cause-and-effect relationships** in a plot can help you understand the author's themes. As you read, use a graphic organizer like the one shown.

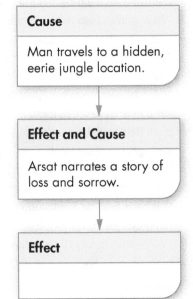

Cause
Man travels to a hidden, eerie jungle location.

Effect and Cause
Arsat narrates a story of loss and sorrow.

Effect

Vocabulary

invincible (in vin′ sə bəl) *adj.* unconquerable (p. 1222)

propitiate (prō pish′ ē āt) *v.* win the goodwill of; appease (p. 1222)

conflagration (kän′ flə grā′ shən) *n.* great fire (p. 1224)

imperturbable (im′ pər tʉr′ bə bəl) *adj.* calm; not easily ruffled (p. 1237)

garrulous (gar′ ə ləs) *adj.* talkative (p. 1239)

derided (di rīd′ id) *v.* made fun of; ridiculed (p. 1241)

Joseph Conrad

(1857–1924)

Author of **"The Lagoon"**

It is accomplishment enough to become one of the most distinguished novelists of your age, but to do so in your third language is an achievement almost without parallel. Born in Poland, Joseph Conrad mastered English only after acquiring Polish, his native language, and French.

At Sea in the World Orphaned at the age of eleven, Conrad fled his Russian-occupied homeland when he was sixteen. He landed first in France and later in England. He spent the next six years as an apprentice seaman. The voyages Conrad made to the corners of the globe—Asia, Africa, and South America—became the vivid settings of much of his fiction. In 1886, he became a master mariner and an English citizen.

A Storytelling Life Conrad published his first novel, *Almayer's Folly,* when he was in his late thirties. Three masterpieces followed: *Lord Jim* (1900); *Youth,* a collection of shorter pieces that includes his famous short story "Heart of Darkness" (1902); and *Nostromo* (1904).

Although many of Conrad's works may be read as thrilling tales of the sea, the notion of "voyage" in a work by Conrad translates to a voyage of self-discovery. The question of loyalty, so crucial for the survival of a ship's crew, appears as a question of the general frailty of human relationships and the limits of self-knowledge. The menacing jungles, vast oceans, and exotic people that confront the characters become metaphors for the hidden depths of the self. Telling tales set around the globe, Conrad charts a geography of the human soul.

THE
LAGOON

Joseph Conrad

BACKGROUND Between 1883 and 1888, Conrad sailed the Malay Archipelago—a group of Pacific islands that includes the Philippines and Indonesia—in British merchant ships. He used the knowledge he acquired of the region—of its language, landscape, and customs—to enrich his seafaring tales. It is likely that Captain William Lingard, revered as a spellbinding storyteller among sailors of the Malay settlements, was the model for Marlowe, who appears as the narrator of several Conrad stories.

The white man, leaning with both arms over the roof of the little house in the stern of the boat, said to the steersman—

"We will pass the night in Arsat's clearing. It is late."

The Malay[1] only grunted, and went on looking fixedly at the river. The white man rested his chin on his crossed arms and gazed at the wake of the boat. At the end of the straight avenue of forests cut by the intense glitter of the river, the sun appeared unclouded and dazzling, poised low over the water that shone smoothly like a band of metal. The forests, somber and dull, stood motionless and silent on each side of the broad stream. At the foot of big, towering trees trunkless nipa palms rose from the mud of the bank, in bunches of leaves enormous and heavy, that hung unstirring over the brown swirl of eddies. In the stillness of the air every tree, every leaf, every bough, every tendril of creeper and every petal of minute blossoms seemed to have been bewitched into an immobility perfect and final. Nothing moved on the river but the eight paddles that rose flashing regularly, dipped together with a single splash; while the steersman swept right and left with a periodic and sudden flourish of his blade describing a glinting semicircle above his head. The churned-up water frothed alongside with a confused murmur. And the white man's canoe, advancing up stream in the short-lived disturbance of its own making,

---

1. **Malay** (mā´ lā) native of the Malay peninsula in Southeast Asia.

seemed to enter the portals[2] of a land from which the very memory of motion had forever departed.

The white man, turning his back upon the setting sun, looked along the empty and broad expanse of the sea-reach. For the last three miles of its course the wandering, hesitating river, as if enticed irresistibly by the freedom of an open horizon, flows straight into the sea, flows straight to the east—to the east that harbors both light and darkness. Astern of the boat the repeated call of some bird, a cry discordant and feeble, skipped along over the smooth water and lost itself, before it could reach the other shore, in the breathless silence of the world.

The steersman dug his paddle into the stream, and held hard with stiffened arms, his body thrown forward. The water gurgled aloud; and suddenly the long straight reach seemed to pivot on its center, the forests swung in a semicircle, and the slanting beams of sunset touched the broadside of the canoe with a fiery glow, throwing the slender and distorted shadows of its crew upon the streaked glitter of the river. The white man turned to look ahead. The course of the boat had been altered at right-angles to the stream, and the carved dragonhead of its prow was pointing now at a gap in the fringing bushes of the bank. It glided through, brushing the overhanging twigs, and disappeared from the river like some slim and amphibious creature leaving the water for its lair in the forests.

---

2. **portals** (pôr′təlz) *n.* doors.

▲ **Critical Viewing**
Judging from this photograph, would it be difficult to escape from an enemy in jungle territory? Why or why not?
[Make a Judgment]

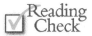

Reading Check

What is the white man's destination?

The Lagoon **1221**

The narrow creek was like a ditch: tortuous, fabulously deep; filled with gloom under the thin strip of pure and shining blue of the heaven. Immense trees soared up, invisible behind the festooned draperies of creepers. Here and there, near the glistening blackness of the water, a twisted root of some tall tree showed amongst the tracery of small ferns, black and dull, writhing and motionless, like an arrested snake. The short words of the paddlers reverberated loudly between the thick and somber walls of vegetation. Darkness oozed out from between the trees, through the tangled maze of the creepers, from behind the great fantastic and unstirring leaves; the darkness, mysterious and invincible; the darkness scented and poisonous of impenetrable forests.

The men poled in the shoaling[3] water. The creek broadened, opening out into a wide sweep of a stagnant lagoon. The forests receded from the marshy bank, leaving a level strip of bright green, reedy grass to frame the reflected blueness of the sky. A fleecy pink cloud drifted high above, trailing the delicate coloring of its image under the floating leaves and the silvery blossoms of the lotus. A little house, perched on high piles, appeared black in the distance. Near it, two tall nibong palms, that seemed to have come out of the forests in the background, leaned slightly over the ragged roof, with a suggestion of sad tenderness and care in the droop of their leafy and soaring heads.

The steersman, pointing with his paddle, said, "Arsat is there. I see his canoe fast between the piles."

The polers ran along the sides of the boat glancing over their shoulders at the end of the day's journey. They would have preferred to spend the night somewhere else than on this lagoon of weird aspect and ghostly reputation. Moreover, they disliked Arsat, first as a stranger, and also because he who repairs a ruined house, and dwells in it, proclaims that he is not afraid to live amongst the spirits that haunt the places abandoned by mankind. Such a man can disturb the course of fate by glances or words; while his familiar ghosts are not easy to propitiate by casual wayfarers upon whom they long to wreak the malice of their human master. White men care not for such things, being unbelievers and in league with the Father of Evil, who leads them unharmed through the invisible dangers of this world. To the warnings of the righteous they oppose an offensive pretense of disbelief. What is there to be done?

So they thought, throwing their weight on the end of their long poles. The big canoe glided on swiftly, noiselessly, and smoothly, toward Arsat's clearing, till, in a great rattling of poles thrown down, and the loud murmurs of "Allah[4] be praised!" it came with a gentle knock against the crooked piles below the house.

---

3. shoaling shallow.
4. Allah (al′ ə) Muslim name for God.

The boatmen with uplifted faces shouted discordantly, "Arsat! O Arsat!" Nobody came. The white man began to climb the rude ladder giving access to the bamboo platform before the house. The juragan[5] of the boat said sulkily, "We will cook in the sampan,[6] and sleep on the water."

"Pass my blankets and the basket," said the white man curtly.

He knelt on the edge of the platform to receive the bundle. Then the boat shoved off, and the white man, standing up, confronted Arsat, who had come out through the low door of his hut. He was a man young, powerful, with a broad chest and muscular arms. He had nothing on but his sarong.[7] His head was bare. His big, soft eyes stared eagerly at the white man, but his voice and demeanor were composed as he asked, without any words of greeting—

"Have you medicine, Tuan?"[8]

"No," said the visitor in a startled tone. "No. Why? Is there sickness in the house?"

"Enter and see," replied Arsat, in the same calm manner, and turning short round, passed again through the small doorway. The white man, dropping his bundles, followed.

In the dim light of the dwelling he made out on a couch of bamboos a woman stretched on her back under a broad sheet of red cotton cloth. She lay still, as if dead; but her big eyes, wide open, glittered in the gloom, staring upward at the slender rafters, motionless and unseeing. She was in a high fever, and evidently unconscious. Her cheeks were sunk slightly, her lips were partly open, and on the young face there was the ominous and fixed expression—the absorbed, contemplating expression of the unconscious who are going to die. The two men stood looking down at her in silence.

"Has she been long ill?" asked the traveler.

"I have not slept for five nights," answered the Malay, in a deliberate tone. "At first she heard voices calling her from the water and struggled against me who held her. But since the sun of today rose she hears nothing—she hears not me. She sees nothing. She sees not me—me!"

---

5. **juragan** (jōō rä´ gän) captain or master.
6. **sampan** small flat-bottomed boat with a cabin formed by mats.
7. **sarong** long, brightly colored strip of cloth worn like a skirt.
8. **Tuan** (twan) Malayan for "sir."

Reading Check

What is wrong in Arsat's house?

SHE LAY STILL
AS IF DEAD...

Literary Analysis
Plot Devices Is the narrator of the story closer in point of view to the white man or Arsat? Explain.

Vocabulary
conflagration (kän′ flə grā′ shən) *n.* great fire

He remained silent for a minute, then asked softly—

"Tuan, will she die?"

"I fear so," said the white man sorrowfully. He had known Arsat years ago, in a far country in times of trouble and danger, when no friendship is to be despised. And since his Malay friend had come unexpectedly to dwell in the hut on the lagoon with a strange woman, he had slept many times there, in his journeys up and down the river. He liked the man who knew how to keep faith in council and how to fight without fear by the side of his white friend. He liked him—not so much perhaps as a man likes his favorite dog—but still he liked him well enough to help and ask no questions, to think sometimes vaguely and hazily in the midst of his own pursuits, about the lonely man and the long-haired woman with audacious face and triumphant eyes, who lived together by the forests—alone and feared.

The white man came out of the hut in time to see the enormous conflagration of sunset put out by the swift and stealthy shadows that, rising like a black and impalpable vapor above the treetops, spread over the heaven, extinguishing the crimson glow of floating clouds and the red brilliance of departing daylight. In a few moments all the stars came out above the intense blackness of the earth, and the great lagoon gleaming suddenly with reflected lights resembled an oval patch of night sky flung down into the hopeless and abysmal night of the wilderness. The white man had some supper out of the basket, then collecting a few sticks that lay about the platform, made up a small fire, not for warmth, but for the sake of the smoke, which would keep off the mosquitos. He wrapped himself in his blankets and sat with his back against the reed wall of the house, smoking thoughtfully.

Arsat came through the doorway with noiseless steps and squatted down by the fire. The white man moved his outstretched legs a little.

"She breathes," said Arsat in a low voice, anticipating the expected question. "She breathes and burns as if with a great fire. She speaks not; she hears not—and burns!" He paused for a moment, then asked in a quiet, incurious tone—

"Tuan . . . will she die?"

The white man moved his shoulders uneasily, and muttered in a hesitating manner—

"If such is her fate."

"No, Tuan," said Arsat calmly. "If such is my fate. I hear, I see, I wait. I remember . . . Tuan, do you remember the old days? Do you remember my brother?"

"Yes," said the white man. The Malay rose suddenly and went in.

The other, sitting still outside, could hear the voice in the hut. Arsat said: "Hear me! Speak!" His words were succeeded by a complete silence. "O Diamelen!" he cried suddenly. After that cry there was a deep sigh. Arsat came out and sank down again in his old place.

They sat in silence before the fire. There was no sound within the house, there was no sound near them; but far away on the lagoon they could hear the voices of the boatmen ringing fitful and distinct on the calm water. The fire in the bows of the sampan shone faintly in the distance with a hazy red glow. Then it died out. The voices ceased. The land and the water slept invisible, unstirring and mute. It was as though there had been nothing left in the world but the glitter of stars streaming, ceaseless and vain, through the black stillness of the night.

The white man gazed straight before him into the darkness with wide-open eyes. The fear and fascination, the inspiration and the wonder of death—of death near, unavoidable, and unseen, soothed the unrest of his race and stirred the most indistinct, the most intimate of his thoughts. The ever-ready suspicion of evil, the gnawing suspicion that lurks in our hearts, flowed out into the stillness round him—into the stillness profound and dumb, and made it appear untrustworthy and infamous, like the placid and impenetrable mask of an unjustifiable violence. In that fleeting and powerful disturbance of his being the earth enfolded in the starlight peace became a shadowy country of inhuman strife, a battlefield of phantoms terrible and charming, august⁹ or ignoble¹⁰, struggling ardently for the possession of our helpless hearts. An unquiet and mysterious country of inextinguishable desires and fears.

A plaintive murmur rose in the night; a murmur saddening and startling, as if the great solitudes of surrounding woods had tried to whisper into his ear the wisdom of their immense and lofty indifference. Sounds hesitating and vague floated in the air round him, shaped themselves slowly into words; and at last flowed on gently in a murmuring stream of soft and monotonous sentences. He stirred like a man waking up and changed his position slightly. Arsat, motionless and shadowy, sitting with bowed head under the stars, was speaking in a low and dreamy tone—

". . . for where can we lay down the heaviness of our trouble but in a friend's heart? A man must speak of war and of love. You, Tuan, know what war is, and you have seen me in time of danger seek death as other men seek life! A writing may be lost; a lie may be written; but what the eye has seen is truth and remains in the mind!"

---

9. **august** (ô gust′) *adj.* worthy of great respect; inspiring awe.
10. **ignoble** (ig nō′ bəl) *adj.* of the common people; dishonorable.

Reading Strategy
Identifying Cause-and-Effect Relationships
What causes Arsat to speak to the white man?

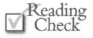
Reading Check
What does Arsat tell Tuan about the woman's health?

"I remember," said the white man quietly. Arsat went on with mournful composure—

"Therefore I shall speak to you of love. Speak in the night. Speak before both night and love are gone—and the eye of day looks upon my sorrow and my shame; upon my blackened face; upon my burnt-up heart."

A sigh, short and faint, marked an almost imperceptible pause, and then his words flowed on, without a stir, without a gesture.

"After the time of trouble and war was over and you went away from my country in the pursuit of your desires, which we, men of the islands, cannot understand, I and my brother became again, as we had been before, the sword bearers of the Ruler. You know we were men of family, belonging to a ruling race, and more fit than any to carry on our right shoulder the emblem of power. And in the time of prosperity Si Dendring showed us favor, as we, in time of sorrow, had showed to him the faithfulness of our courage. It was a time of peace. A time of deer hunts and cock fights; of idle talks and foolish squabbles between men whose bellies are full and weapons are rusty. But the sower watched the young rice shoots grow up without fear, and the traders came and went, departed lean and returned fat into the river of peace. They brought news too. Brought lies and truth mixed together, so that no man knew when to rejoice and when to be sorry. We heard from them about you also. They had seen you here and had seen you there. And I was glad to hear, for I remembered the stirring times, and I always remembered you, Tuan, till the time came when my eyes could see nothing in the past, because they had looked upon the one who is dying there—in the house."

He stopped to exclaim in an intense whisper, "O Mara bahia! O Calamity!" then went on speaking a little louder.

"There's no worse enemy and no better friend than a brother, Tuan, for one brother knows another, and in perfect knowledge is strength for good or evil. I loved my brother. I went to him and told him that I could see nothing but one face, hear nothing but one voice. He told me: 'Open your heart so that she can see what is in it—and wait. Patience is wisdom. Inchi Midah may die or our Ruler may throw off his fear of a woman!'. . . I waited!. . . You remember the lady with the veiled face, Tuan, and the fear of our Ruler before her cunning and temper. And if she wanted her servant, what could I do?

But I fed the hunger of my heart on short glances and stealthy words. I loitered on the path to the bath houses in the daytime, and when the sun had fallen behind the forest I crept along the jasmine hedges of the women's courtyard. Unseeing, we spoke to one another through the scent of flowers, through the veil of leaves, through the blades of long grass that stood still before our lips; so great was our prudence, so faint was the murmur of our great longing. The time passed swiftly . . . and there were whispers amongst women—and our enemies watched—my brother was gloomy, and I began to think of killing and of a fierce death. . . . We are of a people who take what they want—like you whites. There is a time when a man should forget loyalty and respect. Might and authority are given to rulers, but to all men is given love and strength and courage. My brother said, 'You shall take her from their midst. We are two who are like one.' And I answered, 'Let it be soon, for I find no warmth in sunlight that does not shine upon her.' Our time came when the Ruler and all the great people went to the mouth of the river to fish by torchlight. There were hundreds of boats, and on the white sand, between the water and the forests, dwellings of leaves were built for the households of the Rajahs.[11] The smoke of cooking fires was like a blue mist of the evening, and many voices rang in it joyfully. While they were making the boats ready to beat up the fish, my brother came to me and said, 'Tonight!' I looked to my weapons, and when the time came our canoe took its place in the circle of boats carrying the torches. The lights blazed on the water, but behind the boats there was darkness. When the shouting began and the excitement made them like mad we dropped out. The water swallowed our fire, and we floated back to the shore that was dark with only here and there the glimmer of embers. We could hear the talk of slave girls amongst the sheds. Then we found a place deserted and silent. We waited there. She came. She came running along the shore, rapid and leaving no trace, like a leaf driven by the wind into the sea. My brother said gloomily, 'Go and take her; carry her into our boat.' I lifted her in my arms. She panted. Her heart was beating against my breast. I said, 'I take you from those people. You came to the cry of my heart, but my arms take you into my boat against the will of the great!' 'It is right,' said my brother. 'We are men who take what we want and can hold it against many. We should have taken her in daylight.' I said, 'Let us be off'; for since she was in my boat I began to think of our Ruler's many men.

11. **Rajahs** (ra′ jez) Malayan chiefs.

Reading Strategy
Identifying Cause-and-Effect Relationships What causes Arsat to speak to the woman? What is the result of that action?

Reading Check

What do Arsat and his brother decide to do?

"LET IT BE SOON, FOR I FIND NO WARMTH IN SUNLIGHT THAT DOES NOT SHINE UPON HER."

'Yes. Let us be off,' said my brother. 'We are cast out and this boat is our country now—and the sea is our refuge.' He lingered with his foot on the shore, and I entreated him to hasten, for I remembered the strokes of her heart against my breast and thought that two men cannot withstand a hundred. We left, paddling downstream close to the bank; and as we passed by the creek where they were fishing, the great shouting had ceased, but the murmur of voices was loud like the humming of insects flying at noonday. The boats floated, clustered together, in the red light of torches, under a black roof of smoke; and men talked of their sport. Men that boasted, and praised, and jeered—men that would have been our friends in the morning, but on that night were already our enemies. We paddled swiftly past. We had no more friends in the country of our birth. She sat in the middle of the canoe with covered face; silent as she is now; unseeing as she is now—and I had no regret at what I was leaving because I could hear her breathing close to me—as I can hear her now."

He paused, listened with his ear turned to the doorway, then shook his head and went on.

"My brother wanted to shout the cry of challenge—one cry only—to let the people know we were freeborn robbers who trusted our arms and the great sea. And again I begged him in the name of our love to be silent. Could I not hear her breathing close to me? I knew the pursuit would come quick enough. My brother loved me. He dipped his paddle without a splash. He only said, 'There is half a man in you now—the other half is in that woman. I can wait. When you are a whole man again, you will come back with me here to shout defiance. We are sons of the same mother.' I made no answer. All my strength and all my spirit were in my hands that held the paddle—for I longed to be with her in a safe place beyond the reach of men's anger and of women's spite. My love was so great, that I thought it could guide me to a country where death was unknown,

Reading Strategy
Identifying Cause-and-Effect Relationships
What is the effect of the brothers' action? What do you think might happen next?

Literary Analysis
Plot Devices What do the pauses in Arsat's story indicate to the white man and the reader about Arsat's emotional state?

if I could only escape from Inchi Midah's fury and from our Ruler's sword. We paddled with haste, breathing through our teeth. The blades bit deep into the smooth water. We passed out of the river; we flew in clear channels amongst the shallows. We skirted the black coast; we skirted the sand beaches where the sea speaks in whispers to the land; and the gleam of white sand flashed back past our boat, so swiftly she ran upon the water. We spoke not. Only once I said, 'Sleep, Diamelen, for soon you may want all your strength.' I heard the sweetness of her voice, but I never turned my head. The sun rose and still we went on. Water fell from my face like rain from a cloud. We flew in the light and heat. I never looked back, but I knew that my brother's eyes, behind me, were looking steadily ahead, for the boat went as straight as a bushman's dart, when it leaves the end of the sumpitan.[12] There was no better paddler, no better steersman than my brother. Many times, together, we had won races in that canoe. But we never had put out our strength as we did then—then, when for the last time we paddled together! There was no braver or stronger man in our country than my brother. I could not spare the strength to turn my head and look at him, every moment I heard the hiss of his breath getting louder behind me. Still he did not speak. The sun was high. The heat clung to my back like a flame of fire. My ribs were ready to burst, but I could no longer get enough air into my chest. And then I felt I must cry out with my last breath. 'Let us rest!' . . . 'Good!' he answered; and his voice was firm. He was strong. He was brave. He knew not fear and no fatigue . . . My brother!"

---

12. **sumpitan** (sump′ ə tän) Malayan blowgun that discharges poisonous darts.

World
LITERATURE
Connection

Joseph Conrad, International Author
As a child, Jozeph Konrad Nalecz Korzeniowski (1857-1924) moved between cultures and languages. He was born in Berdichev, a city once part of Poland, that was under Russian rule. Polish was his first language, but he also spoke French and Russian.

When he was eleven, Jozeph was orphaned and went to live with his uncle in Switzerland. There he picked up some Italian and German. At seventeen, he shipped out with the French merchant marine. When he was 29, he earned British citizenship and changed his name to Joseph Conrad. Soon after, he settled in Britain.

Conrad did not begin writing until his early thirties, and when he did, he wrote in English. His first novel, *Almayer's Folly*, was published in 1895. Soon Conrad's fiction was published in French translation too. His work influenced leading French writers including André Gide, Marcel Proust, Louis-Ferdinand Céline, André Malraux, and Jean-Paul Sartre.

Connect to the Literature

What evidence of Conrad's ability to learn languages can you find in "The Lagoon"?

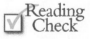

Reading Check

Have Arsat, his brother, and Diamelen escaped the Rajah? Explain.

A murmur powerful and gentle, a murmur vast and faint; the murmur of trembling leaves, of stirring boughs, ran through the tangled depths of the forests, ran over the starry smoothness of the lagoon, and the water between the piles lapped the slimy timber once with a sudden splash. A breath of warm air touched the two men's faces and passed on with a mournful sound—a breath loud and short like an uneasy sigh of the dreaming earth.

Arsat went on in an even, low voice:

"We ran our canoe on the white beach of a little bay close to a long tongue of land that seemed to bar our road; a long wooded cape going far into the sea. My brother knew that place. Beyond the cape a river has its entrance, and through the jungle of that land there is a narrow path. We made a fire and cooked rice. Then we lay down to sleep on the soft sand in the shade of our canoe, while she watched. No sooner had I closed my eyes than I heard her cry of alarm. We leaped up. The sun was halfway down the sky already, and coming in sight in the opening of the bay we saw a prau[13] manned by many paddlers. We knew it at once; it was one of our Rajah's praus. They were watching the shore, and saw us. They beat the gong, and turned the head of the prau into the bay. I felt my heart become weak within my breast. Diamelen sat on the sand and covered her face. There was no escape by sea. My brother laughed. He had the gun you had given him, Tuan, before you went away, but there was only a handful of

---

13. prau (prou) swift Malayan boat with a large sail.

powder. He spoke to me quickly: 'Run with her along the path. I shall keep them back, for they have no firearms, and landing in the face of a man with a gun is certain death for some. Run with her. On the other side of that wood there is a fisherman's house—and a canoe. When I have fired all the shots I will follow. I am a great runner, and before they can come up we shall be gone. I will hold out as long as I can, for she is but a woman—that can neither run nor fight, but she has your heart in her weak hands.' He dropped behind the canoe. The prau was coming. She and I ran, and as we rushed along the path I heard shots. My brother fired—once—twice—and the booming of the gong ceased. There was silence behind us. That neck of land is narrow. Before I heard my brother fire the third shot I saw the shelving shore, and I saw the water again: the mouth of a broad river. We crossed a grassy glade. We ran down to the water. I saw a low hut above the black mud, and a small canoe hauled up. I heard another shot behind me. I thought, 'That is his last charge.' We rushed down to the canoe; a man came running from the hut, but I leaped on him, and we rolled together in the mud. Then I got up, and he lay still at my feet. I don't know whether I had killed him or not. I and Diamelen pushed the canoe afloat. I heard yells behind me, and I saw my brother run across the glade. Many men were bounding after him. I took her in my arms and threw her into the boat, then leaped in myself.

▼ **Critical Viewing**
What aspects of Conrad's story does this photograph capture? **[Connect]**

Reading Check
What instructions does Arsat's brother give him?

"WE RAN OUR CANOE
ON THE WHITE BEACH
OF A LITTLE BAY..."

When I looked back I saw that my brother had fallen. He fell and was up again, but the men were closing round him. He shouted, 'I am coming!' The men were close to him. I looked. Many men. Then I looked at her. Tuan, I pushed the canoe! I pushed it into deep water. She was kneeling forward looking at me, and I said, 'Take your paddle,' while I struck the water with mine. Tuan, I heard him cry. I heard him cry my name twice; and I heard voices shouting, 'Kill! Strike!' I never turned back. I heard him calling my name again with a great shriek, as when life is going out together with the voice—and I never turned my head. My own name! . . . My brother! Three times he called—but I was not afraid of life. Was she not there in that canoe? And could I not with her find a country where death is forgotten—where death is unknown!"

The white man sat up. Arsat rose and stood, an indistinct and silent figure above the dying embers of the fire. Over the lagoon a mist drifting and low had crept, erasing slowly the glittering images of the stars. And now a great expanse of white vapor covered the land; it flowed cold and gray in the darkness, eddied in noiseless whirls round the tree-trunks and about the platform of the house, which seemed to float upon a restless and impalpable illusion of a sea. Only far away the tops of the trees stood outlined on the twinkle of heaven, like a somber and forbidding shore—a coast deceptive, pitiless and black.

Arsat's voice vibrated loudly in the profound peace.

"I had her there! I had her! To get her I would have faced all mankind. But I had her—and—"

His words went out ringing into the empty distances. He paused, and seemed to listen to them dying away very far—beyond help and beyond recall. Then he said quietly—

"Tuan, I loved my brother."

A breath of wind made him shiver. High above his head, high above the silent sea of mist the drooping leaves of the palms rattled together with a mournful and expiring sound. The white man stretched his legs. His chin rested on his chest, and he murmured sadly without lifting his head—

"We all love our brothers."

THEN HE SAID–
"SHE BURNS NO MORE."

Arsat burst out with an intense whispering violence—
"What did I care who died? I wanted peace in my own heart."

He seemed to hear a stir in the house—listened—then stepped in noiselessly. The white man stood up. A breeze was coming in fitful puffs. The stars shone paler as if they had retreated into the frozen depths of immense space. After a chill gust of wind there were a few seconds of perfect calm and absolute silence. Then from behind the black and wavy line of the forests a column of golden light shot up into the heavens and spread over the semicircle of the eastern horizon. The sun had risen. The mist lifted, broke into drifting patches, vanished into thin flying wreaths; and the unveiled lagoon lay, polished and black, in the heavy shadows at the foot of the wall of trees. A white eagle rose over it with a slanting and ponderous flight, reached the clear sunshine and appeared dazzlingly brilliant for a moment, then soaring higher, became a dark and motionless speck before it vanished into the blue as if it had left the earth forever. The white man, standing gazing upward before the doorway, heard in the hut a confused and broken murmur of distracted words ending with a loud groan. Suddenly Arsat stumbled out with outstretched hands, shivered, and stood still for some time with fixed eyes. Then he said—

"She burns no more."

Before his face the sun showed its edge above the treetops, rising steadily. The breeze freshened; a great brilliance burst upon the lagoon, sparkled on the rippling water. The forests came out of the clear shadows of the morning, became distinct, as if they had rushed nearer—to stop short in a great stir of leaves, of nodding boughs, of swaying branches. In the merciless sunshine the whisper of unconscious life grew louder, speaking in an incomprehensible voice round the dumb darkness of that human sorrow. Arsat's eyes wandered slowly, then stared at the rising sun.

"I can see nothing," he said half aloud to himself.

"There is nothing," said the white man, moving to the edge of the platform and waving his hand to his boat. A shout came faintly over the lagoon and the sampan began to glide toward the abode of the friend of ghosts.

"If you want to come with me, I will wait all the morning," said the white man, looking away upon the water.

Reading Strategy
Identifying Cause-and-Effect Relationships
What event causes Arsat to shiver? What else might have caused that reaction?

Reading Check
What happens to Arsat's brother?

"No, Tuan," said Arsat softly. "I shall not eat or sleep in this house, but I must first see my road. Now I can see nothing—see nothing! There is no light and no peace in the world; but there is death—death for many. We were sons of the same mother—and I left him in the midst of enemies; but I am going back now."

He drew a long breath and went on in a dreamy tone:

"In a little while I shall see clear enough to strike—to strike. But she has died, and . . . now . . . darkness."

He flung his arms wide open, let them fall along his body, then stood still with unmoved face and stony eyes, staring at the sun. The white man got down into his canoe. The polers ran smartly along the sides of the boat, looking over their shoulders at the beginning of a weary journey. High in the stern, his head muffled up in white rags, the juragon sat moody, letting his paddle trail in the water. The white man, leaning with both arms over the grass roof of the little cabin, looked back at the shining ripple of the boat's wake. Before the sampan passed out of the lagoon into the creek he lifted his eyes. Arsat had not moved. He stood lonely in the searching sunshine; and he looked beyond the great light of a cloudless day into the darkness of a world of illusions.

Critical Reading

Cite textual evidence to support your responses.

1. **Key Ideas and Details (a)** Why does Arsat ask the white man if he has medicine? **(b) Infer:** What is Arsat's state of mind?

2. **Key Ideas and Details (a)** What does Arsat's brother do while Arsat and Diamelen run to the canoe? **(b) Analyze Cause and Effect:** What motivates Arsat to leave his brother behind? **(c) Speculate:** How else could he have responded, and what might have been the results?

3. **Key Ideas and Details (a) Interpret:** Following Diamelen's death, Arsat says, "I can see nothing," and the white man replies, "There is nothing." What does each statement mean? **(b) Connect:** How might this dialogue relate to the story's final line?

4. **Craft and Structure (a) Analyze:** Find three examples of Conrad's descriptions of sounds, including descriptions of silence and speech. What do these images suggest about the act of storytelling? **(b) Draw Conclusions:** What is Arsat's purpose in telling his story? **(c) Evaluate:** Does he achieve it? Explain.

5. **Integration of Knowledge and Ideas (a) Draw Conclusions:** What do you think Conrad would recommend to people as a way to deal with past mistakes or regrets? **(b) Make a Judgment:** Would you agree? Explain.

JAMES JOYCE

(1882–1941)

Author of **"Araby"**

The Dublin writer James Joyce's innovations in plot, character, and language make him one of the most challenging and distinguished writers of the twentieth century.

Experimentation Joyce's family and teachers wanted him to become a priest, but he pursued his own way as a writer. In 1904, he left Ireland for the continent. Ten years later, he published a landmark collection of short stories entitled *Dubliners.* These deceptively simple tales focus on the psychological conflicts of ordinary people. In the course of each story, the main character is forced to alter his or her perspective on life.

In 1916, Joyce published *A Portrait of the Artist as a Young Man,* a semiautobiographical work. Like Joyce, the novel's main character is in conflict with his Irish roots and chooses to become a writer.

Mature Fiction *A Portrait of the Artist* reveals a heightened awareness of language and an immersion in the minds of characters. Joyce carried these characteristics to a new level in *Ulysses* (1922). A stream-of-consciousness novel that roughly parallels Homer's *Odyssey,* the work presents a day in the life of three Dubliners. *Ulysses* represents a liberation of the novel from old ideas. Using a variety of styles and techniques, it places a new and thoroughly modern emphasis on the play of language.

In his final novel, *Finnegans Wake* (1939), Joyce took his fascination with words a step further. Written in what one scholar terms "a dream language of Joyce's own invention," it explores the author's view of human existence. With such radical innovations, Joyce guaranteed his place as one of the re-inventors of modern fiction.

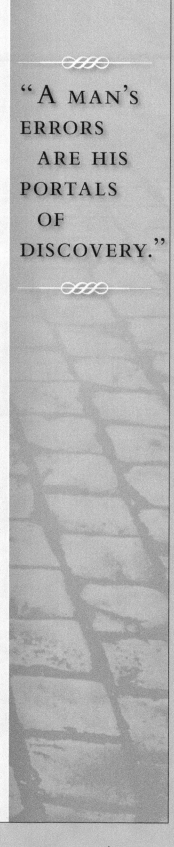

"A MAN'S ERRORS ARE HIS PORTALS OF DISCOVERY."

Araby

JAMES JOYCE

orth Richmond Street, being blind,[1] was a quiet street except at the hour when the Christian Brothers' School set the boys free. An uninhabited house of two stories stood at the blind end, detached from its neighbors in a square ground. The other houses of the street, conscious of decent lives within them, gazed at one another with brown imperturbable faces.

The former tenant of our house, a priest, had died in the back drawing room. Air, musty from having been long enclosed, hung in all the rooms, and the waste room behind the kitchen was littered with old useless papers. Among these I found a few paper-covered books, the pages of which were curled and damp: *The Abbot,* by Walter Scott, *The Devout Communicant* and *The Memoirs of Vidocq.*[2] I liked the last best because its leaves were yellow. The wild garden behind the house contained a central apple tree and a few straggling bushes under one of which I found the late tenant's rusty bicycle pump. He had been a very charitable priest: in his will he had left all his money to institutions and the furniture of his house to his sister.

When the short days of winter came dusk fell before we had well eaten our dinners. When we met in the street the houses had grown somber. The space of sky above us was the color of ever-changing violet and toward it the lamps of the street lifted their feeble lanterns. The cold air stung us and we played till our bodies glowed. Our shouts echoed in the silent street. The career of our play brought us through the dark muddy lanes behind the houses where we ran the gantlet of the rough tribes from the cottages, to the back doors of the dark dripping gardens where odors arose from the ashpits, to the dark odorous stables where a coachman smoothed and combed the horse or shook music from the buckled harness. When we returned to the street, light from the kitchen windows had filled the areas. If my uncle was seen turning the corner we hid in the shadow until we had seen him safely housed. Or if Mangan's sister came out on the doorstep to call her brother in to his tea we watched her from our shadow peer up and down the street. We waited to see whether she would remain or go in and, if she remained, we left our shadow and walked up to Mangan's steps resignedly. She was waiting for us, her figure defined by the light from the half-opened door. Her brother always teased her before he obeyed and I stood by the railings looking at her. Her dress swung as she moved her body and the soft rope of her hair tossed from side to side.

Every morning I lay on the floor in the front parlor watching her door. The blind was pulled down to within an inch of the sash so that I could not be seen. When she came out on the doorstep my heart leaped. I ran to the hall, seized my books and followed her. I kept her brown figure always in my eye and, when we came near the point at

Vocabulary
imperturbable (im´ pər tʉr´ bə bəl) *adj.* calm; not easily ruffled

◀ **Critical Viewing**
Why might the prospect of a fair or bazaar appeal to someone living on a street like this? **[Infer]**

Literary Analysis
Plot Devices What effect does the use of first-person point of view have on your impression of Mangan's sister?

✓ Reading Check
When and where does the story take place?

---

1. **blind** a dead end.
2. ***The Abbot . . . Vidocq*** a historical tale, a religious manual, and the remembrances of a French adventurer, respectively.

which our ways diverged, I quickened my pace and passed her. This happened morning after morning. I had never spoken to her, except for a few casual words, and yet her name was like a summons to all my foolish blood.

Her image accompanied me even in places the most hostile to romance. On Saturday evenings when my aunt went marketing I had to go to carry some of the parcels. We walked through the flaring streets, jostled by drunken men and bargaining women, amid the curses of laborers, the shrill litanies[3] of shop-boys who stood on guard by the barrels of pigs' cheeks, the nasal chanting of street singers, who sang a *come-all-you* about O'Donovan Rossa,[4] or a ballad about the troubles in our native land. These noises converged in a single sensation of life for me: I imagined that I bore my chalice safely through a throng of foes. Her name sprang to my lips at moments in strange prayers and praises which I myself did not understand. My eyes were often full of tears (I could not tell why) and at times a flood from my heart seemed to pour itself out into my bosom. I thought little of the future. I did not know whether I would ever speak to her or not or, if I spoke to her, how I could tell her of my confused adoration. But my body was like a harp and her words and gestures were like fingers running upon the wires.

One evening I went into the back drawing room in which the priest had died. It was a dark rainy evening and there was no sound in the house. Through one of the broken panes I heard the rain impinge upon the earth, the fine incessant needles of water playing in the sodden beds. Some distant lamp or lighted window gleamed below me. I was thankful that I could see so little. All my senses seemed to desire to veil themselves and, feeling that I was about to slip from them, I pressed the palms of my hands together until they trembled, murmuring: *"O love! O love!"* many times.

At last she spoke to me. When she addressed the first words to me I was so confused that I did not know what to answer. She asked me was I going to *Araby.* I forget whether I answered yes or no. It would be a splendid bazaar, she said; she would love to go.

"And why can't you?" I asked.

While she spoke she turned a silver bracelet round and round her wrist. She could not go, she said, because there would be a retreat[5] that week in her convent.[6] Her brother and two other boys were fighting for their caps and I was alone at the railings. She held one of the spikes, bowing her head towards me. The light from the lamp opposite our door caught the white curve of her neck, lit up her hair that rested there and, falling, lit up the hand upon the railing. It fell over one side of her dress and caught the white border of a petticoat, just visible as she stood at ease.

Reading Strategy
Identifying Cause-and-Effect Relationships
What is causing the narrator's distracted behavior? What do you think will happen to him?

Literary Analysis
Plot Devices and Epiphany
In what way might the narrator's comments on his own past thoughts and feelings prepare for an epiphany?

---

3. litanies (lit´ ən ēz) *n* prayers in which a congregation repeats a fixed response; repetitive recitations.
4. come-all-you . . . Rossa opening of a ballad about an Irish hero.
5. retreat *n.* period of retirement or seclusion for prayer, religious study, and meditation.
6. convent *n.* school run by an order of nuns.

"It's well for you," she said.

"If I go," I said, "I will bring you something."

What innumerable follies laid waste my waking and sleeping thoughts after that evening! I wished to annihilate the tedious intervening days. I chafed against the work of school. At night in my bedroom and by day in the classroom her image came between me and the page I strove to read. The syllables of the word *Araby* were called to me through the silence in which my soul luxuriated and cast an Eastern enchantment over me. I asked for leave to go to the bazaar on Saturday night. My aunt was surprised and hoped it was not some Freemason[7] affair. I answered few questions in class. I watched my master's face pass from amiability to sternness; he hoped I was not beginning to idle. I could not call my wandering thoughts together. I had hardly any patience with the serious work of life which, now that it stood between me and my desire, seemed to me child's play, ugly monotonous child's play.

On Saturday morning I reminded my uncle that I wished to go to the bazaar in the evening. He was fussing at the hallstand, looking for the hat brush, and answered me curtly:

"Yes, boy, I know."

As he was in the hall I could not go into the front parlor and lie at the window. I left the house in bad humor and walked slowly toward the school. The air was pitilessly raw and already my heart misgave me.

When I came home to dinner my uncle had not yet been home. Still it was early. I sat staring at the clock for some time and, when its ticking began to irritate me, I left the room. I mounted the staircase and gained the upper part of the house. The high cold empty gloomy rooms liberated me and I went from room to room singing. From the front window I saw my companions playing in the street. Their cries reached me weakened and indistinct and, leaning my forehead against the cool glass, I looked over at the dark house where she lived. I may have stood there for an hour, seeing nothing but the brown-clad figure cast by my imagination, touched discreetly by the lamplight at the curved neck, at the hand upon the railings and at the border below the dress.

When I came downstairs again I found Mrs. Mercer sitting at the fire. She was an old garrulous woman, a pawnbroker's widow, who collected used stamps for some pious purpose. I had to endure the gossip of the tea table. The meal was prolonged beyond an hour and still my uncle did not come. Mrs. Mercer stood up to go: she was sorry she couldn't wait any longer, but it was after eight o'clock and she did not like to be out late, as the night air was bad for her. When she had gone I began to walk up and down the room, clenching my fists. My aunt said:

"I'm afraid you may put off your bazaar for this night of Our Lord."

---

7. **Freemason** Free and Accepted Masons, an international secret society.

Spiral Review

Character Summarize the paragraph that begins "What innumerable follies. . . ." What can you conclude about the narrator's emotional state?

Reading Strategy
Identifying Cause-and-Effect Relationships
Why does the narrator have to wait to go to the bazaar? What effect does his waiting have on his mood?

Vocabulary
garrulous (gar′ ə ləs) *adj.* talkative

Reading Check
What does the narrator promise Mangan's sister?

The Irish Tradition

Joyce's stories are a modern addition to the rich cultural legacy of Ireland. Irish literature began with an oral tradition of epics and flourished through the medieval period. Bede's *History* is a culminating testament to the Irish preservation of learning on the islands—Irish books and Irish teaching flowing into Bede's England made the work possible.

Although the Irish cultural tradition is strong, centuries of rule by the English in Ireland and the Irish struggles against that rule have raised questions of cultural identity. When W. B. Yeats reinvigorated Irish poetry, he helped to launch the Irish Literary Revival. This literary assertion of Irish identity was also a political gesture reinforcing the movement to free Ireland. Since Yeats, writers such as Joyce, Louis MacNeice, and Seamus Heaney have made the Irish identity, as well as the splits it suffered under English rule, a theme for literary exploration.

Connect to the Literature

Which reflects more Irish details: the setting or the narrator? Explain.

At nine o'clock I heard my uncle's latchkey in the hall door. I heard him talking to himself and heard the hall-stand rocking when it had received the weight of his overcoat. I could interpret these signs. When he was midway through his dinner I asked him to give me the money to go to the bazaar. He had forgotten.

"The people are in bed and after their first sleep now," he said.

I did not smile. My aunt said to him energetically:

"Can't you give him the money and let him go? You've kept him late enough as it is."

My uncle said he was very sorry he had forgotten. He said he believed in the old saying: *All work and no play makes Jack a dull boy.* He asked me where I was going and, when I had told him a second time he asked me did I know *The Arab's Farewell to His Steed.*[8] When I left the kitchen he was about to recite the opening lines of the piece to my aunt.

I held a florin[9] tightly in my hand as I strode down Buckingham Street toward the station. The sight of the streets thronged with buyers and glaring with gas recalled to me the purpose of my journey. I took my seat in a third-class carriage of a deserted train. After an intolerable delay the train moved out of the station slowly. It crept onward among ruinous houses and over the twinkling river. At Westland Row Station a crowd of people pressed to the carriage doors; but the porters moved them back, saying that it was a special train for the bazaar. I remained alone in the bare carriage. In a few minutes the train drew up beside an improvised wooden platform. I passed out onto the road and saw by the lighted dial of a clock that it was ten minutes to ten. In front of me was a large building which displayed the magical name.

I could not find any sixpenny entrance and, fearing that the bazaar would be closed, I passed in quickly through a turnstile, handing a shilling to a weary-looking man. I found myself in a big hall girdled at half its height by a gallery. Nearly all the stalls were closed and the greater part of the hall was in darkness. I recognized a silence like that which pervades a church after a service. I walked into the center of the bazaar timidly. A few people were gathered about the stalls which were still open. Before a curtain, over which the words *Café Chantant*[10] were written in colored lamps, two men were counting money on a salver.[11] I listened to the fall of the coins.

---

8. ***The Arab's . . . His Steed*** popular nineteenth-century poem.
9. **florin** two shilling coin of the time.
10. ***Café Chantant*** café with musical entertainment.
11. **salver** tray usually used for the presentation of letters or visiting cards.

Remembering with difficulty why I had come I went over to one of the stalls and examined porcelain vases and flowered tea sets. At the door of the stall a young lady was talking and laughing with two young gentlemen. I remarked their English accents and listened vaguely to their conversation.

"O, I never said such a thing!"

"O, but you did!"

"O, but I didn't!"

"Didn't she say that?"

"Yes. I heard her."

"O, there's a . . . fib!"

Observing me the young lady came over and asked me did I wish to buy anything. The tone of her voice was not encouraging; she seemed to have spoken to me out of a sense of duty. I looked humbly at the great jars that stood like Eastern guards at either side of the dark entrance to the stall and murmured:

"No, thank you."

The young lady changed the position of one of the vases and went back to the two young men. They began to talk of the same subject. Once or twice the young lady glanced at me over her shoulder.

I lingered before her stall, though I knew my stay was useless, to make my interest in her wares seem the more real. Then I turned away slowly and walked down the middle of the bazaar. I allowed the two pennies to fall against the sixpence in my pocket. I heard a voice call from one end of the gallery that the light was out. The upper part of the hall was now completely dark.

Gazing up into the darkness I saw myself as a creature driven and derided by vanity; and my eyes burned with anguish and anger.

▲ **Critical Viewing**
What inferences can you make about people who value objects like the ones shown here? **[Make Inferences]**

Vocabulary
derided (di rīd´ id) *v.* made fun of; ridiculed

Critical Reading ©

1. **Key Ideas and Details** **(a)** What does Mangan's sister do to make a trip to the bazaar so important to the narrator? **(b) Analyze:** Describe three scenes that establish the narrator's feelings for her.

2. **Key Ideas and Details** What features of the Araby bazaar conflict with the narrator's expectations?

3. **Key Ideas and Details** **(a) Draw Conclusions:** What has the narrator lost by the end of the story? **(b) Draw Conclusions:** What might he have gained?

4. **Integration of Knowledge and Ideas** Do the plot devices these writers use, story-within-a-story and epiphany, help convey the pain of wanting something very much and then failing to get it? Explain, using at least three of these Essential Question words: *imply, process, realization, epiphany, story-within-a-story.* *[Connecting to the Essential Question: What is the relationship of the writer to tradition?]*

Cite textual evidence to support your responses.

After You Read   *The Lagoon • Araby*

Literary Analysis

© 1. **Craft and Structure** Conrad uses the **plot device** of a **story-within-a-story** in "The Lagoon." What specific information would you lack if "The Lagoon" had been narrated entirely in the first person by Arsat?

© 2. **Craft and Structure** Why do you think Conrad chose to have Arsat narrate his own story?

© 3. **Key Ideas and Details** (a) Where in "Araby" does the **epiphany** occur? (b) What does the narrator in "Araby" suddenly realize?

© 4. **Integration of Knowledge and Ideas** Explain in what sense the narrator's epiphany in "Araby" is as much a loss of vision as it is a gain of insight.

© 5. **Craft and Structure** Contrast the mood of the parts of "The Lagoon" narrated by Arsat with the mood of the framing story, narrated in the third person.

6. **Comparing Literary Works** Use a chart like the one shown to compare how each story uses plot devices to establish distance between an experience of passion and the act of telling a story about passion.

| Experience of Passion | Distance Between | Circumstances of Storytelling |

7. **Comparing Literary Works** (a) Compare the way that each story creates an "outsider's" perspective on a narrator's obsessive, passionate concerns. (b) Explain how plot devices add to the **theme** of each story.

Reading Strategy

8. **Identify cause and effect** in both stories. (a) What causes Arsat and the youngster in "Araby" to act? (b) In each case, what are the results of those actions?

9. What is the cause of the epiphany in "Araby"?

10. Explain how the story-within-a-story in "The Lagoon" is an effect of the story that frames it.

11. (a) Why do Arsat and the narrator in "Araby" tell the stories they tell? (b) What kind of reception do you think they expect to receive from their audience? Explain your answer.

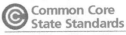
Common Core State Standards

Reading Literature
9. Demonstrate knowledge of eighteenth-, nineteenth- and early-twentieth-century foundational works of American literature, including how two or more texts from the same period treat similar themes or topics. (p. 1243)

Writing
2. Write informative/explanatory texts to examine and convey complex ideas, concepts, and information clearly and accurately through the effective selection, organization, and analysis of content. (p. 1243)

2.b. Develop the topic thoroughly by selecting the most significant and relevant facts, extended definitions, concrete details, quotations, or other information and examples appropriate to the audience's knowledge of the topic. (p. 1243)

5. Develop and strengthen writing as needed by planning, revising, editing, rewriting, or trying a new approach, focusing on addressing what is most significant for a specific purpose and audience. (p. 1243)

9.a. Apply *grades 11–12 Reading standards* to literature. [RL.11-12.9] (p. 1243)

Language
5.b. Analyze nuances in the meaning of words with similar denotations. (p. 1243)

Vocabulary Acquisition and Use

Word Analysis: Latin Root -vinc-

Early in "The Lagoon," you will find the word *invincible,* which means "unconquerable." *Invincible* is formed with the Latin root *-vinc-,* which comes from a Latin verb meaning "to conquer" and "to show conclusively." Some words use a variant spelling such as *-vict-,* which has the same meanings. Use the meaning of the root to define each of the following words. Then, write a sentence using each word appropriately.

1. convict
2. victory
3. vanquish
4. convince
5. evince
6. evict

Vocabulary: Synonyms

Synonyms are words with nearly the same meaning. Write the letter of the word that is a synonym of each word from the vocabulary list on page 1218. Then, explain the differences in meaning between the synonyms.

1. derided: **(a)** ejected, **(b)** exaggerated, **(c)** ridiculed
2. imperturbable: **(a)** calm, **(b)** indifferent, **(c)** ruthless
3. invincible: **(a)** facile, **(b)** warlike, **(c)** unconquerable
4. garrulous: **(a)** coy, **(b)** rich, **(c)** talkative
5. conflagration: **(a)** dispute, **(b)** fire, **(c)** battle
6. propitiate: **(a)** appease, **(b)** refuse, **(c)** resign

Writing

Informative Text James Joyce, an Irish author, and Ernest Hemingway, an American author, wrote several early twentieth-century masterpieces. Find a copy of Hemingway's short story "In Another Country," and read it carefully. Then, write an **essay** comparing and contrasting the first-person narrators in "Araby" and "In Another Country."

Prewriting Start by jotting down your impressions of the narrator in "Araby." Then jot down your impressions of the narrator in "In Another Country." Consider these questions: In what way is each narrator "wounded"? In each story, what events trigger an epiphany, or a moment of sudden insight?

Drafting As you draft your essay, use your prewriting notes as a guide, addressing the details you listed for each narrator. Link these details to broader considerations about how one narrator's characteristics are similar to or different from the other's. Support your ideas with quotations from each story.

Revising Review your draft, making sure that the sentences flow logically and that your ideas are well supported with details. Where evidence is lacking, review the stories to find relevant details to strengthen the support.

Model: Revising to Add Relevant Support

Nearly all the stalls are closed, and he remembers only "with difficulty why I had come...."

In "Araby," the narrator rushes off to the bazaar, but he is disappointed.

Citing specific textual details strengthens writing about literature.

Before You Read

The Rocking-Horse Winner •
A Shocking Accident

Connecting to the Essential Question Both of these stories involve conflicts centering on issues of wealth and class. As you read, find details that show the effect of social position on the characters. These details will help you think about the Essential Question: **How does literature shape or reflect society?**

**Common Core
State Standards**

**Reading Literature
3.** Analyze the impact of the author's choices regarding how to develop and relate elements of a story.

Literary Analysis

In most short stories, the writer explores a **theme,** a central idea or question. Writers often reveal theme through a **symbol,** a person, object, or action that suggests deeper meanings. To identify symbols, look for descriptions that carry special emphasis, such as the underlined words in this passage from "The Rocking-Horse Winner."

> _He knew the horse would take him to where_
> _there was luck,_ if only he forced it. So he
> would mount again, and start on his furious
> ride, hoping at last to get there.

Comparing Literary Works Each of these stories is told from a **third-person point of view,** meaning that the narrator does not take part in the action. As you read, compare how both authors use this point of view to develop their themes, for example, in the way they disclose the thoughts of characters and create symbols to suggest meanings. In addition, ask yourself how the third-person point of view differs in the two stories. Consider, for instance, whether Greene's narrative has the same intensity as Lawrence's.

Reading Strategy

Preparing to Read Complex Texts As you read, use the descriptions, events, and dialogue in the text—and your own background knowledge—to **make predictions** about what might happen. As you continue reading and learn more, you can confirm or revise those predictions. Use a graphic organizer like the one shown.

Detail
Paul misses picking the winner in two races.

↓

Prediction
He will be determined to pick the Derby winner.

↓

Evaluation of Prediction

Vocabulary

discreet (di skrēt´) _adj._ wise; prudent (p. 1247)

obstinately (äb´ stə nət lē) _adv._ in a determined way; stubbornly (p. 1254)

uncanny (un kan´ ē) _adj._ mysterious; hard to explain (p. 1255)

apprehension (ap´ rē hen´ shən) _n._ anxious feeling of foreboding; dread (p. 1263)

embarked (em bärkt´) _v._ engaged in something, such as a conversation (p. 1265)

intrinsically (in trin´ sik lē) _adv._ at its core; innately (p. 1266)

PHLit
Online!
www.PHLitOnline.com

D. H. Lawrence

(1885–1930)

Author of "The Rocking-Horse Winner"

During his lifetime, D. H. Lawrence's literary achievements were overshadowed by controversy. Like Percy Bysshe Shelley and Lord Byron in their day, Lawrence took unorthodox positions on politics and morality that shocked mainstream society.

Early Years Lawrence was born in Eastwood, Nottinghamshire, the son of an almost illiterate coal miner father and a more educated mother. Through her influence, he pursued a scholarship to the Nottingham High School, where he studied from 1898 to 1901. After leaving school for a job as a clerk, he contracted pneumonia and, on recovering, became a teacher.

Lawrence also began to write poems, stories, and novels, and his poetry attracted the attention of the well-known writer and editor Ford Madox Ford. In 1913, Lawrence published his first major novel, *Sons and Lovers,* a thinly disguised autobiography. Two years later, he published *The Rainbow,* which was banned in Britain.

Travels Abroad During World War I, Lawrence and his German wife, Frieda, lived in poverty in England and were unreasonably suspected of being German spies. At the end of the war, they left England and never returned. They traveled to Italy, Ceylon, Australia, Mexico, and the United States, and Lawrence used many of these locales in his fiction. In 1920, he published *Women in Love,* one of his greatest novels. A few years later, although suffering from tuberculosis, he completed *Lady Chatterley's Lover.* Shortly afterward, in the south of France, he died from that disease.

In the years since Lawrence's death, society's views of his writings have changed profoundly. Today, his fiction is widely admired for its vivid settings, fine craftsmanship, and psychological insight.

"THE HUMAN SOUL NEEDS ACTUAL BEAUTY MORE THAN bread."

The Rocking-Horse Winner

D. H. Lawrence

There was a woman who was beautiful, who started with all the advantages, yet she had no luck. She married for love, and the love turned to dust. She had bonny children, yet she felt they had been thrust upon her, and she could not love them. They looked at her coldly, as if they were finding fault with her. And hurriedly she felt she must cover up some fault in herself. Yet what it was that she must cover up she never knew. Nevertheless, when her children were present, she always felt the center of her heart go hard. This troubled her, and in her manner she was all the more gentle and anxious for her children, as if she loved them very much. Only she herself knew that at the center of her heart was a hard little place that could not feel love, no, not for anybody. Everybody else said of her: "She is such a good mother. She adores her children." Only she herself, and her children themselves, knew it was not so. They read it in each other's eyes.

There were a boy and two little girls. They lived in a pleasant house, with a garden and they had discreet servants, and felt themselves superior to anyone in the neighborhood.

Although they lived in style, they felt always an anxiety in the house. There was never enough money. The mother had a small income and the father had a small income, but not nearly enough for the social position which they had to keep up. The father went into town to some office. But though he had good prospects, these prospects never materialized. There was always the grinding sense of the shortage of money, though the style was always kept up.

At last the mother said, "I will see if *I* can't make something." But she did not know where to begin. She racked her brains, and tried this thing and the other, but could not find anything successful. The failure made deep lines come into her face. Her children were growing

◄ **Critical Viewing**
What could someone riding a rocking horse like this one win? **[Speculate]**

Literary Analysis
Theme and Symbol
What ideas about the story's theme does this first paragraph suggest?

Vocabulary
discreet (di skrēt´) *adj.* wise; prudent

Reading Check
What does the mother feel toward her children?

up, they would have to go to school. There must be more money, there must be more money. The father, who was always very handsome and expensive in his tastes, seemed as if he never *would* be able to do anything worth doing. And the mother, who had a great belief in herself, did not succeed any better, and her tastes were just as expensive.

And so the house came to be haunted by the unspoken phrase: *There must be more money! There must be more money!* The children could hear it all the time, though nobody said it aloud. They heard it at Christmas, when the expensive and splendid toys filled the nursery. Behind the shining modern rocking horse, behind the smart doll's house, a voice would start whispering: "There *must* be more money! There *must* be more money!" And the children would stop playing, to listen for a moment. They would look into each other's eyes to see if they had all heard. And each one saw in the eyes of the other two that they too had heard. "There *must* be more money! There *must* be more money!"

It came whispering from the springs of the still-swaying rocking horse, and even the horse, bending his wooden, champing head, heard it. The big doll, sitting so pink and smirking in her new pram,[1] could hear it quite plainly, and seemed to be smirking all the more self-consciously because of it. The foolish puppy, too, that took the place of the teddy bear, he was looking so extraordinarily foolish for no other reason but that he heard the secret whisper all over the house: "There *must* be more money."

Yet nobody ever said it aloud. The whisper was everywhere, and therefore no one spoke it. Just as no one ever says: "We are breathing!" in spite of the fact that breath is coming and going all the time.

"Mother!" said the boy Paul one day. "Why don't we keep a car of our own? Why do we always use uncle's, or else a taxi?"

"Because we're the poor members of the family," said the mother.

"But why *are* we, mother?"

"Well—I suppose," she said slowly and bitterly, "it's because your father has no luck."

The boy was silent for some time.

"Is luck money, mother?" he asked, rather timidly.

"No, Paul! Not quite. It's what causes you to have money."

"Oh!" said Paul vaguely. "I thought when Uncle Oscar said *filthy lucker,* it meant money."

"*Filthy lucre* does mean money," said the mother. "But it's lucre, not luck."

"Oh!" said the boy. "Then what *is* luck, mother?"

"It's what causes you to have money. If you're lucky you have money. That's why it's better to be born lucky than rich. If you're rich, you may lose your money. But if you're lucky, you will always get more money."

---

1. pram baby carriage.

Literary Analysis
Theme and Symbol
How does this secret whispering help reveal a potential theme?

" THERE **MUST** BE MORE
money!
THERE **MUST** BE MORE
money!"

"Oh! Will you! And is father not lucky?"

"Very unlucky, I should say," she said bitterly.

The boy watched her with unsure eyes.

"Why?" he asked.

"I don't know. Nobody ever knows why one person is lucky and another unlucky."

"Don't they? Nobody at all? Does *nobody* know?"

"Perhaps God! But He never tells."

"He ought to, then. And aren't you lucky either, mother?"

"I can't be, if I married an unlucky husband."

"But by yourself, aren't you?"

"I used to think I was, before I married. Now I think I am very unlucky indeed."

"Why?"

"Well—never mind! Perhaps I'm not really," she said.

The child looked at her, to see if she meant it. But he saw, by the lines of her mouth, that she was only trying to hide something from him.

"Well, anyhow," he said stoutly, "I'm a lucky person."

"Why?" said his mother, with a sudden laugh.

He stared at her. He didn't even know why he had said it.

"God told me," he asserted, brazening[2] it out.

"I hope He did, dear!" she said, again with a laugh, but rather bitter.

"He did, mother!"

"Excellent!" said the mother, using one of her husband's exclamations.

The boy saw she did not believe him; or rather, that she paid no attention to his assertion. This angered him somewhere, and made him want to compel her attention.

Reading Strategy
Making and Confirming Predictions Based on what you have read, what do you think Paul will do? Why do you think so?

He went off by himself, vaguely, in a childish way, seeking for the clue to "luck." Absorbed, taking no heed of other people, he went about with a sort of stealth, seeking inwardly for luck. He wanted luck, he wanted it, he wanted it. When the two girls were playing dolls, in the nursery, he would sit on his big rocking horse, charging madly into space, with a frenzy that made the little girls peer at him uneasily. Wildly the horse careered, the waving dark hair of the boy tossed, his eyes had a strange glare in them. The little girls dared not speak to him.

When he had ridden to the end of his mad little journey, he climbed down and stood in front of his rocking horse, staring fixedly into its lowered face. Its red mouth was slightly open, its big eye was wide and glassy bright.

"Now!" he would silently command the snorting steed. "Now take me to where there is luck! Now take me!"

And he would slash the horse on the neck with the little whip he had asked Uncle Oscar for. He *knew* the horse could take him to

Reading Check
What does Paul do to find "the clue to 'luck'"?

---

2. brazening (brā´ zən iŋ) *v.* daring boldly or shamelessly.

where there was luck, if only he forced it. So he would mount again, and start on his furious ride, hoping at last to get there. He knew he could get there.

"You'll break your horse, Paul!" said the nurse.

"He's always riding like that! I wish he'd leave off!" said his elder sister Joan.

But he only glared down on them in silence. Nurse gave him up. She could make nothing of him. Anyhow he was growing beyond her.

One day his mother and his Uncle Oscar came in when he was on one of his furious rides. He did not speak to them.

"Hallo! you young jockey! Riding a winner?" said his uncle.

"Aren't you growing too big for a rocking horse? You're not a very little boy any longer, you know," said his mother.

But Paul only gave a blue glare from his big, rather close-set eyes. He would speak to nobody when he was in full tilt. His mother watched him with an anxious expression on her face.

At last he suddenly stopped forcing his horse into the mechanical gallop, and slid down.

"Well, I got there!" he announced fiercely, his blue eyes still flaring, and his sturdy long legs straddling apart.

"Where did you get to?" asked his mother.

"Where I wanted to go to," he flared back at her.

"That's right, son!" said Uncle Oscar. "Don't you stop till you get there. What's the horse's name?"

"He doesn't have a name," said the boy.

"Gets on without all right?" asked the uncle.

"Well, he has different names. He was called Sansovino last week."

"Sansovino, eh? Won the Ascot.[3] How did you know his name?"

"He always talks about horse races with Bassett," said Joan.

<blockquote>"AREN'T YOU GROWING TOO BIG FOR A rocking horse?"</blockquote>

The uncle was delighted to find that his small nephew was posted with all the racing news. Bassett, the young gardener who had been wounded in the left foot in the war, and had got his present job through Oscar Cresswell, whose batman[4] he had been, was a perfect blade of the "turf."[5] He lived in the racing events, and the small boy lived with him.

Oscar Cresswell got it all from Bassett.

"Master Paul comes and asks me, so I can't do more than tell him, sir," said Bassett, his face terribly serious, as if he were speaking of religious matters.

"And does he ever put anything on a horse he fancies?"

"Well—I don't want to give him away—he's a young sport, a fine sport, sir. Would you mind asking him yourself? He sort of takes a

Literary Analysis
Theme and Symbol
Bassett and the small boy "lived" in the racing events. What might this detail suggest about their lives?

---

3. **Ascot** major English horse race.
4. **batman** British military officer's orderly.
5. **blade . . . "turf"** horse-racing fan.

pleasure in it, and perhaps he'd feel I was giving him away, sir, if you don't mind."

Bassett was serious as a church.

The uncle went back to his nephew, and took him off for a ride in the car.

"Say, Paul, old man, do you ever put anything on a horse?" the uncle asked.

The boy watched the handsome man closely.

"Why, do you think I oughtn't to?" he parried.

"Not a bit of it! I thought perhaps you might give me a tip for the Lincoln."[6]

The car sped on into the country, going down to Uncle Oscar's place in Hampshire.

"Honor bright?" said the nephew.

"Honor bright, son!" said the uncle.

"Well, then, Daffodil."

"Daffodil! I doubt it, sonny. What about Mirza?"

"I only know the winner," said the boy. "That's Daffodil!"

"Daffodil, eh?"

There was a pause. Daffodil was an obscure horse comparatively.

"Uncle!"

"Yes, son?"

"You won't let it go any further, will you? I promised Bassett."

"Bassett be hanged, old man! What's he got to do with it?"

"We're partners! We've been partners from the first! Uncle, he lent me my first five shillings, which I lost. I promised him, honor bright, it was only between me and him: only you gave me that ten-shilling note I started winning with, so I thought you were lucky. You won't let it go any further, will you?"

The boy gazed at his uncle from those big, hot, blue eyes, set rather close together. The uncle stirred and laughed uneasily.

"Right you are, son! I'll keep your tip private. Daffodil, eh! How much are you putting on him?"

"All except twenty pounds," said the boy. "I keep that in reserve."

The uncle thought it a good joke.

"You keep twenty pounds in reserve, do you, you young romancer? What are you betting, then?"

"I'm betting three hundred," said the boy gravely. "But it's between you and me, Uncle Oscar! Honor bright?"

The uncle burst into a roar of laughter.

"It's between you and me all right, you young Nat Gould,"[7] he said, laughing. "But where's your three hundred?"

---

6. **Lincoln** major English horse race.
7. **Nat Gould** famous English sportswriter and authority on horse racing.

Reading Strategy
Making and Confirming Predictions Which horse do you think will do better? Why?

Reading Check

What kind of a partnership does Paul have with Bassett?

"Bassett keeps it for me. We're partners."

"You are, are you! And what is Bassett putting on Daffodil?"

"He won't go quite as high as I do, I expect. Perhaps he'll go a hundred and fifty."

"What, pennies?" laughed the uncle.

"Pounds," said the child, with a surprised look at his uncle. "Bassett keeps a bigger reserve than I do."

Between wonder and amusement, Uncle Oscar was silent. He pursued the matter no further, but he determined to take his nephew with him to the Lincoln races.

"Now, son," he said, "I'm putting twenty on Mirza, and I'll put five for you on any horse you fancy. What's your pick?"

"Daffodil, uncle!"

"No, not the fiver on Daffodil!"

"I should if it was my own five," said the child.

"Good! Good! Right you are! A fiver for me and a fiver for you on Daffodil."

Literary Analysis
Theme, Symbol, and Third-Person Point of View What does the narrator suggest about Paul's need by describing his eyes as "blue fire"?

The child had never been to a race meeting before, and his eyes were blue fire. He pursed his mouth tight, and watched. A Frenchman just in front had put his money on Lancelot. Wild with excitement, he flayed his arms up and down, yelling *Lancelot! Lancelot!* in his French accent.

Daffodil came in first, Lancelot second, Mirza third. The child, flushed and with eyes blazing, was curiously serene. His uncle brought him five five-pound notes: four to one.

"What am I to do with these?" he cried, waving them before the boy's eyes.

"I suppose we'll talk to Bassett," said the boy. "I expect I have fifteen hundred now; and twenty in reserve; and this twenty."

His uncle studied him for some moments.

"Look here, son!" he said. "You're not serious about Bassett and that fifteen hundred, are you?"

"Yes, I am. But it's between you and me, uncle! Honor bright!"

"Honor bright all right, son! But I must talk to Bassett."

Reading Strategy
Making and Confirming Predictions Based on what you have read, who do you think picks the winning horses? Why?

"If you'd like to be a partner, uncle, with Bassett and me, we could all be partners. Only you'd have to promise, honor bright, uncle, not to let it go beyond us three. Bassett and I are lucky, and you must be lucky, because it was your ten shillings I started winning with. . . ."

Uncle Oscar took both Bassett and Paul into Richmond Park for an afternoon, and there they talked.

▶ **Critical Viewing**
Which details in this picture convey the feverish excitement that Paul and Bassett feel about horse racing? **[Analyze]**

"It's like this, you see, sir," Bassett said. "Master Paul would get me talking about racing events, spinning yarns, you know, sir. And he was always keen on knowing if I'd made or if I'd lost. It's about a year since, now, that I put five shillings on Blush of Dawn for him— and we lost. Then the luck turned, with that ten shillings he had

"Daffodil CAME IN FIRST, LANCELOT SECOND, MIRZA THIRD."

from you, that we put on Singhalese. And since that time, it's been pretty steady, all things considering. What do you say, Master Paul?"

"We're all right when we're *sure*," said Paul. "It's when we're not quite sure that we go down."

"Oh, but we're careful then," said Bassett.

"But when are you *sure*?" smiled Uncle Oscar.

"It's Master Paul, sir," said Bassett, in a secret, religious voice. "It's as if he had it from heaven. Like Daffodil now, for the Lincoln. That was as sure as eggs."

"Did you put anything on Daffodil?" asked Oscar Cresswell.

"Yes, sir. I made my bit."

"And my nephew?"

Bassett was obstinately silent, looking at Paul.

"I made twelve hundred, didn't I, Bassett? I told uncle I was putting three hundred on Daffodil."

"That's right," said Bassett, nodding.

"But where's the money?" asked the uncle.

"I keep it safe locked up, sir. Master Paul, he can have it any minute he likes to ask for it."

"What, fifteen hundred pounds?"

"And twenty! And *forty*, that is, with the twenty he made on the course."

"It's amazing!" said the uncle.

"If Master Paul offers you to be partners, sir, I would, if I were you; if you'll excuse me," said Bassett.

Oscar Cresswell thought about it.

"I'll see the money," he said.

They drove home again, and sure enough, Bassett came round to the garden house with fifteen hundred pounds in notes. The twenty pounds reserve was left with Joe Glee, in the Turf Commission deposit.

"You see, it's all right, uncle, when I'm *sure!* Then we go strong, for all we're worth. Don't we, Bassett?"

"We do that, Master Paul."

"And when are you sure?" said the uncle, laughing.

"Oh, well, sometimes I'm *absolutely* sure, like about Daffodil," said the boy, "and sometimes I have an idea; and sometimes I haven't even an idea, have I, Bassett? Then we're careful, because we mostly go down."

"You do, do you! And when you're sure, like about Daffodil, what makes you sure, sonny?"

"Oh, well, I don't know," said the boy uneasily. "I'm sure, you know, uncle; that's all."

"It's as if he had it from heaven, sir," Bassett reiterated.

"I should say so!" said the uncle.

But he became a partner. And when the Leger was coming on, Paul was "sure" about Lively Spark, which was a quite inconsiderable horse. The boy insisted on putting a thousand on the horse, Bassett went for five hundred, and Oscar Cresswell two hundred. Lively

Vocabulary
obstinately (äb′ stə nət lē) *adv.* in a determined way; stubbornly

Spark came in first, and the betting had been ten to one against him. Paul had made ten thousand.

"You see," he said. "I was absolutely sure of him."

Even Oscar Cresswell had cleared two thousand.

"Look here, son," he said, "this sort of thing makes me nervous."

"It needn't, uncle! Perhaps I shan't be sure again for a long time."

"But what are you going to do with your money?" asked the uncle.

"Of course," said the boy, "I started it for mother. She said she had no luck, because father is unlucky, so I thought if *I* was lucky, it might stop whispering."

"What might stop whispering?"

"Our house! I *hate* our house for whispering."

"What does it whisper?"

"Why—why"—the boy fidgeted—"why, I don't know! But it's always short of money, you know, uncle."

"I know it, son, I know it."

"You know people send mother writs, don't you, uncle?"

"I'm afraid I do," said the uncle.

"And then the house whispers like people laughing at you behind your back. It's awful, that is! I thought if I was lucky . . ."

"You might stop it," added the uncle.

The boy watched him with big blue eyes, that had an uncanny cold fire in them, and he said never a word.

"Well then!" said the uncle. "What are we doing?"

"I shouldn't like mother to know I was lucky," said the boy.

"Why not, son?"

"She'd stop me."

"I don't think she would."

"Oh!"—and the boy writhed in an odd way—"I *don't* want her to know, uncle."

"All right, son! We'll manage it without her knowing."

They managed it very easily. Paul, at the other's suggestion, handed over five thousand pounds to his uncle, who deposited it with the family lawyer, who was then to inform Paul's mother that a relative had put five thousand pounds into his hands, which sum was to be paid out a thousand pounds at a time, on the mother's birthday, for the next five years.

"So she'll have a birthday present of a thousand pounds for five successive years," said Uncle Oscar. "I hope it won't make it all the harder for her later."

Paul's mother had her birthday in November. The house had been "whispering" worse than ever lately, and even in spite of his luck, Paul could not bear up against it. He was very anxious to see the effect of the birthday letter, telling his mother about the thousand pounds.

When there were no visitors, Paul now took his meals with his parents, as he was beyond the nursery control. His mother went into

> "OUR HOUSE!
>
> I **HATE** OUR HOUSE FOR
>
> *whispering.*"

Vocabulary
uncanny (un kan′ ē) *adj.*
mysterious; hard to explain

Reading Check

Why does Paul want to win money?

Reading Strategy
Making and Confirming Predictions How do you think Paul's mother will react to the letter about the money? Why?

town nearly every day. She had discovered that she had an odd knack of sketching furs and dress materials, so she worked secretly in the studio of a friend who was the chief "artist" for the leading drapers. She drew the figures of ladies in furs and ladies in silk and sequins for the newspaper advertisements. This young woman artist earned several thousand pounds a year, but Paul's mother only made several hundreds, and she was again dissatisfied. She so wanted to be first in something, and she did not succeed, even in making sketches for drapery advertisements.

She was down to breakfast on the morning of her birthday. Paul watched her face as she read her letters. He knew the lawyer's letter. As his mother read it, her face hardened and became more expressionless. Then a cold, determined look came on her mouth. She hid the letter under the pile of others, and said not a word about it.

"Didn't you have anything nice in the post for your birthday, mother?" said Paul.

"Quite moderately nice," she said, her voice cold and absent.

She went away to town without saying more.

But in the afternoon Uncle Oscar appeared. He said Paul's mother had had a long interview with the lawyer, asking if the whole five thousand could not be advanced at once, as she was in debt.

"What do you think, uncle?" said the boy.

"I leave it to you, son."

"Oh, let her have it, then! We can get some more with the other," said the boy.

"A bird in the hand is worth two in the bush, laddie!" said Uncle Oscar.

"But I'm sure to *know* for the Grand National; or the Lincolnshire; or else the Derby.[8] I'm sure to know for *one* of them," said Paul.

So Uncle Oscar signed the agreement, and Paul's mother touched the whole five thousand. Then something very curious happened. The voices in the house suddenly went mad, like a chorus of frogs on a spring evening. There were certain new furnishings, and Paul had a tutor. He was *really* going to Eton,[9] his father's school, in the following autumn. There were flowers in the winter, and a blossoming of the luxury Paul's mother had been used to. And yet the voices in the house, behind the sprays of mimosa and almond blossom, and from under the piles of iridescent cushions, simply trilled and screamed in a sort of ecstasy: "There *must* be more money! Oh-h-h! There *must* be more money! Oh, now, now-w! now-w-w—there *must* be more money!—more than ever! More than ever!"

It frightened Paul terribly. He studied away at his Latin and Greek with his tutors. But his intense hours were spent with Bassett. The

> " DIDN'T YOU HAVE ANYTHING NICE IN THE POST FOR YOUR BIRTHDAY, mother?"

Reading Strategy
Making and Confirming Predictions How accurate was your prediction about Paul's mother's reaction? How do you think Paul will respond to this result?

---

8. **Grand National . . . Derby** major English horse races.
9. **Eton** prestigious private school in England.

Grand National had gone by: he had not "known," and had lost a hundred pounds. Summer was at hand. He was in agony for the Lincoln. But even for the Lincoln he didn't "know," and he lost fifty pounds. He became wild-eyed and strange, as if something were going to explode in him.

"Let it alone, son! Don't you bother about it!" urged Uncle Oscar. But it was as if the boy couldn't really hear what his uncle was saying.

"I've got to know for the Derby! I've *got* to know for the Derby!" the child reiterated, his big blue eyes blazing with a sort of madness.

His mother noticed how overwrought he was.

"You'd better go to the seaside. Wouldn't you like to go now to the seaside, instead of waiting? I think you'd better," she said, looking down at him anxiously, her heart curiously heavy because of him.

But the child lifted his uncanny blue eyes.

"I couldn't possibly go before the Derby, mother!" he said. "I couldn't possibly!"

"Why not?" she said, her voice becoming heavy when she was opposed. "Why not? You can still go from the seaside to see the Derby with your Uncle Oscar, if that's what you wish. No need for you to wait here. Besides, I think you care too much about these races. It's a bad sign. My family has been a gambling family, and you won't know till you grow up how much damage it has done. But it has done damage. I shall have to send Bassett away, and ask Uncle Oscar not to talk racing to you, unless you promise to be reasonable about it; go away to the seaside and forget it. You're all nerves!"

"I'll do what you like, mother, so long as you don't send me away till after the Derby," the boy said.

"Send you away from where? Just from this house?"

"Yes," he said, gazing at her.

"Why, you curious child, what makes you care about this house so much, suddenly? I never knew you loved it!"

He gazed at her without speaking. He had a secret within a secret, something he had not divulged, even to Bassett or to his Uncle Oscar.

But his mother, after standing undecided and a little bit sullen for some moments, said:

"Very well, then! Don't go to the seaside till after the Derby, if you don't wish it. But promise me you won't let your nerves go to pieces! Promise you won't think so much about horse racing and *events*, as you call them!"

"Oh, no!" said the boy, casually. "I won't think much about them, mother. You needn't worry. I wouldn't worry, mother, if I were you."

"If you were me and I were you," said his mother, "I wonder what we should do!"

"But you know you needn't worry, mother, don't you?" the boy repeated.

"I should be awfully glad to know it," she said wearily.

Literary Analysis
Theme, Symbol, and Third-Person Point of View If the story were told from Paul's point of view, would you know about the mother's "curiously heavy" feelings concerning Paul? Why or why not?

Reading Check
What present does Paul give his mother?

"Oh, well, you *can*, you know. I mean you *ought* to know you needn't worry!" he insisted.

"Ought I? Then I'll see about it," she said.

Paul's secret of secrets was his wooden horse, that which had no name. Since he was emancipated from a nurse and a nursery governess, he had had his rocking horse removed to his own bedroom at the top of the house.

"Surely you're too big for a rocking horse!" his mother had remonstrated.

"Well, you see, mother, till I can have a *real* horse, I like to have *some* sort of animal about," had been his quaint answer.

"Do you feel he keeps you company?" she laughed.

"Oh, yes! He's very good, he always keeps me company, when I'm there," said Paul.

So the horse, rather shabby, stood in an arrested prance in the boy's bedroom.

The Derby was drawing near, and the boy grew more and more tense. He hardly heard what was spoken to him, he was very frail, and his eyes were really uncanny. His mother had sudden strange seizures of uneasiness about him. Sometimes, for half an hour, she would feel a sudden anxiety about him that was almost anguish. She wanted to rush to him at once, and know he was safe.

Two nights before the Derby, she was at a big party in town, when one of her rushes of anxiety about her boy, her firstborn, gripped her heart till she could hardly speak. She fought with the feeling, might and main, for she believed in common sense. But it was too strong. She had to leave the dance and go downstairs to telephone to the country. The children's nursery governess was terribly surprised and startled at being rung up in the night.

"Are the children all right, Miss Wilmot?"

"Oh yes, they are quite all right."

"Master Paul? Is he all right?"

"He went to bed as right as a trivet.[10] Shall I run up and look at him?"

"No!" said Paul's mother reluctantly. "No! Don't trouble. It's all right. Don't sit up. We shall be home fairly soon." She did not want her son's privacy intruded upon.

"Very good," said the governess.

It was about one o'clock when Paul's mother and father drove up to their house. All was still. Paul's mother went to her room and slipped off her white fur cloak. She had told her maid not to wait up for her. She heard her husband downstairs, mixing a whisky-and-soda.

And then, because of the strange anxiety at her heart, she stole upstairs to her son's room. Noiselessly she went along the upper corridor. Was there a faint noise? What was it?

---

10. right as a trivet perfectly right.

She stood, with arrested muscles, outside his door, listening. There was a strange, heavy, and yet not loud noise. Her heart stood still. It was a soundless noise, yet rushing and powerful. Something huge, in violent, hushed motion. What was it? What in God's name was it? She ought to know. She felt that she *knew* the noise. She knew what it was.

Yet she could not place it. She couldn't say what it was. And on and on it went, like madness.

Softly, frozen with anxiety and fear, she turned the door handle.

The room was dark. Yet in the space near the window, she heard and saw something plunging to and fro. She gazed in fear and amazement.

Then suddenly she switched on the light, and saw her son, in his green pajamas, madly surging on his rocking horse. The blaze of light suddenly lit him up, as he urged the wooden horse, and lit her up, as she stood, blond, in her dress of pale green and crystal, in the doorway.

"Paul!" she cried. "Whatever are you doing?"

"It's Malabar!" he screamed, in a powerful, strange voice. "It's Malabar!"

His eyes blazed at her for one strange and senseless second, as he ceased urging his wooden horse. Then he fell with a crash to the ground, and she, all her tormented motherhood flooding upon her, rushed to gather him up.

But he was unconscious, and unconscious he remained, with some brain fever. He talked and tossed, and his mother sat stonily by his side.

"Malabar! It's Malabar! Bassett, Bassett, I *know* it's Malabar!"

So the child cried, trying to get up and urge the rocking horse that gave him his inspiration.

"What does he mean by Malabar?" asked the heart-frozen mother.

"I don't know," said the father, stonily.

"What does he mean by Malabar?" she asked her brother Oscar.

"It's one of the horses running for the Derby," was the answer.

And, in spite of himself, Oscar Cresswell spoke to Bassett, and himself put a thousand on Malabar: at fourteen to one.

The third day of the illness was critical: they were watching for a change. The boy, with his rather long, curly hair, was tossing ceaselessly on the pillow. He neither slept nor regained consciousness, and his eyes were like blue stones. His mother sat, feeling her heart had gone, turned actually into a stone.

Literary Analysis
Theme and Symbol
In what way is the rocking horse connected with the whispering of the house?

Reading Strategy
Making and Confirming Predictions What do you think will happen to Paul?

Reading Check
Why is Paul especially tense just before the Derby?

"It's Malabar!
BASSETT, BASSETT, I KNOW
IT'S MALABAR!"

In the evening, Oscar Cresswell did not come, but Bassett sent a message, saying could he come up for one moment, just one moment? Paul's mother was very angry at the intrusion, but on second thoughts she agreed. The boy was the same. Perhaps Bassett might bring him to consciousness.

The gardener, a shortish fellow with a little brown moustache and sharp little brown eyes, tiptoed into the room, touched his imaginary cap to Paul's mother, and stole to the bedside, staring with glittering, smallish eyes at the tossing, dying child.

"Master Paul!" he whispered. "Master Paul! Malabar came in first all right, a clean win. I did as you told me. You've made over seventy thousand pounds, you have; you've got over eighty thousand. Malabar came in all right, Master Paul."

"Malabar! Malabar! Did I say Malabar, mother? Did I say Malabar? Do you think I'm lucky, mother? I knew Malabar, didn't I? Over eighty thousand pounds! I call that lucky, don't you, mother? Over eighty thousand pounds! I knew, didn't I know I knew? Malabar came in all right. If I ride my horse till I'm sure, then I tell you, Bassett, you can go as high as you like. Did you go for all you were worth, Bassett?"

"I went a thousand on it, Master Paul."

"I never told you, mother, that if I can ride my horse, and *get there*, then I'm absolutely sure—oh, absolutely! Mother, did I ever tell you? I *am* lucky!"

"No, you never did," said the mother.

But the boy died in the night.

And even as he lay dead, his mother heard her brother's voice saying to her: "My God, Hester, you're eighty-odd thousand to the good, and a poor devil of a son to the bad. But, poor devil, poor devil, he's best gone out of a life where he rides his rocking horse to find a winner."

Spiral Review
Character What difficult problem does Paul face throughout the story?

Critical Reading

1. Key Ideas and Details (a) From the point of view of Paul's mother, what is the main problem of the family? **(b) Infer:** What does the mother's statement that the father is "unlucky" suggest about her values?

2. Key Ideas and Details (a) Over the course of the story, how does Paul react to the house's "whispers"? **(b) Analyze Cause and Effect:** Why is he affected as he is?

3. Key Ideas and Details (a) What does Uncle Oscar say at the end of the story? **(b) Interpret:** Do you think Uncle Oscar is speaking for the author? Why or why not?

4. Integration of Knowledge and Ideas What, if anything, is more important than the luck and money that Paul's mother wanted so desperately?

Cite textual evidence to support your responses.

GRAHAM GREENE

(1904-1991)

Author of "A Shocking Accident"

The search for salvation, a theme addressed by poets like T. S. Eliot, is a central concern in the fiction of novelist Graham Greene. Like Eliot, Greene was a religious convert who wrote works exploring pain, fear, despair, and alienation.

Journalism and Travel The son of a school-master, Greene was born in Berkhamsted in Hertfordshire. He converted to Roman Catholicism after studying at Oxford University. Then, he began working as a copy editor in London and married. Eventually, he became a traveling freelance journalist.

Thrillers and More His journalism helped him develop the powers of observation, sensitivity to atmosphere, and simplicity of language that became hallmarks of his fiction. While traveling, he was able to scout out locations for his stories and novels.

Some of these novels, such as *Orient Express* (1932), he called "entertainments." These were an unusual type of thriller that went beyond the genre in its concern with moral issues.

Even more deeply involved with spiritual crisis, however, were such Greene classics as *Brighton Rock* (1938), *The Power and the Glory* (1940), and two novels set in Africa, *The Heart of the Matter* (1948) and *A Burnt-Out Case* (1961). In these works, Greene's concern with salvation burns with intensity.

Psychological Insight Greene's best fiction focuses on the psychology of human character rather than on plot. Many of his protagonists are people without roots or beliefs—people in pain. They may be odd, but they almost always excite the reader's curiosity and pity—and, almost always, Greene treats them with compassion as they strive to achieve salvation.

A SHOCKING ACCIDENT

GRAHAM GREENE

I

Jerome was called into his housemaster's room in the break between the second and the third class on a Thursday morning. He had no fear of trouble, for he was a warden—the name that the proprietor and headmaster of a rather expensive preparatory school had chosen to give to approved, reliable boys in the lower forms (from a warden one became a guardian and finally before leaving, it was hoped for Marlborough or Rugby, a crusader). The housemaster, Mr. Wordsworth, sat behind his desk with an appearance of perplexity and apprehension. Jerome had the odd impression when he entered that he was a cause of fear.

"Sit down, Jerome," Mr. Wordsworth said. "All going well with the trigonometry?"

"Yes, sir."

"I've had a telephone call, Jerome. From your aunt. I'm afraid I have bad news for you."

"Yes, sir?"

"Your father has had an accident."

"Oh."

▲ **Critical Viewing**
What role do you think a pig like the one shown will play in this story? **[Predict]**

Vocabulary
apprehension (ap´ rē hen´ shən) *n.* anxious feeling of foreboding; dread

Reading Check
Why is Jerome not afraid of being called to the housemaster's room?

A Shocking Accident **1263**

Mr. Wordsworth looked at him with some surprise. "A serious accident."

"Yes, sir?"

Jerome worshipped his father: the verb is exact. As man re-creates God, so Jerome re-created his father—from a restless widowed author into a mysterious adventurer who traveled in far places—Nice, Beirut, Majorca, even the Canaries. The time had arrived about his eighth birthday when Jerome believed that his father either "ran guns" or was a member of the British Secret Service. Now it occurred to him that his father might have been wounded in "a hail of machine-gun bullets."

Mr. Wordsworth played with the ruler on his desk. He seemed at a loss how to continue. He said, "You knew your father was in Naples?"

"Yes, sir."

"Your aunt heard from the hospital today."

"Oh."

Mr. Wordsworth said with desperation, "It was a street accident."

"Yes, sir?" It seemed quite likely to Jerome that they would call it a street accident. The police, of course, had fired first; his father would not take human life except as a last resort.

"I'm afraid your father was very seriously hurt indeed."

"Oh."

"In fact, Jerome, he died yesterday. Quite without pain."

"Did they shoot him through the heart?"

"I beg your pardon. What did you say, Jerome?"

"Did they shoot him through the heart?"

"Nobody shot him, Jerome. A pig fell on him." An inexplicable convulsion took place in the nerves of Mr. Wordsworth's face; it really looked for a moment as though he were going to laugh. He closed his eyes, composed his features, and said rapidly, as though it were necessary to expel the story as rapidly as possible, "Your father was walking along a street in Naples when a pig fell on him. A shocking accident. Apparently in the poorer quarters of Naples they keep pigs on their balconies. This one was on the fifth floor. It had grown too fat. The balcony broke. The pig fell on your father."

Mr. Wordsworth left his desk rapidly and went to the window, turning his back on Jerome. He shook a little with emotion.

Jerome said, "What happened to the pig?"

Literary Analysis
Theme and Symbol
Do you think that the way Jerome's father died could be symbolic? Why or why not?

"WHAT HAPPENED TO THE PIG?"

2

This was not callousness on the part of Jerome as it was interpreted by Mr. Wordsworth to his colleagues (he even discussed with them whether, perhaps, Jerome was not yet fitted to be a warden). Jerome was only attempting to visualize the strange scene and to get the details right. Nor was Jerome a boy who cried; he was a boy who brooded, and it never occurred to him at his preparatory school that the circumstances of his father's death were comic—they were still part of the mystery of life. It was later in his first term at his public school, when he told the story to his best friend, that he began to realize how it affected others. Naturally, after that disclosure he was known, rather unreasonably, as Pig.

Unfortunately his aunt had no sense of humor. There was an enlarged snapshot of his father on the piano: a large sad man in an unsuitable dark suit posed in Capri with an umbrella (to guard him against sunstroke), the Faraglioni rocks forming the background. By the age of sixteen Jerome was well aware that the portrait looked more like the author of *Sunshine and Shade* and *Rambles in the Balearics* than an agent of the Secret Service. All the same, he loved the memory of his father: he still possessed an album filled with picture-postcards (the stamps had been soaked off long ago for his other collection), and it pained him when his aunt embarked with strangers on the story of his father's death.

"A shocking accident," she would begin, and the stranger would compose his or her features into the correct shape for interest and commiseration. Both reactions, of course, were false, but it was terrible for Jerome to see how suddenly, midway in her rambling discourse, the interest would become genuine. "I can't think how such things can be allowed in a civilized country," his aunt would say. "I suppose one has to regard Italy as civilized. One is prepared for all kinds of things abroad, of course, and my brother was a great traveler. He always carried a water-filter with him. It was far less expensive, you know, than buying all those bottles of mineral water. My brother always said that his filter paid for his dinner wine. You can see from that what a careful man he was, but who could possibly have expected when he was walking along the Via Dottore Manuele Panucci on his way to the Hydrographic Museum that a pig would fall on him?" That was the moment when the interest became genuine.

Jerome's father had not been a distinguished writer, but the time always seems to come, after an author's death, when somebody thinks it worth his while to write a letter to *The Times Literary Supplement* announcing the preparation of a biography and asking to see any letters or documents or receive any anecdotes from friends of the dead man. Most of the biographies, of course, never appear—one

Spiral Review

Context What conclusions can you draw about the nuances in meaning of the word *disclosure* by analyzing the paragraph?

Vocabulary

embarked (em bärkt′) *v.* engaged in something, such as a conversation

Reading Check

What happened to Jerome's father?

wonders whether the whole thing may not be an obscure form of blackmail and whether many a potential writer of a biography or thesis finds the means in this way to finish his education at Kansas or Nottingham. Jerome, however, as a chartered accountant, lived far from the literary world. He did not realize how small the menace really was, nor that the danger period for someone of his father's obscurity had long passed. Sometimes he rehearsed the method of recounting his father's death so as to reduce the comic element to its smallest dimensions—it would be of no use to refuse information, for in that case the biographer would undoubtedly visit his aunt, who was living to a great old age with no sign of flagging.

It seemed to Jerome that there were two possible methods—the first led gently up to the accident, so well prepared that the death came really as an anticlimax. The chief danger of laughter in such a story was always surprise. When he rehearsed this method Jerome began boringly enough.

"You know Naples and those high tenement buildings? Somebody once told me that the Neapolitan always feels at home in New York just as the man from Turin feels at home in London because the river runs in much the same way in both cities. Where was I? Oh, yes, Naples, of course. You'd be surprised in the poorer quarters what things they keep on the balconies of those skyscraping tenements—not washing, you know, or bedding, but things like livestock, chickens or even pigs. Of course the pigs get no exercise whatever and fatten all the quicker." He could imagine how his hearer's eyes would have glazed by this time. "I've no idea, have you, how heavy a pig can be, but those old buildings are all badly in need of repair. A balcony on the fifth floor gave way under one of those pigs. It struck the third-floor balcony on its way down and sort of ricocheted into the street. My father was on the way to the Hydrographic Museum when the pig hit him. Coming from that height and that angle it broke his neck." This was really a masterly attempt to make an intrinsically interesting subject boring.

The other method Jerome rehearsed had the virtue of brevity.

"My father was killed by a pig."

"Really? In India?"

"No, in Italy."

"How interesting. I never realized there was pig-sticking in Italy. Was your father keen on polo?"

In course of time, neither too early nor too late, rather as though, in his capacity as a chartered accountant, Jerome had studied the statistics and taken the average, he became engaged to be married: to a pleasant fresh-faced girl of twenty-five whose father was a doctor in Pinner. Her name was Sally, her favorite author was still Hugh

Vocabulary
intrinsically (in trin′ sik lē) *adv.* at its core; inherently; innately

Walpole, and she had adored babies ever since she had been given a doll at the age of five which moved its eyes and made water. Their relationship was contented rather than exciting, as became the love affair of a chartered accountant; it would never have done if it had interfered with the figures.

One thought worried Jerome, however. Now that within a year he might himself become a father, his love for the dead man increased; he realized what affection had gone into the picture-postcards. He felt a longing to protect his memory, and uncertain whether this quiet love of his would survive if Sally were so insensitive as to laugh when she heard the story of his father's death. Inevitably she would hear it when Jerome brought her to dinner with his aunt. Several times he tried to tell her himself, as she was naturally anxious to know all she could that concerned him.

"You were very small when your father died?"

"Just nine."

"Poor little boy," she said.

"I was at school. They broke the news to me."

"Did you take it very hard?"

"I can't remember."

"You never told me how it happened."

"It was very sudden. A street accident."

"You'll never drive fast, will you, Jemmy?" (She had begun to call him "Jemmy.") It was too late then to try the second method—the one he thought of as the pig-sticking one.

They were going to marry quietly at a registry-office and have their honeymoon at Torquay. He avoided taking her to see his aunt until a week before the wedding, but then the night came, and he could not have told himself whether his apprehension was more for his father's memory or the security of his own love.

The moment came all too soon. "Is that Jemmy's father?" Sally asked, picking up the portrait of the man with the umbrella.

"Yes, dear. How did you guess?"

"He has Jemmy's eyes and brow, hasn't he?"

"Has Jerome lent you his books?"

"No."

"I will give you a set for your wedding. He wrote so tenderly about his travels. My own favorite is *Nooks and Crannies*. He would have had a great future. It made that shocking accident all the worse."

"Yes?"

Reading Strategy
Making and Confirming Predictions How do you think Sally will react to the story of Jerome's father's death? What impact will that have on Jerome?

Reading Check

What two methods of narrating his father's death does Jerome rehearse?

"IT WAS VERY SUDDEN. A STREET ACCIDENT."

How Jerome longed to leave the room and not see that loved face crinkle with irresistible amusement.

"I had so many letters from his readers after the pig fell on him." She had never been so abrupt before.

And then the miracle happened. Sally did not laugh. Sally sat with open eyes of horror while his aunt told her the story, and at the end, "How horrible," Sally said. "It makes you think, doesn't it? Happening like that. Out of a clear sky."

Jerome's heart sang with joy. It was as though she had appeased his fear forever. In the taxi going home he kissed her with more passion than he had ever shown, and she returned it. There were babies in her pale blue pupils, babies that rolled their eyes and made water.

"A week today," Jerome said, and she squeezed his hand. "Penny for your thoughts, my darling."

"I was wondering," Sally said, "what happened to the poor pig?"

"They almost certainly had it for dinner," Jerome said happily and kissed the dear child again.

Literary Analysis
Theme and Symbol
What does the contrast between Sally's reaction and those of other characters suggest about the theme?

"WHAT HAPPENED TO THE POOR PIG?"

Critical Reading

1. **Key Ideas and Details** How does Jerome protect himself from the embarrassing aspects of the death?

2. **Key Ideas and Details** **(a)** How does Sally react when she hears the story? **(b) Infer:** What does Sally's reaction reveal to Jerome about her character? **(c) Draw Conclusions:** Are Jerome's conflicts about his father's death resolved at the end of the story? Why or why not?

3. **Integration of Knowledge and Ideas** One implication of the "shocking accident" might be that what happens in life is basically beyond our control. Do you agree with this idea? Why or why not?

4. **Integration of Knowledge and Ideas** Does the uniqueness of the main character in either or both of the stories suggest a message about society? Explain. In your response, use at least two of these Essential Question words: *emotion, spontaneity, conventional, trait.* [Connecting to the Essential Question: How does literature shape or reflect society?]

Cite textual evidence to support your responses.

After You Read

The Rocking-Horse Winner ▪ A Shocking Accident

Literary Analysis

1. Key Ideas and Details Using the terms *love* and *money*, state a central question, issue, or concern that expresses one of the **themes** in "The Rocking-Horse Winner."

2. Integration of Knowledge and Ideas Complete a chart like this with **(a)** passages illustrating the **symbolic** meanings of the rocking horse and **(b)** explanations linking these meanings to the theme.

Symbolic Meanings	Passages That Illustrate	Links to Overall Theme
• Frantic effort to satisfy an unsatisfiable need • Frightening power of desires and wishes		

3. Key Ideas and Details For "A Shocking Accident," explain how the accident might symbolize either of these meanings: **(a)** that which makes no sense; **(b)** that which is unacceptable according to upper-class notions.

4. Key Ideas and Details Use the symbolic meanings of the accident to state the theme of "A Shocking Accident."

5. Craft and Structure For both "The Rocking-Horse Winner" and "A Shocking Accident," identify two passages that show the use of the **third-person point of view.**

6. Comparing Literary Works In which story does the third-person point of view work more effectively to reveal the theme? Explain, citing details from the stories.

7. Comparing Literary Works In which story is the third-person narrative more like a fairy tale and in which is it more like an anecdote? Explain.

Reading Strategy

8. (a) If "The Rocking-Horse Winner" continued, **predict** how Paul's mother might act in the future. **(b)** What information in the story and in your own *background knowledge* leads you to make that prediction?

9. What do you think Jerome would have done if Sally had responded with amusement to the story of his father's death? Explain.

10. Which story ending surprised you more? Why?

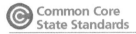

**Common Core
State Standards**

Writing
3. Write narratives to develop real or imagined experiences or events using effective technique, well-chosen details, and well-structured event sequences. *(p. 1270)*
5. Develop and strengthen writing as needed by planning, revising, editing, rewriting, or trying a new approach, focusing on addressing what is most significant for a specific purpose and audience. *(p. 1270)*

Language
4.a. Use context as a clue to the meaning of a word or phrase. *(p. 1270)*

Integrated Language Skills

Vocabulary Acquisition and Use

Word Analysis: Anglo-Saxon prefix *un-*

Lawrence describes Paul's eyes as having an "uncanny" fire. The prefix *un-* means "not" or "the opposite or reversal of an action." It is used with adjectives, such as *unavailable* ("not available"), and verbs, such as *unlock* ("to reverse the action of locking"). The prefix comes from Anglo-Saxon, a Germanic language that is the basis for English. Write an original sentence that shows your understanding of the meaning of each of these words that begin with the prefix *un-*:

1. unhinge
2. unavoidable
3. unrecognized
4. unclasp
5. unsure
6. unchecked

Vocabulary: Context Clues

The context in which an unfamiliar word appears can give you clues to the word's meaning. For each sentence, explain how a context clue helps you identify the meaning of the italicized word from the vocabulary listed on page 1244.

1. The story was *intrinsically* boring, but the storyteller's style made it gripping.
2. The investigator's *discreet* queries raised no suspicions.
3. The camel *obstinately* refused to budge despite the owner's many efforts.
4. Reunited after ten years, the two sisters *embarked* on recounting their lives.
5. The dark clouds gave the worried farmer a feeling of *apprehension*.
6. Her *uncanny* ability to predict the future defied all logic.

Writing

Narrative Text Filmmakers use dialogue, images, and sounds to create symbols in films. Write a **script for a scene** from one of the stories. Include descriptions of the scenery, dialogue, and directions regarding shots, camera movement, and scene changes. Use some of the terms explained in the chart below.

Shots	Camera Movement	Scene Changes
• **Wide shot:** Camera captures a large area • **Medium shot:** Camera sees objects and surroundings • **Close-up:** Camera focuses on one object	• **Crane:** Camera moves in and out and up and down • **Pan:** Camera moves from side to side • **Zoom:** Camera moves in for a closer view	• **Dissolve:** Image grows faint as new image emerges • **Fade-out:** Image fades to black • **Montage:** Quick succession of unrelated images

Prewriting Choose the scene to script. Identify the symbols in that scene and their meaning. Decide how you want those symbols to appear.

Drafting Write a draft of your script. Be sure to describe what the camera sees, the movements of the characters, and the way the symbols will look. Include dialogue, indicating which character is speaking. Embellish your script with notes on how the scene should be shot and edited.

Revising Review your draft, making sure that the scene flows well, that directions are clear, and that you use the symbols effectively. Ensure that the descriptions and dialogue accurately and faithfully present the story.

Conflicts at
Home and Abroad

PART
3

Connecting to the Essential Question War can lead soldiers to write powerful prose and poetry. As you read, notice details that show the impact of the war on these poets. Doing so will help you think about the Essential Question: **How does literature shape or reflect society?**

Literary Analysis

The **tone** of a literary work is the writer's attitude toward the readers and the subject. A writer's choice of words and details conveys the tone of the work. For example, in these lines from Rupert Brooke's "The Soldier," the underlined words and phrases communicate a tone of patriotic devotion and wistful memory:

> Her sights and sounds; *dreams happy as her day*;
> And *laughter*, learnt of *friends*; and *gentleness*,
> In *hearts at peace*, under an *English heaven*.

Comparing Literary Works In a way, these selections are like letters sent home by soldiers during World War I. These "letters" each contain central messages, or **themes,** about the war for those back in England, removed from the fighting. In figuring out these messages, use tone as a clue. Identify words and phrases that reveal each writer's attitude about the war and toward civilian readers. Then, compare and contrast the different writers' messages.

Reading Strategy

 Preparing to Read Complex Texts Because writers often suggest rather than state elements like theme and speaker, readers must **infer the essential message,** or make educated guesses based on clues in the text. Use a chart like the one shown to make inferences about the essential message of these poems.

Vocabulary

stealthy (stel′ thē) *adj.* secretive; furtive (p. 1276)

ghastly (gast′ lē) *adj.* extremely horrible; frightening (p. 1276)

desolate (des′ ə lit) *adj.* deserted; forlorn (p. 1276)

mockeries (mäk′ ər ēz) *n.* futile or disappointing efforts; ridicule (p. 1277)

pallor (pal′ ər) *n.* lack of color; paleness (p. 1277)

**Common Core
State Standards**

Reading Literature
4. Analyze the impact of specific word choices on meaning and tone, including words with multiple meanings or language that is particularly fresh, engaging, or beautiful.

Passage

"think only this of me"

Thoughts About Clues

His personal history does not matter

Inference About Essential Message

www.PHLitOnline.com

RUPERT BROOKE   *(1887–1915)*

Author of *"The Soldier"*

Rupert Brooke had striking good looks, personal charm, and high intelligence. Before World War I began, Brooke had already established himself as a serious poet. He traveled a great deal, writing essays as well as poetry. When war broke out in 1914, he joined the Royal Navy. Tragically, he died from blood poisoning while on a mission to defeat the Turks.

Brooke's war sonnets, traditional and idealistic, were among the last from the soldier-poets of World War I to express wholehearted patriotism. The prolonged, inhuman slaughter of trench warfare extinguished the idealism of many of them.

SIEGFRIED SASSOON   *(1886–1967)*

Author of *"Wirers"*

Born into a wealthy family in Kent, England, Siegfried Sassoon published poetry while still in his twenties. In 1914, he joined the army and showed such reckless courage in battle that he earned the nickname "Mad Jack," along with a medal for gallantry.

By 1916 or 1917, though, Sassoon's attitude toward war had changed. He began to write starkly realistic "trench poems" about war's agonies. He was wounded early in 1917 and, while recovering, wrote a statement condemning the war. Partly to defuse his criticism and partly to protect him from its consequences, he was placed in a hospital for victims of shell shock.

Sassoon survived the war and lived almost fifty years longer, but he wrote little to match his wartime verses.

WILFRED OWEN   *(1893–1918)*

Author of *"Anthem for Doomed Youth"*

Always interested in literature, Wilfred Owen studied at London University and joined the army in 1915. He was wounded three times in 1917 and won a medal for outstanding bravery in 1918. Owen's work became grittier and angrier under the influence of Siegfried Sassoon, whom he had met at a military hospital in 1917. It was a terrible loss to English poetry when Owen was killed in battle just one week before the end of the war.

Owen was unknown as a poet until Sassoon published a collection of his work, *Poems*, in 1920. Today, Owen is regarded as one of the greatest war poets in the English language.

THE SOLDIER

RUPERT BROOKE

BACKGROUND

World War I (1914–1918) pitted Great Britain, France, Russia, Japan, Italy, and, later, the United States (the Allies) against Germany, Austria-Hungary, and Turkey (the Central Powers). The war was fought not only in Europe but also in regions like the Middle East and Asia Minor. Typical of this conflict, especially in Western Europe, was trench warfare. Armies faced each other in defensive trenches protected by barbed wire. Periodically, one army would attack another in the face of machine-gun and artillery fire. Such warfare and the illnesses resulting from life in filthy trenches led to a total loss of about 8.5 million soldiers.

If I should die, think only this of me:
　　That there's some corner of a foreign field
That is forever England. There shall be
　　In that rich earth a richer dust concealed;
5 A dust whom England bore, shaped, made aware,
　　Gave, once, her flowers to love, her ways to roam,
A body of England's, breathing English air,
Washed by the rivers, blest by suns of home.

And think, this heart, all evil shed away,
10　　A pulse in the eternal mind, no less
　　　　Gives somewhere back the thoughts by England given;
Her sights and sounds; dreams happy as her day;
　　　　And laughter, learnt of friends; and gentleness,
　　　　In hearts at peace, under an English heaven.

Literary Analysis
Tone What are three adjectives that describe the tone of this poem? Explain.

Critical Reading

© **1. Key Ideas and Details (a)** How does the speaker ask his readers to remember him, should he die? **(b) Infer:** Why would the speaker go off to war, knowing he could be killed?

© **2. Key Ideas and Details (a)** Name some of the things England has given the speaker. **(b) Interpret:** What is the "richer dust" to which the speaker refers?

© **3. Key Ideas and Details (a)** In lines 9 and 10, what does the speaker say his "heart" will become? **(b) Interpret:** What does the speaker mean by this statement?

© **4. Integration of Knowledge and Ideas** Brooke's attitude has been called a "ridiculous anachronism"—something outdated—in the face of modern warfare. Do you agree or disagree? Why?

Cite textual evidence to support your responses.

WIRERS[1]

SIEGFRIED SASSOON

▲ **Critical Viewing**
Which details in this photograph support Sassoon's depiction of warfare? Explain. **[Connect]**

Vocabulary
stealthy (stel´ thē)
adj. secretive; furtive

ghastly (gast´ lē)
adj. extremely horrible; frightening

desolate (des´ ə lit)
adj. deserted; forlorn

"Pass it along, the wiring party's going out"—
And yawning sentries mumble, "Wirers going out."
Unraveling; twisting; hammering stakes with muffled thud,
They toil with stealthy haste and anger in their blood.

5　The Boche[2] sends up a flare. Black forms stand rigid there,
Stock-still like posts; then darkness, and the clumsy ghosts
Stride hither and thither, whispering, tripped by clutching
　　snare
Of snags and tangles.
　　　　　Ghastly dawn with vaporous coasts
10　Gleams desolate along the sky, night's misery ended.

Young Hughes was badly hit; I heard him carried away,
Moaning at every lurch; no doubt he'll die today.
But *we* can say the front-line wire's been safely mended.

---

1. **Wirers** soldiers who were responsible for repairing the barbed-wire fences that protected the trenches in World War I.
2. **Boche** (bōsh) French slang for a German soldier.

ANTHEM FOR DOOMED YOUTH

WILFRED OWEN

What passing-bells for these who die as cattle?
Only the monstrous anger of the guns.
Only the stuttering rifles' rapid rattle
Can patter out their hasty orisons.[1]
5 No mockeries for them from prayers or bells,
Nor any voice of mourning save the choirs—
The shrill, demented choirs of wailing shells;
And bugles calling for them from sad shires.[2]

What candles may be held to speed them all?
10 Not in the hands of boys, but in their eyes
Shall shine the holy glimmers of good-byes.
The pallor of girls' brows shall be their pall;
Their flowers the tenderness of patient minds,
And each slow dusk a drawing-down of blinds.

---

1. **orisons** (ôr´ i zəns) *n.* prayers.
2. **shires** (shīrz) *n.* any of the counties of England.

Critical Reading

© **1. Key Ideas and Details (a)** In "Wirers," what happens in the course of the mission? **(b) Draw Conclusions:** What is the speaker's attitude toward the mission and toward the war? Explain.

© **2. Key Ideas and Details (a)** In lines 9–14 of "Anthem for Doomed Youth," what conventional signs of mourning are mentioned? **(b) Analyze:** What do Owen's suggested replacements for these signs have in common?

© **3. Integration of Knowledge and Ideas** Do you think Sassoon's poem affected the attitude of British readers toward the war? Explain your answer, using two of these Essential Question words: *position, destructive, factors, influence, support. [Connecting to the Essential Question: How does literature shape or reflect society?]*

Cite textual evidence to support your responses.

Literary Analysis

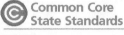

Common Core State Standards

Writing
1. Write arguments to support claims in an analysis of substantive topics or texts, using valid reasoning and relevant and sufficient evidence. *(p. 1279)*

Language
5. Demonstrate understanding of figurative language, word relationships, and nuances in word meanings. *(p. 1279)*

1. Craft and Structure Using a chart like the one shown, briefly describe the **tone** in two or three key passages from each poem.

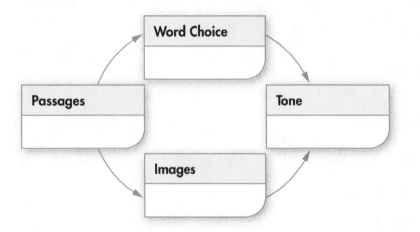

2. Craft and Structure **(a)** Of the three selections, which is the least angry in tone? Explain. **(b)** Which is the most sarcastic? Explain.

3. Craft and Structure **(a)** Which of the selections has the most surprising tone or mixture of tones? Why? **(b)** What is less surprising about the tone or tones of the other selections?

4. Integration of Knowledge and Ideas For English civilians of the time, which of these selections probably conveyed the most positive message about the war? Explain.

5. Integration of Knowledge and Ideas **(a)** Which poems are most concerned with war's destruction? Explain. **(b)** Which criticize how the war is being run? Explain.

6. Comparing Literary Works Compare the attitudes these writers have toward civilian readers.

7. Key Ideas and Details What do you think is Owen's purpose in altering funeral rituals in lines 9–14 of "Anthem for Doomed Youth"? Explain your reasoning.

Reading Strategy

8. Infer the essential message of "Wirers," explaining what details led you to your conclusion.

9. (a) Infer the essential message of "The Soldier" and "Anthem for Doomed Youth" and explain what details led you to that conclusion. **(b)** If Brooke had lived longer and experienced more of the war, do you think he would have produced poetry more like Owen's? Explain your answer.

Integrated Language Skills

© Vocabulary Acquisition and Use

Word Analysis: Anglo-Saxon roots -ghast-, -ghost-

In "Wirers," Sassoon refers to the "ghastly" dawn. *Ghastly* comes from an Anglo-Saxon root, *-ghast-*, that means "to terrify." The same root also appears as *-ghost-*, which means "the spirit of a dead person," which can terrify the living. Use your understanding of these roots to determine the meaning of these words. Then use them in a sentence.

1. aghast

2. ghostly

3. ghosting

4. ghastful

Vocabulary: Synonyms

Synonyms are words that have similar meanings. Write the letter of the word that is the synonym of each word from the vocabulary list on page 1272. Then, explain the differences in meaning between the synonyms.

1. desolate: **(a)** crowded, **(b)** forlorn, **(c)** happy

2. ghastly: **(a)** frightening, **(b)** ghostly, **(c)** shocking

3. mockeries: **(a)** bravery, **(b)** praise, **(c)** ridicule

4. pallor: **(a)** care, **(b)** paleness, **(c)** friends

5. stealthy: **(a)** furtive, **(b)** honest, **(c)** smart

Writing

© **Argumentative Text** When Irish poet William Butler Yeats selected poems for an anthology of modern English poetry, he left out Brooke, Sassoon, and Owen. Yeats explained his action this way: "I have a distaste for certain poems written in the midst of the great war. . . . The writers . . . were . . . officers of exceptional courage . . . but . . . passive suffering is not a theme for poetry." Write an **essay** that responds to Yeats based on your reading of these poets, particularly Sassoon and Owen. Cite evidence from the poems to support your point about the merits—or lack of merit—of these poets.

Prewriting Note uses of imagery, language, or ideas in the poems that reflect poetic skill or communicate important messages. Review your examples to see if they mainly support or refute Yeats's claim, and decide whether you agree or disagree with his view.

Drafting Begin your draft by summarizing Yeats's position and stating your response to it. Use detailed evidence and examples from the poems to support your points.

Revising Review your draft, highlighting generalizations and looking for supporting details for each. Where details are lacking, add them. Make sure that all quotations are accurate and properly referenced.

> **Clearly Stating Your Response**
> ● As I will demonstrate, Yeats misreads poems like "Wirers" when he dismisses them as representing "passive suffering."

Stating a position early and supporting it with evidence gives a clear picture of the argument.

CONNECTING WAR WRITINGS PAST AND PRESENT

Wilfred Owen, British soldier and poet killed in battle one week before the end of World War I in 1918, wrote that "War and the Pity of War" were his chosen subject. The blogger Riverbend's subject is also the pity of war, a war that has forced her and her family, Iraqi Muslims, to realize that they must abandon their home in Baghdad, a city that in 2007 has all but disappeared into violence. Owen uses the traditional poetic form to describe the threat of "The shrill, demented choirs of wailing shells" in "Anthem for Doomed Youth." Riverbend's April 26, 2007 Web journal entry may be prose, yet it is just as fear-based: "It's difficult to decide which is more frightening—car bombs and militias, or having to leave everything you know and love. . . ."

Both writers are in their 20's when they confront the reality of war. Worlds of difference separate them—gender, religion, geography, technology, the patriotism of an enlisted soldier versus the witness a civilian woman must bear to the chaos surrounding her home—yet their concerns are remarkably similar: death, and the death of a way of life. Riverbend, 24 when she began to chronicle the details of daily life in her gripping blog, known in book form as *Baghdad Burning*, writes anonymously because, "I wouldn't feel free to write otherwise. . . ." Owen, at least, knows nothing of that kind of fear and publishes signed poetry describing the horror of what he witnesses. Both doomed soldier-poet and determined prose writer document events that overtake them, in the most effective and persuasive style they know.

RIVERBEND, AUTHOR OF

BAGHDAD BURNING

"I am female, Iraqi, and 24. I survived the war." With these words, the blogger who calls herself Riverbend begins her online journal one Sunday in August 2003. "That's all you need to know. That's all that matters these days," she writes. Her postings have been compiled into two books, *Baghdad Burning*, published in 2005, and *Baghdad Burning II*, which appeared the following year. Riverbend has become something of a blog celebrity, supplying her readers with a comprehensive local Iraqi view of the war. In fact, her blog has journeyed from cyberspace to the printed page to the stage, debuting in New York in 2005 in a blending of documentary drama and blog that became a play.

No journalist, Riverbend, who explains that she was forced from her job as a computer programmer, nonetheless exhibits a journalist's ability to describe everything around her, from the horror of looking for a missing neighbor to power failures that keep her from her computer. Her perspective is personal and her weapons are words, which survive beyond immediate events, just as the words of the war poets of World War I do.

"RIVERBEND" IS A STORYTELLER. HER "BAGHDAD BURNING" BLOG IS ONE PART ANNE FRANK, ANOTHER PART SCHEHERAZADE AND "A THOUSAND AND ONE ARABIAN NIGHTS."

— FROM CYBERSPACE
[PROMOTION BY HER PUBLISHER]

BAGHDAD BURNING

FROM THURSDAY, APRIL 26, 2007

I remember Baghdad before the war—one could live anywhere. We didn't know what our neighbors were—we didn't care. No one asked about religion or sect. No one bothered with what was considered a trivial topic: are you Sunni or Shia? You only asked something like that if you were uncouth and backward. Our lives revolve around it now. Our existence depends on hiding it or high-lighting it—depending on the group of masked men who stop you or raid your home in the middle of the night.

On a personal note, we've finally decided to leave. I guess I've known we would be leaving for a while now. We discussed it as a family dozens of times. At first, someone would suggest it tentatively because, it was just a preposterous idea—leaving one's home and extended family—leaving one's country—and to what? To where?

Since last summer, we had been discussing it more and more. It was only a matter of time before what began as a suggestion—a last case scenario—soon took on solidity and developed into a plan. For the last couple of months, it has only been a matter of logistics. Plane or car? Jordan or Syria? Will we all leave together as a family? Or will it be only my brother and I at first?

After Jordan or Syria—where then? Obviously, either of those countries is going to be a transit to something else. They are both overflowing with Iraqi refugees, and every single Iraqi living in either country is complaining of the fact that work is difficult to come by, and getting a residency is even more difficult. There is also the little problem of being turned back at the border. Thousands of Iraqis aren't being let into Syria or Jordan—and there are no definite criteria for entry, the decision is based on the whim of the border patrol guard checking your passport.

An airplane isn't necessarily safer, as the trip to Baghdad International Airport is in itself risky and travelers are just as likely to be refused permission to enter the country (Syria and Jordan) if they arrive by airplane. And if you're wondering why Syria or Jordan, because they are the only two countries that will let Iraqis in without a visa. Following up visa issues with the few functioning embassies or consulates in Baghdad is next to impossible.

So we've been busy. Busy trying to decide what part of our lives to leave behind. Which memories are dispensable? We, like many Iraqis, are not the classic refugees—the ones with only the clothes on their backs and no choice. We are choosing to leave because the other option is simply a continuation of what has been one long nightmare—stay and wait and try to survive.

On the one hand, I know that leaving the country and starting a new life somewhere else—as yet unknown—is such a huge thing that it should dwarf every trivial concern. The funny thing is that it's the trivial that seems to occupy our lives. We discuss whether to take photo albums or leave them behind. Can I bring along a stuffed animal I've had since the age of four? Is there room for E.'s guitar? What clothes do we take? Summer clothes? The winter clothes too? What about my books? What about the CDs, the baby pictures?

The problem is that we don't even know if we'll ever see this stuff again. We don't know if whatever we leave, including the house, will be available when and if we come back. There are moments when the injustice of having to leave your country, simply because someone got it into his head to invade it, is overwhelming. It is unfair that in order to survive and live normally, we have to leave our home and what remains of family and friends… And to what?

It's difficult to decide which is more frightening—car bombs and militias, or having to leave everything you know and love, to some unspecified place for a future where nothing is certain.

… WE'VE FINALLY DECIDED TO LEAVE

Critical Reading

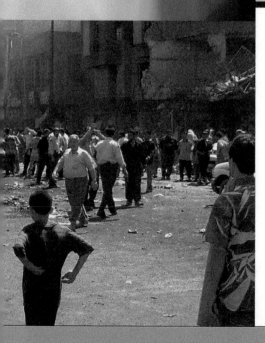

1. **(a)** Why did Riverbend's family originally think leaving Iraq was a "preposterous" idea? **(b) Assess:** Was their idea to leave Iraq "preposterous"? Explain.

2. **(a)** What are the difficulties Riverbend anticipates her family will encounter as they try to leave Iraq?
   (b) Infer: How does Riverbend feel about these difficulties? Explain.

3. **(a)** What items might Riverbend's family take when they leave Iraq? **(b) Interpret:** Why does Riverbend's family want to bring these items?

Use these questions to focus a class discussion of "Baghdad Burning":

4. What can readers who are not involved in a war learn from the writings of Riverbend?

5. How is a blog posted on the Internet different from published essays, stories, or memoirs? How is it similar?

Primary Sources

Speech
Wartime Speech

Memorandum
Evacuation Scheme

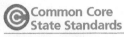Common Core
State Standards

About the Text Forms

A **speech** is an oral presentation on an important issue. Three elements of a speech are its *purpose,* the reason for its presentation; its *occasion,* the event that inspires it; and its *audience,* those who hear it at the time it is delivered or who hear or read it later. In the World War II era, before television, radio listeners were the largest audience for the speeches of national leaders and other important figures. Such speeches can be valuable primary sources in showing how both the authorities and the general public perceived and responded to events.

A **government memorandum** is a brief official message that summarizes reasons for a particular action and gives instructions on how it is to be performed. Since they affected large numbers of people, government memorandums from the past can be valuable primary sources about events and practices of those times.

Reading Informational Text
2. Determine two or more central ideas of a text and analyze their development over the course of the text, including how they interact and build on one another to provide a complex analysis; provide an objective summary of the text.
6. Determine an author's point of view or purpose in a text in which the rhetoric is particularly effective, analyzing how style and content contribute to the power, persuasiveness, or beauty of the text.

Reading Strategy

The central idea, or essential message, of a text is the main point the author expresses. It is closely tied to the author's purpose and his or her point of view on the issue. These texts, written during a period of crisis, reflect their authors' urgent purposes, including the need to ensure the public's willingness to endure hardship for the sake of survival and victory.

As you **determine the essential messages** of these documents, notice the *rhetorical devices and features* that the writers use to emphasize their *main points.*

For example, analyze Churchill's speech for **rhetorical devices** like *parallelism,* the use of similar grammatical structures to express ideas in a memorable way. Also analyze the speech for *emotional appeals,* such as the use of charged words like "victory." Analyze the memorandum for **text features** like headings and lists. Use a chart like the one shown to identify the essential message and the supporting devices and features.

 How does literature shape or reflect *society?*

Winston Churchill was an inspirational leader at a time of great suffering for the British people. As you read, consider how his speech helped shape the public reaction to the hardships of World War II.

Note-Taking Guide

Primary-source documents are a rich source of information for researchers. As you read these documents, use a note-taking guide like the one shown here to organize relevant and accurate information.

1 Type of Document
   ☐ Newspaper Article ☐ Letter ☐ Diary ☐ Speech ☐ Map
   ☐ Government Document ☐ Advertisement ☐ Memorandum ☐ Other

2 Date of Document _____

3 Author _____
   Author's Position _____

4 Original Audience _____

5 Purpose and Importance

   a What was the original purpose? _____
      Write down two details that support your answer. _____
      _____

   b List two important ideas, statements, or observations from this document.
      _____
      _____

   c What does this document show about the time and place in which it
      was composed? _____
      _____
      _____

Reading Strategy
Determine the Essential Message
Identifying the sources' main points and supporting features and devices will help you appreciate their purposes.

This guide was adapted from the **U.S. National Archives** document analysis worksheet.

Vocabulary

intimidated (in tim´ ə dāt əd) *v.* made afraid; frightened (p. 1288)

endurance (en door´ əns) *n.* ability to last or continue (p. 1288)

formidable (fôr´ mə də bəl) *adj.* causing fear or dread; hard to overcome (p. 1288)

invincible (in vin´ sə bəl) *adj.* unconquerable (p. 1288)

retaliate (ri tal´ ē āt´) *v.* fight in order to pay back an injury or wrong (p. 1289)

humanitarian (hyoo man´ ə ter´ ē ən) *adj.* acting to help humanity, especially by easing pain and suffering (p. 1291)

allocation (al´ ō kā´ shən) *n.* setting apart for a specific purpose; fixing the location of (p. 1291)

THE STORY BEHIND THE DOCUMENTS

Sir Winston Churchill

radio microphone

Sir Winston Churchill (1874–1965) first won fame as a soldier and journalist in colonial India and South Africa. His war-hero status earned him a seat in Parliament and several government posts, but he was out of power by the 1930s, when his repeated warnings about the dangers of Nazi Germany went unheeded. Only after World War II broke out did the British turn to the man who had been right about the Nazis all along. Churchill became prime minister in May of 1940 and went on to play a key role in the Allied victory five years later.

Churchill was a gifted orator who made dozens of memorable **speeches.** Many of these were delivered to Parliament or other live audiences and also broadcast on the radio; others were radio addresses made directly to the public. In the dark days of the war, when most of Europe had fallen and Britain faced the Nazis alone, it sometimes seemed that the fate of freedom itself depended on the gruff voice of the prime minister, infusing his fellow citizens with the strength and courage to endure.

In the autumn of 1940, a few months after the fall of France, the Germans concentrated their efforts on air attacks on Britain, hoping to bomb the nation into submission. In anticipation of the bombing attacks—and before the war actually began—the British government made plans for the evacuation of children, hospital patients, and some others in the urban areas likely to be targeted by German bombs. The British Ministry of Health outlined the evacuation plan in a 1939 **government memorandum.**

Evacuation was voluntary, but with the bombs flying, few families refused to participate. Because the likely targets for German bombs were factories, docks, and other industrial areas, the majority of the evacuated children were from poor working-class families who generally live in such areas. They were sent to the less populated countryside to live with farmers and villagers of the more prosperous middle class. The result was culture shock—but a culture shock that ultimately brought Britain closer together.

WARTIME SPEECH

Sir Winston Churchill
BBC, London, 19 May 1940

I speak to you for the first time as Prime Minister in a solemn hour for the life of our country, of our Empire, of our Allies, and, above all, of the cause of Freedom. A tremendous battle is raging in France and Flanders.[1] The Germans, by a remarkable combination of air bombing and heavily armored tanks, have broken through the French defenses north of the Maginot Line,[2] and strong columns of their armored vehicles are ravaging the open country, which for the first day or two was without defenders. They have penetrated deeply and spread alarm and confusion in their track. Behind them there are now appearing infantry in lorries,[3] and behind them, again, the large masses are moving forward. The regroupment of the French armies to make head against, and also to strike at, this intruding wedge has

---

1. **Flanders** (flan′ dərz) region in northwest Europe, on the North Sea, that includes northern France and much of Belgium.
2. **Maginot** (mazh′ ə nō′) **Line** heavy fortifications built before World War II on the eastern frontier of France, in an unsuccessful effort to prevent a German invasion.
3. **infantry in lorries** (lôr′ ēz) foot soldiers in trucks.

▼ **Primary Source: Photographs**
Sir Winston Churchill is shown here making a radio broadcast. In what ways does the presentation of a radio speech differ from a speech given in person? **[Compare and Contrast]**

Reading Check

According to Churchill, what military victories have the Germans won?

F is for **FRANCE**
which we helped
to defend

Vocabulary
intimidated (in tim´ ə dāt əd)
v. made afraid; frightened

endurance (en door´ əns)
n. ability to last or continue

formidable (fôr´ mə də bəl)
adj. causing fear or dread;
hard to overcome

invincible (in vin´ sə bəl)
adj. unconquerable

Primary Source
Speech What do Churchill's
words in the third paragraph
show about his opinion of
the "concrete lines"
of defense?

been proceeding for several days, largely assisted by the magnificent efforts of the Royal Air Force.

We must not allow ourselves to be intimidated by the presence of these armored vehicles in unexpected places behind our lines. If they are behind our Front, the French are also at many points fighting actively behind theirs. Both sides are therefore in an extremely dangerous position. And if the French Army, and our own Army, are well handled, as I believe they will be; if the French retain that genius for recovery and counter-attack for which they have so long been famous; and if the British Army shows the dogged endurance and solid fighting power of which there have been so many examples in the past—then a sudden transformation of the scene might spring into being.

It would be foolish, however, to disguise the gravity of the hour. It would be still more foolish to lose heart and courage or to suppose that well-trained, well-equipped armies numbering three or four millions of men can be overcome in the space of a few weeks, or even months, by a scoop, or raid of mechanized vehicles, however formidable. We may look with confidence to the stabilization of the Front in France, and to the general engagement of the masses, which will enable the qualities of the French and British soldiers to be matched squarely against those of their adversaries. For myself, I have invincible confidence in the French Army and its leaders. Only a very small part of that splendid army has yet been heavily engaged; and only a very small part of France has yet been invaded. There is good evidence to show that practically the whole of the specialized and mechanized forces of the enemy have been already thrown into the battle; and we know that very heavy losses have been inflicted upon them. No officer or man, no brigade or division,[4] which grapples at close quarters with the enemy, wherever encountered, can fail to make a worthy contribution to the general result. The Armies must cast away the idea of resisting behind concrete lines or natural obstacles, and must realize that mastery can only be regained by furious and unrelenting assault. And this spirit must not only animate the High Command, but must inspire every fighting man.

In the air—often at serious odds—often at odds hitherto[5] thought overwhelming—we have been clawing down three or four to one of our enemies; and the relative balance of the British and German Air Forces is now considerably more favorable to us than at the beginning of the battle. In cutting down the German bombers, we are fighting our own battle as well as that of France. My confidence in our ability to fight it out to the finish with the German Air Force has

---

4. brigade or division large units of soldiers.
5. hitherto (hith´ ər too) *adv.* until this time.

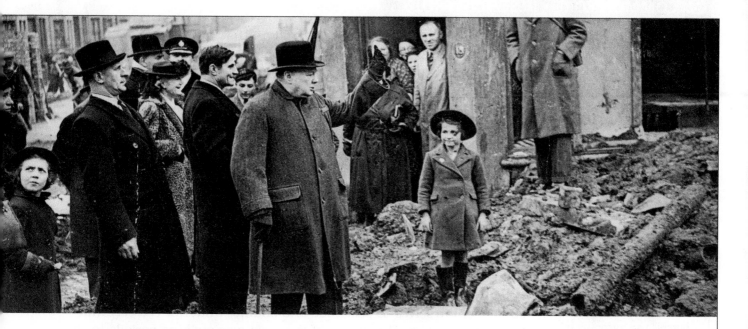

been strengthened by the fierce encounters which have taken place and are taking place. At the same time, our heavy bombers are striking nightly at the taproot of German mechanized power, and have already inflicted serious damage upon the oil refineries on which the Nazi effort to dominate the world directly depends.

We must expect that as soon as stability is reached on the Western Front, the bulk of that hideous apparatus of aggression which gashed Holland into ruin and slavery in a few days, will be turned upon us. I am sure I speak for all when I say we are ready to face it; to endure it; and to retaliate against it—to any extent that the unwritten laws of war permit. There will be many men, and many women, in this island who when the ordeal comes upon them, as come it will, will feel comfort, and even a pride—that they are sharing the perils of our lads at the Front—soldiers, sailors and airmen, God bless them—and are drawing away from them a part at least of the onslaught they have to bear. Is not this the appointed time for all to make the utmost exertions in their power? If the battle is to be won, we must provide our men with everincreasing quantities of the weapons and ammunition they need. We must have, and have quickly, more airplanes, more tanks, more shells, more guns. There is imperious need for these vital munitions.[6] They increase our strength against the powerfully armed enemy. They replace the wastage of the obstinate struggle; and the knowledge that wastage will speedily be replaced enables us to draw more readily upon our reserves and throw them in now that everything counts so much.

Our task is not only to win the battle—but to win the War. After this battle in France abates its force, there will come the battle for

◀▲ **Primary Source: Art and Photographs** What mood about the war does the poster (left page) convey to British citizens? Does the photo above show Churchill conveying a similar mood? Explain. **[Compare and Contrast]**

Vocabulary
retaliate (ri tal´ ē ət´) v. fight in order to pay back an injury or wrong

☑ Reading Check

What does Churchill say is the advantage of "the general engagement of the masses"?

---

6. imperious (im pir´ ē əs) . . . **munitions** (myo͞o nish´ ənz) urgent need for these vital weapons and ammunition.

our island—for all that Britain is, and all that Britain means. That will be the struggle. In that supreme emergency we shall not hesitate to take every step, even the most drastic, to call forth from our people the last ounce and the last inch of effort of which they are capable. The interests of property, the hours of labor, are nothing compared with the struggle for life and honor, for right and freedom, to which we have vowed ourselves.

I have received from the Chiefs of the French Republic, and in particular from its indomitable Prime Minister, M. Reynaud,[7] the most sacred pledges that whatever happens they will fight to the end, be it bitter or be it glorious. Nay, if we fight to the end, it can only be glorious.

Reading Strategy
Determining the Essential Message What is the main point of this paragraph? What rhetorical devices does Churchill use to convey this point?

▼ **Primary Source: Photograph** What does Churchill say have been the effects of having a strong air force with planes like the spitfire pictured here?
[Analyze Causes and Effects]

Having received His Majesty's commission, I have found an administration of men and women of every party and of almost every point of view. We have differed and quarreled in the past; but now one bond unites us all—to wage war until victory is won, and never to surrender ourselves to servitude and shame, whatever the cost and the agony may be. This is one of the most awe-striking periods in the long history of France and Britain. It is also beyond doubt the most sublime. Side by side, unaided except by their kith and kin in the great Dominions and by the wide Empires which rest beneath their shield—side by side, the British and French peoples have advanced to rescue not only Europe but mankind from the foulest and most soul-destroying tyranny which has ever darkened and stained the pages of history. Behind them—behind us—behind the armies and fleets of Britain and France—gather a group of shattered States and bludgeoned[8] races: the Czechs, the Poles, the Norwegians, the Danes, the Dutch, the Belgians—upon all of whom the long night of barbarism will descend, unbroken even by a star of hope, unless we conquer, as conquer we must; as conquer we shall.

Today is Trinity Sunday.[9] Centuries ago words were written to be a call and a spur to the faithful servants of Truth and Justice; "Arm yourselves, and be ye men of valor, and be in readiness for the conflict; for it is better for us to perish in battle than to look upon the outrage of our nation and our altar. As the Will of God is in Heaven, even so let it be."[10]

---

7. **M. Reynaud** (rā nō') Paul Reynaud (1878-1966), French politician who served as France's prime minister from March to June of 1940, when France fell to the Germans.
8. **bludgeoned** (bluj' ənd) *adj.* beaten. Churchill goes on to name the people of nations that have been overrun by the Germans.
9. **Trinity Sunday** Christian holy day on the eighth Sunday after Easter.
10. **"Arm . . . be"** a quotation from the first book of Maccabees 3:58, a book that is part of Roman Catholic versions of the Bible but not Jewish and Protestant versions.

EVACUATION SCHEME

Memo. Ev. 4
GOVERNMENT EVACUATION SCHEME

MEMORANDUM.

4. The objective has been therefore to provide facilities for the removal from certain large crowded areas, in which the effects of air attack would be most serious, of certain groups of people whose removal is desirable on both national and humanitarian grounds, and to transfer them to districts where the primary purpose of dispersal can be achieved. This has involved an order of priority as regards both the classes of persons to be transferred and the towns to be evacuated, and the provisional allocation of other districts as receiving areas.

Priority classes.

5. The classes of person to whom priority is to be given under the Government Scheme are:—

    (1) school children in organized units in charge of their teachers;

    (2) children of pre-school age accompanied by their mothers or other persons responsible for looking after them;

    (3) expectant mothers;

    (4) the adult blind and cripple population so far as removal may be feasible.

The information to be given should include information as to the points of assembly and the amount and kind of hand luggage which can be conveyed. A full list should include the child's gas mask, a change of underclothing, night-clothes, house-shoes or plimsolls, spare stockings or socks, a toothbrush, comb, towel and handerkerchiefs, a warm coat or mackintosh, and a packet of food for the day. The children should be sent away wearing their thickest and warmest footwear.

Reading Strategy
Determining the Essential Message
What text features, such as fonts, heads, and design, are used to convey the essential message of this memorandum?

Vocabulary
humanitarian (hyo͞o man´ ə ter´ ē ən) *adj.* acting to help humanity, especially by easing pain and suffering

allocation (al´ ō kā´ shən) *n.* setting apart for a specific purpose; fixing the location of

Critical Reading

Ⓒ 1. **Key Ideas and Details** **(a)** What major new development in the war does Churchill report in the beginning of his speech? **(b) Analyze:** What answer does Churchill provide to any concerns that this development might cause?

Ⓒ 2. **Key Ideas and Details** **(a)** According to the memorandum, what is the "primary purpose" of the evacuation? **(b) Interpret:** What are the "national and humanitarian grounds" for the evacuation?

Cite textual evidence to support your responses.

PHOTOGRAPHS
OF THE LONDON BLITZ

Churchill's promise of "conflict" in his Wartime Speech of May 19, 1940, was grimly fulfilled during the German bombing attack on London known as the Blitz (from the German *blitzkrieg*, meaning "lightning warfare"). The Blitz, which lasted from September 7, 1940, to May 11, 1941, caused many casualties and resulted in the damage or destruction of more than a million houses. Nevertheless, this bombardment strengthened rather than undermined Britain's resolve to fight. The photographs on this page show some of the physical effects of the Blitz.

▶ **Primary Source: Art and Photographs** What story do the poster (above) and the photographs (right) tell you about the effects of the Blitz on England and its citizens? **[Interpret]**

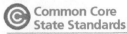
Speech • Memorandum

Comparing Primary Sources

Refer to your Note-Taking Guide to complete these questions:

1. (a) What is the specific occasion and purpose for Churchill's **speech** and the events to which the **government memorandum** responds? **(b)** What future occasion do both documents anticipate?

2. (a) Summarize one or more essential messages expressed in each document. **(b)** How is each document, in its own way, part of the British war effort?

3. (a) Who was the intended audience for each document? **(b)** What details and language used in each document reflect that audience? Use this chart to gather ideas and examples.

ⓒ Vocabulary Acquisition and Use

Antonyms For each word, choose the letter of its antonym, or opposite, and explain your choice.

1. intimidated: **(a)** astounded **(b)** soothed **(c)** yelled **(d)** arose

2. endurance: **(a)** disobedience **(b)** devotion **(c)** stability **(d)** brevity

3. formidable: **(a)** strong **(b)** weak **(c)** scary **(d)** lengthy

4. invincible: **(a)** conquerable **(b)** triumphant **(c)** wise **(d)** printable

Content-Area Vocabulary Indicate whether each statement is true or false and explain your answer.

5. Someone who wants revenge will not seek to *retaliate*.

6. A *humanitarian* effort does little to help others.

7. When you make an *allocation* of funds, you put the money aside for a specific purpose.

Etymology Study *Allocation* contains the Latin root *-loc-*, which means "place." When you make an *allocation*, you set something apart in a particular place or location. Explain the meaning of the following words, which also contain the Latin root *-loc-*. Then, use each word in a sentence.

dislocate	locality	locomotive
local	locomotion	relocate

ⓒ **Common Core**
State Standards

Writing

7. Conduct short as well as more sustained research projects to answer a question or solve a problem; narrow or broaden the inquiry when appropriate; synthesize multiple sources on the subject, demonstrating understanding of the subject under investigation. *(p. 1295)*

8. Gather relevant information from multiple authoritative print and digital sources, using advanced searches effectively; assess the strengths and limitations of each source in terms of the task, purpose, and audience; integrate information into the text selectively to maintain the flow of ideas, avoiding plagiarism and overreliance on any one source and following a standard format for citation. *(p. 1295)*

Language

6. Acquire and use accurately general academic and domain-specific words and phrases, sufficient for reading, writing, speaking, and listening at the college and career readiness level.

Research Task

Topic: Great Speeches

When Winston Churchill's speech beamed out on radio waves in 1940, it relied solely on the power of spoken words to connect with listeners. Twenty-five years later, Lyndon Johnson's "we shall overcome" speech to Congress, urging passage of civil rights legislation, was televised. Today, politicians' speeches can also be viewed on the Internet. How do various media affect the coverage—and the formality and tone—of major speeches like these?

Assignment: Create a **multimedia presentation** in which you analyze media coverage of a major contemporary speech. Focus on how the presentation varies in different media—newspapers, magazines, radio, television, and the Internet. Consider such factors as bias and different audiences and purposes for the coverage.

Formulate a research plan. First, select the speech on which you will focus. Identify the different types of media used to cover the speech. Choose three types of media coverage you wish to research. Then, formulate questions such as these:

- Which medium is most complete and clear in its coverage?
- For each medium, how do different audiences and purposes affect the bias, formality, and tone of the coverage?
- Which medium seems the most unbiased? Explain.

Gather sources. Using print, broadcast, library, and online sources, research coverage of the speech. Keep accurate notations of the sources of all written, visual, and audio material to document your research.

Synthesize information. Based on your research plan, compare and contrast coverage of the speech. Pay special attention to changes in formality and tone across the various media.

Organize and present ideas. Use visuals, such as stills from a television report; sound, such as recording of a radio broadcast; and text to present your analysis. Tell the audience what to look for before showing each example. Then, present your analyses and conclusions.

Model: Presenting a Media Analysis

Step 1: Introduction	Listen for words: "thrilling occasion."
Step 2: Example	Show video clip.
Step 3: Analysis	Denotation and connotation of "thrilling occasion" show reporter may favor the speaker.
Step 4: Conclusion	This news outlet may be biased.

On March 15, 1965, President Lyndon Johnson urged Congress to pass a major civil rights bill.

RESEARCH TIP

In addition to the verbal commentary on the speech, pay attention to nonverbal elements such as music, sound effects, and displayed symbols.

Use a checklist like the one shown to prepare a well-organized multimedia presentation.

Research Checklist

- ☐ Have I answered all the questions in my research plan?
- ☐ Have I properly identified every visual and audio excerpt in my presentation?
- ☐ Have I analyzed each medium's coverage objectively?
- ☐ Do my conclusions proceed logically from my analyses?

Connecting to the Essential Question In this story, a woman's state of mind is affected by wartime conditions. As you read, note details of wartime conditions in the story. These details will help you think about the Essential Question: **What is the relationship between literature and place?**

Literary Analysis

During World War II, life in England was severely disrupted. Routines were changed, and anxiety replaced trust. The usual sights and sounds of daily life became doubtful, dangerous, even deadly.

In this historical context, a ghost story is right at home. A **ghost story** is a tale in which part of the past—typically, a dead person—seems to appear in the present. Ghost stories include these elements:

- An eerie or mysterious atmosphere
- The suggestion that supernatural forces are at work
- Eerie events that may have a natural explanation

A ghost story may include a **flashback,** a scene that interrupts a narrative to relate events that occurred in the past. Ghost stories may create uncertainty or an unresolved tension through **ambiguity**—the effect of two or more different possible interpretations. As you read, note how Bowen uses flashback and ambiguity to develop elements of the story.

Reading Strategy

Preparing to Read Complex Texts "The Demon Lover" enables you to **relate a literary work to a primary-source document.** Bowen's fiction takes place in the real world described by Winston Churchill in his speech beginning on page 1287. As you read Bowen's story, use a graphic organizer like the one shown to relate Mrs. Drover's private battle to the public battle in Churchill's speech.

Vocabulary

spectral (spek´ trəl) *adj.* ghostly (p. 1300)

dislocation (dis´ lō kā´ shən) *n.* condition of being out of place (p. 1303)

arboreal (är bor´ ē´ əl) *adj.* of, near, or among trees (p. 1303)

circumscribed (sur´ kəm skrībd´) *adj.* limited; having a definite boundary (p. 1303)

aperture (ap´ ər chər´) *n.* opening (p. 1305)

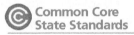

Common Core State Standards

Reading Literature
3. Analyze the impact of the author's choices regarding how to develop and relate elements of a story or drama.

	Literary Work: Demon Lover	Primary Source: Wartime Speech
Source of Fear	Ghostly lover	German army
Atmosphere		
Weapons		
Tactics		
Main Goal		
End Result		

www.PHLitOnline.com

Author of "The Demon Lover"

The fiction of Elizabeth Bowen is distinguished by her subtle observation of landscape, by her innovative and believable use of the supernatural, and by her haunting portrayal of England during one of the darkest eras of the country's history—World War II.

From Life Into Art Early in life, Bowen suffered serious losses. Her father had a breakdown when she was seven years old and was confined to an institution. When Bowen was thirteen, her mother died. As an adult, Bowen was to write about such experiences of the denial of emotion and the helplessness of the heart to understand itself or others in the absence of love. In her characters' insecure lives, in the damage that is done them when their feelings are not acknowledged, one can still trace the marks left by Bowen's own early abandonment.

A Writer's Life Bowen's one ambition was to write, and her family's money was enough to support her as she wrote her first short stories. Her first collection, published in 1923, received little attention. Through the 1930s, she perfected her craft, publishing regularly. In 1938, she completed *The Death of the Heart,* one of her best-known works. The novel is about the disillusionment of an innocent teenage girl, taken in by uncaring relatives after her mother's death.

The War and After During the war, Bowen observed England's hardships keenly and with compassion. She incorporated the brutal realities of the war—air raids, blackouts, betrayal—into some of her best stories. By using a wartime setting and playing on the heightened emotions and perceptions people have at such times, Bowen exposed the innermost workings of her characters' minds.

After the war, Bowen widened her literary activities to include literary criticism and book reviews. Her later novels exhibit a more symbolic, more poetic style than her earlier works. Bowen defined the novel as the "non-poetic statement of poetic truth." Guided by the hardships she had undergone, working in a deceptively simple style, she achieved this goal admirably.

Elizabeth BOWEN (1899–1973)

The DEMON LOVER

Elizabeth Bowen

BACKGROUND World War II was a fact of daily life in the London of the 1940s. After decisive victories in Europe, Germany determined to break Britain with a steady bombardment focused on London. During the Blitz, from September 1940 to May 1941, German planes dropped bombs on the city almost every night. Whole communities were evacuated periodically, leaving street after street of deserted buildings. Elizabeth Bowen lived in London during this time, and the eerie quality of "The Demon Lover" stems from her experience of a time when war's horrors had become all too "ordinary."

Toward the end of her day in London Mrs. Drover went round to her shut-up house to look for several things she wanted to take away. Some belonged to herself, some to her family, who were by now used to their country life. It was late August; it had been a steamy, showery day: at the moment the trees down the pavement glittered in an escape of humid yellow afternoon sun. Against the next batch of clouds, already piling up ink-dark, broken chimneys and parapets stood out. In her once familiar street, as in any unused channel, an unfamiliar queerness had silted up; a cat wove itself in and out of railings, but no human eye watched Mrs. Drover's return. Shifting some parcels under her arm, she slowly forced round her latchkey in an unwilling lock, then gave the door, which had warped, a push with her knee. Dead air came out to meet her as she went in.

The staircase window having been boarded up, no light came down into the hall. But one door, she could just see, stood ajar, so she went quickly through into the room and unshuttered the big window in there. Now the prosaic woman, looking about her, was more perplexed than she knew by everything that she saw, by traces of her long former habit of life—the yellow smoke stain up the white marble mantel-piece, the ring left by a vase on the top of the escritoire,[1] the bruise in the wallpaper where, on the door being thrown open widely, the china handle had always hit the wall. The piano, having gone away to be stored, had left what looked like claw marks on its part of the parquet.[2] Though not much dust had seeped in, each object wore a film of another kind; and, the only ventilation being the chimney, the whole drawing room smelled of the cold hearth. Mrs. Drover put down her parcels on the escritoire and left the room to proceed upstairs; the things she wanted were in a bedroom chest.

She had been anxious to see how the house was—the part-time caretaker she shared with some neighbors was away this week on his holiday, known to be not yet back. At the best of times he did not look in often, and she was never sure that she trusted him. There were some cracks in the structure, left by the last bombing, on which she was anxious to keep an eye. Not that one could do anything—

A shaft of refracted daylight now lay across the hall. She stopped dead and stared at the hall table—on this lay a letter addressed to her.

She thought first—then the caretaker *must* be back. All the same, who, seeing the house shuttered, would have dropped a letter in at the box? It was not a circular, it was not a bill. And the post office redirected, to the address in the country, everything for her that came through the post. The caretaker (even if he *were* back) did not know she was due in London today—her call here had been planned to be a surprise—so his negligence in the manner of this letter, leaving it to wait in the dusk and the dust, annoyed her. Annoyed, she picked up the letter, which bore no stamp. But it cannot be important, or they would know . . . She took the letter rapidly upstairs with her, without a stop to look at the writing till she reached what had been her bedroom, where she let in light. The room looked over the garden and other gardens: the sun had gone in; as the clouds sharpened and lowered, the trees and rank lawns seemed already to smoke with dark. Her reluctance to look again at the letter came from the fact that she felt intruded upon—and by someone contemptuous of her ways. However, in the tenseness preceding the fall of rain she read it: it was a few lines.

> DEAR KATHLEEN,
> You will not have forgotten that today is our anniversary, and the day we said. The years have gone by at once slowly and fast. In view of the fact that nothing has changed, I shall rely upon you to

---

1. **escritoire** (es´ krǝ twär´) *n.* a writing desk or table.
2. **parquet** (pär kā´) *n.* flooring of inlaid woodwork in geometric forms.

Reading Strategy
Relate to Primary Source Documents Winston Churchill described "the gravity of the hour." How does the historical situation contribute to Mrs. Drover's anxiety?

Literary Analysis
The Ghost Story
How does Bowen prepare the reader for the suggestion that there is something supernatural about the letter?

Reading Check

What does Mrs. Drover unexpectedly discover in her vacant house?

War and Literature
In "The Demon Lover," Bowen hardly mentions World War II—the war appears only as the implied explanation for the Drovers' flight from their home. Bowen's story, though, captures the oppressive atmosphere of the Blitz, a time when familiar routines were routinely shattered by blackouts, airraid sirens, and explosions. The menace Mrs. Drover confronts is not a bombing raid, but like the Blitz itself, it is a menace that lurks behind the most ordinary scenes.

Literary works that reflect events of the day may satisfy a reader's need to find sense in the jumble of historical events. At the same time, these works may challenge events, refusing to assent to the values they represent. In her portrait of Mrs. Drover, who lives a life cracked by war, Bowen may be suggesting that our world is haunted by madness, a madness that spawned two world wars less than thirty years apart.

Connect to the Literature

Which details in the description of Mrs. Drover show the effects of war and a difficult life?

Literary Analysis
Flashback What clues in the text signal the beginning of the flashback?

Vocabulary
spectral (spek´ trəl) *adj.* ghostly

keep your promise. I was sorry to see you leave London, but was satisfied that you would be back in time. You may expect me, therefore, at the hour arranged. Until then . . . K.

Mrs. Drover looked for the date: it was today's. She dropped the letter onto the bedsprings, then picked it up to see the writing again—her lips, beneath the remains of lipstick, beginning to go white. She felt so much the change in her own face that she went to the mirror, polished a clear patch in it and looked at once urgently and stealthily in. She was confronted by a woman of forty-four, with eyes starting out under a hatbrim that had been rather carelessly pulled down. She had not put on any more powder since she left the shop where she ate her solitary tea. The pearls her husband had given her on their marriage hung loose round her now rather thinner throat, slipping into the V of the pink wool jumper her sister knitted last autumn as they sat round the fire. Mrs. Drover's most normal expression was one of controlled worry, but of assent. Since the birth of the third of her little boys, attended by a quite serious illness, she had had an intermittent muscular flicker to the left of her mouth, but in spite of this she could always sustain a manner that was at once energetic and calm.

Turning from her own face as precipitately as she had gone to meet it, she went to the chest where the things were, unlocked it, threw up the lid and knelt to search. But as rain began to come crashing down she could not keep from looking over her shoulder at the stripped bed on which the letter lay. Behind the blanket of rain the clock of the church that still stood struck six—with rapidly heightening apprehension she counted each of the slow strokes. "The hour arranged . . . My God," she said, "*What hour*? How should I . . .? After twenty-five years. . . ."

The young girl talking to the soldier in the garden had not ever completely seen his face. It was dark; they were saying good-bye under a tree. Now and then—for it felt, from not seeing him at this intense moment, as though she had never seen him at all—she verified his presence for these few moments longer by putting out a hand, which he each time pressed, without very much kindness, and painfully, on to one of the breast buttons of his uniform. That cut of the button on the palm of her hand was, principally, what she was to carry away. This was so near the end of a leave from France that she could only wish him already gone. It was August 1916. Being not kissed, being drawn away from and looked at intimidated Kathleen till she imagined spectral glitters in the place of his eyes. Turning away and looking back up the lawn she saw, through branches of trees, the drawing-room window alight; she caught a breath for the

▲ **Critical Viewing** In what ways is the mood or atmosphere of the story reflected in this painting? **[Interpret]**

▲ **Critical Viewing**
Which details in this painting suggest the dusty, abandoned quality of Mrs. Drover's room? **[Analyze]**

Literary Analysis
Ambiguity In what two ways might Kathleen's fiancé's remarks be interpreted?

moment when she could go running back there into the safe arms of her mother and sister, and cry: "What shall I do, what shall I do? He has gone."

Hearing her catch her breath, her fiancé said, without feeling: "Cold?"

"You're going away such a long way."

"Not so far as you think."

"I don't understand?"

"You don't have to," he said. "You will. You know what we said."

"But that was—suppose you—I mean, suppose."

"I shall be with you," he said, "sooner or later. You won't forget that. You need do nothing but wait."

Only a little more than a minute later she was free to run up the silent lawn. Looking in through the window at her mother and sister, who did not for the moment perceive her, she already felt that unnatural promise drive down between her and the rest of all humankind. No other way of having given herself could have made her feel so apart, lost and foresworn. She could not have plighted a more sinister troth.

Kathleen behaved well when, some months later, her fiancé was reported missing, presumed killed. Her family not only supported her but were able to praise her courage without stint because they could not regret, as a husband for her, the man they knew almost nothing about. They hoped she would, in a year or two, console herself—and had it been only a question of consolation things might have gone much straighter ahead. But her trouble, behind just a little grief, was a complete dislocation from everything. She did not reject other lovers, for these failed to appear: for years she failed to attract men—and with the approach of her thirties she became natural enough to share her family's anxiousness on this score. She began to put herself out, to wonder; and at thirty-two she was very greatly relieved to find herself being courted by William Drover. She married him, and the two of them settled down in this quiet, arboreal part of Kensington; in this house the years piled up, her children were born and they all lived till they were driven out by the bombs of the next war. Her movements as Mrs. Drover were circumscribed, and she dismissed any idea that they were still watched.

As things were—dead or living the letter writer sent her only a threat. Unable, for some minutes, to go on kneeling with her back exposed to the empty room, Mrs. Drover rose from the chest to sit on an upright chair whose back was firmly against the wall. The desuetude[3] of her former bedroom, her married London home's whole air of being a cracked cup from which memory, with its reassuring power, had either evaporated or leaked away, made a crisis—and at just this crisis the letter writer had, knowledgeably, struck. The hollowness of the house this evening canceled years on years of voices, habits and steps. Through the shut windows she only heard rain fall on the roofs around. To rally herself, she said she was in a mood—and, for two or three seconds shutting her eyes, told herself that she imagined the letter. But she opened them—there it lay on the bed.

On the supernatural side of the letter's entrance she was not permitting her mind to dwell. Who, in London, knew she meant to call at the house today? Evidently, however, this had been known. The caretaker, *had* he come back, had had no cause to expect her: he would have taken the letter in his pocket, to forward it, at his own time, through the post. There was no other sign that the caretaker had been in—but, if not? Letters dropped in at doors of deserted houses do not fly or walk to tables in halls. They do not sit on the dust of empty tables with the air of certainty that they will be found. There is needed some human hand—but nobody but the caretaker had a key. Under circumstances she did not care to consider, a house can be entered without a key. It was possible that she was not alone now. She might be being waited for, downstairs. Waited for—until when? Until "the hour arranged." At least that was not six o'clock; six has struck.

She rose from the chair and went over and locked the door.

The thing was, to get out. To fly? No, not that: she had to catch

---

3. desuetude (des´ wi tood´) *adj.* condition of not being used any more.

Reading Check
What happens to Kathleen's fiancé after he returns to war?

Literary Analysis
The Ghost Story
In this paragraph, how do
Mrs. Drover's fear of the
supernatural and her attention to practical details blur
the lines between the familiar
world and the unknown?

her train. As a woman whose utter dependability was the keystone of her family life she was not willing to return to the country, to her husband, her little boys and her sister, without the objects she had come up to fetch. Resuming work at the chest she set about making up a number of parcels in a rapid, fumbling-decisive way. These, with her shopping parcels, would be too much to carry; these meant a taxi—at the thought of the taxi her heart went up and her normal breathing resumed. I will ring up the taxi now; the taxi cannot come too soon; I shall hear the taxi out there running its engine, till I walk calmly down to it through the hall. I'll ring up—But no: the telephone is cut off . . . She tugged at a knot she had tied wrong.

The idea of flight . . . He was never kind to me, not really. I don't remember him kind at all. Mother said he never considered me. He was set on me, that was what it was—not love. Not love, not meaning a person well. What did he do, to make me promise like that? I can't remember—But she found that she could.

She remembered with such dreadful acuteness that the twenty-five years since then dissolved like smoke and she instinctively looked for the weal[4] left by the button on the palm of her hand. She remembered not only all that he said and did but the complete suspension of *her* existence during that August week. I was not myself—they all told me so at the time. She remembered—but with one white burning blank as where acid has dropped on a photograph: *under no conditions* could she remember his face.

So wherever he may be waiting, I shall not know him. You have no time to run from a face you do not expect.

The thing was to get to the taxi before any clock struck what could be the hour. She would slip down the street and round the side of the square to where the square gave on the main road. She would return in the taxi, safe, to her own door, and bring the driver into the house with her to pick up the parcels from room to room. The idea of the taxi driver made her decisive, bold; she unlocked her door, went to the top of the staircase and listened down.

She heard nothing—but while she was hearing nothing the passé[5] air of the staircase was disturbed by a draft that traveled up to her face. It emanated from the basement: down there a door or window was being opened by someone who chose this moment to leave the house.

The rain had stopped; the pavements steamily shone as Mrs. Drover let herself out by inches from her own front door into the empty street. The unoccupied houses opposite continued to meet her look with their damaged stare. Making toward the thoroughfare and the taxi, she tried not to keep looking behind. Indeed, the silence was so intense—one of those creeks of London silence exaggerated this summer by the damage of war—that no tread could have gained on hers unheard. Where her street debouched on the square where people went on living, she

---

4. weal *n.* raised mark, line, or ridge on the skin caused by an injury.
5. passé (pa sä′) *adj.* stale.

grew conscious of, and checked, her unnatural pace. Across the open end of the square two buses impassively passed each other; women, a perambulator,[6] cyclists, a man wheeling a barrow signalized, once again, the ordinary flow of life. At the square's most populous corner should be—and was—the short taxi rank. This evening, only one taxi —but this, although it presented its blank rump, appeared already to be alertly waiting for her. Indeed, without looking round the driver started his engine as she panted up from behind and put her hand on the door. As she did so, the clock struck seven. The taxi faced the main road. To make the trip back to her house it would have to turn—she had settled back on the seat and the taxi *had* turned before she, surprised by its knowing movement, recollected that she had not "said where." She leaned forward to scratch at the glass panel that divided the driver's head from her own.

The driver braked to what was almost a stop, turned round and slid the glass panel back. The jolt of this flung Mrs. Drover forward till her face was almost into the glass. Through the aperture driver and passenger, not six inches between them, remained for an eternity eye to eye. Mrs. Drover's mouth hung open for some seconds before she could issue her first scream. After that she continued to scream freely and to beat with her gloved hands on the glass all round as the taxi, accelerating without mercy, made off with her into the hinterland of deserted streets.

---

6. perambulator *n.* baby carriage.

Reading Strategy
Relate to a Primary Source
What effect does the war have on what Mrs. Drover sees and hears in the street?

Vocabulary
aperture (ap´ ər chər´) *n.* opening

Critical Reading

© **1. Key Ideas and Details (a)** Why is the appearance of the letter in Mrs. Drover's house unexpected? **(b) Infer:** Why is she so upset by it?

© **2. Key Ideas and Details (a)** Before returning to the war, what had Mrs. Drover's fiancé promised her? **(b) Analyze:** Identify three points at which she feels she is being watched, and describe what each moment adds to the story.

© **3. Key Ideas and Details (a) Analyze:** Identify three references in the story to "traces," marks left behind by objects or actions. **(b) Interpret:** In what sense are ghosts and memories also traces? **(c) Draw Conclusions:** How do the references to traces suggest and support the story's theme?

© **4. Integration of Knowledge and Ideas** Beyond the physical effects of war on the home front, what emotional effects of the war does Bowen's story suggest? In your response, use at least two of these Essential Question words: *alter, vulnerable, unresolved.* [Connecting to the Essential Question: What is the relationship between literature and place?]

Cite textual evidence to support your responses.

Literary Analysis

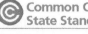

**Common Core
State Standards**

Writing
3.c. Use a variety of
techniques to sequence events
so that they build on one
another to create a coherent
whole and build toward a
particular tone and outcome.
(p. 1307)

3.d. Use precise words
and phrases, telling details,
and sensory language to
convey a vivid picture of the
experiences, events, setting,
and/or characters. *(p. 1307)*

Language
4.a. Use context as a clue
to the meaning of a word or
phrase. *(p. 1307)*

1. **Key Ideas and Details** Bowen uses a historical period—the World War II home front—to create a haunting atmosphere of silence and emptiness. Identify three eerie details that show how ordinary life was affected during this period.

2. **Craft and Structure** A **ghost story** often suggests that supernatural forces are at work. Explain how Bowen creates that suggestion with each of the following sentences:

    a) ". . . no human eye watched Mrs. Drover's return."

    b) "Dead air came out to meet her as she went in."

    c) "She could not have plighted a more sinister troth."

    d) "On the supernatural side of the letter's entrance she was not permitting her mind to dwell."

3. **Integration of Knowledge and Ideas** A ghost story often keeps open the possibility that all the eerie events it recounts have a completely natural explanation. Explain all the events of "The Demon Lover" with completely natural causes.

4. **Craft and Structure** The **flashback** that returns Mrs. Drover and the reader to 1916 suggests an explanation for her state of mind in 1940. **(a)** What does the flashback tell you about Mrs. Drover? **(b)** In what sense is she "haunted" by an unresolved problem in her past?

5. **Craft and Structure** Bowen maintains **ambiguity**—the effect of two or more different interpretations—throughout the story. Use a chart like the one shown to interpret a word, an action, and an image in more than one way.

	Interpretation 1	Interpretation 2
Word		
Action		
Image		

Reading Strategy

6. **Relate a literary work to a primary-source document** by assessing Churchill and Bowen's sense of the power of the spoken word. **(a)** What do you think were some of the effects of a wartime radio broadcast? **(b)** What effect does Bowen create by emphasizing the intense silence of the city?

7. In his wartime speech, Winston Churchill says, "We must not allow ourselves to be intimidated by the presence of these armored vehicles in unexpected places behind our lines." Explain how Elizabeth Bowen, in her wartime story of terror, uses an "armored vehicle" and "unexpected" events to intimidate her main character.

Vocabulary Acquisition and Use.

Word Analysis: Cognates

Cognates are words derived from the same original form. Cognates are often easy to spot because they have parts that look and sound alike.

Spectral, meaning "ghostly," is a cognate of *specter*, a word for "ghost." Both *specter* and *spectral* derive from the Latin word *spectrum*, meaning "appearance." When Isaac Newton experimented with light, he examined the spectrum, the colored bands that are visible when white light is refracted through a prism. Now a spectrum refers to any wide range, such as a spectrum of opinions.

Answer these questions:

1. Would you expect a *specter* to have a lively and vivid appearance? Why or why not?
2. If a store offers you a *spectrum* of choices, would you be a happier shopper? Explain.
3. If a landscape is described as *spectral,* what might it look like?

Vocabulary: Context Clues

Words take on meaning depending upon context—the meanings of the words around them. You can often use context clues to determine the meaning of an unfamiliar word.

Review the vocabulary list on page 1296. Then, in your notebook, explain whether the italicized word in each of the sentences below is used correctly, based on its context.

1. I was relieved when I touched not a *spectral* presence, but solid flesh.
2. Given the pollution in the world's waterways, I am surprised that more *arboreal* species are not endangered.
3. Take whatever you wish; my generosity is strictly *circumscribed*.
4. The letter fit through the *aperture*.
5. The doctor has caused a permanent *dislocation* of your shoulder; you should feel fine in a day or two.

Writing

Narrative Text Write a **sequel** to "The Demon Lover," answering the question *What happened next?* Continue the narrative logically. To ensure that your sequel also maintains the uneasy atmosphere that Bowen creates, use plenty of sensory details. Include an *interior monologue*—a speech that occurs only silently in a character's mind—to depict a character's feelings.

Prewriting Jot down questions that "The Demon Lover" leaves unanswered. Then, suggest answers to these questions. Select a few of these answers as a starting point.

Drafting Outline the events in your story in a logical way. As you draft, fill in background from the original story wherever you think it is necessary. In the interior monologue, include only what the character might know or feel.

Model: Revising to Add Sensory Details

fog-enshrouded   blood-curdling
As the taxi went down the street, the driver gave a laugh.

> Sensory details make writing more vivid and interesting for the reader.

Revising Make sure that the events in your story are in the correct order. If you have used a *flashback*, make sure the reader knows where it begins and ends. Add sensory details to make the sights, sounds, and smells of a scene and the specific actions, movements, gestures, and feelings of the characters as vivid as possible.

Connecting to the Essential Question Each of these poets juxtaposes an image of war with an image of another kind. As you read, notice images in the poems that reveal wartime attitudes. Recognizing these attitudes will help you think about the Essential Question: **How does literature shape or reflect society?**

Literary Analysis

A **theme** is the central idea, message, or insight that a literary work reveals. A **universal theme** is a message about life that is expressed regularly in many different cultures and time periods. For example, the power of love amid the horror of war is a universal theme because every culture and age has experienced it. In every war, the fierce fighter who kills and dies on a battlefield is also someone's beloved, someone's parent, someone's friend. As Keith Douglas expresses it,

> *For here the lover and killer are mingled*
> *who had one body and one heart.*

Comparing Literary Works In the twentieth century, authors who use the universal theme of love and war often express the theme with irony. **Irony** is a discrepancy or a contradiction between appearance and reality, between expectation and outcome, or between what is directly stated and what is really meant. As you read, identify examples of irony and consider what they suggest about the author's point of view.

Reading Strategy

© **Preparing to Read Complex Texts** Each poet has a purpose in juxtaposing contrasting images of love and war. By **understanding the author's purpose,** you will gain an insight into love, war, or life in general. For example, the poet may want to celebrate the power of an undying love or lament the power of a death-dealing war. Use a graphic organizer like this one to help clarify each author's purpose.

Vocabulary

combatants (kəm bat´ 'nts) *n.* fighters (p. 1310)

sprawling (sprôl´ iˆŋ) *v.* spread out (p. 1310)

abide (ə bīd´) *v.* stay, remain (p. 1312)

eloquent (el´ ə kwənt) *adj.* beautifully expressive (p. 1313)

**Common Core
State Standards**

Reading Literature
6. Analyze a case in which grasping point of view requires distinguishing what is directly stated in a text from what is really meant.

Image of Love

Image of War

↓

Purpose of Contrast

KEITH DOUGLAS

(1920–1944)

Author of "Vergissmeinnicht"

Keith Douglas grew up wanting to be a soldier and needing to be a writer. As a boy at boarding school, he wrote poems and trained to become a military officer. When World War II erupted in 1939, Douglas immediately enlisted.

In 1942, when the tank battle of El Alamein began to rage in the desert, Douglas left his post, stole a truck, and drove out to join the fighting. The long battle left thousands of Allied and German troops killed and wounded. "Vergissmeinnicht" ("Forget me not") is Douglas's poetic response to his unforgettable discovery of one German corpse.

On D-Day, June 6, 1944, he commanded a tank troop in the main assault in Normandy. Near the little French village of St. Pierre, on June 9, a mortar shell killed him instantly.

ALUN LEWIS

(1915–1944)

Author of "Postscript: For Gweno"

Born and raised in Wales, Alun Lewis began writing poems in college. He planned to become a teacher, but World War II intervened. Faced with the likelihood of being drafted, Lewis enlisted in 1940 but continued to write, and his collection *Raider's Dawn* appeared in 1942. He also wrote many emotional letters to his wife, Gweno, letters that helped him deal with frequent bouts of depression.

Posted to India in 1942, Lewis became deeply affected by Buddhist principles that coincided with his already strong impulses toward pacifism and social justice. Resistant to military life and reluctant to kill, he found in Buddhism "humility without submission . . . a service of perfect freedom." Lewis died in Burma in 1944.

HENRY REED

(1914–1986)

Author of "Naming of Parts"

One poem—"Naming of Parts"—made Henry Reed famous. Readers immediately recognized its authentic voice and responded to its powerful opposition—life and love versus the mechanics of war and death. The poem became the best known verse inspired by the war, and for decades Reed struggled to become known for his other writing.

During the war, Reed served as a translator and as a cryptographer in Naval Intelligence. He survived World War II and forged a successful career writing radio plays and book reviews. In 1970, he published *Lessons of the War;* however, Reed never again wrote anything with the iron bite of "Naming of Parts."

Vergissmeinnicht[1]

KEITH DOUGLAS

BACKGROUND World War I—the brutal experience that purged all the "romance" from the idea of war—provided the central subject for poets like Wilfred Owen. World War II poets Keith Douglas, Alun Lewis, and Henry Reed left moving verses that testify to the continuing influence of violent conflict on the literary imagination.

Vocabulary
combatants (kəm bat´ 'nts) *n.* fighters

sprawling (sprôl´ iŋ) *v.* spread out

Three weeks gone and the combatants gone,
returning over the nightmare ground
we found the place again, and found
the soldier sprawling in the sun.

5 The frowning barrel of his gun
overshadowing. As we came on
that day, he hit my tank with one
like the entry of a demon.

---

1. German for "forget me not."

10　Look. Here in the gunpit spoil
　　the dishonored picture of his girl
　　who has put: *Steffi. Vergissmeinnicht*
　　in a copybook gothic script.

　　We see him almost with content
15　abased, and seeming to have paid
　　and mocked at by his own equipment
　　that's hard and good when he's decayed.

　　But she would weep to see today
　　how on his skin the swart flies move;
　　the dust upon the paper eye
20　and the burst stomach like a cave.

　　For here the lover and killer are mingled
　　who had one body and one heart.
　　And death who had the soldier singled
　　has done the lover mortal hurt.

Literary Analysis
Universal Theme
What universal theme does the picture of the girl signal?

Reading Strategy
Analyze Author's Purpose
What is the author's purpose in commenting on the soldier's equipment?

Literary Analysis
Universal Theme
Why is the theme expressed in the final two lines a *universal* theme?

Critical Reading ©

1. **Key Ideas and Details** **(a)** What personal object does the speaker find on the body of the German soldier? **(b) Analyze:** What insight does the object lead the speaker to realize?

2. **Integration of Knowledge and Ideas** **(a)** Despite his unemotional tone throughout the poem, what speculation does the speaker make about the girl's response? **(b) Infer:** What does his speculation reveal about human sympathy? **(c) Generalize:** What does his speculation say about the universal theme of love and war?

Cite textual evidence to support your responses.

POSTSCRIPT: FOR GWENO

Alun Lewis

If I should go away,
Beloved, do not say
"He has forgotten me."
For you abide, A singing rib within my dreaming side;
5   You always stay.
And in the mad tormented valley
Where blood and hunger rally
And Death the wild beast is uncaught, untamed,
Our soul withstands the terror
10   And has its quiet honor
Among the glittering stars your voices named.

Critical Reading

Cite textual evidence to support your responses.

1. **Key Ideas and Details** **(a)** Where does the speaker expect to be going? **(b) Interpret:** What gives the speaker the courage to make the journey?

2. **Integration of Knowledge and Ideas** **(a) Take a Position:** Is this poem specific to World War II, or could it have been written during any war? **(b) Defend:** Support your position with two strong reasons.

NAMING of PARTS

HENRY REED

Today we have naming of parts. Yesterday,
We had daily cleaning. And tomorrow morning,
We shall have what to do after firing. But today,
Today we have naming of parts. Japonica
5 Glistens like coral in all of the neighboring gardens,
     And today we have naming of parts.

This is the lower sling swivel. And this
Is the upper sling swivel, whose use you will see,
When you are given your slings. And this is the piling swivel,
10 Which in your case you have not got. The branches
Hold in the gardens their silent, eloquent gestures,
     Which in our case we have not got.

Vocabulary
eloquent (el′ ə kwent) *adj.*
beautifully expressive

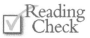

Reading
Check

What does the author say
"we" will do "tomorrow"?

This is the safety-catch, which is always released
With an easy flick of the thumb. And please do not let me
15 See anyone using his finger. You can do it quite easy
If you have any strength in your thumb. The blossoms
Are fragile and motionless, never letting anyone see
  Any of them using their finger.

And this you can see is the bolt. The purpose of this
20 Is to open the breech, as you see. We can slide it
Rapidly backwards and forwards: we call this
Easing the spring. And rapidly backwards and forwards
The early bees are assaulting and fumbling the flowers:
  They call it easing the Spring.

25 They call it easing the Spring: it is perfectly easy
If you have any strength in your thumb: like the bolt,
And the breech, and the cocking-piece, and the point of balance,
Which in our case we have not got; and the almond-blossom
Silent in all of the gardens and the bees going backwards and
  forwards,
30 For today we have naming of parts.

Critical Reading

Cite textual evidence to support your responses.

1. **Key Ideas and Details (a)** What two contrasting actions are taking place in the poem? **(b) Infer:** What associations do you think the speaker makes with each of the contrasting actions?

2. **Key Ideas and Details (a) Assess:** Which one of the contrasting actions does the author prefer? **(b) Interpret:** How can you tell?

3. **Integration of Knowledge and Ideas** What larger social comment is the poet making?

4. **Integration of Knowledge and Ideas** In these three poems, how are vital social bonds affected, or annihilated, by war? Explain. In your response, use at least two of these Essential Question words: *humane, empathy, disconnect, relationship.* *[Connecting to the Essential Question: How does literature shape or reflect society?]*

Literary Analysis

1. Craft and Structures Using a chart like the one shown, identify a word, phrase, or image from each poem that conveys its **universal theme.** Then state the universal theme it conveys.

Poem	Word, Phrase, or Image	Universal Theme
"Vergissmeinnicht"		
"Postscript: For Gweno"		
"Naming of Parts"		

Common Core State Standards

Writing
2. Write informative/ explanatory texts to examine and convey complex ideas, concepts, and information clearly and accurately through the effective selection, organization, and analysis of content.

2. Craft and Structure Compare and contrast the poets' use of **irony** in "Vergissmeinnicht" and "Naming of Parts."

Reading Strategy

3. In "Vergissmeinnicht," what is the **author's purpose** in calling the German girl's photograph "dishonored" (line 10)?

4. In "Naming of Parts," the author gives two different meanings of "easing the spring"—one military (line 22), one drawn from nature (line 24). What is his purpose in doing so?

PERFORMANCE TASKS
Integrated Language Skills

Vocabulary Acquisition and Use

An analogy compares two relationships to show their basic similarity. For each item below, analyze the relationship between the first and second words. Then, select the word that best completes each analogy.

1. combatants : soldiers :: poets :
   a. writers   **b.** boxers   **c.** flyers   **d.** drivers

2. sprawling : condensed :: gigantic :
   a. scary   **b.** warlike   **c.** normal   **d.** tiny

3. abide : continue :: assist :
   a. destroy   **b.** ignore   **c.** help   **d.** accompany

4. eloquent : awkward :: faithful :
   a. loyal   **b.** charming   **c.** foolish   **d.** traitorous

Writing

Informative Text Imagine that you work for a foundation that gives a prize for Best War Poem. Write a **memo** stating the criteria for winning the prize. One of your criteria, for example, might be that the poem must convey a universal theme or that it must use irony effectively. Use a memo format.

Connecting to the Essential Question Cultural conflict is central in "Shooting an Elephant" and in "No Witchcraft for Sale." As you read, notice details of cultural conflict in these two selections. Doing so will help you think about the Essential Question: **How does literature shape or reflect society?**

Literary Analysis

Cultural conflict is the struggle between different social, economic, and historical attitudes and beliefs. *Conflict* is the word commonly applied to such situations. However, other words may be more useful and accurate than *conflict*—outright opposition and struggle—to describe what people experience in such a narrative: *difference, shock, ignorance, misunderstanding, misinterpretation, resistance.* As you read, be alert to subtle shades of thoughts and emotions when two cultural traditions meet.

Stories of cultural conflict often abound in **irony. Verbal irony** is saying something that contradicts what one means or believes. In a cultural conflict, verbal irony may be used for self-protection. **Situational irony** occurs when something happens that contradicts the expectations of characters, readers, or audience. In a cultural conflict, situations may become ironic when an action is not in keeping with a group's attitudes or beliefs. Further, through their use of irony, writers can convey their own nuanced points of view on cultural conflict. As you read, make inferences about the author's point of view by interpreting irony.

Reading Strategy

 Preparing to Read Complex Texts Both "Shooting an Elephant" and "No Witchcraft for Sale" involve themes of cultural conflict. As you read the selections, use a graphic organizer like the one shown to **analyze and evaluate the similar themes.**

Vocabulary

imperialism (im pir′ ē əl iz em) *n.* creating and maintaining an empire; controlling other countries (p. 1320)

despotic (des pät′ ik) *adj.* with absolute power, like a tyrant (p. 1320)

dominion (də min′ yən) *n.* rule, authority (p. 1322)

reverently (re′ və rənt lē) *adv.* with great respect (p. 1329)

incredulously (in krej′ yoo ləs lē) *adv.* with doubt or disbelief (p. 1334)

skeptical (skep′ ti kəl) *adj.* doubting (p. 1334)

Common Core State Standards

Reading Informational Text

3. Analyze a complex set of ideas or sequence of events and explain how specific individuals, ideas, or events interact and develop over the course of a text.

"Shooting an Elephant"	"No Witchcraft for Sale"
Source of Conflict	Source of Conflict
Details of Conflict	Details of Conflict
Result of Conflict	Result of Conflict

www.PHLitOnline.com

GEORGE ORWELL

1903-1950

Author of "Shooting an Elephant"

Becoming an Officer Orwell was born Eric Blair in colonial India, was educated in England, and then joined the Imperial Police in Burma. Orwell was keenly aware of the inequities of imperialism. As an officer of the Burmese police, he headed a native-born police force of 13,000. Among the 90 officers, Englishmen held almost all the top ranks—a few white men governing 13 million Asians.

Disillusioned In 1928, after five years of service as an imperial police officer, the disillusioned Orwell resigned. His first novel, *Burmese Days* (1934), describes these bitter years. "Shooting an Elephant," one of his most famous essays, is based on a defining experience from this period.

Becoming George Orwell Orwell seemed to have a talent for immersing himself in difficult situations and then writing about them with extraordinary insight. Every book that emerged from an Orwell experience was a one-of-a-kind classic. In *Down and Out in Paris and London* (1933), for example, Orwell describes what it is like to be poor in two big cities. After his journeys on the seamier side of things, he published and lived under a new name: George Orwell.

Adventuring During the 1930s, Orwell gave himself to political causes. During the Spanish Civil War (1936–1939), he fought for democracy with anarchists and socialist Republicans. His book on that crisis, *Homage to Catalonia* (1938), is a gripping adventure story, one in which the narrator's cool presence of mind allows him to recall in precise detail his experience of being wounded.

A Political Prophet During World War II, Orwell wrote political and literary journalism. In 1945, he published *Animal Farm*, a satirical fable attacking both fascism and communism. In 1949, he shared a dark vision of the future in his novel *1984*, in which a dictator rules by controlling all thought and language. The year 1984 has passed, but George Orwell's lifelong commitment to political freedom and to the honest use of language is as relevant as ever.

GEORGE ORWELL

SHOOTING AN ELEPHANT

In Moulmein, in lower Burma, I was hated by large numbers of people—the only time in my life that I have been important enough for this to happen to me. I was subdivisional police officer of the town, and in an aimless, petty kind of way anti-European feeling was very bitter. No one had the guts to raise a riot, but if a European woman went through the bazaars alone somebody would probably spit betel juice over her dress. As a police officer I was an obvious target and was baited whenever it seemed safe to do so. When a nimble Burman tripped me up on the football field and the referee (another Burman) looked the other way, the crowd yelled with hideous laughter. This happened more than once. In the end the sneering yellow faces of young men that met me everywhere, the insults hooted after me when I was at a safe distance, got badly on my nerves. The young Buddhist priests were the worst of all. There were several thousands of them in the town and none of them seemed to have anything to do except stand on street corners and jeer at Europeans.

All this was perplexing and upsetting. For at that time I had already made up my mind that imperialism was an evil thing and the sooner I chucked up my job and got out of it the better. Theoretically—and secretly, of course—I was all for the Burmese and all against their oppressors, the British. As for the job I was doing, I hated it more bitterly than I can perhaps make clear. In a job like that you see the dirty work of Empire at close quarters. The wretched prisoners huddling in the stinking cages of the lockups, the gray, cowed faces of the long-term convicts, the scarred buttocks of the men who had been flogged with bamboos—all these oppressed me with an intolerable sense of guilt. But I could get nothing into perspective. I was young and ill educated and I had had to think out my problems in the utter silence that is imposed on every Englishman in the East. I did not even know that the British Empire

◀ **Critical Viewing**
Does this photograph depict a useful beast or a dangerous menace? Explain. **[Make a Judgment]**

Literary Analysis
Cultural Conflict and Irony Explain the situational irony in the statement "I was all for the Burmese and all against their oppressors, the British."

Reading Check
According to Orwell, how do the Burmese view the English?

Reading Strategy
Analyze and Evaluate Similar Themes
What result of long cultural conflict does Orwell say is now taking place?

Vocabulary
imperialism (im pir´ ē əl iz´əm) *n.* creating and maintaining an empire, especially by controlling other countries

despotic (de spät´ ik) *adj.* with absolute power, like a tyrant

is dying, still less did I know that it is a great deal better than the younger empires that are going to supplant it. All I knew was that I was stuck between my hatred of the empire I served and my rage against the evil-spirited little beasts who tried to make my job impossible. With one part of my mind I thought of the British Raj[1] as an unbreakable tyranny, as something clamped down, *in saecula saeculorum*,[2] upon the will of prostrate peoples; with another part I thought that the greatest joy in the world would be to drive a bayonet into a Buddhist priest's guts. Feelings like these are the normal byproducts of imperialism; ask any Anglo-Indian official, if you can catch him off duty.

One day something happened which in a roundabout way was enlightening. It was a tiny incident in itself, but it gave me a better glimpse than I had had before of the real nature of imperialism—the real motives for which despotic governments act. Early one morning the subinspector at a police station the other end of the town rang me up on the phone and said that an elephant was ravaging the bazaar. Would I please come and do something about it? I did not know what I could do, but I wanted to see what was happening and I got onto a pony and started out. I took my rifle, an old .44 Winchester and much too small to kill an elephant, but I thought the noise might be useful *in terrorem*.[3] Various Burmans stopped me on the way and told me about the elephant's doings. It was not, of course, a wild elephant, but a tame one which had gone "must."[4] It had been chained up, as tame elephants always are when their attack of "must" is due, but on the previous night it had broken its chain and escaped. Its mahout,[5] the only person who could manage it when it was in that state, had set out in pursuit, but had taken the wrong direction and was now twelve hours' journey away, and in the morning the elephant had suddenly reappeared in the town. The Burmese population had no weapons and were quite helpless against it. It had already destroyed somebody's bamboo hut, killed a cow and raided some fruit stalls and devoured the stock; also it had met the municipal rubbish van and, when the driver jumped out and took to his heels, had turned the van over and inflicted violences upon it.

The Burmese subinspector and some Indian constables were waiting for me in the quarter where the elephant had been seen. It was a very poor quarter, a labyrinth of squalid bamboo huts, thatched with palm leaf, winding all over a steep hillside. I remember that it was a cloudy, stuffy morning at the beginning of the rains. We began

---

1. **Raj** (räj) rule.
2. *in saecula saeculorum* (in sē´ kōō lə sē´ kōō lour´ əm) Latin for "forever and ever."
3. *in terrorem* Latin for "for terror."
4. **must** into a dangerous, frenzied state.
5. **mahout** (mə hōōt´) elephant keeper and rider.

questioning the people as to where the elephant had gone and, as usual, failed to get any definite information. That is invariably the case in the East; a story always sounds clear enough at a distance, but the nearer you get to the scene of events the vaguer it becomes. Some of the people said that the elephant had gone in one direction, some said that he had gone in another, some professed not even to have heard of any elephant. I had almost made up my mind that the whole story was a pack of lies, when we heard yells a little distance away. There was a loud scandalized cry of "Go away, child! Go away this instant!" and an old woman with a switch in her hand came round the corner of a hut, violently shooing away a crowd of naked children. Some more women followed, clicking their tongues and exclaiming; evidently there was something that the children ought not to have seen. I rounded the hut and saw a man's dead body sprawling in the mud. He was an Indian, a black Dravidian[6] coolie,[7] almost naked, and he could not have been dead many minutes. The people said that the elephant had come suddenly upon him round the corner of the hut, caught him with its trunk, put its foot on his back and ground him into the earth. This was the rainy season and the ground was soft, and his face had scored a trench a foot deep and a couple of yards long. He was lying on his belly with arms crucified and head sharply twisted to one side. His face was coated with mud, the eyes wide open, the teeth bared and grinning with an expression of unendurable agony. (Never tell me, by the way, that the dead look peaceful. Most of the corpses I have seen looked devilish.) The friction of the great beast's foot had stripped the skin from his back as neatly as one skins a rabbit. As soon as I saw the dead man I sent an orderly to a friend's house nearby to borrow an elephant rifle. I had already sent back the pony, not wanting it to go mad with fright and throw me if it smelled the elephant.

The orderly came back in a few minutes with a rifle and five cartridges, and meanwhile some Burmans had arrived and told us that the elephant was in the paddy fields[8] below, only a few hundred yards away. As I started forward practically the whole population of the quarter flocked out of the houses and followed me. They had seen the rifle and were all shouting excitedly that I was going to shoot the elephant. They had not shown much interest in the elephant when he was merely ravaging their homes, but it was different now that he was going to be shot. It was a bit of fun to them, as it would be to

---

6. **Dravidian** (drə vid´ ē ən) belonging to the race of people inhabiting southern India.
7. **coolie** laborer.
8. **paddy fields** rice fields.

LITERATURE IN CONTEXT

Vocabulary of Empire
The key terms in Orwell's political vocabulary often have Latin origins:

- *Imperialism* comes from a Latin word for "command" or "empire."

- *Dominion* comes from a Latin word meaning "lord" or "master."

Supporters of British imperialism may have chosen Latinate words to describe the British Empire as a way of suggesting a comparison with the glory of the Roman Empire. However, critics like Orwell seized the word *imperialism*, and it gained strongly negative connotations.

Some meanings reflect history inaccurately. In an irony that Orwell would have appreciated, the word *despot* is derived from a Greek term for "ruler." Even though our ideas of democracy come from ancient Greece, where some rulers strove for democratic goals, the term has come to describe the opposite of a democratic leader—an oppressive tyrant.

Connect to the Literature

In what ways does the narrator fail to embody words like *imperialism* and *despotic*?

Reading Check

What has the elephant done that shows how dangerous it is?

Literary Analysis
Irony How does Orwell's description of the crowd's reaction create situational irony?

an English crowd; besides they wanted the meat. It made me vaguely uneasy. I had no intention of shooting the elephant—I had merely sent for the rifle to defend myself if necessary— and it is always unnerving to have a crowd following you. I marched down the hill, looking and feeling a fool, with the rifle over my shoulder and an ever-growing army of people jostling at my heels. At the bottom, when you got away from the huts, there was a metaled road[9] and beyond that a miry waste of paddy fields a thousand yards across, not yet plowed but soggy from the first rains and dotted with coarse grass. The elephant was standing eight yards from the road, his left side toward us. He took not the slightest notice of the crowd's approach. He was tearing up bunches of grass, beating them against his knees to clean them, and stuffing them into his mouth.

I had halted on the road. As soon as I saw the elephant I knew with perfect certainty that I ought not to shoot him. It is a serious matter to shoot a working elephant—it is comparable to destroying a huge and costly piece of machinery—and obviously one ought not to do it if it can possibly be avoided. And at that distance, peacefully eating, the elephant looked no more dangerous than a cow. I thought then and I think now that his attack of "must" was already passing off; in which case he would merely wander harmlessly about until the mahout came back and caught him. Moreover, I did not in the least want to shoot him. I decided that I would watch him for a little while to make sure that he did not turn savage again, and then go home.

But at that moment I glanced round at the crowd that had followed me. It was an immense crowd, two thousand at the least and growing every minute. It blocked the road for a long distance on either side. I looked at the sea of yellow faces above the garish clothes—faces all happy and excited over this bit of fun, all certain that the elephant was going to be shot. They were watching me as they would watch a conjurer about to perform a trick. They did not like me, but with the magical rifle in my hands I was momentarily worth watching. And suddenly I realized that I should have to shoot the elephant after all. The people expected it of me and I had got to do it; I could feel their two thousand wills pressing me forward, irresistibly. And it was at this moment, as I stood there with the rifle in my hands, that I first grasped the hollowness, the futility of the white man's dominion in the East. Here was I, the white man with his gun, standing in front of the unarmed native crowd—seemingly the leading actor of the piece; but in reality I was only an absurd puppet pushed to and fro by the will of those yellow faces behind. I perceived in this moment that when the white man turns tyrant it is his own freedom that he destroys. He becomes a sort of hollow, posing dummy, the conventionalized figure

Vocabulary
dominion (də min′ yən) *n.* rule, authority

Literary Analysis
Irony What ironic observation does Orwell share here?

---

9. metaled road road in which the pavement is reinforced with metal strips.

"BUT I DID NOT WANT TO SHOOT THE ELEPHANT."

of a sahib.[10] For it is the condition of his rule that he shall spend his life in trying to impress the "natives," and so in every crisis he has got to do what the "natives" expect of him. He wears a mask, and his face grows to fit it. I had got to shoot the elephant. I had committed myself to doing it when I sent for the rifle. A sahib has got to act like a sahib; he has got to appear resolute, to know his own mind and do definite things. To come all that way, rifle in hand, with two thousand people marching at my heels, and then to trail feebly away, having done nothing—no, that was impossible. The crowd would laugh at me. And my whole life, every white man's life in the East, was one long struggle not to be laughed at.

But I did not want to shoot the elephant. I watched him beating his bunch of grass against his knees with that preoccupied grandmotherly air that elephants have. It seemed to me that it would be murder to shoot him. At that age I was not squeamish about killing animals, but I had never shot an elephant and never wanted to. (Somehow it always seems worse to kill a *large* animal.) Besides, there was the beast's owner to be considered. Alive, the elephant was worth at least a hundred pounds, dead, he would only be worth the value of his tusks, five pounds, possibly. But I had got to act quickly. I turned to some experienced-looking Burmans who had been there when we arrived, and asked them how the elephant had been behaving. They all said the same thing: he took no notice of you if you left him alone, but he might charge if you went too close to him.

---

10. sahib (sä ib) Indian word for European gentleman.

Reading Strategy
Analyze and Evaluate Similar Themes
What is the "mask" Orwell wears, and why must he wear it?

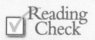

Reading Check

What is the main reason Orwell feels he must shoot the elephant?

▲ **Critical Viewing**
Judging from the details
in this photograph,
what made Orwell
(third from left in back
row) and his fellow
officers conspicuous and
therefore possible targets
for ridicule? **[Analyze]**

It was perfectly clear to me what I ought to do. I ought to walk
up to within, say, twenty-five yards of the elephant and test his
behavior. If he charged, I could shoot; if he took no notice of me, it
would be safe to leave him until the mahout came back. But also I
knew that I was going to do no such thing. I was a poor shot with a
rifle and the ground was soft mud into which one would sink at every
step. If the elephant charged and I missed him, I should have about
as much chance as a toad under a steamroller. But even then I was
not thinking particularly of my own skin, only of the watchful yellow
faces behind. For at that moment, with the crowd watching me, I was
not afraid in the ordinary sense, as I would have been if I had been
alone. A white man mustn't be frightened in front of "natives"; and so,
in general, he isn't frightened. The sole thought in my mind was that
if anything went wrong those two thousand Burmans would see me

pursued, caught, trampled on, and reduced to a grinning corpse like that Indian up the hill. And if that happened it was quite probable that some of them would laugh. That would never do. There was only one alternative. I shoved the cartridges into the magazine and lay down on the road to get a better aim.

The crowd grew very still, and a deep, low, happy sigh, as of people who see the theater curtain go up at last, breathed from innumerable throats. They were going to have their bit of fun, after all. The rifle was a beautiful German thing with cross-hair sights. I did not then know that in shooting an elephant one would shoot to cut an imaginary bar running from ear hole to ear hole. I ought, therefore, as the elephant was sideways on, to have aimed straight at his ear-hole; actually I aimed several inches in front of this, thinking the brain would be further forward.

When I pulled the trigger I did not hear the bang or feel the kick—one never does when a shot goes home—but I heard the devilish roar of glee that went up from the crowd. In that instant, in too short a time, one would have thought, even for the bullet to get there, a mysterious, terrible change had come over the elephant. He neither stirred nor fell, but every line of his body had altered. He looked suddenly stricken, shrunken, immensely old, as though the frightful impact of the bullet had paralyzed him without knocking him down. At last, after what seemed a long time—it might have been five seconds, I dare say—he sagged flabbily to his knees. His mouth slobbered. An enormous senility[11] seemed to have settled upon him. One could have imagined him thousands of years old. I fired again into the same spot. At the second shot he did not collapse but climbed with desperate slowness to his feet and stood weakly upright, with legs sagging and head drooping. I fired a third time. That was the shot that did for him. You could see the agony of it jolt his whole body and knock the last remnant of strength from his legs. But in falling he seemed for a moment to rise, for as his hind legs collapsed beneath him he seemed to tower upward like a huge rock toppling, his trunk reaching skyward like a tree. He trumpeted, for the first and only time. And then down he came, his belly toward me, with a crash that seemed to shake the ground even where I lay.

I got up. The Burmans were already racing past me across the mud. It was obvious that the elephant would never rise again, but he was not dead. He was breathing very rhythmically with long rattling gasps, his great mound of a side painfully rising and falling. His mouth was wide open—I could see far down into caverns of pale pink

---

11. **senility** (si nil´ ə tē) *n.* mental deterioration due to old age.

Literary Analysis
Irony Why is Orwell's comment "That would never do" an example of verbal irony?

Reading Strategy
Analyze and Evaluate Similar Themes What does this long description of the elephant's death reveal about the cultural conflict Orwell faces?

Reading Check

What happens to the elephant after Orwell's first shot?

throat. I waited a long time for him to die, but his breathing did not weaken. Finally I fired my two remaining shots into the spot where I thought his heart must be. The thick blood welled out of him like red velvet, but still he did not die. His body did not even jerk when the shots hit him, the tortured breathing continued without a pause. He was dying, very slowly and in great agony, but in some world remote from me where not even a bullet could damage him further. I felt that I had got to put an end to that dreadful noise. It seemed dreadful to see the great beast lying there, powerless to move and yet powerless to die, and not even to be able to finish him. I sent back for my small rifle and poured shot after shot into his heart and down his throat. They seemed to make no impression. The tortured gasps continued as steadily as the ticking of a clock.

In the end I could not stand it any longer and went away. I heard later that it took him half an hour to die. Burmans were bringing dahs[12] and baskets even before I left, and I was told they had stripped his body almost to the bones by the afternoon.

Afterward, of course, there were endless discussions about the shooting of the elephant. The owner was furious, but he was only an Indian and could do nothing. Besides, legally I had done the right thing, for a mad elephant has to be killed, like a mad dog, if its owner fails to control it. Among the Europeans opinion was divided. The older men said I was right, the younger men said it was a shame to shoot an elephant for killing a coolie, because an elephant was worth more than any Coringhee[13] coolie. And afterward I was very glad that the coolie had been killed; it put me legally in the right and it gave me a sufficient pretext for shooting the elephant. I often wondered whether any of the others grasped that I had done it solely to avoid looking a fool.

12. **dahs** (däz) knives.
13. **Coringhee** (cor in′ gē) Southern Indian.

Reading Strategy

Analyze and Evaluate Similar Themes Read the first sentence of the paragraph beginning "In the end." How does Orwell's individual response mirror the end of the entire colonial enterprise?

Critical Reading

Cite textual evidence to support your responses.

© **1. Key Ideas and Details** **(a)** Why did the Burmese hate George Orwell? **(b) Analyze:** Why does this hatred cause conflict in him? **(c) Interpret:** What does this internal conflict show about Orwell?

© **2. Key Ideas and Details** **(a)** Why does Orwell think that the elephant need not be killed? **(b) Analyze:** What is the main factor in Orwell's decision to shoot the elephant? **(c) Interpret:** What does this decision, and his honesty about it, reveal about his character?

Doris Lessing
(b. 1919)

Author of "No Witchcraft for Sale"

Freely admitting her deep desire to influence others through her works of fiction, Doris Lessing has said that publishing a story or novel is "an attempt to impose one's personality and beliefs on other people. If a writer accepts this responsibility, he must see himself . . . as an architect of the soul."

Exposing Injustice One of the ways that Lessing fulfills this responsibility is by writing about social injustice, challenging ideas of race and women's roles. Her own experiences give her a unique perspective on the problems caused when cultures conflict. In much of her writing, Lessing explores the intricate connections between personal experience and political reality.

She was born in Persia (now Iran), the daughter of a British bank clerk. When she was five, her family moved to the British colony of Rhodesia (now the independent country of Zimbabwe) in southcentral Africa. Her memoir *Under My Skin* (1994) describes some ways that Europeans mistreated Africans, displacing them from their lands and suppressing their traditions.

Experience Shapes a Writer Lessing's talent for writing developed as a response to a variety of experiences, including a childhood she described as a mixture of some pleasure and much pain. Strictly disciplined by her mother at home and by teachers at school, the young Lessing sought refuge in reading and in explorations of nature.

Personal and Political Themes The turbulent influences that drove Lessing to write also taught her about the relationship between individuals and society. *The Golden Notebook* (1962), Lessing's best-known novel, explores social issues through one woman's persistent search for identity. The dominant theme in her works is the free woman who struggles for individuality and equality despite social assumptions and pressures. Lessing's fiction earned her the Nobel Prize for Literature in 2007.

No Witchcraft for Sale

Doris Lessing

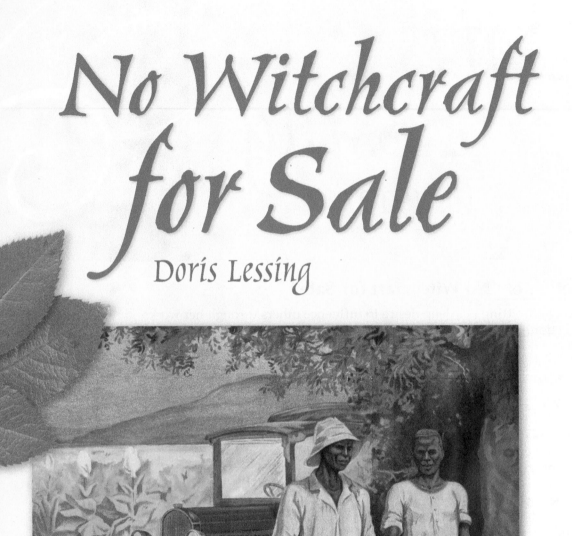

BACKGROUND

Doris Lessing's family moved to Southern Rhodesia (now Zimbabwe) in 1924. For two decades, British control had been forcing two vastly different cultures to live together. Every day, white European values and attitudes met face to face with black African values and attitudes. Traditions and beliefs inevitably clashed. However, although each culture exhibited distinctive characteristics, they also shared some fundamental cultural assumptions.

The Farquars had been childless for years when little Teddy was born; and they were touched by the pleasure of their servants, who brought presents of fowls and eggs and flowers to the homestead when they came to rejoice over the baby, exclaiming with delight over his downy golden head and his blue eyes. They congratulated Mrs. Farquar as if she had achieved a very great thing, and she felt that she had—her smile for the lingering, admiring natives was warm and grateful.

Later, when Teddy had his first haircut, Gideon the cook picked up the soft gold tufts from the ground, and held them reverently in his hand. Then he smiled at the little boy and said: "Little Yellow Head." That became the native name for the child. Gideon and Teddy were great friends from the first. When Gideon had finished his work, he would lift Teddy on his shoulders to the shade of a big tree, and play with him there, forming curious little toys from twigs and leaves and grass, or shaping animals from wetted soil. When Teddy learned to walk it was often Gideon who crouched before him, clucking encouragement, finally catching him when he fell, tossing him up in the air till they both became breathless with laughter. Mrs. Farquar was fond of the old cook because of his love for her child.

There was no second baby; and one day Gideon said: "Ah, missus, missus, the Lord above sent this one; Little Yellow Head is the most good thing we have in our house." Because of that "we" Mrs. Farquar felt a warm impulse toward her cook; and at the end of the month she raised his wages. He had been with her now for several years; he was one of the few natives who had his wife and children in the compound and never wanted to go home to his kraal,[1] which was some hundreds of miles away. Sometimes a small piccanin who had been

---

1. **kraal** (kräl) village of South African natives, usually fenced in with a stockade.

◀ **Critical Viewing**
Using this picture and the title, predict what this story will be about.
[Predict]

Vocabulary
reverently (rev´ ər ənt lē) *adv.* with great respect

Reading Check

What is Gideon's role in the Farquar household?

born the same time as Teddy, could be seen peering from the edge of the bush, staring in awe at the little white boy with his miraculous fair hair and Northern blue eyes. The two little children would gaze at each other with a wide, interested gaze, and once Teddy put out his hand curiously to touch the black child's cheeks and hair.

Gideon, who was watching, shook his head wonderingly, and said: "Ah, missus, these are both children, and one will grow up to be a baas, and one will be a servant"; and Mrs. Farquar smiled and said sadly, "Yes, Gideon, I was thinking the same." She sighed. "It is God's will," said Gideon, who was a mission boy. The Farquars were very religious people; and this shared feeling about God bound servant and masters even closer together.

Teddy was about six years old when he was given a scooter, and discovered the intoxications of speed. All day he would fly around the homestead, in and out of flowerbeds, scattering squawking chickens and irritated dogs, finishing with a wide dizzying arc into the kitchen door. There he would cry: "Gideon, look at me!" And Gideon would laugh and say: "very clever, Little Yellow Head." Gideon's youngest son, who was now a herdsboy, came especially up from the compound to see the scooter. He was afraid to come near it, but Teddy showed off in front of him. "Piccanin," shouted Teddy, "get out of my way!" And he raced in circles around the black child until he was frightened, and fled back to the bush.

"Why did you frighten him?" asked Gideon, gravely reproachful.[2]

Teddy said defiantly: "He's only a black boy," and laughed. Then, when Gideon turned away from him without speaking, his face fell. Very soon he slipped into the house and found an orange and brought it to Gideon, saying: "This is for you." He could not bring himself to say he was sorry; but he could not bear to lose Gideon's affection either. Gideon took the orange unwillingly and sighed. "Soon you will be going away to school, Little Yellow Head," he said wonderingly, "and then you will be grown up." He shook his head gently and said, "And that is how our lives go." He seemed to be putting a distance between himself and Teddy, not because of resentment, but in the way a person accepts something inevitable. The baby had lain in his arms and smiled up into his face: the tiny boy had swung from his shoulders and played with him by the hour. Now Gideon would not let his flesh touch the flesh of the white child. He was kind, but there was a grave formality in his voice that made Teddy pout and sulk away. Also, it made him into a man: with Gideon he was polite, and carried himself formally, and if he came into the kitchen to ask for something, it was in the way a white man uses toward a servant, expecting to be obeyed.

But on the day that Teddy came staggering into the kitchen with his fists to his eyes, shrieking with pain, Gideon dropped the pot full of hot soup that he was holding, rushed to the child, and forced aside

---

2. reproachful (ri prōch′ fəl) *adj.* expressing blame.

Reading Strategy
Analyze and Evaluate Similar Themes What cultural values do the Farquars and Gideon share?

Literary Analysis
Cultural Conflict How do Gideon and Teddy manage the differences in their social status to protect their vulnerable emotions?

his fingers. "A snake!" he exclaimed. Teddy had been on his scooter, and had come to a rest with his foot on the side of a big tub of plants. A treesnake, hanging by its tail from the roof, had spat full into his eyes. Mrs. Farquar came running when she heard the commotion. "He'll go blind," she sobbed, holding Teddy close against her. "Gideon, he'll go blind!" Already the eyes, with perhaps half an hour's sight left in them, were swollen up to the size of fists: Teddy's small white face was distorted by great purple oozing protuberances.[3] Gideon said: "Wait a minute, missus, I'll get some medicine." He ran off into the bush.

Mrs. Farquar lifted the child into the house and bathed his eyes with permanganate.[4] She had scarcely heard Gideon's words; but when she saw that her remedies had no effect at all, and remembered how she had seen natives with no sight in their eyes, because of the spitting of a snake, she began to look for the return of her cook, remembering what she heard of the efficacy[5] of native herbs. She stood by the window, holding the terrified, sobbing little boy in her arms, and peered help-lessly into the bush. It was not more than a few minutes before she saw Gideon come bounding back, and in his hand he held a plant.

"Do not be afraid, missus," said Gideon, "this will cure Little Yellow Head's eyes." He stripped the leaves from the plant, leaving a small white fleshy root. Without even washing it, he put the root in his mouth, chewed it vigorously, and then held the spittle there while he took the child forcibly from Mrs. Farquar. He gripped Teddy down between his knees, and pressed the balls of his thumbs into the swollen eyes, so that the child screamed and Mrs. Farquar cried out in protest: "Gideon, Gideon!" But Gideon took no notice. He knelt over the writhing child, pushing back the puffy lids till chinks of eyeball showed, and then he spat hard, again and again, into first one eye, and then the other. He finally lifted Teddy gently into his mother's arms, and said: "His eyes will get better." But Mrs. Farquar was weep-ing with terror, and she could hardly thank him: it was impossible to believe that Teddy could keep his sight. In a couple of hours the swellings were gone: the eyes were inflamed and tender but Teddy could see. Mr. and Mrs. Farquar went to Gideon in the kitchen and thanked him over and over again. They felt helpless because of their gratitude: it seemed they could do nothing to express it. They gave Gideon presents for his wife and children, and a big increase in wages, but these things could not pay for Teddy's now completely cured eyes. Mrs. Farquar said: "Gideon, God chose you as an instrument for His goodness," and Gideon said: "Yes, missus, God is very good."

Now, when such a thing happens on a farm, it cannot be long before everyone hears of it. Mr. and Mrs. Farquar told their neighbors and the story was discussed from one end of the district to the other. The

Reading Strategy
Analyze and Evaluate Similar Themes When Teddy is injured, what do the reactions of Mrs. Farquar and Gideon show about their cultural differences and similarities?

Reading Check
How is Teddy injured and who heals him?

---

3. **protuberances** (prō tōō´ bər əns iz) *n.* bulges; swellings.
4. **permanganate** (pər maŋ´ gə nāt´) salt of permanganic acid.
5. **efficacy** (ef´ li kə sē) *n.* power to produce intended effects.

▶ **Critical Viewing**
How does the landscape in
this picture contrast with
the "bush" into which
Gideon ventures for Teddy's
medicine? **[Distinguish]**

bush is full of secrets. No one can live in Africa, or at least on the veld,[6] without learning very soon that there is an ancient wisdom of leaf and soil and season—and, too, perhaps most important of all, of the darker tracts of the human mind—which is the black man's heritage. Up and down the district people were telling anecdotes, reminding each other of things that had happened to them.

"But I saw it myself, I tell you. It was a puff-adder bite. The kaffir's[7] arm was swollen to the elbow, like a great shiny black bladder. He was groggy after half a minute. He was dying. Then suddenly a kaffir walked out of the bush with his hands full of green stuff. He smeared something on the place, and next day my boy was back at work, and all you could see was two small punctures in the skin."

This was the kind of tale they told. And, as always, with a certain amount of exasperation, because while all of them knew that in the

---

6. veld in South Africa, open grassy country, with few bushes and almost no trees.
7. kaffir's belonging to a black African; in South Africa, a contemptuous term.

bush of Africa are waiting valuable drugs locked in bark, in simple-looking leaves, in roots, it was impossible to ever get the truth about them from the natives themselves.

The story eventually reached town; and perhaps it was at a sundowner party, or some such function, that a doctor, who happened to be there, challenged it. "Nonsense," he said. "These things get exaggerated in the telling. We are always checking up on this kind of story, and we draw a blank every time."

Anyway, one morning there arrived a strange car at the homestead, and out stepped one of the workers from the laboratory in town, with cases full of test-tubes and chemicals.

Mr. and Mrs. Farquar were flustered and pleased and flattered. They asked the scientist to lunch, and they told the story all over again, for the hundredth time. Little Teddy was there too, his blue eyes sparkling with health, to prove the truth of it. The scientist explained how humanity might benefit if this new drug could be offered for sale; and the Farquars were even more pleased: they were kind, simple people, who liked to think of something good coming about because of them. But when the scientist began talking of the money that might result, their manner showed discomfort. Their feelings over the miracle (that was how they thought of it) were so strong and deep and religious, that it was distasteful to them to think of money. The scientist, seeing their faces, went back to his first point, which was the advancement of humanity. He was perhaps a trifle perfunctory:[8] it was not the first time he had come salting the tail of a fabulous bush secret.[9]

Eventually, when the meal was over, the Farquars called Gideon into their living room and explained to him that this baas, here, was a Big Doctor from the Big City, and he had come all that way to see Gideon. At this Gideon seemed afraid; he did not understand; and Mrs. Farquar explained quickly that it was because of the wonderful thing he had done with Teddy's eyes that the Big Baas had come.

Gideon looked from Mrs. Farquar to Mr. Farquar, and then at the little boy, who was showing great importance because of the occasion. At last he said grudgingly:[10] "The Big Baas want to know what medicine I used?" He spoke

---

8. **perfunctory** (pər fuŋk´ tə rē) *adj.* done without care or interest.
9. **salting . . . bush secret** allusion to the humorous and ironic advice given to children about how to catch a bird—by putting salt on its tail. In other words, the scientist does not really expect to capture a valuable bit of information.
10. **grudgingly** (gruj´ ing ly) *adv.* in a reluctant manner

Vocabulary
incredulously (in krej′ oo
ləs lē) *adv.* with doubt or
disbelief

incredulously, as if he could not believe his old friends could so betray him. Mr. Farquar began explaining how a useful medicine could be made out of the root, and how it could be put on sale, and how thousands of people, black and white, up and down the continent of Africa, could be saved by the medicine when that spitting snake filled their eyes with poison. Gideon listened, his eyes bent on the ground, the skin of his forehead puckering in discomfort. When Mr. Farquar had finished he did not reply. The scientist, who all this time had been leaning back in a big chair, sipping his coffee and smiling with skeptical good humor, chipped in and explained all over again, in different words, about the making of drugs and the progress of science. Also, he offered Gideon a present.

There was silence after this further explanation, and then Gideon remarked indifferently that he could not remember the root. His face was sullen and hostile, even when he looked at the Farquars, whom he usually treated like old friends. They were beginning to feel annoyed; and this feeling annulled[11] the guilt that had been sprung into life by Gideon's accusing manner. They were beginning to feel that he was unreasonable. But it was at that moment that they all realized he would never give in. The magical drug would remain where it was, unknown and useless except for the tiny scattering of Africans who had the knowledge, natives who might be digging a ditch for the municipality in a ragged shirt and a pair of patched shorts, but who were still born to healing, hereditary healers, being the nephews or sons of the old witch doctors whose ugly masks and bits of bone and all the uncouth[12] properties of magic were the outward signs of real power and wisdom.

Spiral Review
Social Criticism In this
portrayal of Gideon's
reaction, what point
might the author be
making about rela-
tions between those
who ruled Rhodesia
and those whom they
excluded from power?

The Farquars might tread on that plant fifty times a day as they passed from house to garden, from cow kraal to mealie field, but they would never know it.

But they went on persuading and arguing, with all the force of their exasperation; and Gideon continued to say that he could not remember, or that there was no such root, or that it was the wrong season of the year, or that it wasn't the root itself, but the spit from his mouth that had cured Teddy's eyes. He said all these things one after another, and seemed not to care they were contradictory. He was rude and stubborn. The Farquars could hardly recognize their gentle, lovable old servant in this ignorant, perversely obstinate African, standing there in front of them with lowered eyes, his hands twitching his cook's apron, repeating over and over whichever one of the stupid refusals that first entered his head.

Literary Analysis
Irony Why is Gideon's
statement, "I will show you
the root," an example of
verbal irony?

And suddenly he appeared to give in. He lifted his head, gave a long blank angry look at the circle of whites, who seemed to him like a circle of yelping dogs pressing around him, and said: "I will show you the root."

They walked single file away from the homestead down a kaffir path. It was a blazing December afternoon, with the sky full of hot

---

11. annulled (ə nuld′) *v.* did away with; neutralized.
12. uncouth (un kooth′) *adj.* uncultured; crude; strange.

rain clouds. Everything was hot: the sun was like a bronze tray whirling overhead, there was a heat shimmer over the fields, the soil was scorching underfoot, the dusty wind blew gritty and thick and warm in their faces. It was a terrible day, fit only for reclining on a verandah with iced drinks, which is where they would normally have been at that hour.

From time to time, remembering that on the day of the snake it had taken ten minutes to find the root, someone asked: "Is it much further, Gideon?" And Gideon would answer over his shoulder, with angry politeness: "I'm looking for the root, baas." And indeed, he would frequently bend sideways and trail his hand among the grasses with a gesture that was insulting in its perfunctoriness. He walked them through the bush along unknown paths for two hours, in that melting destroying heat, so that the sweat trickled coldly down them and their heads ached. They were all quite silent: the Farquars because they were angry, the scientist because he was being proved right again; there was no such plant. His was a tactful silence.

At last, six miles from the house, Gideon suddenly decided they had had enough; or perhaps his anger evaporated at that moment. He picked up, without an attempt at looking anything but casual, a handful of blue flowers from the grass, flowers that had been growing plentifully all down the paths they had come.

He handed them to the scientist without looking at him, and marched off by himself on the way home, leaving them to follow him if they chose.

When they got back to the house, the scientist went to the kitchen to thank Gideon: he was being very polite, even though there was an amused look in his eyes. Gideon was not there. Throwing the flowers casually into the back of his car, the eminent visitor departed on his way back to his laboratory.

Gideon was back in his kitchen in time to prepare dinner, but he was sulking. He spoke to Mr. Farquar like an unwilling servant. It was days before they liked each other again.

The Farquars made inquiries about the root from their laborers. Sometimes they were answered with distrustful stares. Sometimes the natives said: "We do not know. We have never heard of the root." One, the cattle boy, who had been with them a long time, and had grown to trust them

▼ **Critical Viewing**
Is this the way you pictured the landscape through which Gideon led the Farquars and the scientist? Explain.
[Relate]

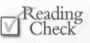
Reading
Check

What does Gideon give the scientist?

a little, said: "Ask your boy in the kitchen. Now, there's a doctor for you. He's the son of a famous medicine man who used to be in these parts, and there's nothing he cannot cure." Then he added politely: "Of course, he's not as good as the white man's doctor, we know that, but he's good for us."

After some time, when the soreness had gone from between the Farquars and Gideon, they began to joke: "When are you going to show us the snake-root, Gideon?" And he would laugh and shake his head, saying, a little uncomfortably: "But I did show you, missus, have you forgotten?"

Much later, Teddy, as a schoolboy, would come into the kitchen and say: "You old rascal, Gideon! Do you remember that time you tricked us all by making us walk miles all over the veld for nothing? It was so far my father had to carry me!"

And Gideon would double up with polite laughter. After much laughing, he would suddenly straighten himself up, wipe his old eyes, and look sadly at Teddy, who was grinning mischievously at him across the kitchen: "Ah, Little Yellow Head, how you have grown! Soon you will be grown up with a farm of your own . . ."

Critical Reading

Cite textual evidence to support your responses.

1. **Key Ideas and Details (a)** What is Teddy's nickname and how does he get it? **(b) Infer:** How does this nickname emphasize the differences between the Farquars and their servants?

2. **Key Ideas and Details (a)** How does Gideon save Teddy's sight? **(b) Interpret:** In what way does this incident reveal an aspect of Gideon previously unknown to the Farquars?

3. **Key Ideas and Details (a) Analyze:** What effect does the scientist's visit have on the Farquars' relationship with Gideon? **(b) Draw Conclusions:** Why does Gideon refuse to share his knowledge?

4. **Key Ideas and Details** What do Gideon's last words to Teddy mean?

5. **Integration of Knowledge and Ideas** Do you think Gideon's decision to withhold information about the plant is justified? Explain.

6. **Integration of Knowledge and Ideas** What insights do Orwell's essay and Lessing's story provide into how people deal with cultural differences? Use three of these Essential Question words in your answer: *differentiate, respond, acquiesce, integrity, understanding, humor. [Connecting to the Essential Question: How does literature shape or reflect society?]*

Literary Analysis

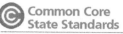
Common Core State Standards

1. Key Ideas and Details **Cultural conflict** often results when individuals or groups do not share a basic value or attitude with another individual or group. Use a chart like the one shown to identify the values in conflict in these selections.

What Orwell does not share with the Burmese	What the Burmese do not share with Orwell	What Gideon does not share with the Farquars	What the Farquars do not share with Gideon

2. Key Ideas and Details Refusal to betray values, traditions, or even history often causes cultural conflict. Gideon "could not believe his old friends could so betray him." Explain how Orwell, Gideon, and the Farquars all try to avoid some kind of betrayal.

3. Key Ideas and Details **Situational irony** results when expectations are not met. **(a)** Identify an example of situational irony in each of these selections. **(b)** What point of view about cultural conflict is revealed by each author's use of irony?

4. Craft and Structure Lessing builds **verbal irony** into the title of her story. Why is the title ironic?

5. Integration of Knowledge and Ideas Orwell conveys the theme of cultural conflict through nonfiction, Lessing through fiction. Which type of writing do you think suits the theme better? Why?

Writing
2. Write informative/explanatory texts to examine and convey complex ideas, concepts, and information clearly and accurately through the effective selection, organization, and analysis of content. (p. 1338)
2.d. Use precise language, domain-specific vocabulary, and techniques such as metaphor, simile, and analogy to manage the complexity of the topic. (p. 1338)

Language
4.a. Use context as a clue to the meaning of a word or phrase. (p. 1338)

Reading Strategy

6. "Shooting an Elephant" and "No Witchcraft for Sale" offer an opportunity to **analyze and evaluate similar themes. (a)** How does Orwell's cultural background determine his actions against the elephant? **(b)** How does Gideon's cultural background determine his actions with the medicinal plant?

7. Cultural norms are sometimes contrary to what some people consider common sense. **(a)** In what way could common sense have solved Orwell's cultural conflict? **(b)** How could common sense have solved the conflict between Gideon and the Farquars?

8. Evaluate the degrees of success in resolving cultural conflict that is shown in these two selections. Who, in your opinion, does the best job—Orwell, Gideon, or the Farquars? Give reasons for your evaluation.

Integrated Language Skills

Vocabulary Acquisition and Use

Word Analysis: Etymology of Political Science and History Terms

The etymology—the word origin—of a political science or history term is often tied to social and political events in the distant past. A powerful leader, an economic program, a war, a migration—all can give birth to words that enter the language and remain current.

For example, in the nineteenth century, when the British Empire was flourishing, the policy of *imperialism* was taken for granted. *Imperialism* derives from the Latin word for empire, *imperium*. Someone who supported such a policy of domination of weaker countries was an *imperialist*.

Write the definition of each of the following political science or history terms. Then, check each word in a dictionary to determine its etymology.

1. colonialism
2. democracy
3. communism

Vocabulary: Contextual Meaning

Select the word from the list on page 1316 that best completes each sentence. Use the meaning of the context to support your choice.

1. The scientist was _____ about the plant's medicinal value; he doubted it would work.
2. She handled the delicate sculpture _____ in honor of the brilliant artist who had made it.
3. His cruel and _____ behavior included imprisoning all his political opponents.
4. They controlled everything, and their _____ stretched from the river in the east to the mountains in the west.
5. He replied _____ because he could not believe the responses that he was hearing.
6. The effects of empire-building can still be seen in those countries that survived centuries of _____.

Writing

Explanatory Text In "Shooting an Elephant," Orwell must perform a violent act that he does not want to perform. In "No Witchcraft for Sale," the Farquars cannot understand Gideon's uncooperativeness, and he feels betrayed by them. In an **essay,** offer a solution to one of these problems.

Prewriting Reread both selections, jotting down details that both clarify the problems and suggest possible solutions.

Drafting In the introductory paragraph, state the problem accurately, identifying the causes of the problem and touching on your proposed solution. In the body of your essay, elaborate on your proposed solution, offering evidence that it will work and connecting it with the problem. Support your discussion of the problem and the solution with *accurate and detailed references* to the text.

Revising Be sure that you provide the possible effects of your proposed solution. Also, make sure that you have used precise language to clarify the causes of the problem.

> **Model: Identify the Causes of the Problem**
> Orwell's **problem is caused by** his position of authority conflicting with his personal beliefs. His position forces him to wear a "mask" and be something he is not. **As a result,** he faces the conflict of either sacrificing his authority or compromising his beliefs.

Precise language clarifies the sources of a problem.

Conventions and Style: Variety in Sentence Beginnings

To avoid monotony in your sentences, use a variety of structures, lengths, and beginnings.

You can vary the beginnings of your sentences in a number of ways. The following chart illustrates a variety of sentence beginnings.

Subject	The elephant destroyed a hut, a cow, and a van in its rage.
Prepositional phrase	In its rage, the elephant destroyed a hut, a cow, and a van.
Participle	Enraged, the elephant destroyed a hut, a cow, and a van.
Adverb	Angrily, the elephant destroyed a hut, a cow, and a van.
Infinitive	To shoot the elephant was not what Orwell wanted to do.
Subordinate clause	As the elephant raged through the town, it destroyed a hut, a cow, and a van.

You may also invert normal sentence order so that the verb comes before the subject.

Normal Order (subject before verb): The elephant was eating grass in the field.

Inverted Order: There was the elephant eating grass in the field.

Practice Rewrite each sentence to begin with the item indicated in parentheses.

1. With gifts of chickens and flowers, the servants showed their delight in the baby. (subject)
2. Teddy, laughing, enjoyed being tossed in the air in play. (participle)
3. Respected and loved, Gideon was a valued servant. (subject)
4. Teddy sped around the homestead riding his scooter. (participle)
5. Shrieking with pain, Teddy staggered into the kitchen. (subject)
6. The plants held valuable secrets in their leaves, roots, and bark. (prepositional phrase)
7. A wind was blowing grit in their faces. (inverted order)
8. Gideon said he didn't remember to avoid answering the questions. (infinitive)
9. The crowd yelled loudly and laughed at Orwell. (adverb)
10. The crowd was behind as he pursued the elephant. (subordinate clause)

Ⓔ Writing and Speaking Conventions

A. Writing Write sentences beginning with the following words or phrases.

1. With insults   2. Gideon   3. Followed
4. As he had always done   5. Carefully

Example: With insults
Sentence: With insults, the fans showed their dislike of the English.

B. Speaking Think of a conflict between two groups that you have read or heard about. Write and present to the class a headline and a brief news story to explain the conflict. Use at least three different kinds of sentence beginnings and one sentence with inverted order.

PH | WRITING COACH

Further instruction and practice are available in *Prentice Hall Writing Coach.*

Connecting to the Essential Question Travelers to distant places usually acquire something meaningful from their experience. It may be tangible, like a souvenir, or intangible, like a memory. As you read, notice details in the stories that suggest how people determine the values of things, places, or even other people. These observations will help you think about the Essential Question: **What is the relationship between literature and place?**

Literary Analysis

Every **historical period** is characterized by certain views and values, which are reflected in the literature of the period.

During the *colonial era,* a few powerful countries controlled the destiny of colonies that they "owned." Some supported this arrangement, while others opposed it. Following are ways in which this political conflict and other results of colonialism are reflected in stories like those by Gordimer and Naipaul:

Setting	Exotic settings in distant colonies Non-English vocabulary in descriptions
Characterization	Use of racial domination as a motive Characters becoming aware of other cultures
Conflict	Antagonism caused by cultural differences Feelings of inferiority in colonized culture

Reading Strategy

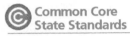 **Preparing to Read Complex Texts** As you read, **apply your background knowledge of a historical period** in order to analyze a setting, character, or conflict. Ask yourself, for example, "What historical fact or political situation or assumption explains this situation?" Make inferences and support them with evidence. Use a graphic organizer like the one shown.

Vocabulary

impressionistic (im presh ən is´ tik) *adj.* conveying a picture through quickly sketched suggestions of details (p. 1343)

segmented (seg´ ment id) *adj.* divided into joined parts (p. 1345)

atrophy (a´ trə fē) *v.* waste away (p. 1346)

patronize (pā´ trən īz) *v.* be a customer of a particular merchant or store (p. 1353)

distill (di stil´) *v.* obtain the essential part (p. 1353)

keenly (kēn´ lē) *adv.* sharply; intensely (p. 1354)

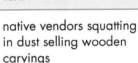 **Common Core State Standards**

Reading Literature
1. Cite strong and thorough textual evidence to support analysis of what the text says explicitly as well as inferences drawn from the text, including determining where the text leaves matters uncertain.

Text

native vendors squatting in dust selling wooden carvings

Interpretation

Africans were so poor that they had to sell handmade artifacts to eke out a living.

Historical Background

Apartheid policies oppressed the black African majority.

www.PHLitOnline.com

NADINE GORDIMER

(B. 1923)

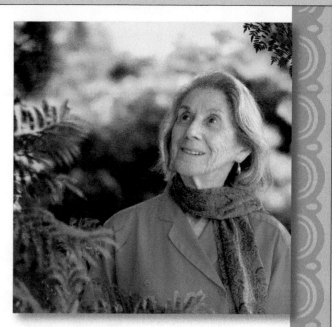

Author of "The Train from Rhodesia"

The fiction of Nadine Gordimer has been shaped by her life in South Africa and by her firm opposition to the former government's policy of apartheid, an institutional form of racial separation and prejudice. In her longer works, as well as in her short stories, she has had a great deal to say about racial division and its harmful effects on both the oppressed and the oppressor. The South African government responded by banning some of her work. Nevertheless, Gordimer has built an international reputation as a writer.

Small Town Origins Gordimer was born in Springs, South Africa, a small town near Johannesburg. Her mother took her out of the local private school when she was eleven. From then until she was sixteen, she "read tremendously" and wrote much fiction. She published her first adult short story, "Come Again Tomorrow," when she was fifteen.

Literary Success *The Soft Voice of the Serpent* (1952) was the first collection of her stories to be published in the United States. Following the critical success of that book, Gordimer's stories appeared in leading American magazines such as *The New Yorker, The Atlantic Monthly,* and *Harper's Magazine.* These stories often describe the entrapment of whites who inherited political and economic power in the closed society of South Africa under apartheid. Frequently, as in "The Train from Rhodesia," she builds a tale around a fleeting but sharply focused moment of insight.

"Luminous Symbol" Until she was thirty, Gordimer had never been outside South Africa. Since then, however, she has traveled widely and lectured in a number of top United States universities, including Princeton, Columbia, and the University of Michigan. She has also won a great many literary awards, including the Nobel Prize for Literature in 1991. Called by one observer "a luminous symbol of at least one white person's understanding of the black man's burden," she is without doubt one of the leading novelists writing in English.

This story is set at a time when South Africa and Rhodesia (now Zimbabwe) enforced policies of racial separation, called apartheid in South Africa, ensuring the continued privileges of a white minority and its domination over the black majority.

THE
TRAIN
FROM
Rhodesia

NADINE GORDIMER

The train came out of the red horizon and bore down toward them over the single straight track. The stationmaster came out of his little brick station with its pointed chalet roof, feeling the creases in his serge uniform in his legs as well. A stir of preparedness rippled through the squatting native vendors waiting in the dust; the face of a carved wooden animal, eternally surprised, stuck out of a sack. The stationmaster's barefoot children wandered over. From the gray mud huts with the untidy heads that stood within a decorated mud wall, chickens, and dogs with their skin stretched like parchment over their bones, followed the piccanins[1] down to the track. The flushed and per-spiring west cast a reflection, faint, without heat, upon the station, upon the tin shed marked "Goods," upon the walled kraal,[2] upon the gray tin house of the stationmaster and upon the sand, that lapped all around, from sky to sky, cast little rhythmical cups of shadow, so that the sand became the sea, and closed over the children's black feet softly and without imprint.

The stationmaster's wife sat behind the mesh of her veranda. Above her head the hunk of a sheep's carcass moved slightly, dan-gling in a current of air.

They waited.

The train called out, along the sky; but there was no answer; and the cry hung on: I'm coming . . . I'm coming . . .

The engine flared out now, big, whisking a dwindling body behind it; the track flared out to let it in.

Creaking, jerking, jostling, gasping, the train filled the station.

Here, let me see that one—the young woman curved her body farther out of the corridor window. Missus? smiled the old boy, look-ing at the creatures he held in his hand. From a piece of string on his gray finger hung a tiny woven basket; he lifted it, questioning. No, no, she urged, leaning down towards him, across the height of the train, towards the man in the piece of old rug; that one, that one, her hand commanded. It was a lion, carved out of soft dry wood that looked like spongecake; heraldic, black and, white, with impressionistic detail burnt in. The old man held it up to her still smiling, not from the heart, but at the customer. Between its Vandyke[3] teeth, in the mouth opened in an endless roar too terrible to be heard, it had a black tongue. Look, said the young husband, if you don't mind! And round the neck of the thing, a piece of fur (rat? rabbit? meerkat?); a real mane, majestic, tell-ing you somehow that the artist had delight in the lion.

All up and down the length of the train in the dust the artists sprang, walking bent, like performing animals, the better to exhibit the fantasy held toward the faces on the train. Buck, startled and stiff, staring with round black and white eyes. More lions, standing erect, grappling with strange, thin, elongated warriors who clutched

1. **piccanins** *n.* native children.
2. **kraal** (kräl) *n.* fenced-in enclosure for cattle or sheep.
3. **Vandyke** (van dīk´) *adj.* tapering to a point, like a Vandyke beard.

◀ **Critical Viewing**
What does the landscape surrounding the tracks in the photo tell you about the area through which the train is traveling? [Infer]

Literary Analysis
Historical Period and Setting Identify three details of the setting that indicate the economic condition of the native Africans.

Vocabulary
impressionistic (im presh ən is´ tik) *adj.* conveying a picture through quickly sketched suggestions of details

Reading Check
What attracts the interest of the young woman on the train?

History Connection

Apartheid

In Gordimer's story, the interactions between white passengers and black vendors reflect the social regime called apartheid ("apartness" in the language of Dutch South Africans). Under apartheid in South Africa, blacks were restricted to living in certain areas. To travel through a white area, they were required to carry passes—even if they worked every day in such areas. Public places—such as schools, restaurants, and hotels—were segregated by law. Whites lived as privileged rulers in the country. Blacks lived for the most part in poverty, stripped of political power. It was only in the closing decades of the twentieth century that blacks, after violent struggles, gained political rights in South Africa and Rhodesia.

Connect to the Literature

Besides language, what other barriers exist between the young woman and the artists?

Reading Strategy

Apply Background Knowledge How do the relative positions of the characters—the whites up on the train, the black natives on the ground—symbolize the policies of apartheid?

spears and showed no fear in their slits of eyes. How much, they asked from the train, how much?

Give me penny, said the little ones with nothing to sell. The dogs went and sat, quite still, under the dining car, where the train breathed out the smell of meat cooking with onion.

A man passed beneath the arch of reaching arms meeting gray-black and white in the exchange of money for the staring wooden eyes, the stiff wooden legs sticking up in the air; went along under the voices and the bargaining, interrogating the wheels. Past the dogs; glancing up at the dining car where he could stare at the faces, behind glass, drinking beer, two by two, on either side of a uniform railway vase with its pale dead flower. Right to the end, to the guard's van, where the stationmaster's children had just collected their mother's two loaves of bread; to the engine itself, where the stationmaster and the driver stood talking against the steaming complaint of the resting beast.

The man called out to them, something loud and joking. They turned to laugh, in a twirl of steam. The two children careered over the sand, clutching the bread, and burst through the iron gate and up the path through the garden in which nothing grew.

Passengers drew themselves in at the corridor windows and turned into compartments to fetch money, to call someone to look. Those sitting inside looked up: suddenly different, caged faces, boxed in, cut off, after the contact of outside.

There was an orange a piccanin would like. . . . What about that chocolate? It wasn't very nice. . . .

A young girl had collected a handful of the hard kind, that no one liked, out of the chocolate box, and was throwing them to the dogs, over at the dining car. But the hens darted in, and swallowed the chocolates, incredibly quick and accurate, before they had even dropped in the dust, and the dogs, a little bewildered, looked up with their brown eyes, not expecting anything.

—No, leave it, said the girl, don't take it. . . .

Too expensive, too much, she shook her head and raised her voice to the old boy, giving up the lion. He held it high where she had handed it to him. No, she said, shaking her head. Three-and-six?[4] insisted her husband, loudly. Yes baas! laughed the old man. Three-and-six? —The young man was incredulous. Oh leave it—she said. The young man stopped. Don't you want it? he said, keeping his face closed to the old man. No, never mind, she said, leave it. The old native kept his head on one side, looking at them sideways, holding the lion. Three-and-six, he murmured, as old people repeat things to themselves.

---

4. three-and-six three shillings and sixpence.

The young woman drew her head in. She went into the coupé[5] and sat down. Out of the window, on the other side, there was nothing; sand and bush; a thorn tree. Back through the open doorway, past the figure of her husband in the corridor, there was the station, the voices, wooden animals waving, running feet. Her eye followed the funny little valance of scrolled wood that outlined the chalet roof of the station; she thought of the lion and smiled. That bit of fur round the neck. But the wooden buck, the hippos, the elephants, the baskets that already bulked out of their brown paper under the seat and on the luggage rack! How will they look at home? Where will you put them? What will they mean away from the places you found them? Away from the unreality of the last few weeks? The young man outside. But he is not part of the unreality; he is for good now. Odd . . . somewhere there was an idea that he, that living with him, was part of the holiday, the strange places.

▲ **Critical Viewing**
How do the figures in this photo compare with the lion figurine described in the story? **[Compare and Contrast]**

Outside, a bell rang. The stationmaster was leaning against the end of the train, green flag rolled in readiness. A few men who had got down to stretch their legs sprang onto the train, clinging to the observation platforms, or perhaps merely standing on the iron step, holding the rail; but on the train, safe from the one dusty platform, the one tin house, the empty sand.

There was a grunt. The train jerked. Through the glass the beer drinkers looked out, as if they could not see beyond it. Behind the flyscreen, the stationmaster's wife sat facing back at them beneath the darkening hunk of meat.

There was a shout. The flag drooped out. Joints not yet coordinated, the segmented body of the train heaved and bumped back against itself. It began to move; slowly the scrolled chalet moved past it, the yells of the natives, running alongside, jetted up into the air, fell back at different levels. Staring wooden faces waved drunkenly, there, then gone, questioning for the last time at the windows. Here, one-and-six baas!—As one automatically opens a hand to catch a thrown ball, a man fumbled wildly down his pocket, brought up the shilling and sixpence and threw them out; the old native, gasping, his skinny toes splaying the sand, flung the lion.

The piccanins were waving, the dogs stood, tails uncertain, watching the train go: past the mud huts, where a woman turned to look, up from the smoke of the fire, her hand pausing on her hip.

The stationmaster went slowly in under the chalet.

The old native stood, breath blowing out the skin between his

Vocabulary
segmented (seg´ ment id) *adj.* divided into joined parts

Reading Check
Why does the girl decide to leave the lion?

---

5. coupé (kōō pā´) *n.* half-compartment at the end of a train, with seats on only one side.

The Train from Rhodesia **1345**

ribs, feet tense, balanced in the sand, smiling and shaking his head. In his opened palm, held in the attitude of receiving, was the retrieved shilling and sixpence.

The blind end of the train was being pulled helplessly out of the station.

The young man swung in from the corridor, breathless. He was shaking his head with laughter and triumph. Here! he said. And waggled the lion at her. One-and-six!

What? she said.

He laughed. I was arguing with him for fun, bargaining—when the train had pulled out already, he came tearing after. . . . One-and-six baas! So there's your lion.

She was holding it away from her, the head with the open jaws, the pointed teeth, the black tongue, the wonderful ruff of fur facing her. She was looking at it with an expression of not seeing, of seeing something different. Her face was drawn up, wryly, like the face of a discomforted child. Her mouth lifted nervously at the corner. Very slowly, cautious, she lifted her finger and touched the mane, where it was joined to the wood.

But how could you, she said. He was shocked by the dismay of her face.

Good Lord, he said, what's the matter?

If you wanted the thing, she said, her voice rising and breaking with the shrill impotence of anger, why didn't you buy it in the first place? If you wanted it, why didn't you pay for it?

Why didn't you take it decently, when he offered it? Why did you have to wait for him to run after the train with it, and give him one-and-six? One-and-six!

She was pushing it at him, trying to force him to take it. He stood astonished, his hands hanging at his sides.

But you wanted it! You liked it so much?

—It's a beautiful piece of work, she said fiercely, as if to protect it from him.

You liked it so much! You said yourself it was too expensive—

Oh you—she said, hopeless and furious. You. . . . She threw the lion onto the seat.

He stood looking at her.

She sat down again in the corner and, her face slumped in her hand, stared out of the window. Everything was turning around inside her. One-and-six. One-and-six. One-and-six for the wood and the carving and the sinews of the legs and the switch of the tail. The mouth open like that and the teeth. The black tongue, rolling, like a wave. The mane round the neck. To give one-and-six for that. The heat of shame mounted through her legs and body and sounded in her ears like the sound of sand pouring. Pouring, pouring. She sat there, sick. A weariness, a tastelessness, the discovery of a void made her hands slacken their grip, atrophy emptily, as if the hour was not worth their grasp. She was feeling like this again. She had thought it was something to do with singleness, with being alone and belonging too much to oneself.

THE TRAIN HAD CAST THE STATION *like a skin.*

She sat there not wanting to move or speak, or to look at anything, even; so that the mood should be associated with nothing,
no object, word or sight that might recur and so recall the feeling
again. . . . Smuts blew in grittily, settled on her hands. Her back
remained at exactly the same angle, turned against the young man
sitting with his hands drooping between his sprawled legs, and the
lion, fallen on its side in the corner.

The train had cast the station like a skin. It called out to the sky,
I'm coming, I'm coming; and again, there was no answer.

▲ **Critical Viewing**
How does the facial
expression of the woman in
the photo reflect the feelings
of the woman in the story?
[Connect]

Critical Reading

ⓒ 1. **Key Ideas and Details** **(a)** Who comes to meet the train from
Rhodesia? **(b) Infer:** What does the interaction between these
people and the passengers indicate about the story's theme?

ⓒ 2. **Key Ideas and Details** **(a) Analyze:** Why does the lion impress
the young woman? **(b) Interpret:** Why is the young woman
angry when her husband bargains for and obtains the lion at
a low price?

ⓒ 3. **Key Ideas and Details** **(a) Draw Conclusions:** What have the
husband and the wife discovered about each other by the end of
the story? **(b) Speculate:** How might their marriage fare, given this
episode? Explain.

ⓒ 4. **Integration of Knowledge and Ideas** What do you think the
train and the station symbolize in this story?

*Cite textual
evidence to
support your
responses.*

V. S. NAIPAUL

Author of "B. Wordsworth"

V. S. Naipaul, who grew up in Trinidad, has earned a reputation as a brilliant writer of fiction and nonfiction books about colonialism, exile, and issues of identity in the contemporary world. Although some writers have accused him of taking a snobbish attitude toward Third World cultures, he was awarded the Nobel Prize in Literature in 2001.

A "Many-Sided Background" Naipaul, whose family came from India, was born in Trinidad, then a part of the British West Indies. There, he grew up in the Hindu culture and attended British schools. These experiences, combined with living in England and traveling all over the world, make up what Naipaul calls his "many-sided background."

In his book of autobiographical writings, *Finding the Center: Two Narratives* (1984), Naipaul recounts how his grandfather came to Trinidad as an indentured laborer. The terms of indenture were not always strictly followed, and members of the Indian community faced many frustrations as a result. The next generation fared somewhat better; Naipaul's father became a popular journalist with the main Trinidadian newspaper.

Explorations in Writing Even as a student, Naipaul shared his father's talent for writing, and he won a scholarship to Oxford University. While in his final year there, he learned that his father had died. Naipaul's family wanted him to return to Trinidad, but he decided to remain in Britain. He soon found work in London writing about the West Indies for radio.

Far from home, he began to write stories that drew on his memories of Trinidad. Those early stories, including "B. Wordsworth," were eventually collected in *Miguel Street* (1959). In these tales, a young narrator describes the comic and absurd elements of growing up in the West Indies. To gain a full perspective of the community, he created a "narrator more in tune with the life of the street than I had been."

"Fiction Never Lies" *A House for Mr. Biswas* (1961) combines the comic perspective of his early tales with poignant and universal themes to tell the story of a man similar to his father. Naipaul returned to his own youth in the novelistic memoir *A Way in the World* (1994). In justifying his choice of fictional accounts over autobiography, Naipaul explains that "an autobiography can distort, facts can be realigned. But fiction never lies. It reveals the writer totally."

1348 A Time of Rapid Change (1901–Present)

B. WORDSWORTH

V.S. NAIPAUL

BACKGROUND THIS STORY IS SET IN TRINIDAD, PROBABLY IN THE 1940S. TRINIDAD, WHICH BECAME INDEPENDENT IN 1962, HAD BEEN A BRITISH COLONY SINCE 1802. FROM 1845 TO 1917, IT RECEIVED INDENTURED WORKERS EMIGRATING FROM INDIA. NAIPAUL'S GRANDFATHER HAD BEEN SUCH A WORKER, BORROWING MONEY FOR PASSAGE AND LABORING FOR YEARS TO PAY OFF THE DEBT. WITH A DIVERSE POPULATION AND WITH THE CULTURE OF BRITAIN, THE COLONIAL POWER, HELD UP AS "SUPERIOR," CULTURAL IDENTITY AND NAMES WERE KEY ISSUES IN TRINIDAD.

Three beggars called punctually every day at the hospitable houses in Miguel Street. At about ten an Indian came in his dhoti[1] and white jacket, and we poured a tin of rice into the sack he carried on his back. At twelve an old woman smoking a clay pipe came and she got a cent. At two a blind man led by a boy called for his penny.

▲ Critical Viewing
What does this picture reveal about a Caribbean setting? **[Infer]**

---

1. dhoti (dō´ tē) traditional loincloth worn by Hindu men.

"I WANT TO WATCH YOUR BEES."

Sometimes we had a rogue.[2] One day a man called and said he was hungry. We gave him a meal. He asked for a cigarette and wouldn't go until we had lit it for him. That man never came again.

The strangest caller came one afternoon at about four o'clock. I had come back from school and was in my home-clothes. The man said to me, "Sonny, may I come inside your yard?"

He was a small man and he was tidily dressed. He wore a hat, a white shirt and black trousers.

I asked, "What you want?"

He said, "I want to watch your bees."

We had four small gru-gru palm trees[3] and they were full of uninvited bees.

I ran up the steps and shouted, "Ma, it have a man outside here. He say he want to watch the bees."

My mother came out, looked at the man and asked in an unfriendly way, "What you want?"

The man said, "I want to watch your bees."

His English was so good, it didn't sound natural, and I could see my mother was worried.

She said to me, "Stay here and watch him while he watch the bees."

The man said, "Thank you, Madam. You have done a good deed today."

He spoke very slowly and very correctly as though every word was costing him money.

We watched the bees, this man and I, for about an hour, squatting near the palm trees.

The man said, "I like watching bees. Sonny, do you like watching bees?"

I said, "I ain't have the time."

He shook his head sadly. He said, "That's what I do, I just watch. I can watch ants for days. Have you ever watched ants? And scorpions, and centipedes, and congorees[4]—have you watched those?"

I shook my head.

I said, "What you does do, mister?"

He got up and said, "I am a poet."

I said, "A good poet?"

He said, "The greatest in the world."

"What your name, mister?"

"B. Wordsworth."

"B for Bill?"

"Black. Black Wordsworth. White Wordsworth[5] was my brother.

Literary Analysis
Historical Period and Setting
What does the regular appearance of the beggars suggest about social conditions at this time?

Spiral Review
Characterization
What do B. Wordsworth's claims establish about his character?

---

2. **rogue** (rōg) *n.* wandering beggar or tramp; scoundrel.
3. **gru-gru** (grōō′ grōō′) **palm trees** West Indian palms that yield edible nuts.
4. **congorees** (kän′ gər ēz) Conger or Congo eels; large, scaleless eels found in the warm waters of the West Indies.
5. **White Wordsworth** English Romantic poet William Wordsworth (1770–1850).

We share one heart. I can watch a small flower like the morning glory and cry."

I said, "Why you does cry?"

"Why, boy? Why? You will know when you grow up. You're a poet, too, you know. And when you're a poet you can cry for everything."

I couldn't laugh.

He said, "You like your mother?"

"When she not beating me."

He pulled out a printed sheet from his hip-pocket and said, "On this paper is the greatest poem about mothers and I'm going to sell it to you at a bargain price. For four cents."

I went inside and I said, "Ma, you want buy a poetry for four cents?"

My mother said, "Tell that blasted man I haul his tail away from my yard, you hear."

I said to B. Wordsworth, "My mother say she ain't have four cents."

B. Wordsworth said, "It is the poet's tragedy."

And he put the paper back in his pocket. He didn't seem to mind.

I said, "Is a funny way to go round selling poetry like that. Only calypsonians[6] do that sort of thing. A lot of people does buy?"

He said, "No one has yet bought a single copy."

"But why you does keep on going round, then?"

He said, "In this way I watch many things, and I always hope to meet poets."

I said, "You really think I is a poet?"

"You're as good as me," he said.

And when B. Wordsworth left, I prayed I would see him again.

About a week later, coming back from school one afternoon, I met him at the corner of Miguel Street.

He said, "I have been waiting for you for a long time."

I said, "You sell any poetry yet?"

He shook his head.

He said, "In my yard I have the best mango tree in Port-of-Spain.[7] And now the mangoes are ripe and red and very sweet and juicy. I have waited here for you to tell you this and to invite you to come and eat some of my mangoes."

He lived in Alberto Street in a one-roomed hut placed right in the center of the lot. The yard seemed all green. There was the

Reading Strategy
Apply Background Knowledge Based on what you know of Romantic poets, what quality of William Wordsworth does B. Wordsworth especially admire?

Literary Analysis
Historical Period and Setting How does background information about calypsonians clarify B. Wordsworth's profession?

Reading Check

How does the narrator meet B. Wordsworth?

---

6. **calypsonians** (kə lip sō′ nē ənz) those who sing calypso songs; the characteristic satirical street singers of Trinidad.
7. **Port-of-Spain** seaport capital of Trinidad and Tobago.

big mango tree. There was a coconut tree and there was a plum tree. The place looked wild, as though it wasn't in the city at all. You couldn't see all the big concrete houses in the street.

He was right. The mangoes were sweet and juicy. I ate about six, and the yellow mango juice ran down my arms to my elbows and down my mouth to my chin and my shirt was stained.

My mother said when I got home, "Where you was? You think you is a man now and could go all over the place? Go cut a whip for me."

She beat me rather badly, and I ran out of the house swearing that I would never come back. I went to B. Wordsworth's house. I was so angry, my nose was bleeding.

B. Wordsworth said, "Stop crying, and we will go for a walk."

I stopped crying, but I was breathing short. We went for a walk. We walked down St. Clair Avenue to the Savannah and we walked to the race-course.

B. Wordsworth said, "Now, let us lie on the grass and look up at the sky, and I want you to think how far those stars are from us."

I did as he told me, and I saw what he meant. I felt like nothing, and at the same time I had never felt so big and great in all my life. I forgot all my anger and all my tears and all the blows.

When I said I was better, he began telling me the names of the stars, and I particularly remembered the constellation of Orion the Hunter,[8] though I don't really know why. I can spot Orion even today, but I have forgotten the rest.

Then a light was flashed into our faces, and we saw a policeman. We got up from the grass.

The policeman said, "What you doing here?"

B. Wordsworth said, "I have been asking myself the same question for forty years."

We became friends, B. Wordsworth and I. He told me, "You must never tell anybody about me and about the mango tree and the coconut tree and the plum tree. You must keep that a secret. If you tell anybody, I will know, because I am a poet."

I gave him my word and I kept it.

I liked his little room. It had no more furniture than George's front room,[9] but it looked cleaner and healthier. But it also looked lonely.

One day I asked him, "Mister Wordsworth, why you does keep

Literary Analysis
Historical Period, Setting, and Characterization
What does the wild array of trees suggest about B. Wordsworth's character?

Reading Strategy
Apply Background Knowledge Explain how B. Wordsworth's knowledge of the names of the stars links him with poets of the past.

---

8. **constellation of Orion** (ō rī´ ən) **the Hunter** group of stars named after a mythological giant who was killed accidentally by the goddess of hunting, Diana.
9. **George's front room** George is a character in one of the companion stories in Naipaul's book, *Miguel Street.*

all this bush in your yard? Ain't it does make the place damp?"

He said, "Listen, and I will tell you a story. Once upon a time a boy and girl met each other and they fell in love. They loved each other so much they got married. They were both poets. He loved words. She loved grass and flowers and trees. They lived happily in a single room, and then one day, the girl poet said to the boy poet, 'We are going to have another poet in the family.' But this poet was never born, because the girl died, and the young poet died with her, inside her. And the girl's husband was very sad, and he said he would never touch a thing in the girl's garden. And so the garden remained, and grew high and wild."

I looked at B. Wordsworth, and as he told me this lovely story, he seemed to grow older. I understood his story.

We went for long walks together. We went to the Botanical Gardens and the Rock Gardens. We climbed Chancellor Hill in the late afternoon and watched the darkness fall on Port-of-Spain, and watched the lights go on in the city and on the ships in the harbor.

He did everything as though he were doing it for the first time in his life. He did everything as though he were doing some church rite.

He would say to me, "Now, how about having some ice cream?"

And when I said, yes, he would grow very serious and say, "Now, which café shall we patronize?" As though it were a very important thing. He would think for some time about it, and finally say, "I think I will go and negotiate the purchase with that shop."

The world became a most exciting place.

One day, when I was in his yard, he said to me, "I have a great secret which I am now going to tell you."

I said, "It really secret?"

"At the moment, yes."

I looked at him, and he looked at me. He said, "This is just between you and me, remember. I am writing a poem."

"Oh." I was disappointed.

He said, "But this is a different sort of poem. This is the greatest poem in the world."

I whistled.

He said, "I have been working on it for more than five years now. I will finish it in about twenty-two years from now, that is, if I keep on writing at the present rate."

"You does write a lot, then?"

He said, "Not any more. I just write one line a month. But I make sure it is a good line."

I asked, "What was last month's good line?"

He looked up at the sky, and said, *"The past is deep."*

I said, "It is a beautiful line."

B. Wordsworth said, "I hope to distill the experiences of a

Reading Strategy

Apply Background Knowledge Based on folk tales and fairy tales you know, how does B. Wordsworth deliberately make his story sound like an ancient tale?

Vocabulary

patronize (pā´ trən īz) *v.* to be a customer of a particular merchant or store

distill (di stil´) *v.* to obtain the essential part

Reading Check

What does B. Wordsworth do when the narrator, angry and crying, comes to see him?

Politics and Fiction

Because V. S. Naipaul's stories and novels examine how characters are affected by their societies, they are sometimes described as political fiction. The tradition of fiction that addresses political and social issues is a long one. British writer Thomas More published one of the first political novels, *Utopia,* in 1516. Eighteenth-century French writer Voltaire wrote *Candide,* one of the most famous political satires of all time. Russian author Leo Tolstoy took on Napoleon's invasion of Russia in *War and Peace,* and in the 1920s Franz Kafka addressed the issue of nightmarish government bureaucracies in *The Trial.*

More recently, novels by Latin American and Caribbean authors, including Juan Rulfo, Jacques Roumain, Carlos Fuentes, Isabel Allende, Julia Alvarez, and Edwidge Danticat, have dealt with political upheavals in their countries. Fiction by Chinua Achebe, Nadine Gordimer, and Ngugi wa Thiong'o has responded to the political turmoil of the African continent. Novels by Naguib Mahfouz, Ahdah Soueif, Anton Shammas, and Amos Oz speak about society in the Middle East.

Connect to the Literature

In what way does "B. Wordsworth" raise political or social questions?

Vocabulary

keenly (kēn´ lē)
adv. sharply; intensely

whole month into that single line of poetry. So, in twenty-two years, I shall have written a poem that will sing to all humanity."

I was filled with wonder.

Our walks continued. We walked along the sea-wall at Docksite one day, and I said, "Mr. Wordsworth, if I drop this pin in the water, you think it will float?"

He said, "This is a strange world. Drop your pin, and let us see what will happen."

The pin sank.

I said, "How is the poem this month?"

But he never told me any other line. He merely said, "Oh, it comes, you know. It comes."

Or we would sit on the sea-wall and watch the liners come into the harbor.

But of the greatest poem in the world I heard no more.

I felt he was growing older.

"How you does live, Mr. Wordsworth?" I asked him one day.

He said, "You mean how I get money?"

When I nodded, he laughed in a crooked way.

He said, "I sing calypsoes in the calypso season."

"And that last you the rest of the year?"

"It is enough."

"But you will be the richest man in the world when you write the greatest poem?"

He didn't reply.

One day when I went to see him in his little house, I found him lying on his little bed. He looked so old and so weak, that I found myself wanting to cry.

He said, "The poem is not going well."

He wasn't looking at me. He was looking through the window at the coconut tree, and he was speaking as though I wasn't there. He said, "When I was twenty I felt the power within myself." Then, almost in front of my eyes, I could see his face growing older and more tired. He said, "But that—that was a long time ago."

And then—I felt it so keenly, it was as though I had been slapped by my mother. I could see it clearly on his face. It was there for everyone to see. Death on the shrinking face.

He looked at me, and saw my tears and sat up.

He said, "Come." I went and sat on his knees.

He looked into my eyes, and he said, "Oh, you can see it, too. I always knew you had the poet's eye."

He didn't even look sad, and that made me burst out crying loudly.

He pulled me to his thin chest, and said, "Do you want me to tell you a funny story?" and he smiled encouragingly at me.

But I couldn't reply.

He said, "When I have finished this story, I want you to promise that you will go away and never come back to see me. Do you promise?"

I nodded.

He said, "Good. Well, listen. That story I told you about the boy poet and the girl poet, do you remember that? That wasn't true. It was something I just made up. All this talk about poetry and the greatest poem in the world, that wasn't true, either. Isn't that the funniest thing you have heard?"

But his voice broke.

I left the house, and ran home crying, like a poet, for everything I saw.

I walked along Alberto Street a year later, but I could find no sign of the poet's house. It hadn't vanished, just like that. It had been pulled down, and a big, two-storied building had taken its place. The mango tree and the plum tree and the coconut tree had all been cut down, and there was brick and concrete everywhere.

It was just as though B. Wordsworth had never existed.

"I WANT YOU TO PROMISE THAT YOU WILL GO AWAY AND NEVER COME BACK TO SEE ME."

Critical Reading

Cite textual evidence to support your responses.

1. **Key Ideas and Details (a)** What reason does B. Wordsworth give for wanting to come into the boy's yard? **(b) Compare and Contrast:** How is B. Wordsworth different from the other visitors who are described?

2. **Key Ideas and Details** What does B. Wordsworth mean when he calls the boy "a poet"?

3. **Key Ideas and Details** B. Wordsworth "did everything as though he were doing it for the first time." In what way does this help make B. Wordsworth "a poet"?

4. **Key Ideas and Details (a) Infer:** What do you think B. Wordsworth's motivation is for spending time with the boy? **(b) Draw Conclusions:** What does the boy gain from knowing B. Wordsworth?

5. **Integration of Knowledge and Ideas** Does B. Wordsworth's name reflect the harmful effects of colonialism on the identity of colonized peoples? Explain, using at least two of these Essential Question words: *authenticity, inherent, identity, influence.* *[Connecting to the Essential Question: What is the relationship between literature and place?]*

Literary Analysis

**Common Core
State Standards**

1. Key Ideas and Details Gordimer and Naipaul use works of art (a carving, a poem) to show how **colonialism** affected people's values. Use a graphic organizer to compare the values placed on the carving in "The Train from Rhodesia" and the poem in "B. Wordsworth."

Carving	Value to Carver	Value to Husband	Value to Wife
Poem	Value to Poet	Value to Townspeople	Value to Boy

2. Integration of Knowledge and Ideas The carving is purchased cheaply and thrown into a corner. The poem of B. Wordsworth is stunted and never even comes into being. What do the fates of these objects say about colonialism?

3. Craft and Structure In "The Train from Rhodesia," the train itself is a major element of the *setting*. How might Gordimer be using "the segmented body of the train" to make a comment about colonialism?

4. Integration of Knowledge and Ideas Explain how the internal **conflict** experienced by the wife in "The Train from Rhodesia" reflects the external conflict created by colonialism and apartheid.

5. Integration of Knowledge and Ideas The *characterization* of B. Wordsworth presents him as a man who lives in two worlds, British and Trinidadian. Do you think this aspect of colonialism helped or hindered his development as a poet? Explain.

6. Analyze Visual Information What qualities of Naipaul does the caricature of him on this page emphasize?

Writing
3. Write narratives to develop real or imagined experiences or events using effective technique, well-chosen details, and well-structured event sequences. *(p. 1357)*

3.d. Use precise words and phrases, telling details, and sensory language to convey a vivid picture of the experiences, events, setting, and/or characters. *(p. 1357)*

Language
4.b. Identify and correctly use patterns of word changes that indicate different meanings or parts of speech. *(p. 1357)*

Reading Strategy

7. In "The Train from Rhodesia," the husband manifests historical European assumptions about the colonial situation. Explain how the wife, by contrast, represents a twentieth-century sensibility.

8. William Wordsworth was a prolific writer who produced thousands of pages of lyric, narrative, and autobiographical poems. In Naipaul's story, B. Wordsworth is barely able to write one line per month. When you **apply this background knowledge,** what comment do you think Naipaul is making?

9. (a) Based on these two stories and your knowledge of history, which aspect of colonialism was most harmful to colonized people? **(b)** Was any aspect of colonialism positive? Explain.

10. Based on these two stories and your background knowledge, what important lessons do you think the nations of the world have learned about the relationships of colonized and colonizing peoples?

▼ David Levine caricature of V. S.Naipaul, Nov. 1, 2001.
http://www.nybooks.com/gallery/1851

Integrated Language Skills

Ⓔ Vocabulary Acquisition and Use

Word Analysis: Patterns of Word Changes

Words often follow patterns as they change in function and in meaning. The word *patron*, for example, comes from a Latin root meaning "protector," "defender," or "father." Its various forms reflect these meanings.

- A *patron* (noun) of the arts is someone wealthy who supports artists.
- To *patronize* (verb) is to be kind but snobbish. *Patronize* also means to shop regularly in a particular store.
- *Patronage* (noun) is the power to grant political jobs or favors. *Patronage* also means business that customers give a store.

Complete each sentence using one of the following words: *patron, patronize, patronage*.

1. Some believe that _____ leads to corruption in politics.
2. A _____ of the arts, she gave generously to the orchestra.
3. I always _____ that vegetable market.

Vocabulary: Analogies

Analogies show the relationships between pairs of words. Complete each analogy using a word from the vocabulary list on page 1340. In each, your choice should create a word pair that matches the relationship between the first two words given. Then, explain your answers.

1. impressionistic : scientific :: subjective :
   a. objective   **b.** perspective   **c.** effective
   d. ineffective
2. segmented : separated :: fulfilled :
   a. abandoned   **b.** emptied   **c.** satisfied
   d. split
3. atrophy : develop :: grow :
   a. invest   **b.** decay   **c.** mature   **d.** enlarge
4. patronize : patron :: advertise :
   a. store   **b.** product   **c.** customer   **d.** advertiser
5. distill : dilute :: destroy :
   a. create   **b.** smash   **c.** distribute   **d.** invent
6. keenly : intensely :: boldly :
   a. beautifully   **b.** cowardly   **c.** bravely
   d. awkwardly

Writing

Ⓔ **Narrative Text** The narrator of Naipaul's story will never forget the remarkable B. Wordsworth. Write a **biographical sketch** of a remarkable person you have known or met, using yourself as a first-person narrator.

Prewriting Jot down the traits that make your subject remarkable. Select a scene or an event that reveals this person's memorable personality.

Drafting As a first-person narrator, write an account of the scene. Like Naipaul, characterize your subject using your reactions and your subject's specific actions and words. Communicate the signficance of the scene or event to your audience.

Model: Revising to Add Precise Details as Support

resonant   lilting
Mrs. Walcott's ̲pleasant voice and ̲Jamaican accent made
̲like a melody. On that occasion, she declared,
"Hear the sounds behind the sounds."
everything she said sound ̲true.

The writer replaces vague language with precise adjectives and a simile and adds a vivid quotation.

Revising Review your account to replace vague adjectives with precise ones and add dialogue that conveys the flavor of the subject's personality.

Connecting to the Essential Question Historical, political, and cultural events—important ones and trivial ones—can become part of tradition. As you read, notice historical events mentioned in the poems. These events will help you think about the Essential Question: **What is the relationship of the writer to tradition?**

Literary Analysis

It is important to analyze the clarity and consistency of political assumptions in a work of literature. You may, for example, apply a **political critique** to Derek Walcott's exploration of literary tradition. A political critique examines political influences and implications in a work of art, raising questions such as these:

- What political events have influenced a work of art?
- What political beliefs affect the writer's attitudes?
- Who "owns" a work of art?
- Who has the right to judge a work of art?
- What political or cultural experience must people have in order to appreciate a work of art?

Walcott's poems include **allusions**—references to persons, places, events, and artworks—that may help readers apply a political critique. Allusions use the past to gain perspective on the present. An allusion often implies that the writer and the reader "own" a common culture by jointly participating in it. Interpreting an allusion in a specific part of a poem helps you understand the meaning of the entire work.

Reading Strategy

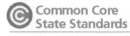 **Preparing to Read Complex Texts** Sometimes you can **repair comprehension by understanding allusions.** To understand Walcott's responses in *Midsummer,* you need to know that the Brixton riots erupted in London among Caribbean immigrants. You might find such information in footnotes, side glosses, background features, reference books, or the Internet. Use a chart like the one shown.

Vocabulary

antic (an´ tik) *adj.* odd and funny; silly (p. 1361)

rancor (raŋ´ kər) *n.* continuing, bitter hate or ill will (p. 1361)

eclipse (i klips´) *n.* dimming or extinction of power or glory (p. 1361)

inducted (in duk´ tid) *v.* brought formally into an organization (p. 1361)

Common Core State Standards

Reading Literature
3. Analyze the impact of the author's choices regarding how to develop and relate elements of a story or drama.

Passage

…a Brixton riot tunneled by water hoses;…

Background Information

Residents of the South London district of Brixton rioted in April 1981.

Interpretation

"Tunneled by water hoses": The police sprayed rioters with high-pressure water from firehoses to disperse them.

PHLit
Online!
www.PHLitOnline.com

Derek Walcott

(b. 1930)

Author of *Midsummer*, XXIII • *Omeros*, Chapter XXVIII

Derek Walcott, one of the most renowned contemporary poets writing in English, has roots in two worlds. Both of his grandmothers were descendants of enslaved Africans, and both of his grandfathers were white colonials. He owes allegiance to his own rich native traditions, which can be traced back to African sources, yet he is also drawn to Western traditions that hearken back to ancient Greece. These foundations support the contexts of his poems, which carry a reader from Tropical Trinidad to ancient Greece to Shakespeare's England.

Early Poetry Walcott was born on the Caribbean Island of St. Lucia, where he spoke both the island dialect and English. He graduated from the University of the West Indies. Precocious and prolific, eighteen-year-old Walcott published the first of his many volumes of poetry, *Twenty-five Poems*, by using two hundred dollars that he borrowed, to print and distribute it on the street.

In 1959, Walcott, also an accomplished playwright, founded the Trinidad Theatre Workshop with his twin brother, Roderick. In his dramatic works, he explores his Caribbean roots more deeply than he does in his poetry. His play *Dream on Monkey Mountain*, a folk drama, won an Obie in 1971. More recently, Walcott collaborated with songwriter and composer Paul Simon on a Broadway musical, *The Capeman* (1997).

High Honors Walcott's 1990 book *Omeros*, which draws on the epics of the ancient Greek poet Homer, ensured him the Nobel Prize for Literature in 1992, making Walcott the first native Caribbean writer ever to win a Nobel Prize for literature. The Swedish Academy, when granting the award, concluded that "West Indian culture has found its great poet."

> **"**
> I come
> from
> a place
> that
> likes
> grandeur.
> **"**

from Midsummer XXIII

Derek Walcott

▲ Critical Viewing
What can you tell from
this photo about the mood
surrounding the Brixton
riots? [Draw Conclusions]

Literary Analysis
**Political Critique of
Art** Explain how Walcott's
mix of images—lemmings,
leaves, chains, whips—
suggests his mixed feelings
and divided loyalties.

BACKGROUND In colonial times, British settlers brought
enslaved Africans to work on their plantations in the West Indies.
These slaves were freed in the 1830s, and in the 1960s and
1970s, the islands won their independence. Many present-day
West Indians have emigrated to Britain in search of opportunity,
only to encounter prejudice and hardships. Their frustrations
erupted in the April 1981 riots in the neighborhood of Brixton,
London, to which Walcott reacts in "Midsummer, XXIII."

With the stampeding hiss and scurry of green lemmings,
midsummer's leaves race to extinction like the roar
of a Brixton riot tunneled by water hoses;
they seethe towards autumn's fire—it is in their nature,
5 being men as well as leaves, to die for the sun.
The leaf stems tug at their chains, the branches bending
like Boer cattle under Tory whips that drag every wagon
nearer to apartheid.[1] And, for me, that closes

---

1. **Boer** (bör) **cattle . . . apartheid** In the 1600s, the Boers, people of Dutch descent, colonized South Africa, where apartheid (racial segregation) was later practiced. The Tories
   held power in Britain when it won control of South Africa in the Boer War (1899–1902).

the child's fairy tale of an antic England—fairy rings,
10   thatched cottages fenced with dog roses,
a green gale lifting the hair of Warwickshire.
I was there to add some color to the British theater.
"But the blacks can't do Shakespeare, they have no experience."
This was true. Their thick skulls bled with rancor
15   when the riot police and the skinheads exchanged quips
you could trace to the Sonnets,[2] or the Moor's eclipse.[3]
Praise had bled my lines white of any more anger,
and snow had inducted me into white fellowships,
while Calibans[4] howled down the barred streets of an empire
20   that began with Caedmon's raceless dew,[5] and is ending
in the alleys of Brixton, burning like Turner's ships.[6]

---

2. **the Sonnets** William Shakespeare's sequence of 154 sonnets, noted for their passionate, often witty inquiries into love and rivalry.

3. **the Moor's eclipse** In Shakespeare's *Othello,* Othello the Moor (a black North African) is destroyed by the scheming of his white lieutenant, Iago.

4. **Calibans** Caliban is a deformed creature in Shakespeare's play *The Tempest.* Enslaved by the enchanter Prospero, Caliban has been interpreted as a native who rebels against his island's "colonizer," Prospero.

5. **Caedmon's** (kad´ mənz) **raceless dew** poetry written by the earliest known English poet, Caedmon (seventh century).

6. **Turner's ships** British artist J. M. W. Turner (1775–1851) rendered atmospheric oil paintings of, among other subjects, ships burning in battle.

Vocabulary

antic (an´ tik) *adj.* odd and funny; silly

rancor (raŋ´ kər) *n.* continuing, bitter hate or ill will

eclipse (i klips´) *n.* dimming or extinction of power or glory

inducted (in dukt´ id) *v.* brought formally into an organization

Reading Strategy

Repair Comprehension by Understanding Allusions Some of Turner's paintings showed ships that carried slaves. How does this information help explain Walcott's final sentence?

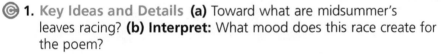

Critical Reading

1. **Key Ideas and Details (a)** Toward what are midsummer's leaves racing? **(b) Interpret:** What mood does this race create for the poem?

2. **Key Ideas and Details (a)** What event "closes" for the speaker "the child's fairy tale of an antic England"? **(b) Infer:** Why is this event disillusioning? **(c) Connect:** Why does Walcott's reason for being in England at the time make the event especially significant for him?

3. **Key Ideas and Details (a) Draw Conclusions:** What does the speaker mean when he says that the "empire / . . . is ending / in the alleys of Brixton"? **(b) Connect:** What common idea or pattern connects the midsummer leaves, Walcott's disillusionment, and the crisis in England?

4. **Integration of Knowledge and Ideas** Judging by the poem, has Walcott come to terms with belonging to both black and white traditions? Explain.

5. **Integration of Knowledge and Ideas** Do you think black artists such as Walcott should withdraw from "white fellowships" to protest racial injustices? Explain.

Cite textual evidence to support your responses.

▲ **Critical Viewing**
How is this picture, painted by Walcott himself, similar or different from images evoked in the poem? **[Compare and Contrast]**

from Omeros

from CHAPTER XXVIII

Derek Walcott

Now he heard the griot[1] muttering his prophetic song
of sorrow that would be the past. It was a note, long-drawn
and endless in its winding like the brown river's tongue:

"We were the color of shadows when we came down
5 with tinkling leg-irons to join the chains of the sea,
for the silver coins multiplying on the sold horizon,

and these shadows are reprinted now on the white sand
of antipodal[2] coasts, your ashen ancestors
from the Bight of Benin, from the margin of Guinea.[3]

10 There were seeds in our stomachs, in the cracking pods
of our skulls on the scorching decks, the tubers[4]
withered in no time. We watched as the river-gods

changed from snakes into currents. When inspected,
our eyes showed dried fronds[5] in their brown irises,
15 and from our curved spines, the rib-cages radiated

like fronds from a palm-branch. Then, when the dead
palms were heaved overside, the ribbed corpses
floated, riding, to the white sand they remembered,

Literary Analysis
Political Critique of Art What political assumption is Walcott making by featuring the song of the griot?

Reading Check
To what does the griot compare the enslaved people?

---

1. **griot** (grē′ ō) *n.* in West African cultures, a poet/historian/performer who preserves and passes on the oral tradition.
2. **antipodal** (an tip′ ə dəl) *adj.* situated on opposite sides of the earth.
3. **the Bight** (bīt) **of Benin** (be nēn′) . . . **Guinea** (gin′ ē) area of west central Africa that came to be known as the Slave Coast.
4. **tubers** (tōōb′ ərz) *n.* thick, fleshy parts of underground stems, such as potatoes.
5. **fronds** (frändz) *n.* leaves of a palm; also the leaflike parts of seaweed.

to the Bight of Benin, to the margin of Guinea.
20   So, when you see burnt branches riding the swell,
     trying to reclaim the surf through crooked fingers,

after a night of rough wind by some stone-white hotel,
past the bright triangular passage of the windsurfers,
remember us to the black waiter bringing the bill."

25   But they crossed, they survived. There is the epical splendor.
     Multiply the rain's lances, multiply their ruin,
     the grace born from subtraction as the hold's iron door

rolled over their eyes like pots left out in the rain,
and the bolt rammed home its echo, the way that thunder-
30   claps perpetuate their reverberation.

So there went the Ashanti one way, the Mandingo another,
the Ibo another, the Guinea.[6] Now each man was a nation
in himself, without mother, father, brother.

---

6. **the Ashanti** (ə shan′ tī) . . . **the Mandingo** (man din′ gō) . . . **the Ibo** (ē′ bō′) . . . **the Guinea** (gin′ ē) names of West African peoples.

Critical Reading

Cite textual evidence to support your responses.

1. **Key Ideas and Details (a)** What event does the griot describe? **(b) Analyze:** How does the griot use plant imagery to link past and present?

2. **Key Ideas and Details (a)** What happens to members of the different West African peoples once they are brought across the sea? **(b) Interpret:** What does Walcott mean when he says, "Now each man was a nation / in himself"?

3. **Integration of Knowledge and Ideas** In this excerpt, does Walcott pass too quickly over the suffering inflicted by the slave trade? Explain.

4. **Integration of Knowledge and Ideas** Does Walcott effectively use traditions to address current controversies? Explain. In your response, use at least two of these Essential Question words: *origins, endurance, situation.* [*Connecting to the Essential Question: What is the relationship of the writer to tradition?*]

Literary Analysis

Common Core State Standards

1. Integration of Knowledge and Ideas Apply a **political critique** to Walcott's poems. First, identify their political stances, such as interpretations of history and individual actions. Then evaluate those stances for clarity, consistency, and reasonableness. Use a graphic organizer like the one shown.

Stance on...	Clarity	Consistency	Reasonableness
Slavery:			
Brixton Riot:			
Participating in Theater:			

2. Integration of Knowledge and Ideas In *Omeros*, Walcott makes the assumption that Homer, part of the European tradition, can be incorporated into the West Indian tradition. In what sense might a great artist of the past belong to everyone?

Writing
7. Conduct short as well as more sustained research projects to answer a question or solve a problem.

Reading Strategy

3. In *Midsummer, XXIII*, how does **repairing your comprehension by understanding the allusion** to Caliban help you to appreciate Walcott's deeply mixed feelings about the Brixton riots?

PERFORMANCE TASKS
Integrated Language Skills

Vocabulary Acquisition and Use

Select the letter of the word that is a synonym for each of the words on the vocabulary list on page 1358.

1. antic: (a) oppositional **(b)** dangerous **(c)** disappointing **(d)** zany

2. rancor: (a) joyfulness **(b)** musicality **(c)** hatred **(d)** frustration

3. eclipse: (a) outburst **(b)** conflagration **(c)** extinction **(d)** omission

4. inducted: (a) anticipated **(b)** initiated **(c)** concluded **(d)** generalized

Writing

Informative Text Walcott's poems conjure up scenes. Plan a **multimedia presentation** of one of his poems. Identify print and nonprint media you would use to present the poem's images, speakers, rhythms, and language. Once you have organized your selected media, write responses to these questions:

- How would the media bring out qualities the poem possesses?
- What new qualities would the media add to the poem?
- How would the media help an audience to appreciate the poem?

Connecting to the Essential Question Seamus Heaney and Eavan Boland accept that the past is always reappearing in our lives. As you read, notice details in the poems that show how the past can still be present. These details will help you think about the Essential Question: **How does literature shape or reflect society?**

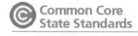

Common Core State Standards

Reading Literature
4. Analyze the impact of specific word choices on meaning and tone, including words with multiple meanings or language that is particularly fresh, engaging, or beautiful.

Literary Analysis

To create a literary work, a writer makes choices about diction and style.

- **Diction** is a writer's typical choice of words—formal or informal, abstract or concrete, scholarly or folksy.
- **Style** encompasses a writer's whole manner of expression. It includes word choice, forms, rhythms, themes, and imagery.

A poem is a work in words, and style and diction—both formed from patterns of words—are crucial to the meaning and tone of a poem. As you read, identify the characteristics of Heaney's and Boland's styles.

One element of Heaney's style is his frequent use of traditional forms. "Two Lorries," for example, is a **sestina,** an old French form consisting of six six-line stanzas and a final stanza of three lines. The end words of each of the first six stanzas are the same but are arranged differently in each stanza. All six end words also reappear in the final stanza. As you read, consider how this form adds to the effect of the poem.

Reading Strategy

Passage

I wanted to grow up and plow,
To close one eye, stiffen my arm.
All I ever did was follow
In his broad shadow
round the farm.

↓

Main Points

Son following his father; looking up to him; wanting to be like him.

↓

Summary

I wanted to be a farmer, like my father.

Preparing to Read Complex Texts To *determine the main idea* of a poem, it can be helpful to **summarize** it. Summarizing is restating key points in brief. Use a chart like the one shown to summarize the poems or individual stanzas in them.

Vocabulary

furrow (fur′ ō) *n.* narrow groove made in the ground by a plow (p. 1369)

nuisance (nōō′ səns) *n.* act, thing, or condition causing trouble (p. 1369)

inklings (iŋk′ liŋz) *n.* indirect suggestions; vague ideas (p. 1374)

mortal (môr′ təl) *adj.* of that which must eventually die (p. 1375)

ordeal (ôr dēl′) *n.* difficult or painful experience that tests one (p. 1375)

www.PHLitOnline.com

Author of "Follower" • "Two Lorries"

Born in County Derry, Northern Ireland, Seamus Heaney has devoted much of his poetry to the life and history of his homeland. He is a gifted traditionalist whom the American poet Robert Lowell called "the most important Irish poet since Yeats." Heaney has earned that high praise with visionary books of poetry, like *Seeing Things* (1991) and *The Spirit Level* (1996), and with his brilliant lectures on poetry, collected in *The Redress of Poetry* (1995).

A Happy Childhood The eldest of nine children, Heaney spent a happy childhood on a farm that had been in his family for generations. He has said that his deep regard for tradition grew from his early experiences in the countryside.

Leaving Home Heaney first published as an undergraduate at Queen's University in Belfast, Northern Ireland. In 1972, having struggled with the role of the artist in Northern Ireland's troubled political climate, he left and settled in the independent Irish Republic. His departure was called an artistic necessity by some and by others a betrayal. Heaney nevertheless remains the leading Irish poet—Republican or Northern.

Popular Success Heaney's accessible and deeply felt poetry has achieved a popularity that is rare among modern poets. Readers around the world have generated a strong demand for his poems, including his best-selling translation of *Beowulf* (2000). His readings are well attended by enthusiastic fans.

Since 1984, he has been Boylston Professor of Rhetoric and Poetry at Harvard. From 1989 to 1994 he also held the chair of Professor of Poetry at Oxford. In 1995, Heaney received the Nobel Prize for Literature.

Seamus Heaney

(b. 1939)

> "Between my finger and my thumb The squat pen rests. I'll dig with it."

Follower

Seamus Heaney

My father worked with a horse plow,
His shoulders globed like a full sail strung
Between the shafts and the furrow.
The horses strained at his clicking tongue.

5 An expert. He would set the wing
And fit the bright steel-pointed sock.
The sod rolled over without breaking.
At the headrig, with a single pluck

Of reins, the sweating team turned round

10 And back into the land. His eye
Narrowed and angled at the ground,
Mapping the furrow exactly.

I stumbled in his hobnailed wake,
Fell sometimes on the polished sod;
15 Sometimes he rode me on his back
Dipping and rising to his plod.

I wanted to grow up and plow,
To close one eye, stiffen my arm.
All I ever did was follow
20 In his broad shadow round the farm.

I was a nuisance, tripping, falling,
Yapping always. But today
It is my father who keeps stumbling
Behind me, and will not go away.

Vocabulary
furrow (fur´ ō) *n.* narrow groove made in the ground by a plow

nuisance (noo´ səns) *n.* act, thing, or condition causing trouble

◀ **Critical Viewing**
Which details in this picture convey the relationship described in the poem? **[Connect]**

Reading Strategy
Summarizing
Summarize the final stanza in one sentence.

Critical Reading

1. **Key Ideas and Details** **(a)** In "Follower," what is the father doing? **(b) Interpret:** Why does the boy want to "close one eye" and "stiffen" his arm?

2. **Craft and Structure** **(a)** Give two examples of precise words Heaney uses to describe tools, actions, or other things associated with farming. **(b) Analyze:** How does the use of such words help convey the child's fascination with his father's life?

3. **Key Ideas and Details** **(a) Compare and Contrast:** How does the relationship between father and son shift at the end of "Follower"? **(b) Draw Conclusions:** What difference between his childhood view of his father and his own experience of adulthood does the speaker see?

4. **Integration of Knowledge and Ideas** Do people's relations with their parents always leave lasting marks or burdens? Explain.

Cite textual evidence to support your responses.

Two Lorries

SEAMUS HEANEY

It's raining on black coal and warm wet ashes.
There are tire-marks in the yard, Agnew's old lorry[1]
Has all its cribs down and Agnew the coalman
With his Belfast accent's sweet-talking my mother.
5   Would she ever go to a film in Magherafelt?
But it's raining and he still has half the load

To deliver farther on. This time the lode
Our coal came from was silk-black, so the ashes
Will be the silkiest white. The Magherafelt
10 (Via Toomebridge) bus goes by. The half-stripped lorry
With its emptied, folded coal-bags moves my mother:
The tasty ways of a leather-aproned coalman!

And films no less! The conceit of a coalman . . .
She goes back in and gets out the black lead
15 And emery paper, this nineteen-forties mother,
All business round her stove, half-wiping ashes
With a backhand from her cheek as the bolted lorry
Gets revved and turned and heads for Magherafelt

And the last delivery. Oh, Magherafelt!
20 Oh, dream of red plush and a city coalman
As time fastforwards and a different lorry
Groans into shot, up Broad Street, with a payload
That will blow the bus station to dust and ashes . . .
After that happened, I'd a vision of my mother,

◀ **Critical Viewing**
Identify ways in which this photograph, like Heaney's poem, conveys both the everyday and unusual.
[Interpret]

Literary Analysis
Diction and Style How does Heaney's repeated use of the word "Oh" help to convey the poem's meaning?

Reading Check
What does the coalman invite the speaker's mother to do?

---

1. lorry truck.

25 A revenant[2] on the bench where I would meet her
In that cold-floored waiting-room in Magherafelt,
Her shopping bags full up with shoveled ashes.
Death walked out past her like a dust-faced coalman
Refolding body-bags, plying his load
30 Empty upon empty, in a flurry

Of motes and engine-revs, but which lorry
Was it now? Young Agnew's or that other,
Heavier, deadlier one, set to explode
In a time beyond her time in Magherafelt . . .
35 So tally bags and sweet-talk darkness, coalman.
Listen to the rain spit in new ashes

As you heft a load of dust that was Magherafelt,
Then reappear from your lorry as my mother's
Dreamboat coalman filmed in silk-white ashes.

Reading Strategy
Summarizing The second half of the poem is Heaney's vision of his mother. Summarize his vision.

---

2. revenant (rev´ ə nənt) *n.* one who returns; ghost.

Critical Reading ©

Cite textual evidence to support your responses.

© **1. Key Ideas and Details (a)** What are the two incidents described in "Two Lorries"? **(b) Analyze:** What details connect the two?

© **2. Key Ideas and Details (a) Infer:** How is the coalman who "sweet-talk[s]" Heaney's mother a threat to the young Heaney? **(b) Connect:** What connection can you find between this threat and the threat of terrorism in Northern Ireland, Heaney's "motherland"?

© **3. Integration of Knowledge and Ideas (a) Hypothesize:** In Heaney's view, what might the coalman's invitation to a movie, not meant or taken seriously, have in common with the promises and results of terrorist politics? **(b) Compare and Contrast:** What differences distinguish the two?

© **4. Integration of Knowledge and Ideas (a) Draw Conclusions:** Judging from "Two Lorries," how would you describe Heaney's attitude toward the Irish conflicts? **(b) Evaluate:** Do you think that writing a poem like "Two Lorries" is a form of political activism? Explain.

EAVAN BOLAND
(b. 1944)

Author of "Outside History"

Eavan Boland was born in Dublin, the capital of the Republic of Ireland. Her father was a diplomat who, she says, "recognized the importance of poetry to civilization." Her mother was a painter, who also "was totally in tune with what poetry tried to do."

Away From Ireland During much of Boland's early life, she was away from Ireland. When she was five, her father became ambassador to Great Britain and the family moved to London. Later, Boland was sent to school in New York City. There, she experienced anti-Irish hostility and felt "a great sense of isolation." Returning to Ireland when she was fifteen, Boland found "a great imaginative release."

A Personal Yet Public Poet Since 1967, she has published several acclaimed volumes of poetry, including *The War Horse* (1975), *In Her Own Image* (1980), *Night Feed* (1982), and *In a Time of Violence* (1994). Boland's poetry is notable for its intense focus on her personal experiences—she freely shares incidents from her life to uncover universal themes and insights. Her 1995 collection of essays, *Object Lessons: The Life of the Woman and Poet in Our Time*, combines her explorations of history, autobiography, and poetry. In addition to publishing poetry, she writes reviews and teaches at universities in both England and the United States.

Married to a novelist and the mother of two daughters, Boland often writes about domestic life, but she shuns the label "woman poet." She says poetry should create only statements that are "bound to be human." Unwilling to yoke poetry to a political program, she notes that "My poetry begins for me where certainty ends."

"What is a colony if not the brutal truth that when we speak the graves open. And the dead walk?"

Starry Night Over the Rhone River, Vincent van Gogh, Musée d'Orsay, Paris, France

OUTSIDE HISTORY

Eavan Boland

There are outsiders, always. These stars—
these iron inklings of an Irish January,
whose light happened

thousands of years before
5   our pain did: they are, they have always been
outside history.

They keep their distance. Under them remains
a place where you found
you were human, and

10 a landscape in which you know you are mortal.
And a time to choose between them.
I have chosen:

Out of myth into history I move to be
part of that ordeal
15 whose darkness is

only now reaching me from those fields,
those rivers, those roads clotted as
firmaments[1] with the dead.

How slowly they die
20 as we kneel beside them, whisper in their ear.
And we are too late. We are always too late.

---

1. firmaments *n.* the heavens.

◄ **Critical Viewing**
Compare the stars in the painting with those in the poem. Do both suggest the eternal, or does one suggest the explosive? **[Compare and Contrast]**

Vocabulary
mortal (môr´ təl) *adj.* of that which must eventually die

ordeal (ôr dēl´) *n.* difficult or painful experience that tests one

Reading Strategy
Summarizing After the colon in line 12, Boland tells what she has "chosen." Summarize her choice.

Critical Reading

1. Key Ideas and Details (a) What is the speaker viewing at the opening of the poem? **(b) Interpret:** Why does the speaker claim this sight is "outside history"?

2. Key Ideas and Details (a) Interpret: According to the speaker, what two things lie under the stars? **(b) Interpret:** Why must the speaker choose between them?

3. Craft and Structure (a) Analyze: What image does the speaker use to contrast the "ordeal" of history with the stars? **(b) Infer:** Who are "the dead" in line 18? **(c) Interpret:** Is acknowledging the dead a way of becoming part of the "ordeal"? Explain.

4. Integration of Knowledge and Ideas In writing this poem, does Boland become part of a larger "ordeal," or is that itself a myth? Explain.

5. Integration of Knowledge and Ideas How might an author justify remaining uninvolved in a conflict? Use three of these Essential Question words in your answer: *cite, doubt, position, rationalize, hindsight. [Connecting to the Essential Question: What is the relationship between literature and place?]*

Cite textual evidence to support your responses.

Literary Analysis

1. Craft and Structure Explain how Heaney's **diction** and **style** in "Follower" fit the subject of the poem.

2. Craft and Structure Complete this chart to analyze Boland's style in "Outside History." Then, summarize the distinctive elements of her style.

	Diction	Imagery	Rhythm/Rhyme	Form
Examples				
Summary of element				

3. Craft and Structure **(a)** What restrictions might the **sestina** form in "Two Lorries" place on Heaney? **(b)** What advantages might the form have?

4. Craft and Structure **(a)** How do Heaney's diction and style help him to re-create the past? Explain, using examples. **(b)** How does Boland make abstract ideas of history vivid?

Reading Strategy

5. Summarize "Two Lorries." Then, use your summary as a basis for stating the *main idea* of the poem.

6. Write a summary of "Outside History." Then, use your summary as a basis for stating the main idea of the poem.

PERFORMANCE TASKS
Integrated Language Skills

Vocabulary Acquisition and Use

Identify the vocabulary word from page 1366 to fill in each blank. Use the contextual meaning of the paragraph to guide your choices.

When Heaney followed his father around the farm, he may have made a ___**1**___ of himself. However, the boy's tripping over a ___**2**___ was probably more a source of amusement than an ___**3**___ for his father. One thing is certain, no ___**4**___ that his father was ___**5**___ had yet reached young Seamus.

Writing

Explanatory Text Use print or online resources to write **directions for traveling** by car from Belfast along the beautiful Antrim coast of Ireland. Identify and record streets, highways, and distances, and note beautiful sights along the route. Include a graphic with compass directions as well as ordered steps—what to do first, second, third, etc.

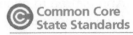

Common Core State Standards

Writing
2. Write informative/explanatory texts to examine and convey complex ideas, concepts, and information clearly and accurately through the effective selection, organization, and analysis of content.

The Postmodern and Beyond

Before You Read

Come and Go • That's All

Connecting to the Essential Question The plays of Samuel Beckett and Harold Pinter convey a sense of bewilderment amid the ordinary events of daily life. As you read, notice details in these plays that show how they differ from plays of the past. These details will help you think about the Essential Question: **What is the relationship of the writer to tradition?**

Common Core State Standards

Reading Literature
3. Analyze the impact of the author's choices regarding how to develop and relate elements of a story or drama.

Literary Analysis

Beckett and Pinter are major figures in the literary movement called **Theater of the Absurd.** The attitude of Absurdist writers is that human life has no inherent meaning and that human actions have essentially no purpose.

The techniques and characteristics of Theater of the Absurd grew directly out of these major themes and issues of the post–World War II era:

- After the horrors of World War II, the only possible way of living seemed to be a mixture of despair and humor.
- After decades of dealing with huge social issues—poverty, war, fascism, the Holocaust—writers turned inward to private, personal, familial, and everyday situations.
- After Modernism, many writers believed that the old structures of dramatic expression were no longer useful forms for a play.
- After centuries of manipulating language and style, writers began to mistrust language itself and its ability to communicate.

Look for moments in the plays that mix despair and humor or that seem to indicate that language has lost its power.

Character

↓

Situation You Expect
Situation in the Play

↓

Dialogue You Expect
Dialogue in the Play

Reading Strategy

Preparing to Read Complex Texts To recognize the absurdities in Theater of the Absurd, **compare and contrast literary elements.** Traditionally, characters, situations, and dialogue make logical sense, but in Theater of the Absurd, playwrights develop and relate these elements to defy logic and expectations. Use a chart like the one shown to compare and contrast characters, situations, and dialogue in an Absurdist play.

Vocabulary

undeterminable (un di tʉr´ min ə bl) *adj.* impossible to identify (p. 1380)

clasped (klaspt) *v.* held tightly (p. 1380)

appalled (ə pôld´) *n.* shocked; filled with horror (p. 1380)

resume (ri zoom´) *v.* continue (p. 1381)

SAMUEL BECKETT

1906-1989

Author of "Come and Go"

As a boy in Dublin, Ireland, young Samuel Beckett loved sports and languages, and, after studying at Trinity College in Dublin, he became as fluent in French as he was in English. In the late 1920s, Beckett settled in Paris, and throughout his life wrote novels and plays in both languages, often serving as his own translator. A major writer in the Modernist tradition, he was a friend of James Joyce and a brilliant critic of Marcel Proust.

Teacher and Resister For a while, Beckett taught French literature at Trinity College, and during World War II he worked as a courier for the French Resistance. He suffered terribly from depression, and during the war he wrote "to stay sane." Though he did travel in Europe and America, Beckett's life was primarily secluded and intensely private.

"TRY AGAIN. FAIL AGAIN. FAIL BETTER."

Waiting for Godot Beckett became suddenly famous in 1952 with what is still his best-known work, *Waiting for Godot*. In this revolutionary play, two tramps wait for someone named Godot. In the course of the play, their actions and inaction, their words spoken and left unspoken, their hesitant gestures and unmade decisions raise many disturbing questions about the meaning and value of human action—or its lack of meaning and value. Godot never arrives.

Prose Poetry Beckett's other major works include the trilogy of novels *Molloy, Malone Dies,* and *The Unnameable* (1951–1955) and the play *Endgame* (1957). Increasingly minimalistic, he developed a more and more compressed mode of expression as well as sparer and shorter forms—dramaticules (like "Come and Go") and micro-narratives. In effect, his distilled writing became a new kind of dramatic prose poetry. Beckett was awarded the Nobel Prize for literature in 1969.

COME AND GO

SAMUEL BECKETT

A DRAMATICULE

FOR JOHN CALDER

CHARACTERS

FLO
VI
RU

(Ages undeterminable)

Sitting center side by side stage right to left FLO, VI *and* RU. *Very erect, facing front, hands* clasped *in laps.*

Silence.

VI: When did we three last meet?

RU: Let us not speak.
[*Silence.*
Exit VI *right.*
Silence.]

FLO: Ru.

RU: Yes.

FLO: What do you think of Vi?

RU: I see little change. [FLO *moves to center seat, whispers in* RU's *ear.* Appalled.] Oh! [*They look at each other.* FLO *puts her finger to her lips.*] Does she not realize?

Vocabulary
undeterminable (un de tur′ min e bl) *adj.* impossible to identify
clasped (klaspt) *v.* held tightly

Reading Strategy
Compare and Contrast Literary Elements
How is the setting different from a traditional setting?

Literary Analysis
Theater of the Absurd
Why is Ru appalled at the whispered secret?

Vocabulary
appalled (u pawld′) *n.* shocked; filled with horror

FLO: God grant not.

> [*Enter* VI. FLO *and* RU *turn back front,* resume *pose.* VI *sits right. Silence.*]
> Just sit together as we used to, in the playground at Miss Wade's.

RU: On the log.

> [*Silence.*
> *Exit* FLO *left.*
> *Silence.*]
> Vi.

VI: Yes.

RU: How do you find Flo?

VI: She seems much the same. [RU *moves to centre seat, whispers in* VI'*s ear. Appalled.*] Oh! [*They look at each other.* RU *puts her finger to her lips.*] Has she not been told?

RU: God forbid.

> [*Enter* FLO, RU *and* VI *turn back front resume pose.* FLO *sits left.*]
> Holding hands . . . that way.

FLO: Dreaming of . . . love.

> [*Silence.*
> *Exit* RU *right.*
> *Silence.*]

VI: Flo.

FLO: Yes.

VI: How do you think Ru is looking?

FLO: One sees little in this light. [VI *moves to centre seat, whispers in* FLO'*s ear. Appalled.*] Oh! [*They look at each other.* VI *puts her finger to her lips.*] Does she not know?

VI: Please God not.

> [*Enter* RU. VI *and* FLO *turn back front, resume pose.* RU *sits right. Silence.*]
> May we not speak of the old days? [*Silence.*] Of what came after? [*Silence.*] Shall we hold hands in the old way?
>
> [*After a moment they join hands as follows:* VI'*s right hand with* RU'*s right hand,* VI'*s left hand with* FLO'*s left hand,* FLO'*s right hand with* RU'*s left hand,* VI'*s arms being above* RU'*s left arm and* FLO'*s right arm. The three pairs of clasped hands rest on the three laps.*
> *Silence.*]

FLO: I can feel the rings.

> [*Silence.*]
> CURTAIN

ONE SEES LITTLE IN THIS LIGHT

Successive positions

1	FLO	VI	RU
2	⌈FLO		RU
	⌊	FLO	RU
3	VI	FLO	RU
4	⌈VI		RU
	⌊VI	RU	
5	VI	RU	FLO
6	⌈VI		FLO
	⌊	VI	FLO
7	RU	VI	FLO

Hands

RU   VI   FLO

Lighting

Soft, from above only and concentrated on playing area. Rest of stage as dark as possible.

Costume

Full-length coats, buttoned high, dull violet (Ru), dull red (Vi), dull yellow (Flo). Drab nonde-script hats with enough brim to shade faces. Apart from colour differentiation three figures as alike as possible. Light shoes with rubber soles. Hands made up to be as visible as possible. No rings apparent.

Seat

Narrow benchlike seat, without back, just long enough to accommodate three figures almost touching. As little visible as possible. It should not be clear what they are sitting on.

Exits

The figures are not seen to go off stage. They should disappear a few steps from lit area. If dark not sufficient to allow this, recourse should be had to screens or drapes as little visible as possible. Exits and entrances slow, without sound of feet.

Ohs

Three very different sounds.

Voices

As low as compatible with audibility. Colorless except for three 'ohs' and two lines following.

Literary Analysis
Theater of the Absurd
Why do you think the women cross hands?

I CAN FEEL THE RINGS.

Cite textual evidence to support your responses.

Critical Reading

1. **Key Ideas and Details (a)** How do the women sit on the stage? **(b) Interpret:** What do their posture and gestures suggest about their lives?

2. **Key Ideas and Details (a)** What happens each time one woman exits? **(b) Speculate:** What do you think each woman whispers?

3. **Key Ideas and Details (a)** Identify one line in which each woman shows she is thinking about the past. **(b) Speculate:** If the women were to "speak of the old days," what do you think they might say?

4. **Integration of Knowledge and Ideas** How do the notes add to your understanding of the play?

Harold Pinter *1930-2008*

Author of "That's All"

Although as a student his favorite authors were novelists—Franz Kafka and Ernest Hemingway—it was drama that most fascinated Harold Pinter. Born in East London, he acted in school plays, studied for two years at London's Royal Academy of Dramatic Art, and even worked as an actor on BBC radio. During the 1950s, Pinter acted and toured with several theater companies, learning the stagecraft and absorbing the dramatic forms and traditions that he would so radically alter.

Plays and Screenplays Pinter produced his first major play, *The Birthday Party*, in 1958, and a string of masterpieces followed: *The Dumb Waiter* (1959), *The Caretaker* (1960), and *The Homecoming* (1965). He has written the screenplays of numerous movies, including *The Servant* (1963), *Betrayal* (1983), and *Sleuth* (2007). Perhaps his greatest screenplay, an adaptation of Marcel Proust's *In Search of Lost Time*, was never filmed, though it was performed on stage in 2000.

Nobel Prize Pinter has also directed many plays and served as an associate director of the National Theatre. The award of the Nobel Prize for Literature in 2005 recognized his wide-ranging accomplishment, his technical innovation, and his profound contribution to the ability of drama to express some of the deepest anxieties of the twentieth and twenty-first centuries.

Menacing Silence Pinter usually presents his audiences with common speech and common situations that mask unnameable fears and forces. Menace always looms in a Pinter drama. Tense silence plays a major role. As in "That's All," Pinter's people may engage in small talk, but behind the banality lie loss, emptiness, deception, delusion, and despair.

"Apart from the known and the unknown, what else is there?"

That's All

Harold Pinter

MRS. A.: I always put the kettle on about that time.

MRS. B.: Yes. (*Pause.*)

MRS. A.: Then she comes round.

MRS. B.: Yes. (*Pause.*)

MRS. A.: Only on Thursdays.

MRS. B.: Yes. (*Pause.*)

MRS. A.: On Wednesdays I used to put it on. When she used to come round. Then she changed it to Thursdays.

MRS. B.: Oh yes.

MRS. A.: After she moved. When she used to live round the corner, then she always came in on Wednesdays, but then when she moved she used to come down to the butcher's on Thursdays. She couldn't find a butcher up there.

MRS. B.: No.

MRS. A.: Anyway, she decided she'd stick to her own butcher. Well, I thought, if she can't find a butcher, that's the best thing.

MRS. B.: Yes. (*Pause.*)

MRS. A.: So she started to come down on Thursdays. I didn't know she was coming down on Thursdays until one day I met her in the butcher.

MRS. B.: Oh yes.

MRS. A.: It wasn't my day for the butcher, I don't go to the butcher on Thursdays.

MRS. B.: No, I know. (*Pause.*)

MRS. A.: I go on Friday.

MRS. B.: Yes. (*Pause.*)

MRS. A.: That's where I see you.

MRS. B.: Yes. (*Pause.*)

MRS. A.: You're always in there on Fridays.

MRS. B.: Oh yes. (*Pause.*)

MRS. A.: But I happened to go in for a bit of meat, it turned out to be a Thursday. I wasn't going in for my usual weekly on Friday. I just slipped in, the day before.

MRS. B.: Yes.

MRS. A.: That was the first time I found out she couldn't find a butcher up there, so she decided to come back here, once a week, to her own butcher.

Reading Strategy
Compare and Contrast Literary Elements
How do the names of the characters contrast with the names of characters in traditional plays?

Literary Analysis
Theater of the Absurd
Summarize the event that Mrs. A. relates. What makes it "absurd"?

Reading Strategy
Compare and Contrast Literary Elements
What do Mrs. B.'s responses suggest about her character?

Reading Check
What day does Mrs. A. go to the butcher?

Literary Analysis
Theatre of the Absurd
Why does Mrs. A. keep elaborating on her topic?

MRS. B.: Yes.

MRS. A.: She came on Thursday so she'd be able to get meat for the weekend. Lasted her till Monday, then from Monday to Thursday they'd have fish. She can always buy cold meat, if they want a change.

MRS. B.: Oh yes. (*Pause.*)

MRS. A.: So I told her to come in when she came down after she'd been to the butcher's and I'd put a kettle on. So she did. (*Pause.*)

MRS. B.: Yes (*Pause.*)

MRS. A.: It was funny because she always used to come in Wednesdays. (*Pause.*) Still, it made a break. (*Long pause.*)

MRS. B.: She doesn't come in no more, does she? (*Pause.*)

MRS. A.: She comes in. She doesn't come in so much, but she comes in. (*Pause.*)

MRS. B.: I thought she didn't come in. (*Pause.*)

MRS. A.: She comes in. (*Pause.*) She just doesn't come in so much. That's all.

Literary Analysis
Theater of the Absurd
What do Mrs. B.'s last two responses reveal about communication?

Critical Reading

Cite textual evidence to support your responses.

© 1. **Key Ideas and Details** (a) Who are Mrs. A. and Mrs. B. talking about? (b) **Interpret:** Why are they talking about her?

© 2. **Craft and Structure** (a) What stage direction follows most of Mrs. B.'s responses? (b) **Analyze:** What important quality does the stage direction add to the sketch?

© 3. **Key Ideas and Details** On the surface, the characters speak only ordinary chitchat or small talk. What do you think lies behind the surface of their chat?

© 4. **Integration of Knowledge and Ideas** What comment about the state of contemporary culture do you think Pinter is making? Explain.

© 5. **Integration of Knowledge and Ideas** In "That's All," Pinter reduces setting, plot, and characterization to the barest minimum. What effect do you think this has on the audience? Use three of these Essential Question words in your answer: *participate, essentials, imaginative, possibilities, unadorned.* [*Connecting to the Essential Question: What is the relationship of the writer to tradition?*]

Literary Analysis

1. Craft and Structure Conflict lies at the heart of drama, but **Theater of the Absurd** deals with conflict in unusual ways. Use a graphic organizer like this one to analyze how Beckett's and Pinter's characters respond to conflict.

	Conflict	Characters' Actions	Resolution
Come and Go			
That's All			

2. Craft and Structure How do the titles of Beckett's and Pinter's short plays help to convey their themes?

Reading Strategy

3. Summarize the plot of "Come and Go." Then, **compare and contrast the literary element**—plot—with the plot of a traditional play.

4. Traditionally, dialogue can establish setting, reveal character, advance the plot, and convey the theme of a play. What does the dialogue accomplish in "That's All"?

PERFORMANCE TASKS
Integrated Language Skills

Vocabulary Acquisition and Use

Select the word from the list on page 1378 that best completes each sentence. Then, use the context to explain your choices.

1. The workers stopped for lunch, but they planned to _____ at one o'clock.

2. Her locket meant a lot to him, so he _____ it tightly in his hand.

3. The audience was _____ by the shocking and outrageous show.

4. The sign was badly damaged, making the name of the town _____.

Writing

Narrative Text Write a **scene from an absurd drama** set in a school. Convey a Beckettian or Pinteresque sense of bewilderment or futility with these literary elements:

- Hopeless or confused characters
- Commonplace situations
- Banal dialogue and silence

Common Core State Standards

Writing
3. Write narratives to develop real or imagined experiences or events using effective technique, well-chosen details, and well-structured event sequences.

Do Not Go Gentle into That Good Night • Fern Hill • The Horses

Common Core State Standards

Reading Literature
2. Determine two or more themes or central ideas of a text and analyze their development over the course of the text, including how they interact and build on one another to produce a complex account.

Connecting to the Essential Question In "Fern Hill," poet Dylan Thomas vividly describes a natural setting he remembers from childhood. As you read, consider the connections between nature and the insights the poems convey. These connections will help you think about the Essential Question: **What is the relationship between literature and place?**

Literary Analysis

Style refers to the characteristic way in which a writer writes. A poet's style is based on elements such as word choice, tone or attitude, line length, stanza form, pace, and sound devices or patterns of sound. Thomas and Hughes have very different styles, Thomas tumbling his words out in a rush, Hughes creating separate little pulses of images:

- Thomas: *"All the sun long it was running, it was lovely, . . ."*
- Hughes: *"Not a leaf, not a bird"*

Thomas's tumbled words fit into strict patterns, however. In "Fern Hill" he uses nine-line stanzas in which the line lengths form a pattern. "Do Not Go Gentle into That Good Night" is a **villanelle,** a nineteen-line poem in which the rhymed first and third lines repeat regularly to help form the rhyme scheme *aba aba aba aba aba abaa*. In contrast, "The Horses" by Ted Hughes is **free verse,** poetry with no fixed pattern.

As you read, consider all the elements of each poet's style. Also consider how the style of each poem suits its **themes**—its central ideas or concerns.

Reading Strategy

Ⓒ Preparing to Read Complex Texts Different poems often express similar themes in different ways. To **evaluate the poet's expression of themes,** follow these three steps:

1. Identify two or more themes, or central ideas, of the poem.
2. Identify the details that work together to develop these themes, and consider how the themes interact to suggest a deeper meaning.
3. Evaluate how effectively those details communicate the themes. Use a chart like the one shown to help you organize your ideas.

Themes

Details That Convey Themes

Effectiveness

Vocabulary

grieved (grēvd) *v.* felt deep sorrow for; mourned (p. 1390)

spellbound (spel´ bound) *adj.* held by a spell; enchanted; magical (p. 1393)

tortuous (tôr´chōo wəs) *adj.* full of twists or curves (p. 1397)

dregs (dregz) *n.* particles of solid matter that settle in the bottom of a liquid; remnants; residue (p. 1397)

Dylan Thomas *(1914–1953)*

Author of "Do Not Go Gentle into That Good Night" • "Fern Hill"

Playful with language and exuberant about life, Thomas gained remarkable popularity in his lifetime. However, he also had a darker side, evident in his poems of death and the loss of childhood innocence.

A Young Poet Dylan Thomas was born in Swansea in southwestern Wales, an industrial city. However, he often visited his maternal grandfather's farm, which he describes in "Fern Hill." With the encouragement of his father, an English teacher, he became interested in poetry at an early age. Before turning twenty, he had already written—at least in early form—many of his best-known poems. As a teenager, he also produced source books of ideas that served as a basis for later works.

Journeys Abroad At the age of twenty-one, Thomas went to London, where he worked in journalism, broadcasting, and filmmaking for a number of years. In 1940, he published a collection of humorous stories about his childhood and youth, *Portrait of the Artist as a Young Dog*. In 1950, he made the first of four trips to the United States. Audiences here embraced him not only for his theatrical readings of his poems but also for the freshness and complexity of his poetic voice.

Though he continued to publish poetry, two of the later works for which he is best known are prose: *Under Milkwood*, a "play for voices," and "A Child's Christmas in Wales," a memoir.

An Artist's Problems Although acclaimed at an early age, Thomas struggled with poverty and alcoholism through most of his adult life. He died while on tour in the United States, where he had planned to collaborate on an opera with Igor Stravinsky.

Do Not Go Gentle into That Good Night

Dylan Thomas

Do not go gentle into that good night,
Old age should burn and rave at close of day;
Rage, rage against the dying of the light.

Though wise men at their end know dark is right,
5   Because their words had forked no lightning they
Do not go gentle into that good night.

Good men, the last wave by, crying how bright
Their frail deeds might have danced in a green bay,
Rage, rage against the dying of the light.

10   Wild men who caught and sang the sun in flight,
And learn, too late, they grieved it on its way,
Do not go gentle into that good night.

Grave men, near death, who see with blinding sight
Blind eyes could blaze like meteors and be gay,
15   Rage, rage against the dying of the light.

And you, my father, there on the sad height,
Curse, bless, me now with your fierce tears, I pray.
Do not go gentle into that good night.
Rage, rage against the dying of the light.

Vocabulary
grieved (grēvd) *v.* felt deep sorrow for; mourned

Literary Analysis
Style and Theme/ Villanelle How does the last line of each stanza stop the movement of the poem and help stress the poem's theme?

Critical Reading

Cite textual evidence to support your responses.

1. **Key Ideas and Details (a)** Whom does the speaker address in the poem? **(b) Infer:** What is the "good night" to which the speaker refers?

2. **Key Ideas and Details (a)** What four types of men does the poem identify and describe? **(b) Interpret:** What regrets does each of these men have as he comes to the end of his life?

3. **Key Ideas and Details (a) Interpret:** What general advice about life and death is the speaker giving in lines 3, 9, 15, and 19? **(b) Analyze:** Considering the speaker's advice in these lines, why do you think he refers to the night as "good"?

DYLAN THOMAS
AND POETRY IN PERFORMANCE

Dylan Thomas grew up in Wales, a country famous for its rich verbal culture. People spent hours conversing over their dinner tables, joking on street corners, and reciting poetry in their neighborhood pubs. As a boy, Thomas listened intently. Soon, rivers of words were pouring out of him too. By his early twenties, he was reading poetry in a musical, booming voice on British radio. A decade later, Thomas toured the United States, performing poetry to huge audiences.

Thomas was not the first lively poet to perform in America. In the 1920s, Langston Hughes and others had read their poems to jazz. Thomas, however, was the first to draw a large following, and he paved the way for performances by the Beat poets in the 1950s. Today, poets and rap artists like those shown here perform in theaters, clubs, and on the electronic media. They are participating in the revival of the spoken word that Dylan Thomas helped to start.

Punk singer and poet Patti Smith performing on *Saturday Night Live*

Poet Miguel Algarin, founder of The Nuyorican Poets Café, a home for poetry in performance on New York's Lower East Side for more than three decades

Rap star Saul Williams in performance

Dylan Thomas

CONNECT TO THE LITERATURE

How does reading Dylan Thomas's poetry aloud differ from reading it silently on the page?

Fern Hill

Dylan Thomas

Now as I was young and easy under the apple boughs
About the lilting house and happy as the grass was green,
        The night above the dingle starry,
            Time let me hail and climb
5   Golden in the heydays of his eyes,
And honored among wagons I was prince of the apple towns
And once below a time I lordly had the trees and leaves
            Trail with daisies and barley
        Down the rivers of the windfall light.

10 And as I was green and carefree, famous among the barns
About the happy yard and singing as the farm was home,
        In the sun that is young once only,
            Time let me play and be
        Golden in the mercy of his means,
15 And green and golden I was huntsman and herdsman, the calves
Sang to my horn, the foxes on the hills barked clear and cold,
            And the sabbath rang slowly
        In the pebbles of the holy streams.

All the sun long it was running, it was lovely, the hay
20 Fields high as the house, the tunes from the chimneys, it was air
            And playing, lovely and watery
            And fire green as grass.
        And nightly under the simple stars
As I rode to sleep the owls were bearing the farm away,
25 All the moon long I heard, blessed among stables, the nightjars[1]
            Flying with the ricks,[2] and the horses
            Flashing into the dark.

And then to awake, and the farm, like a wanderer white
With the dew, come back, the cock on his shoulder; it was all
30   Shining, it was Adam and maiden,
            The sky gathered again
        And the sun grew round that very day.
So it must have been after the birth of the simple light
In the first, spinning place, the spellbound horses walking warm
35   Out of the whinnying green stable
            On to the fields of praise.

---

1. **nightjars** *n.* common nocturnal birds, named for the whirring sound that the male makes.
2. **ricks** *n.* haystacks.

◀ **Critical Viewing** What does the image suggest about the relationship of the poem to childhood? **[Infer]**

Literary Analysis
Style and Theme How does Thomas's tumbling rush of words contrast with the type of stanzas he uses?

Vocabulary
spellbound (spel´bound) *adj.* held by a spell; enchanted; magical

Reading Check
What jobs does the narrator have with the calves and foxes?

And honored among foxes and pheasants by the gay house
Under the new made clouds and happy as the heart was long,
   In the sun born over and over,
40   I ran my heedless ways,
   My wishes raced through the house-high hay
And nothing I cared, at my sky blue trades, that time allows
In all his tuneful turning so few and such morning songs
   Before the children green and golden
45   Follow him out of grace,

Nothing I cared, in the lamb white days, that time would take me
Up to the swallow thronged loft by the shadow of my hand,
   In the moon that is always rising,
        Nor that riding to sleep
50   I should hear him fly with the high fields
And wake to the farm forever fled from the childless land.
Oh as I was young and easy in the mercy of his means,
      Time held me green and dying
   Though I sang in my chains like the sea.

Reading Strategy
Evaluating Expression of Theme How does the imagery in this stanza communicate the idea that childhood has fled? Cite details to support your evaluation.

Critical Reading

Cite textual evidence to support your responses.

1. **Key Ideas and Details (a)** Which two colors does the speaker use to describe himself in youth? **(b) Interpret:** What do the colors suggest that he feels about his childhood?

2. **Key Ideas and Details (a)** Paraphrase the last stanza. **(b) Analyze:** What change in mood occurs here? **(c) Infer:** What is the reason for the change?

3. **Key Ideas and Details** What is the meaning of lines 53–54?

4. **Key Ideas and Details (a)** What stages of life does the poem contrast? **(b) Draw Conclusions:** What attitude does the poem express toward the different stages of life?

5. **Integration of Knowledge and Ideas** Into what important stages would you divide human life? Explain.

Ted Hughes

(1930–1998)

Author of "The Horses"

Born in rural West Yorkshire, Ted Hughes spent much of his youth hunting and fishing with his brother. These experiences contributed to his lifelong interest in the beauty and violence of nature, recurring themes in his work.

Hughes and His Father It would be a mistake, however, to ignore the violence of World War I as an influence on Hughes. He was born well after the war, but his father had had a traumatic experience in that conflict. He was among a handful of men to survive the destruction of his regiment. Hughes once said that as a child, he was strongly affected by his father's silence about this experience.

Hughes himself served in the Royal Air Force and then studied archaeology and anthropology at Pembroke College, Cambridge, where he met the American poet Sylvia Plath. He married Plath in 1956, but they later separated.

A Variety of Work Hughes is best known for his volumes of poetry *Hawk in the Rain, Crow,* and *Moortown.* In these and other works, he uses free verse and powerful, direct speech to express a yearning for a lost wholeness with the natural world. In exploring this theme, which appears in "The Horses," he was strongly influenced by the prose and poetry of D. H. Lawrence.

Hughes was a versatile writer who, in addition to poetry and fiction, wrote books for children. He even wrote a play in a language he invented. One of his final publications was *Tales from Ovid* (1997), a translation of many verse stories from the Latin poet Ovid's *Metamorphoses.* Hughes was poet laureate of England from 1984 until his death.

The Horses

BACKGROUND Although both Thomas and Hughes wrote of nature, they approached it differently. Thomas was fascinated by nature's double face, life and death, as demonstrated in the line "Time held me green and dying" from "Fern Hill." Hughes was often closely attuned to nature's remote, primitive, nonhuman beauty, as in "The Horses."

I climbed through woods in the hour-before-dawn dark.
Evil air, a frost-making stillness,

Not a leaf, not a bird—
A world cast in frost. I came out above the wood

5   Where my breath left tortuous statues in the iron light.
But the valleys were draining the darkness

Till the moorline—blackening dregs of the brightening gray—
Halved the sky ahead. And I saw the horses:

Huge in the dense gray—ten together—
10   Megalith-still.[1] They breathed, making no move,

With draped manes and tilted hind-hooves,
Making no sound.

I passed: not one snorted or jerked its head.
Gray silent fragments

15   Of a gray silent world.

I listened in emptiness on the moor-ridge.
The curlew's[2] tear turned its edge on the silence.

---

1. Megalith-still still as the huge stones left by ancient peoples, such as those at Stonehenge.
2. curlew's (kʉr´ lōōz) *n.* of a large, brownish wading bird with long legs.

Literary Analysis
Style and Theme Identify three short bursts of images that help Hughes convey his theme.

Vocabulary
tortuous (tôr´chōō wəs) *adj.* full of twists or curves

dregs (dregz) *n.* particles of solid matter that settle in the bottom of a liquid; remnants; residue

▼ **Critical Viewing**
Compare and contrast the horses in the poem with those in the picture. **[Compare and Contrast]**

Reading Check
What are the horses doing when Hughes sees them?

Slowly detail leafed from the darkness. Then the sun
Orange, red, red erupted

20 Silently, and splitting to its core tore and flung cloud,
Shook the gulf open, showed blue,

And the big planets hanging—
I turned

Stumbling in the fever of a dream, down towards
25 The dark woods, from the kindling tops.

And came to the horses.
                              There, still they stood,
But now steaming and glistening under the flow of light,

Their draped stone manes, their tilted hind-hooves
Stirring under a thaw while all around them

30 The frost showed its fires. But still they made no sound.
Not one snorted or stamped,

Their hung heads patient as the horizons,
High over valleys, in the red leveling rays—

In din of the crowded streets, going among the years, the faces,
35 May I still meet my memory in so lonely a place

Between the streams and the red clouds, hearing curlews,
Hearing the horizons endure.

Reading Strategy
Evaluating Expression of Theme Contrast the images in lines 34–35 with earlier images. How effective is the contrast in helping to express the poem's theme?

Critical Reading

Cite textual evidence to support your responses.

1. **Key Ideas and Details** **(a) Summarize:** Sum up what occurs in the course of the poem. **(b) Draw Conclusions:** What view of nature do these events suggest? Explain.

2. **Key Ideas and Details** **(a)** What wish does the speaker make at the end of the poem? **(b) Analyze:** Why do you think he makes this wish?

3. **Integration of Knowledge and Ideas** Which details of setting convey Thomas's and Hughes's ideas? Use at least two of these Essential Question words in your response: *dramatic, visual, emphasize.* *[Connecting to the Essential Question: What is the relationship between literature and place?]*

Literary Analysis

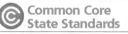

Common Core State Standards

Writing
4. Produce clear and coherent writing in which the development, organization, and style are appropriate to task, purpose, and audience.

1. Craft and Structure Fill in a chart like the one shown here to illustrate key aspects of Thomas's **style.** Then explain how these aspects convey the **theme** in "Fern Hill."

Aspect of Style	Examples
Tumbles out words in a rush	
Uses complex poetic forms	

2. Craft and Structure Fill out a chart for Hughes like the one above, and include his use of **free verse**. Then explain how aspects of Hughes's style help express the theme in "The Horses."

Reading Strategy

3. How does the **villanelle's** repetition in "Do Not Go Gentle into That Good Night" help Thomas to **express his theme**?

4. Of "Fern Hill" and "The Horses," which do you think expresses its theme more effectively? Cite details to support your opinion.

PERFORMANCE TASKS
Integrated Language Skills

Vocabulary Acquisition and Use

Use a word from the vocabulary list on page 1388 to complete each sentence, and explain your choice. Use each word only once.

1. Instead of an easy path, we took a _____ route.

2. The _____ remained in the bottom of the cup.

3. When their beloved leader died, the whole nation _____.

4. She was _____ by the wizard's chant.

Writing

Poem **Parody** is writing that imitates and exaggerates an author's style and themes for humorous purposes. Write a **poem** that is a **parody** of the work of either Thomas or Hughes. Choose a subject or theme that exaggerates a subject from one of the poet's, and imitate and exaggerate that poet's imagery, word choice, tone, and sentence lengths or rhythms. For example, to exaggerate Thomas's style, you might make the tumble of words come even faster.

Connecting to the Essential Question Twentieth-century poets were often torn between traditional and new styles of poetry. Which would you have chosen, and why? As you read, consider the choices each poet has made to follow or break with traditions in form and content. Noting these choices will help you think about the Essential Question: **What is the relationship of the writer to tradition?**

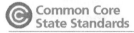

Common Core State Standards

Reading Literature
5. Analyze how an author's choices concerning how to structure specific parts of a text contribute to its overall structure and meaning as well as its aesthetic impact.

Literary Analysis

Before the twentieth century, most English-language poetry used a regular pattern of rhythm, or **meter.** The basic unit of meter is a **foot,** a group of one or more stressed, marked (´), and unstressed (˘) syllables.

- An **iamb** is one unstressed followed by one stressed syllable (˘ ´)
- A **trochee** is one stressed followed by one unstressed syllable (´ ˘)

Meter is described by its prevalent type of foot and number of feet per line. Three feet in a line is called *trimeter;* four feet, *tetrameter;* five feet, *pentameter;* six feet, *hexameter.* Thus, "An Arundel Tomb," with most lines containing four iambs, uses *iambic tetrameter*:

> Thĕ éarl ănd cóuntĕss lié ĭn stóne, . . .

In the twentieth century, many poets abandoned the tradition of meter and instead used **free verse,** poetry without a regular pattern of rhythm or rhyme. Peter Redgrove uses free verse in "On the Patio."

Comparing Literary Works Compare and contrast the ways in which rhythm contributes to the **dramatic structure** of these poems—the use of contrasts to build toward a climax. Also, consider the ways in which the rhythm reinforces meaning and gives aesthetic pleasure.

Reading Strategy

Preparing to Read Complex Texts The best way to understand a poem is to **read it in sentences.** Focus on the units of thought, not on the rhythm or line breaks. As a reminder, use signs like these to mark the ends of lines in a copy of the poem.

Sign	Means
→	Continue without pause
↱	Pause for comma, dash, or semicolon and continue
⯃	Full stop for period

Vocabulary

effigy (ef´ i jē) *n.* portrait or statue of a person (p. 1403)

supine (soo͞´ pīn´) *adj.* lying on the back (p. 1403)

fidelity (fə del´ ə tē) *n.* faithfulness (p. 1403)

larking (lärk´ iŋ) *n.* free-spirited, whimsical fun (p. 1408)

www.PHLitOnline.com

Philip Larkin
(1922–1985)

Author of "An Arundel Tomb" • "The Explosion"

Philip Larkin turned what could have been a discouragement into a reason for developing poetic skill and emotional restraint. As a child in Coventry, England, his home life was dominated by a father who held him accountable to rigid standards. Larkin escaped from these pressures by building a private childhood world rich in creativity and imagination.

Yeats Versus Hardy After graduating from St. John's College, Oxford, Larkin worked as a librarian for Hull University Library, a job he held for many years. His first book of poems, *The North Ship,* shows the strong influence of William Butler Yeats, but an encounter with Thomas Hardy's *Collected Poems* had a profound impact on Larkin. Larkin said, "When I came to Hardy it was with the sense of relief that I didn't have to try to jack myself up to a concept of poetry that lay outside my own life—this is perhaps what I felt Yeats was trying to make me do."

Deprivation Versus Daffodils Reflecting on his life, Larkin metaphorically explained how he drew inspiration from his difficult experiences when he told an interviewer, "Deprivation is for me what daffodils were for Wordsworth."

Although Larkin also developed a lifelong interest in jazz, which he came to love "even more than poetry," it was his clear-eyed, honest poetry, combining conversational language with well-crafted forms, that won him international fame. His poetry speaks of day-to-day realities, sometimes discouragingly, but is quietly haunted by realities beyond everyday life.

> "Life has a practice of living you, if you don't live it."

An Arundel Tomb
Philip Larkin

BACKGROUND THE PHOTOGRAPH ABOVE SHOWS THE INSPIRATION FOR "AN ARUNDEL TOMB": A TABLE TOMB IN CHICHESTER CATHEDRAL, SUSSEX, THAT DATES TO THE FOURTEENTH CENTURY. BURIED IN THE TOMB ARE RICHARD FITZALAN, EARL OF ARUNDEL, AND HIS SECOND WIFE ELEANOR, A MEMBER OF THE PROMINENT HOUSE OF LANCASTER. SIMPLE STONE EFFIGIES OF THE COUPLE LAY SIDE BY SIDE ON TOP OF THE TOMB, THE DETAILS WORN DOWN AND BLURRY, WITH RICHARD REACHING OVER TO HOLD HIS WIFE'S HAND.

Literary Analysis
Free Verse and Meter
How do the meters of lines 1 and 2 differ?

Side by side, their faces blurred,
The earl and countess[1] lie in stone,
Their proper habits[2] vaguely shown
As jointed armor, stiffened pleat,
5 And that faint hint of the absurd—
The little dogs under their feet.

---

1. countess *n.* The wife of an earl is called a countess.
2. habits *n.* clothes worn for a particular activity or occasion.

Such plainness of the pre-baroque[3]
Hardly involves the eye, until
It meets his left-hand gauntlet,[4] still
10 Clasped empty in the other; and
One sees, with a sharp tender shock,
His hand withdrawn, holding her hand.

They would not think to lie so long.
Such faithfulness in effigy
15 Was just a detail friends would see:
A sculptor's sweet commissioned grace
Thrown off in helping to prolong
The Latin names around the base.

They would not guess how early in
20 Their supine stationary voyage
The air would change to soundless damage,
Turn the old tenantry[5] away;
How soon succeeding eyes begin
To look, not read. Rigidly they

25 Persisted, linked, through lengths and breadths
Of time. Snow fell, undated. Light
Each summer thronged the glass. A bright
Litter of birdcalls strewed the same
Bone-riddled ground. And up the paths
30 The endless altered people came,

Washing at their identity.
Now, helpless in the hollow of
An unarmorial age, a trough
Of smoke in slow suspended skeins[6]
35 Above their scrap of history,
Only an attitude remains:

Time has transfigured them into
Untruth. The stone fidelity
They hardly meant has come to be
40 Their final blazon[7], and to prove
Our almost-instinct almost true:
What will survive of us is love.

◀ **Critical Viewing**
Do engraved images such as the one on this tombstone always become an "untruth" in relation to life—as Larkin's poem seems to claim? **[Relate]**

Vocabulary

effigy (ef′ i jē) *n.* portrait, statue, or other likeness of a person

supine (sōō′ pīn′) *adj.* lying on the back

Reading Strategy

Reading Poetry in Sentences Identify the full sentence in which line 25 appears.

Vocabulary

fidelity (fə del′ ə tē) *n.* faithfulness

---

3. pre-baroque (prĕ′ bə rōk′) *adj.* predating the Baroque Period (c. 1600–1750), when tombstone carvings along with other art and architecture grew far more ornate.
4. gauntlet (gônt′ or gänt′lĭt) *n.* armored glove.
5. tenantry *n.* peasants farming the nobles' land.
6. skeins (skānz) *n.* loosely coiled bunches of thread or yarn.
7. blazon (blā′ zən) *n.* coat of arms, emblem of a noble family.

THE EXPLOSION

PHILIP LARKIN

Literary Analysis
Meter and Free Verse
What is the meter of the lines in the first stanza? Explain.

On the day of the explosion
Shadows pointed towards the pithead:[1]
In the sun the slagheap slept.[2]

Down the lane came men in pitboots
5 Coughing oath-edged talk and pipe-smoke,
Shouldering off the freshened silence.

One chased after rabbits; lost them;
Came back with a nest of lark's eggs;
Showed them; lodged them in the grasses.

---

1. **pithead** *n.* the entrance to a coal mine.
2. **slagheap** *n.* a large mound of waste material dug up from a coal mine.

10   So they passed in beards and moleskins,[3]
      Fathers, brothers, nicknames, laughter,
      Through the tall gates standing open.

      At noon, there came a tremor; cows
      Stopped chewing for a second; sun,
15   Scarfed as in a heat-haze, dimmed.

      The dead go on before us, they
      Are sitting in God's house in comfort,
      We shall see them face to face—

      Plain as lettering in the chapels
20   It was said, and for a second
      Wives saw men of the explosion

      Larger than in life they managed—
      Gold as on a coin, or walking
      Somehow from the sun towards them,

25   One showing the eggs unbroken.

---

3. moleskins garments, especially trousers, of heavy cotton.

Literary Analysis
Meter and Free Verse
What is the prevalent foot in this poem? How many feet does it typically have in each line?

Critical Reading

1. **Key Ideas and Details (a)** Describe the physical position of the sculptured couple in "An Arundel Tomb." **(b) Interpret:** What is the "supine stationary voyage" they have made?

2. **Key Ideas and Details (a)** What detail of the Arundel tomb catches the speaker's eye? **(b) Interpret:** What does he mean when he says that time has transfigured the couple into untruth?

3. **Key Ideas and Details (a)** Where are the men in "The Explosion" going? **(b) Infer:** What happens to them?

4. **Key Ideas and Details (a)** What events in "The Explosion" are said to last for a second? **(b) Connect:** What does the contrast between the things that take a second in the fifth and seventh stanzas suggest about life? **(c) Interpret:** What might the lark's egg symbolize about life?

5. **Integration of Knowledge and Ideas** What do both poems say about the traditional poetic subject of love? In your response, use at least two of these Essential Question words: *endure, transform, conventional.* [*Connecting to the Essential Question: What is the relationship of the writer to tradition?*]

Cite textual evidence to support your responses.

Peter Redgrove

(1932–2003)

Author of "On the Patio"

Like William Blake, a visionary poet with whom he is sometimes compared, Peter Redgrove does not fit into the usual categories. He lived at a distance from the literary hub of London—in Falmouth, Cornwall, the southwestern tip of England. Redgrove lived at an imaginative distance from London as well, rejecting the drab, everyday qualities so prevalent in many post-World War II British poems.

Transformation Through Imagination In his poetry, novels, television scripts, and nonfiction works, Redgrove celebrates our power to reimagine and transform our lives. His rich visual imagery reflects a heightened awareness that borders on the mystical as he speaks for stones or sees the world through the eyes of a wandering dog.

Redgrove's poems have been widely acclaimed in England, and he was the recipient of the 1997 Queen's Medal for Poetry.

STEVIE SMITH

(1902–1971)

Author of "Not Waving but Drowning"

Stevie Smith's poems cannot be easily classified. They are modeled, however, on familiar forms—hymns, popular songs, and nineteenth-century British and American poems. Using simple forms and language, she often evokes despair, perhaps relying on the poetic statement of bleak feelings to cleanse or banish them from life.

Auntie Lion The author of this unusual body of work was born Florence Margaret Smith in Hull, Yorkshire. Due to her mother's ill health, she was raised mostly by her beloved Auntie Lion, with whom she continued to live in a northern London suburb even as an adult. While working for a magazine, Smith wrote three novels and nine collections of poems.

Poems and Doodles Smith's poems can be humorous, macabre, surprising, and childlike, and she often illustrates them with sketches or doodles that echo her playful rhythms.

Some critics suggest that her work cunningly satirizes conventional forms of poetic expression, such as the hymn and the nursery rhyme, and adds dark new depths and keen irony to these traditional forms.

On the Patio

Peter Redgrove

A wineglass overflowing with thunderwater
Stands out on the drumming steel table

Among the outcries of the downpour
Feathering chairs and rethundering on the awnings.

5 How the pellets of water shooting miles
Fly into the glass of swirl, and slop

Over the table's scales of rust
Shining like chained sores,

Because the rain eats everything except the glass
10 Of spinning water that is clear down here

But purple with rumbling depths above, and this cloud
Is transferring its might into a glass

In which thunder and lightning come to rest,
The cloud crushed into a glass.

15 Suddenly I dart out into the patio,
Snatch the bright glass up and drain it,

Bang it back down on the thundery steel table for a refill.

Reading Strategy
Reading Poetry in Sentences As you read the poem, at the end of which lines should you come to a complete stop?

Critical Reading

© **1. Key Ideas and Details** **(a)** Describe the scene depicted in "On the Patio." **(b) Connect:** How do the images in the poem link what occurs above with what occurs below?

© **2. Key Ideas and Details** **(a)** What does the speaker do at the end of the poem? **(b) Interpret:** What attitude toward life does the speaker's final gesture symbolize, or represent?

Cite textual evidence to support your responses.

NOT WAVING BUT DROWNING

STEVIE SMITH

Nobody heard him, the dead man,
But still he lay moaning:
I was much further out than you thought
And not waving but drowning.

5   Poor chap, he always loved larking
And now he's dead
It must have been too cold for him his heart gave way,
They said.

Oh, no no no, it was too cold always
10 (Still the dead one lay moaning)
I was much too far out all my life
And not waving but drowning.

Vocabulary
larking (lärk´ iŋ) *n.* free-spirited, whimsical fun

Critical Reading

Cite textual evidence to support your responses.

1. **Key Ideas and Details (a)** What does the dead man moan in the first stanza? **(b) Infer:** How do others misinterpret his gestures?

2. **Key Ideas and Details (a) Compare and Contrast:** What do others say about the cold, and what does the dead man say? **(b) Interpret:** What does the line "I was much too far out all my life" mean? **(c) Analyze:** How does the speaker's relationship to society relate to drowning?

3. **Integration of Knowledge and Ideas** How is the subject matter of these poems like and unlike that of traditional poetry from earlier centuries? In answering, use at least two of these Essential Question words: *ironic, atypical,* and *perspective.* **[Connecting to the Essential Question: What is the relationship of the writer to tradition?]**

Literary Analysis

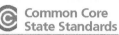

1. Craft and Structure (a) Identify the traditional **meter** in Larkin's poems. **(b)** Explain how breaks in the metrical pattern stress key ideas and build to a climax in the poem's **dramatic structure.** Use a chart like this to help you.

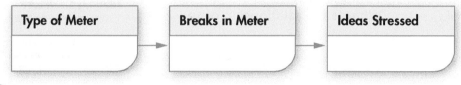

Type of Meter	Breaks in Meter	Ideas Stressed

2. Craft and Structure Explain how the use of **free verse** suits the content of "On the Patio."

3. Craft and Structure Traditional ballads often use four-line stanzas in which unrhymed lines of iambic tetrameter alternate with rhymed lines of iambic trimeter. How does Smith's poem modify this traditional ballad stanza?

4. Comparing Literary Works Compare and contrast the ways in which these poems use rhythm to enhance their dramatic structure.

Reading Strategy

5. In **reading in sentences** lines 19–31 of "An Arundel Tomb," where should you make a full stop?

6. As you read lines 19–25 of "The Explosion," where should you pause or stop, and for how long?

Common Core State Standards

Writing
3.e. Provide a conclusion that follows from and reflects on what is experienced, observed, or resolved over the course of the narrative.

PERFORMANCE TASKS
Integrated Language Skills

Vocabulary Acquisition and Use

For each word, choose the letter of its antonym, or opposite, and explain your choice.

1. effigy: **(a)** scarecrow **(b)** original **(c)** likeness

2. supine: **(a)** neat **(b)** upright **(c)** sloppy

3. fidelity: **(a)** disloyalty **(b)** cowardice **(c)** faithfulness

4. larking: **(a)** mischief **(b)** laziness **(c)** toil

Writing

Narrative Text Write a **reflective essay** in which you explain how an ordinary incident in your experience has taken on meaning as a general lesson about life. Begin by describing the incident. Then move from the specific to the general, providing a conclusion that explores the broader meaning of the incident.

Connecting to the Essential Question In their poems, Penelope Shuttle and Carol Ann Duffy adapt the traditional form of the elegy to suit their purposes. To what degree do you think a modern poet should draw on tradition? As you read, consider the degree to which each poet draws on poetic traditions of the past. These connections will help you think about the Essential Question: **What is the relationship of the writer to tradition?**

Literary Analysis

Form refers to the way a poem is organized. Some types of poems have a **fixed form**—a set number of lines or stanzas that usually follow a set pattern of rhyme and meter. *Sonnets, villanelles,* and *haiku* are examples. For instance, a *Shakespearean,* or *English, sonnet* has fourteen lines that break into three quatrains, or four-line stanzas, and a final couplet. The pattern of end rhymes is usually *abab cdcd efef gg,* and the meter is usually iambic pentameter. "Prayer" by Carol Ann Duffy is a Shakespearean sonnet.

Some types of poems have a **free form,** or no set pattern to follow. Instead, the poet is free to establish his or her own pattern or to use free verse with no pattern at all. Penelope Shuttle's "In the Kitchen" is such a free-form poem.

Comparing Literary Works Both Duffy's poem and Shuttle's are elegiac. In other words, they are written in the spirit of **elegies,** poems mourning the loss of someone or something. Compare and contrast these elegiac poems by considering who or what is being mourned and in how formal a manner.

Reading Strategy

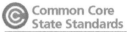 **Preparing to Read Complex Texts** To appreciate the form of a poem and better understand how the structure of specific parts contributes to its overall structure and meaning, **recite the poem aloud.** Listen especially for *parallel structures* or other repeated structures. Use a chart like the one shown to identify the parallel structures.

Vocabulary

utters (ut´ ərz) *v.* speaks (p. 1413)

scales (skālz) *n.* sequences of musical tones arranged to have a rising or falling pitch (p. 1413)

lustrous (lus´ trəs) *adj.* gleaming; shining (p. 1414)

steadfastly (sted´ fast´ lē) *adv.* in a firm manner; without wavering (p. 1414)

Common Core State Standards

Reading Literature
5. Analyze how an author's choices concerning how to structure specific parts of a text contribute to its overall structure and meaning as well as its aesthetic impact.

Parallel Structures	Effect on Meaning
• ironing-board thanks . . . • fridge hums . . . • chair recites . . .	Personified kitchen items give support to speaker.

CAROL ANN DUFFY

(b. 1955)

Author of **"Prayer"**

One of contemporary Britain's most highly regarded poets, Carol Ann Duffy grew up in Staffordshire, England, to which her family moved from Scotland when she was just four years old. Her father was an unusual man—a machine fitter with the electric company, he also ran for Parliament and managed a local soccer team. Encouraged to follow her own path, Duffy studied philosophy at the University of Liverpool and then moved to London, where she worked as poetry editor for *Ambit* magazine. In 1996, she returned to northern England to teach poetry at Manchester Metropolitan University.

Dramatic Poetry A talented playwright as well as a poet, Duffy uses her dramatic skills in her verse, displaying a strong sense of dramatic timing and a deep understanding of human behavior. She also experiments with traditional poetic forms. "I write quite a lot of sonnets," she once noted. "I think of them almost as prayers: short and memorable, something you can recite."

PENELOPE SHUTTLE

(b. 1947)

Author of **"In the Kitchen"**

Penelope Shuttle won her first poetry award when she was in her twenties and has been writing ever since. One source of inspiration has been Cornwall, the remote, rocky coastal area of southwestern England to which she moved in 1970; another has been her husband, the noted poet Peter Redgrove, with whom she coauthored a book of poetry, two novels, and two works of nonfiction.

Poetry as Consolation Shuttle nursed her husband through years of debilitating illness until his death in 2003. During that harrowing time and in the aftermath of her great loss, poetry has provided an outlet for her emotions and a spur for entering the world again. "My years as a carer for Peter and the sadness of witnessing his decline," she observes, "were a time when I fought off depression and anger, not always successfully, but turned to poetry as a channel for and transformer of such emotions." Many of the poems Shuttle wrote in this period, including "In the Kitchen," appear in her collection *Redgrove's Wife* (2006).

PRAYER

CAROL ANN DUFFY

Some days, although we cannot pray, a prayer
utters itself. So, a woman will lift
her head from the sieve of her hands and stare
at the minims[1] sung by a tree, a sudden gift.

5 Some nights, although we are faithless, the truth
enters our hearts, that small familiar pain;
then a man will stand stock-still,[2] hearing his youth
in the distant Latin chanting[3] of a train.

Pray for us now. Grade I piano scales
10 console the lodger looking out across
a Midlands[4] town. Then dusk, and someone calls
a child's name as though they named their loss.

Darkness outside. Inside, the radio's prayer—
Rockall. Malin. Dogger. Finisterre.[5]

---

1. **minims** *n.* half notes in music.
2. **stock-still** *adj.* as still as a stock, or wooden block; perfectly motionless.
3. **Latin chanting** prayers in Latin.
4. **Midlands** *n.* the industrial middle of England.
5. **Rockall . . . Finisterre** (fin´ is târ´) Four places in the familiar listing of coastal areas traditionally named in shipping forecasts heard on British radio.

Vocabulary

utters (ut´ ərz) *v.* speaks

scales (skālz) *n.* sequences of musical tones arranged to have a rising or falling pitch

◄ **Critical Viewing**
Could this painting be said to represent the nights "we are faithless" described in the poem? Explain. **[Connect]**

Literary Analysis
Fixed and Free Forms Describe the pattern of rhyme and meter in this sonnet.

Critical Reading

1. Key Ideas and Details (a) What can the speaker and others not do on some days? **(b) Infer:** What is the woman trying to do in lines 2–3? Explain.

2. Key Ideas and Details (a) Generalize: Given what they cannot do on some days and nights, what do the speaker and others take comfort in instead? **(b) Support:** Cite images that support your generalization.

3. Integration of Knowledge and Ideas (a) Compare and Contrast: In what way are the words on the radio like a prayer? **(b) Analyze:** How do these words and all the other sounds that people hear in the poem relate to modern life? **(c) Interpret:** What does the poem imply about faith and modern life?

Cite textual evidence to support your responses.

In the Kitchen
PENELOPE SHUTTLE

A jug of water
has its own lustrous turmoil

The ironing-board thanks god
for its two good strong legs and sturdy back

5 The new fridge hums like a maniac
with helpfulness

I am trying to love the world
back to normal

The chair recites its stand-alone prayer
10 again and again

The table leaves no stone unturned
The clock votes for the separate burial of hearts

I am trying to love the world
and all its 8000 identifiable languages

15 With the forgetfulness of a potter
I'm trying to get the seas back on the maps
where they belong,

secured to their rivers

20 The kettle alone knows the good he does,
here in the kitchen, loving the world,
steadfastly loving

See how easy it is, he whistles

Vocabulary
lustrous (lus′ trəs) *adj.*
gleaming; shining

Reading Strategy
Reciting Poetry
Aloud Recite lines 7-8.
Which other lines in the
poem parallel these lines?

Vocabulary
steadfastly
(sted′ fast′ lē) *adv.* in a firm
manner; without wavering

Critical Reading

1. Key Ideas and Details (a) What does the speaker say she is trying
to do? **(b) Infer:** Why is she paying so much attention to the objects
in her kitchen?

2. Integration of Knowledge and Ideas Are Duffy's sonnet and
Shuttle's free-verse poem equally effective as elegies? Explain. Use
two of these Essential Question words in your response: *crafted, contemporary, faith.* **[Connecting to the Essential Question: What is
the relationship of the writer to tradition?]**

Cite textual
evidence to
support your
responses.

Literary Analysis

1. Craft and Structure Use a chart like this one to show how the two poems are like and unlike a traditional **elegy.**

Traditional Elegy	"Prayer"	"In the Kitchen"
Is about a great loss		
Mourns a death		
Uses a formal, sad, solemn tone		
Draws universal lessons		

2. Craft and Structure (a) In terms of both structure and content, how is "Prayer" like and unlike a traditional Shakespearean sonnet? **(b)** Given its content, why do you think Duffy chose to write this poem in sonnet form?

Reading Strategy

3. Recite aloud "In the Kitchen" to help you recognize the parallel structures in the poem. What are the two main parallel structures?

4. (a) Explain how the second stanza of "Prayer" parallels the first. **(b)** What parallel structures occur in the final couplet of "Prayer"? How would you read these lines aloud?

PERFORMANCE TASKS
Integrated Language Skills

Vocabulary Acquisition and Use

Indicate whether each statement is true or false, and explain your answer.
   1. Some people use a special rinse to make their hair more *lustrous.*
   2. A hesitant coward *steadfastly* defends others.
   3. When there is total silence, no one *utters* a sound.
   4. *Scales* on a piano are little weights that press down inside when someone plays the keyboard.

Writing

Informative Text Imagine that you must give a **brief introduction to a radio spot** in which both these poems will be read. Using a style that will hook your audience, write an introduction that meets your purpose of providing listeners with the information they will need to understand and appreciate these particular poems and their authors.

Common Core State Standards

Writing
2.a. Introduce a topic; organize complex ideas, concepts, and information so that each new element builds on that which precedes it to create a unified whole.

ANITA DESAI INTRODUCES
"A Devoted Son"

The Long and Short of Novels and Stories

I have always thought of myself as a novelist. What I like is to write slowly, at length, feeling my way as I go, getting to know my characters and following them through their lives. Such books take three, four, or five years to write, and I am happy to live inside them for that time.

A Short Story Captures a Moment, an Episode They are draining to write, though, and in between novels, it is a relief to write short pieces. This also throws me a different challenge: to put everything I want to say into a few pages, perhaps just one scene, and make my point sharply and concisely. Writing a short story is more like writing a poem than a novel. It captures a moment, an episode. It leads no further. It is complete in itself.

These moments come to me as one lives one's days—passing sensations or impressions. Often they don't seem important at the time. Often they are forgotten. But some stay in the mind, keep resurfacing in the memory, teasing and haunting one. Why? Mostly they are little things—words you heard someone say as you stood in line for coffee, an object you saw in your grandmother's house, a field or a bridge you passed in a train. Why do they linger in the mind? What do they mean? What is their significance?

Planting the Seeds of Stories In order to find out, I scribble down a few lines about them on a piece of paper. I put it away with other scraps of paper that live in a file. They may

About the Author

Anita Desai's novel *Baumgartner's Bombay* won the *Hadassah* Prize. Her latest novel, *The Zigzag Way*, was published in 2004.

stay there a long time, even years. Then one day I take them out and find that one is ready, ripe. It is as if they were seeds I planted that are now ready to come bursting out of the earth. In winding a story around them, I understand at last what they meant.

The Seed for "A Devoted Son" "A Devoted Son" occurred to me when I heard an old white-haired neighbor sing a hymn in ringing tones at a ceremony that was being held in his house for his newborn grandson. The old man often embarrassed his family by wandering about the streets and accosting people with wild language and gestures. It was said of him that he had lost his mind when he had to flee his country, leaving his home and lands behind. His son and daughter-in-law took care of him, but it must have been difficult. Yet he was capable of singing, in that incredibly moving way, a hymn of praise to God.

I wanted to capture that duality of human nature, of human life. Nothing is so simple as it seems; everything is complex, mysterious. Yet art—music, literature—can render it so that it becomes utterly pure, clear, and transparent.

▶ **Critical Viewing**
What messages about human nature and life does this picture capture? **[Interpret]**

Critical Reading

1. **Key Ideas and Details (a)** What challenge does writing a short story pose for Desai? **(b) Infer:** How does she feel about such a challenge?

2. **Key Ideas and Details (a)** Where does Desai discover the ideas that eventually become stories? **(b) Interpret:** In your own words, explain why she does not develop these ideas immediately.

As You Read "A Devoted Son" . . .

3. **Integration of Knowledge and Ideas** As you read, consider ways in which "A Devoted Son" is similar to and different from the circumstances that first prompted Desai to write this story.

4. **Integration of Knowledge and Ideas** Explore ways in which "A Devoted Son" supports Desai's claim that literature can render the complexities in life so that they become "utterly pure, clear, and transparent."

Cite textual evidence to support your responses.

" Nothing is so simple as it seems; everything is complex, mysterious."

Connecting to the Essential Question In this story set in India, a father's attempt to help his son succeed backfires in unpredictable ways. As you read "A Devoted Son," notice details about changing social attitudes in India. Your ideas will help you respond to the Essential Question: **How does literature shape or reflect society?**

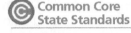

Common Core State Standards

Reading Literature
3. Analyze the impact of the author's choices regarding how to develop and relate elements of a story or drama.

Literary Analysis

The plots of many stories center on **generational conflicts,** differences between older and younger generations. Sometimes these differences are based on personality, but often social factors play a role. For example, a parent's traditional values may conflict with a child's modern ones.

The way characters respond to these and other conflicts often depends on whether the characters can change and grow.

- **Static characters** are those who do not change in the course of a work. They often represent a social role or a particular trait or attitude.
- **Dynamic characters** are those who undergo a major change. They may change by choice or may have change thrust upon them.

As you read, consider why the author chose to present both static and dynamic characters in this story.

Reading Strategy

Preparing to Read Complex Texts Whether a character is static or dynamic, you will understand his or her behavior better if you **identify the causes of the character's actions.** Use a chart like this to record behavior and its causes for the two main characters in "A Devoted Son."

Vocabulary

exemplary (eg zem′ plə rē) *adj.* worthy of serving as a model (p. 1421)

filial (fil′ ē əl) *adj.* of or due from a son or a daughter (p. 1421)

encomiums (en kō′ mē əmz) *n.* formal expressions of great praise (p. 1422)

complaisant (kəm plā′ zənt) *adj.* agreeable; willing to please (p. 1422)

fathom (fa*th*′ əm) *v.* understand thoroughly (p. 1423)

www.PHLitOnline.com

ANITA DESAI

(b. 1937)

Author of "A Devoted Son"

Anita Desai's father was Indian and her mother, German. This unusual heritage may have contributed to her understanding of people from many different cultures. She displays this understanding in finely crafted novels and short stories about conflicts among characters of different generations and backgrounds. These works of fiction have gained her a reputation as one of the most gifted Indian novelists writing in English.

A Diverse Heritage Desai was born in the northern Indian town of Mussoorie, located at the foot of the Himalaya Mountains. She grew up in the old section of Delhi, India's capital city. "There were a great many books in the house and we were all bookworms," Desai recalls.

Choosing a Language Because of its unique heritage, Desai's family spoke three languages: Hindi, English, and German. Desai first learned English at school. When asked why she chose to write in it, Desai explained, "It seemed to me the language of books. I just went on writing it because I always wanted to belong to this world of books." Desai became part of a new development in Indian literature—the Indian writing in English.

Recognition A precocious writer, Desai finished her first English story when she was seven and published for the first time when she was nine. After graduating from Delhi University, the newly married Desai joined the Writers Workshop in Calcutta. In 1963, she published her first novel, *Cry the Peacock,* a portrayal of the despair of a young married woman. This novel was followed by *Bye-Bye, Blackbird* (1968), *Fire on the Mountain* (1977), and *Clear Light of Day* (1980). This last novel, a study of complex family relationships, was nominated for England's prestigious Booker Prize. In many works, she with a quiet power explores the struggle of women in Indian culture to deal with the roles imposed on them by tradition.

> "My style of writing is to allow the story to unfold on its own."

ANITA DESAI

A Devoted Son

BACKGROUND *Since India won its independence from Britain in 1947, modernization has resulted in dramatic contrasts between old and new. In this story, Anita Desai dramatizes the conflict between the traditional respect shown parents, symbolized in the custom of touching one's father's feet, and the modern education that parents strive for their children to acquire.*

Anita Desai
Author's Insight
It is the custom to show respect for one's elders by bending to touch their feet, a custom observed more frequently in old-fashioned families, less so in modern, Westernized ones.

Reading Strategy
Identifying Causes of Characters' Actions
Why did Rakesh's parents sacrifice for him?

When the results appeared in the morning papers, Rakesh scanned them barefoot and in his pajamas, at the garden gate, then went up the steps to the verandah[1] where his father sat sipping his morning tea and bowed down to touch his feet.

"A first division, son?" his father asked, beaming, reaching for the papers.

"At the top of the list, papa," Rakesh murmured, as if awed. "First in the country."

Bedlam broke loose then. The family whooped and danced. The whole day long visitors streamed into the small yellow house at the end of the road to congratulate the parents of this *Wunderkind,*[2] to slap Rakesh on the back and fill the house and garden with the sounds and colors of a festival. There were garlands and halwa,[3] party clothes and gifts (enough fountain pens to last years, even a watch or two), nerves and temper and joy, all in a multicolored whirl of pride and great shining vistas newly opened: Rakesh was the first son in the family to receive an education, so much had been sacrificed in order to send him to school and then medical college, and at last the fruits of their sacrifice had arrived, golden and glorious.

---

1. **verandah** (və ran'də) *n.* partly enclosed porch or balcony along the outside of a building; also spelled veranda.
2. ***Wunderkind*** (voon'dər kint') *n.* person who achieves remarkable success at an early age.
3. **halwa** (häl vä') *n.* Middle Eastern sweet made from sesame flour and honey; also spelled halvah or halva.

◀ **Critical Viewing**
Identify two details in this photograph that illustrate the story's theme of the conflict between the modern and the traditional.
[Interpret]

To everyone who came to him to say "*Mubarak*,[4] Varmaji, your son has brought you glory," the father said, "Yes, and do you know what is the first thing he did when he saw the results this morning? He came and touched my feet. He bowed down and touched my feet." This moved many of the women in the crowd so much that they were seen to raise the ends of their saris[5] and dab at their tears while the men reached out for the betel-leaves[6] and sweetmeats that were offered around on trays and shook their heads in wonder and approval of such exemplary filial behavior. "One does not often see such behavior in sons any more," they all agreed, a little enviously perhaps. Leaving the house, some of the women said, sniffing, "At least on such an occasion they might have served pure *ghee*[7] sweets," and some of the men said, "Don't you think old Varma was giving himself airs? He needn't think we don't remember that he comes from the vegetable market himself, his father used to sell vegetables, and he has never seen the inside of a school." But there was more envy than rancor in their voices and it was, of course, inevitable—not every son in that shabby little colony at the edge of the city was destined to shine as Rakesh shone, and who knew that better than the parents themselves?

And that was only the beginning, the first step in a great, sweeping ascent to the radiant heights of fame and fortune. The thesis he wrote for his M.D. brought Rakesh still greater glory, if only in select medical circles. He won a scholarship. He went to the USA (that was what his father learnt to call it and taught the whole family to say—not America, which was what the ignorant neighbors called it, but, with a grand familiarity, "the USA") where he pursued his career

Literary Analysis
Generational Conflict Is there a generational conflict between Rakesh and his father at this point in the story? Explain.

Vocabulary
exemplary (eg zem′ plə rē) *adj.* worthy of serving as a model

filial (fil′ ē əl) *adj.* relating to a son or a daughter

☑ Reading Check

Why is Rakesh's family celebrating?

---

4. **Mubarak** (mu bär′ək) greeting meaning "blessed one." The word, originally from Arabic, has become part of some languages spoken in India.
5. **saris** (sä′rēz) *n.* traditional garments worn by Indian women, consisting of lengths of cotton, silk, or other cloth wrapped around the waist and draped over one shoulder.
6. **betel-leaves** (bēt′l) *n.* leaves from an evergreen shrub, usually wrapped around seeds from that shrub and commonly chewed in Asia.
7. **ghee** (gē) *n.* clarified butter, often used in Indian cooking.

Vocabulary

encomiums (en kō′ mē əmz) *n.* formal expressions of great praise

Anita Desai

Author's Insight I wanted to draw a quick sketch of a small town and its rather run-down outlying areas to show the humble beginnings of the famous man. Although he is exceptional in the eyes of his family and neighbors, he may not be so in the outer world. His light shines especially strong in this shabby setting.

Vocabulary

complaisant (kəm plā′ zənt) *adj.* agreeable; willing to please

Reading Strategy

Identifying Causes of Characters' Actions Why does Rakesh take his parents to the clinic? What probably causes his fame to dim somewhat soon after that?

Anita Desai

Author's Insight Acquiring a house and car are still signs of success in a country with much poverty.

in the most prestigious of all hospitals and won encomiums from his American colleagues which were relayed to his admiring and glowing family. What was more, he came *back*, he actually returned to that small yellow house in the once-new but increasingly shabby colony, right at the end of the road where the rubbish vans[8] tipped out their stinking contents for pigs to nose in and rag-pickers to build their shacks on, all steaming and smoking just outside the neat wire fences and welltended gardens. To this Rakesh returned and the first thing he did on entering the house was to slip out of the embraces of his sisters and brothers and bow down and touch his father's feet.

As for his mother, she gloated chiefly over the strange fact that he had not married in America, had not brought home a foreign wife as all her neighbors had warned her he would, for wasn't that what all Indian boys went abroad for? Instead he agreed, almost without argument, to marry a girl she had picked out for him in her own village, the daughter of a childhood friend, a plump and uneducated girl, it was true, but so old-fashioned, so placid, so complaisant that she slipped into the household and settled in like a charm, seemingly too lazy and too good-natured to even try and make Rakesh leave home and set up independently, as any other girl might have done. What was more, she was pretty—really pretty, in a plump, pudding way that only gave way to fat—soft, spreading fat, like warm wax—after the birth of their first baby, a son, and then what did it matter?

For some years Rakesh worked in the city hospital, quickly rising to the top of the administrative organization, and was made a director before he left to set up his own clinic. He took his parents in his car—a new, sky-blue Ambassador[9] with a rear window full of stickers and charms revolving on strings—to see the clinic when it was built, and the large sign-board over the door on which his name was printed in letters of red, with a row of degrees and qualifications to follow it like so many little black slaves of the regent.[10] Thereafter his fame seemed to grow just a little dimmer—or maybe it was only that everyone in town had grown accustomed to it at last—but it was also the beginning of his fortune for he now became known not only as the best but also the richest doctor in town.

However, all this was not accomplished in the wink of an eye. Naturally not. It was the achievement of a lifetime and it took up Rakesh's whole life. At the time he set up his clinic his father had grown into an old man and retired from his post at the kerosene dealer's depot at which he had worked for forty years, and his mother died soon after, giving up the ghost with a sigh that sounded positively happy, for it was her own son who ministered to her in her last illness and who sat pressing her feet at the last moment—such a son as few women had borne.

---

8. **rubbish vans** garbage trucks.
9. **Ambassador** popular model of car manufactured by Hindustan Motors of India.
10. **regent** (rē′ jənt) *n.* ruler; governor.

For it had to be admitted—and the most unsuccessful and most rancorous of neighbors eventually did so—that Rakesh was not only a devoted son and a miraculously good-natured man who contrived somehow to obey his parents and humor his wife and show concern equally for his children and his patients, but there was actually a brain inside this beautifully polished and formed body of good manners and kind nature and, in between ministering to his family and playing host to many friends and coaxing them all into feeling happy and grateful and content, he had actually trained his hands as well and emerged an excellent doctor, a really fine surgeon. How one man—and a man born to illiterate parents, his father having worked for a kerosene dealer and his mother having spent her life in a kitchen—had achieved, combined and conducted such a medley of virtues, no one could fathom, but all acknowledged his talent and skill.

It was a strange fact, however, that talent and skill, if displayed for too long, cease to dazzle. It came to pass that the most admiring of all eyes eventually faded and no longer blinked at his glory. Having retired from work and having lost his wife, the old father very quickly went to pieces, as they say. He developed so many complaints and fell ill so frequently and with such mysterious diseases that even his son could no longer make out when it was something of significance and when it was merely a peevish whim. He sat huddled on his string bed most of the day and developed an exasperating habit of stretching out suddenly and lying absolutely still, allowing the whole family to fly around him in a flap, wailing and weeping, and then suddenly sitting up, stiff and gaunt, and spitting out a big gob of betel-juice as if to mock their behavior.

He did this once too often: there had been a big party in the house, a birthday party for the youngest son, and the celebrations had to be suddenly hushed, covered up and hustled out of the way when the daughter-in-law discovered, or thought she discovered, that the old man, stretched out from end to end of his string bed, had lost his pulse; the party broke up, dissolved, even turned into a band of mourners, when the old man sat up and the distraught daughter-in-law received a gob of red spittle right on the hem of her organza[11] sari. After that no one much cared if he sat up crosslegged on his bed, hawking and spitting, or lay down flat and turned gray as a corpse. Except, of course, for that pearl amongst pearls, his son Rakesh.

It was Rakesh who brought him his morning tea, not in one of the china cups from which the rest of the family drank, but in the old man's favorite brass tumbler, and sat at the edge of his bed, comfortable and relaxed with the string of his pajamas dangling out from under his fine lawn night-shirt, and discussed or, rather, read out the morning news to his father. It made no difference to him that his father made no response apart from spitting. It was Rakesh, too, who,

---

11. **organza** (ôr gan′zə) *n.* stiff sheer fabric.

Vocabulary
fathom (fa*th*′ əm)
v. understand thoroughly

Anita Desai
Author's Insight He shows his bitterness and spite at the good health still enjoyed by the young.

Reading Check

Whom does Rakesh marry?

on returning from the clinic in the evening, persuaded the old man to come out of his room, as bare and desolate as a cell, and take the evening air out in the garden, beautifully arranging the pillows and bolsters on the divan[12] in the corner of the open verandah. On summer nights he saw to it that the servants carried out the old man's bed onto the lawn and himself helped his father down the steps and onto the bed, soothing him and settling him down for a night under the stars.

All this was very gratifying for the old man. What was not so gratifying was that he even undertook to supervise his father's diet. One day when the father was really sick, having ordered his daughter-in-law to make him a dish of *soojie*[13] *halwa* and eaten it with a saucerful of cream, Rakesh marched into the room, not with his usual respectful step but with the confident and rather contemptuous stride of the famous doctor, and declared, "No more *halwa* for you, papa. We must be sensible, at your age. If you must have something sweet, Veena will cook you a little *kheer*,[14] that's light, just a little rice and milk. But nothing fried, nothing rich. We can't have this happening again."

The old man who had been lying stretched out on his bed, weak and feeble after a day's illness, gave a start at the very sound, the tone of these words. He opened his eyes—rather, they fell open with shock—and he stared at his son with disbelief that darkened quickly to reproach. A son who actually refused his father the food he craved? No, it was unheard of, it was incredible. But Rakesh had turned his back to him and was cleaning up the litter of bottles and packets on the medicine shelf and did not notice while Veena slipped silently out of the room with a little smirk that only the old man saw, and hated.

Halwa was only the first item to be crossed off the old man's diet. One delicacy after the other went—everything fried to begin with, then everything sweet, and eventually everything, everything that the old man enjoyed.

The meals that arrived for him on the shining stainless steel tray twice a day were frugal to say the least—dry bread, boiled lentils, boiled vegetables and, if there were a bit of chicken or fish, that was boiled too. If he called for another helping—in a cracked voice that quavered theatrically—Rakesh himself would come to the door, gaze at him sadly and shake his head, saying, "Now, papa, we must be careful, we can't risk another illness, you know," and although the daughter-in-law kept tactfully out of the way, the old man could just see her smirk sliding merrily through the air. He tried to bribe his grandchildren into buying him sweets (and how he missed his wife now, that generous, indulgent and illiterate cook), whispering, "Here's fifty paise,"[15] as he stuffed the coins into a tight, hot fist.

Literary Analysis
Static and Dynamic Characters Does Rakesh's stride show a change in his character? In what way is he still the ideal son?

Anita Desai
Author's Insight By this act I want to show Rakesh taking over the role of the senior in the family and his father's shock at realizing he must relinquish it.

Literary Analysis
Generational Conflict
What role do traditional values play in the conflict that arises between Rakesh and his father?

Anita Desai
Author's Insight In a traditional, well-ordered family, defiance is not permitted, so little acts of rebellion have to be devised.

---

12. divan (dē´van´ or di van´) *n.* long backless sofa on which pillows or bolsters are usually arranged to support the back.
13. soojie *n.* Indian term for semolina, a coarse grain usually made from wheat; often spelled sooji or suji.
14. kheer (kir) *n.* rice pudding traditionally served as a dessert in southern India.
15. paise (pī´ se) *n.* plural of paisa, Indian money equal to 1/100 of a rupee.

"Run down to the shop at the crossroads and buy me thirty paise worth of *jalebis*,[16] and you can spend the remaining twenty paise on yourself. Eh? Understand? Will you do that?" He got away with it once or twice but then was found out, the conspirator was scolded by his father and smacked by his mother and Rakesh came storming into the room, almost tearing his hair as he shouted through compressed lips, "Now papa, are you trying to turn my little son into a liar? Quite apart from spoiling your own stomach, you are spoiling him as well—you are encouraging him to lie to his own parents. You should have heard the lies he told his mother when she saw him bringing back those *jalebis* wrapped up in filthy newspaper. I don't allow anyone in my house to buy sweets in the bazaar,[17] papa, surely you know that. There's cholera[18] in the city, typhoid, gastroenteritis— I see these cases daily in the hospital, how can I allow my own family to run such risks?" The old man sighed and lay down in the corpse position. But that worried no one any longer.

There was only one pleasure left in the old man now (his son's early morning visits and readings from the newspaper could no longer be called that) and those were visits from elderly neighbors. These were not frequent as his contemporaries were mostly as decrepit and helpless as he and few could walk the length of the road to visit him any more. Old Bhatia, next door, however, who was still spry enough to refuse, adamantly, to bathe in the tiled bathroom indoors and to insist on carrying out his brass mug and towel, in all seasons and usually at impossible hours, into the yard and bathe noisily under the garden tap, would look over the hedge to see if Varma were out on his verandah and would call to him and talk while he wrapped his *dhoti*[19] about him and dried the sparse hair on his head, shivering with enjoyable exaggeration. Of course these conversations, bawled across the hedge by two rather deaf old men conscious of having their entire households overhearing them, were not very satisfactory but Bhatia occasionally came out of his yard, walked down the bit of road and came in at Varma's gate to collapse onto the stone plinth built under the temple tree.[20] If Rakesh was at home he would help his father down the steps into the garden and arrange him on his night bed under the tree and leave the two old men to chew betel-leaves and discuss the ills of their individual bodies with combined passion.

"At least you have a doctor in the house to look after you," sighed Bhatia, having vividly described his martyrdom to piles.[21]

---

16. *jalebis* (jä leb'ēz) *n.* Indian sweets made by frying a coil of batter and then soaking it in syrup.
17. **bazaar** (bə zär') *n.* open-air market.
18. **cholera** (käl'ər ə) . . . **typhoid** (tī'foid), **gastroenteritis** dangerous infectious diseases causing fever or intestinal problems.
19. *dhoti* (dō'tē) *n.* cloth worn by Hindu men in India, with the ends passing through the legs and tucked in at the waist.
20. **stone . . . tree** stone slab beneath the frangipani, an erect tree often grown in temple gardens in India.
21. **piles** *n.* hemorrhoids.

Reading Strategy
Identifying Causes of Characters Actions What does Rakesh's decision to forbid his father sweets cause his father to do?

Anita Desai
Author's Insight Bathing outdoors is what one might do when living on a farm or a village. Naturally, it cannot be done in a city. I wanted to show how my characters are people still making the transition from one to the other.

Reading Check
What does Varma complain about to his friend?

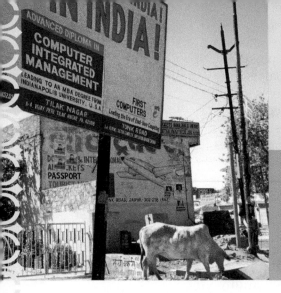

Is it possible, even in this evil age, for a son to refuse his father food?

Anita Desai

Author's Insight
Her refusal is an incredible act of disobedience by a younger member of the family to an elder. I wanted to show the daughter-in-law as belonging to a traditional family but breaking out of it when she can.

Literary Analysis
Static and Dynamic Characters In whose view has Rakesh's "sterling personality and character" undergone "a curious sea change"? Explain.

"Look after me?" cried Varma, his voice cracking like an ancient clay jar. "He—he does not even give me enough to eat."

"What?" said Bhatia, the white hairs in his ears twitching. "Doesn't give you enough to eat? Your own son?"

"My own son. If I ask him for one more piece of bread, he says no, papa, I weighed out the *ata*[22] myself and I can't allow you to have more than two hundred grams of cereal a day. He *weighs* the food he gives me, Bhatia—he has scales to weigh it on. That is what it has come to."

"Never," murmured Bhatia in disbelief. "Is it possible, even in this evil age, for a son to refuse his father food?"

"Let me tell you," Varma whispered eagerly. "Today the family was having fried fish—I could smell it. I called to my daughter-in-law to bring me a piece. She came to the door and said no. . . ."

"Said no?" It was Bhatia's voice that cracked. A *drongo*[23] shot out of the tree and sped away. *"No?"*

"No, she said no, Rakesh has ordered her to give me nothing fried. No butter, he says, no oil. . . ."

"No butter? No oil? How does he expect his father to live?"

Old Varma nodded with melancholy triumph. "That is how he treats me—after I have brought him up, given him an education, made him a great doctor. Great doctor! This is the way great doctors treat their fathers, Bhatia," for the son's sterling personality and character now underwent a curious sea change. Outwardly all might be the same but the interpretation had altered: his masterly efficiency was nothing but cold heartlessness, his authority was only tyranny in disguise.

There was cold comfort in complaining to neighbors and, on such a miserable diet, Varma found himself slipping, weakening and soon becoming a genuinely sick man. Powders and pills and mixtures were not only brought in when dealing with a crisis like an upset stomach

---

22. ata (ä´te) *n.* type of flour used in India.
23. drongo *n.* black bird with a long forked tail.

◀ **Critical Viewing**
Why would Varma be tempted by an open-air market, like the one shown here? **[Analyze]**

but became a regular part of his diet—became his diet, complained Varma, supplanting the natural foods he craved. There were pills to regulate his bowel movements, pills to bring down his blood pressure, pills to deal with his arthritis and, eventually, pills to keep his heart beating. In between there were panicky rushes to the hospital, some humiliating experience with the stomach pump and enema, which left him frightened and helpless. He cried easily, shriveling up on his bed, but if he complained of a pain or even a vague, gray fear in the night, Rakesh would simply open another bottle of pills and force him to take one. "I have my duty to you papa," he said when his father begged to be let off.

"Let me be," Varma begged, turning his face away from the pills on the outstretched hand. "Let me die. It would be better. I do not want to live only to eat your medicines."

"Papa, be reasonable."

"I leave that to you," the father cried with sudden spirit. "Leave me alone, let me die now, I cannot live like this."

"Lying all day on his pillows, fed every few hours by his daughter-in-law's own hand, visited by every member of his family daily—and then he says he does not want to live 'like this,'" Rakesh was heard to say, laughing, to someone outside the door.

"Deprived of food," screamed the old man on the bed, "his wishes ignored, taunted by his daughter-in-law, laughed at by his grand-children—*that* is how I live." But he was very old and weak and all anyone heard was an incoherent croak, some expressive grunts and cries of genuine pain. Only once, when old Bhatia had come to see him and they sat together under the temple tree, they heard him cry, "God is calling me—and they won't let me go."

The quantities of vitamins and tonics he was made to take were not altogether useless. They kept him alive and even gave him a kind of strength that made him hang on long after he ceased to wish to hang on. It was as though he were straining at a rope, trying to break it, and it would not break, it was still strong. He only hurt himself, trying.

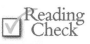

Reading Check

What becomes a regular part of Varma's diet?

In the evening, that summer, the servants would come into his cell, grip his bed, one at each end, and carry it out to the verandah, there sitting it down with a thump that jarred every tooth in his head. In answer to his agonized complaints they said the doctor sahib[24] had told them he must take the evening air and the evening air they would make him take—thump. Then Veena, that smiling, hypocritical pudding in a rustling sari, would appear and pile up the pillows under his head till he was propped up stiffly into a sitting position that made his head swim and his back ache.

"Let me lie down," he begged. "I can't sit up any more."

"Try, papa, Rakesh said you can if you try," she said, and drifted away to the other end of the verandah where her transistor radio vibrated to the lovesick tunes from the cinema[25] that she listened to all day.

So there he sat, like some stiff corpse, terrified, gazing out on the lawn where his grandsons played cricket,[26] in danger of getting one of their hard-spun balls in his eye, and at the gate that opened onto the dusty and rubbish-heaped lane but still bore, proudly, a newly touched-up signboard that bore his son's name and qualifications, his own name having vanished from the gate long ago.

At last the sky-blue Ambassador arrived, the cricket game broke up in haste, the car drove in smartly and the doctor, the great doctor, all in white, stepped out. Someone ran up to take his bag from him, others to escort him up the steps. "Will you have tea?" his wife called, turning down the transistor set. "Or a Coca-Cola? Shall I fry you some samosas?"[27] But he did not reply or even glance in her direction. Ever a devoted son, he went first to the corner where his father sat gazing, stricken, at some undefined spot in the dusty yellow air that swam before him. He did not turn his head to look at his son. But he stopped gobbling air with his uncontrolled lips and set his jaw as hard as a sick and very old man could set it.

"Papa," his son said, tenderly, sitting down on the edge of the bed and reaching out to press his feet.

Old Varma tucked his feet under him, out of the way, and continued to gaze stubbornly into the yellow air of the summer evening.

"Papa, I'm home."

Varma's hand jerked suddenly, in a sharp, derisive movement, but he did not speak.

"How are you feeling, papa?"

Then Varma turned and looked at his son. His face was so out of control and all in pieces, that the multitude of expressions that crossed it could not make up a whole and convey to the famous man exactly what his father thought of him, his skill, his art.

"I'm dying," he croaked. "Let me die, I tell you."

---

24. sahib (sä´ib´, hib´, ēb´, or hĭb´) Indian term of respect.
25. cinema (sin´ə mə) *n.* movies.
26. cricket *n.* open-air game played between two teams using balls and bats.
27. samosas (sə mō´səz) *n.* fried triangular Indian pastries containing vegetables or meat.

"Papa, you're joking," his son smiled at him, lovingly. "I've brought you a new tonic to make you feel better. You must take it, it will make you feel stronger again. Here it is. Promise me you will take it regularly, papa."

Varma's mouth worked as hard as though he still had a gob of betel in it (his supply of betel had been cut off years ago). Then he spat out some words, as sharp and bitter as poison, into his son's face. "Keep your tonic—I want none—I want none—I won't take any more of—of your medicines. None. Never," and he swept the bottle out of his son's hand with a wave of his own, suddenly grand, suddenly effective.

His son jumped, for the bottle was smashed and thick brown syrup had splashed up, staining his white trousers. His wife let out a cry and came running. All around the old man was hubbub once again, noise, attention.

He gave one push to the pillows at his back and dislodged them so he could sink down on his back, quite flat again. He closed his eyes and pointed his chin at the ceiling, like some dire prophet, groaning, "God is calling me—now let me go."

Literary Analysis
Static and Dynamic Characters Compare the father's character at the end of the story with that of the betel-juice spitter of earlier scenes.

Anita Desai
Author's Insight
According to Hindu belief, a human life is divided into four stages—that of a student, a householder, a pilgrim, and, finally, a hermit. This belief is ingrained in the father, who sees the natural cycle thwarted by his son's modern ways, and chafes against it.

Critical Reading ©

Cite textual evidence to support your responses.

© **1. Key Ideas and Details (a)** According to Varma, what is the first thing Rakesh does upon seeing his excellent exam results? **(b) Infer:** At this point in the story, what values does Rakesh's behavior reflect? **(c) Infer:** How does Varma feel about his son at this point in the story?

© **2. Integration of Knowledge and Ideas (a) Evaluate:** After Rakesh becomes a doctor, would you say his behavior toward his father remains devoted? Explain. **(b) Generalize:** What does the story suggest about the relationship between devotion and compassion in caring for others?

© **3. Integration of Knowledge and Ideas (a) Analyze:** Explain the irony of the title from Varma's perspective. **(b) Generalize:** In what ways is this conflict specifically Indian and in what ways is it universal?

© **4. Integration of Knowledge and Ideas (a) Evaluate:** Do you think Rakesh's behavior is truly devoted? Explain. **(b) Generalize:** What lessons about hopes or expectations does the story teach to parents like Varma and to people in general?

© **5. Integration of Knowledge and Ideas** What does the story show about traditional values and changing times in India? Explain, using at least three of these Essential Question words: *respectful, clash, modernization,* and *westernization. [Connecting to the Essential Question: How does literature shape or reflect society?]*

Literary Analysis

1. **Key Ideas and Details** **(a)** Name three things about which Rakesh and Varma come to disagree. **(b)** How do these disagreements reflect a **generational conflict** central to the story?

2. **Integration of Knowledge and Ideas** **(a)** In what ways is the story's generational conflict specific to the Indian setting? **(b)** In what ways is it more universal?

3. **Craft and Structure** Use a chart like this one to compare and contrast Varma and Rakesh in the beginning, middle, and end of the story. Which of the two do you think is a more **dynamic character**? Why?

Character	Beginning	Middle	End
Varma			
Rakesh			

4. **Key Ideas and Details** By the end of the story, what new perspective has Varma developed on his "devoted son"?

5. **Craft and Structure** Are Rakesh's mother and wife **static** or **dynamic characters**? Cite story details to explain your classifications.

6. **Craft and Structure** How does Desai use static and dynamic characters to explore ideas about traditional beliefs in the modern world? Use the characters' dialogue to support your answer.

7. **Integration of Knowledge and Ideas** Would it be possible to show a generational conflict using static characters only? Why or why not?

Reading Strategy

8. **(a) Identify the causes** that lead to the family's sacrifices for Rakesh's education. **(b)** Was this decision unwise? Explain.

9. Explain the causes of each of these actions on the part of Varma or Rakesh:
   (a) Varma hosts a party for the neighbors.
   (b) Rakesh touches his father's feet.
   (c) Varma "goes to pieces."
   (d) Rakesh puts his father on a strict diet.
   (e) Varma smashes the tonic his son brings him.

10. **(a)** In what sense does Varma cause his own problems in this story? **(b)** What role do his traditional values play in causing his problems?

Common Core
State Standards

Writing
1.a. Introduce precise, knowledgeable claim(s), distinguish the claim(s) from alternate or opposing claims, and create an organization that logically sequences claim(s), counterclaims, reasons, and evidence. *(p. 1431)*

1.b. Develop claim(s) and counterclaims fairly and thoroughly, supplying the most relevant evidence for each while pointing out the strengths and limitations of both in a manner that anticipates the audience's knowledge level, concerns, values, and possible biases. *(p. 1431)*

Language
4.a. Use context as a clue to the meaning of a word or phrase. *(p. 1431)*

Integrated Language Skills

Vocabulary Acquisition and Use

Vocabulary Lesson: Latin Root *-fil-*

The word *filial,* meaning "relating to a son or a daughter," contains the Latin root *-fil-,* which means "son or daughter." The same root occurs in the word *affiliate*, which goes back to a Latin word *affiliare,* meaning "to adopt as a son or daughter."

Forms of the word *affiliate* are often used in the fields of *history* and *political science.* Explain the meaning of each form of *affiliate* used in the following sentences, using a dictionary if necessary. Then, use the forms in sentences of your own.

1. With which political party is he *affiliated*?
2. She is an *affiliate* of the Whig party.
3. Is that nation in one of the international alliances, or is it *unaffiliated*?
4. What is your political *affiliation*?

Vocabulary: Context Clues

Context clues are words and phrases in a text that help you reason out the meaning of an unfamiliar word. Use context clues in the sentences below to choose the word from the vocabulary list on page 1418 that best completes the meaning. Then, explain how you arrived at your answers.

1. Rakesh was a(n) _____ student, earning the best grades in his division.
2. He was also a model of _____ devotion, showing much respect to his parents.
3. His father received many _____ for raising such a wonderful son.
4. Rakesh's wife was an easygoing, _____ local girl who tried hard to please her in-laws.
5. Varma could not _____ how Rakesh made him so unhappy when for years he had seemed such a devoted son.

Writing

Argumentative Text On page 1417, Anita Desai explains the original inspiration of this story. Write an **essay** comparing her original concept with the final product and arguing either that her original plan was fulfilled or that it fell short.

Prewriting Reread the story, jotting down details that do and do not conform to Desai's original concept. Evaluate whether or not the story as a whole effectively illustrates the original concept.

Drafting

- Begin by quoting Desai's original plan of capturing "that duality of human nature" and showing that "nothing is so simple as it seems."
- State whether Desai's story lives up to her plan.
- Defend your opinion by citing details from the story.

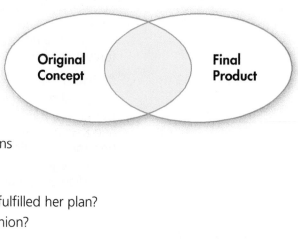

Original Concept · Final Product

Revising If your answer to any of the following questions is "no," make suitable revisions:

- Did I accurately state Desai's original plan?
- Did I clearly state my opinion of whether or not she fulfilled her plan?
- Did I provide enough story details to support my opinion?

"In this world without quiet corners, there can be no easy escapes from history, from hullabaloo, from terrible unquiet fuss."

— SALMAN RUSHDIE

Arundhati Roy

Contemporary British Fiction

A popular World War II song promised "love and laughter and peace ever after" when the world was free again. The truth was that years of air-raids, rationings, casualties, and bombed cities had worn out British citizens. The air breathed by modern writers now seemed stale and rarified. In the 1940s and 50s a new Britain began to emerge—one more critical of class privileges and more multicultural in make-up. This Britain looked different and sounded different. Contemporary British literature reflects this difference. Even more recently, British fiction has explored what it means to live in the consumerist, technological postmodern age, "wired" for fast connection—if not always for satisfying human relationships.

The Sun Never Sets on the British Empire At the height of its imperial power, Great Britain held great influence over its colonies and in world affairs. Throughout the twentieth century, British colonies demanded independence, and England's power waned. Numerous important British authors have written works that re-imagine major historical events in order to re-evaluate the effect they had on British society. Kazuo Ishiguro, a Japanese-born writer who settled in Britain at the age of five, wrote *The Remains of the Day*. Set on an English estate just before World War II and narrated by a butler who serves his master so well he cannot see the master's flaws, the novel chronicles the erosion of the British upper-class influence in domestic and world affairs. Pat Barker's trilogy of books about World War I (*Regeneration*, *The Eye in the Door*, *The Ghost Road*) shows the effects of the war on women and on members of the working class. Ian McEwan's *Atonement* sets its story in World War II and explores the British class system, showing how the life of a servant's son is forever changed by a careless lie.

"Glocal" Britain After World War II, any citizen from the British Commonwealth could immigrate to the United Kingdom, and numerous people from India, Bangladesh, South Africa, the Caribbean, Hong Kong, Nigeria, and Kenya resettled, particularly in London. England's capital city quickly became a teeming mixture of various ethnic identities, with a diversity of languages, customs, and religions. The epic novels of Salman Rushdie, an Indian-British novelist, are among the most critically acclaimed of the past 25 years. *Midnight's Children*, Rushdie's most popular work, tells the story of 1001 children born within an hour of India's independence and endowed with super powers. Rushdie's novels, which mix East and West, natural and supernatural, and the tragic and the comic, have influenced a generation of younger writers, including Zadie Smith. Smith, a woman of Jamaican and English heritage, also continues the great urban comic tradition of Charles Dickens. Her novels *White Teeth* and *On Beauty* celebrate the rich possibilities of hybrid ethnic identities and cross-cultural exchange in contemporary "glocal" (global and local) England.

Common Core State Standards

SL.11-12.1.a, SL.11-12.1.b, SL.11-12.1.c, SL.11-12.1.d
[For the full wording of the standards, see the standards chart in the front of your textbook.]

The Empire Writes Back On the other hand, writers from former colonies, such as South Africa's J. M. Coetzee and India's Arundhati Roy, depict the disfiguring legacies of colonialism in their novels. Both are considerably less optimistic about how deeply or quickly humans can recover from experiences of prejudice, conflict, or violence. Ireland, Great Britain's oldest colony and closest neighbor, continues to produced gifted writers, including Roddy Doyle, whose novels often are set in working class Dublin. Doyle has comically rewritten the pivotal event of Irish rebellion, the 1916 Easter Uprising in *A Star Called Henry*.

Hyperreality British literature also reflects the changes brought about by the computer age and by new scientific technologies. Kazuo Ishiguro's novel *Never Let Me Go* describes what seems like a fairly typical English boarding school—until the reader realizes that the students are clones. Ian McEwan's *Saturday* begins with the world's most famous 9/11 image, a plane off-course, and reflects on how life has changed in the United Kingdom since it supported the American occupation of Iraq. Nick Hornby's *About a Boy* examines the connection between loneliness and acquisitiveness, of living amid lots of great stuff—the best musical equipment, the fastest computers—but still not achieving the kind of human connections that make life meaningful.

Roddy Doyle

Zadie Smith

Speaking and Listening: Discussion

Comprehension and Collaboration With a small group, conduct a **panel discussion** on new British fiction, particularly any of the authors mentioned in this feature. As a group, choose an author and conduct research. Then, assign roles and responsibilities for each panelist. For example, decide who will introduce, moderate, and conclude the discussion.

During the discussion, work to clarify each others' ideas in a respectful manner, especially when there are disagreements. Invite questions and comments from the audience, and respond thoughtfully.

Connecting to the Essential Question In this story, social status plays a role in a couple's decisions about their son's boarding school. As you read, consider what the story shows about the social attitudes of Charlie's parents and future schoolmates. Your ideas will help you respond to the Essential Question: **How does literature shape or reflect society?**

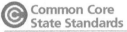

Common Core State Standards

Reading Literature
3. Analyze the impact of the author's choices regarding how to develop and relate elements of a story or drama.

Literary Analysis

Characterization is the creation and development of a character. In **direct characterization,** the writer explicitly states a character's traits. For example, in a story about a knight, the author may directly state "The knight was cruel and violent." In **indirect characterization,** the writer provides details from which you infer the character's traits: "'Do as I say or I'll chop off your heads,' the knight sneered to the children."

Characterization often helps point to a story's **theme.** For example, the story about the knight may express a theme such as "Cruelty and violence are wrong" or "Cruelty and violence may backfire."

In "Next Term, We'll Mash You," the author uses mostly indirect characterization to portray a boy and his parents. As you read, use the details—particularly the *dialogue,* or characters' spoken words—to determine the traits and attitudes of these characters. Also consider how those traits and attitudes relate to the story's theme.

Reading Strategy

Preparing to Read Complex Texts The society in which a work is produced or set usually influences that work. When you **evaluate social influences of the period,** you determine the value of social trends, ideas, or attitudes that a work's characters, plot, or setting reveals. Use a diagram like this to help you evaluate the contemporary British social influences in Lively's story.

Vocabulary

subdued (səb do͞od´ *or* dyo͞od´) *adj.* less intense; softened (p. 1436)

dappled (dap´ əld) *adj.* covered with spots of shade or anything else of a different color (p. 1438)

assessing (ə ses´ iŋ) *v.* determining the value of (p. 1439)

homespun (hōm´ spun´) *adj.* plain; homely (p. 1439)

condescension (kän´ di sen´ shən) *n.* an attitude of lowering oneself to deal with others not considered one's equal; haughtiness (p. 1440)

haggard (hag´ ərd) *adj.* wild-eyed or tired looking; gaunt (p. 1442)

PENELOPE LIVELY

(B. 1933)

Author of "Next Term, We'll Mash You"

One of contemporary Britain's most acclaimed fiction writers, Penelope Lively was born in Cairo, Egypt, when it was still an outpost of the British Empire. In 1945, when she was twelve years old, her parents sent her to a boarding school in Sussex, an English county south of London. For someone who had grown up in the multicultural world of British Egypt, England seemed an alien place. "There were all sorts of codes that I couldn't follow," she recalls; "I was always getting things wrong." Only later did Lively come to realize that being forced to observe English society as an outsider probably helped hone her skills as a writer.

A Late Bloomer After studying history in college, Lively married and began to raise a family. She gave no thought to becoming a writer until, in her late thirties, she tried her hand at writing a book for children. Several more children's books followed until, in 1977, she published her first novel for adults, *The Road to Lichfield*. That book, like much of Lively's fiction, explores the relationship between memory and the past, a subject that had interested Lively since her college days as a student of history.

Crafting the Past Lively sets some of her fiction in the Egypt of her childhood and has also written a nonfiction memoir about growing up there. Her 1987 novel *Moon Tiger*, which earned her Britain's prestigious Booker Prize, is about a historian who grew up in Egypt and decides to write a novel about it. Popular with critics as well as everyday readers, Lively is often praised for her polished, evocative prose, in which not a word is wasted. "Next Term, We'll Mash You" is from her 1986 story collection *Pack of Cards*.

> **"IN WRITING FICTION I AM TRYING TO IMPOSE ORDER UPON CHAOS, TO GIVE STRUCTURE AND MEANING TO WHAT IS APPARENTLY RANDOM."**

NEXT TERM, WE'LL MASH YOU

PENELOPE LIVELY

> **BACKGROUND** FOR CENTURIES, THE BRITISH UPPER CLASS HAS SENT ITS SONS TO EXCLUSIVE PRIVATE SCHOOLS (KNOWN IN BRITAIN AS "PUBLIC SCHOOLS") LIKE ETON, HARROW, OR WESTMINSTER, FOLLOWED BY STUDY AT ONE OF BRITAIN'S TWO MOST PRESTIGIOUS UNIVERSITIES, OXFORD OR CAMBRIDGE. SO EXCLUSIVE ARE THESE PUBLIC SCHOOLS THAT A FAMILY EXPECTING TO SEND A SON TO ONE OFTEN PUTS HIM DOWN ON A FUTURE ATTENDANCE LIST AT BIRTH. CHARLES MANDERS, THE BOY IN THE STORY, WILL BE ENTERING SCHOOL AS PART OF THE "LOWER THIRD"——THE AGE EQUIVALENT OF AN AMERICAN STUDENT STARTING THE EIGHTH GRADE.

Vocabulary
subdued (səb do͞od´ *or* dyo͞od´) *adj.* less intense; softened

Inside the car it was quiet, the noise of the engine even and subdued, the air just the right temperature, the windows tight-fitting. The boy sat on the back seat, a box of chocolates, unopened, beside him, and a comic, folded. The trim Sussex landscape flowed past the windows: cows, white-fenced fields, highly-priced period houses. The sunlight was glassy, remote as a coloured photograph. The backs of the two heads in front of him swayed with the motion of the car.

His mother half-turned to speak to him. "Nearly there now, darling."

The father glanced downwards at his wife's wrist. "Are we all right for time?"

"Just right. Nearly twelve."

"I could do with a drink. Hope they lay something on."

"I'm sure they will. The Wilcoxes say they're awfully nice people. Not really the schoolmaster-type at all, Sally says."

The man said, "He's an Oxford chap."

"Is he? You didn't say."

"Mmn."

"Of course, the fees are that much higher than the Seaford place."

"Fifty quid[1] or so. We'll have to see."

The car turned right, between white gates and high, dark, tight-clipped hedges. The whisper of the road under the tyres changed to the crunch of gravel. The child, staring sideways, read black lettering on a white board: "St Edward's Preparatory School. Please Drive Slowly'. He shifted on the seat, and the leather sucked at the bare skin under his knees, stinging.

The mother said, "It's a lovely place. Those must be the playing-fields. Look, darling, there are some of the boys.' She clicked open her handbag, and the sun caught her mirror and flashed in the child's eyes; the comb went through her hair and he saw the grooves it left, neat as distant ploughing.

"Come on, then, Charles, out you get."

The building was red brick, early nineteenth century, spreading out long arms in which windows glittered blackly. Flowers, trapped in neat beds, were alternate red and white. They went up the steps, the man, the woman, and the child two paces behind.

The woman, the mother, smoothing down a skirt that would be ridged from sitting, thought: I like the way they've got the maid all done up properly. The little white apron and all that. She's foreign, I suppose. Au pair.[2] Very nice. If he comes here there'll be Speech Days[3] and that kind of thing. Sally Wilcox says it's quite dressy—she got that cream linen coat for coming down here. You can see why it costs a bomb. Great big grounds and only an hour and a half from London.

---

1. quid *n.* slang for pounds, the chief monetary unit of Britain.

2. Au pair (ō per´) someone—often a student from a foreign country—who helps with the housework in exchange for room and board.

3. Speech Days special days for presenting awards in schools, usually marked by ceremony and speeches.

▲ **Critical Viewing**
Compare and contrast the author's description of the landscape in the first paragraph with the landscape shown in this image. **[Compare and Contrast]**

Literary Analysis
Characterization and Theme What do the mother's thoughts about the school reveal about the kind of person she is? To what story theme might this characterization point?

✓ **Reading Check**

Where are Charles's parents taking him?

▲ **Critical Viewing**
What sort of effect would a room like the one shown have on a person's perception of a new place? **[Relate]**

Vocabulary
dappled (dap' əld) *adj.* covered with spots of shade or anything else of a different color

"I LIKE THE ATMOSPHERE, DON'T YOU, JOHN?"

They went into a room looking out into a terrace. Beyond, dappled lawns, gently shifting trees, black and white cows grazing behind iron railings. Books, leather chairs, a table with magazines—*Country Life, The Field, The Economist.* "Please, if you would wait here. The Headmaster won't be long."

Alone, they sat, inspected. "I like the atmosphere, don't you, John?"

"Very pleasant, yes. Four hundred a term, near enough. You can tell it's a cut above the Seaford place, though, or the one at St Albans. Bob Wilcox says quite a few City people send their boys here. One or two of the merchant bankers, those kind of people. It's the sort of contact that would do no harm at all. You meet someone, get talking at a cricket match[4] or what have you . . . Not at all a bad thing."

"All right, Charles? You didn't get sick in the car, did you?"

The child had black hair, slicked down smooth to his head. His ears, too large, jutted out, transparent in the light from the window, laced with tiny, delicate veins. His clothes had the shine and crease of newness. He looked at the books, the dark brown pictures, his parents, said nothing.

"Come here, let me tidy your hair."

The door opened. The child hesitated, stood up, sat, then rose again with his father.

"Mr and Mrs Manders? How very nice to meet you—I'm Margaret Spokes, and will you please forgive my husband who is tied up with some wretch who broke the cricket pavilion window and will be just a few more minutes. We try to be organised but a schoolmaster's day is

---

4. cricket match game of cricket, a popular British outdoor sport played with balls and bats on an area called a pitch.

always just that bit unpredictable. Do please sit down and what will you have to revive you after that beastly drive? You live in Finchley, is that right?"

"Hampstead, really," said the mother. "Sherry would be lovely." She worked over the headmaster's wife from shoes to hairstyle, pricing and assessing. Shoes old but expensive—Russell and Bromley. Good skirt. Blouse could be Marks and Sparks[5]—not sure. Real pearls. Super Victorian ring. She's not gone to any particular trouble—that's just what she'd wear anyway. You can be confident, with a voice like that, of course. Sally Wilcox says she knows all sorts of people.

The headmaster's wife said, "I don't know how much you know about us. Prospectuses[6] don't tell you a thing, do they? We'll look round everything in a minute, when you've had a chat with my husband. I gather you're friends of the Wilcoxes, by the way. I'm awfully fond of Simon—he's down for Winchester, of course, but I expect you know that."

The mother smiled over her sherry. Oh, I know that all right. Sally Wilcox doesn't let you forget that.

"And this is Charles? My dear, we've been forgetting all about you! In a minute I'm going to borrow Charles and take him off to meet some of the boys because after all you're choosing a school for him, aren't you, and not for you, so he ought to know what he might be letting himself in for and it shows we've got nothing to hide."

The parents laughed. The father, sherry warming his guts, thought that this was an amusing woman. Not attractive, of course, a bit homespun, but impressive all the same. Partly the voice, of course; it takes a bloody expensive education to produce a voice like that. And other things, of course. Background and all that stuff.

"I think I can hear the thud of the Fourth Form coming in from games, which means my husband is on the way, and then I shall leave you with him while I take Charles off to the common-room."[7]

For a moment the three adults centred on the child, looking, judging. The mother said, "He looks so hideously pale, compared to those boys we saw outside."

"My dear, that's London, isn't it? You just have to get them out, to get some colour into them. Ah, here's James. James—Mr and Mrs Manders. You remember, Bob Wilcox was mentioning at Sports Day . . ."

The headmaster reflected his wife's style, like paired cards in Happy Families.[8] His clothes were mature rather than old, his skin well-scrubbed, his shoes clean, his geniality untainted by the least

Vocabulary
assessing (ə ses´ iŋ) *v.*
determining the value of

Vocabulary
homespun (hōm´ spun´)
adj. plain; homely

Reading
Check

Where are the Manders from?

---

5. **Marks and Sparks** nickname for Marks & Spencer, well-known British department store chain that generally sells less expensive items than, for example, the shoe store Russell and Bromley.
6. **Prospectuses** (prō or prə spek´ təs əz) *n.* statements, often in booklet form, outlining the attractions of a business or an institution such as a school.
7. **common-room** room where students relax and socialize.
8. **Happy Families** British version of the card game Go Fish, played with a special deck of forty-four cards depicting the mother, father, son, and daughter in eleven families.

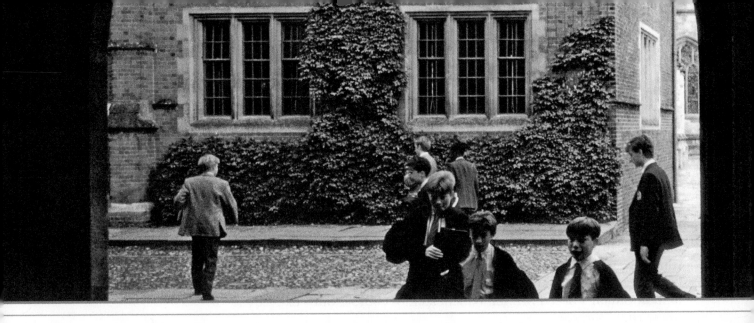

Vocabulary
condescension
(kän´ di sen´ shən) *n.* an attitude of lowering oneself to deal with others not considered one's equal; haughtiness

▲ Critical Viewing
What do you think Charles's experience will be in a school like the one shown in these photographs? **[Speculate]**

Literary Analysis
Characterization
What do the details about the headmaster's wife and the students' behavior toward her show about the kind of person she is?

condescension. He was genuinely sorry to have kept them waiting, but in this business one lurches from one minor crisis to the next . . . And this is Charles? Hello, there, Charles. His large hand rested for a moment on the child's head, quite extinguishing the thin, dark hair. It was as though he had but to clench his fingers to crush the skull. But he took his hand away and moved the parents to the window, to observe the mutilated cricket pavilion, with indulgent laughter.

And the child is borne away by the headmaster's wife. She never touches him or tells him to come, but simply bears him away like some relentless tide, down corridors and through swinging glass doors, towing him like a frail craft, not bothering to look back to see if he is following, confident in the strength of magnetism, or obedience.

And delivers him to a room where boys are scattered among inky tables and rungless chairs and sprawled on a mangy carpet. There is a scampering, and a rising, and a silence falling, as she opens the door.

"Now this is the Lower Third, Charles, who you'd be with if you come to us in September. Boys, this is Charles Manders, and I want you to tell him all about things and answer any questions he wants to ask. You can believe about half of what they say, Charles, and they will tell you the most fearful lies about the food, which is excellent."

The boys laugh and groan; amiable, exaggerated groans. They must like the headmaster's wife: there is licensed repartee.[9] They look at her with bright eyes in open, eager faces. Someone leaps to hold the door for her, and close it behind her. She is gone.

The child stands in the center of the room, and it draws in around him. The circle of children contracts, faces are only a yard or so from him; strange faces, looking, assessing.

---

9. licensed repartee (rep´ ər tē´) witty replies permitted or encouraged by the students.

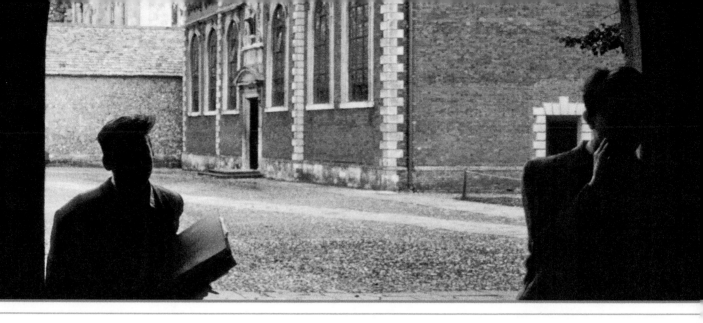

Asking questions. They help themselves to his name, his age, his school. Over their heads he sees beyond the window an inaccessible world of shivering trees and high racing clouds and his voice which has floated like a feather in the dusty schoolroom air dies altogether and he becomes mute, and he stands in the middle of them with shoulders humped, staring down at feet: grubby plimsolls[10] and kicked brown sandals. There is a noise in his ears like rushing water, a torrential din out of which voices boom, blotting each other out so that he cannot always hear the words. Do you? they say, and Have you? and What's your? and the faces, if he looks up, swing into one another in kaleidoscopic patterns and the floor under his feet is unsteady, lifting and falling.

And out of the noises comes one voice that is complete, that he can hear. "Next term, we'll mash you,' it says. "We always mash new boys."

And a bell goes, somewhere beyond doors and down corridors, and suddenly the children are all gone, clattering away and leaving him there with the heaving floor and the walls that shift and swing, and the headmaster's wife comes back and tows him away, and he is with his parents again, and they are getting into the car, and the high hedges skim past the car windows once more, in the other direction, and the gravel under the tyres changes to black tarmac.

"Well?"

"I liked it, didn't you?" The mother adjusted the car around her, closing windows, shrugging into her seat.

"Very pleasant, really. Nice chap."

"I liked him. Not quite so sure about her."

"It's pricey, of course."

"All the same . . ."

---

10. **plimsolls** (plim' səlz) n. British term for sneakers.

"NEXT TERM, WE'LL MASH YOU. WE ALWAYS MASH NEW BOYS."

Reading Check

To whom does the headmaster's wife introduce Charles?

Reading Strategy
Evaluate Social Influences of the Period What social influences prompt the father to think the high school fees are "money well spent"?

Vocabulary
haggard (hag´ ərd) *adj.* wild-eyed or tired looking; gaunt

"Money well spent, though. One way and another."

"Shall we settle it, then?"

"I think so. I'll drop him a line."

The mother pitched her voice a notch higher to speak to the child in the back of the car. "Would you like to go there, Charles? Like Simon Wilcox. Did you see that lovely gym, and the swimming-pool? And did the other boys tell you all about it?"

The child does not answer. He looks straight ahead of him, at the road coiling beneath the bonnet of the car. His face is haggard with anticipation.

"MONEY WELL SPENT, THOUGH. ONE WAY AND ANOTHER."

Critical Reading

Cite textual evidence to support your responses.

1. **Key Ideas and Details (a)** To what school is the Manders family going? **(b) Analyze:** What do the descriptions of the headmaster and his wife show about the kind of school it is?

2. **Key Ideas and Details (a) Summarize:** What do Charles's parents like about the school? **(b) Evaluate:** Do the parents seem properly concerned with Charles's education and happiness? Explain your opinion.

3. **Key Ideas and Details (a)** According to one boy, what do students in the Lower Third always do to newcomers? **(b) Infer:** What does the boy's warning suggest that school will be like for Charles?

4. **Integration of Knowledge and Ideas** What does this story show about class and its effects on British society? Explain, using at least two of these Essential Question words in your answer: *prestige, access, influential,* and *status.* [Connecting to the Essential Question: How does literature shape or reflect society?]

Literary Analysis

© 1. Craft and Structure Choose one character, and show how the author uses **indirect characterization** to reveal what the character is like.

© 2. Craft and Structure Explain how **characterization** reflects the story's **themes.** First, identify details that point to a particular trait or attitude in character. Then, show how the portrayal of that trait or attitude reflects a theme. Use a chart like this:

| Character/Detail | → | Trait or Attitude | → | Theme |

Reading Strategy

3. (a) What **social trends** does the story seem to be criticizing through the characters of the parents? **(b)** What social trends might it be criticizing through the characters of the students?

4. Based on this story, how does class seem to affect the British education system?

PERFORMANCE TASKS
Integrated Language Skills

© Vocabulary Acquisition and Use

Complete the following analogies, using the words from the vocabulary list on page 1434. Use each word only once, and explain your choice.

1. *Counting* is to *enumeration* as _____ is to *evaluation.*

2. *Glamorous* is to *supermodel* as _____ is to *frump.*

3. *Courage* is to *hero* as _____ is to *snob.*

4. *Striped* is to *lines* as _____ is to *spots.*

5. *Loud* is to *scream* as _____ is to *whisper.*

6. *Skinny* is to *thin* as _____ is to *worn.*

Writing

© Argumentative Text Write a **magazine advertisement** for St. Edward's Preparatory School that would attract a couple like the Manders. Think about the persuasive techniques you might employ. To what emotions should you appeal? What tone and language should you use? Would the Manders respond to a **bandwagon** approach ("everybody's doing it"), or to **testimonials,** in which people of stature praise the school? Write your final copy along with a description of visuals that would accompany the text.

© Common Core State Standards

Writing
4. Produce clear and coherent writing in which the development, organization, and style are appropriate to task, purpose, and audience.

Connecting to the Essential Question Arthur C. Clarke challenges the idea that humans can truly conquer space. As you read, notice how Clarke's views are affected by the physical nature of outer space. Your ideas will help you respond to the Essential Question: **What is the relationship between literature and place?**

Literary Analysis

An **argumentative essay** is a short nonfiction piece that argues a particular position. It may develop a number of central ideas that reinforce each other. It typically displays some or all of these features:

- A clear statement of the author's position
- A formal, informative tone
- Carefully researched facts that support general statements
- Ringing phrases to make the argument memorable
- Appeals to reason and/or emotion to convince readers
- Details that address reader concerns and counterclaims
- Clarification of unfamiliar concepts or a refinement of familiar ones

One way to clarify unfamiliar concepts is to use **analogies,** or extended comparisons of an unfamiliar idea to a familiar one. To refine the meaning of a familiar term, the author may apply the term repeatedly, using examples, counterexamples, and definitions to shape readers' understanding of the term. To advance his argument, Clarke refines the meaning of terms such as *space* and *distance*.

Reading Strategy

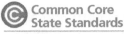 **Preparing to Read Complex Texts** **Applying an expository critique** means evaluating the power and truthfulness of an author's argument. As you read, use a checklist like the one shown to prepare an expository critique of Clarke's argument. Use textual evidence to support your inferences.

Vocabulary

ludicrous (lōō′ di krəs) *adj.* absurd; ridiculous (p. 1446)

irrevocable (ir rev′ ə kə bəl) *adj.* unable to be undone or canceled (p. 1447)

instantaneous (in′ stən tā′ nē əs) *adj.* done or happening in an instant (p. 1449)

enigma (e nig′ mə) *n.* riddle; puzzling situation; mystery (p. 1450)

inevitable (in ev′ i tə bəl) *adj.* unavoidable; certain to happen (p. 1451)

Common Core State Standards

Reading Informational Text

2. Determine two or more central ideas of a text and analyze their development over the course of the text, including how they interact and build on one another to provide a complex analysis; provide an objective summary of the text.

4. Determine the meaning of words and phrases as they are used in a text, including figurative, connotative, and technical meanings; analyze how an author uses and refines the meaning of a key term or terms over the course of a text.

Criteria	Evaluation
Power of arguments	
Validity and truthfulness of arguments	
Appeal to friendly readers	
Appeal to hostile readers	
Anticipation of reader concerns	

www.PHLitOnline.com

Arthur C. Clarke

Author of "We'll Never Conquer Space"

With more than one hundred million copies of his books in print worldwide, Arthur C. Clarke may have been the most successful science-fiction writer of all time. The extensive appeal of his books is probably due to their distinctive combination of technical expertise and touches of poetry.

A Scientific Start As a child, Clarke's natural curiosity led him to explore science and space with unflagging enthusiasm. He created his own map of the moon based on observations he made with a homemade telescope. At the age of twelve, when he started to read a magazine called *Amazing Stories,* Clarke discovered science fiction.

Imagining Satellites During World War II, Clarke's interest in scientific matters led to his service as a radar instructor in the Royal Air Force. At the end of the war, he drew on his wartime experience and his passion for space in an article for *Wireless World* magazine. The piece, entitled "Extra-Terrestrial Relays" (see page 1455) explained how television and telephone signals could be bounced off relay stations—satellites—sent into orbit by rocket. Clarke described, in essence, the methods used today for television and other broadcasting. Many consider Clarke "the godfather of global communication."

A Writer's Perspective From the early 1950s, Clarke worked full time as a writer, producing more than seventy works of fiction and non-fiction. One of his earliest stories, "The Sentinel" (1951), provided the germ of an idea for the epic film *2001: A Space Odyssey* (1968). Clarke summarized the film as an exploration of "man's place in the pecking order of cosmic intelligence."

Exploration of the Possible Clarke established credibility with his audience through an impressive command of science. However, while his speculations are grounded in hard facts, he turns them to lyrical, romantic ends in his science-fiction works. Challenging the notion that science fiction is escapism, Clarke asserted that the genre is "virtually the only kind of writing that's dealing with real problems and possibilities. . . ."

"The only way of finding the limits of the possible is by going beyond them into the impossible."

Conquer Space

Arthur C. Clarke

Background Clarke wrote this essay in 1960, at the brink of the era of space exploration. Three years earlier, in 1957, Sputnik had become the first satellite launched into space. The year after Clarke wrote the essay, in 1961, Alan Shepard became the first American to enter space. Over the next decades, human beings were to land on the moon (1969) and explore Mars via remote probes (1997). Yet Clarke's caution about the limits on the human conquest of space has yet to be tested.

Vocabulary
ludicrous (lo͞o di krəs) *adj.* absurd; ridiculous

▲ **Critical Viewing**
Does this picture support or challenge Clarke's statement, "Man will never conquer space"? Explain. **[Connect]**

Man will never conquer space. Such a statement may sound ludicrous, now that our rockets are already 100 million miles beyond the moon and the first human travelers are preparing to leave the atmosphere. Yet it expresses a truth which our forefathers knew, one we have forgotten—and our descendants must learn again, in heart-break and loneliness.

Our age is in many ways unique, full of events and phenomena which never occurred before and can never happen again. They distort our thinking, making us believe that what is true now will be true forever, though perhaps on a larger scale. Because we have annihilated distance on this planet, we imagine that we can do it once again. The facts are far otherwise, and we will see them more clearly if we forget the present and turn our minds towards the past.

To our ancestors, the vastness of the earth was a dominant fact controlling their thoughts and lives. In all earlier ages than ours, the world was wide indeed, and no man could ever see more than a tiny fraction of its immensity. A few hundred miles—a thousand, at the most—was infinity. Only a lifetime ago, parents waved farewell to their emigrating children in the virtual certainty that they would never meet again.

And now, within one incredible generation, all this has changed. Over the seas where Odysseus wandered for a decade, the Rome-Beirut Comet whispers its way within the hour. And above that, the closer satellites span the distance between Troy and Ithaca[1] in less than a minute.

Psychologically as well as physically, there are no longer any remote places on earth. When a friend leaves for what was once a far country, even if he has no intention of returning, we cannot feel that same sense of irrevocable separation that saddened our forefathers. We know that he is only hours away by jet liner, and that we have merely to reach for the telephone to hear his voice.

In a very few years, when the satellite communication network is established, we will be able to see friends on the far side of the earth as easily as we talk to them on the other side of the town. Then the world will shrink no more, for it will have become a dimensionless point.

Forever Too Large

But the new stage that is opening up for the human drama will never shrink as the old one has done. We have abolished space here on the little earth; we can never abolish the space that yawns between the stars. Once again we are face to face with immensity and must accept its grandeur and terror, its inspiring possibilities and its dreadful restraints. From a world that has become too small, we are moving out into one that will be forever too large, whose frontiers will recede from us always more swiftly than we can reach out towards them.

Consider first the fairly modest solar, or planetary, distances which we are now preparing to assault. The very first Lunik[2] made a substantial impression upon them, traveling more than 200 million miles from the earth—six times the distance to Mars. When we have harnessed nuclear energy for spaceflight, the solar system will contract until it is little larger than the earth today. The remotest of the

Reading Strategy
Applying an Expository Critique What is the effect of Clarke's suggesting—in the first paragraph—that his own argument may sound ludicrous?

Vocabulary
irrevocable (ir rəv´ ə kə bəl) *adj.* unable to be undone or canceled

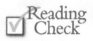
Reading Check
What effect does Clarke say technology is having on distances on Earth?

---

1. **Odysseus . . . Troy and Ithaca** Odysseus was the King of Ithaca and hero of Homer's *Odyssey.* Troy and Ithaca are the ancient cities marking the beginning and end of his wanderings across the Mediterranean Sea in the *Odyssey.* The Comet was an airplane, one of the fastest at the time the essay was written.
2. **Lunik** name given by American journalists to Luna I, an unmanned Soviet space probe of 1959.

▼ **Critical Viewing** What does Clarke say are the limitations of today's radio equipment like the dish shown below? **[Support]**

It will never be possible to converse with anyone on another planet.

planets will be perhaps no more than a week's travel from the earth, while Mars and Venus will be only a few hours away.

This achievement, which will be witnessed within a century, might appear to make even the solar system a comfortable, homely place, with such giant planets as Saturn and Jupiter playing much the same role in our thoughts as do Africa or Asia today. (Their qualitative differences of climate, atmosphere and gravity, fundamental though they are, do not concern us at the moment.) To some extent this may be true, yet as soon as we pass beyond the orbit of the moon, a mere quarter-million miles away, we will meet the first of the barriers that will separate the earth from her scattered children.

The marvelous telephone and television network that will soon enmesh the whole world, making all men neighbors, cannot be extended into space. It will never be possible to converse with anyone on another planet.

Do not misunderstand this statement. Even with today's radio equipment, the problem of sending speech to the other planets is almost trivial. But the messages will take minutes—sometimes hours—on their journey, because radio and light waves travel at the same limited speed of 186,000 miles a second.

Twenty years from now you will be able to listen to a friend on Mars, but the words you hear will have left his mouth at least three minutes earlier, and your reply will take a corresponding time to reach him. In such circumstances, an exchange of verbal messages is possible—but not a conversation.

Even in the case of the nearby moon, the 2½ second time-lag will be annoying. At distances of more than a million miles, it will be intolerable.

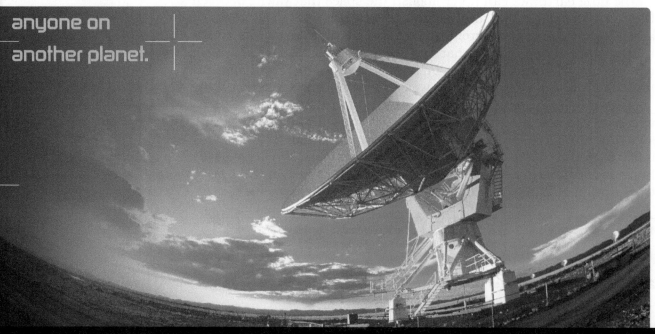

"Time Barrier"

To a culture which has come to take instantaneous communication for granted, as part of the very structure of civilized life, this "time barrier" may have a profound psychological impact. It will be a perpetual reminder of universal laws and limitations against which not all our technology can ever prevail. For it seems as certain as anything can be that no signal—still less any material object—can ever travel faster than light.

The velocity of light is the ultimate speed limit, being part of the very structure of space and time. Within the narrow confines of the solar system, it will not handicap us too severely, once we have accepted the delays in communication which it involves. At the worst, these will amount to 20 hours—the time it takes a radio signal to span the orbit of Pluto, the outermost planet.

Between the three inner worlds the earth, Mars, and Venus, it will never be more than 20 minutes—not enough to interfere seriously with commerce or administration, but more than sufficient to shatter those personal links of sound or vision that can give us a sense of direct contact with friends on earth, wherever they may be.

It is when we move out beyond the confines of the solar system that we come face to face with an altogether new order of cosmic reality. Even today, many otherwise educated men—like those savages who can count to three but lump together all numbers beyond four—cannot grasp the profound distinction between solar and stellar space. The first is the space enclosing our neighboring worlds, the planets; the second is that which embraces those distant suns, the stars, and it is literally millions of times greater.

There is no such abrupt change of scale in terrestrial affairs. To obtain a mental picture of the distance to the nearest star, as compared with the distance to the nearest planet, you must imagine a world in which the closest object to you is only five feet away—and then there is nothing else to see until you have traveled a thousand miles.

Many conservative scientists, appalled by these cosmic gulfs, have denied that they can ever be crossed. Some people never learn; those who 60 years ago scoffed at the possibility of flight, and ten (even five!) years ago laughed at the idea of travel to the planets, are now quite sure that the stars will always be beyond our reach. And again they are wrong, for they have failed to grasp the great lesson of our age—that if something is possible in theory, and no fundamental scientific laws oppose its realization, then sooner or later it will be achieved.

One day, it may be in this century, or it may be a thousand years from now, we shall discover a really efficient means of propelling our space vehicles. Every technical device is always developed to its limit (unless it is superseded by something better) and the ultimate speed for spaceships is the velocity of light. They will never reach that goal, but they will get very close to it. And then the nearest star will be less than five years' voyaging from the earth.

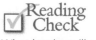

Finding a Place in the World

Clarke's essay poses the question, What is the place of humanity in the universe? With each shift in history, the literature of the British tradition has returned to this question—whether it is in the mingled yearnings for home and for the sea in the Anglo-Saxon poem "The Seafarer" (p. 20) or in Bede's definition of England as a homeland (p. 84) or in Milton's cosmic explorations in *Paradise Lost* (p. 524). Swift brought his satirical eye to the question in *Gulliver's Travels* (p. 606), finding that we are neither small enough (nor unreasonable enough) for Lilliput nor big enough (nor good enough) for Brobdingnag. Sydney Smith took on the issue in perhaps its smallest form: How physically comfortable can we be in the world? (see p. 1065).

Many of these writers, like Clarke, uncover a kind of universal human homelessness—a way in which the world leaves us with persistent, unsatisfied desires or unanswered questions. By affirming this condition, these writers remind us of our limits and challenge us to celebrate the life they define.

Connect to the Literature

What effect does the complexity of the universe have on our own sense of size? Explain.

Vocabulary
enigma (e nig´ mə) *n.* riddle; puzzling situation; mystery

Our exploring ships will spread outwards from their home over an ever-expanding sphere of space. It is a sphere which will grow at almost—but never quite—the speed of light. Five years to the triple system of Alpha Centauri, 10 to the strangely-matched doublet Sirius A and B, 11 to the tantalizing enigma of 61 Cygni,[3] the first star suspected to possess a planet. These journeys are long, but they are not impossible. Man has always accepted whatever price was necessary for his explorations and discoveries, *and the price of Space is Time.*

Even voyages which may last for centuries or millennia will one day be attempted. Suspended animation has already been achieved in the laboratory, and may be the key to interstellar travel. Self-contained cosmic arks which will be tiny traveling worlds in their own right may be another solution, for they would make possible journeys of unlimited extent, lasting generation after generation.

The famous Time Dilation effect predicted by the Theory of Relativity,[4] whereby time appears to pass more slowly for a traveler moving at almost the speed of light, may be yet a third. And there are others.

Looking far into the future, therefore, we must picture a slow (little more than half a billion miles an hour!) expansion of human activities outwards from the solar system, among the suns scattered across the region of the galaxy in which we now find ourselves. These suns are on the average five light-years apart; in other words, we can never get from one to the next in less than five years.

To bring home what this means, let us use a down-to-earth analogy. Imagine a vast ocean, sprinkled with islands—some desert, others perhaps inhabited. On one of these islands an energetic race has just discovered the art of building ships. It is preparing to explore the ocean, but must face the fact that the very nearest island is five years' voyaging away, and that no possible improvement in the technique of ship-building will ever reduce this time.

In these circumstances (which are those in which we will soon find ourselves) what could the islanders achieve?

---

3. **Alpha Centauri . . . 61 Cygni** Alpha Centauri is a system of three stars in the constellation of the Centaur; one of these, Proxima Centauri, is the star closest to Earth besides the sun. Sirius, known as the Dog Star, is the brightest star in Earth's sky; it is actually two stars orbiting each other, one of which (Sirius B), is only as big as the earth. 61 Cygni is a binary star in the constellation Cygnus, the Swan.

4. **Theory of Relativity** In physics, the theory that measurements of an object's physical properties will vary depending on the relative motion of the observer and the observed object: Only the speed of light is constant. One consequence of the theory is that time, as measured by an external observer, will slow down on an object moving close to the speed of light. In theory, a person traveling near the speed of light would age at a slower rate than a person traveling more slowly (the "Time Dilation effect" referred to by Clarke).

Man has always accepted whatever price was necessary for his explorations and discoveries, and the price of Space is Time.

After a few centuries, they might have established colonies on many of the nearby islands and have briefly explored many others. The daughter colonies might themselves have sent out further pioneers, and so a kind of chain reaction would spread the original culture over a steadily expanding area of the ocean.

But now consider the effects of the inevitable, unavoidable time-lag. There could be only the most tenuous contact between the home island and its offspring. Returning messengers could report what had happened on the nearest colony—five years ago. They could never bring information more up to date than that, and dispatches from the more distant parts of the ocean would be from still further in the past—perhaps centuries behind the times. There would never be news from the other islands, but only history.

Vocabulary
inevitable (in ev´ i tə bəl)
adj. unavoidable; certain to happen

Critical Reading

1. Key Ideas and Details (a) What reason does Clarke offer for claiming that a true conversation with someone on another planet is impossible? **(b) Classify:** What distinction does Clarke make between exchanging messages and having a conversation?

Cite textual evidence to support your responses.

2. Key Ideas and Details (a) Compare and Contrast: According to Clarke, how is conquering space different from conquering regions of the Earth? **(b) Infer:** What implications does Clarke think that conquering space would have for human society?

3. Integration of Knowledge and Ideas What broader lesson about human limitations does Clarke's essay contain?

4. Integration of Knowledge and Ideas How does Clarke's view of space as a "place" inform the argument he makes? In your response, use at least two of these Essential Question words: *interplanetary, stellar, limitation.* **[Connecting to the Essential Question: What is the relationship between literature and place?]**

WHERE IS OUR ISLAND HOME?

In the Venerable Bede's *History of the English Church and People*, England makes its debut on the world stage as a remote but fertile island in the North Atlantic. To Arthur C. Clarke, writing well over a thousand years later, the Earth itself is an island home in an unimaginably vast ocean of space.

Is home the Milky Way Galaxy?

Is home the planet Earth?

Is home the British Isles?

Is home the city of London?

CONNECT TO THE LITERATURE

As your eye moves upward on the page, consider how Clarke might answer the questions about a Londoner's Home.

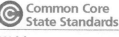

Literary Analysis

1. Key Ideas and Details (a) Summarize the argument that Clarke makes in this **argumentative essay.** Explain how the two central ideas of limits to communication and expanding exploration build on each other. **(b)** What facts and reasons does he provide to support his argument? Use a chart like this to gather your ideas.

Argument:	
Facts	Reasons

2. Craft and Structure (a) Explain Clarke's **analogy** involving islands in the ocean. **(b)** What general point does Clarke make with the analogy?

3. Craft and Structure (a) Explain how Clarke refines the term *space* in the essay, leading to the distinction between solar and stellar space. **(b)** In what way does his refinement of the term support his argument?

4. Integration of Knowledge and Ideas Has Clarke made a persuasive argument about the impossibility of conquering space? Explain.

Reading Strategy

5. (a) In **applying an expository critique** to this essay, what logical and emotional appeals would you cite as especially effective? **(b)** What ringing phrases make the essay memorable?

6. Explain how well Clarke addresses counterclaims to his argument.

PERFORMANCE TASKS
Integrated Language Skills

Vocabulary Acquisition and Use

For each word, choose the letter of its antonym, and explain your choice.

1. ludicrous: **(a)** sensible **(b)** puzzling **(c)** unwise **(d)** tiresome
2. irrevocable: **(a)** tangible **(b)** changeable **(c)** laughable **(d)** doable
3. instantaneous: **(a)** momentous **(b)** large **(c)** wasteful **(d)** slow
4. enigma: **(a)** explanation **(b)** complexity **(c)** puzzle **(d)** stain
5. inevitable: **(a)** wishful **(b)** hopeless **(c)** avoidable **(d)** endurable

Writing

Informative Text Write a brief **essay** in which you *verify and clarify* the facts and explanations that Clarke provides. Using reliable print or online sources, confirm the distances, times, and other factual information in the essay. Remember to attribute your sources of information.

Common Core State Standards

Writing
2. Write informative/ explanatory texts to examine and convey complex ideas, concepts, and information clearly and accurately through the effective selection, organization, and analysis of content.

Analyzing Functional and Expository Texts

Technical Article • Press Release

About the Texts

A **technical article** provides information on a scientific or technological subject. Many technical articles propose new ideas or announce breakthroughs in research. They often include statistical information and factual details explaining the idea; charts, graphs, illustrations, and other visual aids; and conclusions, references, appendices, and footnoted commentary.

A **press release** is a document that an organization sends to the news media to announce developments or events. Written to influence as well as inform media coverage, press releases contain these features:

- An extended headline or subhead summarizing the announcement

- Together with the date of the release, a brief description of key facts answering questions like *Who?, What?, When?, Where?, Why?,* and *How?*

- Supporting quotations from experts or those involved in the project

Reading Strategy

Informational writing uses *text structures* such as cause-and-effect relationships, which show how one thing brings about another. Consequently, **analyzing cause-and-effect relationships** can help you better understand an informational document. As you read, look for explanations of how a particular event or situation produced or might produce particular effects. Use a chart like the one shown to help you identify causes and effects.

Event	Causes	Effects

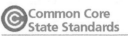

**Common Core
State Standards**

**Reading Informational Text
5.** Analyze and evaluate the effectiveness of the structure an author uses in his or her exposition or argument, including whether the structure makes points clear, convincing, and engaging.

Content-Area Vocabulary

These words appear in the selections that follow. They may also appear in other content-area texts:

satellite (sat´ ʻl it) *n.* a man-made object that revolves around the Earth or another celestial body to relay data

atmosphere (at´ məs fir´) *n.* the mass of gas surrounding any star or planet

velocity (və läs´ ə tē) *n.* the speed and direction of a moving object

orbits (ôr´bits) *n.* paths of celestial bodies revolving around other bodies, like planets or stars

In this article, Clarke proposed a new form of world-wide communication based on "stationary" artificial satellites that could hover in place above a single spot on the Earth. Today, such satellite communication is common, but it was a revolutionary idea when scientist and science-fiction writer Arthur C. Clarke first proposed it in the October, 1945, issue of the journal *Wireless World*. (October, 1945, pp. 305–308).

Extra-Terrestrial Relays:
Can Rocket Stations Give
World-wide Radio Coverage?

By Arthur C. Clarke

> The author is suggesting that the answer to the question in the title is yes. He is also implying that the article will reveal the cause-and-effect chain leading to such "radio coverage."

. . . A rocket which achieved a sufficiently great speed in flight outside the earth's atmosphere would never return. This "orbital" velocity is 8 km per sec (5 miles per sec), and a rocket which attained it would become an artificial satellite, circling the world for ever with no expenditure of power—a second moon, in fact. . . .

> The author makes a prediction that, if true, will make possible the kind of rocket stations he refers to in his title.

It will be possible in a few more years to build radio controlled rockets which can be steered into such orbits beyond the atmosphere and left to broadcast scientific information back to the earth. A little later, manned rockets will be able to make similar flights with sufficient excess power to break the orbit and return to earth.

There are an infinite number of possible stable orbits, circular and elliptical, in which a rocket would remain, if the initial conditions were correct. The velocity of 8 km/sec. applies only to the closest possible orbit, one just outside the atmosphere . . .

> The fact the author points out in this paragraph is extremely important and lays the causal basis for his proposal.

It will be observed that one orbit, with a radius of 42,000 km, has a period of exactly 24 hours. A body in such an orbit, if its plane coincided with that of the earth's equator, would revolve with the earth and would thus be stationary above the same spot on the planet. It would remain fixed in the sky of a whole hemisphere and unlike all other heavenly bodies would neither rise nor set. A body in a smaller orbit would revolve more quickly than the earth and so would rise in the west, as indeed happens with the inner moon of Mars.

Using material ferried up by rockets, it would be possible to construct a "space station" in such an orbit. The station could be provided with living quarters, laboratories and everything needed for the comfort of its crew, who would be relieved and provisioned by a regular rocket service. This project might be undertaken for purely scientific reasons as it would contribute enormously to our knowledge of astronomy, physics, and meteorology. . . .

Although such an undertaking may seem fantastic, it requires for its fulfillment rockets only twice as fast as those already in the design stage. Since the gravitational stresses involved in the structure are negligible, only the very lightest materials would be necessary and the station could be as large as required.

Let us now suppose that such a station were built in this orbit. It could be provided with receiving and transmitting equipment . . . and could act as a repeater to relay transmissions between any two points on the hemisphere beneath . . .

A single station could only provide coverage to half the globe, and for a world service three would be required, though more could be readily utilized. Figure 3 shows the simplest arrangement. The stations would be arranged approximately equidistantly around the earth . . .

> Diagrams and captions help readers to imagine what the author describes.

Figure 3. The stations in the chain would be linked by radio or optical beams and thus any conceivable beam or broadcast service could be provided. . . .

Conclusion

> The author summarizes the advantages of "the space station," which can also be thought of as a series of results.

Briefly summarized, the advantages of the space station are as follows:

(1) It is the only way in which true world coverage can be achieved for all possible types of service.

(2) . . . an almost unlimited number of channels available would be.

(3) The power requirements are extremely small . . . Moreover, the cost of the power would be very low.

(4) However great the initial expense, it would only be a fraction of that required for the world networks replaced, and the running costs would be incomparably less.

Contact:

Jen O'Leary (SSEC)

Russ Dengel (SSEC)

Weather in the palm of your hand

10 January 2006

Dengel created and maintains the PDA Animated Weather service known as PAW, which provides real time weather information in a format accesible to PDAs.

MADISON—Weather lovers have a new tool at hand to obtain weather information on demand through a PDA-friendly weather Web service created by Russ Dengel at the University of Wisconsin-Madison.

Dengel's PDA Animated Weather service, known as PAW, benefits a diverse community from long-haul truck drivers to firefighters in Puerto Rico to commuters trying to get to work safely on a snowy morning. The free service allows PDA users to access real-time radar and satellite weather images and forecasts whenever and wherever. "It's like a meteorologist's dream," says Dengel, a senior information technologist at UW-Madison's Space Science and Engineering Center, where he has access to numerous products.

Dengel frequently updates and expands the service's capabilities to meet the needs of his users. "I want to show people what's possible," Dengel says. PAW users can choose from a multitude of geographic regions and data options, including functions like animation, zoom and roam. Dengel creates these products using data from SSEC's Data Center.

Recently, he tailored the service to meet the needs of the fire department in Puerto Rico. Dengel set up a radar loop centered on San Juan and added satellite data showing clouds over the area. The PAW, he discovered, is "a fairly decent unit for first responders." He plans to continue to work with fire fighters in Puerto Rico to help them get the most out of the PAW service. Dengel also accommodated the fire department in Boise, ID by outfitting PAW with region-specific radar products.

Working with the Wisconsin Department of Transportation, Dengel now offers a PAW version of the DOT's winter road condition information. He created an option that permits users to superimpose road conditions on top of current satellite and radar images. By giving "motorists all the information they need to make good decisions," Dengel makes PAW invaluable to "the average Joe who's driving to work every morning."

Winter weather in Wisconsin inspired Dengel to develop PAW. Waiting for a flight out of the Milwaukee airport last winter, Dengel checked the weather in Madison using a service on his cell phone to get an idea of how long it would take to get from the Madison airport to his home in a suburb. While the mobile service indicated no snow in Madison, Dengel arrived to find three inches of snow on the ground and flakes falling rapidly.

When he made it into work at the Space Science and Engineering Center, Dengel decided to create a small Web site that allowed him to access radar images using a PDA. In the company of many weather enthusiasts, Dengel expanded the program to meet the needs of several co-workers. However, Dengel soon found out that "nothing can hide on the Web."

Only a few months after Dengel made himself a system with a few radar images, hundreds of people from all walks of life began to adopt PAW. With the help of co-workers Bill Bellon and Jerry Robaidek, Dengel created and continues to maintain a dynamic site for the PAW products. In August, over two thousand Web users landed at PAW's humble internet home. During December, the site received over 100,000 hits. The amount of Web traffic reflects the value of the PAW service.

New users keep picking up PAW products and spreading word of the site's usefulness. In response to feedback and suggestions from these users, Dengel constantly adds new products and features. He aims to increase functionality for private pilots and other speciality users. "I'm a meteorologist and I like looking at weather," says Dengel. "I found a lot of people like me."

These paragraphs explain what caused Russ Dengel to develop the PDA-friendly weather Web service.

Critical Reading

1. **(a)** What central question does the technical article ask and answer? **(b)** How does Clarke build support for his response to the question? **(c)** Is the structure he uses effective for communicating his response to the question clearly? Explain.

2. **(a)** What concepts explained verbally does the diagram illustrate? **(b)** According to Clarke, what advantages would ensue from this technology?

3. **(a)** Based on the press release, what prompted Dengel to create the PAW service? **(b)** What is the basic premise of this service? **(c)** What caused Dengel to add new features to this service?

4. **Content-Area Vocabulary (a)** The word *atmosphere* derives from the Greek root *-sphere-*, which means "globe, ball" Explain how the meaning of the Greek root informs the meaning of *atmosphere*. **(b)** Define the following words derived from the same Latin word: *spherical, hemisphere,* and *stratosphere*. **(c)** Use a dictionary to verify your definitions.

Common Core State Standards

Writing
2. Write informative/ explanatory texts to examine and convey complex ideas, concepts, and information clearly and accurately through the effective selection, organization, and analysis of content.

Language
4.d. Verify the preliminary determination of the meaning of a word or phrase.

Timed Writing

Informative Text [40 minutes]

Format

In an **analytical essay,** you break a topic into smaller, meaningful segments and discuss them in a logical order. Support your ideas with sound reasons and evidence.

Write an **analytical essay** in which you explain the different uses and the benefits of satellite technology you read about in the technical article and the press release. You should use examples from the documents, but you may also draw on your knowledge of other areas in which the technology is used. Gather ideas by **synthesizing ideas and making logical connections** between the technical article and the press release.

Academic Vocabulary

When you **synthesize ideas and make logical connections,** you reach conclusions based on the relationship between the two texts.

5-Minute Planner

Complete these steps before you begin to write:

1. Read the prompt carefully and list key words.

2. Scan the text for details that relate to the prompt. **TIP** As you scan, take quick notes by jotting down key words and phrases rather than full sentences.

3. Before writing, sketch a rough outline to guide your work.

4. Reread the prompt, and begin drafting your essay.

In the British journalistic tradition, writers are encouraged to inject their personality into their reporting and to express their *opinions*.

New British Nonfiction: Writing About the World Beyond Britain

Sofka Zinovieff

Simon Schama

Historical Background As early as 1611, when Thomas Coryat published *Coryat's Crudites,* a food lover's travel guide to France and Italy, intrepid travelers from the British Isles were writing about the world beyond their shores. The golden age of travel writing was in Victorian times. One of the most famous authors was Sir Richard Burton, an army captain and adventurer who, in 1849, wrote a guidebook to Goa, India, where he had been stationed. He followed it up with works about Africa, Latin America, the Nile Basin, and the Islamic holy city of Mecca. Scottish author Robert Louis Stevenson, best known today for *Treasure Island,* also published colorful travelogues about his trips to France, California, Hawaii, and the Samoan Islands.

By this time, men were not the only ones traveling and writing about their voyages. Lady Anne Blunt went with her husband to the Middle East to buy horses and ended up writing *Bedouin Tribes of the Euphrates*. Mary Kingsley traveled alone to Africa and wrote the best-selling *Travels in West Africa*. Most astonishing of all was writer, political strategist, and spy Gertrude Bell. Bell published *Syria: The Desert and the Sown,* which brought images of Arabian deserts into many English parlors. Along with T. E. Lawrence, known as "Lawrence of Arabia," she helped engineer the Arab revolt against the Ottoman Empire during World War I, and then drew up the borders for modern Iraq.

Britain's role as the dominant colonial power of the nineteenth century enabled many of its writers to travel the world with relative ease, often by working for their government. Some, like Gertrude Bell, embraced the ideology of the British Empire; others energetically questioned it. All were motivated by a deep curiosity about the wider world.

Current Nonfiction In the twentieth and twenty-first centuries, British writers have continued to explore the world and to consider Britain's role in it. Working as newspaper reporters, travel writers, book authors, and essayists, they have tackled war and peace, culture and politics. Britain's flourishing publishing industry has encouraged many writers to produce carefully observed, insightful nonfiction and has provided a market for them. With one-fifth the population of the United States, Britain publishes more new book titles every year than any other country.

Today, many of the finest nonfiction writers in the English language are British. Their work can be found in newspapers, magazines, Web sites, and books. It runs the gamut from wryly nostalgic books like *Outposts: Journeys to the Surviving Relics of the British Empire* by author Simon Winchester to the sharply critical reportage of journalist Robert Fisk, author of *The Great War for Civilization: The Conquest of the Middle East.*

Newspapers and Magazines In the British journalistic tradition, writers are encouraged to inject their personality into their reporting and to express their opinions. Newspapers like *The Times, The Independent,* and *The Guardian* have nurtured writers with strong voices and helped fuel debate about many international issues.

Magazines have also contributed to the rich nonfiction tradition. One, *Granta,* has had an especially big impact by running long pieces by people who travel the world and report from their very personal perspectives. "Britain is particularly good at narrative writing, and *Granta* has played a major part in the rise of nonfiction amid what is perceived as literature," said Ian Jack, who edited the magazine for twelve years. The thoughtful personal pieces in *Granta* by writers such as James Fenton, Dilip Hiro, Jenny Diski, Simon Schama, and Sofka Zinovieff have shown that fine reporting can be a literary form.

British reportage and writing about the world is as exciting now as ever before. Those publishing today range across several generations, from writers like Jan Morris, who began her career covering the Middle East just after World War II to Robert MacFarlane, who published his first book, *Mountains of the Mind,* in 2003. American readers will discover that while we share a common language, these writers speak in a distinctly British voice.

Robert MacFarlane

Speaking and Listening: Research

© **Comprehension and Collaboration** Besides writing for newspapers, magazines, and Web sites, many British nonfiction writers have published books. Compile an **annotated bibliography** of five books by contemporary British writers who have explored beyond British shores and whose books you might like to read. Briefly explain your choices. Your annotated bibliography should include the book title, its author, and your comments.

To find books for your bibliography, use the Internet. You can browse the Web sites of British publications to find writers whose books have been reviewed recently. Following are the names of some prominent nonfiction writers you might want to research:

Julian Barnes	Pico Iyer	Jan Morris
Liam D'Arcy Brown	Ian Jack	Simon Schama
Jenny Diski	Robert MacFarlane	Tahir Shah
James Fenton	Catherine Merridale	Simon Winchester
Robert Fisk	Anne Mustoe	Gary Younge
Dilip Hiro	Tim Moore	Sofka Zinovieff

Connecting to the Essential Question What makes a popular song popular? To what extent does pop music reflect popular culture in general? As you read, think about the broader points that Hornby makes about pop music and popular culture in general. Your ideas will help you respond to the Essential Question: **How does literature shape or reflect society?**

Literary Analysis

A **personal essay** is a short nonfiction prose piece offering the writer's personal observations on a particular subject. It typically contains some or all of these features:

- A friendly, informal tone, with easy humor
- Opinions about the subject
- Details that reveal the writer's life or personality
- Comments on life in general

Notice not only what Hornby's essay says about pop music but also what it reveals about Hornby himself and about life in general.

Reading Strategy

 Preparing to Read Complex Texts To present their opinions convincingly, essayists often use a variety of arguments and strategies. For example, they may do the following:

- Appeal to emotions based on common experiences
- Anticipate and refute opinions different from their own
- Use logic to argue particular points
- Use humor to make their arguments appealing

  Outlining the arguments and strategies will help you understand the essayist's points. Use an outline form like the one shown. Then, evaluate the effectiveness of the essay's organizational structure by considering how clearly and effectively Hornby communicates his ideas.

Vocabulary

inane (in ān´) *adj.* lacking sense; foolish; silly (p. 1464)

incessant (in ses´ ənt) *adj.* seeming as if it will never stop; endless; continual (p. 1464)

cynically (sin´ i klē) *adv.* in a way that denies people's sincerity or good intentions (p. 1464)

languor (laŋ´ gər) *n.* lack of vitality; sluggishness (p. 1465)

anemic (ə nē´ mik) *adj.* lacking vigor; weak; lifeless (p. 1465)

disposable (di spō´ zə bəl) *adj.* able to be discarded; having only a short period of usefulness (p. 1465)

Common Core State Standards

Reading Informational Text
5. Analyze and evaluate the effectiveness of the structure an author uses in his or her exposition or argument, including whether the structure makes points clear, convincing, and engaging.

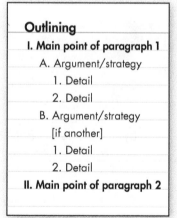

Outlining
I. Main point of paragraph 1
  A. Argument/strategy
    1. Detail
    2. Detail
  B. Argument/strategy
    [if another]
    1. Detail
    2. Detail
II. Main point of paragraph 2

www.PHLitOnline.com

Nick Hornby

(b. 1957)

Author of "I'm Like a Bird"

Work, romance, parenthood, pop music, sports—these are some of the everyday subjects that Nick Hornby explores in his fiction and nonfiction. A noted commentator on popular culture, Hornby has won fame on both sides of the Atlantic for his ability to capture, with sympathy and humor, the ordinary concerns and anxieties of contemporary life.

A Disconcerting Childhood Hornby learned something about anxiety in his own childhood. The son of Sir Derek Hornby, a wealthy and influential businessman, Nick Hornby was raised by his schoolteacher mother after his parents divorced. Yet periodically he left his normal middle-class existence to visit the exotic world his father inhabited. "I never wanted to be in that world," Hornby once told an interviewer. "I was much happier with my mates at home."

From Books to Screen The dual nature of Hornby's life is evident in *Fever Pitch* (1992), the book that established his writing career. An autobiographical work focusing on his obsession with a London soccer team called Arsenal, *Fever Pitch* was hugely popular in Britain, where it was made into a 1997 film starring Colin Firth. Some years later, Jimmy Fallon starred in an American version in which the team was changed to baseball's Boston Red Sox.

Other Hornby books adapted for film include *High Fidelity* (1995), which draws on another of Hornby's passions, popular music; and *About a Boy* (1998), which explores the relationship between aimless Will Freeman and the twelve-year-old boy who claims him as a mentor.

Writing for Charity Hornby faced anguish in his relationship with his own son when Danny was diagnosed as autistic. Determined to do something about this development disorder, Hornby in 1997 helped found TreeHouse, a London school for autistic children. Among his fundraising ventures, he persuaded a number of talented writers to contribute to *Speaking with the Angel* (2000), a story collection he edited, which was then sold to benefit the TreeHouse project.

" It seemed obvious to me that popular culture is an important part of all our lives and it should have some kind of reflection in the books we are reading. "

3. "I'm Like a Bird"
Nick Hornby

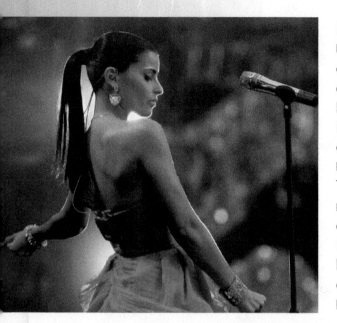

BACKGROUND *31 Songs*, published under the title *Songbook* in the United States, is a collection of Hornby's essays that each focus on a different popular song. In explaining his choices, Hornby notes, "All I have to say about these is that I love them, and want to sing along to them, and force other people to listen to them, and get cross when these other people don't like them as much as I do." The songs are in many different styles by a wide range of performers, including Nelly Furtado, a Canadian singer of Portuguese background (pictured left). "I'm Like a Bird," the Furtado song Hornby profiles in this essay, comes from her first album, *Whoa, Nelly!*, and won the 2002 Grammy for Best Female Pop Vocal Performance.

O h, of course I can understand people dismissing pop music. I know that a lot of it, nearly all of it, is trashy, unimaginative, poorly written, slickly produced, inane, repetitive, and juvenile (although at least four of these adjectives could be used to describe the incessant attacks on pop that you can still find in posh magazines and newspapers); I know, too, believe me, that Cole Porter was "better" than Madonna or Travis,[1] that most pop songs are aimed cynically at a target audience three decades younger than I am, that in any case the golden age was thirty-five years ago and there has been very little of value since. It's just that there's this song I heard on the radio, and I bought the CD, and now I have to hear it ten or fifteen times a day . . .

---

1. Travis Scottish folk rock band that grew extremely popular in the British Isles.

That's the thing that puzzles me about those who feel that contemporary pop (and I use the word to encompass soul, reggae, country, rock—anything and everything that might be regarded as trashy) is beneath them, or behind them, or beyond them—some preposition denoting distance, anyway: Does this mean that you never hear, or at least never enjoy, new songs, that everything you whistle or hum was written years, decades, centuries ago? Do you really deny yourselves the pleasure of mastering a tune (a pleasure, incidentally, that your generation is perhaps the first in the history of mankind to forgo) because you are afraid it might make you look as if you don't know who Harold Bloom[2] is? Wow. I'll bet you're fun at parties.

The song that has been driving me pleasurably potty recently is "I'm Like a Bird" by Nelly Furtado. Only history will judge whether Ms. Furtado turns out to be any kind of artist, and though I have my suspicions that she will not change the way we look at the world, I can't say that I'm very bothered: I will always be grateful to her for creating in me the narcotic need to hear her song again and again. It is, after all, a harmless need, easily satisfied, and there are few enough of those in the world. I don't even want to make a case for this song, as opposed to any other—although I happen to think that it's a very good pop song, with a dreamy languor and a bruised optimism that immediately distinguishes it from its anemic and stunted peers. The point is that a few months ago it didn't exist, at least as far as we are concerned, and now here it is, and that, in itself, is a small miracle.

Dave Eggers[3] has a theory that we play songs over and over, those of us who do, because we have to "solve" them, and it's true that in our early relationship with, and courtship of, a new song, there is a stage which is akin to a sort of emotional puzzlement. There's a little bit in "I'm Like a Bird," for example, about halfway through, where the voice is double-tracked on a phrase, and the effect—especially on someone who is not a musician, someone who loves and appreciates music but is baffled and seduced by even the simplest musical tricks—is rich and fresh and addictive.

Sure, it will seem thin and stale soon enough. Before very long I will have "solved" "I'm Like a Bird," and I won't want to hear it very much anymore—a three-minute pop song can only withhold its mysteries for so long, after all. So, yes, it's disposable, as if that makes any difference to anyone's perceptions of the value of pop music. But then, shouldn't we be sick of the *Moonlight* Sonata by now? Or *Christina's World?*[4] Or *The Importance of Being Earnest?* They're

2. **Harold Bloom** (b. 1930) Yale University professor who has written and edited numerous books on English literature.
3. **Dave Eggers** (b. 1970) American author whose publishing company published Hornby's *Songbook.*
4. **Christina's World** famous painting by American artist Andrew Wyeth (b. 1917).

Reading Strategy
Outlining Arguments and Strategies
What logical and emotional appeals does Hornby use to make his argument about pop music more convincing?

Vocabulary
languor (laŋ´ gər) *n.* lack of vitality; sluggishness

anemic (ə nē´ mik) *adj.* lacking vigor; weak; lifeless

disposable (di spō´ zə bəl) *adj.* able to be discarded; having only a short period of usefulness

Reading Check
What song is "driving" Hornby "potty"?

empty! Nothing left! We sucked 'em dry! That's what gets me: The very people who are snotty about the disposability of pop will go over and over again to see Lady Bracknell say "A handbag?" in a funny voice.[5] They don't think that joke's exhausted itself? Maybe disposability is a sign of pop music's maturity, a recognition of its own limitations, rather than the converse. And anyway, I was sitting in a doctor's waiting room the other day, and four little Afro-Caribbean girls, patiently sitting out their mother's appointment, suddenly launched into Nelly Furtado's song. They were word perfect, and they had a couple of dance moves, and they sang with enormous appetite and glee, and I liked it that we had something in common, temporarily; I felt as though we all lived in the same world, and that doesn't happen so often.

A couple of times a year I make myself a tape to play in the car, a tape full of all the new songs I've loved over the previous few months, and every time I finish one I can't believe that there'll be another. Yet there always is, and I can't wait for the next one; you need only a few hundred more things like that, and you've got a life worth living.

Literary Analysis
Personal Essay What does the last paragraph reveal about Hornby? At what broader comment about life does the final sentence hint?

5. **Lady Bracknell . . . voice** In *The Importance of Being Earnest,* Lady Bracknell's line "A handbag?" has become very famous.

Critical Reading ©

Cite textual evidence to support your responses.

© 1. **Key Ideas and Details (a)** What is Hornby's definition of contemporary pop music? **(b) Infer:** Who does he suggest regards this music as "trashy"? **(c) Analyze:** Does he share this negative opinion? Explain.

© 2. **Key Ideas and Details (a) Summarize:** What does Hornby like about Nelly Furtado's "I'm Like a Bird"? **(b) Connect:** How does Dave Eggers's theory help explain Hornby's reaction to the song?

© 3. **Key Ideas and Details (a)** What three works of music, art, and literature does Hornby contrast with pop music?
(b) Interpret: What is his view of the cultural establishment's reactions to these works?

© 4. **Key Ideas and Details (a) Summarize:** Sum up the incident with the four little girls in the doctor's waiting room. **(b) Generalize:** What does the incident suggest about the cultural value of pop music in general?

© 5. **Integration of Knowledge and Ideas** What comment does this essay make about the cultural establishment? Explain. In your response, use at least two of these Essential Question words: *intellectual, condescending, elitist, offend. [Connecting to the Essential Question: How does literature shape or reflect society?]*

Literary Analysis

1. Key Ideas and Details What does this **personal essay** reveal about Hornby's background, personality, and outlook? Gather your ideas and details on a chart like the one below.

Autobiographical and Other Details	What They Reveal or Suggest

2. Key Ideas and Details Which details help Hornby achieve the informal tone and easy humor typical of personal essays? Cite at least five examples.

3. Integration of Knowledge and Ideas What does the essay suggest about life in general? Show how the essay's details lead to at least two broader comments on life.

Reading Strategy

4. (a) Outline the arguments and strategies of Hornby's opening paragraph. What criticisms of popular music does he anticipate? **(b)** How does the paragraph's last sentence refute those criticisms?

5. (a) What emotional appeals support Hornby's views on the value of pop music? **(b)** What logical explanation does he also offer?

PERFORMANCE TASKS
Integrated Language Skills

Vocabulary Acquisition and Use

Use a word from the vocabulary list to complete each sentence and explain your choice. Use each word only once.

1. That remark is _____; why don't you say something sensible?

2. Unlike real china, paper plates are _____.

3. The voice of the ailing patient was quite _____.

4. "All people are dishonest," she said _____.

5. The _____ chirping of crickets gave me a headache.

6. I had no energy; the hot weather put me in a state of _____.

Writing

Informative Text Write the "liner notes" that might appear in the packaging of a recording of your favorite song. Your notes should give technical details about the composition, instrumentation, and performance of the song. They should also draw on ideas about music that Hornby expresses.

Common Core State Standards

Writing
2. Write informative/ explanatory texts to examine and convey complex ideas, concepts, and information clearly and accurately through the effective selection, organization, and analysis of content.

Write a Short Story

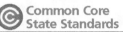 **Common Core State Standards**

Short Story A short story can be set in any time and place, from historic Athens to a future settlement orbiting Jupiter. It can tell about any conflict, from a minor disagreement to a major battle. All short stories do not follow the same plan, but many focus on a single event that reveals an insight about a main character. When you follow the steps in this workshop, you will create an effective short story that brings to life a fictional world.

Assignment Write a short story that tells about a fictional character who faces a compelling conflict.

What to Include Your short story should have these elements:

- A setting that presents a time and place, using concrete sensory details
- A main character who experiences a conflict, or problem to be solved
- A plot that includes a clear sequence of events related to the conflict
- Dialogue that reveals personality and moves the plot forward
- Effective pacing and plot devices, like flashback and foreshadowing

To preview the criteria on which your short story may be assessed, see the rubric on page 1475.

Writing

3. Write narratives to develop real or imagined experiences or events using effective techniques, well-chosen details, and well-structured event sequences.

3.a. Engage and orient the reader by setting out a problem, situation, or observation and its significance, establishing one or multiple point(s) of view, and introducing a narrator and/or characters; create a smooth progression of experiences or events.

3.b. Use narrative techniques, such as dialogue, pacing, description, reflection, and multiple plot lines, to develop experiences, events, and/or characters.

To see how a short-story writer combines elements, read this excerpt from a story in this textbook (p. 1436). In a few lines, the writer establishes the setting and introduces two characters, using dialogue to reveal their relationship.

from: "Next Term, We'll Mash You"

The car turned right, between white gates and high, dark, tight-clipped hedges. The whisper of the road under the tires changed to the crunch of gravel. The child, staring sideways, read black lettering on a white board: "St Edwards's Preparatory School. Please Drive Slowly." He shifted on the seat, and the leather sucked at the bare skin under his knees, stinging.

The mother said, "It's a lovely place. Those must be the playing-fields. Look, darling, there are some of the boys." She clicked open her handbag, and the sun caught her mirror and flashed in the child's eyes; the comb went through her hair and he saw the grooves it left, neat as distant ploughing.

WRITE GUY
Jeff Anderson, M.Ed.

What Do You Notice?

Read the highlighted sentence several times. Then, with a partner, discuss the qualities that make it special. You might consider the following elements:

- Word choice
- Sentence length
- Use of punctuation
- Vivid details

Share your group's observations with the class.

Prewriting and Planning

Choosing Your Topic

To choose a topic for your short story, use one of these strategies:

- **Draw a setting.** A unique setting can trigger story ideas. Sketch any setting: historic, realistic, or fantastic. Then, consider characters and a conflict that might go with the setting you have drawn.

- **Choose a real-life inspiration.** Your story might be loosely based on an event from real life, either one from your own experience or something you heard about in the news or read in a history book. Jot down elements that inspire you and list ways you might change or expand them in a fictional story.

Narrowing Your Topic

Create a story chart. A short story should follow a clear narrative. Using a story chart will help you focus your tale by planning the four stages of a story.

Use your chart to decide whether you will *foreshadow,* or give hints about what will happen. You might also choose to use *flashbacks,* which give readers information about events that happened before the beginning of the story.

Climax
Reya discovers that everyone in town is covering up a crime.

No one speaks to her. Reya begins to think they have a secret.

Rising Action

Falling Action

Exposition
Reya moves to a small town and feels very isolated.

Resolution
Reya exposes the crime and becomes a popular hero.

Gathering Details

Improvise dialogue. Using a character's thoughts and words can help you move your story in an entertaining way. Role-playing alone or with a partner can help you generate ideas for dialogue.

- *Dialogue* between two or more characters can reveal character traits and move the plot forward.

- If you decide to use a first-person point of view, an *interior monologue,* or stream of thoughts and feelings going through the narrator's mind, can reveal his or her reactions to present or remembered events.

Role-play the parts of your characters to find their speech patterns and ways of talking. You can make audio recordings of your improvisations to capture specific words and phrases.

Drafting

Common Core State Standards

Writing
3.d. Use precise words and phrases, telling details, and sensory language to convey a vivid picture of the experiences, events, setting, and/or characters.

Shaping Your Writing

Establish a tense and point of view. Decide if you will tell your story using the past or present tense. Also, choose the narrative point of view from the options shown in this chart.

Narrator	Description	Example
First-person	The story is told by one of the characters involved. You might choose the main character, or a minor character who observes and comments on the action.	*I was sure I could be a great artist, despite what anyone thought.*
Third-person omniscient	The narrator is outside the story and knows everything that happened.	*Vic was a talented art student, but Mr. Watts doubted his dedication.*
Third-person limited	The narrator is outside the story but knows only what one character does and thinks.	*Vic knew he could be a great artist. But what did Mr. Watts think?*

Remember your audience. Think about what your audience needs to know as you are drafting your story. Ask yourself these questions:

- Have I included enough information to make the setting, characters, and conflict clear?
- Am I explaining everything completely, including why characters do what they do?

Providing Elaboration

Show; do not tell. Short stories are more engaging and involving when the writer shows what is happening rather than simply telling one event after another. As you draft, think of ways you can show what your characters are like and what they do. As you draft, look for opportunities to show by using dialogue, sensory language, or specific images.

Telling	*The crowd reacted angrily to the mayor's speech.*
Showing	*The mayor was only through half his speech when the shouting began. Soon, the mayor's soft voice was drowned out by the loud cries from the audience.*

Model: Showing, Not Telling

Her fingers were mottled with ink from the fierceness with which she dotted her *i's* and crossed her *t's* as page after page of final exams was blanketed with precise small lettering.

The writer shows us evidence of her character's strong concentration, rather than simply telling us that she was a hard worker.

Writers on Writing

Anita Desai On Writing Vivid Descriptions

Anita Desai is the author of *A Devoted Son* (p. 1420).

My most vivid memory of childhood in India is of the heat and stillness of summer afternoons when we could do nothing but lie under a slowly revolving fan and read, or doze, waiting for the release brought by the cooler air of evening,

When I wrote a story about children's play—how intense it is and how seriously children take it—I started with an evocation of that heat and stillness. Then the children's games could erupt out of it noisily, almost violently, as a contrast.

> *"I started with an evocation of that heat and stillness."*
> —Anita Desai

from *Games at Twilight*

They faced the afternoon. It was too hot. Too bright. The white walls of the veranda glared stridently in the sun. The bougainvillea hung about it, purple and magenta, in livid balloons. The garden outside was like a tray made of beaten brass, flattened out on the red gravel and the stony soil in all shades of metal—aluminum, tin, copper and brass. No life stirred at this arid time of day—the birds still drooped, like dead fruit, in the papery tents of the trees; some squirrels lay limp on the wet earth under the garden tap. The outdoor dog lay stretched as if dead on the veranda mat, his paws and ears and tail all reaching out like dying travelers in search of water. He rolled his eyes at the children—two white marbles rolling in the purple sockets, begging for sympathy—and attempted to lift his tail in a wag but could not. It only twitched and lay still.

Then, perhaps roused by the shrieks of the children, a band of parrots suddenly fell out of the eucalyptus tree, tumbled frantically in the still, sizzling air, then sorted themselves out into battle formation and streaked away across the sky.

I needed bright, glaring colors to emphasize the heat of summer.

Metal can become white-hot in the sun, so I named different metals to convey that impression of heat.

I needed images of the inactivity and passivity that great heat imposes on one, so all the creatures I named are described as comatose.

Then, out of all that stillness, I wanted action to burst forth, startling the reader.

Revising

Revising Your Overall Structure

Using snapshots to grab the reader's attention. Think of each episode in your story as a photograph of a moment in time. Review your scenes to identify places where the view could be made clearer. Add details like these to make the picture more vivid:

- Descriptive language that is precise and evocative
- Sensory language (appeal to senses of sight, touch, hearing, taste, or smell)
- Figurative language (similes, metaphors, personification) to explain what events, people, and setting are like

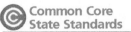

Common Core State Standards

Writing
5. Develop and strengthen writing as needed by revising, rewriting, or trying a new approach, focusing on addressing what is most significant for a specific purpose and audience.

Language
2. Demonstrate command of the conventions of standard English capitalization, punctuation, and spelling when writing.

Model: Revising to Create Snapshots

perched on a bleached-white oak log,
trapped by some long-ago flood on
On the longest day of the year, Rose sat ⋀ near the riverbank,
waiting for the boy. Minutes passed. He was late, and, as
her mind listlessly created teasing rebukes, her ears caught
faint moan   , long and seductive and inhuman
a ⋀ sound in the distance ⋀.

Where is Rose sitting? What sound does she hear?

Peer Review Exchange drafts with a partner. Identify two or three episodes in your partner's story that feel too short or somewhat vague. Consider how envisioning a snapshot of each episode will help the writer add effective details.

Revising Your Word Choice

Check for consistency. Your story could be confusing if you have unintentional shifts in tense or perspective.

Tense. Review your verb tenses. For example, if you are telling the story in the present tense, check that you have not slipped into the past by mistake.	***Narrative point of view.*** Be sure your narrative point of view is consistent. If you are using a first-person narrator, do not slip into the third-person.
Replace: I tried the door, but I'm locked inside. **With**: I tried the door, but I was locked inside.	**Replace**: We did not trust the newcomer, so they kept her under close surveillance. **With**: We did not trust the newcomer, so we kept her under close surveillance.

Developing Your Style

Using Punctuation in Dialogue

Dialogue shows what people say—the punctuation in dialogue can help to show how they say it. The punctuation at the end of a sentence helps to indicate the tone of a sentence. Other forms of punctuation help readers hear the rhythms and pauses of natural speech. Follow these strategies to use punctuation effectively.

You might also use these punctuation strategies in your narration if your story has a first-person point of view.

Find It in Your Reading

Review the dialogue in "Next Term, We'll Mash You" by Penelope Lively.

1. Look for examples of dialogue that are especially vivid or effective.

2. Explain how the punctuation contributes to the effect of each example.

Rule	Example
Use commas to indicate short pauses.	"Well, sure, we can do that."
Use ellipses to show a longer pause or hesitation. Ellipsis points can also suggest a voice trailing off.	"Yes. . . I suppose that's right." "Maybe we should. . ."
Use a dash to indicate a sudden stop, such as an interruption.	"Hey —" "Wait! Don't forget to —"
Use italics to emphasize a word.	"*What* are you doing here?" "What are you doing *here*?"
Use apostrophes to show dropped letters in dialect.	"That's nothin' special."

3. **Discuss:** Choose a line of dialogue from the story and consider how adding a dash or ellipsis points would affect the impact of the line. Read both the original sentence and your revised version aloud to a partner. Without looking at your writing, can your partner tell what punctuation you added?

Apply It to Your Writing

To improve the dialogue in your story, follow these steps:

1. Read each line aloud. Listen for whether or not it sounds natural. Consider adding punctuation to indicate natural pauses in your character's voice.

2. Decide if there is more than one possible reading for the line. For important lines, consider using italics to show which word the character emphasizes.

3. Be careful not to overuse special punctuation, such as ellipsis points, dashes, and italics. Limit exclamation points, as well—they're more effective when used sparingly. Reread all of the dialogue in your story, paying attention to the balance of punctuation.

PH WRITING COACH

Further instruction and practice are available in *Prentice Hall Writing Coach*.

A Love Story

At eighteen, Rose had spent twelve years in the brick school that would catch the summer wind blowing in from the farmland, coating the last week of June in a haze of warm animals and clover. The wooden desks, scarred with jagged hearts and the initials of long-gone students, began to sweat furniture polish, and she could smell the cloying pine scent in her hands even over the heady outdoor mixture. Her fingers were mottled with ink from the fierceness with which she dotted her *i*'s and crossed her *t*'s as page after page of final exams was blanketed with precise small lettering.

> Elizabeth uses sensory language to establish the setting, and, at the end of the paragraph, reveals character through action.

She loved a boy, too, who had a solemn blue gaze and gentle words. They would meet barefoot at the great flat rock on the shore of the creek and wade until their clothes clung to their shaking frames, forcing them to lie in the sun, touching hands, hips, mouths. The fabric would wrinkle and tear, stiff strong fibers meeting stiffer, stronger stone, and the sun would fade the dye, aging their apparel to the nebulous clothing of romantic watercolors. Rose's affection for this boy was simple, an adoration of his smile, his voice, his rough strong hands. She loved his bouquets of wildflowers and the way his hair smelled after he had picked them. She loved how her cheek fit perfectly against his collarbone. She loved him.

> Notice how in this paragraph, Elizabeth conveys emotion through sensory details.

On the longest day of the year, Rose sat perched on a bleached-white oak log, trapped by some long-ago flood on the riverbank, waiting for the boy. Minutes passed. He was late, and, as her mind listlessly created teasing rebukes, her ears caught a faint moan in the distance, long and seductive and inhuman. Senses blazing, she slipped off her seat and plunged through the verdant forest, forcing away from the smell of water to the scent of mystery. Again, the sound came, louder and shriller, and she redoubled her struggle through the undergrowth, small branches whipping across her face. A rhythmic pounding could be felt through the soil, in her heart. It was ahead of her, the moaning and the pounding and a fierce sensation of speed and power.

Bursting through the last line of oaks, she almost fell gasping to her knees in bewilderment. A train, acres long, was ripping across the landscape, in a place where she could only remember ferns and dragonflies and dust in sunlight. And, miraculously, there was a tiny wooden depot and platform clinging next to the tracks; a sign hanging from the window proclaimed "TICKETS" in scarlet paint. Rose staggered over to the building, mind racing but filled with a steadily growing warmth. There was no attendant at the window, only a stack of handwritten slips that said, simply, "Admit One." Vaguely wondering when the next train arrived, she took one and leaned against the rough wall, twisting the slip idly through her fingers until it was soft and powdery.

> The details in this section are symbolic. They point to a resolution of the conflict, which involves the loss of the relationship.

Minutes or hours later, a vermillion engine roared into the station, and Rose clambered into a car and slipped into a seat without hesitation. The boy was across the aisle from her, looking out the opposite window. They smiled nervously at each other, eyes flicking back and forth over the other's features, but neither spoke or moved. Trying to recall his name as the train lurched forward, she found it gone.

> Elizabeth reveals the outcome of the relationship through showing, not telling.

Editing and Proofreading

Focus on punctuation in dialogue. Use quotation marks only for direct quotations. Check that you have used commas and capital letters correctly.

> **Direct Quotation:** *"We're gonna win for sure," said Max.*
> **Indirect Quotation:** *Max thought we would certainly win.*

Focus on spelling. To add *-ing, -ish,* or *-ist* to words that end in *y,* keep the *y* and add the suffix. For example, *worry* becomes *worrying, gray* becomes *grayish,* and *essay* becomes *essayist.*

Spiral Review: Conventions Earlier in this unit, you learned about avoiding sentence fragments and run-ons (p. 1151) and using transitional expressions to show the relationship between two ideas (p. 1169). Review your writing. Make sure you have used at least two transitional expressions to relate ideas.

Publishing, Presenting, and Reflecting

Consider one of the following ways to share your writing:

Record your story. Rehearse your story alone or with a group of classmates. Look for ways to communicate both the narration and dialogue using effective intonation, pauses, and pacing. Make an audio recording of your final reading, and make the recording available for others to borrow.

Create a layout. Use desktop-publishing software to create a final layout for your story, including appropriate illustrations, as well as margins that are not too wide and an effective type design for the title and text.

Reflect on your writing. Jot down your thoughts about the experience of writing a short story. Begin by answering this question: What did you learn about yourself as a writer while creating a short story?

Rubric for Self-Assessment

Evaluate your short story using the following criteria and rating scale, or, with your classmates, determine your own reasonable evaluation criteria.

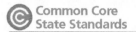

Common Core State Standards

Writing
5. Develop and strengthen writing as needed by editing, focusing on addressing what is most significant for a specific purpose and audience.

Language
2.b. Spell correctly.

PH WRITING COACH

Further instruction and practice are available in *Prentice Hall Writing Coach.*

Criteria	Rating Scale
	not very *very*
Focus: How well do you tell a clear story from beginning to end?	1 2 3 4 5
Organization: How effectively do the events in your story build to a strong climax and satisfying resolution?	1 2 3 4 5
Support/Elaboration: How well do you use dialogue to reveal characters' actions and personalities?	1 2 3 4 5
Style: How effective are your sentences and their punctuation, both in dialogue and narration?	1 2 3 4 5
Conventions: How correct is your use of grammar, especially the punctuation of dialogue?	1 2 3 4 5

Compare Media Coverage of Same Event

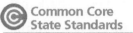

Common Core State Standards

In today's fast-paced world, coverage of news events bombards us from print media like newspapers and magazines and nonprint media like television, radio, and the Internet. News media are the vehicles that bring us our daily dose of current events. Of course, in today's world, it is hard to limit ourselves to one dose per day. As you navigate the world of news media, it is important to understand that facts are not just facts; how stories are covered shapes public understanding of current events.

Speaking and Listening
2. Integrate multiple sources of information presented in diverse formats and media in order to make informed decisions and solve problems, evaluating the credibility and accuracy of each source and noting any discrepancies among the data.

Print Media Formats

Print news media relies primarily on text to deliver information. There are two basic types of print news media:

- **Newspapers** are often published daily. The constant deadlines require stories to be concise and fact-driven. Newspapers often provide objective, unbiased reporting, but opinion pieces such as editorials take up a large portion of papers. Because many newspapers serve a local audience, they focus on local news and have a close relationship with their readers.

- **Magazines,** also known as periodicals or journals, appear less frequently than newspapers. This allows writers to deliver an in-depth analysis of an event and to inject commentary and opinions into a story. Visual elements, such as pictures and graphics, have a more prominent role. Most magazines serve a national audience and focus on national events.

News Coverage

Before you analyze the coverage of an event, you should assess the media source. Use a chart like the one below:

Factors of Print News Coverage	
Purpose	Most news articles are written to inform, but some media makers may also want to influence opinion or entertain. The purpose of a story will affect the information the reporter writes and the editors include.
Author's Perspective	News articles are meant to be objective. Sometimes, however, a writer may omit certain facts or emphasize others that implicitly express an opinion or shape a particular perception.
Audience	Some publications target specific populations and cater to the interests, needs, or even biases of those groups. Understanding the target audience can help you identify possible slants in the presentation of a news story.

Elements of News Presentations

As you read a print media source, notice how the following elements affect your understanding of a story:

- **Headline:** This provides basic information and sets the tone of the story. Look for *charged language*—words with strong positive or negative connotations.

- **Visual elements:** Images and photos affect how a reader understands a story.

- **Placement of story:** Editors will emphasize a story's importance by placing it on the front page of the newspaper.

- **Duration of coverage:** The length of time a story is covered—one day, a week, a month—also indicates its importance.

Activities: Compare Media Coverage

© **Comprehension and Collaboration** For both activities, use an evaluation form like the one shown below.

A. Select a news event, and examine its coverage in three different newspapers or magazines. Look for similarities and differences in the ways each outlet approaches its coverage, and examine how the coverage emphasizes different elements.

Evaluation Form for Print Media Coverage

News Event: _____

Three Sources in Which It Is Covered: _____

Intended Audience of Each Publication: _____

How are the headlines different? _____

Are the stories placed differently? Explain. _____

Do any of the stories seem to favor one side? Explain. _____

What information is the same? What is different? _____

How does each story provide a different understanding of the event? _____
_____

B. Find coverage of the same event in broadcast media (television or radio). Compare the broadcast coverage to the print media versions of the story. Determine if specific information was added or omitted. Write a paragraph explaining your findings.

Cognates and Borrowed Words

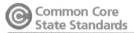

Common Core
State Standards

Cognates are words that share origins and meanings with words in other languages. These words are often spelled similarly. For example, *candeur* in French and *candor* in English are cognates. Both are derived from the Latin word *candere,* meaning "honesty."

English also has many borrowed words that have been taken intact from other languages. Some of these words are so familiar that English speakers often do not realize their foreign origins. Study the borrowed words in the chart below.

Language
4.a. Use context as a clue to the meaning of a word or phrase.
4.c. Consult general and specialized reference materials, both print and digital, to find the pronunciation of a word or determine or clarify its precise meaning, its part of speech, its etymology, or its standard usage.

French	German	Indian	Italian	Native American	West Indian
envoy	frankfurter	bungalow	alfresco	caribou	barbecue
potpourri	hamburger	cashmere	fiasco	chipmunk	canoe
rendezvous	rucksack	jungle	incognito	moccasin	maize

Practice

Directions: Identify the source of each borrowed word and use it in a sentence. If necessary, use a dictionary to aid you.

1. blitz
2. toboggan
3. kowtow
4. chocolate
5. banana
6. pundit
7. chili
8. boomerang
9. hammock
10. algebra

Directions: Find a newspaper or magazine article and identify five or more borrowed words in it. Then, trace the origin of three of these words.

Vocabulary Acquisition and Use: Context Clues

Context clues are words or phrases that help readers clarify the meanings of unfamiliar words in a text. By using context clues, you can determine the word or words that complete a sentence. Sentence Completion questions appear in most standardized tests. These questions test your vocabulary skills as well as your understanding of sentence structure. In these types of questions, you are given sentences with one or more missing words. Your task is to use the context to choose the correct word or words to complete each sentence logically. Try this strategy: (1) Read the sentence. (2) Read *all* of the answer choices, and mark those that might work. (3) Of the ones you marked, choose the answer that works best.

Practice

This exercise is modeled after the Sentence Completion exercises that appear in the Critical Reading section of the SAT.

Directions: Each of the following sentences is missing one or two words. Choose the word or set of words that best completes each sentence.

Test-Taking Tip
Work on the sentence completion questions before the passage-based reading questions. They take less time.

1. The determined __?__ of the Roman Empire brought an army of 40,000 men to England in 42 A.D.
   A. conflagration
   B. aperture
   C. languor
   D. imperialism
   E. condescension

2. The British tribesman were terrifying __?__ when they painted their bodies blue for battle.
   A. combatants
   B. upbraidings
   C. enigmas
   D. effigies
   E. inklings

3. The conquered British natives were somewhat __?__ and did little to overthrow their invaders.
   A. complaisant
   B. exemplary
   C. lustrous
   D. despotic
   E. circumscribed

4. The Romans' __?__ need to spread their form of civilization spurred them to build baths and ampitheaters in every land they conquered.
   A. inane
   B. incessant
   C. impressionistic
   D. invincible
   E. desolate

5. The Roman roads remain a __?__ wonder, raised up out of the landscape with rock dug from __?__ on either side of the road bed.
   A. supine . . . encomiums
   B. filial . . . mockeries
   C. undeterminable . . . tendrils
   D. topographical . . . furrows
   E. transient . . . intrigues

6. __?__ citizens from all walks of life __?__ the baths, less for cleanliness than to socialize.
   A. Garrulous . . . patronized
   B. Vivacious . . . endowed
   C. Clamorous . . . distilled
   D. Segmented . . . eclipsed
   E. Irrevocable . . . recalled

Test-Taking Practice

Critical Reading: Short Reading Passages

The **short reading passages** of standardized tests ask you to read selections that may only be a paragraph or two in length or about 100 words. They may be poetry or fiction selections, or readings from natural science, social studies, and the humanities. They may include narrative, expository, and argumentative elements. The majority of the questions require extended reasoning in which you analyze and synthesize information. You will also be required to comment on the assumptions and the style of the author.

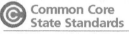

Common Core
State Standards

RL.11-12.1, RL.11-12.2, RL.11-12.4; W.11-12.5; L.11-12.3, L.11-12.3.a
[For the full wording of the standards, see the standards chart in the front of your textbook.]

Practice

The following exercise is modeled after the SAT Short Passage Critical Reading section.

Directions: Read the following passage, taken from "An Arundel Tomb" by Philip Larkin. Then, choose the best answer to each question.

> Side by side, their faces blurred,
> The earl and countess lie in stone,
> Their proper habits vaguely shown
> As jointed armor, stiffened pleat,
> 5 And that faint hint of the absurd—
> The little dogs under their feet.
>
> Such plainness of the pre-baroque
> Hardly involves the eye, until
> It meets his left-hand gauntlet, still
> 10 Clasped empty in the other; and
> One sees, with a sharp tender shock,
> His hand withdrawn, holding her hand.
>
> They would not think to lie so long.
> Such faithfulness in effigy
> 15 Was just a detail friends would see:
> A sculptor's sweet commissioned grace
> Thrown off in helping to prolong
> The Latin names around the base.

Strategy

- **Read carefully** to find text directly related to the question.
- **Avoid being misled** by an answer that looks correct but is not supported by information directly stated.
- When you match specific details in the text to what a question is asking, you have proof of your answer.

1. What basic philosophy does the poet assume?
   A. belief in reincarnation
   B. rebirth after death
   C. eternal life
   D. sacredness in natural things
   E. the absence of God

2. Why does the author make an allusion to the "pre-baroque" in line 7?
   A. to emphasize the tomb's lack of ornamentation
   B. to contrast the time period in which the author writes to the time of the pre-baroque
   C. to suggest the beliefs and customs of the pre-baroque
   D. to compare the Roman period to the Baroque
   E. to allow readers to consider how the earl felt

3. In line 16, the word *commissioned* most nearly means
   A. friendly
   B. paid for
   C. uncompensated
   D. skilled
   E. offered up

4. It can be inferred that the earl and countess are
   A. knights
   B. still alive
   C. married
   D. unhappy
   E. Romans

5. In line 2, how does the figurative language of the poet "the earl and countess lie in stone" compare to the flashback in line 16?
   A. The sculptor's distortion has carried through to today.

B. The poet gives life to them and brings the sculptor back to life.
   C. The poet suggests that the sculptor made them lie in peace.
   D. The sculptor has outlived both the earl and countess in stone.
   E. The earl and countess lie inside of stone while the sculptor is forgotten.

6. Answering which of these questions would increase your comprehension of the poem?
   A. What do the other tombs in Arundel look like?
   B. What does "jointed armor, stiffened pleat" mean?
   C. How would the sculptor know what they looked like?
   D. Why would someone feel "sharp tender shock"?
   E. Who is really buried in this tomb?

7. What clues does the poet give to place the subject matter in its historical period?
   A. armor, gauntlet
   B. hint of the absurd
   C. effigy, detail
   D. faithfulness in effigy
   E. pleat, dogs

8. The main idea of the poem would most likely be which of the following?
   A. The sculptor was trying to protect their Latin names.
   B. The earl and the countess never expected to live on so long.
   C. The affection of the long dead husband and wife is surprising.
   D. The plainness of the tomb and its inhabitants shocks.
   E. Little dogs do not belong on the tomb of a ruler.

Grammar and Writing: Improving Paragraphs

Improving Paragraphs exercises often appear in the writing sections of standardized tests. They are made up of a reading passage with numbered sentences. The passages are usually drafts of student essays that contain errors in grammar, style, and usage. For each question, you must decide which of five possible answers will best correct the given sentence.

Practice

This exercise is modeled after the Improving Paragraphs portion of the SAT Writing Test.

Directions: Questions 1–6 refer to the following draft of a student essay.

⌐1⌐ The Romans enjoyed a prosperous and peaceful existence in Britain, they did not extend their rule into Scotland and Wales. ⌐2⌐ They neglected to settle these areas, farm lands held greater interest, and it was too hard to settle these hostile landscapes. ⌐3⌐ Two-thirds of the troops in Rome guarded Wales alone to keep warlike tribes at bay.

⌐4⌐ Stable society in Britain allowed the establishment of the villas of the wealthy who had grown fabulously rich in the grain trade. ⌐5⌐ Most villas began as simple farm compounds. ⌐6⌐ Yet before long, they featured **stone walls, water running through pipes, a way to heat the rooms, multiple rooms, bathing in bath houses**, and mosaics. ⌐7⌐ A golden age of villa building ensued with details only great fortunes could afford. ⌐8⌐ Highly elaborate and complex mosaic decorations were often found in the finest homes.

⌐9⌐ A central forum with a town hall and merchant's trading area was a feature of most towns. ⌐10⌐ Other improvements included small theaters for plays, larger amphitheaters for gladiator combat, and baths for men and women. ⌐11⌐ Because nothing was too good for the Romans living in Britain.

> ### Strategy
>
> ***Focus only on the answers provided.***
> As you read, you will notice errors. Do not edit these errors the way you might improve them. Select the best of the answer choices.

1. Which revision is most needed in sentence 1?
   A. (As it is now)
   B. The Romans enjoyed a prosperous and peaceful existence in Britain they did not extend their rule into Scotland and Wales.
   C. The Romans enjoyed a prosperous and peaceful existence in Britain. They did not extend their rule into Scotland and Wales.
   D. The Romans enjoyed a prosperous and peaceful existence in Britain, in addition to which they did not extend their rule into Scotland and Wales.
   E. They did not extend their rule into Scotland and Wales. The Romans enjoyed a prosperous and peaceful existence in Britain.

2. To add rhythm and emphasize key ideas, what would be the best version of sentence 2?

A. (As it is now)

B. They neglected to settle these areas. They thought farm lands held greater interest. It was too hard to conquer these hostile landscapes.

C. They neglected to settle these areas, felt farm lands held greater interest, and believed it was too hard to conquer these hostile landscapes.

D. They neglected to settle these areas, they felt farm lands held greater interest, and they believed it was too hard to settle these hostile landscapes.

E. These areas they neglected to settle, farm lands held greater interest, it was too hard to conquer hostile landscapes.

3. Which is the best version of the underlined portion of sentence 6?

A. (As it is now)

B. stone walls, water, heating, multiple rooms, bathing

C. walls made of stone, water running through pipes, heating in the rooms, multiple rooms, bathing in bath houses

D. stone walls, piped water, a way to heat multiple rooms, bathing in bath houses

E. stone walls, water pipes, a heating system, multiple rooms, bath houses

4. Which transition would show the relationship between sentences 7 and 8?

A. moreover

B. for example

C. nevertheless

D. all in all

E. consequently

5. Which sentence would be the best transition between the second and third paragraphs?

A. Life in the towns changed greatly under Roman rule.

B. Villas were not the only signs of increased wealth in Britain.

C. Only Romans living abroad could afford to live in the cities.

D. The effects of Roman civilization greatly altered Britain.

E. The first step to conquering Britain was to change its people.

6. Which part of sentence 10 should be revised to help the essay best express equal ideas?

A. (As it is now)

B. "smaller open-air theaters for religious festivals, pantomime, and plays,"

C. "larger amphitheaters for gladiator combats and executions,"

D. "and open baths for men and women"

E. "as well as"

🕐 Timed Writing: Position Statement [25 minutes]

In the final stanza of Philip Larkin's poem "An Arundel Tomb," after examining the weathered stone remnants of a culture dating from nearly two centuries earlier, he concludes, "What will survive of us is love."

Write an essay in which you agree or disagree with Larkin's poetic prediction. Provide reasons why your opinions are correct based on your encounters with elements of today's culture, like art and science, as well as your personal philosophy. Feel free to speculate what, if anything, will survive of our culture. This assignment is similar to the Essay portion of the SAT Writing section.

> **Academic Vocabulary**
>
> **Perspective** is both a way of looking at things and a personal definition. In your essay, discuss the author's perspective before stating your opinion.

Performance Tasks

Follow the instructions to complete the tasks below as required by your teacher. As you work on each task, incorporate both general academic vocabulary and literary terms you learned in this unit.

> ## Ⓒ Common Core State Standards
>
> **RL.11-12.2, RL.11-12.3, RL.11-12.4, RL.11-12.6; RI.11-12.2, RI.11-12.5; W.11-12.1, W.11-12.2, W.11-12.4, W.11-12.9.a, W.11-12.9.b; SL.11-12.4, SL.11-12.6**
>
> [For the full wording of the standards, see the standards chart in the front of your textbook.]

Writing

Ⓒ Task 1: Literature [RL.11-12.3; W.11-12.2, W.11-12.9.a]

Analyze a Key Narrative Element

*Write an **essay** in which you analyze the development of a key narrative element in a story from this unit.*

- Identify the story you will discuss and provide a brief summary.

- Explain which key narrative element—setting, characters, conflict, or plot sequence—you will analyze in depth.

- Analyze how the author introduces and develops the narrative element you have chosen as a focus. Discuss specific literary techniques, such as the use of descriptive language or dialogue, the author uses to establish this narrative component and engage the reader.

- Discuss the interactions between the narrative element that is your focus and other critical aspects of the story. For example, consider whether the setting is a source of conflict.

- Quote details from the story that support your analysis. Provide smooth transitions that clearly connect the details you cite.

Ⓒ Task 2: Literature [RL.11-12.2; W.11-12.4, W.11-12.9.a]

Analyze Themes in Literature

*Write an **essay** in which you analyze the development of two or more themes in a literary work from this unit.*

- Explain which literary work you will discuss. Introduce your analysis by summarizing the work and clearly identifying two distinct themes it conveys.

- Explain how the author develops the themes over the course of the work. For example, consider descriptions of the setting, characters' actions and reactions, and specific events. Also, consider symbols, imagery, or other literary elements that add to the development of two or more themes.

- Explain how the two themes interact and build on one another throughout the work.

- Express a clear thesis and supply relevant evidence from the story to support your interpretation. Clearly link textual evidence to your ideas.

- Develop and organize your ideas logically to produce coherent and clear support for your analysis.

Ⓒ Task 3: Informational Text [RI.11-12.5; W.11-12.1, W.11-12.9.b]

Analyze and Evaluate Structure

*Write an **essay** in which you analyze and evaluate the structure of a nonfiction work from this unit.*

- State which work you chose and briefly summarize the author's purpose and central ideas.

- Provide an outline or description of the structure of its exposition or argument. Consider whether the structure involves a formal pattern of organization, such as compare and contrast, cause and effect, or main idea and supporting details.

- Evaluate the clarity and logic of the structure, identifying whether it makes the author's ideas clear, convincing, and engaging.

- State a clear main idea, or thesis, and develop and organize your argument logically. Cite specific details from the text as support, and use appropriate transitions to link your ideas.

- End with a conclusion that follows from and supports your evaluation of the author's choices concerning structure.

Speaking and Listening

Analyze Development of Central Ideas

With a partner, deliver a **presentation with visuals** *in which you analyze the development of two central ideas in a nonfiction work from this unit.*

- To prepare, choose a work and analyze two or more central ideas it expresses. Determine whether the author has used a clear formal structure or a variety of structures. Note how ideas are introduced, developed, and refined and how specific supporting ideas relate to the main ideas. Explain how the central ideas combine to create a complex account or analysis.

- Capture your ideas in a combination of notes for your own use during the presentation and visuals to share with your audience. Consider such visuals as an idea web, a cause-and-effect chart, an outline, or a sequence-of-events chart. In addition, consider providing copies of annotated or highlighted text.

- Introduce your presentation by stating which work you chose and providing a brief summary. Then, present your analysis with accompanying visual elements.

- As you speak, use academic and content-area vocabulary accurately to clarify ideas and maintain a formal tone.

Analyze Word Choice, Meaning, and Tone

Deliver an **oral presentation** *in which you analyze the relationship between word choice, tone, and meaning in a literary work from this unit.*

- Identify which work you chose and explain why the author's use of language merits deeper analysis.

- Provide a general description of the types of language—complex, simple, figurative, technical, descriptive, etc.—the author uses in the work.

- Explain the author's overall tone, as well as any changes in tone that occur throughout the work.

- Cite specific examples of each broad type of language you noted. Interpret figures of speech and explain nuances and connotations in word meanings. Discuss how each example you cite adds to the overall meaning and tone of the work.

- As you present your work, take your audience's needs into account. Set a pace, neither too slow nor too fast, that allows you to communicate ideas clearly while maintaining listeners' interest.

Analyze Complex Point of View

Deliver an **analysis and assessment** *of the point of view in a literary work from this unit.*

- Identify a literary work from this unit in which the author's point of view is complicated by the use of satire, irony, understatement, or another literary construct in which stated meaning and actual meaning differ. Explain which story you chose and why you chose it.

- Briefly summarize the work. Identify the specific passages or sections you will analyze in depth.

- Discuss how irony, understatement, satire, or tone function in the work by exploring the differences between surface meanings and actual meanings. Explain how these double meanings help to express the author's point of view, or perspective.

- Cite specific details from the text that support your ideas.

- Use formal English as you present your analysis.

What is the relationship between literature and place?

Lives and Places Groups of writers often "belong" to a place because their work reflects its characters, settings, conflicts, or ideals.

Assignment Write a short **collective biography** of a group of British writers that is defined by a place. For example, consider writers associated with the English countryside or with a neighborhood in London; writers who lived in Ireland or Wales; or writers who fought on the battlefields of World War I. Research the lives of the writers in that place, and relate the place to the literary works created there.

Featured Titles

In this unit, you have read a variety of literature of the modern and postmodern periods. Continue to read works related to this era on your own. Select books that you enjoy, but challenge yourself to explore new topics, new authors, and works offering varied perspectives or approaches. The titles suggested below will help you get started.

LITERATURE

Heart of Darkness **and** The Secret Sharer
Joseph Conrad

Fiction *Heart of Darkness* reveals the darkness within the human spirit during an ominous journey to the heart of the colonial African jungle. "The Secret Sharer" tells the tale of the promising journey of a young sea captain who finds help from an unexpected source.

[Conrad's short story "The Lagoon" appears on page 1220 of this book. Build knowledge by reading more fiction by this author.]

The Importance of Being Earnest
Oscar Wilde   EXEMPLAR TEXT ©

Drama Mistaken identities, clever plot twists, and witty dialogue will keep you entertained as you read this popular comedy of manners by Oscar Wilde. Look beneath the surface and you will find an incisive satire of late-Victorian British society.

Early Short Stories: 1883–1888
Anton Chekhov
Modern Library, 1999   EXEMPLAR TEXT ©

Short Stories This collection of seventy early short stories by Russian writer Anton Chekhov, which includes the masterful story "Home," demonstrates the author's artistry at revealing the breadth of human emotions through seemingly ordinary experiences.

White Teeth
Zadie Smith

Novel After fighting together for the British army in World War II, Archibald Jones and Samad Iqbal settle in London. This extraordinary novel, which tells the story of Archibald's and Samad's lives, is an exploration of immigrant experiences, family, poverty, and friendship.

INFORMATIONAL TEXTS

Historical Texts

Testament of Youth
Vera Brittain
WN, 2009

Autobiography In 1915, Vera Brittain was about to return for her second year as a student at Oxford University. Instead, with the outbreak of World War I, she became a nurse and served through much of the war. In this much-admired memoir, she tells the story of a generation forever affected by the tragic conflict.

All Art Is Propaganda: Critical Essays
George Orwell
First Mariner Books, 2009   EXEMPLAR TEXT ©

Criticism Orwell critiques literary figures such as T. S. Eliot and Graham Greene and presents his views on everything from greed and politics to poverty and homelessness. Included in the book is the essay "Politics and the English Language."

[Orwell's essay "Shooting an Elephant" appears on page 1318 of this book. Build knowledge by reading more nonfiction by this author.]

Once There Was a War
John Steinbeck

Journalism In 1943, journalist John Steinbeck was on assignment for *The New York Herald Tribune* in Italy, North Africa, and England during the London blitz. In his dispatches, he focuses on the human impacts of the war.

Contemporary Scholarship

Yeats
Harold Bloom
Oxford University Press, 1972

Literary Criticism Bloom presents his insightful interpretations of William Butler Yeats's poems and plays, and explains how Yeats was influenced by the writers of the Romantic movement. A must-read for anyone interested in learning more about the work of Yeats.

Preparing to Read Complex Texts

Reading for College and Career In both college and the workplace, readers must analyze texts independently, draw connections among works that offer varied perspectives, and develop their own ideas and informed opinions. The questions shown below, and others that you generate on your own, will help you more effectively read and analyze complex college-level texts.

**Common Core
State Standards**

Reading Literature/Informational Text
10. By the end of grade 12, read and comprehend literature, including stories, dramas, and poems and literary nonfiction, at the high end of the grades 11-CCR text complexity band independently and proficiently.

When reading analytically, ask yourself...

- What idea, experience, or story seems to have compelled the author to write? Has the author presented that idea, experience, or story in a way that I, too, find compelling?

- How might the author's era, social status, belief system, or personal experiences have affected the point of view he or she expresses in the text?

- How do my circumstances affect what I understand and feel about this text?

- What key idea does the author state explicitly? What key idea does he or she suggest or imply? Which details in the text help me to perceive implied ideas?

- Do I find multiple layers of meaning in the text? If so, what relationships do I see among these layers of meaning?

- How do details in the text connect or relate to one another? Do I find any details unconvincing, unrelated, or out of place?

- Do I find the text believable and convincing?

Key Ideas and Details

- What patterns of organization or sequences do I find in the text? Do these patterns help me understand the ideas better?

- What do I notice about the author's style, including his or her diction, uses of imagery and figurative language, and syntax?

- Do I like the author's style? Is the author's style memorable?

- What emotional attitude does the author express toward the topic, the story, or the characters? Does this attitude seem appropriate?

- What emotional attitude does the author express toward me, the reader? Does this attitude seem appropriate?

- What do I notice about the author's voice—his or her personality on the page? Do I like this voice? Does it make me want to read on?

Craft and Structure

- Is the work fresh and original?

- Do I agree with the author's ideas entirely, or are there elements I find unconvincing?

- Do I disagree with the author's ideas entirely, or are there elements I can accept as true?

- Based on my knowledge of British literature, history, and culture, does this work reflect the British tradition? Why or why not?

Integration of Ideas

Resources

English Glossary

Essential Question vocabulary appears in **blue type**. High-utility Academic vocabulary is <u>underlined</u>.

A

abasement (uh BAYS muhnt) *n.* condition of being put down or humbled

abated (uh BAYT ihd) *v.* lessened

abide (uh BYD) *v.* to stay; remain

absolution (AB suh LOO shuhn) *n.* act of freeing someone of a sin or criminal charge

acceded (ak SEED uhd) *v.* yielded; agreed

accounts (uh KOWNTS) *n.* records of money received and paid out; financial records

adjure (uh JUR) *v.* request solemnly; appeal to earnestly

admonish (ad MON ihsh) *v.* caution

adroitly (uh DROYT lee) *adv.* with physical or mental skill

adulterations (uh duhl tuh RAY shuhnz) *n.* impurities; added ingredients that are improper or inferior

adversary (AD vuhr sehr ee) *n.* opponent; enemy

<u>**advocate**</u> (AD vuh kayt) *v.* speak or write in support of

affably (AF uh blee) *adv.* in a friendly manner

affinities (uh FIHN uh teez) *n.* family connections; sympathies

affluence (AF loo uhns) *n.* abundant wealth

ague (AY gyoo) *n.* a chill or fit of shivering

alderman (AWL duhr muhn) *n.* chief officers in a shire or county

alters (AWL tuhrz) *v.* changes

amiable (AY mee uh buhl) *adj.* friendly; agreeable

amorous (AM uhr uhs) *adj.* full of love or desire

anarchy (AN uhr kee) *n.* absence of government; disorder

anatomize (uh NAT uh myz) *v.* to dissect in order to examine structure

ancestral (an SEHS truhl) *adj.* inherited

anemic (uh NEE mihk) *adj.* lacking power, vigor, vitality, or colorfulness; listless; weak

<u>**annotate**</u> (AN uh tayt) *v.* note or mark with explanation

antic (AN tihk) *adj.* odd and funny; silly

antidote (AN tee doht) *n.* something that works against an unwanted condition; remedy

aperture (AP uhr chur) *n.* opening

apothecary (uh POTH uh kehr ee) *n.* pharmacist; druggist

appalled (uh PAWLD) *v.* filled with consternation or dismay

appendage (uh PEHN dihj) *n.* something added on

apprehension (ap rih HEHN shuhn) *n.* anxious feeling of foreboding; dread

apprehensions (ap rih HEHN shuhnz) *n.* fears; concerns

approbation (AP ruh BAY shuhn) *n.* official approval or sanction

arboreal (ahr BAWR ee uhl) *adj.* of, near, or among trees

<u>**articulate**</u> (ahr TIHK yuh layt) *v.* express clearly

artifice (AHR tuh fihs) *n.* skill; the product of skill, especially a skillful deception

artificiality (AHR tuh fihsh ee AL uh tee) *n.* unnatural; unreal

aspire (uh SPYR) *v.* have high ambitions; yearn or seek after

assault (uh SAWLT) *v.* violently attack

assessing (uh SEHS ihng) *v.* to estimate the value of (property) for taxation

assiduous (uh SIHJ oo uhs) *adj.* constant in application or attention

assignations (AS ihg NAY shuhn) *n.* appointments to meet

asunder (uh SUHN duhr) *adj.* into parts or pieces

atrophy (AT ruh fee) *v.* to waste away

augment (awg MEHNT) *v.* make greater; enlarge

authentic (aw THEHN tihk) *adj.* genuine; real

avarice (AV uhr ihs) *n.* greed

averred (uh VURD) *v.* stated to be true

awe (aw) *n.* mixed feeling of reverence, fear, and wonder

B

balm (bahm) *n.* ointment or other thing that heals or soothes

bar (bahr) *n.* one of the vertical lines dividing written music into equal sections called measures

beliefs (bih LEEFS) *n.* what is held to be true

bequeath (bih KWEETH) *v.* hand down as an inheritance

bilious (BIHL yuhs) *adj.* peevish; irritable; crank

blight (blyt) *n.* condition of withering

blithe (blyTH) *adj.* cheerful

boundary (BOWN duhr ee) *n.* limiting line; border

breach (breech) *n.* breaking or being broken; failure to observe the terms of an agreement

brink (brihngk) *n.* edge; margin

burden (BUR duhn) *n.* something that weighs one down; a heavy load or responsibility

C

cadence (KAY duhns) *n.* measured movement

caprices (kuh PREES ez) *n.* whims

capitalism (KAP uh tuh lihz uhm) *n.* economic system in which private individuals or groups of individuals own land, factories, and other means of production

<u>**categorize**</u> (KAT uh guh ryz) *v.* place in related groups

censure (SEHN shuhr) *v.* strongly disapprove; condemn

certify (SUR tuh fy) *v.* declare a thing true or accurate; verify; attest

<u>**characterize**</u> (KAR ihk tuh ryz) *v.* describe features, qualities, or traits

chronicle (KRON uh kuhl) *n.* historical record of events in chronological order

chrysalis (KRIHS uh lihs) *n.* the third stage in the development of a moth or butterfly

circumscribed (SUR kuhm skrybd) *v.* limited; having a definite boundary

<u>**cite**</u> (syt) *v.* quote from a text

city (SIHT ee) *n.* large and heavily populated town

clamorous (KLAM uhr uhs) *adj.* loud and confused; noisy

<u>**clarify**</u> (KLAR uh fy) *v.* make clear

clasped (klaspt) *v.* firmly grasped or gripped

classics (KLAS ihks) *n.* books or paintings of the highest quality

<u>**classify**</u> (KLAS uh fy) *v.* assign to a category

climacteric (kly MAK tuhr ihk) *n.* any critical period

colonize (KOL uh nyz) *v.* establish a settlement

combatants (KOM buh tuhnts) *n.* fighters

combustible (kuhm BUHS tuh buhl) *adj.* capable of being ignited and burned; flammable

commentary (KOM uhn TEHR ee) *n.* a series of comments

commission (kuh MIHSH uhn) *n.* authorization; act of giving authority to an individual

commodity (kuh MOD uh tee) *n.* product that is bought or sold

English Glossary **R1**

compassionate (kuhm PASH uh niht) *adj.* sympathizing

compile (kuhm PYL) *v.* put together

complaisant (kuhm PLAY zuhnt) *adj.* agreeable; willing to please

comprised (kuhm PRYZD) *v.* consisted of; included

concord (KON kawrd) *n.* friendly relations; harmony

condescension (kon dih SEHN shuhn) *n.* a patronizing act

conflagration (KON fluh GRAY shuhn) *n.* great fire

conflict (KON flihkt) *n.* a fight or struggle

conjecture (kuhn JEHK chuhr) *v.* guess

connote (kuh NOHT) *v.* suggest or convey

conquest (KON kwehst) *n.* act of conquering

consciousness (KON shuhs nihs) *n.* state of being aware

constituency (kuhn STIHCH oo uhn see) *n.* the people making up a body of voters

construct (kuhn STRUHKT) *v.* build by fitting parts together systematically

contemporary (kuhn TEHM puh rehr ee) *adj.* belonging to the same period of time

contemptuous (kuhn TEHMP choo uhs) *adj.* scornful

contend (kuhn TEHND) *v.* assert or argue

contention (kuhn TEHN shuhn) *n.* dispute; argument

contentious (kuhn TEHN shuhs) *adj.* quarrelsome

contextualize (kuhn TEHKS choo uh lyz) *v.* place information within a larger background

contrite (kuhn TRYT) *adj.* willing to repent or atone

controversy (KON truh vur see) *n.* act of arguing a question about which differences of opinion exist

contusions (kuhn TOO zhuhnz) *n.* an injury in which the skin is not broken; a bruise

conventional (kuhn VEHN shuh nuhl) *adj.* acting or behaving according to commonly accepted or approved ways

coordinate (koh AWR duh nayt) *v.* relate or link

country (KUHN tree) *n.* land; nation

covetousness (KUHV uh tuhs nuhs) *n.* greediness

conviction (kuhn VIHK shuhn) *n.* belief; faith

countenance (KOWN tuh nuhns) *n.* face

courtly (KAWRT lee) *adj.* elegantly dignified; polite

cower (KOW uhr) *v.* crouched, as from fear or cold

coyness (KOY nuhs) *n.* shyness; aloofness, often as part of a flirtation

credulity (kruh DOO luh tee) *n.* tendency to believe too readily

credulous (KREHJ uh luhs) *adj.* tending to believe too readily

critique (krih TEEK) *v.* examine critically; review

cultivated (KUHL tuh vay tihd) *v.* grown

cynically (SIHN uh kuhl ee) *adv.* like or characteristic of a cynic; distrusting or disparaging the motives of other

D

dappled (DAP uhld) *adj.* a spot or mottled marking, usually occurring in clusters

dauntless (DAWNT lihs) *adj.* fearless; cannot be intimidated

debate (dih BAYT) *v.* discuss opposing reasons

deduce (dih DOOS) *v.* infer from a general principle

deference (DEHF uhr uhns) *n.* courteous regard or respect

deficient (dih FIHSH uhnt) *adj.* lacking an essential quality

define (dih FYN) *v.* tell the qualities that make something what it is

deftly (DEHFT lee) *adv.* with ease and quickness

deism (DEE ihz uhm) *n.* belief in God on the evidence of reason and nature

deliberation (dih lihb uh RAY shuhn) *n.* careful consideration and discussion before reaching a decision

delirious (dih LIHR ee uhs) *adj.* having hallucinations; ranting

demonstrate (DEHM uhn strayt) *v.* show by reasoning or examples

denote (dih NOHT) *v.* refer to clearly

depict (dih PIHKT) *v.* portray an image using words

depredation (dep ruh DAY shuhn) *n.* a predatory attack; a raid

derided (dih RYD ihd) *v.* made fun of; ridiculed

design (dih ZYN) *v.* condescend; lower oneself

desolate (DEHS uh liht) *adj.* deserted; forlorn

despondent (dih SPON duhnt) *adj.* hopeless; dejected

despotic (dehs POT ihk) *adj.* tyrannical

destitute (DEHS tuh toot) *adj.* lacking

destruction (dih STRUHK shuhn) *n.* act of destroying

devise (dih VYZ) *v.* work out or create; plan

diffusive (dih FYOO sihv) *adj.* tending to spread out

disabused (dihs uh BYOOZ) *v.* freed from false ideas

discern (duh ZURN) *v.* recognize as separate or different

discreet (dihs KREET) *adj.* wise; prudent

discretion (dihs KREHSH uhn) *n.* care in what one does and says; good judgment; prudence

dislocation (dihs loh KAY shuhn) *n.* condition of being out of place

dispensation (dihs puhn SAY shuhn) *n.* religious system or beliefs

disposable (dihs POH zuh buhl) *adj.* free for use; available

dissatisfaction (dihs sat ihs FAK shuhn) *n.* state of being discontent

dissect (dih SEHKT) *v.* analyze and interpret minutely

distemper (dihs TEHM puhr) *n.* infectious disease such as the plague

distill (dihs TIHL) *v.* to obtain the essential part

divine (duh VYN) *adj.* heavenly; holy

dominion (duh MIHN yuhn) *n.* rule or power over a territory; authority or control

dominions (duh MIHN yuhnz) *n.* governed territories or lands

dowry (DOW ree) *n.* property brought by a woman's family to her husband upon their marriage

dregs (drehgz) *n.* a small amount; a residue

E

eclipse (ih KLIHPS) *v.* dimming or extinction of power or glory

economic (ee kuh NOM ihk) *adj.* having to do with the management of the income

edit (EHD iht) *v.* alter, adapt, or refine

effigy (EHF uh jee) *n.* portrait or statue of a person

electors (ih LEHK tuhrz) *n.* those who vote

eloquent (EHL uh kwuhnt) *adj.* beautifully expressive

eludes (ih LOODZ) *v.* avoids or escapes

embarked (ehm BAHRKT) *v.* engaged in something, such as a journey

embellishments (ehm BEHL ihsh muhnts) *n.* decorative touches; ornamentation

eminent (EHM uh nuhnt) *adj.* noteworthy; of high rank; distinguished

empire (EHM pyr) *n.* group of nations or states under one ruler or government

encomiums (ehn KOH mee uhmz) *n.* formal expressions of great praise

endeavored (ehn DEHV uhrd) *n.* made a serious attempt; tried

enhance (ehn HANS) *v.* improve or heighten

enigma (ih NIHG muh) *n.* riddle; perplexing statement, person, or situation

entreated (ehn TREET uhd) *v.* begged; pleaded with

enumerate (ih NOO muh rayt) *v.* specify a list

epic (EHP ihk) *n.* long poem that tells of the adventures of one or more great heroes

equate (ih KWAYT) *v.* consider one thing the same as another

equivocate (ih KWIHV uh kayt) *v.* to use terms that have two or more meanings to mislead purposely or deceive

escapade (EHS kuh payd) *n.* adventurous action, especially one that breaks ordinary rules of conduct

esteemed (ehs TEEMD) *adj.* highly respected; held in high regard

etymology (eht uh MOL uh jee) *n.* the study of word origins

evaluate (ih VAL yoo ayt) *v.* determine something's significance, worth, or condition

evanescence (ehv uh NEHS uhns) *n.* vanishing or tendency to vanish

evoke (ih VOHK) *v.* draw out a reaction

exemplary (ehg ZEHM pluhr ee) *adj.* of that which should serve as a model

exile (EHG zyl) *v.* force a person to leave home or country

exotic (ehg ZOT ihk) *adj.* from a foreign country

expedient (ehk SPEE dee uhnt) *n.* device used in an emergency

expiated (EHKS pee ayt uhd) *v.* atoned; made amends for, especially by suffering

extract (ehk STRAKT) *v.* draw out information

extravagant (ehk STRAV uh guhnt) *adj.* going beyond reasonable limits; excessive

F

fantastic (fan TAS tihk) *adj.* very fanciful; unbelievably good

fastidious (fas TIHD ee uhs) *adj.* particular; difficult to please

fate (fayt) *n.* destiny

fathom (FATH uhm) *v.* understand thoroughly

fervent (FUR vuhnt) *adj.* having great warmth of feeling

fidelity (fy DEHL uh tee) *n.* faithfulness

filial (FIHL ee uhl) *adj.* expected of a son or a daughter

form (FAWR myuh layt) *v.* give shape to

format (FAWR mat) *v.* arrange according to a plan

formulate (FAWR myuh layt) *v.* express fully and clearly; devise

fortitude (FAWR tuh tood) *n.* courage; strength to endure

fracture (FRAK chuhr) *n.* the act of breaking; state of being broken

frugally (FROO guhl ee) *adv.* in a way that is careful with money

furrow (FUR oh) *n.* narrow groove made in the ground by a plow

G

gall (gawl) *n.* bitter feeling; deep spite

galled (gawld) *adj.* injured or made sore by rubbing or chafing

galleons (GAL ee uhnz) *n.* large sailing ships used for war or trade

garnished (GAHR nihsht) *v.* decorated; trimmed

garrulous (GAR uh luhs) *adj.* talkative

gaunt (gawnt) *adj.* thin and bony, as from great hunger or age

geography (jee OG ruh fee) *n.* surface features of a place or region

ghastly (GAST lee) *adj.* terrible; very bad

gleaned (gleend) *v.* collected from bit by bit, as when gathering stray grain after a harvest

gout (gowt) *n.* a mass or splash, as of blood; spurt

grandeur (GRAN juhr) *n.* splendor; magnificence

gravity (GRAV uh tee) *n.* weight; seriousness

grievances (GREE vuhns ez) *n.* circumstances that cause people to complain

grieved (greevd) *v.* felt deep grief for; mourned

guile (gyl) *n.* artful trickery

H

haggard (HAG uhrd) *adj.* appearing worn and exhausted; gaunt

harbingers (HAHR bihn juhrz) *n.* forerunners

heedless (HEED lihs) *adj.* not taking notice; inattentive

highlight (HY lyt) *v.* emphasize

hoary (HAWR ee) *adj.* white or gray with age

homespun (hohm spuhn) *adj.* spun or made at home; plain

hypothesize (hy POTH uh syz) *v.* suggest a possible explanation

I

ideal (y DEE uhl) *n.* perfect type

idealism (y DEE uh lihz uhm) *n.* a belief in or pursuit of things as they should be

ignoble (ihg NOH buhl) *adj.* not noble; common

ignominy (IHG nuh mihn ee) *n.* humiliation; dishonor

illumine (ih LOO muhn) *v.* light up

illusion (ih LOO zhuhn) *n.* appearance or feeling that misleads because it is not real

immigrant (IHM uh gruhnt) *n.* person who comes into a foreign country to live

immortal (ih MAWR tuhl) *adj.* living or lasting forever; not dying

impediments (ihm PEHD uh muhnts) *n.* obstacles

imperceptibly (ihm puhr SEHP tuh buhl ee) *adv.* without being noticed

imperial (ihm PIHR ee uhl) *adj.* of an empire; having supreme authority

imperialism (ihm PIHR ee uh lihz uhm) *n.* policy of forming an empire by conquest and colonization

impertinence (ihm PUR tuh nuhns) *n.* rudeness; impudence

imperturbable (ihm puhr TUR buh buhl) *adj.* calm; not easily ruffled

implored (ihm PLAWRD) *v.* begged earnestly

importuning (ihm pawr TOON ihng) *v.* pleading with

impressionistic (ihm prehsh uh NIHS tihk) *adj.* conveying a picture through quickly sketched suggestions of details

impudence (IHM pyuh duhns) *n.* lack of shame; rudeness

impulse (IHM puhls) *n.* force driving forward

inane (ihn AYN) *adj.* lacking sense, significance, or ideas; silly

incessant (ihn SEHS uhnt) *adj.* continuing without interruption; ceaseless

incitement (ihn SYT muhnt) *n.* act of urging; encouragement

inconstancy (ihn KON stuhn see) *n.* fickleness; changeableness

inconstantly (ihn KON stuhnt lee) *adv.* changeably; in a fickle way

incredulously (ihn KR uh luhs lee) *adv.* in a manner expressing doubt or disbelief

independence (ihn dih PEHN duhns) *n.* freedom from the control of others

indignant (ihn DIHG nuhnt) *adj.* outraged; filled with righteous anger

indissoluble (ihn dih SOL yuh buhl) *adj.* not able to be dissolved or undone

inducted (ihn DUHKT ihd) *v.* brought formally into an organization

industry (IHN duh stree) *n.* any branch of business, trade, or manufacture

inevitable (ihn EHV uh tuh buhl) *adj.* unavoidable; certain to happen

infamy (IHN fuh mee) *n.* very bad reputation; disgrace; dishonor

infirmity (n FUR muh tee) *n.* physical or mental defect; illness

ingenuous (ihn JEHN yoo uhs) *adj.* naïve; simple

ingratiating (ihn GRAY shee ay tihng) *adj.* charming; agreeable; pleasing

inheritance (ihn HEHR uh tuhns) *n.* act of inheriting

inklings (IHNGK lihngz) *n.* indirect suggestions; vague ideas

innumerable (ih NOO muhr uh buhl) *adj.* too many to count

insatiableness (ihn SAY shuh buhl nuhs) *n.* the quality of being impossible to fill

instantaneous (IHN stuhn TAY nee uhs) *adj.* done or happening in an instant

integrate (IHN tuh grayt) *v.* bring together distinct parts

intemperance (ihn TEHM puhr uhns) *n.* lack of restraint

interpret (ihn TUR priht) *v.* explain the meaning

interpretation (ihn tur pruh TAY shuhn) *n.* act of explaining

interred (ihn TURD) *v.* buried in the earth

intrigues (ihn TREEGZ) *n.* plots or schemes

intrinsically (ihn TRIHN suh kuhl ee) *adv.* at its core; inherently; innately

invasion (ihn VAY zhuhn) *n.* entering by force

invincible (ihn VIHN suh buhl) *adj.* unconquerable

irrevocable (ih REHV uh kuh buhl) *adj.* unable to be undone or cancelled

isolation (y suh LAY shuhn) *n.* state of being completely separated from others

J

judicious (joo DIHSH uhs) *adj.* showing good judgment

K

keenly (KEEN lee) *adv.* sharply; intensely

ken (kehn) *n.* range of sight or knowledge

kindred (KIHN drihd) *n.* a person's relatives collectively

kingdoms (KIHNG duhm) *n.* countries that are governed by a king or queen

L

label (LAY buhl) *v.* describe or designate

laity (LAY uh tee) *n.* those not initiated into a priesthood

lament (luh MEHNT) *v.* to express grief over; to mourn

lamentable (LAM uhn tuh buhl) *adj.* causing grief; distressing

lamentations (lam uhn TAY shuhnz) *n.* expressions of grief or mourning

languish (LANG gwihsh) *v.* become weak; droop; suffer from longing

languished (LANG gwihsht) *v.* weakened; dulled

languor (LANG guhr) *n.* lack of energy or vitality; sluggishness

largesse (LAHR jihs) *n.* nobility of spirit

larking (LAHRK ihng) *v.* free-spirited, whimsical fun

legacy (LEHG uh see) *n.* money or other property left to a person by the will of someone who has died

lintel (LIHN tuhl) *n.* horizontal bar above a door

loathsome (LOHTH suhm) *adj.* disgusting

loyalties (LOY uhl teez) *n.* loyal feelings or behaviors; faithfulness

loyalty (LOY uhl tee) *n.* loyal feeling or behavior; faithfulness

ludicrous (LOO duh kruhs) *adj.* absurd; ridiculous

lustrous (LUHS truhs) *adj.* having luster; shining; luminous

M

macadam (muh KAD uhm) *n.* the broken stone used in making a road

madrigals (MAD ruh guhlz) *n.* short love poems set to music

magistrate (MAJ uh strayt) *n.* a local official who administers the law or serves as a judge

malevolence (muh LEHV uh luhns) *n.* ill will; spitefulness

malicious (muh LIHSH uhs) *adj.* deliberately harmful; destructive

massive (MAS ihv) *adj.* big and solid; bulky

measure (MEHZH uhr) *n.* a section of written music between two vertical lines called bars; a bill, resolution, or something else proposed or enacted to improve a situation

melodious (muh LOH dee uhs) *adj.* sweet-sounding; tuneful

melody (MEHL uh dee) *n.* a sequence of single tones that together create a tune or song

migrated (MY grayt uhd) *v.* moved from one region or country to another

mobility (moh BIHL uh tee) *n.* ability to move

mockeries (MOK uhr eez) *n.* futile or disappointing efforts; ridicule

modernization (mod uhr nuh ZAY shuhn) *n.* bringing up to the present ways or standards

monarch (MON uhrk) *n.* country ruled by one person

monotonous (muh NOT uh nuhs) *adj.* without variation

morose (muh ROHS) *adj.* gloomy; sullen

mortal (MAWR tuhl) *adj.* of that which must eventually die

multitudinous (muhl tuh TOO duh nuhs) *adj.* existing in great numbers

munificence (myoo NIHF uh suhns) *n.* lavish generosity

N

nature (NAY chuhr) *n.* all things except those made by man

nimble (NIHM buhl) *adj.* able to move quickly and lightly

nocturnal (nok TUR nuhl) *adj.* occurring at night

notorious (noh TAWR ee uhs) *adj.* widely but unfavorably known; having a bad reputation

nuisance (NOO suhns) *n.* act, thing, or condition causing trouble

O

obdurate (OB duhr iht) *adj.* stubborn

obedience (oh BEE dee uhns) *n.* the act of following orders or instructions

obliquely (uh BLEEK lee) *adv.* at a slant; indirectly

obscure (uhb SKYUR) *adj.* not easily seen; not generally known

obscure (uhb SKYUR) *v.* making difficult to see

obstinate (OB stuh niht) *adj.* stubborn; dogged

obstinately (OB stuh niht lee) *adv.* in a determined way; stubbornly

officious (uh FIHSH uhs) *adj.* meddlesome

ordeal (awr DEEL) *n.* difficult or painful experience that tests one

order (AWR duhr) *n.* way one thing follows another

orthodox (AWR thuh doks) *adj.* conforming to established beliefs

outcast (OWT KAST) *n.* person cast out from home and friends

outline (OWT LYN) *v.* develop a general plan

P

pallor (PAL uhr) *n.* unnatural lack of color; paleness

palpable (PAL puh buhl) *adj.* capable of being touched or felt

palpitation (pal puh TAY shuhn) *n.* an unusually or abnormally rapid or violent beating of the heart

paltry (PAWL tree) *adj.* practically worthless; insignificant

paradox (PAR uh doks) *n.* statement that may be true but seems to say two opposite things

paraphrase (PAR uh frayz) *v.* reword something spoken or written

pastoral (PAS tuhr uhl) *n.* simple or naturally beautiful like the country

pathos (PAY thos) *n.* quality that evokes sorrow or compassion

patronize (PAY truh nyz) *v.* to be a customer of a particular merchant or store

penury (PEHN yuhr ee) *n.* poverty

perceive (puhr SEEV) *v.* recognize through the senses

peril (PEHR uhl) *n.* exposure to harm or injury

pernicious (puhr NIHSH uhs) *adj.* causing great injury, destruction, or ruin; fatal; deadly

phantasm (FAN taz uhm) *n.* supernatural form or shape; ghost; figment of the imagination

philosophy (fuh LOS uh fee) *n.* system for guiding life

piety (PY uh tee) *n.* devotion to religion

platitude (PLAT uh tood) *n.* commonplace or overused statement

plebeian (plih BEE uhn) *adj.* common; not aristocratic

power (POW uhr) *n.* strength or force

predominance (prih DOM uh nuhns) *n.* superiority

predominant (prih DOM uh nuhnt) *adj.* foremost; powerful

prefiguring (pree FIHG yuhr ihng) *v.* resembling and so suggesting beforehand

prenatal (pree NAY tuhl) *adj.* existing or taking place before birth

presumed (prih ZOOMD) *v.* taken for granted; assumed

presumption (prih ZUHMP shuhn) *n.* audacity

prevail (prih VAYL) *v.* to succeed; become dominant; win out

prevarication (pree VAR uh KAY shuhn) *n.* evasion of truth

prime (prym) *n.* best stage of a thing or process

pristine (PRIHS teen) *adj.* original; unspoiled

probe (prohb) *v.* search into and explore thoroughly

prodding (PROD ihng) *v.* poking, jabbing, seeking

prodigal (PROD uh guhl) *adj.* recklessly wasteful

prodigious (pruh DIHJ uhs) *adj.* enormous; huge

profanation (PROF uh NAY shuhn) *n.* action showing disrespect for something sacred

proferring (PROF uhr ihng) *n.* offering

profuse (pruh FYOOS) *adj.* abundant; pouring out

progress (PROG rehs) *n.* growth; improvement

promontories (PROM uhn tawr eez) *n.* peaks of high land sticking out into a body of water

prophet (PROF iht) *n.* person who tells what will happen

propitiate (pruh PIHSH ee ayt) *v.* win the good-will of; appease

propose (pruh POHZ) *v.* set forth a plan or intention

propriety (pruh PRY uh tee) *n.* quality or condition of being proper

prosper (PROS puhr) *v.* to thrive

prowess (PROW ihs) *n.* heroism; distinction

prudence (PROO duhns) *n.* careful management of resources; economy

pulp (puhlp) *n.* the soft, juicy, edible part of a fruit

purge (purj) *v.* purify; cleanse

R

rancor (RANG kuhr) *n.* ill will; continuing and bitter hate

ransacked (RAN sakt) *v.* searched through to find goods to rob; Looted

rapture (RAP chuhr) *n.* joy; great pleasure

rapturous (RAP chuhr uhs) *adj.* filled with joy and love; ecstatic

rational (RASH uh nuhl) *adj.* sensible; reasonable

realms (rehlmz) *n.* regions under the rule of a king or queen

rebellious (rih BEHL yuhs) *adj.* defying authority

rebuild (ree BIHLD) *v.* build or create again

rebuke (rih BYOOK) *v.* criticize strongly

recall (rih KAWL) *v.* remember

reckoning (REHK uhn ihng) *n.* accounting

recoil (rih KOYL) *v.* to draw back in fear, surprise, or disgust

recommend (rehk uh MEHND) *v.* suggest favorably

recompense (REHK uhm pehns) *n.* payment in return for something

recount (rih KOWNT) *v.* tell in detail

reform (rih FAWRM) *v.* make better

reformation (REHF uhr MAY shuhn) *n.* change for the better; improvement

refractory (rih FRAK tuhr ee) *adj.* hard to manage; stubborn

refute (rih FYOOT) *v.* prove wrong

reiterate (ree IHT uh rayt) *v.* state or do over again

relates (rih LAYTS) *v.* tells

remnant (REHM nuhnt) *n.* what is left over; remainder

Renaissance (REHN uh sahns) *n.* great revival of art and learning in Europe during the 1300s, 1400s, and 1500s

reparation (rehp uh RAY shuhn) *n.* compensation for a wrong

reprove (rih PROOV) *v.* to disapprove of strongly; censure

requiem (REHK wee uhm) *n.* musical composition honoring the dead

resolution (rehz uh LOO shuhn) *n.* a resolve or determination

resume (rih ZOOM) *v.* to take up or go on with again after interruption

reticent (REHT uh suhnt) *adj.* silent; reserved

reverence (REHV uhr uhns) *n.* deep respect

reverently (REHV uhr uhnt lee) *adv.* with deep respect or awe

revolution (rehv uh LOO shuhn) *n.* complete overthrow of an established government or political system

righteousness (RY chuhs nihs) *n.* the character-istic of acting in a just, virtuous manner

risible (RIHZ uh buhl) *adj.* prompting laughter

rites (ryts) *n.* ceremonies; rituals

role (rohl) *n.* part or function assumed by any person or thing

roused (rowzd) *v.* stirred up

rue (roo) *n.* sorrow; regret

rummage (RUHM ihj) *v.* to search thoroughly or actively through

S

sanguine (SANG gwihn) *adj.* confident; cheerful

satiety (suh TY uh tee) *n.* state of being filled with enough or more than enough

sauntered (SAWN tuhrd) *v.* walked at an unhur-ried pace

scales (skaylz) *n.* thin, platelike pieces on an animal or plant

schism (SIHZ uhm) *n.* division of a group into factions

scope (skohp) *n.* range of perception or understanding

scurry (SKUR ee) *v.* to run hastily; to scamper

segmented (SEHG muhnt uhd) *v.* divided into joined parts

semblance (SEHM bluhns) *n.* appearance; image

sentinel (SEHN tuh nuhl) *n.* person or animal that guards

sepulcher (SEHP uhl kuhr) *n.* tomb

sequestered (sih KWEHS tuhrd) *v.* kept apart from others

shrill (shrihl) *adj.* high and sharp in tone; high-pitched

sinews (SIHN yooz) *n.* tendons

sinuous (SIHN yu uhs) *adj.* bending; winding

skeptical (SKEHP tuh kuhl) *adj.* doubting; not easily persuaded

smudge (smuhj) *n.* a smear or stain of dirt

sojourn (SOH jurn) *n.* short stay someplace; visit

solace (SOL ihs) *n.* comfort; relief

solicitous (suh LIHS uh tuhs) *adj.* showing care or concern

sordid (SAWR dihd) *adj.* dirty

sound (sownd) *adj.* healthy; undamaged

sovereign (SOV ruhn) *adj.* supreme in power, rank, or authority

specious (SPEE shuhs) *adj.* deceptively attractive or valid; false

spectral (SPEHK truhl) *adj.* ghostly

spellbound (SPEHL BOWND) *adj.* bound by or as if by a spell

spirit (SPIHR iht) *n.* immaterial part of man

sprawling (SPRAWL ihng) *adj.* spread out

stagnant (STAG nuhnt) *adj.* motionless; foul

stature (STACH uhr) *n.* height; level of achievement

stead (stehd) *n.* position being filled by a replacement

steadfastly (STEHD fast lee) *adv.* fixed in direction; steadily directed

stealthy (STEHL thee) *adj.* secretive; furtive; sly

stoic (STOH ihk) *n.* person indifferent to joy, grief, pleasure, or pain

struggle (STRUHG uhl) *v.* work hard against difficulties

subdued (suhb DOOD) *adj.* quiet; inhibited; repressed; controlled

substantial (suhb STAN shuhl) *adj.* having substance, large in size or strength

succor (SUHK uhr) *v.* help; aid; relief

suffused (suh FYOOZD) *v.* spread throughout; filled

sulk (suhlk) *v.* to show resentment by refusing to interact with others

sullen (SUHL uhn) *adj.* gloomy; dismal

sundry (SUHN dree) *adj.* various; miscellaneous

supine (soo PAHYN) *adj.* lying on the back

supplication (suhp luh KAY shuhn) *n.* act of praying or pleading

surmise (suhr MYZ) *n.* imaginings; speculation; guess

sustenance (SUHS tuh nuhns) *n.* food or money to support life

symbolize (SIHM buh lyz) *v.* represent a thing or concept

symmetry (SIHM uh tree) *n.* balanced form; the beauty resulting from such balance

syntax (SIHN taks) *n.* the study of sentence structure

T

tarry (TAR ee) *v.* to delay or linger

technology (tehk NOL uh jee) *n.* science of the mechanical and industrial arts

teeming (TEE mihng) *v.* filled to overflowing

temperate (TEHM puhr iht) *adj.* mild

tempestuous (tehm PEHS chu uhs) *adj.* turbulent; stormy

tenacity (tih NAS uh tee) *n.* persistence; stubbornness

terrestrial (tuh REHS tree uhl) *adj.* relating to the earth or to this world

topographical (top uh GRAF uh kuhl) *adj.* representing the surface features of a region

tortuous (TAWR chu uhs) *adj.* full of twists, turns, or bends; twisting, winding, or crooked

traditional (truh DIHSH uh nuhl) *adj.* customary

transformation (trans fuhr MAY shuhn) *n.* act or process of changing

transgress (tranz GREHS) *v.* violate a law or command

transgressed (tranz GREHST) *v.* overstepped or broke (a law or commandment)

tranquil (TRANG kwuhl) *adj.* calm; serene; peaceful

transcendent (tran SEHN duhnt) *adj.* exceeding beyond all limits

transient (TRAN shuhnt) *adj.* temporary; passing

treachery (TREHCH uhr ee) *n.* betrayal of trust, faith, or allegiance

treasons (TREE zuhnz) *n.* betrayals of one's country or oath of loyalty

trends (trehndz) *n.* general directions; fashions or styles

trepidation (TREHP uh DAY shuhn) *n.* trembling

tribe (tryb) *n.* group of people united by race and customs

trifles (TRY fuhlz) *n.* things of little value or importance

truculent (TRUHK yuh luhnt) *adj.* cruel; fierce

tumid (TOO mihd) *adj.* swollen

tumult (TOO muhlt) *n.* noisy commotion, often caused by a crowd

turbid (TUR bihd) *adj.* muddy or cloudy; stirred up and confused

turmoil (TUR moyl) *n.* a state of great commotion, confusion, or disturbance

tyrants (TY ruhnts) *n.* cruel, oppressive rulers

U

uncanny (uhn KAN ee) *adj.* mysterious; hard to explain

undeterminable (uhn dih TUR muh nuh buhl) *adj.* not able to be decided or settled

ungenial (uhn JEEN yuhl) *adj.* disagreeable; characterized by bad weather

upbraidings (uhp BRAY dihngz) *n.* stern words of disapproval; scoldings

urban (UR buhn) *adj.* that is or has the essential characteristics of a city

utters (UHT uhrz) *v.* sends forth with the voice

V

vales (vaylz) *n.* valleys; hollows; depressed stretches of ground

valor (VAL uhr) *n.* courageous behavior; bravery

values (VAL yooz) *n.* principles

venerable (VEHN uhr uh buhl) *adj.* commanding respect because of age, character, or social rank

verge (vurj) *n.* edge; rim

vindication (vihn duh KAY shuhn) *n.* act of providing justification or support for

vintage (VIHN tihj) *n.* wine of fine quality

vivacious (vy VAY shuhs) *adj.* lively, spirited

vulnerable (VUHL nuhr uh buhl) *adj.* exposed to attack or harm

W

wallowed (WOL ohd) *v.* rolled around in mud, water, etc.

wan (won) *adj.* sickly pale; faint or weak

waning (WAY nihng) *v.* gradually becoming dimmer or weaker

welfare (WEHL FAIR) *n.* condition of being well; health

winsome (WIHN suhm) *adj.* having a charming appearance or way

wither (WIHTH uhr) *v.* fade or waste away

wreath (reeth) *n.* circle of flowers

writhes (rythz) *v.* twists and turns the body, as in agony

writhing (RYTH ihng) *n.* twisting or turning motion

Spanish Glossary

El vocabulario de Pregunta Essential aparece en **azul**. El vocabulario academico de alta utilidad está <u>subrayado</u>.

A

abasement / humillación *s.* condición de ser degradado o rebajado

abated / disminuido *v.* reducido

abide / permanecer *v.* quedarse; mantenerse

absolution / absolución *s.* acto de librar a alguien de un pecado o acusación criminal

acceded / accedió *v.* cedió; acordó

accounts / cuentas *s.* registros de dinero recibido y pagado; registros financieros

adjure / implorar *v.* solicitar solemnemente; conjurar seriamente

admonish / amonestar *v.* advertir

adroitly / diestramente *adv.* con destreza física o mental

adulterations / adulteraciones *s.* impurezas; ingredientes agregados que son inadecuados o inferiores

adversary / adversario *s.* opositor; enemigo

<u>**advocate / abogar**</u> *v.* hablar o escribir en apoyo de

affably / afablemente *adv.* de manera amistosa

affinities / afinidades *s.* conexiones familiares; simpatías

affluence / opulencia *s.* riqueza abundante

ague / escalofrío *s.* enfriamiento o estremecimiento

alderman / concejal *s.* funcionario principal en un pueblo o condado

alters / altera *v.* cambia

amiable / amigable *adj.* amistoso; afable

amorous / amoroso *adj.* lleno de amor o deseo

anarchy / anarquía *s.* ausencia de gobierno; desorden

anatomize / anatomizar *v.* disecar a fin de examinar su estructura

ancestral / ancestral *adj.* heredado

anemic / anémico *adj.* que le falta fuerza, vigor, vitalidad o colorido; desganado; débil

<u>**annotate / anotar**</u> *v.* hacer anotaciones o señalar con una explicación

antic / bufonesco *adj.* raro y cómico; ridículo

antidote / antídoto *s.* algo que sirve para combatir una condición no deseada; remedio

aperture / abertura *s.* orificio

apothecary / boticario *s.* farmacéutico; titular de droguería

appalled / pasmó *v.* que se llenó de consternación o desaliento

appendage / apéndice *s.* algo que se agrega

apprehension / aprensión *s.* sentimiento ansioso de presentimiento; pavor

apprehensions / aprensiones *s.* temores; preocupaciones

approbation / aprobación *s.* aceptación o ratificación oficial

arboreal / arbóreo *adj.* de, cerca o entre los árboles

articulate / articular *v.* expresar claramente

artifice / artificio *s.* habilidad; el producto de una destreza, especialmente un engaño astuto

artificiality / artificialidad *s.* que no es natural; irreal

aspire / aspirar *v.* tener grandes ambiciones; desear o buscar

assault / asaltar *v.* atacar violentamente

assessing / avaluando *v.* estimando el valor (de una propiedad) para fines de impuestos

assiduous / asiduo *adj.* constante en cuanto a aplicación o atención

assignations / asignaciones *s.* citas que deben cumplirse

asunder / en partes *adj.* roto en partes o pedazos

atrophy / atrofiar *v.* deteriorar

augment / aumentar *v.* hacer más grande; expandir

authentic / auténtico *adj.* genuino; real

avarice / avaricia *s.* codicia

averred / afirmó *v.* verificó

awe / asombro *s.* sensación mixta de reverencia, temor y asombro

B

balm / bálsamo *s.* ungüento u otra cosa que sana o alivia

bar / barra *s.* una de las líneas verticales que divide la música escrita en secciones iguales llamadas compases

bequeath / heredar *v.* pasar como una herencia

beliefs / creencias *s.* lo que uno sostiene que es cierto

bilious / colérico *adj.* malgeniado; irritable; malhumorado

blight / plaga *s.* condición de estar marchito

blithe / alegre *adj.* Animado

boundary / límite *s.* línea divisoria; frontera

breach / ruptura *s.* rompimiento o estar roto; dejar de cumplir con los términos de un acuerdo

brink / borde *s.* orilla; margen

burden / carga *s.* algo que pone un peso sobre uno; una pesada obligación o responsabilidad

C

cadence / cadencia *s.* movimiento medido

capitalism / capitalismo *s.* sistema económico en el cual personas particulares o grupos de personas son propietarias de tierras, fábricas y otros medios de producción.

caprices / caprichos *s.* extravagancias

<u>**categorize / categorizar**</u> *v.* colocar en grupos relacionados

censure / censurar *v.* desaprobar con firmeza; condenar

certify / certificar *v.* declarar que una cosa es cierta o exacta; verificar; atestar

<u>**characterize / caracterizar**</u> *v.* describir aspectos, cualidades o rasgos

chronicle / crónica *s.* registro histórico de eventos en orden cronológico

chrysalis / crisálida *s.* la tercera fase en el desarrollo de una polilla o mariposa

circumscribed / circunscrito *v.* delimitado; que tiene un lindero definido

<u>**cite / citar**</u> *v.* referirse a un texto

city / ciudad *s.* pueblo grande densamente poblado

clamorous / clamoroso *adj.* bullicioso y confuso; ruidoso

<u>**clarify / aclarar**</u> *v.* poner en claro

clasped / agarrado *v.* sujetado o estrechado firmemente

classics / clásicos *s.* libros o pinturas de las más alta calidad

<u>**classify / clasificar**</u> *v.* asignar a una categoría

climacteric / crisis s. cualquier período crítico

colonize / colonizar v. establecer un asentamiento

combatants / combatientes s. luchadores

combustible / combustible adj. capaz de ser encendido y quemado; inflamable

commentary / comentario s. serie de observaciones

commission / comisión s. autorización; acto de dar autoridad a un individuo

commodity / mercancía s. producto que es comprado o vendido

compassionate / compasivo adj. simpatizante con

compile / compilar v. reunir

complaisant / complaciente adj. afable; dispuesto a agradar

comprised / comprendió v. consistió de; incluyó

concord / concordia s. relaciones amistosas; armonía

condescension / condescendencia s. el acto o instancia de condescender

conflagration / conflagración s. gran incendio

conflict / conflicto s. lucha o contienda

conjecture / conjeturar v. adivinar

connote / connotar v. sugerir o comunicar

conquest / conquista s. acto de conquistar

consciousness / conciencia s. estar consciente de

constituency / distrito electoral s. la gente que compone un grupo de votantes

construct / construir v. colocar partes sistemáticamente para armar algo

contemporary / contemporáneo adj. que pertenece al mismo período de tiempo

contemptuous / desdeñoso adj. despreciativo

contend / contender v. aseverar o disputar

contention / contienda s. disputa, argumento

contentious / contencioso adj. disputador

contextualize / contextualizar v. colocar información dentro de un plano más amplio

contrite / contrito adj. dispuesto a arrepentirse o a expiar

controversy / controversia s. acto de disputar un tema sobre el cual existen varios puntos de vista

contusions / contusiones s. herida en la que la piel no se rompe; magulladura

conventional / convencional adj. que actúa o se comporta de manera usualmente aceptada o aprobada

conviction / convicción s. creencia; fe

coordinate / coordinar v. relacionar o vincular

countenance / semblante s. cara

country / país s. territorio; nación

courtly / cortésmente adj. elegantemente digno; decoroso

covetousness / codicia s. avaricia

cower / agachar v. encogerse, como de miedo o frío

coyness / modestia s. timidez; afectación, a menudo como parte de un coqueteo

credulity / credulidad s. tendencia a creer con demasiada facilidad

credulous / crédulo adj. que tiende a creer con demasiada facilidad

critique / criticar v. examinar críticamente, revisar

cultivated / cultivó v. sembró

cynically / cínicamente adv. semejante o característico de un cínico; desconfiado o que menosprecia los motivos de otro

D

dappled / manchado adj. pinto o moteado, usualmente en montones

dauntless / intrépido adj. valiente; que nada le intimida

debate / debatir v. discutir razonamientos opuestos

deduce / deducir v. inferir algo de un principio general

deference / deferencia s. consideración o respeto hacia otros

deficient / deficiente adj. que carece de una cualidad esencial

define / definir v. mencionar las cualidades que describen algo

deftly / diestramente adv. con facilidad y rapidez

deism / deísmo s. creencia en Dios basada en la evidencia de la razón y la naturaleza

deliberation / deliberación s. consideración y discusión cuidadosa antes de tomar una decisión

delirious / delirante adj. que tiene alucinaciones; desvariado

demonstrate / demostrar v. mostrar usando el razonamiento o ejemplos

denote / denotar v. referirse claramente a algo

depict / representar v. describir una imagen utilizando palabras

depredation / depredación s. un ataque predatorio; pillaje

derided / mofó v. burló; ridiculizó

deign / dignarse v. condescender; rebajarse a

desolate / desolado adj. desierto; solitario

despondent / desalentado adj. desanimado; abatido

despotic / despótico adj. tiránico

destitute / desprovisto adj. Carente

destruction / destrucción s. el acto de destruir

devise / idear v. inventar o crear; planear

diffusive / difusivo adj. tendiente a esparcirse

disabused / desengañó v. liberó de ideas falsas

discern / discernir v. reconocer como separado o diferente

discreet / discreto adj. sabio; prudente

discretion / discreción s. cuidado en lo que uno hace y dice; buen criterio; prudencia

dislocation / dislocación s. condición de estar fuera de lugar

dispensation / designio divino s. sistema religioso o creencias

disposable / disponible adj. libre para usar; a disposición

dissatisfaction / descontento s. estado de disgusto

dissect / disecar v. analizar e interpretar minuciosamente

distemper / distémper s. enfermedad infecciosa, como la plaga

distill / destilar v. obtener la parte esencial

divine / divino adj. celestial; sagrado

dominion / dominio s. soberanía o poder sobre un territorio; autoridad o control

dominions / dominios s. territorios o tierras gobernadas

dowry / dote s. propiedad que aporta la familia de la mujer a su marido cuando se casan

dregs / vestigios s. una pequeña cantidad; residuo

E

eclipse / eclipsar v. desvanecer o extinguir el poder o la gloria

economic / económico adj. relacionado al manejo de los ingresos

edit / editar v. alterar, adaptar o refinar

effigy / efigie s. retrato o estatua de una persona

electors / electores s. aquellos que votan

eloquent / elocuente adj. bellamente expresivo

eludes / elude v. evita o escapa

embarked / enfrascó v. que participó en algo, como en una conversación

embellishments / adornos *s.* toques decorativos; ornamentos

eminent / eminente *adj.* notable; de algo rango; distinguido

empire / imperio *s.* grupo de naciones o estados bajo un solo soberano o gobierno

encomiums / encomios *s.* expresiones formales de gran elogio

endeavored / esforzó *s.* hizo un intento serio; trató

enhance / realzar *v.* mejorar o elevar

enigma / enigma *s.* acertijo; declaración, persona o situación perpleja

entreated / suplicó *v.* imploró; rogó

enumerate / enumerar *v.* especificar en una lista

epic / epopeya *s.* poema largo sobre las aventuras de uno o más grandes héroes

equate / igualar *v.* considerar que una cosa es igual que otra

equivocate / emplear lenguaje ambiguo *v.* usar términos que tienen dos o más significados para despistar intencionalmente o engañar

escapade / escapada *s.* aventura, especialmente una que rompe con las reglas normales de conducta

esteemed / estimado *adj.* altamente respetado; tener en alta estima

etymology / etimología *s.* el estudio de los orígenes de las palabras

evaluate / evaluar *v.* establecer el significado, valor o condición de algo

evanescence / desvanecimiento *s.* desaparición o tendencia a desaparecer

evoke / evocar *v.* provocar una reacción

exemplary / ejemplar *adj.* dícese de algo que podría servir de modelo

exile / exiliar *v.* obligar a una persona a abandonar su hogar o país

exotic / exótico *adj.* de un país extranjero

expedient / recurso *s.* dispositivo usado en una emergencia

expiated / expió *v.* reparó; dio cumplida satisfacción, especialmente mediante el sufrimiento

extract / extraer *v.* sonsacar información

extravagant / extravagante *adj.* ir más allá de los límites razonables; excesivo

F

fantastic / fantástico *adj.* muy extravagante; increíblemente bueno

fastidious / quisquilloso *adj.* exigente; difícil de satisfacer

fate / sino *s.* destino

fathom / comprender *v.* entender cabalmente

fervent / ferviente *adj.* tener gran calidez de sentimientos

fidelity / fidelidad *s.* lealtad

filial / filial *adj.* lo que se espera de un hijo o hija

form / moldear *v.* dar forma a

format / formatear *v.* disponer de acuerdo a un plan

formulate / formular *v.* expresar completa y claramente; idear

fortitude / fortaleza *s.* valor; fuerza para resistir

fracture / fractura *s.* el acto de quebrar; condición de estar roto

frugally / frugalmente *adv.* forma de ser cuidadoso con el dinero

furrow / surco *s.* carril angosto hecho en la tierra con un arado

G

gall / amargura *s.* sentimiento amargo; rencor profundo

galled / irritado *adj.* lastimado o excoriado por rozadura

galleons / galeones *s.* grandes veleros usados para la guerra o el comercio

garnished / adornó *v.* decoró; guarneció

garrulous / gárrulo *adj.* parlanchín

gaunt / demacrado *adj.* flaco y huesudo, como por desnutrición o edad avanzada

geography / geografía *s.* aspectos de la superficie de un lugar o región

ghastly / horriblemente *adv.* terriblemente; muy malo

gleaned / espigó *v.* juntó poco a poco, como cuando se recolecta granos que quedan después de una cosecha

gout / gota *s.* una masa o salpicadura de un líquido como la sangre

grandeur / grandeza *s.* esplendor; magnificencia

gravity / gravedad *s.* peso; seriedad

grievances / agravios *s.* circunstancias que hacen que la gente se queje

grieved / afligió *v.* sintió mucho pesar; lamentó

guile / maña *s.* embuste habilidoso

H

haggard / demacrado *adj.* que aparenta estar consumido y agotado; ojeroso

harbingers / precursores *s.* heraldos

heedless / incauto *adj.* descuidado; desatento

highlight / realzar *v.* destacar

hoary / canoso *adj.* blanco o encanecido con la edad

homespun / doméstico *adj.* hilado o hecho en casa

hypothesize / formular una hipótesis *v.* sugerir una explicación posible

I

ideal / ideal *s.* modelo de perfección

idealism / idealismo *s.* acto de descuidar asuntos prácticos por seguir los ideales

ignoble / innoble *adj.* que no es noble; plebeyo

ignominy / ignominia *s.* humillación; deshonra

illumine / iluminar *v.* alumbrar

illusion / ilusión *s.* apariencia o sentimiento que engaña porque no es real

immigrant / inmigrante *s.* persona que llega a vivir a un país extranjero

immortal / inmortal *adj.* que vive o perdura para siempre; que no muere

impediments / impedimentos *s.* obstáculos

imperceptibly / imperceptiblemente *adv.* sin que se note

imperial / imperial *adj.* de un imperio; que tiene autoridad suprema

imperialism / imperialismo *s.* política de crear un imperio por medio de la conquista y la colonización

impertinence / impertinencia *s.* descortesía; insolencia

imperturbable / imperturbable *adj.* calmado; que no se enfada fácilmente

implored / imploró *v.* rogó seriamente

importuning / importunando *v.* insistiendo con

impressionistic / impresionista *adj.* que comunica un dibujo mediante sugerencias de detalles con un trazo rápido

impudence / impudencia *s.* falta de vergüenza; descortesía

impulse / impulso *s.* fuerza que empuja hacia adelante

inane / vacío *adj.* que le falta sentido, significado o ideas; necio

incessant / incesante *adj.* que continúa sin interrupción; perenne

incitement / incitación *s.* acto de apremiar; estímulo

inconstancy / inconstancia *s.* inestabilidad; veleidad

inconstantly / inconstantemente *adv.* inestablemente; veleidosamente

incredulously / incrédulamente *adv.* de forma que expresa duda o escepticismo

independence / independencia *s.* estar libre del control de los demás

indignant / indignado *adj.* enfurecido; lleno de cólera justa

indissoluble / indisoluble *adj.* que no puede ser disuelto o deshecho

inducted / admitió *v.* introdujo formalmente a una organización

industry / industria *s.* cualquier rama empresarial, comercial o manufacturera

inevitable / inevitable *adj.* ineludible; que sucederá con seguridad

infamy / infamia *s.* muy mala reputación; desgracia; deshonra

infirmity / enfermedad *s.* defecto físico o mental; dolencia

ingenuous / ingenuo *adj.* inocente; sencillo

ingratiating / congraciador *adj.* encantador; ameno; complaciente

inheritance / herencia *s.* acto de heredar

inklings / indicios *s.* sugerencias indirectas; ideas vagas

innumerable / innumerable *adj.* mucha cantidad para contar

insatiableness / insaciabilidad *s.* la cualidad de ser imposible de satisfacer

instantaneous / instantáneo *adj.* que se hace o sucede en un instante

integrate / integrar *v.* reunir partes distintas

intemperance / intemperancia *s.* falta de moderación

interpret / interpretar *v.* explicar el significado

interpretation / interpretación *s.* el acto de explicar

interred / sepultó *v.* enterró

intrigues / intrigas *s.* tramas o maquinaciones

intrinsically / intrínsecamente *adv.* en su meollo; inherentemente; de manera innata

invasion / invasión *s.* entrar a la fuerza

invincible / invencible *adj.* inconquistable

irrevocable / irrevocable *adj.* incapaz de ser deshecho o cancelado

isolation / aislamiento *s.* acto de estar completamente separado de los demás

J

judicious / juicioso *adj.* que muestra buen criterio

K

keenly / profundamente *adv.* agudamente; intensamente

ken / vista *s.* alcance de la vista o comprensión

kindred / parentela *s.* el grupo de parientes de una persona

kingdoms / reinos *s.* países bajo el mandato de un rey o una reina

L

label / calificar *v.* describir o designar

laity / laicos *s.* aquéllos que no pertenecen al sacerdocio

lament / lamentar *v.* expresar dolor; afligirse

lamentable / lamentable *adj.* que causa dolor; perturbador

lamentations / lamentaciones *s.* expresiones de dolor o aflicción

languish / languidecer *v.* debilitar; marchitar; suspirar por

languished / languideció *v.* se debilitó; se entorpeció

languor / languidez *s.* falta de energía o vitalidad; lentitud

largesse / generosidad *s.* nobleza de espíritu

larking / retozar *v.* divertirse despreocupada y caprichosamente

legacy / legado *s.* dinero u otras pertenencias heredadas a una persona por voluntad de alguien que haya muerto

lintel / dintel *s.* barra horizontal sobre una puerta

loathsome / repulsivo *adj.* repugnante

loyalties / lealtades *s.* sentimientos o comportamientos leales; fidelidad

loyalty / lealtad *s.* sentimiento o comportamiento leal; fidelidad

ludicrous / risible *adj.* absurdo; ridículo

lustrous / lustroso *adj.* que tiene lustre; brillante; luminoso

M

macadam / macadán *s.* piedra quebrada que se usa para hacer una calle con el mismo nombre

madrigals / madrigales *s.* poemas cortos de amor con música

magistrate / magistrado *s.* un funcionario local que hace cumplir la ley o funge como juez

malevolence / malevolencia *s.* mala voluntad; despecho

malicious / malicioso *adj.* deliberadamente dañino; destructivo

massive / masivo *adj.* grande y sólido; voluminoso

measure / medida *s.* una sección de música escrita entre dos líneas verticales llamadas barras; ley, resolución o algo parecido que se propone o ratifica para mejorar una situación

melodious / melodioso *adj.* de sonido placentero; armonioso

melody / melodía *s.* secuencia de tonos solos que juntos crean una tonada o canción

migrated / emigró *v.* que se mudó de una región o país a otro

mobility / movilidad *s.* habilidad de movimiento

mockeries / burlas *s.* esfuerzos fútiles o decepcionantes; ridículo

modernization / modernización *s.* llevar a la actualidad las costumbres o normas

monarch / monarca *s.* persona que gobierna un país

monotonous / monótono *adj.* sin variación

morose / malhumorado *adj.* triste; adusto

mortal / mortal *adj.* dícese de todo lo que eventualmente morirá

multitudinous / numeroso *adj.* que existe en grandes cantidades

munificence / munificencia *s.* esplendidez

N

nature / naturaleza *s.* todas las cosas, excepto aquellas creadas por el hombre

nimble / ágil *adj.* capaz de moverse rápidamente y con ligereza

nocturnal / nocturno *adj.* que ocurre de noche

notorious / notorio *adj.* ampliamente conocido pero desfavorablemente; que tiene una mala reputación

nuisance / fastidio *s.* acto, cosa o condición que causa molestia

O

obdurate / inexorable *adj.* obstinado

obedience / obediencia *s.* el acto de seguir órdenes o instrucciones

obliquely / oblicuamente *adv.* sesgadamente; indirectamente

obscure / oscuro *adj.* que no se ve fácilmente; que por lo general no se conoce

obscure / oscurecer *v.* que hace difícil ver

obstinate / obstinado *adj.* testarudo; terco

obstinately / obstinadamente *adv.* de forma determinante; testarudamente

officious / oficioso *adj.* entremetido

ordeal / prueba severa *s.* experiencia difícil o penosa que lo pone a uno a prueba

order / orden *s.* manera en que una cosa sigue después de otra

orthodox / ortodoxo *adj.* que se conforma a las creencias establecidas

outcast / desterrado *s.* persona exiliada de su hogar y amistades

outline / esbozar *v.* desarrollar un plan general

P

pallor / palor *s.* falta no natural de color; palor

palpable / palpable *adj.* capaz de ser tocado o sentido

palpitation / palpitación *s.* latido del corazón inusual o anormalmente rápido o violento

paltry / miserable *adj.* prácticamente inútil; insignificante

paradox / paradoja *s.* afirmación que puede ser verdadera pero pareciera expresar dos cosas opuestas

paraphrase / parafrasear *v.* poner en otras palabras algo dicho o escrito

pastoral / pastoral *s.* simple o naturalmente bello, como el campo

pathos / patetismo *s.* cualidad que evoca tristeza o compasión

patronize / frecuentar *v.* ser cliente asiduo de un determinado negocio o almacén

penury / penuria *s.* pobreza

perceive / percibir *v.* reconocer a través de los sentidos

peril / peligro *s.* exposición a situación peligrosa o arriesgada

pernicious / pernicioso *adj.* que causa un gran daño, destrucción o ruina; fatal; mortal

pernicious / pernicioso *adj.* que causa un gran daño, destrucción o ruina; mortal

phantasm / fantasma *s.* forma o figura sobrenatural; espectro; producto de la imaginación

philosophy / filosofía *s.* sistema que sirve de guía para la vida

piety / piedad *s.* devoción a una religión

platitude / perogrullada *s.* declaración que carece de autoridad

plebeian / plebeyo *adj.* común; no aristocrático

power / poder *s.* fuerza o vigor

predominance / predominio *s.* superioridad

predominant / predominante *adj.* en primer lugar; poderoso

prefiguring / prefigurando *v.* que se parece, por lo que se sugiere de antemano

prenatal / prenatal *adj.* que existe o tiene lugar antes del nacimiento

presumed / presumió *v.* que dio por sentado; supuso

presumption / presunción *s.* atrevimiento

prevail / prevalecer *v.* tener éxito; obtener el dominio; terminar ganando

prevarication / engaño *s.* evasión de la verdad

prime / plenitud *s.* la mejor etapa de una cosa o proceso

pristine / prístino *adj.* original; intacto

probe / indagar *v.* investigar y explorar minuciosamente

prodding / aguijoneando *v.* picando, punzando, buscando

prodigal / pródigo *adj.* despilfarrador

prodigious / prodigioso *adj.* enorme; inmenso

profanation / profanación *s.* acción que muestra irreverencia hacia algo sagrado

proferring / ofrecimiento *s.* ofrenda

profuse / profuso *adj.* abundante; que se derrama

progress / progreso *s.* crecimiento; mejora

promontories / promontorios *s.* colinas de tierras altas que se introducen en una masa de agua

prophet / profeta *s.* persona que dice lo que ocurrirá

propitiate / propiciar *v.* ganarse la buena voluntad de; aplacar

propose / proponer *v.* presentar un plan o intención

propriety / propiedad *s.* cualidad o condición de ser correcto

prosper / prosperar *v.* medrar

prowess / proeza *s.* heroísmo; distinción

prudence / prudencia *s.* cuidadoso manejo de recursos; economía

pulp / pulpa *s.* la parte suave, jugosa y comestible de una fruta

purge / purgar *v.* purificar; limpiar

R

rancor / rencor *s.* mala voluntad; odio amargo y persistente

ransacked / saqueó *v.* buscó por todo para hallar bienes para robar; pilló

rapture / éxtasis *s.* embeleso; gran placer

rapturous / extasiado *adj.* lleno de embeleso y amor; extático

rational / racional *adj.* sensato; razonable

realms / reinos *s.* regiones bajo el gobierno de un rey o reina

rebellious / rebelde *adj.* que desafía a la autoridad

rebuild / reconstruir *v.* construir o crear de nuevo

rebuke / increpar *v.* criticar fuertemente

recall / recordar *v.* rememorar

reckoning / cálculo *s.* contabilidad

recoil / recular *v.* retroceder por temor, sorpresa o disgusto

recommend / recomendar *v.* sugerir favorablemente

recompense / recompensar *v.* pagar en compensación por algo

recount / narrar *v.* contar con detalles

reform / reformar *v.* mejorar

reformation / reforma *s.* cambio positivo; mejora

refractory / recalcitrante *adj.* difícil de manejar; terco

refute / refutar *v.* demostrar lo contrario

reiterate / reiterar *v.* decir o hacer de nuevo

relates / relata *v.* cuenta

remnant / remanente *s.* lo que queda; residuo

renaissance / renacimiento *s.* gran renacer del arte y de los conocimientos en Europa durante los siglos XIV, XV y XVI

reparation / reparación *s.* compensación por un mal

reprove / criticar v. desaprobar con firmeza; censurar

requiem / réquiem s. composición musical para honrar a los muertos

resolution / resolución s. propósito o determinación

resume / reasumir v. asumir de nuevo o continuar con algo después de una interrupción

reticent / discreto adj. callado; reservado

reverence / reverencia s. respeto profundo

reverently / reverentemente adv. con profundo respeto o admiración

revolution / revolución s. derrocamiento total de un gobierno o sistema político establecido

righteousness / rectitud s. la característica de actuar de forma justa y virtuosa

risible / risible adj. que causa risa

rites / ritos s. ceremonias; rituales

role / papel s. rol o función desempeñada por una persona o cosa

roused / suscitó v. agitó

rue / desilusión s. tristeza; arrepentimiento

rummage / registrar v. buscar detenidamente o activamente

S

sanguine / optimista adj. confiado; esperanzado

satiety / saciedad s. condición de estar lleno con suficiente o más que suficiente

sauntered / deambuló v. caminó a un paso pausado

scales / escamas s. parte delgada, escariosa o membranosa de una planta, como la bráctea de un amento o candelilla

schism / cisma s. separación de un grupo en facciones

scope / alcance s. rango de percepción o entendimiento

scurry / escabullir v. correr rápidamente; escurrirse

segmented / segmentó v. dividió en partes unidas

semblance / apariencia s. aspecto exterior; imagen

sentinel / centinela s. persona o animal que vigila

sepulcher / sepulcro s. tumba

sequestered / secuestró v. mantuvo alejado de los demás

shrill / agudo adj. tono alto y agudo; estridente

sinews / tendones s. fibras

sinuous / sinuoso adj. ondulado; tortuoso

skeptical / escéptico adj. dudoso; que no se persuade fácilmente

smudge / mancha s. un tiznajo o mancha de tierra

sojourn / estada s. corta estadía en algún lugar; visita

solace / solaz s. confortación; desahogo

solicitous / solícito adj. que muestra interés o preocupación

sordid / sórdido adj. sucio

sound / íntegro adj. sano; ileso

sovereign / soberano adj. supremo en poder, rango o autoridad

specious / especioso adj. engañosamente atractivo o válido; falso

spectral / espectral adj. fantasmal

spellbound / encantado adj. atado como por un hechizo

spirit / espíritu s. parte inmaterial del ser humano

sprawling / extendido adj. irregular y grande

stagnant / estancado adj. estático; fétido

stature / estatura s. altura; nivel de realización

stead / lugar s. posición ocupada por un reemplazo

steadfastly / resueltamente adv. con dirección fija; dirigido con firmeza

stealthy / furtivo adj. secreto; clandestino; disimulado

stoic / estoico s. persona indiferente a la alegría, pena, placer o dolor

struggle / luchar v. esforzarse para vencer vicisitudes

subdued / reprimido adj. quieto; inhibido, dominado; controlado

substantial / sustancial adj. que tiene sustancia; grande en tamaño o fuerza

succor / socorrer v. ayudar; asistir; aliviar

suffused / bañó v. se dispersó por todo; llenó

sulk / enfurruñar v. mostrar resentimiento, rehusándose a interactuar con otros

sullen / malhumorado adj. triste; sombrío

sundry / diversos adj. varios; misceláneos

supine / supino adj. que yace sobre su espalda

supplication / súplica s. acto de rezar o rogar

surmise / conjetura s. imaginación; especulación; suposición

sustenance / sustento s. alimento o dinero para subsistir

symbolize / simbolizar v. representar una cosa o un concepto

symmetry / simetría s. forma balanceada; la belleza que resulta de un balance tal

syntax / sintaxis s. el estudio de la estructura de las oraciones

T

tarry / aguardar v. demorarse o quedarse atrás

technology / tecnología s. ciencia de las artes industriales y mecánicas

teeming / rebosar v. llenar hasta que se desborda

temperate / temperado adj. leve

tempestuous / tempestuoso adj. turbulento; tormentoso

tenacity / tenacidad s. persistencia; terquedad

terrestrial / terrestre adj. relativo a la tierra o a este mundo

topographical / topográfico adj. que representa las características superficiales de una región

tortuous / tortuoso adj. lleno de curvas, vueltas o giros; que es sinuoso, curveado o torcido

traditional / tradicional adj. habitual

transformation / transformación s. acto o proceso de cambio

transgress / transgredir v. violar una ley u orden

transgressed / transgredió v. propasó o violó (una ley o mandamiento)

tranquil / tranquilo adj. calmado; sereno; apacible

transcendent / trascendente adj. que excede todos los límites

transient / pasajero adj. temporal; transitorio

treachery / engaño s. el acto de traicionar la confianza, fe o lealtad

treasons / traiciones s. deslealtades hacia su propio país o hacia un juramento de lealtad

trends / tendencias s. direcciones generales; modas o estilos

trepidation / trepidación s. estremecimiento

trifles / bagatelas s. cosas de poco valor o importancia

truculent / truculento adj. cruel; feroz

tumid / túmido adj. hinchado

tumult / tumulto s. conmoción ruidosa, a menudo causada por una muchedumbre

turbid / turbio adj. lodoso o lechoso; revuelto y confuso

turmoil / disturbio s. estado de gran conmoción, confusión o alboroto

tyrants / tiranos s. gobernantes crueles y opresivos

U

uncanny / extraño *adj.* misterioso; difícil de explicar

undeterminable / indeterminable *adj.* no determinable; incierto

ungenial / desfavorable *adj.* desagradable; caracterizado por el mal tiempo

upbraidings / reproches *s.* palabras fuertes de desaprobación; regaños

urban / urbano *adj.* que es o posee las características principales de una ciudad

utters / pronuncia *v.* transmite con la voz

V

vales / valles *s.* hondonadas; hundimientos; depresiones en la superficie terrestre

valor / valor *s.* comportamiento valeroso; coraje

values / valores *s.* valor real; precio correcto

venerable / venerable *adj.* que exige respeto debido a edad, carácter o posición social

verge / borde *s.* filo; margen

vindication / reivindicación *s.* acto de dar justificación o apoyo por

vintage / vendimia *s.* vino de alta calidad

vivacious / vivaz *adj.* vivaracho, fogoso

vulnerable / vulnerable *adj.* expuesto a ataque o perjuicio

W

wallowed / revolcó *v.* rodó por el fango, agua, etc.

wan / pálido *adj.* con palidez enfermiza; desfallecido o débil

waning / menguando *v.* haciendo gradualmente más oscuro o débil

welfare / bienestar *s.* condición de estar bien; salud

winsome / atractivo *adj.* que tiene una apariencia o comportamiento encantador

wither / marchitar *v.* languidecer o deteriorarse

wreath / corona *s.* círculo de flores

writhes / retuerce *v.* que tuerce y contorsiona el cuerpo, como en agonía

writhing / retorciendo *v.* haciendo movimientos de retorcimiento y contorsión

Life of the English Language

The life of every language depends on the people who use it. Whenever you use English by asking a question, talking on the phone, going to a movie, reading a magazine, or writing an e-mail, you keep it healthy and valuable.

Using a Dictionary

Use a **dictionary** to find the meaning, the pronunciation, and the part of speech of a word. Consult a dictionary also to trace the word's *etymology,* or its origin. Etymology explains how words change, how they are borrowed from other languages, and how new words are invented, or "coined."

Here is an entry from a dictionary. Notice what it tells about the word *anthology.*

> **anthology** (an thäl′ə jè) *n., pl.* –gies [Gr. anthologia, a garland, collection of short poems < *anthologos*, gathering flowers < *anthos*, flower + *legein*, to gather] a collection of poems, stories, songs, excerpts, etc., chosen by the compiler.

Dictionaries provide the *denotation* of each word, or its objective meaning. The symbol < means "comes from" or "is derived from." In this case, the Greek words for "flower" and "gather" combined to form a Greek word that meant a garland, and then that word became an English word that means a collection of literary flowers—a collection of literature like the one you are reading now.

Using a Thesaurus

Use a **thesaurus** to increase your vocabulary. In a thesaurus, you will find synonyms, or words that have similar meanings, for most words. Follow these guidelines to use a thesaurus:

- Do not choose a word just because it sounds interesting or educated. Choose the word that expresses exactly the meaning you intend.
- To avoid errors, look up the word in a dictionary to check its precise meaning and to make sure you are using it properly.

Here is an entry from a thesaurus. Notice what it tells about the word *book.*

> **book** *noun* A printed and bound work: tome, volume. See WORDS.
> **book** *verb* **1.** To register in or as if in a book: catalog, enroll, inscribe, list, set down, write down. *See* REMEMBER. **2.** To cause to be set aside, as for one's use, in advance: bespeak, engage, reserve. *See* GET.

If the word can be used as different parts of speech, as book can, the thesaurus entry provides synonyms for the word as each part of speech. Many words also have connotations, or emotional associations that the word calls to mind. A thesaurus entry also gives specific synonyms for each connotation of the word.

Activity Look up the words *knight* and *chivalry* in a dictionary. **(a)** What are their etymologies? **(b)** Explain what their etymologies reveal about the development of English. Then, check the word *chivalry* in a thesaurus. **(c)** What are two synonyms for this word? **(d)** In what way do the connotations of the synonyms differ?

The Origin and Development of English

Old English English began about the year 500 when Germanic tribes settled in Britain. The language of these peoples—the Angles, Saxons, and Jutes—combined with Danish and Norse when Vikings attacked Britain and added some Latin elements when Christian missionaries arrived. The result was Old English, which looked like this:

> Hwaet! We Gar-Dena   in gear-dagum,
> peod-cyninga,   prym gefrunon,
> hu da aepelingas   ellen fremedon!

These words are the opening lines of the Old English epic poem *Beowulf,* probably composed in the eighth century. In modern English, they mean: "Listen! We know the ancient glory of the Spear-Danes, and the heroic deeds of those noble kings!"

Middle English The biggest change in English took place after the Norman Conquest of Britain in 1066. The Normans spoke a dialect of Old French, and Old English changed dramatically when the Normans became the new aristocracy. From about 1100 to 1500, the people of Britain spoke what we now call Middle English.

> A Knyght ther was, and that a worthy man,
> That fro the tyme that he first bigan
> To riden out, he loved chivalrie,
> Trouthe and honour, fredom and curtesie.

These lines from the opening section of Chaucer's *Canterbury Tales* (c. 1400) are much easier for us to understand than the lines from *Beowulf.* They mean: "There was a knight, a worthy man who, from the time he began to ride, loved chivalry, truth, honor, freedom, and courtesy."

Modern English During the Renaissance, with its emphasis on reviving classical culture, Greek and Latin languages exerted a strong influence on the English language. In addition, Shakespeare added about two thousand words to the language. Grammar, spelling, and pronunciation continued to change. Modern English was born.

> *But soft! What light through yonder window breaks?*
> *It is the East, and Juliet is the sun!*

These lines from Shakespeare's *Romeo and Juliet* (c. 1600) need no translation, although it is helpful to know that "soft" means "speak softly." Since Shakespeare's day, conventions of usage and grammar have continued to change. For example, the *th* at the ends of many verbs has become *s*. In Shakespeare's time, it was correct to say "Romeo *hath* fallen in love." In our time, it is right to say "he *has* fallen in love." However, the changes of the past five hundred years are not nearly as drastic as the changes from Old English to Middle English, or from Middle English to Modern English. We still speak Modern English.

Old Words, New Words

Modern English has a larger vocabulary than any other language in the world. The *Oxford English Dictionary* contains about a half million words, and it is estimated that another half million scientific and technical terms do not appear in the dictionary. Here are the main ways that new words enter the language:

- **War**—Conquerors introduce new terms and ideas—and new vocabulary, such as *anger,* from Old Norse.

- **Immigration**—When large groups of people move from one country to another, they bring their languages with them, such as *boycott,* from Ireland.

- **Travel and Trade**—Those who travel to foreign lands and those who do business in faraway places bring new words back with them, such as *shampoo,* from Hindi.

- **Science and Technology**—In our time, the amazing growth of science and technology adds multitudes of new words to English, such as *Internet.*

English is also filled with **borrowings,** words taken directly from other languages. Sometimes borrowed words keep basically the same meanings they have in their original languages: *pajamas* (Hindi), *sauna* (Finnish), *camouflage* (French), *plaza* (Spanish). Sometimes borrowed words take on new meanings. *Sleuth,* for example, an Old Norse word for trail, has come to mean the person who follows a *trail*—a detective.

Mythology contributed to our language too. Some of the days of the week are named after Norse gods—Wednesday was Woden's Day, Thursday was Thor's Day. Greek and Roman myths have given us many words, such as *jovial* (from Jove), *martial* (from Mars), *mercurial* (from Mercury), and *herculean* (from Hercules).

Americanisms are words, phrases, usages, or idioms that originated in American English or that are unique to the way Americans speak. They are expressions of our national character in all its variety: *easy as pie, prairie dog, bamboozle, panhandle, halftime, fringe benefit, bookmobile, jackhammer, southpaw, lickety split.*

Activity Look up the following words in a dictionary. Describe the ways in which you think these words entered American English.

sabotage   burrito   moccasin   mecca   megabyte

The Influence of English

English continues to have an effect on world cultures and literature. There are about three hundred million native English speakers, and about the same number who speak English as a second language. Although more people speak Mandarin Chinese, English is the dominant language of trade, tourism, international diplomacy, science, and technology.

Language is a vehicle of both communication and culture, and the cultural influence of English in the twenty-first century is unprecedented in the history of the world's languages. Beyond business and science, English spreads through sports, pop music, Hollywood movies, television, and journalism. A book that is translated into English reaches many more people than it would in its native language alone. Perhaps most significantly, English dominates the Internet. The next time you log on, notice how many Web sites from around the world also have an English version. The global use of English is the closest the world has ever come to speaking an international language.

Activity Choose one area of culture—such as sports, fashion, the arts, or technology—and identify three new words that English has recently added to the *world's* vocabulary. **(a)** How do you think non-English speakers feel about the spread of English? **(b)** Do you think English helps to bring people together? Why or why not?

Tips for Improving Fluency

When you were younger, you learned to read. Then, you read to expand your experiences or for pure enjoyment. Now, you are expected to read to learn. As you progress in school, you are given more and more material to read. The tips on these pages will help you improve your reading fluency, or your ability to read easily, smoothly, and expressively. Use these tips as you read daily.

Keeping Your Concentration

One common problem that readers face is the loss of concentration. When you are reading an assignment, you might find yourself rereading the same sentence several times without really understanding it. The first step in changing this behavior is to notice that you do it. Becoming an active, aware reader will help you get the most from your assignments. Practice using these strategies:

- Cover what you have already read with a note card as you go along. Then, you will not be able to reread without noticing that you are doing it.
- Set a purpose for reading beyond just completing the assignment. Then, read actively by pausing to ask yourself questions about the material as you read. Check the accuracy of your answers as you continue to read.
- Use the Reading Strategy instruction and notes that appear with each selection in this textbook.
- Look at any art or illustrations that accompany the reading and use picture clues to help your comprehension.
- Stop reading after a specified period of time (for example, 5 minutes) and summarize what you have read. To help you with this strategy, use the Reading Check questions that appear with each selection in this textbook. Reread to find any answers you do not know.

Reading Phrases

Fluent readers read phrases rather than individual words. Reading this way will speed up your reading and improve your comprehension. Here are some useful ideas:

- Experts recommend rereading as a strategy to increase fluency. Choose a passage of text that is neither too hard nor too easy. Read the same passage aloud several times until you can read it smoothly. When you can read the passage fluently, pick another passage and keep practicing.
- Read aloud into a tape recorder. Then, listen to the recording, noting your accuracy, pacing, and expression. You can also read aloud and share feedback with a partner.
- Use the *Pearson Prentice Hall Literature Audio Program Hear It!* to hear the selections read aloud. Read along silently in your textbook, noticing how the reader uses his or her voice and emphasizes certain words and phrases.
- Set a target reading rate. Time yourself as you read and work to increase your speed without sacrificing the level of your comprehension.

Understanding Key Vocabulary

If you do not understand some of the words in an assignment, you may miss out on important concepts. Therefore, it is helpful to keep a dictionary nearby when you are reading. Follow these steps:

- Before you begin reading, scan the text for unfamiliar words or terms. Find out what those words mean before you begin reading.
- Use context—the surrounding words, phrases, and sentences—to help you determine the meanings of unfamiliar words.
- If you are unable to understand the meaning through context, refer to the dictionary.

Paying Attention to Punctuation

When you read, pay attention to punctuation. Commas, periods, exclamation points, semicolons, and colons tell you when to pause or stop. They also indicate relationships between groups of words. When you recognize these relationships you will read with greater understanding and expression. Look at the chart below.

Punctuation Mark	Meaning
comma	brief pause
period	pause at the end of a thought
exclamation point	pause that indicates emphasis
semicolon	pause between related but distinct thoughts
colon	pause before giving explanation or examples

Using the Reading Fluency Checklist

Use the checklist below each time you read a selection in this textbook. In your Language Arts journal or notebook, note which skills you need to work on and chart your progress each week.

Reading Fluency Checklist
❑ Preview the text to check for difficult or unfamiliar words.
❑ Practice reading aloud.
❑ Read according to punctuation.
❑ Break down long sentences into the subject and its meaning.
❑ Read groups of words for meaning rather than reading single words.
❑ Read with expression (change your tone of voice to add meaning to the word).

Reading is a skill that can be improved with practice. The key to improving your fluency is to read. The more you read, the better your reading will become.

Approaches to Criticism

By writing **criticism**—writing that analyzes literature—readers share their responses to a written work. Criticism is also a way for a reader to deepen his or her own understanding and appreciation of the work, and to help others to deepen theirs.

The information in this handbook will guide you through the process of writing criticism. In addition, it will help you to refine your critical perceptions to ensure that you are ready to produce work at the college level.

Understanding Criticism

There are a few different types of criticism. Each can enhance understanding and deepen appreciation of literature in a distinctive way. All types share similar functions.

The Types of Criticism

Analysis Students are frequently asked to analyze, or break into parts and examine, a passage or a work. When you write an analysis, you must support your ideas with references to the text.

Archetypal Criticism Archetypal criticism evaluates works of literature by identifying and analyzing the archetypes contained within them. An archetype, sometimes called a "universal symbol," is a plot, character, symbol, image, setting, or idea that recurs in the literature of many different cultures. Archetypes and patterns of archetypes can be seen as representing common patterns of human life and experience.

Biographical Criticism Biographical criticism uses information about a writer's life to shed light on his or her work.

Historical Criticism Historical criticism traces connections between an author's work and the events, circumstances, or ideas that shaped the writer's historical era.

Political Criticism Political criticism involves viewing an author's work with a focus on political assumptions and content—whether explicit or implicit—and, possibly, assessing the political impact of the work. Similar to historical criticism, political criticism draws connections between an author's work and the political issues and assumptions of the times.

Philosophical Criticism In philosophical criticism, the elements of a literary work such as plot, characters, conflict, and motivations are examined through the lens of the author's philosophical arguments and stances. The critic taking a philosophical approach will analyze philosophical arguments presented in a literary work and determine how those arguments have molded the work.

The Functions of Criticism

Critical writing serves a variety of important functions:

Making Connections All criticism makes connections between two or more things. For instance, an analysis of a poem may show similarities among different images.

Making Distinctions Criticism must make distinctions as well as connections. In an analysis of a poem, a critic may distinguish between two possible purposes for poetry: first, to create an enduring image and, second, to present a deeper meaning.

Achieving Insight By making connections and distinctions, criticism achieves insight. An analysis of a poem may reach the insight that the poem stands on its own as a work of beauty apart from any deeper meaning.

Making a Judgment Assessing the value of a work is an important function of criticism. A critic may assess a work by comparing it with other works and by using a standard such as enjoyment, insight, or beauty.

"Placing" the Work Critics guide readers not by telling them *what* to think but by giving them *terms in which to think*. Critical writing may help readers apply varied perspectives to illuminate different aspects of a work.

Writing Criticism

Like all solid writing, a work of criticism presents a thesis (a central idea) and supports it with arguments and evidence. Follow the strategies below to develop a critical thesis and gather support for it.

Formulate a Working Thesis

Once you have chosen a work or works on which to write, formulate a working thesis. First, ask yourself questions like these:

- What strikes you most about the work or the writer that your paper will address? What puzzles you most?

- In what ways is the work unlike others you have read?

- What makes the techniques used by the writer so well-suited to (or so poorly chosen for) conveying the theme of the work?

Jot down notes answering your questions. Then, reread passages that illustrate your answers, jotting down notes about what each passage contributes to the work. Review your notes, and write a sentence that draws a conclusion about the work.

Gather Support

Taking Notes From the Work
Once you have a working thesis, take notes on passages in the work that confirm it. To aid your search for support, consider the type of support suited to your thesis, as in the chart.

Conducting Additional Research If you are writing biographical or historical criticism, you will need to consult sources on the writer's life and era. Even if you are writing a close analysis of a poem, you should consider consulting the works of critics to benefit from their insights and understanding.

If your thesis concerns . . .	look for support in the form of . . .
Character	• dialogue • character's actions • writer's descriptions of the character • other characters' reactions to the character
Theme	• fate of characters • patterns and contrasts of imagery, character, or events • mood • writer's attitude toward the action
Style	• memorable descriptions, observations • passages that "sound like" the writer • examples of rhetorical devices, such as exaggeration and irony
Historical Context	• references to historical events and personalities • evidence of social or political pressures on characters • socially significant contrasts between characters (for example, between the rich and the poor)
Literary Influences	• writer's chosen form or genre • passages that "sound like" another writer • events or situations that resemble those in other works • evidence of an outlook similar to that of another writer

Take Notes

Consider recording notes from the works you are analyzing, as well as from any critical works you consult, on a set of note cards. A good set of note cards enables you to recall details accurately, to organize your ideas effectively, and to see connections between ideas.

One Card, One Idea If you use note cards while researching, record each key passage, theme, critical opinion, or fact on a separate note card. A good note card includes a brief quotation or summary of an idea and a record of the source, including the page number, in which you found the information. When copying a sentence from a work, use quotation marks and check to make sure you have copied it correctly.

Coding Sources Keep a working bibliography, a list of all works you consult, as you conduct research. Assign a code, such as a letter, to each work on the list. For each note you take, include the code for the source.

Coding Cards Organize your note cards by labeling each with the subtopic it concerns.

Present Support Appropriately

As you draft, consider how much support you need for each point and the form that support should take. You can provide support in the following forms:

- **Summaries** are short accounts in your own words of important elements of the work, such as events, a character's traits, or the writer's ideas. They are appropriate for background information.

- **Paraphrases** are restatements of passages from a work in your own words. They are appropriate for background and for information incidental to your main point.

- **Quotations of key passages** are direct transcriptions of the writer's words, enclosed in quotation marks or, if longer than three lines, set as indented text. If a passage is crucial to your thesis, you should quote it directly and at whatever length is necessary.

Quotations of multiple examples are required to support claims about general features of a work, such as a claim about the writer's ironic style or use of cartoonlike characters.

DOs and DON'Ts of Academic Writing

Avoid gender and cultural bias. Certain terms and usages reflect the bias of past generations. To eliminate bias in any academic work you do, edit with the following rules in mind:

- **Pronoun usage** When referring to an unspecified individual in a case in which his or her gender is irrelevant, use forms of the pronoun phrase *he or she*. Example: "A lawyer is trained to use his or her mind."

- **"Culture-centric" terms** Replace terms that reflect a bias toward one culture with more generally accepted synonyms. For instance, replace terms such as primitive (used of hunting-gathering peoples), the Orient (used to refer to Asia), and Indians (used of Native Americans), all of which suggest a view of the world centered in Western European culture.

Avoid plagiarism. Presenting someone else's ideas, research, or exact words as your own is plagiarism, the equivalent of stealing or fraud. Laws protect the rights of writers and researchers in cases of commercial plagiarism. Academic standards protect their rights in cases of academic plagiarism.

To avoid plagiarism, follow these practices:

- Read from several sources.

- Synthesize what you learn.

- Let the ideas of experts help you draw your own conclusions.

- Always credit your sources properly when using someone else's ideas to support your view.

By following these guidelines, you will also push yourself to think independently.

Forming Your Critical Vocabulary

To enhance your critical perceptions—the connections you find and the distinctions you make—improve your critical vocabulary. The High-Utility Academic Words that appear in this textbook and are underlined in the Glossary (pp. R1–R13) are useful in critical writing.

In research writing, cite your sources. In the body of your paper, provide a footnote, an endnote, or an internal citation, identifying the sources of facts, opinions, or quotations. At the end of your paper, provide a bibliography or a Works Cited list, a list of all the sources you cite. Follow an established format, such as Modern Language Association (MLA) Style or American Psychological Association (APA) Style.

Works Cited List (MLA Style)

A Works Cited list must contain accurate information sufficient to enable a reader to locate each source you cite. The basic components of an entry are as follows:

- Name of the author, editor, translator, or group responsible for the work
- Title
- Place and date of publication
- Publisher

For print materials, the information required for a citation generally appears on the copyright and title pages of a work. For the format of Works Cited list entries, consult the examples at right and in the chart on page R22.

Parenthetical Citations (MLA Style)

A parenthetical citation briefly identifies the source from which you have taken a specific quotation, factual claim, or opinion. It refers the reader to one of the entries on your Works Cited list. A parenthetical citation has the following features:

- It appears in parentheses.
- It identifies the source by the last name of the author, editor, or translator.
- It gives a page reference, identifying the page of the source on which the information cited can be found.

Punctuation A parenthetical citation generally falls outside a closing quotation mark but within the final punctuation of a clause or sentence. For a long quotation set off from the rest of your text, place the citation at the end of the excerpt without any punctuation following.

Special Cases

- If the author is an organization, use the organization's name, in a shortened version if necessary.
- If you cite more than one work by the same author, add the title or a shortened version of the title.

Sample Works-Cited Lists

Carwardine, Mark, Erich Hoyt, R. Ewan Fordyce, and Peter Gill. *The Nature Company Guides: Whales, Dolphins, and Porpoises.* New York: Time-Life, 1998.
"Discovering Whales." 18 Oct. 1999.
    <http://whales.magna.com.au/DISCOVER>.

Neruda, Pablo. "Ode to Spring." *Odes to Opposites.* Trans. Ken Krabbenhoft. Ed. and illus. Ferris Cook. Boston: Little, 1995.
The Saga of the Volsungs. Trans. Jesse L. Byock. London: Penguin, 1990.

List an anonymous work by title.

List both the title of the work and the collection in which it is found.

Sample Parenthetical Citations

It makes sense that baleen whales such as the blue whale, the bowhead whale, the humpback whale, and the sei whale (to name just a few) grow to immense sizes (Carwardine, Hoyt, and Fordyce 19–21). The blue whale has grooves running from under its chin to partway along the length of its underbelly. As in some other whales, these grooves expand and allow even more food and water to be taken in (Ellis 18–21).

Author's last name

Page numbers where information can be found

MLA Style for Listing Sources

Book with one author	Pyles, Thomas. *The Origins and Development of the English Language.* 2nd ed. New York: Harcourt, 1971.
Book with two or three authors	McCrum, Robert, William Cran, and Robert MacNeil. *The Story of English.* New York: Penguin, 1987.
Book with an editor	Truth, Sojourner. *Narrative of Sojourner Truth.* Ed. Margaret Washington. New York: Vintage, 1993.
Book with more than three authors or editors	Donald, Robert B., et al. *Writing Clear Essays.* Upper Saddle River: Prentice, 1996.
Single work in an anthology	Hawthorne, Nathaniel. "Young Goodman Brown." *Literature: An Introduction to Reading and Writing.* Ed. Edgar V. Roberts and H. E. Jacobs. Upper Saddle River: Prentice, 1998. 376–385. [Indicate pages for the entire selection.]
Introduction to a work in a published edition	Washington, Margaret. Introduction. *Narrative of Sojourner Truth.* By Sojourner Truth. Ed. Washington. New York: Vintage, 1993. v–xi.
Signed article from an encyclopedia	Askeland, Donald R. "Welding." *World Book Encyclopedia.* 1991 ed.
Signed article in a weekly magazine	Wallace, Charles. (2000, February 14). A Vodacious Deal. *Time* 14 Feb. 2000: 63.
Signed article in a monthly magazine	Gustaitis, Joseph. "The Sticky History of Chewing Gum." *American History* Oct. 1998: 30–38.
Newspaper	Thurow, Roger. "South Africans Who Fought for Sanctions Now Scrap for Investors." *Wall Street Journal* 11 Feb. 2000: A1+. [For a multipage article that does not appear on consecutive pages, write only the first page number on which it appears, followed by the plus sign.]
Unsigned editorial or story	"Selective Silence." Editorial. *Wall Street Journal* 11 Feb. 2000: A14. [If the editorial or story is signed, begin with the author's name.]
Signed pamphlet or brochure	[Treat the pamphlet as though it were a book.]
Work from a library subscription service	Ertman, Earl L. "Nefertiti's Eyes." *Archaeology* Mar.–Apr. 2008: 28–32. *Kids Search.* EBSCO. New York Public Library. 18 June 2008 <http://www.ebscohost.com>.
Filmstrips, slide programs, videocassettes, DVDs, and other audiovisual media	*The Diary of Anne Frank.* Dir. George Stevens. Perf. Millie Perkins, Shelley Winters, Joseph Schildkraut, Lou Jacobi, and Richard Beymer. 1959. DVD. Twentieth Century Fox, 2004.
CD (with multiple publishers)	Simms, James, ed. *Romeo and Juliet.* By William Shakespeare. CD-ROM. Oxford: Attica Cybernetics; London: BBC Education; London: Harper, 1995.
Radio or television program transcript	"Washington's Crossing of the Delaware." Host Liane Hansen. Guest David Hackett Fischer. *Weekend Edition Sunday.* Natl. Public Radio. WNYC, New York. 23 Dec. 2003. Transcript.
Internet Web page	"Fun Facts About Gum." National Association of Chewing Gum Manufacturers. 19 Dec. 1999 <http://www.nacgm.org/consumer/funfacts.html>. [Indicate the date you accessed the information. Content and addresses at Web sites change frequently.]
Personal interview	Smith, Jane. Personal interview. 10 Feb. 2000.

APA Style for Listing Sources

Book with one author	Pyles, T. (1971). *The origins and development of the English language* (2nd ed.). New York: Harcourt Brace Jovanovich.
Book with two or three authors	McCrum, R., Cran, W., & MacNeil, R. (1987). *The story of English.* New York: Penguin Books.
Book with an editor	Truth, S. (1993). *Narrative of Sojourner Truth* (M. Washington, Ed.). New York: Vintage Books.
Book with more than three authors or editors	Donald, R. B., Morrow, B. R., Wargetz, L. G., & Werner, K. (1996). *Writing clear essays.* Upper Saddle River, NJ: Prentice Hall. [With eight or more authors, abbreviate all authors after the sixth as "et al."]
Single work from an anthology	Hawthorne, N. (1998). Young Goodman Brown. In E. V. Roberts, & H. E. Jacobs (Eds.), *Literature: An introduction to reading and writing* (pp. 376–385). Upper Saddle River, NJ: Prentice Hall.
Introduction in a published edition	Washington, M. (1993). Introduction. In M. Washington (Ed.), S. Truth, *Narrative of Sojourner Truth* (pp. v–xi). New York: Vintage Books.
Signed article from an encyclopedia	Askeland, D. R. (1991). Welding. In *World Book Encyclopedia.* (Vol. 21, pp. 190–191). Chicago: World Book.
Signed article in a weekly magazine	Wallace, C. (2000, February 14). A vodacious deal. *Time, 155,* 63. [The volume number appears in italics before the page number.]
Signed article in a monthly magazine	Gustaitis, J. (1998, October). The sticky history of chewing gum. *American History, 33,* 30–38.
Newspaper	Thurow, R. (2000, February 11). South Africans who fought for sanctions now scrap for investors. *Wall Street Journal,* pp. A1, A4. [If an article appears on discontinuous pages, give all page numbers and separate the numbers with a comma.]
Unsigned editorial or story	Selective silence [Editorial]. (2000, February 11). *Wall Street Journal,* p. A14.
Signed pamphlet	Pearson Education. (2000). *LifeCare* (2nd ed.) [Pamphlet]. New York: Smith, John: Author.
Work from a library subscription service	Ertman, Earl L. (2008, March–April). "Nefertiti's Eyes." *Archaeology, 61,* 28–32. Retrieved June 18, 2008, from EBSCO Science Reference Center database.
Filmstrips, slide programs, videocassettes, DVDs, and other audiovisual media	Wallis, H. B. (Producer), & Curtiz, M. (Director). (1942). *Casablanca* [Motion picture]. United States: Warner.
Radio or television program transcript	Hackett Fisher, D. (Guest), Hansen, L. (Host). (2003, December 23). Washington's crossing of the Delaware. [Radio series installment]. *Weekend Edition Sunday.* New York: National Public Radio. Retrieved March 6, 2008 from http://www.npr.org/templates/story/story.php?storyId=1573202
Internet	National Association of Chewing Gum Manufacturers. (1999).Retrieved December 19, 1999, from http://www.nacgm.org/consumer/funfacts.html [References to Websites should begin with the author's last name, if available. Indicate the site name and the available path or URL address.]
CD	Shakespeare, W. (1995). *Romeo and Juliet.* (J. Simms, Ed.) [CD-ROM] Oxford: Attica Cybernetics.
Personal interview	[APA states that, since interviews (and other personal communications) do not provide "recoverable data," they should only be cited in text.]

Literary Terms

ALLEGORY An *allegory* is a literary work with two or more levels of meaning—a literal level and one or more symbolic levels. The events, settings, objects, or characters in an allegory—the literal level—stand for ideas or qualities, such as goodness, tyranny, salvation, and so on. Allegorical writing was common in the Middle Ages. Spenser revived the form in *The Faerie Queene,* and John Bunyan revived it yet again in *The Pilgrim's Progress.* Some modern novels, such as George Orwell's *Animal Farm,* can be read as allegories.

ALLITERATION *Alliteration* is the repetition of initial consonant sounds in accented syllables. Coleridge uses the alliteration of both *b* and *f* sounds in this line from "The Rime of the Ancient Mariner":

> The fair breeze blew, the white foam flew.

Especially in poetry, alliteration is used to emphasize and to link words, as well as to create musical sounds.

See also *Anglo-Saxon Poetry.*

ALLUSION *Allusion* is a reference to a well-known person, place, event, literary work, or work of art.

AMBIGUITY *Ambiguity* is the effect created when words suggest and support two or more divergent interpretations. Ambiguity may be used in literature to express experiences or truths that are complex or even contradictory. For instance, the title of Elizabeth Bowen's short story "The Demon Lover," on page 1298, is ambiguous: It can refer either to the main character, who is a lover of a "demon" (a past love that she has not resolved), to the past that haunts her, or to her demonic lover, a ghost who haunts her. This ambiguous use of words reflects a larger ambiguity in the story.

See also *Irony.*

ANALOGY An *analogy* is an extended comparison of relationships. It is based on the idea or insight that the relationship between one pair of things is like the relationship between another pair. Unlike a metaphor, another form of comparison, an analogy involves an explicit comparison, often using the word *like* or *as.*

See also *Metaphor* and *Simile.*

ANAPEST See *Meter.*

ANGLO-SAXON POETRY The rhythmic poetry composed in the Old English language before A.D. 1100 is known as *Anglo-Saxon poetry.* It generally has four accented syllables and an indefinite number of unaccented syllables in each line. Each line is divided in half by a caesura, or pause, and the halves are linked by the alliteration of two or three of the accented syllables. The following translation from "Wulf and Eadwacer" shows the alliteration and caesuras used in Anglo-Saxon poetry:

> I waited for my Wulf // with far-Wandering yearnings,
> When it was rainy weather // and I sat weeping.

Anglo-Saxon poetry was sung or chanted to the accompaniment of a primitive harp; it was not written but was passed down orally.

See also *Alliteration, Caesura,* and *Kenning.*

ARCHETYPAL LITERARY ELEMENTS *Archetypal literary elements* are patterns in literature found around the world. For instance, the occurrence of events in threes is an archetypal element of fairy tales. Certain character types, such as mysterious guides, are also archetypal elements of such traditional stories. According to some critics, these elements express in symbolic form truths about the human mind.

ARGUMENT See *Persuasion.*

ASSONANCE *Assonance* is the repetition of vowel sounds in stressed syllables containing dissimilar consonant sounds. Robert Browning uses assonance in this line in "Andrea del Sarto":

> Ah, but man's reach should exceed his grasp. . . .

The long *e* sound is repeated in the words *reach* and *exceed.* The syllables containing these sounds are stressed and contain different consonants: *r-ch* and *c-d.*

See also *Consonance.*

BALLAD A *ballad* is a song that tells a story, often about adventure or romance, or a poem imitating such a song. Most ballads are divided into four- or six-line stanzas, are rhymed, use simple language, and depict dramatic action. Many ballads employ a repeated refrain. Some use incremental repetition, in which the refrain is varied slightly each time it appears.

BLANK VERSE *Blank verse* is unrhymed poetry usually written in iambic pentameter (see Meter). Occasional variations in rhythm are introduced in blank verse to create emphasis, variety, and naturalness of sound. Because blank verse sounds much like ordinary spoken English, it is often used in drama, as by Shakespeare, and in poetry.

See also *Meter.*

CAESURA A *caesura* is a natural pause in the middle of a line of poetry. In Anglo-Saxon poetry, a caesura divides each four-stress line in half and thus is essential to the rhythm.

See also *Anglo-Saxon Poetry.*

CARPE DIEM A Latin phrase, *carpe diem* means "seize the day" or "make the most of passing time." Many great literary works have been written with the *carpe diem* theme.

CHARACTER The personality that takes part in the action of a literary work is known as a character. Characters can be classified in different ways. A character who plays an important role is called a *major character.* A character who does not is called a *minor character.* A character who plays the central role in a story is called the **protagonist.** A character who opposes the protagonist is called the **antagonist.** A **round character** has many aspects to his or her personality. A **flat character** is defined by only a few qualities. A character who changes is called **dynamic;** a character who does not change is called **static.**

See also **Characterization.**

CHARACTERIZATION **Characterization** is the act of creating and developing a character. A writer uses **direct characterization** when he or she describes a character's traits explicitly. Writers also use **indirect characterization.** A character's traits can be revealed indirectly in what he or she says, thinks, or does; in a description of his or her appearance; or in the statements, thoughts, or actions of other characters.

See also **Character.**

CLIMAX The **climax** is the high point of interest or suspense in a literary work. Often, the climax is also the crisis in the plot, the point at which the protagonist changes his or her understanding or situation. Sometimes, the climax coincides with the **resolution,** the point at which the central conflict is ended.

See also **Plot.**

COMEDY A **comedy** is a literary work, especially a play, that has a happy ending. A comedy often shows ordinary characters in conflict with their society. Types of comedy include **romantic comedy,** which involves problems among lovers, and the **comedy of manners,** which satirically challenges the social customs of a sophisticated society. Comedy is often contrasted with tragedy, in which the protagonist meets an unfortunate end.

See also **Drama** and **Tragedy.**

CONCEIT A **conceit** is an unusual and surprising comparison between two very different things. This special kind of metaphor or complicated analogy is often the basis for a whole poem. During the Elizabethan Age, sonnets commonly included Petrarchan conceits. **Petrarchan conceits** make extravagant claims about the beloved's beauty or the speaker's suffering, with comparisons to divine beings, powerful natural forces, and objects that contain a given quality in the highest degree. Spenser uses a Petrarchan conceit when he claims in Sonnet 1, on page 254, that the "starry light" of his beloved's eyes will make his book happy when she reads it. Seventeenth-century **metaphysical** poets used elaborate, unusual, and highly intellectual conceits, as in the conceit of the compass in John Donne's "A Valediction: Forbidding Mourning," on page 484.

See also **Metaphor.**

CONFLICT A **conflict** is a struggle between opposing forces. Sometimes, this struggle is internal, or within a character. At other times, the struggle is external, or between the character and some outside force. The outside force may be another character, nature, or some element of society such as a custom or a political institution. Often, the conflict in a work combines several of these possibilities.

See also **Plot.**

CONNOTATION **Connotation** refers to the associations that a word calls to mind in addition to its dictionary meaning. For example, the words *home* and *domicile* have the same dictionary meaning. However, the first has positive connotations of warmth and security, whereas the second does not.

See also **Denotation.**

CONSONANCE **Consonance** is the repetition of final consonant sounds in stressed syllables containing dissimilar vowel sounds. Samuel Taylor Coleridge uses consonance in these lines from "The Rime of the Ancient Mariner," on page 820:

a frightful fie**nd** / Doth close behi**nd** him tread.

Fiend and the stressed syllable in *behind* have the same final consonat sounds but different vowel sounds.

See also **Assonance.**

COUPLET A **couplet** is a pair of rhyming lines written in the same meter. A **heroic couplet** is a rhymed pair of iambic pentameter lines. In a **closed couplet,** the meaning and syntax are completed within the two lines. These lines from Alexander Pope's "An Essay on Criticism" are a closed heroic couplet:

True ease in writing comes from art, not chance,
As those move easiest who have learned to dance.

Shakespearean sonnets usually end with heroic couplets.

See also **Sonnet.**

DACTYL See **Meter.**

DENOTATION **Denotation** is the objective meaning of a word—that to which the word refers, independent of other associations that the word calls to mind. Dictionaries list the denotative meanings of words.

See also **Connotation.**

DIALECT **Dialect** is the form of a language spoken by people in a particular region or group. Dialects differ from one another in grammar, vocabulary, and pronunciation.

DIALOGUE **Dialogue** is a conversation between characters. Writers use dialogue to reveal character, to present events, to add variety to narratives, and to interest readers. Dialogue in a story is usually set off by quotation marks and paragraphing. Dialogue in a play script generally follows the name of the speaker.

DIARY A **diary** is a personal record of daily events, usually written in prose. Most diaries are not written for publication; sometimes, however, interesting diaries or diaries written by influential people are published. One example of a published diary is that of Samuel Pepys, a selection from which appears on page 571.

See also **Journal.**

DICTION **Diction** is a writer's word choice. It can be a major determinant of the writer's style. Diction can be described as formal or informal, abstract or concrete, plain or ornate, ordinary or technical.

See also **Style.**

DIMETER See *Meter.*

DRAMA A *drama* is a story written to be performed by actors. It may consist of one or more large sections, called acts, which are made up of any number of smaller sections, called scenes.

Drama originated in the religious rituals and symbolic reenactments of primitive peoples. The ancient Greeks, who developed drama into a sophisticated art form, created such dramatic forms as tragedy and comedy.

The first dramas in England were the miracle plays and morality plays of the Middle Ages. Miracle plays told biblical stories. Morality plays, such as *Everyman,* were allegories dealing with personified virtues and vices. The English Renaissance saw a flowering of drama in England, culminating in the works of William Shakespeare, who wrote many of the world's greatest comedies, tragedies, histories, and romances. During the Neoclassical Age, English drama turned to satirical comedies of manners that probed the virtues of upper-class society. In the Romantic and Victorian ages, a few good verse plays were written, including Percy Bysshe Shelley's *The Cenci* and *Prometheus Unbound.* The end of the nineteenth and beginning of the twentieth centuries saw a resurgence of the drama in England and throughout the English-speaking world. Great plays of the Modern period include works by Bernard Shaw, Christopher Fry, T. S. Eliot, Harold Pinter, and Samuel Beckett.

DRAMATIC MONOLOGUE A *dramatic monologue* is a poem in which an imaginary character speaks to a silent listener. Robert Browning's "My Last Duchess," on page 978, is a dramatic monologue.

ELEGY An *elegy* is a solemn and formal lyric poem about death. It may mourn a particular person or reflect on a serious or tragic theme, such as the passing of youth or beauty. See Thomas Gray's "Elegy Written in a Country Churchyard," on page 666.

See also *Lyric Poem.*

END-STOPPED LINE An *end-stopped line* is a line of poetry concluding with a break in the meter and in the meaning. This pause at the end of a line is often punctuated by a period, comma, dash, or semicolon. These lines from "Away, Melancholy," by Stevie Smith, are end-stopped:

> Are not the trees green,
> The earth as green?
> Does not the wind blow,
> Fire leap and the rivers flow?

See also *Run-on Line.*

EPIC An *epic* is a long narrative poem about the adventures of gods or of a hero. *Beowulf,* on page 40, is a *folk epic,* one that was composed orally and passed from storyteller to storyteller. The ancient Greek epics attributed to Homer—the *Iliad* and the *Odyssey*—are also folk epics. The *Aeneid,* by the Roman poet Virgil, and *The Divine Comedy,* by the Italian poet Dante Alighieri, are examples of literary epics from the Classical

and Medieval periods, respectively. John Milton's *Paradise Lost,* a selection from which appears on page 524, is also a literary epic.

Epic conventions are traditional characteristics of epic poems, including an opening statement of the theme; an appeal for supernatural help in telling the story (an invocation); a beginning *in medias res* (Latin: "in the middle of things"); catalogs of people and things; accounts of past events; and descriptive phrases.

See also *Kenning.*

EPIGRAM An *epigram* is a brief statement in prose or in verse. The concluding couplet in an English sonnet may be epigrammatic. An essay may be written in an epigrammatic style.

EPIPHANY *Epiphany* is a term introduced by James Joyce to describe a moment of insight in which a character recognizes a truth. In Joyce's "Araby," on page 1236, the boy has an epiphany when he sees the falsity of his dream.

EPITAPH An *epitaph* is an inscription written on a tomb or burial place. In literature, epitaphs include serious or humorous lines written as if intended for such use, like the epitaph in Thomas Gray's "Elegy Written in a Country Churchyard," on page 666.

ESSAY An *essay* is a short nonfiction work about a particular subject. Essays are of many types but may be classified by tone or style as formal or informal. Addison's breezy style and tongue-in-cheek descriptions make "The Aims of *The Spectator,*" on page 682, an instance of an informal essay. An essay is often classed by its main purpose as descriptive, narrative, expository, argumentative, or persuasive.

EXTENDED METAPHOR See *Metaphor.*

FICTION *Fiction* is prose writing about imaginary characters and events. Some writers of fiction base their stories on real events, whereas others rely solely on their imaginations.

See also *Narration* and *Prose.*

FIGURATIVE LANGUAGE *Figurative language* is writing or speech not meant to be interpreted literally. Poets and other writers use figurative language to paint vivid word pictures, to make their writing emotionally intense and concentrated, and to state their ideas in new and unusual ways. Among the figures of speech making up figurative language are hyperbole, irony, metaphor, metonymy, oxymoron, paradox, personification, simile, and synecdoche.

See also the entries for individual figures of speech.

FOLKLORE The stories, legends, myths, ballads, riddles, sayings, and other traditional works produced orally by illiterate or semiliterate peoples are known as *folklore.* Folklore influences written literature in many ways. The beheading contest in *Sir Gawain and the Green Knight,* on page 170, is an example of folklore.

FOOT See *Meter.*

FREE VERSE *Free verse* is poetry not written in a regular, rhythmical pattern, or meter. Instead of having metrical feet and lines, free verse has a rhythm that suits its meaning and that uses the sounds of spoken language in lines of different lengths. Free verse has been widely used in twentieth-century poetry. An example is "The Galloping Cat," by Stevie Smith:

> All the same I
> Intend to go on being
> A cat that likes to
> Gallop about doing good
> So
> Now with my bald head I go,
> Chopping the untidy flowers down, to and fro.

GOTHIC *Gothic* is a term used to describe literary works that make extensive use of primitive, medieval, wild, mysterious, or natural elements. Gothic novels, such as Mary Wollstonecraft Shelley's *Frankenstein,* the Introduction to which appears on page 760, often depict horrifying events set in gloomy castles.

HEPTAMETER See *Meter.*

HEXAMETER See *Meter.*

HYPERBOLE *Hyperbole* is a deliberate exaggeration or overstatement. In "Song," on page 482, John Donne uses this figure of speech:

> When thou sigh'st, thou sigh'st not wind,
> but sigh'st my soul away

See also *Figurative Language.*

IAMBIC PENTAMETER See *Meter.*

IMAGE An *image* is a word or phrase that appeals to one or more of the senses—sight, hearing, touch, taste, or smell. In a famous essay on *Hamlet*, T. S. Eliot explained how a group of images can be used as an "objective correlative." By this phrase, Eliot meant that a complex emotional state can be suggested by images that are carefully chosen to evoke this state.

See also *Imagery.*

IMAGERY *Imagery* is the descriptive language used in literature to re-create sensory experiences. Imagery enriches writing by making it more vivid, setting a tone, suggesting emotions, and guiding readers' reactions.

IRONY *Irony* is the general name given to literary techniques that involve surprising, interesting, or amusing contradictions. In **verbal irony**, words are used to suggest the opposite of their usual meaning. In **dramatic irony**, there is a contradiction between what a character thinks and what the reader or audience knows to be true. In **irony of situation**, an event occurs that directly contradicts expectations.

JOURNAL A *journal* is a daily autobiographical account of events and personal reactions. Daniel Defoe adapted this form to fictional use in *A Journal of the Plague Year,* an excerpt from which appears on page 590.

See also *Diary.*

KENNING A *kenning* is a metaphorical phrase used in Anglo-Saxon poetry to replace a concrete noun. In "The Seafarer," on page 20, the cuckoo is called "summer's sentinel" and the sea, "the whale's home."

See also *Anglo-Saxon Poetry* and *Epic.*

LEGEND A *legend* is a widely told story about the past that may or may not be based in fact. A legend often reflects a people's identity or cultural values, generally with more historical truth than that in a myth. English legends include the stories of King Arthur (retold in *Morte d'Arthur,* a selection from which appears on page 185) and Robin Hood.

See also *Myth.*

LETTER A *letter* addresses a specific person or group and is meant to be read within a specific time.

LYRIC POEM A *lyric poem* is a poem expressing the observations and feelings of a single speaker. Unlike a narrative poem, it presents an experience or a single effect, but it does not tell a full story. Types of lyric poems include the elegy, the ode, and the sonnet.

METAPHOR A *metaphor* is a figure of speech in which one thing is spoken of as though it were something else, as in "death, that long sleep." Through this identification of dissimilar things, a comparison is suggested or implied.

An **extended metaphor** is developed at length and involves several points of comparison. A mixed metaphor occurs when two metaphors are jumbled together, as in "The thorns of life rained down on him."

A **dead metaphor** is one that has been so overused that its original metaphorical impact has been lost. Examples of dead metaphors include "the foot of the bed" and "toe the line."

See also *Figurative Language.*

METAPHYSICAL POETRY The term **metaphysical poetry** describes the works of such seventeenth-century English poets as Richard Crashaw, John Donne, George Herbert, and Andrew Marvell. Characteristic features of metaphysical poetry include intellectual playfulness, argument, paradoxes, irony, elaborate and unusual conceits, incongruity, and the rhythms of ordinary speech. Examples of metaphysical poems in this textbook include Donne's "Song," on page 482, and Marvell's "To His Coy Mistress," on page 506.

METER *Meter* is the rhythmical pattern of a poem. This pattern is determined by the number and types of stresses, or beats, in each line. To describe the meter of a poem, you must scan its lines. Scanning involves marking the stressed and unstressed syllables, as follows:

> Ĭ wĕen | thăt, whĕn | thĕ grăve's | dărk wăll
> Dĭd first | hĕr form | rĕtain,
> Thĕy thought | thĕir hearts | cŏuld ne'er | rĕcall
> Thĕ light | ŏf joy | ăgain.

—Emily Brontë, "Song"

As you can see, each stressed syllable is marked with a slanted line (ˊ) and each unstressed syllable with a horseshoe symbol (˘). The stresses are then divided by vertical lines into groups called feet. The following types of feet are common in English poetry:

1. **Iamb:** a foot with one unstressed syllable followed by one stressed syllable, as in the word **afraid**
2. **Trochee:** a foot with one stressed syllable followed by one unstressed syllable, as in the word **heather**
3. **Anapest:** a foot with two unstressed syllables followed by one stressed syllable, as in the word **disembark**
4. **Dactyl:** a foot with one stressed syllable followed by two unstressed syllables, as in the word **solitude**
5. **Spondee:** a foot with two stressed syllables, as in the word **workday**
6. **Pyrrhic:** a foot with two unstressed syllables, as in the last foot of the word **unspeak | ably**
7. **Amphibrach:** a foot with an unstressed syllable, one stressed syllable, and another unstressed syllable, as in the word **another**
8. **Amphimacer:** a foot with a stressed syllable, one unstressed syllable, and another stressed syllable, as in **up and down**

A line of poetry is described as **iambic, trochaic, anapestic,** or **dactylic** according to the kind of foot that appears most often in the line. Lines are also described in terms of the number of feet that occur in them, as follows:

1. **Monometer:** verse written in one-foot lines:

> Sound the Flute!
> Now it's mute.
> Birds delight
> Day and Night.

> —William Blake, "Spring"

2. **Dimeter:** verse written in two-foot lines:

> Ŏ Rose | thŏu art sick.
> The ĭnvis | ĭble worm.
> That flies | ĭn the night
> Ĭn the how | lĭng storm:
> Has found | out thy bed
> Ŏf crim | sŏn joy: . . .

> —William Blake, "The Sick Rose"

3. **Trimeter:** verse written in three-foot lines:

> Ĭ went | tŏ the Gard | ĕn of Love
> And saw | whăt Ĭ nev | ĕr had seen:
> Ă Chap | ĕl wăs built | ĭn the midst,
> Where Ĭ used | tŏ play | ŏn the green.

> —William Blake, "The Garden of Love"

4. **Tetrameter:** verse written in four-foot lines:

> Ĭ wand | ĕr thro' | each chart | ĕr'd street
> Near where | the chart | ĕr'd Thames |
> does flow
> And mark | ĭn ev | ĕry face | Ĭ meet
> Marks ŏf | weakness, | marks ŏf | woe.

> —William Blake, "London"

A six-foot line is called a **hexameter.** A line with seven feet is a **heptameter.**

A complete description of the meter of a line tells both how many feet there are in the line and what kind of foot is most common. Thus, the stanza from Emily Brontë's poem, quoted at the beginning of this entry, would be described as being made up of alternating iambic tetrameter and iambic trimeter lines. Poetry that does not have a regular meter is called **free verse.**

See also **Free Verse.**

METONYMY **Metonymy** is a figure of speech that substitutes something closely related for the thing actually meant. In the opening line of "The Lost Leader," Robert Browning says, "Just for a handful of silver he left us," using "silver" to refer to money paid for a betrayal.

See also **Figurative Language.**

MIRACLE PLAY See **Drama.**

MOCK EPIC A **mock epic** is a poem about a trivial matter written in the style of a serious epic. The incongruity of style and subject matter produces comic effects. Alexander Pope's "The Rape of the Lock," on page 632, is a mock epic.

See also **Epic.**

MODERNISM **Modernism** describes an international movement in the arts during the early twentieth century. Modernists rejected old forms and experimented with the new. Literary Modernists—such as James Joyce, W. B. Yeats, and T. S. Eliot—used images as symbols. They presented human experiences in fragments, rather than as a coherent whole, which led to new experiments in the forms of poetry and fiction.

MONOLOGUE A **monologue** is a speech or performance given entirely by one person or by one character.

See also **Dramatic Monologue** and **Soliloquy.**

MOOD **Mood,** or **atmosphere,** is the feeling created in the reader by a literary work or passage. Mood may be suggested by the writer's choice of words, by events in the work, or by the physical setting. Nadine Gordimer begins "The Train from Rhodesia," on page 1342, with a description of the hot, sandy train station that sets a mood mixing boredom and confinement with the eager expectation of the train.

See also **Setting** and **Tone.**

MORALITY PLAY See *Drama.*

MYTH A *myth* is a fictional tale, originally with religious significance, that explains the actions of gods or heroes, the causes of natural phenomena, or both. Allusions to characters and motifs from Greek, Roman, Norse, and Celtic myths are common in English literature. In addition, mythological stories are often retold or adapted.

See also *Legend.*

NARRATION *Narration* is writing that tells a story. The act of telling a story is also called narration. The *narrative,* or story, is told by a character or speaker called the *narrator.* Biographies, autobiographies, journals, reports, novels, short stories, plays, narrative poems, anecdotes, fables, parables, myths, legends, folk tales, ballads, and epic poems are all narratives, or types of narration.

See also *Point of View.*

NARRATIVE POEM A *narrative poem* is a poem that tells a story in verse. Three traditional types of narrative poems include ballads, epics, and metrical romances.

NATURALISM *Naturalism* was a literary movement among writers at the end of the nineteenth century and during the early decades of the twentieth century. The Naturalists depicted life in its grimmer details and viewed people as hopeless victims of natural laws.

See also *Realism.*

NEOCLASSICISM *Neoclassicism* was a literary movement of the late seventeenth and the eighteenth centuries in which writers turned to classical Greek and Roman literary models and standards. Like the ancients, Neoclassicists, such as Alexander Pope, stressed order, harmony, restraint, and the ideal. Much Neoclassical literature dealt with themes related to proper human conduct. The most popular literary forms of the day—essays, letters, early novels, epigrams, parodies, and satires—reflected this emphasis.

See also *Romanticism.*

NONFICTION *Nonfiction* is prose writing that presents and explains ideas or tells about real places, objects or events. To be classified as nonfiction, a work must be true.

NOVEL A *novel* is an extended work of fiction that often has a complicated plot, many major and minor characters, a unifying theme, and several settings. Novels can be grouped in many ways, based on the historical periods in which they are written (such as Victorian), on the subjects and themes that they treat (such as Gothic or regional), on the techniques used in them (such as stream of consciousness), or on their part in literary movements (such as Naturalism or Realism). Among the early novels were Samuel Richardson's *Pamela* and *Clarissa* and Henry Fielding's *Tom Jones.* Other classic English novels include Jane Austen's *Pride and Prejudice,* Sir Walter Scott's *Waverley,* Charles Dickens's *David Copperfield,* and George Eliot's *The Mill on the Floss.* Major twentieth-century novelists include James Joyce, Virginia Woolf, D. H. Lawrence, Henry James, Graham Greene, and Patrick White. A *novella*—for example, Joseph Conrad's *Heart of Darkness*—is not as long as a novel but is longer than a short story.

OBJECTIVE CORRELATIVE See *Image.*

OCTAVE See *Stanza.*

ODE An *ode* is a long, formal lyric poem with a serious theme. It may have a traditional structure with stanzas grouped in threes, called the *strophe,* the *antistrophe,* and the *epode.* Odes often honor people, commemorate events, or respond to natural scenes.

See also *Lyric Poem.*

ONOMATOPOEIA *Onomatopoeia* is the use of words that imitate sounds. Examples of such words are *buzz, hiss, murmur,* and *rustle.* Onomatopoeia is used to create musical effects and to reinforce meaning.

ORAL TRADITION *Oral tradition* is the body of songs, stories, and poems preserved by being passed from generation to generation by word of mouth. Among the many materials composed or preserved through oral tradition in Great Britain are *Beowulf,* on page 40, and the folk ballads on pages 205–211. In his *Morte d'Arthur,* a selection from which begins on page 185, Sir Thomas Malory drew on Arthurian legends from the oral tradition. Shakespeare drew on materials from the oral tradition to create the sprites and fairies of *A Midsummer Night's Dream* and the witches of *Macbeth,* on page 322. Folk epics, ballads, myths, legends, folk tales, folk songs, proverbs, and nursery rhymes are all products of the oral tradition.

See also *Ballad, Folklore, Legend,* and *Myth.*

OXYMORON An *oxymoron* is a figure of speech that fuses two contradictory ideas, such as "freezing fire" or "happy grief," thus suggesting a paradox in just a few words.

See also *Figurative Language* and *Paradox.*

PARABLE A *parable* is a short, simple story from which a moral or religious lesson can be drawn. The most famous parables are those in the New Testament, an example of which appears on page 302.

PARADOX A *paradox* is a statement that seems to be contradictory but that actually presents a truth. In "Love's Growth," John Donne presents the following paradox:

Methinks I lied all winter, when I swore
My love was infinite, if spring make it more.

Because a paradox is surprising or even shocking, it draws the reader's attention to what is being said.

See also *Figurative Language* and *Oxymoron.*

PARODY A *parody* is a humorous imitation of another work or of a type of work.

PASTORAL *Pastoral* refers to literary works that deal with the pleasures of a simple rural life or with escape to a simpler place and time. The tradition of pastoral literature began in ancient Greece with the poetic idylls of Theocritus. The Roman poet Virgil also wrote a famous collection of pastoral poems, the *Eclogues.*

During the European Renaissance, pastoral writing became quite popular. Two famous examples are *The Countess of Pembroke's Arcadia,* by Sir Philip Sidney, and Christopher Marlowe's "The Passionate Shepherd to His Love," on page 266.

Today, the term *pastoral* is commonly applied to any work in which a speaker longs to escape to a simpler rural life. By this definition, both William Wordsworth's "The World Is Too Much With Us," on page 790, and William Butler Yeats's "The Lake Isle of Innisfree," on page 1141, are pastoral poems.

PENTAMETER See *Meter.*

PERSONIFICATION *Personification* is a figure of speech in which a nonhuman subject is given human characteristics. Percy Bysshe Shelley uses personification in these lines:

> Swiftly walk o'er the western wave,
> Spirit of the Night!

Effective personification of things or ideas makes their qualities seem unified, like the characteristics of a person, and their relationship with the reader seem closer.

See also *Figurative Language* and *Metaphor.*

PERSUASION *Persuasion* is writing or speech that attempts to convince a reader to think or act in a particular way. Persuasion is used in advertising, in editorials, in sermons, and in political speeches. An *argument* is a logical way of presenting a belief, conclusion, or stance. A good argument is supported with reasoning and evidence.

PLOT *Plot* is the sequence of events in a literary work. The two primary elements of any plot are characters and a conflict. Most plots can be analyzed into many or all of the following parts:

1. The *exposition* introduces the setting, the characters, and the basic situation.
2. The *inciting incident* introduces the central conflict and develops the rising action.
3. During the *development,* or rising action, the conflict runs its course and usually intensifies.
4. At the *climax,* the conflict reaches a high point of interest or suspense.
5. The *denouement,* or *falling action,* ties up loose ends that remain after the climax of the conflict.
6. At the *resolution,* the story is resolved and an insight is revealed.

There are many variations on the standard plot structure. Some stories begin *in medias res* ("in the middle of things"), after the inciting incident has already occurred. In some stories, the expository material appears toward the middle, in flashbacks. In many stories, there is no denouement. Occasionally, the conflict is left unresolved.

POETRY *Poetry* is one of the three major types, or genres, of literature, the others being prose and drama. Poetry defies simple definition because there is no single characteristic that is found in all poems and not found in all nonpoems.

Often, poems are divided into lines and stanzas. Poems such as sonnets, odes, villanelles, and sestinas are governed by rules regarding the number of lines, the number and placement of stressed syllables in each line, and the rhyme scheme. In the case of villanelles and sestinas, the repetition of words at the ends of lines or of entire lines is required. (An example of a sestina, Seamus Heaney's "Two Lorries," appears on page 1370. An example of a villanelle, Dylan Thomas's "Do Not Go Gentle into That Good Night," appears on page 1390.) However, some poems are written in free verse. Most poems make use of highly concise, musical, and emotionally charged language. Many also use imagery, figurative language, and devices of sound like rhyme.

Types of poetry include *narrative poetry* (ballads, epics, and metrical romances); *dramatic poetry* (dramatic monologues and dramatic dialogues); *lyrics* (sonnets, odes, elegies, and love poems); and *concrete poetry* (a poem presented on the page in a shape that suggests its subject).

POINT OF VIEW The perspective, or vantage point, from which a story is told is its *point of view.* If a character within the story narrates, then it is told from the *first-person point of view.* If a voice from outside the story tells it, then the story is told from the *third-person point of view.* If the knowledge of the storyteller is limited to the internal states of one character, then the storyteller has a *limited point of view.* If the storyteller's knowledge extends to the internal states of all the characters, then the storyteller has an *omniscient point of view.*

POLITICAL COMMENTARY *Political commentary* offers opinions on political issues, building arguments on evidence and assumptions. Using writing forms such as speeches, poems, and letters, commentators seek to persuade using persuasive devices such as rhetorical questions and balanced clauses.

PROSE *Prose* is the ordinary form of written language and one of the three major types of literature. Most writing that is not poetry, drama, or song is considered prose. Prose occurs in two major forms: fiction and nonfiction.

PSALM A *psalm* is a sacred song or lyric poem in praise of God.

PYRRHIC See *Meter.*

QUATRAIN See *Stanza.*

REALISM *Realism* is the presentation in art of details from actual life. During the last part of the nineteenth century and the first part of the twentieth, Realism enjoyed considerable popularity among writers in the English-speaking world. Novels often dealt with grim social realities and presented realistic portrayals of the psychological states of characters.

REFRAIN A *refrain* is a regularly repeated line or group of lines in a poem or song.

See also *Ballad.*

REGIONALISM *Regionalism* is the tendency to confine one's writing to the presentation of the distinct culture of an area, including its speech, customs, and history. For example, the Brontës wrote about Yorkshire, Thomas Hardy wrote about Dorset and Wessex, and D. H. Lawrence wrote about Nottinghamshire.

RHYME *Rhyme* is the repetition of sounds at the ends of words. *End rhyme* occurs when rhyming words appear at the ends of lines. *Internal rhyme* occurs when rhyming words fall within a line. *Exact rhyme* is the use of identical rhyming sounds, as in *love* and *dove*. *Approximate,* or *slant*, *rhyme* is the use of sounds that are similar but not identical, as in *prove* and *glove*.

RHYME SCHEME *Rhyme scheme* is the regular pattern of rhyming words in a poem or stanza. To indicate a rhyme scheme, assign a different letter to each final sound in the poem or stanza. The following lines from Charlotte Brontë's "On the Death of Anne Brontë" have been marked:

There's little joy in life for me,	a
And little terror in the grave;	b
I've lived the parting hour to see	a
Of one I would have died to save.	b

RHYTHM See *Meter.*

ROMANCE A *romance* is a story that presents remote or imaginative incidents rather than ordinary, realistic experience. The term *romance* was originally used to refer to medieval tales of the deeds and loves of noble knights and ladies. These early romances, or tales of chivalry and courtly love, are exemplified by *Sir Gawain and the Green Knight,* on page 170, and by the extract from Malory's *Morte d'Arthur,* on page 185. During the Renaissance in England, many writers, such as Edmund Spenser in *The Faerie Queene,* drew heavily on the romance tradition. From the eighteenth century on, the term *romance* has been used to describe sentimental novels about love.

ROMANTICISM *Romanticism* was a literary and artistic movement of the eighteenth and nineteenth centuries. In reaction to Neoclassicism, the Romantics emphasized imagination, fancy, freedom, emotion, wildness, the beauty of the untamed natural world, the rights of the individual, the nobility of the common man, and the attractiveness of pastoral life. Important figures in the Romantic Movement included William Wordsworth, Samuel Taylor Coleridge, Percy Bysshe Shelley, John Keats, and George Gordon, Lord Byron.

RUN-ON LINE A *run-on line* is a line that does not contain a pause or a stop at the end. It ends in the middle of a statement and a grammatical unit, and the reader must read the next line to find the end of the statement and the completion of the grammatical unit. The beginning of Molly Holden's "The Double Nature of White" illustrates the run-on line:

> White orchards are the earliest, stunning
> the spirit resigned to winter's black, white thorn
> sprays first the bare wet branches of the hedge.

See also *End-Stopped Line.*

SATIRE *Satire* is writing that ridicules or holds up to contempt the faults of individuals or groups. Satires include Jonathan Swift's prose work *Gulliver's Travels*, on page 606, and Alexander Pope's poem *The Rape of the Lock,* on page 632. Although a satire is often humorous, its purpose is not simply to make readers laugh but also to correct the flaws and shortcomings that it points out.

SCANSION *Scansion* is the process of analyzing the metrical pattern of a poem.

See also *Meter.*

SERMON A *sermon* is a speech offering religious or moral instruction. For example, the Sermon on the Mount, on page 301, given by Jesus on a mountain in Galilee, contains the basic teachings of Christianity.

SESTET See *Stanza.*

SETTING The *setting* is the time and place of the action of a literary work. A setting can provide a backdrop for the action. It can be the force that the protagonist struggles against and thus the source of the central conflict. It can also be used to create an atmosphere. In many works, the setting symbolizes a point that the author wishes to emphasize.

See also *Mood* and *Symbol.*

SHORT STORY A *short story* is a brief work of fiction. The short story resembles the longer novel, but it generally has a simpler plot and setting. In addition, a short story tends to reveal character at a crucial moment, rather than to develop it through many incidents.

SIMILE A *simile* is a figure of speech that compares two apparently dissimilar things using *like* or *as.* Christina Rossetti uses simile in "Goblin Market" to describe two sisters:

> Like two blossoms on one stem,
> Like two flakes of new-fallen snow,
> Like two wands of ivory
> Tipped with gold for awful kings.

By comparing apparently dissimilar things, the writer of a simile surprises the reader into an appreciation of the hidden similarities of the things being compared.

See also *Figurative Language.*

SOCIAL COMMENTARY *Social commentary* is writing that offers insight into society, its values, and its customs. For example, Mary Wollstonecraft's *A Vindication of the Rights of Woman* (p. 916) offers social commentary on the debate over women's rights and seeks to attribute this problem to social customs.

SOLILOQUY A *soliloquy* is a long speech in a play or in a prose work made by a character who is alone and thus reveals private thoughts and feelings to the audience or reader. William Shakespeare opens Act III of *Macbeth,* on page 361, with a soliloquy in which Banquo speculates on Macbeth's reaction to the witches' prophecy.

See also *Monologue.*

SONNET A sonnet is a fourteen-line lyric poem with a single theme. Sonnets are usually written in iambic pentameter. The **Petrarchan**, or **Italian sonnet,** is divided into two parts, an eight-line octave and a six-line sestet. The octave rhymes *abba abba*, while the sestet generally rhymes *cde cde* or uses some combination of *cd* rhymes. The octave raises a question, states a problem, or presents a brief narrative, and the sestet answers the question, solves the problem, or comments on the narrative.

The **Shakespearean**, or **English**, **sonnet** has three four-line quatrains plus a concluding two-line couplet. The rhyme scheme of such a sonnet is usually *abab cdcd efef gg*. Each of the three quatrains usually explores a different variation of the main theme. Then, the couplet presents a summarizing or concluding statement.

The **Spenserian** sonnet has three quatrains and a couplet, but the quatrains are joined by linking rhymes like those of an Italian sonnet. The rhyme scheme of this type of sonnet is *abab bcbc cdcd ee*.

See also *Lyric Poem* and *Sonnet Sequence.*

SONNET SEQUENCE A *sonnet sequence* is a series or group of sonnets, most often written to or about a beloved. Although each sonnet can stand alone as a separate poem, the sequence lets the poet trace the development of a relationship or examine different aspects of a single subject. Examples of sonnet sequences are Sir Philip Sidney's *Astrophel and Stella,* Edmund Spenser's *Amoretti,* and Elizabeth Barrett Browning's *Sonnets from the Portuguese.*

See also *Sonnet.*

SPEAKER The *speaker* is the imaginary voice assumed by the writer of a poem; the character who "says" the poem. This character is often not identified by name but may be identified otherwise. For example, the title of William Blake's poem "The Chimney Sweeper," on page 751, identifies the speaker, a child who gives an account of his life.

Recognizing the speaker and thinking about his or her characteristics are often central to interpreting a lyric poem. In Blake's poem, for instance, the speaker's acceptance of his oppressive life is offered for the reader's evaluation.

See also *Point of View.*

SPONDEE See *Meter.*

SPRUNG RHYTHM The term *sprung rhythm* was used by Gerard Manley Hopkins to describe the idiosyncratic meters of his poems. The rhythm is quite varied and contains such violations of traditional metrical rules as several strong stresses in a row or feet containing more than two weak stresses.

STANZA A *stanza* is a group of lines in a poem, which is seen as a unit. Many poems are divided into stanzas that are separated by spaces. Stanzas often function like paragraphs in prose. Each stanza states and develops one main idea.

Stanzas are commonly named according to the number of lines found in them, as follows:

1. *Couplet:* a two-line stanza
2. *Tercet:* a three-line stanza
3. *Quatrain:* a four-line stanza
4. *Cinquain:* a five-line stanza
5. *Sestet:* a six-line stanza
6. *Heptastich:* a seven-line stanza
7. *Octave:* an eight-line stanza

See also *Sonnet.*

STYLE *Style* is a writer's typical way of writing. Determinants of a writer's style include formality, use of figurative language, use of rhythm, typical grammatical patterns, typical sentence lengths, and typical methods of organization. John Milton is noted for a grand, heroic style that contrasts with John Keats's rich, sensory style and with T. S. Eliot's allusive, ironic style.

See also *Diction.*

SUBLIME The *sublime* is an effect created in literature when a writer confronts a power or mystery in nature that exceeds human understanding. The effect is achieved by representing the infinite or endless in sensory terms, as when Byron characterizes the inexhaustible power of the ocean in the "Apostrophe to the Ocean" in *Childe Harold's Pilgrimage,* on page 856.

SYMBOL A *symbol* is a sign, word, phrase, image, or other object that stands for or represents something else. Thus, a flag can symbolize a country, a spoken word can symbolize an object, a fine car can symbolize wealth, and so on. In literary criticism, a distinction is often made between traditional or conventional symbols—those that are part of our general cultural inheritance—and *personal symbols*—those that are created by particular authors for use in particular works. For example, the lamb in William Blake's poem "The Lamb," on page 748, is a conventional symbol for peace, gentleness, and innocence. However, the tiger in Blake's poem "The Tyger," on page 749, is not a conventional or inherited symbol. Blake created this symbol specifically for this poem.

Conventional symbolism is often based on elements of nature. For example, youth is often symbolized by greenery or springtime, middle age by summer, and old age by autumn or winter. Conventional symbols are also borrowed from religion and politics. For example, a cross may be a symbol of Christianity, or the color red may be a symbol of Marxist ideology.

SYNECDOCHE *Synecdoche* is a figure of speech in which a part of something is used to stand for the whole. In the preface to his long poem entitled *Milton,* William Blake includes these lines: "And did those feet in ancient time / Walk upon England's mountains green?" The "feet" stand for the whole body, and "England's mountains green" stand for England.

See also *Figurative Language.*

SYNTAX *Syntax* is the way words are organized—for example, their order is a sentence or phrase.

TETRAMETER See *Meter.*

THEME *Theme* is the central idea, concern, or purpose in a literary work. In an essay, the theme might be directly stated in what is known as a thesis statement. In a serious literary work, the theme is usually expressed indirectly rather than directly. A light work, one written strictly for entertainment, may not have a theme.

TONE *Tone* is the writer's attitude toward the readers and toward the subject. It may be formal or informal, friendly or distant, personal or pompous. For example, John Keats's tone in his poem "On First Looking into Chapman's Homer," on page 882, is earnest and respectful, while James Boswell's tone in *The Life of Samuel Johnson,* which begins on page 655, is familiar and engaging.

See also *Mood.*

TRADITION In literary study and practice, a *tradition* is a past body of work, developed over the course of history. A literary tradition may be unified by form (the tradition of the sonnet), by language (literature in English), or by nationality (English literature). A tradition develops through the acknowledgment of works, forms, and styles as classic. It also develops through critical reappraisals, as when T. S. Eliot, in the early twentieth century, elevated seventeenth-century poet John Donne out of the shadows of critical obscurity and disfavor. Writers participate in a tradition if only by following conventions about the suitable forms and subjects for literature. They make conscious use of the tradition when they use references, stories, or forms from old literature to give authority to their work. For example, John Milton uses the classical form of the epic in *Paradise Lost,* page 524, to retell the biblical story of the Fall. Writers may also break from a tradition, as when Wordsworth rejects elevated poetic language in favor of conversational speech in poems such as "London, 1802," page 791. A tradition may also be used to question itself. For example, Derek Walcott in the extract from *Midsummer,* page 1360, uses references to Shakespeare's works to question the extent to which he, a black poet, can participate in a tradition largely maintained by white society for white society.

TRAGEDY *Tragedy* is a type of drama or literature that shows the downfall or destruction of a noble or outstanding person, traditionally one who possesses a character weakness called a *tragic flaw.* Macbeth, for example, is a brave and noble figure led astray by ambition. The *tragic hero* is caught up in a sequence of events that inevitably results in disaster. Because the protagonist is neither a wicked villain nor an innocent victim, the audience reacts with mixed emotions—both pity and fear, according to the Greek philosopher Aristotle, who defined tragedy in the *Poetics.* The outcome of a tragedy, in which the protagonist is isolated from society, contrasts with the happy resolution of a comedy, in which the protagonist makes peace with society.

See also *Comedy* and *Drama.*

TRIMETER See *Meter.*

TROCHEE See *Meter.*

VOICE The *voice* of a writer is his or her "sound" on the page. It is based on elements such as word choice, sound devices, pace, and attitude.

College Application Essay

If you are applying for admission to a college, you will probably need to submit an essay as part of your application. This essay will help admissions committee members get a sense of you as a person and as a student. Review the chart at right for general strategies, and follow the guidelines below to produce an effective college application essay.

Selecting a Topic

Read the essay question on the application form with care. Mark key criteria and direction words such as *describe* and *explain*. After you have written a first draft, check to make sure you have met all of the requirements of the question. Your essay has a better chance of succeeding if it meets the requirements exactly.

General Questions About You

The essay question on a college application may be as general as "Describe a significant experience or event in your life and explain its consequences for you." To choose the right topic for such a question, think of an event or experience that truly is meaningful to you—a camping trip, a volunteer event, a family reunion. Test the subject by drafting a letter about it to a good friend or relative. If you find that your enthusiasm for the subject grows as you write, and if your discussion reveals something about your growth or your outlook on life, the topic may be the right one for your essay.

Directed Questions

The essay question on an application may be a directed question, rather than a general question. For instance, you may be asked to select three figures from history you would like to meet and to explain your choices.

In such cases, do not give an answer just because you think it will please reviewers. Rely on your own interests and instincts. Your most convincing writing will come from genuine interest in the subject.

> ### Strategies for Writing an Effective College Application Essay
>
> - **Choose the right topic.** If you have a choice of essay topics, choose one that truly interests you.
> - **Organize.** Use a strong organization that carries the reader from introduction to conclusion.
> - **Begin Strongly.** Open with an introduction that has a good chance of sparking the reader's interest.
> - **Elaborate.** Be sure to explain why the experiences you discuss are important to you or what you learned from them.
> - **Show style.** Bring life to your essay through vivid descriptions, precise word choice, and sophisticated sentence structure, such as parallelism. Consider including dialogue where appropriate.
> - **Close with a clincher.** Write a conclusion that effectively sums up your ideas.
> - **Do a clean job.** Proofread your essay carefully. It should be error-free.

Style

Remember that an essay is a formal document addressed to strangers. Use a formal to semiformal style. Avoid incomplete sentences and slang unless you are using them for clear stylistic effect. Use words with precision, selecting one or two accurate words to express your meaning. Do not use a word if you are unsure of its meaning.

Format

Most applications limit the length of essays. Do not exceed the allowed space or word count. Your college application essay should be neatly typed or printed, using adequate margins. Proofread your final draft carefully. If you submit a separate copy of the essay (rather than writing on the application form), number the pages and include your name and contact information on each page.

Reusing Your Essay

Most students apply to a number of different colleges. Once you have written a strong essay for one application, you may adapt it for others. However, do not submit a single essay to several schools blindly. Always read the application essay question carefully to ensure that the essay you submit fulfills all of its requirements.

Workplace Writing

Job Search Document: Cover Letter

A cover letter is a formal letter in which the writer asks to be considered for a job. It usually accompanies, or "covers," a completed job application, a résumé, or both. A good cover letter relates specifically to the job for which the writer is applying.

Write a Cover Letter

Consider a part-time job or a summer job you would like to have. Then, write a cover letter to accompany a job application. Include a header, an inside address, an introductory paragraph, one or two body paragraphs, a closing paragraph, and a signature. Mention your main qualifications, and explain how they make you a good fit for the job.

Cesar Moreno
000 Park Avenue
San Marcos, Texas 00000
512-000-0000
emailaddress@theinternet.com

January 15, 20—

Barbara Jones, Director
River Place Day Camp
500 S. Camp Street
Austin, TX 00000

Dear Ms. Jones:

I am writing to apply for the position of Activities Coordinator for your summer camp. The job description posted on the Texas Summer Camps job board perfectly parallels my own interests and experience.

As noted on the enclosed résumé, I have four years' experience as a camp counselor, including one as Lead Counselor and one as Assistant Activities Director. In these roles, I learned not only to work as a team leader, but also to help tailor a camp's programs to the needs of its campers. As an education student at Texas State University, I have completed basic education courses as well as electives in counseling, recreational learning, and youth leadership. These courses, along with my volunteer work as an after-school mentor, have sparked my interest in non-classroom education. In fact, I plan to base my entire career on the idea that learning can be fun—and can happen anywhere.

I hope to help make River Place Day Camp a fun, educational, and well-organized experience for both its campers and its staff. I look forward to meeting with you and discussing my qualifications in more detail.

Sincerely,

Cesar Moreno

The heading should include the writer's name, address, phone number, e-mail address, and the date of the letter.

The inside address includes the name, title, and address of the recipient.

The body paragraph describes how the writer's experiences relate specifically to the job responsibilities.

Job Search Document: Résumé

A **résumé** is a written summary or outline of a person's job qualifications. It plays a key part in most career or job searches. An effective résumé has the following elements:

- candidate's name, current address, phone number, and e-mail address;
- educational background, work experience, and other relevant life experiences;
- logical organization;
- clearly labled sections.

Compile a Résumé

Write a résumé to use in a job search. Consider a specific job you would like to pursue. Then, brainstorm for relevant information in your schooling, work experience, including important details and maintaining a professional tone. As you develop your document, experiment with different fonts to create a professional, readable document.

CESAR MORENO
000 Park Avenue
San Marcos, Texas 00000
512-000-0000 • emailaddress@theinternet.com

Place contact information at the top of the résumé.

EDUCATION
- **Texas State University**, San Marcos, TX
  Bachelor of Science in Education
  Expected: May, 20—
- **Austin High School**, Austin, TX
  Graduated with honors, May, 20—

The headings *Education, Work Experience,* and so on indicate that this résumé is organized by topic.

WORK EXPERIENCE
- **Summer 2008–Summer 2010**
  Camp Lazy J, Fredericksburg, TX
  Camp Counselor: Supervised groups of campers aged 8–12. Served as Lead Counselor in 20– and as Assistant Activities Director in 20–.
- **2009–2010**
  YMCA, Austin, Texas
  Life Guard and Swim Instructor: Guarded weekend free-swim sessions and taught beginning and intermediate youth swim classes.

The items under each topic are bulleted and arranged from most to least recent.

VOLUNTEER EXPERIENCE
- **2009–present**
  San Marcos Community Center, San Marcos, TX
  After-School Mentor: Help elementary and middle school students organize and complete schoolwork, develop skills and interests, and resolve personal issues.
- **2008–2009**
  Stepping Up Preschool, Austin, TX
  Teacher's Aide: Assisted in the 3- and 4-year-old classroom; helped plan and execute special summer programs.

ADDITIONAL SKILLS AND CERTIFICATIONS
- CPR certified, 2007 to the present
- Fluent in Spanish
- Proficient in water sports, including rowing, kayaking, and rafting
- Proficient in Microsoft Word, Excel, and PowerPoint
- Completed childcare training course, YMCA, 2007

A résumé should be no longer than a single page.

REFERENCES
Furnished on request.

Job Search Document: Job Application

Many employers require job applicants to complete a **job application.** A job application is a standard form that asks for particular kinds of information, including the candidate's contact information, education, and work experience.

Complete a Job Application

Consider a part-time job you would like to have. Then, copy and complete the job application shown here using your own information.

Employment Application

PERSONAL INFORMATION
Full Name: Cesar Moreno
Address: 000 Park Ave., San Marcos, TX, 00000
Phone Number: (512) 000-0000
E-mail Address: emailaddress@theinternet.com

POSITION AND AVAILABILITY
Position Applied For: Activities Coordinator

EDUCATION

School	Degree/Diploma	Graduation Date
Texas State University	B.S./Education	expected 5/20—
Austin High School	diploma	May, 20—

Additional Skills, Qualifications, Licenses, Training, Awards
CPR and childcare certified, 2007–present Fluent in Spanish

EMPLOYMENT HISTORY
Present/Last Position and Dates: Camp Counselor, Summer 2006–Summer 2009
Employer: Camp Lazy J
Responsibilities: supervised campers aged 8–12
Supervisor: Mr. Smith
May we contact Supervisor? If so, phone number: yes; (512) 000-0000

Previous Position: Lifeguard and Swim Instructor, 2007–2008
Employer: Austin YMCA
Responsibilities: Guarded free-swim sessions; taught youth swim classes
Supervisor: Mrs. Smith
May we contact Supervisor? If so, phone number: yes; (512) 000-0000

Please list additional employment information on a separate sheet of paper.

I certify that the information contained in this application is true and complete. I authorize the verification of any or all information listed above.

Signature: *Cesar Moreno*
Date: January 15, 20—

> Include only relevant information, and condense it to fit the space available.

> Get your former supervisor's permission before responding "yes" to this item.

> The applicant's signature gives the employer permission to check the information provided.

Business Communications: Business Letter

Business letters are formal letters in which the content is other than personal. Whatever the subject, an effective business letter has the following elements:

- a heading, inside address, salutation or greeting, body, closing, and signature
- one of several acceptable formats, including *block format,* in which each part of the letter begins at the left margin, and *modified block format,* in which the heading, closing, and signature are indented to the center of the page
- formal and courteous language

Write a Business Letter

Choose one of the following purposes and write a business letter to accomplish it. Include heading, inside address, salutation, body, closing, and signature. Use polite and formal language.

- complain about poor service in a restaurant
- accompany a short story you hope to have published
- praise the work of an artist or musician
- gain support for a beautification plan in your community

Bright Orange Lodge
000 Orange Dr.
Orchard, FL 00000

May 1, 20—

Tom Manager, Business Manager
Universal Bank, Inc.
00000 Adams Park Drive
Miami, FL 00000

Dear Mr. Manager:

> The inside address includes the name, title, company, and address of the recipient.

I am writing to confirm the reservation you have made for your organization's annual corporate retreat.

Per our phone conversation of April 28, you requested that the Bright Orange Lodge facilities be reserved for Universal Bank, Inc. from Friday, June 10, at 6:00 p.m. to Sunday, June 12, at 3:00 p.m. Facilities are to include the large meeting room, the kitchen, and a block of between 20 and 30 double-occupancy rooms. As we discussed, I anticipate a firm room count from you by the end of this month.

> This letter is organized in modified block format.

Per the same conversation, I understand that Universal Bank is planning to use its own caterers for all meals. Should this change, Bright Orange can provide food services in its main dining hall, but we will need advance notice.

A bill for the above-specified services will be sent to your attention under separate cover.

Thank you for choosing Bright Orange for your corporate retreat. If I can be of any further assistance, or if you have any questions, please contact me directly at (352) 000-0000.

Sincerely,
Pat Brown

Pat Brown
Event Coordinator

> Business letters end with formal closings, such as *Sincerely* or *Respectfully yours,* followed by the writer's signature and typed name.

Business Communications: Memo

A **memo**—short for *memorandum*—is a brief printed message between co-workers. It usually focuses on information necessary for the completion of a particular task or project. An effective memo has the following elements:

- block organization, with each new element beginning at the left margin
- sender's name, intended audience, date, and topic
- clear and brief description, including statement of actions required

MEMO

TO: Members of the Corporate Retreat Staff
FROM: Ann Smith, Vice President
DATE: May 11, 20—
RE: PLANNING SESSION

Our annual corporate retreat is fast approaching. To ensure that all aspects of the retreat are coordinated, let's meet this Friday, May 14, at 9:00 a.m. in the second-floor conference room.

We will discuss the following topics, so please be prepared to report the status of your assigned area of responsibility.

- finalized dates, times, and location of the retreat (Tom)
- schedule of sessions and events (Bruno)
- presenters and topics (Yolanda)
- caterers and pricing (Barry)
- employee communications — invitations, RSVPs, etc. (DeShon)

I appreciate the many hours you have already invested in the planning process, and I hope that our meeting on Friday will be brief and productive.

AS

> Most memos follow this format: To, From, Date, and Re (Regarding). The word *re:* is Latin for "about." It introduces the subject of the memo.

> The body of a memo is brief and informative, and should clearly state a course of action.

> Memos are often initialed (either at the conclusion or next to the "FROM" line) in order to indicate that the contents have been approved by the sender.

Business Communications: E-Mail

An **e-mail** is a message sent through an electronic communication system such as a computer network or the Internet. Like a memo, an e-mail may be sent to many recipients at once; however, an e-mail has the added benefit of traveling instantaneously. It can also be used to send an attachment—a file that travels with the e-mail but that must be opened using a separate application. While e-mail messages are often more casual than memos, a workplace e-mail (unlike a personal e-mail) should maintain an appropriately formal tone.

Write a Memo and an E-mail

Choose one of the topics below and write a memo that states the message quickly and efficiently. Then, recast the memo as an e-mail.

- announcement of an upcoming event to members of a club or organization
- reminder to fellow workers in a gift shop about store procedures
- information about a surprise party for a teacher
- details about transportation to a sports competition

○ ○ ○	
← → [ ] 🔍 [ ]	
Mail Contacts Calendar Notepad	
Send Save as a Draft Spell Check Colors Fonts Cancel	
From: [▲▼]	
To: Tom_Bernard@e-mail, Bruno_Jones@e-mail, Yolanda_Valois@ e-mail, Barry_Tate@e-mail, DeShon_Allen@e-mail	The header of an e-mail is arranged into fields. *CC* stands for "Carbon Copy." A copy of the e-mail will be sent to the address listed in the CC field.
CC: Sara_Hayes@e-mail	
Subject: Friday planning session	
Attach Files [ ] Agenda.doc Agenda.doc	To see the attached document, recipients can double-click on this icon. The file will then open into the word-processing application.
Hi, all—	
Let's meet Friday morning at 9:00 in the 2nd floor conference room to finalize the retreat plans. A meeting agenda is attached.	
Ann	

Business Communications: Meeting Minutes

Meeting minutes are notes that tell what transpired at a meeting: what was said, what was decided, and what was left unresolved. Often, the person taking the minutes will jot down abbreviated notes during the meeting, and then rewrite the minutes afterward to distribute to meeting participants.

Write Meeting Minutes

In a small group, conduct a business meeting. Take notes during the meeting. Afterward, write a set of minutes to distribute to your fellow group members.

Meeting to Finalize Corporate Retreat Plans
Friday, May 14, 20–
Main Office, 2nd Floor Conference Room, 9:00 a.m.

Committee Members Present: Ann Smith, Tom Bernard, Yolanda Valois, DeShon Allen
Committee Members Absent: Bruno Jones
Others Present: Sara Hayes, assistant to Ann Smith

Proceedings:
Meeting called to order at 9:00 a.m. by Ann Smith.
Agenda was distributed by Sara Hayes.

First Agenda Item: Retreat dates, times, and location, presented by Tom Bernard.
   Tom reported that he has received a letter from Bright Orange Lodge that confirms reservation of their retreat facilities for Universal Bank, Inc. from Friday, June 10, at 6:00 p.m. through Sunday, June 12, at 3:00 p.m. A copy of this letter is attached to the minutes.

Second Agenda Item: Schedule of sessions and events, presented by Ann Smith for Bruno Jones.
   Bruno is out of the office today, but e-mailed Ann the finalized retreat schedule. Ann distributed copies of the schedule to all members. MOTION to approve schedule; passed unanimously.

Assessment of the meeting: Members agreed that the retreat promises to be very successful. Jeff congratulated committee members on a job well done.

Meeting adjourned at 10:05 a.m.
Meeting minutes compiled by Sarah Hayes.

The header should include the name of the meeting and its date, location, and time.

These minutes are formatted to show that the meeting followed an agenda.

A *motion* is a proposal to vote on something. All motions and their results should be carefully noted in meeting minutes.

Business Communications: Technical Writing

Technical writing refers to any kind of writing that presents specialized information to help someone perform a task. Scientific reports, troubleshooting guides, assembly instructions, and school handbooks are all examples of technical writing. Although the format varies with the purpose, all technical writing must be clear and easy to use—in other words, "user friendly." It must also be absolutely precise.

Write a Section of a Technical Document

Think of something you know how to do well and write a set of procedures for completing the task. Remember to use specific language that accurately describes the details of the task.

Porterdale Community Library rev. 7/09
Policies and Procedures
Section IV: Collection Maintenance

A page header identifies the publication title, the section, and the revision date.

IV.D. PROCESSING NEW MATERIALS
When new items are delivered to the library, they must be processed, or prepared for use by patrons. The steps for processing a new shipment of items are as follows.

A brief introduction tells the reader what is included in this section.

1. **Before unpacking the items:**
   a. Remove the packing slip from the box.
   b. Find the matching order form in the main filing cabinet. Order forms are filed alphabetically by vendor.

2. **Unpacking the items:**
   a. Check each item against both the order form and the packing slip.
   b. Place a checkmark on each document next to the title of the item.
   c. If all items in the shipment correspond with those on the order form, send the order form and invoice to the business office for payment. The invoice is usually inside the shipment or affixed to the outside in an envelope.
   d. If an item is missing or damaged, make a note and/or set the item aside. (See section IV.B. for Ordering and Returning procedures.)

(To process books, see item 3, below. To process other media items, proceed to item 4 on the following page.)

Cross-references and navigational guides are included to help the reader find additional needed information with ease.

3. **Processing books:**
   a. Attach a bar code label to the upper left-hand corner of the front cover.
   b. Stamp books with the library name on the front inside cover and back inside cover.
   c. Prepare a spine label for books. (See section II.A. for call number designation.) Affix the label to the spine with a label protector.
   d. Enter information for the new item into the library catalog database. (See section III.B. for cataloging procedures.)

Guide to Rubrics

What is a rubric?

A rubric is a tool, often in the form of a chart or a grid, that helps you assess your work. Rubrics are particularly helpful for writing and speaking assignments.

To help you or others assess, or evaluate, your work, a rubric offers several specific criteria to be applied to your work. Then the rubric helps you or an evaluator indicate your range of success or failure according to those specific criteria. Rubrics are often used to evaluate writing for standardized tests.

Using a rubric will save you time, focus your learning, and improve the work you do. When you know what the rubric will be before you begin writing a persuasive essay, for example, you will be aware as you write of specific criteria that are important in that kind of an essay. As you evaluate the essay before giving it to your teacher, you will focus on the specific areas that your teacher wants you to master—or on areas that you know present challenges for you. Instead of searching through your work randomly for any way to improve it or correct its errors, you will have a clear and helpful focus on specific criteria.

How are rubrics constructed?

Rubrics can be constructed in several ways.

- Your teacher may assign a rubric for a specific assignment.

- Your teacher may direct you to a rubric in your textbook.

- Your teacher and your class may construct a rubric for a particular assignment together.

- You and your classmates may construct a rubric together.

- You may create your own rubric with criteria you want to evaluate in your work.

How will a rubric help me?

A rubric will help you assess your work on a scale. Scales vary from rubric to rubric but usually range from 6 to 1, 5 to 1, or 4 to 1, with 6, 5, or 4 being the highest score and 1 being the lowest. If someone else is using the rubric to assess your work, the rubric will give your evaluator a clear range within which to place your work. If you are using the rubric yourself, it will help you make improvements to your work.

What are the types of rubrics?

- A holistic rubric has general criteria that can apply to a variety of assignments. See p. R45 for an example of a holistic rubric.

- An analytic rubric is specific to a particular assignment. The criteria for evaluation address the specific issues important in that assignment. See p. R44 for examples of analytic rubrics.

Sample Analytic Rubrics

Rubric With a 4-point Scale

The following analytic rubric is an example of a rubric to assess a persuasive essay. It will help you evaluate focus, organization, support/elaboration, and style/convention.

	Focus	Organization	Support/Elaboration	Style/Convention
4	Demonstrates highly effective word choice; clearly focused on task.	Uses clear, consistent organizational strategy.	Provides convincing, well-elaborated reasons to support the position.	Incorporates transitions; includes very few mechanical errors.
3	Demonstrates good word choice; stays focused on persuasive task.	Uses clear organizational strategy with occasional inconsistencies.	Provides two or more moderately elaborated reasons to support the position.	Incorporates some transitions; includes few mechanical errors.
2	Shows some good word choices; minimally stays focused on persuasive task.	Uses inconsistent organizational strategy; presentation is not logical.	Provides several reasons, but few are elaborated; only one elaborated reason.	Incorporates few transitions; includes many mechanical errors.
1	Shows lack of attention to persuasive task.	Demonstrates lack of organizational strategy.	Provides no specific reasons or does not elaborate.	Does not connect ideas; includes many mechanical errors.

Rubric With a 6-point Scale

The following analytic rubric is an example of a rubric to assess a persuasive essay. It will help you evaluate presentation, position, evidence, and arguments.

	Presentation	Position	Evidence	Arguments
6	Essay clearly and effectively addresses an issue with more than one side.	Essay clearly states a supportable position on the issue.	All evidence is logically organized, well presented, and supports the position.	All reader concerns and counterarguments are effectively addressed.
5	Most of essay addresses an issue that has more than one side.	Essay clearly states a position on the issue.	Most evidence is logically organized, well presented, and supports the position.	Most reader concerns and counterarguments are effectively addressed.
4	Essay adequately addresses issue that has more than one side.	Essay adequately states a position on the issue.	Many parts of evidence support the position; some evidence is out of order.	Many reader concerns and counterarguments are adequately addressed.
3	Essay addresses issue with two sides but does not present second side clearly.	Essay states a position on the issue, but the position is difficult to support.	Some evidence supports the position, but some evidence is out of order.	Some reader concerns and counterarguments are addressed.
2	Essay addresses issue with two sides but does not present second side.	Essay states a position on the issue, but the position is not supportable.	Not much evidence supports the position, and what is included is out of order.	A few reader concerns and counterarguments are addressed.
1	Essay does not address issue with more than one side.	Essay does not state a position on the issue.	No evidence supports the position.	No reader concerns or counterarguments are addressed.

Sample Holistic Rubric

Holistic rubrics are sometimes used to assess writing assignments on standardized tests.
Notice that the criteria for evaluation are focus, organization, support, and use of conventions.

Points	Criteria
6 Points	• The writing is strongly focused and shows fresh insight into the writing task. • The writing is organized with a logical progression of ideas. • A main idea is fully developed, and support is specific and substantial. • A mature command of the language is evident. • Sentence structure is varied, and writing is free of all but purposefully used fragments. • Virtually no errors in writing conventions appear.
5 Points	• The writing is clearly focused on the task. • The writing is well organized and generally shows a logical progression of ideas. • A main idea is well developed and supported with relevant detail. • Sentence structure is varied, and the writing is free of unintended fragments. • Writing conventions are followed correctly.
4 Points	• The writing is clearly focused on the task, but extraneous material may intrude at times. • Clear organizational pattern is present, though lapses may occur. • A main idea is adequately supported, but development may be uneven. • Sentence structure is generally fragment free but shows little variation. • Writing conventions are generally followed correctly.
3 Points	• Writing is generally focused on the task, but extraneous material may intrude at times. • An organizational pattern is evident, but writing may lack a logical progression of ideas. • Support for the main idea is generally present but is sometimes illogical. • Sentence structure is generally free of fragments, but there is almost no variation. • The work generally demonstrates a knowledge of writing conventions, with occasional misspellings.
2 Points	• The writing is related to the task but generally lacks focus. • There is little evidence of organizational pattern, and there is little sense of cohesion. • Support for the main idea is generally inadequate, illogical, or absent. • Sentence structure is unvaried, and serious errors may occur. • Errors in writing conventions and spellings are frequent.
1 Point	• The writing may have little connection to the task and is generally unfocused. • There has been little attempt at organization or development. • The paper seems fragmented, with no clear main idea. • Sentence structure is unvaried, and serious errors appear. • Poor word choice and poor command of the language obscure meaning. • Errors in writing conventions and spelling are frequent.
Unscorable	The paper is considered unscorable if: • The response is unrelated to the task or is simply a rewording of the prompt. • The response has been copied from a published work. • The student did not write a response. • The response is illegible. • The words in the response are arranged with no meaning. • There is an insufficient amount of writing to score.

Student Model

Persuasive Writing

This persuasive letter, which would receive a top score according to a persuasive rubric, is a response to the following writing prompt, or assignment:

Write a letter to a government official strongly supporting an environmental issue that is important to you and urging the official to take a specific action that supports your cause.

Dear Secretary of the Interior:

It's a normal carefree day in the forest. The birds are singing and all of the animals are relaxing under the refreshing glow of the sun. But suddenly the thunderous sound of a chainsaw echoes throughout the woodlands, and trees fall violently. The creatures of the forest run in terror. Many of these beautiful creatures will starve to death slowly and painfully as their homes are destroyed, and this precious ecosystem will not be able to regrow to its previous greatness for many years to come.

This sad story is a true one in many places around the globe. We must slow deforestation and replant trees immediately to save our breathable air, fertile soil, and fragile ecosystems.

If entire forests continue to be obliterated, less oxygen will be produced and more CO_2 emitted. In fact, deforestation accounts for a quarter of the CO_2 released into the atmosphere each year: about 1–2 billion tons. Forests provide the majority of the oxygen on earth, and if these forests disappear our air will soon be unbreathable.

Second, deforestation results in a loss of topsoil. Many of the companies who are involved in deforestation claim that the land is needed for farms, but deforestation makes the land much less fertile because it accelerates the process of erosion. According to the UN Food and Agriculture Organization, deforestation has damaged almost 6 million square kilometers of soil.

Finally, if cutting doesn't slow, many species will die off and many ecosystems will be destroyed. The 2000 UN Global Environment Outlook says that forests and rain forests have the most diverse plant and animal life in the world. The GEO also notes that there are more than 1,000 threatened species living in the world's forests. Imagine someone destroying all the houses in your neighborhood and leaving all of the residents homeless. This is how it is for the organisms that live in the forests.

In conclusion, deforestation must slow down and trees must be replanted immediately, or we will lose clean air, topsoil, and many precious organisms. Furthermore, a loss in forests will result in a generation that knows very little about nature. So, to prevent the chaotic disturbance of peace in the forests, please do whatever you can to prevent deforestation. Vote YES on any UN bills that would help the condition of our world's forests.

Sincerely Yours,
Jamil Khouri

A descriptive and interesting introduction grabs the reader's attention and shows a persuasive focus.

The writer supports the argument with facts and evidence, and also uses the persuasive appeal to the reader's emotions.

The conclusion restates the argument and presents a call to action.

21st Century Skills

Changing technology creates new ways to communicate. This handbook provides an overview of some ways you can use today's technology to create, share, and find information. You will find brief descriptions of the following topics in this section:

- ✔ Blogs
- ✔ Social Networking
- ✔ Widgets and Feeds
- ✔ Podcasts
- ✔ Wikis
- ✔ Internet Research Guide

BLOGS

A **blog** is a common form of online writing. The word *blog* is a contraction of *Web log*. Most blogs include a series of entries known as posts. The posts appear in a single column and are displayed in reverse chronological order. That means that the most recent post is at the top of the page. As you scroll down, you will find earlier posts.

Blogs have become increasingly popular. Researchers estimate that 75,000 new blogs are launched every day. Blog authors are often called bloggers. They can use their personal sites to share ideas, experiences, and impressions. Because blogs are designed so that they are easy to update, bloggers can post new messages as often as they like, often daily.

Another key component of blogs is interactivity with their audience. Many blogs allow readers to post their responses by using a comments feature found in each new post. Popular blog entries often inspire extended conversations and debates.

Kinds of Blogs

Not all blogs are the same. Many blogs have a single author, but others are group projects.

Blogs also serve a variety of purposes. Here are some common types of blog:

- Personal blogs often have a general focus. Bloggers post about any topic they find interesting in their daily lives.
- Topical blogs focus on a specific theme, such as movie reviews, political news, class assignments, or health care opportunities.
- Open Forum blogs are open to any Internet user.
- Closed Forum blogs are allowed only to members of a site. Bloggers can further limit readership by giving only invited users full access to their site.

Web Safety

Always be aware of the information you post on the Internet. Remember that whatever information you post can be read by everyone with access to that page. Once you post a picture or text, it can be saved on someone else's computer, even if you later remove it.

Using the Internet safely means keeping personal information personal. Do not post sensitive information. Never include your address (e-mail or real), last name, telephone numbers, or mention places you can be frequently found. Do not give out this information for other people. Never give out passwords you use to access other Web sites and do not respond to e-mails from strangers.

Anatomy of a Blog

Here are some of the features you can include in a blog.

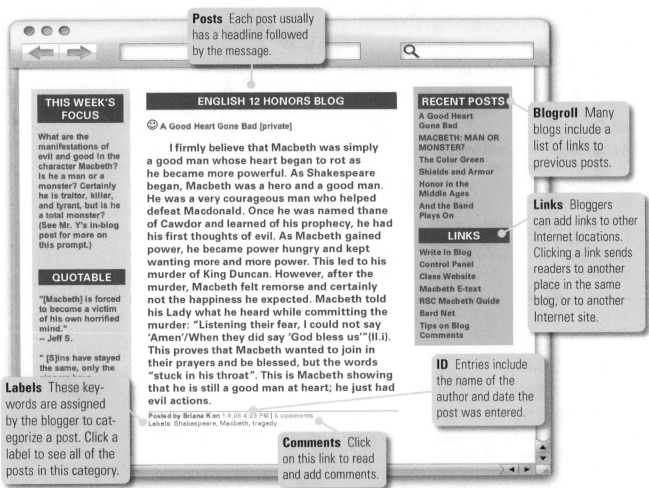

Posts Each post usually has a headline followed by the message.

THIS WEEK'S FOCUS

What are the manifestations of evil and good in the character Macbeth? Is he a man or a monster? Certainly he is traitor, killer, and tyrant, but is he a total monster? (See Mr. Y's in-blog post for more on this prompt.)

QUOTABLE

"[Macbeth] is forced to become a victim of his own horrified mind."
– Jeff S.

" [S]ins have stayed the same, only the

ENGLISH 12 HONORS BLOG

☺ A Good Heart Gone Bad [private]

   I firmly believe that Macbeth was simply a good man whose heart began to rot as he became more powerful. As Shakespeare began, Macbeth was a hero and a good man. He was a very courageous man who helped defeat Macdonald. Once he was named thane of Cawdor and learned of his prophecy, he had his first thoughts of evil. As Macbeth gained power, he became power hungry and kept wanting more and more power. This led to his murder of King Duncan. However, after the murder, Macbeth felt remorse and certainly not the happiness he expected. Macbeth told his Lady what he heard while committing the murder: "Listening their fear, I could not say 'Amen'/When they did say 'God bless us'"(II.i). This proves that Macbeth wanted to join in their prayers and be blessed, but the words "stuck in his throat". This is Macbeth showing that he is still a good man at heart; he just had evil actions.

Posted by Briana K on 1.8.05 4:29 PM | 6 comments
Labels: Shakespeare, Macbeth, tragedy

RECENT POSTS

A Good Heart Gone Bad
MACBETH: MAN OR MONSTER?
The Color Green
Shields and Armor
Honor in the Middle Ages
And the Band Plays On

LINKS

Write In Blog
Control Panel
Class Website
Macbeth E-text
RSC Macbeth Guide
Bard Net
Tips on Blog Comments

Blogroll Many blogs include a list of links to previous posts.

Links Bloggers can add links to other Internet locations. Clicking a link sends readers to another place in the same blog, or to another Internet site.

ID Entries include the name of the author and date the post was entered.

Labels These keywords are assigned by the blogger to categorize a post. Click a label to see all of the posts in this category.

Comments Click on this link to read and add comments.

Creating a Blog

Like any form of writing, blogging is a form of communication. Keep these hints and strategies in mind to help you create an interesting and fair blog:

- Focus each blog entry on a single topic. If you have two ideas you want to write about, create two separate blog entries. This can help readers find topics that interest them.

- Vary the length of your posts. Sometimes, all you need is a line or two to share a quick thought. Other posts will be much longer.

- Make your main ideas pop out by using clear or clever headlines and boldfacing key terms.

- Use labels to categorize entries, allowing readers to find material that interests them.

- Give credit to other people's work and ideas. Mention the names of people whose ideas you are quoting. You can also add a link that will take readers directly to that person's blog or site.

- If you post comments, try to make them brief and polite. Even if you disagree, state the reasons for your disagreement clearly and without exaggeration.

SOCIAL NETWORKING

Social networking refers to any interaction between members of an online community. People can exchange many different kinds of information, from text and voice messages to video images.

Many social network communities, such as MySpace and Facebook, allow users to create permanent pages that describe themselves. Users create home pages to share ideas about their lives and post messages to other members in the network. Each user is responsible for adding and updating the content on his or her profile page. You can create a social network page for an individual or a group, such as a school or special interest club. Many hosting sites do not charge to register, so you can also have fun by creating a page for a pet or a fictional character.

Here are some features you are likely to find on a social network profile:

- A biographical description, including photographs and artwork.

- Lists of favorite things, such as books, movies, music, and fashions.

- Playable media elements, such as videos and sound recordings.

- Message boards, or "walls," in which members of the community can exchange messages.

Privacy in Social Networks

Social networks allow users to decide how open their profiles will be. Be sure to read introductory information carefully before you register at a new site. Once you have a personal profile page, monitor your privacy settings regularly. Remember that any information you post will be available to anyone in your network.

Users often post messages anonymously or using false names, or pseudonyms. People can also post using someone else's name. Judge all information on the net critically. Do not assume that you know who posted information simply because you recognize the name of the post author. The rapid speed of communication on the Internet can make it easy to jump to conclusions. Be careful to avoid this trap.

Think twice before posting anything on a social networking page or blog. Once you have posted a photo or text, it can be saved on someone else's computer. Even if you remove the material later, the Web user still has a copy. Once another user has your photo, he or she might post it to other sites, or alter it using photo editing software. This practice may not be legal, but many users are not familiar with privacy laws, or choose to ignore them.

In fact, the user might not even be a person. A Web crawler is a computer program that browses the Internet and collects and saves data posted on Web sites. Also known as Web spiders or Web robots, these automated programs might gather information for marketing research or targeted sales.

Tips for Sending Effective Messages

Technology makes it easy to share ideas quickly, but writing for the Internet also poses some special challenges. The writing style for blogs and social networks is usually conversational. In blog posts and comments, instant messages, and e-mails, writers express themselves very quickly, using relaxed language, short sentences, and abbreviations. However, in a conversation, we get a lot of information from a speaker's tone of voice and body language. On the Internet, those clues are missing. As a result, Internet writers sometimes use italics or bracketed labels to indicate emotions. An alternative is using emoticons—strings of characters that give visual clues to indicate emotion:

:-) smile (happy)	:-(frown (unhappy)	;-) wink (light sarcasm)

	That's just great!
Direct Tone	That's just great. :-)
	That's just *great.*
	That's just great. ;-)
Sarcastic Tone	<sarcasm> That's just great. <end sarcasm>

Here are some additional strategies you can use for communicating effectively when using technology:

- Reread your messages. Before you click **Send,** read your message through and make sure that your tone will be clear to the reader

- Don't jump to conclusions—ask for clarification first. Make sure you really understand what someone is saying before you respond.

- Remember that during chat sessions, messages often cross. As a result, messages may not always refer to the message immediately above. Read carefully to make sure you understand which topic a message refers to. If you're not sure, say so.

- Avoid using ALL CAPS. Many people feel this is like shouting for an entire conversation.

WIDGETS and FEEDS

A **widget** is a small application that can be found on many blogs, social network profiles, and other Web sites. Each widget performs a specific task. You might find widgets that give weather predictions, offer dictionary definitions or translations, or provide entertainment such as games. Other widgets present a new item each day, such as a joke, vocabulary word, sports photograph, brain teaser, or inspirational quotation.

A **feed** is a special kind of widget. It displays headlines taken from the latest content on a specific media source. Clicking on the headline will take you to the full article. Feeds can connect you to the latest news or sports. Feeds are convenient because they automatically send new data to your web page. You get news when it occurs.

Many social network communities and other Web sites allow you to personalize your home page by adding widgets and feeds. Browse through the options available to find the applications that are most useful to you. Be aware that loading widgets onto your page can affect the speed with which your page loads and updates. Test a new widget for one or two sessions—if you do not like the way it performs, simply delete it.

Widget and feeds on a home page.

PODCASTS

A **podcast** is a digital audio or video recording of a program that is made available on the Internet. Users can replay the podcast on a computer, or download and replay it on a personal audio player. You might think of podcasts as radio or television programs that you create yourself. They can be embedded on a Web site or fed to a Web page through a podcast widget.

Creating an Effective Podcast

To make a podcast, you will need a recording device, such as a microphone or digital video camera, as well as editing software. Open source editing software is widely available and free of charge. Most audio podcasts are converted into the MP3 format. Bulleted list of hints and strategies for creating a podcast that is clear and entertaining (such as rehearsing before recording, preparing a time outline, limiting length, and so on).

- Listen to several podcasts by different authors to get a feeling for the medium. Make a list of features and styles you like, as well as those you want to avoid.

- Test your microphone to find the best recording distance. You will stand close to the microphone so that your voice sounds full, but not so close that you create an echo.

- Create an outline that gives your estimated timing for each element.

- Be prepared before you record. Rehearse, but do not create a script. Podcasts are best when they have a natural, easy flow.

- Talk directly to your listeners. Slow down enough so they can understand you.

- Use software to edit your podcast before publishing it.

WIKIS

A **wiki** is collaborative Web site that lets visitors create, add, remove, and edit content. The term comes from the Hawaiian phrase *wiki wiki,* which means "quick." Web users at a wiki are both the readers and the writers of the site. Some wikis are open to contributions from anyone. Others require visitors to register before they can edit the content.

Wikipedia is a well-known wiki encyclopedia. All of the text was created by people who use the site. Articles are constantly changing, as visitors find and correct errors and improve texts.

Wikis have both advantages and disadvantages as sources of information. They are valuable open forums for the exchange of ideas. The unique collaborative writing process allows entries to change over time. However, entries can also be modified incorrectly. Careless or malicious users can delete good content and add inappropriate or inaccurate information.

You can change the information on a wiki, but be sure your information is correct and clear before you add it. Wikis keep track of all changes, so your work will be recorded and can be evaluated by other users.

Wiki users must agree to use the sites responsibly so they can offer accurate information. As with blogs and social networking pages, the informal nature of wikis can lead to trouble. Remember that all information you post to a wiki—including text or images you erase—can not only be seen but also tracked, since all versions of the wiki are saved for security purposes.

Research and Technology Guide

USING THE INTERNET FOR RESEARCH

Key Word Search

Before you begin a search, you should identify your specific topic. To make searching easier, narrow your subject to a key word or a group of key words. These are your search terms, and they should be as specific as possible. For example, if you are looking for the latest concert dates for your favorite musical group, you might use the band's name as a key word. However, if you were to enter the name of the group in the query box of the search engine, you might be presented with thousands of links to information about the group that is unrelated to what you want to know. You might locate such information as band member biographies, the group's history, fan reviews of concerts, and hundreds of sites with related names containing information that is irrelevant to your search. Because you used such a broad key word, you might need to navigate through all that information before you could find a link or subheading for concert dates. In contrast, if you were to type in "Duplex Arena and [band name]," you would have a better chance of locating pages that contain this information.

How to Narrow Your Search

If you have a large group of key words and still do not know which ones to use, write out a list of all the words you are considering. Once you have completed the list, scrutinize it. Then, delete the words that are least important to your search, and highlight those that are most important.

These **key search connectors** can help you fine-tune your search:

AND: Narrows a search by retrieving documents that include both terms. For example: *baseball* AND *playoffs*

OR: Broadens a search by retrieving documents including any of the terms. For example: *playoffs* OR *championships*

NOT: *Narrows a search by excluding documents containing certain words. For example:* **baseball** NOT **history of**

Tips for an Effective Search

1. Remember that search engines can be case-sensitive. If your first attempt at searching fails, check your search terms for misspellings and try again.

2. If you are entering a group of key words, present them in order from the most important to the least important key word.

3. Avoid opening the link to every single page in your results list. Search engines present pages in descending order of relevancy. The most useful pages will be located at the top of the list. However, read the description of each link before you open the page.

4. Some search engines provide helpful tips for specializing your search. Take the opportunity to learn more about effective searching.

Other Ways to Search

Using Online Reference Sites How you search should be tailored to what you are hoping to find. If you are looking for data and facts, use reference sites before you jump onto a simple search engine. For example, you can find reference sites to provide definitions of words, statistics about almost any subject, biographies, maps, and concise information on many topics. Here are some useful online reference sites:

Online libraries
Online periodicals
Almanacs
Encyclopedias

You can find these sources using subject searches.

Conducting Subject Searches As you prepare to go online, consider your subject and the best way to find information to suit your needs. If you are looking for general information on a topic and you want your search results to be extensive, consider the subject search indexes on most search engines. These indexes, in the form of category and subject lists, often appear on the first page of a search engine. When you click on a specific highlighted word, you will be presented with a new screen containing subcategories of the topic you chose.

Evaluating the Reliability of Internet Resources

Just as you would evaluate the quality, bias, and validity of any other research material you locate, check the source of information you find online. Compare these two sites containing information about the poet and writer Langston Hughes:

Site A is a personal Web site constructed by a college student. It contains no bibliographic information or links to sites that he used. Included on the site are several poems by Langston Hughes and a student essay about the poet's use of symbolism. It has not been updated in more than six months.

Site B is a Web site constructed and maintained by the English Department of a major university. Information on Hughes is presented in a scholarly format, with a bibliography and credits for the writer. The site includes links to other sites and indicates new features that are added weekly.

For your own research, consider the information you find on Site B to be more reliable and accurate than that on Site A. Because it is maintained by experts in their field who are held accountable for their work, the university site will be a better research tool than the student-generated one.

Tips for Evaluating Internet Sources

1. Consider who constructed and who now maintains the Web page. Determine whether this author is a reputable source. Often, the URL endings indicate a source.

   - Sites ending in *.edu* are maintained by educational institutions.

   - Sites ending in *.gov* are maintained by government agencies (federal, state, or local).

   - Sites ending in *.org* are normally maintained by nonprofit organizations and agencies.

   - Sites ending in *.com* are commercially or personally maintained.

2. Skim the official and trademarked Web pages first. It is safe to assume that the information you draw from Web pages of reputable institutions, online encyclopedias, online versions of major daily newspapers, or government-owned sites produce information as reliable as the material you would find in print. In contrast, unbranded sites or those generated by individuals tend to borrow information from other sources without providing documentation. As information travels from one source to another, it could have been muddled, misinterpreted, edited, or revised.

3. You can still find valuable information in the less "official" sites. Check for the writer's credentials, and then consider these factors:

   - Do not be misled by official-looking graphics or presentations.

   - Make sure that the information is updated enough to suit your needs. Many Web pages will indicate how recently they have been updated.

   - If the information is borrowed, notice whether you can trace it back to its original source.

Respecting Copyrighted Material

Because the Internet is a relatively new and quickly growing medium, issues of copyright and ownership arise almost daily. As laws begin to govern the use and reuse of material posted online, they may change the way that people can access or reprint material.

Text, photographs, music, and fine art printed online may not be reproduced without acknowledged permission of the copyright owner.

Tips for Discussing Literature

As you read and study literature, discussions with other readers can help you understand, enjoy, and develop interpretations of what you read. Use the following tips to practice good speaking and listening skills in group discussions of literature.

- ## Understand the purpose of your discussion.

  Your purpose when you discuss literature is to broaden your understanding and appreciation of a work by testing your own ideas and hearing the ideas of others. Be sure to stay focused on the literature you are discussing and to keep your comments relevant to that literature. Starting with one focus question will help to keep your discussion on track.

- ## Communicate effectively.

  Effective communication requires thinking before speaking. Plan the points that you want to make and decide how you will express them. Organize these points in logical order and cite details from the work to support your ideas. Jot down informal notes to help keep your ideas focused.

  Remember to speak clearly, pronouncing words slowly and carefully so that your listeners will understand your ideas. Also, keep in mind that some literature touches readers deeply—be aware of the possibility of counterproductive emotional responses and work to control them.

- ## Make relevant contributions.

  Especially when responding to a short story or a novel, avoid simply summarizing the plot. Instead, consider *what* you think might happen next, *why* events take place as they do, or *how* a writer provokes a response in you. Let your ideas inspire deeper thought or discussion about the literature.

- ## Consider other ideas and interpretations.

  A work of literature can generate a wide variety of responses in different readers—and that can make your discussions really exciting. Be open to the idea that many interpretations can be valid. To support your own ideas, point to the events, descriptions, characters, or other literary elements in the work that led to your interpretation. To consider someone else's ideas, decide whether details in the work support the interpretation he or she presents. Be sure to convey your criticism of the ideas of others in a respectful and supportive manner.

- ## Ask questions and extend the contributions of others.

  Get in the habit of asking questions to help you clarify your understanding of another reader's ideas. You can also use questions to call attention to possible areas of confusion, to points that are open to debate, or to errors in the speaker's points.

  In addition, offer elaboration of the points that others make by providing examples and illustrations from the literature. To move a discussion forward, summarize and evaluate tentative conclusions reached by the group members.

Oral and Visual Communication

You use speaking and listening skills every day. When you talk with your friends, teachers, or parents, or when you interact with store clerks, you are communicating orally. In addition to everyday conversation, oral communication includes class discussions, speeches, interviews, presentations, debates, and performances. The following terms will give you a better understanding of the many elements that are part of communication and help you eliminate barriers to listening by managing any distractions:

Body language refers to the use of facial expressions, eye contact, gestures, posture, and movement to communicate a feeling or an idea.

Connotation is the set of associations a word calls to mind. The connotations of the words you choose influence the message you send. For example, most people respond more favorably to being described as "slim" rather than as "skinny." The connotation of *slim* is more appealing than that of *skinny*.

Eye contact is direct visual contact with another person's eyes.

Feedback is the set of verbal and nonverbal reactions that indicate to a speaker that a message has been received and understood.

Gestures are the movements made with arms, hands, face and fingers to communicate.

Listening is understanding and interpreting sound in a meaningful way. You listen differently for different purposes.

Listening for key information: For example, when a teacher gives an assignment, or when someone gives you directions to a place, you listen for key information.

Listening for main points: In a classroom exchange of ideas or information, or while watching a television documentary, you listen for main points.

Listening critically: When you evaluate a performance, song, or a persuasive or political speech, you listen critically, questioning and judging the speaker's message.

Medium is the material or technique used to present a visual image. Common media include paint, clay, and film.

Nonverbal communication is communication without the use of words. People communicate nonverbally through gestures, facial expressions, posture, and body movements. Sign language is an entire language based on nonverbal communication. Be aware of your nonverbal communication and make sure that your gestures and facial expressions do not conflict with your words.

Projection is speaking in such a way that the voice carries clearly to an audience. It's important to project your voice when speaking in a large space like a classroom or an auditorium.

Viewing is observing, understanding, analyzing, and evaluating information presented through visual means. You might use the following questions to help you interpret what you view:

- What subject is presented?
- What is communicated about the subject?
- Which parts are factual? Which are opinion?
- What mood, attitude, or opinion is conveyed?
- What is your emotional response?

Vocal delivery is the way in which you present a message. Your vocal delivery involves all of the following elements:

Volume: the loudness or quietness of your voice

Pitch: the high or low quality of your voice

Rate: the speed at which you speak; also called pace

Stress: the amount of emphasis placed on different syllables in a word or on different words in a sentence

All of these elements individually, and the way in which they are combined, contribute to the meaning of a spoken message.

Speaking, Listening, and Viewing Situations

Here are some of the many types of situations in which you apply speaking, listening, and viewing skills:

Audience Your audience in any situation refers to the person or people to whom you direct your message. An audience can be a group of people observing a performance or just one person. When preparing for any speaking situation, it's useful to analyze your audience, so that you can tailor your message to them.

Charts and graphs are visual representations of statistical information. For example, a pie chart might indicate how the average dollar is spent by government, and a bar graph might compare populations in cities over time.

Debate A debate is a formal public-speaking situation in which participants prepare and present arguments on opposing sides of a question, states as a **proposition.**

The two sides in a debate are the *affirmative* (pro) and the *negative* (con). The affirmative side argues in favor of the proposition, while the negative side argues against it. Each side has an opportunity for *rebuttal,* in which they may challenge or question the other side's argument.

Documentaries are nonfiction films that analyze news events or other focused subjects. You can watch a documentary for the information on its subject.

Graphic organizers summarize and present information in ways that can help you understand the information. Graphic organizers include charts, outlines, webs, maps, lists, and diagrams. For example, a graphic organizer for a history chapter might be an outline. A Venn diagram is intersecting circles that display information showing how concepts are alike and different.

Group discussion results when three or more people meet to solve a common problem, arrive at a decision, or answer a question of mutual interest. Group discussion is one of the most widely used forms or interpersonal communication in modern society.

Interview An interview is a form of interaction in which one person, the interviewer, asks questions of another person, the interviewee. Interviews may take place for many purposes: to obtain information, to discover a person's suitability for a job or a college, or to inform the public of a notable person's opinions.

Maps are visual representations of Earth's surface. Maps may show political boundaries and physical features and provide information on a variety of other topics. A map's titles and its key identify the content of the map.

Oral interpretation is the reading or speaking of a work of literature aloud for an audience. Oral interpretation involves giving expression to the ideas, meaning, or even the structure of a work of literature. The speaker interprets the work through his or her vocal delivery. **Storytelling,** in which a speaker reads or tells a story expressively, is a form of oral interpretation.

Panel discussion is a group discussion on a topic of interest common to all members of a panel and to a listening audience. A panel is usually composed of four to six experts on a particular topic who are brought together to share information and opinions.

Pantomime is a form of nonverbal communication in which an idea or a story is communicated completely through the use of gesture, body language, and facial expressions, without any words at all.

Political cartoons are drawings that comment on important political or social issues. Often, these cartoons use humor to convey a message about their subject. Viewers use their own knowledge of events to evaluate the cartoonist's opinion.

Readers theatre is a dramatic reading of a work of literature in which participants take parts from a story or play and read them aloud in expressive voices. Unlike a play, however, sets and costumes are not part of the performance, and the participants remain seated as they deliver their lines.

Role play To role-play is to take the role of a person or character and act out a given situation, speaking, acting, and responding in the manner of the character.

Speech A speech is a talk or address given to an audience. A speech may be **impromptu** or **extemporaneous**— delivered on the spur of the moment with no preparation— or formally prepared and delivered for a specific purpose or occasion.

- *Purposes:* the most common purposes of speeches are to persuade, to entertain, to explain, and to inform.

- *Occasions:* Different occasions call for different types of speeches. Speeches given on these occasions could be persuasive, entertaining, or informative, as appropriate.

Visual representation refers to informative texts, such as newspapers and advertisements, and entertaining texts, such as magazines. Visual representations use elements of design—such as texture and color, shapes, drawings, and photographs—to convey the meaning, message, or theme.

Grammar, Usage, and Mechanics Handbook

Parts of Speech

Every English word, depending on its meaning and its use in a sentence, can be identified as one of the eight parts of speech. These are nouns, pronouns, verbs, adjectives, adverbs, prepositions, conjunctions, and interjections.

Understanding the parts of speech will help you learn the rules of English grammar and usage.

Part of Speech	Definition	Examples
Noun	**Names a person, place, or thing**	
Common	• Names any one of a class of persons, places, or things	writer, country, novel
Proper	• Names a specific person, place or thing	Charles Dickens, Great Britain, *Hard Times*
Pronoun	**Stands for a noun or for a word that takes the place of a noun**	
Personal	• Refers to the person speaking (first person); the person spoken to (second person); or the person, place, or thing spoken about (third person)	I, me, my, mine, we, us, our, ours, you, our, yours, he, him, his, she, her, hers, it, its, they, them, their, theirs, myself, ourselves, yourself, yourselves, himself, herself, itself, themselves
Reflexive	• Names the person or thing receiving an action when that person or thing is the same as the one performing the action	"They click upon *themselves*/ As the breeze rises,…" –Robert Frost
Intensive	• Adds emphasis to a noun or pronoun	"The United States *themselves* are essentially the greatest poem…" –Walt Whitman
Demonstrative	• Singles out specific person(s), place(s), or thing(s)	this, that, these, those
Relative	• Begins a subordinate clause and connects it to another idea in the sentence	that, which, who, whom, whose
Interrogative	• Begins a question	what, which, who, whom, whose
Indefinite	• Refers to a person, place, or thing that may or may not be specifically named	another, everyone, nobody, one, both, few, all, most, none

(Parts of Speech continued)

(continued)

Part of Speech	Definition	Examples
Verb	**Expresses time while showing an action, condition, or the fact that something exists**	
Action	• Tells what action someone or something is performing	gather, read, work, jump, imagine, analyze, conclude
Linking	• Connects the subject with another word that identifies or describes the subject	appear, be, become, feel, look, remain, sound, stay, taste
Helping	• Added to another verb to make a verb phrase	be, do, have, should, can, could, may
Adjective	**Used to describe a noun or pronoun or give it a more specific meaning**	*purple* hat, *happy* face, *this* bowl, *three* cars, *enough* food, *a loud* sound
Adverb	**Modifies a verb, an adjective, or another adverb by telling *where, when, how* or *to what extent***	will answer *soon, extremely* sad, calls *more* often
Preposition	**Relates a noun or pronoun that appears with it to another word in the sentence**	Dad made a meal *for* us. We talked *till* dusk. Bo missed school *because of* his illness.
Conjunction	**Connects words or groups of words**	
Coordinating	• Connects equal words or word groups	bread *and* cheese, brief *but* powerful
Correlative	• Used in pairs to connect equal words or word groups	*both* Luis *and* Rosa, neither you nor I
Subordinating	• Indicates the connection between two ideas by placing one below the other in rank or importance	We will miss her *if* she leaves. Hank shrieked *when* he slipped on the ice.
Interjection	**Expresses feeling or emotion**	ah, hey, ouch, well, yippee

Phrases and Clauses

Phrases A **phrase** is a group of words that does not have a subject and verb and that functions as one part of speech.

Prepositional Phrases A **prepositional phrase** is a group of words that includes a preposition and a noun or pronoun.

    before dawn   **as a result of** the rain

An **adjective phrase** is a prepositional phrase that modifies a noun or pronoun.

    Eliza appreciates the beauty of a well-crafted poem.

An **adverb phrase** is a prepositional phrase that modifies a verb, an adjective, or an adverb.

    She reads Spenser's sonnets **with great pleasure.**

Appositive Phrases An **appositive phrase** is a noun or pronoun with modifiers, placed next to a noun or pronoun to add information.

    Mr. Roth, **my music teacher,** is sick.

Verbal Phrases A **participial phrase** is a participle that is modified by an adverb or an adverb phrase or that has a complement. The entire phase acts as an adjective.

    Jenna's backpack, **loaded with equipment,** was heavy.

A **gerund** is a noun formed from the present participle of a verb (ending in *–ing*). A **gerund phrase** is a gerund with modifiers or a complement, all acting together as a noun.

Taking photographs of wildlife **is her main hobby.**

An **infinitive phrase** is an infinitive with modifiers, complements, or a subject, all acting together as a single part of speech.

She tries **to get out into the wilderness often.**

Clauses A **clause** is a group of words with its own subject and verb.

Independent Clauses An independent clause can stand by itself as a complete sentence.

George Orwell wrote with extraordinary insight.

Subordinate Clauses A subordinate clause cannot stand by itself as a complete sentence.

George Orwell, **who wrote with extraordinary insight,** produced many politically relevant works.

An **adjective clause** is a subordinate clause that modifies a noun or pronoun by telling *what kind* or *which one*.

"The Lamb" is the poem **that I memorized for class.**

An **adverb clause** is a subordinate clause that modifies a verb, an adjective, an adverb, or a verbal by telling *where, when, in what way, to what extent, under what condition,* or *why*.

When I recited the poem, Mr. Lopez was impressed.

A **noun clause** is a subordinate clause that acts as a noun.

William Blake survived on **whatever he made as an engraver.**

Sentence Structure

Subject and Predicate A **sentence** is a group of words with two main parts: a *subject* and a *predicate*. Together, these parts express a complete thought.

The **complete subject** tells *whom* or *what* the sentence is about. The **complete predicate** tells what the complete subject of the sentence does or is.

    Complete Subject   **Complete Predicate**

    Both of those girls | have already read *Macbeth*.

The **simple subject** is the essential noun, pronoun, or group of words acting as a noun that cannot be left out of the complete subject. The **simple predicate** is the essential verb or verb phrase that cannot be left out of the complete predicate.

    Simple Subject   **Simple Predicate**

    Both of those girls | **have** already **read** *Macbeth*.

Complements A **complement** is a word or word group that completes the meaning of the predicate. There are five kinds of complements: *direct objects, indirect objects, objective complements, predicate nominatives,* and *predicate adjectives*.

A **direct object** is a noun, a pronoun, or a group of words acting as a noun that receives the action of a transitive verb.

Joseph Addison held important political **posts.**

An **indirect object** is a noun or pronoun that appears with a direct object and names the person or thing that something is given to or done for.

Oxford awarded **Samuel Johnson** an honorary degree. [The direct object is *degree.*]

An **objective complement** is an adjective or noun that appears with a direct object and describes or renames it.

Many consider Shakespeare the greatest **playwright.** [The direct object is *Shakespeare.*]

A **predicate nominative** is a noun or pronoun that appears with a linking verb and tells something about the subject.

"A Modest Proposal" is a **pamphlet.**

A **predicate adjective** is an adjective that appears with a linking verb and describes the subject of the sentence.

"A Modest Proposal" is **satirical.**

Classifying Sentences by Structure

Sentences are often classified according to the kind and number of clauses they contain. The four basic sentence structures are *simple, compound, complex,* and *compound-complex*.

A **simple sentence** consists of one independent clause.

Terrence enjoys modern British literature.

A **compound sentence** consists or two or more independent clauses.

Terrence enjoys modern British literature, but his brother prefers the classics.

A **complex sentence** consists of one independent clause and one or more subordinate clauses.

Terrence, who reads voraciously, enjoys modern British literature.

A **compound-complex sentence** consists of two or more independent clauses and one or more subordinate clauses.

Terrence, who reads voraciously, enjoys modern British literature, but his brother prefers the classics.

Paragraph Structure

An effective paragraph is organized around one **main idea,** which is often stated in a **topic sentence.** The other sentences support the main idea. To give the paragraph **unity,** make sure the connection between each sentence and the main idea is clear.

Usage

Lessons throughout your literature book will help you with many usage problems. See Unit 1 for help with **using coordinating conjunctions** (p. 67) and **using correlative conjunctions** (p. 154). See Unit 2 for help with **using subordinating conjunctions** (p.263) and **using adjective and adverb clauses** (p. 419). In Unit 3 you will find lessons on **comparative and superlative adjectives** and **adverbs** (p. 493), **using participles, gerunds,** and **infinitives** (p. 503), and **misplaced and dangling modifiers** (p. 539). Unit 4 has lessons on the following topics: **introductory phrases** and **clauses** (p. 755), **subject-verb agreement problems** (p. 767), and **pronoun-antecedent agreement problems** (p. 795). See Unit 5 for help with **avoiding shifts in verb tense** (p. 1009) and **using active, not passive, voice** (p. 1085). Go to Unit 6 for lessons on **sentence fragments** and **run-ons** (p. 1151), **transitional expressions** (p. 1169), **using parallel structure** (p. 1207), and **creating sentence variety** (p. 1339).

Unintended Shift in Person

Do not change needlessly from one person to another. Keep the person consistent in your sentences.

Max went to the bakery, but *you* can't buy mints there. [shift from third person to second person]

Max went to the bakery, but **he** can't buy mints there. [consistent]

Modifier Placement

To avoid confusion, a modifying word, phrase, or clause should be placed as close as possible to the word or words it is supposed to modify.

My cousin has a ferret **who works in a pet store.** [misplaced modifier]

My cousin, **who works in a pet store,** has a ferret. [correct placement]

Agreement

Subject and Verb Agreement

A singular subject must have a singular verb. A plural subject must have a plural verb.

Dr. Boone uses a telescope to view the night sky.

The **students use** a telescope to view the night sky.

A phrase or clause that comes between a subject and verb does not affect subject-verb agreement.

His **theory,** as well as his claims, **lacks** support.

Two subjects joined by *and* usually take a plural verb.

The **dog** and the **cats are** healthy.

Two singular subject joined by *or* or *nor* must have a singular verb.

The **dog** or the **cat is** hiding.

Two plural subjects joined by *or* or *nor* must have a plural verb.

The **dogs** and the **cats are** coming home with us.

Pronoun and Antecedent Agreement

Pronouns must agree with their antecedents in number and gender. Use singular pronouns with singular antecedents and plural pronouns with plural antecedents.

Doris Lessing uses **her** writing to challenge ideas about women's roles.

Writers often use **their** skills to effect social change.

Use a singular pronoun when the antecedent is a singular indefinite pronoun such as *anybody, each, either, everybody, neither, no one, one,* or *someone.*

Judge **each** of the articles on **its** merits.

Use a plural pronoun when the antecedent is a plural indefinite pronoun (*both, few, many,* or *several*).

Both of the articles have **their** flaws.

The indefinite pronouns *all, any, more, most, none,* and *some* can be singular or plural depending on the number of the word to which they refer.

Most of the books are in **their** proper places.

Most of the *book* has been torn from **its** binding.

Using Verbs

Principal Parts of Regular and Irregular Verbs

A verb has four principal parts:

Present	Present Participle	Past	Past Participle
learn	learning	learned	learned
discuss	discussing	discussed	discussed
stand	standing	stood	stood
begin	beginning	began	begun

Regular verbs such as *learn* and *discuss* form the past and past participle by adding *–ed* to the present form. **Irregular verbs** such as *stand* and *begin* form the past and past participle in other ways. If you are in doubt about the principal parts of an irregular verb, check a dictionary.

The Tenses of Verbs

The different tenses of verbs indicate the time an action or condition occurred.

The **present tense** is most often used to show one of the following:

Present action or condition:	Jamal **hikes** to the lake. The sky **is** clear.
Regularly occurring action or condition:	Tourists **flock** to the site yearly. **I am** usually tired by 9:00.
Constant action or condition:	The earth **orbits** the sun. Pets **are** good for our health.

The **past tense** is used to express a completed action or condition.

The squirrel **dropped** the nut and **ran** up the tree.

The **present perfect tense** is used to express (1) an action or condition that happened at an indefinite time in the past or (2) an action or condition from the past that is continuing into the present.

We **have seen** improvements in the neighborhood.

The puppy **has been** under the bed all day.

The **past perfect tense** shows an action or condition completed before another past action or condition.

Gerard **had revised** his essay before he turned it in.

The **future tense** is used to show a future action or condition.

The Glazers **will visit** us tomorrow.

The future perfect tense is used to show a future action or condition that is completed before another future action or condition.

Mimi **will have painted** the kitchen by the time we finish the shutters.

Using Modifiers

Degrees of Comparison

Adjectives and adverbs take different forms to show the three degrees of comparison: the *positive*, the *comparative*, and the *superlative*.

Positive	Comparative	Superlative
fast	faster	fastest
crafty	craftier	craftiest
abruptly	more abruptly	most abruptly
badly	worse	worst
much	more	most

Using Comparative and Superlative Adjectives and Adverbs

Use comparative adjectives and adverbs to compare two things. Use superlative adjectives and adverbs to compare three or more things.

Jake practices **more often** than Jamal.

Of everyone in the band, Jake practices **most often.**

Using Pronouns

Pronoun Case

The **case** of a pronoun is the form it takes to show its use in a sentence. There are three pronoun cases: *nominative*, *objective*, and *possessive*.

Nominative	Objective	Possessive
I, you, he, she, it, we, you, they	me, you, him, her, it, us, you, them	my, your, his, her, its, our, their, mine, yours, his, hers, its, ours, theirs

Use the **nominative case** for the *subject* or for a *predicate nominative*.

They are going to the movies. [subject]

The biggest movie fan is **she.** [predicate nominative]

Use the **objective case** for a *direct object*, an *indirect object*, or the *object of a preposition*.

The ending of the play surprised **me.** [direct object]

Mary gave **us** two tickets to the play. [indirect object]

The audience cheered for **him.** [object of preposition]

The **possessive case** is used to show ownership.

The red suitcase is **hers.**

Commonly Confused Words

Diction refers to word choice. The words you choose contribute to the overall effectiveness of your writing. One aspect of diction has to do with choosing between commonly confused words, such as the pairs listed below.

amount, number

Amount refers to quantity or a unit. *Number* refers to individual items that can be counted.

The **amount** of attention that great writers have paid to Faust is remarkable.

A **number** of important English writers have been fascinated by the legend of King Arthur.

bad, badly

Use bad after a linking verb such as *feel, look,* or *seem.* Use *badly* when an adverb is required.

> In "My Last Duchess," the duke does not seem to feel **bad** about the death of his wife.
>
> The announcement of Lady Macbeth's death **badly** unnerves Macbeth.

fewer, less

Use *fewer* for things that can be counted. Use *less* for amounts of quantities that cannot be counted.

> Wordsworth uses **fewer** end-stopped lines than Pope does.
>
> The prodigal son shows **less** respect for the father than the older son does.

lay, lie

Lay is a transitive verb meaning "to set or put something down." Its principal parts are *lay, laying, laid, laid. Lie* is an intransitive verb meaning "to recline." Its principal parts are *lie, lying, lay, lain.*

> Coleridge implies that the mariner's reckless act of killing the albatross **lays** a curse on the crew.
>
> By the end of D.H. Lawrence's story, Paul **lies** dead.

who, whom

Remember to use *who* only as a subject in clauses and sentences and *whom* only as an object.

> V.S. Naipaul, **who** wrote "B. Wordsworth," has also written some well-received novels.
>
> V.S. Naipaul, **whom** many critics have praised as one of the best contemporary writers in English, was born and raised in Trinidad.

Editing For English Language Conventions

Capitalization

First Words

Capitalize the first word of a sentence.

> **S**tories about knights and their deeds interest me.

Capitalize the first word of a direct quotation.

> **S**haron asked, "**D**o you like stories about knights?"

Proper Nouns and Proper Adjectives

Capitalize all proper nouns.

> **T**hames **R**iver   **J**ohn **K**eats   the **R**enaissance

Capitalize all proper adjectives.

> **S**hakespearean play   **D**anish invaders
> **E**lizabethan period   **B**ritish literature

Academic Course Names

Capitalize course names only if they are language courses, are followed by a number, or are preceded by a proper noun or adjective.

> **S**panish   **H**onors Chemistry   **H**istory 101
> **g**eology   **a**lgebra   **s**ocial **s**tudies

Titles

Capitalize titles showing family relationships when they refer to a specific person unless they are preceded by a possessive noun or pronoun.

> **U**ncle Oscar   Mangan's **s**ister   his **a**unt Tessa

Capitalize the first word and all other key words in the titles of books, stories, songs, and other works of art.

> *Frankenstein*   "**S**hooting an **E**lephant"

Punctuation

End Marks

Use a **period** to end a declarative sentence or an imperative sentence.

> We are studying the structure of sonnets.
>
> Read the biography of Mary Shelley.

Use periods with abbreviations.

> D.H. Lawrence   Mrs. Browning

Use a **question mark** to end an interrogative sentence.

> What is Macbeth's fatal flaw**?**

Use an **exclamation mark** after an exclamatory sentence or a forceful imperative sentence.

> That's a beautiful painting**!**   Let me go now**!**

Commas

Use a **comma** before the conjunction to separate two independent clauses in a compound sentence.

> The game was very close**,** but we were victorious.

Use commas to separate three or more words, phrases, or clauses in a series.

> William Blake was a writer**,** artist**,** and printer.

Use a comma after an introductory word, phrase, or clause.

> When Grendel was killed**,** his mother sought revenge.

Use commas to set off nonessential expressions.

> Old English**,** of course**,** requires translation.

Use commas with places and dates.

> Coventry**,** England   September 1**,** 1939

Semicolons

Use a **semicolon** to join closely related independent clauses that are not already joined by a conjunction.

> Tanya likes to write poetry; Heather prefers prose.

Use semicolons to avoid confusion when items in a series contain commas.

> They traveled to London, England; Madrid, Spain; and Rome, Italy.

Colons

Use a **colon** before a list of items following an independent clause.

> Notable Victorian poets include the following: Tennyson, Arnold, Housman, and Hopkins.

Use a colon to introduce an independent clause that summarizes or explains the sentence before it.

> Malcolm loves volunteering: He reads to sick children every Saturday afternoon.

Quotation Marks

Use **quotation marks** to enclose a direct quotation.

> "Short stories," Ms. Hildebrand said, "should have rich, well-developed characters."

An **indirect quotation** does not require quotation marks.

> Ms. Hildebrand said that short stories should have well-developed characters.

Use quotation marks around the titles of short written works, episodes in a series, songs, and titles of works mentioned as parts of collections.

> "The Lagoon"   "Boswell Meets Johnson"

Italics

Italicize the titles of long written works, movies, television and radio shows, lengthy works of music, paintings, and sculptures.

> *Howards End*   *60 Minutes*   *Guernica*

For handwritten material, you can use underlining instead of italics.

> The Princess Bride   Mona Lisa

Dashes

Use **dashes** to indicate an abrupt change of thought, a dramatic interrupting idea, or a summary statement.

> I read the entire first act of *Macbeth*—you won't believe this—in less than an hour.

Parentheses

Use **parentheses** to set off asides and explanations when the material is not essential or when it consists of one or more sentences.

> He listened intently (it was too dark to see who was speaking) to try to identify the voices.

In the example above, the sentence in parentheses interrupts the larger sentence, so it does not have a capital letter and a period. When a sentence in parentheses falls between two other complete sentences, it should start with a capital letter and end with a period.

> The quarterback threw three touchdown passes. (**W**e knew he could do it.) Our team won the game by two points.

Apostrophes

Add an **apostrophe** and an *s* to show the possessive case of most singular nouns and of plural nouns that do not end in *–s* or *–es*.

> Blake's poems   the mice's whiskers

Names ending in *s* form their possessives in the same way, except for classical and biblical names, which add only an apostrophe to form the possessive.

> Dickens's   Hercules'

Add an apostrophe to show the possessive case of plural nouns ending in *–s* and *–es*.

> the girls' songs   the Ortizes' car

Use an apostrophe in a contraction to indicate the position of the missing letter or letters.

> She's never read a Coleridge poem she didn't like.

Brackets

Use **brackets** to enclose a word or words you insert in a quotation when you are quoting someone else.

> Use brackets to enclose a word or words you insert in a quotation when you are quoting someone else.
> Arthur C. Clarke writes about changes in travel: "Over the seas where Odysseus wandered for a decade, the Rome-Beirut Comet [an airplane] whispers its way within the hour."

Ellipses

Use three **ellipses** to indicate where you have omitted words from quoted material.

> Wollestonecraft wrote, "The education of women has of late been more attended to than formerly; yet they are still . . . ridiculed or pitied . . . ."

In the example above, the four dots at the end of the sentence are the three ellipses plus the period from the original sentence.

Spelling

Spelling Rules

Learning the rules of English spelling will help you make **generalizations** about how to spell words.

Rules for Spelling with Word Parts

The three word parts that can combine to form a word are roots, prefixes, and suffixes. Many of these word parts come from the Greek, Latin, and Anglo-Saxon languages.

The **root word** carries a word's basic meaning.

Root and Origin	Meaning	Examples
-leg- (-log-) [Gr.]	to say, speak	*leg*al, *log*ic
-pon- (-pos-) [L.]	to put, place	post*pone*, de*pos*it

A **prefix** is one or more syllables at the beginning of a word. A prefix adds to the meaning of the root.

Prefix and Origin	Meaning	Examples
anti- [Gr.]	against	*anti*pathy
inter- [L.]	between	*inter*national
mis- [A.S.]	wrong	*mis*place

A **suffix** is added to the end of a root word and can change the word's meaning or part of speech.

Suffix and Origin	Meaning	Part of Speech
-ful [A.S.]	full of: scorn*ful*	adjective
-ity [L.]	state of being: advers*ity*	noun
-ize (-ise) [Gr.]	to make: idol*ize*	verb
-ly [A.S.]	in a manner: calm*ly*	adverb

Rules for Adding Suffixes to Root Words

When adding a suffix to a root word ending in *y* preceded by a consonant, change *y* to *i* unless the suffix begins with *i*.

ply + -able = pliable   happy + -ness = happiness
defy + -ing = defying   cry + -ing = crying

For a root word ending in *e*, drop the *e* when adding a suffix beginning with a vowel.

drive + -ing = driving   move + -able = movable
SOME EXCEPTIONS: traceable, seeing, dyeing

For root words ending with a consonant + vowel + consonant in a stressed syllable, double the final consonant when adding a suffix that begins with a vowel.

mud + -y = muddy   submit + -ed = submitted
SOME EXCEPTIONS: mixing, reference

Rules for Adding Prefixes to Root Words

When a prefix is added to a root word, the spelling of the root remains the same.

un- + certain = uncertain   mis- + spell = misspell

With some prefixes, the spelling of the prefix changes when joined to the root to make the pronunciation easier.

in- + mortal = immortal   ad- + vert = avert

Orthographic Patterns

Certain letter combinations in English make certain sounds. For instance, *ph* sounds like *f, eigh* usually makes a long *a* sound, and the *k* before an *n* is often silent.

pharmacy   n**eigh**bor   ac**k**nowledge

Understanding **orthographic patterns** such as these can help you improve your spelling.

Forming Plurals

The plural form of most nouns is formed by adding *–s* or *–es* to the singular.

computer**s**   gadget**s**   Washington**s**

For words ending in *s, ss, x, z, sh, ch*, add *–es*.

circus**es**   tax**es**   wish**es**   bench**es**

For words ending in *y* or *o* preceded by a vowel, add *–s*.

key**s**   patio**s**

For words ending in *y* preceded by a consonant, change the *y* to an *i* and add *–es*.

cit**ies**   enem**ies**   troph**ies**

For most words ending in *o* preceded by consonant, add *–es*.

echo**es**   tomato**es**

Some words form the plural in irregular ways.

oxen   children   teeth   deer

Foreign Words Used in English

Some words used in English are actually foreign words we have adopted. Learning to spell these words requires memorization. When in doubt, check a dictionary.

sushi   enchilada   au pair   fiancé
laissez faire   croissant

Index of Authors and Titles

Note: Page numbers in *italics* refer to biographical information for authors, or commentary on titles or literary and historical issues. Nonfiction and informational text appears in red.

Index of Skills

Reading for Information

Analyzing Functional and Expository Texts

Primary Sources

Reading Strategies

Vocabulary

Essential Question Vocabulary

Grammar, Usage and Mechanics

Thesaurus, 152, 224, **R14**

Topic sentence, **R60**

Transitional expression, 1339

Verb, **R61–62**

Verb tense, 1009

Verb phrase, **R59–60**

Verbs, active/passive voice, 1085

Vocabulary of tragedy, 417

Word Analysis

Etymology study
   allocation, 1294
   anatomize, 793
   concord, 290
   gall, 271
   magistrate, 580
   orthodox, 908
   ransacked, 212

Prefixes
   ab-, 704
   ad-, 704
   an-, 704
   anthrop-, 930
   apo-, 136
   bio-, 930
   con-, 492
   cosmo-, 930
   dis-, 597
   epi-, 930
   equi-, 930
   ex-, 704
   geo-, 930
   mal-, 377
   mono-, 1007
   pro-, 704
   pseudo-, 930
   quadr-, 930
   syn, 704
   thermo-, 930
   un-, 1270

Roots
   -angle-, 930
   -arch-, 704
   -archy-, 1150
   -atomos-, 793
   -chron-, 280
   -cred-, 398
   -derma-, 930
   -dict-, 663, 704
   -doc-, 704
   -doxa-, 908
   -droit-, 197
   -fil-, 1431
   -fract-, 1168
   -ghast-, 1279
   -ghost-, 1279
   -jec-, 627
   -journ-, 851
   -jud-, 704
   -jur-, 704
   -lum-, 537
   -morph-, 930
   -ortho-, 908
   -patron-, 1357
   -photo-, 930

-pod-, 930
-puls-, 879
-sol-, 66
-sphere-, 930
-spir-, 754
-stat-, 306
-stell-, 930
-terr(a)-, 1084
top-, 1186
-trans-, 1205
-turb-, 417
-urbs-, 704
-ven-, 704
-vinc-, 1243
-voc-, 359

Suffixes
   -al, 930
   -an, 704
   -ar, 930
   -ate, 704
   -ation, 704
   -dom, 704
   -ence, 988
   -ic, 930
   -ity, 704
   -logy, 930
   -meter, 930
   -oid, 930
   -ous, 865
   -phobia, 930
   -some, 745
   -tion, 121
   -ty, 704, 930
   -y, 704

Word-phrase relationships, 1051

Writing Applications

Absurd drama scene, 1387

Analytical essay
   archetypal images, 398
   Timed Writing, 291, 1295

Argument, lxx, lxxi

Autobiographical narrative, 766
   Professional Model (Raffel), 217
   Student Model, 220
   Workshop, 214

Biographical essay, 975, 1480

Biographical narrative plan, 492

Biographical sketch, 1357

Blog, 121

Business letter, **R38**

Business memo, 89, **R39**

College application essay, **R34**

Compare-and-contrast essay
   epic settings, 551
   perspectives on home, 226
   reply poems, 271
   social criticism, 1021
   stream of consciousness, 1215
   Timed Writing, 909

Cover letter, **R35**

Critical essay, Timed Writing, 581

Directions for reciting a poem, 676

Editorial, 32, 663

E-mail, 919, **R40**

Essential Question response
   How does literature shape or reflect
      society? 38, 95, 123, 137, 213, 226, 291,
      296, 552, 558, 604, 628, 680, 732, 746,
      866, 909, 910, 958, 997, 1028
   What is the relationship between literature
      and place? 18, 82, 264, 581, 588, 664,
      818, 852, 1040, 1072
   What is the relationship of the writer to
      tradition? 252, 272, 321, 480, 494, 504,
      521, 646, 758, 779, 880, 976, 1086,
      1358, 1444

Expository essay, Essential Question
   response, 213

Historical investigation
   annotated bibliography, 1008
   Professional Model, 1101
   Student Model, 1104
   Workshop, 1096

Interior monologue, 197, 865

Introduction to a radio spot, 1415

Job application, 66, **R37**

Letter of recommendation, 1095

Letter to the editor, 685

Liner notes for a recorded song, 1467

Literary analysis, 706

Magazine advertisement, 1443

Manual for writing sonnets, 262

Meeting minutes, **R41**

Memo, 557, 1315

Mock-heroic poem, 645

Multi-genre analysis, 754

Multi-genre response, 1168

Multimedia presentation
   Professional Model (McCracken), 923
   Student Model, 926
   Workshop, 694

Multimedia presentation plan, 627

News story, 67

Objective summary, lvi, lvii

Parable, 306

Parody, 1399

Persuasive essay, 1112
   Professional Model (Kermode), 445
   Student Model, 448
   Timed Writing, 441, 713, 1027
   Workshop, 442

Persuasive sermon, 136

Persuasive speech, 745

Poem, 1186

Position statement, Timed Writing, 233, 461,
   939, 1487

Problem-and-solution essay, 1338

Public service announcement, 514

Reflective composition, 932

Writing Strategies

Prewriting

Drafting

Revising

More Skills . . .

Test-Taking Practice

Grammar

ACT: English Test, 228, 708, 1114
SAT: Writing, Identifying Sentence Errors, 456
SAT: Writing, Improving Paragraphs, 1482
SAT: Writing, Improving Sentences, 934

Reading

ACT: Natural Science Reading, 226
ACT: Reading Test, Humanities, 706
ACT: Reading Test, Prose Fiction, 1112
SAT: Critical Reading, Long Reading
Passages, 932
SAT: Critical Reading, Paired Passages, 454
SAT: Critical Reading, Short Reading
Passages, 1480

Timed writing:

ACT: Position Statement, 229, 1115
ACT: Persuasive Essay, 709
SAT: Position Statement, 457, 935

Vocabulary in context

SAT: Critical Reading, Sentence Completion,
225, 453, 705, 931, 1111
SAT: Reading Comprehension, Sentence
Completion, 1479

Index of Features

Acknowledgments

Grateful acknowledgment is made to the following for copyrighted material:

Aitken Alexander Associates Ltd "B. Wordsworth" from *Miguel Street* by V. S. Naipaul. Copyright © 1959 by V. S. Naipaul. Used with permission of Aitken Alexander Associates Limited.

Anvil Press Poetry Ltd. "Prayer" from *Mean Time* by Carol Ann Duffy. Published by Anvil Press Poetry in 1993. Copyright © Carol Ann Duffy, 1985, 1987, 1990, 1993, 1994. Used by permission of Anvil Press Poetry.

Georges Borchardt, Inc. From "Disappearing Act" by John Lahr from *The New Yorker*, February 12, 2007. Used by permission of Georges Borchardt, Inc.

Professor Geoffrey Bownas "When I went to visit" by Ki Tsurayuki, "Was it that I went to sleep" by Ono Kamachi, "Once cannot ask loneliness" by Priest Jakuren. Copyright © 1964 by Penguin Books, revised edition 1998. Translation copyright © Geoffrey Bownas and Anthony Thwaite, 1964, 1998. Used by permission of Geoffrey Bownas.

Broadway Video "Where's Frankenstein" from a *Saturday Night Live* episode that originally aired on October 28, 2006, hosted by Hugh Laurie. Copyright © 2006 NBC Studios, Inc. Distributed by Broadway Video Enterprises. Courtesy of Broadway Video Enterprises and NBC Studios, Inc.

Curtis Brown London "Be Ye Men of Valor" (retitled "Wartime Speech"), BBC London, May 19, 1940, from *Blood, Toil, Tears and Sweat: The Speeches of Winston Churchill* edited and with an introduction by David Cannadine. Speeches Copyright © 1989 by Winston Churchill. Used courtesy of Curtis Brown Ltd. on behalf of The Estate of Winston Churchill.

California State Parks Jack London State Historic Park brochure, copyright © 2001 California State Parks. Used by permission of California State Parks.

Cambridge University Press, NY Excerpt from "Letter to Thomas Flower Ellis from Thomas Babington Macaulay on the Passing of the Reform Bill" written in 1831, from *The Selected Letters of Thomas Babington Macaulay,* ed. Thomas Pinney, 5 vols. Used with the permission of Cambridge University Press.

Citysearch.com "A Thoughtful, Poignant, and Chilling Macbeth" October 7, 1999 from *www.shakespearefest.org/macbeth_99.htm#Reviews.* Copyright © Citysearch.com. Citysearch is a registered trademark of Bluefoot Ventures, Inc. and is used under license. Used by permission of Citysearch.com.

Arthur C. Clarke "Extra-Terrestrial Relays" by Arthur C. Clarke from *Wireless World,* October 1945, pp 305-308 © 1945. Used by permission of the author and the author's agents, Scovil Chichak Galen Literary Agency, Inc.

Jonathan Clowes Ltd. "No Witchcraft for Sale," from *African Short Stories* by Doris Lessing. Copyright © 1981 Doris Lessing. Used by kind permission of Jonathan Clowes, Ltd., London, on behalf of Doris Lessing.

Copyright Clearance Center, Inc. for Hearst Communications, Inc. 'Kingdom of Desire' a sensual 'Macbeth' remake Peking opera style" by Robert Hurwitt from San Francisco Chronicle, May 23, 2005, *www.sfgate.com/cgi-bin/article.cgi?f=/c/a/2005/05/23/DDG9LCS1OH1.DTL&hw=kingdom+of+desire&sn=002&sc=981.* Copyright © 2005 by San Francisco Chronicle. Reproduced with permission of San Francisco Chronicle via Copyright Clearance Center.

Cumbria County Council Table of Traffic Flow at Waterhead, Ambleside. A591 from *Transport and Policies 1999/2000, and Local Transport Plan 2001/2–2005/6.* Copyright © Cumbria County Council. Used by permission of Cumbria County Council.

The Charles Dickens Museum Charles Dickens Museum in London Homepage & Online Tour retrieved from *http://www.dickensmuseum.com.* Copyright © 2005 Charles Dickens Museum. Reproduced courtesy of The Charles Dickens Museum, London.

Dorling Kindersley Ltd. "Lancashire and the Lakes" from *DK Eyewitness Travel Guides: Great Britain* by Michael Leapman. Copyright © 1995, 2001 Dorling Kindersley Limited, London. Reproduced by permission of Dorling Kindersley Ltd.

Dutton Signet From *Beowulf* by Burton Raffel, translator. Translation copyright © 1963, renewed © 1991 by Burton Raffel. Used by permission of Dutton Signet, a division of Penguin Group (USA) Inc.

Encyclopædia Britannica Search results: Anglo-Saxon Poetry from *http://search.eb.com/search?query=anglo+saxon+poetry&x=0&y=0.* "English Literature: The Old English Period: Poetry: The major manuscripts" from *http://search.eb.com/eb/article-12747.* Copyright © 2007 by Encyclopædia Britannica. Used with permission from Encyclopædia Britannica, Inc.

Faber and Faber Limited "Journey of the Magi" from *Collected Poems 1909–1962* by T. S. Eliot, copyright 1936, copyright © 1964, 1963 by T. S. Eliot. "The Horses" from *New Selected Poems* by Ted Hughes. Copyright © 1957, 1960 by Ted Hughes. Published in the UK in The Hawk in the Rain by Ted Hughes. "Follower" from *Poems 1965–1975* by Seamus Heaney. Copyright © 1980 by Seamus Heaney. "The Hollow Men" from *Collected Poems 1909–1962* by T. S. Eliot, copyright 1936 and renewed 1964, 1963 by T. S. Eliot. "Two Lorries" from *The Spirit Level* by Seamus Heaney. Copyright © 1996 by Seamus Heaney. "The Explosion" from *Collected Poems* by Philip Larkin. Copyright © 1988, 1989 by the Estate of Philip Larkin. "An Arundel Tomb" from *Collected Poems* by Philip Larkin. Copyright © 1988, 1989 by the Estate of Philip Larkin. "That's All" from *Complete Works: Three* by Harold Pinter. Copyright © 1966 by H. Pinter Ltd. "Not Palaces" by Stephen Spender. From *Collected Poems 1928–1985.* Copyright © 1986 by Stephen Spender. Copyright © 1934 by The Modern Library, Inc. and renewed 1962, 1964, 1986 by Stephen Spender. Used by permission of Faber and Faber.

Farrar, Straus & Giroux, LLC "Follower" from *Poems 1965–1975* by Seamus Heaney. Copyright © 1980 by Seamus Heaney. "The Horses" from *Collected Poems* by Ted Hughes. Copyright © 2003 by The Estate of Ted Hughes. "Two Lorries" from *The Spirit Level* by Seamus Heaney. Copyright © 1996 by Seamus Heaney. "The Explosion" from *Collected Poems* by Philip Larkin. Copyright © 1988, 1989 by the Estate of Philip Larkin. "An Arundel Tomb" from *Collected Poems* by Philip Larkin. Copyright © 1988, 1989 by the Estate of Philip Larkin. "Chapter XXVIII, Part I" from *Omeros* by Derek Walcott. Copyright © 1990 by Derek Walcott. "Midsummer XXIII" from *Collected Poems 1948–1984* by Derek Walcott. Copyright © 1986 by Derek Walcott. Used by permission of Farrar, Straus and Giroux, LLC.

Florida Department of Environmental Protection Marjorie Kinnan Rawlings Historic State Park Brochure from *http://www.floridastateparks.org/marjoriekinnanrawlings/docs/brochure.pdf.* Printed 02/07. Used by permission of Florida Department of Environmental Protection.

Fondo de Cultura Economica From *The Nine Guardians* by Rosario Castellanos, translated by Irene Nicholson. Balún Canán de Rosario Castellanos. D.R. © 1957 Fondo de Cultura Economica. Carretera Picacho-Ajusco 227, C.P. 14200, Mexico, D.F. Used by permission of Fondo de Cultura Económica.

Professor Norman Gash "The case for parliamentary reform: 1831: Lord John Russell: 1 March 1831" by Lord John Russell from *The Age of Peel* by Norman Gash (London, Edward Arnold, 1973) *www.dialspace.dial.pipex.com/town/terrace/adw03/peel/refact/refbill.htm.* Copyright © Norman Gash. "A conservative criticism of parliamentary reform: 1831" by Sir Robert Peel, 2nd Baronet from *The Age of Peel* by Norman Gash (London, Edward Arnold, 1973) *www.dialspace.dial.pipex.com/town/terrace/adw03/peel/refact/refpeel.htm.* Copyright © Norman Gash. Used by permission of Norman Gash.

Greater London Authority From *The Mayor's Annual Report 2004* from *http://www.london.gov.uk/mayor/annual_report/docs/ann_rpt_2004.pdf.* Copyright April 2004, Greater London Authority. Used by permission.

Grove/Atlantic, Inc. "That's All" from *Complete Works: Three* by Harold Pinter. Copyright © 1966 by H. Pinter Ltd. "Come and Go" from Collected Shorter Plays by Samuel Beckett. Copyright © 1968, 1984 by Samuel Beckett. "Next Term We'll Mash You" from *Pack of Cards* by Penelope Lively. Copyright © 1978, 1980 1981, 1982, 1984, 1985, 1986 by Penelope Lively. Used by permission of Grove/Atlantic, Inc.

Grove/Atlantic, Inc. From *Pedro Paramo* by Juan Rulfo, translated by Margaret Sayers Peden. Originally published in Mexico in 1955. English translation by Margaret Sayers Peden. Copyright © 1994 by Northwestern University Press.

J.C. Hall "Vergissmeinnicht" by Keith Douglas from *The Complete Poems of Keith Douglas,* Faber and Faber Ltd. Used by permission of Faber and Faber Ltd. and J.C. Hall.

Harcourt, Inc. Excerpt from *Mrs. Dalloway* by Virginia Woolf, copyright 1925 by Harcourt, Inc. and renewed 1953 by Leonard Woolf. Used by permission of the publisher. "The Hollow Men" from Collected Poems 1909–1962 by T. S. Eliot, copyright 1936 by Harcourt, Inc. and renewed 1964 by T. S. Eliot. "The Lady in the Looking Glass: A Reflection" from *A Haunted House and Other Short Stories* by Virginia Woolf, copyright 1944 and renewed 1972 by Harcourt, Inc. "Shooting an Elephant" from *Shooting an Elephant and Other Essays* by George Orwell, copyright 1950 by Sonia Brownell Orwell and renewed 1978 by Sonia Pitt-Rivers. "Journey of the Magi" from *Collected Poems 1909–1962* by T. S. Eliot, copyright 1936 by Harcourt Brace & Company, copyright © 1964, 1963 by T. S. Eliot. "Charles Baudelaire: L'Invitation au Voyage" from *Things of This World,* copyright © 1956 and renewed 1984 by Richard Wilbur. From A Room of One's Own by Virginia Woolf, copyright 1929 by Harcourt, Inc. and renewed 1957 by Leonard Woolf. Used by permission of the publisher. This material may not be reproduced in any form or by any means without the prior written permission of the publisher.

HarperCollins Publishers, Inc. "A Devoted Son" from *Games at Twilight and Other Stories* by Anita Desai. Copyright © 1978 by Anita Desai. Used by permission of HarperCollins Publishers, Inc.

HarperCollins Publishers, Ltd. UK "Post-Script: For Gweno" from *Raiders' Dawn and Other Poems* by Alun Lewis. First published in March, 1942. Second Impression June, 1942. Third Impression August, 1942. Fourth Impression October, 1943. Fifth Impression 1945. Reprinted 1946. Copyright © Alun Lewis. Used by permission of HarperCollins Publishers Ltd.

A.M. Heath & Company Limited "Shooting an Elephant" from *Shooting an Elephant and Other Essays* by George Orwell. Copyright © George Orwell, 1936. Used by permission of Bill Hamilton as the Literary Executor of the Estate of the Late Sonia Brownell Orwell and Secker & Warburg Ltd.

David Higham Associates Limited "On the Patio" from *Poems 1954–1987* by Peter Redgrove. Copyright © Peter Redgrove, 1959, 1961, 1963, 1966, 1972, 1973, 1975, 1977, 1979, 1981, 1985, 1986, 1987. "A Shocking Accident" from *Collected Stories of Graham Greene* by Graham Greene. Copyright © 1957 by Graham Greene. "In the Kitchen" from *Redgrove's Wife* by Penelope Shuttle. First published 2006 by Bloodaxe Books Ltd. Copyright © Penelope Shuttle 2006. "from Faust" from *Goethe's Faust: Parts I and II* by Louis Macneice. Originally published by Faber and Faber Limited. "Next Term We'll Mash You" from Pack of Cards by Penelope Lively. Copyright © 1978, 1980 1981, 1982, 1984, 1985, 1986 by Penelope Lively. Used by permission of David Higham Associates.

Hughes Network Systems, LLC "Satellite Network Keeps Florida Communicating During Emergencies" from *http://www.hughes.com/HUGHES/Doc/0/P6K0209FS0KK3E3H417TPTVSD6/florida_emergency.pdf.* Used by permission of Hughes Network Systems, LLC, www.hughes.com.

Johnson & Alcock Ltd. (formerly John Johnson Ltd.) "I have visited again" by Alexander Pushkin. Copyright © *The Bronze Horseman: Selected Poems of Alexander Pushkin,* translated by D.M. Thomas, Secker & Warburg UK 1981/Viking US 1982. Used by permission of Johnson & Alcock Ltd.

Alfred A. Knopf, Inc. "The Demon Lover" from *The Collected Stories of Elizabeth Bowen* by Elizabeth Bowen, copyright © 1981 by Curtis Brown Ltd., Literary Executors of the Estate of Elizabeth Bowen. Used by permission of Alfred A. Knopf, a division of Random House, Inc.

Lake District National Park Authority Education Service Tracking Management from *Education Service Traffic Management.* Copyright © Lake District National Park Authority. Used by permission of Lake District National Park Authority.

Barbara Levy Literary Agency "Wirers" from *Collected Poems Of Siegfried Sasson* by Siegfried Sassoon, copyright 1918, 1920 by E. P. Dutton. Used by kind permission of George Sassoon.

MARTA Metropolitan Atlanta Rapid Transit Authority Map and Schedule" from *www.itsmarta.com/getthere/schedules/index-rail.htm.* Copyright © 2004 MARTA. All rights reserved. Used by permission of MARTA.

Metropolitan Transportation Authority Go Metro Map and Metro Red Line East Schedule from *www.mta.net/riding_metro/riders_guide/planning_trip.htm.* Copyright © 2007 LACMTA. Used by permission of Metropolitan Transportation Authority.

Michelin Travel Publications "Tintern Abbey" by Staff from *The Green Guide.* Copyright © Michelin et Cie, proprietaires-editeurs. Used by permission of Michelin Travel Publications.

William Morrow & Company, Inc. From *Neverwhere* by Neil Gaiman. Copyright © 1996, 1997 by Neil Gaiman. Used by permission of HarperCollins Publishers.

NASA Johnson Space Center "Anticipating Earthquakes" by Patrick L. Barry from *www.nasa.gov/vision/earth/environment/earthquakes_prt.htm.* Copyright © National Aeronautics and Space Administration.

The National Archives of the UK "Government Evacuation Scheme (Source 1)" from *Learning Curve: The National Archives of the UK.* www.learningcurve.gov.uk/homefront/evacuation/britain/source1.htm. "The Interrogation of Don Lewes from Cordoba in Andalucia, Simplified Transcript (Source 4)" by from Learning Curve: The National Archives of the UK *www.learningcurve.gov.uk/snapshots/snapshot39/39_images_am/39_trans/SP63_1137Am4_pg1_simp.htm.*

New Beacon Books Ltd. "Time Removed" from *Fractured Circles* by James Berry, published by New Beacon Books Ltd. Copyright © 1979, James Berry. "Freedom" from *Fractured Circles* by James Berry, published by New Beacon Books Ltd. Copyright © 1979, James Berry. From "Lucy: Englan' Lady" from *Lucy's Letter and Loving* by James Berry. Copyright © 1982 by James Berry. First published by New Beacon Books Ltd. in 1982. Used by permission of New Beacon Books, Ltd

New Directions Publishing Corporation "Do Not Go Gentle Into That Good Night" by Dylan Thomas, from *The Poems of Dylan Thomas.* Copyright © 1952 by Dylan Thomas. "Anthem for Doomed Youth" by Wilfred Owen, from *The Collected Poems Of Wilfred Owen,* copyright © 1963 by Chatto & Windus, Ltd. "Jade Flower Palace" by Tu Fu, translated by Kenneth Rexroth from *One Hundred Poems from The Chinese.* Copyright © 1971 by Kenneth Rexroth. "Not Waving But Drowning" by Stevie Smith, from *Collected Poems of Stevie Smith,* copyright © 1972 by Stevie Smith. "Fern Hill" by Dylan Thomas, from *The Poems of Dylan Thomas,* copyright © 1945 by The Trustees for the Copyrights of Dylan Thomas. Used by permission of New Directions Publishing Corp.

The New York Times Agency c/o PARS International "The Scottish Play, Told With Sound and Fury and Puppets" by Lawrence Van Gelder from The New York Times Arts & Culture Section, 4/26/2007 Issue, Page E5, *http://theater2.nytimes.com/2007/04/26/theater/reviews/26macb.html?pagewanted=print. Copyright* © 2007 The New York Times. All rights reserved. Used by permission and protected by the Copyright Laws of the United States. The printing, copying, redistribution, or retransmission of the Material without express written permission is prohibited. www.nytimes.com.

W. W. Norton & Company, Inc. "Outside History" from *Outside History: Selected Poems, 1980–1990* by Eavan Boland. Copyright © 1990 by Eavan Boland. "The Inferno: Canto XXXIV", from *The Divine Comedy* by Dante Alighieri, translated by John Ciardi. Copyright 1954, 1957, 1959, 1960, 1961, 1965, 1967, 1970 by the Ciardi Family Publishing Trust. From *Sir Gawain And The Green Knight: A New Verse Translation* by Marie Borroff, translator. Copyright © 1967 by W.W. Norton & Company, Inc. Used by permission of W.W. Norton & Company, Inc.

The Flannery O'Connor-Andalusia Foundation Andalusia: Home of Flannery O'Connor brochure. Used courtesy of Flannery O'Connor-Andalusia Foundation.

Jen O'Leary "Weather in the Palm of Your Hand" by Jennifer O'Leary, University of Wisconsin-Madison Space Science and Engineering Center from *www.ssec.wisc.edu/media/features/jan10_06.htm*. Used by permission of the author.

Oxford University Press, Inc. "The Wanderer," from *An Anthology of Old English Poetry*, edited and translated by Charles W. Kennedy. Copyright © 1960 by Oxford University Press, Inc. Used by permission of Oxford University Press, Inc.

Oxford University Press, UK "The Naming of Parts," from *A Map of Verona* by Henry Reed, 1946, copyright © by Henry Reed. Used by permission of Oxford University Press, UK.

Oxford University Press, UK "To Lucasta, Going To the Wars" from *The Poems Of Richard Lovelace*, edited by C.H. Wilkinson, copyright © 1953. "To the Virgins, to Make Much of Time" from The Poems of Robert Herrick, edited by L.C. Martin.

Penguin Books Ltd., London "The Wife of Bath's Tale" from *The Canterbury Tales* by Geoffrey Chaucer, translated by Nevill Coghill (Penguin Classics 1951, Fourth revised edition 1977). Copyright 1951 by Nevill Coghill. Copyright © the Estate of Nevill Coghill, 1958, 1960, 1975, 1977. From *A History of The English Church and People* by Bede (pp 37-40), translated by Leo Sherley-Price, revised by R.E. Latham (Penguin Classics 1955, Revised edition 1968). Copyright © Leo Sherley-Price, 1955, 1968. "Prologue" from *The Canterbury Tales* by Geoffrey Chaucer, translated by Nevill Coghill (Penguin Classics 1951, Fourth revised edition 1977). Copyright 1951 by Nevill Coghill. Copyright © the Estate of Nevill Coghill, 1958, 1960, 1975, 1977. "Pardoner's Tale" from *The Canterbury Tales* by Geoffrey Chaucer, translated by Nevill Coghill (Penguin Classics 1951, Fourth revised edition 1977). Copyright 1951 by Nevill Coghill. Copyright © the Estate of Nevill Coghill, 1958, 1960, 1975, 1977. From *The Decameron* by Giovanni Boccaccio, translated with an introduction and notes by G. H. McWilliam (Penguin Classics 1972, Second Edition 1995). Copyright © G. H. McWilliam, 1972, 1995. "Next Term We'll Mash You" from Pack of Cards by Penelope Lively. Copyright © 1978, 1980 1981, 1982, 1984, 1985, 1986 by Penelope Lively. Used by permission of Penguin Group Ltd., UK.

Random House, Inc. "In Memory of W. B. Yeats", copyright 1940 & renewed 1968 by W.H. Auden from *Collected Poems* by W.H. Auden. "Musee des Beaux Arts", copyright 1940 & renewed 1968 by W.H. Auden from *Collected Poems* by W.H. Auden. Used by permission of Random House, Inc. "Home" by Anton Chekhov from *Modern Library*, copyright © 1999 by Random House, Inc.

Riverbend From "Baghdad Burning" by Riverbend (baghdad.burning@gmail.com)from *The Great Wall of Segregation...*, *http://riverbendblog.blogspot.com*, April 26, 2007.

Riverhead Books, an imprint of Penguin Group (USA) Inc. "I'm Like a Bird" from *Songbook* by Nick Hornby, copyright © 2002 by Nick Hornby. Used by permission of Riverhead Books, an imprint of Penguin Group (USA) Inc.

Rogers, Coleridge & White Ltd. "A Devoted Son" from *Games at Twilight and Other Stories* by Anita Desai. Copyright © 1978 Anita Desai. Reproduced by permission of the author c/o Rogers, Coleridge & White Ltd., 20 Powis Mews, London W11 1JN.

Russell & Volkening, Inc. "The Train from Rhodesia" from *Selected Stories* by Nadine Gordimer. Copyright © 1950 by Nadine Gordimer, renewed in 1978 by Nadine Gordimer. Used by the permission of Russell & Volkening as agents for the author.

Scovil Chichak Galen Literary Agency, Inc. "We'll Never Conquer Space" by Arthur C. Clarke, from *Science Digest*, June 1960. Copyright © 1960 by Popular Mechanics Company. Used by permission of the author and the author's agents, Scovil Chichak Galen Literary Agency, Inc.

Scribner, an imprint of Simon & Schuster "The Second Coming" from *The Collected Works of W.B. Yeats, Volume 1: The Poems* edited by Richard J. Finneran. Copyright © 1924 by The Macmillan Company; copyright renewed © 1952 by Bertha Georgie Yeats. Used with the permission of Scribner, an imprint of Simon & Schuster Adult Publishing Group, All rights reserved.

Smithsonian Institution "Recasting Shakespeare's Stage" by Eric Jaffe from *www.smithsonianmag.com/arts-culture/globe.html*. Copyright 2008 Smithsonian Institution. Used with permission from Smithsonian Business Ventures. All rights reserved. Reproduction in any medium is strictly prohibited without permission from Smithsonian Institution. Such permission may be requested from Smithsonian Business Ventures.

Stage Three Music (US) Inc. "Eli, the Barrow Boy" written by Colin Meloy from *Picaresque*. Copyright © 2005 music of Stage Three/Osterozhna! Music (BMI). Used by permission of Stage Three Music (US), Inc.

The Estate of Ann Stanford "The Wife's Lament" by Ann Stanford from *The Women Poets In English: An Anthology*. Copyright © 1972 by Ann Stanford. Used with permission of the Estate of Ann Stanford.

Taylor & Francis From "The Rape Of The Lock", reprinted from *The Poems of Alexander Pope*, edited by John Butt. Reproduced by permission of Taylor & Francis Books UK.

University of California Press & Carmen Balcells Agencia Literaria *Selected Odes of Pablo Neruda*, by Pablo Neruda, translated by Margaret Sayers Peden, copyright © 1990 by the Fundacion Pablo Neruda, published by the University of California Press. All rights reserved.

The University of Chicago Press Excerpt from "Oedipus The King" by Sophocles, D. Grene, trans., from *The Complete Greek Tragedies*, R. Lattimore and D. Grene, eds. Used with permission of The University of Chicago Press.

Ed Victor, Ltd. "Not Palaces" from *Collected Poems 1928–1985* by Stephen Spender, copyright © 2004 by Stephen Spender. Used by permission of Ed Victor Ltd.

Viking Penguin, Inc. "Araby", from *Dubliners* by James Joyce, copyright 1916 by B. W. Heubsch. Definitive text Copyright © 1967 by The Estate of James Joyce. "Wirers" from *Collected Poems Of Siegfried Sasson* by Siegfried Sassoon, copyright 1918, 1920 by E. P. Dutton. Copyright 1936, 1946, 1947, 1948 by Siegfried Sassoon. "The Rocking-Horse Winner" from *Complete Short Stories Of D.H. Lawrence* by D.H. Lawrence. Copyright © 1933 by the Estate of D. H. Lawrence, renewed © 1961 by Angelo Ravagli and C. M. Weekley, Executors of the Estate of Frieda Lawrence. "The Book of Sand", from *Collected Fictions*, by Jorge Luis Borges, translated by Andrew Hurley, copyright © 1998 by Maria Kodama; translation copyright © 1998 by Penguin Putnam, Inc. From "In Athens Once", from *Days Of Obligation* by Richard Rodriguez, copyright © 1992 by Richard Rodriguez. Used by permission of Viking Penguin, a division of Penguin Group (USA) Inc. All rights reserved.

Wake Forest University Press "Carrick Revisited" from *Selected Poems of Louis MacNeice*, edited by Michael Longley. Copyright © Wake Forest University Press, 1990. Used by permission of Wake Forest University Press.

The Arthur Waley Estate Excerpts from *The Analects of Confucius*, translated and annotated by Arthur Waley. Copyright © 1938 by George Allen and Unwin Ltd, London. From "The Book of Songs, Song 34 (Thick Grow the Rush Leaves)" translated by Arthur Waley from *The Book Of Songs*. Copyright © 1919, 1941 by Alfred A. Knopf, Inc. Used by permission of The Arthur Waley Estate.

Wikipedia.org "Zorro" retrieved from http://en.wikipedia.org accessed on 6/6/07. "Space Mirror Memorial" retrieved from http://en.wikipedia.org accessed on 6/15/07. "Davy Crockett" retrieved from http://en.wikipedia.org accessed on 6/18/07.

Yale University Press "The Seafarer" from *Poems from the Old English*, translated by Burton Raffel. Copyright © 1960, 1964; renewed 1988, 1922 by The University of Nebraska Press. Copyright © 1994 by Burton Raffel. Used by permission of Yale University Press.

Note: Every effort has been made to locate the copyright owner of material reproduced on this component. Omissions brought to our attention will be corrected in subsequent editions.

Credits

Photo Credits

Images; **1144**: Underwood & Underwood/CORBIS; **1144**: age fotostock / SuperStock; **1145**: The Image Bank/Getty Images; **1147**: Gilles Mermet / Art Resource, NY; **1147**: Gilles Mermet / Art Resource, NY; **1148**: Gilles Mermet / Art Resource, NY; **1155**: Hulton-Deutsch Collection/CORBIS; **1156**: E.O. HoppÈ/CORBIS; **1158**: Jean Kugler/Getty Images; **1163**: PhotothÈque R. Magritte-ADAGP / Art Resource, NY, ©1998 C. Herscovici, Brussels/ Artists Rights Society (ARS), New York.; **1171**: Bettmann/CORBIS; **1172**: The Granger Collection, New York; **1172**: Bkgrnd Freyda Miller/CORBIS; **1174**: Michael Goldman/Getty Images; **1176**: Art Projects International; **1177**: **1179**: Getty Images; **1180**: Michael St. Maur Sheil/CORBIS; **1182**: Sophie Bassouls/Sygma/CORBIS; **1182**: **1183**: Paul Hardy/CORBIS; **1184**: Paul Hardy/CORBIS; **1187**: © Gilles Mermet / Art Resource; **1188**: Getty Images; **1189**: t. Private Collection, © The Bloomsbury Workshop, London / The Bridgeman Art Library International; **1189**: b. Private Collection, The Stapleton Collection/ The Bridgeman Art Library International; **1189**: **1190**: t. Marilyn Monroe, Andy Warhol, © Andy Warhol Foundation/CORBIS. TM 2006 Marilyn Monroe, LLC by CMG Worldwide, Inc / www.MarilynMonroe.com © Andy Warhol Foundation for the Visual Arts / ARS, New York; **1190**: br. Getty Images; **1190**: bl. **1192**: RÈunion des MusÈes Nationaux / Art Resource, NY; **1193**: **1195**: The Garden of Love, Walter Richard Sickert, Fitzwilliam Museum, Cambridge; **1196**: RÈunion des MusÈes Nationaux / Art Resource, NY; **1197**: age fotostock / SuperStock; **1198**: Private Collection, / The Bridgeman Art Library International; **1200**: Julian Barrow/Getty Images; **1200**: **1201**: Andreas Altwein/dpa/CORBIS; **1210**: b. Library of Congress, Prints & Photographs Division, NYWT&S Collection; **1217**: Getty Images **1219**: Hulton-Deutsch Collection/CORBIS; **1220–1221**: Ron Dahlquist / Super; **1223**: Image1 / SuperStock; **1224–1225**: border Gala / SuperStock; **1226**: Michael Halminski / SuperStock; **1228–1229**: Steve Vidler / SuperStock; **1230–1231**: age fotostock / SuperStock; **1231**: Ben Mangor / SuperStock; **1232**: Digital Vision Ltd. / SuperStock; **1233**: The Granger Collection, New York; **1234**: St. Patrick's Close, Walter Osborne, National Gallery of Ireland; **1235**: Robbie Pleck / SuperStock; **1238**: © The Metropolitan Museum of Art / Art Resource, NY; **1239**: British Museum / Art Resource, NY; **1243**: Bettmann/CORBIS; **1244**: Stockbyte /Getty Images; **1245**: Stockbyte /Getty Images; **1247**: Izzy Schwartz/Getty Images; **1249**: Marvin E. Newman/Getty Images; **1250**: Jonathan Kitchen/ Getty Images; **1251**: C Squared Studios/Getty Images; **1255**: Stockbyte / Getty Images; **1256**: Marvin E. Newman/Getty Images; **1258**: Bettmann/ CORBIS; **1259**: Kevin Summers/Getty Images; **1260**: Kevin Summers/ Getty Images; **1262**: Kevin Summers/Getty Images; **1264**: Beth Dixson/ Getty Images; **1267**: Bildarchiv Preussischer Kulturbesitz / Art Resource, NY; **1269**: t. Michael Nicholson/CORBIS; **1269**: m. Hulton-Deutsch Collection/CORBIS; **1269**: b. The Granger Collection, New York; **1270**: Bettmann/CORBIS; **1271**: t. Nathan Benn/CORBIS; **1272**: Bettmann/ CORBIS; **1276**: Getty Images; **1278–1279**: AFP/Getty Images; **1282**: Bettmann/ CORBIS; **1283**: Snark/Art Resource, NY; **1293**: Hulton-Deutsch Collection/ CORBIS; **1296**: Portrait of N. Pietrunkevic, Nikolai Ge, Scala/Art Resource, NY; **1297**: Sleepless Night, Nikolai Romadin, Scala/Art Resource, NY; **1302–1303**: Hulton-Deutsch Collection/CORBIS; **1305**: b. courtesy of Royal Literary Fund and Special Collections, U of Birmingham; **1306**: Hulton-Deutsch Collection/CORBIS; **1308**: The Art Archive / Imperial War Museum; **1308**: The Art Archive / Imperial War Museum; **1313**: The Granger Collection, New York; **1314**: Paul Souders/ CORBIS; **1319**: Steve McDonough/CORBIS; **1320**: ©Orwell Archive; **1323**: Colin McPherson/CORBIS; **1324**: HIP / Art Resource, NY; **1327**: HIP / Art Resource, NY; **1330**: Private Collection/ The Stapleton Collection/ The Bridgeman Art Library; **1337**: Micheline Pelletier/CORBIS; **1338**: Ron Stroud/Masterfile; **1340**: Jean Miele/CORBIS; **1343**: Peter Turnley/ CORBIS; **1344**: David Bergman/CORBIS; **1355**: BASSOULS SOPHIE/ CORBIS SYGMA; **1356**: ©Bettmann/CORBIS; **1358**: "Boy on a Wall: Rat Island, 1989" from TIEPOLO'S HOUND by Derek Walcott. Copyright © 20 by Derek Walcott. Reprinted ty Permission of Farrar, Straus and Giroux, LLC. From the collection of Michael and Judy Chastanet.; **1358**: Ryan McVay/Getty Images; 1363: ©Smith Richard Frank/CORBIS Sygma; **1366**: Hulton-Deutsch Collection/CORBIS; **1369**: The Irish Times; **1370**: Starry Night, Vincent van Gogh, Digital Image © The Museum of Modern Art/Licensed by SCALA / Art Resource, NY; **1373**: JLImages / Alamy; **1375**: Thierry Orban/CORBIS SYGMA; **1376**: Ulrik Tofte/Getty Images; **1376**: Ulrik Tofte/Getty Images; **1379**: Getty Images; **1380**: Getty Images; **1385**: Getty Images; **1386**: Arthur S. AubryGetty Images; **1388**: Daniel Nevins / SuperStock; **1391**: AP/Wide World Photos; **1392**: Scott Stulberg/CORBIS; **1394**: Scott Stulberg/CORBIS; **1397**: Getty Images; **1398**: image reproduced with the kind permission of the Dean and Chapter of Chichester Cathedral; **1402**: t. Nicolas Elder/Globe Photos; **1402**: b. Hulton-Deutsch Collection/CORBIS; **1403**: GK Hart/Vicky Hart/Getty Images; **1404**: PIER/Getty Images; **1406**: Getty Images; **1407**: t. Colin McPherson/CORBIS; **1407**: b. Getty Images; **1408**: Artkey/ CORBIS; **1408**: Artkey/CORBIS; **1410**: Getty Images; **1410**: Getty Images; **1412**: l. Fridmar Damm/zefa/Corbis; **1412**: r. Colin McPherson/CORBIS; **1413**: istockphoto.com; **1415**: Colin McPherson/CORBIS; **1416**: Franck Guiziou/Hemis/CORBIS; **1417**: Martin Harvey/CORBIS; **1422**: Grace Davies/Omni-Photo Communications, Inc.; **1423**: Blaine Harrington III/ CORBIS; **1431**: Getty Images; **1432**: © David Noton Photography / Alamy; **1434**: © Orit Allush / Alamy; **1434**: © Orit Allush / Alamy; **1436**: Christopher Pillitz/Getty Images; **1438**: Tim Graham/Getty Images; **1441**: William Coupon/CORBIS; **1442**: Steve Nagy/Design Pics/CORBIS; **1443**: NASA/ JPL; **1444**: US Geological Service; **1444**: Hiroyuki Matsumoto /Getty Images; **1448**: AITCH/Getty Images; **1449**: t. CORBIS; **1449**: b. istockphoto. com; **1449**: mb. ESA/K. Horgan/Getty Images; **1449**: mt. DRA/Getty Images; **1459**: mc. PHERSON COLIN/CORBIS SYGMA; **1460**: Luke MacGregor/Reuters/CORBIS; **1462**: Tim Mosenfelder/CORBIS; **1462**: Tim Mosenfelder/CORBIS; **1486**: bcl. ©Bettmann/Corbis

Staff Credits

The people who made up the Pearson Prentice Hall Literature team— representing design, editorial, editorial services, education technology, manufacturing and inventory planning, market research, marketing services, planning and budgeting, product planning, production serv- ices, project office, publishing processes, and rights and permissions— are listed below. Boldface type denotes the core team members.

Tobey Antao, Margaret Antonini, Rosalyn Arcilla, Penny Baker, James Ryan Bannon, Stephan Barth, **Tricia Battipede,** Krista Baudo, Rachel Beckman, Julie Berger, Lawrence Berkowitz, Melissa Biezin, **Suzanne Biron,** Rick Blount, **Marcela Boos, Betsy Bostwick,** Kay Bosworth, Jeff Bradley, Andrea Brescia, Susan Brorein, Lois Brown, **Pam Carey,** Lisa Carrillo, **Geoffrey Cassar,** Patty Cavuoto, Doria Ceraso, Jennifer Ciccone, Jaime Cohen, Rebecca Cottingham, Joe Cucchiara, Jason Cuoco, **Alan Dalgleish, Karen Edmonds, Irene Ehrmann,** Stephen Eldridge, Amy Fleming, Dorothea Fox, Steve Frankel, Cindy Frederick, Philip Fried, Diane Fristachi, Phillip Gagler, **Pamela Gallo,** Husain Gatlin, **Elaine Goldman,** Elizabeth Good, John Guild, Phil Hadad, Patricia Hade, Monduane Harris, Brian Hawkes, Jennifer B. Heart, Martha Heller, John Hill, Beth Hyslip, Mary Jean Jones, Grace Kang, Nathan Kinney, Roxanne Knoll, **Kate Krimsky,** Monisha Kumar, Jill Kushner, Sue Langan, Melisa Leong, Susan Levine, Dave Liston, **Mary Luthi, George Lychock, Gregory Lynch, Joan Mazzeo, Sandra McGloster,** Salita Mehta, Eve Melnechuk, Kathleen Mercandetti, Artur Mkrtchyan, Karyn Mueller, Alison Muff, Christine Mulcahy, Kenneth Myett, Elizabeth Nemeth, Stefano Nese, Carrie O'Connor, April Okano, Kim Ortell, Sonia Pap, Raymond Parenteau, Dominique Pickens, Linda Punskovsky, **Sheila Ramsay,** Maureen Raymond, Mairead Reddin, **Erin Rehill-Seker, Renee Roberts, Laura Ross,** Bryan Salacki, Sharon Schultz, Jennifer Serra, **Melissa Shustyk,** Rose Sievers, Christy Singer, Yvonne Stecky, **Cynthia Summers,** Steve Thomas, Merle Uuesoo, Roberta Warshaw, Patricia Williams, Daniela Velez

Additional Credits

Lydie Bemba, Victoria Blades, Denise Data, Rachel Drice, Eleanor Kostyk, Jill Little, Loraine Machlin, Evan Marx, Marilyn McCarthy, Patrick O'Keefe, Shelia M. Smith, Lucia Tirondola, Laura Vivenzio, Linda Waldman, Angel Weyant